CONDENSED

Gabby's
Wordspeller ©
&
PHONETIC
DICTIONARY

Find your word by the way it sounds

Cross-Reference: find other words that sound the same
Suffixes: see all the word endings
Prefixes: definition/derivative

DIANE FRANK

Summary: Over 35,000 entries of commonly used American English words with multiple misspellings based upon their phonetic sound. Extensive cross-referencing allows for words that are either similar in meaning and/or spelling. Defined Prefixes as well as all Suffix endings for all proper words are easily located. Misspelled words are printed in a second color to allow differentiation from properly spelled words.

Notice of Rights

Notice of Liability

Editor/Author/Publishing/Cover Design by Diane M. Frank
and Gabrielle M. Purcell

Copyright © June, 2009 by DMFrank Publishing
PO Box 412, Rainier, Washington 98576-0412, USA

Library of Congress Cataloging-in-Publication Data
Library of Congress Control Number: 2008900169

Gabby's Wordspeller and Condensed Phonetic Dictionary
Summary: Over 35,000 entries of commonly used American English words with multiple misspellings based upon their phonetic sound. Extensive cross-referencing allows for words that are either similar in meaning and/or spelling. Defined Prefixes as well as all Suffix endings for all proper words are easily located. Misspelled words are printed in a second color to allow differentiation from properly spelled words.

www.gabbyswordspeller.com

ISBN 978-0-9801025-1-2

Manufactured in the United States of America

Second Revised 2-Color Edition

This book

was written for

my daughter, Gabrielle, and

for others of the world who may find

comfort in

using this floatation device as they

embark across the great

sea of the English

language.

About the Author

Diane Frank spent 10 years as a literacy tutor at community colleges in Texas, Alaska and Washington then graduated with a degree in Communications at The Evergreen State College. The school is known nationally for being a liberal arts school using an interdisciplinary approach to learning. This allowed Diane to spend a great deal of her time making use of academic resources, professors, extended scholastic networks and linguists in order to design a multi-functional methodology for a phonetic dictionary. She was able, via the use of a statistics course, to design and implement surveys which employed responses from people of vast geographic and socio-economic backgrounds as well as age and education levels. She was able to conduct a feasibility study into the market, availability of resource tools such as dictionaries and spell-checkers as it relates to their effectiveness in dealing with phonetic spellings. Diane's studies revealed that several 'links' or 'bridges' were absent from reference material available in 1997. Since the release of this new, truly phonetic dictionary and cross-referencer, Diane has discovered that, although it has been 12 years since her original feasibility study, that these same 'bridges' are still sorely lacking from the resource tool market. Thank goodness she kept her nose to the grindstone!

About the Co-Author

Gabrielle Purcell, being true to her dyslexic nature, is brilliant and willfull in her expression. She had tendencies from the onset of birth which would be continuously enlightening to her family and friends. Therefore it came as no small wonder to her as to why someone hadn't developed a dictionary which, 'spelled the words by the way they sound'. This was a logical concept for her and a big 'duh' to the rest of the educated world. The multitude of compliments received since the inception of this book are all truly meant for Gabby, who's willfulness, strength and out-of'-the-box mentality made it all possible!

PREFACE

The height of inspiration that I shared with my daughter was on the one night we decided I should write this book which ran contrary to what was happening in our lives at the time. Because of this night I have come to thank my bicycle accident which I experienced when riding home from college where I was finishing my degree. If not for this accident, which herniated discs in my back and left me nearly debilitated for 1.5 years, this book would not exist today.

During this time of debilitation, I watched my life fall apart and my career come to a screeching halt. It was in this span of time that my daughter, Gabby (who had been diagnosed at 8 with dyslexia) had my full attention one night when she became verbally irate at having to write a two paragraph report for her high school class. I observed helplessly from my bed as she slumped over in my office chair literally crying so hard it was as if her self-esteem had suffered its last straw and was flowing out with her tears. She cried that this task would take her all night and that she had so much other homework still to accomplish. This was her first month as a freshman in high school. And she was right, we had been going through this hell since she started kindergarten and her reading skills were still below a fifth grade level.

Never had I felt so strongly the brutality of feeling so hopeless and powerless all at the same time in my entire life. I was a single mother and my two children meant everything in the world to me. And there we found ourselves, that evening in September 1997, at the lowest point in our lives, all hopes that we would be successful at anything...EVER...was drained...gone! It was in this moment of quiet, as the two of us sat and wept, exhausted with the thoughts of this helplessness in resolving our dilemmas, that Gabby suddenly burst out with the only possible intelligent solution. "Mom! Why don't you write me a dictionary that spells the words the way I hear them so that I can write?" I was stunned, such a sudden change in attitude. So swift that I was taken aback and could only exuberantly and decidedly reply, "Okay, I will".

And that's what I did fulltime for the next year while laid up in my bed watching the rest of the world go by. A kindred soul thought my endeavor worthy enough to purchase me Macintosh's first powerbook. I kept up the "good" work and managed finally to finish this book eleven years later.

I wish to thank...of course, my children who endured our poverty as I typed away. I probably wouldn't be alive today (spared from several hopeless moments during my healing) if it hadn't been for Marshall Alexander Andersen Hatfield whose loving attitude, support, nursing and nurturing earned her the largest angel wings that any human could possibly earn in many lifetimes of good deeds. To my chiropractor, who, unlike the neurosurgeons who said I would never walk again, put me back on my feet within 2 months of my first visit. I thank you all!

FOREWORD

The literal meaning of the word *dyslexia* – from its Greek roots – is "difficulty with words".

Dr. Maryanne Wolfe, author of *Proust and the Squid: The Story and Science of the Reading Brain*, explains, "the more you know about a word, the faster you can read it." Dr. Virginia Berninger, of the University of Washington, has demonstrated that reading fluency is enhanced for dyslexic students through instruction that focuses on the interrelation between the three "forms" shared by each word: the meaning of the word, its visual appearance, and its sound.

Ronald Davis, author of *The Gift of Dyslexia*, builds his program for dyslexia correction upon the insight that word mastery is essential to reading development, using only two essential materials: clay and a dictionary. Students use clay to create three-dimensional models of the meaning of each word, as well as the letters that spell the word. The dictionary is the key to independence: it provides the correct spelling, a key to accurate pronunciation, and all possible definitions and use of each word. The modeling is needed because dyslexic individuals think mostly in pictures, unable to think with words unless they have mental pictures to go along with them. By tapping into the creative process, the Davis program empowers each student with the ability to learn and discover on their own.

But here is where dyslexics encounter their biggest barrier: spelling. The most persistent and pervasive symptom of dyslexia is an orthographic barrier; they have difficulty remembering the conventional spelling of phonetically irregular words. Many educators focus on intensive teaching of phonics, as this provides one avenue for decoding many of the simpler words encountered by beginning readers. English is not a phonetic language, but rather a polyglot and amalgam of words drawn from different languages, often retaining spellings that reflect histories and pronunciations long forgotten.

If you can't spell a word, you cannot find it in a dictionary.

Through brain scans, Dr. Sally Shaywitz of Yale University has shown that dyslexic readers typically underutilize the "visual word form area" of the brain – the part of the visual cortex believed to be involved in instantaneous recognition of whole words. This is the part of the brain that probably stores a picture of the right letters arranged in the right order, the part that is engaged when you choose the correct spelling because it just *looks* right to you.

It isn't that dyslexic writers are unable to spell a word; with their creative problem-solving strengths, they can easily spell the same word half a dozen different ways. As Andrew Jackson once said, "its a damn poor mind that can think of only one way to spell a word." The problem is in figuring out which spelling is the one that everyone else will use and understand.

This is where the most powerful tool – the dictionary – is also the most inaccessible. Because if we err in guessing the first 2 or 3 letters of the word, we will never find it.

And here is where *Gabby's Wordspeller* becomes indispensible – it provides the key to the door that opens the dictionary. It is where all those phonetic decoding skills emphasized by well-meaning primary school teachers can finally be brought to fruition: *krecher* may not be a word, but it *is* a spelling, albeit an incorrect one. In a regular dictionary, it leads us to the Kremlin, which is not where we wanted to go. But Gabby's phonetic dictionary gives us the answer in exactly the place we have gone to find it: "creature."

Suname leads to tsunami. *Fanomanen* takes us to phenomenon. *Ekselerate* turns into accelerate. And pretty soon, the world of words is ours for the taking. If we already know the meaning of the word, that is all that is needed. The correct spelling is there, in a form that we can copy and use.

If our trip to the dictionary is also a search for meaning, or etymology, or information as to usage, or a set of synonyms, then *Gabby's* has opened the door for us. By providing the spelling we need, we can access the larger dictionary or thesaurus which can provide us with whatever information we seek.

This reference book should be in every school library, in every classroom, and at home on every student's desk. It is the key to independence for every learner.

-Abigail Marshall, Author of *The Everything Parent's Guide to Children with Dyslexia* and *When Your Child Has ... Dyslexia*. She also manages the *Dyslexia the Gift* site www.dyslexia.com for Davis Dyslexia Assoc. International.

About Dialects, Annunciation and Pronunciation

Perhaps, in my opinion, there is more emphasis placed upon the problems with spelling as it relates to the 'speller' and their perceived disabilities, when, in actuality, more emphasis could be placed upon annunciation or pronunciation by those who speak the language.

As a child learning EFL (English as a First Language) or a traveler new to this country learning ESL (English as a Second Language) there lies one common trait, hearing the language for the first time on American soil. When it comes to spelling English there are a number of issues facing the speller; hearing difficulties (tones, accents, dialects), sight difficulties (irregular neuronet firing, eye muscle control). These challenges are compounded by someone who speaks the language without articulating, pronunciating or annunciating correctly.

Dialects within the United States alone ranges from hundreds to thousands (depending upon whom is citing the study). It's very challenging to take a spelling test with a new teacher who has a strong southern drawl or to grow up in one region of the country where entire letters are dropped from words, letters such as 'r', 't', 'g' and 'd'. In some regions letters are even added that do not belong to a proper English word such as 'r' or 't' or 'd'. Words such as 'something' turn into 'sumthen' and 'children' into 'chilren'. Parts of the country 'warsh' their clothes. Some English speakers may not use the proper tense of a word and interrelate 'forget' with 'forgot' and 'drank' with 'drunk'.

Confusion goes even further with a new speller when, upon hearing a word taken out of context, may experience the inability to grasp and differentiate how to spell the word. Words spoken and not articulated give rise to synonymous sounding words such as 'petal, pedal and peddle' or 'procession', 'precession' and 'precision'.

It behooves us all to ease off on the pressure we place upon those who are challenged with spelling the written word and take responsibility for how we articulate our speech and stop 'warshing our clothes'!

Diane Frank

~ What Gabby's Wordspeller DOES and DOES NOT do ~

1) **Does not include proper nouns**. Reason; not enough room, this task is left to another resource tool named the 'Encyclopedia'.

2) **Does not differentiate between** a noun, a verb, an adjective, an adverb. Reason; not enough room, this task is left to another resource tool termed a 'standard dictionary'.

3) **Does not have page numbers**. Reason, not enough room, this dictionary is an evolving tool and will be changed each and every printing. When searching for your word, you will be taken directly to where you wish to be. Your search is not for a page number, but an alphabetized word. The margins required to generate page numbers on each page would eliminate 3,000 valuable misspelled words. Gabby's Wordspeller cannot afford to loose a single misspelling. Nor does it care to reduce the size of the text which is currently readable for those who wear reading glasses up to 1.5 magnification lenses (don't need to go looking for those reading glasses)!

4) **Does have 250 pages of misspellings removed** in order to produce a book which is both portable and manageable. Gabby's required condensing, which involved removing 250 pages = approximately 57,000 misspelled words. Gabby's would have been heavy and unmanageable without condensing. This is why every conceivable misspelling is not included. But, with the evolution of this phonetic dictionary over time, each and every misspelled word can be located within one inch up or down from where you 'think' your misspelling should be.

5) **Does not come in digital form (CD)**. The current technology doesn't offer protection on digital copyright. Additionally, to perform a search digitally for a specific misspelling requires ISO codes which have not yet been developed. If there were existing phonetic ISO codes, Gabby's Wordspeller & Phonetic Dictionary would not be in your hands right now!

6) **Does have text turned vertically**. Reason; to fit in as many misspellings as possible within the constraints of a portable book. Once the author dealt with the emotional disturbance that three years of work was not allowed reflection in Gabby's due to the bulky size of the book, 250 pages were removed. This move then illuminated that the cross-referencing tool had become compromised. How to remedy this? The author pondered, as she worked each and everyday replacing misspellings to regain the composure of the cross-reference tool. One particular day, having come to the end of her wits that there were still thousands of words which needed to make their way back into this resource book, she struck upon the idea to turn the text

to a vertical position. "Could a quarter turn of the text make this book work again?" And voila! Once the text was turned, more columns fit into place and 25 valuable pages of misspellings found their way back into Gabby's.

The most redeeming quality of all then came to surface with this move. Not only did this feature allow to the regaining and composure of the cross-referencing sector, but also lent character and greater useability for the word-seeker. Find your word with one hand and write the word with the other hand! What a bonus!

7) **Does require a learning curve**. In order to merge three resource tools into one small book required the use of code. Every stroke of the key requires "space". The one year necessarily spent to edit this book into final form required the removal of superfluous marks. And superfluous marks included redundancy. The repetition of words would only make the book heavy and bulky.

Just as when the Thesaurus first came to our aid and required a 'learning curve', so it is true for Gabby's. As with any other 'tool', Gabby's illicits a 'learning curve'. But use it just three times and you will overcome the curve!

8) **Doesn't state that it actually has 100,000 words between the covers?** In the 12 years performed in creating this phonetic dictionary, the author discovered something about the standard dictionaries. Gabby's provides 35,000 BASE words. Base words meaning 'root' words, which is an important note here. When Gabby's provides a base word, for example "qualify", it lists the word, then adds behind this base word all the possible suffix endings associated with that word. 'Qualify' has 8 suffix endings associated with this base word. When suffix endings are applied they are; *qualified, qualifies, qualifiedly,qualifiedness, qualifier, qualifiable, qualifying* and *qualification*. Did you know that?

Although some of these words are classified as adjectives, the fact remains that the base word and base definition are derivatives of the same. If you visit an average of 5 dictionaries you wouldn't even be able to locate the word *'qualifiedly'* and wouldn't think it was a real word. Perhaps you may consider that you just 'made it up'. Turns out *'qualifiedly'* is a real word, albeit an adjective, but still a word associated with the base definition word, *'qualify'*. BUT, *qualifiedly* will not be listed within some dictionaries (MSN Encarta and Cambridge, for example).

Another illumination is that standard dictionaries who boast 50,000 words are really saying they have spelled out *'qualify'*, *'qualifier'* and *'qualification'* providing the same basic definition for each one. Each of the words are, primarily, the same. So for one base word, a standard dictionary claims it as three separate words (keeping in mind that these three words each have the same derivative).

Gabby's mostly provides base (root) words, then lists all possible suffix endings. Therefore **Gabby's could, conceivably, boast 100,000** words (which a standard dictionary would do). Any English word has an average of three suffix endings or derivatives. Take a spin with a standard dictionary and compare it to Gabby's... word for word and you will be impressed.

9) **Why doesn't Gabby's list some words** that have beginning letters such as 'UN' and 'DE'?

* Prefixes and their importance *

To avoid redundancy, Gabby's only lists base or root words. **If adding a prefix to a base word alters the base words' definition, then it will be treated as a base word in and of itself and will be listed**...such as *'undo'*.

The base word for *'de-ice'* is *'de'* (a prefix) and *'ice'* (a base word). In order to list over 100,000 words and their misspellings required providing a prefix along with it's definition. Gabby's would be a five volume set if' *'undo' 'unchanged'*, *'unlock'*, *'unwind'* and all the other misspelled 'un' + base words were listed along with the misspellings for *'do'*, *'change'*, *'lock'* and *'wind'*.

Therefore when searching for a word that begins with a prefix + a base word...find your base word, then locate the prefix word and you will unravel immediately the spelling and definition for that word. As well, many English words are based in the Latin language. The author studied years of Latin and discovered she is able to understand many words in the romance languages due to recognizing the prefixes. Many standard dictionaries were used to locate and gather all prefixes as well as their definitions...just another little handy tool found in Gabby's Wordspeller!

10) **Does not come in hardbound cover**. Reason; a child will not be able to hold the book and thumb through pages if the cover is not flexible. To compensate for the extensive 'use' the cover will experience, Gabby's comes laminated and perfect-bound. This encourages additional insurance against the book falling apart from constant daily use.

INTRODUCTION

"Gabby's Wordspeller & Phonetic Dictionary" is primarily designed to allow the user to locate their word by the way it sounds (phonetically). As a resource tool, it enables the user with the ability to not only locate their word within seconds...but as a *phonetic* dictionary qualifies it as suitable for ESL, dyslexics and EFL. This reference book (unlike any dictionary ever created) also performs the following functions:

Cross-referencing...(thousands of these cross-references exist in Gabby's)

- *emigrant or immigrant?*
- *gym or gem?*
- *marry or merry?*
- *scene or seen or seine?*
- *pedal or petal or peddle?*
- *carrot or karat or caret or carat?*

Learn how to spell the word correctly the first time you hear it...

korts, spelled phonetically could lend to words such as:	*bol*, spelled phonetically could be...
quartz	ball
courts	bowl
quarts	bawl
chords	bull
cords	

All these words, as well as thousands of other words are cross-referenced extensively throughout the phonetic dictionary.

Gabby's provides short, concise definitions to enable the user to quickly identify which word they wish to spell correctly. This lends the user the ability to then consult a standard dictionary for further definitions if desired.

Misspellings often involve transposing letters which are most commonly misinterpreted in hearing such as:

t	with	*d*	*au*	with	*ow*
b	with	*p*	*ch*	with	*sh*
ph	with	*f*	*ou*	with	*ow*
kn	with	*n*	*th*	with	*f*
qu	with	*kw*	*c*	with	*s*

Another advantage of Gabby's is that it provides suffix endings for over 35,000 commonly used words to include legal, medical and slang. Over 12 notable standard dictionaries were required to retrieve every conceivable suffix ending for each word. No single dictionary performs this added feature. Each book contains an easy to use CD Tutorial for PC which illustrates how to utilize suffix endings. As well, Gabby's has provided all known 'proper' prefix's as well as their definitions.

METHODOLOGY: for misspelled words + base words

RULE #1: If you have a difficult time using this dictionary, refer back to these rules!

RULE #2: Simply look up the word by the way it SOUNDS...not the way it should/would/could be spelled.

RULE #3: Look up the **base** **word**. The base word is the "root" of the word without suffixes added:

> Example: *baged*, bag(gged) / back(ed)
>
>> ~*baged*, is the misspelled word
>>
>> = bag(gged) is "bagged" spelled properly ~bag is the base word to look up in the dictionary to make certain this is the word you want
>>
>> = back(ed) is "backed" spelled properly ~back is the base word to look up in the dictionary to make certain this is the word you want

> Example: *beder*, better / bid(dder) / bitter / bet(ttor)
>
>> ~*beder*, is the misspelled word
>>
>> = better is spelled properly
>>
>> = bid(dder) "bidder" spelled properly~bid is the base word to look up in the dictionary to make certain this is the word you want
>>
>> = bitter is spelled properly
>>
>> = bet(ttor) "bettor" spelled properly~bet is the base word to look up in the dictionary to make certain this is the word you want

> Example: *eksploratory*, explore(ratory)
>
>> ~*eksploratory* is the misspelled word
>>
>> = explore(ratory) "exploratory" spelled properly ~explore is the base word to locate in the dictionary to make certain this is the word you want

METHODOLOGY: for properly spelled words

RULE #1:   If you have a difficult time using this dictionary, refer back to these rules!

RULE #2:   Simply look up the word the way it SOUNDS...not the way it should/would/ could be spelled.

RULE #3:   Suffixes (**Word Endings**):

A.) The <u>asterisk (*)</u> means to add an "s" to the end of the word. **Example: ~ receptionist,*** = receptionist + 's' = receptionists

B.) Go back into the latter part of the base word for a letter which matches the beginning letter of the suffix ending. **Example: paralysis,ytic,yze,yzed,zying,yzation,yzer,** *DEFINITION* = paral<u>ytic</u>, paral<u>yze</u>, paral<u>yzed</u>, paral<u>yzing</u>, paral<u>yzation</u>, paral<u>yzer</u>

C.) The <u>suffix</u> endings, for the word is added onto the end or from a letter in the word.
Examples:

~ **call,***,lled,lling,ller, *DEFINITION*,
ca<u>lled</u>, ca<u>lling</u>, ca<u>ller</u>
(The double 'll' is listed to assure you that there are two 'll's)

~ **balance,***,ed,cing, *DEFINITION*,
balance<u>s</u>, balanc<u>ed</u>, balan<u>cing</u>
(Asterisk (*) means "just add an 's'. The 'ed' comes off the 'e' and the 'cing' comes off the 'c')

~ **immaculate,**ely,eness,acy, *DEFINITION*,
immaculat<u>ely</u>, immaculat<u>eness</u>, immacul<u>acy</u>

~ **reckless,**ssly,ssness, *DEFINITION*,
reckle<u>ssly</u>, reckle<u>ssness</u>
(The double 'ss' is listed to assure you that there are two 'ss')

~ **nag,**gged,gging,ggingly, *DEFINITION*,
na<u>gged</u>, na<u>gging</u>, na<u>ggingly</u>
(The double 'gg' is listed to assure you that there are two 'gg')

~ **adapt,***,ted,ting,tive,tively,tation,table, tability, *DEFINITION*,
adapt<u>s</u>, adap<u>ted</u>, adap<u>ting</u>, adap<u>tive</u>, adap<u>tively</u>, adap<u>tation</u>, adap<u>table</u>, adap<u>tability</u>

RULE #4:   DE... If the word is not listed below, simply remove the first 2 letters - <u>DE</u> - then look up the remainder of the word.

Example: deice, '*de*' means "AWAY FROM/DOWN FROM" then look up the base word 'ice'.

RULE #5:   UN... If the word is not listed below, simply remove the first 2 letters -<u>UN</u>- then look up the remainder of the word.

Example: unfavorable, '*un*' means "NOT/REVERSAL" then look up the base word 'favorable'.

KEY: HOW TO NAVIGATE GABBY'S

ab, PREFIX INDICATING "FROM/AWAY FROM" MOST OFTEN MODIFIES THE WORD

Row 1

aback, su
abak, aba
abal, able
abalishen, abolition
abanden, abandon
abandin, abandon
abandon, *, ned, ning, nment, LEFT ALL ALONE
abart, apart
abaut, about
abawt, about
abbreveashen, abbreviate(tion)
abbreviate, *, ed, ting, tion, TO SHORTEN/CONDENSE
abcerd, absent
abcerd, absurd
abcint, absent
abcurd, absurd
abdicate, *, ed, ting, RELINQUISH
abdikate, abdicate
abdiman, abdomen
abdomen, minn, minally, STOMACH AREA
abducate, abdicate
abduct, *, ted, tin, tee, tion, tor, KIDNAP
abdukate, abdicate
abdukt, abduct
abdumen, abdomen

STOP at end of this page. GO to top of Row 2

abeluty, ability
aberigene, aborigine
aberigine, aborigine
abess, abyss

Row 2

ability, ties, CAPACITY
abiss, abyss
abitchuery, obituary
abituary, ob
able, ly, CAP
ablederate, obliterate
abliveon, oblivion
abnormal, lly, lity, NOT TYPICAL/NATURAL
abnormil, abnorma
abnormul, abnorm
aboard, ONTO SOMETHING SUCH AS VESSEL/TRAIN/ ORGANIZATION (or see abort)
abof, above
abolesh, abolish
abolish, hes, hed, hment, END, TERMINATE
abomanable, abom nable
abolition, *, nist, SOMEONE WHO DESIRES TO END/ TERMINATE SOMETHING
abominable, HORRID
abominuble, abominable
aborchen, abortion
aborchun, abortion
abord, aboard / abort
aboregini, aborigine
aboreginul, aborigine(nal)
aborigine, *, nal, INDIGENOUS, NATIVE
aborijinul, aborigine(nal)

STOP at end of this page. GO to top of Row 3

about, APPROXIMATELY
above, OVER
abowt, about
abpropreate, appropriate

Row 3

abreveat, abreviate
abreveation, abreviate(tion)
abrev, n, abbreviate(tion)
abrid, CONDENSING/REWRITING
abrikot, april
abril, April
abroad, LEFT HOME TO GO OVERSEAS
abrod, abroad
abrol, April
abropt, abrupt
abrowtch, approach
abrul, April
abrupt, tly, tle s, SUDDEN
abscess, sses se
absence, *, NOT PRESENT
   absent(s)
absens, absence (absent(s))
absent, *, ly, te, teeism, INTENTIONALLY UNAVAILABLE (or see absence)
abserd, absur
abserdity, absurd(ity)
abserdly, abs rd(ly)
abses, absces
absilute, absolute
absilutly, absolute(ly)
absins, absence / absent(s)
absint, absent
absintee, absent(ee)
absird, absurd
absirdety, absurd(ity)
absirdly, absurd(ly)
absolute, tely, tion, tism, DEFINITELY
ab, *, bed, bing, bingly, bment, btion, bable, bent, bency, btive, COLLECT
abstain, *, ned, ning, nment, DENY

GO TO THE NEXT PAGE, ROW 4

---

n, abbreviate
abbreviate(tion)
, approximate
pproval

Row 4

"A"

a, PREFIX INDICATING "TO/TOWARDS/AT" MOST OFTEN MODIFIES THE WORD
ab, PREFIX INDICATING "FROM/AWAY FROM" MOST OFTEN MODIFIES THE WORD
aback, SURPRISED
abak, aback
abal, able
abalishen, abolition
abanden, abandon
abandin, abandon
abandon,*,ned,ning,nment, LEFT ALL ALONE
abart, apart
abaut, about
abawt, about
abbreveashen, abbreviate(tion)
abbreviate,*,ed,ting,tion, TO SHORTEN/CONDENSE
abcent, absent
abcerd, absurd
abcint, absent
abcurd, absurd
abdicate,*,ed,ting, RELINQUISH
abdikate, abdicate
abdiman, abdomen
abdomen,minal,minally,minous, STOMACH AREA
abducate, abdicate
abduct,*,ted,ting,tee,tion,tor, KIDNAP
abdukate, abdicate
abdukt, abduct
abdumen, abdomen
abedeinse, obedience
abedience, obedience
abel, able
abelete, ability
abeluty, ability
aberigene, aborigine
aberigine, aborigine
abess, abyss

abetchuery, obituary
abide,*,ed,ding,dingly,ddance, STAY
abidid, abide(d)
abil, able
ability,ties, CAPACITY
abiss, abyss
abitchuery, obituary
abituary, obituary
able,ly, CAPABLE
ablederate, obliterate
abliveon, oblivion
abnormal,lly,lity, NOT TYPICAL/NATURAL
abnormil, abnormal
abnormul, abnormal
aboard, ONTO SOMETHING SUCH AS VESSEL/TRAIN/ ORGANIZATION (or see abort)
abof, above
abolesh, abolish
abolish,hes,hed,hment, END, TERMINATE
abomanable, abominable
abolition,*,nist, SOMEONE WHO DESIRES TO END/ TERMINATE SOMETHING
abominable, HORRID
abominuble, abominable
aborchen, abortion
aborchun, abortion
abord, aboard /abort
aboregini, aborigine
aboreginul, aborigine(nal)
aborigine,*,nal, INDIGINEOUS, NATIVE
aborijinul, aborgine(nal)
aborshun, abortion
abort,*,ted,ting, STOP/QUIT ACTION (or see aboard)
abortion,*, CANCEL PROJECT/PREGNANCY
about, APPROXIMATELY
above, OVER
abowt, about
abpropreate, appropriate

abproximat, approximate
abpruval, approval
abrel, April
abreveashen, abbreviate(tion)
abreveat, abbreviate
abreveation, abbreviate(tion)
abreviate, abbreviate
abridged, SHORTEN BY CONDENSING/REWRITING
abrikot, apricot
abril, April
abroad, LEFT HOME TO GO OVERSEAS
abrod, abroad
abrol, April
abropt, abrupt
abrowtch, approach
abrul, April
abrupt,tly,tless, SUDDEN
abscess,sses,ssed, INFECTION IN THE BONE
absence,*, NOT PRESENT/AVAILABLE (or see absent(s))
absens, absence /absent(s)
absent,*,ly,tee,teeism, INTENTIONALLY UNAVAILABLE (or see absence)
abserd, absurd
abserdity, absurd(ity)
abserdly, absurd(ly)
abses, abscess
absilute, absolute
absilutly, absolute(ly)
absins, absence /absent(s)
absint, absent
absintee, absent(ee)
absird, absurd
absirdety, absurd(ity)
absirdly, absurd(ly)
absolute,tely,tion,tism, DEFINITELY
absorb,*,bed,bing,bingly,bment,btion,bable, bent,bency,btive, COLLECT
abstain,*,ned,ning,nment, DENY

abstane, abstain
abstract,*,ted,ting,tedly,tion,tional,tionist, tionism,tive, *APART FROM, THEORETICAL*
abstrakt, abstract
absulootly, absolute(ly)
absunt, absent
absurd,dly,dity,dities,dness, *CRAZY*
absurdety, absurd(ity)
abtetude, aptitude
abtitude, aptitude
abtumin, abdomen
abuf, above
abul, able
abulishen, abolition
abundance,*,nt,ntly, *PLENTY*
abundince, abundance
abundint, abundance(nt)
aburegene, aborigine
aburijene, aborigine
abuse, abuse
abuse,*,sed,sing,sive,siveness, *TREAT WRONGLY*
abusef, abuse(sive)
abusif, abuse(sive)
abuve, above
abuze, abuse
abyss,ssmal,ssmally, *CHASM, GREAT DEPTH*
abzent, absent
abzilute, absolute
abzint, absent
abzorb, absorb
abzuloot, absolute
abzulute, absolute
ac, *PREFIX INDICATING "TO/TOWARDS/AT" MOST OFTEN MODIFIES THE WORD*
academic,*,ia,cal,cally, *SCHOOLING*
academy,emies, *SPECIAL SCHOOL*
acadume, academy
acadintul, accident(al)
accedental, accident(al)

accelarate, accelerate
accelerate,*,ed,ting,tion,tor, *QUICKEN, FORCE TO GO/MOVE, GAS PEDAL*
accellrate, accelerate
accent,*, *TONES IN SPEECH, HIGHLIGHTS*
accentuate,*,ted,ting,tion, *EMPHASIZE*
accepshen, except(ion)
accept,*,ted,ting,tingly,tance,table,tably, tability, *APPROVE (or see except)*
acceptinse, accept(ance)
acceshen, access(ion)
accesorize, accessory(rize)
access,sses,ssed,ssing,ssible,ssion, *ENTER*
accessory,ries,rize,rizing, *ADDITIONAL*
accident,*,tal,tally, *INVOLUNTARILY*
acclimate,*,ed,ting,tion,tize, *ACCUSTOMED*
acomedashen, accommodate(tion)
accomodation, accommodate(tion)
accommodate,*,ting,tion,tive, *ASSIST*
accompany,nies,nied,nying,niment,nist, *GOES ALONG WITH*
accompeny, accompany
accomplise,*, *PARTICIPATED IN A CRIME*
accomplish,hes,hed,hing,hment, *GOAL/IDEA ACHIEVED*
accomudation, accommodate(tion)
account,*,ted,ting,tant,tance,tancy,table, tability, *RESPONSIBLE/LIABLE FOR*
accuate,*,ted,ting,tion, *INITIATE/BEGIN ACTIVITY*
accudental, accident(al)
accumulate,*,ted,ting,tion,tive,tively,tor, *TO GATHER GROW*
accurate,ely,eness,acy, *CORRECT*
accuse,*,sing,sal,sation,singly,ser, *CHARGE OR IMPLY*
accustom,med, *FAMILIAR, HABITUAL*
ace, *A SCORE IN GAME/ON DIE, TO WIN*
acebt, except /accept
acer, acre

acerens, occur(rrence)
ache,*,ed,hing,hy,hiness, *HURT*
acheeve, achieve
acheve, achieve
acid,*,dic, *CHEMICAL BALANCE*
achieve,*, ed,ving,vment,vable, *GAIN*
achin, action
achual, actual
acidemic, academic
acidental, accident(al)
ack, ache
acknowledge,*,ed,gement,ging,gingly, *RECOGNIZE*
acks, ax /ache(s)
ackses, access
ackses, access/ax(es)/axis
ackseshen, access(ion)
acksesory, accessory
acksglood, exclude
acksul, axil / axle
aclemate, acclimate
aclimate, acclimate
acne, *AFFLICTION OF THE SKIN*
acnolege, acknowledge
acomadashen, accommodate(tion)
acomidate, accommodate
acomidate, accommodate
acomidation, accommodate(tion)
acompany, accompany
acompined, accompany(nied)
acomplise, accomplise
acompuny, accompany
acomudashen, accommodate(tion)
acomudate, accommodate
acount, account
acoustic,*,cal,cally, *OF SOUND*
acquaint,*,ted, *ASSOCIATE WITH*
acquaintance,*,ed, *FAMILIAR*
acquire,*,red,ring,rement, *OBTAIN*
acquisition,*,ned, *ACQUIRED*

acquisitive,*,ely,eness, *READILY ACQUIRES*	**actual**,lly,lity,lization,lize, *REAL*	**add**,*,dded,dding,dditive,ddition,dditional,
acquit,*,tted,tting,ttal,ttance, *ABSOLVES, FREED*	actule, actual	dditionally,ddendum, *INCREASE, PLUS, MORE*
acquittal, *ABSOLVES, FREE OF JUDGEMENT*	acurit, accurate	*THAN BEFORE*
acqwaentense, acquaintance	activate, activate	**addict**,*,ted,ting,tion, *HABITUAL/OBSESSIVE USE*
acqwantinse, acquaintance	actuve, active	**additive**,*, *MORE, AN INCREASE, ADDITIONALLY*
acrabats, acrobat(s)	academic, academic	**address**,ses,sed,sing, *ROUTE/LOCATION OF*
acre,*,eage, *AMOUNT OF LAND*	acult, occult	adebt, adept
acro, *PREFIX INDICATING "END/BEGINNING/HEIGHT"*	acumpany, accompany	adec, attic / addict
MOST OFTEN MODIFIES THE WORD	acumpened, accompany(nied)	adek, attic / addict
acrobat,*,tic, *INVOLVES VARIOUS CONFIGURATIONS*	acupansy, occupancy	adekt, addict
acronym,*, *INITIALS, FIRST LETTER OF WORDS*	**acupuncture**,*,rist, *TREATMENT FOR HEALING BODY*	adelesinse, adolescence
across, *OVER*	acurate, accurate	ademant, adament
acsebt, except / accept	acurens, occur(rrence)	ademint, adament
acsecute, execute	acuse, accuse	ademunt, adament
acsel, excel/accel/axle	acustic, acoustic	adenaficashun, identification
acselurashen, accelerate(tion)	acustumed, accustom(ed)	**adept**,tly,tness, *SKILLFUL*
acsent, accent	**acute**,ely,eness, *SHARP*	adequace, adequacy
acsentric, eccentric	acwatic, aquatic	**adequacy**,cies, *ABILITY*
acsepshen, except(ion)	acwaynt, acquaint	**adequate**,ely,eness, *SUFFICIENT*
acsept, accept / except	acwayntense, acquaintance	adequise, adequacy
acsesurize, accessory(rize)	acwazition, acquisition	adequot, adequate
acshooul, actual	acwifalent, equivalent	adeshen, edition /add(ition)
acshual, actual	acwire, acquire	adetif, additive
acshun, action	acwit, acquit	adetion, edition /add(ition)
acsis, access/ax(es)/axis	acwuzeshun, acquisition	adetude, attitude
acsisory, accessory	acwyre, acquire	adgetate, agitate
acsite, excite	**ad**, *PREFIX INDICATING "TO/TOWARDS" MOST OFTEN*	adgitate, agitate
acskershin, excursion	*MODIFIES THE WORD, SHORT FOR ADVERTISEMENT*	adgrenalin, adrenaline
acspereanse, experience	*(or see "at /add /aid")*	adgudekashen, adjudicate(tion)
act,*,ted,tor,ting, *ACTION*	adacity, audacity	adgust, adjust
actevate, activate	adakit, etiquette	adhear, adhere
acteve, active	adam, atom	**adhere**,*,ed,ring,ent,ence, *STICKS TO*
actin, action	**adamant**,tly, *RELENTLESS*	**adhesion**, *STICKS TO*
action,*,nable,nably, *DOING, MOVEMENT*	**adapt**,*,ted,ting,tive,tively,tation,table,tability,	**adhesive**,*,eness, *STICKS TO*
activate,*,ed,ting,tion, *START*	ter,tor, *ADJUST*	adible, audible
active,ely,vity,veness,vant,vate,vist,vism,	adasity, audacity	adic, attic / addict
MOVING, CAUSE TO ACT	adatif, additive	adict, addict
actovate, activate		**adieu**,*, *GOOD-BYE*
actseed, exceed		adik, attic / addict

advice, RECOMMEND (or see advise)
advikete, advocate
advincher, adventure
advinshure, adventure
advinture, adventure
advirb, adverb
advirsare, adversary
advirse, adverse
advirsere, adversary
advise,*,ed,sing,edly,ement,sor,ser,sory,sable, sably,sability INFORM (or see advice)
advize, advise / advice
advizuble, advise(sable)
advocate,*,ed,ting,tory,acy,tion,tive,tor, SUPPORTER
advukate, advocate
advurb, adverb
advurcity, adverse(sity)
advurs, adverse
advursary, adversary
advursere, adversary
advursle, adverse(ly)
advursudy, adverse(sity)
advurtise, advertise
advurtize, advertise
adwenalin, adrenaline
ael, ail
aem, aim
aemeable, amiable
aengwish, anguish
aenjul, angel
aenkre, angry
aent, aunt / ant
aenus, anus
aenxiatee, anxiety
aepaloge, apology
aerial, BY AIRCRAFT
aero, PREFIX INDICATING "AIR" MOST OFTEN MODIFIES THE WORD

aerobic,*, OXYGEN EXERCISE
aerodynamic,*,cally, AIR MOTION
aerosol,*, COMPRESSED CONTENTS IN A CAN
aesthetic,*,cal,cally, PLEASING TO THE EYES
a∋t, eight/ ate
af, PREFIX INDICATING "TO/TOWARDS" MOST OFTEN MODIFIES THE WORD
afadavit, affidavit
afair, affair
afare, affair
afder, after
afect, effect / affect
afectation, affect(ation)
afection, affection
afed, aphid
afekshen, affection
afekshin, affection
afekt, effect / affect
afektashin, affect(ation)
afektation, affect(ation)
afektion, affection
afemanit, effeminate
afend, offend
afenity, affinity
afense, offense
afensef, offense(sive)
afensif, offense(sive)
afer, affair / ever
afes, office
afeser, office(r)
afeshul, official
afet, aphid
affair, *, BUSINESS
affare, affair
affect,*,ted,ting,ter,tation,tational,tive, CAUSE SOMETHING TO HAPPEN, TRYING TO IMPRESS, PRETENTIOUS (USED AS A VERB) (or see effect)
affection,*,nate,nately,nateness, TO EXPRESS FONDNESS

afeleat, affiliate
afermative, affirm(ative)
affinity, affinity
affinity,*,tive, ATTRACTION
afflict,*,ted,tion,ter,tively, DISTRESS
affidavit,* , LEGALLY BINDING STATEMENT
affiliate,*,ed,ting,tion, ASSOCIATED WITH
affirm,*,med,ming,mative,mation, SUPPORT WITH APPROVAL
affluence,*,ed, ABUNDANCE
affluent,uently, ABUNDANCE
afford,*,ded,dance,dable,dability, SPARE
affront,*,ted,ting, CONFRONT
afie, aphid
afileat, affiliate
afimanit, effeminate
afinity, affinity
afinse, offense
afinsef, offense(sive)
afirm, affirm
afis, office
afiser, office(r)
afishensy, efficiency
afishinsy, efficiency
afishul, official
afishuly, official(lly)
afit, aphid
aflict, afflict
aflikt, afflict
afloat, FLOATING
aflot, afloat
afluent, affluent
afluense, affluence
afluinse, affluence
aford, afford
aforduble, afford(able)
afortuble, afford(able)
afore, PREFIX INDICATING "BEFORE" MOST OFTEN MODIFIES THE WORD

afraid, *FEARFUL*
afrayed, afraid
afrebaudy, every(body)
afrewar, every(where)
afrewer, every(where)
afront, affront
afrunt, affront
after, *PREFIX INDICATING "AFTER" MOST OFTEN*
   MODIFIES THE WORD
after,rward, *FOLLOWING*
aftur, after
afud, aphid
afudavit, affidavit
afurmative, affirm(ative)
afus, office
afuser, office(r)
afut, afoot
ag, agri, agro, *PREFIX INDICATING "SOIL/FIELD"*
   MOST OFTEN MODIFIES THE WORD
ag, age / egg
again, *REPEAT*
against, *TOWARD, FACING, OPPOSITE OF FLOW*
agany, agony
agasent, adjacent
agasint, adjacent
agd, age(d)
age,*,ed,ging,eless, *MEASURE OF TIME*
agen, again /age(ging)
agenda,*, *SCHEDULE/FORMAT/PLAN*
agene, agony
agenst, against
agent,*,ncy, *CATALYST, INTRODUCED TO PERFORM A*
   TASK
agenta, agenda
ageny, agony
agetat, agitate
agetiv, adjective
agern, adjourn
agewdicate, adjudicate

aggravate,*,ed,ting,tingly, *AGITATE*
aggravation, *AGITATE*
aggresef, aggressive
aggresefly, aggressive(ly)
aggreshen, aggression
aggresive, aggressive
aggression,*, *OFFENSIVE/ROUGH/FORCEFUL*
aggressive,ely,eness,ssor, *OFFENSIVE*
aggretion, aggression
agile,lity,eness, *LIMBER, FLEXIBLE*
aginda, agenda
aginst, against
agint, agent
aginy, agony
agirn, adjourn
agitate,ed,ting,tor,tion,tive,edly, *AROUSE,*
   AGGRAVATE, AGGRESSIVE STIMULATION
ago, *PAST*
agony,nies,nize,nized,nizing, *SUFFER*
agorn, adjourn
agravashen, aggravation
agravate, aggravate
agravation, aggravation
agrecultsher, agriculture
agree,*,eed,eeing,eement,eeable,eeably,
   CONSENT TO
agrekulcher, agriculture
agrenalin, adrenaline
agresef, aggressive
agreshen, aggression
agresif, aggressive
agresifle, aggressive(ly)
agresion, aggression
agresiv, aggressive
agression, aggression
agressive, aggressive
agressive, aggressive
agretion, aggression
agricultcher, agriculture
agriculture,*,ral,rist,ralist, *FARMING*

agrikultcher, agriculture
agruvashen, aggravation
agruvate, aggravate
agruvate, aggravate
agruvation, aggravation
agsberament, experiment
agsblane, explain
agsebt, except / accept
agseed, exceed
agsept, except / accept
agsersize, exercise
agsert, exert
agspel, expel
agsplan, explain
agsplisit, explicit
agstend, extend
agstereor, exterior
agsternal, external
agstinkt, extinct
agstreem, extreme
agsturnal, external
agucolture, agriculture
agudecate, adjudicate
agudikate, adjudicate
agul, agile
agune, agony
agunt, agent
aguny, agony
agust, adjust /August
agustible, adjust(able)
agutate, agitate
agutev, adjective
agzemt, exempt
ahead, *COMING UP*
ahed, ahead
aid,*,ding, *HELP*
ail,*,ling,lmnet, *SICK/NOT WELL* (or see ale)
aile, aisle

aim, *,med,ming,mless,mlessly,mlessness,
  FOCUS ON A POINT, DIRECT ATTENTION
air, *,red,ring,rless, *SPACE, A GAS/AURA* (or see
  are/heir/err)
airborne, *OFF THE GROUND*
airea, area
airloom, heirloom
airobic, aerobic
airodynamic, aerodynamic
airoganse, arrogance
airport, *,*, *AIRCRAFT BASE*
aisle, *,ed, *PASSAGEWAY*
ait, eight / ate
aj, age / edge
ajasent, adjacent
ajasint, adjacent
ajative, adjective
aje, age
ajenda, agenda
ajent, agent
ajern, adjourn
ajetate, agitate
ajewdicat, adjudicate
ajewdikashen, adjudicate(tion)
ajil, agile
ajilety, agile(lity)
ajinda, agenda
ajint, agent
ajitate, agitate
ajodikate, adjudicate
ajorn, adjourn
ajourn, adjourn
ajrenalin, adrenaline
ajrenulin, adrenaline
ajudikate, adjudicate
ajul, agile
ajunt, agent
ajurn, adjourn
ajust, adjust

ajustible, adjust(able)
ajutev, adjective
ak, ache
akademe, academy
akademic, academic
akadume, academy
akamidate, accommodate
akashenul, occasion(al)
akcelaration, accelerate(tion)
akchen, action
akchuel, actual
akchun, action
akedemik, academic
aker, acre
akerens, occur(rrence)
akewpunksher, acupuncture
akews, accuse
akewsashen, accuse(sation)
akidemic, academic
aklemate, acclimate
aklumate, acclimate
aknaulig, acknowledge
akne, acne
aknolege, acknowledge
akod, echo(ed)
akomedashen, accommodate(tion)
akomidate, accommodate
akomidation, accommodate(tion)
akomodate, accommodate
akompaned, accompany(nied)
akompeny, accompany
akomplis, accomplise
akomudate, accommodate
akonume, economy
akorinse, occur(rrence)
akount, account
akr, acre
akrabatek, acrobat(ic)
akree, agree

akronem, acronym
akross, across
aks, ax /ache(s)
aksald, excel(lled) /accel(lled)
akschange, exchange
aksd, ax(ed)
aksedent, accident
akseed, exceed
aksel, excel/ accel/ axle
akselarashen, accelerate(tion)
akselarate, accelerate
akselaratur, accelerate(tor)
akseld, excel(lled) /accel(lled)
akselerate, accelerate
akselirashen, accelerate(tion)
akseluratur, accelerate(tor)
aksent, accent
aksentric, eccentric
aksentuate, accentuate
aksepshen, except(ion)
aksept, accept / except
akseptense, accept(ance)
akseptid, accept(ed)
akseptinse, accept(ance)
akses, access/ ax(es)/ axis
aksesares, accessory(ries)
aksesarize, accessory(rize)
aksesd, access(ed)
aksesible, access(ible)
aksesirize, accessory(rize)
aksesory, accessory
aksesuble, access(ible)
aksesurize, accessory(rize)
aksglude, exclude
aksglute, exclude
akshen, action
akshin, action
akshual, actual
akshuat, actuate

alege, allege
alegense, allegiance
alein, alien
aleinashen, alien(ation)
aleinate, alien(ate)
alejanse, allegiance
alekate, allocate
alekshen, elect(ion)
alekt, elect
alektrician, electrician
alektrik, electric
alektrishen, electrician
alemenade, eliminate
alemony, alimony
aleon, alien
alergic, allergy
alerges, allergy(gies)
alert,*,ted,ting,tness, *NOTIFY*
alesit, illicit
aleun, alien
aleunashen, alien(ation)
aleunate, alien(ate)
aleus, alias
alev, olive
aleveate, alleviate
aleven, eleven
aleviate, alleviate
alevin, eleven
alevinth, eleven(th)
alevon, eleven
aley, alley
alf, elf
alfabedikul, alphabet(ical)
alfabet, alphabet
alfibetize, alphabet(ize)
alfubedikul, alphabet(ical)
alfubutize, alphabet(ize)
algae, *WATER ORGANISM*
algebra,aic,aical,aically, *TYPE OF MATH*

algubra, algebra
ali, ally
alians, alliance
alias,ses, *ANOTHER NAME*
alibi,*, *EXCUSE*
alicate, allocate
alid, ally(lied)
aliderate, illiterate
alien,*,nate,nation,nable, *FOREIGNER* (or see alliance)
alienashen, alien(ation)
alif, olive
aligater, alligator
aligatur, alligator
align,*,ned,ning,nment, *STRAIGHTEN*
alikate, allocate
alike, *SIMILAR*
alimenate, eliminate
alimony, *MONETARY ALLOWANCE AFTER DIVORCE*
aline, align
alinment, align(ment)
alirt, alert
alis, ally(lies)
alisit, illicit
aliterate, illiterate
alunate, alien(ate)
alive, *NOT DEAD, HAS SPIRIT*
alja, algae
aljebra, algebra
aljibra, algebra
alk, elk
alkali,ine,inity,loid, *CHEMICAL BALANCE*
alkohol, alcohol
alkove, alcove
alkuhol, alcohol
all, *EVERYTHING* (or see ail /ale /awl)
allege,*,ed,ging,edly, *ASSERT*
allegiance,nt, *LOYALTY*

allelo, alleo, allo, *PREFIX INDICATING "OTHER/ALTERNATE" MOST OFTEN MODIFIES THE WORD*
allergy,gies, *SENSITIVE/REACTION TO*
allergic, *SENSITIVE/REACTION TO*
alleviate,*,ed,ting,tion,tive,tory, *RELIEVE*
alley,*,yway, *PASSAGEWAY*
alliance,*,ied,ies, *JOIN*
alligator,*, *LARGE REPTILE*
allocate,*,ed,tion, *ASSIGN*
allow,*,ed,wing,wable, *PERMIT*
allowance,*, *PERMITTED, ALLOTTED*
alloy,*, *METALS TOGETHER*
alltogether, altogether
allude,*,ed,ding,usion,usive, *CASUALLY MAKE REFERENCE TO* (or see elude)
allusion,ive, *TO MENTION INDIRECTLY/CASUALLY* (or see elusion or illusion)
allusive, *TO MENTION INDIRECTLY/CASUALLY* (or see elusive)
allure,*,ed,ring,ement,ringly, *TEMPT*
ally,llies,llied,llying, *UNITED*
almanac,*, *BOOK WITH INFORMATION AS IT RELATES TO SPACE AND STARS*
alminak, almanac
almonak, almanac
almost, *CLOSE*
almozt, almost
almunak, almanac
alokate, allocate
alone, *NO ONE, NOTHING ELSE*
aloore, allure
aloosuf, allude(usive) /elude(usive)
alosiv, allude(usive) /elude(usive)
alow, allow
alowins, allowance
alowy, alloy
aloy, alloy
alphabet,tic,tical,tize,tizes,tized,tizing,tization,tizer, *ENGLISH LETTERS TO FORM WORDS*

alphebetical, alphabet(ical)
alphubedikul, alphabet(ical)
already, BY THIS TIME
also, INCLUDED, ALONG WITH
alt, alti, alto, PREFIX INDICATING "HIGH" MOST
   OFTEN MODIFIES THE WORD
altar,*, PLATFORM FOR WORSHIP (or see alter/alder)
alter,*,res,red,ring,ration, TO SLIGHTLY CHANGE/
   MODIFY (or see alder or altar)
alterashen, alter(ation)
alternate,*,ely,ting,tely,tion,tive,tively, TO GO
   BACK AND FORTH BETWEEN, ROTATE
alternative,*,ely, CHOICES/OPTIONS
alternutiv, alternative
altetude, altitude
although, EVEN THOUGH
altir, alder /altar /alter
altirashen, alter(ation)
altiration, alter(ation)
altird, alter(ed)
altirnetly, alternate(ly)
altirnitef, alternative
altirnutiv, alternative
altitude,*, HEIGHT
altogether, IN ONE PLACE
altur, alder /altar /alter
alturashen, alter(ation)
alturation, alter(ation)
alturd, alter(ed)
alturnetly, alternate(ly)
alturnutiv, alternative
altwogether, altogether
aluby, alibi
alucate, allocate
alude, elude
alufent, elephant
alugable, eligible
alujen, illusion /allusion /elusion
alukate, allocate

alumenum, aluminum
aluminate, illuminate
aluminum, A METAL
alumony, alimony
alumunum, aluminum
alure, allure
alurgik, allergic
alurjik, allergic
alurt, alert
alusif, allude(usive) /elude(usive)
alusion, allude(usion) /illusion /elude(usion)
alusov, allude(usive) /elude(usive)
aluv, olive
always, FOREVER (or see aim)
alwaz, always
aly, ally
alyan, alien
alyke, alike
am, PRESENT TENSE OF "BE" (or see aim)
amachur, amateur
amaculet, immaculate
amakewlit, immaculate
amakulit, immaculate
amasher, amateur
amateur,*,rish,rishly, NONPROFESSIONAL
amatur, amateur
amaunt, amount
amawntuble, amount(able)
amaze,*,ed,edly,zing,zingly,ement, IMPRESS
ambechis, ambitious
ambeshun, ambition
ambeshusnes, ambitious(ness)
ambetious, ambitious
ambi, PREFIX INDICATING "BOTH/AROUND" MOST
   OFTEN MODIFIES THE WORD
ambichen, ambition
ambiches, ambitious
ambishisnes, ambitious(ness)
ambishun, ambition

ambishus, ambitious
ambishusnes, ambitious(ness)
ambition,*, DESIRE TO ACHIEVE A GOAL
ambitious, ambitious
ambitious,sly,sness, STRIVING DILIGENTLY
   TOWARDS A GOAL
amblanse, ambulance
amblins, ambulance
ambolanse, ambulance
amboosh, ambush
amboshd, ambush(ed)
ambulance,*,atory, RESCUE VEHICLE
ambulence, ambulance
ambush,hes,hed,ment, ENTRAP
ambushd, ambush(ed)
ambutashen, amputate(tion)
ame, aim
ameable, amiable
ameba, amoeba
amechur, amateur
amedeat, immediate
ameds, emit /omit
ameible, amiable(ly)
amekibul, amicable
amekuble, amicable
amend,*,ded,ding,dment,dable,datory, REPAIR
amense, immense
amenus, ominous
amepa, amoeba
amergensee, emergency
amerse, immerse
ameshen, omission /emission
ameteut, immediate
amethist, amethyst
amethyst,*, PURPLE QUARTZ
amertize, amortize
ameuble, amiable /amiable(ly)
amewsd, amuse(d)
amewsmint, amuse(ment)

amiable,eness,ly,bility, GOOD-NATURED
amicable,ly, bility, FRIENDLY
amichure, amateur
amikable, amicable
amikuble, amicable
amind, amend
amindment, amend(ment)
aminse, immense
aminus, ominous
amirse, immerse
amishen, omission /emission
amit, emit /omit
amithist, amethyst
amitz, emit /omit
amiuble, amiable(ly)
ammonea, ammonia
ammonia,ic, A GAS
amne, omni
amnevore, omnivore
amnivore, omnivore
amochure, amateur
amoeba,*,bic, ANIMAL
among,gst, IN THE MIDST OF, WITH OTHERS
amonia, ammonia
amonkst, among(st)
amonya, ammonia
amortize,*,zable,tization, IN LOAN CALCULATION
amount,*,ted,ting,table, SUM
amownt, amount
ampetate, amputate
ampeutashen, amputate(tion)
ampewtation, amputate(tion)
amphi, PREFIX INDICATING "BOTH/AROUND" MOST OFTEN MODIFIES THE WORD
ampition, ambition
amplafikashen, amplify(fication)
amplefy, amplify
amplifucation, amplify(fication)

amplify,fies,fied,fier,ying,ficate,fication, MAGNIFY SOUND
amplufikashen, amplify(fication)
amplufy, amplify
amputashen, amputate(tion)
amputate,*,ed,ting,tion,tee, REMOVE LIMB FROM MAIN TORSO
amrold, emerald
amruld, emerald
amune, immune
amunety, immune(nity)
amung, among
amunity, immune(nity)
amunkst, among(st)
amunxt, among(st)
amurgensee, emergency
amurse, immerse
amuse,*,ed,sing,ement, ENTERTAIN
amuthist, amethyst
amuze, amuse
amuzment, amuse(ment)
amythest, amethyst
an, PREFIX INDICATING "TO/TOWARDS" MOST OFTEN MODIFIES THE WORD
ana, PREFIX INDICATING "UP/BACK/AGAIN" MOST OFTEN MODIFIES THE WORD
anadot, anecdote
anal,lly, NEAR/INVOLVING THE ANUS (or see annul)
analesis, analysis
analigy, analogy
analize, analyze
analog,gous,gously, TYPE OF WAVE/SOUND
analogy,gies,gous,gously, LIKENESS
analysis, BREAKDOWN TO STUDY
analyst, PERSON WHO STUDIES DETAILS
analyze,*,ed,zing,er, STRICT EXAMINATION/ STUDY
anamashen, animate(tion)
anamation, animate(tion)
anamulistik, animal(istic)

anarchy,hies,hism,hist,histic,hic,hical,hically, NO GOVERNMENT
anarkey, anarchy
anasthesia, anesthesia
anatomy,mic,mical,mically, COMPLETE STRUCTURE OF A BODY
anbroder, embroider
ancestor,*,ry,tral,trally, LINEAGE
anchor,*,red,ring,raged, STABILITY
ancient,*,tness, OLD, GREAT IN AGE
ancorij, encourage /anchor(age)
and, WORD USED AS A CONJUNCTION, THIS PLUS THAT, ALSO, INCLUDING (or see ant /aunt /end)
andanger, endanger
andefir, endeavor
andevur, endeavor
andlis, endless
andure, endure
ane, any
anebody, anybody
anecdote,*, ,tal, STORY (or see antidote)
anedotul, anecdote(tal)
anedot, anecdote /antidote
anekdote, anecdote
anel, anal /annul
anelog, analog
anelyze, analyze
anemal, animal
anemashen, animate(tion)
anemate, animate
anemation, animate(tion)
aneme, enemy
anemek, anemic
anemia, BLOOD HAS A DEFICIENCY/NEED (or see enema or enigma)
anemic,cally, BLOOD HAS A DEFICIENCY/NEED
anemul, animal
anemulestik, animal(istic)
anerjetek, eneroetic

anewity, annuity
anes, anus
aneshil, initial
anesthesia, *AN ANASTHETIC*
anesthetic,*,cally,ist, *PAIN KILLER*
anesthetize,*,ed,zing, *TO DULL PAIN WITH DRUG*
anesthezia, anesthesia
anesthutize, anesthetize
anew, *FRESH/NEW START*
anezthetic, anesthetic
anforse, enforce
angaje, engage
angel,*,lic, *SPIRITUAL BEING* (or see angle)
angelek, angel(ic)
anger,*,red,gry, *MAD*
angil, angel /angle
angir, anger
angle,*,ed,ling,er, *HINT,SLANT/TILT* (or see angel)
angrafe, engrave
angrave, engrave
angre, angry
angrele, angrily
angreust, angry(riest)
angri, angry
angrily,iness, *OF ANGER*
angryest, angry(riest)
angsiute, anxiety
anguish,ed,hed,hing, *SORROW*
angul, angle /angel
angwish, anguish
angziute, anxiety
anialate, annihilate
anidot, anecdote /antidote
anidotul, antidote
anikdote, anecdote(tal)
anil, anal /annul
anilate, annihilate

anilize, analyze
anilog, analog
anilyze, analyze
animal,*,listic, *NOT HUMAN*
animashen, animate(tion)
animate,*,ed,ting,tion, *LIVELY, AS IF REAL*
animea, anemia /enema
animul, animal
animulistek, animal(istic)
anis, anus
anishal, initial
anisthedek, anesthetic
anisthetic, anesthetic
anisthezia, anesthesia
anitiate, initiate
aniulate, annihilate
anjekshen, inject(ion)
anjel, angel
anjelik, angel(ic)
anjil, angel
anjoiment, enjoy(ment)
anjul, angel
anker, anchor
ankureg, anchor(age)
ankor, anchor
ankoreg, encourage /anchor(age)
ankreust, angry(riest)
ankry, angry
ankurig, encourage /anchor(age)
anlarje, enlarge
anliten, enlighten
anmal, animal
annihilate,*,ed,tion,tor, *DESTROY*
announce,*,ed,cing,ement,er, *DECLARE*
annoy,*,yed,ying,yance, *IRRITATE*
annoyents, annoy(ance)
annual,*,lly,lize, *YEARLY*
annuely, annual(lly)
annuity,ties, *ANNUAL STIPEND/PAYMENT*

annul,led,lment, *VOID, REVOKE* (or see anal)
anoed, annoy(ed)
anoent, anoint
anogreashen, inaugurate(tion)
anogreation, inaugurate(tion)
anoint,*,ted, *TO SELECT/CONSECRATE*
anonemous, anonymous
anonemusly, anonymous(ly)
anonimous, anonymous
anonimusly, anonymous(ly)
anonseate, enunciate
anonymous,sly,sness,mity, *NOT KNOWN*
anorgee, energy
anorgetek, energetic
anorkey, anarchy
anormis, enormous
anormus, enormous
another, *ADDITIONAL*
anothir, another
anounce, announce
anounse, announce
anowe, annoy
anownse, announce
anoy, annoy
anoyance, annoy(ance)
anoyd, annoy(ed)
anrich, enrich
anrol, enroll
anrold, enroll(ed)
anser, answer
anseruble, answer(able)
ansestor, ancestor
anshent, ancient
anshunt, ancient
ansiklopedea, encyclopedia
ansir, answer
ansistor, ancestor
ansur, answer
ansuruble, answer(able)

answer,*,red,ring,rable,rably, SOLUTION
ant,*, SMALL SIX-LEGGED INSECT (or see and/aunt)
antagonize,*,ist,istic,istically, ENEMY/OPPOSITION
ante, PREFIX INDICATING "BEFORE/PRECEDING" MOST
   OFTEN MODIFIES THE WORD
ante,*, POKER EXPRESSION, TO PRECEDE/COME
   BEFORE (or see aunt(ie) or anti)
antebiotik, antibiotic
antebyotik, antibiotic
antecepate, anticipate
antefreeze, antifreeze
antefreze, antifreeze
antehistamene, antihistamine
antehistumene, antihistamine
anteke, antique
antekwedy, antique(uity)
antekwity, antique(uity)
antelope,*, MAMMAL
antena, antenna
antenna, DEVICE TO ATTRACT SIGNALS/FREQUENCY
antesapashen, anticipate(tion)
antesepate, anticipate
antesupation, anticipate(tion)
anthem,*, SONG
anthim, anthem
anti, OPPOSE/DISAGREE (or see aunt(ie) /ante)
anti, PREFIX INDICATING "AGAINST" MOST OFTEN
   MODIFIES THE WORD
antibiotic,*,cally, MANMADE CHEMICAL
anticepate, anticipate
anticipate,*,ed,ting,tion,tive,tory, EXPECT
antidote,*,tal,tally, USED TO REVERSE EFFECTS OF
   POISON (or see anecdote)
antifreeze, SUBSTANCE TO PREVENT FREEZING
antihistamine, INACTIVATES HISTAMINE
antikwedy, antique(uity)
antilope, antelope
antina, antenna
antique,*,ed,ely,uity,uate,uated, ANCIENT

antiquedy, antique(uity)
antisapashen, anticipate(tion)
antisupation, anticipate(tion)
antonym,*,mic,mous, WORDS WITH OPPOSITE
   MEANINGS
antorse, endorse /indoors
antser, answer
antulope, antelope
anu, anew
anual, annual
anuale, annual(lly)
anudot, anecdote
anuel, annual
anuety, annuity
anuile, annual(lly)
anul, annul
anulise, analyze
anulyze, analyze
anumashen, animate(tion)
anumate, animate
anumation, animate(tion)
anumel, animal
anumilestik, animal(istic)
anunseade, enunciate
anurgee, energy
anurjetek, energetic
anus, LOWER ORIFICE
anustheshu, anesthesia
anusthetik, anesthetic
anuzthetek, anesthetic
anvilope, envelope
anvirunmint, environment
anvy, envy
anwritch, enrich
anxiety,ties,ious,iously,iousness, UNEASINESS
any,ybody,yhow,ymore,yone,ything,yway,
   ywhere,ytime, SOME AT RANDOM
anybody,dies, ANY PERSON

anyual, annual
aoch, ouch
ap, PREFIX INDICATING "TO/TOWARDS" MOST OFTEN
   MOST OFTEN MODIFIES THE WORD
apademic, epidemic
apaloge, apology
aparatus, apparatus
apareshun, apparition
aparint, apparent
aparition, apparition
apart, MAKE INTO SEPARATE PIECES
apartment,*, ROOMS IN DWELLING
apartmint, apartment
apasenter, epicenter
apathy, INDIFFERENT, NO EMOTION
apathetic,cal, INDIFFERENT, NO EMOTION
apatight, appetite
apatit, appetite
apdoman, abdomen
apdukt, abduct
apduman, abdomen
apeal, appeal
apearance, appearance
apeel, appeal
apel, apple
apendektumy, appendectomy
apenyun, opinion
aperal, apparel
aperant, apparent
aperatus, apparatus
aperishen, apparition
aperition, apparition
aperul, apparel
apesode, episode
apethetik, apathetic
apetight, appetite
apetit, appetite
aphed, aphid
aphid,*, INSECT

apidemic, epidemic	apoentment, appointment	**appreciate**,*,ed,ting,tion,tory,tive,able,*GRATEFUL*
apindectemy, appendectomy	apoint, appoint	**apprehend**,*,ded,ding,nsive,nsively,nsion,
apineun, opinion	apointment, appointment	nsible,nsibly, *TO SEIZE, BE CAUTIOUS*
apinyun, opinion	apol, apple	**apprentice**,*,ed,cing,eship *LEARNER/IN TRAINING*
apiretion, apparition	apolegize, apology(gize)	appresif, oppress(ive)
apithetik, apathetic	**apology**,gies,gize,gizes,gized,gizing,getic, *ASK*	appripo, apropos
apitite, appetite	*FORGIVENESS*	**approach**,hes,hed,hing, *ADVANCE TOWARDS,*
aplakashen, application	apoluge, apology	*NEARING*
aplaud, applaud	apologize, apology(gize)	appropo, apropos
aple, apple	aponent, opponent	**appropriate**,*,ted,ting,ely,eness, *PROPER TO,*
aplecable, applicable	aponit, appoint	*BELONGS ALONG WITH, IN CHARACTER WITH*
aplecant, applicant	apose, oppose	**approve**,*,ed,ving,val,vable,vingly, *ACCEPTANCE*
aplecator, application	**apostrophe**,*, , *SYMBOL IN ENGLISH LANGUAGE*	*COMMENDATION*
aplekant, applicant	aposum, opossum	**approximate**,ed,ely,ting,tion, *AROUND/SOMEWHAT*
aplekashen, application	apoynt, appoint	apprupo, apropos
aplekator, applicator	apoze, oppose	apracot, apricot
aplekuble, applicable	**apparatus**,ses, *EQUIPMENT*	appraisal, appraisal
apli, apply	**apparel**, *CLOTHING*	apral, April
aplianse, appliance	**apparent**,tly, *CLEAR*	aprapo, apropos
aplicable, applicable	**apparition**,*, *SPIRIT*	apprazul, appraisal
aplicant, applicant	**appeal**,*,led,ling,lingly,lable, *CALL FOR MERCY,*	apreciate, appreciate
aplicator, applicator	*VIEW FAVORABLY*	aprehend, apprehend
aplid, apply(lied)	**appearance**,*, , *BECOME VISIBLE*	aprehind, apprehend
apliderate, obliterate	**appendectomy**,mies, *REMOVE APPENDIX FROM BODY*	aprekot, apricot
aplikashen, application	**appetite**,*,ising,izer, *DESIRE, A HUNGER, A FOOD*	aprel, April
aplikation, application	**applaud**,*,ded,ding,use,, *USE HANDS TO CLAP*	apren, apron
aplikator, applicator	**applause**, *ACCLAIM, USE HANDS TO CLAP*	aprentis, apprentice
aplikuble, applicable	**apple**,*, *FRUIT*	apres, oppress
apliveon, oblivion	**appliance**,*, *SPECIALIZED TOOL/MACHINE TO*	apresheate, appreciate
aplod, applaud	*PERFORM SPECIFIC TASKS*	appreshen, oppress(ion)
aplos, applause	**applicable**,eness,ly, *RELEVANT, USEFUL*	apresif, oppress(ive)
aplukant, applicant	**applicant**,*, *CANDIDATE FOR EMPLOYMENT*	**apricot**,*, *FRUIT*
aplukashen, application	**application**,*, *FORM TO APPLY FOR WORK*	aprikot, apricot
aplukation, application	**applicator**,*,ting, *USED TO APPLY SOMETHING*	**April**, *MONTH OF THE YEAR*
aplukator, applicator	**apply**,lies,lied,lying, *PUT ON*	aprin, apron
aply, apply	**appoint**,*,ted,ting,tee, *ASSIGN, DESIGNATE*	aprintise, apprentice
apodimic, epidemic	**appointment**,*, *AN ASSIGNED TIME*	apripo, apropos
apoent, appoint	**appraisal**,*,ser,sement, *EVALUATION*	aproach, approach
	apprapo, apropos	aproch, approach

aprol, April
apron,*, *CLOTHING PROTECTOR*
apropos, *SUITABLE IN A PARTICULAR SITUATION/TIME*
apropreate, appropriate
appropriate, appropriate
aprotch, approach
aproval, approval
aproxemat, approximate
aproxemation, approximate(tion)
aproximate, approximate
aproximation, approximate(tion)
apruful, approval
aprul, April
aprupo, apropos
apruvel, approval
apsalutly, absolute(ly)
apsens, absence / absent(s)
apsent, absent
apsentee, absent(ee)
apserd, absurd
apserdle, absurd(ly)
apshen, option
apsiloot, absolute
apsins, absence / absent(s)
apsintee, absent(ee)
apsird, absurd
apsoloot, absolute
apsolute, absolute
apsorb, absorb
apstane, abstain
apstract, abstract
apstrukshen, abstract(ion)/obstruct(ion)
apsulootly, absolute(ly)
apsulute, absolute
apsulutly, absolute(ly)
apsurd, absurd
apsurdly, absurd(ly)
aptetood, aptitude
aptetude, aptitude

aptikate, abdicate
aptimen, abdomen
aptitewd, aptitude
aptitude,*,dinal,dability, *TENDENCY TOWARDS,*
        AFFINITY FOR
aptomen, abdomen
aptumen, abdomen
apul, apple
aputhetik, apathetic
aputit, appetite
apuzit, oppose(site)
apzorb, absorb
aqaint, acquaint
aqefir, aquifer
aqire, acquire
aqua,ueous, *WATER, TO DO WITH WATER, A COLOR*
aquaduct, aqueduct
aquaent, acquaint
aquafer, aquifer
aquaint, acquaint
aquareum, aquarium
aquarium,*, *FISH CONTAINER*
aquatic,*, *IN WATER*
aqueduct,*, *WATER CHANNEL*
aqufer, aquifer
aquifer,*,rous, *PROVIDES WATER*
aquipd, equip(pped)
aquivalint, equivalent
aqute, acute
aqwazitun, acquisition
aqwire, acquire
aqwit, acquit
aqwuzishen, acquisition
ar, are /heir /air /our /hour
ara, array /aura
arachnid,*,noid, *WINGLESS ANTHROPODS*
aradekate, eradicate
aradic, erratic /erotic
aradikashen, eradicate(tion)

aradikate, eradicate
araign, arraign
araignment, arraign(ment)
arain, arraign
arainment, arraign(ment)
arakned, arachnid
arange, arrange
arangment, arrange(ment)
aranj, arrange
aranment, arraign(ment)
arase, erase
arashinal, irrational
aratic, erratic
araudik, erotic
aray, array
arayn, arraign
araze, erase
arbetrate, arbitrate
arbitrate,*,ed,ting,al,ary,arily,ariness,ament,
        tion,tive,tor, *DETERMINE*
arborne, airborne
arbutrashen, arbitrate(tion)
arc,*, *PART OF A CURVE* (or see ark or arch)
arcade,*,dia, *OF GAMES OR ARCHED PASSAGEWAY*
arch, *PREFIX INDICATING "CHIEF/ BEGINNING" MOST*
        OFTEN MODIFIES THE WORD
arch,hes,hed,hing, *CURVED BEND* (or see ark/arc)
archaek, archaic
archaic, *OLD-FASHIONED, ANCIENT*
archeology,gist,gical, *STUDY OF PEOPLE*
archer,*,ry, *ONE WHO USES BOWS AND ARROWS*
archetekt, architect
archiology, archeology
archir, archer
architect,*,ture,tural, *BUILDER*
archive,*,val,vist, *PLACE OF PUBLIC RECORDS*
archur, archer
arctic, *NORTH POLE*
ardefishal, artificial

arku, argue
arkumint, argument
arkutekshur, architect(ure)
arkyve, archive
arloom, heirloom
arm,*,med,ming,mament, *APPENDAGE ON UPPER TORSO, TO TAKE UP WEAPONS*
arme, army
armes, army(mies)
armonica, harmonica
army,mies, *MANY BODIES*
arn, iron
arnamint, ornament
arnge, orange
arnje, orange
arnt, aren't
arnument, ornament
aro, arrow
aroara, aurora
arobek, aerobic
arobik, aerobic
arochun, erosion
arode, erode
arodik, erotic
arodynamic, aerodynamic
aroganse, arrogance
arogate, irrigate
arogent, arrogance(nt)
arogint, arrogance(nt)
aroma,*,atic,tize, *ODOR, SMELL*
aromadek, aroma(tic)
arond, errand
aronic, ironic
aror, error
arora, aurora
aroshen, erosion
aroshin, erosion
around, *HERE AND THERE*

argeumint, argument
argew, argue
argkeumint, argument
argue,*,ed,uing,uable,uably, *DEBATE, DISCUSS*
argument,*,tation,tative,tum, *DEBATE, DISCUSS*
arguous, arduous
arguwus, arduous
aria, area
arid,dity, *PARCHED*
arie, awry
arife, arrive
ariful, arrive(val)
arigate, irrigate
arigenashen, originate(tion)
ariginul, origin(al)
arijinul, origin(al)
arind, errand
arint, aren't
ariplasible, irreplacable
arir, error
arisol, aerosol
aristocrat,*,tic,acy, *WEALTHY UPPER CLASS*
arithmetic,*, *MATH*
arivd, arrive(d)
arive, arrive
arivul, arrive(val)
arjuwus, arduous
ark,*, *BOX/CHEST/CUPBOARD/BOAT*(or see arc/arch)
arkade, arcade
arkaek, archaic
arkaik, archaic
arkeoligy, archeology
arketekt, architect
arkeu, argue
arkiology, archeology
arkitect, architect
arkiteksher, architect(ure)
arkive, archive
arktic, arctic

ardekle, article
ardent,tly, *PASSIONATE*
ardery, artery
ardest, artist
ardewous, arduous
ardgewus, arduous
ardifishel, artificial
ardikle, article
ardint, ardent
ardiry, artery
ardist, artist
ardjewous, arduous
ardufishul, artificial
ardukle, article
arduous,sly,sness, *DIFFICULT*
ardury, artery
are, *TO BE, IS* (or see air/heir/hour/our)
area,*,al, *RANGE OF CONCEPT/EVENT/OPERATION*
arear, arrear
ared, arid
aregate, irrigate
aregenashen, originate(tion)
aregeno, oregano
aregenul, origin(al)
arejenul, origin(al)
arekshin, erect(ion)
arekt, erect
arena,*, *ENCLOSED SPACE*
arend, errand
aren't, *CONTRACTION OF THE WORDS "ARE NOT"*
areplasible, irreplacable
areprochible, irreproachable
arer, error / arrear
arest, arrest
arestokrat, aristocrat
arethmatic, arithmetic
areu, area
areul, aerial
arezt, arrest

arouse,*,ed,sing,sal, *TO AWAKEN, STIMULATE, BRING TO ACTION*
arouzel, arouse(sal)
arow, arrow
arownd, around
arowsul, arouse(sal)
arowze, arouse
arport, airport
arraign,*,ned,ning,nment, *ANSWER INDICTMENT*
arrange,*,ed,ging,ement,er, *ADJUST, SITUATE*
arranment, arraign(ment)
array, *ORDER*
arrear,*,rage, *PAST DUE*
arrest,*,ted,ting,tingly, *SUSPEND, CAPTURE*
arrive,*,ed,ting,val, *PRESENT AT DESTINATION*
arrogance,nt,ntly, *OVERLY SELF-IMPORTANT*
arrow,*, *SHAFT WITH POINT*
arrowgance, arrogance
arsen, arson
arson,*,nist, *MALICIOUS/INTENTIONAL BURNING*
arsunest, arson(ist)
art,*, tist,tistry,ty,tistic,tistical,tistically,tisan,tful, tfully,tfulness,tless,tlessly,tlessness,tly, tiness, *METHOD OF EXPRESSION*
arteculate, articulte
artefishel, artificial
artekewlate, articulate
artekulashen, articulate(tion)
artekulate, articulate
artelury, artillery
artereal, arterial
arterial,*, *PATH FOR FLOW*
artery,ries, *CHANNEL FOR TRANSPORTATION*
artesdik, artist(ic)
artest, artist
artestek, artist(ic)
arthridek, arthritis(ic)
arthridis, arthritis
arthritis,tic, *INFLAMMATION*

article,*, *PART, ONE OF SEVERAL (TOO MANY DEFINITIONS PLEASE SEE STANDARD DICTIONARY)*
articulate, articulate
articulate,*,ed,ting,tion,tely, *INTEGRATE, SPECIFIC*
artificial,lly, *SIMULATED, NOT REAL*
artifishul, artificial
artik, arctic
artikel, article
artikewlate, articulate
artikulashen, articulate(tion)
artikulate, articulate
artillery,*, *FOR WEAPONS*
artireal, arterial
artiry, artery
artisdik, artist(ic)
artist,*,tistic,tistically, *SKILLED*
artistek, artist(ic)
artsh, arch
artsher, archer
artucle, article
artufishul, artificial
artury, artery
arubshen, erupt(ion) /irrupt(ion)
arubt, erupt /irrupt
arubtif, erupt(ive) /irrupt(ive)
arugate, irrigate
arupshen, erupt(ion) /irrupt(ion)
arupt, erupt /irrupt
aruptif, erupt(ive) /irrupt(ive)
aruption, erupt(ion) /irrupt(ion)
arye, awry
aryve, arrive
as, *PREFIX INDICATING "TO/TOWARDS" MOST OFTEN MODIFIES THE WORD*
asaeal, assail
asaee, essay
asail, assail
asalt, assault
asasen, assassin

asault, assault
asay, essay
asbekt, aspect
asberashun, aspiration
asberegus, asparagus
asbeshulee, especially
asbestos, *TYPE OF FIBER*
asbir, aspire
asburin, aspirin
ascape, escape
ascend,*,ded,ding,dment,dable,dance,dancy, dence,dant, *DOMINANT, RISING ABOVE, GO UP (or see assent or ascent)*
ascendant,*,nce, *DOMINANT, RISE ABOVE OTHERS*
ascension,nal, *TO GO UP*
ascent,*,ted,ting, *MOTION UPWARDS (or see assent or ascend)*
ascertain,*,ned,ning, *MAKE SURE*
ascind, ascend
asdeem, esteem
ased, acid
asemble, assemble /assembly
asemetric, asymmetric
asemewlate, assimilate
asemulate, assimilate
asend, ascend
asendent, ascendant
asense, essence
asenshil, essential
asent, ascent /assent
asential, essential
asershen, assert(ion)
asert, assert
asertane, ascertain
asertif, assert(ive)
asertion, assert(ion)
asesible, access(ible)
asesment, assessment
asest, assist

asesuble, access(ible)
asexual, *NOT SEXUAL*
asfalt, asphalt
asfault, asphalt
asfikseate, asphyxiate
asfixiate, asphyxiate
asfolt, asphalt
ashamed,dly, *TOUCHED BY SHAME, NOT PROUD*
ashamt, ashamed
asheeve, achieve
ashirense, assure(rance)
ashtarik, asterisk
ashuranse, assure(rance)
asid, acid /aside
aside, *SEPARATE FROM*
asiduous, assiduous
asign, assign
asignment, assignment
asijuous, assiduous
asilum, asylum
asim, awesome
asimble, assemble
asimetric, asymmetric
asimilate, assimilate
asimulate, assimilate
asind, ascend
asindent, ascendant
asine, assign
asinment, assignment
asinse, essence
asinshul, essential
asint, ascent / assent
asirshen, assert(ion)
asirt, assert
asirtane, ascertain
asirtev, assert(ive)
asist, assist
askalador, escalator
askalater, escalator

askape, escape
askort, escort
askulader, escalator
asleep, *DORMANT STATE*
asmu, asthma
asocheate, associate
asociate, associate
asolt, assault
asorded, assorted
asorted, assorted
asosheate, associate
asoshiate, associate
asparagus, *VEGETABLE*
aspect,*, *OUTLOOK*
aspekt, aspect
asperagus, asparagus
asperashun, aspiration
asperation, aspiration
asperen, aspirin
asperugus, asparagus
aspeshilee, especially
aspeshulee, especially
aspestus, asbestos
asphalt, *MINERAL PITCH*
asphixiate, asphyxiate
asphyxiate,*,ed,ting,tion, *OF BREATHING*
aspirashun, aspiration
aspiration,*,nal, *AMBITION, OF BREATHING (TOO MANY DEFINITIONS, PLEASE SEE STANDARD DICTIONARY)*
aspire,*,ed,ring,er,ration,rational,rant, *GOAL, DESIRE*
aspirin,*, *PAIN RELIEVER*
asprashun, aspiration
aspren, aspirin
aspurashun, aspiration
aspuration, aspiration
aspuren, aspirin
assall,lable,lant, *IMPACT UPON*

assasin, assassin
assassin,*,nate,nation, *TO MURDER, A MURDERER*
assault,*,ted,ting, *ATTACK WITH INTENT TO HARM*
assemble,*ed,ling,lage,ly, *PUT TOGETHER*
assent,ted, *AGREEMENT* (or see ascent)
assert,*,ted,ting,tion,table,ter,tive,tively, tiveness, *INSIST*
assessment,*, *APPRAISAL*
asset,*, *POSSESS SOMETHING VALUABLE*
assiduous,sly, *DILIGENT*
assign,*,ned,ning, *APPORTION*
assignment,*, *ASSIGNED WORK*
assimilate,*,ed,ting,tion, *MAKE INTO, BECOME LIKE*
assint, assent
assist,*,ted,ting,tant,tance, *HELP*
associate,*,ed,ting,tion, *CONNECTION TO*
assorted,ting,tment, *VARIOUS TYPES*
assume,*,ed,ming,mable,mably, *SUPPOSE A FACT*
assumption,*,ive, *TAKE FOR GRANTED*
assure,*,ed,rance, *CERTAINTY*
asteem, esteem
astemate, estimate
asterik, asterisk
asterisk, *LITTLE TEXT STAR*
asteroed, asteroid
asteroid, *PERTAINING TO STAR*
asthetik, aesthetic
asthma,atic,atical,atically, *DIFFICULTY BREATHING*
asthmu, asthma
astimate, estimate
astonesh, astonish
astonish,hes,hed,hing,hment, *SURPRISE/ IMPRESS*
astragen, estrogen
astral,ly, *STELLAR*
astrawneme, astronomy
astrek, asterisk
astrengent, astringent
astrenjint, astringent
astrenot, astronaut

astres, estrus	**at**, *PREFIX INDICATING "TO/TOWARDS" MOST OFTEN MODIFIES THE WORD* (or see ate /eight /add)	atgust, adjust
astrik, asterisk	atach, attach	athear, adhere
astringent,*,ncy,tly, *Acrid*	atack, attack	**atheist**,ism,tic,tical,tically, *DISBELIEF IN A GOD*
astrinot, astronaut	ataen, attain	athek, ethic
astris, estrus	atain, attain	athere, adhere
astroed, asteroid	atak, attack	athesif, adhesive
astrol, astral	atament, adament	athic, ethic
astrology, astrology	ataminit, adament	athiest, atheist
astrology,ger,gic,gical,gically,gist, *PREDICT THE FUTURE WITH THE STARS*	atane, attain	athik, ethic
astronaut,*, *PERSON OF SPACE FLIGHT*	atatch, attach	athleat, athlete
astroneme, astronomy	atcheeve, achieve	**athlete**,*,tic,tics,tically, *SPORTS TRAINED, ATHLETE*
astronomic,mical,mically, *OF NUMEROUS/GREAT PROPORTION*	atec, attic /addict	athnek, ethnic
astronomy,mer,mers, *OBSERVE CELESTIAL BODIES*	ated, add(ed)	athnuk, ethnic
astronot, astronaut	atek, attic /addict	athorety, authority
astronume, astronomy	atekwase, adequacy	athrek, etheric
astroyd, asteroid	atembt, attempt	athrik, etheric
astrugen, estrogen	atemobel, automobile	athuk, ethic
astrul, astral	atempt, attempt	atic, attic /addict
astrunot, astronaut	atemt, attempt	atid, add(ed)
astumate, estimate	atenchin, attention	atikit, etiquette
astural, astral	atend, attend	atikwuse, adequacy
asturik, asterisk	atendens, attend(ance)	atikwit, adequate
asturisk, asterisk	atendent, attend(ant)	atimant, adament
asum, awesome /assume	atenshin, attention	atimint,adament
asumetric, asymmetric	atentef, attentive	atimt, attempt
asumpshen, assumption	atention, attention	atinchon, attention
asumption, assumption	atentive, attentive	atind, attend
asunse, essence	atequasy, adequacy	atinshun, attention
asurans, assure(rance)	ateqwit, adequate	atipecle, atypical
asurants, assure(rance)	aternal, eternal	atipikul, atypical
asurshen, assert(ion)	aterney, attorney	atiquit, adequate
asurtif, assert(ive)	atesy, odyssey	atiquot, adequate
asylom, asylum	atetif, additive	atire, attire
asylum, *REFUGE FOR DESTITUTE*	atetude, attitude	atisum, autism
asymetric, asymmetric	atgasent, adjacent	atitif, additive
asymmetric,rY, *OFF-BALANCE*	atgasint, adjacent	atitude, attitude
	atgern, adjourn	atmechen, admission
	atgewdikate, adjudicate	atmedid, admit(tted)
		atmenester, administer

atmenustrashen, administrate(tion)
atmeshen, admission
atmesphere, atmosphere
atmichen, admission
atmided, admit(tted)
atminaster, administer
atminastrashin, administrate(tion)
atminuster, administer
atminustrashen, administrate(tion)
atmird, admire(d)
atmire, admire
atmisef, admission(ive)
atmisfeer, atmosphere
atmishun, admission
atmisphere, atmosphere
atmisuble, admissible
atmit, admit
atmosfear, atmosphere
atmosphere,ric,rical,rically, AROUND A PLANET
atmusfeer, atmosphere
atmusphere, atmosphere
atmyre, admire
atobiografy, autobiography
atograf, autograph
atolesence, adolescence
atom,*,mic,mically,mize,mizer, PARTICLES OF ELEMENT
atomadik, automatic
atomatik, automatic
atomobel, automobile
atonal,*,lity,listic,lly, CANNOT HEAR TRUE TONES
atone,*,eable,nable,ement, MAKE UP FOR/AMEND
atonime, autonomy
atonome, autonomy
atorney, attorney
atracshun, attraction
atract, attract
atraction, attraction
atrakshun, attraction

atrakt, attract
atraktif, attract(ive)
atrebute, attribute
atrefee, atrophy
atrenalyne, adrenaline
atrenulen, adrenaline
atress, address
atreum, atrium
atribute, attribute
atriem, atrium
atrifee, atrophy
atriss, address
atrium,*, GLASS ROOM
atrocious,sly,sness, OUTRAGEOUS
atrocity,ties, OUTRAGEOUS
atrocius, atrocious
atrofee, atrophy
atrophy,hied,hic, DEGENERATE
atrosety, atrocity
atroshus, atrocious
atrufee, atrophy
atsetera, etcetera
atsheve, achieve
attach,hes,hed,hing,hment, FASTEN
attack,*,ked,king, ASSAIL
attain,*,ned,ning, GAIN
attempt,*,ted,ting, TRY TO ACCOMPLISH
attemt, attempt
attenchon, attention
attend,*,ded,ding,dance,dant, ACCOMPANY, GO TO
attention,ive, FOCUS ON
attentive,ively, FOCUS ON
attic,*, IN THE ROOF (or see addict)
attichon, attention
attinchon, attention
attire,*,ed,ring, APPAREL
attitude,*,dinal, MENTAL POSTURE
attorney,*, REPRESENTATIVE OF LAW
attotode, attitude

attract,*,ted,ting,tive,tively, TO DRAW TOWARDS
attraction,*, DRAWN TOWARDS
attribute,*,ed,ting,tion, TO CREDIT
atukit, etiquette
atulesense, adolescence
atum, atom /autumn
atument, adament
aturnal, eternal
aturney, attorney
atutif, additive
atutode, attitude
atvacate, advocate
atvanse, advance
atvantech, advantage
atvanteg, advantage
atvantuge, advantage
atvencher, adventure
atvenshure, adventure
atverb, adverb
atversare, adversary
atverse, adverse
atversery, adversary
atvertize, advertise
atvincher, adventure
atvinsher, adventure
atvirb, adverb
atvirsary, adversary
atvirse, adverse
atvise, advice /advise
atvisuble, advise(sable)
atvize, advise /advice
atvokate, advocate
atvukate, advocate
atvurb, adverb
atvurcity, adverse(sity)
atvurse, adverse
atvursle, adverse(ly)
atvurtize, advertise
atypical, IRREGULAR

auch, ouch
aucshen, auction
auction,*,neer,ning, *SELL BY BID*
aud, odd /ought /out
audacity,ious,iously,iousness, *OVER-BOLD*
audasity, audacity
audeance, audience
audeble, audible
audem, autumn
audeo, audio
auder, otter /outer
audeshun, audition
audet, audit
audetoreum, auditorium
audetorium, auditorium
audety, odd(ity)
audfit, outfit
audiance, audience
audible,ly,bility,eness, *WELL HEARD*
audience,*, *GROUP WHO OBSERVES*
audio, *HEAR*
audir, otter /outer
audishun, audition
audit,*,ted,ting,tor, *UNDER EXAMINATION*
audition,*,ned,ning, *SUBMIT TO EXAMINATION*
auditorium,*, *FOR PUBLIC AUDIENCE*
audity, odd(ly)
audle, odd(ly)
audobyogerfey, autobiography
audrage, outrage
auel, owl
auger,*, *TOOL TO BORE SOMETHING*
augir, auger
augment,*,ted,ting,tation, *INCREASE SIZE*
augre, auger
August, *A MONTH IN THE YEAR*
auil, owl
aukshun, auction
auktober, October

aukward, awkward
aukwurd, awkward
aul, owl /all /awl
auldir, alder /altar /alter
auldur, alder /altar /alter
aulfubet, alphabet
aulso, also
aulternate, alternate
aultirnetly, alternate(ly)
aultogethur, altogether
aulturnate, alternate
aulways, always
auneng, awning
aunt,*,tie, *SISTER OF MOTHER/FATHER* (or see ant)
auntefrese, antifreeze
aupoyntmint, appointment
aupshen, option
aur, hour /our /oar
aura,*,al,ric, *LIGHT FIELD*
aurajin, origin
aurekel, auricle /oracle
auri, awry
aurickle, auricle /oracle
auricle,cular, *OF THE EAR* (or see oracle)
aurikel, auricle /oracle
aurk, arc /ark
aurle, hour(ly)
auroara, aurora
aurora,*,al, *RADIANT EMISSION*
ausem, awesome
ausim, awesome
auspicious,sly,sness, *FAVORABLE*
auspishus, auspicious
auspitious, auspicious
austear, austere
austeere, austere
austere,ely, *HARSH*
ausum, awesome
aut, out /ought

autem, autumn
autemobel, automobile
auteo, audio
auter, otter /outer
autfit, outfit
autgo, outgo
authentic,cly,cally,city,cate,cation,cator, *VALID, NOT FICTITIOUS/FAKE*
auther, author
authintik, authentic
authir, author
author,*,red, *CREATOR/ORIGINATOR*
authoretarian, authoritarian
authoritarian, *DICTATORIAL*
authority,ties,tative,tatively, *EXERCISES COMMAND*
autim, autumn
autio, audio
autir, otter /outer
autism,stic, *BRAIN ACTIVITY IMBALANCE*
autlaw, outlaw
autlet, outlet
autline, outline
autluk, outlook
autly, odd((ly)
auto, *PREFIX INDICATING "OF OR BY ONESELF" MOST OFTEN MODIFIES THE WORD*
autobiografy, autobiography
autobiography,hies,her,hical,hically, *WRITTEN BY ONESELF*
autobyografy, autobiography
autograf, autograph
autograph,*,hed,hing, *AUTHOR'S SIGNATURE*
automadik, automatic
automatic,*,cally,ion, *SELF-CONTROLLING, PERFORMS THRU PROGRAMMING*
automobel, automobile
automobile,*, *PERSONAL TRANSPORTATION*
autoname, autonomy
autonime, autonomy

avrige, average
avucate, advocate
avukodo, avocado
avulanch, avalanche
avundful, eventful
avurb, adverb
avurij, average
avurse, adverse
avurtize, adverstise
await,*,ted,ting, *TO EXPECT*
awake,*,en,ening,king, *FROM SLEEP*
award,*,ded,ding, *A PRIZE*
aware,eness, *CAUTIOUS*
awate, await
away, *SOMEWHERE ELSE*
awayt, await
awcshen, auction
awd, odd /ought /out
awdacity, audacity
awdasety, audacity
awdeanse, audience
awdeble, audible
awdege, outage
awdeje, outage
awdeo, audio
awder, outer /otter
awdet, audit
awdete, odd(ity)
awdetoreum, auditorium
awdible, audible
awdir, outer /otter
awdishun, audition
awdit, audit
awdition, audition
awditorium, auditorium
awdity, odd(ity)
awdline, outline
awdur, outer /otter
awe,*,ed, *TAKEN ABACK, STUNNED*

awesome,ely,eness, *IMPRESSIVE*
awfil, awful
awful,lly,lness, *DREADFUL*
awger, auger
awgest, August
awgir, auger
awgist, August
awgment, augment
awgmint, augment
awgre, auger
awgur, auger
awgusd, August
awgust, August
awhile, *FOR SOME TIME NOW*
awil, awhile
awkewpie, occupy
awkshun, auction
awkupy, occupy
awkward,dly,dness, *BUNGLING OR EMBARRASSING*
awl,*, *TOOL FOR SEWING LEATHER* (or see owl /all)
awlso, also
awning,*, *ROOF OVERHANG*
aword, award
awrekt, erect
awrickle, auricle
awrie, awry
awrikle, auricle
awroara, aurora
awrode, erode
awrora, aurora
awru, aura
awry, *OFF COURSE*
awsem, awesome
awsome, awesome
awspeshus, auspicious
awspitious, auspicious
awstear, austere
awsteer, austere
awsum, awesome

awt, out /ought
awtem, autumn
awter, otter /outer
awtesm, autism
awtfit, outfit
awtgo, outgo
awthentik, authentic
awthintik, authentic
awthir, author
awthority, authority
awtim, autumn
awtir, otter /outer
awtism, autism
awtitorium, auditorium
awtizm, autism
awtlaw, outlaw
awtlet, outlet
awtleng, outlying
awtline, outline
awtluk, outlook
awtlying, outlying
awtobiografy, autobiography
awtopse, autopsy
awtpost, outpost
awtput, output
awtrage, outrage
awtragus, outrage(ous)
awtrite, outright
awtset, outset
awtside, outside
awtskurt, outskirt
awtsmart, outsmart
awtum, autumn
awtur, outer /otter
awtwerd, outward
awtwit, outwit
awtwurd, outward
awul, owl

ax,xes,xed,xing, A TOOL WITH A SHARP BLADE FOR CHOPPING WOOD (or see ache(s) or axis)
axcebt, except /accept
axcedent, accident
axceed, exceed
accelerate, accelerate
axchange, exchange
axchoole, actual
axcident, accident
axclude, exclude
axcurshin, excursion
axebt, except / accept
axent, accent
axepshen, except(ion)
axeptinse, accept(ance)
axesory, accessory
axess, access
axglood, exclude
axicute, execute
axil,*, ANGLE BETWEEN STEM/BRANCH (or see axle)
axint, accent
axis,xes, A PIVOTAL POINT ON WHICH SOMETHING IS CENTERED (or see ax(es))
axkerjen, excursion
axklude, exclude
axkuze, excuse
axle,*, ROD WITH TWO WHEELS ATTACHED(or see axil)
axol, axil /axle
axplan, explain
axsedintal, accident(al)
axseed, exceed
axselense, excellent
axseluratur, accelerate(tor)
axsenshuate, accentuate
axsent, accent
axsentuate, accentuate
axsept, accept /except
axseptense, accept(ance)
axseptinse, accept(ance)

axses, access /ax(es) /axis
axsesares, accessory(ries)
axsesori, accessory
axsesurize, accessory(rize)
axshule, actual
axshun, action
axsident, accident
axsidental, accident(al)
axsidint, accident
axsint, accent
axsintuate, accentuate
axst, ax(ed)
axsudentul, accident(al)
axturnal, external
axual, actual
axuel, actual
axukute, execute
axul, axil /axle
axule, actual
azbekt, aspect
azberigus, asparagus
azbestus, asbestos
azburashun, aspiration
azdragen, estrogen
azemulate, assimilate
azendent, ascendant
azertane, ascertain
azfalt, asphalt
azfault, asphalt
azfikseate, asphyxiate
azfolt, asphalt
azide, aside
azilum, asylum
azinment, assignment
azinshul, essential
azma, asthma
azmu, asthma
azpekt, aspect
azpir, aspire

azpren, aspirin
azspect, aspect
azteem, esteem
azthma, asthma
aztonesh, astonish
aztral, astral
aztranaut, astronaut
aztrawneme, astronomy
aztrengent, astringent
aztringent, astringent
aztroid, asteroid
aztrol, astral
aztrolegy, astrology
aztronume, astronomy
aztrul, astral
aztrunot, astronaut
azumshin, assumption
azurtane, ascertain

"B"

ba, bay
babby, baby
babe, baby
babesit, babysit
baby,bies,bied, INFANT
babysit,*,tter,tting, WATCH OTHERS CHILDREN
bacen, bacon
bach, back /batch /badge /bash /bake
bachelor,*, NON-MARRIED MAN
bachiler, bachelor
bachuler, bachelor
bacin, bacon
back,*,ked,king,ker, GO TO THE PREVIOUS/PAST, IN THE REAR OF (or see bake)
backward,*,dness, IN REVERSE
backwurd, backward

bacon, SALTED HOG MEAT/FAT
bacos, because
bacter, bacteri, bacterio, PREFIX INDICATING
  "BACTERIA" MOST OFTEN MODIFIES THE WORD
bacteria, al, ium, MICROSCOPIC ORGANISM
bactirea, bacteria
bactireul, bacteria(l)
bad, dly, NOT GOOD (or see bat or bade)
badchelor, bachelor
badder, batter
bade, ed, PAST TENSE OF "BID", TO TELL
badel, battle
bader, batter
badery, battery
badge, *, INSIGNIA
badger, *, red, ring, TO HECKLE SOMEONE, AN ANIMAL
badiry, battery
badje, badge
badjur, badger
badle, battle
badol, battle
badore, battery
badre, battery
badshelor, bachelor
badul, battle
baduly, body(dily)
badur, batter
badury, battery
bae, bay
baege, beige
baej, beige
bael, bail /bale
baenkwit, banquet
baet, bait /bate
bafal, befall
bafileon, pavilion
bafol, befall
bag, *, gged,gging,gger,ggy, A CONTAINER TO HOLD
  ITEMS (or see back /beige /batch /badge)

bagage, baggage
bagd, bag(gged) /back(ed)
bage, badge /beige /bag(ggy)
baged, bag(gged) /back(ed)
bagege, baggage
bageje, baggage
bagel, *, ROLL WITH A HOLE
bagener, begin(nner)
bager, bag(gger) /badger
baggage, LUGGAGE
bagige, baggage
bagil, bagel
baginer, begin(nner)
bagir, badger /bag(gger)
bagle, bagel
baguj, baggage
bagul, bagel
bagur, bag(gger) /badger
bahaver, behavior
bahavior, behavior
bahind, behind
baige, beige
baije, beige
bail, *, led, LIBERATE, REMOVE FROM (or see bale)
bailef, bailiff
bailif, bailiff
bailiff, *, CIVIL OFFICER OR FUNCTIONARY
bainquet, banquet
bair, bear /bare
bait, *, ted, ting, LURING TO CATCH (or see bate)
baj, badge /beige /batch
bajer, badger
bak, back /bake
bakd, bake(d) /back(ed)
bake, *, ed, king, er, COOK FOOD IN AN OVEN (or see back)
bakeeny, bikini
baken, bacon
bakene, bikini

bakery, ries, WHERE PASTRIES ARE BAKED
bakin, bacon
bakini, bikini
bakiry, bakery
bakose, because
bakry, bakery
bakt, bake(d) /back(ed)
bakterea, bacteria
baktereul, bacteria(l)
baktirea, bacteria
bakuj, baggage
bakwerd, backward
bakwird, backward
bakwurd, backward
bal, ball /bale /bail /bawl
bala, ballet
balad, ballad /ballade
balance, *, ed, cing, EQUILIBRIUM, CENTERED
balarena, ballerina
balat, ballot /ballad /ballade
balay, ballet
balcene, balcony
balcony, nies, PORCH ABOVE THE FIRST STORY ON A
  BUILDING
balcuny, balcony
bald, ding, dness, LOOSING HAIR (or see bold/
  ball(ed) /bale(d) /bail(ed))
bale, *, ed, ling, er, TO BUNDLE (or see bail)
baled, bale(d) /bail(ed) /ballad / ballade
baleef, belief
baleeve, believe
balef, bailiff
balens, balance
balerena, ballerina
balestic, balistic
balet, ballet /ballot /ballad /ballade
baleve, believe
balevuble, believe(vable)
balid, ballad /ballade
balif, bailiff

balins, balance
balirena, ballerina
balistic,* *PROJECTILE IN AIR*
balit, ballot /ballet
balkeny, balcony
balkune, balcony
ball,* lled,lling, *ROUND OBJECT FOR THROWING/ SPORTS, A FORMAL DANCE STYLE* (or see bawl/ bail/ bale)
ballad,* dic,dist,dry, *SIMPLE SONG/POEM* (or see ballade)
ballade,* *SPECIFIC STYLE OF POEM/MUSICAL PIECE* (or see ballad)
balled, ballad /ballade /ball(ed)
ballerina,* *FEMALE DANCER*
ballid, ballad /ballade
ballet,* *CLASSICAL DANCE* (or see ballot)
balloon,* ned,ning, *FULL OF AIR*
ballot,* ted,ting,ter, *OF VOTING*
balm,* *OINTMENT FROM PLANTS*
balme, balmy
balmy, mier,miest,mily,miness, *OF WARM/ MILD CLIMATE*
balo, below /bellow /billow
balonee, bologna /baloney
baloney, *NONSENSE, MEAT* (or see bologna)
balong, belong
baloom, bloom
baloon, balloon
balot, ballot / ballet
balow, below / billow /bellow
bals, bowels /ball(s) /bale(s) /bail(s)
baluf, bailiff
balume, bloom
balune, balloon
balunse, balance
balurena, ballerina
banana,* *EDIBLE FRUIT*

band,* ded,ding, *COLLECTION OF PERFORMING MUSICIANS, TO BE GROUPED/BOUND TOGETHER*
bandage,* ed,ging, *FOR REPAIRING WOUNDS*
baneeth, beneath
baner, banner
banesh, banish
banevulense, benevolence
banign, benign
banine, benign
banir, banner
banish,* hed,hment,*CONDEMNED TO EXILE*
bankrupsee, bankruptcy
bankrupt,cy,cies, *BROKE TO THE BANK, CAN'T PAY*
bankwit, banquet
banner,* *TYPE OF SIGN*
banquet,* *FEAST WITH FRIENDS*
banquit, banquet
banur, banner
baptesm, baptism
baptism,* mal, *REBIRTHING RITUAL*
baptize,* ed,zing, *REBIRTHING RITUAL*
baptizm, baptism
bar, rred,rring, *LONG/FLAT SECTION/COUNTER (TOO MANY DEFINITION, PLEASE SEE STANDARD DICTIONARY)* (or see bare or bear)
barack, barrack
barbarian,* ic, *UNCIVILIZED PERSON*
barbekew, barbecue
barbeku, barbecue
barbecue,* ed,uing, *GRILLED MEAT*
barbeque, barbecue
barber,* *CUTS HAIR*
barberean, barbarian
barberian, barbarian
barbetchuet, barbiturate
barbichuit, barbiturate
barbique, barbecue
barbir, barber
barbitchuet, barbiturate
barbiturate,* *SEDATIVE DRUG*

barbur, barber
barder, barter
bardur, barter
bare,* ring,rren, *WITHOUT COVER* (or see bear/ berry/ bury)
bareave, bereave
bareck, barrack
bareeve, bereave
bareft, bereft
barel, barrel
baren, barren
bareng, bearing /bar(rring) /bare(ring)
barestur, barrister
baret, barrette / beret
baretone, baritone
bareur, barrier
bargain,* ned,ning, *AFFORDABLE DEAL*
barge,* ed,ging *FLAT-BOTTOM BOAT, BEHAVE LIKE A BOAT*
bargen, bargain
bargun, bargain
bargund, bargain(ed)
baricade, barricade
barier, barrier
barikade, barricade
baril, barrel
barin, barren
baring, bearing /bare(ring) /bar(rring)
barister, barrister
baristur, barrister
barit, barrette / beret
baritone,* *DEEP TONE*
barje, barge
baro, barrow / borrow
baro, bary, *PREFIX INDICATING "PRESSURE/WEIGHT" MOST OFTEN MODIFIES THE WORD* (or see barrow or borrow)
baroge, barrage
baroje, barrage

barol, barrel
barometer,tric, *INSTRUMENT MEASURING PRESSURE*
baromiter, barometer
baron, barren
barow, borrow /burrow /borough
barrack,ed, *LODGE FOR MANY PEOPLE*
barrage,ed, *ALL AT ONCE*
barrel,*,ed,ling, *DRUM OR GREAT SPEED*
barren,ly,ness, *UNFERTILE*
barrette,*, *CLASP* (or see beret)
barricade,*,ded,ding, *BLOCK AGAINST*
barrier,*, *OBSTRUCTION*
barring, *EXCEPTING, REFUSAL*
barrister,*, *LAWYER*
barrow, *CASTRATED HOG* (or see borrow)
bartender,*, *TENDS BAR*
barter,*,red,ring, *TRADE*
bartinder, bartender
bartur, barter
baruton, baritone
bary, berry /bury
bas, base /bass
basball, baseball
basboll, baseball
base,*,ed,sing,eless, *A FOUNDATION, FORM IN BASEBALL* (or see bass)
baseach, beseech
baseball, *SPORT*
baseech, beseech
basek, basic
basekly, basic(ally)
basel, basil
basement,*, *UNDER HOUSE*
basen, basin
bases, basis /base(s)
baset, bassett
bashfel, bashful
bashful, *SHY*

basi, baso, *PREFIX INDICATING "BOTTOM/ BASE" MOST OFTEN MODIFIES THE WORD*
basic,*,cally, *FUNDAMENTAL*
baside, beside
basik, basic
basikly, basic(ally)
basil, *HERB*
basin,*, *SHAPED LIKE BOWL*
basis, *ON WHICH IT STANDS* (or see base(s))
basit, bassett
basket,*, *WOVEN CONTAINER*
baskit, basket
baskut, basket
basmant, basement
basmint, basement
basoon, bassoon
bass, *A FISH, STRINGED INSTRUMENT, A LEVEL OF TONE* (or see base)
bassett, *DOG, HOUND*
bassoon, *HORN*
basuk, basic
basul, basil
basun, basin
basune, bassoon
basurk, berserk
basus, basis /base(s)
basut, bassett
bat,*,tted,tting,tter, *STUFFING, A TOOL USED IN BASEBALL, TO HIT* (or see bate /bait)
batch,hes,hed,hing, *INCREMENTS/CERTAIN AMOUNTS OF SOMETHING AT A TIME* (or see badge)
batcheler, bachelor
batchuler, bachelor
bate,*,ed,ting, *DECREASE, HOLD BACK* (or see bait)
batel, battle
baten, batten
batenshul, potential
bater, batter
batery, battery

bath,*,hroom, *A PLACE TO WASH, TO IMMERSE IN LIQUID* (or see bathe)
bathe,*,ed,hing, *TO WASH UP, IMMERSE IN LIQUID* (or see bath)
batil, bottle /battle
batin, batten
batinshul, potential
batiry, battery
batle, battle
baton,*, *WAND*
batore, battery
batre, battery
batrothed, betrothed
batshelor, bachelor
batshiler, bachelor
batter,*,red,ring, *FRYING MIXTURE, BASEBALL PLAYER, TO BE ATTACKED*
batten, *SECURE/STRENGTHEN, WOOD STRIPS* (or see bat(tting))
battery,ies, *APPLIES TO MILITARY, MECHANICAL, ELECTRICAL, BASEBALL*
battle,*,ed,ling, *FIGHT BETWEEN TWO FORCES*
batul, battle
batur, batter
batury, battery
batween, between
baul, ball /bawl /bail /bale
baulm, balm
baulme, balmy
baund, bound
baut, bought /bout
bautel, bottle
bavileon, pavilion
bawdil, bottle
bawildre, bewilder
bawilder, bewilder
bawl,*,led,ling,ler, *WEEP, SHOUT AT* (or see ball)
bawls, bawl(s) /bowel(s) /ball(s)
bawnd, bound
bawnse, bounce /bound(s)

bawntee, bounty
bawntiful, bountiful
bay,*, RELATES TO WINDOW, BARN, DOG HOWLING, SHIP HOSPITAL, AIRCRAFT, SHRUB, OCEAN INLET
bayle, bail / bale
bayond, beyond
bayou, OUTLET OF WATER
bayu, bayou
bazaar,*, SALE OF ARTICLES (or see bizarre)
bazel, basil
bazen, basin
bazil, basil
bazin, basin
bazul, basil
bazurk, berserk
bazzar, bizzare / bazaar
be, A VERB EXPRESSING PRESENT TENSE (or see bee)
be, PREFIX INDICATING "COMPLETELY/ INTENSELY" MOST OFTEN MODIFIES THE WORD
beach,es,ed, SHORELINE (or see beech)
beacon,*, SIGNAL (or see beckon)
bead,*,ded,ding, ROUNDED FORM/OBJECT
beafy, beefy
beagle,*, DOG
beagul, beagle
beak,* BIRD BILL
beaker,*, VESSEL
beam,*,med,ming, TO SHINE, LINEAR SUPPORT
bean,*, VEGETABLE, TO HURT (or see been/bin)
bear,*,ring,rish,rishly, ANIMAL, PUT PRESSURE ON/ AGAINST (or see bare /beer /bearing)
bearable, TOLERABLE
beard,*,ded, MALE FACIAL HAIR
bearing,*, SUPPORTS, PRESSURE, MACHINE PART, HEADING (or see bare(ring))
beast,*,tly,liness, ANIMA
beat,*,ting, THRASH/STRIKE/HIT (or see beet)
beau,*, BOYFRIEND (or see bow or bough)
beautician,*, HAIRDRESSER

beautiful, EYE PLEASER
beautishun, beautician
beauty,ies,tify,tifully,tious,tification, PLEASING TO THE SENSES, GMP
beaver,*, ANIMAL
bebleografy, bibliography
became, PAST TENSE OF "BECOME"
because, THE REASON FOR
becin, beckon /beacon /bacon
becon, beckon /beacon /bacon
beckon,*,ned,ning, TO SUMMON/CALL FORTH, ENTICE TO COME (or see beacon/bacon)
beckun, beckon/beacon/bacon
become,*,ming,became, GOING TO BE (or see became)
becon, beckon /beacon /bacon
becos, because
becum, become
becun, beckon /beacon /bacon
becuz, because
bed,*,dded,dding, SOMETHING TO SLEEP/ LIE DOWN UPON (or see bead /bet /bit)
beded, bet(tted) /bed(dded) /bead(ed)
beder, better /bid(dder) /bitter /bet(ttor)
bedid, bet(tted) /bed(dded)
bedil, beetle
bedir, better /bid(dder) /bitter /bet(ttor)
bedraggled, MUSSED UP
bedragled, bedraggled
bedraguled, bedraggled
bedridden, CONFINED TO BED
bedriden, bedridden
bedritin, bedridden
bedrothed, betrothed
bedspread,*, BED COVER
bedspred, bedspread
bedud, bet(tted) / bed(dded)
bedul, beetle

bedur, better /bid(dder) /bitter /bet(ttor)
bedwritin, bedridden
bee,*, FURRY INSECT (or see "be")
beech, TREE (or see beach)
beedil, beetle
beedul, beetle
beef, beef
beef,fy,finess,fed,fing, FLESHY, MEAT FROM BOVINE, TO COMPLAIN
beek, beak
beeker, beaker
beekin, beacon
beem, beam
been, PAST TENSE OF "BE" (or see bean)
beeng, being
beer,*, FERMENTED BREW (or see bear)
beerd, beard
beest, beast
beestro, bistro
beet,*, A VEGETABLE (or see beat)
beetle,*, BUG
beetul, beetle
beever, beaver
befall, OCCUR
befol, befall
before, PREVIOUS
befour, before
befrend, befriend
befriend,*,ded, MAKE FRIENDS WITH
befrind, befriend
beg,*,gged,gging, PLEAD (or see big or beach)
begar, beggar
begen, begin
begenir, begin(nner)
beger, beggar
beggar,*, ONE WHO BEGS
beggir, beggar
beggur, beggar
begil, beagle

belevuble, believe(vable)
belief,*, _FAITH, HOPE_
believe,*,ed,ving,vable, _FAITH, HOPE_
believeable, believe(vable)
beligerent, belligerent
belise, police
belittle,*,ed,ling,ement, _TO INSULT_
belle, belly
belligerent,tly,nce,ncy, _WAR-LIKE AGGRESSIVENESS_
bellow,*,wed,wing, _DEEP ROAR, INSTRUMENT (or see below or billow)_
belly,llies, _ABDOMEN_
belo, bellow /below /billow
belonee, bologna / baloney
belong,*,ging,gings, _HAVE RIGHTS TO_
beloon, balloon
below, _BENEATH, LOWER (or see bellow /billow)_
belt,*,ted,ting, _STRAP TO WEAR AROUND THE WAIST, PUNCH/HIT SOMETHING (or see built)_
belurds, billiards
belyon, billion
bemt, beam(ed)
ben, been /bin /bean
benafactor, benefactor
benaficial, beneficial
benaficiary, beneficiary
benafishiary, beneficiary
benafishul, beneficial
benafit, benefit
benansa, bonanza
benanu, banana
bench,hes,hed, _RELATES TO LAW, GEOLOGY, SPORTS_
bend,*,ding,nt, _CROOK/ANGLE (or see bent /bind)_
bended, bent
bendid, bent
bene, _PREFIX INDICATING "GOOD/WELL" MOST OFTEN MODIFIES THE WORD_
beneath, _UNDER, LOWER_
beneeth, beneath

benefactor,*, tion, _CONTRIBUTOR_
beneficial,lly, _HELPFUL_
beneficiary,ries, _ONE WHO BENEFITS FROM_
benefishiery, beneficiary
benefishul, beneficial
benefit,*,ted,ting, _TO SERVE_
benevolence, benevolence
benevolence,nt,ntly, _BIG HEARTED_
benevulense, benevolence
benge, binge
benifactor, benefactor
benificial, beneficial
benificiary, beneficiary
benifisheary, beneficiary
benifishul, beneficial
benifit, benefit
benign,nity,nities,nly, _KINDLY_
benine, benign
benje, binge
bent, _PAST TENSE OF" BEND"_
bented, bent
benufactor, benefactor
benuficial, beneficial
benuficiary, beneficiary
benufisheary, beneficiary
benufishul, beneficial
benufit, benefit
beond, beyond
ber, burr /bear /bare /beer
berbin, bourbon
berch, birch
berd, bird / beard
berden, burden
berdinsum, burden(some)
bere, berry /bury /bare /bear
bereave,*,ed,ving,ement, _ANGUISH OVER LOSS_
bereble, bearable
berecade, barricade
bereft, _LACKING/LOSS/DEPRIVED_
berek, barrack

begin,*,nning,gan,nner, _TO START_
beginer, begin(nner)
begir, beggar
begle, beagle
begul, beagle
begur, beggar
begutre, bigotry
behaf, behalf
behalf, _ON THE PART OF_
behaveor, behavior
behavior,ism, _MANNERISMS, ATTITUDE_
behavyur, behavior
behind, _TO THE BACK_
behoof, behoove
behoove,*,ed,ving, _TO BE PROPER_
behufe, behoove
behuve, behoove
beige, _COLOR_
being,*,gness, _EXISTS_
bekame, became
beken, beckon /beacon /bacon
beker, beaker
bekin, beckon /beacon /bacon
bekom, become
bekon, beckon /beacon /bacon
bekos, because
bekum, become
bekur, beaker
bekus, because
bekuz, because
beladed, belated
beladid, belated
belated,dly, _OVERDUE_
belatide, belated
beld, build /bill(ed) /built
bele, belly
belegarant, belligerent
beleon, billion
belerds, billiards

berekad, barricade
berekade, barricade
berel, barrel
beren, barren
bereng, bearing /bare(ring)
berer, bear(er) /barrier
berestur, barrister
beret,*, CLOTH CAP (or see barrette)
beretone, baritone
bereul, burial
bereur, barrier
bergendy, burgundy
bergler, burglar
bergundy, burgundy
berial, burial
berible, bearable
bericade, barricade
berick, barrack
berier, barrier
berikade, barricade
beril, barrel
berin, barren
bering, bearing
berister, barrister
beristur, barrister
beritone, baritone
berkler, burglar
berlap, burlap
berlesk, burlesque
berly, burly
berm,*,med, SLOPED SOIL
bern, burn
bernt, burnt
bero, barrow /burrow /burro /borough
berog, barrage
beroj, barrage
berol, barrel
beron, barren

berow, barrow /borrow
berp, burp
berry,ries, FRUIT (or see bury)
bersaverense, persevere(rance)
berserk, VIOLENT FRENZY
berst, burst
berth,*, PLACE TO SETTLE INTO/SLEEP (or see birth)
berthday, birthday
beruble, bearable
berubul, bearable
berukad, barricade
berul, barrel
berston, baritone
berry, berry /bury
bes, bee(s) /best
besar, bizarre /bazaar
besd, best /beast
bese, busy
beseach, beseech
beseech,her,hingly, IMPLORE
beserk, berserk
beside,*, ALONGSIDE, AS WELL AS
besk, bisque
besket, biscuit
besque, bisque
best,*, PAST TENSE OF "BETTER" (or see beast)
bestro, bistro
besy, busy
bet,*,tted,tting,ttor, TO PLACE A WAGER IN ORDER TO WIN SOMETHING (or see beet/ beat/ bed/ bed)
beted, bet(tted) / bed(dded)
beter, better /bid(dder) /bitter /bet(ttor)
betid, bet(tted) / bed(dded)
betir, better /bid(dder) /bitter /bet(ttor)
beton, baton
betor, better /bid(dder) /bitter /bet(ttor)
betray,yal,yer, VIOLATION OF TRUST
betrothed, ENGAGEMENT TO SOMEONE
better,rment, MORE SUPERIOR (or see bet(ttor))

betud, bet(tted) / bed(dded)
between, IN THE MIDDLE OF HERE AND THERE
beudful, beautiful
beudiful, beautiful
beudy, beauty
beugl, bugle
beurd, beard
beuro, bureau
beurocrasy, bureaucracy
beut, butte
beuteshun, beautician
beutiful, beautiful
beuty, beauty
bevarige, beverage
bevel,*,led,ling, INCLINED SURFACE
beverage,*, FLAVORED LIQUID TO DRINK
bevil, bevel
bevir, beaver
bevirage, beverage
bevle, bevel
bevol, bevel
bevrag, beverage
bevrig, beverage
bevul, bevel
bevur, beaver
beware, CAUTION
bewere, beware
bewhere, beware
bewhove, behoove
bewilder,*,red,ring,ringly,rment, CONFUSE
bewt, butte
bewte, beauty
bewteful, beautiful
bewteshin, beautician
bewyon, bouillon
beyeng, being
beyond, OUT OF REACH
beyut, butte
bezar, bizarre /bazaar

bezd, best / beast
bezerk, berserk
bi, bin, bis, PREFIX INDICATING "TWO/TWICE" MOST
   OFTEN MODIFIES THE WORD (or see by/bye)
bialegy, biology
bianeal, biennial /biannual
bianel, biennial /biannual
biannual, TWICE A YEAR (or see biennial)
bianuel, biannual
bianyual, biannual
bias, PREFERENCE TOWARDS/FOR
bibleografy, bibliography
bibleogrufy, bibliography
biblio, PREFIX INDICATING "BOOK" MOST OFTEN
   MODIFIES THE WORD
bibliography,hies,hic,hical, LIST OF PRINTED
   MATERIAL
bicame, became
bicentenial, bicentennial
bicentennial,*, TWO HUNDRED YEAR MARK
biceps, muscles
bicker,*,red,ring, ARGUE
bicos, because
bicus, because
bicycle,*,ed,ling,list, TWO-WHEEL TRANSPORTATION
bid,*,dder,dding, TO TELL, BE TOLD, BID FAREWELL,
   WAGER SOMETHING TO GAIN SOMETHING ELSE (or
   see bite/ bitter/ bit/ bed /bide)
bidder, bitter / bid(der) /bite(r)
bide,*,ed,ling, WAIT, WITHSTAND (or see bid/bite)
bider, bite(r) / bid(dder) /bitter
bidragled, bedraggled
bidraguled, bedraggled
bidtrothed, betrothed
bieng, buy(ing)
bienial, biennial /biannual
biennial, TWO YEARS (or see biannual)
bifal, befall
bifocals, TWO-PART LENS

bifocul, bifocals
bifokul, bifocals
bifol, befall
bifore, before
bifour, before
bifrend, befriend
big,gger,ggest,ggy, LARGE (or see beg)
bigetree, bigotry
bigetry, bigotry
bigotry, NARROW-MINDED
bigutry, bigotry
bihalf, behalf
bihind, behind
bikame, became
bikeeny, bikini
biker, bike(r) / bike(r)
bike,*,ed,king,er, 2 WHEEL TRANSPORTATION
bikini,*, TWO-PIECE BATHING SUIT
bikose, because
bikum, become
bikur, bicker /bike(r)
bikus, because
bilak, black
bilanear, bilinear
bilards, billiards
bilateral, BOTH SIDES
bilatirul, bilateral
bild, build / bill(ed) /built
bile, FLUID MADE BY THE LIVER (or see bill)
biled, build / bill(ed) /built
bileef, belief
bileeve, believe
bilenear, bilinear
bilengual, bilingual
bilengwul, bilingual
bileon, billion
bilerds, billiards
bileve, believe
bilevuble, believe(vable)

biliards, billiards
bilinear, TWO LINES
bilingual, SPEAKS TWO LANGUAGES
bilingwal, bilingual
bilion, billion
bill,*,lled,lling, TOTAL COSTS (or see bile)
billiards, POOL GAME
billion,*,naire, ONE THOUSAND MILLION
billow,*,wed,wing,OF WIND(or see below/bellow)
bilo, billow/ below/ bellow
bilonee, baloney /bologna
bilong, belong
bilow, below /billow /bellow
bilt, built /build
bilurds, billiards
bilyon, billion
bimonthly, TWICE A MONTH
bimonthly, bimonthly
bin,*, COMPARTMENT FOR STORAGE (or see been)
binanu, banana
binanzu, bonanza
binary,ries, UNITS OF TWO
binch, bench
bind,*,ded,ding,dingly,der, HOLD THINGS TOGETHER
bineeth, beneath
binefacter, benefactor
binery, binary
binevilense, benevolence
binevulense, benevolence
binge,*,ed,ging, SPREE
binign, benign
binine, benign
binje, binge
binocular,*, DEVICE THAT MAGNIFIES FOR BOTH EYES
binokuler, binocular
binomeal, binomial
binomial,*, HAS TWO NAMES/TERMS
binoquler, binocular
bint, bent

bitray, betray
bitrothed, betrothed
bitter, *UNPLEASANT (or see bid(dder) or bite(r))*
bitur, bitter/ bid(dder)/ bite(r)
bitween, between
bius, bias
biusfere, biosphere
biusphere, biosphere
biwelder, bewilder
biwilder, bewilder
biyopse, biopsy
biyorethum, biorhythm
biyou, bayou
biyu, bayou
biyus, bias
bizar, bizarre/ bazaar
bizarre,ely,eness, *PECULIAR (or see bazaar)*
bizee, busy
bizerk, berserk
bizurk, berserk
bizzar, bizzare/ bazaar
black,*,ken,kened,ker,kest, *COLOR*
bladder, *HOLDS URINE/LIQUIDS*
blade,*, *USED TO SLICE/CUT*
blader, bladder
bladur, bladder
blaenkit, blanket
blair, blare
blak, black
blam, blame
blame,*,ed,ming,mable,eful,eless,elessly, elessness, *WHAT/WHO IS RESPONSIBLE*
bland,ly, *EXPRESSIVELY FLAT*
blank, *NOTHING*
blanket,*,ted,ting, *COVER*
blankit, blanket
blare,*,ed,ring, *SOUND LOUDLY*
blasa, plaza
blase, blaze

birkler, burglar
birlesk, burlesque
birlup, burlap
birm, berm
birn, burn
birnt, burnt
biro, burro /burrow /borough
birometer, barometer
birp, burp
birst, burst
birth,*, hed,hing, *PHYSICAL BODY BECOMES VISIBLE (or see berth)*
birthday,*,*, *DATE OF BIRTH*
bisar, bizarre /bazaar
biscuit,*, *NORMALLY GOES WITH GRAVY, A SOFT ROLL*
biscut, biscuit
biseach, beseech
biseech, beseech
bisekul, bicycle
bisenteneal, bicentennial
biseps, biceps
bisicle, bicycle
biside, beside
bisikul, bicycle
bisintineal, bicentennial
bisk, bisque
biskit, biscuit
biskut, biscuit
bisness, business
bisnis, business
bisque, *OF SPORTS, A SOUP*
bistro, *NIGHTCLUB*
bisurk, berserk
bisy, busy
bit,*, *TINY INCREMENTS OF SOMETHING, TOOL FOR DRILLING,PAST TENSE OF "BITE"(or see bite/bid)*
bite,*,ting,ter, *USE OF MOUTH AS A TOOL(or see bit)*
biter, bitter /bid(dder) /bite(r)
biton, baton

binufakter, benefactor
binufishal, beneficial
binufishary, beneficiary
binufit, benefit
binury, binary
bio, *PREFIX INDICATING "LIFE" MOST OFTEN MODIFIES THE WORD*
biocide,dal, *CIVILIZATION CHOKING OFF IT'S OWN LIFE SUPPLY*
biofisics, biophysics
biofizecs, biophysics
biografee, biography
biografue, biography
biography,hies, *STORY OF PEOPLE'S HISTORY*
biology,gical,gically,gist, *STUDY OF LIFE*
biophisics, biophysics
biophysics, *STUDY OF LIFE*
biopsy,sies, *STUDY OF TISSUE*
biorethum, biorhythm
biorhythm, *BIOLOGICAL RHYTHM*
biorithum, biorhythm
biorythm, biorhythm
biorythm, biorhythm
bios, bias
biosfeare, biosphere
bioside, biocide
biosphere, *ALL THAT SUPPORTS LIFE ON EARTH*
bipardesan, bipartisan
bipardisan, bipartisan
bipartisan, *TWO SIDES SHARING SAME PURPOSE*
bir, burr
birben, bourbon
birch, *A TREE*
bird,*, *ANIMAL WITH WINGS/FEATHERS*
birden, burden
birdensum, burden(some)
birdinsum, burden(some)
biret, barrette /beret
birglur, burglar
birgundy, burgundy

blasem, blossom
blasfemus, blasphemy(mous)
blasfemy, blasphemy
blasma, plasma
blasphemy,mous, *SPEAK BADLY OF SOMEONE*
blast, blasto, *PREFIX INDICATING "GERM/ BUD" MOST OFTEN MODIFIES THE WORD*
blast,ted,ting, *BURSTING FORCE/RUSH*
blastek, plastic
blastik, plastic
blatebus, platypus
blater, bladder
blatibus, platypus
blaus, blouse
blawse, blouse
blaze,*,ed,zing,er, *FLAME, HORSE MARK, PROCLAIM, SPORT COAT*
blazu, plaza
blea, plea
bleach,es,hed, *TO MAKE WHITE*
bleachers, *SEATS FOR SPECTATORS*
bleed,*,der,ding,bled, *LOOSE BLOOD, ALLOW RELEASE OF FLUID*
bleak,kish,kly,kness, *PALLID, DESOLATE, STARK*
bleech, bleach
bleechers, bleachers
bleef, belief
bleek, bleak
blemish,hes,hed, *DEFECT ON A SURFACE*
blemp, blimp
blend,*,ded,ding, *MIX*
blenk, blink
bler, blur
bless,ses,sed,sing, *FAVOR UPON* (or see bliss)
blester, blister
blew, *TO DO WITH AIR, PAST TENSE OF "BLOW"* (or see blue)
blezurd, blizzard
blight,*,, *DESTROYED BY ORGANISM* (or see plight)

blimp,* *HELIUM BALLOON*
blind,*,ded,ding,ders, *WITHOUT SIGHT, WINDOW COVERING* (or see blend)
blink,*,ked,king, *TO OPEN/CLOSE/OPEN*
blinker,*,, *TURN INDICATOR*
blir, blur
blis, bliss
blisful, bliss(ful)
bliss,sful,sfully,sfullness, *EXTREMELY HAPPY* (or see bless)
blister,*,red,ring, *SORE*
blisurd, blizzard
blite, blight
blizzard,*,, *VIOLENT STORM*
blo, blow / below
bloan, blown
bloat,*,ted,ting, *SWELL* (or see blot)
block,*,ked,king,kage, *IN PATHWAY*
blockade,*,, ed,ding, *OBSTRUCT TRAVEL*
blod, blood /bloat /blown
blog,*,gged,gging,gger, *COMPUTER INTERNET TERM* (or see block)
blok, block /blog
blokade, blockade
blonde,*, *A COLOR*
blone, blown
blont, blonde
blood,*,ded,dy,dily,dless,diness, *BODY FLUID CARRYING NUTRIENTS*
blooish, blue(uish)
bloom,*,med,ming, *OPEN UP*
blosim, blossom
blossom,*,med,ming, *FLOURISH*
blosum, blossom
blot,*,tted,tting,tter, *SPOT, STAIN* (or see bloat or blood)
blouse,es, *WOMAN'S SHIRT*
blouze, blouse

blow,*,wing,blew,wn, *FORCEFUL AIR CURRENT* (or see below)
blown, *TO DO WITH AIR, PAST TENSE OF "BLOW"*
blowse, blouse
blu, blue /blew
blubber,ry, *WHALE FAT, SOBBING*
blubur, blubber
blud, blood
blue,*,uish, *COLOR* (or see blew)
bluesh, blue(uish)
bluff,*,ffed,ffing,ffer, *A CLIFF, TO PRETEND/FAKE*
blume, bloom
blunder,*,red,ring, *BUNGLES*
blunt,*,tly,tness, *DULL*
bluper, blubber
blupir, blubber
blur,*,rred,rring,rry, *INDISTINCT/FUZZY*
blush,hes,hed,hing, *PHYSICAL RESPONSE IN THE CHEEKS*
blut, blood
bluty, blood(y)
bo, bough /bow /beau
boar,*, *SWINE, PIG* (or see bore)
board,*,ded,ding, *MILLED WOOD, FURNISH WITH FOOD* (or see bore(d))
boast,*,ted,ting,tful,tfully, *TO BRAG, COMPLIMENT*
boat,*,ting,ter, *VESSEL IN WATER*
bob,*,bbed,bbing, *TO MOVE UP AND DOWN* (or see bobbin or bop)
bobbin,*, *SEWING TOOL* (or see bop(pping))
bobd, bop(pped) /bob(bbed)
boben, bobbin /bob(bbing)
bobin, bobbin /bob(bbing)
bobt, bop(pped) /bob(bbed)
bochulism, botulism
bocks, box
bodchulism, botulism
boddle, bottle

bode,*, PAST TENSE OF "BIDE" TO WAIT (or see body or bought)
bodeese, bodice /body
bodel, bottle
bodely, body(dily)
bodem, bottom
bodes, body(dies) /bodice
bodice, WOMAN'S GARMENT FOR UPPER TORSO
bodim, bottom
bodis, body(dies) /bodice
bodjulism, botulism
bodle, bottle
bodul, bottle
bodulism, botulism
bodum, bottom
body,dies,dily, THE PHYSICAL FORM WHICH HOUSES A SPIRIT/LIFE (or see bodice)
boe, boy /buoy
boee, boy /buoy
boel, boil
boent, buoyant
boestures, boisterous
boeul, boil
boeunse, buoyant(ncy)
boi, boy / buoy
boil,*,led,ling, BRING LIQUID TO STEAM TEMPERATURE
boiunse, buoyant(ncy)
bok, book /poke
boka, bouquet
boks, box
boisterous,sly,sness, ROWDY
bol, ball /bowl /bawl /bull
bolb, bulb
bolbus, bulbous
bold,der,dest,dly,dness, BRAVE, STANDS OUT (or see bolt)
bolder, boulder /bold(er)
bole, bowl /ball /bawl /bully
bolef, belief

boletin, bulletin
boletle, belittle
boleve, believe
bolidel, belittle
boligerant, belligerent
bolistic, balistic
bolit, bullet
boliten, bulletin
bolivard, boulevard
bolk, bulk
boll, bowl /ball /bawl
bollion, bullion / bouillon
bolm, balm
bolme, balmy
bolmy, balmy
bologna, MIXTURE OF MEAT TYPES (or see baloney)
bolonee, baloney /bologna
bolster,*,red,ring, SUPPORT
bolt,*,ted,ting, SECURES, THREADED ROD WITH HEAD (or see bold)
bolter, boulder /bold(er)
bolyon, bullion /bouillon
bom, balm / bomb
bomb,*,bed,bing, EXPLOSIVE DEVICE
bomirang, boomerang
bon, bone
bona fide, GENUINE
bonanza, BONUS DEAL
bond,*,ded,ding,dage, TO JOIN/ATTACH TO, TIE UP
bone fide, bona fide
bone,*,ey, SKELETAL
boni fide, bona fide
bonu fide, bona fide
bony, bone(y)
bonyon, bunion
book,*,ked,king,kish,kishly,kishness, BOUND PAPER WITH A COVER, TO RESERVE A PLACE
bookie,*, BOOKS BETS
booky, bookie

boomerang,*, ARTICLE FOR SPORT
boomurang, boomerang
boose, booze / buzz
boost, TO LIFT (or see boast or bust)
boosum, bosom
boot,*, OVER ANKLE SHOE (or see butte)
booteek, boutique
booth,hes, PRIVATE STALL/AREA
bootshur, butcher
booy, buoy
booyon, bouillon / bullion
booze, HARD LIQUOR (or see buzz)
bop,*,pped,pping, TO HIT/WHACK (or see bob)
boped, bop(pped) /bob(bbed)
bopt, bop(pped) /bob(bbed)
boquet, bouquet
bor, boar /bore /bar
borbon, bourbon
bord, board / bore(d)
bordem, boredom
border,*,red,ring, TO LIMIT
bordim, boredom
bordor, border
bordum, boredom
bordur, border
bore,*,ed,ring, PIERCE/PUNCTURE/DRILL, LACKS INTEREST, PAST TENSE OF "BEAR" (or see boar)
boredom, DOLDRUMS, LACK OF INTEREST
boren, barren / beret
boret, barrette / beret
borin, borne / born
born, BROUGHT INTO EXISTENCE (or see borne)
borne, SUFFIX MEANING TO BE CARRIED OR MOVED BY A PARTICULAR THING (or see born)
boro, PREFIX INDICATING "BORON" MOST OFTEN MODIFIES THE WORD (or see borrow/borough)
borot, borrow(ed)
borough,*, SELF-GOVERNING TOWN (or see burrow /burro /borrow)

borrow, borrow/ burrow/ borough
borrow,*,wed,wing,wer, LOAN (or see burrow)
bort, bore(d) /board
borter, border
bortur, border
bose, bough(s) /bow(s) /bossy
bosed, boss(ed)
boseness, boss(iness)
boshel, bushel
bosiness, boss(iness)
bosom,*,med, WOMEN'S BREASTS
boss,sses,ssed,ssing,ssy, TO ORDER SOMEONE TO DO SOMETHING, ONE IN CHARGE
bossom, bosom
bossy,siness, DOMINEERING
bost, boast / boss(ed) /boost
bosy, bossy
bot, boat /bought
botany,nic,nical,nist, OF PLANTS
botcher, butcher
botchulism, botulism
bote, boat /bought
boteek, boutique
botel, bottle
botem, bottom
botes, body(dies) /bodice
both, TWO TOGETHER (or see booth)
bother,*,red,ring,rsome, ANNOY
botil, bottle
botim, bottom
botiney, botany
botle, bottle
botney, botany
botom, bottom
botshulism, botulism
bottle,*,ed,ling,er, GLASS CONTAINER
bottom,*,med,ming,mless, BASE
botul, bottle
botulism, FOOD POISONING

botum, bottom
boty, body
bough,*,hed, BUNCHED FLOWERS, TREE BRANCHES, PART OF A SHIP (or see bow or beau)
bought, PURCHASED, PAST TENSE OF "BUY" (or see bout)
bouillon, BROTH (or see bullion)
boulder,*, LARGE ROCK (or see bold)
boulevard,*, AVENUE
boulion, bouillon /bullion
boulse, bowels /bowl(s)
bounce,*,ed,cing,cy,er,REBOUND, UP/DOWN ACTION JUMP, DESTINY
bound,*,ded,dless,dlessly,dlessness, TO HOLD, CAPTURE, PLENTY, ABUNDANCE
boundary,ries, A LIMIT OR BORDERLINE
bounsy, bounce(y)
bountiful,lly,lness, PLENTIFUL
bounty,ties,tied,tiful,teous, PAYMENT/REWARD FOR CAPTURE, PLENTY, ABUNDANCE
bouquet, BUNCH OF FLOWERS
bourbon, WHISKEY
bourgeoisie, WEALTHY MIDDLE CLASS
bout,*, A SPELL OF, TEMPORARY EXPERIENCE
boutique,*, WOMEN'S CLOTHING
bouwls, bowels
bow,*,wed,wing, TO BEND, HAIR ORNAMENT, FOR INSTRUMENT/ARROW (or see bough /beau)
bowels, INTESTINES OF ANYTHING
bowkay, bouquet
bowl,*,led,ling,ler, ROUND VESSEL, GAME OF BALLS WITH PINS (or see ball or bawl)
bowlder, boulder / bold(er)
bownd, bound
bowndee, bounty
bowndeful, bountiful
bowndury, boundary
bowndy, bounty
bownse, bounce /bound(s)
bownsee, bounce(cy)

bowntee, bounty
bownteful, bountiful
bownts, bounce /bound(s)
bowt, bout
bowteek, boutique
box,xes,xing,xy, SQUARE SHAPED CONTAINER, SPORT
boy,*, yish,yishly, YOUNG MALE (or see buoy)
boyant, buoyant
boyint, buoyant
boyle, boil
boysterus, boisterous
boyunse, buoyant(ncy)
bra,*, WOMEN'S UNDERGARMENT
brace,*,ced,cing, SUPPORT (or see brass /braise)
bracelet,*, WRIST ORNAMENT
bracket,*,ting, FIXTURE TO ATTACH TO, TO ENCLOSE WITHIN
brade, braid
brael, brail /braille
braen, brain
braes, brace /braise
braf, brave
brag,*,gged,gging, TO BOAST/PRAISE
braget, braggart
braggart,*, ONE WHO BOASTS
bragirt, braggart
braid,*,ded,ding, TO INTERTWINE TOGETHER
brail, OF BOATS, BIRD, FISH (or see braille)
braille, TEXT FOR THE BLIND (or see brail)
brain,*,nless,ny, THINKING PART/MASS IN THE SKULL
braise,*,ed,sing, TO BROWN MEAT AND COVER TO COOK (or see brace)
brake,*,ed,king, TO STOP, HOLD BACK (or see break)
braket, bracket
brakible, breakable
brakit, bracket
brakley, broccoli
brakuble, breakable

bral, brail /braille /brawl
brane, brain
brankeal, bronchial
bras, brace /brass /braise /bra(s)
braslet, bracelet
brass,SY, *METAL, MILITARY OFFICERS*
brathren, brethren
brau, bra
braud, broad
braukle, broccoli
braun, brown /brawn
braus, browse /brow(s)
brave,*,-er,-est,ery, *COURAGEOUS*
braw, bra
brawkley, broccoli
brawl,*,, *LOUD FIGHT*
brawn, *MUSCLES* (or see brown)
brawnkeul, bronchial
brawnkitis, bronchitis
brawnze, bronze
brayed, braid
brayel, brail /braille
braz, braise /brace /bra(s)
breach,hes,hed,hing, *BREAK CONTRACT/AGREEMENT*
bread,ded,ding,dth, *BAKED DOUGH* (or see bred or breed)
breadth, *THE EXTENT/DISTANCE/BROADNESS* (or see breath)
brej, bridge
break,*,-king,kage,ker,broke, *COME APART* (or see brake)
breakable, *CAN COME APART*
breakuble, breakable
breast,*,-ted, *BOSOM*
breath,hes,hed,hing,less,lessly, *INHALE, EXHALE AIR* (or see breadth)
brec, brick
brech, breach

bred, *PASTE TENSE OF "BREED", HAVING MATED* (or see bread/ breed/ barette)
breed,*,-ding, *TO MATE FOR PROCREATION, A TYPE/ CLASSIFICATION* (or see bred or bread)
breef, brief
breeng, bring
breenk, brink
breeth, breath
breeve, bereave
breeze,*, -ed,zing,zily,zy, *GENTLE WIND*
bref, brief
brege, bridge
breif, brief
brej, bridge
brek, brick
breluns, brilliance
brelyans, brilliance
brem, brim
breng, bring
brenk, brink
brese, breeze
brest, breast
bret, barrette /beret /breed /bread
breth, breath /breadth
brethless, breath(less)
brethlis, breath(less)
brethren, *PLURAL FOR BROTHER*
brethrin, brethren
brew,*,-wed,wing, *A DRINK CONCOCTION*
breze, breeze
bribe,*,-ed,bing,ery, *REWARD FOR CORRUPTION*
brick,*,-ked, *CLAY BLOCK*
bride,*,-dal, *FEMALE GETTING MARRIED*
bridegroom,*, , *MARRYING MALE*
bridesmaid,*, , *ATTENDS BRIDE*
bridge,*,-ed,ging, *LINK FOR TRAVEL*
bridgeroom, bridegroom
bridgrum, bridegroom

bridle,*,-ed,ling, *FOR RESTRAINT (HORSES)* (or see brittle)
bridmade, bridemaid
bridol, bridle / brittle
bridsmaid, bridemaid
bridul, bridle / brittle
brief,*,-fed,fing, *SHORT/SWEET/TO THE POINT, UNDERWEAR*
brig, bridge
bright,*,-ter,test,tly,tness, *STRONG LIGHT ENERGY*
brij, bridge
brik, brick
brileans, brilliance
briliance, brilliance
brilliance,nt,ntly, *INTENSE LIGHT ENERGY*
brim,*,-mmed,mming, *THE EDGE/RIM OF SOMETHING*
bring,*,-ging,brought, *BEAR FORTH*
brink, *NEAR THE EDGE*
brit, bright / bride
britesmade, bridemaid
britle, bridle / brittle
brittle,eness, *CRISP* (or see bridle)
britul, bridle / brittle
broad,dly,den,dness, *AS IN WIDTH OR BREADTH*
broadcast,*,-ted,ting,ter, *ANNOUNCE, SCATTER*
broccoli or brocoli, *VEGETABLE*
brochere, brochure
brochure,*, , *PAMPHLET*
brocoli, broccoli
brod, broad /brought /brood
brodkast, broadcast
broeel, broil
broel, broil
broil,*,-led,ling, *WAY TO COOK*
brok, broke
broke,en, *PAST TENSE OF "BREAK", NO MONEY*
brokle, broccoli
brokley, broccoli
brol, brawl

bron, brawn /brown
brona, prana /piranha
bronceal, bronchial
bronch, bronchi, broncho, *PREFIX INDICATING*
  "BRONCHIAL" MOST OFTEN MODIFIES THE WORD
broncheul, bronchial
bronchial,lly, *OF THE AIR/BREATHING PASSAGES*
bronchitis, *BREATHING PROBLEM*
bronckial, bronchial
bronkeul, bronchial
bronkites, bronchitis
bronse, bronze
bronze,ed,zing, *METALLIC*
brood,*,ding,dingly, *CONCERNING OFFSPRING IN A*
  GROUP, TO GRIEVE, TO SET ON EGGS
broodel, brutal
brook,*, *STREAM*
broom,*, *FOR SWEEPING*
broonet, brunet
brootal, brutal
brootle, brutal
bropane, propane
brosher, brochure
broshur, brochure
broth, *SOUP*
brother,*,rly, *MALE SIBLING*
brought,*, *PAST TENSE OF "BRING"*
brow,*, *ABOVE EYES* (or see browse)
browl, brawl
brown,*,ned,ning, *COLOR* (or see brawn)
browse,*,ed,sing,er, *GLANCE/PERUSE/CASUALLY GO*
  THROUGH (or see brow(s))
broyl, broil
brud, brood
brudel, brutal
brue, brew
bruise,*,ed,sing, *A BLOW TO, DAMAGED TISSUE*
bruke, brook
brume, broom

brunet, brunet
brunet, *DARK COLOR*
brunkitis, bronchitis
brunnet, brunet
'bruse, bruise
brush,hes,hed,hing, *ENCOUNTER, HAIR TOOL,*
  BUSHES
brutal,lly,lize,lization,lity, *SAVAGE*
bruther, brother
brutil, brutal
bruz, bruise
brydgroom, bridegroom
brydle, bridle / brittle
brydsmade, bridemaid
bryt, bright
bubble,*,ed,ling,er, *AIR, GAS GLOBULES*
bubil, bubble
buble, bubble
bucame, became
bucher, butcher
buchur, butcher
buck,*,ked,king, *UNSEAT RIDER, MALE DEER,DOLLAR*
bucket,*, *A CONTAINER*
buckil, buckle
buckit, bucket
buckle,*,ed,ling, *TO SECURE, OR TAKE SHAPE OF*
bud,*,dded,dding, *READY TO OPEN, FULL OF FUTURE*
  POTENTIAL (or see butt/ butte/ but)
budder, butter
buddy,ddies,ddied,ddying, *SOMEONE YOU*
  BEFRIEND, TRAVEL ALONGSIDE (or see beauty)
bude, buddy / beauty
budeful, beautiful
buden, button
buder, butter
budge,*,ed,ging, *TO MOVE*
budget,*,ted,ting,ter,tary, *RATION A SPECIFIC*
  AMOUNT FOR EXPENDITURES
budi, buddy / beauty

budiful, beautiful
budin, button
budj, budge
budler, butler
budok, buttock
budres, buttress
budris, buttress
budrothed, betrothed
buduk, buttock
budy, buddy /beauty
buee, buoy
bufa, buffet
bufal, befall
bufalo, buffalo
bufer, buffer
buffalo,*, *ANIMAL*
buffer,*,red,ring, *ABSORBS SHOCK, POLISHES*
buffet,*, *SELF-SERVE RESTAURANT*
bufilo, buffalo
bufir, buffer
bufol, befall
bufrend, befriend
bufulo, buffalo
bufur, buffer
buge, budge
bugel, bugle
bugener, begin(nner)
buget, budget
bugil, bugle
bugin, begin
bugit, budget
bugle,*, *INSTRUMENT*
bugul, bugle
bugwazee, bourgeoisie
buhaf, behalf
buhind, behind
build,*,der,ding,lt, *CONSTRUCT* (or see built)
built, *PAST TENSE OF "BUILD"*
buj, budge

bujet, budget
bujit, budget
bujwazee, bourgeoisie
buk, buck /book
bukame, became
buke, bookie
bukel, buckle
bukene, bikini
buket, bucket
bukie, bookie
bukil, buckle
bukit, bucket
bukaus, because
bukos, because
bul, bull
bulated, belated
bulaten, bulletin
bulatide, belated
bulavard, boulevard
bulb,*,bous, OF PLANTS, GLASS GLOBES WITH FILAMENTS
bulbus, bulbous
bulch, bulge
bulck, bulk
bule, bully
buledul, belittle
buleef, belief
buleeve, believe
bulef, belief
bulegirant, belligerent
buleon, bullion /bouillon
bulese, police
bulet, bullet
buletin, bulletin
bulevard, boulevard
buleve, believe
bulevuble, believe(vable)
bulge,*,ed,ging, SWELL OUT
buligerant, belligerent

buljurent, belligerent
bulion, bullion /bouillon
bulistic, balistic
bulit, bullet
bullten, bulletin
bulitel, belittle
bulivard, boulevard
bulje, bulge
bulk,ky,kiness, MASS OF SOMETHING
bull,*, MALE ANIMAL
bullet,*, PROJECTILE
bulletin,*, DOCUMENT
bullion, OF GOLD (or see bouillon)
bully,llies,llied,llying, INTIMIDATOR
bullyon, bouillon /bullion
bulo, blow /below
bulonee, baloney /bologna
bulong, belong
buloon, balloon
bulow, below /bellow /billow
bulp, bulb
bulune, balloon
buluvard, boulevard
buly, bully
bulyon, bullion /bouillon
bumbelbee, bumblebee
bumblebee,*, BIG BEE
bumer, bummer
bumerang, boomerang
bumir, bummer
bummer, OF QUARRY, NOT HAPPY
bumur, bummer
bumurang, boomerang
bunana, banana
bunansa, bonanza
bunch,hes,hed,hing, MORE THAN A FEW IN THE GROUP
bundle,*,ed,ling,er, TO GROUP/BIND TOGETHER
bune, bunny
buneeth, beneath

buneon, bunion
bunevilance, benevolence
bungil, bungle
bungle,*,ed,ling, MESS-UP
bunie, bunny
bunine, benign
bunion or bunyon, BUMP ON TOE
bunny,nies, RABBIT
bunsh, bunch
buny, bunny
bunyun, bunion
buond, beyond
buoy,*, FLOATING DEVICE
buoyant,ncy, TO FLOAT
bur, burr
burave, brave
burbon, bourbon
burch, birch
burd, bird
burden,*,ned,ning,nsome, HEAVY LOAD
burdensum, burden(some)
burdin, burden
burdinsum, burden(some)
burdon, burden
bureal, burial
bureau,*, A DRESSER, GOVERNMENT DEPARTMENT
bureaucracy,cies,at, GOVERNMENT ADMINISTRATION
bureeve, bereave
bureft, bereft
buret, barrette /beret
bureve, bereave
burgendy, burgundy
burgeois, bourgeois
burglar,*,ry,ries,rize, ROBBERY
burglir, burglar
burgundy, A COLOR, A WINE
burial,*, BURYING DECEASED
burileans, brilliance
buring, bring

busil, bustle
busim, bosom
business,es, *A SERVICE*
busle, bustle
busness, business
busniss, business
bust,*,ted,ting,tie,tier, *HEAD AND SHOULDERS, WOMEN'S BREASTS, CAUGHT RED-HANDED* (or see boost/ burst/ bus(ssed))
bustle,*,ed,ling, *HURRIES ABOUT, FOR SKIRTS*
busul, bustle
busum, bosom
busurk, berserk
busy,sies,sier,siest, *ENGROSSED*
but, *A PREPOSITION MEANING "EXCEPT/ DIFFERENCE"* (or see but /butte /bud /boot)
butcher,*,red,ring, *CUT UP*
bute, boot /but /butt /butte
buted, butt(ed) /bud(dded)
buteek, boutique
buteful, beautiful
buten, button
butenchul, potential
buter, butter
buth, booth
buti, buddy /beauty
butid, butt(ed) /bud(dded)
butiful, beautiful
butike, boutique
butin, button
butinchul, potential
butir, butter
butishun, beautician
butler,*, *MALE SERVANT*
butlur, butler
butok, buttock
buton, baton /button
butra, betray
butres, buttress

burite, bright
burkler, burglar
burlap, *WOVEN HEMP/JUTE*
burlee, burly
burlesk, burlesque
burlesque,er, *MOCKERY*
burlip, burlap
burly, *BIG MUSCULAR BODY*
burm, berm
burn,*,ned,ning,burnt, *SCORCH*
burnt, *BEEN BURNED, PAST TENSE OF "BURN"*
buro, burro /burrow /borough /bureau
burocrasy, bureaucracy
burog, barrage
buromiter, barometer
burp,*,ped,ping, *BELCH*
burr,*, *PRICKLY SEED, ROUGH EDGES*
burro,*, *DONKEY* (or see burrow or borough)
burrow,*,wed,wing, *LODGE INTO HOLE* (or see burro or borough)
burst,*,ted,ting, *ERUPT*
burth, berth /birth
burthday, birthday
bury,ries,ried,rying, *PUT IN GROUND* (or see berry)
bus,sses,ssed,ssing, *LARGE VEHICLE TO TRANSPORT MANY PASSENGERS, CARRIER OF INFORMATION*
busar, bizarre /bazaar
busd, bust /boost /bus(ssed)
busdid, bust(ed) /burst
busech, beseech
buseech, beseech
busel, bustle
busem, bosom
buserd, buzzard
buses, bus(sses)
bushel,*, *MEASUREMENT OF AMOUNT*
bushil, bushel
buside, beside

butris, buttress
butrothed, betrothed
buts, butt(s) /bud(s) /boot(s)
butsher, butcher
butshir, butcher
butt,*,tted,tting, *REAR END/BOTTOM OF SOMETHING, FORCE UPON, "BUTT-IN"*(or see bud/but/butte or butt)
butte,*, *HILL/MOUNTAIN WITH FLAT TOP* (or see but or butt)
butter,ry, *CHURNED FROM MILK*
buttock,*, *RUMP*
button,*,ned,ning, *FIXTURE FOR CLOTHING*
buttress, *TO STRENGTHEN*
butuk, buttock
butween, between
buty, buddy /beauty
buvileon, pavilion
buware, beware
buwee, buoy
buwelder, bewilder
buwildre, bewilder
buwro, bureau
buwte, beauty
buy,*,ying,bought, *PURCHASE* (or see bye/by/bi)
buyent, buoyant
buyint, buoyant
buyond, beyond
buzar, bizarre /bazaar
buze, booze /buzz
buzerd, buzzard
buzerk, berserk
buzum, bosom
buzurk, berserk
buzzard,*, *CARNIVOROUS BIRD*
by, *ALONGSIDE* (or see bye /bi /buy)
by, bye, *PREFIX INDICATING "NEAR/SECONDARY" MOST OFTEN MODIFIES THE WORD*(or see bye/bi/buy)
bye, *AS IN GOOD-BYE* (or see by/bi/buy)
byeneul, biennial /biannual

byker, bike(r)
bysenteneal, bicentennial
byu, bayou

"C"

cabage, cabbage
cabaret,*, *TYPE OF MUSICAL SHOW*
cabbage,*, *VEGETABLE*
cabdive, captive
cabduve, captive
cabel, cable
caben, cabin
caberay, cabaret
cabich, cabbage
cabige, cabbage
cabin,*, *RUSTIC STRUCTURE*
cabinet,*,,try, *STORAGE WITH DOORS, POLITICAL
    ADVISORY*
cabiret, cabaret
cabitch, cabbage
cable,*,ed,ling, *WIRE ROPE, CONNECTION*
cabnet, cabinet
cabnit, cabinet
caboose,*, *LAST CAR ON A TRAIN*
cabsel, capsule
cabshure, capture
cabten, captain
cabture, capture
cabtuve, captive
cabul, cable
cabuse, caboose
cac, caco, *PREFIX INDICATING "HARSH/ BAD" MOST
    OFTEN MODIFIES THE WORD*
cache,*,ed,hing, *TO HIDE ITEMS IN* (or see cash or
    catch)
cacher, catcher

cachup, ketchup /catsup
cackle,*,ed,ling, *SHRILL SOUND/LAUGH*
cacoon, cocoon
cactis, cactus
cactus,is,ti, *DESERT PLANT*
cadaver,*,ric, *LIFELESS BODY*
caddie, caddy
caddy or caddie,*, *PERSON WHO CARRIES CLUBS IN
    GOLF, BOX*
cadee, caddy
cadence, *MARCHING RHYTHM*
cader, cater
caderact, cataract
cadet,*, *TRAINING FOR SERVICE*
cadilist, catalyst
cadilog, catalog
cadinse, cadence
cadle, cattle
cadul, cattle
cadulist, catalyst
cadulog, catalog
cadur, cater
caduract, cataract
caf, calf /cave
cafa, cafe
cafe,*, *SMALL RESTAURANT* (or see coffee or calf)
cafeene, caffeine
cafene, caffein
cafeteria,*, *SELF-SERVE RESTAURANT*
caffeine,nated,nism, *STIMULANT AND DIURETIC*
cafine, caffein
cafiteria, cafeteria
cafs, calves /cave(s)
cafutirea, cafeteria
cage,*,ed,ging, *FOR CONFINEMENT*
cagwal, casual
cahoot,*,, *IN PARTNERSHIP*
cahute, cahoot
cainker, canker /chancre

cairfree, carefree
cairful, careful
caje, cage
cajewul, casual
cajole,*,ed,ling, *COAX*
cajwul, casual
cake,*,ed,king, *BAKED SWEET DOUGH, ACT LIKE CAKE*
cakel, cackle
caktis, cactus
caktus, cactus
caky, khaki
cal, call /cowl /kale
calamity,ties,tous, *DISASTER*
calcilate, calculate
calcilus, calculus
calcium, *ELEMENT ON EARTH*
calculate,*,ed,ting,tingly,tion,tor, *TO MENTALLY/
    MATHEMATICALLY ESTIMATE/FIGURE*
calculus,les, *MATH LANGUAGE*
cale, kale
caleflower, cauliflower
calek, colic
calendar,*, *REGISTER OF MONTHS/DAYS OF THE YEAR*
    (or see calender or colander)
calender,*,rer, *PRESS/ROLLER FOR PAPER OR CLOTH*
    (or see calendar or colander)
calendula, *MEDICINAL FLOWER*
caler, collar /call(er)
cales, callous /callus
calesthenics, calisthenics
calf,|ves, *YOUNG ANIMAL, LOWER PORTION OF LEG*
caliber or calibre,*, *OF MEASUREMENT, DIAMETER*
    (or see caliper)
calibrate,*,ed,ting,tion,tor, *DETERMINE/SET
    MEASUREMENT/SIZE*
calibre, caliber
calidiscope, kaleidoscope
califlower, cauliflower
calinder, calendar /calender /colander

calindula, calendula
caliper or calliper,*, *INSTRUMENT FOR MEASURING* (or see caliber)
calire, calorie
calis, callous /callus
calisthenics, *EXERCISES*
calk, *DEVICE FOR SHOES* (or see caulk)
calkilate, calculate
calkulus, calculus
call,*,lled,lling,ller, *ATTEMPT TO CONTACT/INVITE SOMEONE TO ANSWER/RESPOND* (or see cowl)
calleague, colleague
callous or callus,ses,sed,sly,sness, *HARDENED/ROUGH AREA ON SKIN/PLANT*
calm,mes,med,ming,mly,mative,mness, *TO SOOTHE* (or see come)
calorie,*,ric,rically,rific,ize, *UNIT OF MEASUREMENT FOR FOOD*
calostomy, colostomy
calseum, calcium
caluber, caliber
calubrate, calibrate
calunder, colander
caluper, caliper
calur, collar / call(er)
calury, calorie
calus, callous /callus
calusthenics, calisthenics
calves, *PLURAL FOR THE WORD "CALF"*
came, *PAST TENSE OF "COME", CHANNEL USED FOR MANUFACTURING*
camel,*, *ANIMAL*
camendible, commendable
camenduble, commendable
camera,*, *TAKES PHOTOS*
camfor, camphor
caminduble, commendable
camofloje, camouflage
camouflage,*,ed,ging, *DISGUISED*

campaign,*,ned,ning, *ACTION TO INFLUENCE*
campane, campaign
camphor,raceous, *FROM TREES, MEDICINAL*
campis, campus
campus,es, *SCHOOL GROUNDS*
camra, camera
camuflodge, camouflage
camul, camel
camunicate, communicate
camunity, community
camute, commute
can,*,nned,nning,nner, *ABLE TO, TIN VESSEL* (or see cane)
canabus, cannabis
canal,*, *WHERE FLUIDS FLOW*
canary,ries, *ISLAND BIRD* (or see cannery)
cancel,*,lled,lling,llation,*DELETE,RENDER NULL/VOID*
cancelation, cancel(llation)
cancer,ous, *DISEASE*
cancur, chancre /canker
candedate, candidate
candid,dly,dness, *FRANK*
candidate,*,acy,acies, *SEEKS OFFICE*
candle,*,ed,ling, *WAX WITH WICK*
candudite, candidate
candul, candle
candy,dies,died, *SWEET TREAT*
cane,*,ned, *STICK OF WOOD/SUGAR*
canebulize, cannibal(ize)
caneon, canyon
canery, cannery / canary
canesis, kinesis
cangaroo, kangaroo
canibal, cannibal
canibis, cannabis
canikcanik, kinnikinnick
canin, cannon / canine
canine,*, *DOG*
canion, canyon

canipe, canopy
caniry, cannery / canary
canister,*, *CONTAINER*
canker,*,rous, *DISEASE, SORE* (or see chancre)
cannabis, *A USEFUL PLANT*
cannery,ries, *PLACE WHICH CANS FOOD*
cannibal,*,lism,lize,*EATS FLESH OF ITS OWN SPECIES*
cannon,*, *WEAPON*
canon, cannon
canopy,pies,pied,ying, *COVERING FOR SHELTER*
canseld, cancel(lled)
canser, cancer
cansil, cancel
cansilashen, cancel(llation)
cansir, cancer
cansul, cancel
cansulation, cancel(llation)
cansuld, cancel(lled)
can't, *CONTRACTION OF THE WORDS "CAN NOT"*
cantaloup or cantaloupe,*, *EDIBLE FRUIT*
canted, candid
canteen,*, *CONTAINER FOR LIQUIDS*
cantelope, cantaloup
cantena, cantina
canter,*, *SPEED OF HORSE*
cantidit, candidate
cantilope, cantaloup
cantina,*, *SALOON, BAG FOR SADDLE*
cantul, candle
cantulope, cantaloup
cantur, canter
canty, candy
canubelize, cannibal(ize)
canubil, cannibal
canubis, cannabis
canupe, canopy
canuster, canister
canvas, *WOVEN HEMP/NATURAL FIBERS* (or see canvass)

canvass,ser, TO SOLICIT (or see canvass)
canvis, canvas / canvass
canvus, canvass / canvas
canyon,*, DEEP VALLEY
capability,ties, CAPACITY, ABILITY, SKILL
capable,eness,ly, CAPACITY, ABILITY, SKILL
capacity,ties, STATUS OF, AMOUNT
capasety, capacity
capdivate, captivate
capdof, captive
capduvate, captivate
capebilety, capability
capedul, capital /capitol
capedulism, capitalism
capelary, capillary
capetul, capital /capitol
capetulesm, capitalism
capillary,ries, OF THE BODY
capital, LARGE, MAIN, TOP (or see capitol)
capitalism,st,ize,ization, PRIVATE/FREE ENTERPRISE
capitol, CENTER OF GOVERNMENT (or see capital)
capshun, caption
capshur, capture
capsile, capsule
capsize,ed,zing,zable, OVERTURN A BOAT
capsule,*,lar,lize, MATERIAL BEING CONTAINED
captain,*, ONE WHO COMMANDS
captin, captain
caption,*,ned, HEADING OR TITLE
captivate,*,ed,ting, CHARMED
captive,*,vity, CONTROLLED
captun, captain
capture,*,ed,ring,er, TAKE BY FORCE
captuvate, captivate
captuve, captive
capubility, capability
capuble, capable
capudul, capital /capitol
capudulesm, capitalism

capulary, capillary
caput, kaput
caracter, character
caramel,*,led,ling,lize, CANDY
caroke, karaoke
carat,*, 200 MILLIGRAMS (or see caret /carrot/ karat)
caravan,*,ned,ning, GROUP OF VEHICLES/TRAVELERS
carbarator, carburetor
carbender, carpenter
carberator, carburetor
carbin, carbon
carbinete, carbonate
carbirater, carburetor
carbon,*,nize, FORMS ORGANIC COMPOUNDS
carbonate,*,tion, SALT OR GAS
carbunete, carbonate
carburetor,*, HEART OF COMBUSTIBLE ENGINE
carcass,sses, EXTERNAL REMAINS OF ANYTHING
carcino, PREFIX INDICATING "CANCER" MOST OFTEN MODIFIES THE WORD
carcinogen,*,nic, CANCER CAUSING
carcus, carcass
card,*,ded,ding, STIFF PAPER, ASKED FOR I.D. (or see cart)
cardboard, THICK PAPER
cardeac, cardiac
cardenul, cardinal
cardi, cardio, PREFIX INDICATING "HEART" MOST OFTEN MODIFIES THE WORD
cardiac, OF THE HEART
cardillege, cartilage
cardin, carton
cardinal,*, A BIRD, RANK IN CATHOLIC CHURCH
cardulege, cartilage
care,*,ed,ring, CONCERN OVER (or see carry)
careboo, caribou
caredge, carriage
careen,*,ned,ning, LEAN TO ONE SIDE

career,*, PROFESSION
carefree, WITHOUT CARE
careful,lly,lness, WITH CARE
carege, carriage
careless,ssly,ssness, NOT WITH CARE
caremel, caramel
careoke, karaoke
caress,sses,ssed,ssing,ssingly,ssive, PET/STROKE SMOOTHLY/GENTLY
caret,*, PROOFREADING MARK (or see carrot/ carat /caret /karat)
careur, carrier
carful, careful
cargo,oes,os, FREIGHT ON VESSEL
cariage, carriage
carib, carob
caribou, reindeer
caricature,*,ed,ring, EXAGGERATED IMITATION
carie, carry
carier, carrier
carige, carriage
carioke, karaoke
carisma, charisma
carit, carat /caret /carrot /karat
carivan, caravan
carkis, carcass
carkus, carcass
carlis, careless
carma, karma
carmel, caramel
carmil, caramel
carmu, karma
carmul, caramel
carnashun, carnation
carnation,*, FLOWER
carnival,*, TRAVELING AMUSEMENT SHOW
carnivore,*,rous, EATS FLESH
carnuvil, carnival
carnuvore, carnivore

carob, *LOCUST BEAN RESEMBLING CHOCOLATE*
caroberate, corroborate
carode, corrode
caroke, karaoke
carol,*,led,ling, *SONGS*
carosell, carousel
carosene, kerosene
carot, carat /caret /carrot /karat
caroty, karate
carouse,*,sing, *UNDESIRABLE DRUNKEN BEHAVIOR*
carousel,*, *MERRY-GO-ROUND*
carpenter,*,try, *BUILDS WITH WOOD*
carpet,*,ted,ting, *SOFT FLOOR COVERING*
carpinder, carpenter
carpinter, carpenter
carpit, carpet
carriage,*, *PULLED FOUR-WHEELED CART*
carrier,*, *ONE WHO TRANSPORTS*
carrot,*, *VEGETABLE* (or see carat /caret/ karat)
carry,rries,rried,rrying,rrier, *TO TRANSPORT*
carsenagen, carcinogen
carsinugen, carcinogen
cart,*,ted,ting, *VEHICLE FOR TRANSPORT*
cartilage, *SOFT BONE IN THE BODY*
cartin, carton
cartnul, cardinal
carton,*, *PAPER BOX*
cartoon,*,nist, *ANIMATED CARICATURES*
cartrege, cartridge
cartridge,*, *REFILLABLE/ REPLACEABLE CONTAINER*
cartrige, cartridge
cartulige, cartilage
cartun, carton /cartoon
carubu, caribou
carudge, carriage
carusen, kerosene
carve,*,ed,ving,er, *TO SHAPE WITH KNIFE*
cary, carry
cascade,*,ed,ding, *LIKE A WATERFALL*

cascara, *TREE*
case,*,ed,sing, *CERTAIN NUMBER OF ITEMS CON-TAINED TOGETHER (TOO MANY DEFINITIONS PLEASE SEE STANDARD DICTIONARY)*
caseng, casing
caseno, casino
caserole, casserole
casete, cassette
cash,hed,hing, *MONETARY/MONEY* (or see cache)
cashere, cashier
cashew,*, *NUT*
cashier,*, *HANDLES MONEY*
cashmere, *GOAT WOOL*
cashu, cashew
casil, castle
casing,*, *COVERING OR SUPPORT*
casino,*, *FOR GAMBLING*
casirole, casserole
casiroll, casserole
cask,*, *KEG FOR LIQUIDS*
caskade, cascade
caskera, cascara
casket,*, *COFFIN*
caskit, casket
casserole,*, *MIXTURE OF FOOD INTO ONE DISH*
cassette,*, *AUDIO CARTRIDGE*
cast,*,ting, *TO THROW AWAY FROM (TOO MANY DEFINITIONS, PLEASE SEE STANDARD DICTIONARY)*
castle,*, *FORTRESS*
castrate,*,ed,ting, *REMOVE REPRODUCTIVE ORGANS*
casual,lly,lness, *BY CHANCE, RELAXED*
casul, castle
caswal, casual
cat, cata, cath, kata, *PREFIX INDICATING "APART/DOWN" MOST OFTEN MODIFIES THE WORD*
cat,*, *ANIMAL*
catalog,*,ged,ging, *LIST IN ORDER*
catalyst,*, *STIMULUS*
catapult,*,ted,ting, *TO BE HURLED*

cataract,*, *EYE DISEASE OR WATERFALL*
catastrophe,*, *DISASTER*
catch,es,hing,caught, *CAPTURE* (or see cache)
catcher,*, *BASEBALL FIELD POSITION*
catchup, ketchup /catsup
catechism, *TEACHING OF CHRISTIAN PRINCIPLES*
catalog, catalog
catepiler, caterpillar
catepiller, caterpillar
catepult, catapult
cater,*,red,ring, *PROVIDE FOR*
cateract, cataract
caterpillar,*, *WORM*
catilist, catalyst
catilog, catalog
catipiler, caterpillar
catipult, catapult
caturact, cataract
catle, cattle
catsup, ketchup
cattle, *DOMESTIC BEEF, BOVINE*
catukism, catechism
catulist, catalyst
catulog, catalog
catupiler, caterpillar
catupult, catapult
caturact, cataract
caucus,ses, *NOMINATION PARTY*
caught, *PAST TENSE OF "CATCH",OBTAINED* (or see cot)
caul, call /cowl
cauliflower, *VEGETABLE*
caulk,*,ked,king, *FILL SEAMS/JOINTS* (or see calk)
cause,ed,sing,sal,sation, *BRING ABOUT*
caustic,cally,city, *CORROSIVE CHEMICAL*
caut, caught /cot
caution,*,ned,ning,nary, *BEWARE*
cautious,sly,ness, *PREPARED FOR DANGER*
cava, kava
cavalry,ries, *MOUNTED SOLDIERS*
cave,*, *HOLE IN EARTH*
cavern,*,nous, *HOLLOW IN EARTH*
cavety, cavity

cavilry, cavalry
cavirn, cavern
cavity,ties,tate,tation, *HOLLOWED OUT AREA, DECAYED TOOTH*
cavs, calves /cave(s)
cavu, kava
cavulry, cavalry
cavurn, cavern
cawcus, caucus
cawl, call / cowl
cawshis, cautious
cawshun, caution
cawt, caught / cot
cayenne, *HOT PEPPER*
cayning, canine
cazual, casual
cease,ses,ed,sing,eless,elessly, *STOP (or see "sea(s)/seize/ see(s)")*
cechup, ketchup / catsup
ceel, keel
cegar, cigar
ceiling,*, *OVERHEAD IN ROOM (or see seal)*
cel, cell/ seal/ sell
celabent, celibant
celary, celery
celebrate,*,ed,ting,tion,tive,tory,ant, *REJOICE*
celebrity,ties, *PERSON WELL EXPOSED TO THE PUBLIC*
celery, *VEGETABLE*
celestial,*,lly, *SPIRITUAL, NOT PHYSICAL ON THIS PLANE*
celibacy,ant, *ABSENT FROM SEXUAL ACTIVITY*
celibant,acy, *ABSENT FROM SEXUAL ACTIVITY*
celibent, celibant
celibrate, celebrate
celinder, cyclinder
celing, ceiling /seal(ing)
cell,*,llular, *OF STRUCTURES/SCIENCE (or see sell or sail)*
cellar,*, *STORAGE UNDERGROUND (or see sell)*

cellophane, *PLASTIC WRAP*
cellular, *OF COMMUNICATIONS OR SCIENCE*
cellulite, *FAT POCKETS IN THE BODY*
cellulose, *CARBOHYDRATE*
celophane, cellophane
celseus, celsius
Celsius, *METHOD OF REPORTING TEMPERATURE*
celt,*,tic, *TOOL, GROUP OF PEOPLE, LANGUAGE*
celubasy, celibacy
celubent, celibant
celubint, celibant
celubrate, celebrate
celular, cellular
celulite, cellulite
celulose, cellulose
cement, *MIXTURE OF MATERIALS WHICH HARDENS*
cemetary,ries, *GRAVEYARD*
cemutary, cemetary
cenameter, centimeter
cendral, central
cenik, cynic
cenikal, cynical
cenima, cinema
cense, since /sense /sense /cent(s) /scent(s)
censeer, sincere
censhury, century
censor,*,red,ring,rship,rable,rship,rious,riousl, riousness,sure, *CONTROL INFORMATION (or see sensor)*
census, *SURVEY (or see sense(s))*
cent, centi, *PREFIX INDICATING "HUNDRED/ HUNDREDTH" MOST OFTEN MODIFIES THE WORD*
cent,*, *MONEY (or see scent or sent)*
centennial,*, *100 YEARS*
center,*,red,ring, *THE MIDDLE*
centigrade,*, *WAY OF REPORTING TEMPERATURE*
centimeter,*, *MORE THAN 0.39 OF AN INCH*
centinial, centennial
centipede,*, *POISONOUS BUG*

central,lly,lity,lism,lize,lization, *FOCUS BETWEEN TWO OR MORE*
centri, centro, *PREFIX INDICATING "CENTER" MOST OFTEN MODIFIES THE WORD*
centrul, central
centry, sentry
centigrade, centigrade
centumeter, centimeter
centupede, centipede
century,ries, *100 YEAR MARK*
ceramic,*, *CLAY-FIRING METHOD*
cerashen, serrate(tion)
ceration, serrate(tion)
cerb, curb
cerculate, circulate
cercumcise, circumcise
cercumfurens, circumference
cercumstance, circumstance
cerdify, certify
cerdle, curdle
cereal, *EDIBLE GRAIN*
cerebr, cerebro, *PREFIX INDICATING "BRAIN" MOST OFTEN MODIFIES THE WORD*
ceremony,nies,nial,nially,nious, *FORMAL GROUP GATHERING*
cereul, cereal
cereur, carrier
cerf, curve
cerfew, curfew
cerfue, curfew
cericuture, caricature
cerikulum, curriculum
cerimony, ceremony
cerisel, carousel
cerit, carat/caret /carrot/ karat
cerivan, caravan
cerklar, circular
cerkomferinse, circumference
cerkumsize, circumcise

cerkus, circus
cerl, curl
cernil, colonel / kernel
cerol, carol
cerosene, kerosene
cerse, curse
cersif, cursive
certain,nly,nty, *FOR SURE*
certale, curtail
certan, curtain
certificasion, certificate(tion)
certificate,*,ed,ting,tion,*VALIDATION FOR LEARNING*
certify,fies,fied,fying,fier,fiable,fiably, *MAKE CERTAIN, A LEGAL DOCUMENT*
certin, certain
certsy, curtsy
certul, curdle
cerunsy, currency
cerunt, currant /current
cerus, cirrus / scirrhus
cerusel, carousel
ceruvan, caravan
cerve, curve
cervix,*,ical, *OF THE NECK*
cervuchure, curvature
cery, curry /carry
ceshel, seashell
cest, cyst
cesta, siesta
cew, cue
cfood, seafood
cfud, seafood
chader, chatter
chado, shadow
chaf, chafe /chaff
chafd, shaft /chafe(d) /chaff(ed)
chafe,*,ed,fing, *ANNOYED/IRRITATED, RUBBED UNTIL SORE (or see shaft or chaff)*

chaff,*,ffed,ffing, *TO TEASE/JOKE WITH SOMEONE (or see chafe)*
chafs, chafe(s) /chaff(s)
chaft, shaft /chafe(d) /chaff(ed)
chain,*,ned,ning, *LINKS PUT/HOOKED TOGETHER*
chair,*, *FURNITURE*
chak, chalk /choke /shock /chock
chakra,*, *CENTERS IN BODY*
chalenge, challenge
chalinge, challenge
chalk,*,ked,king,ky, *LIMESTONE*
challenge,*,ed,ging,gable,er, *TEST OF SKILLS*
champagne, *EFFERVESCENT WINE*
champane, champagne
champeon, champion
champion,*,ned,ning, *WINS CONTEST OF SKILL*
chanal, channel
chance,*,ed, *A GAMBLE*
chancre,*,rous, *ULCERATION ON THE SKIN (or see canker)*
chandelier,*, *LAMP WITH MANY ARMS FOR BULBS*
chandulere, chandelier
chane, chain
chanel, channel
change,*,ed,ging,gable, *TRANSFORM*
chanil, channel
channel,*,led,ling,ler, *AVENUE TO RECEIVE*
chant,*,ted,ting,tingly, *RECITE/REPEAT WORDS IN VERBAL RHYTHM (or see chain(ed))*
chanse, chance /chant(s)
chanul, channel
chaos,otic, *APPEARS TO US TO BE DISORGANIZED*
chap,*,pped,pping, *dry/rough skin, leather pant*
chapel,*, *for rituals*
chaplain,*, *PERFORMS RITUAL SERVICES*
chaplan, chaplain
chapter,*, *SECTION OF PRINT, COLLEGE OR SCHOOL*
chapul, chapel

character,*,ristic,ristically,rize,rization, *PERSONALITY/ QUALITIES*
charade,*,*, *PANTOMIME GAME*
charcoal,*,led, *ORGANIC SUBSTANCE IN EARTH*
charder, charter
chare, chair
charecter, character
charge,*,ed,er,ging,eable, *APPLY TOWARDS CREDIT, CREATE POWER, ENERGIZE, APPLY FORCE*
charguble, charge(able)
charidy, charity
charisma,atic, *INSPIRATIONAL QUALITY*
charitable,ly, *GIVING*
charity,ties,table, *GIVING UNCONDITIONALLY*
charj, charge
charjur, charge(r)
charjuble, charge(able)
charm,*,med,ming,mingly,mer, *ALLUREMENT, LUCKY OBJECT*
chart,*,ted,ting, *PLOT OUT*
charter,*,red,ring, *CONTRACT, OUTLINE*
charutable, charitable
chas, chase /chaste
chasd, chaste /chase(d)
chase,*,ed,sing, *PURSUE TO CAPTURE (or see chaste)*
chasem, chasm
chasim, chasm
chasm,*,mic, *DEEP VOID*
chassis, *FRAME OF VEHICLE*
chaste,er,est,ely,eness, *SIMPLE, PLAIN, FAITHFUL (or see chase(d))*
chasum, chasm
chasy, chassis
chater, chatter /shatter
chatter,*,red,ring, *TALK TOO MUCH ABOUT UNINTERESTING TOPICS*
chauffeur,*, *DESIGNATED DRIVER*
chauk, chalk, choke /shock /chock

chayos, chaos
chazm, chasm
chazum, chasm
cheap,per,pest,ply,pens, *LOW COST*
cheat,*,ted,ting,ter, *DISHONEST ACQUISITION*
check,*,ked,king,ker,kers,kered, *BANK DRAFT, A MARK, TO MAKE CERTAIN, A GAME, ALTERNATING COLORED BOXES*
cheef, chief
cheep, cheap
cheese, *CURDLED MILK*
cheet, cheat
chef,*, *HEAD COOK*
chek, check
chekan, chicken
chekurs, check(ers)
cheldren, children
chelenge, challenge
chelren, children
chemical,*, *OF CHEMISTRY*
chemistry, *MOTHER OF SCIENCE*
chemney, chimney
chemotherapy, *RADIATION TREATMENT*
chemucal, chemical
chemustry, chemistry
chen, chin
chep, cheap /sheep
cher, share /chair
cherch, church
cheridy, charity
cheritable, charitable
cherity, charity
cherle, sure(ly)
chern, churn
chese, cheese
chest, schist
chevolry, chivalry
chevulry, chivalry
chew,*,wed,wing,wable, *GRIND WITH TEETH*

chewt, shute /chute
chic, *STYLISH*
chick,*, *YOUNG BIRD, GIRL*
chicken,*, *FOWL, BIRD*
chicory, *HERB*
chief,*, *HIGHEST AUTHORITY*
chik, chick
chiken, chicken
chikury, chicory
child, *YOUNG PERSON*
children, *YOUNG PEOPLE*
chilostomy, colostomy
chilren, children
chimney,*, *SMOKE STACK*
chimotherapy, chemotherapy
chimukul, chemical
chin,*, *POINT OF JAW (or see shin or shine)*
chirch, church
chirle, sure(ly)
chiro, *PREFIX INDICATING "HAND" MOST OFTEN MODIFIES THE WORD*
chiropractor,tic, *REALIGNS BONES OF BODY FOR HEALTH*
chirtch, church
chisel,*,led,ling, *TOOL FOR FORMING SHAPES*
chist, schist
chivalry,rous, *COURTEOUS AND HELPFUL GENTELMAN*
chizt, schist
chizul, chisel
chlor, chloro, *PREFIX INDICATING "GREEN/ CHLORINE" MOST OFTEN MODIFIES THE WORD*
chlorene, chlorine
chlorine,nate,idize, *CHEMICAL IRRITANT*
chocolate, *FROM CACAO NUT*
choice,*, *SELECTION*
choir,*, *SINGING GROUP*
chock,*,ked,king, *TO BLOCK/ SECURE/ BRACE (or see choke/ chalk/ shock)*
chok, chalk /choke /shock /chock

choke,*,ed,king,kingly,er, *RESTRICTED SUPPLY OF AIR/MOVEMENT(or see chalk/shock/chock)*
choklit, chocolate
choklut, chocolate
chokra, chakra
chol, chole, *PREFIX INDICATING "BILE/GALLBLADDER" MOST OFTEN MODIFIES THE WORD*
cholesterol, *NATURALLY PRESENT IN THE BODY*
cholk, chalk
cholostemy, colostomy
choo, chew / shoe
choose,*, *PICK ONE OVER THE OTHER (or see chew(s) or chose)*
chor, chore /shore
choral, *OF A CHOIR (or see coral/ corral /chorale)*
chorale, *A HYMN OF SIMPLE TUNE (or see choral/ corral /coral)*
chord,*, *OF MUSICAL NOTES (or see cord or short)*
chore,*, *SMALL TASKS (or see shore)*
chorn, shorn
chorus, *A UNION OF PERFORMERS (or see course)*
chorz, chore(s) /shard(s)
chose,en, *HAVING SELECTED, PAST TENSE OF "CHOOSE" (or see choose)*
chow main, chow mein
chow mein, *FOOD*
choyse, choice
chrapnul, shrapnel
christmas, *A RELIGIOUS HOLIDAY*
chrom, chromo, *PREFIX INDICATING "COLOR/ CHROMIUM" MOST OFTEN MODIFIES THE WORD*
chrome,ed,ming, *METALLIC*
chromizone, chromosome
chromosome,*, *IN ALL BODIES*
chronic,cally, *CONTINUOUS*
chronicle,*,ed,ling, *LIST OF FACTS*
chronological,lly, *ORGANIZE BY DATES*
chrys, chryso, *PREFIX INDICATING "GOLD" MOST OFTEN MODIFIES THE WORD*

chrysanthemum,*,* FLOWER
chue, chew
chugar, sugar
chugur, sugar
chural, choral /coral /corral /chorale
church,hes,hy, FOR RELIGIOUS PURPOSES
churle, sure(ly)
churn,*,ned,ning, FAT, MILK SEPARATION
chuse, choose /chew(s)
chute,*,ed,ting, RAPID/STEEP DESCENT (or see shoot)

cianide, cyanide
ciburnetiks, cybernetics
ciclist, cyclist
cid, kid / kite
cider, STRONG JUICE
cidur, cider
cigar,*, ROLLED TOBACCO
cigarette,* OF TOBACCO
cilinder, cylinder
cilosal, colossal
ciment, cement
cinch,hes,hed,hing, FIRM GRIP ON, EASILY ACHIEVED, FOR CERTAIN (or see singe)
cinda, kind of
cinder,*, CHARRED SUBSTANCE (or see send)
cinduf, kind of
cine, PREFIX INDICATING "MOTION PICTURE" MOST OFTEN MODIFIES THE WORD
cinema,*,atic, MOTION-PICTURE
cinery, canary / cannery
cinima, cinema
cinnamon, SPICE FROM TREE BARK
cinspirusy, conspiracy
cinstrucshen, construction
cintential, centennial
circle,*,ed,ling, ROUND FIGURE/SHAPE
circompherence, circumference

circuit,*,try, MAKES THE ROUNDS, GOES AROUND, NETWORK
circular,*,, GOES AROUND IN THE SHAPE OF A CIRCLE
circulate,*,ed,ting,tion, FLOWING/MOVING
circum, PREFIX INDICATING "AROUND" MOST OFTEN MODIFIES THE WORD
circumcise,sion, REMOVAL OF FORESKIN ON PENIS
circumference, DISTANCE/LINE AROUND A CIRCLE
circumstance,*,ntial,ntiate, INCIDENT
circus,ses, ENTERTAINING PERFORMANCE IN TENTS
cirkumsize, circumcise
cirnel, colonel / kernel
ciroberate, corroborate
cirrus, CLOUD TYPE/SHAPE (or see scirrhus)
cirteus, courteous
cirus, cirrus / scirrhus
cirvature, curvature
cis, PREFIX INDICATING "ON THIS SIDE" MOST OFTEN MODIFIES THE WORD
cist, BURIED IN STONE (or see cyst)
citashun, citation
citation,*, A SUMMONS
cite,*,ed,ting, OFFICIALLY CALL FORTH (or see site)
citizen,*,nry,nship, MEMBER OF, WITH PRIVILEDGES
citres, citrus
citric, ACID FROM FRUIT
citrus, FRUIT
citusin, citizen
city,ties, METROPOLIS
ciunide, cyanide
civic, CITIZENSHIP
civil, OF STATE OR COMMUNITY
civilean, civilian
civilian,*,, NOT MILITARY CITIZENS
civul, civil
ciyen, cayenne
clae, clay
claim,*,med,ming, ASSERT POSSESSION OF (or see clam)

clairvoyance,nt, THOSE WHO CHANNEL INFORMATION
clam,*,mmed,mming, SHELLFISH (or see claim)
clamp,*,ped,ping, PINCH TOGETHER
clan, BODIES OF LIKE-MINDED INDIVIDUALS
clandestine,ely,eness, WITH DECEPTION IN MIND
clandustine, clandestine
clap,*,pped,pping,pt, SOUND, GONORRHEA
clarical, clerical
clarify,fies, GIVE SPECIFIC MEANING TO
clarity, MAKE CLEAR
clarvoyants, clairvoyance
claset, closet
clash,hes,hed,hing, COLLIDE, LOUD SOUND
clasha, cliche
clasic, classic
clasify, classify
clasp,*,ped,ping, HOLD
class,ses, GROUPED TOGETHER DUE TO SIMILARITIES
classic,*,cal,cally, WITHSTOOD TEST OF TIME
classify,fies,fied,fication, ABLE TO PLACE INTO A GROUP
clasuc, classic
clause,*,sal, STIPULATION (or see claw(s))
claustrophobia, FEAR OF COZY/TIGHT PLACES
claustrophobic, FEAR OF COZY/TIGHT PLACES
claw,*,wed,wing, HOOKED, FINGERLIKE (or see clause)
clawsit, closet
clawzet, closet
clay, SOIL FROM EARTH
clean,*,ned,ning,ner,nly,liness, UNSOILED
cleanse,*,sed,sing, MAKE CLEAN
clear,*,red,ring, FREE OF OBSTRUCTION
clearance,*, TO CLEAR OF
cleat,*, FOR TRACTION, STRENGTH
cleen, clean
cleer, clear
cleerance, clearance
cleff, cliff

clek, click /clique
clen, clean
clench,hes,hed,hing,her, TO HOLD/GRASP TIGHTLY (or see clinch)
cleng, cling
clenik, clinic
clenz, cleanse
clep, clip
clere, clear
clerense, clearance
clergy,gies, ORDAINED BY CHRISTIANS
clerical, OFFICE WORKER
clerity, clarity
clerk,*,kly, PERFORMS GENERAL DUTIES
clervoyanse, clairvoyance
clesha, cliche
clet, cleat
cletoras, clitoris
clever,rly,rness, INGENIOUS
clew, clue
cliant, client
cliche,*, STEREOTYPICAL PHRASE
click,*,ked,king,ker, SNAPPING NOISE, FIT WELL TOGETHER (or see clique)
client,*,tele, CUSTOMER
cliff,*, STEEP ROCK FACE
clik, click
clim, climb
climate,*, WEATHER OR ATMOSPHERE CONDITION
climax,actic, GREATEST HEIGHT
climb,*,bed,bing,bable,MOMENTUM UPWARDS,GO UP
clim, climb
climute, climate
clinch,hes,hed,hing,her, TO RESOLVE, FASTEN/HOLD (or see clench)
cling,*,ged,ging,ger, ATTACH TIGHTLY TO
clinic,*,cal, PLACE FOR EXAMINATION
clip,*,pped,pping, CUT OFF OR OUT, A TACKLE

clique,*,uish,ey, A SELECT GROUP
clirge, clergy
clirk, clerk
clisha, cliche
clitoris,ral, POINT FOR FEMININE AROUSAL
cloak,*,ked,king, A GARMET OR TO CONCEAL, DIGUISE (or see clock)
clobber,*,red,ring, TO BEAT UP
clober, clobber
clock,*,ked,king, KEEP TIME (or see cloak)
clofe, clove
clofur, clover
cloger, closure
cloister,*,red,ring, OF BUILDINGS, TO ENCLOSE
clojer, closure
clok, clock / cloak
clone,*,ed,ning, REPLICAS
clos, clothes /claw(s) /close /clause
close,*,ed,sing,er,est, SHUT DOWN, NEAR TO (or see close or clothes)
closet,*,ted,ting, SMALL PRIVATE SPACE
closher, closure
closir, close(r) /closure
closline, clothesline
closturfobeu, claustrophobia
closur, close(r) /closure
closure,*, CONCEAL, SHUT DOWN (or see close(r))
clot,*,tted,tting, LUMP, MASS OF MATTER
cloted, clot(tted)
cloth,he,hes,hed,hing, WOVEN FIBERS INTO MATE-RIAL, USED FORCLOTHING (or see close)
clothes, OUTER/UNDER GARMENTS FOR THE BODY (or see close)
clothesline,*, LINE FOR HANGING GARMENTS/CLOTHES ON
clothsline, clothesline
cloud,*,dy,ded,ding,diness, SMOKE, WATER PARTICLES, OBSCURES VISION
cloun, clown

clout, INFLUENCE, TO STRIKE (or see cloud)
clove,*, OF A PLANT, FORM OF MEASUREMENT
clover,*, HERBAL PLANT
clow, claw
clowd, cloud
clown,*,ned,ning,nish, FUNNY, GOOFY, NOT NORMAL, SOMETIMES RIDICULOUS /OBNOXIOUS
clows, clothes /claw(s) /close /clause
clowsit, closet
clowt, clout
cloyster, cloister
cloz, clothes/claw(s)/close/clause
clozer, close(r) /closure
clozir, close(r) /closure
clozline, clothesline
clozur, close(r) / closure
club,*,bbed,bbing, GROUP MEMBERSHIP, AN INSTRUMENT USED AS A WEAPON
cluch, clutch
cluder, clutter
clue,*,ed,uless, HINT
clump,*,ped,ping,py, COLLECTION OF/INTO A MASS
clumsy,sily,siness, AWKWARDLY DONE
clumze, clumsy
clurgy, clergy
cluster,*,red,ring,ry, GROUPINGS TOGETHER
clutch,hes,hed,hing, USED TO CHANGE GEARS IN TRANSMISSION, GRASP FIRMLY, GROUP OF EGGS
cluter, clutter
clutorus, clitoris
clutter, CONFUSING SIGHT OR NOISE
co, col, com, con, cor, PREFIX INDICATING "WITH/TOGETHER" MOST OFTEN MODIFIES THE WORD
co-op, COMMUNITY-OWNED BUSINESS, A COOPERATIVE (or see coop or coup)
coach,hes,hed,hing, TO GUIDE OTHERS
coagulate,*,ed,ting,tion, TO THICKEN, FORM CLOTS
coal,*, ORGANIC SUBSTANCE IN THE EARTH

coalition,*,ned,nist, *VOLUNTARY GATHERING OF PEOPLE FOR A CAUSE*
coar, core /corp
coarse,er,est,ely,eness, *HARSH, ABRASIVE, ROUGH (or see course)*
coast,*,ted,ting, *BETWEEN LAND AND WATER, TO BE MOVING WITHOUT PROPULSION (or see cost)*
coaster,*, *TO SET DRINKS ON (TOO MANY DEFINITIONS, PLEASE SEE STANDARD DICTIONARY)*
coat,*,ted,ting, *OUTER GARMENT FOR WARMTH*
coax,xes,xed,xing, *TO PERSUADE/INFLUENCE*
cob,*, *TUBULAR IN SHAPE (TOO MANY DEFINITIONS, PLEASE SEE STANDARD DICTIONARY)*
cobalt, *CHEMICAL, BLUE COLORING*
cobolt, cobalt
cobra,*, *SNAKE*
cobweb,*, *SPIDER'S WEB*
cocaine, *NARCOTIC DRUG*
cocane, cocaine
coch, coach
cock,*,ky, *A ROOSTER, OF MASCULINE SUGGESTION (or see cook)*
cockroach,hes, *INFESTATING INSECT*
cocktail,*, *ALCOHOLIC BEVERAGES*
cocoa, *FROM THE CACAO SEED*
coconut,*, *FRUIT*
cocoon,*, *HOME SPUN BY LARVAE*
coctale, cocktail
cocunut, coconut
cocus, caucus
code,*,ded,ding, *LANGUAGE*
codeine, *DRUG FROM OPIUM*
coden, cotton /codeine
codien, codein
codin, cotton /codeine
coduge, cottage
coed,*, *BOTH SEXES*
coel, coil
coelate, collate

coen, coin
coencident, coincident
coenside, coincide
coensident, coincident
coerce,*,ed,cing,cible,cion,cive,civeness,cively, *FORCE INTO COMPLIANCE*
cofe, cove /coffee /cough
cofen, coffin /cough(ing)
cofert, covert /cover(ed)
cof cough
coffee, *BEVERAGE (or see cove)*
coffin,*, *BOX FOR TRANSPORT, CASKET*
cofin, coffin /cough(ing)
cofy, coffee
cognative, cognitive
cogneshun, cognition
cognisant, cognizant
cognition, *PERCEPTIVE/AWARE (or see cognizant)*
cognitive,ely,vism, *COME TO KNOW THROUGH PERCEPTION/REASONING*
cognizant,nce,able, *PERCEPTIVE/AWARE*
cognutev, cognitive
cohabitate,*,ed,ting,tion, *DWELL/LIVE TOGETHER*
cohabutate, cohabitate
coherent,nce,ncy, *WORKS CONSISTENTLY/ PREDICTABLY*
coherse, coerce
cohesive,ely,eness,ion, *BONDS TOGETHER*
cohesuf, cohesive
cohort,*, *CO-PARTNER*
cohurse, coerce
coil,*,led,ling, *SPIRAL SHAPE*
coin,*,ned,nage, *METAL USED FOR MONEY*
coincide,*,ed,ding, *AGREE*
coincident,nce,tal, *CHANCE HAPPENING*
cok, cook /cock
cokane, cocaine
cokes, coax
cokie, cookie

cokroch, cockroach
coktale, cocktail
col, *PREFIX INDICATING "INTESTINES" MOST OFTEN MODIFIES THE WORD (or see call/cowl/coal)*
coladerul, colateral
colage, collage
colamedy, calamity
colander,*, *STRAINER*
colapse, collapse
colapsuble, collapse(sible)
colar, collar /call(er)
colard, collard greens
colate, collate
colateral,lly,lize, *USED TO GUARANTEE/SECURE A LOAN*
cold,der,dest,dly, *OPPOSITE OF HOT (or see colt)*
coldslaw, coleslaw
cole, coal /call
coleage, colleague
colect, collect
colection, colleciton
colector, collector
colege, college
colegiate, collegiate
colekshin, collection
colem, column
colen, colon
colenise, colonize
coleny, colony
coler, color /cooler /collar
coleshun, collision /coalition
coleslaw, *CABBAGE SALAD*
colic, *PAIN CAUSED BY ACID IN THE INTESTINES*
colide, collide
coliflower, cauliflower
colijin, collision
colim, column
colinary, culinary
coliny, colony

colk, calk /caulk
collaborate,*,ed,ting,tion,tive,tively, *COOPERATE*
collage,*, *MIXED MEDIA ART*
collander, colander
collapsable, collapse(sible)
collapse,*,ed,sing,sable, *BREAK DOWN*
collar,*,red, *RIM ON SHIRT, BELT FOR NECK*
collard greens, *VEGETABLE*
collate,*,ed,ting,tion, *MERGE, COMPARE*
colleague,*,* *ASSOCIATE*
collect,*,ted,ting,tive,tor, *GATHER*
collection,*, *ACT OF GATHERING THINGS*
college,*, *HIGHER EDUCATION*
collegiate,* *OF COLLEGE AND, OR STUDENTS*
collide,*,ed,ding, *RUN INTO*
collision,*,* *ACT OF RUNNING INTO*
colm, calm
colmenate, culminate
colo, *PREFIX INDICATING "INTESTINES" MOST OFTEN MODIFIES THE WORD*
cologne,*, *TOILET WATER* (or see colon)
colon, *INTESTINES, PUNCTUATION IN TEXT* (or see cologne)
coloneal, colonial
colonel,*, *U.S. MILITARY OFFICER* (or see kernel)
colonial,list,lism, *FIRST EUROPEANS TO AMERICA*
colonize,*,ed,zing, *FIRST SETTLERS*
colony,nies, *ACCUMULATION OF SIMILAR PEOPLES*
color,*,red,ring,ful, *HUES OF LIGHT SPECTRUM*
colossal, *GREAT MAGNITUDE*
colostomy,mies, *INVOLVES INTESTINES/ANUS*
colpret, culprit
colt,*, *THE YOUNG OF SOME IN ANIMAL KINGDOM* (or see cold)
coltivate, cultivate
coltsfoot, *USEFUL HERB*
coltuvate, cultivate
coluge, college

column,*,ned,nar,nist, *VERTICAL PILLARS OR ROWS, WRITTEN ARTICLE*
colun, colon
colunise, colonize
coluny, colony
colunise, colonize
colurd, collard greens
colvert, culvert
com, calm /come /comb /cum
com, con, cor, co, col, *PREFIX INDICATING "WITH/ TOGETHER" MOST OFTEN MODIFIES THE WORD*
coma,*, *UNCONSCIOUSNESS* (or see comma)
comand, command
comander, commander
comasery, commissary
comb,*,bed,bing, *TOOL FOR HAIR* (or see come)
combat,*,ted,ting,ting,tant,tive, *OPPOSE*
combination,*,tive,able, *UNIFY*
combine,*,ed,ning, *COME TOGETHER, FARM MACHINE*
combunashen, combination
combunation, combination
combustchen, combustion
combustible,bility,eness, *POTENTIAL TO IGNITE INTO FLAMES*
combustion,ive, *CHEMICAL REACTION, FIRE/OXYGEN*
come,*,ming,came, *RESPOND, GO TOWARDS* (or see comb or cum)
comec, comic
comedeun, comedian
comedian,*,ienne, *AMUSING ENTERTAINER*
comedy,dic, *HUMOROUS ACCOUNTS*
comemorate, commemorate
comence, commence
comendable, commendable
comendation, commendation
comenduble, commendable
comensirate, commensurate
comensurate, commensurate
coment, comment

comentator, commentator
coments, commence /comment(s)
comerbund, cummerbund
comerce, commerce
comercial, commercial
comerse, commerce
comershul, commercial
comeshen, commission
comeshener, commissioner
comet,*, *SPACE MATTER AND ICE AT HIGH SPEED* (or see commit)
comete, committee
cometioner, commissioner
cometment, commitment
comewn, commune
comfert, comfort
comfort,*,ted,ting,ter, *RELIEF, CALM, PLEASANT*
comfortable,ly, *RELIEF, CALM, PLEASANT*
comfurter, comfort(er)
comic,*,cal, *FUNNY, HUMOROUS*
comidore, commodore
comidy, comedy
comimurate, commemorate
comin, common
comindation, commendation
cominduble, commendable
cominsirate, commensurate
comint, comment
comintator, commentator
comirse, commerce
comirshul, commercial
comisary, commissary
comishen, commission
comishener, commissioner
comisioner, commissioner
comissary, commissary
comission, commission
comit, comet / commit
comitee, committee

comition, commission
comitioner, commissioner
comitment, commitment
comittee, committee
comity, comedy
comloda, cum laude
comma,*, *PUNCTUATION* (or see coma)
command,*,ded,ding, *DOMINATING, DIRECTING*
commander,*,*, *DOMINANCE, MILITARY*
commemorate,*,ed,ting,tive, *HONORING SOMEONE OR SOMETHING OF THE PAST*
commence,*,ed,cing,ment, *TO BEGIN*
commendable,eness,ly, *PRAISEWORTHY*
commendation,*,*, *PRAISE*
commensurate,ely,tion, *EQUAL/CORRESPONDS TO*
comment,*,ted,ting,tary, *MAKE REMARKS, GIVE OPINION*
commentator,*,tate, *ONE WHO GIVES OPINIONS/REMARKS*
commerce, *EXCHANGING WARES OR GOODS*
commercial,*,lize,lization, *ADVERTISEMENTS, ABOUT TRADE*
commisary, commissary
commision, commission
commissary,ries, *MILITARY STORE*
commission,*,ned,ning, *ALLOTTED SUM OR PERCENT, DELEGATE*
commissioner,*,*, *POSITION OF AUTHORITY*
commit,*,tted,tting, *RELEGATE, ENTRUST*
commitee, committee
commitment,*, *OBLIGATED, ENTRUSTED TO SOMEONE OR SOMETHING*
committee,*,*, *SELECTED GROUP TO DO WORK*
commodity,ties, *OBJECT FOR TRADE*
commodore,*,*, *MILITARY OFFICER*
common,*,nly,ness, *FAMILIAR*
communal,*,*, *OF COMMUNITY*
commune,*,*, *COLLECTION OF PEOPLE WITH SIMILAR IDEAS/VALUES*

communicable, *PASSED ON, TO BE COMMUNICATIVE*
communicate,*,ed,ting,tion,tive,tively, tiveness, *EXCHANGE INFORMATION*
communion, *CHRISTIAN RITUAL*
communism, *TYPE OF GOVERNMENT*
communist,*,tic, *ADVOCATE OF COMMUNISM*
community,ties, *ASSOCIATION OF SIMILAR PEOPLES*
commute,*,ed,ting,*INTERCHANGE,DISTANCE TRAVEL*
comodity, commodity
comodore, commodore
comon, common
compact,*,ted,ting, *SMALLEST DIMENSION POSSIBLE*
companeon, companion
companion,*,ship, *MATE/PARTNER*
company,nies, *ASSOCIATION OF INDIVIDUALS*
comparable,ly,eness,bility, *SIMILAR, ALIKE*
compare,*,ed,ring,arative,aratively,rable,rably, *PARALLEL EXAMINATION*
comparison,*,*, *ENGAGING EXAMINATION*
compartment,*,tal,tally,talize,talized,talizing, *SECTIONED SEPARATELY*
compashinet, compassionate
compasionate, compassionate
compass,ses, *DIRECTION FINDER*
compassionate,ely, *TAKE PITY ON*
compatible,bility,bilities, *AGREEABLE*
compedidor, competitor
compeditor, competitor
compel,*,lled,lling,llingly, *DRIVEN TO, AN URGING/DESIRE*
compelation, compellation
compellation,*,*, *NAME, DENOMINATION*
compensate,*,ed,ting,tion,tory, *MAKE UP FOR*
compeny, company
comper, compare
comperison, comparison
comperuble, comparable
compete,*,ed,ting,tition, *BE BETTER THAN*
competence,cy, *BEING ADEQUATE*

competishen, competition
competition,*, *MATCH FOR SKILL TESTING*
competitor,*, *ONE WHO COMPETES*
compilashun, compellation
compile,*,ed,ling,lation, *BRING/PUT TOGETHER*
compinsate, compensate
compitance, competence
compizishen, composition
complacence,cy,cies,nt,ntly, *HAPPY WITH SELF* (or see complaisance)
complain,*,ned,ning,nt,ner, *FIND FAULT*
complaisance,nt, *DESIRE TO PLEASE, CIVIL* (or see complacence)
complasens,complacence/complaisance
complekate, complicate
compleks, complex
complekshin, complexion
complement,*,tal,tary,tation, *WHEN ADDED MAKES COMPLETE* (or see compliment)
compleshin, completion
complete,*,ed,ting,tly, *CONCLUDE, FINISH*
completion, *CONCLUDE/FINISH*
complex,xes,xity,*COMBINATION OF INTERCONNECTED PARTS*
complexion,*,ned, *SKIN PHYSICAL CHARACTERISTIC*
compli, comply
complicashin, complication
complicat, complicate
complicate,*,ed,ting, *MORE TO CONSIDER*
complication,*,*, *ADDITIONAL INVOLVEMENT/ CONSIDERATION*
complikashun, complication
complikat, complicate
compliment,*,ted,ting,tary, *PRAISE, EXPRESS ADMIRATION* (or see complement)
complucashun, complication
complukate, complicate
compliment, complement /compliment
comply,lies,ying, *CONFORM*
component,*,*, *PHASE/PART OF SOMETHING*

compose, *, ed, sing, er, TO FORM
composite, *, PARTS OF THE WHOLE
composition, *, IDENTIFY/ARRANGE PARTS OF THE WHOLE
compost, *, ted, ting, RECYCLING ORGANIC MATTER
composure, *, CENTERED STATE OF MIND
compound, *, ded, ding, ADDITIONAL PARTS, TO ADD TO THE WHOLE
compownd, compound
compoze, compose
compramise, compromise
comprehend, *, ded, GRASP, UNDERSTAND
comprehenshun, comprehension
comprehensible, bility, eness, ABLE TO GRASP/UNDERSTAND
comprehension, ive, ively, UNDERSTAND/GRASP
compreshun, compression
compress, ses, sed, sing, sible, sibility, COMPACT, CONDENSE
compression, nal, REDUCING VOLUME
compressor, *, MACHINE THAT CONDENSES/REDUCES
compretion, compression
compromise, *, ed, sing, OUTCOME IMPERFECT, AGREE FOR THE SAKE OF BEING AGREEABLE
comprumize, compromise
comptroller, *, CONTROLLER OF FINANCES
compuder, computer
compulashun, compellation
compulshun, compulsion
compulsion, *, IRRESISTIBLE URGE TO ACT
compulsive, ely, eness, GIVEN TO ACT ON URGES
compulsory, rily, REINFORCED FACT
compultion, compulsion
compusition, composition
computashun, computation
computation, *, nal, ive, ively, TO RECKON/ESTIMATE
compute, *, ed, ting, table, FIGURE DATA, ESTIMATE
computer, *, rize, rized, rization, ELECTRONIC DATA PROCESSOR

computishen, competition
compuzishen, composition
comrade, *, ery, dship, CLOSE ASSOCIATES
comtroler, comptroller
comudoor, commodore
comunal, communal
comune, commune /common
comunecuble, communicable
comunete, community
comunicable, communicable
comunicate, communicate
comunion, communion
comunism, communism
comunist, communist
comunity, community
comurse, commerce
comurshal, commercial
comusery, commissary
comute, commute
con, com, cor, co, col, PREFIX INDICATING "WITH/TOGETHER" MOST OFTEN MODIFIES THE WORD
con, *, nned, nning, TO TRICK (or see cone)
conceal, *, led, ling, lment, TO HIDE FROM SIGHT
concede, *, ed, ding, YIELD (or see conceit)
conceit, ted, VAIN (or see concede)
conceivable, bility, eness, ly, ABILITY TO UNDERTAND, IMAGINE
conceive, *, ed, ving, A THOUGHT WHICH BECOMES UNDERSTAND, IMAGINE
concentrate, *, ed, ting, tion, FOCUS, CONDENSE
concept, *, tive, tively, IDEA/PLAN
conception, nal, MOMENT OF CREATION
conceptual, lism, lise, lly, THOUGHTS BECOMING
concern, *, ned, ning, ment, WORRIED ABOUT NEGATIVE OUTCOME, INTEREST IN
concert, *, ted, ting, PLAN/WORK/ACT TOGETHER IN MUSIC/THEATER
concesion, concession
concession, *, TO PART WITH SOME CONTROL, SELL UNDER AUTHORITY

conset, conceit / concede
consev, concieve
conch, hes, A SHELL, OF DOME
concheinchus, conscientious
conchis, conscious
conchuse, conscious
concierge, OVERSEES GATES/ENTRYWAYS
concise, ely, eness, TO THE POINT WITH FEW WORDS
conclude, *, ed, ding, WRAP-UP, SUMMARIZED ENDING
conclugen, conclusion
conclusion, *, FINALIZE, END
conclusion, conclusion
conclusion, conclusion
concoct, *, ted, ting, PUTTING TOGETHER IDEAS
concrete, ely, eness, HARDENED GRAVEL MIXTURE
concussion, *, sive, INJURY FROM IMPACT
concution, concussion
condemn, *, ned, ning, STEP TOWARDS ELIMINATION
condensashen, condensation
condensation, *, GAS REDUCED TO LIQUID
condense, *, ed, er, sing, REDUCE
condescend, ding, dingly, TALK DOWN TO SOMEONE, TREAT AS AN INFERIOR
condesend, condescend
condewit, conduit
condimeneum, condominium
condiment, *, SPICES, SAUCES
condinsashen, condensation
condinsation, condensation
condisend, condescend
condishen, condition
condition, *, ned, ning, nal, TO FORCE INTO ANOTHER FORM, RESTRUCTURE
condolence, *, SYMPATHY FOR SOMEONE'S PAIN
condom, *, COVER FOR PENIS
condomeneum, condominium
condominium, *, FORM OF APARTMENTS
condone, *, ed, ning, FORGIVE
conduct, *, ted, ting, ESCORT, TRANSPORT, BEHAVIOR
conductor, *, rial, rship, TRANSMITS, LEADS, GUIDES

conduit, CHANNEL FOR ENERGY, FLUIDS, ETC.
condukter, conductor
condum, condom
condument, condiment
condunsation, condensation
cone,*, GEOMETRIC SHAPE OF MANY THINGS
conect, connect
conekshen, connection
confection,*,nary,nery,ner, A DESSERT
confederate,*,acy,tion, UNITED ALLIANCE
confedont, confidant
confeduret, confederate
confedy, confetti
confekshen, confection
conference,*, MEETING FOR DISCUSSION
confermation, confirmation
confesion, confession
confess,sses,ssed,ssing,ssor, DISCLOSE
  INFORMATION, ADMIT FACTS
confession,*,nal, ADMIT INVOLVEMENT
confetion, confection
confetti, PARTY MATERIAL
confetty, confetti
confety, confetti
confidant,*,confidante', TRUSTED PERSON (or see
  confident)
confide,*,ed,ding, SHARE THOUGHTS WITH SOMEONE
confidence,nt,ntial, TRUST
confidenshul, confidential
confidential,lly, PRIVATE
confidont, confidant
configerashun, configuration
configuration,*, ARRANGEMENT OF PARTS
confine,*,ed,ning,nment, RESTRICTED, IMPRISONED
confinement, BEING RESTRICTED, IMPRISONED
confinmint, confinement
confrents, conference
confirm,*,med,ming, TO VALIDATE
confirmation,*,ive, ACT OF VALIDATION

conflict,*,ted,ting, GOES AGAINST
conform,*,med,ming,mer,mist,mism, TO TAKE ON
  ANOTHER FORM
confront,*,ted,ting, FACE, ENCOUNTER
confudense, confidence
confujen, confusion
confuranse, conference
confurmashun, confirmation
confuse,*,ed,sing, DIS-ORDER, OFF-CENTER
confusion, STATE OF DIS-ORDER, OFF-CENTER
conger, conjure
conglomerate,*,ed,ting, GATHERED INTO MASS
congradulashen, congratulation
congratulate,*,ed,ting,tion, WISH ONE WELL,
  COMPLIMENT
congratulation,*, EXPRESS WISHING ONE WELL,
  COMPLIMENT
congregate,*,ed,ting, GATHERING, ASSEMBLY
congregation,*,nal, TO GATHER, ASSEMBLY
congress,ssional,ssionally, LEGISLATIVE ASSEMBLY
  TO PROMOTE A GROUPS INTERESTS
congrewint, congruent
congrigate, congregate
congris, congress
congruent,nce,ncy,ntly, AGREEMENT, CONSISTENCY
congrugashun, congregation
congrugate, congregate
conifer,*, TREE GROUP
conjugal,lity,lly, RELATION WITH PARTNER/MATE
conjunction,*,nal,nally, UNIFICATION, BRING
  TOGETHER
conjunkshen, conjunction
conjure,*,ed,ring, CREATE/CONSPIRE
conker, conquer
conklude, conclude
conkrete, concrete
conkur, conquer
conkushen, concussion
conkwest, conquest

connect,*,ted,ting,tive,tivity, BOND ASSOCIATE/
  BRING TOGETHER
connection,*, ACT OF BRINGING TOGETHER/BOND
conphert, comfort
conquer,*,red,ring, OBTAIN BY FORCE
conquest,*, WIN BY WILL
consalidate, consolidate
conscientious,sly,sness, WITH UNSELFISH MOTIVES
conscious,sly,sness, AWARE OF PHYSICAL REALITY
conseal, conceal
consecutive,ely,eness, DIRECTLY FOLLOWING
  ANOTHER
conseed, concede
consel, conceal/ council/ counsel
conseet, conceit
conseevable, conceivable
conseeve, conceive
consekcutive, consecutive
consemate, consummate
consensus,ual,ually, AGREEMENT, MUTUAL CONSENT
consent,*,ted,ting, YIELD OR COMPLY
consentrate, concentrate
consepshun, conception
consept, concept
conseption, conception
conseptual, conceptual
consequence,*, REACTION TO AN ACTION
consern, concern
consert, concert
conservation,nist,nism, TO PRESERVE/ PROTECT
conservative,*, PRACTICES RESTRAINT
conseshun, concession
consetion, concession
conseve, conceive
consider,*,red,ring,able,ation, ENGAGE IN
  THOUGHT
consierge, concierge
consignment,*, GIVING SOMEONE A PERCENT FOR
  SELLING YOUR WARES

consikwense, consequence
consilation, consolation
consimate, consummate
consinent, consonant
consinment, consignment
consintrate, concentrate
consiquence, consequence
consise, concise
consist,*,ted,ting,tent, COMPOSED OF
consistency,cies, HOW FLUID, VISCOUS
consolation,*, TO OFFER SOLACE/ SUPPORT FOR EFFORT (or see constellation)
console,*,ed,ling, SOOTHE, OFFER SUPPORT, CABINET FOR ELECTRONICS
consolidate,*,ed,ting,tion, PUT ALL TOGETHER
consonant,*, LETTERS IN ENGLISH WORDS THAT AREN'T VOWELS
consoom, consume
conspearusy, conspiracy
conspicuous,sly,sness, OBVIOUS, STRIKING
conspikuos, conspicuous
conspikyous, conspicuous
conspiracy,cies, A GROUP OF PEOPLE PLOTTING AN EVENT TO UPSET STATUS QUO
constancy, DILIGENT/REPEATEDLY CONSISTENT
constant,*,tly, UNIFORM, UNCHANGING
constatushen, constitution
constellation,*, NAME FOR GROUPED CELESTIAL STARS (or see consolation)
constense, constancy
constilashen, constellation
constilation, constellation
constint, constant
constipashen, constipation
constipation, RESTRICTED BOWEL MOVEMENT
constitushen, constitution
constitution,*,nal, WRITTEN RULES/PRINCIPLES/ REGULATIONS

constrict,*,ted,ting,tion,tive, PREVENT FROM PROPER MOVEMENT
construct,*,ted,ting,tive, MOLD/FORM/CREATE
construction,nal,nally, BUILDING/FORMING
constulashen, constellation
constulation, constellation
constupashen, constipation
consukwinse, consequence
consulashen, consolation
consulation, consolation
consult,*,ted,ting,tant,tation, COMMUNICATE WITH SOMEONE WHO IS SEEKING ADVICE
consultashen, consult(ation)
consumate, consummate
consume,*,ed,er,erism,ming,mable, DECOMPOSE OR DESTROY, INGEST, MAKE USE OF
consummate,*,ed,ting, COMPLETE, FULFILL
consumpshen, consumption
consumption,tive, WHAT'S BEEN DESTROYED, DECOMPOSED
consumshen, consumption
consunent, consonant
consurt, concert
consurvashenm, conservation
contact,*,ted,ting, TOUCHING, ASSOCIATION WITH
contagious,sly,sness, SPREAD TO OTHERS
contain,*,ned,ning,ner,nment, HOLD WITHIN
contaminate,*,ed,ting,ant,tion, SOMETHING INCLUDED WHICH DOESN'T BELONG AT ALL
contemplate,*,ed,ting,tive,tively,tiveness, TO OBSERVE THOROUGHLY
contemporary,ries,riness, REFLECTIVE OF CURRENT TIMES
contempt,tible,table,bleness,tibly,tuous,tuously, tuousness, THE STATE OF BEING DISHONORED/ DISRESPECTED
contend,*,ded,ding,der, CHOOSE OR FORCED TO DEAL WITH, FACE OFF

content,ted,tedly,tedness,tment, THAT WHICH IS CONTAINED WITHIN, SATISFIED
contenual, continual
contenuense, continuance
contenuisly, continue(uously)
contenule, continual
contest,*,ted, DISPUTE, FOR SUPERIORITY
context,ture, INTERWOVEN MEANING IN TEXT
contimplate, contemplate
contimporary, contemporary
continent,*,tal, LAND MASS
contingent,*,nce,ncy, MAY HAPPEN IF...
continet, continent
contint, content
continuance, POSTPONEMENT TO CONTINUE AT A FUTURE DATE
continuants, continuance
continue,*,ed,uing,ual,ually,uation,uouse, uouesly, KEEP GOING
contorshenist, contortionist
contortionist,*, FLEXIBLE ACTS WITH THE BODY
contour,*,red,ring, THE SHAPE/FORM OF OUTLINE
contra, contro, PREFIX INDICATING "AGAINST" MOST OFTEN MODIFIES THE WORD
contraception,ive, FOR PREVENTION OF PREGNANCY
contract,*ted,ting,tor,tual,tive, WRITTEN OBLIGATION OF SERVICE
contraction,*,nal,nary, MUSCLES TIGHTENING, COMBINATION OF WORDS
contradict,*,ted,ting,tion,tory, CONTRARY/ OPPOSE/DENY
contrak, contract
contrakshen, contraction
contrary,ries,riness,riety, PROVE OPPOSITE, DENY
contrast,*,ted,ting,tingly, COMPARING DIFFERENCES
contraversy, controversy
contrebute, contribute
contrery, contrary
contribute,*,ed,ting,tion,tive,tory, GIVE, LEND

contrition, *AMENDING SIN WITH PRAYER*
control,*,lled,lling, *ATTEMPT TO GAIN ORDER*
controversy,sies,sial, *DIFFERENCE IN OPINION, DEBATE*
contrudik, contradict
contrusepshun, contraception
contumplate, contemplate
contunent, continent
conture, contour
conufir, conifer
conva, convey
convalescence,nt, *RECOVERING HEALTH*
convelesents, convalescence
convene,*,ed,ning, *CALL TO APPEAR, MEET*
convenient,nce, *EASE OF FACILITIES, COMFORT*
convense, convinse
convention,*,nal, *PEOPLE GATHERING, AN ASSEMBLY*
convenyant, convenient
convenyut, convenient
conversashen, conversation
converse,es,sing,sant, *EXCHANGE INFORMATION, MADE OPPOSITE/REVERSE*
conversation,nal,nally,nalist, *COMMUNICATING THOUGHTS*
conversion,*, *CHANGED IN ONE FORM OR ANOTHER*
convert,*,ted,ting,ter, *OF CHANGE, TRANSFORM*
convict,*,ted,ting,tion, *HAVING BEEN FOUND GUILTY/AT FAULT*
convince,*,ed,cing, *TO PERSUADE SOMEONE TO YOUR OPINION*
convulesense, convalescence
convulesents, convalescence
convulgin, convulsion
convulshen, convulsion
convulsion,*,sive, *INTENSE MUSCLE CONTRACTION*
convurgin, conversion
convursashen, conversation
conversation, conversation
coocoo, cuckoo

cood, could
coodent, couldn't
cooger, cougar
cook,*,ked,king, *PREPARE FOOD*
cookie,*,*, *SWEET CAKE TREAT*
cool,lly,lness, *BETWEEN WARM/COLD TEMPERATURE, EXPRESSION OF APPRECIATION*
cooler,*, *COLD CONTAINER FOR FOOD*
coom lada, cum laude
coop,ped, *SMALL CAGE FOR SMALL ANIMALS (or see co-op or coup)*
cooperate,*,*,ed,ting,tive, *UNITE TO PRODUCE*
coordinate,*,*,ed,ting,tion, *ORGANIZE FOR DESIRED RESULTS, LINE SYSTEM*
cooth, couth
cope,*,ed,ping, *TO DEAL WITH STRESS, SHAPE/MATCH*
copeur, copy(pier)
coper, copper
copper,RY, *METAL*
copulate,*,ed,ted,tion, *PHYSICAL SEXUAL UNITY*
copur, copper
copy,pies,pied,ying, *TO REPRODUCE*
cor, core /car
coral, *OCEAN REEF ANIMALS*
cord,*, *STRANDS WOVEN OR TWISTED TOGETHER (or see chord /quart(s) /quartz)*
cordaroy, corduroy
cordial,lity,lness,lly, *GRACIOUS, KIND, A LIQUEUR*
cordinate, coordinate
cordunate, coordinate
corduroy, *RIBBED MATERIAL*
core,*,ed,ring, *THE CENTER OF (or see corp)*
corect, correct
corelate, correlate
corespond, correspond
corgul, cordial
coridor, corridor
corigate, corrugate
corilate, correlate

coriner, coroner
coriner, coronary
coris, chorus / course
corispond, correspond
corjil, cordial
cork,*,ked, *BARK FROM A TREE (or see quark)*
corn,*, *GRAIN, ON TOE*
cornea,al, *PART OF EYE*
corner,*,red,ring, *WHERE WALLS OR LINES MEET, NO WAY OUT*
cornia, cornea
cornikopea, cornucopia
cornucopia, *HORN OF PLENTY*
coroborate, corroborate
corode, corrode
coronary,ries, *HEART ARTERIES*
coroner,*, *INVESTIGATES SUSPICIOUS DEATHS*
corp,*, *NUMBER OF PEOPLE WORKING TOGETHER (or see core)*
corparul, corporal
corpirate, corporate
corporal, *OF THE PHYSICAL BODY*
corporate,ed,ting,tion, *UNITE MANY INTO ONE*
corpse,*, *DEAD BODY*
corpural, corporal
corpurate, corporate
corral,*, *FENCED ENCLOSURE FOR ANIMALS (or see coral)*
correct,*,ted,ting,tly,tiontable,tible,tness,tor,tively, *TO SET RIGHT OR STRAIGHT*
correlate,*,ed,ting,tion, *IF ONE... THEN THE OTHER*
correspond,*,ded,ding,dence, *SIMILAR/RELATED TO, COMMUNICATE WITH*
corridor,*, *NARROW PASSAGE*
corroborate,*,ed,ting,tion,tive,tory, *CAN BACK UP THE TRUTH WITH EVIDENCE*
corrode,*,ed,ding,osion,osive, *CHEMICAL EROSION, EATEN AWAY*
corrugate,ed,ting, *ALTERNATING BENDS, FORMS*

corrupt,*,ted,ting,tion,tible,tibility,tibleness, tibly,tness, *TO NEGATIVELY STEER OF COURSE*
corsage,*,, *FLOWERS TO WEAR, BODICE*
corse, course /coarse /core(s)
corsoge, corsage
cort, cord /court /quart
cort-marshul, court-martial
corts, cord(s) /court(s) /quart(s)
corudoor, corridor
corugate, corrugate
corul, choral /coral /corral /chorale
corulate, correlate
corunary, coronary
coruner, coroner
corupt, corrupt
coruspond, correspond
cos, cause
cosee, cozy
coshen, caution
coshis, cautious
coshun, caution
cosmic,cally, *NOT OF THIS PHYSICAL PLANE*
cosmopolitan, *BELONGS TO THE WORLD, NO ATTACHMENT*
cosmos, *UNIVERSAL HARMONY*
cost,*,ting,tly, *EXPENSE (or see coast /cause(d))*
coster, coaster
costic, caustic
costoom, costume
costume,*,, *GARMENTS TO SUIT A CHARACTER TYPE*
cosy, cozy
cot,*, *FOLDING BED (or see caught /coat)*
cotage, cottage
cotej, cottage
coten, cotton
coton, cotton
cottage,*,, *SMALL DWELLING*
cotton, *PLANT WHICH CLOTH IS PRODUCED FROM*
cotuge, cottage

couch,hes,hed, *FURNITURE, PUT-DOWN*
cougar,*,, *animal*
cough,*,hed,hing, *FORCEFULLY EXPEL AIR FROM LUNGS*
cought, caught /cot /cough(ed)
could, *PAST TENSE OF "CAN"*
couldn't, *CONTRACTION OF THE WORDS "COULD NOT"*
coulishun, coalition
council,*, *A GROUP MEETING TO DISCUSS OR MAKE DECISIONS (or see counsel)*
counsel,*,led,lling, *GIVES ADVISE, PROVIDES INFORMATION (or see council)*
counside, coincide
count,*,ted,ting, *ADD THE NUMBER OF THINGS*
counter,*, *PREFIX INDICATING "AGAINST" MOST OFTEN MODIFIES THE WORD*
counter,*,red,ring,rance, *SURFACE FOR SERVING, SOMETHING THAT COUNTS, OPPOSING MOVE*
country,ries, *OUT OF THE CITY, COLLECTION OF STATES, NATION OF PEOPLE*
county,ties, *A GEOGRAPHICAL AREA*
coup, *QUICK/SUCCESSFUL MOVE (or see coop)*
couple,*, ed,ling, *PARTNERS*
coupler,*,,ling, *DEVICE FOR CONNECTING*
coupon,*,, *REDEEM FOR CASH VALUE*
coupurate, cooperate
courage,eous,eously,eousness, *BRAVE IN FACING DANGER*
courier,*,, *MESSENGER*
course,*, *PATH, IDEA, CONCEPT TO FOLLOW (or see coarse)*
court,*,ted,ting, *ENCLOSED AREA, HALL OR CHAMBER FOR SPORTS OR CIVIC ACTIVITIES*
court-martial,led,ling, *MILITARY TRIAL*
courteous,sly,sness, *POLITE*
courtesy,sies, *POLITE BEHAVIOR*
cousin,*,, *KINSHIP, RELATIVE*
cout, caught /cot
couth, *SOPHISTICATED*

cova, kava
cove,*, ed,ving, *NOOK, CAVE (or see coffee)*
covenant,*,, *AGREEMENT, CONTRACT TO KEEP PROMISE*
cover,*,red,ring, *TO HIDE OR PROTECT*
coverage, *ACT OF HIDING OR BEING PROTECTED*
covert,tly,tness, *UNDER COVER, DISGUISED, SHELTERED*
covet, *DESIRE WITHOUT REGARDS TO CONSEQUENCE*
covunent, covenant
covurt, covert
cow,*, *THE FEMININE OF VARIOUS SPECIES*
coward,*,dly,dliness,dice, *CANNOT BRAVELY FACE DANGER*
cowch, couch
cowculus, calculus
cowerd, coward
cowkulate, calculate
cowl,*,ling, *A HOOD (or see call)*
cownder, counter
cownsul, council /counsel
cownt, count
cowntur, counter
cownty, county
cowurd, coward
coxs, coax
coz, cause
cozmic, cosmic
cozmopoletin, cosmopolitan
cozmos, cosmos
cozy,zies,zily,ziness, *COMFORTABLE, CONTENT, SNUG*
crab,*, *CRUSTACEAN, HARD SHELLED OCEAN ANIMAL*
crack,*,ked,king, *TO SPLIT APART, SLANG FOR A SERIOUSLY ADDICTIVE DRUG, A SOUND*
cracker,*,, *YEASTLESS BISCUIT, FIREWORKS*
crackle,*,ed,ling, *SOUND, GLAZE ON POTTERY*
crader, crater / creator
cradle,*,ed,ling,*BED FOR INFANT,HOLD IN ARMS,TOOL*
cradul, cradle

crafe, crave
craft,*,ted,ting, *SKILL USING HANDS, VESSEL FOR TRAVEL*
crain, crane
craink, crank
crak, crack
crakel, crackle
craker, cracker
cral, crawl
cram,*,mmed,mming, *TO FORCE INTO A SPACE*
cramp,*,ped,ping, *CONFINES, MUSCLE CONTRACTIONS*
crampt, cramp(ed)
cranberry,ries, *EDIBLE BERRY*
crane,*,ed,ning, *MACHINE, STRETCH*
craneum, cranium
crani, cranio, *PREFIX INDICATING "SKULL" MOST OFTEN MODIFIES THE WORD*
cranium,*,ia, *SKULL*
crank,*,ked,king,ky, *TOOL, SOMEONE IRRITABLE*
cranny,nies, *CREVICE, NOOK, CRACK*
crany, cranny
craon, crayon
crap,*,pped,pping,ppy, *GAME OF DICE, TIRED OUT* (or see crepe)
crape, crepe /crap(ppy)
crase, crazy
crash,hes,hed,hing, *SOUND, TO RUN INTO, OFF OF SOMETHING*
crass,sness, *COARSE, THICK, DENSE*
crate,*, ed,ting, *BOX, BOX UP*
crater,*,red,ral, *BOWL-SHAPE DEPRESSION, CONCAVE* (or see creator)
craul, crawl
crave,*,ed,ving, *TO YEARN, DESIRE HEAVILY*
crawl,*,led,ling, *ON HANDS AND KNEES, MOVE SLOWLY, CROUCHED POSITION*
crayon,*, *WAX PENCIL*
crazy, *INSANE, INFATUATED*

creader, creator
creak,*,ked,king, *NOISE* (or see creek)
creal, creel
cream,my,mily,miness, *FROM MILK, TO WHIP ON SOMEONE* (or see creme)
creap, creep
crease,*,ed,sing, *MAKE FOLDED LINES, MARK IN*
creashun, create(tion)
creasul, creosole
create,*,ed,ting,tive,tively,tiveness,tion, *MAKE THOUGHTS PHYSICAL REALITY*
createf, create(tive)
creator,*,*, *ONES WHO MAKE THOUGHTS PHYSICAL REALITIES*
creature,*,ely, *SOMETHING OTHER THAN HUMAN, ANIMATE, INANIMATE*
creb, crib
crebeg, cribbage
crecher, creature
crededer, creditor
credential,*,*, *TO VALIDATE CONFIDENCE, ASSURE OF AUTHENTICITY*
creder, critter
credible,ly,bility,eness, *WORTHY/BELIEVABLE*
credider, creditor
credinshul, credential
credisize, criticize
credit,*,ted,ting,table, *RECORD OF HANDLING OTHER'S MONEY/SPENDING/EARNINGS, ACCOUNT TO BORROW AGAINST*
creditor,*, *ONE WHOM MONEY IS OWED TO*
creduble, credible
creducal, critical
creecher, creature
creek,*, *SMALL STREAM/TRIBUTARY* (or see creak)
creel, *FISH BASKET, OF SEWING MACHINES*
creen, careen
creenkul, crinkle

creep,*,ped,ping,py, *SOMETHING WHICH CAUSES FEARFUL SENSATION, TO SNEAK UP IN CROUCHED POSTURE*
creisote, creosote
creke, creak /creek
crekit, cricket
cremate,*,ed,ting,tor, *BURN A BODY TO ASH*
creme, *LIKE CREAM* (or see cream)
cremenul, criminal
cremson, crimson
creng, cringe
crenj, cringe
crenkle, crinkle
creosole, *BLACK, FROM TAR AND RESIN* (or see creosote)
creosote, *FROM WOOD TAR USED FOR PRESERVATIVE, ANTISEPTIC* (or see creosole)
crepe,*, *THIN PAPER, FABRIC* (or see creep)
creple, cripple
creptic, cryptic
crescendo,*,di, *GRADUAL/GROWING/INCREASING*
crescent,*, *SHAPE OF QUARTER MOON*
crescross, crisscross
crese, crease
cresendo, crescendo
cresent, crescent /croissant
crest,*,ted,ting, *TOP/CROWN/PEAK*
cresunt, crescent /croissant
creteek, critique
creteke, critique
cretik, critic
cretisize, criticize
creusol, creosole
creusote, creosote
crevasse,ed,sing, *FISSURE OF GLACIER/RIVER* (or see crevice)
crevice,*, *CRACK/FISSURE* (or see crevasse)
crevus, crevasse crevice
crew,*, *GANG/BODY OF PEOPLE* (or see cruise)

crewd, crude
crews, cruise /crew(s)
crewsade, crusade
crewshul, crucial
crewsufix, crucifix
crewton, crouton
crib,*,bbed,bbing, ENCLOSURE/CONTAINER, CHEAT SHEET
cribage, cribbage
cribbage, GAME, CARDS
cribd, crib(bbed)
cribeg, cribbage
cricket,*, INSECT
crid, cried
crider, critter
cridik, critic
criducal, critical
cridusize, criticize
cried, PAST TENSE OF "CRY"
cries, PAST TENSE OF "CRY"
criket, cricket
crime,*, ACT AGAINST MAN'S LAWS
crimenal, criminal
criminal,*,lly, ONE WHO VIOLATED MAN'S LAWS
crimson, COLOR
cringe,*,ed,ging, RECOIL IN POSTURE, RETRACT
crinj, cringe
crinkle,*,ed,ling, NOISE, CRUMPLE
criple, cripple
cripple,*,ed,ling, LAME, DISABLE
criptic, cryptic
criscross, crisscross
crisis,ses, TURNING POINT IN LIFE
crisont, croissant
crisp,ply,piness,py, BRITTLE, FRESH
crisscross,sses,ssed,ssing, TWO LINES THAT INTERSECT TO FORM AN "X"
cristal, crystal
cristashen, crustacean

criter, critter
critic,*, ONE WHO PASSES JUDGEMENT
critical,cally,calness, BEING JUDGEMENTAL
criticize,*,ed,zing,ism, TO PROVIDE PERSONAL JUDGEMENT
critique,*,ed,uing, PROVIDE WRITTEN OPINION
critter,*, NON-HUMAN CREATURE
criz, cries
croak,*,ked,king, FROG SOUND, TO DIE
croan, crone
crochet,*,ted,ting, KNIT WITH NEEDLE
crock,*,kery, KETTLE, POT, DEROGATORY RESPONSE (or see croak)
crocodile,*, LARGE BROWN REPTILE
crok, crock /croak
crokedile, crocodile
croket, croquet /croquette
crokudile, crocodile
crol, crawl
crone,*, AGED WOMAN
crony,nies, FRIENDS, BUDDIES
crook,*, ked,kedly,kedness, DISHONORABLE PERSON, A BEND, HOOK
croose, cruise /crew(s)
crop,*, pped,pping, YIELD IN FIELD, SUDDEN APPEARANCE
croquet, GAME (or see croquette)
croquette, PREPARED FOOD (or see croquet)
croshay, crochet
cross,sses,ssed,ssing, TWO LINES PERFORMING INTERSECTION
crotch,hless, WHERE LEGS MEET THE TORSO, FORK OF SOMETHING
crouch,hes,hed,hing, HUDDLE, SQUAT, CRINGE
croud, crowd
crouton, SMALL TOAST
crow,*,wed,wing, BOAST, ROOSTER SOUND

crowch, crouch
crowd,*,ded,ding, BODIES CLOSE TOGETHER
crowkus, crocus
crown,*,ned,ning, PEAK, CREST, TOP, HEAD ADORNMENT
crowshay, crochet
crowtch, crouch
cru, crew
cruch, crutch
crucial, UPMOST IMPORTANCE
crucifix,xion, PERTAINING TO CHRISTIAN CROSS
crude,er,est,ely,eness,NEED FURTHER DEVELOPMENT
crudenshul, credential
crudinshuls, credential(s)
crue, crew
cruise,*,ed,sing,er, MOVE ABOUT IN CAR OR BOAT FOR PLEASURE (or see crew)
cruke, crook
cruks, crux
crumb,*,bly, TINY BITS OF SOMETHING
crumble,*,ed,ling, FALL APART IN PIECES
crumple,*,ed,ling, WRINKLE, SQUEEZE OR FORM CREASES
crunch,hes,hed,hing,hy, TO BREAK, WRINKLE
crupt, corrupt
crusade,*,ed,ding, MOVEMENT WITH ASSERTIVE INTENT
cruse, cruise /crew(s)
crusendo, crescendo
crush,hes,hed,hing,her, TO SMASH
crushul, crucial
crust,*,ty,ted,tal,tless, PASTRY LINING
crustacean,*,eous, WATER ANIMAL, ANTHROPOD
crutch,hes, TOOL FOR SUPPORT
cruteek, critique
cruteke, critique
cruton, crouton
crux,xes, TROUBLE, CROSS

cry,ries,ried,ying, *VERBAL SOUND, EMOTIONAL RELEASE*
cryptic,cal,cally, *CODES TO CONCEAL OR HIDE*
crysis, crisis
crystal,*,lize, *OF OR LIKE CLEAR QUARTZ ROCK*
cshel, seashell
cu, cue
cubby,bies, *SMALL, SNUG SPACE*
cube,*,ed, *SHAPE WHERE ALL SIDES THE SAME, MATHEMATICAL EXPRESSION (or see cubby)*
cubek, cubic
cubekle, cubicle
cubic, *OF A CUBE, MATHEMATICAL EXPRESSION*
cubicle,*, *AREA SECTIONED OFF, SMALL SPACE*
cubird, cupboard
cuburd, cupboard
cubuse, caboose
cuckoo,*,oed,oing, *BIRD, CRAZY*
cucu, cuckoo
cucumber,*,*, *VEGETABLE*
cucune, cocoon
cud, *WHAT A COW CHEWS (or see could /cue(d)/ cute)*
cudaver, cadaver
cuddle,*,ed,ling, *HOLD SNUGGLY*
cudent, couldn't
cudet, cadet
cudint, couldn't
cudle, cuddle
cue,*,ed,uing, *SIGNAL/SIGN, SOMETHING WHICH DISTINGUISHES*
cuepon, coupon
cufer, cover
cuferege, coverage
cuff,*,fed,fing, *FIST BLOW, ON SLEEVES, ON CREDIT, RESTRAINT FOR WRISTS*
cuger, cougar
cugole, cajole
cuisine, *FINE COOKING*

cuk, cook /cock
cuke, cook /cookie
cukoon, cocoon
cuku, cuckoo
cukumber, cucumber
cul-de-sac,*, *BULB SHAPE AT END WITH EXIT AND ENTRANCE BEING THE SAME*
culamity, calamity
culander, colander
culapse, collapse
culcher, culture
culejet, collegiate
culekshun, collection
culekt, collect
culektur, collector
culenary, culinary
culendjula, calendula
culer, color /cooler
culide, collide
culidescope, kaleidoscope
culinary, *ART OF FOOD PREPARATION*
culindula, calendula
culishun, collision
culition, collision
culmenate, culminate
culminate,*,ed,ting,tion, *CLIMAX/GREAT HEIGHT*
culoge, collage
culone, cologne /colon
culoneul, colonial
culor, color
culostimy, colostomy
culosul, colossal
culprit,*, *ONE WHO COMMITTED AN OFFENSE*
culsher, culture
cult, *GROUP OF PEOPLE WITH FIRM RELIGIOOUS BELIEFS*
cultavashen, cultivate(tion)
cultivashen, cultivate(tion)
cultivate,*,ed,ting,tion, *DEVELOP/FACILITATE GROWTH OF SOMETHING*

cultsher, culture
culture,*,ral,rally, *ESSENCE OF A GROUP/SOCIETY, NURTURING*
culvert,*, *A DRAIN*
cum laude, *METHOD OF COMPARING GRADUATES AGAINST ONE ANOTHER*
cum, *WITH/TOGETHER, A SECRETION (or see come)*
cumaletive, cumulative
cumand, command
cumander, commander
cumberbun, cummerbund
cumberbund, cummerbund
cumbine, combine
cumbuschen, combustion
cumbustible, combustible
cumdean, comedian
cumemorate, commemorate
cumenduble, commendable
cumenserite, commensurate
cuments, commence
cumerbund, cummerbund
cumershal, commercial
cumfert, comfort
cumfertible, comfortable
cuminduble, commendable
cumishen, commission
cumishioner, commissioner
cumitee, committee
cumitment, commitment
cumlota, cum laude
cummerbund,*, *BAND FOR WAIST WORN WITH FORMALS*
cumnee, company
cumodity, commodity
cumpartment, compartment
cumpashunet, compassionate
cumpass, compass
cumpatuble, compatibility
cumpedidor, competitor
cumpel, compel

cumpeny, company
cumperible, comparable
cumperison, comparison
cumpete, compete
cumpetitor, competitor
cumpile, compile
cumplane, complain
cumplasens,complacence/complaisance
cumplecshun, complexion
cumpleks, complex
cumpleshun, completion
cumplete, complete
cumply, comply
cumponent, component
cumpose, compose
cumposier, composure
cumposit, composite
cumpownd, compound
cumpreshun, compression
cumpresor, compressor
cumpress, compress
cumpuder, computer
cumpulsery, compulsory
cumpulshun, compulsion
cumpulsuve, compulsive
cumpute, compute
cumputer, computer
cumulative,ely,eness, ACCUMULATION/COLLECTS
cumunal, communal
cumunikable, communicable
cumunyon, communion
cunal, canal
cunclude, conclude
cunclution, conclusion
cuncoct, concoct
cundem, condemn
cundense, condense
cundinse, condense
cundishen, condition

cundition, condition
cundolense, condolence
cundone, condone
cundukt, conduct
cunekshen, connection
cunekt, connect
cunfecshin, confection
cunferm, confirm
cunfeshun, confession
cunfess, confess
cunfetion, confetion
cunfetty, confetti
cunfide, confide
cunfiguration, configuration
cunfine, confine
cunfinment, confinement
cunfirm, confirm
cunflict, conflict
cunform, conform
cunfront, confront
cunfugin, confusion
cunfuse, confuse
cunfusion, confusion
cunglomurete, conglomerate
cungradulashen, congratulation
cungratshulate, congratulate
cungruint, congruent
cuning, cunning
cunjunkshen, conjunction
cunklusion, conclusion
cunkokt, concoct
cunkushun, concussion
cunning,gly,gness, CRAFTY, SKILLFUL
cunseed, concede
cunseel, conceal
cunseet, conceit
cunseeve, conceive
cunseevuble, conceivable
cunsent, consent

cunsepshual, conceptual
cunsepshun, conception
cunseption, conception
cunservutive, conservative
cunsinment, consignment
cunsise, concise
cunsist, consist
cunsistency, consistency
cunsiter, consider
cunsole, console
cunsoludate, consolidate
cunsoom, consume
cunsoul, console
cunspikuos, conspicuous
cunstrict, constrict
cunstrucshen, construction
cunstruct, construct
cunsult, consult
cunsurn, concern
cuntamunate, contaminate
cuntane, contain
cuntemporary, contemporary
cuntemt, contempt
cuntend, contend
cuntent, content
cuntenuense, continuance
cuntest, contest
cuntrakshen, contraction
cuntree, country
cuntrery, contrary
cuntrishen, contrition
cuntrol, control
cunvekt, convict
cunvence, convince
cunvene, convene
cunvenshen, convention
cunvenyent, convenient
cunvergin, conversion
cunvershen, conversion

cunvert, convert
cunvulgin, convulsion
cunvulshen, convulsion
cup,*,pped,pping, *VESSEL OR SHAPE LIKE SMALL BOWL* (or see coop)
cupasity, capacity
cupboard,*, *CABINET IN KITCHEN*
cupcake,*, *SMALL CAKE*
cupe, coop
cupil, couple
cupler, coupler
cupon, coupon
cupul, couple
curabirate, corroborate
curable,bility,eness,ly, *CAN BE CURED*
curader, curator
cural, corral
curamic, ceramic
curant, currant / current
curator,*, *APPOINTED BY COURT, OVERSEER*
curb,*,bed,bing, *FOR RESTRAINT, TO PROTECT SOMETHING*
curcle, circle
curcumsize, circumcise
curd,*, *USED TO MAKE CHEESE* (or see cure(d))
curdesy, courtesy
curdeus, courteous
curdisy, courtesy
curdle,*,ed,ling, *COAGULATING*
cure,*,ed,ring,rative, *TAKE BACK TO EQUILIBRIUM, HEALTHY STATE*
cureen, careen
cureer, career
curege, courage
curekt, correct
curekulum, curriculum
curency, currency
curensy, currency
curent, currant / current

cureosedy, curiosity
cureosity, curiosity
curess, caress
cureur, courier
cureus, curious
cureusol, creosole
curf, curve
curfew,*, *A TIME TO BE OFF THE STREETS*
curfu, curfew
curiculum, curriculum
curier, courier
curige, courage
curiosity,ties, *ACT OF BEING CURIOUS*
curious,sly,sness, *INQUISITIVE, QUESTIONING*
curl,*,led,ling,ler,ly, *A TWIST, LOOP, RINGLET*
curnol, colonel / kernel
curnul, colonel / kernel
curoberate, corroborate
curoborate, corroborate
curode, corrode
curoty, karate
curowse, carouse
currant, *FRUIT, BERRY* (or see current)
currency,cies, *MONEY*
current,*,tly,tness, *PRESENT FLOW OF, AS IN RIVER OR AIR* (or see currant)
curriculum,*,lar, *LEARNING COURSES*
curry,rried,rric, *SPICE*
curse,ed,sing,edness, *SWEAR*
cursive,ely, *FLOWING HAND WRITING*
curtail,lment, *SHORTEN*
curtain,*, *TEMPORARY DIVIDER OR CLOTH PROTECTION*
curtale, curtail
curten, curtain
curtesy, courtesy
curteus, courteous
curtisy, courtesy
curtsy,sies,sied,ying, *FEMALE BOW TO AUDIENCE*
curtul, curdle
curuge, courage

curvature,*, *PROFILE OF SHAPE*
curve,*,ed,ving, *BEND WITH NO ANGLES*
curvechure, curvature
cury, curry
cus, cuss
cusen, cousin
cuset, cassette
cushen, cushion
cushion,*,ned,ning, *PADDING TO SOFTEN, FORM OF PROTECTION*
cusin, cousin
cusp,*,ped,pated, *INTERSECTION OF TWO ARCS, CURVES*
cuspid,*,dal,dated, *TOOTH*
cuss,sses,ssed, *TO CURSE*
custard,*, *DESSERTS*
custedy, custody
custodian,*,nship, *GUARDIAN*
custody,dies,dial, *UNDER CARE OF GUARDIAN, IMPRISONED*
custom,*,mable, *TRADITION, HABIT*
customary,ries,rily,riness,*ROUTINE,TRADITIONALLY*
customer,*, *CLIENT, PURCHASER*
customize,*,ed,zing,zation, *INDIVIDUAL SHAPE OR DESIGN FOR DESIRED RESULTS*
cut,*,tter, *CAUSE SEPARATION* (or see cud or cute)
catastrufe, catastrophe
cute,er,test,tie, *APPEALING TO THE EYE, SHREWD*
cuth, couth
cuticle,*, *AROUND NAILS AND CELLS*
cutlary, cutlery
cutlery, *CUTTING TOOL, KNIVES*
cutukle, cuticle
cuvenent, covenant
cuver, cover
cuvit, covet
cuvridge, coverage
cuzen, cousin
cuzn, cousin

cwuzene, cuisine
cyanide, ELEMENT FOR POISON/EXTRACTING GOLD
cybernetics, STUDY OF COMMUNICATIONS SYSTEMS
cyborg,*, HUMAN MODIFIED INTO PARTIAL ROBOT
cycle,*,ed,ling, REPEATING INTERVALS, A COURSE OF EVENTS, REVOLUTIONS
cyclist,*, THOSE WHO RIDE TWO-WHEELED BIKES
cyclone,*,nic,nal,nically, CONICAL SHAPED WIND STORM
cylanoid, solenoid
cylinder,*,dric,drical, GEOMETRIC SHAPE WHICH MAY BE MOBILE OR STATIONERY
cymbal,*,list, MUSICAL INSTRUMENT (or see symbol)
cynic,*,cism, DISBELIEVER
cynical,lly,lness, BEING A DISBELIEVER
cyst,tic, SACK OF FLUID
czar,*, RULER OF PEOPLE

"D"

da, day
dabate, debate
dab,*,bbed,bbing,bber, BLOT/DIP/BARELY TOUCH
dabble,*,ed,ling, PARTICIPATE WITHOUT SERIOUS COMMITMENT
dabelatate, debilitate
dabilutate, debilitate
dable, dabble
dabre, debris
daciduous, deciduous
daclare, declare
dacree, decree
dacrepit, decrepit
dada, data
dadu, data
dadukt, deduct

daduse, deduce
dae, day
daedy, deity
dafalt, default
dafeet, defeat
dafenative, definitive
dafensable, defensible
dafense, defense
dafeshansy, deficiency
dafiants, defiance
dafide, divide
dafie, defy
daficnse, defiance
dafinative, definitive
dafindant, defendant
dafine, define
dafinse, defense
dafinsible, defensible
dafishantsy, deficiency
dafishensy, deficiency
dafishent, deficient
dafoleate, defoliate
daform, deform
dafray, defray
dafrod, defraud
dafumation, defamation
dafunkt, defunct
dafur, defer
dafuze, diffuse
dafy, defy
dagavoo, deja vu
dager, dagger
dagger,*, SHARP INSTRUMENT
dagree, degree
daidy, deity
daily,lies, EVERY DAY (or see dally or dale)
dainty,tily,tiness, FRAGILE, DELICATE
dair, dare
dairy,ries, WHERE MILK IS

daity, deity
dajavu, deja vu
daklare, declare
dakline, decline
dakree, decree
dakrepit, decrepit
dal, dale /dowel /doll
dalay, delay
dale,*, VALLEY (or see daily /dalles /dell)
daleburite, deliberate
dalectable, delectable
dalema, dilemma
dalenkwent, delinquent
dalenquent, delinquent
dalereus, delirious
daleshus, delicious
delete, delete
dalfin, dolphin
daliberate, deliberate
dalima, dilemma
dalinquent, delinquent
dalishus, delicious
dalite, delight /daylight
daliver, deliver
dalles, SHALLOW RIVER ROCK BOTTOM WITH RAPIDS (or see dowel or doll)
dally,llies,llied,llying, TO DABBLE IN, NOT SERIOUS (or see dale or daily)
daloot, dilute
dalugen, delusion
daluks, deluxe
dalushen, delusion
dalute, dilute
daluxe, deluxe
daly, daily /dally /dale
dam,*,mmed,mming, BARRIER AGAINST WATER (or see damn)
damage,*,ed,ging, TO HARM/ALTER NEGATIVELY
damand, demand

dameg, damage	danote, denote	darelik, derelict
damenish, diminish	danse, dance	darevutive, derivative
dameno, domino	dante, dainty	darier, derriere
damenor, demeanor	danty, dainty	darivadev, derivative
damenshen, dimension	daoderant, deodorant	darivative, derivative
damented, demented	daoderize, deodorize	darive, derive
damention, dimension	daparsher, departure	**dark**,*,ker,kest,ken,kened, *OPPOSITE OF LIGHT*
damenyen, dominion	dapart, depart	**darling**,*,gly,gness, *SOMEONE ENDEARING/ BELOVED*
damestic, domestic	dapartment, department	**darn**, *TO SEW, SHORT FOR "OH, TOO BAD…"*
damig, damage	daparture, departure	**dart**,*,ted,ting, *OF SPORT, MOVE WITH QUICK SPEED*
daminish, diminish	dapend, depend	darulik, derelict
damino, domino	dapikt, depict	dary, dairy
daminyun, dominion	dapind, depend	das, day(s) /daze
damize, demise	dapindant, dependant	dasblay, display
damn,*,ned,ning,nable,nation, *EXPRESSION OF FRUSTRATION (or see dam)*	dapindence, dependence	dasburse, disperse
damolish, demolish	dapleshin, depletion	dascrepshun, description
damonik, demon(ic)	daplete, deplete	dasdrakt, distract
damp,per,pest, *MOIST*	daploma, diploma	dasdrust, distrust
dampen,ned,ning, *TO MOISTEN*	daplomacy, diplomacy	dase, daisy /daze
damper,*, *CONTROLS FLOW*	daplorable, deplorable	dasease, decease /disease
dampin, dampen	daplore, deplore	daseet, deceit
dampun, dampen	daport, deport	daseeve, deceive
dampur, damper	dapose, depose	dasegin, decision
damsel,*, *YOUNG WOMAN*	daposit, deposit	dasel, dazzle
damsul, damsel	dapresheate, depreciate	dasember, December
damug, damage	dapreshen, depression	dasenagrate, disintegrate
damzul, damsel	dapress, depress	dasend, descend
dance,*,ed,cing,er, *TO BODILY MOVE TO MUSIC*	daprive, deprive	dasendent, descendant
dandreff, dandruff	darbe, darby	dasentugrate, disintegrate
dandriff, dandruff	**darbies,** *HANDCUFFS*	daservise, disservice
dandruff, *FLAKEY SKIN ON SCALP*	**darby**,bies, *PLASTERER'S TOOL*	dasesd, decease(d) /disease(d)
danger,*,rous,rously,rness, *BEWARE OF IMMINENT HARM*	**dare**,*,ed,ring, *HAVE COURAGE TO CHALLENGE (or see dairy)*	dasese, decease /disease
dangle,*,er,ling,lingly, *TO SWING FREELY*	dareair, derriere	daset, deceit
dangul, dangle	darect, direct	dasetful, deceit(ful)
danjur, danger	darection, direction	daseve, deceive
dank,kly,kness, *UNPLEASANTLY DAMP*	darectory, directory	**dash**,hes,hed,hing, *SMALL AMOUNT OF, QUICKLY IN SHORT TIME, TEXT TYPE*
danominashun, denomination	darekshun, direction	dasidewus, deciduous
	darektory, directory	dasifur, decipher

dasigen, decision
dasijen, decision
dasile, docile
dasimbur, December
dasinagrate, disintegrate
dasinshent, dissentient
dasipher, decipher
dasiple, disciple
daskripshen, description
daskwalefy, disqualify
dasmiss, dismiss
dasosheate, dissociate
daspare, despair
daspense, dispense
daspensible, dispensable
dasperse, disperse
daspikable, despicable
daspize, despise
dasplay, display
daspondent, despondent
daspose, dispose
daspute, dispute
dasrebututble, disreputable
dasrobe, disrobe
dastardly,dliness, COWARDLY
dasteengwish, distinguish
dastengwesh, distinguish
dastenkt, distinct
dastill, distill
dastingwish, distinguish
dastirdly, dastardly
dastort, distort
dastract, distract
dastress, distress
dastroy, destroy
dasturb, disturb
dasturdly, dastardly
dasul, dazzle
dat, date

data, FACTS, INFORMATION
dataunt, detente
date,*, ed,ting, TIME REFERENCE
detective, detective
datekt, detect
datektif, detective
datektor, detector
datenshin, detention
daterant, deterrent
datereate, deteriorate
daterent, deterrent
datereorate, deteriorate
datergent, detergent
determinent, determine(nt)
datont, detente
datu, data
daturgent, detergent
daturjent, detergent
daturmen, determine
daturmenashen, determination
daturmenint, determine(nt)
daug, dog
daughter,*, FEMALE BORN/LEGALLY ENDOWED TO MOTHER AND/OR FATHER
daul, dowel /doll
daulur, dollar
daun, dawn/ don/ down
daus, douse /dowse
dausil, docile
dauter, daughter
dautful, doubt(ful)
davegen, division
davejin, division
davelop, develop
daversidy, diversity
daversudy, diversity
davert, divert
davide, divide
davigen, division

davine, divine
davision, division
davize, device
davoid, devoid
davorse, divorce
davoshen, devotion
davout, devout
davurt, divert
davurzade, diversity
dawn,*,ned,ning, MORNING DAYBREAK (or see don or down)
dawrekt, direct
daws, douse /dowse
day,*, SUNRISE TO SUNRISE (or see daze)
dayede, deity
dayity, deity
dayjavue, deja vu
daytont, detente
daze,ed, NOT OF CLEAR THINKING, CONFUSED (or see daisy or day(s))
dazeese, disease /daisy(s)
dazel, dazzle
dazzle,*, ed,ling, INFLUENCE BY UNUSUAL MEASURES
=====================
DE......If the word is not listed below, simply remove the first 2 letters -DE- then look up the remainder of the word.
Example: de-ice, "de" means "away from/down from". Then look up the word "ice".
de, PREFIX INDICATING "AWAY FROM/DOWN FROM/ REVERSE/NEGATIVE" MOST OFTEN MODIFIES THE WORD
deacon,*,ness,nry,nries, OFFICIAL OF A CHURCH
deactivate,*,ed,ting, STOP ACTION, DISSOLVE
deactovate, deactivate
dead,dly,lier,liest,ly PAST TENSE OF "DIE", NO LONGER ALIVE/FUNCTIONAL (or see deed/did)
deaden,ner,ning, TO SEEM DEAD, NUMB (or see did(n't))

deadleist, dead(liest)
deaf,fen,fening,feningly,fness,fly, *LOSS OF THE ABILITY TO HEAR*
deakon, deacon
deaktevat, deactivate
deaktuvate, deactivate
deal,*,ler,ling,dealt, *ARRANGEMENT BETWEEN PEOPLE, DO IN CARD GAME (or see dell or dill)*
dealed, dealt
dealt, *PAST TENSE OF "DEAL"*
deam, deem
dean,*, *HEAD OF FORMAL GROUP (or see den)*
deanky, dinkey
deap, deep
dear,rly,rness, *HEARTFELT (or see deer)*
death,hless,hly, *WHEN THE SPIRIT LEAVES THE BODY*
debach, debauch
debate,*,ed,ting, *ARGUE FACTS*
debauch,hes,hment,hery,heries, *CORRUPT, CHANGED FROM ORIGINAL DIRECTION*
debauchury, debauch(ery)
debelutat, debilitate
debenar, debonair
debet, debit
debilitate,*,ed,ting, *NOT UP TO PAR, WEAKEN*
debinar, debonair
debit,*,ted,ting, *A DEBT OWING*
debloma, diploma
deblomusy, diplomacy
deboch, debauch
debochury, debauch(ery)
debonair, *CHARMING, LIKABLE, AIR OF CLASS*
deboner, debonair
debotch, debauch
debre, debris
debris, *GARBAGE, RUBBISH*
debry, debris
debt,*,ted, *IN THE STATE OF OWING TO ANOTHER*
debth, depth

debtor, *ONE WHO OWES ANOTHER (or see detour or deter)*
debude, deputy
debunair, debonair
debunar, debonair
debut, *FIRST SHOWING TO THE PUBLIC (or see debit)*
debutize, deputize
debuty, deputy
dec, deca, deka, *PREFIX INDICATING "TEN" MOST OFTEN MODIFIES THE WORD (or see deck)*
decade,*, *TEN YEARS (or see decay(ed))*
decadent,nce,ncy,tly,*ON THE DECLINE/DETERIORATE*
decal,*, *IMAGE OF PICTURE OR WORDS*
decanter,*, *VESSEL FOR STORAGE*
decapitate,*,ed,tion, *LOSS OF HEAD*
decate, decade /decay(ed)
decay,*,yed,ying, *DETERIORATE, CHANGE FROM ONE FORM TO ANOTHER*
decease,*,ed, *TO PASS AWAY, DEPART FROM THIS PHYSICAL REALITY (or see disease)*
deceit,tful,tfully,tfullness,*TO PURPOSELY MISLEAD*
deceive,*,ed,ving,vingly,vable,vably,vableness, vability, *TO PURPOSELY MISLEAD*
decelerate,*,ed,ting, *TO DECREASE SPEED*
December, *MONTH OF A YEAR*
decency,cies, *WHAT'S PROPER*
decent,tly,tness, *RESPECTABLE (or see descent)*
decentralize,*,ed,zing, *TAKE FROM A FEW AND GIVE TO MANY, TO SHARE AROUND*
deception,*,ive,ively,iveness, *THE ACT OF PURPOSELY MISLEADING*
deci, *PREFIX INDICATING "TENTH" MOST OFTEN MODIFIES THE WORD*
decibel,*, *MEASUREMENT OF SOUND WAVES*
decide,*,ed,ding,edly, *FORM A CONCLUSION, PICK AN OPTION*
decerate, decorate
dech, ditch
dechonary, dictionary

deciduous, *SHEDS ITS LEAVES IN THE FALL*
decifur, decipher
decimal,*,lize,lized,lizing, *A POINT TO SEPARATE NUMBERS*
decimate,*,ed,ting, *TO DESTROY, KILL ONE IN TEN*
decimber, December
decipher,*,red,ring, *TO DECODE*
decision,*,ive, *FINAL CONCLUSION*
deck,*,ked,king, *OUTDOOR FLOOR*
decksterity, dexterity
declaration,*,ive,tory, *ANNOUNCEMENT, MAKE A STATEMENT*
declare,*,ed,ring,rable,edly, *TO STATE/ANNOUNCE*
declaration, declaration
decline,*,ed,ning,nation,nate, *DOWNWARD BEND OR SLOPE*
decompose,*,ed,sing, *DECAY, TO TRANSFORM TO BASIC ELEMENTS*
decon, deacon
decorashun, decoration
decorate,*,ed,ting,tor, *ADORN, ORNAMENTAL*
decoration, *ADORNMENT, ORNAMENTAL*
decorative, *ADORNMENT, ORNAMENTAL*
decoy,*, *A FAKE TO FOOL OR MISLEAD*
decrative, decorative
decrease,*,ed,sing, *BECOME LESS THAN THE ORIGINAL*
decree,*, eed,eeing,eeable, *JUDICIAL/ AUTHORITATIVE DECISION*
decrepit,tness,tly,tude,tate,tation, *WEAK/WORN/ WASTED*
decrese, decrease
decudent, decadent
decumpose, decompose
ded, dead /deed /did
dedakashun, dedication
dedakate, dedicate
deden, didn't /den /deaden
dedicate,*,ed,ting,tory,tive, *APPROPRIATE, DEVOTE*

dedication,*,nal, *APPROPRIATE, DEVOTE*
dedin, deaden
dedinate, detonate
dedlee, dead(ly)
dedleist, dead(liest)
dedleur, dead(lier)
dedly, dead(ly)
dedlyest, dead(liest)
dednate, detonate
dedo, ditto
dedonate, detonate
dedor, debtor
dedriment, detriment
dedrument, detriment
deduce,*,ed,cing, *DRAW CONCLUSION FROM EVIDENCE*
deduct,*,ted,ting,table,tion,tive, *SUBTRACT, TAKE AWAY*
dedukashun, dedication
dedukate, dedicate
dedun, deaden
deed,*,ded, *AN ACT /CONTRACT /AGREEMENT (or see dead)*
deel, deal
deeled, dealt
deem,*,med, *JUDGED/BELIEVED/THOUGHT*
deen, dean /den
deenge, dinghy /dingy
deenky, dinkey
deep,per,pest,ply,pen,penly,pened,pness, *BEYOND THE SURFACE, GREAT IN DIMENSION*
deer, *ANIMAL (or see dear)*
def, deaf
deface,*,ed,cing, *ALTER THE FACE/FRONT OF*
defakate, defecate
defakt, default
defamation,tory, *INTENT TO INJURE ANOTHER'S CHARACTER*
defanishun, definition

defanit, definite
defasit, deficit
defastate, devastate
default,*,ted, *LEGALLY FAILING TO ANSWER, FAIL AN AGREEMENT*
defeat,*,ted,ting,tism,tist, *OVERCOME, OVERTHROW*
defecate,*,ed,ting, *CLEAR THE BOWELS*
defect,*,ted, *NOT USEFUL AS INTENDED, MARRED*
defective,ion,ely,eness, *NOT USEFUL AS INTENDED*
defekate, defecate
defekt, defect
defektive, defective
defemation, defamation
defend,*,ded,ding, *PROTECT*
defendant,*, *ONE WHO DEFENDS/PROTECTS AGAINST*
defenishun, definition
defense,*,sive,eless,elessly,elessness, *PROTECT AGAINST ATTACK*
defensible,eness,bility,ly, *ABLE TO DEFEND*
defenutef, definitive
defer,*,rred,rring,rrable,rrence,rrent, *DELAY, POST-PONE, YIELD TO ANOTHER (or see differ)*
deferensheate, differentiate
deferentiate, differentiate
defesit, deficit
defews, diffuse
defi, defy
defiance,nt,ntly, *CHALLENGE, RESIST, OPPOSE*
deficate, defecate
deficiency,cies, *SHORT OF EXPECTATIONS/NEEDS, NOT ENOUGH*
deficient,tly, *LESS THAN EXPECTED/NEEDED*
deficit,*, *OWE MORE THAN WHAT'S AVAILABLE*
defide, divide
defients, defiance
defikate, defecate
defimation, defamation
defind, defend
defindant, defendant

define,*,ed,ning, *SET BOUNDARIES/RULES/BORDERS*
defineshun, definition
definetion, definition
definite,ely,eness,tive, *FOR SURE, ABSOLUTELY*
definition,*,nal, *STATEMENT DESCRIBING BOUND-ARIES/ RULES/ BORDERS*
definitive,ely,eness, *FOR CERTAIN, FINAL*
definute, definite
defir, defer /differ
defishant, deficient
defishantsy, deficiency
defisit, deficit
defistate, devastate
deflate,*,ed,ting, *REMOVE VOLUME OR FULLNESS*
deflect,*,ted,ting,tive,tor,tion, *RICHOCHET OFF/ ALTER COURSE/DIRECTION OF SOMETHING*
defoleate, defoliate
defoliate,*,tion,tor, *LOSS OF LEAVES FROM PLANT*
deforestation,*, *REMOVE TREES FROM FOREST*
deforistashun, deforestation
deform,*,med,ming,mation,medly,medness, mity, *OF UNUSUAL/ABNORMAL FORM*
deforustashin, deforestation
defostate, devastate
defraud,*,ded,dation, *ROB OF RIGHTS/PROPERTY*
defray,yal,yment,yable, *MONETARY COMPENSATION OR ARRANGEMENT*
defrense, difference
defrent, different
defrod, defraud
defukate, defecate
defumashun, defamation
defunct, *NO LONGER IN USE*
defuneshun, definition
defunetle, definite(ly)
defunishun, definition
defunit, definite
defur, defer /differ
defurinse, difference

defuse, diffuse
defusit, deficit
defustate, devastate
defuze, diffuse
defy,fies,fied,fying, *TO RESIST/DARE/CHALLENGE*
degekt, deject
degenerate,*,ed,ting,tive,acy,ely,eness, *BECOME LESS, OPPOSITE OF GETTING BETTER*
deginerate, degenerate
degit, digit
degradashen, degrade(dation)
degrade,*,ed,ding,dation, *TO LOWER RANK IN STANDARDS/GRADE*
degree,*,ed, *MEASUREMENT OF STANDARD/ANGLES, SUM OF*
degrudashen, degrade(dation)
dehidrate, dehydrate
dehydrate,*,ed,ting,tion, *REMOVE MOISTURE FROM*
deity,ties, *SUPREME BEING*
deja vu, *SEEN BEFORE*
deject,*,ted,ting,tedly,tedness,tion, *DISPIRIT, DISCOURAGE*
dejenurate, degenerate
dejinurate, degenerate
dejit, digit
dek, deck
deka, decay
dekad, decay(ed) /decade
dekadint, decadent
dekal, decal
dekantur, decanter
dekaputate, decapitate
dekay, decay
deken, deacon
dekerashun, decoration
dekerate, decorate
dekin, deacon
deklare, declare
dekleration, declaration

dekline, decline
deklurashun, declaration
dekompose, decompose
dekon, deacon
dekorashun, decoration
dekorate, decorate
dekoy, decoy
dekradashen, degrade(dation)
dekrative, decorative
dekree, decree
dekrepit, decrepit
dekrese, decrease
dekrutive, decorative
dekshunare, dictionary
deksterudy, dexterity
dekstrus, dexterous
dektion, diction
dekudent, decadent
dekumpose, decompose
dekun, deacon
dekurashun, decoration
dekurater, decorate(tor)
del, deal/ dell/ dill
delacatesen, delicatessen
delacit, delicate
delacusy, delicacy
delagation, delegation
delakatesen, delicatessen
delaket, delicate
delay,*,yed,ying, *DETAIN, HINDER, PROLONG*
deld, dealt
dele, deli
deleburant, deliberate
delecacy, delicacy
delectable,*,eness,bility,ly, *HIGHLY PLEASURABLE*
deled, dealt
delegate,*,ed,ting, *APPOINT AS REPRESENTATIVE, ENTRUST*
delegation,*, *TO DELEGATE, ASSEMBLY OF PEOPLE*

delekt, delict
delenkwent, delinquent
delenquent, delinquent
deler, deal(er)
delereus, delirious
delete,*,ed,ting,tion, *TO REMOVE, UNDO*
delf, delve
deliberate,eness,ely,tion, *PURPOSEFUL/CAREFULLY THOUGHT OUT*
deliburate, deliberate
delicacy,cies, *OF REFINED QUALITY IN TASTE*
delicate,ely,eness, *FRAGILE, FINE QUALITY, CHOICE*
delicatesen,*, *STORE WITH VARIETY OF PREPARED FOODS/MEATS*
delicious,sly,sness, *EXQUISITE TASTE, HAPPY TO TASTE BUDS*
delict,*, *MISDEMEANOR, OFFENSE*
deligation, delegation
delight,*,ted,ting,tful,tedly,tfully,fullness, *PRO-VIDE GREAT SATISFACTION (or see daylight)*
delikatesen, delicatessen
delinquent,tly,ncy,ncies, *FAILURE TO SATISFY AGREEMENT ON TIME*
delir, deal(er)
delirious,sly,sness, *IRRATIONAL BEHAVIOR*
delishus, delicious
delite, delight / daylight
deliver,*,red,ring,ry,rable, *TO SEND/PRESENT ITEMS SUCH AS GOODS/THOUGHTS/ARTICLES*
dell, *A HOLLOW/VALLEY (or see deal or dill)*
deloot, dilute
delor, deal(er)
delt, dealt
delugashun, delegation
delugen, delusion
delukatesen, delicatessen
delukit, delicate
deluks, deluxe
delukusy, delicacy

denje, dingy
denky, dinkey
denominator, denominator
denomination, *, nal, nally, nism, ive, tor, *SPECIES OF THE WHOLE, SEPARATE BUT SAME*
denominator, *, *OF FRACTIONS*
denote, *, ed, ting, ement, tive, table, tative, tatively, *DESIGNATED, SYMBOLISES*
dense, er, est, ely, eness, sify, *THICK/COMPACT, CLOSE TOGETHER*
density, ties, *THICK/COMPACT/CLOSE TOGETHER*
dent, denti, *PREFIX INDICATING "TOOTH" MOST OFTEN MODIFIES THE WORD*
dent, *, *IMPRESSION/HOLLOW (or see didn't/dint)*
dental, lize, lization, *OF TEETH*
dentist, *, try, *DOCTOR FOR TEETH*
denture, *, *ARTICIFIAL TEETH*
denum, denim
denur, dinner
deny, nies, nied, ying, *NOT ADMIT, WON'T CLAIM*
deoderint, deodorant
deoderize, deodorize
deodorant, *HIDES ODOR/SMELLS*
deodorize, *, ed, zing, *REMOVE ODOR/SMELL*
deoksidize, deoxidize
deoksudize, deoxidize
deoxidize, *, ed, zing, *REMOVE OXYGEN*
dep, deep /dip
depart, *, ted, ting, *GO AWAY FROM*
department, *, *SECTIONS OF THE WHOLE, A SUBSET*
departure, *, *TO GO AWAY FROM, LEAVE*
depazishen, deposition
depend, *, ded, ding, dable, dably, dability, *RELY ON*
dependant, *, *RELATIONSHIP TO OTHER THINGS (or see dependent)*
dependence, cy, cies, *OF RELYING ON*
dependent, *, *SUPPORTED BY OTHERS (or see dependant)*
deper, dipper

democrat, *, *ONE IN PARTY WHO WORKS FOR SOCIAL EQUALITY FOR ALL*
democratic, ize, ization, *PROCESS OF WORKING TOWARDS SOCIAL EQUALITY FOR ALL*
demography, hic, hical, hically, *STATISTICS OR RECORDS OF PUBLIC VITAL INFORMATION*
demokrasy, democracy
demokrat, democrat
demokratic, democratic
demokruse, democracy
demolish, hes, hed, hing, *DESTROY, RUIN*
demolition, *, *ACT OF DESTROYING/RUINING*
demon, *, nic, cal, cally, ization, ize, *EVIL*
demonek, demon(ic)
demonstrate, *, ed, ting, tion, *HOW TO, EXPLAIN CLEARLY/DELIBERATELY*
demple, dimple
demugog, demagogue
demuleshin, demolition
demun, demon
demunstrate, demonstrate
demunstrashen, demonstrate(tion)
demur, dimmer
den, *, *CONCEALED HIDEOUT, COZY/TUCKED AWAY PLACE*
denacher, denature
denature, *, ed, ring, *ROB OF NATURAL COMPOSURE*
dencher, denture
dendr, dendri, dendrok, *PREFIX INDICATING "TREE" MOST OFTEN MODIFIES THE WORD*
dendrite, *, *PATHWAYS OF NEURONS CARRYING IMPULSES IN THE BRAIN*
deng, ding
denge, dingy /dinghy
dengle, dangle
denial, *, able, *REFUSE, DENY*
deni, deny
denim, *, *HEAVY COTTON FABRIC*
denir, dinner
deniul, denial

delur, deal(er)
delusion, nal, *PAST TENSE OF "DELUDE", BEING MISLED, HAVING FALSE IMPRESSION*
delute, dilute
deluxe, *, *FINEST QUALITY*
delve, *, ed, ving, *TO BURY/DIG INTO*
dem, deem /dim
demacrasy, democracy
demacrat, democrat
demagogue, *, guery, gic, gical, *LEADER WHO USES POPULAR EMOTIONS*
demagrafy, demography
demakratic, democratic
demalishun, demolition
demand, *, ded, ding, *COMMAND/INSIST ON FULFILLMENT OF DESIRES*
demarcation, *, *SETTING BOUNDARIES, ESTABLISHING GUIDELINES*
demarkashun, demarcation
demble, dimple
demean, *, ned, ning, *HUMILIATE*
demeanor, *CONCERNING BEHAVIOR/CONDUCT*
demented, *CRAZY, UNPOPULAR BEHAVIOR/THOUGHTS*
demer, dimmer
demestek, domestic
demi, *PREFIX INDICATING "HALF/PARTLY" MOST OFTEN MODIFIES THE WORD*
demigog, demagogue
demikrat, democrat
demilaturise, demilitarize
demilitarize, *, ed, zing, zation, *REMOVE MILITARY*
demiluturise, demilitarize
demin, demon
deminstrate, demonstrate
demir, dimmer
demise, ed, sing, *TRANSFER, PASSED FROM THIS REALITY*
demobilize, *, ed, zing, zation, *DISARM, DISBAND*
democracy, cies, *BY AND FOR ALL PEOPLE*

depewtise, deputize
depict,*,ted,ting, SHAPE/FORM/CREATE IMAGE
depir, dipper
deplete,*,ed,ting,tive, USE TO THE END, RUNNING OUT OF
depletion, THE ACT OF RUNNING OUT OF
diploma, diploma
diplomacy, diplomacy
diplomat, diplomat
deplorable,ly,bility,eness, LAMENT
deplore,ed,ring, LAMENT
depo, depot
depoortashen, deportation
depor, deep(er)
deport,*,ted,ting,ment, TO BE EXPELLED, SENT FROM COUNTRY
deportation, ACT OF SENDING FROM THE COUNTRY
deportee,*,, ONE WHO WAS DEPORTED FROM COUNTRY
depose,sable, WRITE OR SPEAK UNDER OATH
deposit,*,ted,ting,tor, TO PUT SOMETHING OF VALUE INTO SAFEKEEPING
deposition,*,, STATEMENT UNDER OATH
depot,*,, LOADING/UNLOADING STATION FOR TRANSPORT
depravashen, deprivation
depravation, deprivation
depreciate,*,ed,ting,able,tion,tive,tingly, ESTIMATE OF LOWER VALUE
depresheate, depreciate
depreshen, depression
depresion, depression
depress,sses,ssed,ssing, LOWER IN ELEVATION, LOW IN HOPE/FAITH
depression,*,, A LOW/SLUGGISH SPELL
deprivation,ive, LACK OF ACCESS TO
deprive,*,ed,ving,vable,val, PREVENT FROM HAVING ACCESS TO
depruvashen, deprivation
depth,*,, A MEASURE DOWNWARDS OR INTO

depude, deputy
depudise, deputize
depudize, deputize
depur, dipper
depusishen, deposition
deputize,*,,ed,zing, APPOINT AS DEPUTY
deputy,ties,tize, AGENT OF THE LAW
depuzishen, deposition
der, dear /deer /dare
derable, durable
derallik, derelict
derashen, duration
deration, duration
derdee, dirty
dere, dairy
derear, derrier
derekshen, direction
derektury, directory
derelict,*,tion, SOMEONE OR SOMETHING LEFT WITHOUT A GUIDE
deress, duress
derible, durable
derick, derrick
derier, derriere
derik, derrick
dering, during /dare(ring)
derivative,*,ely,ion,ional, ROOT/ORIGIN OF
derive,*,ed,ving,vable, FROM THE ORIGINAL, DESCENDED FROM
derma, dermat, dermato, PREFIX INDICATING "SKIN" MOST OFTEN MODIFIES THE WORD
dermutidis, dermatitis
derrick,*,, TOWERLIKE EQUIPMENT WITH A CENTRAL POST
derriere,*,, REAR END
dert, dirt
derty, dirty
derubil, durable
deruble, durable

derulik, derelict
dery, dairy
desabelity, disability
desable, disable
desacrate, desecrate
desadvantage, disadvantage
desagre, disagree
desalinate,ed,ting,azation, REMOVE SALT FROM
desalow, disallow
desalugen, disillusion
desalunate, desalinate
desaplen, discipline
desapoint, disappoint
desaprove, disapprove
desaray, disarray
desarm, disarm
desarmament, disarmament
desaster, disaster
desavantage, disadvantage
desbaleef, disbelief
desband, disband
desbar, disbar
desbatch, dispatch
desblay, display
desbondent, despondent
desbozul, disposal
desburse, disperse
desbute, dispute
desbuzishun, disposition
descard, discard
desc, desk/disk/disc
descard, discard
descend,*,ded,ding,dible,dable, TO STEP DOWN FROM, DOWNWARD
descendant,*,dent, PREVIOUS/PRIOR TO THE CURRENT GENERATION, IN RELATION TO
descent, PAST TENSE FOR THE WORD "DESCEND", A STEP DOWN (or see decent)
descharge, discharge

desclose, disclose
descontenue, discontinue
descord, discord
descotek, discotheque
descover, discover
descredit, discredit
descremenate, discriminate
descrepensy, discrepancy
descrete, discreet/discrete
descretion, discretion
describe,*,ed,bing,bable, TO EXPLAIN DETAILS OF
    SOMETHING
descripshen, description
description,*,ive, GIVE DETAILS TO, EXPLAIN
descumfert, discomfort
descushen, discussion
descust, disgust
desdanation, destination
desdane, disdain
desdaste, distaste
desdent, distant
desdint, distant
desdiny, destiny
desditute, destitute
desdort, distort
desdrabute, distribute
desdrakt, distract
desdrust, distrust
desdunashun, destination
desduny, destiny
desdurb, disturb
desdutute, destitute
desease, disease
deseble, decibel
desecrate,*,ed,ting, TO TREAT WHAT'S SACRED TO
    OTHERS AS UNSACRED
desee, dizzy
deseese, decease /disease
deseet, deceit

desegon, decision
desegregate,ed,ting,tion, UNDO RACIAL
    SEGREGATION
desegrigate, desegregate
desegrugate, desegregate
deselarate, decelerate
deselurate, decelerate
desemate, decimate
desember, December
desemul, decimal
desend, descend
desendent, descendant
desenherit, disinherit
desensee, decency
desent, decent /descent
desentralise, decentralize
desepshun, deception
deseption, deception
desern, discern
desert,*, LAND LACKING LUSH VEGETATION, TO LEAVE
    WITHOUT PERMISSION (or see dessert)
deserve,*,ed,ving,edly, REWARD/PUNISHMENT FOR
    ACT/THOUGHT/DEED
deservise, disservice
desesd, decease(d) /disease(d)
deset, deceit
desetful, deceit(ful)
deseve, deceive
desfegure, disfigure
desfigure, disfigure
desfunction, dysfunction
desfunkshen, dysfunction
desgard, discard
desgarge, discharge
desgise, disguise
desgrase, disgrace
desgreshun, discretion
desgruntle, disgruntle
desgus, discus /discuss

desgust, disgust /discuss(ed)
desguys, disguise
desh, dish
desharden, dishearten
desharten, dishearten
deshevel, dishevel
deshonest, dishonest
deshonorable, dishonorable
desible, decibel
desicrate, desecrate
desid, decide
desidewus, deciduous
desifer, decipher
design,*,ned,ning, CREATION OF A MODEL, OUTLINE/
    PLAN FOR SOMETHING
designate,*,ed,ting,tion,tive,tory,tor, TO ASSIGN/
    APPOINT
designer,*, ONE WHO CREATES DESIGNS
desijen, decision
desijues, deciduous
desil, diesel
desilat, desolate
desimal, decimal
desimanate, disseminate
desimate, decimate
desimbark, disembark
desimber, December
desind, descend
desine, design
desiner, designer
desinfect, disinfect
desingage, disengage
desinsee, decency
desint, decent /descent
desintary, dysentery
desintegrate, disintegrate
desintralise, decentralize
desinugrate, disintegrate
desipher, decipher

desipul, disciple
desirable,*,bility,eness,ly, *LIKE TO HAVE*
desire,*,ed,ring, *A WISH/WANT/COMPULSION FOR*
desiruble, desirable
desisev, decision(ive)
desk,*, *FURNITURE* (or see disc or disk)
deskard, discard
deskerege, discourage
desklame, disclaim
deskonekt, disconnect
deskontenue, discontinue
deskord, discord
deskover, discover
deskredit, discredit
deskremenate, discriminate
deskrepincy, discrepancy
deskribe, describe
deskripshen, description
deskunekt, disconnect
deskurege, discourage
deskus, discus / discuss
deskust, disgust / discuss(ed)
deskushun, discussion
deskuver, discover
deskwalefy, disqualify
deslocate, dislocate
desleksea, dyslexia
deslexia, dyslexia
deslocate, dislocate
deslodge, dislodge
deslog, dislodge
deslokate, dislocate
desmantul, dismantle
desmanul, dismantle
desmay, dismay
desmiss, dismiss
desmount, dismount
desmownt, dismount
desmul, dismal

desobay, disobey
desobedeanse, disobedience
desociate, dissociate
desolate,eness,tion, *DESERTED, EMPTY OF*
desolenate, desalinate
desolve, dissolve
deson, disown
desonerible, dishonorable
desonest, dishonest
desont, decent / descent
desorder, disorder
desorderly, disorderly
desoreint, disorient
desosheate, dissociate
desown, disown
despair,ring,ringly, *DEEPLY TROUBLED, HOPELESS*
desparashin, desperation
despare, despair
desparedy, disparity
despatch, dispatch
despense, dispense
despensible, dispensable
desperashun, desperation
desperate,ely,eness, *OF FEELING FRANTIC, GIVEN*
    TO HOPELESSNESS
desperation, *BEYOND REGARD FOR HOPE*
desperit, desperate
desperity, disparity
desperse, disperse
despicable,eness,ly, *BEING WORTHLESS/ NO GOOD*
despikable, despicable
despinse, dispense
despinsuble, dispensable
despise,*,ed,sing,sable, *VERY LOW OPINION OF,*
    STRONG DISLIKE
desplased, displaced
desplay, display
desplejur, displease(sure)
desplesher, displease(sure)

despondent,ncy,tly,ding, *SEVERELY DISPIRITED/*
    DEPRESSED
desposal, disposal
desposeshun, disposition
desposition, disposition
desposuble, disposable
despraporshen, disproportion
desproportion, disproportion
despurashin, desperation
despurit, desperate
despusishun, disposition
despute, dispute
desputable, dispute(table)
despuzition, disposition
desqualify, disqualify
desqwalefy, disqualify
desregard, disregard
desrepare, disrepair
desreputable, disreputable
desrespect, disrespect
desrespkt, disrespect
desrobe, disrobe
desrubshen, disruption
desrubt, disrupt
desrupshen, disruption
desrupt, disrupt
desruption, disruption
dessert,*, *A TASTY SWEET DISH FOLLOWING MAIN*
    COURSE (or see desert)
destanashin, destination
destanation, destination
destance, distance
destane, disdain
destany, destiny
destaste, distaste
destemper, distemper
destenkt, distinct
destense, distance
destent, distant

desterb, disturb
destill, distill
destimper, distemper
destination,*, ARRIVAL POINT
destinct, distinct
destint, distant
destiny,ned,ning,nies, FATE, OVERALL ARRIVAL POINT
destitute,*,tion, WITHOUT POSSESSION OF, HOMELESS
destort, distort
destrabute, distribute
destract, distract
destrekt, district
destrikt, district
destroy,*,yed,ying,yer,OBLITERATE/RUIN/DEMOLISH
destruct,*,ted,ting,tible,tibility, DESTROY A MISSILE AFTER IT'S LAUNCHED
destruction, ACT OF RUINING/DEMOLISHING
destructive,ely,eness,vity, OBLITERATE/RUIN/ DEMOLISH
destrukshen, destruction
destruktive, destructive
destruktof, destructive
destrust, distrust
destulashen, distill(ation)
destunashin, destination
destuny, destiny
destutute, destitute
desuade, dissuade
desubel, decibel
desubility, disability
desucrate, desecrate
desugree, disagree
desukrate, desecrate
desul, diesel
desulit, desolate
desulow, disallow
desumal, decimal

desumate, decimate
desumbark, disembark
desunt, decent /descent
desupeer, disappear
desupoent, disappoint
desuprove, disapprove
desurn, discern
desurt, desert /dessert
desurve, deserve
deswade, dissuade
det, debt
detach,hes,hed,hing,ment, PULL AWAY FROM, SEPARATE
detail,*,led,ling, EXACT PARTICULARS
detain,*,ned,ning,nee, TO KEEP FROM GOING, HOLD BACK/DELAY
detakashun, dedication
detakate, dedicate
detale, detail
detane, detain
detauks, detox
detch, ditch
detect,*,ted,ting,table,tible,tion, UNCOVER, SENSE, DISCOVER
detective,*, ONE WHO UNCOVERS FACTS, DISCOVERS
detector,*, A DEVICE WHICH SENSES/DISCOVERS
detekt, detect
detektif, detective
detektur, detector
deten, deaden
detenate, detonate
detenshen, detention
detente,*, CEASE-FIRE, LESSENING OF TENSIONS BETWEEN WARRING PEOPLE
detention,*, FORCED CONFINEMENT
deter,*,rred,rring, ATTEMPT TO RESTRAIN FROM (or see detour or debtor)
deterant, deterrent
detereate, deteriorate

deterent, deterrent
detergent,*, CHEMICAL CLEANSER
deteriorate,*,ed,ting,tion, LOOSE FORM/ FUNCTION
determenent, determine(nt)
determination,*, DECIDED, DECISION, STRONG DESIRE FOR ACCOMPLISHMENT
determine,*,ed,ning,nism,nist,nistic,nable, nistically,edly,edness,er,nant,nate,nation, native, THINK OUT, PLAN A COURSE OF ACTION
deterrent,nce, PAST TENSE FOR "DETER", USED TO PREVENT OR RESTRAIN
detest,*,table,tableness,tability,tably,tation, EXTREME DISLIKE, DISAGREE WITH
deteur, detour /debtor /deter
deth, death
deticashun, dedication
deticate, dedicate
detikashun, dedication
detikate, dedicate
detin, deaden
detinate, detonate
detinshun, detention
detir, debtor /detour /deter
detirmenedly, determine(dly)
detirmenent, determine(nt)
detly, dead(ly)
detnate, detonate
deto, ditto
detoks, detox
detoksefy, detoxify
detoksuficashen, detoxification
detonate,*,ed,ting,able,table,tion, CAUSE TO EXPLODE
detont, detente
detor, debtor /detour /deter
detour,*,red, STEER FROM PRIMARY PATH/ ROAD
detox, SLANG FOR "DETOXIFY", ELIMINATE CHEMICALS FROM THE BODY SYSTEM

detoxicate,*,ed,ting,tion, *DETOXIFY, REMOVE IMPURITIES*
detoxify, *REMOVAL OF IMPURITIES FROM BODY*
detract,*,ted,ting,tion, *TAKES AWAY FROM*
detrament, detriment
detriment,*,tal,tally, *COULD HARM, NEGATIVE INPUT*
detrument, detriment
dets, debt(s)
detukashun, dedication
detukate, dedicate
detunate, detonate
detur,deter /detour /debtor
deture, detour /debtor /deter
deturgent, detergent
deturmen, determine
deturmenashen, determination
deturmenent, determine(nt)
deturmenism, determine(nism)
deturminent, determine(nt)
deuce,*,ed,edly, *TWO DOTS ON DICE, GAMBLING EXPRESSION* (or see duce)
deva, *ENTITY OF GOOD SPIRITS* (or see diva)
devadend, dividend
devastate,*,ed,ting,tive,tion,*TOTAL DISARRAY/ CHAOTIC ARRANGEMENT/UNRECOGNIZABLE*
deveanse, deviance
deveant, deviant
deveashen, deviation
deveat, deviate
deveation, deviation
deveents, deviance
devegen, division
devel, devil
develop,*,ped,ping,per,ment, *GATHERING OF THOUGHTS AND PLANS TOGETHER INTO ONE*
devestate, devastate
deveunse, deviance
deveunt, deviant
deviance,CY, *UNACCEPTABLE BEHAVIOR*

deviant,*,deviate, *THOSE WHO DISPLAY UNACCEPTABLE BEHAVIOR*
deviate,*,ed,ting,tion, *TO STEER OFF THE PATH*
deviation,*, *TO DEVIATE, BE DEVIANT*
device, *SOMETHING DESIGNED TO BE USED AS A TOOL/AID* (or see devise)
devide, divide
devidend, dividend
devil,*,lish,lishly,led,ling, *FOOD PROCESS, MAN'S CREATION OF A BEING TO BE FEARED*
devine, divine
devise,*,ed,sing,er, *OF WILLS/PROPERTY, TO CREATE* (or see device)
devistate, devastate
devize, devise /device
devoid, *ABSENCE OF, EMPTY*
devol, devil
devorse, divorce
devoshen, devotion
devostate, devastate
devotion,*,lism,list,nal,nally, *DEDICATED, LOYAL*
devout,tly,tness, pious, *EARNEST TO RELIGION*
devoyd, devoid
devu, deva /diva
devudend, dividend
devul, devil
devursity, diversity
devurt, divert
devustate, devastate
dew, *MOISTURE OUTDOORS WHICH COLLECTS INTO DROPS* (or see do/due/doe)
dewal, dual /duel
dewdle, doodle
dewet, duet
dewing, doing
dewl, duel /dual
dewo, duo
dewplekate, duplicate
dewplex, duplex

dewse, duce /deuce /due(s)
dewsh, douche
dex, deck(s) /dig(s)
dexshen, diction
dexshunery, dictionary
dexterity, *MENTAL/PHYSICAL SKILL*
dextero, dextr, dextro, *PREFIX INDICATING "RIGHT" MOST OFTEN MODIFIES THE WORD*
dexterous, *OF DEXTERITY*
dextrus, dexterous
dezal, diesel
dezaster, disaster
deze, dizzy
dezeez, disease
dezert, desert /dessert
dezerve, deserve
dezignate, designate
dezine, design
deziner, designer
dezirable, desirable
dezire, desire
dezklose, disclose
dezmay, dismay
dezmul, dismal
dezolve, dissolve
dezordurly, disorderly
dezposuble, disposable
dezrepare, disrepair
dezugnate, designate
dezul, diesel
dezurt, desert /dessert
dezurve, deserve
di, dif, dis, *PREFIX INDICATING "FROM/AWAY/ NEGATIVE" MOST OFTEN MODIFIES THE WORD*
dia, *PREFIX INDICATING "ACROSS/ THROUGH" MOST OFTEN MODIFIES THE WORD*
diabalekle, diabolical
diabedik, diabetic
diabetes, *IMBALANCE IN GLUCOSE LEVELS*

diabetic, SOMEONE WITH GLUCOSE IMBALANCE
diabolical,lly,lness, OF BEING DIABOLIC, EVIL
diafram, diaphragm
diagenul, diagonal
diagnose,*,ed,sing,stic, TO STUDY THE NATURE OF A PROBLEM
diagnosis, OPINION ON THE NATURE OF A PROBLEM
diagnul, diagonal
diagnule, diagonal(lly)
diagonal,lly, OPPOSITE, CATY-CORNER FROM
diagram,*,mmed,mming,mmatic,mmatical, mmatically, DRAWING
dial,*,led,ling, FACE OF WATCH, PLACE A PHONE CALL
dialect,*,tal,tally,tic,tician,ticism,tical,tically, THE WAY THE LANGUAGE IS SPOKEN
dialogue,*,ed,uing,gist,gistic,gistically, VERBAL COMMUNICATION BETWEEN ENTITIES
diameter,*,ric,rical,tral,trically, STRAIGHT LINE THROUGH THE CENTER OF A CIRCULAR SHAPE LEAVING EQUAL PARTS
diamider, diameter
diamond,*,ed, CUT STONE INTO GEM/SHAPE/PATTERN
diaper,*,red, ABSORBENT PANTS FOR FLUIDS
diaphragm,*,matic,matically, A DIVISION BETWEEN TWO THINGS, CONTRACEPTIVE DEVICE
diarea, diarrhea
diaretik, diuretic
diarrhea,al,hoeic,hoetic, ANAL EXCREMENT OF AB-NORMAL FLUID CONSISTENCY/FREQUENCY
diary,ries, LOG/JOURNAL OF THOUGHTS EACH DAY
diatery, dietary
dibate, debate
dibauch, debauch
dibelutate, debilitate
diber, dipper / diaper
diblomu, diploma
diblomusy, diplomacy
dibochury, debauch(ery)

dibs, SLANG FOR LAYING A CLAIM, SMALL MONETARY PARTICIPATION
dibur, dipper / diaper
dicanter, decanter
dice,*, PLURAL FOR "DIE", TWO CUBES WITH VARIETY OF DOTS, TO CHOP UP
dicey,er,eist, IFFY/RISKY WITH ELEMENT OF DAMAGE
dicember, December
dich, ditch
dicker,*,red,ring, RALLY TO STRIKE A DEAL
dicrepit, decrepit
dicshen, diction
dicshunairy, dictionary
dictate,*,ed,ting,tor, TO ORDER/COMMAND/RULE/ GIVE ORDERS
dictation, WRITE DOWN WHAT IS BEING SAID
dictatorial,ry,lly,lness,OPPRESSIVE, AUTHORITARIAN
diction, A WAY OF SPEAKING, ENUNCIATION
dictionary,ries, WORDS WITH DEFINITIONS ARRANGED ALPHABETICALLY
did,does, PAST TENSE OF "DO"(or see dead /died)
diden, didn't / deaden
didn't, CONTRACTION OF THE WORDS "DID NOT "(or see dent/deaden)
dido, ditto
didukt, deduct
diduse, deduce
die,*,ed, TO BE DEAD/CEASE TO BE ALIVE, AN ENGRAVED STAMP, A PUNCHED OUT TEMPLATE, CUBE USED FOR GAMING (or see dye)
diegnosus, diagnosis
dielekt, dialect
diere, diary
diesel,*,lized,lizing, TYPE OF ENGINE/FUEL
diet,*,ted,ting,tary, SPECIFIC FOOD/BEVERAGE
dietary,ries, A SYSTEM OF FOOD FOR TYPES OF PEOPLE
dif, dis, di, PREFIX INDICATING "FROM/AWAY/ NEGATIVE" MOST OFTEN MODIFIES THE WORD
difadend, dividend

difalt, default
difase, deface
dife, dive
difeet, defeat
difinitive, definitive
difekult, difficult
difense, defense
difensible, defensible
difer, defer /differ
diferense, difference
diferensheate, differentiate
diferently, different(ly)
difeshensy, deficiency
difews, diffuse
differ, TO NOT BE ALIKE
differantly, different(ly)
difference,*,ed,cing, QUALITIES NOT ALIKE
different,tly,tness,tial, NOT THE SAME
differentiate,*,ed,ting,tion, TO OUTLINE DIFFERENCES
difficult,ty,ties, NOT EASY TO PERFORM
diffuse,*,ed,sing,ely,eness,er,sive, ELIMINATE FOCUS BY SPREADING OUT, TO END PRESSURE
difficult, difficult
difinse, defiance
difikult, difficult
difine, define
difir, defer /differ
difishant, deficient
difoleate, defoliate
difor, differ /defer
diforensheate, differentiate
diforent, different
diform, deform
difraud, defraud
difray, defray
difrense, difference
difrent, different
difrod, defraud

difucult, difficult
difukult, difficult
difunkt, defunct
difur, defer /differ
difurense, difference
difurensheate, differentiate
difurensheate, differentiate
difurent, different
difurently, different(ly)
difurinsheate, differentiate
difurintly, different(ly)
difuse, diffuse
dify, defy
digesgen, digestion
digest,*,ted,ting,tible,tibility,tibleness,tive,tively tiveness, CONSUME/PROCESS, SUMMARIZATIONS
digestev, digest(tive)
digestif, digest(tive)
digestion, CONSUME AND PROCESS
digestuf, digest(tive)
digestyon, digestion
diget, digit
digit,*,tize,talize,talization, COUNTING/MEASURING
dignafid, dignified
dignafied, dignified
dignified, STATELY IN FIGURE OR FORM, HONORABLE
dignosis, diagnosis
dignufied, dignified
digrade, degrade
digree, degree
digres, digress
digress,ssion,ssive,ssional,ssively,ssiveness, WANDER OFF MAIN COURSE OR SUBJECT
dijest, digest
dijestev, digest(tive)
dijeston, digestion
dijet, digit
dika, decay
dikad, decay(ed)

dikanter, decanter
dikdutoreal, dictatorial
diker, dicker
diklar, declare
diklin, decline
dikrepit, decrepit
dikshen, diction
dikshenare, dictionary
dikshun, diction
dikshunare, dictionary
diksterity, dexterity
diktashen, dictation
diktate, dictate
diktater, dictate(tor)
diktation, dictation
diktatur, dictate(tor)
diktion, diction
diktionery, dictionary
diktutoreal, dictatorial
dil, dial / dill
dilagense, diligence
dilajense, diligence
dilate,*,ed,ting,tion,tability,table,tably,tingly,tive, EXPAND/SWELL/BROADEN
dilatont, diletante
dilay, delay
dilectable, delectable
diledaly, dilydaly
dilekt, delict
dilema, dilemma
dilemma,atic, NOT A SITUATION OF CHOICE
dilenkwent, delinquent
dilenquent, delinquent
dilereus, delirious
diletante,*,tish,teism, A DABBLER FOR AMUSEMENT
dilete, delete
diletont, diletante
dilidaly, dilydaly
diligence,nt,tly, STEADY PERSEVERANCE, CONSTANT

dilikt, delict
diliver, deliver
dill, AN HERB (or see dial or deal)
dilledaly, dilydaly
diloot, dilute
dilugen, delusion
dilugense, diligence
dilugent, diligence(nt)
dilujents, diligence
diluks, deluxe
dilur, deal(er)
dilushen, delusion
dilute,*,ed,ting,eness,tion, TO WEAKEN THE STRENGTH OF
dilutont, diletante
diluxe, deluxe
dilydaly,ying, TO WASTE TIME
dim,*,mmed,mming,mly,mness,mmer,mmest, BETWEEN BRIGHT AND DARK ..CLOSER TO DARK (or see dime)
dimagog, demagogue
dimand, demand
dimble, dimple
dime,*, A COIN (or see dim)
dimean, demean
dimeanor, demeanor
dimen, demean
dimend, diamond
dimension,*,nless,nal,nality,naly, MORE THAN ONE LAYER
dimentchen, dimension
dimented, demented
dimer, dimmer
dimestek, domestic
diminish,hes,hed,hing, TO LESSEN/MAKE SMALLER
dimize, demise
dimmer,*, LESSEN BRIGHTNESS
dimografy, demography
dimokresy, democracy

dimolish, demolish
dimolishin, demolition
dimond, diamond
dimonek, demon(ic)
dimple,*,ed,ling, *A DEPRESSION INTO SURFACE, INDENTATION*
dimukratic, democratic
dimulishun, demolition
dimunstrate, demonstrate
dimur, dimmer
din, den /dine /didn't
dinamek, dynamic
dinamic, dynamic
dinamite, dynamite
dinasor, dinosaur
dinasty, dynasty
dincher, denture
dindrite, dendrite
dine,*,ed,ning, *TO EAT*
diner,*, *PLACE TO EAT (or see dinner)*
dinesor, dinosaur
dinet, dinette
dinette, *DINING ROOM/PLACE NEAR KITCHEN TO EAT*
ding,*,gged, *BELL SOUNDS, INDENTATIONS/MARKS*
dingee, dinghy / dingy
dinghy,hies, *SMALL BOAT/VESSEL ON WATER (or see dingy)*
dingy,gies,giness,gily, *DIM/MURKY, NOT VIBRANT (or see dinghy or dinkey)*
dinie, deny
dinisor, dinosaur
dinje, dingy
dinkey, *QUITE SMALL/TINY*
dinner,*, *EVENING MEAL (or see diner)*
dinomenashin, denomination
dinomenator, denominator
dinominashan, denomination
dinomite, dynamite
dinosaur,*, *PREHISTORIC CREATURES*

dinostea, dynasty
dinote, denote
dinse, dense
dinsity, density
dint, *MAKE A MARK/DENT (or see dent/didn't)*
dintal, dental
dintist, dentist
dinture, denture
dinumite, dynamite
dinur, diner / dinner
dinusor, dinosaur
dinusty, dynasty
dioreu, diarrhea
dip,*,pper,pped,pping, *SLIGHTLY IMMERSE/ DECLINE/ GO INTO*
diparsher, departure
dipart, depart
dipartment, department
diparture, departure
dipend, depend
dipendant, dependant
dipendence, dependence
diper, diaper / dipper
dipleshin, depletion
diplete, deplete
diploma,*, *DOCUMENT FOR COMPLETION OF COURSE/SCHOOL*
diplomacy, *SKILLFUL NEGOTIATIONS*
diplomat,*,tic,tics,cally,ist, *PERSON WHO PERFORMS TACTFUL NEGOTIATIONS*
diplorable, deplorable
diplore, deplore
diport, deport
dipose, depose
diposit, deposit
dipozishen, deposition
dipper,*, *SPOON WITH HANDLE, A BIRD (or see diaper)*
dipres, depress

dipresheate, depreciate
dipreshen, depression
dipresion, depression
diprive, deprive
dipur, diaper / dipper
dirashen, duration
dirdee, dirty
dire,ely,eness, *EXTREME, DISASTROUS*
direct,*,ted,ting,tly,tness,tor, *AIM FOR/WITH, OF COMMANDS*
direction,*,nal, *WAVE/SIGNALS IN SPACE*
directory,ries, *BOOK WITH ALPHABETICAL LISTINGS*
direkshen, direction
direktory, directory
direng, during
diress, duress
drive, derive
dirmatites, dermatitis
dirmutitis, dermatitis
dirt, *SOILED, SOIL (earth)*
dirty,tied,tier,tiest,ying,tily,tiness, *UNCLEAN*
dis, *PREFIX INDICATING "NOT/OPPOSITE/LACK OF" MOST OFTEN MODIFIES THE WORD*
disabelity, disability
disability,ties,blement, *UNABLE TO PERFORM AT NECESSARY CAPACITY*
disable,*,ed,ling, *CANNOT PERFORM, DISCONNECT*
disadvantage,*,ed,ging,eous, *A DIFFICULTY/ CHALLENGE IN ACCOMPLISHING SUCCESS/GOAL*
disagree,*,ed,eing,ement,eable,eably, eableness, *TO NOT AGREE WITH*
disakree, disagree
disallow,wance,wable, *NOT ALLOWED*
disalow, disallow
disalugen, disillusion
disalujen, disillusion
disalusion, disillusion
disaper, disappear
disaplen, discipline

disappear,*,red,ring,rance, VANISH FROM SIGHT
disappoint,*,ed,ting,tment, HOPES NOT REALIZED
disapprove,*,ed,ving,val,vingly, DOESN'T CARE FOR/APPROVE OF
disaray, disarray
disarm,med,ming, REMOVE POWER/WEAPONS
disarmament, ACT OF DISARMING
disarray, DISORDERED/JUMBLED
dissasociate, dissociate
disaster,*,trous,trously, MISFORTUNE, CALAMITY, EXTENSIVE DAMAGE
disavantage, disadvantage
disbaleef, disbelief
disband,ded,dment, DISMISSED FROM GROUP OR MILITARY
disbar,rred,rring, REMOVED FROM LEGAL COURT OR PRACTICE
disbatch, dispatch
disbelief,*,eve,eved,eving,ever, DOESN'T BELIEVE TO BE TRUE
disberse, disperse
disbileef, disbelief
disblay, display
disblese, displease
disbolef, desbelief
disbondent, despondent
disbose, dispose
disbozishun, disposition
disbozul, disposal
disbraporshen, disproportion
disbuleef, desbelief
disburse, disperse
disbusishun, disposition
disbute, dispute
disbuzishun, disposition
disc,*, COMPUTER/MUSIC STORAGE DEVICES, SECTIONS IN THE SPINE, BRAKE PARTS (or see disk)
discard,*,ded,ding, TO RID OF/THROW AWAY

discern,ning,nible,nable,nibleness,nibly, nableness,nably,nment, PERCEIVE ONE FROM ANOTHER, SEE A DIFFERENCE
dich, ditch / dish
discharge,*,ed,ging,eable,er, TO RELEASE FROM
disciple,*, ONE WHO FOLLOWS A TEACHER
discipline,*,ed,ning,nable,narian,nary,er,nal, CONTROL/TRAIN TO PERFORM SPECIFICALLY
disclaim,med,ming,mer, NOT LAY CLAIM TO, DISOWN/DENY RESPONSIBILITY OF
disclose,*,ed,sing,sure,ser, REVEAL/MAKE KNOWN
discombobulate,*,ed,ting, DISTURB, PERPLEX
discomfort,ting, UNCOMFORTABLE, UNHAPPY
disconnect,*,ted,ting,tion,tedly,tedness, BE REMOVED FROM CONNECTION WITH
discontinue,*,ed,uing,uance,uation,uity, ABANDON, CEASE, STOP THE USE OF
discord,dance,dancy,dancies,dant,dantly, NOT IN HARMONY WITH, DISAGREE WITH
discotek, discotheque
discotheque,*, NIGHTCLUB WITH MUSIC
discount,*,ted,ting, MAKE LESS, REDUCE PRICE OF
discourage,*,ed,ging,ement,gingly, LESSEN HOPES OF ACCOMPLISHING
discover,*,red,ring,rer,ry,ries, TO FIND, REALIZE
discownt, discount
discredit,table,tably, GIVE NO CREDIT TO, DISBELIEF
discreet,tly,tness, GUARDED, CAUTIOUS (or see discrete)
discremente, discriminate
discrepancy,cies,nt,ntly, DIFFERENCE BETWEEN
discrete, SEPARATE PARTS, DISTINCT (or see discreet)
discretion,nary,nal, MAKE INDIVIDUAL JUDGEMENT, BEING DISCREET
discribe, describe
discriminate,*,ed,ting,ant,able,ely,tion,tive, tor,tory,atively, USING DIFFERENCE AGAINST, CHOOSE ONE OVER ANOTHER

discrepshen, description
discumbobulate, discombobulate
discumfert, discomfort
discunect, disconnect
discuntenue, discontinue
discurage, discourage
discus,ses, USED FOR THROWING (or see discuss)
discuss,sses,ssed,ssing,ssable, CONVERSATION TO EXAMINE SUBJECT (or see discus)
discussion,*, ACT OF CONVERSATION TO EXAMINE SUBJECT
discust, disgust
discuver, discover
disdain,nful,nfully,nfulness, SCORN, CONTEMPT FOR, REJECT
disdent, distant
disderb, disturb
disdort, distort
disdrabushen, distribute(tion)
disdrabute, distribute
disdrakt, distract
disdrebute, distribute
disdress, distress
disdrubute, distribute
disdrust, distrust
disdulashen, distill(ation)
disdurb, disturb
dise, dice /dizzy /dicey
disease,*,ed,sing, BLOCK OF ENERGY ALLOWING TISSUE BREAKDOWN VIA MINUTE ORGANISMS
disect, dissect
diseese, decease / disease
diseet, deceit
diseeve, deceive
disekt, dissect
disembark,*,kation,kment, MOVE FROM SHIP TO SHORE
disembur, December
diseminate, disseminate

disenagrate, disintegrate
disend, descend
disendant, descendant
disenfect, disinfect
disengage,*,ed,ging,ement, SET FREE FROM BEING ATTACHED
disenherit, disinherit
disenshent, dissentient
disenshint, dissentient
disentary, dysentery
disentient, dissentient
diseplen, discipline
disepoint, disappoint
diseray, disarray
disern, discern
diservice, disservice
disesd, decease(d) / disease(d)
diset, deceit
disetful, deceit(ful)
diseve, deceive
disfigure,*,ed,ring,ration,ement, CAUSING UNSIGHTLY APPEARANCE
disfunction, dysfunction
disfunkshon, dysfunction
disgarge, discharge
disgise, disguise

disgrace,*,ed,cing,eful,efully,efulness, SHAME, DISHONOR
disgretion, discretion
disgruntle,ed,ling,ement, NOT CONTENTED, UNGRATIFIED
disguise,*,ed,sing,sable,er, MASK TRUE IDENTITY
disgus, discuss /discus
disgust,*,ted,ting,tful,tingly, REPUGNANT, AWFUL (or see discuss(ed))
dish,hes, VESSEL GENERALLY FOR FOOD(or see ditch)
disharten, dishearten
dishearten,ned,ning, LOOSE SPIRIT/HOPE/COURAGE
dishevel,led,lled,lment,llment, MESSED UP, UNTIDY

dishonest,tly,ties, BEING DECEITFUL, NOT HONEST
dishonorable,ly,eness, UNRESPECTABLE, NOT HONORABLE
disidvantege, disadvantage
disifer, decipher
disilushen, disillusion
disillusion,ned,nment, NO LONGER UNDER ILLUSION, KNOWING
disimanate, disseminate
disimbark, disembark
disimbur, December
disinfect,*,ted,ting,tant,tion, CLEANSE AWAY UNWANTED MICROORGANISMS
disingage, disengage
disinherit,*,ted,tance, REMOVED FROM A WRITTEN WILL
disintegrate,*,ed,ting,tion,tor, TO FALL APART
disintery, dysentery
disiplen, discipline
disipul, disciple
disisev, decision(ive)
disk,*, FLAT/CIRCULAR, FLOWER HEAD, STEEL BLADE (or see disc or desk)
diskard, discard
diskeruge, discourage
disklame, disclaim
disklose, disclose
diskomfurt, discomfort
diskonect, disconnect
diskontenue, discontinue
diskord, discord
diskotek, discotheque
diskover, discover
diskownt, discount
diskredit, discredit
diskrepincy, discrepancy
diskreshun, discretion
diskrete, discreet/discrete
diskribe, describe

diskripshen, description
diskumbobulate, discombobulate
diskumfert, discomfort
diskunekt, disconnect
diskuntenue, discontinue
diskurege, discourage
diskus, discus /discuss
diskust, disgust /discuss(ed)
diskuver, discover
diskwalefy, disqualify
diskwolify, disqualify
disleksea, dyslexia
dislexia, dyslexia
dislocate,*,ed,ting,tion, MOVE FROM ORIGINAL PLACE
dislodge,*,ed,ging,gment, MOVE FROM FIXED POSITION
dismal,lly, DEPRESSING/GLOOMY
dismanle, dismantle
dismantle,*,ed,ling, REMOVE, TAKE APART
dismanul, dismantle
dismay,*,yed,ying,yingly, DISTRESS, DREAD, DISILLUSIONED
dismbark, disembark
dismiss,sses,ssed,ssing,ssal,ssion, PERMIT TO LEAVE, REMOVE, DISCHARGE
dismount,*,ted,ting, REMOVE FROM POSITION
dismownt, dismount
dismul, dismal
disoba, disobey
disobdeinse, disobedience
disobedience,nt,ntly, REFUSE TO BE CONTROLLED
disobey,*,yed,ying, TO BE BEYOND CONTROL
disociate, dissociate
disolfe, dissolve
disolve, dissolve
dison, disown
disonerible, dishonorable
disonist, dishonest

disonurable, dishonorable
disorder,red,redly,redness, NOT ORGANIZED
disorderly, NOT PROPER ORDER
disoreint, disorient
disorient,*,ted,ting,tate,tated,tation, LOSS OF PERCEPTION, CONFUSED
disown,ned, RELEASE OWNERSHIP OF
dispair, despair
dispare, despair
disparity,ties, GAP BETWEEN, INEQUALITY
disparody, disparity
disparty, disparity
dispatch,hes,hed,hing,her, SEND SOMEONE OUT
dispensable,bility,eness, CAN BE DISCARDED
dispense,*,ed,sing,sation, TO DISTRIBUTE
disperse,*,ed,sing,edly,sible, SCATTER INTO VARIOUS DIRECTIONS
disperudy, disparity
dispeutible, dispute(table)
dispewt, dispute
dispikuble, despicable
dispinsable, dispensable
dispize, despise
displace,*,ed,cing,eable,ement, NOT IN PLACE OR POSITION NORMALLY FOUND
display,*,yed,ying, ON SHOW, EXHIBITION
displease,*,ed,sing,sure, NOT TO SOMEONE'S SATISFACTION
displejur, displease(sure)
displese, displease
displesher, displease(sure)
dispondent, despondent
disposable,*, CAN DISCARD/THROW AWAY
disposal,ability,ableness, ABILITY TO ARRANGE, ORGANIZE, MAKE USE OF
dispose,*,ed,sing,sition, TO RID OF, ORGANIZE
disposition, ATTITUDE, INCLINATION
dispraporshen, disproportion

disproportion,nal,nate,nately, NOT IN RELATION TO ITSELF OR ITS SURROUNDINGS
disput, dispute
dispute,*,ed,ting,table,tability, DEBATE
disputuble, dispute(table)
disqard, discard
disqualify,fies,fied,ying,fication, DISBAR, REMOVE FROM COMPETITION
disregard,*,ded,ding, PAY NO NOTICE OR ATTENTION TO
disrepair, NEED TO BE FIXED
disreputable,eness,bility,ly, OF POOR REPUTATION/CHARACTER
disrespect,*,table,tful,tfully,tfulness, SHOW NO HONOR/RESPECT
disrobe,*,ed,bing, UNDRESS, REMOVE GARMENTS
disrupt,*,ted,ting,tion,tive,tiveness,tively, INTERRUPT, CAUSE CHAOS
disruption, interrupt, CAUSE CHAOS
dissect,*,ted,ting,tion,tor, CRITICALLY EXAMINE, TAKE APART
disseminate,*,ed,ting,tion,tive,tor, TO PASS ON, SPREAD
dissentient,*, DISAGREE WITH MAJORITY OPINION
disservice, UNWANTED SERVICE
dissociate,*,ed,ting,tion, STOP ASSOCIATING WITH
dissolve,*,ed,ving,vable,ent, BREAK AWAY TO NOTHING, DISAPPEAR
dissuade,*,ed,ding,dable,er,asion,sive, SWAY SOMEONE AWAY FROM INTENDED IDEA/PATH
distalashen, distill(ation)
distance,*,ed,cing, TIME/SPACE IN BETWEEN
distane, disdain
distanst, distance(d)
distant,tly, REMOVED IN MIND OR BODY FROM THIS PLACE OR TIME
distaste,eful,efully,efulness, DOESN'T LIKE THE WAY IT APPEALS TO THE SENSES
disteengwish, distinguish

distemper, CONTAGIOUS DISEASE IN ANIMALS, OF PAINTING
distance, distance
distengwish, distinguish
distenkt, distinct
distent, distant
disterb, disturb
distill,lled,lling,llation,llate, SEPARATION, CONDENSATION OF LIQUID
distimper, distemper
distinct,tly,tness,tion,tive,tively, CONTRAST, DISTINGUISHED, DIFFERENT
distinguish,hed,hes,hing,hable,hably,hableness DIFFERENCE/UNIQUENESS
distort,*,ted,ting,tion,tional, WARP/TWIST/ CONFUSE FROM NATURAL/PROPER FORM
distrabushen, distribute(tion)
distrabute, distribute
distract,*,ted,ting,tingly,tedly,tive,tion, DEVIATE FROM ORIGINAL FOCUS/INTENT
distrekt, district
distress,ssed,ssing, GREAT NEED, PAIN OR GRIEF
distribute,*,ed,ting,tion,tional,tive,tively, tiveness, TO SPREAD AROUND, PASS ALONG
district,*, A SPECIFIC AREA OF TERRITORY/LAND
distroy, destroy
distruction, destruction
distructive, destructive
distrukshen, destruction
distruktof, destructive
distrust,*,ted,ting,tful,tfully,tfulness, NOT TRUST OR HAVE CONFIDENCE IN
distulashen, distill(ation)
distunst, distance(d)
disturb,*,bed,bing,bance, TO MAKE IRREGULAR, INTERRUPT
disuade, dissuade
disbiluty, disability
disugre, disagree

disugree, disagree
disulow, disallow
disulugen, disillusion
disumbark, disembark
disupeer, disappear
disuplen, discipline
disupoint, disappoint
disuprove, disapprove
disuray, disarray
disurn, discern
disurvuse, disservice
diswade, dissuade
ditch,hes,hed,hing, *A GULLEY IN THE EARTH, SKIP OUT OF SCHOOL, LEAVE SOMEONE*
ditect, detect
ditective, detective
ditector, detector
diteeriorate, deteriorate
ditekt, detect
ditektur, detector
diterent, deterrent
ditereorate, deteriorate
ditermenint, determine(nt)
dito, ditto
ditrakt, detract
ditto,*,, *COPY, DUPLICATE, SAME BACK TO YOU*
diturgent, detergent
diturmenism, determine(nism)
diubolikul, diabolical
diufram, diaphragm
diugnose, diagnose
diugram, diagram
diul, dial
diulekt, dialect
diulog, dialogue
diure, diary
diurea, diarrhea
diuretek, diuretic
diuretic, *INCREASES THE ELIMINATION OF LIQUID*

diureuh, diarrhea
diutery, dietary
diva, *GODDESS* (or see deva)
divadend, dividend
dive,*,ving,er,dove, *TO PLUNGE HEAD-FIRST INTO ANYTHING*
divelop, develop
diversion,*,, *CHANGE COURSE OR DIRECTION*
diversity, *TO BE DIFFERENT*
divert,*,ted,ting,tingly,tive, *CHANGE COURSE OR DIRECTION*
divide,*,ed,ding, *SEPARATE, CREATE PARTS*
dividend,*,, *A NUMBER THAT CAN BE DIVIDED BY ANOTHER NUMBER*
divine,ely,eness,nity, *OF A HIGH DEGREE, SUPREME, ABOVE AVERAGE* (or see define)
divise, device /devise
division,*,nal, *SEPARATE PARTS WITHIN THE WHOLE*
divize, devise
divoid, devoid
divorce,*,ed,cing,eable,ement, *FORMAL DIVISION OR SEPARATION FROM*
divoshen, devotion
divout, devout
divu, diva /deva
divudend, dividend
divurshen, diversion
divursity, diversity
divurt, divert
diyul, dial
dizalujen, disillusion
dizastur, disaster
dizeez, disease
dizeembark, disembark
dizemunate, disseminate
dizinfect, disinfect
dizmantul, dismantle
dizmul, dismal
dizobay, disobey

dizolve, dissolve
dizorder, disorder
dizordurly, disorderly
dizposuble, disposable
dizrepare, disrepair
dizrespekt, disrespect
dizumbark, disembark
dizuray, disarray
dizzy,zier,ziest,zily,zied,zying, *FUZZY, DISORIENTED, UNFOCUSED*
do,oing,done,oable,did, *THE ACT OF* (or see dew/ due /doe /dough)
doal, dual /duel
dobul, double
docile,ely,lity, *OF RECEPTIVE/ACCEPTABLE ATTITUDE, ABLE TO CONFORM*
dock,*,ked,king, *TYPE OF HERB BEHAVIOR, LOADING PLATFORM FOR VESSELS, TO REMOVE*
doctor,*,red,ring, *ONE WHO REPAIRS BODILY INJURY*
doctrine,nal,nality,nally,naire, *DOGMATIC TEACHING OF BELIEFS/VALUES*
doctrenul, doctrine(nal)
document,*,ted,ting,tary,tation,tary,taries, *PAPERS WHICH STATE EVIDENCE*
documentary,ries, *FACTS FOR PUBLIC VIEWING*
dodad, doodad
doder, daughter
doderize, deodorize
dodge,*,ed,ging,er, *MOVES ASIDE, SHIFTS FROM PREDICTED POSITION* (or see dog)
dodil, doodle
dodul, doodle
dodurent, deodorant
doe, *FEMALE OF SHEEP/ GOAT/ DEER/ RABBIT/ ANTELOPE* (or see do or dough)
does, *DOING CURRENTLY* (or see due(s)/doe(s)/ dose/do)
doel, duel /dual
doeng, doing

doesn't, CONTRACTION OF THE WORDS "DOES NOT"
doet, duet
dog, IN CANIS ANIMAL FAMILY (or see dodge)
doge, dodge /dog
doil, duel /dual
doing,done, CURRENTLY IN THE ACT OF
doje, dodge
dok, dock
dokewment, document
dokter, doctor
doktren, doctrine
dokument, document
dol, doll /dole /dual /duel
dolar, dollar
dolcimer, dulcimer
dole,*,ed,ling,eful,lness, DEAL/GIVE-OUT PORTION OUT (or see dolly)
doler, dollar
dolfen, dolphin
dolfin, dolphin
dolir, dollar
doll,*,lly,llish,llishly,llishness, A TOY, CUTE LOOKING (or see dole)
dollar,*, U.S. MONEY/BILL
dolly,lies, OBJECT WITH WHEELS FOR MOVING THINGS, TOOL FOR VARIOUS TRADES, A DOLL
dolsemer, dulcimer
dolsumer, dulcimer
dom, dome/ doom/ dumb
domain,*,anial, TERRITORY/PROPERTY WITH BOUNDARIES
domane, domain
domanet, dominant
domanet, dominant
domasile, domicile
dome,*,ed,ming, HALF CIRCLE/180° (or see dumb or doom)
domenate, dominate
domenint, dominant

domenion, dominion
domeno, domino
domenyen, dominion
domestic,cally,cate,cated,cable,cation,city,cities cize, FORCED TO CONFORM TO HUMAN USE
domicile,liary,liate,liation, HOME/ RESIDENCE
dominant,nce,ncy, AUTHORITY, RULE
dominate,*,ed,ting,tion,tive,tor, POWER OVER, OVERRULER
dominion,*,ium, CONTROL OVER TERRITORY, OWNERSHIP OF
dominish, diminish
domino,es, MASQUERADE COSTUME, GAME
domnate, dominate
domonent, dominant
domonent, dominant
domosile, domicile
domunate, dominate
domunent, dominant
domunet, dominant
domusile, domicile
don't, CONTRACTION FOR WORDS "DO NOT"
don,*,nned,nning, TO PUT ON, ADDED TO NAME (or see dawn or done)
donate,*,ed,ting,tion,tor, A GIFT, PERHAPS WITH STRINGS ATTACHED
dond, don't
done, PAST TENSE OF "DO", TASK/JOB COMPLETED
doner, donor
donkey,*, AN ANIMAL
donor,*,rship, SOMEONE WHO GIVES SOMETHING AWAY
dont, don't
donur, donor
donut, doughnut
dooal, duel /dual
dood, dude
doodad,*, GADGET, DECORATION
doode, duty
doodle,*,ed,ling, IDLY SKETCH, DRAW

doom,med, THE END OF
doon, dune
doop, dupe
door,*,rway, OBJECT WHICH SEPARATES TWO SIDES WHEN CLOSED
dormetory, dormitory
dorsal, dorsal
doose, duce /deuce /due(s)
doosh, douche
doote, duty
dooz, due(s)
dope,*, ed,ping,er,ey, SLANG FOR DRUGS, NOT SMART
doplex, duplex
doplicate, duplicate
duplicate, duplicate
dor, door
dormant,ncy, ASLEEP
dormatory, dormitory
dormet, dormant
dormetory, dormitory
dormint, dormant
dormitory,ries, A LARGE PLACE WITH MANY ROOMS FOR SLEEPING/LIVING
dormut, dormant
dormutory, dormitory
dorsal,lly, ON THE BACK
dorsil, dorsal
dorsul, dorsal
dos, does /doze /due(s) /dowse
dosable, disable
dosach, dosage
dosage,*, AMOUNT OF DRUG
dosberse, disperse
dosblased, displaced
dosblay, display
dosbose, dispose
doscremenate, discriminate
doscrete, discreet / discrete
dosderb, disturb
dosdrakt, distract

dosdrebute, distribute
dosdress, distress
dosdrust, distrust
dosdurb, disturb
dose,*,ed,sing, *SPECIFIC AMOUNT OF SOMETHING (or see doze /due(s))*
dosech, dosage
dosege, dosage
dosej, dosage
dosemanate, disseminate
dosembur, December
dosent, doesn't
dosenugrate, disintegrate
doser, dozer
dosfigyer, disfigure
dosgreshun, discretion
dosgruntle, disgruntle
dosh, douche
dosich, dosage
dosige, dosage
dosij, dosage
dosil, docile
dosimbur, December
dosimer, dulcimer
dosin, dozen
doskrete, discreet /discrete
dospinse, dispense
displaced, displaced
dosplay, display
dosplease, displease
dospose, dispose
dosposuble, disposable
dospozul, disposal
dosputuble, dispute(table)
dosqualify, disqualify
dosreputuble, disreputable
dosrupshen, disruption
dosrupt, disrupt
dostengwish, distinguish

dosterb, disturb
dostingwish, distinguish
dostract, distract
dostress, distress
dostrust, distrust
dosuj, dosage
dosul, docile
dot,*,tted,tting, *ROUND SPOTS (or see dote)*
dote,*,ed,ting,tingly, *TO WATCH OVER, OVERSEE CLOSELY (or see dot or doubt)*
doted, dot(tted) /dote(d)
doter, daughter
dotur, daughter
double,*,ed,ling,eness,ly, *TWICE AS MANY AS THE ORIGINAL*
doubt,*,ted,ting,table,tingly,tful,tfully,tless, tlessly, *NOT COMPLETELY BELIEVABLE*
douche,*,ed,hing, *INTRODUCING FLUID INTO CAVITY OF BODY*
dough,hie, *PASTY /TACKY MIXTURE, MONEY*
doughnut,*, *ROUND PASTRY WITH HOLE*
doul, dual /duel /dowel /dole
doun, down
douse,*,ed,sing,er, *OR DOWSE, TO SMOTHER/ PUT OUT/EXTINQUISH (same as dowse)*
dout, doubt
dove,*, *PAST-TENSE OF "DIVE", A BIRD*
dovegin, division
dovine, divine
dovorse, divorce
dow, dough /doe
dowel,*,led,ling, *USED LIKE A NAIL/PIN/SCREW*
dowen, doing
dowl, dowel
down, *OPPOSITE OF UP, FEATHERS OF A FOWL*
downut, doughnut
dows, douse /dowse
dowse,*,ed,sing, or douse, *SMOTHER/PUT OUT/ EXTINGUISH (same as douse)*

dowt, doubt
dowtful, doubt(full)
doz, doze /does /dose
doze,*,ed,zing,zy,zily,ziness, *TO SLEEP LIGHTLY (or see dose)*
dozen, *TWELVE OF SOMETHING*
dozent, doesn't
dozer,*, *HEAVY EQUIPMENT WHICH MOVES EARTHEN MATERIAL*
drad, dread
draft,*,ted,ting,ty, *A LIGHT BREEZE, TO PULL/ DRAW FROM*
drag,*,gged,gging,ggingly, *SLIDE/PULL WITH DIFFICULTY, PULLING WITHOUT LIFTING, MEN IN WOMEN'S CLOTHING*
dragen, dragon
dragenfly, dragonfly
dragin, dragon
draginfly, dragonfly
dragon,*,nish, *MYTHICAL ANIMAL*
dragonfly,lies, *INSECT*
draik, drake
drain,*,ned,ning,nage, *FLUID/ENERGY FLOWING AWAY FROM, OUTLET*
drake,*, *INSECT FOR BAIT, MALE IN DUCK FAMILY*
drama,*,atic,atics,atically,atize,atization,aturgy, atist,*GIVEN TO THEATER/PLAYS/CHARACTERROLES*
dran, drain
drank, *PASTE TENSE OF "DRINK"*
draot, drought
drape,*,ed,ping,ery,eries, *HANGING CLOTH USED TO VEIL SOMETHING FROM SIGHT OR TO ENHANCE*
drapir, dropper
drapur, dropper
dras, dress
drastic,cally, *SEVERELY*
draul, droll /drawl
draun, drawn /drown
drauper, dropper

drause, drowsy
draw,*,wing,drawn, *TO BRING FORTH FROM OUT OF SIGHT, BRING TOWARDS*
drawin, drawn
drawl,ler,lingly, *TO DRAG VOWELS OUT SLOWLY IN SPEAKING* (or see droll)
drawn, *PAST TENSE OF "DRAW"* (or see drown)
drawnd, drown(ed)
drawpur, dropper
drawt, drought
dread,*,ded,ding,dful,dfully,dfulness, *COMPLETE APPREHENSION IN FACING A SITUATION*
dream,*,med,ming,mnt,mless,mlessly, mlessness,mful,mfully,mfulness, *IMAGINE, THINK, ENVISION*
dreary,rily,riness, *GLOOMY*
drebul, dribble
drebuld, dribble(d)
drech, dredge
dred, dread
dredge,*,ed,ging, *TO GATHER OBJECTS UP FROM THE BOTTOM OF A BODY OF WATER WITH TOOLS/ MACHINERY*
dreem, dream
dreft, drift
dreg, dredge
dreid, dried
drej, dredge
drel, drill
drem, dream
drench,hes,hed,hing, *SOAKING WET*
drenk, drink
drenker, drinker
drep, drip
drery, dreary
dres, dress
dreser, dresser
dress,*,sses,ssed,sser,ssing, *TO PUT ON CLOTHING*

dresser, *ONE WHO HELPS OTHERS DRESS IN COS-TUMES, A CABINET WITH DRAWERS*
dresur, dresser
drewl, drool
drewp, droop
drezur, dresser
dri, dry
dribble,*,ed,ling, *SMALL OR SHORT AMOUNT OF ANYTHING*
dribul, dribble
drid, dried
dried, *PAST TENSE OF "DRY"*
drier,dryer, *"MORE" DRY*
driest, *"MOST" DRY*
drift,*,ted,ting,ter,tingly,tless,ty, *AMBLES ABOUT/ AROUND/ AWAY WITH EASE*
drill,*,lled,lling,ller, *TO BORE, MAKE OPENINGS*
drinch, drench
drink,*,king,kable,drank,ker, *TO TAKE IN LIQUIDS*
drinker,drunk, *ONE WHO OVER INDULGES IN ALCOHOL*
drip,*,pped,pping,ppy, *FALLING DROPS OF FLUID*
drire, dreary
dris, dry(ries)
driur, drier / dryer
drive,*,ving,en,drove,er, *TO MOVE/PUSH/RIDE SOMETHING ALONG*
drizzle,*,ed,ling, *VARIETY OF RAINFALL*
dro, draw
drofe, drove
drol, drawl /droll
droll,ller,llest,llness,lly, *ODDLY HUMOROUS* (or see drawl)
droma, drama
dron, drawn /drown
drone,*,ed,ning,ningly,er, *STEADY ONE-TONE SOUND, A BEE, INCAPABLE OF FREE WILL/ THOUGHT*
drool,*,led,ling, *SALIVA COMING FROM MOUTH*

droop,*,ped,ping,pingly,py, *TO LAY FORWARD LAZILY, SLUMP*
drop,*,pped,pping, *LIQUID FALLING IN BLOBS, LET SOMETHING GO*
droper, dropper
dropir, dropper
dropper,*,rful, *AN INSTRUMENT WHICH ALLOWS A DROP AT A TIME*
dropur, dropper
drought,ty, *LONG PERIODS OF TIME WITHOUT WATER*
droun, drown
drouse, drowsy
drout, drought
drouze, drowsy
drove,*, *PAST TENSE OF "DRIVE", MANY OF SOMETHING*
drow, draw
drown,*,ned,ning, *INTAKE OF WATER WHICH MAY KILL* (or see drawn)
drowsy,sily,siness, *NEARING SLEEP*
drowt, drought
droz, draw(s)
druch, drudge
drudge,ery,eries,gingly, *MENIAL/DULL WORK*
druel, drool
drug,*,gged,gging,ggey, *CHEMICALS* (or see drudge)
drugd, drug(gged) /drudge(d)
druge, drudge /drug
druj, drudge
druk, drug
drul, drool
drum,*,mmed,mming,mmer, *PERCUSSION INSTRUMENT, A LURING SOUND OR ACTION*
drumd, drum(mmed)
drumer, drum(mmer)
drunk,*, *PAST TENSE OF "DRINK", SOMEONE WHO DRINKS TOO MUCH ALCOHOL*
drupe, droop

drus, dress
dry,*, ries,ried,ying,yer, *TO REMOVE MOISTURE*
dryd, dried
dryest, driest
dryur, drier /dryer
du, dew/ due/ do
duable, do(able) /due(able)
dual,*,lity,lly,lism, *TWO WORKING THE SAME, DOUBLE (or see duel)*
duat, duet
dub,*, bbed,bbing, *TITLE OR NAME BESTOWED ON YOU BY ANOTHER, SOUND RECORDING*
dubate, debate
dubilutate, debilitate
duble, double
dublikate, duplicate
dubol, double
dubry, debris
dubul, double
ducanter, decanter
duce,*, *DICTATOR (or see deuce)*
duch, douche
duck,*,ked,king, *TO STOOP/TUCK/DIVE, FOWL/BIRD (or see duct)*
ducline, decline
duct,*,tless, *CABLE OR CHANNEL FOR MOVING THINGS ALONG (or see duck(ed))*
dud,*, *DOESN'T WORK, CLOTHES (or see dude)*
dudad, doodad
dude,*, *TOURIST ON A RANCH, INFORMAL TEENAGE REFERENCE TO ONE ANOTHER*
duded out, *DRESSED SNAZZY*
dudil, doodle
dudol, doodle
dudy, duty
due,*, *OUTSTANDING DEBT, DATE IT IS PAYABLE UPON (or see dew or do)*
dueble, do(able) /due(able)

duel,*,list,ler, *DISPUTE/FIGHT BETWEEN TWO PEOPLE/FACTIONS (or see dual)*
duen, doing
dueng, doing
duet,*, *TWO VOICES/INSTRUMENTS PERFORMING TOGETHER*
duf, dove
dufalt, default
dufase, deface
dufeet, defeat
dufel, duffel
dufenative, definitive
dufendant, defendant
dufense, defense
dufensible, defensible
duffel, *CANVAS/WOOL MATERIAL*
duffil, duffel
duffle, duffel
dufianse, defiance
dufide, divide
dufil, duffel
dufinative, definitive
dufine, define
dufishant, deficient
dufishensy, deficiency
dufle, duffel
dufol, duffel
dufray, defray
duful, duffel
dufunkt, defunct
dufy, defy
dugrade, degrade
dugree, degree
duible, do(able) /due(able)
duil, dual /duel
duin, doing
duing, doing
duk, duck /duke /duct
duka, decay

dukanter, decanter
dukd, duck(ed) /duct /duke(d)
duke,*,ed,king, *FISTS, POSITION UNDER THAT OF PRINCE (or see duck or duct)*
dukline, decline
dukrepit, decrepit
dukt, duck(ed) /duct /duke(d)
dul, dual /duel /dull
dulay, delay
dulcimer,*, *STRINGED INSTRUMENT*
dulectable, delectable
dulema, dilemma
dulereus, delirious
dulete, delete
dulever, deliver
duliburate, deliberate
dulicacy, delicacy
dulimu, dilemma
dulishus, delicious
dulite, delight /daylight
duliver, deliver
dull,*,lled,lling,llish,llness,llard, *WITHOUT SHINE OR ATTRACTIVENESS, BORING (or see duel/dual)*
dulsemur, dulcimer
dulsimer, dulcimer
dulujen, delusion
duluxe, deluxe
dum, doom /dumb
dumand, demand
dumb,*,ber,best,bing,bly,bness, *CANNOT SPEAK*
dumbling, dumpling
dume, dummy /doom
dumean, demean
dumeener, demeanor
dumenish, diminish
dumenshen, dimension
dumention, dimension
dumenyen, dominion
dumer, dumb(er)

dumes, dummy(mies)
dumesdek, domestic
dumest, dumb(est)
dumestic, domestic
dumie, dummy
duminish, diminish
duminted, demented
dumir, dumb(er)
dumist, dumb(est)
dumize, demise
dummy,mmies,mmied,mmying, *ONE BEING MANIPULATED INTO ACTION/MOTION, A MANNEQUIN/PUPPET*
dumonik, demon(ic)
dumor, dumb(er)
dump,*,ped,ping, *TO HEAVILY FALL, BE DROPPED*
dumpling,*, *DOUGHBALLS EATEN IN SAUCE*
dumur, dumb(er)
dumy, dummy
dun, done /dune
dune,*, *MOUND/HILL OF SAND*
dung,gy, *MANURE* (or see dunk)
dungaree,*, *HEAVY COTTON CLOTHING*
dungeree, dungaree
dunguree, dungaree
dunie, deny
dunk,*,ked,king, *TO DIP INTO* (or see dung)
dunomenator, denominator
dunomunashin, denomination
dunote, denote
duo,duet, *A PAIR*
duol, dual /duel
duparsher, departure
dupart, depart
dupartment, department
duparture, departure
dupe,*,ed,ping, *TO TRICK/DECEIVE*
dupend, depend
dupendant, dependant

dupendence, dependence
dupikt, depict
dupind, depend
duplacate, duplicate
dupleshin, depletion
duplete, deplete
duplex,xes,xity, *TWO WORKING IDENTICALLY, SIDE-BY-SIDE*
duplicate,*,ed,ting,tion,tor,*COPY OF THE ORIGINAL*
duplokate, duplicate
diploma, diploma
duplomusy, diplomacy
duplorable, deplorable
duplore, deplore
dupose, depose
dupozishen, deposition
dupozit, deposit
dupresheate, depreciate
duprive, deprive
durable,bility,eness,ly, *USEFUL MANY TIMES*
durashen, duration
duration, *FROM NOW UNTIL...*
durdee, dirty
durebul, durable
durect, direct
durection, direction
durectory, directory
durekshun, direction
durekt, direct
durektory, directory
dureng, during
duress, *UNDER STRESS, RESTRAINED FROM FREEDOM*
durible, durable
during, *AT THE SAME TIME*
durivadive, derivative
durivative, derivative
durive, derive
durmatites, dermatitis
durt, dirt

durty, dirty
dus, does /due(s) /deuce
dusabiludy, disability
dusable, disable
dusaster, disaster
dusblay, display
dusbose, dispose
dusbute, dispute
discrete, discreet / discrete
discretion, discretion
duscuss, discuss
dusdane, disdain
dusderb, disturb
dusdort, distort
dusdrakt, distract
dusdrebute, distribute
duse, does /due(s) /deuce
dusese, decease /disease
duseft, deceive(d)
dusembur, December
dusemunate, disseminate
dusenagrate, disintegrate
dusendent, descendant
dusent, doesn't
duses, decease /disease /deuce(s)
dusest, decease(d) /disease(d)
duset, deceit
dusetful, deceit(ful)
dusevd, deceive(d)
duseve, deceive
duseze, disease
dusfegure, disfigure
dusgard, discard
dusgise, disguise
dusgrase, disgrace
dush, douche
dushevul, dishevel
dusidewus, deciduous
dusimanate, disseminate

dusimbur, December
dusin, dozen
dusinagrate, disintegrate
dusindent, descendant
dusint, doesn't
dusipul, disciple
dusk,ky,kily,kiness, *END OF DAY BEFORE NIGHTFALL*
duskremanate, discriminate
duskrepensy, discrepancy
duskrete, discreet /discrete
duskribe, describe
duskripshen, description
duskust, disgust
duskuver, discover
duskwolify, disqualify
duslocate, dislocate
dusloge, dislodge
dusmanul, dismantle
dusmay, dismay
dusmiss, dismiss
dusmownt, dismount
dusolfe, dissolve
dusoreant, disorient
duspensible, dispensable
duspeut, dispute
duspinse, dispense
dusplay, display
dusplease, displease
duspose, dispose
dusposil, disposal
dusposuble, disposable
dusregard, disregard
dusrobe, disrobe
dust,ty,tless,tily,tiness, *TINY PARTICLES OF MATTER*
dustane, disdain
duste, dust(y)
dusteengwish, distinguish
dustenkt, distinct
dusterb, disturb

dustill, distill
dustingwish, distinguish
dustort, distort
dustract, distract
dustress, distress
dustroy, destroy
dustrukshen, destruction
duswrubshen, disruption
duswrubt, disrupt
dutektur, detector
dutenshin, detention
dutereate, deteriorate
dutereorate, deteriorate
duterint, deterrent
dutermin, determine
duterminashen, determination
duturgent, detergent
duty,ties,tiful,tifully,tifulness,teous, *OBLIGATION, RESPONSIBILITY, NECESSARY*
duv, dove
duvejin, division
duvelup, develop
duversity, diversity
duvide, divide
duvigen, division
duvigin, division
duvijen, division
duvine, divine
duvise, device
duvize, device
duvoid, devoid
duvorse, divorce
duvoshen, devotion
duvursedy, diversity
duwen, doing
dux, duck(s) /duct /duke(s)
duz, due(s) /does
duzaster, disaster
duzent, doesn't

duzeze, disease
duzin, dozen
duzint, doesn't
duzolve, dissolve
duzoreint, disorient
duzen, dozen
dwarf,fed,fing,fish,fishly,fishness,fism,rves, rved, *STUNTED FROM FULL GROWTH*
dwarves,ed,en, *MORE THAN ONE DWARF (or see dwarf)*
dwell,*,lled,lling, *DELAY, LINGER*
dwendle, dwindle
dwindle,*,ed,ling, *SHRINK, DEGENERATE, SHRIVEL*
dworf, dwarf
dyagnol, diagonal
dyagnose, diagnose
dyalekt, dialect
dyameter, diameter
dyatery, dietary
dye,*,ed,ying,er,yable, *STAIN/COLOR/PIGMENTS TO APPLY* (or see die or di)
dyet, diet
dyetery, dietary
dyignose, diagnose
dying, *TOWARDS DEATH, TRANSFORMATION*
dyke,*, *MASCULINE LESBIAN* (or see dike)
dylate, dilate
dynamic,*,ism, *MOTION OF HIGH ENERGY*
dynamite,tic,er, *EXPLOSIVES*
dynasty, ties, *STRING OF HEREDITARY RULERS*
dypur, diaper /dipper
dyre, dire
dys, *PREFIX INDICATING "BAD" MOST OFTEN MODIFIES THE WORD* (or see die(s) or dice)
dysekt, dissect
dysentery,ric, *INFECTIOUS DISEASE*
dyslexia,ic, *TIMING IN CORPUS CALLOSUM NEURON SIGNALS WHICH AFFECTS COMMUNICATION BETWEEN BRAIN HEMISPHERES*

dysfunction,*,nal, *NOT ACTING WITHIN IDEAL LIMITS*
dyufram, diaphragm
dyul, dial
dyulog, dialogue
dyureuh, diarrhea

"E"

each, *ONE APIECE, TREATED INDIVIDUALLY*
eager,rly,ness, *MOTIVATED, VERY INTERESTED*
eagle,*, *BIRD*
ear,*, *GROWTH ON HEAD TO HEAR WITH*
earing, earring
early,lier,liest,liness, *PRIOR TO ORIGINAL TIME*
earn,*,ner,ning, *REWARD FOR SERVICE/LABOR (or see urn)*
ernest,tly,tness, *SINCERE FEELINGS, EFFORT, MONEY TRANSACTION TO HOLD CONTRACT*
earring,*, *EAR ADORNMENT*
earth,hen,hly, *OUR PLANET*
east,tern,ternly,tward, *COMPASS DIRECTION*
ease,*,eful,efully, *WITHOUT STRAIN TO PERFORM, UNDERSTAND (or see easy)*
easel,*, *TRIPOD TO HOLD WORKBOARDS, ETC.*
easement,*,*, *LEGAL USE/RIGHTS TO SOMETHING, TO HELP MAKE EASIER*
easily,iness, *NO DIFFICULTY*
easy, *NOT DIFFICULT OR HARD (or see ease)*
eat,*,ten,ting,table, *TO INGEST*
eaves, *OVERHANG OF A BUILDING*
eaze, ease /easy
eb, ebb
ebademik, epidemic
ebasode, episode
ebb,*,bbing, *TO FALL/SINK/RECEDE*
ebdikate, abdicate
ebdumin, abdomen
ebedemek, epidemic

eberigenie, aborgine
ebide, abide
ebirijeny, aborigine
ebiss, abyss
ebnormul, abnormal
ebolish, abolish
ebomenable, abominable
ebominable, abominable
ebony, *BLACK WOOD*
ebord, aboard /abort
ebort, abort /aboard
ebowt, about
ebreveate, abbreviate
ebrod, abroad
ebstain, abstain
ebundinse, abundance
ebune, ebony
ebuve, above
academic, academic
eccentric,cally,city,cities, *ODD, NOT OF THE NORM*
ech, each /etch /edge /itch
echd, itch(ed) /etch(ed)
echo,oes,oed,oing, *REPETITIVE SOUNDS BOUNCING BACK TOWARDS ORIGINATOR*
echu, issue
echud, issue(d)
eckbrest, express(ed)
eckdravert, extrovert
ecksdreem, extreme
ecksploit, exploit
eclectic,cally,cism, *COMPILATION OF OTHERS WORK/VARIOUS SOURCES*
eclectic, eclectic
eclepse, eclipse
eclipse,*,ed,sing,ptic, *SHADOW CAST BY PLANETARY BODIES BLOCKING ANOTHER PLANETARY BODY*
ecnolege, acknowledge
eco, *PREFIX INDICATING "ECOLOGY" MOST OFTEN MODIFIES THE WORD (or see echo)*

ecoli, *A BACTERIA, PROPERLY SPELLED E COLI*
ecology,gical,gically,gist, *SCIENCE ON ORGANISMS IN THE ENVIRONMENT*
ecology, ecology
economy,mies,mic,mics,mical,mize, *GOODS AND MONEY*
economy, economy
ecosfere, ecosphere
ecosistem, ecosystem
ecosphere, *BREATHABLE AREA FOR LIFE*
ecosystem,*, *ORGANISMS INTERACTING TO CREATE ENVIRONMENT*
equit, acquit
ecsclimashin, exclamation
ecsebt, except /accept
ecselerate, accelerate
ecsempt, exempt
ecsepshen, except(ion)
ecsite, excite
ecsklumashen, exclamation
ecspekt, expect
ecstasy,sies,atic,atically, *JUBILANT, IN BLISS*
ecsteengwish, extinguish
ecstuse, ecstasy
ecto, *PREFIX INDICATING "OUTSIDE" MOST OFTEN MODIFIES THE WORD*
ecute, acute
ecwashin, equation
ecwatic, aquatic
ecwilebreum, equilibrium
eczema,atous, *SKIN IRRITATION FROM BACTERIA*
eczima, eczema
ed, eat /eight /ate
edable, edible
edakit, etiquette
edapd, adapt
edapt, adapt
edatur, editor
edch, etch /edge /itch

eddy,ddies,ddied,ying, CIRCULAR MOVING CURRENT IN WATER/AIR
ede, eddy
edel, it'll
edelescense, adolescence
edelt, adult
edept, adept
edeshen, edition /add(ition)
edet, edit
edeut, idiot
edge,*,ed,ging,gy,giness, POINT OF ANGLE WHERE ONE ANGLE DROPS OFF AT
edgust, adjust
edhere, adhere
edible,lity,eness, CAN BE SAFELY EATEN
edikit, etiquette
edikshen, addict(ion)
edil, it'll
edishen, edition / add(ition)
edit,*,ted,ting, MAKE READY FOR PUBLICATION
edition,*, ONE OUT OF A SET OF A PUBLISHED VOLUME (or see addition)
editor,*,rial,rially,rialist,rialize, DIRECTOR/ PREPARER OF WRITTEN MATERIAL
editur, editor
edj, etch /edge /itch
edjust, adjust
edmechen, admission
edmichen, admission
edmire, admire
edmishun, admission
edmit, admit
edobt, adopt
edolt, adult
edoo, adieu
edopt, adopt
edore, adore
edorn, adorn

edrenulin, adrenalin
edres, address
edsedura, etcetera
edself, itself
edsedura, etcetera
edsh, etch /edge /itch
edu, adieu
eduble, edible
educate,*,ed,ting,tion,tional,tive,tor, INSTRUCT
edukit, etiquette
edul, it'll
edulescense, adolescence
edult, adult
edut, edit
edvantij, advantage
edverse, adverse
edvirse, adverse
edvise, advise /advice
edvurse, adverse
edy, eddy
edzetera, etcetera
eel,*, OCEAN FISH
eet, eat /yet
ef, if /eve
efact, effect /affect
efadent, evident
efaire, affair
efakt, effect /affect
efal, evil
efalushin, evolution
efan, even
efar, ever
efare, affair
efect, effect /affect
efegy, effigy
efekt, effect /affect
efektive, effect(ive) /affect(ive)
efeminate, effeminate
efeminit, effeminate

efen, even
efening, evening
efenity, affinity
efer, ever /affair
efert, effort
efervesant, effervescent
efervescent, effervescent
effect,*,ted,ting,tive,tiveness,tual,tually, tualness,tuate,tuation, RESULT, FULFILL MENT ACCOMPLISHMENT (or see affect)
effeminate,acy,acies,ely,eness, OF FEMININE PERSUASION
effervescent,nce,tly, GASEOUS BUBBLES, STRONG FEELINGS
efficiency,cies,nt, PRODUCE WELL IN SHORT PERIOD OF TIME, TYPE OF LIVING QUARTERS
effigy,gies, SOMETHING CONSTRUCTED IN HUMAN LIKENESS
effort,*,tless,tlessly,tlessness, ATTEMPT TO PRODUCE, SHOW SKILLS/TALENTS
eficiency, efficiency
efident, evident
efigy, effigy
efil, evil
eflushen, evolution
efin, even
efinity, affinity
efir, ever
efirvesant, effervescent
efishensy, efficiency
efisiancy, efficiency
eflikt, afflict
eflot, afloat
efluinse, affluence
efning, evening
efodent, evident
efol, evil
efolushin, evolution
efolve, evolve

efon, even
efoot, afoot
efor, ever
eford, afford
efort, effort
efrad, afraid
efrebote, every(body)
efreda, every(day)
efree, every
efrething, every(thing)
efrewer, every(where)
efrewun, every(one)
efriwun, every(one)
efryday, every(day)
efront, affront
efrunt, affront
efudent, evident
efugy, effigy
eful, evil
efulushun, evolution
efur, ever
efurt, effort
efurvesant, effervescent
efut, afoot
eg, edge /egg /etch /itch
egajurate, exaggerate
egalatarian, egalitarian
egalitarian,*,nism, *EQUALITY OF ALL PEOPLES /*
  REPTILES
egalutarean, egalitarian
egekt, eject
egenst, against
eger, eager
egern, adjourn
egg,*,gged,gging, *PRODUCED BY FOWL /BIRD /*
eginst, against
egle, eagle
egneranse, ignorant(nce)
egneshin, ignition

egneus, igneous
egnide, ignite
egnishin, ignition
egnite, ignite
egnorants, ignorant(nce)
egnor, ignore
egnurant, ignorant
ego, ago
ego,*,oism,oist,oistical,oistically, *PART OF US THAT*
  IS SELF-SERVING/FEARFUL (or see echo)
egotistic,cal,cally,ism, *CENTERED ON ONESELF*
egre, agree
egresiv, aggressive
egsabishen, exhibit(ion)
egsagurate, exaggerate
egsajurate, exaggerate
egsakt, exact
egsample, example
egsaspurate, exasperate
egsastshin, exhaust(ion)
egsbereanse, experience
egsberimentashen, experiment(ation)
egsbire, expire
egsblan, explain
egsblod, explode
egsblor, explore
egsbloshen, explosion
egsbort, export
egsboz, expose
egsbres, express
egsburt, expert
egscavate, excavate
egsdra, extra
egsdreem, extreme
egsebit, exhibit
egsebt, except /accept
egseed, exceed
egsempt, exempt
egsemshen, exempt(ion)

egsepshen, except(ion)
egsept, except /accept
egsersize, exercise
egsert, exert
egsesif, excess(ive) /access(ive)
egsest, exist
egsglumashen, exclamation
egshale, exhale
egsibeshen, exhibit(ion)
egsibit, exhibit
egsilarate,exhilarate /accelerate
egsile, exile
egsima, eczema
egsimt, exempt
egsist, exist
egsistens, exist(ence)
egsit, exit
egskershun, excursion
egskurshen, excursion
egskuvate, excavate
egsorsize, exercise
egsost, exhaust
egsostshen, exhaust(ion)
egsotic, exotic
egspadishen, expedition
egspand, expand
egspect, expect
egspel, expel
egspense, expense
egsperament, experiment
egspereanse, experience
egspinse, expense
egspirashen, expire(ration)
egspire, expire
egsplanashen, explanation
egsplane, explain
egsplesit, explicit
egsplod, explode
egsplor, explore

egsplorashen, explore(ration)
egsploratory, explore(ratory)
egsplosean, explosion
egsplunashen, explanation
egsport, export
egsportashen, export(ation)
egspos, expose
egspres, express
egspurashen, expire(ration)
egspurt, expert
egsqwizit, exquisite
egstengwish, extinguish
egstend, extend
egstenkt, extinct
egstereor, exterior
egsternul, external
egstinkt, extinct
egstra, extra
egstrakt, extract
egstravert, extrovert
egstrem, extreme
egstremly, extreme(ly)
egstrivurt, extrovert
egsturnal, external
egsubishen, exhibit(ion)
egsulent, excellent
egsurshen, exert(ion)
egsurt, exert
egszemt, exempt
egukate, educate
egul, eagle
egur, eager
egzajurate, exaggerate
egzakt, exact
egzample, example
egzema, eczema
egzershin, exert(ion)
egzile, exile
egzilurate, exhilarate /accelerate

egzima, eczema
egzimpt, exempt
egzimt, exempt
egzist, exist
egzit, exit
egzotek, exotic
egzurshen, exert(ion)
egzursize, exercise
egzurtion, exert(ion)
ehed, ahead
eight,ty,teen,tieth, ENGLISH NUMBER (or see ate)
eighteen,nth,nths, ENGLISH NUMBER
eil, aisle
ej, edge /etch /itch
ejakt, eject
eject,*,ted,ting,tion,tor,tors, FORCED TO LEAVE/ BE EXPELLED
ejekt, eject
ejenda, agenda
ejern, adjourn
ejorn, adjourn
ejrenalin, adrenaline
ejukate, educate
ejusduble, adjust(able)
ejust, adjust
ekademe, academy
ekadume, academy
ekcesori, accessory
ekchange, exchange
eklektic, eclectic
eklipse, eclipse
ekliptik, eclipse(ptic)
eknolege, acknowledge
eknurint, ignorant
eko, echo /ego
ekod, echo(ed)
ekology, ecology
ekolugy, ecology
ekonimy, economy

ekonume, economy
ekosestum, ecosystem
ekosfere, ecosphere
ekosistem, ecosystem
ekosphere, ecosphere
eknor, ignore
eksagerashen, exaggerate(tion)
eksajurashen, exaggerate(tion)
eksakute, execute
eksalant, excellent
eksalins, excel(llence)
eksamenashen, examine(nation)
eksaminashen, examine(nation)
eksample, example
eksapurashen, exasperate(tion)
eksaqute, execute
eksated, exit(ed)
eksberament, experiment
eksbire, expire
eksblan, explain
eksblanashen, explanation
eksblinashen, explanation
eksblod, explode
eksblor, explore
eksblorashen, explore(ration)
eksbloshen, explosion
eksbloytashen, exploit(ation)
eksbortashen, export(ation)
eksbos, expose
eksbres, express
eksburashen, expire(ration)
eksburt, expert
ekscerjen, excursion
ekschange, exchange
eksclemashin, exclamation
ekscurshin, excursion
ekscuse, excuse
eksdra, extra
eksdravirt, extrovert

eksdreem, extreme
eksebit, exhibit
eksebt, except /accept
eksekute, execute
eksel, excel /accel
ekselarashen, accelerate(tion)
ekselen, excel(lled) /accel(lled)
ekselense, excellent
ekselerashen, accelerate(tion)
ekselerate, accelerate
ekselurashen, accelerate(tion)
ekselurate, accelerate
ekseluratur, accelerate(tor)
eksentrek, eccentric
eksentrik, eccentric
eksepshen, except(ion)
ekseptense, accept(ance)
ekserpt, excerpt
eksert, exert
ekses, excess /access
eksesif, excess(ive) /access(ive)
eksesis, excess(es) /access(es)
eksesori, accessory
eksfoleate, exfoliate
eksglud, exclude
eksglumashen, exclamation
eksglut, exclude
ekshale, exhale
eksibishen, exhibit(ion)
eksibit, exhibit
eksilarat, exhilarate /accelerate
eksile, exile
eksilens, excel(llence)
eksimpt, exempt
eksimshen, exempt(ion)
eksinshuate, accentuate
eksintrik, eccentric
eksirpt, excerpt
eksistens, exist(ence)

eksit, exit /excite
eksitment, excite(ment)
eksklumashen, exclamation
ekskurshen, excursion
ekskuse, excuse
ekskuvaded, excavate(d)
ekskuvashen, excavate(tion)
ekskuvate, excavate
ekskwisit, exquisite
eksolent, excellent
eksorbeint, exorbitant
eksorbident, exorbitant
eksorsize, exercise
ekspadishen, expedition
ekspand, expand
ekspedishen, expedition
ekspekt, expect
ekspektashen, expect(tation)
ekspektent, expect(ant)
ekspel, expel
ekspend, expend
ekspense, expense
ekspensef, expensive(sive)
eksperament, experiment
ekspereanse, experience
ekspert, expert
ekspinse, expense
ekspire, expire
eksplan, explain
eksplanashen, explanation
eksplicit, explicit
eksplinashen, explanation
eksplisit, explicit
eksplisitly, explicit(ly)
eksplod, explode
eksploet, exploit
eksploit, exploit
eksplor, explore
eksplorashen, explore(ration)

eksploratory, explore(ratory)
eksployt, exploit
eksplunashen, explanation
eksport, export
eksportashen, export(ation)
ekspos, expose
ekspres, express
eksqus, excuse
ekstend, extend
ekstengwish, extinguish
ekstereur, exterior
ekstind, extend
ekstinkt, extinct
ekstra, extra
ekstrakt, extract
ekstrem, extreme
ekstremle, extreme(ly)
ekstruvert, extrovert
eksturnal, external
ekstuse, ecstasy
eksubishen, exhibit(ion)
eksulant, excellent
eksulashen, exhale(lation)
eksulins, excellent(nce)
eksuqushen, execute(tion)
eksuqution, execute(tion)
eksurpt, excerpt
eksurshen, exert(ion)
eksursize, exercise
eksurt, exert
eksuvashen, excavate(tion)
ekuate, equate
ekute, acute
ekwabil, equable
ekwable, equable
ekwade, equity
ekwader, equator
ekwal, equal
ekwalete, equality

ekwaliz, equal(ize)
ekwashin, equation
ekwashun, equation
ekwate, equate /equity
ekwatur, equator
ekwaul, equal
ekwebul, equable
ekwel, equal
ekwelebreum, equilibrium
ekwenoks, equinox
ekwenox, equinox
ekwevalent, equivalent
ekwil, equal
ekwinoks, equinox
ekwinox, equinox
ekwip, equip
ekwipment, equip(ment)
ekwit, acquit
ekwity, equity
ekwivulent, equivalent
ekwolity, equality
ekwoliz, equal(ize)
ekwotek, aquatic
ekwuble, equable
ekwude, equity
ekwul, equal
ekwuliz, equal(ize)
ekwunox, equinox
el, eel /ail /ill
elegible, eligible
elagint, elegant
elamintry, elementary
elamtry, elementary
elarm, alarm
elastic,*,city, STRETCHES OUT/SHRINKS BACK
elastrate, illustrate
elate,*,ed,tion, RAISED MOOD /SPIRIT
elavashen, elevate(tion)
elavater, elevate(r)
elbow,*,wed,wing, JOINT IN THE ARM

elbum, album
elchuhol, alcohol
elder,*,est,rly, ONE WHO HAS LIVED MORE YEARS
    THAN OTHERS (or see alder)
eldur, elder
elect,*,ted,ting,tion,tions,table, TO MAKE A CHOICE
elective,*,ely,eness, OPTION TO CHOOSE
elector,*,tral,rate, VOTERS
electric,cal,cals,cally,city,ify,ro, FREQUENCY/
    ENERGY EXISTING IN ALL PARTICLES
electrician,*, PEOPLE WHO WORK WITH WIRES/
    ELECTRICITY
electrishun, electrician
electro, PREFIX INDICATING "ELECTRIC" MOST OFTEN
    MODIFIES THE WORD
electron,*,ic,ics, A CHARGED PARTICLE
eledge, allege
ele, alley
elefint, elephant
elegable, eligible
eleganse, allegiance
elegant,tly,nce, BEAUTIFUL/CLASSY
elege, allege
elegul, illegal
elejense, allegiance
elekt, elect
elektev, elective
elektric, electric
elektrician, electrician
elektrishen, electrician
elekul, illegal
elemanate, eliminate
element,*,tal,tary,BASIC, FUNDAMENTAL
elementary, FIRST AND BASIC
elephant,*, AN ANIMAL
elere, allure
elergik, allergic
elert, alert
elevashen, elevate(tion)

elevate,*,ed,ting,tion, RAISE HORIZONTAL LEVEL
eleveate, alleviate
eleven,nth,nths, AN ENGLISH NUMBER
elevin, eleven
elevinth, eleven(th)
elf,elves,fin,fish, IMAGINARY ENTITIES
elfs, elf(lves)
elgebra, algebra
elianse, alliance
eliderate, illiterate
elifent, elephant
eligable, eligible
eligent, elegant
eligible,*,bility,bilities, POTENTIAL TO BE CHOSEN
elimenate, eliminate
eliminate,*,ed,ting,tion, GET RID OF, DISPOSE
elimony, alimony
eline, align
elipse, ellipse
eliset, illicit
elisit, illicit
elistrate, illustrate
elipsus, ellipsis
eliturate, illiterate
elivashen, elevate(tion)
elive, alive
elk, IN THE DEER FAMILY
ellipse,ptic,ptical, OVAL SHAPE
ellipsis, SYMBOL (...) USED IN PLACE OF A WORD
ellisit, illicit
elnes, ill(ness)
elogekul, illogical
elogicul, illogical
elongate,*,ed,ting,tion,TO LENGTHEN/MAKE LONGER
elood, elude
eloor, allure
eloosuf, allude(usive) /elude(usive)
eloot, elude
elorm, alarm

elovate, elevate
eloy, alloy
elso, also
eltetude, altitude
eltitude, altitude
elude,*,ed,ding,usive,usion, *GET AWAY /NOT BE PERCEIVED (or see allude)*
elufint, elephant
elugable, eligible
elugant, elegant
elugint, elegant
elumenade, illuminate
elumentary, elementary
elumenum, aluminum
eluminate, illuminate
elumintry, elementary
eluminum, aluminum
elumony, alimony
elure, allure
elugent, elegant
elugens, elegant(nce)
elurgik, allergic
elurjik, allergic
elurt, alert
elushun, illusion, illusion /allusion /elusion
elusion,ive, *GET AWAY/NOT BE PERCEIVED (or see allusion or illusion)*
elusive, *GET AWAY/NOT BE PERCEIVED (or see allusive)*
elustrate, illustrate
eluvashen, elevate(tion)
eluvate, elevate
em, en, *PREFIX INDICATING "INTO /ON /PUT INTO" MOST OFTEN MODIFIES THE WORD*
emachure, amateur
emaculet, immaculate
emage, image
emagenashen, imagine(ation)
emagrant, immigrant /emigrant

emagrashen, immigrate(tion)
emagrate, immigrate
emagrunt, immigrant /emigrant
emagunashen, imagine(ation)
emaj, image
emajinashen, imagine(nation)
emakewilt, immaculate
emakulit, immaculate
emancipate,*,ed,ting,tion, *FREE FROM BONDAGE*
emanent, eminent /imminent
emanit, imminent
emansepade, emancipate
emansipate, emancipate
ematashin, imitate(tion)
ematate, imitate
ematation, imitate(tion)
emature, immature
embankment,*, *A BURM/MOUND*
embargo,oes, *RESTRICT FROM PORTS*
embaris, embarrass
embark,*,ked,king, *PREPARING TO TAKE A JOURNEY*
embarrass,sses,ssed,ssing,ssingly,ssment, *UNDESIRABLY EXPOSED*
embassy,sies, *SAFE PLACE WITHIN ANOTHER COUNTRY*
embed,*,dded,dding, *SINK INTO UNTIL FLUSH*
ember,*, *SPARK/COAL FROM FIREWOOD*
emberis, embarrass
embilukil, umbilical
embishun, ambition
emblem,*, *A SYMBOL OR FIGURE*
emblie, imply
emblum, emblem
emboss,sses,ssed,ssing, *IMPRINT INTO*
embostur, imposter
embrace,*,ed,cing, *TO HOLD DEAR*
embrase, embrace
embreo, embryo
embroeder, embroider
embroider,*,red,ring, *STITCH WITH NEEDLE/THREAD*

embrufe, improve
embrufment, improve(ment)
embryo,*,onic,ology,ologist, *SOMETHING GROWING INSIDE BEFORE IT EMERGES*
embtee, empty
embulense, ambulance
embur, ember
embush, ambush
embuzishun, impose(sition)
emcompruble, incomparable
emcumblete, incomplete
emeable, amiable
emedeat, immediate
emej, image
emend, amend
emense, immense
emerald, *A COLOR, A GEMSTONE*
emerge,*,ed,ging,ence,ent,encies, *TO COME FROM WITHIN, ERUPT*
emergency,cies, *TO BE DEALT WITH IMMEDIATELY*
emerjensee, emergency
emeshen, emission /omission
emfadek, emphatic
emfusis, emphasis
emigrant,*, *LEAVE A COUNTRY TO GO TO ANOTHER (or see immigrant)*
emigrate,*,ed,ting,tion, *LEAVE A COUNTRY TO GO TO ANOTHER (or see immigrate)*
emigrunt, immigrant /emigrant
emij, image
emind, amend
eminent, imminent
eminent,tly, *SOMEONE WHO ACHIEVED BEYOND OTHERS (or see imminent)*
eminse, immense
eminge, emerge
emission,*, *SOMETHING DISCHARGED, PUT INTO CIRCULATION (or see omission)*

emit,*,tted,tting, *DISCHARGE, PUT OUT A FREQUENCY* (or see omit)
emitate, imitate
emitation, imitate(tion)
emochun, emotion
emonent, eminent /imminent
emonia, ammonia
emoral, immoral
emordul, immortal
emortal, immortal
emortalety, immortal(ity)
emortalidy, immortal(ity)
emorul, immoral
emoshin, emotion
emotion,*,nal,nally,nality,nless,nalize,ive, *CHEMICALS RELEASED BY WHAT WE ARE THINKING THAT CREATES EMOTION*
emownt, amount
empact, impact
empakt, impact
emparetive, imperative
emparor, emperor
emparative, imperative
emperfect, imperfect
emperor,*, *RULER OF PEOPLE/LAND*
empersenate, impersonate
empersonal, impersonal
empersonashen, impersonate(tion)
empersonate, impersonate
emphasis,ses,sed,sing,ize,ized,izing, *PLACE GREAT IMPORTANCE IN/UPON*
emphatic,cally, *PLACE GREAT IMPORTANCE IN/UPON*
emphisis, emphasis
empire,*, *REGION OF PEOPLE/LAND RULED BY AN EMPEROR*
empirer, emperor
emplament, implement
emplant, implant
emplicate, implicate

emplication, implicate(tion)
emploe, employee / employ
emploer, employer
employ,*,yed,ying,yable,yability, *USE SOMETHING/SOMEONE TO COMPLETE A TASK WHICH MAY/MAY NOT INVOLVE MONEY* (or see employee)
employee,*, *SOMEONE WHO IS LEGALLY HIRED AND WORKS FOR PAY* (or see employ)
employer,*, *SOMEONE WHO PAYS SOMEONE ELSE TO WORK*
employment,*, *BEING HIRED TO WORK*
emplucashen, implicate(tion)
emplucate, implicate
emplument, implement
emply, imply
empofuresh, impoverish
empolite, impolite
empolse, impulse
emport, import
emportashen, import(ation)
empose, impose
emposible, impossible
emposter, imposter
emposuble, impossible
empound, impound
empoverish, impoverish
empoze, impose
empraktecul, impractical
emprapuble, improbable
emprasise, imprecise
empravize, improvise
empravise, imprecise
empregnable, impregnable
empregnate, impregnate
empregnuble, impregnable
emprent, imprint
empres, empress / impress
empreshen, impress(sion)

empresise, imprecise
empresive, impress(sive)
empresont, imprison(ed)
empress, impress
empress,ses, *FEMALE RULER OF EMPIRE* (or see impress)
empretion, impress(sion)
emprint, imprint
emprison, imprison
emprobable, improbable
empromptu, impromptu
empromtu, impromptu
empropable, improbable
emproper, improper
emprove, improve
emprovement, improve(ment)
emprovisation, improvise(sation)
emprovize, improvise
emprovusashen, improvise(sation)
emprufe, improve
emprus, empress /impress
empruve, improve
empruvize improvise
emptee, empty
empty,ties,tied,tying,tiness, *REMOVE CONTENTS FROM SOMETHING*
empulite, impolite
empulse, impulse
empulsef, impulse(sive)
empulsive, impulse(sive)
empurfekt, imperfect
empuror, emperor
empursenate, impersonate
empursonal, impersonal
emput, input
emputate, amputate
empuzishen, impose(sition)
emruld, emerald
emte, empty

emuch, image
emug, image
emugrant, immigrant /emigrant
emugrashen, immigrate(tion) /emigrate(tion)
emugrate, immigrate
emugrent, emigrant /immigrant
emuj, image
emulate,*,ed,ting,tion, STRIVE TO LIVE UP TO
emune, immune
emunety, immune(nity)
emunezashen, immunize(zation)
emunise, immunize
emurg, emerge
emurgensee, emergency
emurse, immerse
emutashin, imitate(tion)
emutate, imitate
emuze, amuse
en, em,PREFIX INDICATING "INTO/ON/PUT INTO" MOST OFTEN MODIFIES THE WORD (or see prefix in/un/inn)
enabiledy, inability
enability, inability
enabishen, inhibit(ion)
enable,*,ed,ling,EMPOWER/AID SOMEONE/ SOMETHING TO PERFORM MORE EFFICIENTLY (or see unable)
enabul, enable /unable
enaccessible, inaccessible
enact,*,ted,ting,tment, TO PERFORM OR MAKE INTO
enaction, inaction
enacuracy, inaccuracy(acy)
enacurate, innacurate
enadequate, inadequate
enadequit, inadequate
enadmisable, inadmissable
enadukwit, inadequate
enadverdent, inadvertent
enadvirdent, inadvertent

enadvisable, inadvisable
enaksesible, inaccessible
enakshen, inaction
enakt, enact
enakurite, innacurate
enalegy, analogy
enalesis, analysis
enaleuble, inalienable
enalienable, inalienable
enaligy, analogy
enaliuble, inalienable
enalugy, analogy
enamel,*,led,ling, PAINT, COATING USED FOR PROTECTION
enanemit, inanimate
enanimate, inanimate
enapal, enable /unable
enappreciative, inappreciative
enapproachable, inapproachable
enappropriate, inappropriate
enaprochible, inapproachable
enapropriate, inappropriate
enapul, enable /unable
enaquerisy, inaccurate(acy)
enaqurite, innacurate
enarkey, anarchy
enarup, interrupt
enasinse, innocence
enate, innate
enatequit, inadequate
enatible, inaudible
enatmisable, inadmissable
enatvirdent, inadvertent
enatvisable, inadvisable
enatvurtent, inadvertent
enaudible, inaudible
enauf, enough
enaugurate, inaugurate
enavadif, innovate(tive)

enbankment, embankment
enbark, embark
enbasee, embassy
enbed, embed
enberis, embarrass
enblem, emblem
enboss, emboss
enbrase, embrace
enbroder, embroider
encandescent, incandescent
encapable, incapable
encapacitate, incapacitate
encapuble, incapable
encarnate, incarnate
encarsurate, incarcerate
encenerate, incinerate
encentive, incentive
enception, incept(ion)
encereg, encourage /anchor(age)
ench, inch
enchant,*,ted,ting,tment, DELIGHT, FASCINATE
enchor, anchor
enchur, ensure /insure
encircle,*,ed,ling, SURROUND WITH A CIRCLE
enclanation, incline(nation)
encline, incline
enclood, include
enclose,*,ed,sing,sment,sure, SURROUND/KEEP IN
encloser, enclose(sure)
enclosment, enclose(ment)
enclude, include
enclunashen, incline(nation)
enclusef, inclusive
enclusion, inclusion
encoherent, incoherent
encombatent, incompetent
encome, income
encomparable, incomparable
enclusef, inclusive

enclusion, inclusion
encompass,*,sses,ssed,ssing, *ITEMS WITHIN A CIRCLE*
encompatible, incompatible
encompetent, incompetent
encomplete, incomplete
encompruble, incomparable
enconclusef, inconclusive
enconclusive, inconclusive
enconsiderate, inconsiderate
enconsistent, inconsistent
enconvenient, inconvenient
encoragable, incorrigible
encore,*, , *ASKED TO PERFORM MORE BY AN AUDIENCE*
encorij, encourage /anchor(age)
encorporate, incorporate
encorrect, incorrect
encounter,*,red,ring, *TO EMBARK UPON SOMETHING/SOMEONE*
encourage,*,ed,ging,ement, *INSTILL FAITH/HOPE*
encrease, increase
encredible, incredible
enkredulus, incredulous
encremenate, incriminate
encrement, increment
encriminate, incriminate
encubate, incubate
encumbent, incumbent
encumpatable, incompatible
encumplete, incomplete
encunkiusif, inconclusive
encunsestant, inconsistent
encunveneunt, inconvenient
encupasitate, incapacitate
encupasity, incapacitate
encur, incur
encurable, incurable
encuragable, incorrigible

encureje, encourage /anchor(age)
encurekt, incorrect
encurej, encourage /anchor(age)
encurig, encourage /anchor(age)
encyclopedia,*, *REFERENCE SOURCE THAT DEFINES/ EXPLAINS THINGS THAT ARE NOUNS*
end,*,ded,ding, *NO MORE, OVER (or see "and")*
endanger,*,red,ring,rment, *IN HARM'S WAY, NEEDS PROTECTION*
endangurment, endanger(ment)
endanjer, endanger
endakashen, indicate(tion)
endapendense, independent(nce)
endasishen, indecision
endavigual, individual
endear,*,red,ring,rment, *VERY FOND OF*
endeavor,*,red,ring, *TO SET ABOUT THE TASK TO DO SOMETHING*
endebted, indebted
endecashen, indicate(tion)
endecision, indecision
endecisive, indecisive
endecks, index
endeed, indeed
endefanete, indefinite
endefinite, indefinite
endefir, endeavor
endefur, endeavor
endefurent, indifferent
endego, indigo
endent, indent
endentashen, indent(ation)
endependense, independent(nce)
endependent, independent
ender, inter /enter
enderfere, interfere
endesent, indecent
endeted, indebted
endever, endeavor

endex, index
endicashen, indicate(tion)
endicate, indicate
endifrent, indifferent
endigo, indigo
endisisuf, indecisive
endite, indict
endless,ssly,ssness, *WILL NEVER STOP*
endlis, endless
endo, *PREFIX INDICATING "INSIDE" MOST OFTEN MODIFIES THE WORD*
endocrine, *OF THE GLANDS IN THE BODY*
endoer, endure
endoose, induce
endors, indoor(s)
endorse,*,ed,sing,ement, *TO SUPPORT OR AFFIRM IN WRITING (or see indoor(s))*
endostry, industry
endrukit, intricate
enduce, induce
endulge, indulge
endulgense, indulge(nce)
endukren, endocrine
endupendent, independent
endur, inter /enter /endure
endure,*,ed,ring,rance,rable,rably, *TO PUT UP WITH OR TOLERATE*
enduse, induce
enduseshin, indecision
endustreul, industrial
endustry, industry
enduztreal, industrial
ene, any
enebody, anybody
eneduble, inedible
eneg, inning
enegma, enigma /enema
enema,*, *RECTAL CLEANSING (or see anemia/ enigma)*

enemik, anemic
enemut, intimate
enemy,mies, A FOE, NOT FRIENDS WITH
eneng, inning
enept, inept
ener, inner
enercom, intercom
enerconnect, interconnect
enerelate, interrelate
energetic,cally, TO HAVE LOTS OF ENERGY
energy, HAVING ENOUGH POWER TO DO SOMETHING
enerject, interject
enerjetek, energetic
enerkorse, intercourse
enerlude, interlude
enermedeary, intermediary
enermingle, intermingle
enermission, intermission
enermost, innermost
enernashenul, international
enernet, internet
enersculastic, interscholastic
enersection, innersection
enersekshen, innersection
enersperse, intersperse
enerstate, interstate
enert, inert
enervene, intervene
enervue, interview
enervul, interval
enerwoven, interwoven
enescapable, inescapable
enesense, innocence
enesheation, initiate(tion)
enesthezia, anesthesia
eneviduble, inevitable
enevitable, inevitable
enexpensive, inexpensive
enexperience, inexperience

enfachuashen, infatuate(tion)
enfachuate, infatuate
enfallible, infallible
enfaltrate, infiltrate
enfaluble, infallible
enfansy, infant(ncy)
enfant, infant
enfantry, infantry
enfatchuashen, infatuate(tion)
enfatuate, infatuate
enfecshus, infect(ious)
enfect, infect
enfekshen, infect(ion)
enfekt, infect
enfeltrate, infiltrate
enfenativly, infinite(tively)
enfentre, infantry
enfereorety, inferior(ity)
enferior, inferior
enfestructure, infrastructure
enfeureate, infuriate
enfiltrate, infiltrate
enfinetly, infinite(ly)
enfinite, infinite
enfirmary, infirmary
enfirmation, inform(ation)
enfistructure, infrastructure
enflammation, inflammation
enflashen, inflate(tion)
enflate, inflate
enfleksuble, inflexible
enflemashen, inflammation
enflewanse, influence
enflexible, inflexible
enflicked, inflict
enflict, inflict
enflimation, inflammation
enflimshen, inflammation
enfluensable, influence(able)

enfluence, influence
enflumation, inflammation
enforce,*,ed,cing,ement,er, SUPPORT, TO BACK
enform, inform
enformal, informal
enformant, informant
enformation, inform(ation)
enfraction, infraction
enfrakshen, infraction
enfrared, infrared
enfrastructure, infrastructure
enfrekwent, infrequent
enfrequent, infrequent
enfrured, infrared
enfugen, infuse(sion)
enfujen, infuse(sion)
enfultrate, infiltrate
enfunsy, infant(ncy)
enfunt, infant
enfuntre, infantry
enfuriate, infuriate
enfurmashen, inform(ation)
enfurmery, infirmary
enfuse, infuse
enfushen, infuse(sion)
engage,*,ed,ging,ement, TO PUT INTO MOTION, DIRECT ATTENTION
enge, inch
engect, inject
engection, inject(ion)
engekshen, inject(ion)
engen, engine
engeneer, engineer
engenious, ingenious
engenuity, ingenuity
engenyus, ingenious
enger, injure / anger
engest, ingest
enget, ingot

engine,*, *MACHINE/DEVICE USED FOR POWER/ PROPELLING*

engineer,*,red,ring, *PUT ITEMS TOGETHER TO BECOME SOMETHING ELSE*

enginuety, ingenuity
engoement, enjoy(ment)
engoeuble, enjoy(able)
engoiment, enjoy(ment)
engolf, engulf
engot, ingot
engoy, enjoy
engoyuble, enjoy(able)
engrain, ingrain

engrave,*,ed,ving,er, *TO MARK/CARVE TEXT/ SYMBOLS INTO SOMETHING*

engredient, ingredient
enguish, anguish

engulf,*,fed,fing, *TAKE IN, OVERCOME*

engun, engine
enguneer, engineer
engury, injure(ry)
engustes, injustice
engut, ingot
enhabetent, inhabit(ant)
enhabit, inhabit
enhabitency, inhabit(ancy)
enhalant, inhalant
enhalation, inhale(lation)
enhale, inhale

enhance,*,ed,cing,ement, *MAKE MORE APPEALING*

enharent, inherent
enharet, inherit
enharitance, inherit(ance)
enharmonic, inharmonic
enhebit, inhibit
enhelashen, inhale(lation)
enherent, inherent
enherit, inherit
enheritance, inherit(ance)

enhewmane, inhumane
enhibishen, inhibit(ion)
enhibit, inhibit
enhosbatalety,inhospitable(ality)
enhosbitable, inhospitable
enhubishen, inhibit(ion)
enhulashen, inhale(lation)
enhumane, inhumane
eni, any
enialate, annihilate
enibishen, inhibit(ion)
enibode, anybody
enielate, annihilate
enig, inning

enigma,*,atic, *not explainable, not understood (or see enema or anemia)*

enigrate, integrate
enima, enema /anemia
enime, enemy
enimut, intimate
enindashen, inundate(tion)
enindate, inundate
ening, inning
enipropreut, inappropriate
eniquality, inequal(ity)
eircom, intercom
enirelate, interrelate
enirgetek, energetic
enirgy, energy
enirlude, interlude
enirmission, intermission
enirnet, internet
enirsculastic, interscholastic
enirsection, innersection
enirtwine, intertwine
enirupt, interrupt
enirvene, intervene
enirview, interview
enirvue, interview

enishiashen, initiate(tion)
enishul, initial
enisthezia, anesthesia
enitial, initial
enitiate, initiate
enitiation, initiate(tion)
eniulate, annihilate
enje, inch
enjecshen, inject(ion)
enjekt, inject
enjen, engine
enjeneer, engineer
enjenuedy, ingenuity
enjenuity, ingenuity
enjest, ingest
enjin, engine
enjineer, engineer
enjoement, enjoy(ment)

enjoy,*,yed,ying,yment,yable, *APPRECIATE*

enjoyuble, enjoy(able)
enjuner, engineer
enjure, injure
enjustice, injustice
enk, ink
enkapasitate, incapacitate
enkapasity, incapacitate
enkarserade, incarcerate
enker, anchor /incur
enkerej, encourage /anchor(age)
enkewbate, incubate
enklin, incline
enkling, inkling
enklood, include
enklose, enclose
enkloshur, enclose(sure)
enkloze, enclose
enklud, include
enklunashen, incline(nation)
enklusev, inclusive

enklushen, inclusion
enkompus, encompass
enkomputent, incompetent
enkonsistent, inconsistent
enkore, encore
enkoreg, encourage /anchor(age)
enkoreguble, incorrigible
enkorpurate, incorporate
enkownter, encounter
enkreduble, incredible
enkreese, increase
enkremunate, incriminate
enkrument, increment
enkum, income
enkumbent, incumbent
enkumpatuble, incompatible
enkumpus, encompass
enkunsiduret, inconsiderate
enkunsistent, inconsistent
enkunvenyunt, inconvenient
enkupasitate, incapacitate
enkurable, incurable
enkurekt, incorrect
enkwesishun, inquisition
enkwire, inquire(ry)
enkwisative, inquisitive
enland, inland
enlarge,*,ed,ging,ement,er,*MAKE BIGGER/GREATER*
enlargment, enlarge(ment)
enlarje, enlarge
enlaw, in-law
enles, unless
enlest, enlist
enlet, inlet
enlighten,*,ned,ning,nment, *ACHIEVE GREATER*
   KNOWLEDGE
enlist,*,ted,ting,tment, *SIGN-UP, JOIN SOMETHING*
enliten, enlighten
enlund, inland

enmachure, immature
enmade, inmate
enmate, inmate
enmature, immature
ennacurate, innacurate
enner, inner
enoberative, inoperable(ative)
enocence, innocence
enocreate, inaugurate
enodible, inaudible
enof, enough
enogreashen, inaugurate(tion)
enogreate, inaugurate
enogurate, inaugurate
enonimus, anonymous
enonseade, enunciate
enoperable, inoperable
enopurtune, inopportune
enopurative, inoperable(ative)
enopurtunity, inopportune(nity)
enorgetek, energetic
enorgy, energy
enormis, enormous
enormous,sly, *GIGANTIC/BIGGEST*
enormus, enormous
enosent, innocence(nt)
enotable, inaudible
enouf, enough
enough, *TIME TO STOP*
enovadef, innovate(tive)
enovate, innovate
enovative, innovate(tive)
enowe, annoy
enownse, announce
enoy, annoy
enoyens, annoy(ance)
enpatient, inpatient
enpersonate, impersonate
enpli, imply

enpolite, impolite
enpolse, impulse
enpose, impose
enposibul, impossible
enposter, imposter
enposuble, impossible
enpound, impound
enpoverish, impoverish
enpownd, impound
enpractical, impractical
enprasise, imprecise
enpravize, improvise
enprecise, imprecise
enprecise, imprecise
enpregnable, impregnable
enpregnate, impregnate
enpreshen, impress(sion)
enpresise, imprecise
enpresive, impress(sive)
enpressed, impress(sed)
enprint, imprint
enprison, imprison
enprobuble, improbable
enpromptu, impromptu
enpromtu, impromptu
enpropable, improbable
enproper, improper
enprove, improve
enprovement, improve(ment)
enprovisation, improvise(sation)
enprovise, improvise
enprovusashen, improvise(sation)
enprufe, improve
enpruve, improve
enpruvize improvise
enpulite, impolite
enpulse, impulse
enpulsef, impulse(sive)
enpulsive, impulse(sive)
enput, input

enqubate, incubate
enquesidev, inquisitive
enquire, inquire
enquisadev, inquisitive
enquisition, inquisition
enquisitive, inquisitive
enquizeshen, inquisition
enraj, enrage
enrage, *, ed,ging,ement, *GREAT ANGER/RAGE*
enrech, enrich
enrich, hes,hed,hing,hment, *MAKE BETTER/FINER*
enjekshen, interject(ion)
enrol, enroll
enroll, *,led,ling,lment, *JOIN, ENLIST*
enrolment, enroll(ment)
ensabordinate, insubordinate
ensadent, incident
ensafishent, insufficient
ensakure, insecure
ensakuredy, insecure(rity)
ensakurity, insecure(rity)
ensalate, insulate
ensane, insane
ensanetashen, insanitary(ation)
ensanety, insane(nity)
ensanidy, insane(nity)
ensanitary, insanitary
ensanitashen, insanitary(ation)
ensasheuble, insatiable
ensatiable, insatiable
ensaulvent, insolvent
ensbarashen, inspire(ration)
enscribe, inscribe
enscription, inscription
ensebordinate, insubordinate
enseam, inseam
ensect, insect
ensecticide, insecticide
ensecure, insecure

ensedent, incident
ensedius, insidious
ensegnea, insignia
ensegnifukent, insignificant
ensejen, incision
ensekt, insect
ensektaside, insecticide
enselashen, insulate(tion)
ensemanation, inseminate(tion)
ensem, inseam
enseminate, inseminate
ensen, ensign
ensenarate, incinerate
ensense, incense
ensenseer, insincere
ensensible, insensible
ensensitive, insensitive
ensentive, incentive
ensentuf, incentive
ensenuashen, insinuate(tion)
ensenuate, insinuate
ensepshen, incept(ion)
ensept, incept
enserekshen, insurrection
ensermowntible, insurmountable
ensershen, insert(ion)
ensert, insert
ensest, incest / insist
ensh, inch
ensher, ensure / insure
enshiranse, insure(rance)
enshree, entry / entree
enshure, insure
enshurence, insure(rance)
enside, inside
ensident, incident
ensidious, insidious
ensidnea, insignia
ensigen, incision

ensight, insight
ensign, *, *MILITARY RANK*
ensignia, insignia
ensignifukent, insignificant
ensiklopedia, encyclopedia
ensikure, insecure
ensikuredy, insecure(rity)
ensilate, insulate
ensilin, insulin
ensimanashen, inseminate(tion)
ensimanate, inseminate
ensiklopedia, encyclopedia
ensin, ensign
ensinarate, incinerate
ensincere, insincere
ensinsative, insensitive
ensinse, incense
ensinsuble, insensible
ensinuashen, insinuate(tion)
ensinuate, insinuate
ensirection, insurrection
ensishen, incision
ensist, insist
ensistent, insistent
ensite, inside / insight
ensiteful, insight(ful)
ensiteus, insidious
ensition, incision
enskribe, inscribe
enskripshen, inscription
ensoluble, insoluble
ensolvable, insolvable
ensolvent, insolvent
ensomnia, insomnia
ensovent, insolvent
ensoyuble, insoluble
ensparashen, inspire(ration)
enspecshen, inspect(ion)
enspect, inspect

enspection, inspect(ion)
enspekshen, inspect(ion)
enspekt, inspect
enspire, inspire
enspuration, inspire(ration)
enstall, install
enstance, instance
enstant, instant
enstantaneous, instantaneous
enstatute, institute
enstatution, instute(tion)
enstead, instead
ensted, instead
enstenked, instinct
enstense, instance
enstetushen, instute(tion)
enstigate, instigate
enstill, instill
enstinct, instinct
enstinse, instance
enstintaneusly, instantaneous(ly)
enstitute, institute
enstol, install
enstolashen, install(ation)
enstrament, instrument
enstriment, instrument
enstrucshen, instruct(ion)
enstruct, instruct
enstruction, instruct(ion)
enstrukt, instruct
enstrument, instrument
enstrumental, instrument(al)
enstugate, instigate
enstunt, instant
enstuntly, instant(ly)
ensubordinate, insubordinate
ensucure, insecure
ensufishent, insufficient
ensugnifakent, insignificant

ensulate, insulate
ensulation, insulate(tion)
ensulin, insulin
ensult, insult
ensunseer, insincere
ensure, insure
ensure,*,ed,ring, *GUARANTEE/PROMISE* (or see insure)
ensurkle, encircle
ensurmountable, insurmountable
ensurrection, insurrection
ensurshen, insert(ion)
ensurt, insert
ensyklopedia, encyclopedia
ent, end /and
entacate, indicate
entact, intact
entaferance, interfere(rance)
entager, integer
entagral, integral
entagrate, integrate
entak, intact / intake
entalect, intellect
entalectual, intellect(ual)
entamet, intimate
entangible, intangible
entangle,*,ed,ling,ement, *TO GET MIXED UP IN*
entanjuble, intangible
entatee, entity
enteger, integer
entegral, integral
entegrate, integrate
entegrity, integrity
entegrude, integrity
entekashen, indicate(tion)
entelagents, intelligent(nce)
entellect, intellect
entelugint, intelligent
entenation, intonate(tion)

entend, intend
entense, intense
entenshin, intent(ion)
entensity, intense(sity)
entensuve, intense(sive)
entent, intent
enter, entero, *PREFIX INDICATING "INTESTINE" MOST OFTEN MODIFIES THE WORD*
enter,*,red,ring, *GO INTO*
entercede, intercede
entercept, intercept
entercom, intercom
enterconnect, interconnect
entercourse, intercourse
enterd, enter(ed)
enterfere, interfere
enterference, interfere(rance)
entergekshen, interject(ion)
enterim, interim
enterior, interior
enterject, interject
enterlock, interlock
enterlude, interlude
entermediary, intermediary
entermingle, intermingle
entermission, intermission
entern, intern
enternal, internal
enternational, international
enternet, internet
enterogate, interrogate
enterpreneur, entrepreneur
enterpret, interpret
enterpretation, interpretation
enterprise,*,sing,*USE AMBITION TO TAKE ON RISKS*
enterrelate, interrelate
enterrogate, interrogate
enterrupt, interrupt
enterscholastic, interscholastic

entersperse, intersperse
enterstate, interstate
entertain,*,ned,ning,nment,ner, *AMUSE/ENGAGE*
  SOMEONE
entertainer, entertain(er)
entertainment, entertain(ment)
entertwine, intertwine
enterval, interval
entervene, intervene
enterview, interview
enterwoven, interwoven
entestine, intestine
entety, entity
entever, endeavor
enthooseastik, enthuse(siastic)
enthrall,*,led,ling, *OVERWHELMED WITH AWE*
enthrol, enthrall
enthuse,ed,siasm,siastic,siastically, *TO HAVE*
  INTEREST/ENERGY FOR
enthuseastek, enthuse(siastic)
enthuziazm, enthuse(siasm)
entice,*,ed,cing, *APPEAL TO, ALLURE, SUCCUMB TO*
entid, end(ed)
entidle, entitle
entiger, integer
entigo, indigo
entigral, integral
entigration, integrate(tion)
entil, until
entilect, intellect
entimadate, intimidate
'entimate, intimate
entimidate, intimidate
entina, antenna
entinse, intense
entinsive, intense(sive)
entint, intent
entintion, intent(ion)
entire,ely,ety, *COMPLETE, THE WHOLE THING*

entirest, interest
entirle, entire(ly)
entirnet, internet
entirpreneur, entrepreneur
entirprize, enterprise
entirprutashen, interpretation
entirty, entire(ty)
entisepate, anticipate
entitle,*,ed,ling,ement, *RIGHTS, AUTHORITY TO*
entity,ties, *A BEING WITH HUMAN FORM*
entlis, endless
ento, into
entoishen, intuit(ion)
entolerable, intolerable
entonate, intonate
entoor, endure
entoxicate, intoxicate
entra, entree
entraduction, introduce(ction)
entraduse, introduce
entrakit, intricate
entramural, intramural
entrance,ed,cing, *PLACE/WAY TO GET IN*
entranet, intranet
entrapreneur, entrepreneur
entraspect, introspect
entravenous, intravenous
entray, entree
entree,*, *A MEAL, FOOD SERVING* (or see entry)
entrege, intrigue
entrense, entrance
entrensic, intrinsic
entrepreneur,*,rial,rialism,rism,rship, *ONE WHO*
  RISKS FINANCING A NEW BUSINESS/ENTERPRISE
entres, entry(ries) /entree(s)
entrest, interest
entricate, intricate
entrigue, intrigue
entrinsic, intrinsic

entroduce, introduce
entrospect, introspect
entrovert, introvert
entrude, intrude
entrudukshen, introduce(ction)
entruduse, introduce
entrugen, instrusion
entrumural, intramural
entrunse, entrance
entrupreneur, entrepreneur
entrushen, intrusion
entrust,*,ted,ting, *LEAVE THE CARE OF SOMETHING/*
  SOMEONE TO ANOTHER (or see interest)
entry,ries,rant, *OPENING GOING IN, ENTER INTO* (or
  see entree)
entuative, intuit(ive)
entufere, interfere
entuger, integer
entugrate, integrate
entuishen, intuit(ion)
entuit, intuit
entunate, intonate
entur, enter
enturem, interim
enturlock, interlock
enturpreneur, entrepreneur
enturn, intern
enturnal, internal
enturnalize, internal(ize)
enturpret, interpret
enturprise, enterprise
entursept, intercept
enturtane, entertain
enturtaner, entertain(er)
enturtanment, entertain(ment)
entutes, entity(ties)
entyre, entire
enubelidy, inability
enubishen, inhibit(ion)

enuf, enough
enume, enemy
enunciate,*,ed,ting, SPEAK CLEARLY/SPECIFICALLY
enundate, inundate
enunseate, enunciate
enupresheative, inappreciative
enprochible, inapproachable
enpropreut, inappropriate
enur, inner
enurcom, intercom
enurelate, interrelate
enurgee, energy
enurgekshen, interject(ion)
enurim, interim
enurjetek, energetic
enurlude, interlude
enurmediary, intermediary
enurmingle, intermingle
enurmission, intermission
enurmost, innermost
enurnet, internet
enursculastic, interscholastic
enursecshen, intersection
enursperse, intersperse
enurt, inert
enurupt, interrupt
enurval, interval
enurvene, intervene
enurview, interview
enurvue, interview
enurwoven, interwoven
enuscapuble, inescapable
enusense, innocence
enusent, innocence(nt)
enuther, another
enuvate, innovate
envade, invade
envalid, invalid
envalope, envelope

envaluable, invaluable
envariable, invariable
envashen, invasion
envasion, invasion
envatashen, invitation
envate, invade
envaulve, involve
enve, envy
enved, envy(vied)
envelope,*,ed,ping,ement, TO ENCLOSE/ WRAP TO
PROTECT SOMETHING
envensable, invincible
envenshen, invent(ion)
envent, invent
enventory, inventory
enverdebrae, invertebrate
envereably, invariable(ly)
envert, invert
envertebrate, invertebrate
enves, envy(vies)
envest, invest
envestagashen, investigate(tion)
envestigate, investigate
envestmant, invest(ment)
enveuble, enviable
enveus, envious
enviable, SOMEONE WISHING THEY HAD
envigorate, invigorate
envilope, envelope
envincible, invincible
envintory, inventory
enviormental, environment(al)
envious, BEING JEALOUS
environment,*,tal,tally, EXTERIOR SURROUNDINGS
envisability, invisible(bility)
envisible, invisible
envitation, invitation
envizable, invisible
envoice, invoice

envoluntary, involuntary
envolve, involve
envoyse, invoice
envulid, invalid
envurdabrae, invertebrate
envurt, invert
envy,vies,vied,vious,viously,viousness,viable,
WANT SOMETHING THAT SOMEONE ELSE HAS
enward, inward
enword, inward
enwrech, enrich
enwrich, enrich
enwroll, enroll
eny, any
enzerkle, encircle
enzide, inside
ep, epi, PREFIX INDICATING "OVER/NEAR" MOST OFTEN
MODIFIES THE WORD
epademic, epidemic
epareshin, apparition
eparition, apparition
epart, apart
epartmint, apartment
epasenter, epicenter
epasode, episode
epazode, episode
epeal, appeal
epeel, appeal
eperatus, apparatus
eperinse, appearance
eperint, apparent
eperul, apparel
epicenter,*, CENTRAL SPOT OF EARTHQUAKE
epidemic,*, MANY LIVES AT RISK IN AN AREA
episode,*, PARTS OF AN ONGOING SHOW
epizode, episode
epliense, appliance
eplod, applaud
eply, apply

eqwel, equal
eqwerium, aquarium
er, PREFIX INDICATING EMPHASIS ON THE ACTIVITY OR DOING OF A VERB (or see ear/err/air/heir)
erabrochuble, irreproachable
eradesent, iridescent
eradic, erratic / erotic
eradicate,*,ed,ting,tion, ELIMINATE, DISPOSE
eradukashen, eradicate(tion)
eragardles, irregardless
eragashen, irrigate(tion)
eragate, irrigate
eragation, irrigate(tion)
eraguardless, irregardless
erain, arraign
erakned, arachnid
eran, arraign
erand, errand
erange, arrange
erangment, arrange(ment)
eranment, arraign(ment)
eraplasible, irreplacable
eraprochuble, irreproachable
erasbonsuble, irresponsible
erasbonzuble, irresponsible
erase,*,ed,sing,er,eable, ELIMINATE COMPLETELY
erashinul, irrational
erasistible, irresistible
erasol, aerosol
eraspective, irrespective
eraspektif, irrespective
erasponsuble, irresponsible
erasponzuble, irresponsible
eratashen, irritate(tion)
eratate, irritate
eratible, irritable
eratic, erratic / erotic
erational, irrational
eratrevible, irretrievable

eraudik, erotic
eravokable, irrevocable
eray, array
erayn, arraign
erazestuble, irresistible
erazistuble, irresistible
erb, herb
erbal, herb(al)
erbashis, herb(aceous)
erbel, herb(al)
erbivore, herbivore
erborne, airborne
erbul, herb(al)
erbulism, herb(alism)
erbulist, herb(alist)
erchen, urchin
erchin, urchin
erea, area
erebrochuble, irreproachable
erect,*,ted,ting,tion, SET STRAIGHT UP, RAISE
ered, arid
eredesent, iridescent
ereer, arrear
eregardles, irregardless
eragashen, irrigate(tion)
eregate, irrigate
eregation, irrigate(tion)
eregeno, oregano
eregewler, irregular
eregler, irregular
erekshen, erect(ion)
erelavense, irrelevant(nce)
erelavent, irrelevant
ereluvense, irrelevant(nce)
ereluvint, irrelevant
erena, arena
ereng, earring
ereperuble, irreparable
erepirable, irreparable

epodemec, epidemic
epoint, appoint
epointment, appointment
epoynt, appoint
epoyntment, appointment
eprasal, appraisal
epreciate, appreciate
eprentis, apprentice
epresheate, appreciate
eprintise, apprentice
epruvel, approval
epsorb, absorb
epstane, abstain
epsurd, absurd
eptikate, abdicate
epusode, episode
epzorb, absorb
epzurd, absurd
equable,ly,bility,eness, IS EQUAL TO, SAME IN VALUE, UNIFORM
equal,*,led,ling,able,lize,lizes,lizer,lizing,lization, SAME AS, EQUIVALENT, UNIFORM
equality, OF BEING THE SAME, EQUIVALENT
equate,*,ed,ting, COMPARE/BALANCE/MAKE UNIFORM
equation,*, BALANCE OF BOTH SIDES
equator,*, ONE OF TWO HALVES OF A PLANET/STAR
equel, equal
equi, PREFIX INDICATING "EQUAL" MOST OFTEN MODIFIES THE WORD
equil, equal
equilibrium, balance
equinox,es, WHEN DAY/NIGHT ARE IN EQUAL PARTS
equip,*,pped,pment, TO MAKE READY FOR A TASK, EVENT
equity,ties, HOW MUCH YOU OWN, JUSTICE/RIGHTS
equivalent,tly,ncy, THE SAME AS, EQUAL
equivilense, equivalent(ncy)
eqwareum, aquarium
eqwashin, equation

erisol, aerosol
erispective, irrespective
erispektif, irrespective
erisponsuble, irresponsible
eristocrat, aristocrat
eritate, irritate
erithmatic, arithmetic
eritrevuble, irretrievable
erive, arrive
erivokuble, irrevocable
erizisduble, irresistible
erj, urge
erjense, urge(nce) /urge(ncy)
erjinse, urge(nce) /urge(ncy)
erjint, urge(nt)
erk, irk
erle, early
erloom, heirloom
erly, early
ern, earn /urn
ernest, earnest
ero, arrow
erobik, aerobic
erochun, erosion
erode,*,ed,ding,osion, *WEAR, WEAR, WASH AWAY*
erodik, erotic
erodynamic, aerodynamic
eroganse, arrogance
erogate, irrigate
erogint, arrogance(nt)
eroma, aroma
eromadek, aroma(tic)
erond, errand
eronic, ironic
eror, error
erosbonsuble, irresponsible
erosion, *WEARING, WASHING AWAY*
erosponsuble, irresponsible
erote, erode

ereprochible, irreproachable
erepruble, irreparable
erepurable, irreparable
erekshen, erect(ion)
ereng, earring
erer, error
eresistible, irresistible
erespective, irrespective
erest, arrest
erestokrat, aristocrat
eretashen, irritate(tion)
eretibul, irritable
eretrevible, irretrievable
eretrievable, irretrievable
ereu, area
ereul, aerial
erevocable, irrevocable
erg, urge
ergense, urge(ncy)
ergent, urge(nt)
erginsy, urge(ncy)
ergint, urge(nt)
eri, awry
eribrochuble, irreproachable
erid, arid
eridesent, iridescent
erift, arrive(d)
erigardles, irregardless
erigashen, irrigate(tion)
erigate, irrigate
erigation, irrigate(tion)
eriguardless, irregardless
erind, errand
ering, earring /err(ing)
eriplasible, irreplacable
eriproachable, irreproachable
erir, error
erisbonsuble, irresponsible
erisistible, irresistible

erotic,ca,cally, *SEXUAL AROUSAL/SENSATION*
erosponzuble, irresponsible
err, *SHORT FOR ERROR, TO MAKE A MISTAKE* (or see ear /air /heir)
errand,*, *TRAVEL TO PERFORM A TASK*
erratate, irritate
erratic,cally, *SUDDEN UNPREDICTABLE MOVEMENTS, THOUGHTS*
errogate, irrigate
error,*, *NOT CORRECT*
ershen, urchin
erashunal, irrational
ertearial, arterial
erth, earth
erubt, erupt /irrupt
erubtif, erupt(ive) /irrupt(ive)
erubtion, erupt(ion) /irrupt(ion)
erugardles, irregardless
erugashen, irrigate(tion)
erugate, irrigate
erugation, irrigate(tion)
eruguardless, irregardless
eruplasuble, irreplacable
eruprochuble, irreproachable
erupshen, erupt(ion) /irrupt(ion)
erupt,*,ted,ting,tion,tive,tively,tible, *FORMING BULGE WHICH OPENS/BURSTS* (or see irrupt)
eruptif, erupt(ive) /irrupt(ive)
erur, error
erusbonsuble, irresponsible
erusistible, irresistible
erusol, aerosol
eruspective, irrespective
eruspektif, irrespective
erusponsuble, irresponsible
erutashen, irritate(tion)
erutate, irritate
erutible, irritable
erutrevible, irretrievable

esiguous, assiduous
esfikseat, asphyxiate
esfixeat, asphyxiate
esil, easel
esilum, asylum
esily, easily
esimble, assemble
esimelate, assimilate
esimetric, asymmetric
esind, ascend
esindant, ascendant
esine, assign
esinment, assignment
esinse, essence
esinshul, essential
esent, ascent /assent
esirt, assert
esist, assist
eskape, escape
eskort, escort
eskulater, escalator
esleep, asleep
esm, ism
esment, easement
esmint, easement
esofigus, esophagus
esnt, isn't
esolt, assault
esophagus,*, *TUBE IN THE THROAT*
esorted, assorted
esosheate, associate
esoshiate, associate
esoteric,cal,cally, *KNOWLEDGE GAINEC BY A FEW*
especially, *PARTICULARLY, MOST CERTAINLY*
esperugus, asparagus
espeshulee, especially
espir, aspire
essay,*, *WRITE ABOUT A SPECIFIC POINT/THING*

essence,*, *THE AMBIANCE OR BASIC SENSE OF THE OVERALL*
essential,*,lly, *MUST HAVE, MOST IMPORTANT*
est, east
estableshment, establish(ment)
establish,es,ed,hing,hment, *TO CREATE A BASIS, BEGINNING*
estamashen, estimate(tion)
esteem, esteem
esteem,*,med,ming, *BEST REGARDS FOR, ADMIRE*
esteengwish, extinguish
estem, esteem
estemut, estimate
estern, east(ern)
estimashen, estimate(tion)
estimate,*,ed,ting,tion,able,ably,ableness, *TO APPROXIMATE BASED ON KNOWLEDGE*
estirle, east(erly)
estonesh, astonish
estragen, estrogen
estrawlegy, astrology
estrengent, astringent
estringent, astringent
estris, estrus
estrogen, *A HORMONE CREATED BY FEMALES BEGINNING AT PUBERTY*
estrology, astrology
estronume, astronomy
estrugen, estrogen
estrus,rum,ual, *WHEN CONCEPTION IS POSSIBLE*
estumashen, estimate(tion)
estumit, estimate
esturle, east(erly)
esue, issue
esuense, issue(uance)
esuinse, issue(uance)
esul, easel
esume, assume
esunse, essence

erutuble, irritable
eruvokuble, irrevocable
eruzistuble, irresistible
es, is/ ease
esa, essay
esael, assail
esail, assail
esalt, assault
esanse, essence
esasen, assassin
esault, assault
esay, essay
esbeshulee, especially
escalate,*,ed,ting,tor, *TO RISE*
escalator,*, *A CONVEYOR WHICH CARRIES/MOVES ITEMS/PEOPLE*
escape,*,ed,ping, *TO GET AWAY FROM WITHOUT PERMISSION*
escort,*,ted,ting, *SOMEONE WHO ACCOMPANIES TO ASSIST*
esculator, escalator
esdeem, esteem
ese, ease /easy
esemble, assemble
esemulate, assimilate
esence, essence
esend, ascend
esenshul, essential
esent, ascent /assent
esential, essential
esert, assert
esesmint, assessment
eshamed, ashamed
esherance, assure(rance)
eshew, issue
eshu, issue
eshurance, assure(rance)
eside, aside
esidjewus, assiduous

esylum, asylum
et, eat/eight/ate
etable, edible
etach, attach
etack, attack
etaen, attain
etak, attack
etalek, italic
etane, attain
etatch, attach
etcetera, etc.(et cetera), *MORE OF THE SAME*
etch,hes,hed,hing, *CARVE INTO(or see edge /itch)*
ete, eddy
etempt, attempt
etemt, attempt
etenchin, attention
etend, attend
etenshin, attention
etenshun, attention
eternal,llly,nity,nize, *FOREVER*
etheric, *ALL THINGS AROUND AND BEYOND THE EARTH*
ethic,*,cal,cally, *JUDGEMENT OF CONDUCT/ BEHAVIOR*
ethnac, ethnic
ethnic,*,*GROUP OF PEOPLE WITH THE SAME LANGUAGE, TRAITS*
ethnuk, ethnic
ethrik, etheric
ethuk, ethic
etikit, etiquette
etimt, attempt
etinchon, attention
etinshun, attention
etiquette, *RULES OF PROPER BEHAVIOR*
etire, attire
etrakshun, attraction
etrakt, attract
etroshus, atrocious
etself, itself
etsetara, etcetera

etsulf, itself
eturnal, eternal
eturney, attorney
eu, ewe/ you/ yew
eu, *PREFIX INDICATING "GOOD" MOST OFTEN MODIFIES THE WORD*
eucalyptus, *A TREE*
euforia, euphoria
eul, eel
eunaform, uniform
euphoria,ic, *FEELS JOYFUL/UNREAL*
euraneum, uranium
eurinery, urinary
eutopea, utopia
evacuate, evacuate
evacuate,*,ed,ting,tion, *TO EMPTY FROM A PLACE AS EXPECTED*
evade,*,ed,ding,asion, *TO NOT BE/ THINK/ BEHAVE AS EXPECTED*
evadins, evident(nce)
evakuashen, evacuate(tion)
evakuate, evacuate
evale, evil(lly)
evaluashen, evaluate(tion)
evaluate,*,ed,ting,tion, *TO STUDY/REVIEW FOR FINAL JUDGEMENT*
evalushen, evolution
evalutionery, evolution(ary)
evan, even
evanly, even(ly)
evaperate, evaporate
evaperation, evaporate(tion)
evaporate,*,ed,ting,tion, *LIQUID/SOLID CONVERTED INTO GAS*
evapurashen, evaporate(tion)
evapurate, evaporate
evarewer, every(where)
evasef, evasion(ive)
evashen, evasion
evasion,ive, *TO NOT BE/THINK/BEHAVE AS EXPECTED*

evate, evade
evedins, evident(nce)
evekshin, evict(ion)
evekt, evict
even,*,ed,ning,nly,nness,ntuality, *LEVEL WITH (TOO MANY DEFINITIONS PLEASE SEE STANDARD DICTIONARY)*
evendful, eventful
evening,*, *AFTER 6 O'CLOCK P.M.*
evenshuele, event(ually)
event,*,tual,tually,tful,tfully,tfullness, *SOMETHING OUT OF THE ORDINARY, WILL HAPPEN IN THE FUTURE*
eventful,llly, *SOMETHING OUT OF THE ORDINARY*
eventualy, event(ually)
ever,rmore, *AT ANY TIME*
everewar, every(where)
evervesent, effervescent
every,yone,ything,ybody,ywhere,yday, *ALL*
eves, eaves
evict,*,ted,ting,tion, *TO FORCIBLY REMOVE*
evidens, evident(nce)
evident,*,tly,dance, *PROOF OF BEING SEEN, UNDERSTOOD*
evikshen, evict(ion)
eviktion, evict(ion)
evil,*,lly,lness, *OPPOSITE OF LOVE, THREATENING*
evilitionary, evolution(ary)
evin, even
evindful, eventful
evinly, even(ly)
evinshuale, event(ually)
evint, event
evintualy, event(ually)
evir, ever
evneng, evening
evning, evening
evol, evil
evolushenary, evolution(ary)

evolution,*,nary, *THE ACT OF EVOLVING*
evolvd, evolve(d)
evolve,*,ed,ving, *ADAPT, GAIN WISDOM, TRANSFORM*
evon, even
evoneng, evening
evor, ever
evre, every
evrebode, every(body)
evreda, every(day)
evretheng, every(thing)
evrewer, every(where)
evrewun, every(one)
evriwun, every(one)
evry, every(one,thing,body,where,day)
evryday, every(day)
evrywere, every(where)
evs, eaves
evudens, evident(nce)
evudins, evident(nce)
evudintly, evident(ly)
evul, evil
evule, evil(lly)
evulushin, evolution
evuneng, evening
evunle, even(ly)
ew, ewe /you /yew
eway, away
ewe,*, *FEMALE SHEEP (or see you or yew)*
ewrekt, erect
ex, *PREFIX INDICATING "FORMER/OUTSIDE/ EXTERNAL" MOST OFTEN MODIFIES THE WORD*
exact,tly,tness,ted,ting, *SPECIFICALLY*
exagerate, exaggerate
exageration, exaggerate(tion)
exaggerate,*,ted,ting,tion, *TO STRETCH, ELONGATE THE TRUE FORM*
exajurashen, exaggerate(tion)
exakude, execute
exakushen, execute(tion)

exale, exhale
examenashen, examine(nation)
examine,*,ed,ning,nation, *TO CLOSELY/CAREFULLY OBSERVE*
example,*, *SIMILAR TO, USED TO DESCRIBE*
exampul, example
examunashen, examine(nation)
exaqushen, execute(tion)
exasperate,*,ed,ting,tion, *GREATLY ANNOY/ANGER*
exaspiration, exasperate
exaspurate, exasperate
exaustshen, exhaust(ion)
exblanashen, explanation
exblode, explode
exbloetashen, exploit(ation)
exblor, explore
exbloshun, explosion
exblunashen, explanation
exborashen, expire(ration)
exbort, export
exbortashen, export(ation)
exbos, expose
express, express
exburashen, expire(ration)
excavate,*,ed,ting,tion, *TO DIG FOR SOMETHING*
exceed,*,ded,ding,dingly,*DO MORE THAN EXPECTED THAN NORMAL/AVERAGE* (or see accel)
excel,*,lled,lling,llence,llency, *PERFORM BETTER*
exceluration, accelerate(tion)
excellent,tly,tly, *OUTSTANDING*
excelurashen, accelerate(tion)
exceluration, accelerate(tion)
excenshuate, accentuate
excentuate, accentuate
excepshen, except(ion)
except,*,ted,ting,tion,tional, *THIS BUT NOT THAT, EXTRACT FROM* (or see accept)
excerpt,*,ted, *A SMALL PART OF THE WRITTEN WHOLE*
excesory, accessory

excesorize, accessory(rize)
excess,*,ses,sive,sively, *MORE THAN ENOUGH (or see access)*
exchange,*,ed,ging, *TO TRADE*
excinshuate, accentuate
excite,*,ed,ting,ement,table,tability,tableness, *AROUSE, FEEL TINGLY INSIDE*
exclamation,*,ms,med, *DISPLAY OF FORCE/ ENTHUSIASM/WILLFULLNESS, PUNCTUATED WITH AN EXCLAMATION POINT*
excloot, exclude
exclude,*,ded,ding,sive,sively,usion,usions, *NOT INCLUDED AS PART OF SOMETHING OR GROUP*
excursion,*, *A SHORT TRIP, CHEAP FARE*
excuse,*,ed,sing, *REASONS FOR A PROBLEM BEING*
excuvashen, excavate(tion)
excuvation, excavate(tion)
exdravert, extrovert
exdruvirt, extrovert
execute,*,ed,ting,tion, *TO FOLLOW, ENFORCE A PLAN TO KILL WITH UNNATURAL METHODS*
exelarate, exhilarate /accelerate
exema, eczema
exempt,ted,ting,tion, *SET FREE, EXCUSE FROM DUTY/TAXES/RULES/LEGAL HOLDINGS*
exemshen, exempt(ion)
exenshen, except(ion)
exercise,*,ed,sing, *MENTAL/PHYSICAL ACTIVITY FOR IMPROVEMENT* (or see exercise)
exert,*,ted,ting,tion, *PUT FORTH POWER/ENERGY*
exest, exist
exfoliate,*,ed,ling,tion, *LAYERS LIFTING OFF*
exhale,*,ed,ling,lation, *TO BREATH OUT*
exhaust,*,ted,ting,tive,tion, *TO RUN OUT OF, DISCHARGE/FUMES FROM A MOTOR*
exhaustein, exhaust(ion)
exhibit,*,ted,ting,tion, *ON SHOW*
exhilarate,*,ed,ting,tion, *REFRESHING, EXCITING (or see accelerate)*

expense , expense
exsplod , explode
exstase , ecstasy
exstend , extend
exstengwish , extinguish
extract , extract
extravert , extrovert
extreamly , extreme(ly)
extremly , extreme(ly)
exstusee , ecstasy
exsubishen , exhibit(ion)
exsulens , excell(ence)
exsulent , excellent
exsuqushen , execute(tion)
exsurpt , excerpt
exteenkt , extinct

extend,*,ded,ding,nsion,nsive,nsively, TO STRETCH, ADD BEYOND WHAT IS ALREADY
extenquish , extinguish
exterior, OUTSIDE LAYER
external,llly, OUTSIDE OF SOMETHING OR SOMEONE
extinct,tion, DOES NOT EXIST ANY LONGER
extinguish,hes,hed,hing, TO PUT OUT, END
extra, exstro, PREFIX INDICATING "OUTSIDE/
BEYOND" MOST OFTEN MODIFIES THE WORD
extra *, MORE OF THE SAME
extract,*,ted,ting,tion, TO TAKE/DRAW FROM
extravurt , extrovert
extreamly , extreme(ly)
extreme,*,ely,mism, OF THE GREATEST/MOST
extro, exstra, PREFIX INDICATING "OUTSIDE/
BEYOND" MOST OFTEN MODIFIES THE WORD
extrovert,*,ted,tly, OUTGOING/GREGARIOUS
exukushen , execute(tion)
exuqushen , execute(tion)
exqute , execute
exursize , exercise
exurt , exert
exurtion , exert(ion)

exzamen , examine
exzema , eczema
eye,*,ed,ying, ORGAN OF SIGHT (or see "I")
eyebrow,*,hes, HAIR AROUND TOP OF EYES
eyelash,hes, HAIR ON EYELIDS
ez , ease / easy
ezale , easily
ezay , essay
ezbeshulee , especially
ezdragen , estrogen
eze , easy /ease
ezel , easel
ezinshil , essential
ezkort , escort
ezment , easement
ezoteric , esoteric
ezperagus , asparagus
ezsperugus , asparagus
eztablush , establish
ezteem , esteem
eztimate , estimate
eztonish , astonish
eztrawlegy , astrology
eztrogin , estrogen
eztrus , estrus
ezul , easel
ezule , easily

"F"

fabewlus , fabulous
fabewlusly , fabulous(ly)
fable,*, MYTH/LEGEND/STORY
fabrecation , fabricate(tion)
fabrek , fabric
fabrekashin , fabricate(tion)
fabrekate , fabricate

fabric,*, THREADS WOVEN TOGETHER
fabricate,*,ed,ting,tion, TO CREATE, CHANGE FROM
ONE MATERIAL FORM TO ANOTHER
fabrukashen , fabricate(tion)
fabrukate , fabricate
fabuaree , February
fabul , fable
fabules , fabulous / fable(s)
fabulis , fabulous
fabulous,sly, EXCELLENT, WONDERFUL
fabulus , fabulous
fabulusly , fabulous(ly)
facade,*, FALSE FRONT, PHONY
face,*,ed,cing,cial, EXTERIOR FRONT, ON FRONT OF
HEAD (or see phase)
facelty , faculty
facet,*, ONE PLANE/FACE/SIDE OUT OF MANY
facetious,sly, NOT SERIOUS, BEING AMUSING
fachel , facial
fachen , fashion
fachinuble , fashion(able)
fachul , facial
fachun , fashion
fachunible , fashion(able)
facial,*, HAVING TO DO WITH THE FACE
facilitate,*,ed,ting,tion, HELP/ENABLE SUCCESS
facshun , faction
fact,*,tual,tually,tualness, FOR REAL, TRUE
(or see fake(d) /fax/ face(d))
faction,*,nal,nally,nalism, OF MATH, PART OF A
LARGER GROUP
faculty,ties, SKILL OR ABILITY, TEACHING STAFF
fad,*, CURRENT STYLE (or see fade or fate)
fade,*,ed,ding, LOOSE COLOR/PICTURE (or see fate)
fadel , fatal
fadul , fatal
faer , fire
fag,ggot, BUNDLE OF STICKS, CIGARETTE
Fahrenheit, OF THERMOMETERS/TEMPERATURE

fas, phase /face
fasecian, physician
fased, face(d) /fast /phase(d)
fasek, physique /physic
fasel, fossil
faselisd, fossil(ized)
faselitashen, facilitate(tion)
faselitation, facilitate(tion)
faselutate, facilitate
fasener, fastener
faseque, physique
faseshan, physician
fasfate, phosphate
fash, fish
fashel, facial
fashen, fashion
fashenuble, fashion(able)
fashil, facial
fashin, fashion
fashinuble, fashion(able)
fashion,*,ned,ning,nable, *CLOTHING STYLES WITHIN A CERTAIN TIMEFRAME*
fashul, facial
fashun, fashion
fashunebul, fashion(able)
fasician, physician
fasik, physic /physique
fasil, fossil
fasilatashen, facilitate(tion)
fasilatat, facilitate
fasilatation, facilitate(tion)
fasilitate, facilitate
fasiner, fastener
fasing, face(cing) /phase(ing)
fasique, physique
fast,*,ter,ting, *RATE OF SPEED, TO NOT EAT FOOD*
fastener,*, *BUTTONS, ZIPPERS, SNAPS, CLOSURE*
fasul, fossil

fat,tter,ttest,tten,ttening,tty, *LAYER OF FOOD STORE IN MOST LIVING THINGS* (or see fad/fade/fate)
fatal,lly,lity,lities,list, *LIFE THREATENING*
fate,*,ed,eful,efully,eness, *THE BELIEF THAT EVENTS ARE PRE-PLANNED*
fath, faith
father,*,red,ring, *MALE PARENT, NAME FOR A PRIEST*
fathom,*, *MEASUREMENT FOR THE OCEAN DEPTH, DEEP TO UNDERSTAND*
fathur, feather /father
fatigue, fatigue
fatigue,ed, *EXHAUSTION, WEARY*
faucet,*, *PLUMBING DEVICE FOR WATER/LIQUIDS*
faul, foul /fowl /fall
fault,*,ty,tless,tlessly,tily,tly,tiness,tful, *SOMETHING OR SOMEONE TO BLAME, A PROBLEM*
faun,*, *HALF GOAT HALF HUMAN* (or see fawn)
fauna, *ANIMALS OF A REGION*
faund, found
faundashen, foundation
faundation, foundation
faundry, foundry
faunt, found
fauntry, foundry
fausel, fossil
fausfate, phosphate
fausit, faucet
fausphate, phosphate
fauster, foster
fausul, fossil
fauxpas, *ALSO FAUX PAS, A BLUNDER*
faveret, favorite
favor,*,red,ring,rable,rably,rite,rful,rless, *PREFERANCE FOR*
fawcet, faucet
fawdur, fodder
fawel, foul /fowl
fawl, foul /fowl
fawlust, foul(est)

fawn,*, *BABY DEER* (or see faun)
fawnd, fond /found
fawndashen, foundation
fawnt, font /found
fawntry, foundry
fawsel, fossil
fawsilized, fossil(ized)
fawsul, fossil
fawt, fought
fawul, foul /fowl
fax,xes,xed,xing, *SEND A LETTER BY PHONE* (or see facts)
faze, phase
fazek, physique
fazeshan, physician
fe, fee
fear,*,red,ring,rful,rless, *AFRAID, POWERLESSNESS*
feasent, pheasant
feast,*,ted,ting, *GREAT AMOUNT OF FOOD*
feasta, fiesta
feat,*, *PERFORM WITH UNUSUAL ABILITY* (or see feet)
feather,*,red,ring, *BIRD CLOTHES, A DECORATIVE EFFECT*
feature,*,ed,ring, *SPECIAL*
feb, fib
February, *MONTH OF THE YEAR*
febuaree, February
febwuaree, February
fech, fetch
fecher, feature
fecster, fixture
fed, *PAST TENSE OF "FEED"*
fedarashen, federation
fedaration, federation
fedarul, federal
federal,*,lly, *NATIONAL GOVERNMENT*
federation,*, *GROUP OF PEOPLE FORMING UNION*
fediration, federation
fedle, fiddle

fedler, fiddle(r)
fedul, fiddle
fedulize, fertile(lize)
fedurashen, federation
fee,*, COST FOR/TO DO SOMETHING
feecher, feature
feed,*,ding,der,fed, GIVE FOOD TO (or see feet)
feel,*,felt,ling,lings, USE OF TOUCH/EMOTIONS TO SENSE ENVIRONMENT
feeld, field
feer, fear
feest, feast
feesta, fiesta
feet, MORE THAN ONE FOOT (or see feat)
fefer, fever
feferish, fever(ish)
fefir, fever
fefiresh, fever(ish)
fefor, fever
feftee, fifty
fefteen, fifteen
feften, fifteen
fefth, fifth
feftinth, fifteen(th)
feftis, fifty(ties)
fefty, fifty
fefur, fever
fefurish, fever(ish)
feg, fig
fegen, fission
feger, figure
feianse, fiance'
feild, field
fejon, fission
feks, fix
feksdur, fixture
feksher, fixture
fekshun, fiction
fekst, fix(ed)

fekster, fixture
feksus, fix(es)
fekure, figure
felade, fillet
feladendron, philodendron
felanthrepy, philanthropy
felanthropist, philanthropy(pist)
felay, fillet
feld, felt /field /fill(ed)
feldur, filter
fele, fillet /filly
fell, PAST TENSE OF "FALL" (or see fill)
felm, film
felosofy, philosophy
felt, PAST TENSE OF "FEEL", CRUSHED WOOL/COTTON (or see field)
felter, filter
felthe, filthy
feludindron, philodendron
felurmonek, philharmonic
female,*, THE FEMININE, LIFE GIVER
femanen, feminine
femelear, familiar
feminine, THE COMPLIMENT OF MASCULINE
femunin, feminine
fen, fin
fence,*,ed,cing,er, OUTSIDE BARRIER/WALL, A SPORT
fench, finch
fender,*, PART OF A BICYCLE/VEHICLE, A SCREEN, A GUITAR
fenedic, phonetic
fenesh, finish
fenetick, phonetic
fenger, finger
fengernail, fingernail
fengerprint, fingerprint
fengur, finger
fenish, finish

fenker, finger
fenkerprint, fingerprint
fenkur, finger
fenomanen, phenomenon
fenomena, phenomenon
fenominul, phenomenal
fense, fence
fensh, finch
fentur, fender
feonsa, fiance'
fepuary, February
fepyuery, February
fer, fear /for /fir /fur /far /fair /fare
ferbed, forbid
ferbedin, forbid(dden)
ferbid, forbid
ferdelize, fertile(lize)
ferdul, fertile
ferdulizashen, fertile(lization)
fere, ferry/ fairy/ furry
ferefur, forever
ferenhite, Fahrenheit
feres, ferry(ries) /fairy/fairy(ries)
feret, ferret
ferever, forever
fergave, forgave
fergetful, forget(ful)
fergif, forgive
fergifness, forgive(ness)
fergit, forget
fergitful, forget(ful)
fergive, forgive
fergivnes, forgive(ness)
fergot, forgot
fergoten, forgot(tten)
feriner, foreign(er)
ferius, furious
ferlough, furlough
ferlow, furlough

ferm, firm
fermaledy, formal(ity)
fermality, formal(ity)
fermashen, formation
fermation, formation
ferment,*,ted,ting,table,tability,tative, MOVING TOWARDS FERMENTATION
fermentation,nal, ENZYMATIC/CELLULAR REACTION
fern,*, A PLANT
fernachur, furniture
fernecher, furniture
fernes, furnace
fernis, furnace
fernish, furnish
ferniture, furniture
fernus, furnace
fernush, furnish
fero, pharoah /furrow
ferochusle, ferocious(ly)
ferocious,sly,sness, FIERCE, INTENSE
feroshusle, ferocious(ly)
ferotious, ferocious
ferow, furrow /pharoah
ferr, ferri, ferro, ferroso, PREFIX INDICATING "IRON" MOST OFTEN MODIFIES THE WORD
ferret,*, MEMBER OF THE WEASEL FAMILY
ferry,rries,rried,rrying BOAT THAT CROSSES WATER CARRYING THINGS (or see fairy or furry)
fers, fierce /fear(s) /first
fersake, forsake
fersakin, forsake(n)
fersd, first
ferse, fierce
fersest, fierce(st)
fersly, fierce(ly)
fersnis, fierce(ness)
ferst, first
ferther, farther /further
ferthur, farther /further

fertile,lize,lizer,lizing,lization, ABLE/READY TO PRODUCE, PREPARE FOR PRODUCTION
fertulize, fertile(lize)
ferut, ferret
fery, ferry /fairy /furry
ferys, ferry(ries) / fairy(ries)
fesasist, physicist
feseks, physics
fesent, pheasant
fesh, fish
fesical, physical
fesics, physics
fesik, physique
fesikle, physical
fesilatashen, facilitate(tion)
fesilatate, facilitate
fesilatation, facilitate(tion)
fesint, pheasant
fesiology, physiology
fesishen, physician
fesode, facade
fest, fist
festaful, festival
festival,*, A CELEBRATION
festofil, festival
fesunt, pheasant
fet, feet /feat /feed /fed
fetarashen, federation
fetarashen, federation
fetaration, federation
fetch,hes,hed,hing, TO GET AND BRING BACK
feteg, fatigue
feth, fifth
fethur, feather
fetirashen, federation
fetler, fiddle(r)
feturation, federation
feture, feature
feu, few
feucher, future

feud,*,ding, A LONGSTANDING QUARREL/FIGHT
feul, fuel
feuld, field
feum, fume
feumegat, fumigate
feumigate, fumigate
feumugation, fumigate(tion)
feuree, fury / furry
feurius, furious
feus, fuse
feut, feud
fever,*,rish, BODY TEMPERATURE TOO HIGH
fevir, fever
fevirish, fever(ish)
fevur, fever
fevurish, fever(ish)
few, MORE THAN TWO
fewchur, future
fewd, feud
fewgitive, fugitive
fewmigashen, fumigate(tion)
fewmigate, fumigate
fewmigate, fumigate
fewmigation, fumigate(tion)
fewnarul, funeral
fewreus, furious
fews, fuse
fewton, futon
fewul, fuel
fex, fix
fext, fix(ed)
feyuree, fury
fezek, physique
fezent, pheasant
fezeology, physiology
fezeshan, physician
fezik, physique
fezint, pheasant
fezunt, pheasant
fiance', HUMAN TO BE MARRIED

fiar, fire
fib,*, bber,bbing, TO TELL A LIE
fiber,*,rous, PLANT MATERIAL (or see fib(bber))
fibre, fiber
fibrus, fiber(ous)
fibur, fiber
ficshen, fiction
ficster, fixture
fiction,*,nal, STORIES/BOOKS ABOUT MADE UP CHARACTERS
fiddle,*,er,ling, AN INSTRUMENT
fider, fight(er) /fit(tter)
fidir, fight(er) /fit(tter)
fidle, fiddle
fidlur, fiddle(r)
fidor, fight(er) /fit(tter)
fidul, fiddle
fidur, fight(er) /fit(tter)
field,*, LAND WITH FEW IF NO TREES
fierce,er,est,ely,eness, DANGEROUS, THREATENING
fiesta,*, CELEBRATION
fife, five
fifteen,nth, NUMBER
fiftees, fifty(ties)
fiften, fifteen
fiftenth, fifteen(th)
fiftes, fifty(ties)
fifth,*, ONE-FIFTH OF FIVE PARTS
fifty,ties,tieth, A NUMBER
fig,*, A FRUIT
figen, fission
figeur, figure
figeurene, figurine
fight,*,ter,ting, STRUGGLE, BATTLE BETWEEN
figure,*,ed,ring,rine,rines, SHAPE/FORM OF SOME-THING, NUMBERS (TOO MANY DEFINITIONS PLEASE SEE STANDARD DICTIONARY)
figurine,*, SHAPE/FORM OF SOMETHING
fijon, fission

fikchen, fiction
fiks, fix /fig(s)
fikshin, fiction
fikshur, fixture
fikster, fixture
fiksus, fix(es)
fikt, fix(ed)
fikur, figure
fil, fill /fell /file /feel
filade, fillet
filadendron, philodendron
filadindron, philodendron
filanthrepy, philanthropy
filanthropist, philanthropy(pist)
filarmonek, philharmonic
filasofical, philosophy(hical)
fild, file(d)/ field/ fill(ed)
fildur, filter
file,*, ed,ling, TO ORGANIZE, TOOL TO GRIND, FORM A LINE (or see fill /fillet /filly)
filermonek, philharmonic
filet, fillet
filhermonic, philharmonic
filings, file(lings) / feel(ings)
fill,*,lled,lling,ller, MAKE OPPOSITE OF EMPTY (or see file or fell)
fillet,*,ted,ting, ALSO FILET, BONES REMOVED FROM FISH/ANIMALS (TOO MANY DEFINITIONS, PLEASE SEE STANDARD DICTIONARY)
filly,llies, YOUNG FEMALE HORSE
film,*,med,ming,mation, A COATING, A MOVING PICTURE
filodendron, philodendron
filosofy, philosophy
filosophy, philosophy
filt, file(d) /field /fill(ed)
filter,*,red,ring, USED TO SEPARATE OR SORT
filthy,hier,hiest, DIRTIEST OF THE DIRTY, NASTY
filudendron, philodendron

filurmonic, philharmonic
fily, filly
fimilear, familiar
fin,*, EXTRUSION FOR WEAVING THROUGH AIR OR WATER (or see fine)
final,*,lly,le,list, THE END, THE LAST
finance,*,cial,cials,cially, ABOUT MONEY
finants, finance
finch,es, A BIRD
find,*,der,ding, REVEAL THE UNSEEN/UNKNOWN
findur, fender /find(er)
fine,*,er,est,ed,ning,ely, THIN, VERY NICE, MONETARY PUNISHMENT (or see fin)
finedik, phonetic
finel, final / fennel
finely, fine(ly) /final(lly)
fines, finesse/ fine(s)/ fine(st)
finesh, finish
finesse,*, HANDLE WITH SKILL/CONTROL/ DELICATELY (or see fine(st))
finetic, phonetic
finger,*,red,ring, ON THE HAND, USE THE HAND, EXTRUSION
fingernail,*, ON THE FINGER
fingerprint,*,ted,ting, ON THE FINGER
finish,es,hed,hing,her, TO COMPLETE
finker, finger
finkerprint, fingerprint
finle, final /fennel
finol, final /fennel
finomanen, phenomenon
finomena, phenomenon
finominul, phenomenal
finse, fence
finsh, finch
fintur, fender
finul, final / fennel
finuly, final(lly)
fionsa, fiance'

fiper, fiber
fipur, fiber
fir,*, AN EVERGREEN TREE (or see fire /fur /for)
firbed, forbid
firbedin, forbid(dden)
firbiten, forbid(dden)
firdul, fertile
fire,*, ed,ring, CHEMICAL REACTION THAT BURNS, TAKE
   JOB AWAY, EMOTIONAL (or see far or furry)
firefur, forever
firevur, forever
firgave, forgave
firgefnis, forgive(ness)
firget, forget
firgetful, forget(ful)
firgitful, forget(ful)
firgive, forgive
firgot, forgot
firgoten, forgot(tten)
firlow, furlough
firm,*,med,ming, BETWEEN SOFT/HARD, CAPITALIST
   GROUP
firmaledy, formal(ity)
firmality, formal(ity)
firmashen, formation
firmation, formation
firment, ferment
firn, fern
firnes, furnace
firnus, furnace
firochusle, ferocious(ly)
firoshis, ferocious
firoshusle, ferocious(ly)
firow, furrow
firsaken, forsake(n)
first,*, BEFORE ALL
firtalize, fertile(lize)
firtul, fertile
firy, furry

fisasist, physicist
fisealugist, physiology(gist)
fisecal, physical
fisek physic /physique
fiseks, physics
fiseolagekul, physiology(gical)
fiseologikul, physiology(gical)
fiseologist, physiology(gist)
fiseology, physiology
fiseshan, physician
fish,*,hed,hing,hy, VERTEBRATE IN WATER, CATCH FISH
   IN WATER
fishen, fission /fish(ing)
fishun, fission /fish(ing)
fisician, physician
fisics, physics
fisicul, physical
fisik, physique
fisiologest, physiology(gist)
fision, fission
fisishen, physician
fisode, facade
fisots, facade(s)
fission, USE HEAT TO SPLIT AN ATOMS NUCLEUS
fist,*,ted, CLOSED HAND, AN EXPRESSION
fit,*,tted,tting,tter,ttest, SOMETHING THAT WEARS
   WELL, EMOTIONAL OUTBURST (or see fight)
fite, fight
fiteg, fatigue
fiter, fight(er) /fit(tter)
fith, fifth
fitler, fiddle(r)
fitlur, fiddle(r)
fitur, fight(er) / fit(tter)
five,*, AN ENGLISH NUMBER
fix,xes,xed,xing,xate,xation,xative, INTENSE
   FOCUS, TO REPAIR
fixture,*, PERMANENTLY FASTENED
fizasist, physicist

fizek, physique
fizeolagekul, physiology(gical)
fizeolagist, physiology(gist)
fizeology, physiology
fizeshan, physician
fizesist, physicist
fizik, physique
fiziks, physics
fiziologest, physiology(gist)
flabides, phlebitis
flabites, phlebitis
flabodumy, phlebotomy
flabotimest, phlebotomy(mist)
fladery, flattery
flafur, flavor
flag,*,gged,gging, MATERIAL WITH A SYMBOL, TO
   WAVE SOMEONE OVER, TO TAG SOMEONE
flail,*,led,ling, THRASH ABOUT, A TOOL FOR
   THRASHING GRAIN
flair,*, APTITUDE/KNACK FOR,DEMEANOR(or see flare)
flale, flail
flamable, flammable
flame,*,ed,ming, TIP OF FIRE, SUDDEN ERUPTION
flamingo,*, A BIRD, DANCE
flammable,*,bility, CAN CATCH ON FIRE
flanel, flannel
flank,*, ked,king, THE REAR, SIDES
flannel,*, COTTON MATERIAL
flap,*,pped,pping, WAVE ABOUT, REMOVABLE COVER
flare,*,ed,ring, SHOOTING LIGHT, TO SPREAD OUT (or
   see flair)
flash,hes,hed,hing,her, LIGHTS FOR A BRIEF
   MOMENT, TATTOO LINGO
flat,*,tten,tter,ttest, THIN, HORIZONTAL, OFF KEY
flatery, flattery
flattery, PRAISE THAT'S NOT SINCERE OR SERIOUS
flaus, floss /flaw(s)
flavor,*,red,ring,rful,rless, PERCEIVED BY
   TASTEBUDS ON THE TONGUE

flaw,*,wed,wless, NOT RIGHT (or see flow)
flawer, flour /flower
flawnder, flounder
fle, flea /fle
flea,*, A TINY BUG (or see flee)
flebidis, phlebitis
flebitis, phlebitis
flebodumy, phlebotomy
flecks, fleck(s) /flex
fled, PAST TENSE OF "FLEE" (or see fleet)
flee,*,ed,eing, RUN AWAY (or see flea)
fleece,es,ed,cing, SHEEP COAT, COAT MATERIAL
fleet,*,ter,test,ting,tingly, GROUP OF BOATS, MOVE
  SWIFTLY, QUICKLY
flegm, phlegm
fleks, flex /fleck(s)
flem, phlegm
flemingo, flamingo
flemsy, flimsy
flench,flinch
fleng, fling
flent, flint
flep, flip
fleper, flipper
flert, flirt
flery, flurry
flese, fleece /flea(s)
flesh,hy,hier,hiest, SOFT AND FIRM PARTS OF FRUIT
  AND ANIMALS
flete, fleet
flew, PAST TENSE OF "FLY" (or see flu or flue)
flewid, fluid
flex,xes,xed,xing,xible, TO BEND, TEMPORARILY
  BEND (or see fleck(s))
fli, fly
fliar, flier /fly(er)
flibidis, phlebitis
flibitis, phlebitis
flibodumy, phlebotomy

flibotimest, phlebotomy(mist)
flick,*,ker,king,kered,kering, SNAP, CANDLE FLAME
  ACTION
flid, flew /flight
flier,*, A PIECE OF PAPER WITH INFORMATION TO BE
  CIRCULATED (or see fly(er))
flight,*,, TO TRAVEL THROUGH THE AIR
flik, flick
flim, phlegm
flimengo, flamingo
flimsy,sier,siest, LIGHTWEIGHT, DELICATE
flinch,hes,hed,hing, TO JERK
fling,*,ging,lung, THROW/CAST AWAY, A CAREFREE
  TIME
flint,*, USED TO START FIRE
flip,*,pped,pping, ALTERNATING SIDES WHILE IN THE
  AIR
fliper, flipper
flipper,*, MOVEABLE EXTRUSION ON ANIMALS FOR
  MOVEMENT, MANMADE FOOT PADDLES
flirt,*,ting, TEASING/TOYING WITH
flit,*,tted,tting, DART IN/OUT (or see flight)
fliur, flier /fly(er)
flo, flow
float,*,ted,ting, STAYS ON TOP OF LIQUID/AIR,
  BUOYANT
flock,*,ked,king, GROUP TOGETHER
flod, flood
flok, flock
flone, flown
flood,*,ded,ding, TOO MUCH WATER
flook, fluke
floor,*,red,ring, A SURFACE TO WALK ON
floot, flute
flop,*,pped,pping,ppy, FALL FLAT DOWN, LOOSE
flor, floor
floral,*, FLOWERS
floresent, flourescent
floresh, flourish

florish, flourish
florist,*, WORKS WITH FLOWERS
floss,sses,ssed,ssing,WAY TO CLEAN BETWEEN TEETH
flot, float
flounder,*,red,ring, FISH, STRUGGLE FOR PROPER
  STANCE
flour, GRINDING GRAIN TO POWDER (or see flower)
flourescent, ILLUMINATING LIGHT
flouride,*,date,dation, GAS, CHEMICAL ADDED TO
  WATER CONSIDERED POISONOUS
flourish,es,hed,hing, GROW HEALTHY AND STRONG
flow,*,wed,wing, STEADILY MOVING ALONG,
  MOVEMENT
flower,*,red,ring, PLANT, PART OF PLANT WHICH
  PREPARES THE SEED (or see flour)
flown, PAST TENSE OF "FLY"
flownder, flounder
flu,*,, A VIRUS (or see flew or flue)
flubotemist, phlebotomy(mist)
flubotemy, phlebotomy
flucshuate, fluctuate
fluctuate,*,ed,ting,tion, TO MOVE BACK AND FORTH
  IN DEGREES
flud, flood
fludder, flutter
fluder, flutter
flue,* CHIMNEY PIPE (or see flew or flu)
flued, fluid
fluff,*,fed,fing,fy, LIGHTEN UP BY SHAKING
fluid,*, LIQUID STATE
fluke,*, UNUSUAL OCCURANCE, PART OF A FISH, PART
  OF AN ANCHOR
flumengo, flamingo
flung, PAST TENSE OF "FLING" (or see flunk)
fluoro, fluo, fluor, PREFIX INDICATING "FLOURINE"
  MOST OFTENMODIFIES THE WORD
fluresh, flourish
flurish, flourish
flurry,rries, SPORADIC, FAST SNOW/BEHAVIOR

flurt, flirt	foel, foil / foal	fomy, foam(y)
flurry, flurry	foeul, foil	fon, fun /phone /fawn /faun
flush,hes,hed,hing,hable, *RID OF SOMETHING*	**fog**,gged,gging,ggy, *A MISTY CLOUD*	fona, fauna
fluster,*,red,ring, *CONFUSED, NERVOUS*	**foil**,*,ed,ling,ler, *THIN SHEETS OF METAL, TRICKED*	fonagraf, phonograph
flute,*,ed,ting,tist, *AN INSTRUMENT, A DESIGN*	fok, folk /fog	foncshin, function
flutter, flutter	fokes, focus	**fond**,der,dest,dly, *ATTRACTED TO* (or see font or phone(d))
flutter,*,red,ring, *BACK AND FORTH OR UP AND DOWN VIGOROUSLY*	fokis, focus	fondumentle, fundamental
fly,lies,flew,ying,yer, *AIRBORNE, INSECT* (or see flier)	foks, folk(s) /fox	fone, phone /funny /phony
fo, foe /faux	fokus, focus	fonedik, phonetic
foal,*,led,ling, *YOUNG ANIMAL*	fol, foal /fool /full /fall	fonegraf, phonograph
foal(ed), foal(ed)	folanthrapy, philanthropy	fonek, phonic
foam,*,med,ming,my, *ENCASED POCKETS OF AIR*	**fold**,*,ded,ding,dable, *BEND/CREASE OVER* (or see foal(ed) /fool(ed) /fault)	fonetic, phonetic
fobea, phobia	**folder**,*, *FOLDED SHEET TO HOLD PAPERS*	fonic, phonic
fobia, phobia	foldur, folder	fonigraf, phonograph
focis, focus	foleg, foliage	fonik, phonic
focks, fox	folej, foliage	fonkshen, function
focus,es,sed,sing, *CONCENTRATE ONLY ON ONE THING OR THOUGHT, HAVE NO THOUGHTS*	folesee, fallacy	**font**,*, *SIZE/STYLE OF LETTERS, BASIN* (or see fond)
fod, food	folesh, fool(ish)	fontementul, fundamental
fodagraf, photo(graph)	folfill, fulfill	fonugraf, phonograph
fodar, fodder	foliage, plants	**food**,*, *WHAT IS CHEWED/SWALLOWED FOR SUSTENANCE*
fodasenthesis, photosynthesis	folig, foliage	**fool**,*,led,ling,lingly,lish,lishness, *DOESN'T COMPREHEND THE SITUATION*
fodasinthesis, photosynthesis	folij, foliage	
fodder,*, *FOOD FOR CATTLE*	folish, fool(ish)	foome, fume
fodegraf, photo(graph)	**folk**,*,ksy, *STYLE OF MUSIC, THE PARENTS/PEOPLE*	foonrul, funeral
foder, fodder	folksee, folk(sy)	**foot**,ting,tage, *ATTACHED TO LEG, FIRM SPOT, U.S. MEASUREMENT OF LENGTH*
fodigraf, photo(graph)	**follow**,*,wed,wing,wer, *ONE BEHIND ANOTHER*	footon, futon
fodir, fodder	**folly**,llies, *FOOLISH*	fophade, phosphate
fodisinthasis, photosynthesis	folo, follow	**for**, *PREFIX INDICATING "AWAY/OFF/EXTREMELY" MOST OFTEN MODIFIES THE WORD, ALSO MEANS, GIVE TOWARDS, BELONGS TO* (or see fore or four)
fodo, photo	foloer, follow(er)	
fodograf, photo(graph)	folowir, follow(er)	**forage**,*,ed,ging,er, *TO SEARCH FOR*
fodon, photon /futon	fols, false /foal(s) /fall(s)	foram, forum
fodosinthesis, photosynthesis	folt, foal(ed) /fold /foal(ed)	foran, foreign
fodugraf, photo(graph)	folter, folder	foraner, foreign(er)
fodur, fodder	foltur, folder	forasdry, forest(ry)
fodusinthesis, photosynthesis	foly, folly	forast, forest
foe,*, *AN ADVERSARY* (or see faux)	folze, false	
	fome, foam /foam(y)	
	fomileur, familiar	

forastir, forest(er)
forbedin, forbid(dden)
forbet, forbid
forbetin, forbid(dden)
forbid,*,dden,dding,ddingly,forbade, NOT ALLOWED
forbiten, forbid(dden)
force,*,ed,cing,eful,efully,efulness, A PUSH OR PULL WITH INTENSE ENERGY
forchanet, fortunate
forchen, fortune
forchun, fortune
forchunet, fortunate
forchunitly, fortunate(ly)
fordafid, fortify(fied)
forde, forty
fordeath, fortieth
fordeen, fourteen
fordefication, fortification
fordefid, fortify(fied)
fordefy, fortify
fordeith, forty(tieth)
fordifid, fortify(fied)
fordify, fortify
fordufecashen, fortification
fordufid, fortify(fied)
fordufy, fortify
fordyeth, fortieth
fore, PREFIX INDICATING "BEFORE/IN FRONT" MOST OFTEN MODIFIES THE WORD, FRONT OF A VESSEL (or see four or for)
foreg, forage
foreign,ner,ners, NOT FAMILIAR, FROM ANOTHER PLACE
forein, foreign
forem, forum
foren, foreign
forenir, foreign(er)
foresdashen, forest(ation)

foresdry, forest(ry)
foreside, LAND ALONG THE OCEAN, THE FRONT OF SOMETHING (or see foresight)
foresight,*,ted,tedly,tedness, KNOW/THINK BEFOREHAND (or see farsight)
foresite, foresight
forest,*,ted,tal,tial,tation,ter,try, LAND MADE UP OF WILD ANIMALS/PLANTS, LARGE/HEAVILY WOODED/TREED AREA
forestashen, forest(ation)
foresteul, forest(ial)
forestur, forest(er)
forever, ON AND ON WITHOUT END
foreword,*, INTRODUCTORY WRITING (or see forward)
forfat, forfeit
forfeit,*,ted,ting,ture, FORCED TO LET GO OF
forfut, forfeit
forg, fork
forgave, PAST TENSE FOR THE WORD "FORGIVE"
forge,*,ed,ging, FAKE COPY, SOFTEN METAL BY FIRE
forget,*,tting,tful, CHOOSE NOT TO/CAN'T REMEMBER
forgifnes, forgive(ness)
forgit, forget
forgitful, forget(ful)
forgive,*,en,ving,eness,forgave, GIVEN MERCY, PARDON, EXCUSED
forgot,tten, PAST TENSE OF "FORGET"
forgoten, forgot(tten)
forige, forage
forim, forum
forin, foreign
foriner, foreign(er)
forisdashen, forest(ation)
forisdry, forest(ry)
forist, forest
foristation, forest(ation)
foristir, forest(er)
foristry, forest(ry)

forje, forge
fork,*,ed,king, TOOL FOR EATING/WORKING, SPLIT IN THE PATH
forlow, furlough
form,*,med,ming,mation,mative,mational, matively, SHAPE/TEMPLATE/DESIGN (or see forum or farm)
formad, format
formaded, format(tted)
formader, format(tter)
formadid, format(tted)
formal,*,lly,lity,lities,lize,lization,lizer, PROPER, DONE WITH CERTAIN RULES, DRESS-UP OCCASSION
formalesation, formal(ization)
formalidy, formal(ity)
formalise, formal(ize)
formaluzashen, formal(ization)
formaly, formal(lly) /former(ly)
formashen, formation
format,*,tted,tting,tter, SPECIFIC PROTOCOL/ DESIGN/SHAPE/STRUCTURE MOST OFTEN USED
formated, format(tted)
formater, format(tter)
formatif, form(ative)
formation,*, MADE/ENCOURAGED INTO A SHAPE
formativly, form(atively)
formel, formal
formelize, formal(ize)
formely, formal(lly)
former,*,rly, PREVIOUSLY, USED TO BE
formetive, form(ative)
formewla, formula
formewlashen, formula(tion)
formil, formal
formily, formal(lly) /former(ly)
formir, former
formirly, former(ly) /formal(lly)
formitevly, form(atively)
formitive, form(ative)

formle, formal
formolezashen, formal(ization)
formolize, formal(ize)
formotivly, form(atively)
formt, form(ed)
formul, formal
formula,*, ate,ated,ating,ation,aic,aically,arize, arizer,lism, SPECIFIC MIXTURE OF MOLECULES
formulashen, formula(tion)
formule, formal(lly)
formulisashen, formal(ization)
formulise, formal(ize)
formulu, formula
formuluzashen, formal(ization)
formuly, formal(lly)
formur, former
formurly, former(ly)
formutef, form(ative)
formutivly, form(atively)
forogt, forage(d)
foroshus, ferocious
fors, force /four(s) /farce
forsake,*, en,king,forsook, ABANDON, QUIT
forsakin, forsake(n)
forshen, fortune
forside, foreside / foresight
forsite, foresight / foreside
fort,*, tify, A STRUCTURE OR AREA TO BE PROTECTED
fortafid, fortify(fied)
fortchunetly, fortunate(ly)
forte, forty
forteen, fourteen
forteeth, forty(tieth)
fortenth, fourteenth
forteficashen, fortification
fortefid, fortify(fied)
fortefy, fortify
fortens, fourteen(s)
forteuth, forty(tieth)

fortewnit, fortunate
forth,hright, MOVEMENT FORWARD (or see fourth)
fortieth,*, AN ENGLISH NUMBER
fortification,*, PROTECTING AN AREA/STRUCTURE, TO STRENGTHEN/IMPROVE UPON
fortifid, fortify(fied)
fortify,fied,fying, STRENGTHEN/ADD/IMPROVE UPON
fortifyed, fortify(fied)
fortinth, fourteenth
fortufecation, fortification
fortufid, fortify(fied)
fortufy, fortify
fortunate,ely, SELF-CREATED OPPORTUNITY
fortune,*, GREAT WEALTH
fortunetly, fortunate(ly)
fortunit, fortunate
fortunitly, fortunate(ly)
forty,ties,tieth, AN ENGLISH NUMBER
fortyeth, forty(tieth)
foruge, forage
forujt, forage(d)
forum,*, GROUP OF PEOPLE IN DISCUSSION
forun, foreign
foruner, foreign(er)
forusdashen, forest(ation)
forusdry, forest(ry)
forust, forest
forustashen, forest(ation)
foruster, forest(er)
forustre, forest(ry)
forward,*, ded,ding,dly,dness, GO AHEAD, BE FRANK (or see foreword)
forwurd, forward /foreword
fos, foe(s) / faux
fosal, fossil
fosder, foster
fosdur, foster
fosel, fossil
foselisd, fossil(ized)

foset, faucet
fosfade, phosphate
fosfate, phosphate
fosil, fossil
fosilisd, fossil(ized)
fosphate, phosphate
fossil,*, lize,lized,lization, CARBON MATTER TURNED TO STONE
foster,*, red,ring, PLACEBO PARENT
fosul, fossil
fosulisd, fossil(ized)
fosulzd, fossil(ized)
fosut, faucet
fot, foot /food /fought
fotagraf, photo(graph)
fotar, fodder
fotasinthesis, photosynthesis
fotegraf, photo(graph)
foter, fodder
fother, father
fotigraf, photo(graph)
fotigue, fatigue
fotir, fodder
foto, photo
fotograf, photo(graph)
foton, photon /futon
fotosinthesis, photosynthesis
fotugraf, photo(graph)
fotur, fodder
fotusinthesis, photosynthesis
fought, PAST TENSE OF "FIGHT"
foul,*, led,ling,ler,lest, OFFENSIVE, OUTSIDE OF THE RULES (or see fowl)
found,ded,der,ding, PAST TENSE OF "FIND", ONE WHO DISCOVERED/LOCATED FIRST, INITIAL DATE OF DISCOVERY
foundashen, foundation
foundation,*, nal, BASE/BASIS FOR A BUILDING/ CORPORATION/BUSINESS/FRIENDSHIP

foundry,*,ries, *WHERE METAL IS MELTED*
fountain,*, *STATUE OR STRUCTURE SHOOTING WATER*
fountin, fountain
four,*,rth, *AN ENGLISH NUMBER* (or see fore or for)
fourest, forest
fourever, forever
fourfit, forfeit
fourgave, forgave
fourget, forget
fourgive, forgive
fourgot, forgot
fourmadur, format(tter)
fourmalize, formal(ize)
fourmashin, formation
fourmer, former
fourmul, formal
fours, force / four(s)
fourteen,*, *AN ENGLISH NUMBER*
fourteenth,*, *AN ENGLISH NUMBER, ONE OF 14*
fourth,*, *AN ENGLISH NUMBER, ONE TO FOUR PARTS*
   (or see forth)
fourtinth, fourteenth
fourwurd, forward
fow, foe / faux
fowel, foul /fowl
fowks, fox
fowl,*, *WILD BIRD* (or see foul or foal)
fowlest, foul(est)
fowlust, foul(est)
fownd, found
fowndashun, foundation
fowndation, foundation
fowndre, foundry
fownt, found
fowntin, fountain
fowt, fought
fowul, foul /fowl
fox,es, *A FURRY ANIMAL*
foyl, foil

fozdur, foster
fozel, fossil
fozter, foster
fracshen, fraction
fracshenal, fraction(al)
fracsher, fracture
fraction,*,nal,nally,nary, *PART OF THE WHOLE* (or
   see friction or fracture)
fractioneal, fraction(al)
fracture,*,ed,ring, *A BREAK, BROKEN* (or see
   fraction)
frad, afraid /fray(ed) /freight
fraded, freight(ed)
frader, freighter
fradewlent, fraud(ulent)
fradewlently, fraud(ulently)
frael, frail
fraeltee, frail(ty)
fragelidy, fragile(lity)
frageled, freight(ed)
fragile,ely,lity, *DELICATE*
fragment,*,tal,ted,ting,tation,*PIECE OF THE WHOLE*
fragmint, fragment
fragmintashen, fragment(ation)
fragmintul, fragment(al)
fragrance,*, *A SMELL, AROMA*
fragrant,*, *A SMELL, AROMA*
fragrinse, fragrance
fragrint, fragrant
fragul, fragile
fraight, freight
fraighter, freighter
frail,ler,lest,lty, *VERY DELICATE*
frailtee, frail(ty)
frait, freight
frajilety, fragile(lity)
frajiludy, fragile(lity)
frajul, fragile
frakchen, fraction

frakment, fragment
frakmentashen, fragment(ation)
frakmentul, fragment(al)
frakmint, fragment
frakmintul, fragment(al)
frakshenul, fraction(al)
fraksher, fracture
frakshin, fraction
frakshur, fracture
fraktionul, fraction(al)
frakul, freckle
frale, frail
fralest, frail(est)
fralic, frolic
fraluc, frolic
frame,*,ed,ming,ers, *STRUCTURE TO ENCASE
   SOMETHING, CRIMINAL ACT*
framur, frame(r)
franc,*, *FRENCH MONEY* (or see frank)
frandekly, frantic(ally)
frandikly, frantic(ally)
frank,ker,kest,kly, *HONEST, OPEN EXPRESSION* (or
   see franc)
frankist, frank(est)
frankle, frank(ly)
frantek, frantic
frantekly, frantic(ally)
frantic,cally, *ANXIOUS, DISORDER, WILDLY RUNNING
   ABOUT*
frantikly, frantic(ally)
frash, fresh
frate, freight
frater, freighter
fratid, freight(ed)
fraud,*,dly,dulent,dulently, *TRICKING/CHEATING*
fraul, frail
frauler, frail(er)
fraulist, frail(est)
fraultee, frail(ty)

fraun, frown
frauns, frown(s)
frawd, fraud
frawdly, fraud(ly)
frawn, frown
fraxshen, fraction
fre, free /fray
freak,*,ked,king,ky, SHOCKING OR ODD, UNUSUAL
freaze, freeze
frechen, fresh(en)
frecher, fresh(er)
frechin, fresh(en)
frechnur, fresh(ener)
frechun, fresh(en)
freckle,*,ed, BEAUTY SPOT ON SKIN
frection, friction
fred, free(d) / fret
fredem, freedom
fredum, freedom
free,*,ed,eing,ely, LIBERTY
freedom,*, TO HAVE LIBERTY
freedum, freedom
freekwensee, frequency
freekwint, frequent
freekwintly, frequent(ly)
freeky, freak(y)
freese, freeze
freetim, freedom
freetum, freedom
freeze,*,zing,zable,froze, LIQUID TO SOLID, WATER
        AT 32°F, 0°C
freg, fridge
freged, frigid
freghted, freight(ed)
fregit, frigid
freight,*,ted,ting,ter, GOODS BEING TRANSPORTED
freighter,*, SHIP CARRYING CARGO
freigter, freighter
freiht, freight

frej, fridge
frejid, frigid
frek, freak
frekal, freckle
frekol, freckle
frekqint, frequent
frekqintly, frequent(ly)
frekshen, friction
frekul, freckle
frekwensee, frequency
frekwent, frequent
frekwently, frequent(ly)
freky, freak(y)
frely, free(ly)
French, A NATIONALITY (or see fringe)
frend, friend
frendlenes, friend(liness)
frendle, friend(ly)
frendleist, friend(liest)
frendleur, friend(lier)
frenge, fringe /French
frenj, fringe /French
frense, frenzy
frent, friend
frentleist, friend(liest)
frentleur, friend(lier)
frently, friend(ly)
frenzy,zied,zies, CHAOTIC EXCITEMENT
frequency,cies, DISTANCE/NUMBER OF TIMES
        BETWEEN WAVE PEAKS
frequent,ly, HOW OFTEN
freqwensee, frequency
freqwint, frequent
freqwintly, frequent(ly)
fres, freeze /free(s) /frizz
frese, freeze /frizz(y)
fresh,*,her,hest,hen,hener,hly, PEAK CONDITION
freshenur, fresh(ener)
freshin, fresh(en)

freshir, fresh(er)
freshnur, fresh(ener)
freshon, fresh(en)
freshur, fresh(er)
frestrate, frustrate
fretem, freedom
freter, freighter
fretim, freedom
fretum, freedom
frevolus, frivolous
frevulus, frivolous
frewgul, frugal
frewktose, fructose
frez, freeze /frizz /free(s)
freze, frizz(y) /freeze /free(s)
fri, fry
fricshen, friction
friction,nal,nless, RESISTANCE BETWEEN TWO THINGS
        (or see fraction)
frid, fried / fright
Friday,*, A DAY OF THE WEEK
friden, frighten
fridgarator, refrigerate(tor)
fridge,*, SLANG FOR REFRIGERATOR
fridy, Friday
fried, PAST TENSE OF "FRY", COOK IN SKILLET
friend,*,dly,dlier,dliest,dliness,FRIENDSHIP,
        MUTUAL INTEREST/ADMIRATION
frier, fry(er)
fries,ed, COOK IN SKILLET, GET TOO HOT
frig, fridge
frigarador, refrigerate(tor)
friged, frigid
frigerator, refrigerate(tor)
friget, frigid
fright,tful,tless, SUDDEN FEAR
frighten,*,ned,ning, TO SUDDENLY SCARE SOMEONE
frigid,dly,dness,kity, STIFF/COLD
frigirator, refrigerate(tor)

frigit, frigid
frij, fridge
frijik, frigid
frikshen, friction
frikshenles, friction(less)
frikshenul, friction(al)
friktion, friction
friktional, friction(al)
frin, fright /friend
frind, friend
frindleist, friend(liest)
frindlenes, friend(liness)
frindleur, friend(lier)
frindly, friend(ly)
fringe,*,ed,ging, *DECORATIVE EDGE, ON THE OUTSIDE EDGE* (or see French)
frinj, fringe / French
frinsy, frenzy
frint, friend
frintleist, friend(liest)
frintleur, friend(lier)
frintly, friend(ly)
frinzy, frenzy
fris, fries /frizz
frisy, frizz(y)
frit, fried / fright
friten, frighten
frivolous,sly,sness,lty, *SILLY, NOT SERIOUS*
frivulus, frivolous
friz, frizz /freeze /fries
frize, frizz(y) /fries
frizy, frizz(y)
frizz,zzes,zzed,zzing,zzy, *KINKY/WAVY* (or see freeze or fries)
frock, frog
frod, fraud
frodewlint, fraud(ulent)
frodewlintly, fraud(ulently)

frodth, froth
frodulent, fraud(ulent)
frodulently, fraud(ulently)
frog,*,ggy, *AN AMPHIBIAN*
frogle, frugal
frogy, frog(ggy)
frojewlint, fraud(ulent)
frojewlintly, fraud(ulently)
frojiledy, fragile(lity)
frojulent, fraud(ulent)
frojulently, fraud(ulently)
frok, frog
frolek, frolic
frolic,*,ced,cing, *PLAY LIGHTHEARTED, ROMP HAPPILY*
froluc, frolic
from, *WHERE IT WAS BEFORE*
frond, front
frondeer, frontier
front,*,ted,ting, *OUTSIDE FACING, GIVE IN ADVANCE*
fronteer, frontier
frontid, front(ed)
frontier,*, *FRINGE OR EDGE OF A PLACE OR IN INFORMATION*
froogle, frugal
frooishen, fruition
froot, fruit
frosd, frost /froze
frosdee, frost(y)
fros, froze
frosen, froze(n)
frosin, froze(n)
frost,*,ted,ting,ty,tless,(frostbite) *COATING OF SOMETHING ON OBJECT, ICE,ICING ON CAKES* (or see froze)
froth,*,hed,hing,hy, *FOAM*
frowd, fraud
frown,*,ned,ning, *MOUTH TURNED DOWN, DOESN'T APPROVE*

frozd, frost /froze
froze,en, *PAST TENSE OF "FREEZE"*
frozen, *PAST TENSE OF "FREEZE"*
fructose, *NATURAL SUGAR*
frude, fruit
frueshin, fruition
frug, frog
frugal,lly,lity,lities,lness, *VERY LITTLE WASTE*
frugelidy, fragile(lity)
frugiledy, fragile(lity)
frugle, frugal
fruishin, fruition
fruit,*,tful,ty,tless, *SEED BEARING PART PRODUCED BY FEMALE PLANTS, SWEET AND SILLY*
fruition, *A REALIZATION/REWARD FOR EFFORT/ ACCOMPLISHMENT*
frujilety, fragile(lity)
frujiludy, fragile(lity)
fruktose, fructose
frum, from
frund, front
frundeer, frontier
frunt, front
frunteer, frontier
frushtrate, frustrate
frustrate,*,ed,ting,tion, *SHAKEN BY LACK OF KNOWLEDGE OR INFORMATION*
frute, fruit
fry,ries,ried,ying,yer, *COOK IN SKILLET, GET TOO HOT, GET IN TROUBLE*
fryday, Friday
fryde, Friday /fried
fu, few
fucher, future
fud, feud /food /foot
fudch, fudge
fudge,*,ed,ging, *CHOCOLATE DESSERT,EXAGGERATE THE TRUTH*
fudon, futon

fued, feud
fuel,*,,led,ling, *USED TO POWER THINGS*
fug, fudge
fugative, fugitive
fugitive,*,, *RUNAWAY, ROAMS*
fugt, fudge(d)
fujative, fugitive
fuj, fudge
fuil, fuel
ful, fool /full /fuel
fulad, fillet
fulanthrapist, philanthropy(pist)
fulanthrapy, philanthropy
fulate, fillet
fulay, fillet
fuld, fool(ed) /fuel(ed)
fule, fuel /fool /full /full(lly)
fuled, fool(ed) /fuel(ed)
fuler, full(er)
fulesh, fool(ish)
fulest, full(est)
fulfill,*,,led,ling,lment, *CONTENT, HAVE WHAT WAS WANTED*
fulir, full(er)
fulish, fool(ish)
fulist, full(est)
full,ler,lest,lly, *HOLDING THE MOST IT CAN HOLD*
fulor, full(er)
fulosofy, philosophy
fulur, full(er)
fulust, full(est)
fuly, full(y)
fum, fume
fumbel, fumble
fumbil, fumble
fumble,*,,ed,ling, *DROP SOMETHING ACCIDENTALLY, DROP A BALL DURING PLAY*
fumbol, fumble
fume,*,,ed,ming, *TO EMIT STEAM/GAS/SMOKE, SMELL*

fumegashen, fumigate(tion)
fumegate, fumigate
fumegation, fumigate(tion)
fumelear, familiar
fumigashen, fumigate(tion)
fumigate,*,,ed,ting,tion, *TO FLOOD/OVER-WHELM WITH SMOKE/GAS*
fumpl, fumble
fumugation, fumigate(tion)
fun,nny,nnier,nniest, *HAPPINESS, PLAYFUL*
funal, funeral
funarul, funeral
funcshenul, function(al)
funcshin, function
function,*,,ned,ning,nal, *SERVE, HAVE OPERATIONAL, PERFORM*
functionul, function(al)
functshen, function
fund,*,,ded,ding,der, *PUT MONEY TOWARDS, HOLDS MONEY FOR PURPOSE*
fundamental,*,,lly, *NECESSARY*
fundemintol, fundamental
fundumintel, fundamental
fundur, fund(er)
funedic, phonetic
fune, funny
funeir, fun(nnier)
funeist, fun(nniest)
funel, funnel
funeor, fun(nnier)
funeral,*,, *EVENT HONORING THE DEAD*
funes, finesse / fun(nnies)
funetic, phonetic
funeur, fun(nnier)
fungis, fungus
fungus (from fungi) *NOT A PLANT BUT IS LIVING AND GROWS*
funie, funny
funies, fun(nnies)

funiest, fun(nniest)
funil, funnel
funior, fun(nnier)
funiral, funeral
funkshenul, function(al)
funkshin, function
funkshunal, function(al)
funkus, fungus
funle, funnel
funnel,*,,led,ling, *CONE SHAPE WITH HOLE IN MIDDLE*
funnil, funnel
funny,nnies,nnier,nniest, *CREATES SMILE OR LAUGHTER, HUMOR*
funol, funnel
funomenal, phenomenal
funominul, phenomenal
funrul, funeral
funt, fund
funtamental, fundamental
funy, funny
funyer, fun(nnier)
funyest, fun(nniest)
funyur, fun(nnier)
fur,*,,rred,rring,rry, *HAIR ON ANIMAL (or see for/ fury)*
furbed, forbid
furbedin, forbid(dden)
furbet, forbid
furbid, forbid
furbiten, forbid(dden)
furdal, fertile
furdalize, fertile(lize)
furdelize, fertile(lize)
furdil, fertile
furdulizashen, fertile(lization)
fure, fury /furry
furefir, forever
furefur, forever
furesteul, forest(ial)

fureus, furious
furever, forever
furgave, forgave
furgefnis, forgive(ness)
furget, forget
furgetful, forget(ful)
furgitful, forget(ful)
furgive, forgive
furgivnes, forgive(ness)
furgot, forgot
furgotin, forgot(tten)
furious,sly, *BEYOND ANGRY*
furlough,*, *A LEAVE OF ABSENCE*
furlow, furlough
furm, firm
furmaledy, formal(ity)
furmality, formal(ity)
furmashen, formation
furmation, formation
furment, ferment
furn, fern
furnace,*, *HEATER*
furnacher, furniture
furnature, furniture
furnish,es,hed,hing, *PLACE FURNITURE INTO A ROOM*
furniture,*, *OBJECTS/ARTICLES PLACED IN A ROOM FOR COMFORT*
furnusher, furniture
furochusle, ferocious(ly)
furod, furrow(ed)
furoshus, ferocious
furoshusle, ferocious(ly)
furot, furrow(ed)
furotious, ferocious
furow, furrow
furrow,*,wed,wing, *A TRENCH IN THE SOIL, WRINKLE IN BROW*
furry,rrier,rriest, *HAIRY* (or see fury)
fursake, forsake

fursaken, forsake(n)
furst, first
furtal, fertile
further,red,ring,(furthest) *MORE THAN FAR* (or see farther)
furtile, fertile
furtile, fertile(lize)
furtulize, fertile(lize)
fury,ries, *RAGE* (or see furry)
fuse,*,ed,sing,eable, *ITEM WHICH PROTECTS FROM FIRE HAZARD, USED TO IGNITE EXPLOSIVES, MELT ITEMS TOGETHER* (or see fuss or fuzz)
fuseir, fuss(ier) /fuzz(ier)
fuseist, fuss(iest) /fuzz(iest)
fusek, physique
fuselitate, facilitate
fuselitation, facilitate(tion)
fuseur, fuss(ier) /fuzz(ier)
fusher, future
fusilatashen, facilitate(tion)
fusilatate, facilitate
fusilatation, facilitate(tion)
fusines, fuss(iness) /fuzz(iness)
fusod, facade
fuss,*,sses,ssed,ssing,ssy,ssily,ssiness, *TO FOCUS ON MINOR DETAILS* (or see fuse or fuzz)
fusy, fussy /fuzz(y)
fut, food /foot /feud
futch, fudge
futeg, fatigue
futj, fudge
futon,*, *A CUSHION/MATTRESS WITH HEAVY COTTON BATTING* (or see photon)
futsher, future
future,*, *A TIME AFTER NOW*
fuz, fuzz /fuse /fuss
fuzd, fuse(d) /fuss(ed)
fuze, fuse/ fuss(y) /fuzz(y)
fuzed, fuse(d) /fuss(ed)
fuzeir, fuss(ier) /fuzz(ier)

fuzek, physique
fuziest, fuss(iest) /fuzz(iest)
fuzines, fuss(iness) /fuzz(iness)
fuzt, fuse(d) /fuss(ed)
fuzyest, fuss(iest) /fuzz(iest)
fuzynes, fuss(iness) /fuzz(iness)
fuzz,zzy,zzies,zzier,zziest,zziness, *FUR/OTHER MATERIAL, BLURRY TO THE EYES* (or see fuse or fuss)
fuzzyness, fuss(ines) /fuzz(iness)

"G"

gach, gauge
gader, gaiter
gadget,*, *AN ITEM USED AS A TOOL*
gaf, golf /gave
gafel, gavel
gaful, gavel
gag,*,gged,gging, *NEARLY CHOKE, TO KEEP SOMEONE FROM SPEAKING* (or see guage or jag)
gagd, gag(gged) /guage(d) /jiag(gged)
gage, gauge
gagels, goggles
gaget, gadget
gail, jail /gale
gain,*,,ned,ning,nful,nfully, *BENEFIT, IMPROVE*
gait,*, *DISTANCE BETWEEN FOOTSTEPS* (or see gate)
gaiter,*, *WRAP FOR LEGS BELOW THE KNEE, SLANG FOR ALLIGATOR*
gaje, gauge
gajit, gadget
gakass, jackass
gal,*, *REFERENCE TO A FEMALE* (or see gall/gale/jail)
galactic, *THE MILKY WAY, GALAXY*
galan, gallon
galant, gallant
galashes, galoshes

galaxy,xies, *PLANETS/STARS WITHIN A SYSTEM*
galeksy, galaxy
gale,*, *STRONG WINDS (or see gal /galley /jail)*
galen, gallon
galent, gallant
galep, gallop
galery, gallery
galexy, galaxy
galey, galley
galf, golf
galie, galley
galin, gallon
galip, gallop
galiry, gallery
gallant,tly,try, *COURAGEOUS, STATELY, AMOROUS, IN REFERENCE TO MALES*
gallen, gallon
gallery,ries, *SHOWCASE FOR ART (TOO MANY DEFINITIONS, PLEASE SEE PROPER DICTIONARY)*
galley,*, *KITCHEN IN A VESSEL, ANCIENT BOAT*
gallon,*, *U.S.MEASURE FOR LIQUID*
gallop,*,ped,ping, *GAIT OF A HORSE OR ANIMAL*
gallows, *STRUCTURE FROM WHICH PEOPLE WERE HUNG TO DEATH*
galoshes, *RUBBER BOOTS*
galows, gallows
galre, gallery
galun, gallon
galup, gallop
galury, gallery
galy, galley /July /jelly
gam, jam /jamb /game
gamble,*,ed,ling,er, *BET MONEY ON NUMBERS*
game,*,ming,er, *COMPETITION TO WIN*

gamet, gamut
gamut, *FULL SCALE OF MUSICAL NOTES, THE WHOLE RANGE OF THINGS*
gander,*, *MALE GOOSE*
gane, gain
ganedic, genetic
gang,*,ged,ging, *GROUP OF PEOPLE/THINGS WITH COMMONALITY*
ganitor, janitor
gantlet, gauntlet
gap,*,pped,pping, *A SPACE, BREAK IN CONTINUITY (or see gape)*
gape,ped,ping,pingly, *NORMALLY CONCERNS THE MOUTH OPENING WIDE (or see gape)*
gar, jar
garage,*, ed, *STRUCTURE INTENDED FOR VEHICLES*
garantee, guarantee
garbage, *TRASH*
gard, guard
garden,*,ned,ning,ner, *GROWING PLANTS*
gardeun, guardian
gardian, guardian
garela, gorilla /guerilla
garentee, guarantee
gargen, jargon
gargle,*,ed,ling, *RINSE THE THROAT WITH LIQUID*
gargoele, gargoyle
gargoyle,*, *CARVED GOTHIC FIGURES*
garila, gorilla /guerilla
garland,*, *PLANT ITEMS WOVEN TOGETHER*
garlic, *EDIBLE BULB FROM PLANT*
garment,*, *CLOTHING*
garnish,hes,hed,hing, *DECORATIVE FOOD USED TO ACCENT FOOD, TO PORTION OUT*
gart, guard
garteun, guardian
gas,ses,ssed,ssing,seous, *NOT LIQUID OR SOLID*
gasoline, *USED TO POWER MOTORS*
gasp,*,ped,ping, *STRUGGLE FOR AIR*

gastr, gastro, *PREFIX INDICATING "STOMACH" MOST OFTEN MODIFIES THE WORD*
gasture, gesture
gasuntite, gesundheit
gate,*,ted, *CLOSURE TO MONITOR EXIT/ENTRANCE*
gater, alligator /gaiter
gather,*,red,ring, *COLLECT TOGETHER*
gator, alligator /gaiter
gaudy, *OUTRAGEOUS STYLE NAMED AFTER FAMOUS ARCHITECT IN BARCELONA*
gauge,*,ed,ging, *MEASURE FOR THINGS SUCH AS VOLUME/SIZE (OR SEE JAUNT)*
gaunt,tly,tness, *HAGGARD/THIN, LACKING AVERAGE PRESSURE*
gauntlet,*, *CHALLENGE*
gaurantee, guarantee
gaus, gauze
gauze, *CLOTH FOR BANDAGES*
gava, java
gave, *PAST TENSE OF "GIVE"*
gavel,*, *WOODEN HAMMER USED IN COURTROOMS*
gaw, jaw
gawalk, jaywalk
gawn, gown
gawok, jaywalk
gawul, jowl
gay,*,yly, *BRIGHT, HAPPY, HOMOSEXUAL*
gaywalk, jaywalk
gaywok, jaywalk
gaz, jazz /gaze /guaze
gaze,*,ed,zing, *A LONG LOOK AT (or see gauze)*
gazuntite, gesundheit
ge, geo, *PREFIX INDICATING "EARTH" MOST OFTEN MODIFIES THE WORD*
geagrafee, geography
gear,*,red,ring, *INTERLOCKING NOTCHED RINGS WHICH DRIVE MACHINES*
geburish, jibber(ish)
gedo, ghetto

geneol, genial
geens, jean(s) /gene(s)
geese, MORE THAN ONE GOOSE
gef, give
geffy, jiffy
geft, gift
gegle, giggle /jiggle
gel,*,led,ling,llable, SEMI-SOFT/FIRM SUBSTANCE (or see jell/ jail/ gal)
gelatin,*,nous, LIKE JELLO
geld, guild/ guilt/ jell(ed)
gele, jelly
geletin, gelatin
gelt, guilt/ jilt/ jell(ed)/ guild
gelty, guilt(y)
gelus, jealous
gelutin, gelatin
gely, July /jelly
gem,*, STONE, JEWEL (or see gym)
gemek, gimmick
gemik, gimmick
gemmy, jimmy
gemnaseum, gymnasium
gemnast, gymnast
gen, gene /jean
genarate, generate
genaration, generation
genarulize, general(ize)
genarus, generous
gene pig, guinea pig
gene,*, STRING OF CHROMOSOMES (or see jean)
genedic, genetic
general,*,lly,lize,lization, ENCOMPASSES MANY THINGS, A MILITARY OFFICER
generate,*,ed,ting, CREATE, PRODUCE
generation,*, PEOPLE BORN IN GROUPS AT SAME TIME
generator,*, MACHINE THAT CREATES AC ENERGY
generic,*, GENERAL NAME BRAND/CLASSIFICATION
generous,sly,sity, GIVE AWAY WHAT CAN BE SPARED

genetic,*, STUDY OF GENES AND ASSOCIATED PARTICLES
geneul, genial
geneus, genius
genial,lly, WELCOMING, DOESN'T APPEAR JUDGEMENTAL
genie,*, MAGIC ENTITY IN A BOTTLE
geniral, general
genirus, generous
genius,ses,sness, CAPABLE OF DEEP THINKING
genjur, ginger
genle, gentle
genome,*, STUDY OF HUMAN GENES AND ALL ASSOCIATED INTERACTIONS
genre',*, DIFFERENT STYLES/MEDIUM, EXPRESSION FOR ART, MUSIC
gentle,er,est,tility,eness, KIND IN BEHAVIOR, NON-THREATENING
gentul, gentle
genuine,ely,eness, TRUTHFUL, REAL
genrul, general
genurul, general
genurus, generous
genyus, genius
geo, ge, PREFIX INDICATING "EARTH" MOST OFTEN MODIFIES THE WORD
geography,hies,hic,hical, THE STUDY OF EVERYTHING ON THE SURFACE OF THE EARTH
geology,gies,gical,gic,gist, STUDY OF THE EARTH'S CRUST
geometry,ries,ric,rical, VARIOUS SHAPES/SYMBOLS/ LINES/ANGLES
gep, gyp
gepardy, jeopardy
gepsee, gypsy
gepsum, gypsum
gerantee, guarantee

gerbil,*, A SMALL RODENT
gere, gear / jury
geresdikshen, jurisdiction
gergul, gurgle
gerila, gorilla /guerilla
gerk, jerk
gerky, jerky
gerl, girl
gerlfrend, girlfriend
germ,*, BACTERIA
germinate,*,ed,ting,tion, SEED BEGINNING TO GROW
gernal, journal
gernalist, journal(ist)
gerne, journey /gurney
gernulest, journal(ist)
gerny, gurney /journey
gerter, girder
gerth, girth
gerunte, guarantee
gerur, juror
gery, jury
gesd, guest /guess(ed) /jest
gese, geese /guess
gesoontite, gesundheit
gess, guess
gest, guest /guess(ed) /jest
gest, jest /just /guest /guess(ed)
gesture,*,ed,ring, BODILY MOTIONS
gesundheit, WISHING GOOD HEALTH TO SOMEONE WHO SNEEZED (German)
gesuntite, gesundheit
get,*,tter,tting, TO TAKE IN, HAVE IT (or see jet)
gete, jetty
geter, jitter
geto, ghetto
getsam, jetsam
gety, jetty
gev, give

gewdeshal, judicial
gewdishes, judicious
gewel, jewel
gewly, July
gewn, June /goon
gews, juice
geyser,*, *WATER WHICH SHOOTS UP FROM A HOLE IN THE EARTH*
ghetto,*, *A SECTION OF LAND WHERE OVERCROWDING IS A RESULT OF DISCRIMINATION*
ghost,*,tly, *SPIRITS WHICH PROVE TO EXIST BUT ARE INVISIBLE TO US*
gi, guy
giant,*, *HUGE, ENORMOUS*
gib, jib /jibe
gibe, jibe
giberish, jibber(ish)
gide, guide
gidense, guidance
gif, give
giffy, jiffy
gift,*,ted,ting, *TO GIVE SOMETHING WITHOUT EXPECTATIONS OF RETURN*
gig,*, *ARRANGEMENT FOR MUSICAL PERFORMANCE (or see jig)*
giga, *PREFIX INDICATING "ONE BILLIONTH" MOST OFTEN MODIFIES THE WORD*
gigantic, *INCREDIBLY HUGE, ENORMOUS*
gigger, jigger
giggle,*,ed,ling,*STYLE OF LAUGHING (or see jiggle)*
gigle, giggle
gigsaw, jigsaw
gilatnus, gelatin(ous)
gild, guild /guilt /jell(ed)
gildy, guilt(y)
giloshes, galoshes
gilt, guild /guilt /jell(ed)
gilty, guilt(y)
gily, July / jelly

gim, gem /gym
gimik, gimmick
gimmick,*,ky, *TRICK, ATTENTION GETTER*
gimmy, jimmy
gimnaseum, gymnasium
gimnast, gymnast
ginarashin, generation
ginarate, generate
ginarator, generator
ginarulize, general(ize)
ginarus, generous
gine pig, guinea pig
ginerik, generic
ginetic, genetic(s)
ginger,rly, *EDIBLE PLANT, TO BE CAUTIOUS*
gingle, jingle
ginks, jinx
ginokologist, gynecologist
ginucalugist, gynecologist
ginuen, genuine
ginul, gentle
ginurulize, general(ize)
ginus, genus
giologee, geology
giometry, geometry
gip, gyp
gipsee, gypsy
gipsum, gypsum
girate, gyrate
girble, gerbil
girder,*, *BEAM USED FOR HORIZONTAL BRACING IN BUILDINGS*
girgul, gurgle
girl,*,ly, *YOUNG FEMALE PERSON*
girlfriend,*, *A GIRL WHO IS ALSO A FRIEND*
girm, germ
girmanate, germinate
girmalist, journal(ist)
girney, gurney /journey

girnul, journal
ginnul, general
girth,*,*WIDTH OF SOMETHING ACROSS,CIRCUMFERENCE*
giry, jury
giser, geyser
gisuntite, gesundheit
git, get
gito, ghetto
gitter, jitter
give,*, ving,en, *PROVIDE OR PRESENT SOMETHING EXPECTING NOTHING IN RETURN (or see jive)*
gizer, geyser
gizuntite, gesundheit
glacier,*,ial, *ICE,FROZEN WATER AROUND MOUNTAIN*
glad,dder,ddest,dly, *PLEASED*
glair, glare
glamour,rous,rously,rize, *ALLURING, BEWITCHING*
glance,*,ed,cing, *A QUICK LOOK*
gland,*,dular,dulous, *ORGANS IN THE BODY*
glare,*,ed,ring, *A SHARP LOOK WITH THE EYES, INTENSE LIGHT*
glas, glass /glaze
glaser, glacier /glazer
glasher, glacier
glass,ses,sy, *HARD/FLAT/FRAGILE SUBSTANCE MADE WITH MIXTURE OF MINERALS/CHEMICALS*
glaze,*,ed,zing,er, *A COATING OF SUBSTANCE ON SOMETHING*
glazr, glaze(r)
gleam,*,med,ming,my,mier,miest, *A BRIEF MOMENT IN APPEARANCE*
glech, glitch
gleder, glitter
gledur, glitter
glee,eful,efully, *WITH JOY, EXUBERANCE*
gleful, glee(ful)
glemmer, glimmer
glempse, glimpse
glent, glint

gloss,sy,sed, SHINE UP
glossary,ries, AREA IN SOME BOOKS WITH DEFINITIONS
glote, gloat /glow(ed)
glove,*,ed, COVERING FOR HANDS
glow,*,wed,wing, TO BE LITE FROM WITHIN, INTERNAL LIGHT
gluco, glyco, PREFIX INDICATING "SUGAR" MOST OFTEN MODIFIES THE WORD
glucose, SUGAR, SYRUP
glue,*,ed,uing, TYPE OF LIQUID USED TO STICK THINGS TOGETHER, STUCK TO SOMETHING
gluecose, glucose
glufs, glove(s)
glukose, glucose
glum,mly,mness,mmer,mmest, DISAPPOINT, NEGATIVE PERSPECTIVE, APPEARS TO BE NO SOLUTION, SULLEN (or see gloom)
glumy, glum(mmy) /gloom(y)
glutinous,sity,sness,sly, STICKS TOGETHER, LIKE GLUE
gluvs, glove(s)
glyco, gluco, PREFIX INDICATING "SUGAR" MOST OFTEN MODIFIES THE WORD
gnaw,*,wed,wing, MOUTH OR CHEW ON SOMETHING GENTLY
gnome,*, A SMALL HUMAN ENTITY WHICH ONLY SOME PEOPLE CAN SEE
go,oes,oing, READY/SET/MOVE, MOBILIZE TO ANOTHER PLACE
goal,*, SOMETHING TO ACHIEVE/GO FOR, ATTEMPT TO REACH
goalie,*, SOMEONE WHO DEFENDS AGAINST SOMEONE WHO WANTS TO MAKE POINTS IN A GAME
goat,*, AN ANIMAL
goatee,*, A BEARD SHAVED TO A POINT
gobble,*,ed,ling, TO EAT VERY QUICKLY
goble, gobble
goblet,*, A DRINKING VESSEL

goblin,*, AN ENTITY ONLY SOME PEOPLE CAN SEE
gobul, gobble
god, CREATES ALL THINGS SEEN AND UNSEEN (or see good or got)
goddess, FEMALE ENTITY WHO CO-CREATES
goden, gotten
gody, gaudy
goen, join
goent, joint /join(ed)
goes, FORM OF "GO", IS MOVING TO ANOTHER SPACE OR ATTITUDE
goest, joist
gof, golf
gofener, governor
gofer, gopher /golfer
gofeul, jovial
gofur, gopher
gog, jog
gogels, goggles
goger, jog(gger)
gogir, jog(gger)
goggles, SAFETY EYE PROTECTION
gogils, goggles
goguls, goggles
gogur, jog(gger)
goin, join
goke, joke /jockey
goky, jockey
gol, goal
golaktik, galactic
gold, A PRECIOUS METAL
golden, THE COLOR OF GOLD
goldun, golden
gole, goal /goalie /golly /jolly
golf,*,fed,fing,fer, A SPORT
golie, goal/ goalie /golly /jolly
golly, VERBAL EXPRESSION OF SURPRISE (or see goalie or jolly)
goloshes, galoshes

glesen, glisten
glesten, glisten
gletch, glitch
gleu, glue
glew, glue
glich, glitch
glide,*,ed,ding,er, TO MOVE SMOOTHLY WITHOUT RESISTANCE
glider, glide(r) /glitter
glimer, glimmer
glimmer,*,red,ring, A DIM LIGHT
glimpse,*,ed,sing, SLIGHT GLANCE, SEE BRIEFLY
glint,*,ted,ting, A TWINKLE, SPARKLE
glisen, glisten
glisten,*,ned,ning, TO REFLECT LIGHT, SHINY
glitch,hes, MONKEYWRENCH IN THE PLANS, PROBLEM IN THE OPERATION OF
glite, glide
gliter, glitter /glide(r)
glitter,*,red,ring, SHINY SPECKS, FLECKS OF LIGHT (or see glider)
gliture, glitter /glide(r)
glo, glow
gloat,*,ted,ting, OVERLY PROUD OF AN ACCOMPLISHMENT
global,lly,lize,lization, TO INCORPORATE THE GLOBE, INCLUDE THE WORLD
globe,*, THE SHAPE AND PICTURE OF THE WORLD
globel, global
globul, global
glofs, glove(s)
glomp,*,ped,ping, MANY THINGS WHICH GRAB, STICK ONTO SOMETHING AT THE SAME TIME
gloo, glue
gloom,*,med,ming,my,mily, DULL SENSE OF FEAR
glorify,fies,fied,fying,fication, WORSHIP
glorufy, glorify
glory,ries,rify, IN HONOR, PRAISE
glosery, glossary

golt, jolt / gold
golten, golden
goly, jolly /golly /goalie
gondes, jaundice
gone,er, PAST TENSE OF "GO", ALREADY LEFT
goner,*, SOMEONE WHO IS GONE OR IN TROUBLE
gong,*, A MUSICAL INSTRUMENT
gonir, gone(r)
gont, jaunt /gaunt /join(ed)
gontlet, gauntlet
gonur, gone(r)
good,dy,dly,dness, ACCEPTABLE
good-bye,*, FAREWELL, EXPRESSION FOR LEAVING
goods, STUFF, STUFF FOR SALE
gooly, July
goon,*, THUG, A DERAGATORY NAME FOR SOMEONE
goose, A FEMALE BIRD, SQUEEZE SOMEONE (or see juice)
goot, jute
gopher,*, A RODENT, SOMEONE WHO GOES TO PICK-UP SOMETHING
gord, gourd /guard
gorela, gorilla /guerilla
gorge,*,ed,ging, TO STUFF, GEOLOGICAL FORMATION
gorgeous, SOMETHING VERY ATTRACTIV
gorgis, gorgeous
gorgus, gorgeous
gorilla,*, A MAMMAL (or see guerilla)
gorj, gorge
gorjus, gorgeous
gorma, gourmet
gos, goes /gauze
gosep, gossip
gosepd, gossip(ed)
gosip, gossip
gospel,*, PARTS OF THE BIBLE
gossip*,ped,ping, WORDS SAID ABOUT SOMEONE WHO ISN'T AROUND TO HEAR
gost, ghost

gosup, gossip
got,tten, PAST TENSE OF "GET", ACQUIRED SOMETHING DIDN'T HAVE BEFORE (or see goat /god /jot)
gote, goat /goatee
gotee, goatee
goten, gotten
goth,hic, DARK FORM OF SELF EXPRESSION, MEDIEVAL THEME
gothec, gothic
gotin, gotten
gotten, PAST TENSE OF "GET/GOT"
goty, gaudy
gouge,*,ed,ging, MAKE HOLES OR GROOVES INTO
goun, gown
gourd,*, FRUIT FROM A PLANT
gourmet,*, ONE WHO UNDERSTANDS FINE FOODS
goverment, government
govern,*,ned,ning, CONTROLLING ENTITIES WHO UPHOLD, CREATE RULES
government,*,tal, GROUP OF PEOPLE WHO RULE, UPHOLDS RULES FOR A PEOPLE
governor,*, STATE ELECTED POLITICIAN
goveul, jovial
govirment, government
govnur, governor
gowge, gouge
gown,*, FULL LENGTH DRESS, ROBE
gownse, jounce
gowul, jowl
goy, joy
goyful, joy(ful)
goyn, join
goynt, joint /join(ed)
goyus, joy(us)
goz, goes /gauze
grab,*,bbed,bbing,bby, TAKE ROUGHLY/QUICKLY
grace,*,ed,cing,eful,efully,efullness, ELEGANCE (or see graze)
grachus, gracious

gracious,sly,sness, PERFORM ELEGANTLY
grade,*,ed,ding, LEVEL IN LEARNING, DEGREES, STEPS (or see grate)
gradetude, gratitude
gradify, gratify
graditude, gratitude
gradjual, gradual
gradual,lly, MOVEMENT A BIT AT A TIME
graduation,*, CEREMONY CELEBRATING COMPLETION
graf, graph
grafe, grave
grafek, graphic
graffiti,to, PICTURES/WORDS PLACED/PAINTED IN PUBLIC PLACES WITHOUT PERMISSION
grafic, graphic
grafite, graphite /graffiti /gravity
grafity, gravity /graffiti
graft,*,ted,ting, TO ATTACH PART OF A LIVE THING TO PART OF ANOTHER LIVE THING
grafudy, gravity
grafux, graphic
grain,*, EDIBLE PLANT
grajual, gradual
grajuashen, graduation
gram,*, MEASURE OF WEIGHT
grammar,*,mmatical,mmacality,mmaticalness, WORDS AND THE WAY THEY ARE USED BY PEOPLE
grand,der,dest,deur,diose, OF GREAT STATURE, IMMENSE, BEST THERE IS (or see grant)
gran, grain
grandure, grand(eur) /grand(er)
granet, granite
granite, IGNEOUS ROCK
granola, DRIED GRAIN AND FRUIT MIXED TOGETHER
grant,*,ted,ting, GIVE WHAT WAS ASKED FOR
granut, granite
grape,*, FRUIT OF THE VINE
grapefruit,*, CITRUS FRUIT
grapevine,*, VINE OF A FRUIT

grapfruit, grapefruit
grapfrut, grapefruit
graph,*,hed,hing, TO PLOT ON, SHOWS CHANGES IN NUMBERS
graphic,*, VISUAL ART BY PEOPLE OR COMPUTER
graphite, TYPE OF ROCK
grapvine, grapevine
grase, grace /graze
grashis, gracious
grasp,*,ped,ping, GET A FIRM HOLD OF SOMETHING
grass,ses, PLANT
grat, great /grate /grade
grate,*,ed,ting, FABRICATED METAL OR STEEL, SOMETHING IRRITATING(or see great/ grade)
grateful,lly,llness, APPRECIATIVE
gratetude, gratitude
gratify,fies,fied,fying,fication, FULFILLING, PLEASURABLE
gratitude,*, APPRECIATION
graul, growl
grave, gravy
grave,*,er,est, WHERE SOMETHING IS BURIED, SERIOUS SITUATION
gravedy, gravity
gravel,led,ling, SMALL ROCKS
gravitation,nal,nally,tive, THE ACT OF BEING AFFECTED BY GRAVITY
gravity, POWERFUL FORCE KEEPING THINGS FROM FLOATING INTO SPACE
gravul, gravel
gravy,vies, THICK SAUCE
grawl, growl
grawnd, ground
gray,*,ying,yer,ying, COLOR, FROM AGING
graze,*,ed,zing, HOW HERD ANIMALS EAT (or see grace)
grease,*,ed,sing,sy,sier,siest,eless, FROM ANIMAL FAT, USE FOR MOVING MACHINE PARTS

great,*,ter,test,tly, HIGH ON THE SCALE OF IMPRESSIVE (or see grate)
gred, grid / greed
gredy, grit(tty) /greedy
greed,*,dy,dier,diest, TAKE MORE THAN NEED /greedy
greef, grief
green,*,ner,nest, COLOR, PLANTS
greese, grease
greet,*,ted,ting, TO WELCOME
greeve, grieve
greeze, grease
grefiti, graffiti
grell, grill
grem, grim /grime
gren, grin /green
grenola, granola
grep, grip
greshus, gracious
gret, grit /greet /greed
grety, grit(tty)
grew, PAST TENSE OF "GROW"
grewsome, gruesome
greze, grease
grid,*, PERPENDICULAR LINES
griddle,*,ed,ling, FLAT COOKING UTENSIL
gride, grit(tty)
gridul, griddle
grief, DEEP SADNESS (or see grieve)
grieve,*,ed,ving,vance, MOURNING A LOSS
grifete, graffiti
grill,*,led,ling, COOK ON METAL GRID OVER COALS
grim,mmer,mmest,mly,mmness, STUBBORN, VIRTUALLY UNCHANGABLE (or see grime)
grime,*,ed,ming,grimy, DIRT/GREASE/SOOT
grimy, DIRT/GREASE/SOOT
grin,*,ned,ning, SMILE BROADLY
grind,*,ded,ding, TO MILL/CHOP/SMASH/PULVERIZE (or see grin(nned))
grinola, granola

grip,*,pped,pping,pper, FIRMLY GRASP, HAND HOLD (or see gripe)
gripe,*,ping, VERBALLY COMPLAINING TO SOME OTHER THAN THE INTENDED RECIPIENT (or see grip)
grit,*,tty,tier,tiest, TINY GRANULES OF VARIETY OF MATERIAL, GROUND CORN
grital, griddle
gritle, griddle
grity, grit(tty)
gro, grow
groan,*,ned,ning, MOAN FROM PAIN
grocery,*, FOOD, NON-FOODS BOUGHT FROM STORE
grofe, grove
groggy,gier,giest, NOT QUITE AWAKE, STUPOR
grone, groan
groof, groove
groom,*,med,ming,mer, MALE GETTING MARRIED, TO CLEAN THE BODY
groove,*,ed,ving,vy,vier,viest, LONG INDENTATION IN SOMETHING, GET IN-STEP TO BE COOL
grope,*,ed,ping,per, TO AIMLESSLY ATTEMPT TO GRASP WITH HAND
grosery, grocery
grosry, grocery
gross,ssed,ssing,sser,ssest,ssly,ssness, SUM BEFORE EXPENDITURES, MEASUREMENT OF WEIGHT, DISTASTEFUL, REPULSIVE
grotesk, grotesque
grotesque,*,ely,eness, UGLY, DESPICABLE
groth, growth
grouch,hes,hy,hier,hiest, UNREASONABLY IRRITATED
groul, growl
ground,*,ded,ding,der, THE EARTH, FEET PLANTED SOLIDLY, BE ON THE EARTH'S SURFACE
group,*,ped,ping, TO PUT SIMILAR OBJECT, THINGS, PEOPLE TOGETHER
grouse,*, GAME BIRD (or see gross)
grove,*, A FIELD WHERE TREES WITH EDIBLE FRUIT IS GROWN

grow,*,wing,wn,grew, *GETTING BIGGER/TALLER*
growch, grouch
growl,*,led,ling, *VERBAL WARNING COMING FROM DEEP IN THE THROAT*
grown, *PAST TENSE OF "GROW"* (or see groan)
grownd, ground
grows, grow(s) /grouse /gross
growth,*, *COMPARE SIZE OR AMOUNT OF SOMETHING GROWING*
groz, gross /grow(s) /grouse
grub,*,bby,bbier,bbiest, *SLANG FOR FOOD, DIRTY AND MESSY*
grudge,*,er,gingly, *SOMEONE WHO WON'T FORGIVE SOMEONE ELSE*
gruel, *RUNNY/SLOPPY BOWL OF FOOD*
grueling, *HARD AND TEDIOUS*
gruesome,ely,eness, *AWFUL*
gruf, groove
grufede, graffiti
gruff,fer,fest,fness,fy, *RUDE AND ROUGH*
grufiti, graffiti
grug, grudge
gruj, grudge
grumble,*,ed,ling, *LOW/IRRITABLE MUMBLING, STOMACH SOUNDS WHEN HUNGRY*
grunola, granola
grunt,*,ted,ting, *SOUND MADE WHEN LIFTING/WHEN UNABLE TO RESPOND VERBALLY*
grupe, group
grusome, gruesome
guage, gauge
guantlet, gauntlet
guarantee,*,eed,eeing, *BACK UP A CLAIM, WITHOUT A DOUBT*
guard,*,ded,ding, *PROTECT AGAINST INVADER*
guardian,*,nship, *PROTECTOR*
guaze, gauze
gubalee, jubilee
gubelashen, jubilant(ation)

gubilation, jubilant(ation)
gud, good /gut
gud-by, good-bye
guder, gutter
gudge, judge
gudishal, judicial
gudishes, judicious
gudo, judo
guds, goods /gut(s)
guel, jewel
guerilla,*, *PEOPLE WHO HIDE WHEN FIGHTING* (or see gorilla)
guess,ses,sed,sing, *TAKE A GAMBLE AT THE PROPER ANSWER, DON'T KNOW ANSWER*
guest,*, *STAYING TEMPORARILY AT A PLACE THAT IS NOT YOURS* (or see guess(ed))
gufener, governor
gufner, governor
gug, jug /judge
guggle, juggle
gugul, juggle
guidance, *RECEIVE DIRECTION*
guide,*,ded,ding,dance, *SHOW THE WAY*
guil, jewel
guild,*, *COOPERATIVE GROUP OF PEOPLE WITH A PARTICULAR INTEREST*
guilt,*,ty, *BEING OR FEELING RESPONSIBLE FOR AN ACTION*
guinea pig,*, *A RODENT*
gul, gull /jewel /joule
gulactic, galactic
gulaktek, galactic
gulatnus, gelatin(ous)
guleble, gull(ible)
guloshes, galoshes
gull,*,llery,lled,lling,llible,llibility,llibly, *TYPE OF BIRD, TO BE TRICKED/DECEIVED*
gulp,*,ped,ping, *TAKE IN A LARGE MOUTHFUL*
guly, July

gum,*,mmed,mming,my, *SOMETHING CHEWABLE, RUBBERY, FROM A TREE*
gumble, jumble
gump, jump
gun,*,nned,nning, *A FIRING WEAPON, TO STEP ON THE ACCELERATOR, TO SHOOT SOMEONE* (or see goon or June)
gune, June /goon
gungle, jungle
gungul, jungle
guniur, junior
guleble, gull(ible)
gunk, junk
gunker, junk(er)
gunkie, junkie
gunkshen, junction
gunksher, juncture
gunyer, junior
guppy,pies, *FISH*
gurbel, gerbil
gurder, girder
gure, jury
gurer, juror
guresdiction, jurisdiction
gurgle,*,ed,ling, *SOUNDS COMING FROM THE THROAT, BUBBLING SOUND*
guri, jury
gurk, jerk
gurilla, guerilla /gorilla
gurk, jerk
gurl, girl
gurlfrend, girlfriend
gurm, germ
gurmenate, germinate
gurnelist, journal(ist)
gurney,*, *A COT OR STRETCHER TO CARRY BODIES* (or see journey)
gurmol, journal
gurter, girder

gurth, girth
gus, goose /juice
gusd, gust /just
gusdefecation, justify(fication)
gusdefiable, justifiable
gusdes, justice
gusdify, justify
guse, goose /juice
gusee, juicy
gush,hes,hed,hing, TO SPEW FORTH IN SUDDEN BURST
gust,*,ting, BIG BLOWS IN BURSTS, IRRATIC/HIGH WINDS (or see just)
gustefy, justify
gustes, justice
gustification, justify(fication)
gut,*,tted,tting, INSIDES OF LIVING THINGS, TO REMOVE INSIDES (or see good/jewt/jut)
gute, jute
gutir, gutter
guto, judo
gutter,*, ALONG ROOFS FOR RAIN COLLECTION
guverment, government
guviner, governor
guvinile, juvenile
guy,*, males, wire or rope used to support or steady something
guynacologist, gynecologist
guynicologist, gynecologist
gy, guy
gym,*, A PLACE TO WORK-OUT (or see gem)
gymnasium,*, A BUILDING WHERE PEOPLE DO PHYSICAL ACTIVITIES
gymnast,*,tics, ONE WHO PRACTICES THE ART OF MANIPULATING THEIR BODIES
gyn, gynaeco, gyne, gyneco, gyneco, gyno, PREFIX INDICATING "FEMALE" MOST OFTEN MODIFIES THE WORD

gynecologist,*,gy, THE SCIENCE OF, ONE WHO STUDIES WOMEN'S ORGANS
gyp,*,ped,ping, TO CHEAT/STEAL
gypsum, CHALKY ROCK
gypsy,sies, PEOPLE WHO CHOOSE TO BE ON THE FRINGE OF SOCIETY FOR WHATEVER REASON
gyrate,*, ed,ting, TO SPIRAL

"H"

ha, hay /hey
habachi, hibachi
habe, happy
haben, happen
habin, happen
habit,*,tual, DOING THE SAME THING OVER AND OVER
habitat,*, NATURAL HOME FOR LIVING THINGS
habitual,*, SOMEONE WHO DEALS WITH MANY HABITS
habochi, hibachi
haby, happy
hach, hatch /hash /hack
hachet, hatchet
hachit, hatchet
hack,*,ked,king,ker, THE ENTERING OF PRIVATE DATA ON COMPUTERS, CHOP AT
hactare, hectare'
had, PAST TENSE FOR THE WORD "HAVE" (or see hat)
hadn't, CONTRACTION OF THE WORDS "HAD NOT"
hadur, hot(tter)
hael, howl
haf, half/ have/ halve
hafen, haven /heaven
hafhasert, haphazard

hafhazard, haphazard
hafhazurdle, haphazard(ly)
hafint, haven't
hafnt, haven't
hafun, haven /heaven /have(ving)
hagerd, haggard
haggard,*,dly, ROUGH, WORN
hagurd, haggard
haiku, FORM OF JAPANESE POETRY
hail,led,ling, RAIN IN THE FORM OF ICE, LOUD VOCAL WELCOME (or see hale)
hainger, hanger
hainkerchef, handerkerchief
hair,ry,rier,riest, STRANDS OF WHICH GROW FROM THE SKIN (or see hare or heir)
hak, hawk / hack
hakd, hack(ed)
haker, hack(er)
haktare, hectare'
hal, PREFIX INDICATING "SALT/HALOGEN" MOST OFTEN MODIFIES THE WORD (or see hall/ hale/ hail/ haul/ howl)
halareus, hilarious
hale,*,er,est,eness, TO COMPLY (or see hall/ haul/ hail/ holly)
halegram, hologram
halekopter, helicopter
haleluya, hallelujah
half,fness, WHOLE MADE INTO TWO PARTS (or see have or halve)
halfhasard, haphazard
halfhasurdly, haphazard(ly)
halibut, A FISH
hall,*, (hallway) NARROW CORRIDOR WITH DOORS INSIDE A BUILDING (or see haul or hail)
hallelujah,*, REJOICE
halloween,*, A HOLIDAY
halm, helm

halo, PREFIX INDICATING "SALT/HALOGEN" MOST OFTEN MODIFIES THE WORD
halo,*, REFLECTS THE LITE COMING FROM WITHIN SOMEONE (or see hollow or hello)
halokost, holocaust
halow, hollow /halo
halowen, halloween
halp, help
halpful, helpful
halt,*,ted,ting, STOP NOW (or see haul(ed))
halter,*, GEAR FOR A HORSE
halubet, halibut
halugram, hologram
halve,*,ed,ving, TO SEPARATE ONE INTO TWO PARTS (or see have)
haly, holly
ham,*,mmed,mming, PORK, TO BE GOOFY
hamak, hammock
hambergur, hamburger
hamburger,*, BEEF GROUND UP
hamer, hammer
hamileate, humiliate
hammer,*,red,ring,FORCE SOMETHING IN,HANDTOOL
hammock,*, WOVEN FABRIC STRETCHED BETWEEN TWO TREES TO LYING UPON
hamogenize, homogenize
hamper,*,red,ring, PUT CLOTHES INTO, GET IN THE WAY OF PROGRESS
hamster,*, A RODENT
hamuk, hammock
hamur, hammer
hand,*,ded,ding,dful,dy, AT THE END OF THE ARM WITH FINGERS ON IT
hande, handy
handeist, handy(diest)
handel, handle
handeur, handy(dier)
handicap,*, pped, UNABLE TO FUNCTION AT FULL CAPACITY, CHALLENGED

handil, handle
handkerchief,*, SQUARE CLOTH
handle,*,ed,ling,er, FOR HANDS OR WITH HANDS
handmade, MADE BY HAND NOT BY MACHINE
handout,*, TO GIVE SOMETHING TO SOMEONE WHO IS IN NEED
handul, handle
handy,dier,diest, SOMETHING EASILY AVAILABLE
hang,*ged,ging,ger, SECURE SOMETHING ABOVE THE FLOOR ALLOWING FOR A VERTICAL POSITION
hangar,*, PLACE FOR LARGE TRANSPORTATION VESSELS (or see hanger)
hanger,*, FOR SUSPENSION OFF THE GROUND (or see hangar)
hank, hang
hankerchif, handkerchief
hant, hand
hantecap, handicap
hantel, handle
hantil, handle
hantmade, handmade
hantowt, handout
hantul, handle
hanty, handy
hapale, happy(pily)
hape, happy
hapeir, happy(pier)
hapeist, happy(piest)
hapele, happy(pily)
hapen, happen
hapenes, happy(piness)
hapeur, happy(pier)
haphazard,dly,DO THINGS UNSAFELY, DISORGANIZED
hapie, happy
hapile, happy(pily)
hapin, happen
hapines, happy(piness)
happen,*,ned,ning, AN EVENT THAT HAS OCCURRED

happy,ppier,ppiest,ppily,ppiness, BEING JOYFUL IN LIFE
hapule, happy(pily)
hapun, happen
hapy, happy
hapyer, happy(pier)
hapyest, happy(piest)
hapynes, happy(piness)
har, hair/ heir/ hare
harass,sses,ssed,ssing,ssment, AGGRAVATE BEYOND NORMAL
haray, hurrah
harbor,*,red,ring, WHERE BOATS DOCK, HOLD ONTO
hard,der,dest,den, CHALLENGING, DENSE, SOLID (or see heart)
hardily, heart(ily)
hardles, heartless
hardly, BARELY, NOT QUITE
hardship,*, TOUGH TIMES
hardware,*, TOOLS, USE TO BUILD WITH, REPAIR MATERIAL
hardy,dier,diest,diness, STRONG AND CAPABLE
hardyness, hardy(diness)
hare,*, A WILD RABBIT (or see hair(y) or here)
haredetary, hereditary
haredity, heredity
haree, hair(y)
harefy, horrify
harendous, horrendous
harendus, horrendous
harer, horror
haretitary, hereditary
haretity, heredity
hareur, hair(ier)
hareust, hair(iest)
harfest, harvest
harifik, horrify(fic)
harindus, horrendous
harison, horizon

harm,*,med,ming,mful,mless, *TO INJURE*
harmeny, harmony
harmfel, harm(ful)
harminy, harmony
harmlis, harm(less)
harmonica,*,, *MUSICAL INSTRUMENT*
harmonize,*, ed,zing, *SYNCHRONIZE SOUNDS*
harmony,nies, *VARIETY OF DIFFERENT THINGS VIBRATING AT A COMPATIBLE FREQUENCY*
harmuny, harmony
harness,sses,ssed,ssing, *HOLD ONTO, GET HOLD OF*
harnis, harness
harnus, harness
haroek, hero(ic)
haroen, heroine
haroik, hero(ic)
haroin, heroine
harp,*,ped,ping, *MUSICAL INSTRUMENT, TO NAG*
harpoon,*,ned,ning, *TO STAB WITH A LONG METAL POLE WITH BARB ON THE END*
harpsicord,*,, *A MUSICAL INSTRUMENT*
harsh,her,hest,hly, *STERN AND ROUGH*
hat, hard /heart
harteist, heart(iest) /hard(iest)
harteur, heart(ier) /hard(ier)
harth, hearth
hartily, heart(ily)
hartiness, hardy(diness)
hartles, heartless
hartlus, heartless
hartly, hardly
hartship, hardship
hardware, hardware
harty, heart(y) /hardy
haruble, horrible
harvest,*,ted,ting,ter, *BRING IN RIPENED FOOD*
hary, hair(y)
has, *ACQUIRED*
hasard, hazard

hase, haze /haze(y)
hasel, hazel
hasen, hasten
hash,hes,hed,hing, *A FOOD, TO TALK IT OVER*
hasil, hassle
hasn't, *CONTRACTION OF THE WORDS "HAS NOT"*
haspitality, hospitality
hassle,*, ed,ling, *TO AGITATE*
haste,ey, *DO IT QUICKLY*
hasten,ned,ning, *TO SPEED UP*
hasul, hassle /hazel
hat,*, *COVERING FOR HEAD (or see had/hate)*
hatch,hes,hed,hing, *COVER OF STORAGE AREA, LIVE THINGS COMING FROM EGGS*
hatchet,*,, *SMALL AX*
hate,*,ed,ting,eful,tred, *MOST OPPOSITE FROM LOVE*
hauder, hot(tter)
hauefur, however
haughty,ty,tier,tiest,tily,tiness, *ACTING AS IF BETTER THAN OTHERS*
hauk, hawk /hock
haul,*,led,ling, *TRANSPORT A LOAD (or see hall)*
hauleluea, hallelujah
haulo, hollow
haulter, halter
haultur, halter
haunch,hes, *PART OF REAR LEGS ON ANIMALS*
haund, hound
haunt,*,ted,ting, *TO SPOOK*
haups, hops
haured, horrid
haurur, horror
haus, house
hausd, house(d)
hauspus, hospice
haustej, hostage
haustel, hostel /hostile
haustig, hostage
haut, hot

hauvel, hovel
hauztul, hostel /hostile
hav, halve/ have/ half
havd, halve(d)
have, *TO POSSESS, ACQUIRE (or see half or halve)*
haven't, *CONTRACTION OF THE WORDS "HAVE NOT"*
haven,*, *A SAFE PLACE (or see heaven or have(ving))*
havin, haven /heaven
havint, haven't
havs, halve(s)
havun, haven /heaven
haw, how
hawever, however
hawk,*, *A BIRD*
hawl, howl /haul
hawle, holly
hawnd, hound
hawnt, hound
hawvul, hovel
hay,*,ying, *DRY GRASS, ALFALFA, WORKING WITH HAY (or see hey)*
haz, has /haze
hazard,*,dly,dous, *DANGEROUS*
haze,*,ed,zing,zy, *SMOKE, MIST, DUST, BLURRY*
hazel, *A PLANT, A COLOR (OR SEE HASSLE)*
haznt, hasn't
hazurd, hazard
he, *A MALE*
head,*,ded,ding,der, *BODY PART ON TOP OF SHOULDERS, ON TOP OF, LEADING*
heal,*,led,ling,ler, *TO CURE, SOMEONE WHO CURES, MEND (or see heel or he'll)*
health,hy,hier,hiest, *OF SOUND BODY/MIND*
heap,*,ped,ping, *TO MOUND UP*
hear,*,ring,rd, *SOUND IN EARS (or see here)*
heard, *PAST TENSE FOR "HEAR "(or see herd)*
hearsay, *GOSSIP*
hearse, *A VEHICLE FOR MOVING CASKETS*

hearst, hearse
heart,*,ty,tier,tiest,tily,tiness, *AN ORGAN IN A BODY (or see hard)*
hearth,*, *SURROUNDING A FIREPLACE*
heartless,ssly,ssness, *CRUEL*
heat,*,ted,ting,er,rtless, *WARM, FOR MAKING WARM (or see heed or he'd)*
heave,*,ed,ving, *TO THRUST SOMETHING HEAVY USING FORCE*
heaven,*,nly, *A EUPHORIC STATE OF MIND, DIVINE*
heavy,vier,viest,ily,viness, *OF GREAT WEIGHT*
hebachi, hibachi
hebnutize, hypnotize
heckle,ed,ling,er, *ANNOYING NOISES AND WORDS AIMED AT A SPEAKER*
hecksugon, hexagon
heckup, hiccup
hectare',*,', *METRIC MEASUREMENT, 2.5 ACRES*
hectic, *CONFUSING RUSH*
hecto, *PREFIX INDICATING "ONE HUNDRED" MOST OFTEN MODIFIES THE WORD*
he'd, *CONTRACTION OF THE WORDS "HE WOULD, HE HAD" (or see heed/ head/ he'd/ hit)*
hed, head/ hit/ he'd/ head/ heed
hedch, hitch /hedge
hedeus, hideous
hedge,*,ed,ging, *BUSHES, TO TRIM BY CUTTING*
hedid, heed(ed)/ heat(ed)/ head(ed)
hedud, heed(ed)/ heat(ed)/ head(ed)
heed,*,ded,ding, *PAY ATTENTION, TAKE NOTICE OF (or see heat/ he'd/ heed)*
heef, heave
heel,*,led,ling, *PART OF THE FOOT (or see heal or he'll)*
heep, heap
heet, heat
hefen, heaven
hefer, heifer
hefon, heaven

hefur, heifer
hefy, heavy
heg, hedge
heifer,*, *IMMATURE COW*
height,*,ten, *MEASURE TOP TO BOTTOM,MAKE TALLER*
heigth, height
heimlek, heimlich
heimlich, *A MANEUVER WHICH CLEARS WINDPIPE FOR BREATHING*
heir,*, *ONE WHO RECEIVES MONEY/PROPERTY SOMEONE BEQUEATHED THEM UPON THEIR DEATH (or see hair/ heir/ air/ err)*
heirloom,*, *SOMETHING PRECIOUS HANDED DOWN TO FOLLOWING GENERATIONS*
heiten, height(en)
heith, height
heithen, height(en)
hej, hedge
heksigon, hexagon
heksugon, hexagon
hektare, hectare'
hektik, hectic
hekul, heckle
hekup, hiccup
hel, heel/ hell /heal /he'll /hill
helakopter, helicopter
helareus, hilarious
held, *PAST TENSE OF "HOLD"*
heleom, helium
helicopter,*, *FLYING MACHINE*
helio, *PREFIX INDICATING "SUN" MOST OFTEN MODIFIES THE WORD*
helium, *A GAS*
hell,*,llish,llishly, *AN IMAGINARY PLACE OF GREAT DISCOMFORT (or see he'll/ heal/ heel)*
he'll, *CONTRACTION OF THE WORDS "HE WILL" (or see hell/ heal/ heel)*
hello, *AMERICAN GREETING*
helm,*, *STEERING PART OF A BOAT*

helmet,*, *A PROTECTIVE COVER FOR THE HEAD*
helo, hello
help,*,ped,ping, *SOMEONE OR SOMETHING BEING AIDED*
helpful,lly,lness, *THOSE WHO AID OTHERS*
helpfulnes, helpful(ness)
helpless,sly,sness, *UNABLE TO AID ONESELF*
helt, held / hilt
helth, health
hem,*,mmed,mming, *HAVING TO DO WITH BORDERS ON THINGS (or see him or hymn)*
hemi, *NAME BRAND*
hemi, *PREFIX INDICATING "HALF" MOST OFTEN MODIFIES THE WORD*
hemisphere,*, *ONE HALF OF EARTH*
hemo, *PREFIX INDICATING "BLOOD" MOST OFTEN MODIFIES THE WORD*
hemosfere, hemisphere
hemp,*, *A PLANT USEFUL FOR CLOTHING/ MATERIAL/ROPE/PAPER*
hemself, himself
hen,*, *FEMALE CHICKEN*
hena, henna
hence,*, *THEREFORE, AND SO*
hender, hinder
hendrance, hindrance
henge, hinge
henje, hinge
henna, *PLANT FOR DYING HAIR/FABRIC, FOR TEMPORARY TATTOOS*
hens, hen(s) /hence
hent, hint
hep, heap /hip
hepacrite, hypocrite
hepakrete, hypocrite
hepatitis, *ILLNESS CAUSED BY VIRUS*
hepnosis, hypnosis
hepnutize, hypnotize
hepokrite, hypocrite

hepopotamus, hippopotamus
hepothesis, hypothesis
hept, hepta, PREFIX INDICATING "SEVEN" MOST OFTEN MODIFIES THE WORD
hepy, hip(py)
her,*, IN REFERRING TO A FEMALE (or see hear/ here/ hair/ hare/ heir)
heracane, hurricane
herass, harass
herb,*,bal,baceous,lism,balist, PLANTS FOR HEALING/COOKING WITH (THE "H" IS SILENT)
herbavor, herbivore
herbivore,*,ous, PLANT EATING ANIMAL (THE "H" IS SILENT)
herbulist, herb(alist)
herd,*,ded,ding, ANIMALS GATHERED INTO A GROUP FOR MOVING (or see heard or hurt)
herdle, hurdle /hurtle
herdul, hurdle /hurtle
here,*, IN THIS VICINITY, WHERE YOU ARE (or see hear/ hair(y)/ hare)
hered, hurry(ried)
hereditary,rily,riness, ABLE TO BE PASSED ON FROM ONE GENERATION TO ANOTHER
heredity,ties, PASSED DOWN THROUGH GENERATIONS
hereist, hair(iest)
herendus, horrendous
heresay, hearsay
hereur, hair(ier)
hericane, hurricane
herison, horizon
herizun, horizon
hermit,*, A RECLUSE, HERMIT CRAB, A CRUSTACEAN
hero,oes,oic,oine, BRAVE ACT TO SAVE SOMETHING ALIVE FROM PERIL OR DEATH
heroek, hero(ic)
heroine, DRUG TO EASE PAIN, ADDICTIVE, MANMADE
hers, hearse /her(s)
herself,lves, SHE ALONE

herst, hearse
hert, hurt/ heard/ herd
hertful, hurt(ful)
herth, hearth
hertle, hurdle /hurtle
hertul, hurdle /hurtle
hery, hair(y) /hurry
herz, her(s)/ here's/ hearse
he's, CONTRACTION OF THE WORDS, "HE IS"
hes, his/ hiss/ he's
hesatashen, hesitate(tion)
hesatation, hesitate(tion)
hesdorean, historian
hesdorik, historic
hesdory, history
hesdurekteme, hysterectomy
hesetashen, hesitate(tion)
hesetation, hesitate(tion)
hesitant,tly,tation, PAUSE TO CONSIDER BEFORE CONTINUING, CONSIDERING BEFORE STARTING
hesitashen, hesitate(tion)
hesitate,*,ted,ting,tingly, TAKE A PAUSE BEFORE CONTINUING
hesterektomy, hysterectomy
hestorian, historian
hestorical, historic(al)
hestorik, historic
hestory, history
hesutashen, hesitate(tion)
hesutation, hesitate(tion)
het, head/ hit/ he'd/ heat/ heed
hetch, hitch
hetero, PREFIX INDICATING "OTHER/ DIFFERENT" MOST OFTEN MODIFIES THE WORD
heteus, hideous
hetid, heed(ed)/ heat(ed)/ head(ed)
hetud, heed(ed)/ heat(ed)/ head(ed)
heu, hue /who
heug, huge

heuj, huge
heumen, human
heve, heave /heavy
hevin, heaven
hevy, heavy
hew, hue /who
hewman, human /humane
hewmer, humor
hewmid, humid
hewmileate, humiliate
hex, PREFIX INDICATING "SEX" MOST OFTEN MODIFIES THE WORD
hexagon,*, SIX-SIDED FIGURE/SHAPE
hey, AN EXCLAMATION FOR GREETING OR FOR SURPRISE, WAY OF GREETING (or see hay)
hezetante, hesitant
hezitate, hesitate
hezutashen, hesitate(tion)
hi, A WELCOME GREETING (or see high)
hibachi,ies, ROUND COOKING GRILL
hiberacteve, hyperactive
hibernate,ed,ting,tion, TO SLEEP OVER THE WINTER
hibochi, hibachi
hibred, hybrid
hibrud, hybrid
hiccup,*,pped,pping, THROAT MUSCLE IN TEMPORARY SPASM
hid,dden, IN HIDING, PAST TENSE OF "HIDE", STORED FROM EYESIGHT (or see hit)
hidch, hitch /hedge
hide,*,ding, TO STORE FROM EYESIGHT, SKIN OFF OF ANIMAL (or hid or height)
hiden, hid(den)
hideous,sly,sness, FRIGHTFULLY UGLY
hideout,*, WHERE SOMEONE GOES TO HIDE
hidout, hideout
hidrant, hydrant
hidrent, hydrant
hidroelectric, hydroelectric

hidrophonic, hydrophonic
hidroponic, hydrophonic
hidrugen, hydrogen
hieroglyphs,hic, CARVED, PAINTED SYMBOLS FROM PAST PEOPLES
hif, hive
hifen, hyphen
hifenate, hyphen(ate)
hifer, heifer
hifin, hyphen
higene, hygiene
higenist, hygiene(nist)
high,*,her,hest,hly, ALTITUDE BETWEEN THE GROUND AND SPACE, A EUPHORIC SENSE UNDER THE INFLUENCE OF A HALLUCINOGEN (or see hi)
hijack,*,ked,king, TAKE VEHICLE/VESSEL BY FORCE
hijene, hygiene
hike,*,ked,king, TO WALK ON ROUGH, NATURAL TERRAIN
hikoo, haiku
hiku, haiku
hikup, hiccup
hilarious,sly, ABSOLUTELY FUNNY
hill,* MOUNDS ON THE EARTH (or see he'll)
hilt,*, SWORD OR DAGGER HANDLE, COMPLETELY AND ABSOLUTELY
him, REFERENCE TO MALE OVER THERE, MALE/THIRD PERSON (or see hem or hymn)
hime, hemi
himesfere, hemisphere
himesphere, hemisphere
himlek, heimlich
himluk, heimlich
himp, hemp
himself, HIS OWN SELF
hin, hen
hince, hence
hind, THE REAR PORTION OF AN ANIMAL

hinder,*,red,ring, IN THE WAY OF PROGRESS OR SUCCESS
hindrance,*, IN THE WAY OF PROGRESS/SUCCESS
hinge,*,ed,ging, SWINGS BY WAY OF A PIN ENCASED IN A HINGE
hinje, hinge
hinse, hence
hint,*,ted,ting, TINY PORTION OF THE FULL FACT
hip,*,ppy, THE PELVIC AREA ON PEOPLE AND ANIMALS, TO BE COOL AND, OR INDIFFERENT TO SOCIAL PRESSURES
hipadrete, hypocrite
hipatidus, hepatitis
hipauthusis, hypothesis
hipawthusis, hypothesis
hipe, hype / hip
hiperactive, hyperactive
hiperactuve, hyperactive
hipernate, hibernate
hipnosis, hypnosis
hipnosus, hypnosis
hipnutise, hypnotize
hipocrite, hypocrite
hipokrit, hypocrite
hipotenuse, hypotenuse
hipothurmeu, hypothermia
hipothusis, hypothesis
hippopotamus,*, LARGE/HEAVY HERBIVORE
hir, her/ hire/ here
hiracane, hurricane
hirass, harass
hird, heard/ herd/ hurt/ hire(d)
hirdul, hurdle / hurtle
hire,*,ed,ring, PAID TO WORK (or see high(er))
hirison, horizon
hirmet, hermit
hiro, hero
hiroek, hero(ic)
hiroglifs, hieroglyphs

hiroin, hero(ine) / heroin
hirs, hearse/ her(s)/ hire(s)
hirself, herself
hirst, hearse
hirt, hurt/ heard/ herd
hirtul, hurdle / hurtle
hirz, her(s)/ hearse/ hire(s)
his, BELONGS TO HIM (or see hiss)
hisderektomy, hysterectomy
hisdorean, historian
hisdoric, historic
hisdurekteme, hysterectomy
hisetate, hesitate
hiss,ses,sed,sing, SOUND A SNAKE OR STEAM MAKES (or see his)
hist, histo, PREFIX INDICATING "LIVING TISSUE" MOST OFTEN MODIFIES THE WORD
histare, history
histere, history
historian,*, PEOPLE WELL STUDIED IN HISTORY
historic,cal,cally, AN EVENT IN THE PAST WORTH REMEMBERING
history,ries, THE PAST
histrektomy, hysterectomy
histure, history
histurektemy, hysterectomy
hit,*,tting, TO STRIKE A BLOW (or see height/ hid/ hide)
hitch,hes,hed,hing, TO JOIN TWO THINGS TOGETHER BY WAY OF (or see hedge)
hite, height /hide
hiten, height(en) /hid(dden)
hiteout, hideout
hiteus, hideous
hith, height
hithen, height(en)
hitout, hideout
hitun, height(en)
hive,*, BUMPS ON A PERSON, HOME OF BEES OR WASPS

ho, hoe/ who/ hue
hoard,*,ded,ding, *TO STOCKPILE MORE GOODS THAN NECESSARY*
hoarse,er,est, *THE WAY ONE TALKS AFTER GETTING OVER A COLD OR FLU (or see horse)*
hoax,es, *A TRICK IN DECEPTION*
hobble,*,ed,ling, *WALK WITH A LIMP*
hobby,ies, *A PASTTIME*
hobe, hope / hobby
hobful, hope(ful)
hobil, hobble
hobless, hope(less)
hobt, hop(pped) /hope(d)
hobul, hobble
hoby, hobby
hockey, *A SKATING SPORT*
hod, *HOLDER FOR MORTAR (or see hot or hold)*
hodel, hotel
hoder, hot(tter)
hodir, hot(tter)
hody, haughty
hoe,*,ed,oing, *A HAND TOOL (or see whore)*
hoest, hoist
hof, huff
hofel, hovel
hofer, hover
hoful, hovel
hofur, hover
hog,*, *A PIG, SOMEONE WHO EATS LIKE A PIG*
hoist,*,ted,ting, *LIFT OR RAISE UP*
hok, hawk / hock
hoks, hoax / hock(s)
hoky, hockey
hol, hole/ whole/ haul/ hall
hold,*,ding, *KEEP FROM MOVING/FALLING, TO GRASP, KEEP STILL*
holder, halter / hold(er)
holder,*,*, *SOMETHING THAT HOLDS THINGS*

hole,*,ed, *AN OPENING/SPACE/ORIFICE/GAP (or see holy/ holly/ whole(y)/ wholly)*
holegram, hologram
holeist, holy(liest)
holer, holler
holeur, holy(lier)
holey, wholly/ whole(y)/ holy
holiday,*, *A DAY OF REMEMBERANCE OR HONORING*
holigram, hologram
holl, hall/ haul/ whole/ hole
holler,*,red,ring, *YELLING/CALLING LOUDLY*
hollow,*,wed,wing, *TO DIG OR CARVE OUT SO INSIDE IS EMPTY (or see halo)*
holly,ies, *PLANT (or see holy/hole/whole/wholly)*
holo, *PREFIX INDICATING "WHOLE" MOST OFTEN MODIFIES THE WORD (or see hollow/hello)*
holocaust,*, *DEVASTATING DESTRUCTION OF PEOPLE/PLACES*
hologram,*, *A THREE DIMENSIONAL ILLUSION, VISUAL REFLECTED BY LASERS*
holow, hollow
holoween, halloween
holsal, wholesale
holsel, wholesale
holsem, wholesome
holsome, wholesome
holster,*, *HOLDER FOR A PISTOL*
holsum, wholesome
holt, hold /halt /haul(ed)
holter, halter /hold(er)
holuday, holiday
holugram, hologram
holur, holler
holy,lier,liest, *SACRED (or see hole/ holly/ wholly/ hole(y)/ whole(y))*
hom, whom /home
homade, homemade
home,*,ey, *A PLACE WHERE SOMEONE LIVES*
homeless, *HAVING NO HOME*

homely, *PERSON WHO IS WITHDRAWN/ SHY*
homemade, *NOT MADE BY A MACHINE IN A FACTORY*
homeny, hominy
homeo, homo, *PREFIX INDICATING "THE SAME" MOST OFTEN MODIFIES THE WORD*
homer,*, *HOME RUN IN BASEBALL*
homevur, whomever
homey, *HOME BOY*
hominy, *GROUND CORN*
homir, homer
homless, homeless
homly, homely
homo, homeo, *PREFIX INDICATING "THE SAME" MOST OFTEN MODIFIES THE WORD*
homogenize,*,ed,zing, *CREAM/MILK MIXED TOGETHER*
homur, homer
homy, homey
honch, haunch /hunch
hond, hone(d) /haunt
hondred, hundred
hone,*,ed,ning, *TO SHARPEN (or see honey)*
honer, honor
honerary, honorary
honest,ty,tly, *TRUTHFUL ("H" IS SILENT)*
honey,*, *A LIQUID FROM NECTAR MADE BY BEES*
honeymoon,*,ned,ning, *WHAT A COUPLE HAS AFTER THEIR WEDDING*
honist, honest
honk,*,ked,king, *A HORN SOUND, SOUND A GOOSE MAKES*
honker, hunk(er) /honk
honor,*,red,ring,rable,rably, *RESPECT, STRONG MORAL INTEGRITY ("H" IS SILENT)*
honorary, *AWARD OF HONOR ("H" IS SILENT)*
hont, haunt /hone(d) /hunt
hontred, hundred
honur, honor
honymoon, honeymoon

hoo, hue /who
hood,*,ded, JACKET/HAT COMBINATION, ENGINE COVER ON CAR, IN THE NEIGHBORHOOD (or see hoot or who'd)
hooever, whoever
hoof,*, fed,fing,ves,ved, FEET OF SOME ANIMALS
hook,*, ked,king, A CURVED TOOL WITH SHARP TIP FOR GRABBING
hoomever, whomever
hoop,*,ped,ping, THINGS THAT ARE A CIRCLE USED AS A TOOL OR TOY (or see hop)
hooray, hurrah
hoos, who's/ whose/ hue(s)
hoot,*,ted,ting, SOUND OWL MAKES, FOND EXPRESSION TOWARDS SOMEONE (or see hood/who'd)
hoove,*, ed, MORE THAN ONE HOOF
hop,*,pped,pping, TO JUMP UP AND DOWN, WHAT A RABBIT DOES (or see hope)
hopd, hop(pped) /hope(d)
hope,*, ed,ping,eful,eless, WISH FOR SOMETHING (or see hop/ hops/ hobby)
hopful, hope(ful)
hopless, hope(less)
hops, A GRAIN (or see hope(s))
hopscotch, GAME
hopskoch, hopscotch
hor, whore
horafid, horrify(fied)
horascope, horoscope
hord, hoard/ hard/ horde/ horrid
horde,*, MANY THINGS OR PEOPLE ALL TOGETHER AT ONCE, SWARMS OF (or see hard or horrid)
hordervs, h'ordeuvres
h'ordeuvres, APPETIZERS
hordurves, h'ordeuvres
hored, hoard /horrid /horde
horefik, horrify(fic)
horefy, horrify
horendous, horrendous

horer, horror
horescope, horoscope
horesontul, horizontal
horible, horrible
horify, horrify
horir, horror
horiscope, horoscope
horizon,*, WHERE THE SUN/MOON RISES/SETS
horizontal,lly, POSITION SITUATED LINEAR WITH THE HORIZON
hormeny, harmony
hormful, harm(ful)
hormles, harm(less)
hormone,*, nal,noid, CHEMICALS MANUFACTURED BY THE BODY (pineal gland)
hormuny, harmony
horn,*, ned,ning, INSTRUMENT PLAYED BY BLOWING, USED FOR SOUND ON VEHICLES AND VESSELS
horne, horny
hornet,*, LARGE VOLATILE WASP
horny, MADE OF HORN, SLANG FOR CERTAIN DESIRES
horoscope,*, USING THE STARS TO GUESS THE FUTURE
horrendous,sly, TERRIBLE, DREADFUL
horrible,ly, AWFUL, UGLY, HORRENDOUS
horrify,fies,fied,fying,fic, VERY FRIGHTENING, BEYOND SCARY
horror,*, OVERPOWERING/UNIMAGINABLE FEAR
horse,*, ed,sing, ANIMAL(or see hoarse or horror)
hort, horde
horuble, horrible
horufid, horrify(fied)
horufy, horrify
horur, horror
horuscope, horoscope
horusontel, horizontal
hos, hoe(s) /hose /who's /hue(s) /whose
hosbedul, hospital
hosbetality, hospitality

hosbidul, hospital
hosbitality, hospitality
hosbituble, hospitable
hosbitul, hospital
hosdege, hostage
hosdej, hostage
hosdel, hostel /hostile
hosdji, hostage
hosdul, hostel /hostile
hose,*, ed,sing,RUBBER TUBE(or see whose/who's)
hospetable, hospitable
hospetality, hospitality
hospetul, hospital
hospitable,ly,leness, KIND/FRIENDLY TO GUESTS
hospital,*,lize,lized,lizing, PLACE FOR SICK AND INJURED PEOPLE
hospitality,ties, KINDNESS TO GUESTS
host,*,ted,ting,tess, TO SPONSOR, ONE WHO ENTERTAINS/IS IN CHARGE
hostage,*, PERSON HELD AGAINST THEIR WILL
hostel,*, SHELTERS AROUND THE WORLD WHERE PEOPLE TRAVELING MAY STAY FOR CHEAP (or see hostile)
hoster, holster
hostes, host(ess)
hostige, hostage
hostile,lity,lities, ACTS AGGRESSIVE/ ANGRY (or see hostel)
hostis, host(ess)
hostle, hostile /hostel
hostul, hostel /hostile
hostus, host(ess)
hot,tter,ttest,ttest, CAN BURN, WARMER THAN WARM, IN REFERENCE TO SOMEONE VERY ATTRACTIVE (or see hod)
hotel,*, BUILDINGS WITH ROOMS FOR TRAVELERS TO STAY THE NIGHT
hoter, hot(tter)
hotur, hot(tter)

hoty, haughty
houefur, however
houl, howl /haul
hound,*, *TO AGITATE SOMEONE, BE PERSISTENT LIKE A HOUND DOG ON A SCENT, A DOG*
hour,*,rly, *60 SECONDS ("h" IS SILENT)(or see our)*
house,*,ed,sing, *STRUCTURE/DWELLING TO LIVE IN*
hovel,*, *A TINY DWELLING, SMALL OPEN STRUCTURE*
hover,*,red,ring, *TO FLOAT ABOVE FOR A PERIOD OF TIME WITHOUT MOVING, TO FLOAT ABOVE*
hovil, hovel
hovul, hovel
hovur, hover
how, *EXPLAIN THE WAY SOMETHING IS SAID OR DONE, QUESTION THE WAY SOMETHING HAPPENS*
however, *IN ANY EVENT, ON THE OTHER HAND, STILL*
howl,*,led,ling, *SOUND DOG MAKES, A LOUD SOUND*
hownd, hound
hownt, hound
howse, house
hox, hoax /hock(s)
hoz, hose/ hoe(s)/ who's/ whose
hozbetuble, hospitable
hozdul, hostel /hostile
hozpetality, hospitality
hozpitable, hospitable
hozt, host
hoztus, host(ess)
hu, hue /who
hub,*, *THE CENTER OF SOMETHING WHICH HOLDS IT ALL TOGETHER, KEEPS IT MOVING*
hubcap,*, *COVER FOR WHEELS, COVERS THE HUB*
huch, hutch /huge /hush
huckleberry,ries, *AN EDIBLE BERRY*
hud, hood/ hoot/ who'd
huddle,*,ed,ling, *FORM/HUNCH INTO A TIGHT GROUP*
hude, hood/ hoot/ who'd
hudel, huddle

hue,*, *SHADES, DEGREES OF THE SAME COLOR (or see who)*
huever, whoever
huf, hoof /huff /hoove
hufd, huff(ed) /hoove(d)
hufed, huff(ed) /hoove(d)
huff,*,ffed,ffing, *DEEP GASPS FOR AIR, DEEP BREATH OUT*
hug,*,gged,gging,ggable,ggably, *WRAP ARMS AROUND SOMEONE OR SOMETHING WITH GOOD INTENT (or see huge)*
hugable, hug(ggable)
hugd, hug(gged)
huge,ely,eously,eness, *ENORMOUS IN BULK, TAKES UP ALOT OF SPACE (or see hutch)*
hugible, hug(ggable)
hugt, hug(gged)
huguble, hug(ggable)
huj, huge
huk, hook
hukd, hug(gged)
hukeble, hug(ggable)
huklbery, huckleberry
hukt, hook(ed) /hug(gged)
hul, hull /who'll
hulareus, hilarious
hull,*, *MAINFRAME/COVER (or see who'll)*
hum, whom
hum,*,mmed,mming, *A SOUND MADE WITH LIPS PURSED (or see whom)*
human,*,men,noid,nity,nness,nism,nist,nistic, ntarian,ntarianism,nize,nization,nly,nizer, *HOMO SAPIEN BEING (or see humane)*
humane,ely, *BE FAIR, CIVILIZED, REFINED (or see human)*
humble,*,ed,ling, *NOT SELF-RIGHTEOUS, ISN'T FLAGRANTLY PROUD OR OPINIONATED*
humbul, humble
humdinger, *OUTSTANDING*

humed, humid
humeleate, humiliate
humen, human
humenbird, hummingbird
humengbird, hummingbird
humer, humor /hummer
humerus, humor(ous)
humes, hummus /humus
humever, whomever
humid,dity,dify,dification,dly, *MOISTURE IN THE AIR*
humiliate,*,ed,ting,tion, *BELITTLED, ATTACK ON SELF-ESTEEM, HARSH JUDGEMENT*
humin, human
huminbird, hummingbird
humis, hummus /humus
hummer,*, *A TYPE OF TRUCK*
hummingbird,*, *TINY BIRD*
hummus, *CHICKPEA, GARBONZO MIXTURE FOR AN EDIBLE SPREAD (or see humus)*
humor,*,red,ring,rous,rously, *FUNNY (or see hummer)*
hump,*,ped,ping, *A BUMP, WHAT A MALE DOG DOES*
humple, humble
humud, humid
humur, humor /hummer
humus, *ORGANIC RICH SOIL (or see hummus)*
hunch,hes,hed,hing, *BENT OVER, HAVE AN IDEA*
hundred,*,dth, *100, A NUMBER USED IN THE U.S.*
hunemoon, honeymoon
hung, *PAST TENSE OF "HANG"*
hunger,*,red,ring,gry,grily,griness,*TO NEED/WANT SOMETHING DESPERATELY (or see hunker)*
hungry,rier,riest, *NEED FOOD*
hunk,*,ker, *CHUNK OF SOMETHING (or see hung or honk)*
hunker, hunk(er)
hunsh, hunch
hunt,*,ted,ting,ter, *TO PURSUE TO LOCATE*
huntch, hunch

hydrophonic,*, USE OF WATER WITH ADDED VITAMINS/MINERALS TO FEED ROOT PLANTS INSTEAD OF SOIL
hydroponic, hydrophonic
hyfen, hyphen
hygene, hygiene
hygiene,nist, CARE FOR THE EXTERIOR OF THE BODY
hygro, PREFIX INDICATING "MOISTURE" MOST OFTEN MODIFIES THE WORD
hyjack, hijack
hyke, hike
hymn,*,nal, RELIGIOUS SONG (or see him or hem)
hypawthusis, hypothesis
hype, EXAGGERATING (or see hip)
hyper, PREFIX INDICATING "ABOVE/OVER" MOST OFTEN MODIFIES THE WORD
hyperactive,vity, UNFOCUSED ENERGY
hypernate, hibernate
hyperthermia, hypothermia
hypethermia, hypothermia
hyphen,nate, A MARK WHICH SHOWS CONNECTION BETWEEN TWO WORDS
hyphenate, hyphen(ate)
hypnosis, SLIP TO A PLACE IN THE SUBCONSCIOUSE MIND
hypnotize,*,ed,zing, BE TALKED INTO A SUBCONSCIOUSE STATE OF MIND
hypo, PREFIX INDICATING "BELOW/UNDER" MOST OFTEN MODIFIES THE WORD
hypocrite,*,tical,ticly,isy,isies, SOMEONE WHO SAYS ONE THING BUT DOES ANOTHER, LYING
hypotenuse, LONGEST SIDE OF TRIANGLE, USUALLY THE BASE
hypothermia, BODY BELOW NORMAL TEMPERATURE
hypothesis,ses, A THEORY FORMED DUE TO LACK OF INFORMATION OR TIME
hypothusis, hypothesis
hysdurekteme, hysterectomy

husband,*,dman, PARTNER OF A WIFE, MARRIED TERM
husbend, husband
husbind, husband
hush,hes,hed,hing, BEING TOLD TO BE QUIET WITH A SOUND, GET SILENT
husk,*,ked,king, PROTECTIVE SHELLS ON THE FRUIT FROM PLANTS, TO REMOVE HUSKS
husky,kies,kier,kiest, A DOG, SOMEONE WHO IS LARGER IN SIZE AND MUSCLE THAN PEERS
husle, hustle
husler, hustle(r)
huspend, husband
hustle,*,ed,ling,er, GET A MOVE ON IT, SOMEONE WHO GAMBLES AT POOL
hut,*, RAMSHACKLE STRUCTURE, WORD USED IN FOOTBALL (or see hoot)
hutch,hes, CAGE FOR ANIMALS, TO HOLD DISHES
hutel, huddle
hutul, huddle
huv, hoove
huz, who's/ whose/ hue's
huzbend, husband
huze, hue(s)/ who's/ whose
huzpend, husband
hybernate, hibernate
hybred, hybrid
hybrid,*, OFFSPRING FROM TWO ANIMALS OR PLANTS
hydr, hydro, PREFIX INDICATING "WATER/ LIQUID" MOST OFTEN MODIFIES THE WORD
hydrant,*, CAP FOR ACCESS TO STORED WATER
hydraulic,*, USE OF LIQUID UNDER PRESSURE TO MAKE PARTS MOVE
hydrint, hydrant
hydroelectric,cal,cally, USED TO RUN MACHINES VIA WATER PRESSURE THROUGH GENERATORS
hydrogen, A GAS, MORE OF THIS CHEMICAL THAN ANY OTHER ON THE PLANET

huntret, hundred
huntrid, hundred
huny, honey
hunymoon, honeymoon
hup, hoop /hub
hupcap, hubcap
hur, her
huracane, hurricane
hurass, harass
hurb, herb
hurbavore, herbivore
hurd, heard/ herd/ hurt
hurdid, herd(ed) /hurt(ed)
hurdle,*,ed,ling, JUMP OVER OBSTACLES (or see hurtle)
hure, hurry
huredetary, hereditary
hureditare, hereditary
huredity, heredity
huricane, hurricane
hurifek, horrify(fic)
hurisun, horizon
hurizen, horizon
hurmit, hermit
huroik, hero(ic)
hurrah,*, YELL FOR JOY
hurricane,*, HIGH WINDS E FROM THE SEAS
hurried, hurry(ried)
hurry,ries,ried,rying, TO GO FASTER THAN NORMAL
hurs, hearse /her(s)
hurself, herself
hurst, hearse
hurt,*,ting,tful, PAIN, OR CAUSES PAIN (or see herd or heard)
hurtle,*,ed,ling, TO THROW OR FLING VIOLENTLY/ WITH GREAT FORCE (or see hurdle)
hury, hurry
hurz, her(s) /hearse
hus, hue(s)/ who's/ whose

"I"

I, PERSONAL POSSESSIVE FOR "ME" (or see eye)
ial, aisle
ibrau, eyebrow
ibreveate, abbreviate
ibreviate, abbreviate
ibrow, eyebrow
ice,*, ed,cing,cy, FROZEN WATER
ich, itch
ichu, issue
ichuense, issue(uance)
ichuinse, issue(uance)
icing, TOPPING FOR BAKED GOODS
icon,*, nic,nical, SMALL PICTURES OR SYMBOLS THAT
ARE REPRESENTATIVE
icselerate, accelerate
icy,icier,iciest, FROZEN WATER
icycle,*, FROZEN ICE SHAPED LIKE DAGGERS
I'd, CONTRACTION OF THE WORDS "I WOULD, I COULD,
I SHOULD, I HAD"
id, BASED ON FREUD'S EGO THEORY (or see eye(d)
idapt, adapt
idch, itch
idea,*, al,ally, A THOUGHT, THE BEST THOUGHT
idel, it'll /idle /idol
idem, item
idemize, item(ize)
idenfy, identify
idenity, identity
identical,lly,lness, EXACTLY THE SAME
identification,*, PICTURE OR LEGAL DOCUMENT
PROVING WHO A PERSON IS (I.D.)
identify, fies, fied, fying, TO RECOGNIZE

identity, ties, A CHARACTERISTIC WHICH IDENTIFIES
ONE FROM ANOTHER
idenufi, identify
ideo, PREFIX INDICATING "IDEA" MOST OFTEN MODIFIES
THE WORD (or see idio)
ideut, idiot
idim, item
idimise, item(ize)
idinefy, identify
idinety, identity
idintekul, identical
idintufecation, identification
idio, PREFIX INDICATING "PRIVATE/ INDIVIDUAL/
PROPER" MOST OFTEN MODIFIES THE WORD
(or see ideo)
idiot,*, tic, ACTS LIKE A FOOL
idle,*, er,ling, RUN IN NEUTRAL, SITTING WITHOUT
MOVING (or see idol or it'll)
idmire, admire
idmit, admit
idmyre, admire
idol,*, ADMIRED BY MANY (or see idle)
idolt, adult
idoo, adieu
idself, itself
idsetura, etcetera
idsulf, itself
idu, adieu
idul, idol /idle /it'll
idult, adult
idum, item
idvanse, advance
idvantige, advantage
idvize, advise /advice
ie, eye
iel, aisle /I'll
ieng, eye(ying)
if, THEN THIS IF NOT THAT, IT COULD BE THIS OR THAT
BASED ON WHETHER

ife, ivy /iffy
ifekt, effect /affect
iffy,ffier,ffiest, PROBABILITY IT WILL/WILL NOT HAPPEN
ifre, ivory
ifree, every
ifry, ivory
ify, ivy /iffy
ig, il, im, in, ir, PREFIX INDICATING "NOT" MOST
OFTEN MODIFIES THE WORD
igalatarian, egalitarian
igalutarean, egalitarian
igloo,*, DOME DWELLING BUILT OF ICE BLOCKS
iglu, igloo
ignarent, ignorant
igneous, OLD ROCK FORMED BY HIGH HEAT
ignerants, ignorant(nce)
ignerent, ignorant
igneus, igneous
ignide, ignite
ignishin, ignition
ignite,*, ed,ting,tion, SPARK TO MAKE IT START,
START A FIRE
ignition,*, ELECTRICAL SPARK TO START AN ENGINE
ignorant,ntly,ance, LACKING INFORMATION
ignor, ignore
ignore,*, ed,ring, PURPOSELY NOT PAY ATTENTION
ignurent, ignorant
igree, agree
igsajurate, exaggerate
igsakt, exact
igsample, example
igsberament, experiment
igsblod, explode
igsbozishen, expose(sition)
igsebshen, except(ion)
igsebt, except /accept
igsempt, exempt
igsept, except /accept
igsert, exert

I'll, CONTRACTION OF THE WORDS "I WILL" (or see aisle or ill)

ill,lness, NOT WELL

illegal,lly,lity, AGAINST THE LAW, NOT LEGAL

illicit,tly,tness, PROHIBITED BY LAW, NOT ALLOWED

illisit, illicit

illiterate, HARDLY ABLE TO READ AND WRITE, NOT EDUCATED

illogical,lly, NOT LOGICAL, NOT REALISTIC

illuminate,*,ed,ting,tion, TO ENLIGHTEN, INFORM

illusion,*,nal,nary,nist,nism, SENSE SOMETHING AS IF IT WERE PHYSICAL/REAL (or see allude(usion) or elude(usion))

illustrate,*,ed,ting,tion,tor, DRAW A PICTURE, ONE WHO DRAWS

ilness, ill(ness)

ilogikul, illogical

ilorm, alarm

ilongate, elongate

ilude, elude

ilujen, illusion /allusion /elusion

ilumenade, illuminate

iluminate, illuminate

ilnus, ill(ness)

ilund, island

ilur, allure

ilushen, illusion, illusion /allusion /elusion

ilusion, illusion, illusion /allusion /elusion

ilusive, elusive

ilustrate, illustrate

ilute, elude

I'm, CONTRACTION OF THE WORDS "I AM"

im, in, il, ir, PREFIX INDICATING "NOT/ IN/ INTO/ON" MOST OFTEN MODIFIES THE WORD

imaculet, immaculate

image,*,ging,gination,ginative, A PICTURE REAL OR IN THE MIND

imagenashen, imagine(nation)

imaginashen, imagine(nation)

imagrant, immigrant /emigrant

imagrate, immigrate /emigrate

imagrent, emigrant /immigrant

imagunashen, imagine(nation)

imaj, image

imajenashen, imagine(nation)

imanint, eminent /imminent

imansopate, emancipate

imatashin, imitate(tion)

imatate, imitate

imature, immature

imbankment, embankment

imbargo, embargo

imbark, embark

imbasee, embassy

imbeded, embed(dded)

imbelikul, umbilical

imberis, embarrass

imbet, embed

imbilakul, umbilical

imblim, emblem

imboss, emboss

imbrase, embrace

imbreo, embryo

imbrorder, embroider

imbrufment, improve(ment)

imbtee, empty

imbur, ember

imbuse, embassy

imeduetly, immediate(ly)

imediate, immediate

imenent, imminent

imense, immense

imerg, emerge

imergency, emergency

imerse, immerse

imertality, immortal(ity)

imetashen, imitate(tion)

imeteut, immediate

imfasis, emphasis

imfusis, emphasis

imigrant, immigrant /emigrant

imigrashen, immigrate(tion) /emigrate(tion)

imigrate, immigrate /emigrate

imigration, immigrate(tion) /emigrate(tion)

imigrunt, immigrant /emigrant

iminent, imminent

iminse, immense

imitate,*,ed,ting,tion,tive, TO COPY, FAKES

imkombutent, incompetent

immaculate,ely,eness,acy, NO SPOTS/STAINS/ MARS/FLAWS

immature,ely,eness,rity, NOT OLD ENOUGH, NOT MATURE, NOT GROWN, FOOLISH

immediate,ely,eness, RIGHT NOW

immense,ely,eness, GREAT IN SIZE, HUGE, VAST

immerse,es,ed,sing,sion,sionist, SINK INTO LIQUID/THOUGHT/ACTIVITY

immigrant,*, SOMEONE WHO GOES TO ANOTHER COUNTRY (or see emigrant)

immigrate,*,ed,ting,tion, TO GO TO ANOTHER COUNTRY (or see emigrate)

imminent,tly,ncy,tness, IT WILL HAPPEN NO MATTER HOW LONG IT TAKES, INEVITABLE

immoral,lly,lity,lities, NOT PROPER/MORAL/ DECENT

immortal,lly,lity, EXISTS FROM NOW ON, NEVER ENDING

immune,nity,nities, FREE FROM, EXEMPT, HEALTHY

immunize,*,ed,zing,zation,PHARMACEUTICALS INTRODUCED INTO THE BODY TO FIGHT MICRO ORGANISMS WHICH MAY/MAY NOT INVADE BODY

imochen, emotion

imochun, emotion

imoral, immoral

imordle, immoral

imortaledy, immortal(ity)

imortality, immortal(ity)

imorul, immoral

imownt, amount

impact,*,ted,ting,tion,*TWO BODIES OF MASS COL-LIDING INTO ONE ANOTHER, SIZEABLE EFFECT*

imparer, emperor

imparutev, imperative

impashent, impatient

impatient,nce,tly, *NOT PATIENT, UNABLE TO RELAX*

imperative,*,val,ely,eness, *ABSOLUTELY ESSENTIAL, NECESSARY*

imperfect,tly,ness,tion, *NOT AS GOOD AS COULD BE*

imperor, emperor

impersonal,lly,lity,lities,lize, *NOT ATTACHED IN A PERSONAL WAY, ABSENCE OF PERSONAL FEELINGS*

impersonate,*,ed,ting,tion, *TO ACT/BEHAVE LIKE SOMEONE ELSE*

imphasis, emphasis

impire, empire

implamint, implement

implant,*,ted,ting, *TO INSTILL IDEAS OR THOUGHTS, REPLACE BODY ORGAN WITH ANOTHER ONE*

implecate, implicate

implement,*,ted,ting,tal,tation, *SOMETHING USED AS A TOOL, TO INCORPORATE INTO*

implicate,*,ed,ting,tion, *BE TANGLED/ INVOLVED IN, SUSPECTED PARTICIPATION*

imploe, employee / employ

imploer, employer

imploy, employ / employee

imployer, employer

implucate, implicate

implucation, implicate(tion)

implument, implement

imply,lied,ying,lication, *SUGGESTING SOMETHING OR SOMEONE IS RESPONSIBLE*

impolite,ely,eness, *RUDE/FRANK/IMPERSONAL/ HONEST*

impolse, impulse

impolsive, impulse(sive)

import,*,ted,ting,tion,table,tability, *BRING INTO THE COUNTRY FROM ANOTHER COUNTRY*

impose,*,ed,sing,sition, *TO INTERRUPT, SUGGESTED REFERENCE, UNWELCOME INCLUSION*

imposebul, impossible

impossible,ly,bility,eness, *NOT POSSIBLE, COULD NEVER HAPPEN*

imposter,*, *UNWELCOME INCLUSION, BE WHERE ONE IS NOT WANTED, ILLEGITIMATE*

impound,*,ded,ding, *TAKE AWAY/CONFISCATE/ HOLD LAWFULLY*

impoverish,hed,her,hment, *MARGINALIZED, UN-ABLE TO ADEQUATELY SUPPORT ONESELF*

impovuresh, impoverish

impoze, impose

impractical,able,ability,ableness, *NOT PRACTICAL/ LOGICAL FOR SITUATION*

impraktecle, impractical

imprecise,ely,eness,sion, *NOT PRECISE/FACTUAL*

impregnable,bility,eness,ly, *NOT ABLE TO MOVE PENETRATE/GET INTO*

impregnate,*,ed,ting,tor,able, *TO INTRO-DUCE/INJECT INTO, MAKE PREGNANT, INFUSE*

impregnuble, impregnable

imprent, imprint

impress,sses,ssed,ssing,ssion,ssionable, ssionability,ssionableness,ssionist,ssionism, ssionistic,ssive,ssively,ssiveness,ssible, ssibility, *FAVORABLY AFFECTED*

impretion, impress(sion)

imprint,*,ted,ting,ter, *PRINT/STAMP INTO, TO LODGE/INSTLL INTO MEMORY*

imprison,ned,ning,nment,ner, *PLACE INTO PRISON, CONFINE, INCARCERATE*

improbable,ly,bility,eness, *HIGHLY UNLIKELY, NOT NORMALLY POSSIBLE, MOST LIKELY NOT*

impromptu, *OFF THE TOP OF YOUR HEAD, SPUR OF THE MOMENT IDEA*

improper,rly,rness, *NOT PROPER/ACCEPTABLE*

impropuble, improbable

improve,*,ed,ving,er,ement,vable,vability, *MAKE BETTER THAN BEFORE, TOWARDS PERFECTION*

improvise,*,ed,sing,er,sation,sational,sator, satorial, *MAKE IT UP AS YOU GO, IMPROMPTU*

improvusashen, improvise(sation)

impruf, improve

impte, empty

impulite, impolite

impulse,*,sion,sive,sively,siveness, *SUDDEN ACT/ MOVEMENT WITHOUT APPARENT THOUGHT*

impurer, emperor

impurfekt, imperfect

impursenate, impersonate

impursonal, impersonal

impursonation, impersonat(tion)

impuseshen, impose(sition)

imput, input

imruld, emerald

imte, empty

imug, image

imugrant, immigrant /emigrant

imugrashen, immigrate(tion) /emigrate(tion)

imugrate, immigrate

imugrent, immigrant /emigrant

imuj, image

imune, immune

imunent, eminent /imminent

imunezashen, immunize(zation)

imunezation, immunize(zation)

imunise, immunize

imunity, immune(nity)

imunize, immunize

imurgency, emergency

imurse, immerse

imurtalety, immortal(ity)

imutashin, imitate(tion)

imutation, imitate(tion)

in, *CONTAINED/BELONGS WITHIN, CONFINED, ENTER, POPULAR NOW, INCLUSION (or see inn)*

in, ig, il, im, ir, *PREFIX INDICATING "NOT" MOST OFTEN MODIFIES THE WORD (or see prefix "un"/"en")*

inabel, enable / unable

inability, ties, *UNABLE, NOT ABLE TO, WITHOUT CAPACITY TO*

inabishen, inhibit(ion)

inable, enable / unable

inabul, enable / unable

inabler, enable(r)

inaccessable, bility, eness, ly, *CANNOT BE OBTAINED, UNREACHABLE, NO ACCESS*

inacsesable, inaccessible

inact, enact

inaction,*, *NO ACTION, IDLE*

inacurate, innacurate

inadequate, ely, eness, acy, acies, *NOT ENOUGH, INADEQUATE, LACKING*

inadmissable, bility, bly, *NOT ALLOWED TO ENTER, NOT ADMISSABLE*

inadvertent, tly, nce, ncy, ncies, *NOT PAYING ATTENTION, NOT DIRECT/STRAIGHTFORWARD*

inadvisable, bility, *ADVISE/RECOMMEND AGAINST, BEST NOT TO DO/SAY SOMETHING*

inakd, enact

inakshen, inaction

inaleable, inalienable

inaleuble, inalienable

inalienable, ly, bility, *CANNOT TAKE AWAY*

inalisis, analysis

inamet, intimate

inamul, enamel

inanimate, ely, eness, *NOT ANIMATE, USUALLY AN OBJECT WHICH DOESN'T ACT OR MOVE*

inaple, enable / unable

inappreciative, able, ably, eness, also unappreciative, *NOT APPRECIATED, ACTIONS NOT REGARDED AS USEFUL/NECESSARY*

inapproachable, *NOT ACCESSIBLE/APPROACHABLE, UNREACHABLE*

inappropriate, ely, eness, *NOT PROPER/ APPROPRIATE/ACCEPTABLE AT THE MOMENT*

inapul, enable /unable

inaqurite, innacurate

inasinse, innocence

inate, innate

inatequit, inadequate

inatible, inaudible

inatly, innate(ly)

inatmissable, inadmissable

inatvertense, inadvertent

inatvizable, inadvisable

inatvurtent, inadvertent

inaudible, ly, bility, *NOT ABLE TO HEAR, NOT AUDIBLE, CAN'T BE HEARD*

inaugurate,*, ed, ting, tion, tor, al, *FORMALLY INSTALL/BEGIN, ADDRESS TO THE PUBLIC*

inbankment, embankment

inbaris, embarrass

inbark, embark

inbasee, embassy

inbed, embed

inberis, embarrass

inbet, embed

inblem, emblem

inblum, emblem

inbosd, emboss(ed)

inboss, emboss

inbrase, embrace

inbreo, embryo

inbrorder, embroider

incadesent, incandescent

incandescent, tly, *A BULB TYPE WITH A FILAMENT THAT HEATS UP, BRIGHT/SHINING LITE*

incapable, ly, eness, bility, *NOT CAPABLE/ABLE TO, DON'T HAVE WHAT IT TAKES TO ACCOMPLISH*

incapacitate, ed, tion, *OUT OF ORDER, UNABLE TO FUNCTION AS USUAL, LACKING POWER TO*

incarcerate,*, ed, ting, tion, *SENTENCED TO CONFINEMENT*

incarnate,*, ed, ting, tion, *TAKE ON PHYSICAL FORM*

incarserate, incarcerate

incense, ed, sing, *AROMATIC PRESSED POWDER FOR BURNING*

incenurate, incinerate

incerense, insure(rance)

incentive,*, *A MOTIVATION FOR PERFORMING A TASK*

incept, tor, tion, tive, tively, *FROM THE BEGINNING, MOMENT OF CREATION*

incepshen, incept(ion)

incest, tuous, tuously, tuousness, *SEX AMONGST THE FAMILY IF RELATED BY BLOOD*

inch, hes, hed, hing, *A U.S. MEASUREMENT*

inchant, enchant

inchantmint, enchant(ment)

inchoy, enjoy

inchur, ensure /insure /injure

incident,*, nce, ntal, ntally, *HAPPENING ATTACHED TO A LARGER EVENT, DISTINCT BUT SEEMINGLY MINOR*

incinerate,*, ed, ting, tor, tion, *TO BURN, COOKS TO ASHES WITH FIRE*

incircle, encircle

incision,*, sed, *MAKE A CUT INTO*

incline,*, ed, ning, nation, *A GRADUALLY ELEVATED PLANE, TO GO UP, MOST LIKELY TO*

inclood, include

inclose, enclose

incloser, enclose(sure)

inclosment, enclose(ment)

inclozur, enclose(sure)

include,*,ed,ding,usion,usive,usively,usiveness, dible,dable, ADD/INVOLVE SOMETHING INTO GROUP OF OTHER THINGS

inclusef, inclusive

inclushen, include(usion)

inclusion,*,ive, ADD/INVOLVE SOMETHING INTO GROUP OF OTHER THINGS

inclusive,ely,eness, ADD/INVOLVE SOMETHING INTO GROUP OF OTHER THINGS

incoherent,tly,nce,ncy,ncies, UNABLE TO COMPREHEND UNDERSTAND, CANNOT COMMUNICATE LOGICALLY/UNDERSTANDABLE

incombutent, incompetent

income,*,ming, MONEY COMING IN

incomparable,bility,bly, NOTHING TO COMPARE TO

incompas, encompass

incompatible,bility,bleness,bly, NOT ABLE TO GET ALONG WITH, TOO MANY DIFFERENCES

incompetent,nce,ncy,ntly, NOT ABLE TO COMPETE/ KEEP UP, LACKS QUALIFICATIONS

incomplete,*,ed,ely,eness,etion, NOT COMPLETE, NEEDS MORE TO FINISH

incompruble, incomparable

inconclusive,ely,eness, NO FINAL RESULTS, NO CERTAIN ANSWERS

inconsiderate,ely,eness,tion,ably,ableness, NOT CONCERNED WITH SOMEONE'S EMOTIONAL REACTION OR WELL BEING

inconsistent,tly,ncy,ncies, DOESN'T PERFORM STEADILY/PREDICTABLY

inconvenient,tly,nce,ncy,ncies, DOESN'T FIT INTO THE PLAN CAUSING DELAY OF FINISHING, NOT ON THE WAY THERE, UNPLANNED

incorect, incorrect

incoriguble, incorrigible

incorporate,*,ed,ting,able,ation,ative,ator, TO INCLUDE INTO THE WORKINGS OF, BROUGHT INTO A LARGER BODY, UNITE, COMBINE

incorrect,tly,tness, NOT EXACT/FACTUAL/SUITABLE

incorrigible,bility,eness,ly, NOT ABLE TO BE CORRECTED/REFORMED TO MEET EXPECTED STANDARDS

incorugible, incorrigible

incounter, encounter

incownter, encounter

increase,*,ed,sing,singly,sable, TO MAKE MORE THAN THERE WAS, ADD MORE

incredible,ly,lity,eness, ASTONISHING, BEYOND EXPECTATION

incredulous,sly,sness, CROSS BETWEEN INCREDIBLE AND RIDICULOUS

incremenate, incriminate

increment,*,tal,tally, MOVE EXACT AMOUNT IN ONE DIRECTION, INCREASE

incriminate,*,ed,ting,tion, TO ACCUSE OR LEND SUSPICION, CHARGE WITH A CRIME

incruments, increment(s)

incubate,tion,tional,tive,tor, TO PROTECT AN EGG IN PERFECT ENVIRONMENT FOR EMBRYO TO GROW INTO FULL FORM

incumbent,*,ncy,ncies,ntly, FILL A POST OR OFFICE

incumpatuble, incompatible

incunklusef, inconclusive

incunsideret, inconsiderate

incunsistent, inconsistent

incupasitate, incapacitate

incur,rred,rrence, LIABLE FOR, ADDED DEBT IN ORIGINAL LOAN

incurable,bility,eness, SEEMINGLY UNABLE TO CURE, EXTREMELY DIFFICULT TO HEAL

incureg, encourage /anchor(age)

incurekt, incorrect

incurig, encourage /anchor(age)

ind, and /end

indanger, endanger

indangurment, endanger(ment)

indanjer, endanger

indasishen, indecision

indaveguel, individual

indavishual, individual

indebted,dness, OWE SOMETHING TO SOMEONE

indecent,ncy,ncies,ntly, NOT ACCEPTABLE BY SOCIETY'S STANDARDS

indecision, NOT ABLE TO BE FIRM IN MAKING A CHOICE

indecisive,eness,ely, NOT ABLE TO MAKE A FIRM CHOICE

inded, end(ed)

indedud, indebt(ed)

indeed, CERTAINLY, CONFIRMATION

indefer, endeavor

indeferent, indifferent

indeferent, indifferent

indefinite,ely,eness, WITH NO END OR FINAL GOAL, NOT DEFINED

indefur, endeavor

indefurent, indifferent

indefurent, indifferent

indego, indigo

indekat, indicate

indeks, index

indent,*,ted,ting,tation, A DENT IN SOMETHING, DIFFERENT DEPTH FROM REST OF THE SURFACE

independent,*,tly,nce,ncy,ncies, ABLE TO STAND PRIMARILY ON ITS OWN, NOT DEPENDENT

inder, inter /enter

indesent, indecent

indeted, indebted

indever, endeavor

index,xes,xed,xing,xical, TO CATEGORIZE, DIVIDE INTO GROUPS, PROVIDE A NAME FOR EASY RETRIEVAL

indicate,*,ed,ting,tion,tive,tively,tor(y), GIVE A SIGN TOWARDS A DIRECTION, PROVIDES INFORMATION, HELPS IN FIGURING ANSWER

indicater, indicate(tor)

indict,ted,ting,table,ter,tor,tment, CHARGE WITH A CRIME ("C" IS SILENT)

indifferent,tly,tist,tism,nce, *NOT PARTIAL OR CONCERNED WITH CHOICES/ACT/EVENT*
indifrent, indifferent
indigo,*, *DEEP BLUE COLOR, COLOR FROM A PLANT*
indikate, indicate
indintashen, indent(ation)
indite, indict
individual,*,lly,lism,lity,lize,lities,ization,ate, *ON ITS OWN, DOESN'T BELONG TO A GROUP*
indlis, endless
indoctrinate,*,ed,ting,tion,tor, *FORCED TEACHING PRINCIPLES/IDEOLOGY TO ELIMINATE CREATIVE THINKING*
indoer, endure
indoor,*,, *INSIDE A STRUCTURE/DWELLING*
indoose, induce
indorse, endorse /indoor(s)
indorsment, endorse(ment)
indostry, industry
indrakit, intricate
inducate, indicate
induce,*,ed,ement,er,cible, *BRING ON, START/ MAKE HAPPEN*
indulge,*,ed,ging(ly),er,ence,encies,ent,ently, *TO AFFORD ONESELF A DESIRE, SATISFY AN IMPULSE*
indur, inter /enter /endure
induseshin, indecision
industrial,lly,list,lness,lism,lize,lization, *PRODUCTIVE, MANUFACTURES*
industry,ries,rious,riously, *MACHINE/TECHNOLOGY/ MANUFACTURING*
induvijual, individual
inedible, *CANNOT OR SHOULD NOT EAT*
inegma, enigma / enema
inekspensef, inexpensive
inekwality, inequal(ity)
inema, enema / anemia
inemut, intimate

inendashen, inundate(tion)
inendate, inundate
inept,tly,tness,titude, *UNABLE, INCOMPETENT*
inequal,ity,ties, *NOT EQUAL, DIFFERENCES EXIST*
iner, inner
inercom, intercom
inerconnect, interconnect
inerem, interim
inerge, energy
inergetek, energetic
inerject, interject
inerjetek, energetic
inerkorse, intercourse
inerlock, interlock
inerlude, interlude
inermedeary, intermediary
inermingle, intermingle
inermishen, intermission
inermission, intermission
inermost, innermost
inernashenul, international
inernational, international
inernet, internet
interrelate, interrelate
inersculastic, interscholastic
inersection, innersection
inersekshen, innersection
inersperse, intersperse
inert,tly,teness, *VISIBLY INACTIVE, NO APPARENT ACTION/MOVEMENT*
inertwine, intertwine
inerupt, interrupt
inervene, intervene
inerview, interview
inervue, interview
inervul, interval
inerwoven, interwoven
inescapable, *CANNOT ESCAPE*
inesent, innocence(nt)

inesheashen, initiate(tion)
ineshul, initial
inesince, innocence
inesthesia, anesthesia
inetiale, initial(lly)
inetuble, inedible
inetvizable, inadvisable
inevitable,bility,eness,ly, *CANNOT AVOID*
inexcesable, inaccessible
inexpensive,ely,eness,*FAIR PRICE, NOT EXPENSIVE*
inexperience,ed, *DOESN'T HAVE SKILLS TO PERFORM*
infachuashen, infatuate(tion)
infachuate, infatuate
infadek, emphatic
infallible,lity,eness,ly, *FOR CERTAIN*
infaluble, infallible
infant,*,ncy,ncies,thood,tlike, *BABIES UP TO ONE YEAR OLD*
infantry,ries,ymen, *FOOT SOLDIERS*
infatuate,ed,tion,edly, *INSTANTLY ATTRACTED TO WITH WILD ABANDON*
infect,*,ted,tedness,ting,tion,ter,tor,tious, tiously,tiousness,tive, *TO POLLLUTE AN AREA*
infekshus, infect(ious)
infenatively, infinite(tively)
infent, infant
infentry, infantry
inferior,rity,rly,rity, *LESSER THAN ANOTHER, NOT SUPERIOR*
infermashen, inform(ation)
infermury, infirmary
infest,*,ed,ting,tation, *THREATENINGLY OVERWHELM*
infeureate, infuriate
infiltrate,*,ed,ting,tion,tive, *PASS BEYOND BOR- DERS OF A SPACE WHERE UNINVITED*
infinite,ely,eness,tude,tive,tival,tively,ty,ties, *GOES ON AND ON PERHAPS FOREVER*
infirmary,ries, *SITE FOR MEDICAL CARE*
infistructure, infrastructure

inflammation, SWOLLEN TISSUE

inflashen, inflate(tion)

inflate,*,,ed,table,ting,tion,tionism,tionist, TO AIR UP, RAISE, EXPAND/INCREASE

infleksuble, inflexible

inflemashen, inflammation

inflewance, influence

inflexible,bility,eness,ly, WON'T BEND, STUBBORN, NOT FLEXIBLE

inflict,*,,ted,table,ting,tion,ter,tor,tive, TO CAUSE PAIN, TO BRING ABOUT PUNISHMENT

inflimation, inflammation

influence,*,,ed,cing,eable,er,ntial,ntially, TO IMPRESS UPON, ONE WHO IMPRESSES OTHERS, AUTHORITY, POSITION OF POWER, EXERT UPON

inform,*,,med,ming,mation,mer,mative,matively mativeness,matory, OFFER ADVICE/FACTS

informal,lly,lity, NOT FORMAL, RELAXED, COMFORTABLE

informant,*, SOMEONE WHO PROVIDES FACTS TO A LAWFUL ENTITY

inforse, enforce

infra, PREFIX INDICATING "BENEATH" MOST OFTEN MODIFIES THE WORD

infraction,*, BREAK A RULE/LAW/CONTRACT

infrared, A LASER TYPE, A LEVEL OF FREQUENCY NEAR THE COLOR RED

infrastructure, SKELETAL/FOUNDATION OF

infrequent,ncy,tly, OCCASIONALLY

infugen, infuse(sion)

infultrate, infiltrate

infunently, infinite(ly)

infunit, infinite

infunsy, infant(ncy)

infunt, infant

infuntry, infantry

infuriate,*,,ed,ting,tingly,tion,ely, ENRAGE, FURIOUSLY ANGRY

infurmation, inform(ation)

infurmery, infirmary

infuse,*,,ed,sing,sibility,sible,sive,er, LIQUID INTRODUCED/INJECTED INTO ANOTHER LIQUID

infustashen, infestation

infustrukture, infrastructure

ing, inch

ingage, engage

ingaje, engage

inganuity, ingenuity

ingection, inject(ion)

ingekt, inject

ingen, engine

ingeneer, engineer

ingenious, ESPECIALLY CREATIVE IN PERSPECTIVE

ingenuity,ties, ABLE TO USE CREATIVE IMAGINATION

inger, injure

ingery, injure(ry)

ingest,*,,ted,ting,tive,ta, TO SWALLOW, TAKE INTO THROUGH THE MOUTH AND SWALLOWED

inginuity, ingenuity

ingoeuble, enjoy(able)

ingolf, engulf

ingot,*,, MASS OR CHUNK OF METAL

ingoy, enjoy

ingrafe, engrave

ingrain,*,,ned,nedly, ROUTED INTO, CARVED INTO, DEEPLY IMPRESSED WITHIN

ingrave, engrave

ingredient,*, VARIETY OF ELEMENTS COMBINED TO MAKE SOMETHING ELSE

ingulf, engulf

ingun, engine

inguneer, engineer

ingury, injure(ry)

ingustes, injustice

inhabetent, inhabit(ant)

inhabit,*,,ted,ting,tation,table,tancy,tancies, tance,tant, TO OCCUPY, LIVE IN

inhalant,*, A DEVICE FOR BREATHING IN MEDICINE

inhalashin, inhale(lation)

inhale,*, ,ed,ling,lation,lational,er,lator, BREATH IN

inhanse, enhance

inharent, inherent

inharet, inherit

inharitance, inherit(ance)

inharmonic,*,,ious,iously,iousness,ny, TONES NOT PEAKING TOGETHER, FREQUENCY NOT SYNCHRONIZED

inherent,tly, BELONGS AS PART OF THE WHOLE, INSEPARABLE

inheret, inherit

inherit,*,,ted,ting,tor(y),tive,ter,tion, tability,tance, GOODS AND MONEY RECEIVED WHEN SOMEONE DIES

inhewmane, inhumane

inhibit,*,,ted,ting,tor(y),tive,ter,tion, KEEP BACK/ RESTRAINED, TIMID/SLOW TO ACT

inhosbitable, inhospitable

inhospitable,eness,ly,ality, NOT TREATED WARMLY/ FRIENDLY/GENEROUSLY

inhubeshen, inhibit(ion)

inhulashen, inhale(lation)

inhumane,ely, CRUEL

inima, enema /anemia

inime, enemy

inimet, intimate

inmutle, intimate(ly)

ining, inning

inisheation, initiate(tion)

inishul, initial

initial,*,,led,ling,lly,lness,lize, ORIGINALLY, THE BEGINNING, THE FIRST

initiate,*,,ed,ting,tion,tive,tor(y), BREAK INTO NEW KNOWLEDGE, BEGIN SOMETHING NEW

inje, inch

inject,*,,ted,ting,tion,table,tor, INSERT SOMETHING INTO SOMETHING ELSE

injen, engine

injneer, engineer

injeneus, ingenious
injenuidy, ingenuity
injekshen, inject(ion)
injest, ingest
injin, engine
injineer, engineer
injoy, enjoy
injoymint, enjoy(ment)
injoyuble, enjoy(able)
injun, engine
injure,*,ed,ring,ry,rious(ly),rer,riousness, DAMAGE, OFFEND,VIOLATE ANOTHER'S RIGHTS
injustice,*, NOT PLAYING FAIRLY, SOMEONE'S RIGHTS VIOLATED
ink,*,ky,ker,kiness, FLUID USED IN A PEN
inkadesent, incandescent
inkarsurade, incarcerate
inker, incur
inkerej, encourage /anchor(age)
inkewbate, incubate
inkline, incline
inkling, A FEELING/HINT/IDEA
inklood, include
inkloshur, enclose(sure)
inkloze, enclose
inklud, include
inklusev, inclusive
inkompruble, incomparable
inkompus, encompass
inkonsistent, inconsistent
inkoreg, encourage /anchor(age)
inkoreguble, incorrigible
inkorpurate incorporate
inkownter, encounter
inkreduble, incredible
inkredulus, incredulous
inkreese, increase
inkrument, increment
inkum, income

inkumbent, incumbent
inkumblete, incomplete
inkumpatuble, incompatible
inkumplete, incomplete
inkumpus, encompass
inkunsiduret, inconsiderate
inkunvenyunt, inconvenient
inkurect, incorrect
inkwesishun, inquisition
inkwesutev, inquisitive
inkwire, inquire(ry)
inkwisative, inquisitive
inland,der, AWAY FROM THE SEA
inlarge, enlarge
inlargmint, enlarge(ment)
inlarje, enlarge
in-law,*, PEOPLE RELATED BY MARRIAGE
inles, unless
inlest, enlist
inlet,*,ting, RECESS BETWEEN LAND/WATER, INSERTED
inlist, enlist
inliten, enlighten
inlund, inland
inmachure, immature
inmate,*, ONE CONFINED TO PRISON OR JAIL
inmature, immature
inmertaledy, immortal(ity)
inmortalidy, immortal(ity)
inn,*, A DWELLING TO SLEEP FOR THE NIGHT
innacurate,ely,eness,acy,acies, NOT CORRECT/ FACTUAL/ACCURATE
innate,ely,eness, BELONGS WITH THE BODY
inner,rly, TOWARDS THE CENTER (or see inter)
innerlock, interlock
innerlude, interlude
innermingle, intermingle
innermission, intermission
innernational, international

innernet, internet
innerscolastic, interscholastic
innertwine, intertwine
innervene, intervene
inning,*, A SECTION OF PLAY IN A GAME OF SPORTS
innocence,cy,cies, FREE FROM ULTERIOR MOTIVES
innocent,tly,FREE FROM ULTERIOR MOTIVES
innovate,tive,tion,tory,tor, IMPROVE SYSTEM WITH NEW CREATIVE IDEA INSTILLING CHANGE
inoberable, inoperable
inoburatef, inoperable(ative)
inocent, innocence(nt)
inocreate, inaugurate
inoduble, inaudible
inof, enough
inogreashen, inaugurate(tion)
inogreate, inaugurate
inogreation, inaugurate(tion)
inogurate, inaugurate
inonemus, anonymous
inonseate, enunciate
inoperable,ative,ativeness, WILL NOT OPERATE
inopportune,ely,eness,nity, NOT THE BEST TIME TO ENSURE SUCCESS
inopurtune, inopportune
inorge, energy
inorgetek, energetic
inormis, enormous
inormous, enormous
inormus, enormous
inosense, innocence
inosence, innocence
inotable, inaudible
inovadef, innovate(tive)
inovate, innovate(tive)
inovative, innovate(tive)
inownse, announce
inpashent, impatient
inpatient, VISITS HOSPITAL FOR TREATEMENT (or see impatient)
impersonashen, impersonate(tion)

inpersonate, impersonate
inplie, imply
inpolite, impolite
inpolse, impulse
inport, import
inpose, impose
inposebul, impossible
inposition, impose(sition)
inpossible, impossible
inposter, imposter
inpound, impound
inpoverish, impoverish
inpownd, impound
inpractical, impractical
inpragnuble, impregnable
inprasise, imprecise
inpravize, improvise
inprecise, imprecise
inpregnable, impregnable
inpregnate, impregnate
inpregnuble, impregnable
inprent, imprint
inpres, impress /empress
inpresion, impress(sion)
inpresive, impress(sive)
inprint, imprint
inprison, imprison
inprobuble, improbable
inpromptu, impromptu
inpromtu, impromptu
inpropable, improbable
inproper, improper
inprove, improve
inprovement, improve(ment)
improvisation, improvise(sation)
inprovise, improvise
inprufment, improve(ment)
inpruve, improve
inpruvize improvise

inpulse, impulse
inpulsive, impulse(sive)
input, tting, *ADD TO EXISTING INFORMATION*
inquazishen, inquisition
inqubate, incubate
inquire, er,ringly,ry,ries, *TO ASK OF, SEEK FURTHER INFORMATION*
inquisition, nal,nist, *TAKE PEOPLE IN AGAINST THEIR WILL TO INTERROGATE THEM*
inquisitive, ely,eness,tor,torial,rially, *TO SEEK ANSWERS/KNOWLEDGE*
inquizadive, inquisitive
inquizeshen, inquisition
inrage, enrage
inraj, enrage
inrich, enrich
inrol, enroll
inrolmint, enroll(ment)
insabordinate, insubordinate
insacure, insecure
insadent, incident
insafishent, insufficient
insakuredy, insecure(rity)
insalate, insulate
insalin, insulin
insane, ely,eness,nity,nities, *THINK IN UNPOPULAR MODALITY WHICH SEPARATES ONE FROM EVERYONE ELSE, MENTAL HEALTH IN DOUBT*
insanetation, insanitary(ation)
insanifekent, insignificant
insanitary, riness,ation, *UNCLEAN/UNACCEPTABLE FOR GOOD HEALTH*
insarektion, insurrection
insatiable, ey,bility,ate,ately,ateness,iety,eness, *APPETITE FOR SOMETHING THAT CANNOT BE SATIATED/ SATISFIED*
insawyuble, insoluble
insayuble, insoluble
insbarashen, inspire(ration)

insburashen, inspire(ration)
inscribe, *,ed,bing,bable,bableness,ber, *LEAVE A MARK BY ANY METHOD*
inscription, *,nal,nless,ive(ly), *LEAVING A MARK BY MANY METHODS*
inseam, *, *SEAM ON THE INSIDE OF PANTLEGS*
insebordinate, insubordinate
insect, *, *BUGS (or see incest)*
insecticide, *,dal, *CHEMICALS TO KILL BUGS*
insecure, ely,rity,eness, *ILL AT EASE, NOT SECURE/ COMFORTABLE WITH ENVIRONMENT*
insedent, incident
insedius, insidious
inseficient, insufficient
insegnea, insignia
insegnifakent, insignificant
insejen, incision
insekt, insect
insektaside, insecticide
insekurety, insecure(rity)
inselate, insulate
inselation, insulate(tion)
inseminate, *,ed,ting,tion, *INJECT SEMEN INTO*
insen, ensign
insenarade, incinerate
insenea, insignia
insense, incense
insenseer, insincere
insensible, ly,eness,bility,bilities, *NOT MAKING SENSE TO PERCEIVER, MISUNDERSTOOD*
insensitive, eness,vity,ely, *DOESN'T EASILY REACT TO SENSORY INPUT*
insentive, incentive
insentuf, incentive
insenuashen, insinuate(tion)
insenuate, insinuate
inseparable, bility,bly, *WILL NOT BE DISJOINTED OR TAKEN APART*
insepshen, incept(ion)

insept, incept
inseption, incept(ion)
inserekshen, insurrection
inserkle, encircle
insermountable, insurmountable
insert,ter,tion,tional, PLACE INTO ALREADY EXISTING FORM OR METHODOLOGY
inseshun, incision
insest, insist / incest
insestent, insistent
insh, inch
insher, ensure / insure
insherance, insure(rance)
inshree, entry / entree
inshurans, insure(rance)
inshure, insure
insicure, insecure
inside,*,er, INTERIOR OF A FORM (or see insight)
insident, incident
insidious,sly,sness, ILL INTENT DETECTABLE, MANIPULATE TO HARM WITHOUT BEING PERCEIVED AS SO
insidnea, insignia
insiffient, insufficient
insight,tful, ABILITY TO PERCEIVE FUTURE OUTCOMES OF CURRENT EVENT
insignia,*, BADGES OR MEDALS OF HONOR OR AUTHORITY IN MILITARY
insignificant,tly,nce,ncy,ncies, NOT SIGNIFICANT/ NOT IMPORTANT, WORTHY TO CALCULATE IN, NOT IMPORTANT
insiklopedea, encyclopedia
insimanation, inseminate(tion)
insin, ensign
insinarate, incinerate
insincere,ely,rity,rities, NOT SINCERE/TRUTHFUL
insinsative, insensitive
insinseer, insincere
insinsuble, insensible

insintuf, incentive
insinuate,*,ed,ting,tion,tive,tingly,tor, LEADING TOWARDS ACCUSATION, INDIRECTLY IMPLYING
insishen, incision
insist,*,ted,ting,tingly,tent,tently,tence,tency, tencies, MUST HAVE/BE, ABSOLUTE
insite, inside / insight
insiteful, insight(ful)
insiteus, insidious
insition, incision
inskribe, inscribe
inskripshen, inscription
insoluble,bility,eness,bly, WILL NOT DISSOLVE IN LIQUID
insolvable, NOT ABLE TO BE SOLVED, NO ANSWER
insolvent,*,ncy, NOT ENOUGH FLUID CAPITAL TO GET OUT OF DEBT, CANNOT BE LIQUIDATED,
insomnia,ac,ious, PROBLEM SLEEPING
insovable, insolvable
insparation, inspire(ration)
inspect,*,ted,ting,tion,tive,tor,torate,toral,torial torship, EXAMINE FOR FLAWS
insperation, inspire(ration)
inspire,*,ed,ring,ration,er,rational,rationally, ratory,rable, EMPOWER, INSTILL FAITH/ HOPE
instagate, instigate
install,*,lled,lling,llation,ller,llment, PUT SOME- THING OR SOMEONE INTO A PLACE TO PERFORM A FUNCTION, MAKE A PAYMENT (or see instill)
instance,cy, AN EXAMPLE/MOMENT
instant,tly, IN A WINK, RIGHT AWAY
instantaneous,ly,sness, HAPPENED SO QUICKLY THAT TIME COULDN'T BE MEASURED
instatushen, institute(tion)
instatute, institute
instaul, install
instead, IN PLACE OF, A SUBSTITUTE
instegate, instigate
instenked, instinct

instense, instance
instentaneously, instantaneous(ly)
instetution, institute(tion)
instigate,*,ed,ting,tive,tor, PROVOKE, STIR UP, INITIATE AN ACTION
instill,*,lled,lling,llation,ller,llment, INTRODUCE GRADUALLY (or see install)
instinct,*,tual,tive,tively, KNOWINGNESS WE'RE ALL BORN WITH
instinse, instance
instintaneously, instantaneous(ly)
institute,*,tion,tionally,tionalism,tionalist, tionalize, ESTABLISH TO WORK AS A GROUP, FORMAL PLACE OF LEARNING
instol, install
instolashen, install(ation)
instrament, instrument
instriment, instrument
instruct,*,ted,ting,tion,tional,tor,tive,tively, tiveness, PROVIDE KNOWLEDGE TO/FOR OTHERS
instugate, instigate
instrument,*,tal,tally,talist,talism,tality,tation, AN ITEM WHICH MEASURES OR FUNCTIONS AS A DEVICE TO HELP WITH WORK, MUSICAL DEVICE
instulation, install(ation) /instill(ation)
instunlty, instant(ly)
instunle, instant(ly)
instunt, instant
insubordinate,*,ely,tion, DOESN'T SUBMIT TO AUTHORITY
insucure, insecure
insufficient,tly,ncy,ncies,nce, NOT SUFFICIENT, NOT ENOUGH
insugnifakent, insignificant
insukurety, insecure(rity)
insulate,*,ed,ting,tion,tor, LAYER/COAT OF SOMETHING FOR PROTECTION/BARRIER
insulin, SECRETED BY A HORMONE IN THE BODY, A MANMADE CHEMICAL TO TREAT DIABETES

insult, *, ted,ting,tingly,table,ter, *AN ATTEMPT TO LOWER ANOTHER'S SELF ESTEEM*

insunseer, insincere

insure, *, ed,ring,er,rance,rant, *PROTECT AGAINST MONETARY/PROPERTY/JOB LOSS*

insurekshen, insurrection

insurens, insurance

insurkle, encircle

insurmountable, lly, *CANNOT BE ACHIEVED/ OVERCOME*

insurrection, nary,naries,nism,nal,nally, *REVOLT AGAINST FIGURES OF AUTHORITY*

insurshen, insert(ion)

insurt, insert

insyklopedia, encyclopedia

intact, tness, *NOT AFFECTED BY A POTENTIALLY DAMAGING EVENT*

intaferance, interfere(rance)

intagral, integral

intagrate, integrate

intagration, integrate(tion)

intak, intact / intake

intake, *A TUBE OR DEVICE WHICH TAKES IN FLUID OR AIR FOR MECHANICS (or see intact)*

intalect, intellect

intalectual, intellect(ual)

intamit, intimate

intarier, interior

intatee, entity

intecate, indicate

integer, *, *TERM IN MUSIC AND MATH*

integral, lly,lity, *IMPORTANT PART OF THE WHOLE*

integrate, *, ed,ting,tion,tionist,tor, *INCLUDE INTO THE WHOLE, MAKE A PART OF A WHOLE*

integrity, ties, *SOUND PRINCIPLES, HONORABLE*

intellect, tion,tualist,tualistic,lism,tualize,tive, tively,tual,tuality, *ABILITY FOR MENTAL COMPREHENSION*

intelligent, *, nce,tial,tly,tsia, *LEVEL OF ABILITY TO PERFORM COMPLEX REASONING*

intenation, intonate(tion)

intend, *, ded,ding,der,dment, *APPARENT GOAL (or see intent)*

intense, ely,sity,sive,sively,sify,eness,sifier, sification, *FIRM/FORWARD/KEEN/VIGOROUS/ EXTREME*

intenshin, intent(ion)

intent, tly,tness,tion,tional,nally,ned,nless,nality, *THOUGHTFULLY PLAN A COURSE OF ACTION*

inter, *, *PREFIX INDICATING "BETWEEN/AMONG" MOST OFTEN MODIFIES THE WORD (or see intra/enter)*

inter, rred,rring,rment, *TO BURY (or see enter)*

interagate, interrogate

intercede, ed,ding,er, *MEDIATE/FACILITATE*

intercept, *, ted,ting,ter,tion,tive, *PASS BETWEEN/ THROUGH A LINE/OBSTRUCT A LINEAR ACTION*

intercom, *INTERCOMMUNICATION SYSTEM/ COMMUNICATE BY MICROPHONE*

interconnect, *, ted,ting,tion,tedness,tible, table, *TO CONNECT BETWEEN TWO SOURCES*

intercourse, *INTERCHANGE OF FEELINGS/THOUGHTS, COPULATION*

interdisciplinary, rity,rian, *WHEN ALL FIELDS/ SYSTEMS ARE INTERCONNECTED/COMMUNICATING*

interest, *, ted,tedly,ting, *ATTENTIVENESS TO LEARN SOMETHING NEW, LENDERS COLLECT THIS*

interfere, *, ed,ring,ringly,er,ence,ntial, *TO INTERCEPT BETWEEN ONGOING EXCHANGE, PRESENCE OF SLOWS PROGRESS*

interim, *A TEMPORARY PAUSE IN AN ONGOING PROJECT*

interior, *, rity,rly, *INSIDE OF STRUCTURE*

interject, *, ted,ting,torily,tion,tionally,tory, *INTERRUPT WITH INFORMATION*

interlock, *, ked,king,ker, *CHAINLIKE, ONE ENMESHED WITH ANOTHER, PART OF ONE MECHANISM EMBEDDED INTO THE OTHER*

interlude, *, dial, *PAUSE DURING A PERFORMANCE OR ACTIVITY*

intermediary, ries, *FACILITATOR/AMBASSADOR/ AGENT WHO AIDS COMMUNICATION BETWEEN GROUPS*

intermingle, *, ed,ling,ement, *MINGLE TOGETHER, INTERTWINED*

intermission, *, ive, *A BREAK BETWEEN EVENTS/ ACTIVITY/PERFORMANCE*

intern, *, nship,nist,nment, *A STUDENT PRACTICING UNDER SUPERVISION, SOMETHING CONFINED DURING WAR*

internal, lly,lize,lization,lity, *INSIDE A FORM/BODY*

international, le,lity,lly,lism,list,lize,lization, *OUTSIDE NATIONAL BOUNDARIES*

internet, *A COMPUTER WEB WHICH NETS BETWEEN COMPUTERS ALL OVER THE WORLD*

interpret, *, ted,ting,tability,table,ter,tive,tively, *REVIEW FACTS FOR FURTHER CLARIFICATION, BRING ABOUT THE MEANING OF*

interpretation, nal, *ACT OF REVIEWING FACTS FOR FURTHER CLARIFICATION*

interprise, enterprise

interrelate, tion,tionship, *TO RELATE THINGS TOGETHER, SECURE COMMON GROUND BETWEEN TWO THINGS*

interrogate, *, ed,ting,tion,tional,tive,tively,tor, tory,tories, *TRANSMIT A SIGNAL FOR SETTING OFF AN APPROPRIATE RESPONSE, INTENSE QUESTIONING BY AUTHORITIES*

interrupt, *, ted,ting,tion,ter,tive, *HINDER THE PROGRESS OF MOMENTARILY*

interscholastic, *, *ACTIVITIES BETWEEN SCHOOLS*

intersection, *, *POINT WHERE TWO LINE CRISSCROSS, PLACE WHERE OPPOSING LINES CROSS*

intersperse, *, ed,edly,sing,sion, *TO SCATTER, BEING SCATTERED ABOUT*

interstate, *, *HIWAYS BETWEEN STATES, ROADS CONNECTING STATES*

intertane, entertain
intertanment, entertain(ment)
intertwine,*,ed,ning,ningly,ement, TO WEAVE TOGETHER
interupt, interrupt
interval,*, A PAUSE OR GAP BETWEEN
intervene,*,ed,ning,ntion,ntionist,nism,nor, TO INTERFERE, GET BETWEEN
interview,*,wed,wing, QUESTIONING PERSON FOR QUALIFICATIONS OR ANSWERS
interwoven, INTERTWINED, BRAIDED TOGETHER
intestine,*,nal,nally, ORGAN INSIDE BODY WHERE FOOD IS PROCESSED
intety, entity
intever, endeavor
inthooseastik, enthuse(siastic)
inthooziazm, enthuse(siasm)
inthrall, enthrall
inthroll, enthrall
inthuseastek, enthuse(siastic)
inthusiasm, enthuse(siasm)
inticate, indicate
intication, indicate(tion)
intidle, entitle
intiger, integer
intigo, indigo
intil, until
intimadate, intimidate
intimate,ely,er,tion, CLOSE/BONDING, MAKE KNOWN
intimidate,*,ed,ting,tion,tor, ATTEMPT TO LOWER SOMEONE'S SELF ESTEEM OR CONFIDENCE BY APPEARING GREATER THAN THEM
intinse, intense
intinshen, intent(ion)
intire, entire
intirle, entire(ly)
intirlee, entire(ly)
intirsept, intercept
intirty, entire(ty)

intise, entice
intite, entity
intitle, entitle
intlis, endless
into, ENTER /INSIDE
intoishen, intuit(ion)
intolerable,eness,ly,bility,ance,ant,antly, WILL NOT TOLERATE, NOT ABLE TO DEAL WITH
intonate,*,ed,ting,tion,tional,er, ACCENT ON CERTAIN WORDS WHICH AFFECT MEANING
intorse, endorse /indoor(s)
intortane, entertain
intoxicate,*,ed,edly,ting,tingly,ant,tion, DRUNK FROM ALCOHOL, INEBRIATED, HIGH WITH EXCITEMENT
intra, PREFIX INDICATING "INSIDE/WITHIN" MOST OFTEN MODIFIES THE WORD (or see inter)
intradukshen, introduce(ction)
intraduse, introduce
intrakit, intricate
intramural,lly, EVENTS HAPPENING WITHIN, SCHOOL SPORTS
intrance, entrance
intranet,*, A WEB OF NETWORKING WITHIN A CLOSED/ RESTRICTED COMPUTER SYSTEM
intraspect, introspect
intravenous,sly, INJECTING FLUID INTO VEINS
intrees, entry(ries) /entree
intrege, intrigue
intrense, entrance
intrensic, intrinsic
intres, entry(ries) /entree
intrest, interest
intricate,ely,ely,acy,acies,eness, OF THE TINIEST DETAIL
intridukshen, introduce(ction)
intrigue,*,ed,uing,uingly,er, DEEPLY INTERESTED, CAPTIVATED

intrinsic,cal,cally,calness, ABSOLUTELY IMPORTANT, ESSENTIAL, CANNOT DO WITHOUT IT
intro, PREFIX INDICATING "INSIDE/WITHIN" MOST OFTEN MODIFIES THE WORD (or see inter)
introduce,*,ed,cing,er,ction,tory,ctive,ctorily, ACQUAINTING PEOPLE TOGETHER, PRESENT SOMETHING
introduse, introduce
introspect,tion,tional,tive,tiveness, TO GO WITHIN FOR KNOWLEDGE AND ANSWERS
introvert,*,ted,rsion,rsive,sively, SOMEONE WHO SPENDS MOST OF THEIR TIME WITH THEMSELVES, DOESN'T SEEK THE OUTSIDE WORLD FOR ANSWERS
intrude,*,ed,ding,er,usion,usive,usively, usiveness, ENTER WITHOUT INVITATION, FISSURES FILLED WITH MOLTEN LAVA
intrusive,ely, ENTER WITHOUT INVITATION, ROCK FORM
intrusion, ENTER WITHOUT INVITATION, ROCK FORM
intrust, entrust /interest
intry, entry /entree
intuative, intuit(ive)
intufer, interfere
intuger, integer
intugrate, integrate
intuishen, intuit(ion)
intuit,table,tion,tional,tionism,tionalism,tionist, tive,tively,tiveness, A KNOWINGNESS WE ARE ALL BORN WITH, CAN SEE OUR OWN FUTURE
intunate, intonate
intur, enter /inter
inturn, intern
inturnalize, internal(ize)
inturnil, internal
inturpret, interpret
inturpretation, interpretation
inturprise, enterprise

intursede, intercede
intursept, intercept
inturtane, entertain
inturtaner, entertain(er)
inturtanment, entertain(ment)
intutes, entity(ties)
intyre, entire
inubelidy, inability
inubishen, inhibite(tion)
inucent, innocence(nt)
inuf, enough
inume, enemy
inunciate, enunciate
inundate,*,ed,ting,tion,tor(y), OVERWHELMED,
OVERFLOWING, OVER ABUNDANCE
inunseade, enunciate
inupresheative, inappreciative
inuprochible, inapproachable
inupropreut, inappropriate
inur, inner
inurcom, intercom
inurelate, interrelate
inurem, interim
inurge, energy
inujetek, energetic
inurlock, interlock
inurlude, interlude
inurmediary, intermediary
inurmingle, intermingle
inurmission, intermission
inurmost, innermost
inurnashenul, international
inurnet, internet
inursculastic, interscholastic
inursection, intersection
inursperse, intersperse
inurt, inert
inurtwine, intertwine
inurupt, interrupt

inurval, interval
inurvene, intervene
inurvue, interview
inurwoven, interwoven
inuscapable, inescapable
inusense, innocence
inuvate, innovate
invade,*,ed,ding,er, TO OVERWHELM A TERRITORY
OR PEOPLES BY UNWELCOME OCCUPATION, AN
ENEMY WHO ENTERS TO OCCUPY A SYSTEM
invalid,dly,dity,date,dation,dator,dism, NOT
VALID/LEGAL, VOIDED, A PERSON INCAPABLE
OF FUNCTIONING NORMALLY
invalope, envelope
invaluable,eness,ly, WORTH MORE THAN CAN BE
BOUGHT FOR, MOST VALUABLE
invariable,ly,bility,eness, CONSTANT, NEVER
CHANGING
invashen, invasion
invasion,*,ive,iveness, ATTEMPT TO CONQUER IN A
HOSTILE MANNER, HOSTILE OVERTHROW
invatation, invitation
invate, invade
inved, envy(vied)
invee, envy
invegorate, invigorate
invelop, envelope
invensable, invincible
invenshen, invent(ion)
invent,*,ted,ting,tion,tional,tor,table,tive,tively,
tiveness, CREATION FROM THOUGHT
inventory,ries,rial,rialy, A CATALOG/LIST OF GOODS
inverdabrae, invertebrate
inveriably, invariable(ly)
invert,*,ed,tibility,tible,rsion,ter, SWITCH AROUND,
MAKE OPPOSITE, INSIDE OUT
invertebrate,eness,acy, HAS NO SPINE/BACKBONE
inves, envy(vies)
invesible, invisible

invest,*,ted,ting,tment, PUT TIME/MONEY INTO
SOMETHING/PROJECT
investigate,*,ed,ting,tion,tive,tor,tory, SEARCH
FOR CLUES/ANSWERS/SIGNS
investmunt, invest(ment)
invetation, invitation
inveuble, enviable
inveus, envious
invezible, invisible
invigorate,*,ed,ting,ant,tor, BRING EXCITEMENT
TO, RENEW
invilope, envelope
invincible,bility,eness,ly, NOT ABLE TO CONQUER OR
PENETRATE
invintory, inventory
invious, envious
invirenment, environment
invirunmental, environment(al)
invisability, invisible(bility)
invisible,ly,eness,bility, NOT PERCEIVABLE, CANNOT
SEE OR FEEL
invitation,*,nal, ASKED TO COME TO AN EVENT,
WELCOME TO VISIT
invoice,*,ed,cing, A DETAILED BILL DUE AND OWING
involope, envelope
involuntary,rily,riness, DID NOT VOLUNTEER
involve,*,ed,ving,ement,er, BE CAUGHT UP IN,
INTERACTING WITH, OBLIGATE TIME/THOUGHT
invoyce, invoice
invulid, invalid
invurdabrae, invertebrate
invurt, invert
invy, envy
inward,*,dly,dness, FACING TOWARDS THE INSIDE,
ON IN SIDE
inword, inward
inwrech, enrich
inwroll, enroll
iodine, A CHEMICAL ELEMENT

ion,*,nize,nizer,nization, *ATOM/PARTICLE WITH A CHARGE*
ionesfer, ionosphere
ionesphere, ionosphere
ionisfere, ionosphere
ionosphere, *A PROTECTIVE LAYER SURROUNDING THE EARTH ABOVE 43 MILES, HOLES MADE IN IT WITH ROCKETS CREATE OZONE DEPLETION*
iqwantense, acquaintance
ir, *PREFIX INDICATING "NOT" MOST OFTEN MODIFIES THE WORD*
irabrochuble, irreproachable
iradebul, irritable
iradekate, eradicate
iradesent, iridescent
iradic, erratic / erotic
iradubel, irritable
iradukashen, eradicate(tion)
iragardles, irregardless
iragashen, irrigate(tion)
iragate, irrigate
iraguardless, irregardless
iraknid, arachnid
iranment, arraign(ment)
iraplasible, irreplacable
iraproachable, irreproachable
irasbonsuble, irresponsible
irase, erase
irashenul, irrational
irasistible, irresistible
iraspective, irrespective
iraspektif, irrespective
irasponsuble, irresponsible
iratable, irritable
iratashen, irritate(tion)
iratate, irritate
iratation, irritate(tion)
irate, *ANGRY*
iratic, erratic / erotic

irational, irrational
iratrevible, irretrievable
iratuble, irritable
iravokuble, irrevocable
iraze, erase
irazistuble, irresistible
irchin, urchin
irebrochuble, irreproachable
iredescent, iridescent
iredesent, iridescent
iredubel, irritable
iregardless, irregardless
iregashen, irrigate(tion)
iregate, irrigate
iregation, irrigate(tion)
iregeuler, irregular
iregeuleredy, irregular(ity)
iregewler, irregular
ireglur, irregular
ireguardless, irregardless
iregular, irregular
ireguleredy, irregular(ity)
irekshen, erect(ion)
irekt, erect
irelavense, irrelevant(nce)
irelevant, irrelevant
irelevense, irrelevant(nce)
ireluvense, irrelevant(nce)
ireluvint, irrelevant
iren, iron
ireny, irony
ireperuble, irreparable
irepirable, irreparable
ireproachable, irreproachable
ireprochible, irreproachable
irepruble, irreparable
irepurable, irreparable
ires, iris
iresbonsuble, irresponsible

irresistible, irresistible
irespective, irrespective
irespektif, irrespective
iresponsuble, irresponsible
iretashen, irritate(tion)
iretate, irritate
iretibul, irritable
iretreavible, irretrievable
iretrievable, irretrievable
irevocable, irrevocable
irg, urge
irgint, urge(nt)
iribrochuble, irreproachable
irid, irido, *PREFIX INDICATING "IRIS/ RAINBOW" MOST OFTEN MODIFIES THE WORD*
iridescent,nce, *A LIGHT REFLECTION WITH RAINBOW COLORS*
irifd, arrive(d)
iriful, arrive(val)
irigardles, irregardless
irigashen, irrigate(tion)
irigate, irrigate
irigation, irrigate(tion)
irn, iron / earn
iriplasible, irreplacable
iris, *PART OF THE EYE, A FLOWER*
irisbonsuble, irresponsible
irisistible, irresistible
irispective, irrespective
irispektif, irrespective
irisponsuble, irresponsible
iritable, irritable
iritashen, irritate(tion)
iritate, irritate
iritation, irritate(tion)
iritrevible, irretrievable
irivokuble, irrevocable
irizisduble, irresistible
irj, urge

irk,*, ANNOYING
irn, earn /urn /iron
irnd, earn(ed) /iron(ed)
irnest, earnest
irochun, erosion
irode, erode
irodinamic, aerodynamic
irodynamic, aerodynamic
irogate, irrigate
iron,*,ned,ning, A METAL, A TOOL FOR TAKING WRINKLES OUT OF CLOTHES/TOOL FOR GOLF/SMOOTH OUT WRINKLES
irone, irony
ironic,cal,cally,ny,calness, OPPOSITE TO WHAT YOU WOULD EXPECT
irony,nies, ODDLY COINCIDENTAL
irosbonsuble, irresponsible
iroshin, erosion
irosponsuble, irresponsible
irote, erode
irovokuble, irrevocable
irowze, arouse
irragate, irrigate
irragation, irrigate(tion)
irraplasible, irreplacable
irraproachable, irreproachable
irratable, irritable
irratate, irritate
irrate, irate
irrational,lit,lness,lly,lism,list,listic, NOT RATIONAL, NOT ABLE TO PROVE RATIONALE
irregardless, NOT REGARDED, ASIDE FROM THAT
irregate, irrigate
irregation, irrigate(tion)
irregular,*,rly,rity, NOT REGULAR
irrelavent, irrelevant
irrelevant,nce,ncy,ntly, NOT RELEVANT, DOES NOT PERTAIN TO
irrepairable, irreparable

irreparable,bility,eness,ly, CANNOT BE REPAIRED
irreplacable, NOT ABLE TO BE REPLACED
irreplaceable, irreplacable
irreproachable,eness,bility,ly, NOT ABLE TO BE APPROACHED, UNBLEMISHED
irresistible,bility,eness,ly, NOT ABLE TO RESIST
irrespective,ely, NOT TO BE CONSIDERED IN THE EQUATION/CIRCUMSTANCE/EVENT
irresponsible,ly,bility,eness, NOT RESPONSIBLE
irretrievable,bility,eness,ly, NOT ABLE TO BE RETRIEVED/CAPTURED/RELIEVED, LOST
irrevocable,bility,eness,ly, NOT REVERSIBLE, CANNOT BE UNDONE/CHANGED
irridescent, iridescent
irrigate,*,ed,ting,tion,tional,tive,tor, METHOD OF PROVIDING WATER TO
irriplasible, irreplacable
irritable,ly,eness,bility, ANNOY/AGGRAVATE/STIMULATE, INFLAMMED TISSUE
irritate,*,ed,ting,tion,tive,tingly,tor, ANNOY/AGGRAVATE/STIMULATE, INFLAMMED TISSUE
irrogate, irrigate
irrogation, irrigate(tion)
irruplacable, irreplacable
irrupt,*,ted,ting,tion,tive,tively, SUDDENLY/FORCIBLY INVADE/ENTER (or see erupt)
irth, earth
irubshen, erupt(ion) /irrupt(ion)
irubt, erupt /irrupt
irubtif, erupt(ive) /irrupt(ive)
irudebul, irritable
irudibul, irritable
irugardles, irregardless
irugashen, irrigate(tion)
irugate, irrigate
irugation, irrigate(tion)
iruguardless, irregardless
irune, irony
iruplaseble, irreplacable

iruprochuble, irreproachable
irupshen, erupt(ion) /irrupt(ion)
irupt, erupt / irrupt
iruptif, erupt(ive) /irrupt(ive)
iruption, erupt(ion) /irrupt(ion)
irus, iris
irusbonsuble, irresponsible
irusistible, irresistible
iruspective, irrespective
iruspektif, irrespective
irusponsuble, irresponsible
irutashen, irritate(tion)
irutate, irritate
irutation, irritate(tion)
irutrevible, irretrievable
irutrievable, irretrievable
irutuble, irritable
iruvokuble, irrevocable
iruzistuble, irresistible
is, iso, PREFIX INDICATING "EQUAL" MOST OFTEN MODIFIES THE WORD
is, THIRD PERSON SINGULAR, PRESENT IN TIME
isalashen, isolate(tion)
isalation, isolate(tion)
isay, essay
isbeshalee, especially
isbeshulee, especially
iscape, escape
isdeem, esteem
ise, ice /icy /eye(s)
iselate, isolate
iselation, isolate(tion)
isense, essence
isenshil, essential
isential, essential
ishew, issue
ishu, issue
ishuense, issue(uance)
isier, icy(cier)

isikle, icycle
isilate, isolate
isilation, isolate(tion)
ising, icing
isinshul, essential
iskape, escape
iskort, escort
island,*,der, *BODY OF LAND SURROUNDED BY WATER, ONE WHO LIVES ON AN ISLAND*
isofigus, esophagus
ism,*, *A SUFFIX WHICH MEANS A SYSTEM OF PRINCIPLES, A PRACTICE*
isn't, *CONTRACTION OF THE WORDS "IS NOT"*
iso, *PREFIX INDICATING "EQUAL" MOST OFTEN MODIFIES THE WORD*
isolashen, isolate(tion)
isolate,*,ed,ting,tion,tionism,tionist, *TO PREVENT HAVING CONTACT WITH ANOTHER THING*
isoteric, esoteric
ispeshalee, especially
ispeshulee, especially
issuanse, issue(uance)
issue,*,ed,uing,er,uance,uable,uably,*DISTRIBUTE/ HAND OUT INFORMATION, POINT OF MATTER*
issuence, issue(uance)
istablish, establish
istablush, establish
isteem, esteem
istrologe, astrology
isuance, issue(uance)
isue, issue
isuinse, issue(uance)
isulashen, isolate(tion)
isulate, isolate
isulation, isolate(tion)
itach, attach
itak, attack
italic,*,cize,cized,cization, *SLANTED STYLE OF PRINT TO ATTRACT ATTENTION*

italisize, italic(ize)
itch,hes,hed,hing,hiness,hy, *DESIRE TO SCRATCH, A NEED TO SATISFY* (or see etch)
item,*,mize,mizer,mization, *ARTICLE OR UNIT IN A COLLECTION, AN OBJECT*
itenarary, itinerary
itenerary, itinerary
iternul, eternal
iteut, idiot
itinerary,ries,ate,ation, *LIST OF DETAILS PERTAINING TO A TRIP*
itle, idol /idle
it'll, *CONTRACTION OF THE WORDS "IT WILL"*
it's, *CONTRACTION OF THE WORDS "IT IS"*
itself, *ONE ON ITS OWN*
itsetera, etcetera
itul, idol /idle /it'll
itum, item
itumize, item(ize)
iturnal, eternal
iudine, iodine
iul, aisle /I'll
iun, ion
iunizur, ion(izer)
iurn, iron
ivacuate, evacuate
ivade, evade
ivakuashen, evacuate(tion)
ivakuate, evacuate
ivaluashen, evaluate(tion)
ivaluate, evaluate
ivant, event
ivaparate, evaporate
ivaporate, evaporate
I've, *CONTRACTION OF THE WORDS "I HAVE"*
ive, ivy
ivent, event
ivolve, evolve
ivory, *A BONE OR HORN FROM MAMMALS*

ivry, ivory
ivy,vies,vied, *A PLANT*
ixagerate, exaggerate
ixajurate, exaggerate
ixamunashen, examine(nation)
ixempt, exempt
ixemshen, exempt(ion)
ixitment, excite(ment)
ixkershen, excursion
ixklude, exclude
ixklute, exclude
ixkurjen, excursion
ixkus, excuse
ixost, exhaust
ixperiense, experience
ixpire, expire
ixplisitly, explicit(ly)
ixploet, exploit
ixseluratur, accelerate(tor)
izbeshulee, especially
izenshil, essential
izkape, escape
izkort, escort
izoteric, esoteric
iztablish, establish
izteem, esteem

"j"

jack, *PREFIX INDICATING "MALE/LARGE/HEAVY" MOST OFTEN MODIFIES THE WORD*
jackass,es, *MALE DONKEY*
jacket,*,ted,tless, *A COVERING, PROTECTIVE COAT*
jacks, *TOOLS FOR HOLDING UP CARS, A GAME FOR KIDS (TOO MANY DEFINITIONS, PLEASE SEE STANDARD DICTIONARY)*

jail,*, A BUILDING WHERE PEOPLE WHO BREAK LAWS ARE CONFINED
jaket, jacket
jaks, jacks
jale, jail /jelly
jaly, July /July /jelly
jam,*, FRUIT SPREAD, BEING STUCK (or see jamb)
jamb,*, HOLDS A STABLE OPENING FOR A DOOR (or see jam)
janedic, genetics
janewery, January
janitor,*,tial, A CUSTODIAN, SOMEONE WHO SEES TO CLEANING/MAINTENANCE OF PUBLIC BUILDING
January, A MONTH OF THE YEAR
januery, January
janyuery, January
jar,*,rred,rring, STARTLE SOMEONE, WHAT A DOOR IS WHEN IT'S OPEN, GLASS CONTAINER WITH A LID
jargon,*, A DIALECT, THE WAY A LANGUAGE IS SPOKEN
jasture, gesture
jaundice,ed, AN UNHEALTHY BODY CONDITION
jaunt,*, SPONTANEOUS/BRIEF JOURNEY
jau, jaw
java, COMPUTER SOFTWARE, COFFEE BEVERAGE
jaw,*, PART OF THE MOUTH
jawalk, jaywalk
jawolk, jaywalk
jaywalk,*,ked,king,ker, TO CROSS A STREET AT AN INAPPROPRIATE PLACE
jazz,zzes,zzed,zzy, TYPE OF MUSIC, TO MODERNIZE
jealous,sy,sness,sly,sies, EMOTION WHICH ERUPTS WHEN ONE IS INSECURE/FEARFUL
jean,*, THICK FABRIC USED FOR PANTS (or see gene)
jeaneul, genial
jeauluge, geology
jebalashen, jubilant(ation)
jeburish, jibber(ish)
jeneol, genial
jeneus, genius

jeens, jean(s) /gene(s)
jegle, jiggle
jegsaw, jigsaw
jelatin, gelatin
jelatnus, gelatin(ous)
jele, jelly
jelis, jealous
jeliten, gelatin
jell,*,lled,lling,lly,llify, TO SET/BECOME FIRM (or see gel)
jelly, FRUIT SPREAD
jeluten, gelatin
jely, July /jelly
jem, gem /gym
jemmy, jimmy
jemnaseum, gymnasium
jemnast, gymnastics
jen, gene /jean
jenarashin, generation
jenarate, generate
jenarator, generator
jenarus, generous
jeneal, genial
jene, genie
jenerik, generic
jenerul, general
jenerus, generous
jenetic, genetics
jeneus, genius
jengle, jingle
jengur, ginger
jenks, jinx
jenome, genome
jenrul, general
jens, jean(s) /gene(s)
jentul, gentle
jenuen, genuine
jenul, gentle
jenurulize, general(ize)

jenus, genus
jenyus, genius
jeografee, geography
jeometry, geometry
jeopardy,dize,dizes, GREAT RISK OF DANGER IF NOT SKILLFUL ENOUGH
jep, gyp
jepardy, jeopardy
jeperdize, jeopardy(dize)
jepsee, gypsy
jepsum, gypsum
jerbul, gerbil
jeresdikshen, jurisdiction
jerk,*,ked,king,kily,kiness,ky, QUICK MOTION/JOLT
jerky, DRIED MEAT
jermanate, germinate
jernal, journal
jernalist, journal(ist)
jerney, journey
jeror, juror
jery, jury
jest,ter,ting,tingly, IN FUN, TO MAKE LIGHT OF
jesture, gesture
jet stream,*, WIND CURRENT WHICH SPIRALS AROUND SPECIFIC PARTS OF THE EARTH
jet,*,tted,tting, A PLANE, A ROCK, TYPE OF STREAM ACTION (or see get)
jete, jetty
jetsam, WASTE/ITEMS ELIMINATED FROM A JET
jetty,tties, PIER/STRUCTURE AT AN OCEAN SHORE
jety, jetty
jewbalee, jubilee
jewdeshul, judicial
jewdishes, judicious
jewel,*,lry,ler, DECORATIVE ORNAMENTS FOR THE BODY (or see joule)
jewly, July
jewn, June
jewse, juice

jewt, jute
jewvinile, juvenile
jib,*,bbed,bbing,bber, SAIL OF A BOAT, ARM OF A CRANE
jibber,rish, TALKING NONSENSE
jibe,*,ed,bing, SYNCHRONISE, HARMONY
jiffy, DONE FAST
jig,*,gged,gging, A DANCE, FISHING/TOOLING DEVICE, SOMETHING THAT DOESN'T HAVE A NAME "THING AMA JIG" (or see gig)
jigantic, gigantic
jigger, A TOOL, THING THAT DOESN'T HAVE A NAME "A THING AMA JIGGER", MEASURING DEVICE
jiggle,*,ed,ling,ly, ACTION LIKE JELLO IN MOTION, DANCE MOVEMENT (or see giggle)
jigsaw,*,wed,wing, A CUTTING TOOL, A PUZZLE
jilatnus, gelatin(ous)
jilt,ter, discard someone
jily, July /jelly
jim, gem /gym
jimmy,mmies,mmied,ying, FORCE A LOCK TO OPEN
jimnaseum, gymnasium
jimnast, gymnastics
jinarashin, generation
jinarate, generate
jinarator, generator
jinarulize, general(ize)
jinarus, generous
jinerik, generic
jinetic, genetics
jinger, ginger
jingle,*,ed,ling, BELL SOUNDS, BRIEF, CATCHY TUNE
jinks, jinx
jinrul, general
jintul, gentle
jinuen, genuine
jinurulize, general(ize)
jinus, genus
jinx,xed, SOMETHING THAT CAUSES BAD LUCK

jiolugee, geology
jiometry, geometry
jip, gyp
jipsee, gypsy
jipsum, gypsum
jirate, gyrate
jirble, gerbil
jirm, germ
jirmanate, germinate
jirney, journey
jirnul, journal
jirnulist, journal(ist)
jirur, juror
jiry, jury
jitter,*,red,ring,ry, BRIEF BURSTS OF SHAKING OR JIGGLING, A DANCE, FEARFUL REACTION
jive,*, A RHYTHM STYLE OF MUSIC AND ALL ASSOCIATED WITH IT
job,*,bless,blessness, WORKING CONSISTENTLY FOR INCOME
jock,, SOMEONE WHO FOCUSES PRIMARILY ON SPORTS IN SCHOOL
jockey,*,yed,ying, RIDER IN HORSE RACING, META-PHOR FOR GETTING INTO POSITION TO WIN
joee, joy
joen, join
joent, joint /join(ed)
joest, joist
jofeul, jovial
jog,*,gged,gging,gger, TYPE OF RUNNING
jogur, jog(ger)
join,*,ned,ning,nable,ner, BRING TWO OR MORE THINGS TOGETHER IN UNION WHERE TWO INDEPENDENT PIECES ARE BROUGHT TOGETHER, CASUAL PUBLIC FACILITY
joist,*, HORIZONTAL/PARALLEL BOARDS IN A STRUCTURE/FOUNDATION
jok, jock /joke

joke,*,ed,king,kingly,er,ester, COMMENT/STORY INTENDED TO GENERATE LAUGHTER (or see jock)
joky, jockey
jol, joule /jewel
jolee, jolly
jolly,lier,lolliest,lity, MERRY, LIVELY, GAY
jolt,*,ted,ting,ty, A SUDDEN HARSH ACTION
joly, jolly
jondis, jaundice
jont, jaunt/ join(ed)/ joint
jooly, July
joon, June
joot, jute
jop, job
jornul, journal
josel, jostle
josh,hing,her, TEASING WITH GOOD HUMOR
jostle,*,ed,ling,ement,er, TO PUSH/JUMBLE/ SHOVE/BUMP/COLLIDE IN A CROWDED SITUATION
josul, jostle
jot,*,tted,tting, QUICKLY WRITE SOMETHING DOWN, WRITE A QUICK NOTE
jouel, jowl /joule
joule,*, A METHOD OF MEASURING (or see jewel)
jounce,*,ed,cing, TO BOUNCE AROUND
journal,*, lize,lizer,lism, AN ITEMIZED ACCOUNT OF AN EVENT OR SPAN OF TIME
journalist,, ONE WHO DOCUMENTS OR RECOUNTS AN EVENT OR SPAN OF TIME
journey,*,yed,ying, TO TRAVEL OR TAKE A TRIP
joust,*,ted,ting,ter, MEDIEVAL COMBAT
jovial,lity,lness,lly, JOLLY, GOOD CHEER/HUMOR
jow, jaw
jowl,*,led, THE JAW, FISH HEAD (or see joule)
jownse, jounce

joy,yful,yfully,yous,yously,yousness, A PLEASURABLE/UNEMOTIONAL STATE OF BEING, HARMONIOUS FEELING, STATE OF BE-ING
joyes, joy(ous)
joyesly, joy(ously)
joyfil, joy(ful)
joyis, joy(ous)
joyn, join
joynt, joint /join(ed)
joyst, joist
joyusness, joy(ousness)
jubalashen, jubilant(ation)
jubilant,tly,lance,ation,ate,atory, EXHULTANT/TRIUMPHANT/FESTIVE
jubilee,*, A ROWDY/FESTIVE CELEBRATION NORMALLY HONORING A TIMESPAN
juce, juice /juicy
judeshal, judicial
judeshus, judicious
judge,*,ed,ging,ement,emental, MAKING A DECISION BASED ON KNOWN INFORMATION
judicial,lly,ary, ACTS/ADMINISTRATION OF JUDGING
judicious,sly,sness, BEHAVING IN A JUDGEMENTAL FASHION
judo, SELF-DEFENSE SPORT
juel, joule /jewel
jug,*,gful, A LARGE CONTAINER FOR FLUIDS OR LIQUID (or see judge)
juge, jug /judge
juggle,*,ed,ling,er, KEEP OBJECTS AFLOAT IN THE AIR SIMULTANEOUSLY
jugil, juggle
juice,*,er,cy,cier,ciest,eless, LIQUID FROM FRUIT juicy,cier,ciest, edible food laden with moisture
jul, joule /jewel
July, A MONTH OF THE YEAR
jumble,*,ed,ling, TO MIX TOGETHER WITHOUT ORDER

jump,*,ped,ping,py,piness,per, TO TAKE TO THE AIR FOR NANOSECONDS TO DEFY GRAVITY
juncer, junk(er)
junction,*,nal, PLACE WHERE THINGS MEET, TIME/ PLACE INTERCHANGE
juncture,*, ONE POINT WHERE THINGS OR THOUGHTS MEET, PLACE FOR EXCHANGE
June, A MONTH OF THE YEAR
jungle,*,led,ly, PLACE WHERE PLANTS/ANIMALS ARE ABUNDANT/FREE FROM HUMAN RESTRAINT
junior,*, A CLASS LEVEL IN SCHOOL, THE MALE OFFSPRING OF A FATHER
junk,ked,king,ky,ker, OBJECTS CONSIDERED TO BE OF NO VALUE
junke, junkie
junkie,*, PEOPLE WHO ARE WASTED TO DRUGS
junkshen, junction
junksher, juncture
junky, junkie
junyer, junior
juol, jewel /joule
juometree, geometry
jurasdiction, jurisdiction
jurbel, gerbil
jure, jury
juresdiction, jurisdiction
jurisdiction,nal,nally, AN AREA/RANGE CONTROLLED BY PARTICULAR ENTITIES
jurk, jerk
jurky, jerky
jurm, germ
jurmenate, germinate
jurney, journey
jurnil, journal
jurnilist, journal(ist)
juror,*, MEMBER OF A GROUP WHO SITS IN COURT AND JUDGES A DEFENDANT
jurusdikshen, jurisdiction

jury,ries, A GROUP WHO SIT IN COURT AND JUDGES A DEFENDANT
jusd, just
jusdes, justice
jusdifiable, justifiable
jusdify, justify
jusdufecation, justify(fication)
juse, juice /juicy
juser, juice(r)
just,tly,tness, WHAT IS RIGHT BY SOCIAL NORMS
justefiable, justifiable
justefication, justify(fication)
justes, justice
justice,*,eless,elike,ciable,ciability, ONE WHO IS EMPLOYED BY THE GOVERNMENT TO MAKE LAWFUL DECISIONS
justifiable,bility,bleness,ly, DEFENDS THAT THE ACTION REFLECTS THE CAUSE
justify,fies,fied,fying,fyingly,fier,fication, ficative,ficatory, TO DEFEND REACTIONS, TO ARGUE IN DEFENSE OF ACTION OR THOUGHT
jusy, juice(cy)
jut,*,tted,tting, STICKS OUT (or see jute)
jute, PLANT FIBER FOR WEAVING AND BRAIDING
juto, judo
juvenile,*, lism,lity, A YOUTH, IMMATURE
juxta, PREFIX INDICATING "NEAR/CLOSE" MOST OFTEN MODIFIES THE WORD

"K"

kabduve, captive
kaben, cabin
kaberay, cabaret
kabich, cabbage
kabige, cabbage
kabin, cabin

kable, cable
kabnet, cabinet
kabnit, cabinet
kaboose, caboose
kabsher, capture
kabsul, capsule
kabten, captain
kabture, capture
kabul, cable
kabuse, caboose
kach, catch/ cache/ cash
kacher, catcher
kackel, cackle
kadavir, cadaver
kade, caddy
kadence, cadence
kadet, cadet
kadilist, catalyst
kadilog, catalog
kadinse, cadence
kadul, cattle
kadulist, catalyst
kadulog, catalog
kadur, cater
kaduract, cataract
kaf, calf /cave
kafa, cafe
kafe, cafe /coffee
kafene, caffein
kafetirea, cafeteria
kafine, caffein
kafiterea, cafeteria
kafs, calves /cave(s)
kage, cage
kahoot, cahoot
kahute, cahoot
kail, kale
kainker, chancre /canker
kairful, careful

kaje, cage
kajole, cajole
kake, cake /khaki
kakil, cackle
kakoon, cocoon
kaktis, cactus
kakul, cackle
kaky, khaki
kal, kale /call
kale, AN EDIBLE PLANT
kaleidoscope,*,pic,pical,pically, COLORFUL
VIEWING OBJECT
kalek, colic
kalender, calender /calender /colander
kaler, collar /call(er)
kales, callous /callus
kalesterol, cholesterol
kaliber, caliber
kalibrate, calibrate
kalide, collide
kalidoscope, kaleidoscope
kaliflower, cauliflower
kalindula, calendula
kalindur, calendar /calender /colander
kalipur, caliper
kalir, collar /call(er)
kalire, calorie
kalis, callous /callus
kalisthenics, calisthenics
kalk, calk /caulk
kalkilate, calculate
kalkulate, calculate
kalkulus, calculus
kalon, cologne /colon
kaloneil, colonial
kalore, calorie
kalostemy, colostomy
kalqulus, calculus
kalseum, calcium

kaluber, caliber
kalubrate, calibrate
kaluper, caliper
kalury, calorie
kalus, callous /callus
kalusthinics, calisthenics
kalvs, calves
kam, came
kamenduble, commendable
kamfer, camphor
kamil, camel
kaminduble, commendable
kamofloje, camouflage
kampane, campaign
kampus, campus
kamru, camera
kamu, comma
kamul, camel
kamunecate, communicate
kamunety, community
kamute, commute
kancer, cancer /chancre /canker
kanded, candid
kandidat, candidate
kandil, candle
kandy, candy
kane, cane
kanebul, cannibal
kanebulize, cannibal(ize)
kaneon, canyon
kanepy, canopy
kanery, canary /cannery
kanesiology, kinesis(iology)
kanesis, kinesis
kangaroo,*, LARGE MARSUPIAL ANIMAL
kanibul, cannibal
kanibus, cannabis
kanikanik, kinnikinnick
kanin, cannon /canine

kaniry, cannery /canary
kanister, canister
kanker, chancre /canker
kanon, cannon
kanopy, canopy
kanselashin, cancel(llation)
kanseld, cancel(lled)
kansilashun, cancel(llation)
kansild, cancel(lled)
kansir, cancer
kansul, cancel
kansulashen, cancel(llation)
kansult, cancel(lled)
kant, can't
kantalope, cantaloup
kanted, candid
kanteen, canteen
kantelope, cantaloup
kantina, cantina
kantir, canter
kantulope, cantaloup
kantur, canter
kanubelize, cannibal(ize)
kanubis, cannabis
kanuster, canister
kanves, canvas /canvass
kanvus, canvas /canvass
kanyun, canyon
kaos, chaos
kapabul, capable
kapasety, capacity
kapdivate, captivate
kapedul, capital /capitol
kapedulism, capitalism
kapelary, capillary
kapetul, capital /capitol
kapetulesm, capitalism
kapiblety, capability
kapibul, capable

kapilary, capillary
kapoot, kaput
kapshun, caption
kapsil, capsule
kapsize, capsize
kapsul, capsule
kaptin, captain
kaption, caption
kaptuf, captive
kaptun, captain
kaptuvate, captivate
kapubilety, capability
kapubul, capable
kapulery, capillary
kaput, DIED, PASSED OUT, FELL OVER DEAD
kapzize, capsize
karacter, character
karaoke, GAME WHERE SONGS WITHOUT WORDS ARE SUNG TO
karat,*, A MEASUREMENT FOR GEMS AND GOLD (or see karate/ carrot/ carat /caret)
karate, MARTIAL ART FORM (or see karat)
karbin, carbon
karbinete, carbonate
karbon, carbon
karburator, carburetor
kard, card
kardboard, cardboard
kardeac, cardiac
kardenul, cardinal
kardilege, cartilage
kardnul, cardinal
kare, carry /care
karebu, caribou
karecatshure, caricature
kareer, career
karefree, carefree
karekteriz, character(ize)
kareless, careless

kareoke, karaoke
karess, caress
karet, carat/caret /carrot/ karat
kareur, carrier
karevan, caravan
karf, carve
karful, careful
kargo, cargo
karib, carob
kariboo, caribou
karisma, charisma
karit, carat/caret /carrot/ karat
karkes, carcass
karkus, carcass
karlis, careless
karma, A BELIEF
karmil, caramel
karmu, karma
karmul, caramel
karnashun, carnation
karnevul, carnival
karnivore, carnivore
karob, carob
karoburate, corroborate
karode, corrode
karoke, karaoke
karosene, kerosene
karote, karate
karouse, carouse
karpenter, carpenter
karpet, carpet
karpinder, carpenter
karpit, carpet
karsenugen, carcinogen
karsinugin, carcinogen
kart, cart
kartoon, cartoon
kartreg, cartridge
kartrig, cartridge

kartuleg, cartilage
kartune, cartoon
karudge, carriage
karul, carol
karusen, kerosene
karv, carve
kary, carry
kascade, cascade
kase, case
kaseno, casino
kaset, cassette
kash, cash /cache
kasher, cashier
kashmer, cashmere
kashu, cashew
kasine, casino
kasing, casing
kasiroll, casserole
kask, cask
kaskera, cascara
kasket, casket
kast, cast
kastrate, castrate
kasul, castle
kat, cat
katch, cache/ cash/ catch
katelog, catalog
katepiler, caterpillar
katepult, catapult
kater, cater
kateract, cataract
katikism, catechism
katukism, catechism
katulist, catalyst
katulog, catalog
katupiler, caterpillar
katupult, catapult
katurakt, cataract
kau, cow

kaudej, cottage
kaufe, coffee
kaul, call / cowl
kaumu, comma
rausd, cause(d) /cost
kaut, caught /cot
kava, *BEVERAGE FROM PLANT*
kavety, cavity
kavilry, cavalry
kavirn, cavern
kavity, cavity
kavs, calves /cave(s)
kavude, cavity
kavulree, cavalry
kavurn, cavern
kawcus, caucus
kawshun, caution
kawshus, cautious
kawt, caught / cot
kayen, cayenne
kaynine, canine
kayos, chaos
kazual, casual
ke, key
kech, catch
kechen, kitchen
kechup, ketchup /catsup
ked, key(ed) /kid
kednapur, kidnap(pper)
kedny, kidney
kedul, kettle
kedy, kitty
keel,*,led,ling,less, *FALL OVER, STRUCTURAL PART OF A BOAT*
keen,nly,nness,ner, *SHARP IN SENSES, VERY AWARE*
keep,*,per,ping,pable, *TO HOLD ON TO, WITHHOLD FROM SOMEONE, POSSESS*
kek, kick
kel, kill /keel

keld, kill(ed) /kelt
kell, kill
keln, kiln
kelo, kilo
kelowatt, kilowatt
kelp, *WATER PLANT*
kelt, celt/ kilt/ kill(ed)
kelur, kill(er)
kemotherapy, chemotherapy
ken, kin/ keen/ can
kendergarden, kindergarten
kendling, kindle(ling)
kendred, kind(red)
kendul, kindle
kendurgarden, kindergarten
kenel, kennel
kenesiology, kinesis(iology)
kenesis, kinesis
keng, king /kink
kengdum, kingdom
kenikkanik, kinnikinnick
kenk, king /kink
kenly, keen(ly)
kennel,*,led,ling, *FENCING/HOUSING FOR ANIMALS*
kenol, kennel
kensum, consume
kentend, contend
kentenual, continual
kenting, kindle(ling)
kentred, kind(red)
kenturgarden, kindergarten
kenul, kennel
keosk, kiosk
keper, kipper
kepsize, capsize
kepur, kipper
keracter, character
keral, choral/ coral/ corral/ chorale
keraoky, karaoke

kerat, carat/caret /carrot/ karat
keravan, caravan
kerb, curb
kerd, curd
kerdeus, courteous
kerdul, curdle
kerekt, correct
kerekturiz, character(ize)
kereoke, karaoke
kerf, curve
kerfue, curfew
kericuture, caricature
kerier, carrier
kerige, carriage /courage
kerikulum, curriculum
kerioke, karaoke
kerisel, carousel
kerisen, kerosene
kerit, carat/caret /carrot/ karat
kerivan, caravan
kerl, curl
kernal, colonel /kernel
kernel,*,ly, SMALL BITS/SECTIONS OF CORN COB/ NUTS/SEEDS (or see colonel)
kernul, colonel /kernel
keroberate, corroborate
kerol, carol
keroselI, carousel
kerosene, TYPE OF FUEL
kerot, carat/caret /carrot/ karat
keroty, karate
kersanthimum, chrysanthemum
kerse, curse
kersive, cursive
kersoje, corsage
kersuf, cursive
kertale, curtail
kertin, curtain
kertsy, curtsy

kertul, curdle
keruge, courage
kerunsy, currency
kerunt, currant /current
kerupt, corrupt
kerusel, carousel
kerusen, kerosene
keruvan, caravan
kerve, curve
kervicher, curvature
kervuchure, curvature
kery, curry /carry
kes, kiss
kess, kiss
ket, kid/ kit/ kite
ketal, kettle
ketch, catch
ketchen, kitchen
ketcher, catcher
ketchup, TOMATO BASED CONDIMENT (also catsup)
keten, kitten
ketny, kidney
kets, kid(s)/ kit(s)/ kite(s)
kettle,*, LARGE IRON POT, METAL VESSEL WITH ROUNDED BOTTOM AND WIDE TOP
ketul, kettle
kety, kitty
keurader, curator
kew, cue
kewe, kiwi
kewk, cook
key,*,yed, TOOL TO UNLOCK SOMETHING, IMPORTANT INFORMATION TO UNLOCK A MYSTERY
keylo, kilo
keyosk, kiosk
khaki,*, A TYPE OF COTTON PANT, A COLOR
kibuse, caboose
kichen, kitchen

kick,*,ked,king,ker, STRIKE SOMETHING WITH FRONT OF FOOT
kid,*,ddy,dder,dding,ddingly,ddishness,dlike, A YOUNG CHILD/ANIMAL JOKING(or see kite/kit)
kiddy, kitty
kiden, kitten
kidnap,*,pped,pping,pper, ONE WHO STEALS AWAY WITH SOMEONE
kidnaper, kidnap(pper)
kidney,*, ORGANS IN THE BODY
kidny, kidney
kidur, kid(dder)
kidy, kid(ddy) / kitty
kigole, cajole
kijole, cajole
kik, kick
kil, kill
kild, kill(ed) / kilt
kiler, kill(er)
kill,*,lled,ller,lling, TAKE LIFE AWAY FROM
kiln,*, A SPECIAL OVEN WHICH EXCEEDS 1000°
kilo, PREFIX INDICATING "THOUSAND" MOST OFTEN MODIFIES THE WORD
kiloge, collage
kiloneul, colonial
kilor, kill(er)
kilosil, colossal
kilostomy, colostomy
kilowatt, ELECTRICAL MEASUREMENT
kilt,*, SKIRT OF SCOTTISH DESCENT (or see kill(ed))
kilur, kill(er)
kimecul, chemical
kimestry, chemistry
kimponent, component
kimustry, chemistry
kin,*,smen,kinfolk, RELATIVES (or see can)
kinal, canal
kind of, SORT OF, SOMEWHAT

kind,dred,dly,dest,dness,der, *WHAT TYPE, BEING*
  NICE WITHOUT ULTERIOR MOTIVES
kinda, kind of
kindergarten,ner, *A CLASS LEVEL IN SCHOOL*
kindhearted,dly,dness, *A GENTLE SPIRIT*
kindle,*,ed,ling, *MATERIAL USED AS A FIRE STARTER*
kindolense, condolence
kinducter, conductor
kinduf, kind of
kindukt, conduct
kindurgarden, kindergarten
kinery, canary / cannery
kinesis,iology, *STUDY OF HEALTH/MUSCLES OF THE*
  BODY, HEALING USING KINERGETIC STUDY
kinet, kineto, *PREFIX INDICATING "MOTION" MOST*
  OFTEN MODIFIES THE WORD
kinfedy, confetti
kinfes, confess
kinfeshun, confession
kinfetion, confession
king,*,gdom, *RULER IN A MONARCH*
kingradulashun, congratulation
kinikkanik, kinnikinnick
kink,*,ked,king,ky, *SOMETHING THAT KNOT'S UP, A*
  BEND/HOOK IN A LINEAR SYSTEM (or see king)
kinkdom, kingdom
kinol, kennel
kinsole, console
kinspirusy, conspiracy
kinstrucshen, construction
kinstruct, construct
kinsult, consult
kinsumpshen, consumption
kint, kind
kinta, kind of
kintaminate, contaminate
kintergarden, kindergarten
kintred, kind(red)
kinul, kennel

kiosk,*, *INFORMATION STATION*
kiper, kipper
kipper,*, *FISH AND RELATED*
kiral, choral/ coral/ corral/ chorale
kirnel, colonel / kernel
kiroberate, corroborate
kiropraktor, chiropractor
kirote, karate
kirten, curtain
kirteus, courteous
kiruge, courage
kirupraktor, chiropractor
kirvucher, curvature
kis, kiss
kiset, cassette
kiss,sses,ssed,ssing, *USING LIPS FOR TOUCHING*
kit,*, *ACCUMULATION OF ITEMS IN A CONTAINER TO USE*
  FOR A SPECIFIC TASK (or see kite)
kitastrufy, catastrophe
kitchen,*, *PLACE TO PREPARE FOOD*
kite,*, *FRAME WITH COVERING THAT SAILS IN THE WIND*
  BY A STRING (MANY DEFINITIONS PLEASE SEE
  STANDARD DICTIONARY) (or see kit)
kiten, kitten
kitny, kidney
kitten,*, *IMMATURE CAT*
kitty,tties, *IMMATURE CAT, GAMBLING TERM*
kity, kitty
kiwi,*, *FRUIT, BIRD*
kiyen, cayenne
klairvoyants, clairvoyance
klam, clam / claim
klamp, clamp
klan, clan
klandistine, clandestine
klap, clap
klapse, collapse
klaricul, clerical
klarity, clarity

klarvoyuns, clairvoyance
klaset, closet
klash, clash
klasha, cliche
klasic, classic
klasify, classify
klasp, clasp
klass, class
klasuc, classic
klasufy, classify
klaun, clown
klausterfobic, claustrophobic
klaw, claw
klawsit, closet
klawzet, closet
klay, clay
klecter, collector
kleerense, clearance
kleet, cleat
kleff, cliff
klen, clean
klench, clench /clinch
kleng, cling
klenik, clinic
klenikul, clinic(al)
klense, cleanse
klensh, clench /clinch
klenz, cleanse
klep, clip
kler, clear
klerense, clearance
klerge, clergy
klerical, clerical
klerify, clarify
klerity, clarity
klerk, clerk
klervoyents, clairvoyance
klet, cleat
kletorus, clitoris

kode, code	koktale, cocktail	kolm, calm
kodej, cottage	kokunut, coconut	kolmenate, culminate
kodene, codeine	kol, call /cowl	koloj, collage
kodin, cotton	koladerul, collateral	kolostemy, colostomy
koduge, cottage	kolamedy, calamity	kolpret, culprit
koed, coed	kolander, colander	kolsla, coleslaw
koel, coil	kolaps, collapse	kolslow, coleslaw
koen, coin	kolapsubl, collapse(sible)	kolt, cold or colt
koenside, coincide	kolasal, colossal	koltivate, cultivate
koensudent, coincident	kolate, collate	koltsfoot, coltsfoot
kof, cough	kold, cold	koluge, college
kofe, cove/ coffee/ cough	koldsfoot, coltsfoot	kolum, column
kofen, coffin / cough(ing)	kole, coal /call	kolun, colon
kofert, covert	koleage, colleague	kolundir, colander
kofin, coffin / cough(ing)	koleague, colleague	kolune, colony
kofy, coffee	kolecshin, collection	kolunise, colonize
kognativ, cognitive	kolecter, collector	kolur, collar / call(er)
kognisant, cognizant	kolegent, collegiate	kolvurt, culvert
kognishun, cognition	kolekt, collect	kom, calm/ come/ comb
kognition, cognition	kolem, column	koma, coma / comma
kognutiv, cognitive	kolen, colon	komand, command
kohabutate, cohatitate	kolenary, culinary	komander, commander
kohearent, coherent	kolendur, colander	kombat, combat
koherent, coherent	koleng, call(ing) /cowl(ing)	kombenation, combination
kohesuf, cohesive	kolenize, colonize	kombinashun, combination
kohesuve, cohesive	koleny, colony	kombine, combine
kohort, cohort	koler, collar/ call(er)/ cooler	kombunashen, combination
kohurse, coerce	kolerd, collard greens	kombustible, combustible
koil, coil	kolesterol, cholesterol	kombustion, combustion
koin, coin	kolic, colic	komec, comic
koinside, coincide	kolid, collide	komedian, comedian
koinsudent, coincident	koliflower, cauliflower	komedy, comedy
kok, cock / cook	kolige, college	komemerate, commemorate
kokain, cocaine	kolijin, collision	komendable, commendable
kokane, cocaine	kolim, column	komendation, commendation
koko, cocoa	koliny, colony	komenduble, commendable
kokonut, coconut	kolur, cooler /color /collar	komense, commence
kokroch, cockroach	kolishen, coalition	koment, comment
koks, coax	kolk, calk / caulk	komentatur, commentator

koments, commence
komerse, commerce
komershul, commercial
komet, commit /comet
komfert, comfort
komfertible, comfortable
komfurter, comfort(er)
komic, comic
komidy, comedy
komimurate, commemorate
komin, common
komindation, commendation
kominduble, commendable
kominsurate, commensurate
komint, comment
komintator, commentator
komirse, commerce
komirshul, commercial
komisary, commissary
komishner, commissioner
komit, comet / commit
komitee, committee
komitment, commitment
komity, comedy
komloda, cum laude
komodety, commodity
kompact, compact
kompar, compare
komparebul, comparable
kompartment, compartment
kompashunet, compassionate
kompass, compass
kompatibility,compatibility
kompeditor, competitor
kompel, compel
komper, compare
kompete, compete
kompetior, competitor
kompile, compile

kompinsate, compensate
kompitance, competence
kompizishen, composition
komplane, complain
komplasins,complacence/complaisance
komplecshun, complexion
kompleks, complex
kompleshun, completion
komplete, complete
komplukashun, complication
komplukate, complicate
komplumint, complement/compliment
komply, comply
komponent, component
kompose, compose
komposier, composure
komposit, composite
kompost, compost
komposyer, composure
kompound, compound
kompownd, compound
kompramise, compromise
komprehend, comprehend
komprehenshun, comprehension
kompreshun, compression
kompresor, compressor
kompress, compress
kompretion, compression
kompruble, comparable
komprumize, compromise
komptroler, comptroller
kompulsery, compulsory
kompulshun, compulsion
kompulsuve, compulsive
kompultion, compulsion
komputashun, computation
kompute, compute
komputer, computer
komputishen, competition

kompuzishen, composition
komrad, comrade
komtroler, comptroller
komudoor, commodore
komun, common /commune
komune, commune
komunest, communist
komunety, community
komunicate, communicate
komunism, communism
komunul, communal
kon, con / cone
koncesion, concession
konch, conch
koncheinchus, conscientious
konchuse, conscious
konclude, conclude
konclujen, conclusion
konclusion, conclusion
koncution, concussion
kondem, condemn
kondensashen, condensation
kondense, condense
kondesend, condescend
kondewit, conduit
kondimeneum, condominium
kondiment, condiment
kondinsashun, condensation
kondisend, condescend
kondishen, condition
kondition, condition
kondolense, condolence
kondomeneum, condominium
kondone, condone
konduct, conduct
konducter, conductor
konduit, conduit
kondukt, conduct
kondum, condom

kondument, condiment
kone, cone
konekshen, connection
konekt, connect
konfederit, confederate
konfedont, confidant
konfeduret, confederate
konfedy, confetti
konfekshun, confection
konferanse, conference
konferm, confirm
konfermashun, confirmation
konfes, confess
konfeshun, confession
konfesion, confession
konfetty, confetti
konfide, confide
konfidense, confidence
konfidenshul, confidential
konfidential, confidential
konfidont, confidant
konfigurashun, configuration
konfine, confine
konfinment, confinement
konfirents, conference
konfirm, confirm
konfirmashun, confirmation
konfirmation, confirmation
konflict, conflict
konform, conform
konfrunt, confront
konfudense, confidence
konfudenshul, confidential
konfudont, confidant
konfujen, confusion
konfuranse, conference
konfuse, confuse
konfusion, confusion
konger, conjure

konglomurete, conglomerate
kongradulashun, congratulation
kongratshulate, congratulate
kongregashun, congregation
kongres, congress
kongrewint, congruent
kongrigate, congregate
kongris, congress
kongrugate, congregate
kongrugation, congregation
kongruint, congruent
konifur, conifer
konjer, conjure
konjewgul, conjugal
konjugul, conjugal
konjunction, conjunction
konjunkshen, conjunction
konjure, conjure
konk, conch
konker, conquer
konkokt, concoct
konkrete, concrete
konkwest, conquest
konquest, conquest
konsalidate, consolidate
konscientious, conscientious
konsecutive, consecutive
konseed, concede
konsel, conceal /council
konseet, conceit
konseeve, conceive
konseevuble, conceivable
konsemate, consummate
konsent, consent
konsentrate, concentrate
konsepshual, conceptual
konsepshun, conception
konsept, concept
konserge, concierge

konsern, concern
konservation, conservation
konservutive, conservative
konseshun, concession
konsetion, concession
konseve, conceive
konshenshis, conscientious
konsider, consider
konsierge, concierge
konsikwense, consequence
konsimate, consummate
konsinet, consonant
konsinment, consignment
konsintrate, concentrate
konsiquence, consequence
konsise, concise
konsist, consist
konsistency, consistency
konsiter, consider
konsolashen, consolation
konsole, console
konsolidate, consolidate
konsoul, console
konspearusy, conspiracy
konspikuos, conspicuous
konspikyewus, conspicuous
konspirusy, conspiracy
konstancy, constancy
konstant, constant
konstatushen, constitution
konstilashen, constellation
konstinse, constancy
konstint, constant
konstipashen, constipation
konstitushen, constitution
konstrict, constrict
konstrucshen, construction
konstruct, construct
konstulashen, constellation

konstupashen, constipation	kontrusepshun, contraception	kords, cord(s)/chord(s)/court(s)/quart(s)/quartz
konstutushen, constitution	kontumplate, contemplate	kordunate, coordinate
konsukwinse, consequence	kontunent, continent	korduroy, corduroy
konsulashun, consolation	konture, contour	kore, core /corp
konsult, consult	konufir, conifer	korekt, correct
konsumate, consummate	konvene, convene	kores, chorus /course
konsume, consume	konvenyut, convenient	korespond, correspond
konsumshen, consumption	konversashen, conversation	korgil, cordial
konsunet, consonant	konvershen, conversion	korgul, cordial
konsurt, concert	konvert, convert	koridoor, corridor
konsurvashen, conservation	konvict, convict	korigate, corrugate
kontagus, contagious	konvinse, convince	korilate, correlate
kontain, contain	konvinshen, convention	koriner, coroner
kontakt, contact	konvulesents, convalescence	korinery, coronary
kontamenate, contaminate	konvulgin, convulsion	koris, chorus /course
kontane, contain	konvulshen, convulsion	korispond, correspond
kontekst, context	konvursashen, conversation	korjil, cordial
kontemporary, contemporary	konvursation, conversation	kork, cork /quark
kontemt, contempt	kood, could	korn, corn
kontend, contend	kooger, cougar	korner, corner /coroner
kontent, content	kook, cook /cock	korneu, cornea
kontenuel, continual	kookoo, cuckoo	kornikopea, cornucopia
kontest, contest	kooky, cookie	kornukopea, cornucopia
kontimplate, contemplate	kool, cool	kornur, corner /coroner
kontimporary, contemporary	koop, coop /co-op	korode, corrode
kontinet, continent	kooperate, cooperate	korparul, corporal
konting, content	kooshin, cushion	korpirate, corporate
kontinuance, continuance	kooth, couth	korps, corpse
kontorshenist, contortionist	kope, cope /copy	korpural, corporal
kontradik, contradict	koper, copper	korpurate, corporate
kontrak, contract	kopeir, copy(pier)	kors, course /coarse
kontrasepshun, contraception	kopier, copy(pier)	korsd, coarse(d)
kontrast, contrast	kopulate, copulate	korsoge, corsage
kontraversy, controversy	kopur, copper	kort, cord/ court/ quart
kontrebute, contribute	kopy, copy	kort-marshul, court-martial
kontrery, contrary	koral, choral/ coral/ corral/ chorale	korts, quartz/court(s)/quart(s)/cord(s)/chord(s)
kontrishen, contrition	kord, cord /chord /court	korudoor, corridor
kontrol, control	kordaroy, corduroy	korugate, corrugate
kontrudik, contradict	kordinate, coordinate	korul, choral/ coral/ corral/ chorale

korulate, correlate
koruner, coroner
korunery, coronary
korupt, corrupt
korus, chorus /course
koruspond, correspond
korve, carve
kos, cause
kosd, cause(d) /cost /coast /
kosee, cozy
koshin, caution
koshus, cautious
kosmik, cosmic
kosmopolutin, cosmopolitan
kosmos, cosmos
kost, cost/ cause(d)/ coast
koster, coaster
kostic, caustic
kostum, costume
kostyume, costume
kosy, cozy
kot, caught/ cot/ coat
kotage, cottage
kotch, coach
koten, cotton
kotuge, cottage
kouch, couch
koulishun, coalition
kounsil, council /counsel
kount, count
kova, kava
kove, cove
kovenant, covenant
kover, cover
kovit, covet
kovu, kava
kovurt, covert
kow, cow
kowch, couch

kowculus, calculus
kowerd, coward
kowkulate, calculate
kowl, call /cowl
kownder, counter
kownsul, council /counsel
kownt, count
kowntur, counter
kownty, county
kowurd, coward
koyel, coil
koyn, coin
koz, cause
kozd, cause(d) /cost
kozmik, cosmic
kozmopoletin, cosmopolitan
kozmos, cosmos
kozy, cozy
krab, crab
krader, crater /creator
kradul, cradle
kradur, crater /creator
krafe, crave
kraft, craft
krain, crane
kraink, crank
krak, crack
krakel, crackle
kraker, cracker
kral, crawl /corral
kram, cram
kramp, cramp
kranberry, cranberry
krane, crane
kraneum, cranium
krank, crank
krany, cranny
kraon, crayon
krap, crap /crepe

krape, crepe
krasee, crazy
krash, crash
krass, crass
krate, crate
krater, crater /creator
krave, crave
krawnik, chronic
krayon, crayon
krazy, crazy
kreader, creator
kreal, creel
kream, cream /creme
kreap, creep
krease, crease
kreashun, create(tion)
kreasul, creosole
kreate, create
kreatef, create(ive)
kreative, create(tive)
kreator, creator
kreb, crib
krebd, crib(bbed)
krebeg, cribbage
krecher, creature
krededer, creditor
kreder, critter
kredet, credit
kredible, credible
kredider, creditor
kredik, critic
kredisize, criticize
kredit, credit
kreditor, creditor
kreduble, credible
kreecher, creature
kreel, creel
kreen, careen

kraut, *PICKLED CABBAGE*

kreenkul, crinkle
kreep, creep
kreisote, creosote
kreke, creak /creek
krekit, cricket
krel, creel
kremate, cremate
kreme, cream /creme
kremenul, criminal
kreminal, criminal
kremsun, crimson
kreng, cringe
krenj, cringe
krenkle, crinkle
kreple, cripple
kreptic, cryptic
krescross, crisscross
krese, crease
kresendo, crescendo
kresent, crescent
kresont, croissant
kresp, crisp
kress, caress
krest, crest
kreteek, critique
kretik, critic
kretikul, critical
kreusol, creosole
kreusote, creosote
krevas, crevasse /crevice
krevus, crevasse /crevice
krew, crew
krewd, crude
krewshul, crucial
krewsufix, crucifix
krewton, crouton
kri, cry
krib, crib
kribage, cribbage

krid, cried
kridecal, critical
kridenshul, credential
krider, critter
kridesize, criticize
krien, cry(ing)
kriket, cricket
krime, crime
krimenal, criminal
krimson, crimson
kring, cringe
krinj, cringe
kriptic, cryptic
kripul, cripple
krisade, crusade
kriscross, crisscross
krisis, crisis
krismus, christmas
krisont, croissant
krisp, crisp
kristal, crystal
kristashen, crustacean
kritesize, criticize
kritik, critic
kritur, critter
kriz, cries
kroak, croak
kroan, crone
krok, crock /croak
krokedile, crocodile
kroket, croquet /croquette
krokudile, crocodile
krokus, crocus
krol, crawl
krom, chrome /crumb
kromizone, chromosome
krone, crone /crony
krones, crony(s)
kronic, chronic

kronicle, chronicle
kronlogical, chronological
kronucle, chronicle
kronulogikul, chronological
krony, crony
krook, crook
kroose, cruise /crew(s)
krop, crop
kroshay, crochet
kross, cross
krotch, crotch
krouch, crouch
krout, kraut
krow, crow
krowch, crouch
krowd, crowd
krown, crown
krowshay, crochet
krowt, kraut
kru, crew
kruch, crutch
krude, crude
krudenshul, credential
krue, crew
kruke, crook
kruks, crux
krum, crumb
krumble, crumble
krumple, crumple
krunch, crunch
krupt, corrupt
krusade, crusade
kruse, cruise /crew(s)
krusefix, crucifix
krusendo, crescendo
krush, crush
krushul, crucial
krusont, croissant
krust, crust

kumpoze, compose
kumpozer, composure
kumpreshun, compression
kumpresor, compressor
kumpress, compress
kumpuder, computer
kumpulsery, compulsory
kumpulshun, compulsion
kumpuss, compass
kumpute, compute
kumputer, computer
kumulative, cumulative
kumunal, communal
kumuneon, communion
kunal, canal
kundem, condemn
kundinse, condense
kundishen, condition
kundition, condition
kundolense, condolence
kundone, condone
kundukt, conduct
kundukter, conductor
kunekshen, connection
kunekt, connect
kunfekshun, confection
kunferm, confirm
kunfermashun, confirmation
kunfes, confess
kunfeshun, confession
kunfety, confetti
kunfide, confide
kunfigerashun, configuration
kunfine, confine
kunfinment, confinement
kunflict, conflict
kunform, conform
kunfrunt, confront
kunfujen, confusion

kunfuze, confuse
kunglomurete, conglomerate
kungradulashun, congratulation
kungratshulate, congratulate
kungruint, congruent
kunikkunik, kinnikinnick
kuning, cunning
kunjunction, conjunction
kunklude, conclude
kunklujen, conclusion
kunkokt, concoct
kunkushen, concussion
kunning, cunning
kunsecutive, consecutive
kunseed, concede
kunseel, conceal
kunseet, conceit
kunseevable, conceivable
kunseeve, conceive
kunsent, consent
kunsepshual, conceptual
kunsepshun, conception
kunsern, concern
kunseshun, concession
kunsevable, conceivable
kunsider, consider
kunsinment, consignment
kunsirvutive, conservative
kunsise, concise
kunsist, consist
kunsistency, consistency
kunsiter, consider
kunsole, console
kunsoludate, consolidate
kunsoom, consume
kunsoul, console
kunspearucy, conspiracy
kunspikyus, conspicuous
kunstrict, constrict

kunstrucshen, construction
kunstruct, construct
kunsult, consult
kunsume, consume
kunsumshen, consumption
kuntagus, contagious
kuntain, contain
kuntamunate, contaminate
kuntane, contain
kuntemporary, contemporary
kuntemt, contempt
kuntend, contend
kuntent, content
kuntenual, continual
kuntenuense, continuance
kuntenule, continual
kuntest, contest
kuntimporary, contemporary
kuntorshenist, contortionist
kuntrakshen, contraction
kuntree, country
kuntrery, contrary
kuntribute, contribute
kuntrishen, contrition
kuntrol, control
kunveenyut, convenient
kunvene, convene
kunvense, convinse
kunvenshen, convention
kunvenyant, convenient
kunvergin, conversion
kunvershen, conversion
kunvert, convert
kunvict, convict
kunvulgin, convulsion
kunvulshen, convulsion
kup, cup /coop
kupasity, capacity
kupcake, cupcake

kupe, coop
kupil, couple
kupler, coupler
kupon, coupon
kupoot, kaput
kupul, couple
kuput, kaput
kurable, curable
kurader, curator
kural, choral/ coral/ corral/ chorale
kurb, curb
kurd, curd
kurdesy, courtesy
kurdeus, courteous
kurdisy, courtesy
kurdle, curdle
kure, cure
kureen, careen
kureer, career
kurege, courage
kureje, courage
kurekt, correct
kurekulum, curriculum
kurensy, currency
kurent, currant /current
kureosety, curiosity
kureosudy, curiosity
kures, caress
kureur, courier
kureus, curious
kureusol, creosole
kurf, curve
kurfew, curfew
kurfue, curfew
kurige, courage
kurin, curtain
kurinsy, currency
kuriosity, curiosity
kurisma, charisma

kurl, curl
kurnel, colonel /kernel
kuroburate, corroborate
kurode, corrode
kuroky, karaoke
kurote, karate
kuroty, karate
kurowse, carouse
kursanthimum, chrysanthemum
kursathimum, chrysanthemum
kurse, curse
kursif, cursive
kursive, cursive
kursoge, corsage
kurtale, curtail
kurten, curtain
kurtesy, courtesy
kurteus, courteous
kurtin, curtain
kurtle, curdle
kurtse, curtsy
kurupt, corrupt
kurvachure, curvature
kurve, curve
kury, curry
kus, cuss
kusen, cousin
kuset, cassette
kushen, cushion
kusin, cousin
kusp, cusp
kusped, cuspid
kuss, cuss
kustedy, custody
kustem, custom
kustemary, customary
kustemize, customize
kusterd, custard
kustimer, customer

kustodeun, custodian
kustomary, customary
kustomer, customer
kustomize, customize
kut, cut /cat
kutastrufee, catastrophe
kute, cute
kutecle, cuticle
kuth, couth
kutlury, cutlery
kutukle, cuticle
kuvenant, covenant
kuver, cover
kuvit, covet
kuvridge, coverage
kuvunent, covenant
kuzn, cousin
kwack, quack / quake
kwad, quad
kwadrant, quadrant
kwadrunt, quadrant
kwagmire, quagmire
kwaik, quake
kwail, quail
kwaint, quaint
kwak, quack /quake
kwale, quail
kwaledy, quality
kwalefication, qualify(fication)
kwalefikashen, qualify(fication)
kwalefiuble, qualify(fiable)
kwalefiur, qualify(fier)
kwaletatif, quality(tative)
kwalety, quality
kwalifekashen, qualify(fication)
kwalify, qualify
kwalitatif, quality(tative)
kwalitee, quality
kwalm, qualm

kwandery, quandary
kwandree, quandary
kwant, quaint
kwantefy, quantify
kwantem, quanta(tum)
kwantety, quantity
kwantify, quantify
kwantifyer, quantify(fier)
kwantim, quanta(tum)
kwantity, quantity
kwantry, quandary
kwantum, quanta(tum)
kward, quart
kwarder, quarter
kwarderly, quarter(ly)
kwards, quartz /quart(s)
kwardur, quarter
kwardurly, quarter(ly)
kwardz, quartz /quart(s)
kware, quarry
kwarel, quarrel
kwarentene, quarantine
kwaril, quarrel
kwarintene, quarantine
kwark, quark
kwarol, quarrel
kwart, quart
kwarter, quarter
kwarterly, quarter(ly)
kwarts, quartz /quart(s)
kwarul, quarrel
kwary, quarry /query
kwasar, quasar
kwasy, quasi
kwaundre, quandary
kwaure, quarry
kwawrel, quarrel
kwawrul, quarrel
kwawry, quarry

kwaysar, quasar
kwazar, quasar
kwazee, quasi
kwazene, cuisine
kwear, queer
kween, queen
kwefir, quiver
kwefur, quiver
kwek, quick
kwekest, quick(est)
kwekly, quick(ly)
kweky, quick(ie)
kwel, quill
kwelt, quilt
kwench, quench
kwentuplet, quintuplet
kwer, queer
kwerk, quirk
kwerky, quirk(y)
kwery, query
kwes, quiz
kwesden, question
kwesekal, quiz(zzical)
kweshten, question
kwest, quest
kwestenair, question(nnaire)
kwesteun, question
kwestshunar, question(nnaire)
kwestun, question
kwet, quit /quite
kweter, quit(tter) /quiet(er)
kwever, quiver
kwez, quiz
kwezekal, quiz(zzical)
kwezene, cuisine
kwezt, quest
kwiet, quiet
kwietly, quiet(ly)
kwifir, quiver

kwifor, quiver
kwik, quick
kwikest, quick(est)
kwikly, quick(ly)
kwiky, quick(ie)
kwil, quill
kwilt, quilt
kwinch, quench
kwintuplet, quintuplet
kwire, choir
kwirk, quirk
kwiry, query
kwisekal, quiz(zzical)
kwisine, cuisine
kwit, quit / quite
kwiter, quit(tter) /quiet(er)
kwiut, quiet
kwiutly, quiet(ly)
kwiver, quiver
kwiyet, quiet
kwiz, quiz
kwizekal, quiz(zzical)
kwochent, quotient
kwod, quad
kwoda, quota
kwodabul, quote(table)
kwodashen, quote(tation)
kwode, quote
kwodrent, quadrant
kwodu, quota
kwoledy, quality
kwolefikashen, qualify(fication)
kwolefy, qualify
kwoletatif, quality(tative)
kwoletative, quality(tative)
kwolety, quality
kwolification, qualify(fication)
kwolifikashen, qualify(fication)
kwolifiuble, qualify(fiable)

kwolifiur, qualify(fier)
kwolitatif, quality(tative)
kwolitative, quality(tative)
kwolitee, quality
kwolm, qualm
kwolufy, qualify
kwondery, quandary
kwonefy, quantify
kwontefyer, quantify(fier)
kwontem, quanta(tum)
kwontety, quantity
kwontify, quantify
kwontifyer, quantify(fier)
kwontim, quanta(tum)
kwontity, quantity
kwontre, quandary
kwontum, quanta(tum)
kworam, quorum
kword, quart
kworder, quarter
kworderly, quarter(ly)
kwords, quartz /quart(s)
kwordur, quarter
kwordurly, quarter(ly)
kwordz, quartz /quart(s)
kworel, quarrel
kworem, quorum
kworentene, quarantine
kworil, quarrel
kworim, quorum
kworintene, quarantine
kwork, quark
kworol, quarrel
kworom, quorum
kwort, quart
kworter, quarter
kworterly, quarter(ly)
kwortir, quarter
kworts, quartz /quart(s)

kwortur, quarter
kwortz, quartz /quart(s)
kworul, quarrel
kworum, quorum
kworuntene, quarantine
kwoshent, quotient
kwosy, quasi
kwota, quota
kwotabul, quote(table)
kwotashen, quote(tation)
kwotation, quote(tation)
kwote, quote
kwotu, quota
kwozy, quasi
kwurentene, quarantine
kwurintene, quarantine
kwurk, quirk
kwurky, quirk(y)
kwyit, quiet
kwyre, choir

"L"

la, law /lay
labarenth, labyrinth
labedo, libido
label,*,led,ling, A WAY TO REMEMBER/SAVE/ RETRIEVE/CATEGORIZE THINGS
laber, labor
laberatory, laboratory
labeul, labial
labi, labio, PREFIX INDICATING "LIP" MOST OFTEN MODIFIES THE WORD
labial,lly,lize,lization, SOUND, OF THE LIPS, ORGAN PIPE
labido, libido
labil, label

labio, labi, PREFIX INDICATING "LIP" MOST OFTEN MODIFIES THE WORD
labor,*,red,ring,ringly,rious,riously,riousness, rism,rist,rer, PHYSICALLY WORKING
laboratory,ries, PLACE FOR STUDY/ EXPERIMENTS AND OBSERVATION
laborenth, labyrinth
labratory, laboratory
labrinth, labyrinth
labrutory, laboratory
labul, label
labur, labor
labyrinth,*, A MAZE, CHAOTIC CIRCUMSTANCES
lace,*,ed,cing, SECURE SHOES WITH, WOVEN STRING
lacerate,*,ed,ting,tion, GASH OR RIP OPEN, GASH TORN INTO FABRIC OR SKIN
lach, latch
lack,*,ked,king, BELIEF THAT ONE DOES NOT HAVE ENOUGH OF SOMETHING (or see lake)
lackative, laxative
lacker, lacquer
lacks, lax/ lake(s)/ lack(s)
lacktat, lactate
lacquer,*, VARNISH
lacrosse, ORIGINALLY A NATIVE AMERICAN SPORTS GAME
lact,lacti, lacto, PREFIX INDICATING "MILK" MOST OFTEN MODIFIES THE WORD
lactate,*,ed,ting,tion, MILK BEING PRODUCED IN MAMMALS
lactose, SUGAR FROM COW MILK
lad,*, YOUNG MEN (or see laid or late)
ladder,*, TWO POLES WITH RUNGS FOR CLIMBING (or see later)
lade, laid/ lay/ lady/ late
ladel, ladle
laden, BURDENED DOWN, HEAVY LOAD
lader, ladder/ later/ latter
laderal, lateral

laderuly, lateral(ly)
ladery, lottery
lades, lattice / ladie(s) / lettuce
ladetude, latitude
ladir, latter /ladder /later
ladis, lattice / ladie(s)
laditude, latitude
ladle,*, ed,ling, LONG HANDLE SPOON TO SERVE FOOD
ladul, ladle
ladur, later/ ladder/ latter
ladural, lateral
ladutude, latitude
lady,dies, A WOMAN
lae, lay
laed, laid / late
laeng, lay(ing)
laer, layer
laevo, lev, levo, PREFIX INDICATING "COUNTER-
    CLOCKWISE" MOST OFTEN MODIFIES THE WORD
lafdur, laughter
lafender, lavender
laff, laugh
lafter, laughter
lag,*,gged,gging, TO BE SLOWER THAN THE OTHERS,
    SHAPE OR CASING, DELAY
lager, BEER
lagestics, logistic(s)
lagetamate, legitimate
lagicul, logic(al)
lagistics, logistic(s)
lagitamate, legitimate
lagoon,*, ENCLOSED/NEARLY ENCLOSED SMALL BODY
    OF WATER NEAR LARGER BODY OF WATER
lai, lay
laid, PAST TENSE OF "LAY" (or see late)
lain, PAST TENSE OF "LAID" (or see lane)
laing, lay(ing)
laingweg, language
laj, lodge

lajekul, logic(al)
lajistics, logistic(s)
lake,*, LARGE BODY OF WATER FED BY SPRINGS (or
    see lack)
laker, lacquer
lakross, lacrosse
laks, lax/ lake(s)/ lack(s)
laksetif, laxative
laksutef, laxative
laktate, lactate
laktose, lactose
lam, RUNNING FROM TROUBLE (or see lamb or lame)
lama, llama
lamb,*, YOUNG SHEEP (or see lam or lame)
lame,ly,eness, PERMANENTLY INJURED LIMB OR LIMBS
    THAT DON'T WORK (or see lam or lamb)
lamenate, laminate
lament,*,ted,ting,table,tableness,tably,tation,
    MOURN THE LOSS OF SOMEONE, SPEND TIME IN
    THE PAST ON REGRETS
laminate,*, GLUE LAYERS TOGETHER
lamp,*, A LIGHT WITH A SHADE/COVER OVER THE BULB
lamunate, laminate
lance,*, ed,cing,er, MEDIEVAL WEAPON
land,*,ded,ding,dless, EARTH, TO SETTLE ONTO/
    DIVIDE UP/SET ONTO THE EARTH
landern, lantern
landlord,*, OWNER WHO RENTS/LEASES PROPERTY
landscape,*, ed,ping,er, FOLIAGE/FAUNA/TERRAIN
    OF WHAT THE EYE SEES
landslide,*, WHEN LAND BREAKS AWAY FROM OTHER
    LAND DUE TO WATER
lane,*, PASSAGEWAYS/ROADS FOR VEHICLES, PATHS IN
    BOWLING (or see lain)
lanelin, lanolin
language,*, WORDS/MEANS OF COMMUNICATION IN
    DIFFERENT REGIONS
langweg, language
lankwij, language

lanky,kily,iness, TALL AND THIN
lanlord, landlord
lanolin, OIL FROM WOOL
lanqueg, language
lans, lance /lane(s)
lanskap, landscape
lanskapur, landscape(r)
lant, land
lantern,*, FUELED FLAME WITHIN CONTAINER
lantlord, landlord
lantscape, landscape
lantslide, landslide
lanulin, lanolin
lap,*,pped,pping, TO GO AROUND, HOW ANIMALS
    DRINK, CREATED IN SITTING POSITION
lapadary, lapidary
lapel,*, COLLARS
lapidary,ries,rian, CUT/POLISH/ENGRAVE STONES
laprutory, laboratory
lapse,es,sed,sing, SLIPPING INTO, LOOSE A MOMENT
    IN TIME, PAUSE (or see lap(s))
lapudary, lapidary
lard, FAT FROM DEAD PIGS
larel, laurel
larengitis, laryngitis
large,er,est,ely,eness, BIG
larges, largess /large(st)
largess, GENEROUS GIFT OR DONATION EXPECTING
    NOTHING IN RETURNF
largist, large(st)
largly, large(ly)
lariette, laureate
larinex, larynx
larj, large
larjes, largess
lark,*, BIRD, PRANT, ON AN IMPULSE FOR FUN
larniks, larynx
larva,al, BABY INSECT THAT RESEMBLES A WORM
    BEFORE IT BECOMES AN ADULT

larying, laryngo, PREFIX INDICATING "LARYNX/VOCAL ORGAN" MOST OFTEN MODIFIES THE WORD
laryngitis,ic, THROAT INFLAMMATION
larynx, THROAT
lasarate , lacerate
lasd , last /lace(d)
lase , lace/ lace(y)/ lazy
laser,*, A LIGHT FREQUENCY
laserashen , lacerate(tion)
laserate , lacerate
laseration , lacerate(tion)
lash,hes,hed,hing,her, HAIRS ON THE EYE, USE SOMETHING SUCH AS ROPE TO STRIKE OR TIE UP SOMETHING, THRUST OUT WITH ILL INTENT
lasirashen , lacerate(tion)
lasirate , lacerate
lasiration , lacerate(tion)
lasirat , lacerate
lasuration , lacerate(tion)
lasso,oes, SLIDING HOOP OUT OF ROPE
last,*,ted,ting,tly,NOT THE FIRST, WON'T GO AWAY FOR QUITE AWHILE (or see lace(d))
lasuit , lawsuit
lasurashen , lacerate(tion)
lasurat , lacerate
lasute , lawsuit
latch,hes,hed, CLOSURE FOR A DOOR/LID
late,er,ely,eness,tish, NOT ON TIME, OF A PARTICULAR TIME (or see lady/ladder/latter)
laten , laden
latent,tly,ncy, A TIME LAPSE BETWEEN WHEN IT HAPPENED AND THE REACTION
later, FURTHER ALONG IN TIME (or see late/ladder/latter)
lateral,lly, EXTENDS FROM THE SIDE, A MOVEMENT IN A SIDEWAYS DIRECTION
latex,xes,tices, FORM OF MANMADE RUBBER/ PLASTIC USED FOR GLOVES, PAINT, ETC.

lath,*, NARROW STRIPS OF WOOD USED TO BUILD WITH (or see lathe)
lathargic , lethargic
lathe,*, ed,hing, WOOD SHAPING MACHINE (or see lath)
lather,*,red,ring,ry,rer, SOAPY OR FOAMY BUBBLES
latil , ladle
latincy , latent(ncy)
latise , lattice
latitude,*,dinal,dinally, LINES THAT RUN NORTH/SOUTH
latle , ladle
latrine,*, MILITARY WORD FOR TOILET
latter,rly, MORE TOWARDS THE LAST (or see ladder)
lattice,ed, WOOD STRIPS CRISSCROSSED TOGETHER FOR DECORATION
latur , later/ ladder/ latter
latural , lateral
latury , lottery
laty , lady
laugh,hes,hed,hing,hable, TO EXPRESS GLEE VOCALLY IN BURSTS, DISPLAY OF ENJOYMENT
laughter, VOCAL EXPRESSION OF HAPPINESS AND GLEE
laun , lawn
launch,hes,hed,hing,her, PROPEL/SHOOT SOMETHING
launder,*,rer, WASH AND IRON CLOTHING
laundry, CLEANING/CARING OF CLOTHES
laur , layer
laureate,eship, HONORED/DISTINGUISHED POET
laurel, A TREE, REST ON PREVIOUS AWARDS
lausut , lawsuit
lauyer , lawyer
lava, MOLTEN ROCK
lavender, A PLANT
lavesh , lavish
lavinder , lavender
lavish,hes,her,hly,hness,hment, TO BESTOW UPON SOMEONE GIFTS AND OTHER THINGS
lavunder , lavendar

law,*, wful,wfully,wfulness,wless,wlessly, RULES SUPPORTED BY A GOVERNMENT
lawn mower,*, MACHINE FOR MOWING GRASS
lawn,*, GRASSY AREAS
lawnch , launch
lawsuit,*, A CASE BROUGHT BEFORE A JUDGE CONCERNING THE LAW
lawyer,*, PAID PEOPLE TO HELP YOU WITH THE LAWS
lax,xly,xness,xity, RELAXED, NO HURRY (or see lake(s) or lack(s))
laxative,*, PLANT/CHEMICALS FOR RELAXING THE BOWELS
laxsutif , laxative
laxutif , laxative
lay,*, yed,ying, TO SET DOWN AN OBJECT, TO INSTALL, SOMEONE WHO IS TRAINING TO BE AN UPPER RANK, GET SET ASIDE, RECLINE (or see lie)
layer,*,red,ring, THICKNESS OF SOMETHING OVER TOP OF ANOTHER, ONE FRAME OVER OTHERS
laytex , latex
layur , layer / lawyer
lazarashen , lacerate(tion)
laze , lazy
lazer , laser
lazeur , lazy(zier)
lazy,zier,ziest,zily,ziness, NO AMBITION TO DO ANYTHING (or see lace(y))
lbo , elbow
leach,hes,hed,hing, SEEPING LIQUID, LIQUID PERCOLATING (or see leech)
lead,dless,len,der,derless,ding, A HEAVY METAL, SOMEONE WHO TAKES CHARGE OF A SITUATION
leader,*, ONE WHO TAKES CHARGE (or see letter or liter)
leaf,fy, GROWS FROM A TREE
league,*,er, GROUPS PARTICIPATING IN A SIMILAR ACTIVITY DIVIDED INTO REGIONS OR ABILITIES
leak,*,ked,king,kage,ky,kiness, WHEN LIQUID/INFORMATION SEEPS OUT (or see leek)

lean,*,nly,ness, *VERY LITTLE FAT, A VERTICAL POSITION LEANING TOWARDS A HORIZONTAL POSITION (or see lien)*

leap,*,ped,ping,lept, *TO BOUND/JUMP*

lear, leer

learn,*,ned,ning,nable,ner,nedly,nedness, *TO TAKE IN INFORMATION AS KNOWLEDGE*

leary, leery

lease,*,ed,sing, *TO BORROW/USE FOR AWHILE IN EXCHANGE FOR MONEY (or see lees)*

leash,es,hed,hing, *RESTRAINT FOR ANIMALS*

leason, liaison

least,twise, *SMALLEST AMOUNT, GREATER THAN "LESS" (or see lease(ed))*

leasy, lessee

leather,*, *DRIED SKIN FROM ANIMALS*

leave,*,ving,left, *TO GO AWAY, PAST TENSE OF "LEAF", (LEAVES) ON A TREE*

leazon, liaison

lebarul, liberal

lebirate, liberate

lebrul, liberal

leburate, liberate

leburty, liberty

lech, leech

lecture,*,ed,ring,er, *TO SPEAK AT GREAT LENGTH ABOUT SOMETHING BEFORE A GROUP OF PEOPLE*

led, *PAST TENSE OF "LEAD" (or see lid or lead)*

ledal, little

leder, liter/ litter/ letter/ leader

lederary, literary

lederul, literal

ledge,*,er, *A FLAT LANDING ATOP A WALL OR WALL SECTION, A BOOK WHICH KEEPS ACCOUNTING RECORDS, AN OVERHANG*

ledir, leader/ letter/ liter/ litter

ledis, lettuce

leds, let(s) /lead(s)

ledur, liter/ litter/ letter/ leader

ledurasy, literacy

ledus, lettuce

leech,hes, *A BLOOD SUCKING BUG (or see leach)*

leed, lead

leef, leaf / leave

leeg, league

leek, *A VEGETABLE (or see leak)*

leen, lean /lien

leenyency, leniency

leep, leap

leer,*, *A LONG GLANCE WITH MALICIOUS INTENT*

leery, *SUSPICIOUS OF, WARY OF*

lees, *SEDIMENTS OF WINE OR LIQUOR (or see lease)*

leese, lease

leesh, leash

leest, least /lease(d)

leet, lead

leeward, *AWAY FROM THE WIND*

lef, leaf/ live/ leave/ left

lefd, lift/ left/ leaf(ed)/ live(d)

lefee, levee/ levy/ leaf(y)

lefol, level

left,ty, *LEFT VS. RIGHT, PAST TENSE OF "LEAVE", APPEARS TO BE GONE (or see lift/live(d))*

leful, level

leg,*,gged,gging, *EXTREMITY ON THE LOWER END OF THE TORSO, SUPPORT FOR TABLE/CHAIRS, AN EXTENSION (or see league/ledge)*

legacy,cies, *SOMETHING HANDED DOWN FROM PREDECESSORS*

legal,ly,lity,lities,lize,lization,lism, *RULES AS DECIDED BY THE SUPREME COURT*

legament, ligament

leganse, allegiance

lege, ledge / league

legebul, legible

legend,*,dary,daries, *A STORY HANDED DOWN THROUGH HISTORY*

leger, leisure /ledge(r)

legesy, legacy

legible,ly,bility, *WRITING CAPABLE OF BEING READ*

legibul, legible

legido, libido

legind, legend

legion,*,nary,naries, *LARGE GROUP ASSOCIATED WITH THE MILITARY*

legislation, *PASSING AND CREATING LAWS*

legislative,ely, *RELATED TO LAWMAKING*

legislature, *LAWMAKING BRANCH*

legistics, logistic(s)

legisy, legacy

legitimate,acy,ely,eness,tion, *LEGALLY RECOGNIZED*

leguble, legible

legue, league

legul, legal

legulize, legal(ize)

legume,*, *SPECIES OF PLANT*

legun, lesion / legion

leguse, legacy

leguslashen, legislation

leguslative, legislative

leguslature, legislature

legusy, legacy

leisure,ed,eless,ely,rliness,eness, *RELAXED, UNHURRIED*

lejable, legible

lejanse, allegiance

lej, ledge /leech

lejebul, legible

lejen, lesion / legion

lejend, legend

lejer, leisure /ledge(r)

lejibul, legible

lejin, legion /lesion

lejislashen, legislation

lejislative, legislative

lejislature, legislature
lejitamet, legitimate
lejun, legion /lesion
lek, lick/ leak/ leek/ league
leked, lick(ed) /leak(ed)
lekemia, leukemia
leker, liquor /lick(er)
lekoresh, licorice
lekur, liquor /lick(er)
leksher, lecture
lekture, lecture
lekume, legume
lekwefide, liquefy(fied)
lekwid, liquid
lekwidate, liquid(ate)
lekwify, liquefy
lem, limb
lemazene, limousine
lemb, limb
lember, limber
lembo, limbo
lemet, limit
lemfatic, lymph(atic)
lemintation, lament(tation)
lemit, limit
lemitation, limit(ation)
lemon,*,ny,nade, *CITRUS FRUIT, JUICE*
lemune, lemon(y)
lemp, limp
lemphatic, lymph(atic)
lemusine, limousine
lemutation, limit(ation)
lemuzene, limousine
len, lean / lien
lenament, liniment
lend,*,ded,ding,nt,der, *TO LET SOMEONE BORROW*
    (or see lint or lean(ed))
lenear, linear
lenen, linen

leneuge, lineage
leneul, lineal
lenger, linger
lengo, lingo
length,*,hen,hener,hiness,hy, *HOW LONG*
    SOMETHING IS
lenguist, linguist
lenguistics, linguist(ics)
lengwist, linguist
lengwistics, linguist(ics)
leniency,cies,ce,nt,ntly, *NOT RIGID OR TOO STRICT*
lenin, linen /lean(ing)
leniuge, lineage
leniur, linear
lenk, link
lenkage, link(age)
lenker, linger
lenkth, length
lenoleum, linoleum
lenon, linen /lean(ing)
lens,*, *PART OF THE EYE, USED IN GLASSES*
lenseed, linseed
lent,*, *PAST TENSE OF "LEND", LET SOMEONE BORROW, A*
    RELIGIOUS EVENT (or see lint or lean(ed))
lenth, length
lentil,*, *PLANT IN THE LEGUME FAMILY*
lentul, lentil
lenument, liniment
lenyensy, leniency
leotard,*, *HEAVYWEIGHT PANTYHOSE*
lep, lip /leap
lepel, lapel
leper, liquor
lequid, liquid
lequidate, liquid(ate)
lequifide, liquefy(fied)
lequify, liquefy
leranex, larynx
lerch, lurch

lere, leery
lerengitis, laryngitis
leric, lyric
lerinex, larynx
leringitis, laryngitis
lerk, lurk
lern, learn
lernicks, larynx
lery, leery
les, less /lease
lesard, lizard
lesbian,*, *WOMAN WHO PREFERS INTIMATE*
    COMPANIONSHIP WITH ANOTHER WOMAN
lese, lessee
lesee, lessee
lesen, lessen/ lesson/ listen
leser, lesser /lessor
lesh, leash
leshun, lesion
lesin, lessen/ lesson/ listen
lesion,*, *AN INJURED SPOT ON HUMAN TISSUE*
lesir, lesser /lessor
lesless, listless
leson, lessen/ lesson/ listen
lesp, lisp
less,sser, *NOT AS MUCH AS BEFORE OR AS EXPECTED*
lessee,*, *ONE WHO IS LEASING*
lessen, *TAKE SOME AWAY, REMOVE SOME (or see*
    lesson)
lesser, *NOT AS MUCH AS BEFORE, LESS THAN (or see*
    lessor)
lesson,*, *A TEACHING/LEARNING SECTION/SESSION*
    (or see lessen)
lessor,*, *ONE WHO LEASES OUT PROPERTY TO OTHERS*
    (or see lesser)
lest, list / least
lesten, listen
lestless, listless
lesun, lessen/ lesson/ listen

lesur, lesser /lessor
let,*,tting, *PERMIT, ALLOW* (or see led or lead)
leter, liter/ litter/ letter/ leader
leteracy, literacy
leteral, literal
leterally, literal(ly)
leterary, literary
leterature, literature
letes, lettuce
lethal,lly,lity, *DEADLY*
lethargic,cal,cally,gy,gize, *SLEEPY, NO ENERGY, SLUMPED*
lether, leather
lethergy, lethargy
lethul, lethal
letir, liter/ litter/ letter/ leader
letiracher, literature
letis, lettuce
letmus, litmus
letrine, latrine
let's, *CONTRACTION OF THE WORDS "LET US"*
letter,*,red,ring, *SYMBOLS OF THE ALPHABET, PAPER WITH WRITING TO SOMEONE, TO MAKE LETTER SHAPES* (or see leader)
lettuce, *AN EDIBLE PLANT*
letur, liter/ litter/ letter/ leader
leturacher, literature
letus, lettuce
leuc, leuco, leuko, *PREFIX INDICATING "WHITE/ COLORLESS" MOST OFTEN MODIFIES THE WORD*
leukemia,ic, *A FATAL DISEASE*
leutard, leotard
lev, *PREFIX INDICATING "COUNTERCLOCKWISE" MOST OFTEN MODIFIES THE WORD*
levabul, live(vable)
levatate, levitate
leve, leave /levy /levee

levee,*, *TRENCH OR EMBANKMENT FOR CONTROLLING WATER* (or see levy)
level,*,ly,lness,ler, *STRAIGHT UP OR HORIZONTAL, TRUTHFUL WITH SOMEONE*
lever,*,rage, *APPLY PHYSICS/HARDWARE TO LIFT*
levi, levee /levy
levid, livid
levil, level
levitate,*,ed,ting,tion,ty, *DEFY GRAVITY*
levo, *PREFIX INDICATING "COUNTERCLOCKWISE" MOST OFTEN MODIFIES THE WORD*
levor, lever /liver
levs, leave(s)
levuble, live(vable)
levul, level
levur, liver /lever
levury, livery
levutate, levitate
levy,viable,vier, *USED TO COLLECT MONEY* (or see levee)
lew, lieu
lewb, lube
lewbrecashen, lubricate(tion)
lewbrecate, lubricate
lewbrikate, lubricate
lewcid, lucid
lewcratef, lucrative
lewd,dly,dness, *OBSCENE, GIVEN TO LUST AND INDECENCY* (or see loot)
lewdakris, ludicrous
lewducris, ludicrous
lewkrative, lucrative
lewkwarm, lukewarm
lewlu, lulu
lewmenary, luminary
lewmenesense, luminescense
lewmenosity, luminosity
lewmenus, luminous
lewmin, lumen

lewner, lunar
leword, leeward
lewpine, lupine
lewse, loose / lose
lewsid, lucid
lewsun, loose(n)
lewt, loot/ lute/ lewd
lezard, lizard
lezbeun, lesbian
li, lie /lye /lay
liabelity, liable(bility)
liable,bility,bilities, *SOMEONE TO BE BLAMED*
liaison,*, *FORMATION OF DEEP CONNECTION BETWEEN PEOPLE FOR MANEUVERING, BONDING*
liar,*, *SOMEONE WHO DOESN'T TELL THE TRUTH* (or see lyre)
libary, library
libel,lant,lee,lous,lously, *WRITR MALICIOUS WORDS ABOUT SOMEONE ELSE FOR PUBLIC VIEWING* (or see liable)
liberal,*,lly,lness,lism,lism,lity,lities,listic,list, *MODERATE, TOLERANT, OPEN MINDED*
liberate,*, ed,ting,tion,tor, *TO SET FREE*
liberty,ties, *THE ACT OF FREEDOM*
libery, library
libido,dinal,dinally, *THOUGHTS WHICH DRIVE THE SEXUAL IMPULSES*
lible, libel /liable
library,ries, *A PLACE WHICH COLLECTS AND DISSEMINATES WRITTEN HISTORY*
librul, liberal
libul, libel /liable
libural, liberal
license,*,ed,sing,sable,see,er, *A PERMIT TO OPERATE*
lichen,*, *MOSS, A FORM OF PLANT WITH HEALING QUALITIES* (or see liken)
licinse, license
lick,*,ked,king, *USING THE TONGUE* (or see like)

licorice, A PLANT EXTRACT, A CANDY
lid,*,dded,dless, A HINGED OPENING (or see lie(d) or light)
lidegashen, litigate(tion)
lidegate, litigate
lidel, little
lider, liter /litter /light(er)
lideral, literal
liderally, literal(ly)
liderary, literary
liderasy, literacy
liderature, literature
lidigate, litigate
lidul, little
liduracher, literature
lidurally, literal(ly)
lidurare, literary

lie,*,ed,lying, TO NOT TELL THE TRUTH, BODY IN A RECLINED OR FLAT POSITION, INACTIVE POSITION (or see lay or lye)
lieng, lying
lier, liar /lyre
lien, SOMEONE WHO TAKES AWAY PROPERTY FOR MONEY DUE (or see lion)
lieu, INSTEAD OF, IN PLACE OF
lieutenant,*, A MILITARY OFFICER
lifd, lift /live(d)
life, ALL THINGS VISIBLE ARE OF LIFE
lifeble, live(vable)
lifle, live(ly)
lifehood, livelihood
lifehud, livelihood
lift,*,ted,ting, PICK/HOIST UP (or see live(d)/left)
ligality, legal(ity)
ligament,*,tous,tal,tary, FIBROUS TISSUE IN THE BODY
light,*,ted,ting,tly, A WAVE FREQUENCY WE CAN VISIBLY SEE, ILLUMINATING, NOT HEAVY
lightening, ILLUMINATED ELECTRICAL BOLTS IN SKY

lightness, NOT HEAVY, FEATHER WEIGHT, DEGREE OF ILLUMINATION
ligoon, lagoon
ligament, ligament
lik, lick /like
like,*,ed,kable,eness, SIMILAR TO SOMETHING OR SOMEONE ELSE, ENJOY SOMETHING, ATTRACTED TO SOMETHING (or see lick)
liken,*, SIMILAR TO, RESEMBLING (or see lichen or lick(ing))
likeness, SIMILAR TO, RESEMBLING
liker, liquor /lick(er)
likerish, licorice
likewise, SIMILARLY, ALSO
likness, likeness
likoresh, licorice
likt, like(d) /lick(ed)
likuble, like(kable)
likun, liken
likwid, liquid
likwidate, liquid(ate)
likwifide, liquefy(fied)
likwify, liquefy
likwise, likewise
lilac,*, AROMATIC PLANT
liluc, lilac
limazene, limousine
limb,*,bed,bing, BRANCHES OF TREES/ SHRUBS, TO REMOVE BRANCHES/EXTRUSIONS FROM THE BODY TORSO
limber, ABLE TO MOVE BODY SMOOTHLY AND WITH DEXTERITY
limbo, PLACE BETWEEN HERE AND THERE, WITH UNCERTAINTY, A PHYSICAL GAME
lime,*, A CITRUS FRUIT, CAO FOR SETTING BRICKS AND STONE
limelight,*, BEING IN THE SPOTLIGHT
limesine, limousine
limet, limit

limetation, limit(ation)
limfatic, lymph(atic)
limit,*,ted,ting,tation,tless,tative,ter,tary, ONLY GO SO FAR, A FIXED VALUE
limlite, limelight
limon, lemon
limousine,*, LONG AUTOMOBILE FOR TRANSPORTING PEOPLE
limp,*,ped,ping,pingly,ply,per, NOT STIFF /RIGID, LOSS OF FUNCTION, LACK OF WILLFUL CONTROL OVER THE BODY
limphatic, lymph(atic)
limpt, limp(ed)
limusine, limousine
limuzene, limousine
linament, liniment
lind, lend/ lint/ line(d)
line,*,ed,ning,eless,eable,nable, BETWEEN TWO POINTS, RUN PARALLEL, FOR FISHING
lineage,*, OUR ANCESTORS, FAMILY TREE, WHERE WE COME FROM
lineal,lly, HEREDITY FOLLOWING A DIRECT PATH
linear,rly,ation, PATH STRAIGHT AHEAD WITH NO DEVIATION
linen,*, TAN COTTON FABRIC (or see linin)
lineng, lining
liner,*, COATING INSIDE A VESSEL FOR PROTECTION
lineur, linear
linger,*,red,ring,ringly,er, STAY AROUND LONGER, LOITER, WAITING
lingo,oes, WAY TO SAY SOMETHING, UNIQUE METHOD OF COMMUNICATION
linguist,*, ONE WHO SPECIALIZED IN LANGUAGES
linguistic,*,tical,tically,ulate, STUDY OF LANGUAGES AND SPEECH
lingwist, linguist
lingwistics, linguist(ics)
liniment,*, HEALING OINTMENTS
linin, IN CELL NUCLEUS (or see linen or lining)

lining,*, LAYER INSIDE OF EXTERIOR LINING (or see linin or linen)
liniul, lineal
link,*,ked,king,kage,ker, TWO THINGS JOINED TOGETHER
links, lynx /link(s)
linkth, length
linkuge, link(age)
linoleum, FLOOR COVERING
lins, lens / line(s)
linseed, OIL
lint,*,ty,tless, FUZZ FROM MATERIAL (or see lent or line(d))
linth, length
lintul, lentil
linument, liniment
linur, liner
linx, lynx
linz, lens /line(s)
lion,*,ness, A WILD ANIMAL (or see lien)
lior, liar
lip, PREFIX INDICATING "FATTY" MOST OFTEN MODIFIES THE WORD
lip,*,pped,pping,ppy, USING ONLY THE LIPS, MOUTH PARTS ON THE FACE
lipo, PREFIX INDICATING "FATTY" MOST OFTEN MODIFIES THE WORD
liprul, liberal
liger, liquor
liquefy or liquify,fiable,fier,fied,fying, TURN SOLID TO LIQUID
liquid,*,date,dated,dating,dation,dize, FLUID
liquifying, liquefy(ing)
liqoresh, licorice
liquor,*, FERMENTED ALCOHOLIC LIQUID
lir, liar / lyre
lirch, lurch
lirec, lyric
liric, lyric

lirn, learn
lisard, lizard
lisense, license
liserd, lizard
lisles, listless
lison, listen
lisp,*,pingly, PRONUNCIATION IS CHALLENGED BY SHAPE OF TEETH OR JAW MUSCLE FORMATION
list,*,ted,ting, IDENTIFY OBJECTS BY ITEMIZING, ORGANIZING TECHNIQUE
listen,*,ned,ning, TO HEAR AND PAY ATTENTION
listless,ssly,ssness, NO ENERGY, LACKS INTEREST
lisun, listen
lisuns, license
lisurt, lizard
lite, PAST TENSE OF "LIGHT" (or see lid/light/lie(d))
litegation, litigate(tion)
litel, little
litening, lightening
liter,*, METRIC MEASUREMENT (or see litter or light(er))
literacy, ABILITY TO WRITE AND READ
literal,lly,lity,lize,list,listic,lism, QUITE SO, PERFECT INTERPRETATION, REALISTICALLY
literary,rily,riness,ate,ately,ator, OF WRITTEN TEXT, LEARNED, EDUCATED
literature, WRITINGS ABOUT EVERYTHING, TEXT
lithargic, lethargic
lithargy, lethargy
litigate,*,ed,ting,tor,tious, BRING A DISPUTE INTO LAWFUL JUDGEMENT, BROUGHT TO COURT
litigation,*, A LAWSUIT
litle, little
litly, light(ly)
litmus, AN ACID TEST
litness, lightness
litning, lightening
litor, light(er) /litter

litter,*,red,ring, TRASH/GARBAGE WHERE IT DOESN'T BELONG, GROUP OF INFANT ANIMALS IN A CERTAIN SPECIES (or see liter or light(er))
little, SMALL SIZE IN COMPARISON
litul, little
litur, litter/ liter/ light(er)
liturally, literal(ly)
liubility, liable(bility)
liur, liar /lyre
livad, livid
livapul, live(vable)
live,*,ed,ving,ely,vable,eness,vability, A PLACE WHERE YOU DWELL, NOT DEAD, ACTIVE/VITAL
liveable, live(vable)
livebul, live(vable)
livelihood,*, OCCUPATION
livelyhood, livelihood
liver,*, AN ORGAN IN THE BODY
livery, UNIFORM, CARE OF HORSES
livid,dity,dness,dly, FURIOUS, BRUISED FLESH COLOR
livle, live(ly)
livlihood, livelihood
livly, live(ly)
livur, liver
livury, livery
lizard,*, A REPTILE
llama,*, A WOOLY MAMMAL
lo, low
load,*,ded,ding, A WEIGHT/BURDEN, TO HEAP OR PILE INTO A VESSEL, ADD AMMUNITION
loaf,fer, OF BREAD, SOMEONE WHO LIES AROUND DOING NOTHING, A SHOE, FOOD SHAPE
loafer,*, SOMEONE WHO IS LAZY, A SHOE
loam,my, A RICH/ORGANIC SOIL
loan,*,ned,ning, ALLOW SOMEONE TO BORROW SOMETHING (or see lone)
loathe,*,ed,hing,er,hsome, DESPISES, STRONGLY DISLIKES

lob,*, bbed, bbing, *A HIGH, ROUNDED ARCH BY A BALL IN A SPORT (or see lobe or lop)*
lobby, bbies, bbied, ying, *WAITING/ RESTING ROOM, TO COERSE POLITICAL LAWMAKERS FOR VOTES*
lobe,*, ed, bule, *BULBOUS PART OF THE EAR OR A PLANT, ROUND SHAPE (or see lobby)*
lobster,*, *AN EDIBLE CRUSTACEAN*
loby, lobby
loc, lock
locader, locate(tor)
local,lly,le,lism,lity,lities, *IN THE AREA, WITHIN DESIGNATED REGION*
localety, local(ity)
localize,ed,zation, *TO BE LOCATED IN A SPECIFIC REGION, IN THE AREA*
locashen, locate(tion)
locate,*,ed,ting,tion,tive,tor, *TO IDENTIFY A SPECIFIC PLACE*
lobd, lob(bbed)
locemoshen, locomotive
locer, locker
locest, locust
lock,*, ked,king,kage,kable,kless, *A MECHANISM WHICH REQUIRES A KEY, TO SECURE, TO BE INEXCUSABLY INVOLVED, EXCLUDED*
locker,*, *A CONTAINER WITH A LOCK*
locksmith,*, *ONE WHO WORKS WITH LOCKS*
loco, *CRAZY*
locomoshen, locomotion
locomotion, *THE ACT OF MOVING, LOCATING FROM ONE PLACE TO ANOTHER*
locomotive,* *THE BODILY OR PHYSICAL ACT OF MOVEMENT FROM ONE PLACE TO ANOTHER*
locsmith, locksmith
locul, local
loculizashen, localize(zation)
loculize, localize
loculy, local(ly)
locumoshen, locomotion

locomotive, locomotive
locumr, locker
locust,*, *A BUG ("T" IS SILENT)*
lod, load
lodery, lottery
lodge,*,ed,ging,gable,ement, *SOMETHING JAMMED INTO A TIGHT SPACE, HABITATION FOR VISITORS WHO OCCASIONALLY COME FOR THE NIGHT, BRING FORTH ACTION ("D" IS SILENT)*
lodis, lotus
lodury, lottery
lodus, lotus
loen, loin
loer, lower
loest, low(est)
loeul, loyal
lof, loaf
lofa, lava
lofer, loafer
loft,*,ted,ting,ty,tily, *SMALL LANDING ABOVE THE MAIN FLOOR, PROPEL SOMETHING INTO THE AIR*
lofur, loafer
log,*,gged,gging,gger, *MAKE A WRITTEN NOTE OF, PART OF A TREE TRUNK, TO REMOVE TIMBER, MEASURE VELOCITY*
logarithm, *A MATH FUNCTION*
loge, lodge
logec, logic
logecul, logic(al)
loger, log(ger)
logestics, logistic(s)
logic,*,cal,cally,cality,calness, *TO MAKE SENSE OF, BE REASONABLE*
logicul, logic(al)
logir, log(ger)
logistic,*,cal,cally,cian, *ARRANGING ACTIONS TO BENEFIT AN ADDITIONAL ACTION, CALCULATING*
logo,*, *A THEME OR SYMBOL WHICH IDENTIFIES*
logrethm, logarithm

logrythm, logarithm
logur, log(ger)
loin,*, *SECTION OF A BODY*
loir, lower
loiter,*,red,ring, *TO STAND AROUND, HANGING OUT*
lojecul, logic(al)
lojek, logic
lojical, logic(al)
lojik, logic
lok, look / lock
lokality, local(ity)
lokashen, locate(tion)
lokate, locate
lokator, locate(tor)
lokel, local
lokelizashen, localize(zation)
lokelize, localize
lokely, local(ly)
lokemotive, locomotive
loker, locker /look(er)
lokes, locust /look(s) /lock(s)
lokimoshen, locomotive
lokimotev, locomotive
lokir, locker
lokist, locust
loko, loco
loksmeth, locksmith
lokt, lock(ed) /look(ed)
lokul, local
lokule, local(ly)
lokulization, localize(zation)
lokulize, localize
lokumoshen, locomotion
lokumotef, locomotive
lokumotive, locomotive
lokur, locker
lokus, locust
lolegag, lollygag
lolepop lollipop

loligag, lollygag
lollipop,*,lollypop(s), *CANDY*
lollygag,*,gged,gging, *TO LOITER/HANG AROUND DOING NOTHING*
loly, low(ly)
lolypop, lollipop
loma, llama
lombur, lumber
lome, loam
lomy, loam(y)
lon mower, lawn mower
lon, lone /loan /lawn
lonch, launch
londer, launder
londry, laundry
londurer, launder(er)
lone,er,ely,eliness,esome,esomely,esomeness, *ALL BY ITSELF, SINGLED OUT, JUST ONE (or see loan)*
long,ger,gest, *THE LENGTH OR DURATION OF SOMETHING, MEASURE OF TIME*
longatude, longitude
longetudenul, longitude(dinal)
longir, long(er)
longist, long(est)
longitude,*,dinal,dinally, *INVISIBLE LINE ON EARTH THAT RUNS EAST, WEST*
lonir, lone(r)
lonjatude, longitude
lonjetudenul, longitude(dinal)
lonjitude, longitude
lonk, long
lonker, long(er)
lonkist, long(est)
lonly, lone(ly)
lons, lawn(s) /loan(s)
lonsem, lone(some)
lonsum, lone(some)
lonter, launder

lontre, laundry
lonur, lone(r)
loob, lube
loobrucate, lubricate
lood, lewd /load
loodekres, ludicrous
look,*,ked,king,ker, *TO VIEW WITH THE EYES*
lookwarm, lukewarm
looloo, lulu
loom,*,ming, *INTO THE FUTURE, LATER IN TIME, A MACHINE FOR WEAVING YARN OR THREAD (or see loam)*
loomenesent, luminescense(nt)
loomenocity, luminosity
loominesinse, luminescence
loominus, luminous
loomy, loam(y)
loon,*,ny, *A BIRD, BEHAVING GOOFY (or see lune)*
looner, lunar
loop,*,ped,ping,py, *A SEMI-CIRCULAR SHAPE, TO WRAP AROUND, GO AROUND, BEHAVING ODD*
loopen, lupine
loose,*,sing,en,ens,ened,ening, *TO MISPLACE/ FORGET SOMETHING, RELAX HOLD ON, UN-TIGHTEN, SLOPPY, GET RID OF (or see lose)*
loosid, lucid
loot,*,ted,ting,ter, *MONEY OR GOODS, ONE WHO STEALS THINGS (or see lute or lewd)*
looze, loose /lose
lop,*,pped,pping, *ACT OF REMOVING, ROUGHLY (or see lobe)*
lope,*,er,ed,ping, *EASY STRIDES WITH BOUNCE*
lord,*,ded,ding, *MASTER, ONE WHO TAKES OWNERSHIP*
lore,*, *BELIEF IN THE FORM OF A STORY OF THE PAST*
loreate, laureate
lorg, large
loriette, laureate
lorj, large

lort, lord
lorul, laurel
losd, lost
lose,*,er,sing,lost, *PAST TENSE OF "LOST", HAVING LOST (or see loose)*
losenge, lozenge
loshen, lotion
loshin, lotion
losinge, lozenge
losinje, lozenge
losir, lose(r) /loose(r)
loss,es, *TAKEN AWAY, REMOVED*
lost, *PAST TENSE OF "LOOSE", CANNOT BE FOUND*
losuit, lawsuit
losur, lose(r) /loose(r)
losure, lose(r) /loose(r)
losute, lawsuit
lot,*,tted,tting, *WHOLE BUNCH, A SPECIFIC SIZE OF SOMETHING, A SECTION AMONG MANY*
lotery, lottery
lotes, lotus
lothe, loath
lotion,*, *CREAMY LIQUID TO APPLY TO THE BODY*
lotis, lotus
lottery,ries, *GAMBLING*
lotury, lottery
lotus, *A FLOWER, A POSITION, A PLANT*
loud,dly,der,dest, *SOUND THAT IS BEYOND A COMFORTABLE HEARING RANGE*
loul, loyal
lounch, lounge
lounge,*,ed,ging,er, *TO LIE AROUND, RECLINED POSITION, ROOM WHERE PEOPLE REST/RELAX*
lour, lower
louver,*, *SHUTTERS*
lova, lava
love,*,ed,ving,vable,vableness,vably,vability,er, eless, *A SPECIAL AFFECTION FOR*
lovte, loft(y)
lovu, lava

low,west,wly, *CLOSE TO THE BOTTOM OR THE GROUND, LACK OF ENERGY*
lowd, loud
lowder, loud(er)
lowdest, loud(est)
lowen, loin
lower,*,red,ring, *ACT OF LETTING DOWN, CLOSE TO THE BOTTOM OR GROUND, LESSEN*
lownch, lounge
lownge, lounge
lows, low(s) /loathe(s)
lowt, loud /load
lowtest, loud(est)
lowyer, lawyer
lowyul, loyal
loyal,list,lly,lties, *FAITHFUL*
loyer, lawyer
loyn, loin
loyulty, loyal(ty)
loyure, lawyer
lozenge,*,, *THROAT MEDICINE*
lu, lieu
lube,*,bing, *GREASE*
lubracashen, lubricate(tion)
lubracate, lubricate
lubricate,*,ed,ting,tion,ant, *TO GREASE/OIL UP*
luch, lush
lucheus, luscious
luchious, luscious
luchness, lush(ness)
lucid,dity,dness,dly, *A STATE OF BEING BETWEEN HERE AND THERE*
luck,ky,kily,kier,kiest,kless, *GOOD FORTUNE*
luckgerious, luxury(rious)
lucrative,ely,eness, *COULD YIELD PROFIT OR GAIN*
lucwarm, lukewarm
ludakris, ludicrous
lude, lewd/ lute/ loot
ludecris, ludicrous

luder, loot(er)
ludicrous,sly,sness, *RIDICULOUS*
luf, love
lufable, love(vable)
lufer, louver /love(r)
lufless, love(less)
lug,*,gged,gging, *TO CARRY AROUND A HEAVY LOAD, ON A WHEEL, PULL* (or see luck)
lugd, lug(gged)
lugege, luggage
luggage, *TRAVELING BAGS*
lugije, luggage
lugjereus, luxury(rious)
lugjureus, luxury(rious)
lugshureant, luxuriant
lugshureous, luxury(rious)
lugshury, luxury
lugt, lug(gged)
luk, look /luck
lukchury, luxury
luke, luck /luck(y)
lukege, luggage
lukemea, leukemia
lukewarm, *BETWEEN WARM AND HOT*
lukgureus, luxury(rious)
lukiest, luck(iest)
lukige, luggage
lukjereus, luxury(rious)
lukrative, lucrative
luks, look(s) /luck(s)
lukshereant, luxuriant
lukshury, luxury
luksuryant, luxuriant
luky, luck(y)
lull,*,led,ling, *A PAUSE, GENTLY COAX, CAUSE TO RELAX*
lulu,*,, *REAL WINNER*
lumbar, *SECTION IN THE SPINE*

lumber,rer,rman,rless,ring,ringly,ringness, *BOARDS CUT FROM TIMBER*
lume, loom
lumen,*,na,nous, *OF LIGHT, GIVING OFF LIGHT, UNIT OF MEASURE*
lumenary, luminary
lumenesense, luminescense
lumenesent, luminescense(nt)
lumenosidty, luminosity
lument, lament
lumentation, lament(ation)
lumenus, luminous
lumenusly, luminous(ly)
luminary,ries, *GIVING OFF LIGHT*
luminescense,nt, *GIVING OFF LIGHT*
luminosity,ties, *INTENSITY OF LIGHT*
luminous,sly,sness, *AMOUNT OF LIGHT, OF LIGHT*
luminus, lumen(ous)
lump,*,ped,ping,py, *MASS OR AGGREGATE OF SOMETHING*
lun, loon /lune
lunar, *OF THE MOON*
lunch,hed,hes,hing,her,heon, *MEAL BETWEEN BREAKFAST AND DINNER*
lune,nula, *MOON WHEN IT'S NOT FULL* (or see loon)
luney, loon(y) /lune
lung,*, *ORGAN OF THE BODY* (or see lunge)
lunge,*,ed,ging,er, *TO LEAP FORWARD TOWARDS SOMETHING, TO PULL QUICKLY/HARD AGAINST RESTRAINTS*
lunir, lunar
lunje, lunge
lunur, lunar
lupe, loop
lupel, lapel
lupen, lupine
lupine,*,, *A WOLF, A PLANT*
lurch,hes,hed,hing,her, *HANG ABOUT SUSPICIOUSLY, DRUNKEN STAGGER, LEAP INTO ACTION*

lurk,*,ked,king,kingly, STALK/SECRETLY WAIT
lus, loose /lose
luscious,sly,sness, GLORIOUS SENSORY EXPERIENCE OF SOMETHING USING TASTE/SMELL/SIGHT AND/OR TOUCH
lusd, lust
lusder, luster
lusdruss, lust(rous)
luse, loose /lose
lused, lucid
lusen, loose(n)
lush,hly,hness, ABUNDANT, OPULENT FLORAL AND FAUNA, RICH IN FOLIAGE, AN ALCOHOLIC
lusheous, luscious
lushus, luscious
lusid, lucid
lusin, loose(n)
lust,*,ted,ting,tful,tfully,fulness,trous, TEMPORARY INTENSE DESIRE
luster,rless,ring, GLISTENING, WAY LIGHT REFLECTS, AS IF GLOWING, SHINY REFLECTION
lustious, luscious
lusty,tily,tiness, HEARTY AND JOVIAL, ROBUST
lute,*, A MUSICAL INSTRUMENT (or see loot or lewd)
lutenant, lieutenant
luter, loot(er)
lutinant, lieutenant
lutrene, latrine
luv, love
luvabul, love(vable)
luver, louver /love(r)
luvless, love(less)
luxuriant,nce,ncy,tly, VERY HEALTHY, RICHLY ABUNDANT, PROFUSE
luxury,ries,ious,iously,iousness, GREAT RICHNESS, OPULENT, OVERLY ABUNDANT
luz, loose /lose
ly, lye /lie
lye, WOOD ASH FOR SOAP (or see lie)

lying, NOT TELLING THE TRUTH, PAST TENSE OF "LIE"
lymfatic, lymph(atic)
lymph, lympho, PREFIX INDICATING "LYMPH/ YELLOWISH" MOST OFTEN MODIFIES THE WORD
lymph,hatic, FLUID WITH WHITE BLOOD CELLS, OF THE BODY
lympho, lymph, PREFIX INDICATING "LYMPH/ YELLOWISH" MOST OFTEN MODIFIES THE WORD
lynx,xes, A WILD ANIMAL
lyo, lys, PREFIX INDICATING "DISSOLVED/ DISPERSED" MOST OFTEN MODIFIES THE WORD
lyre,*, AN INSTRUMENT (or see liar)
lyric,*, cal,cally,calness,cism,ist, WORDS SANG IN A SONG
lys, lyso,PREFIX INDICATING "DISSOLVED/DISPERSED" MOST OFTEN MODIFIES THE WORD

"M"

ma, may
mab, mob
mabe, maybe
mabilety, mobile(lity)
mac, mach/ make/ mock
macaroni,ies, CHEESY NOODLES
macaroon,*, A COOKIE
macasen, moccasin
macaw,*, A TROPICAL BIRD
mace,ed, SPICE, MEDIEVAL WEAPON,CHEMICAL SPRAY (or see make/ maize/ maze/mase)
mach, AMOUNT OF SPEED (or see make /match/ mock /mash)
machenery, machine(ry)
macherel, mackerel
macherly, mature(ly)
machete,*, A CHOPPING HAND TOOL

machine,*,nability,nable,nate,nation,nator,ery, eries,nist, A DEVICE WITH MOVING PARTS THAT PERFORMS WORK
machurashen, mature(ration)
machure, mature
machuredy, mature(rity)
machuril, mackerel
mack, make /mach /mock
mackerel,*, EDIBLE FISH
macks, max /make(s)
macrame, LACED/WOVEN ROPE
macro, PREFIX INDICATING "DISSOLVED/ DISPERSED" MOST OFTEN MODIFIES THE WORD
macrocosm,*,mic(ally), THE BIG PICTURE, INCORPORATES EVERYTHING BIG AND SMALL
macruma, macrame
macsimul, maximal
macuroni, macaroni
macuroon, macaroon
macusen, moccasin
mad,dder,ddest,dden,ddening,ddeningly,dness, NOT HAPPY, MORE THAN IRRITATED, ANGRY (or see mat /made /maid)
madch, match
made, PAST TENSE OF "MAKE", HAVING CREATED (or see maid or mate)
madekulus, meticulous
madel, model /mottle
madena, matinee
mader, matter /mad(dder)
maderde, maitre d'
madereulise, materialize
madernize, modern(ize)
madernulistic, maternal(istic)
madesenul, medicine(nal)
madina, matinee
madir, mad(dder) /matter
madisenul, medicine(nal)
madist, mad(ddest)

madna, matinee
madnes, mad(dness)
mado, motto
madramony, matrimony
madreark, matriarch
madrearkul, matriarch(al)
madremony, matrimony
madren, matron
madress, mattress
madrexs, matrix
madrearkul, matriarch(al)
madricks, matrix
madrimony, matrimony
madris, mattress
madron, matron
madur, matter /mad(der)
madurde, maitre d'
maer, mayor
maestro,*, MASTER OF ANY MEDIUM RELATED TO ART
mafe, mauve
maferick, maverick
mafrek, maverick
magacul, magic(al)
magazine,*,nist, COMPILED PAGES OF WRITTEN ARTICLES, HAVING TO DO WITH WEAPONS
mager, major
magesine, magazine
magesty, majesty
magestrate, magistrate
maggot,*, LARVA OF AN INSECT
magic,cal,cally,cian,*, DIDN'T VISIBLY WITNESS THE CHANGE OF EVENTS WHICH LED TO AN EVENT
magir, major
magirete, major(ette)
magisty, majesty
magistrate,*,acy, LOCAL OFFICIAL OFFICE
magit, maggot
magizene, magazine
magma,*,ata,atic, MOLTEN ROCK

magnate,*, PROMINENT INDUSTRIALIST (or see magnet))
magnatise, magnetize
magnatisum, magnet(ism)
magnatude, magnitude
magnedic, magnet(ic)
magnefacashen, magnify(fication)
magnefasent, magnificent
magnefesently, magnificent(ly)
magnefiable, magnify(iable)
magnefy, magnify
magnet, magneto, PREFIX INDICATING "MAGNET" MOST OFTEN MODIFIES THE WORD
magnet,*,tic,ticality,tism, DRAWN TO,ORE FROM THE EARTH, TOWARD THE NORTH/SOUTH ENDS (or see magnate)
magnetize,es,zable,zation,zer, BE DRAWN TO, MAKE POLAR
magneto, magnet, PREFIX INDICATING "MAGNET" MOST OFTEN MODIFIES THE WORD
magnetude, magnitude
magnifesent, magnificent
magnificent,nce,cently, SPLENDID
magnify,fies,fied,ying,fiable,fier,fication, TO ENLARGE, GET CLOSER TO, MAKE BIGGER
magnit, magnet /magnate
magnitise, magnetize
magnitude, THE SIZE OR EXTENT OF, THE DEGREE OF
magnufecashen, magnify(fication)
magnufy, magnify
magnutise, magnetize
magnutisum, magnet(ism)
magnutude, magnitude
magoredy, major(ity)
magorete, major(ette)
magority, major(ity)
magot, maggot
maguk, magic
magul, module

maguler, module(lar)
magur, major
magurete, major(ette)
magustrate, magistrate
maguzene, magazine
maid,*,den, ONE WHO CLEANS BEHIND OTHERS FOR A LIVING (or see made or mate)
mail,*,led,ling,ler, SEND A PHYSICAL THING AWAY TO SOMEONE (or see male)
maim,*,med,mer, TO MUTILATE, DESTROY
main,*,nly, THE MOST IMPORTANT ONE, THE ONE THAT STANDS OUT (or see mane)
maingy, mangy
maintain,*,ned,ning,nable, UPKEEP, KEEP IN GOOD REPAIR
maintenance,ed,cing, TO KEEP IN WORKING ORDER, TO FIX, SUPPORT, UPKEEP
maitre d',*, HEADWAITER/HOTEL MANAGER
maize,*, CORN (or see maze)
majek, magic
majer, major
majesty,tic,tical,tically, OF AUTHORITY/GRANDEUR, GREAT IMPRESSION
majewlate, modulate
majir, major
major,rity,rities,rette, THE MOST OF, A MILITARY RANK, FEMALE MARCHER, HIGHES NUMBER OF
majoredy, major(ity)
majulate, modulate
majul, module
majur, major
majustrate, magistrate
mak, mach/ make/ mock
makaril, mackerel
makarony, macaroni
makaroon, macaroon
makaw, macaw
make,*,made,king,er, TO CREATE, BRING TO REALITY (or see moch or mock)

maked, made /mock(ed)
makerony, macaroni
makinate, machine(nate)
makir, make(r)
makirony, macaroni
makremay, macrame
makrocosim, macrocosm
makrumay, macrame
maks, max /make(s) /mock(s)
maksamis, maximize
maksemal, maximal
maksemize, maximize
maksimul, maximal
maksimum, maximum
maksumum, maximum
makuril, mackerel
makurone, macaroni
makusen, moccasin
makzemize, maximize
mal, male, PREFIX INDICATING "BAD" MOST OFTEN MODIFIES THE WORD (or see mall/ maul/ male/ mail)
malable, malleable
maladek, melody(dic)
maladjusted,,tment, NOT SITUATED AS SHOULD BE, IMPROPER ORIENTATION
malado, mulato
malady,,dies, A DISORDER OR CONFLICT BETWEEN THE BODY AND MIND, ABNORMAL ARRANGEMENT
malajusted, maladjusted
malanosis, malanoma(osis)
malaria, DISEASE TRANSPORTED TO HUMANS BY SOME MOSQUITOES
malarkey, DOESN'T APPEAR TO BE THE TRUTH, CALLING A BLUFF
malas, malice
malases, molasses
mald, maul(ed) /mail(ed) /malt

male, mal, PREFIX INDICATING "BAD" MOST OFTEN MODIFIES THE WORD
male,,*,,eness, THE MASCULINE GENDER, THE INSERTION END (or see mail)
maleble, malleable
maledy, malady
malegnent, malignant
malegusted, maladjusted
malegustment, maladjusted(tment)
malejusted, maladjusted
malekule, molecule
malekuler, molecular
malenoma, malanoma
malerd, mallard
malese, malice
malesha, militia
malest, molest
malet, mallet
malevolent,,tly,,nce, MALICIOUS, HATEFUL
malfunction,,*,,ned,,ning, DOESN'T WORK AS IT WAS INTENDED
malfunkshen, malfunction
malible, malleable
malice,,cious,,ciously,,ciousness, DIRECT HATE TOWARDS ANOTHER, EMOTION RELATED TO FEAR AND INSECURITY
malignant,,ncy,,tly, ACT OF BEING MALICIOUS, DANGEROUS GROWTH
maligusted, maladjusted
malinoma, melanoma
malisha, militia
malit, mallet
malitia, militia
mality, malady
mall,,*,, LARGE BUILDING WITH SMALL STORES INSIDE (or see mail/ male/ maul)
mallard,,*,, WILD DUCK
malleable,,lity,,eness, SEEMINGLY STIFF MATERIAL/ METAL THAT'S EASILY WORKED/ MOLDED

mallet,,*,, HAMMER TYPE TOOL
malnerished, malnourished
malnewtrishen, malnutrition
malnourished, NOT ENOUGH NUTRITIONAL FOOD
malnureshed, malnourished
malnutrition, SUFFERING LACK OF NUTRITIOUS FOOD
malodic, melody(dic)
malos, malice
malpractice,,*,,cioner, DR. WHO PRODUCED A FATALITY OR SERIOUS INJURY WHILE PRACTICING
malpraktes, malpractice
malt,,*,,ted,,ty, A FROTHY COLD DRINK (or see maul(ed) or molt)
maluble, malleable
maludy, malady
malugusted, maladjusted
malujusted, maladjusted
malujustment, maladjusted(tment)
malunosis, malanoma(osis)
malurd, mallard
malus, malice
maluṭ, mallet
mama, A MOTHER (or see mamma)
mama, mamma
mamal, mammal
mamalean, mammal(ian)
mam, maim
mamel, mammal
mamento, memento
mamery gland, mammary gland
mameth, mammoth
mamil, mammal
maminto, memento
mamiry gland, mammary gland
mamith, mammoth
mamma, MILK SECRETING BREASTS/TEATS/ORGAN
mammal,,*,,lian, WARM BLOODED ANIMAL THAT GIVES BIRTH TO ITS YOUNG

mammary gland,*, GLANDS IN THE BREAST THAT SECRETES MILK
mammoth, ICE AGE ELEPHANT
mamory gland, mammary gland
mamoth, mammoth
mamt, maim(ed)
mamul, mammal
man, ADULT MALE (or see mane or main)
manacle,*, WRIST RESTRAINTS
manage,*, ed,ging,ement,eable,eableness,er, bility,eably, ABILITY TO DEAL WITH AND ORCHESTRATE AFFAIRS SMOOTHLY
manakin,*, BIRD (or see mannikin/ manikin/ mannequin)
manakure, manicure
manark, monarch
manarkeul, monarch(ial)
manarky, monarch(y)
manase, mayonaise
manchen, mansion
mandala,*, A SYMBOL OF SPIRITUAL SIGNIFICANCE
mandalin, mandolin
mandarin,*, FRUIT
mandate,*, ed,ting, A COMMAND, RULE
mandatory,ries,rily, COMMANDE, ORDERED
mandel, mantel/ mantle
mandelin, mandolin
manderin, mandarin
mandetory, mandatory
manditory, mandatory
mandle, mantel/ mantle
mandola, mandala
mandolin,*, A STRINGED INSTRUMENT
mandrake, AN HERB
mandrel,*, A DEVICE TO AID IN CUTTING A SOLID MATERIAL
mandril, mandrel
mandrul, mandrel
mandul, mantel/ mantle

manduren, mandarin
mandutory, mandatory
mane, HAIR ABOUT THE NECK OF AN ANIMAL (or see main or many)
manea, mania
maneac, maniac
manecure, manicure
manee, many
manefest, manifest
manefesto, manifest(o)
manefold, manifold
manege, manage
managment, management
maneje, manage
manekin, manikin/ manakin/ mannequin
manekul, manacle
manense, maintenance
maner, manner/ manor/ manure
manerism, manner(ism)
manerlee, manner(ly)
maneuver,red,ring,rability,rable,rer, SKILLFUL DISPLAY OF MOVEMENT
manevest, manifest
mang, mange
mange, A SKIN CONDITION
manger, TROUGH FOR ANIMALS
mangle,*, ed,ling,er, TO SHRED/TEAR UP, A LARGE IRON
mango,*, A FRUIT
mangul, mangle
mangy,gily,giness, SHABBY/ILL-KEPT
mania, INTENSE EMOTION
maniac,cal,cally, SOMEONE UNCONTROLLABLE ON A CONTINUOUS BASIS
manicle, manacle
manicure,*,rist, CARING OF FINGERNAILS
manifest,*,ted,ting,ter,tly,tation,tant,to, DESIR-ED RESULT ACHIEVED WITH LITTLE EFFORT

manifold,*,dly,dness, ON A MOTOR, A COPY, TO MULTIPLY
manige, manage
manigment, management
manikin,*, A MOLD OF A BODY FOR CLOTHING DISPLAY (or see manakin or mannequin)
manila, BUFF-COLORED HEMP PAPER
manipulate,table,tive,tory,tion,tor, TO CONTROL ENVIRONMENT/EVENTS
manir, manner/ manor/ manure
manirism, manner(ism)
manirlee, manner(ly)
manj, mange
manjur, manger
manle, main(ly) /man(ly)
mannequin,*, A HUMAN-MADE MODEL OF A HUMAN (or see manakin or manikin)
manner,*,rless,rism,rist, ristic,rly, TO HANDLE ONESELF PROPERLY, TO BE POLITE
manofestation, manifest(ation)
manogumy, monogamy
manolith, monolith
manopuly, monopoly
manor,*, HOME OF MEDIEVAL TIMES (or see manure or manner)
manotny, monotony
manotone, monotone
manotunus, monotony(nous)
manshen, mansion
mansion,*, A VERY LARGE HOME
mantane, maintain
mantanuble, maintain(able)
mantel,*, FIREPLACE SHELF (or see mantle)
mantenanse, maintenance
mantil, mantel /mantle
mantle,*, A CLOAK, A CLOTH SLEEVE FOR A GAS LANTERN (or see mantel)
mantul, mantel /mantle
mantunense, maintenance

manual,*,lly, DIRECTIONS ON HOW TO USE SOME-
    THING, TO DO BY HAND
manucle, manacle
manuel, manual
manuely, manual(ly)
manufacture,*,ed,ring,rer,rable,ral, CREATE
    SOMETHING FROM RAW MATERIALS
manufaksher, manufacture
manufestation, manifest(ation)
manufold, manifold
manuge, manage
manugment, management
manuil, manual
manukin, manakin
manul, mantel /mantle
manur, manner/ manor/ manure
manure,rial,rer, WASTE FROM ANIMALS (or see
    manor or manner)
manurism, manner(ism)
manurly, manner(ly)
manuscript,*,tion, WHAT SOMEONE WRITES THAT
    MAY BECOME A BOOK OR MOVIE
manuskrept, manuscript
manustery, monastery
manuver, maneuver
many, MORE THAN A FEW (or see mini)
manyewfaksher, manufacture
manyual, manual
manyuskrept, manuscript
maonase, mayonaise
maor, mayor
map,*,pped,pping, DIRECTIONS OR GUIDE TO A
    SPECIFIC AREA (or see mop)
mapal, maple
mape, maybe
mapd, map(pped) /mop(pped)
mapel, maple
maple,*, A TREE, SYRUP FROM TREE
mapul, maple

mar,*,rred,rring, TO RUIN/DETRACT FROM (or see
    mare or mayor)
maraje, mirage
marakulus, miracle(culous)
maranad, marinade /marinate
maranate, marinade /marinate
marange, meringue
marathon,*,ner, A LONG DISTANCE EVENT
marbel, marble
marble,*,ed,ling,ly,er,lize, A LITTLE GLASS BALL,
    TYPE OF ROCK, A VISUAL EFFECT
marbul, marble
marc, mark
marcetable, market(able)
march,es,ed,hing, BRISK FORM OF WALKING (or see
    March)
March, NAME OF A MONTH IN THE YEAR (or see
    march)
marchel law, martial law
marchel, martial /marshal
marchen, martian /march(ing)
marchul law, martial law
marchul, martial /marshal
marden, martin
mardene, martini
mardengale, martingale
marder, martyr
mardin, martin
mardine, martini
mardingale, martingale
mardir, martyr
mardur, martyr
mare, marry /merry
mare,*, FEMALE HORSE (or see marry or mayor)
mared, married /mar(rred)
maredean, meridian
mareg, marriage
maregold, marigold
marej, marrieage

marejuana, marijuana
marena, marina
marenad, marinade /marinate
marene, marine
mareonette, marionette
maret, merit
maretime, maritime
maretul, marital
mareunette, marionette
marewana, marijuana
marfelus, marvel(ous)
marfilus, marvel(ous)
margarine, A FAKE BUTTER
margen, margin
margenul, margin(al)
margerem, marjoram
margin,*,nal,nally,nality,nate, SPACE OUTSIDE OF
    THE TEXT/ BORDER AREA
margorem, marjoram
margurim, marjoram
marid, married
maridian, meridian
marig, marriage
marigold,*, A FLOWER
marij, marriage
marijuana, ALSO MARIHUANA,HIGHLY USEFUL MEDIC-
    INAL PLANT WHICH IS CURRENTLY OUTLAWED
    (or see hemp)
marily, merry(rily)
marina,*, FOR BOAT MOORING
marinade,*,ded,ding, SAUCE WITH SPICES THAT
    FISH/MEAT IS SOAKED IN (or see marinate)
marinate,*,ted,ting, THE ACT OF SOAKING FISH OR
    MEAT IN A SAUCE (or see marinade)
marine,er,er's, CONCERNED WITH THE OCEAN /SEA
marionette,*, A PUPPET ON STRINGS
marit, merit
marital,lly, CONCERNING BEING MARRIED
marithon, marathon

maritime, OF THE OCEAN OR SEA
mariwana, marijuana
marjaren, margarine
marjen, margin
marjenul, margin(al)
marjeren, margarine
marjin, margin
marjinul, margin(al)
marjoram,*, HERBAL PLANT
mark,*,ked,king, A GOUGE/LINE/SCRATCH/ IMPRESSION
markee, marquee /marquis
marker,*, A LINE OF MARKATION, A TOOL OR INSTRUMENT THAT MARKS
market,*,ted,ting,table,tability, ABOUT SELLING GOODS
marke, marquee /marquis
markit, market
markt, mark(ed)
markur, marker
marmalade, A FRUIT PRESERVE
marmulade, marmalade
marn, martin /marten
maroon,ned, BE LEFT ABANDONED, STRANDED
marose, morose
marow, marrow
marquee, A BANNER, TENT, SIGN OVER ENTRANCEWAY (or see marquise)
marquis,ses,sate, BRITISH RANK(or see marquee)
marriage,*,eable,eability,eableness, TWO PEOPLE WHO LEGALLY BOND IN MATRIMONY
married, PAST TENSE OF "MARRY"
marrow, INNER BONE, PARTNER, MATE
marry,rries,rried,ying, TWO PEOPLE LEGALLY BONDING (or see merry)
marsh,hes,hy, WETLAND
marshal law, martial law

marshal,lled,lling,lcy,lship, EUROPEAN OFFICER, SIMILAR TO A SHERIFF, TO LEAD, USHER (or see martial)m.f.e.
marshen, martian /march(ing)
marshil, marshal /martial
marshin, martian /march(ing)
marshmallow, A SUGAR SWEET , AN HERBAL PLANT
marshmelow, marshmallow
marshul, marshal /martial
marsoopeal, marsupial
marsupeul, marsupial
marsupial, AN ANIMAL THAT SLEEPS DURING THE DAY
martch, March /march
marten, martin
marten, MEMBER OF THE WEASEL FAMILY (or see martin)
martengale, martingale
marteny, martini
marter, martyr
martial law, PERMANENT MILITARY RULE IN THE U.S.
martial,lism,list,lly,lness, OF WAR (or see marshal)
martian,*, PLANET MARS INHABITANTS
martin,*, A BIRD
martingale,*, A BIRD
martini,*, ALCOHOLIC DRINK
martir, martyr
martur, martyr
martyr,*,rize,rdom, SOMEONE WHO RISKS THEIR LIVES FOR A CAUSE OF THEIR CHOOSING
marune, maroon
marut, merit
marutime, maritime
marvel,*,led,ling,lous,lously,lousness, GREATLY IMPRESSIVE, ATTENTION GETTER
marvelus, marvel(ous)
marvil, marvel
marvilus, marvel(ous)
marvul, marvel

mary, marry /merry
maryonette, marionette
mas, mace /mass /moss
masa, mesa
masacistic, masochism
masacur, massacre
masage, massage
masakistic, masochism(stic)
masakisum, masochism
masakur, massacre
mascara, A DYE PUT ON EYELASHES
mascarade, masquerade
mascot,*, A THING OF LUCK
masculine,ely,eness,nity,nize,nized,nizing, MALE
masd, mast
masdebashen, masturbate(tion)
masdek, mastic
masder, master
masderbade, masturbate
masdereus, mysterious
masdides, mastitis
masdik, mastic
masdir, master
masditis, mastitis
masdurful, master(full)
mase, mace /maize /maze
masectame, mastectomy
masectome, mastectomy
masecur, massacre
masef, massive
masekur, massacre
masen, mason
masenger, messenger
masenry, mason(ry)
maseurse, masseuse
maseve, massive
masgot, mascot
mash,hed,hing,her, TO SHRED, PULVERIZE, SQUISH, TURN TO PASTE, SMASH

match,hes,hed,hing, PAIR UP, PUT SUITABLES TOGETHER, A CHEMICALLY TREATED ITEM USED TO CREATE FLAME

matcherashen, mature(ration)

matchure, mature

mate,*,ed,ting, TO JOIN TOGETHER, METHOD OF PROPOGATION, A CALL IN THE GAME OF CHESS (or see made /maid /matte)

matekulus, meticulous

matena, matinee

mater, matter /mad(dder)

materde, maitre d'

matereul, material

materealise, materialize

material,*,lly,lism,list,listic,listically,lity,lities, lness, NON-VIRTUAL, OF THE PHYSICAL PLANE, OF MASS, OF THE PHYSICAL

materialize,*,ed,zing,zation,er, TO PHYSICALLY APPEAR

maternal,lly,listic,lism, MOTHERING, NURTURING

maternity,ties, A HUMAN STATE OF BEING PREGNANT

mateure, mature

math, LANGUAGE OF NUMBERS

mathematic,*,cal,cally,cian, SCIENCE AND LANGUAGE DEALING WITH NUMBERS

mathology, mythology

matikulus, meticulous

matina, matinee

matinee,*, SPECIFIC AREA OF TIME WHEN A MOVIE IS SHOWN IN A THEATER

matir, mad(dder) /matter

matirde, maitre d'

matireal, material

matirnol, maternal

matirnulistic, maternal(istic)

matist, mad(ddest)

matna, matinee

matne, matinee

matness, mad(ness)

---

massacre,*,ed,ring, KILLING OF SIGNIFICANT AMOUNT AT ONCE

massage,*,ed,ging, MANIPULATE OR RUB SKIN TO AFFECT INTERNAL TISSUE

masseur,*,use, MALE WHO GIVES MASSAGE

masseuse,*,ur, FEMALE WHO GIVES MASSAGE

massiuse, masseuse

massive,ely,eness, OF GREAT QUANTITY, SIZE

massuer, masseur

massuse, masseuse

mast, PART OF SAIL ON VESSEL, HOG FEED (or see mace(d))

mastectomy,mies, BREAST REMOVAL

mastek, mastic

master,*,red,ring,ry,rful,rfully,rliness,rly,rhood, rfulness, ONE WHO IS HIGHLY SKILLFUL/WISE

masterbashen, masturbate(tion)

masterbate, masturbate

mastereus, mysterious

mastic,*, RESIN OR SEALANT FOR PROTECTIVE COAT

mastidis, mastitis

mastique, mystique

mastir, master

mastirbashen, masturbate(tion)

mastirful, master(full)

mastitis,ic, INFLAMED BREAST OR UDDER

masturbate,*,ted,tting,tion, TO STIMULATE ONE'S SEXUAL ORGANS TO AROUSAL/ORGASM

masturly, master(ly)

mastytis, mastitis

masuese, masseuse

masukestik, masochism

masukistic, masochism(stic)

masure, masseur

masuse, masseuse

mat,*,tted,tting, FLAT ITEM FOR DOORSTEPS, FOR DISPLAYING VISUAL IMAGES, A FLAT MESH OF SOME MATERIAL (or see mad /matte /mate)

matabulism, metabolism

---

mashene, machine

mashenery, machine(ry)

mashenest, machine(st)

mashety, machete

mashine, machine

mashinury, machine(ry)

masif, massive

masiker, massacre

masin, mason

masive, massive

mask,* ked,king, COVER UP

maskalen, masculine

maskarade, masquerade

maskarate, masquerade

maskeet, mesquite

maskera, mascara

maskerate, masquerade

masketo, mosquito

maskewlen, masculine

maskot, mascot

maskulen, masculine

maskulin, masculine

maskurade, masquerade

maskurate, masquerade

masochism, st,stic, PATHOLOGICAL SELF-DESTRUCTION

masof, massive

masoge, massage

masoje, massage

masokism, masochism

masokistic, masochism(stic)

masokizum, masochism

mason,*,nry,nries, WORKS WITH STONE

masoose, masseuse

masquerade,*,er,ding, WITH A MASK OR DISGUISE

masquite, mesquite

mass,es, MEASURE OF VOLUME, WEIGHT, ACCUMULATION OF SIGNIFICANT AMOUNT

mato, motto
matramony, matrimony
matrearch, matriarch
matrearchal, matriarch(al)
matreark, matriarch
matreks, matrix
matremony, matrimony
matren, matron
matress, mattress
matrex, matrix
matriarch,*,hal,halism,hate,hy,hies, MOTHER IS
    LEADING ROLE
matricks, matrix
matrimony,*,nies,nial,nially, OF MARRIAGE
matrin, matron
matris, mattress
matrix,es,ices, MYSTERY/LABYRINTH/RIDDLE (TOO
    MANY DEFINITIONS, PLEASE SEE STANDARD
    DICTIONARY)
matron,*,nage,nly,nal,nage,nize, A FEMALE
    CHAPERONE/GUARDIAN/ATTENDANT
matropolis, metropolis
matte, METAL STYLE, NON-GLOSSY SURFACE
matter,*,red, OF IMPORTANCE/ SUBSTANCE/PHYSICAL
    MATERIAL
mattress,ses, BED OF STUFFING FOR SLEEPING ON
matur, matter /mad(der)
maturde, maitre d'
mature,*,ed,ring,rate,ration,rational,rative,ely,
    eness,rity, GROWN TO PHYSICAL PEAK
maturnedy, maternity
maturnity, maternity
maugul, module
maujul, module
maul,*,led, A TOOL, TO PHYSICALLY BATTER, REDUCE
    TO LESSER STATE (or see mall or mole)
maunaz, mayonaise
mausoleum, GRANDIOSE TOMB
mauve, A COLOR

mave, mauve
maverick,*,, RADICALS, ONE'S WHO DON'T FOLLOW
    TRADITIONAL BELIEFS OR VALUES
mavrik, maverick
mavurek, maverick
mawntin, mountain
max,xed,xing, SHORT FOR MAXIMUM
maximal,lly, OF THE MOST POSSIBLE
maximize,*,ed,zing,er, THE MOST POSSIBLE
maximum,*, THE MOST POSSIBLE
May, A MONTH IN THE YEAR (or see may)
may, ALLOWED TO (or see May)
maybe, PERHAPS
maydreark, matriarch
mayenase, mayonaise
mayer, mayor
mayonaise, SPREAD OR SALAD DRESSING FOR FOOD
mayor,*,ral,ralty,ralties, POLITICAL POSITION
mazdek, mastic
mazderful, master(full)
mazdik, mastic
mazdur, master
maze,*,ed,zing,zy, INABILITY TO MOVE OR THINK
    ALONG A CONTINUOUS PATH
mazef, massive
mazeker, massacre
mazektomy, mastectomy
mazif, massive
maziker, massacre
mazonry, mason(ry)
mazt, mast
mazturbate, masturbate
meadow,*, A FIELD GENERALLY WITHOUT TREES
meager,rly,rness, SMALL PORTION/ AMOUNT
meal,*, FOOD, FOOD EATEN AT CERTAIN TIME
mean,*,ning,ningful,ningfully,ningfulness,nt, ILL
    INTENT, EXPRESS THOUGHTS OF HARMFUL
    INTENT, METHOD OF ACHIEVING A GOAL

meant, PAST TENSE OF "MEAN", ATTEMPT TO EXPRESS
    THOUGHTS
mear, mere
measles, A VIRUS
measure,*,ed,ring,rable,rability,rableness,
    rably,ement, USE NUMBERS/WORDS TO
    EXPLAIN SIZE/AMOUNT/DISTANCE
meat,*,ty,tiness, MUSCLE FIBER IN LIVING THINGS,
    EDIBLE PARTS (or see meet)
mecaneks, mechanic(s)
mechanic,*,cal,cally,calness,ist, WORKS WITH
    PARTS WHICH MAKES OBJECTS MOVE, SYSTEM
    OF APPROACH
mechanize,*,ed,zing,zation,istic,istically,er,
    USE MACHINE TO PERFORM A TASK
mechen, mission
mechenary, mission(ary)
med, mid /meet
meda, meta
medabulism, metabolism
medafesic, metaphysic
medafisical, metaphysic(al)
medafore, metaphor
medagashen, mitigate(tion)
medagate, mitigate
medal,*,llic,list,llion, A BADGE, OBJECT FOR AWARD
    (or see metal/ mettle/ meddle/ middle)
medamorfasis, metamorphosis
medaphore, metaphor
medaphysic, metaphysic
medaphysical, metaphysic(al)
medasen, medicine
medashen, medicine
medatashen, meditate(tion)
meddle,*,er, esome,esomeness,esomely, INTER-
    FERE WITH OTHER'S THINGS/AFFAIRS, (or see
    medal /metal /mettle /middle)
medea, media
medeader, mediate(tor)
medean, median

medeashen, mediate(tion)
medeat, mediate
medeator, mediate(tor)
medec, medic
medecal, medical
medefisic, metaphysic
medefore, metaphor
medek, medic
medekal, medical
medekulus, meticulous
medel, medal /metal /mettle /meddle /middle
medemorfasis, metamorphosis
medeokrity, mediocre(rity)
medeor, meteor
medeorite, meteorite
medeorology, meterology
medephore, metaphor
meder, meter
medernedy, maternity
medeorology, meterology
medesin, medicine
medetashen, meditate(tion)
medeum, medium
medeur, meteor
medevul, medieval
medget, midget
media,* , AUDIO/VIDEO COMMUNICATION
median,nly, OF THE MIDDLE, SEPARATION
medical,/*,lly, OF MEDICINE, EXAMINATION
mediate,*,ed,ting,tion,tive,tize,tor,tization, TO
FACILITATE/DIFFUSE BETWEEN TWO OPPOSING
PARTIES OR OBJECTS
medic,* , ONE'S WHO WORK WITH INJURIES, MEDICINE
medical,/*,lly, OF MEDICINE, EXAMINATION
medicine,*,nal,nally,nable, MAN-MADE CHEMICALS
TAKEN INTO THE BODY
medieval,lism,list,list,lly, OF THE MIDDLE AGES
medifiseks, metaphysics
medik, medic

medikulus, meticulous
medil, medal, medal /metal /mettle /meddle /middle
mediocre,rity,rities, BETWEEN POOR AND GOOD
QUALITY, IN-BETWEEN
mediocur, mediocre(rity)
medir, meter
medirology, meterology
medisine, medicine
meditate,*,ed,ting,tion,tative,tatively,tor,
tiveness, BE SILENT/STILL/ELIMINATE THOUGHT
medium,*,mistic, COMMUNICATION USING THE
VIRTUAL FIELD, TRANSLATING INFORMATION
FROM ONE FORM OF MEDIA TO ANOTHER
medjet, midget
medle, medal /metal /mettle /meddle /middle
medo, meadow
medol, medal /metal /mettle /meddle /middle
medow, meadow
medrapolitan, metropolitan
medrek, metric
medric, metric
medropoletan, metropolitan
medst, midst
medtrik, metric
medufore, metaphor
medugation, mitigate(tion)
medukul, medical
medul, medal /metal /mettle /meddle /middle
medulsom, meddle(some)
medumorfasis, metamorphosis
medur, meter
medurology, meterology
medusin, medicine
medutashen, meditate(tion)
medwife, midwife
meek,kly,kness, GENTLE/MILD TEMPERAMENT
meel, meal
meen, mean

meet,*,ting, COME TOGETHER, ARRIVE AT SAME
DESTINATION AND TIME (or see meat)
mega, PREFIX INDICATING "MILLION/VERY LARGE"
MOST OFTEN MODIFIES THE WORD
megalo, PREFIX INDICATING "MILLION/VERY LARGE"
MOST OFTEN MODIFIES THE WORD
meger, meager /measure
megu, mega
megur, measure /meager
meiosis, CELLULAR PROCESS, UNDERSTATEMENT
mejur, measure
mejut, midget
mek, meek
mekanise, mechanize
mekcher, mixture
mekenize, mechanize
meker, meager
mekschur, mixture
mekster, mixture
mekunize, mechanize
mekur, meager
mel, meal / mail
melado, mulato
meladramatic, melodrama(tic)
melady, melody
melameter, milli(meter)
melan, melon
melancholy,lies,lily,liness,lic, DESPONDENT,
DEPRESSED, CONTEMPLATIVE
melanoma,* ,ata,osis, TUMOR, CELLS WITH DARK
PIGMENT
melasecond, millisecond
melatent, militant
melateristic, military(ristic)
melato, mulato
melaturize, military(rize)
meld,*,ded,ding, AS IF TO MELT TOGETHER, BLEND
INTO ONE (or see melt or mill(ed))
meldoo, mildew

meldu, mildew
meledy, melody
melen, melon
melencholy, melancholy
melenkaly, melancholy
melenoma, melanoma
meleonaire, million(aire)
meletary, military
melin, melon
melincholy, melancholy
melinkoly, melancholy
melinoma, malanoma
melisha, militia
melitia, militia
melk, milk
mell, mill
mellapede, millipede
mellow,wly,wness, *BECOME SOFTENED/RELAXED WITHOUT FEAR*
melnutrishen, malnutrition
melo, mellow
melodrama,*,,atic,atically,atics,atist, *EXAGERRATED ACT/EVENT, OVER EMPHASIS*
melody,dies,dic,dical,dically,dious,diousness, *A SERIES OF SOUNDS/FREQUENCY, TUNES IN HARMONY*
melogram, milli(gram)
melon,*, *EDIBLE FRUIT*
melonkoly, melancholy
melow, mellow
melt,*,ted,ting,table,tability,ter, *TO CHANGE FROM SOLID TO LIQUID, CHANGE FORM* (or see meld)
meltary, military
meludrumatek, melodrama(tic)
melugram, milli(gram)
meluleter, milli(liter)
melun, melon
meluncholy, melancholy
melunoma, malanoma

melunosis, malanoma(osis)
melupete, millipede
melusekund, millisecond
melutare, military
melutint, militant
melyonaire, million(aire)
melyun, million
memacree, mimic(ry)
memakry, mimic(ry)
member,*,rship, *PART/PERSON WHICH BELONGS TO LARGER ORGANISM/ORGANIZATION*
membrane,*,,nous,naceous, *LAYER OF THIN TISSUE*
memek, mimic
memento, *ARTICLE/OBJECT REMINDER OF THE PAST*
memerabelia, memorabilia
memerable, memorable
memerize, memorize
memic, mimic
memoir,*,, *PRINTED REMINDER OF THE PAST*
memorabilia, *REMINDERS OF THE PAST*
memorable,eness,ly, *WORTHY OF REMEMBERING*
memorial,list,lly,lize,lization,lizer, *AN OBJECT PLACED IN MEMORY OF THOSE WHO DIED*
memorize,*,ed,zing,zable,er, *STORE INTO MEMORY*
memory,ries, *COLLECTION OF STORED INFORMATION*
memrize, memorize
memruble, memorable
memry, memory
memuk, mimic
memurabilea, memorabilia
memurise, memorize
memwar, memoir
men,*, *HUMAN ADULT MALE* (or see mean)
mens, men(s) /mean(s)
menace,ced,cing, *HARMFUL/THREATENING, A NUISANCE*
menamize, minimize
menamul, minimal
menamuly, minimal(y)

menamum, minimum
menapos, menopause
menarolization, mineral(ization)
menarul, mineral
menarulize, mineral(ize)
menaskewul, minuscule
menastrony, minestrone
menastry, minister(y)
menchen, mention
mend,*,,ded,ding,dable, *TO FIX, REPAIR* (or see mint or meant)
mene, mean /mini
meneacher, miniature
menemize, minimize
menengidos, meningitis
menenjidus, meningitis
menerable, memorable
menerul, mineral
menes, menace
menestrony, minestrone
menestry, minister(y)
menet, minute
meneul, menial
mengul, mingle
meni, mini
menial,lly, *REQUIRES LITTLE THOUGHT*
meniature, miniature
menila, manila
meningitis,ic, *VIRUS OF THE BODY*
menipause, menopause
menipulate, manipulate
menis, menace
menk, mink
menmerable, memorable
mennow, minnow
meno, minnow
menogamy, monogamy
menokside, monoxide

mer, mere /mirror
meracle, miracle
meraculus, miracle(culous)
merage, mirage
meragolt, marigold
meraje, mirage
merakle, miracle
merakulus, miracle(culous)
meral, morale /mural
meraly, merry(rily)
meranade, marinade /marinate
merange, meringue
merathon, marathon
mercantile,lism,list, COMMERCE, TRADE
mercenary,ries,rily,riness, HIRED TO KILL
merchandise,ed,sing,dize,er,izer, GOODS FOR
   RETAIL SALE
merchant,*,table, ONE WHO DEALS IN GOODS FOR
   RETAIL
mercury,rial,ric, A PLANET, BEHAVIOR AS IF RULED BY
   THE PLANET, A METALLIC ELEMENT USED IN
   THERMOMETERS
mercy,cies,ciful,cifully,ciful,ciless,cilessly,
   cilessness, PROVIDE COMPASSION/BENEVOLENCE
   AT A CRUCIAL TIME
merder, murder
merderer, murder(er)
mere,ely, SIMPLY FOR THE REASON OF... (or see
   marry/ merry/ mirror)
mered, married
meredian, meridian
merege, marriage
meregold, marigold
mereinette, marionette
mereje, marriage
merekul, miracle
merenate, marinade /marinate
merene, marine
mereod, myriad

mereonette, marionette
meret, merit
merethon, marathon
meretime, maritime
meretul, marital
mereunette, marionette
merewana, marijuana
merge,*,ed,ging,er,ence, COME TOGETHER AS ONE
meriad, myriad
meridge, marriage
meridian,*,nal,nally, INVISIBLE CIRCLE RUNNING
   AROUND EARTH THROUGH NORTH/SOUTH POLES
merigold, marigold
merijuana, marijuana
merily, merry(rily)
merina, marina
merinade, marinade /marinate
merinate, marinade /marinate
merine, marine
meringue, WHIPPED EGGS
merit,*,ted,tedly,tless,torious, WORTHY OF HONOR
   OR NOTE
merital, marital
merithon, marathon
meritime, maritime
meritol, marital
meriwana, marijuana
merje, merge
merk, murky
merkanteel, mercantile
merkury, mercury
merky, murky
merlen, merlin
merlin, BIRD
mermaid,*, ILLUSIONARY FISH WOMAN
mermer, murmur
mermur, murmur
mero, marrow
meroge, mirage

menopause,sal, STOPPING OF THE MONTHLY
   BLEEDING, ESTROGEN IN FEMALES
menopuly, monopoly
menoscule, minuscule
menotnus, monotony(nous)
menotny, monotony
menoxide, monoxide
menruble, memorable
mense, mince
menses, MENSTRUATION
menshen, mention
mensteration, menstruation
menstral, menstrual /minstrel
menstrashen, menstruation
menstration, menstruation
menstrual,uous,ate,uum, MENSTRUATION (or see
   minstrel)
menstruation, FEMALE MONTHLY UTERUS LINING
   DISCHARGE, A PERIOD
ment, mint/ mend/ meant
mental,lity,lity, THOUGHT, OF THE MIND
menthol, OIL
mention,*, ned,ning,nable,ner, CALLING BRIEF
   ATTENTION TO SOMETHING
mentle, mental
mentor,*, A COACH, GUIDE
mentur, mentor
menu,*, LIST OF RESTAURANT MEALS
menuet, minuet
menumem, minimum
menumly, minimal(y)
menupause, menopause
menure, manure
menus, menace
menustrony, minestrone
menyew, menu
menyewet, minuet
menyon, mignon
meol, meal

meroj, mirage
meror, mirror
merose, morose
merow, marrow
merry,rriment,rrily,rriness, CHEERY, HAPPY
mersenary, mercenary
mershandise, merchandise
mersinary, mercenary
mersy, mercy
merukul, miracle
merur, mirror
mery, marry /merry
mes, meso, PREFIX INDICATING "MIDDLE" MOST
    OFTEN MODIFIES THE WORD
mes, mess
mesa,*, LAND PLATEAU
mesage, message /massage
mesalaneus, miscellaneous
mesals, measles /missile(s)
mesbahave, misbehave
mesbaleef, misbelief
mesbaleve, misbelieve
mescalculate, miscalculate
meschef, mischief
mesconstrue, misconstrue
mesdake, mistake
mesdamener, misdemeanor
mesderius, mysterious
mesdress, mistress
mesdriul, mistrial
mesdufy, mystify
mesdur, mister (Mr.)
mesdury, mystery
meseg, message
mesej, message
mesel, missile
meseness, mess(iness)
mesenger, messenger
mesenturpet, misinterpret

meseur, mess(ier) /masseur
meseust, mess(iest)
mesfet, misfit
mesfire, misfire
mesforshen, misfortune
mesfortune, misfortune
mesgeving, misgiving
mesguge, misjudge
mesh,hes,hed, INTERWOVEN METAL STRANDS TO
    CREATE A BLANKET/NET
meshandle, mishandle
meshap, mishap
meshen, mission
meshenary, mission(ary)
mesher, measure
meshur, measure
mesige, message
mesije, message
mesil, missile
mesils, measles /missile(s)
mesinform, misinform
mesinger, messenger
mesinturpret, misinterpret
mesjef, mischief
mesjug, misjudge
meskalaneus, miscellaneous
meskarege, miscarriage
meskedo, mosquito
meskeet, mesquite
meskenstrew, misconstrue
meskownt, miscount
meskwote, misquote
mesled, misled
mesleed, mislead
mesmach, mismatch
mesmerize,*,ism,ic,ically,ist,zation,er,INTENSELY
    ATTENTIVE TO THE POINT OF EXCLUDING ALL
    OTHER THINGS
mesmurize, mesmerize

mesnomer, misnomer
meso, mes, PREFIX INDICATING "MIDDLE" MOST
    OFTEN MODIFIES THE WORD
mesoje, massage
mespell, misspell
mesplase, misplace
mesprent, misprint
mesprunounce, mispronounce
mesquite, LAND TYPE, A TREE, SHRUB
mesquote, misquote
mesred, misread
mesrepresent, misrepresent
mess,es,ssed,ssing,ssy,ssily,ssiness,ssier,ssiest,
    SLOPPY, DISHEVELED, DISARRAY
message,*, ed,ging, SHORT NOTE OF VOICE/TEXT
messenger,*, ONE WHO DELIVERS A NOTE
messusege, misuse(sage)
mest, mist/ miss(ed)/ mess(ed)
mestake, mistake
mestakin, mistaken
mestamener, misdemeanor
meste, mist(y)
mesteek, mystique
mestefy, mystify
mester, mister (Mr.)
mestereus, mysterious
mestic, mystic
mestides, mastitis
mestify, mystify
mestikul, mystic(cal)
mestireus, mysterious
mestreat, mistreat
mestress, mistress
mestrete, mistreat
mestris, mistress
mestriul, mistrial
mestufy, mystify
mestumener, misdemeanor
mestury, mystery

mesuge, message
mesuje, message
mesulaneus, miscellaneous
mesuls, measles /missile(s)
mesultoe, mistletoe
mesunderstand, misunderstand
mesunderstood, misunderstood
mesure, measure
mesurible, miserable
mesuse, masseuse /misuse
mesuseje, misuse(sage)
mesuze, misuse /masseuse
mesyews, misuse
met, PAST TENSE OF "MEET", (or see mitt /mite/ meet /meat)
meta, PREFIX INDICATING "BEYOND/ CHANGE" MOST OFTEN MODIFIES THE WORD
metabolism,*,izes,ized,izing,ic,ical,ically, THE CONVERSION OF ENERGY IN A LIVING ORGANISM, FUNCTION OF LIFE
metabolism, metabolism
metafisical, metaphysic(al)
metagate, mitigate
metal,*,led,ling,lic,lically, CHEMICAL ELEMENTS FOUND IN THE EARTH (or see mettle/meddle/ medal/middle)
metamorphosis, MAJOR TRANSFORMATION AS A CATERPILLAR TO A BUTTERFLY
metaphor,*,ric,rical,rically, EXPRESSING THOUGHT USING UNCONVENTIONAL COMPARISONS
metaphysic,*,cal,cally, STUDY OF THE SUPERNATURAL, INVISIBLE
metasen, medicine
metatashen, meditate(tion)
mete, meat(y)
metea, media
metean, median
meteashen, mediate(tion)
meteate, mediate

meteator, mediate(tor)
metefisical, metaphysic(al)
metek, medic
metekal, medical
metekulus, meticulous
metel, medal /metal /mettle /meddle
metel, middle
metemorfusis, metamorphosis
meten, mitten
meteokrety, mediocre(rity)
meteokur, mediocre
meteor,*,ric, COMPACTED SAND AND ICE TRAVELING AT HIGH VELOCITY THROUGH SPACE
meteorite,*, METEOR THAT SURVIVES ENTRY THROUGH EARTH'S ATMOSPHERE
meteorology,gic,gical,gically,gist, STUDY OF THE ATMOSPHERE SUCH AS WEATHER/CLIMATE
metephysical, metaphysic(al)
meter,*,red, FORM/INSTRUMENT OF MEASUREMENT
meterology, meterology
metesen, medicine
metetashen, meditate(tion)
meteum, medium
meteurology, meterology
metevul, medieval
meteyorite, meteorite
meth, myth or methanphetamine
meth, SHORT FOR METHAMPHETAMINE
methadone, MAN-MADE DRUG, DOWNER, HIGHLY ADDICTIVE
methakul, myth(ical)
methalogic, mythologic
methamphetamine,*, ABBREVIATION FOR METH, MANMADE CHEMICAL STIMULANT
methane, A GAS
methanfetamene, methamphetamine
methanol, TOXIC LIQUID
methanphetamine, methamphetamine
methasize, myth(icize)

methecul, myth(ical)
methed, method
methedology, method(ology)
methedone, methadone
methemfetamine, methamphetamine
methenphetamine, methamphetamine
methid, method
methidology, method(ology)
method,*,dolical,dolically,dolicalness,dology, dologies,dize,dizer, A SYSTEM/PROCEDURE/ TECHNIQUE
metholugy, mythology
methonol, methanol
methud, method
methudology, method(ology)
methudone, methadone
methunol, methanol
metia, media
metic, medic
metical, medical
meticulous,sly,sness,sity, EXCESSIVE ATTENTION TO DETAIL/CLEANLINESS/EXACTING
metil, medal /metal /mettle /meddle /middle
metin, mitten
meting, meet(ing)
metir, meter
metirology, meterology
metisine, medicine
metitate, meditate
metle, medal /metal /mettle /meddle /middle
meto, meadow
metr, metro, PREFIX INDICATING "WOMB/MOTHER" MOST OFTEN MODIFIES THE WORD
metrapolitan, metropolitan
metric,*,cal,cally,ist, A MEASUREMENT SYSTEM
metropolis,ses, CENTRAL CITY
metropolitan,nism, HUB OF CITY AND THOSE WHO DWELL THERE
metruk, metric

metst, midst
mettle,*, ed,esome, *COURAGEOUS, SPIRITED* (or see medal/ metal /mettle /meddle /middle)
metukul, medical
metul, medal /metal /mettle /meddle /middle
metur, meter
meturnedy, maternity
meturnul, maternal
meturology, meterology
metutashen, meditate(tion)
meuchuel, mutual
meudilate, mutilate
meukus, mucus
meul, meal /mule
meurol, mural
meus, muse
meusikul, music(al)
meut, mute
meutat, mutate
meutene, mutiny
meutilate, mutilate
meutulashen, mutilate(tation)
meuzeim, museum
meuzek, music
meuzeshen, musician
mewfee, movie
mewfuble, move(vable)
mewkus, mucus
mewl, mule
mewn, moon
mewnisapaledy, municipal(ity)
mewnisepal, municipal
mewral, mural
mewrul, mural
mewse, muse/ moose/ mousse
mewseum, museum
mewsik, music
mewt, moot / mute
mewtelate, mutilate

mewteny, mutiny
mewtint, mutant
mewvee, movie
mewvuble, move(vable)
mewzishen, musician
mexcher, mixture
mexter, mixture
mez, mess
mezandul, mishandle
mezdamener, misdemeanor
mezder, mister (Mr.)
mezdery, mystery
mezdumener, misdemeanor
mezfet, misfit
mezfire, misfire
mezforchen, misfortune
mezhap, mishap
mezinform, misinform
mezkwote, misquote
mezled, misled
mezleet, mislead
mezmach, mismatch
mezmurize, mesmerize
meznomer, misnomer
mezpell, misspell
mezplase, misplace
mezprent, misprint
mezred, misread
mezreprezent, misrepresent
mezruble, miserable
meztake, mistake
meztamener, misdemeanor
meztek, mystic
mezter, mister (Mr.)
meztereus, mysterious
meztreat, mistreat
meztress, mistress
meztriul, mistrial
mezuls, measles

mezury, misery
mi, my
mibuleve, misbelieve
mica, *ORGANIC, SILICATE*
michen, mission
michenary, mission(ary)
micks, mix
micrawave, microwave
micro, *PREFIX INDICATING "SMALL" MOST OFTEN MODIFIES THE WORD*
micro, *VERY SMALL*
microbe,bial,bian,bic, *ORGANISMS SEEN ONLY UNDER A MICROSCOPE*
micrometer, *SYSTEM OF MEASUREMENT*
micron, *LATIN FOR SMALL*
microphone,*, *TRANSMITS SOUND*
microscope,*,pic, *INSTRUMENT WHICH ENLARGES FOR VIEWING WITH THE EYES*
microwave,*, *ELECTROMAGNETIC WAVELENGTH, AN APPLIANCE*
micu, mica
mid, *PREFIX INDICATING "HALF/MIDDLE" MOST OFTEN MODIFIES THE WORD* (or see mitt)
midachondria, mitochondria
midagashen, mitigate(tion)
midagate, mitigate
middle, *IN BETWEEN* (or see medal /metal /mettle /meddle)
midegate, mitigate
midegation, mitigate(tion)
mider, miter
midevil, medieval
midget,*, *UNUSUALLY SMALL PERSON*
midigashen, mitigate(tion)
midjet, midget
midle, middle
midochondria, mitochondria
midokondrea, mitochondria
midol, middle

midst, LOCATED IN THE MIDDLE, AMONG
miduchondria, mitochondria
midul, medal /metal /mettle /meddle /middle
midur, miter
midwife,eves,ery, ASSISTS MOTHER THROUGH BIRTHING A CHILD
miff,*,/fed,fiest,fy, BE OFFENDED
miget, midget
might,ty,tier,tiest,tily,tiness, STRENGTH, POWER, PERHAPS (or see mite)
mignon,*, SMALL, DELICATE
migraine,*, A SERIOUS HEADACHE
migrashen, migrate(tion)
migrant,*, ONE WHO IS CONTINUOUSLY MOVING
migrate,*,ed,ting,tion,ant,tor,tory, TO MOVE LOCATION OF HOME BASED UPON THE SEASONS
migro, micro
migrunt, migrant
migrutory, migrate(tory)
mijet, midget
mika, mica
mikaw, macaw
mikcher, mixture
mikount, miscount
mikrafone, microphone
mikrascope, microscope
mikrawave, microwave
mikro, micro
mikrobe, microbe
mikrofone, microphone
mikromeder, micrometer
mikrometer, micrometer
mikron, micron
mikrowave, microwave
mikschur, mixture
mikshter, mixture
mikster, mixture
miku, mica
milado, mulato

milage, mile(age)
milagram, milli(gram)
milaleder, milli(liter)
milaleter, milli(liter)
milameder, milli(meter)
milameter, milli(meter)
milapede, millipede
milarea, malaria
milasecond, millisecond
milasekend, millisecond
milasus, molasses
milatent, militant
milato, mulato
milaturestic, military(ristic)
milaturise, military(rize)
mild,der,dest,dly,dness, PLEASANT (or see milled)
mildew,wy, FUNGI
mildu, mildew
mile,*,eage, U.S. MEASUREMENT FOR DISTANCE
milegram, milli(gram)
milekuler, molecular
milemeder, milli(meter)
mileonaire, million(aire)
milepete, millipede
miler, mill(er)
milesekent, millisecond
milest, molest
miletary, military
mileturezation, military(rization)
miligram, milli(gram)
milileder, milli(liter)
milileter, milli(liter)
milimeter, milli(meter)
milion, million
milionair, million(aire)
milipede, millipede
milipete, millipede
militant,ncy,tness,tly, ORDERLY, BY STRICT RULES

military,ries,rily,rize,rization,rism,rist,ristic,tically,ate,ation, GROUP OF PEOPLE BEING LED WITH STRICT RULES, AN ORDERLY GROUP
militia,*, GROUP ORGANIZED/TRAINED TO FIGHT
milk,ker,ky,kiness, WHITE LIFE-GIVING FLUID EXCRETED BY MOTHERS OF MAMMALS, ANY RESEMBLANCE TO MILK
mill,*,lled,lling,ller, GRINDING OF FOODSTUFF TO GRIND/REMOVE HULL (or see mile)
millaliter, milli(liter)
millameder, milli(meter)
millameter, milli(meter)
milli, igram,iliter,imeter, LATIN = THOUSAND/ THOUSANDTH
milli, PREFIX INDICATING "ONE THOUSANDTH" MOST OFTEN MODIFIES THE WORD
million,*,naire, U.S. NUMBER TO IDENTIFY QUANTITY
millipede,*, INSECT
millisecond,*, METRIC NUMBER
miltary, military
miluge, mile(age)
milugram, milli(gram)
milumeder, milli(meter)
milumeter, milli(meter)
milupede, millipede
milutant, militant
milutare, military
milyen, million
milyonaire, million(aire)
mimakry, mimic(ry)
mimbrane, membrane
mimbur, member
mime,*,ed,ming, ACTOR WHO USES THE BODY TO ACT, COMMUNICATE WITHOUT USING WORDS
mimic,*,ced,cing,cry,cries, TO COPY, IMITATE ANOTHER PERSON
mimorabilia, memorabilia
mimorabul, memorable
mimorealzation, memorial(ization)

mimoreul, memorial
mimorise, memorize
mimory, memory
mimurabilia, memorabilia
mimwar, memoir
minamize, minimize
minamul, minimal
minamum, minimum
minapos, menopause
minaralize, mineral(ize)
minarul, mineral
minaskewul, minuscule
minaskule, minuscule
minaster, minister
minastrony, minestrone
mince,*,ed,cing, CHOP UP FINELY (SUCH AS FOOD)
minchen, mention
mind,*,ded,ding,dful,dfully,dfulness,dless, dlessly,dlessness, PART OF A LIVING THING THAT MAKES THEM AWARE, WHERE THOUGHTS ARE GENERATED (or see mend or mint)
mine,ed,ning,er, PAST TENSE OF "MY", CLAIMING OWNERSHIP, A FORMED TUNNEL INTO THE GROUND WHICH BEARS PRECIOUS ROCKS OR METALS, SUBSURFACE BOMB (or see mind)
mineacher, miniature
mineature, miniature
minemal, minimal
minemize, minimize
minemum, minimum
minengidus, meningitis
mineon, mignon
miner, mine(r) /minor
mineral,*,lize,lizing,lization,lizer, ORGANIC SUBSTANCES
mines, minus /mine(s) /mince /menace
mineskule, minuscule
minester, minister
minestrone, SOUP

minet, minute
mingle,*,ed,ling, TO BE AMONG, ASSOCIATE WITH
mini, LATIN FOR SMALL, SHORT, BRIEF (or see many)
mini, PREFIX INDICATING "SMALL" MOST OFTEN MODIFIES THE WORD
miniature,*,rize,rization, SMALL FORM OF ORIGINAL SIZE
minimal,ly, THE LEAST POSSIBLE
minimize,*,ed,zing, MAKE SMALLER, LESS
minimum,*, THE LEAST POSSIBLE
miniscule, minuscule
minister,*,ry,ries,rial,rially, PREACHING ABOUT RELIGION
miniucher, miniature
mink,*, A RODENT
minnow,*,wed,wing, A VERY SMALL FISH
mino, minnow
minogumy, monogamy
minokside, monoxide
minopos, menopause
minopuly, monopoly
minor,*, BELOW MAJOR, SMALLER THAN, MUSICAL CHORD (or see miner)
minos, minus /miner(s)
minotnus, monotony(nous)
minotny, monotony
minow, minnow
minoxite, monoxide
minse, mince
minses, menses
minshen, mention
minsteration, menstruation
minstral, menstrual /minstrel
minstrel,*, ONE WHO ENTERTAINS WITH POETRY/ SONG (or see minstral)
mint,*,ted,ting, AN HERB, PLACE WHERE COINS ARE MADE (or see meant)
mintalety, mental(ity)
mintel, mental

minter, mentor
minthol, menthol
mintle, mental
mintor, mentor
mintul, mental
minu, menu
minuet,*, SLOW RYTHM IN MUSIC, DANCE
minural, mineral
minure, manure
minus, MATH EXPRESSION, TAKE AWAY/SUBTRACT FROM (or see menace)
minuscule, OF LITTLE IMPORTANCE, TINY
minuskule, minuscule
minustrony, minestrone
minute,*,ely, MEASURE OF TIME, RECORD A MEETING, SLIGHT/SMALL
minuver, maneuver
minyew, menu
minyewet, minuet
minyon, mignon
miosis, meiosis
miracle,*,culous,culously,lousness, EVENT PRECEDED BY MYSTERIOUS ACTIONS, SEEMINGLY IMPOSSIBLE OCCURENCE
miraculus, miracle(culous)
mirage,*, AN OPTICAL ILLUSION
mirakle, miracle
miral, morale or mural
mirange, meringue
mircantile, mercantile
mirchandise, merchandise
mirchant, merchant
miread, myriad
mirekul, miracle
mireod, myriad
mirer, mirror
mirje, merge
mirkanteel, mercantile
mirky, murky

mirlin, merlin
mirmer, murmur
mirmur, murmur
mirmur, murmur
miroge, mirage
miror, mirror
mirose, morose
mirquery, mercury
mirror,*,red,ring, REFLECTION
mirseful, mercy(ciful)
mirsy, mercy
mirukul, miracle
mirur, mirror
mirurd, mirror(ed)
mis, PREFIX INDICATING "BAD/WRONG/ WRONGLY"
    MOST OFTEN MODIFIES THE WORD
misalaneus, miscellaneous
misandul, mishandle
misap, mishap
misbaleef, misbelief
misbaleve, misbelieve
misbehave,*,ed,ving,vior, TO NOT BEHAVE
misbelief, DO NOT BELIEVE
misbelieve, PAST TENSE OF "MISBELIEF"
misbuleef, misbelief
miscalculate,*,ed,ting,tion,tor, NOT PROPER
    CALCULATION
miscarriage,*,ed,ging, LOSS IN CARRYING A FETUS
    TO FULL TERM
miscellaneous, VARIETY OF ELEMENTS/THINGS/
    THAT HAVE NO RELEVANCE TO ONE ANOTHER
mischef, mischief
mischief,evous,ecously,evousness, ACTION/BE-
    HAVIOR THAT CREATES AGITATION FOR OTHERS
misconstrue,*,ed,uing, MISINTERPRETE,
    INCORRECT UNDERSTANDING OF INFORMATION
miscount,*,ted,ting, COUNT DIDN'T COME OUT
    CORRECTLY
miscownt, miscount
misd, miss(ed) /mist

misdacism, mystic(icism)
misdaken, mistaken
misdamener, misdemeanor
misdemeanor,*, CITED FOR NOT OBEYING SET RULES
misdereus, mysterious
misdireus, mysterious
misdress, mistress
misdriul, mistrial
misdrus, mistress
misdufy, mystify
misdur, mister (Mr.)
misdury, mystery
mised, miss(ed) /mist
misel, missile
miself, my(self)
miseltoe, mistletoe
misenform, misinform
misenterpret, misinterpret
miser,rly,rliness, ONE WHO IS OVERLY FEARFUL
    ABOUT USING, SPENDING THEIR MONEY
miserable,ly,eness, EXTREMELY UNCOMFORTABLE,
    FEELING BEYOND CAPACITY
misery,ries, DREADFUL EMOTIONAL OR PHYSICAL
    STATE OF BEING
misfire,*,ed,ring, DIDN'T HIT THE TARGET
misfit,*, DOESN'T QUITE FIT IN WITH THE OTHERS
misfortune,*, UNPLANNED DISTURBING EVENT
misgef, mischief
misgiving,*, GIVEN TO DOUBT OR APPREHENSION IN
    MAKING A JUDGEMENT
misguge, misjudge
mishandle,*,ed,ling, TO NOT TREAT CAREFULLY
mishap,*, EVENT WHICH RENDERS UNCONTROLLABLE
    REACTIONS
mishen, mission
mishenary, mission(ary)
misinform,*,med,mant,mer,mation, NOT
    CORRECT INFORMATION

misinterpret,*,ted,ting,ter,tation, DOESN'T
    REPRESENT THE FACTS
mision, mission
misionary, mission(ary)
misijif, mischief
misjudge,*,ed,ging,ement, MAKE DECISION WITH-
    OUT TAKING ALL FACTS INTO CONSIDERATION
misjuge, misjudge
miskalaneus, miscellaneous
miskalkulate, miscalculate
miskedo, mosquito
miskeet, mesquite
miskerage, miscarriage
miskeruge, miscarriage
miskonstrue, misconstrue
miskownt, miscount
miskunstrew, misconstrue
misle, missile
mislead,*,ding, MANIPULATE INTO UNDESIRABLE
    DIRECTION
misled, PAST TENSE OF MISLEAD
misletoe, mistletoe
mismach, mismatch
mismatch,hes,hed,hing, DO NOT MATCH UP
    TOGETHER
misnomer,*, INCORRECT NAME FOR
misoge, massage
misoje, massage
misspell, misspell
misplace,*,ed,cing,ement, NOT PLACED WHERE IT
    NORMALLY BELONGS
misprint,*,ted, PRINTED INCORRECT INFORMATION
mispronounce,*,ed,cing,ciation, WORD NOT
    SPOKEN CORRECTLY
misprunownse, mispronounce
misquote,*,ed,ting,tation, DIDN'T ACCURATELY
    REFLECT WHAT WAS ACTUALLY SAID
misread,*, TO NOT READ CORRECTLY
misred, misread

misrepresent,*,ted,ting,tation,tative,ter, DOESN'T ACCURATELY REPRESENT
miss,*,sses,ssed,ssing, NOT IN USUAL/PREFERRED PLACE, REFERENCE TO YOUNG UNMARRIED WOMAN
missile,*,ery, A THROWN OR SHOT PROJECTILE WITH INTENT TO INJURE
mission,*,nary,naries, SET OUT TO COMPLETE A TASK AS IF WITH AUTHORITY
misslede, mislead
misspell,*,lled,lling, TO SPELL INCORRECTLY
missusage, misuse(sage)
missuse, misuse
mist,*,ting,ty,tily,tiness, VERY LIGHT SPRAY OF WATER, A HAZE (or see miss(ed))
mistacism, mystic(icism)
mistake,*,en,enly,eness,kable, THINK IT IS SOMETHING IT IS NOT, INCORRECT
mistakuble, mistake(kable)
mistamener, misdemeanor
misteek, mystique
mistefy, mystify
mistek, mystic / mystique
mistektamy, mastectomy
mister, MR. (ABBREVIATION), REFERENCE TO A MAN
mistereus, mysterious
mistic, mystic
misticul, mystic(cal)
mistique, mystique
mistireus, mysterious
mistletoe, PARASITIC PLANT ON A TREE
mistreat,*,ted,ting, TO TREAT SOMETHING, SOMEONE IMPROPERLY
mistress, WOMAN IN POSITION OF COMMAND/RULE
mistret, mistreat
mistrial,*, UNABLE TO MAKE A JUDGEMENT IN A TRIAL DUE TO VARIOUS REASONS
mistro, maestro
mistufy, mystify
misul, missile

misulaneus, miscellaneous
misulf, my(self)
misultoe, mistletoe
misunderstand,*,ding,tood, NOT ABLE TO COMPREHEND/UNDERSTAND
misunderstood, PAST TENSE OF "MISUNDERSTAND"
misur, miser
misuruble, miserable
misury, misery
misus, miss(es)
misuse, masseuse
misuse,*,ed,sing,er,sage, NOT USING PROPERLY
misuze, misuse
mit, mitt /mite /might
mitachondria, mitochondria
mitagashen, mitigate(tion)
mitagate, mitigate
mite,*, TINY INSECT, ANIMAL, SOMETHING TINY (or see might or might(y))
miten, mitten
miter,*,red,ring, REFERENCE TO ANGLES
mitereul, material
miteur, might(ier)
mitevul, medieval
mith, myth
mithakul, myth(ical)
mithalogic, mythologic
mithasize, myth(icize)
mithecul, myth(ical)
mitholagize, mythologic(ize)
mithology, mythology
mitiest, might(iest)
mitigate,able,tion,tive,tor,tory, TO LESSEN A BURDEN OR SEVERITY
mitochondria,ion,al, ORGANELLES WITHIN A CELL WHICH ASSIST IN METABOLISM
mitropolis, metropolis
mitst, midst

mitt,*, A COVERING FOR THE HAND (or see mite or might)
mitten,*, HAND COVERING TO PROTECT SKIN FROM GREAT TEMPERATURE DIFFERENCES
mitul, medal/metal/mettle/meddle/middle
mityest, might(iest)
mix,xes,xed,xing,xer, TO BLEND/STIR VARIOUS ELEMENTS/ARTICLES/INGREDIENTS TOGETHER ELIMINATING ORDER
mixcher, mixture
mixture,*, COMBINE DIFFERENT THINGS TOGETHER CREATING SOMETHING ENTIRELY DIFFERENT
mizconstsrue, misconstrue
mizdakin, mistaken
mizdamener, misdemeanor
mizdereus, mysterious
mizdress, mistress
mizdrus, mistress
mizdur, mister (Mr.)
mizdury, mystery
mizenformation, misinform(ation)
mizenturpret, misinterpret
mizer, miser
mizeruble, miserable
mizfet, misfit
mizfire, misfire
mizforchen, misfortune
mizgeving, misgiving
mizhandul, mishandle
mizhap, mishap
mizinform, misinform
mizkunstrew, misconstrue
mizkwote, misquote
mizled, misled
mizleed, mislead
mizmach, mismatch
miznomer, misnomer
mizpell, misspell
mizplase, misplace

moist, ten,tens,tened,ture,turize,turizer,tness, BETWEEN DRY/WET, MORE THAN DAMP
mojulate, modulate
mojul, module
mojulir, module(lar)
mok, mach/ make/ mock
moka, mocha
mokasen, moccasin
mokery, mock(ery)
mokesin, moccasin
moksy, moxie
moku, mocha
mol, mall/ maul/ mole
molar,*,rity, A TOOTH, CHEMISTRY AMOUNT
molarky, malarkey
molasis, molasses
molasses, RICH/DARK SYRUP
molakul, molecule
molakuler, molecular
mold,*,ded,ding,dy,diness,dable, FUNGI, CONTAINER USED TO MAKE A FORM, USED FOR FRAMING/FINISHING WORK (or see molt or maul(ed))
moldibul, mold(able)
molduble, mold(able)
mole,*,*, A CHEMISTRY MEASUREMENT OF WEIGHT, A RODENT, A BEAUTY MARK, GROWTH ON SKIN
molecule,*,*lar,larly,larlity, TINY PARTICLES WHICH CANNOT BE SEEN, ONLY KNOWN, GROUPS OF TINY INVISIBLE PARTICLES
molekule, molecule
molekuler, molecular
moler, molar
molest,*,ted,ting,ter,tation, TO PHYSICALLY FORCE SOMEONE INTO AN UNACCEPTABLE SITUATION
molikule, molecule
moll, mall/ maul/ mole
mollusk,*,*, INVERTEBRAE GENERALLY WITH SHELLS AND NO SEGMENTS

molt, malt
molt,*,ted,ting,ter, TO SHED OUTER LAYER SUCH AS SKIN (or see mold/ malt/ maul/ maul(ed))
molur, molar
molusk, mollusk
mom,*,*mma,mmy, PARENT WHO PERFORMED THE BIRTHING
moma, mamma
momendus, moment(ous)
moment,*,tary,tarily,tariness,tly,tous,tously, tousness,tum, VERY BRIEF MEASURE/ AMOUNT OF TIME
momentus, moment(ous)
mominshus, moment(ious)
momint, moment
mominterily, moment(arily)
momintum, moment(um)
momintus, moment(ous)
mon, mono, PREFIX INDICATING "ALONG/ONLY/ SINGLE" MOST OFTEN MODIFIES THE WORD
monafilament, monofilament
monagram, monogram
monalith, monolith
monalithic, monolith(ic)
monalogue, monologue
monanukleosis, mononucleosis
monarale, monorail
monarch,*, hal,hial,hally,hianism,hical,hical, hism,hist,histic,hy,hies, LARGE BUTTERFLY, POWERFUL POSITION, SOLE RULER
monark, monarch
monarkial, monarch(ial)
monastery,ries,rial,tic,tical,tically,ticism, PLACE OF ISOLATION
monater, monitor
monatone, monotone
mondane, mundane
Monday,*, A DAY OF THE WEEK
mone, moan

mone, money
monegram, monogram
monelogue, monologue
monenukleosis, mononucleosis
monerale, monorail
monestasism, monastery(tacism)
monestery, monastery
monetary,rily,tize,tization, OF MONEY
monetone, monotone
monetor, monitor
monewment, monument
money,nies, MINTED COIN AND PAPER USED FOR EXCHANGE OF ITEMS OR SERVICES
mongrel,*,ly,lize, MIXED BREED OF DOG
mongril, mongrel
mongrul, mongrel
monie, money
monigram, monogram
monilogue, monologue
moninukleosis, mononucleosis
monirale, monorail
monistery, monastery
monitary, monetary
monitone, monotone
monitor,*,red,ring,ry,rship, ENFORCER OF RULES, A MACHINE THAT READS VITAL LIFE SIGNS
monk,*,khood,kish,kishly,kishness,kery,keries, ONE WHO PRACTICES TO OVERCOME EGO
monkey,kies,ying, ANIMAL, MAMMAL, TO ACT LIKE A MONKEY
mono, mon, PREFIX INDICATING "ALONG/ONLY/ SINGLE" MOST OFTEN MODIFIES THE WORD
mono, SHORT FOR MONONUCLEOSIS
monocular,*, ITEM WHERE ONE EYE CAN SEE MAGNIFICATION
monofilament,*, ONE FILAMENT IN A BULB
monogamy,mous,mic,mist,mistic,mously, mousness, ADULT WHO ACCEPTS ONLY ONE PARTNER

monogram,*,med,ming,matic, *LETTER/CHARACTER REPRESENTING A NAME*
monolith,hic,hically, *SINGLE SKIN, STONE*
monologue,*, *ONE PERSON WHO SPEAKS*
mononucleosis, *ONE-NUCLEUS BLOOD CELLS RESULTANT FROM A VIRUS*
monopoly,lies, *ONE COMPANY DOMINATES LEAVING A PEOPLE NO ABILITY TO CHOOSE*
monorail,*, *A SINGLE RAIL FOR TRAVEL*
monotary, monetary
monotone,*,ed,ning,nic, *ONE TONE*
monotony,nous,nously,nousness, *REPETITION, SAME THING OVER AND OVER AGAIN*
monoxide, *ONE OXYGEN ATOM IN A MOLECULE*
monsoon,*, *GREAT RUSH OF RAIN IN A CERTAIN SEASON WHICH LASTS FOR MONTHS*
monstrasute, monstrosity
monstrausete, monstrosity
monster,*,trous,trously,trousity, trosities, *USED TO DESCRIBE SOMETHING UNUSUAL/FRIGHTENING, NOT NATURAL/NORMAL*
monstres, monstrous
monstrocity, monstrosity
monstrosete, monstrosity
monstrous,osity,osities, *USED TO DESCRIBE SOMETHING UNUSUAL/FRIGHTENING*
monstrosity,sities, *USED TO DESCRIBE SOMETHING UNUSUAL/FRIGHTENING/ABNORMAL*
monstrosete, monstrosity
monstrus, monstrous
monstur, monster
monsune, monsoon
month,*,hly,hlies, *A MEASURE OF TIME WHICH DIVIDES DAYS OF THE YEAR INTO SECTIONS*
monuer, manure
monugram, monogram
monulithic, monolith(ic)
monulogue, monologue

monument,*, tal,tally,talize, *A MARKER/STONE/ARTICLE/STRUCTURE IN HONOR OF SOMEONE/SOMETHING*
monumint, monument
monurale, monorail
monure, manure
monustery, monastery
monutary, monetary
monutone, monotone
mony, money
monyument, monument
monzoon, monsoon
monzter, monster
mood,*,dier,diest,dy,dily,diness, *AN EMOTIONAL STATE OF MIND* (or see moot or mute)
moodyness, mood(iness)
moof, move
moofuble, move(vable)
moon,*,nish,nishly,ny, *LARGEST PLANET SEEN AT NIGHT WHICH IS OPPOSITE FROM THE SUN*
moor,*,red,ring,rage, *A BOG, A PLACE TO DOCK A BOAT, ACT OF DOCKING A SHIP* (or see more)
moose, *A LARGE MEMBER OF THE DEER FAMILY* (or see mouse or mousse)
moot,tness, *UP FOR DISCUSSION WITHOUT DECISION, ARGUABLE, DEBATABLE* (or see mute/mood)
mootiness, mood(iness)
mooty, mood(y)
moove, move
mop,*,pped,pping, *AN ITEM USED WET TO CLEAN FLOORS* (or see mob or map)
mope,*,ed,ping,pingly,pish,pishness, *TO BE DISINTERESTED DUE TO SADNESS OR BEING BORED, TO HAVE LOW SPIRITS* (or see mop)
moped, mop(ped) /mope(d)
mopt, mop(ped) /mope(d)
mor, mar /more /moor

moral,*,lly,lism,list,listic,lize,lization,lizer, lizingly, *ABILITY TO JUDGE/BEHAVE RIGHT FROM WRONG* (or see morale or morel)
morale,lity,lities, *CONDITION OR STATE OF ONE'S ABILITY TO JUDGE/ACT ON THOSE JUDGEMENTS* (or see mural/ moral/ morel)
moralestic, moral(istic)
moraly, moral(ly)
moratorium,*, ry, *A PURPOSELY IMPOSED DELAY FOR AN UNDETERMINED AMOUNT OF TIME*
morbed, morbid
morbedly, morbid(ly)
morbel, marble
morbet, morbid
morbid,dly,dness,dity, *AKIN TO DEATH/DARKNESS*
morbidety, morbid(ity)
morbil, marble
morbit, morbid
morbul, marble
morch, march /March
morchoery, mortuary
morchuery, mortuary
mordar, mortar
mordel, mortal
mordir, mortar
mordul, mortal
morduly, mortal(ly)
mordur, mortar
more,*, *OF A GREATER NUMBER BY COMPARISON TO, GREATER* (or see moor)
morege, moor(age)
morel,*, *EDIBLE MUSHROOM* (or see moral/morale)
morelise, moral(ize)
morelistic, moral(istic)
mores, *SOCIAL ACCEPTANCE*
moretoreum, moratorium
morgage, mortgage
morge, morgue
morgedge, mortgage

morgeje, mortgage
morgen, margin
morgerin, margarine
morgije, mortgage
morgue,*, *PLACE WHERE BODIES WITHOUT SPIRITS ARE TEMPORARILY HELD*
morige, moor(age)
moril, moral /morel
morily, moral(ly)
moritoreum, moratorium
morjaren, margarine
mork, morgue
morn, mourn /morning
mornen, morning /mourn(ing)
morneng, mourn(ing) /morning
mornful, mourn(ful)
mornin, morning /mourn(ing)
morning,*, *MORN, FIRST PART OF THE DAY BEFORE 12 NOON (or see mourn(ing))*
morose,ly,eness,sity, *GLOOMY OR DARK THOUGHTS, IDEAS, BEHAVIOR*
morotoreum, moratorium
morph, morpho, *PREFIX INDICATING "SHAPE/FORM/STRUCTURE" MOST OFTEN MODIFIES THE WORD*
mors, mores
morshuery, mortuary
mortal,*,lly,lity,lities, *RELATED TO DEATH/KILLING/ DYING*
mortaledy, mortal(ity)
mortalidy, mortal(ity)
mortar,*, *MIXTURE USED FOR JOINTS TO HOLD BRICK, VESSEL SHAPE WITH A PESTLE*
mortel, mortal
morter, mortar
mortgage,*,ed,ging,ger,gor, *TITLE/DEED OF PROPERTY HELD BY SOMEONE WHICH REQUIRES MONEY TO OWN/HAVE*
mortil, mortal
mortir, mortar

mortuary,ries, *A FUNERAL HOME*
mortul, mortal
mortur, mortar
morul, moral
morulesm, moral(ism)
morulestic, moral(istic)
morulise, moral(ize)
moruly, moral(ly)
mos, moss or most
mosaic,*,cally,cist, *MANY PIECES PLACED TOGETHER TO FORM A PICTURE*
mosayic, mosaic
mosdereus, mysterious
mosdly, most(ly)
mose, moose /mousse
moseik, mosaic
mosektimy, mastectomy
moshen, motion
moshun, motion
mosk, mosque
moskeet, mesquite
mosketo, mosquito
moskewlur, muscle(cular)
mosly, most(ly)
mosoleum, mausoleum
mosoose, masseuse
mosque,*, *A BUILDING WHERE MUSLIMS PRAY*
mosquito,oes,oey, *AN INSECT WHO SEEKS BLOOD*
mosquler, muscle(cular)
moss,sy,sier,siest, *A PLANT GROWTH*
most,tly, *PAST TENSE OF MORE, THE GREATEST AMOUNT IN COMPARISON TO ANOTHER AMOUNT*
mostache, mustache /moustache
mostash, mustache /moustache
mostectemy, mastectomy
moster, monster
mostereus, mysterious
mostique, mystique
mosuleum, mausoleum

mosuse, masseuse
motafikashen, modify(fication)
motavashen, motive(vation)
motchewlate, modulate
motchulashen, modulate(tion)
motchulate, modulate
mote, *SPECK, PARTICLE (or see moat or mode)*
moteef, motif
motef, motif /motive
motel,*, *LODGING WHERE YOU CAN PARK YOUR VEHICLE NEAR THE DOOR (or see mottle)*
moter, motor
moterashen, moderate(tion)
moteret, moderate
motereul, material
moterise, motor(ize)
motern, modern
moternul, maternal
motevashen, motive(vation)
moth,*, *A NOCTURNAL INSECT*
mother,*,red,ring,rly,rlessness, *ONE WHO HAS GIVEN BIRTH, BACTERIAL COATING ON FERMENTING LIQUIDS, ORIGINATOR OF LIFE*
motif, *RECURRING THEME IN VISUAL PRESENTATION (or see motive)*
motil, model /mottle
motion,*,nal,ned,ning,nless,nlessness, *ACTIVITY, MOVEMENT*
motir, motor
motirn, modern
motivashen, motive(vation)
motive,*,vate,vates,vated,vating,vation, vational,vatative, *ENCOURAGED TO PERFORM ALONG IN A PLANNED DIRECTION (or see motif)*
motle, mottle /model
motled, mottle(d) /model(ed)
moto, motto
motor,*,red,ring,rist,rization,rize,rized,rizing, *AN ENGINE/DEVICE USED TO CREATE MOTION*

mottle,ed,er,ling, SPLOTCHY IN COLOR, PATCHES OF IRREGULAR SHAPES

motto,*, A CONCISE DESCRIPTION OF PRINCIPLE OR PURPOSE

motul, model /mottle
motur, motor
moturashen, moderate(tion)
moturet, moderate
moturise, motor(ize)
moturn, modern
moturnize, modern(ize)
motuv, motive
motuvashen, motive(vation)
motuvate, motive(vate)
moucus, mucous

mound,*,ded,ding, A SMALL HILL/PILE/ HEAP (or see mount)

mount,*,ted,ting, TO SIT ATOP OF, SHORT FOR MOUNTAIN, AFFIX SOMETHING, GET ON TOP OF

mountain,*,neer,nous,nously,nousness, GREAT HILLS OF ORGANIC MATTER, LARGE JUTTING EXTRUSIONS OF EARTH

mounteneer, mountain(eer)
mountin, mountain

mourn,*,ned,ning,ningly,nfully,ner, nfulness, EMOTIONALLY EXPERIENCE LOSS OF SOMETHING (or see morning)

mouse,er,sing,ey, SMALL RODENT (or see moose or mousse)

mousse, DESSERT (or see mouse or moose)

moustache, FACIAL HAIR GROWING ABOVE THE LIP (also spelled mustache)

moutenus, mountain(ous)

mouth,*,hed,hing,her,hful,hfuls,hy, ORIFICE ON THE FACE WHICH MAKES SOUNDS/INGESTS

mov, mauve /move

move,*,ed,ving,vingly,er,vable,vableness, vably,vability,vless,elessly,eless, elessness, ement, TO RELOCATE/CHANGE FROM ONE PLACE/ LOCATION TO ANOTHER

movie,*, PICTURES IN MOTION

movment, move(ment)

mow,*,wed,wing, TO CUT WITH A TOOL OR MACHINE, TO CUT GREAT QUANTITIES AT A TIME

mownd, mound
mownt, mound /mount
mownten, mountain
mowten, mountain
mowteneer, mountain(eer)
mowth, mouth
mowtin, mountain
mowtinus, mountain(ous)

moxie, COURAGE, ASSERTIVE

moxy, moxie
moyeast, moist
moyster, moist(ure)
moysturize, moist(urize)
mozaek, mosaic
mozayic, mosaic
mozed, most
mozly, most(ly)
mozoleum, mausoleum
mozt, most
mozuleim, mausoleum
mt, empty
mubiledy, mobile(lity)
mubility, mobile(lity)
mucaw, macaw

much, AMOUNT OF SOMETHING, SIZEABLE QUANTITY

muchene, machine
muchenist, machine(st)
muchety, machete
muchual, mutual
muchure, mature

muchuredy, mature(rity)
muchurle, mature(ly)
muchyual, mutual

mucus,osity,mucous, SLIPPERY SECRETED SUBSTANCE FOR PROTECTION OF SKIN

mud,dded,dding,ddy, DIRT MIXED WITH WATER (or see mutt)

mudalate, mutilate

muddle,*,ed,ling, TO CONFUSE, MAKE UNCLEAR, MAKE A MESS, CREATE DISORDER

muddy,ddies,ddier,ddiest,ddying,ddily,ddiness, WATER MIXED WITH DIRT

mude, mood/ mute/ muddy
mudel, muddle
mudelate, mutilate
muden, mutton
mudeness, mood(iness)
muder, mutter
mudereul, material
mudereulise, materialize
mudernol, maternal
mudiest, muddy(diest)
mudil, muddle
mudilate, mutilate
mudir, mutter
mudle, muddle
mudon, mutton
mudul, muddle
mudur, mutter
mudy, muddy /mood(y)
mudyest, muddy(diest)
muer, moor
muerege, moor(age)
muf, move /muff
mufan, muffin /move(ving)
mufee, movie
mufen, muffin /move(ving)
muffin, muffin

muffin,*, BAKED DESSERT

muffler,*, USED TO KEEP LOUD NOISES QUIET
mufin, muffin
mufler, muffler
mufment, move(ment)
mufuble, move(vable)
mug,*,gged,gging,gger,ggy, DRINKING VESSEL, SOMEONE WHO ASSAULTS WITH INTENT TO ROB, A FACE, WARM/DAMP/STILL AIR
mugd, mug(gged)
muge, muggy
mugeness, muggy(giness)
mugestekal, majesty(tical)
mugestik, majesty(tic)
muggie, muggy
muggy,ggily,gginess, WARM AND HUMID
mugi, muggy
mugishen, magic(ian)
mugority, major(ity)
mugy, muggy
mugynes, muggy(giness)
muir, moor
mujestical, majesty(tical)
mujishen, magic(ian)
mukaw, macaw
mukus, mucus
mul, mull /mule
mulado, mulato
mularea, malaria
mularky, malarkey
mulasis, molasses
mulato,oes, MIXTURE OF RACES OR BREEDS
mulch,hes,hed,hing, TO TILL UP GROUND, ADD ORGANIC MATERIAL TO SOIL
muldaplekashen, multiplication
muldaplikation, multiplication
muldiply, multiply
mule,*,lish, HYBRID MAMMAL/PLANT, STUBBORN PERSON, SHOE WITHOUT A BACK (or see mull)
mulekuler, molecular

mulest, molest
mulevolens, malevolence
mulevolent, malevolent
mulignant, malignant
mulk, milk
mull,*, A FABRIC, TO STUDY/THINK ABOUT, MUSLIN, HUMUS (or see mule)
multaplekashen, multiplication
multaply, multiply
multch, mulch
multeply, multiply
multi, mult, PREFIX INDICATING "MUCH/ MANY" MOST OFTEN MODIFIES THE WORD
multiplekashen, multiplication
multiplication,tive,tively, THE ACT OF WORKING NUMBERS TIMES NUMBERS
multiply,lied,lying,lier,licity, TO INCREASE NUMBERS BY REPRODUCTION, ADDING NUMBERS TIMES NUMBERS, MATH
mumble,*,ed,ling,er,lingly, TO SPEAK WITHOUT ANNUNCIATION OR UNINTELLIGIBLY, SPEAKING WITHOUT WORDS BEING UNDERSTOOD
mumbul, mumble
mume, mummy
mummy,mmies,mmify,mmification, A DRIED UP CORPSE, WORD FOR MOM IN ENGLAND
mumy, mummy
mumps, A VIRUS WHICH ATTACKS THE THROAT
munarkikul, monarch(ical)
munarky, monarch(y)
mundae, Monday
mundane,ely, ROUTINE
munday, Monday
mune, moon
munee, money
munepulate, manipulate
munesipality, municipal(ity)
munesipul, municipal

municipal,*,lity,lities,lly,lize,lization, TOWN/CITY GOVERNED BY ITS OWN LAWS
munie, money
munila, manila
munipulate, manipulate
munisepal, municipal
munisepality, municipal(ity)
munisipal, municipal
munk, monk
munkee, monkey
munky, monkey
munodnes, monotony(nous)
munogamy, monogamy
munogimy, monogamy
munokside, monoxide
munokuler, monocular
munopuly, monopoly
munorkeul, monarch(ial)
munotny, monotony
munotunus, monotony(nous)
munoxide, monoxide
munsoon, monsoon
munstrocity, monstrocity
munstrosedy, monstrocity
munsune, monsoon
munth, month
munthly, month(ly)
munure, manure
munuver, maneuver
muny, money
muraculus, miracle(culous)
muraje, mirage
murakulus, miracle(culous)
mural,*, LARGE PAINTING APPLIED ONTO A WALL
muraledy, morale(lity)
murality, morale(lity)
murange, meringue
murchandise, merchandise
murchant, merchant

murder,*,red,ring,rer,rous,rousness, TO KILL SOMEONE UNLAWFULLY
murdir, murder
murdur, murder
murege, moor(age)
murel, mural
murena, marina
murene, marine
murge, merge
murgur, merge(r)
muridean, meridian
muril, mural
murina, marina
murine, marine
murje, merge
murk, murky
murkanteel, mercantile
murkery, mercury
murky,kily,kiness, DARK, SILTY OR THICK LIQUID/ AIR, GLOOMY
murlin, merlin
murmade, mermaid
murmer, murmur
murmir, murmur
murmur,*,rer,ring,ringly,rous, A LOW STEADY STREAM OF SOUND, MUFFLED SOUND
muroge, mirage
muroje, mirage
murose, morose
mursenary, mercenary
mursinary, mercenary
mursy, mercy
mursyful, mercy(ciful)
murul, mural
musal, mussel/ muscle/ muzzle
muscle,*,ed,ling,cular,cularity,cularly, THICK TISSUE WHICH MOVES BONES (or see mussel or muzzle)
musdach, moustache

musdake, mistake
musdakin, mistaken
musderd, mustard
musdurd, mustard
muse,*,ed,sing,er,singly, WHAT INSPIRES AN ARTIST, A DEEP THINK/CONTEMPLATION (or see moose/ mouse/ mousse)
musec, music
musecal, music(al)
musecian, musician
musecul, music(al)
musek, music
musektome, mastectomy
musekul, music(al)
musel, mussel/ muscle/ muzzle
museshen, musician
museum,*, A STRUCTURE FOR EXHIBITS OF INTERESTING ITEMS
mushedy, machete
mushene, machine
mushenest, machine(st)
mushete, machete
mushinary, machine(ry)
mushroom,*,med,ming, FUNGI WITH BELL-SHAPED HEAD ON A STEM
mushrum, mushroom
mushual, mutual
music,cal,cally,cality,lness, TONES, SOUNDS PLAYED IN HARMONY ON INSTRUMENTS, PLEASING SOUND TO EARS
musician,*,nly,nship, PROFESSIONALLY INVOLVED IN CREATING MUSIC
musik, music
musil, mussel/ muscle/ muzzle
musishen, musician
muskedo, mosquito
musket, mesquite
muskera, mascara
musketo, mosquito

muskuler, muscle(cular)
musle, mussel/ muscle/ muzzle
muslen, muslin
muslin,*, MEDIUM WEIGHT COTTON CLOTH
musoge, massage
musoje, massage
musol, muscle/ mussel/ muzzle
musoose, masseuse
musquedo, mosquito
musquler, muscle(cular)
mussel,*, EDIBLE MARINE MOLLUSK WITH SHELL (or see muscle or muzzle)
mussle, mussel/ muscle/ muzzle
must, IT HAS TO BE, IMPERATIVE
mustache,*, HAIR ON TOP OF THE UPPER LIP ON ADULT MALES (also spelled moustache)
mustake, mistake
mustakin, mistaken
mustang,*, WILD HORSES
mustard, AN HERB USED AS A CONDIMENT
muster,*,red,ring, TO GATHER/COLLECT/ASSEMBLE
musterd, mustard
mustereus, mysterious
mustir, muster
mustird, mustard
mustireus, mysterious
musturd, mustard
musuese, masseuse
musul, muscle /mussel /muzzle
mususe, masseuse
mut, mutt /mute /mud
mutalate, mutilate
mutashen, mutation
mutate,*,ed,ting,mutative,mutation,mutant, ENDURED CHROMOSOME ALTERATION
mutch, much
mutchuel, mutual
mute,*,ed,ting,ely,eness,tism, NO SPEECH, UNABLE TO SPEAK (or see mutt or moot)

mutelate, mutilate
muten, mutton /mutant
mutent, mutant
muteny, mutiny
muter, mutter
mutereolise, materialize
mutereul, material
muternedy, maternity
muternol, maternal
muternulistek, maternal(istic)
muther, mother
muthor, mother
mutil, muddle
mutilashen, mutilate(tation)
mutilate,*,ed,ting,tion,tor, *TO SHRED, RIP, TEAR BEYOND RECOGNITION*
mutin, mutton
mutireul, material
mutirnil, maternal
mutle, muddle
muton, mutton
mutony, mutiny
mutt,*, *MIXED BREED (or see mute)*
mutter,*,red,ring,ringly, *TO MURMUR, SPEAK LOW AND UNINTELLIGIBLY, UNDECIPHERABLE SPEECH*
mutton,*, *SHEEP MEAT*
mutual,*,lly,lism,list,listic,lity,lize,lization, *CONSENT TO SHARE/AGREE*
mutul, muddle
mutulashen, mutilate(tation)
mutune, mutiny
mutur, mutter
muture, mature /mutter
muty, muddy /mood(y)
muve, move

muvee, movie
muvuble, move(vable)
muzdake, mistake
muzeim, museum
muzektame, mastectomy
muzekul, music(al)
muzel, muzzle
muzeshen, musician
muzeum, museum
muzik, music
muzikul, music(al)
muzishen, musician
muzlen, muslin
muzlin, muslin
muzt, must
muztake, mistake
muzter, muster
muztereus, mysterious
muzul, muzzle
muzzle,*,er, *DEVICE TO RESTRAIN ANIMALS FROM BITING (or see muscle)*
my, *PREFIX INDICATING "MUSCLE" MOST OFTEN MODIFIES THE WORD*
my, *MYSELF, DENOTES OWNERSHIP*
myc, *PREFIX INDICATING "FUNGUS" MOST OFTEN MODIFIES THE WORD*
mycrascope, microscope
mycrobeul, microbe(bial)
mycron, micron
mycrophone, microphone
myder, miter
mydokondrea, mitochondria
mydukondrea, mitochondria
mygrane, migraine
mygrashen, migrate(tion)
mygrate, migrate
mygratory, migrate(tory)
mykrafone, microphone
mykraskope, microscope

mykro, micro
mykrobe, microbe
mykrofone, microphone
mykrometer, micrometer
mykron, micron
mykrowave, microwave
myld, mild
myluge, mile(age)
myme, mime
mynd, mind / mend
myne, mine
myreod, myriad
myriad, *MANY, MORE THAN TEN THOUSAND*
mysdacism, mystic(icism)
mystecal, mystic(cal)
mysteek, mystique
mystereus, mysterious
mysterious,sly,sness, *OF THE UNKNOWN, NOT ENOUGH FACTS TO UNDERSTAND*
mystery,ries, *NOT ENOUGH FACTS TO UNDERSTAND, OF THE UNKNOWN*
mystic,*,cal,cally,lity,lness,cism,ification, *A MYSTERY, THE UNSEEN/UNEXPLAINED*
mystify,fies,fied,fying,fyingly,fication, *PURPOSELY MISLEAD/BE VAGUE*
mystirious, mysterious
mystukul, mystic(cal)
mystury, mystery
mysulf, my(self)
myt, mitt /mite /might
myter, miter
myth,*,hic,hical,hical,hically,hicize,hicizer, *A STORY SURVIVING HISTORY THAT ISN'T CURRENTLY SUPPORTED BY FACT*
mythologic,cal,cally,ist,ger,ize,ized,izing, *OF MYTHS, LEGENDS, FOLKLORE*
mythology,gies, *OF THE UNKNOWN, ATTEMPT TO EXPLAIN THE UNKNOWN*
mytochondrea, mitochondria

mytokondrea , mitochondria

N, SYMBOL FOR NITROGEN, AN INDEFINITE NUMBER IN MATH
nab,*,bbed,bbing,bber, TO GRAB/SEIZE/CATCH UNEXPECTEDLY
naber, neighbor
naberhood, neighbor(hood)
nabir, neighbor
nabken, napkin
nabkin, napkin
nabor, neighbor
naborhud, neighbor(hood)
nabt, nab(bed) / nap(ped)
nabur, neighbor
naburhood, neighbor(hood)
nacessity, necessity
nach, notch
nacheirpath, naturopath
nachen, nation
nachenaluty, nation(ality)
nachenul, nation(al)
nacher, nature
nacheralist, natural(ist)
nacheropethy, naturopath(y)
nacherul, natural
nacheruly, natural(ly)
naches, nauseous
nachinal, nation(al)
nachir, nature
nachon, nation
nachrul, natural
nachur, nature
nachuril, natural
nachurily, natural(ly)

nachuropath, naturopath
nachuropathy, naturopath(y)
nachus, nauseous
nadef, native
nadefly, native(ly)
nadeve, native
nadical, nautical
nadilus, nautilus
nadive, native
naduf, native
nady, naughty /knot(ty)
naefe, naive
naem, name
naeve, naive
naevet, naive(te)
naevly, naive(ly)
nafee, navy
nafegashen, navigate(tion)
nafegubul, navigable
nafel, naval/ navel/ novel
nafigate, navigate
nafigubul, navigable
nafil, naval/ navel/ novel
nafol, naval/ navel/ novel
nafugate, navigate
nafuguble, navigable
naful, naval/ navel/ novel
nafulty, novelty
nafy, navy
nag,*,gged,gging,ggingly, AN ACT PERFORMED REPEATEDLY, IRRITATED BY REPETITION, YOUNG/OLD HORSE
naglekt, neglect
nagosheate, negotiate
nagoshubul, negotiable
nagotiate, negotiate
nagutev, negative
naife, naive
naighbor, neighbor

nail,*,led,ling,ler, SLENDER STEEL WITH POINT/HEAD FOR HAMMERING, PROTECTIVE GROWTH ON FINGERS/TOES
naim, name
naive,ely,eness,ete,ety, TO LACK INFORMATION, CLUELESS
nak, knack
naked,dly,dness, WITHOUT CLOTHES OR COVERING
naket, naked
nakit, naked
nale, nail
nalege, knowledge
namadik, pneumatic / nomad(ic)
name,*,ed,ming,ely,eless,elessly,elessness, LEGAL/PROPER TITLE, WHAT TO CALL SOMETHING/ SOMEONE
namles, name(less)
namly, name(ly)
nane, nanny
nanny,nies, SOMEONE WHO IS HIRED BY A FAMILY TO TAKE CARE OF THE CHILDREN, A FEMALE GOAT
nano, PREFIX INDICATING "ONE BILLIONTH/EXTREMELY SMALL" MOST OFTEN MODIFIES THE WORD
nany, nanny
nap,*,pped,pping,pper, SLEEP BRIEFLY, PILE/CLOTH/ SUBSTANCE/FUZZ (or see knap or nape)
nape, BACK OF NECK(or see nap/knap/knap(ppy))
naped, nab(bed) / nap(ped)
napken, napkin
napkin,*, CLOTH OR PAPER USED AT MEALTIME FOR FACE AND HANDS
nappy, knappy
napt, nab(bed) /nap(ped)
narashen, narrate(tion)
narate, narrate
narative, narrate(tive)
narator, narrate(tor)
narcisim, narcissism
narcissism,st,stic,stically, EXCESSIVE SELF-LOVE

narcistik, narcissism(stic)
narco, PREFIX INDICATING "NARCOTIC/STUPOR/SLEEP" MOST OFTEN MODIFIES THE WORD
narcotic,*,cally,ize,ization, A CHEMICAL WHICH ALTERS BODY METABOLISM
nare, narry
narely, narrow(ly)
narkotek, narcotic
naro, narrow
naroly, narrow(ly)
narowd, narrow(ed)
narrate,*,ed,ting,tion,tional,tive,tively,tor, TO RECOUNT/TELL/RELATE A STORY
narrow,*,wed,wing,wly,wness, NOT AS WIDE AS USUAL/NORMAL, THIN STRIP, MAKE SMALLER
narsesm, narcissism
narsestic, narcissism(stic)
narsistic, narcissism(stic)
narsizm, narcissism
nary, NEVER, NOT
nasal,lity,lism,lly,lize,lization, INVOLVING THE NOSE AND ITS PASSAGEWAYS
nasdeor, nasty(tier)
nasdursheum, nasturtium
nasdy, nasty
nasel, nasal
nasely, nasal(ly)
nasesidy, necessity
nasesitate, necessitate
nashen, nation
nashenaledy, nation(ality)
nashenul, nation(al)
nashinality, nation(ality)
nashonul, nation(al)
nashunaludy, nation(ality)
nashuropathy, naturopath(y)
nasius, nauseous
nastee, nasty
nastershum, nasturtium
nasturtium,*, A FLOWERING PLANT

nasty,tier,tiest,tily, UNDESIRABLE, OBJECTIONABLE, UNACCEPTABLE, NOT PROPER
nat, not /naught /knot /gnat
natcheroputhy, naturopath(y)
natcherul, natural
natchural, natural
natchurely, natural(ly)
natecal, nautical
natef, native
nateuropath, naturopath
nateve, native
natical, nautical
natif, native
natilis, nautilus
nation,*,nal,nally,nalize,nalization,nhood,nless, nalism,nalist,nality,nalities,nalizer, BELONGS DEVOTED/LOYAL TO A PEOPLE/COUNTRY
natiunality, nation(ality)
native,*, ely,eness,vism,vist,vistic,vity,vities, BORN/BELONG TO CERTAIN LAND OR AREA, RACE OF PEOPLES, NOT AN IMMIGRANT
natoreus, notorious
natsher, nature
natsheropethy, naturopath(y)
natshur, nature
natuf, native
natufly, native(ly)
natural,*,lly,lness,lism,list,list,listic,listically, lize,lization,NOT REFINED/MODIFIED/ REARRANGED/CHANGED/MOLDED/MANIPULATED
naturapathy, naturopath(y)
nature,*, BASIC ESSENCE OF THINGS, CHARACTER, COMBINATION OF QUALITIES
naturel, natural
naturilist, natural(ist)
naturopath,*,hy,hic, TREATS ILLNES/INJURIES WITH NATURAL REMEDIES
natuv, native
nau, gnaw/ know/ now

naude, naughty /knot(ty)
naudical, nautical
nauev, naive
naught, NOTHING, NOT, DON'T NEED ANYTHING (or see not or knot)
naughty,tier,tiest,tily,tiness, IMPROPER BEHAVIOR, MISCHIEVOUS (or see knot(ty))
naumune, nominee
nausdalgea, nostalgia
nausdalgik, nostalgic
nausdrel, nostril
nausea,ate,ting,tingly, FEELING ILL IN STOMACH
nauseous,sly,sness, STOMACH FEELING ILL
naushus, nauseous
nausious, nauseous
naustalgea, nostalgia
naustalgik, nostalgic
naustrel, nostril
naut, not /naught /knot
nautch, notch
nautical,ally, OCEAN NAVIGATION
nautilus,ses,li, SPIRAL OCEAN SHELL
nauves, novice
nauvulest, novel(ist)
nauvulte, novelty
navagate, navigate
navagation, navigate(tion)
naval, SHIPS, OF A NAVY (or see navel or novel)
navee, navy
navegable, navigable
navegashen, navigate(tion)
navegate, navigate
navegation, navigate(tion)
navel,*, SPOT ON THE BELLY WHERE THE UMBILICAL CORD WAS SEVERED, MIDDLE OR CENTRAL PLACE (or see naval or novel)
navember, November
navigable,bility,eness,ly,ABLE TO MANEUVER/GUIDE

navigate,*,ed,ting,tion,tional,tion,tionally,tor, *STEER OR MANEUVER, ONE WHO STEERS/ MANEUVERS/GUIDES*
navil, naval/ navel/ novel
navimber, November
navol, naval/ navel/ novel
navugashen, navigate(tion)
navugate, navigate
navugation, navigate(tion)
navugable, navigable
navul, naval/ navel/ novel
navuldy, novelty
navy,vies, *COLLECTION OF SHIPS BELONGING TO A NATION*
naw, gnaw /now
nawleg, knowlege
nawstrel, nostril
nayber, neighbor
nazdeur, nasty(tier)
nazdursheum, nasturtium
nazdy, nasty
nazel, nasal
nazely, nasal(ly)
nazil, nasal
nazily, nasal(ly)
naztersheum, nasturtium
nazty, nasty
near,*,rer,rest,rly,rness, *CLOSE TO*
neat,*,ter,tly,tness, *ORDERLY/ORGANIZED, APPEALING* (or see need/ knead/ knee(d))
nebal, nibble
neber, neighbor
nebir, neighbor
neble, nibble
nebor, neighbor
nebul, nibble
nebur, neighbor
necasery, necessary
necatene, nicotine

neccesary, necessary
neccesitate, necessitate
neccesity, necessity
neccessary, necessary
necdur, nectar
nece, niece
necesary, necessary
necesitate, necessitate
necessary,rily,riness, *MUST BE/HAVE, REQUIRED*
necessatate, necessitate
necessitate,*,ed,ting,tion,tive, *REQUIRED, ESSENTIAL*
necessity,tous,tously,tousness, *REQUIRED, MUST HAVE*
neche, niche
nechel, nickel
necisary, necessary
neck,*,ked,king, *PART OF THE BODY BETWEEN HEAD AND SHOULDERS, PART OF THE SPINE*
necklace,*, *ORNAMENT/ADORNMENT FOR THE NECK*
necklajay, negligee
neckleshay, negligee
neclasha, negligee
necotine, nicotine
necramancer, necromancer
necrimancer, necromancer
necromancer,*,cy,ntic,ntically,*ENTITY/OCCURENCE WHICH REFLECTS OUR GREATEST FEAR, THE DARK/ UNAPPEALING SIDE OF OUR NATURE*
nectar,*, *SWEET JUICE OF A FLOWER*
nectarine,*, *CROSS BETWEEN PEACH/PLUM*
necterene, nectarine
nectir, nectar
nectirene, nectarine
nectur, nectar
necturene, nectarine
ned, need/ neat/ knead/ knee(d)
nede, need(y)
neded, need(ed)/ knead(ded)

nedel, needle /nettle
nedil, needle /nettle
nedle, needle /nettle
nedly, neat(ly)
nedul, needle /nettle
nedwurk, network
nedy, need(y)
nee, knee
need,*,ded,ding,diness,dy,dful,dfully,dfulness, dless, *REQUIRED, ESSENTIAL, MANDATORY* (or see knead/ knee(d)/ neat)
needle,*,ed,ling, *SLENDER METAL PIN WITH A SHARP POINT AT ONE END AND HOLE AT THE OTHER END, FOR SEWING* (or see nettle)
needly, neat(ly)
neel, kneel
neer, near
neerer, near(er)
neerest, near(est)
neerly, near(ly)
nees, niece /knee(s)
nefew, nephew
nefir, never
nefu, nephew
nefur, never
negative,*,ely,eness,vity,vism,vistic, *MINUS, SMALLER THAN THE EYE, IN THE RED, OPPOSITE OF POSITIVE, FILM UNPROCESSED*
negetiv, negative
neghbor, neighbor
neghborhood, neighboor(hood)
negitif, negative
negitive, negative
neglagay, negligee
neglagense, negligence
neglagent, negligence(nt)
neglagible, negligence(gible)
neglagint, negligence(nt)
neglaja, negligee

neglect,*,ted,ting,tful,tfully,tfulness,tor, *NOT BE RESPONSIBLE/TAKE CARE OF*
neglegable, negligence(gible)
neglegense, negligence
negligee,*, *WOMEN'S UNDERGARMENTS*
negligence,*,nt,ntly,gible,gibly,gibility, gibleness, *NOT TAKE CARE OF/BE RESPONSIBLE*
neglijay, negligee
neglijents, negligence
neglisha, negligee
neglugense, negligence
negodev, negative
negosheate, negotiate
negosheuble, negotiable
negoshubul, negotiable
negotef, negative
negotiable,bility, *ABLE TO COME TO AN AGREEMENT*
negotiate,*,ed,ting,tion,tor, *COME TO AN AGREEMENT BY COMMUNICATING*
negudev, negative
negutif, negative
negutive, negative
neibor, neighbor
neighbor,*,rly,rhood, *PEOPLE WHO DWELL NEAR YOU, THOSE WHO LIVE CLOSE TO YOU*
neither, *NOT ONE OR THE OTHER, NOT THIS ONE OR THAT ONE*
nek, neck
nekatene, nicotine
nekdur, nectar
nekil, nickel
neklagent, negligence(nt)
neklajense, negligence
neklasha, negligee
neklegent, negligence(nt)
nekles, necklace
neklesha, negligee
neklijent, negligence(nt)
neklis, necklace

neklisha, negligee
neklus, necklace
nekotene, nicotine
nekramanser, necromancer
nekrumanser, necromancer
nekst, next
nektarine, nectarine
nekter, nectar
nekturene, nectarine
nekul, nickel
nekzd, next
nel, nil /kneel
nemf, nymph
nemfomanea, nymphomania
nemonia, pneumonia
nemph, nymph
nemphomanea, nymphomania
neo, *PREFIX INDICATING "NEW" MOST OFTEN MODIFIES THE WORD*
nep, nip
nepd, nip(pped)
nepe, nip(ppy)
nephew,*, *RELATION BY BLOOD FAMILY*
nephu, nephew
nepil, nipple
nept, nip(pped)
nepul, nipple
nerador, narrrate(tor)
nerashen, narrate(tion)
nerate, narrate
neratek, neurotic
nerative, narrate(tive)
nerator, narrate(tor)
nercher, nurture
nere, near /nary
neresh, nourish
nereshen, narrate(tion)
nerf, nerve
nerfona, nirvana

nerfus, nervous
nerly, near(ly)
nero, narrow
nerodic, neurotic
neroly, narrow(ly)
neron, neuron
nerosis, neurosis
nerotic, neurotic
nerow, narrow
nerse, nurse
nervana, nirvana
nerve,*,eless, *SOFT TISSUE IN THE BODY WHICH RELATE BODY TO BRAIN BY ELECTRICAL IMPULSES, BODY'S FORM OF COMMUNICATION*
nervous,sly,sness, *UNGROUNDED, WORRIED, STRESSED, UNSURE, DOUBTFUL, FEARFUL*
nervus, nervous
nery, nary
nes, knee(s) neice
nesasary, necessary
nesdalgik, nostalgic
nesd, nest
nese, niece
nesesary, necessary
nesessitate, necessitate
nesesudy, necessity
nesil, nestle
nesisary, necessary
nesol, nestle
nesold, nestle(d)
nest,*,ted,ting,ter, *A BIRD'S HOME*
nestalgek, nostalgic
nestle,*,ed,ling,ler, *COZY/SNUGGLE UP AGAINST*
nestursheum, nasturtium
nesul, nestle
net,*,tted,tting,table,tlike, *A WEB, WEAVING OF SOMETHING, COLLECTION OF (or see neat/knit)*
netal, needle /nettle
nete, neat /need(y)

nethur, neither
netil, needle /nettle
netly, neat(ly)
netol, needle /nettle
netorius, notorius
netpiky, nitpick(y)
netsh, niche
nettle, AN HERB (or see needle)
netul, needle / nettle
network,*,ked,king, JOIN/CONNECT TOGETHER
network, network
nety, need(y)
neuder, neuter
neur, neuri, neuro, PREFIX INDICATING "NERVE"
    MOST OFTEN MODIFIES THE WORD
neurodic, neurotic
neuron, OF THE NERVOUS SYSTEM
neurosis, DISORDER OF NERVES/EMOTIONS
neurotic,cally,osis, DISORDER AFFECTING EMOTIONS
    AS IT RELATES TO THE NERVOUS SYSTEM
neuter,*,red,ring, A LIVING THING WITHOUT ABILITY
    TO REPRODUCE
neutral,lity,lly,lism,list,listic,lize, BETWEEN
    EXTREMES/OPPOSITES, IN THE MIDDLE
neutrino,*, TINY UNCHARGED PARTICLE
neutron,*, UNCHARGED PARTICLE IN ATOM
nevember, November
never, NOT EVER
nevimber, November
nevor, never
new,*, wer,west,wish,wly,wness, JUST CAME INTO
    BEING, JUST CREATED (or see knew)
newborn,*, JUST BORN
newcleur, nuclear
newdul, noodle
newdur, neuter
newkleus, nucleus
newlewed, newlywed
newlywed,*, COUPLES IN FIRST YEAR OF MARRIAGE

newmadik, pneumatic /nomad(ic)
newmaril, numeral
newmatek, pneumatic
newmerology, numerology
newmerus, numerous
newmonia, pneumonia
newmurader, numerator
newmurology, numerology
newmurus, numerous
newron, neuron
newsinse, nuisance
newspaper,*, PAPER WITH PRINTED TEXT WHICH
    REPORTS ON EVENTS
newter, neuter
newtral, neutral
newtreint, nutrient
newtreno, neutrino
newtril, neutral
newtrishen, nutrition
newtrishus, nutritious
newtrol, neutral
newtron, neutron
next, FOLLOWS AFTER, COMING UP
nezt, nest
nibble,*,ed,ling, TINY BITE/MORSEL TO EAT
nibul, nibble
nicatene, nicotine
nice,er,est,ety, KIND, THOUGHTFUL, CONSIDERATE,
    APPEALING, PLEASANT
nicesity, necessity
niche,*, A CORNER OF, A LITTLE PLACE CARVED/
    ETCHED OUT OF SOMETHING
nichel, nickel
nicity, nice(ty)
nickel,*,led, U.S. COIN
nicotine, A CHEMICAL SUBSTANCE NATURALLY FOUND
    IN TOBACCO
nid, night
niece,*, A RELATIVE BY BLOOD FAMILY

niese, niece
nif, knife
night,*,tly, THE DARK PART OF A 24 HOUR PERIOD,
    WITHOUT THE SUN (or see knight)
niglekt, neglect
niglekted, neglect(ed)
nigosheate, negotiate
nigosheuble, negotiable
nigotiate, negotiate
nigotiate, negotiate
nikatene, nicotine
nikel, nickel
nikotene, nicotine
niknak, knick knack
nikul, nickel
nikutene, nicotine
nil, NOTHING, NONE (or see kneel)
nilon, nylon
nimf, nymph
nimfomanea, nymphomania
nimonea, pneumonia
nimph, nymph
nimphomania, nymphomania
nindeith, nine(tieth)
nindes, nine(ties)
nindy, nine(ty)
nine,*, er,ety,eties,nth,nteenth,ntieth, ENGLISH
    NUMBER BETWEEN EIGHT AND TEN
ninfomaneac, nymphomania(c)
ninphomania, nymphomania
nintenth, nine(teenth)
ninthe, nine(nth)
ninty, nine(ty)
nintys, nine(ties)
nip,*,pped,pping,pper,ppy, TAKE A LITTLE BITE AT,
    TAKE IN JUST A LITTLE
niped, nip(pped)
niple, nipple

nipple,*, FORMED TIP EXTRUSIONS ON THE CHEST CAVITY, TIP WITH ORIFICE
nipul, nipple
nipy, nip(ppy)
nircher, nurture
nireshment, nourish(ment)
nirfona, nirvana
nirfus, nervous
niron, neuron
nirosis, neurosis
nirse, nurse
nirvana, A STATE OF BLISS WHERE ONE IS TRANSFORMED FROM THE MATERIAL PLANE
nirves, nervous /nerve(s)
nirvus, nervous
nise, nice
nisedy, nice(ty)
niser, nice(r)
nisesity, necessity
nisest, nice(st)
nistalgek, nostalgic
nit,*, PARASITIC LARVAE (or see night /knit /net)
nitch, niche
nite, night /knight /knit
nited, knit(tted) /knight(ed)
nitoreus, notorius
nitpeky, nitpick(y)
nitpick,*,ky, TO BE OVERLY CONCERNED ABOUT MINUTE DETAILS
nitpiky, nitpick(y)
nitr,*, PREFIX INDICATING "NITROGEN" MOST OFTEN MODIFIES THE WORD
nitragen, nitrogen
nitral, nitrile
nitregen, nitrogen
nitrel, nitrile
nitrigen, nitrogen
nitrile, CHEMICAL CLASSIFICATION

nitro,*, PREFIX INDICATING "NITROGEN" MOST OFTEN MODIFIES THE WORD
nitrogen, A GAS
nitrul, nitrile
nitsh, niche
no, NEGATORY (or see know)
nob,*,bby, BUMPS/EXTRUSIONS (or see knob)
nobel, noble
nobelity, nobility
nobil, noble
nobility,ties, SUPERIOR, REPUTABLE, OF QUALITY
noble,*, er,est,esse, OF RANK/REPUTATION, CHEMICALLY INERT
nobody, NO BODY, NO PERSON
noboty, nobody
nobul, noble
noc, nock/ knock/ nook
noch, notch
nochin, notion
nochus, nauseous
nock,*,ked,king, SETTING AN ARROW INTO PLACE ON BOW STRING, PART OF ARROW(or see knock)
noct, nocti, PREFIX INDICATING "NIGHT" MOST OFTEN MODIFIES THE WORD
nocturnal,lity,lly,ne, ACTIVE AT NIGHT
nod,*,dded,dding, AN UP AND DOWN HEAD MOVEMENT (or see not or node)
nodafekashen, notify(fication)
nodch, notch
node,dal,dality, STUMP/BULGE (MANY DEFINITIONS PLEASE SEE STANDARD DICTIONARY) (or see note)
nodefication, notify(fication)
nodefy, notify
nodekul, nautical
nodelus, nautilus
noderize, notarize
nodes, notice /node(s)
nodical, nautical

nodier, naughty(tier)
nodiest, naughty(tiest)
nodify, notify
nodikal, nautical
nodirize, notarize
nodis, notice
nodle, noodle
nodufikashen, notify(fication)
nodufy, notify
nodukul, nautical
nodurise, notarize
nodus, notice
nody, naughty /knot(ty)
noefe, naive
noese, noise/ noise(sy)/ nosey
noeve, naive
noevet, naive(te)
nofa, nova
nofel, novel
nofelty, novelty
nofember, November
nofil, novel
nofilty, novelty
nofu, nova
nogiekted, neglect(ed)
noise,*,eless,elessly,elessness,sy,sily,siness, DISHARMONIC SOUND, AN ALARMING SOUND, OFFENSIVE SOUND
noisey, noise(y)
nok, nock / knock /nook
nokshus, noxious
nokternul, nocturnal
nokturnal, nocturnal
nol, knoll / null
nole, knoll
nolech, knowledge
noleg, knowledge
nolige, knowledge
noll, knoll

nom, gnome
nomad,*,dic,dically,dism, A WANDERER, WITHOUT A PERMANENT HOME (or see pneumatic)
nomadek, pneumatic /nomad(ic)
nomanaded, nominate(d)
nomanate, nominate
nomanee, nominee
'nomat, nomad
nomatic, nomad(ic) /pneumatic
nomenashen, nominate(tion)
nomenate, nominate
nomene, nominee
nominate,*,ted,ting,tion,tive,tor, TO SELECT PEOPLE WHO WILL BE VOTED FOR IN ELECTION
nominee,*, SOMEONE SELECTED TO BE VOTED FOR, ONE WHOM IS SELECTED FOR ELECTION
nomunashin, nominate(tion)
nomunate, nominate
nomunee, nominee
non, PREFIX INDICATING "NOT" MOST OFTEN MODIFIES THE WORD (or see know(n) or none)
noncense, nonsense
nonchalant,tly,nce, CASUAL, UNCONCERNED
nonchelot, nonchalant
nonchilont, nonchalant
nonchulot, nonchalant
none, WITHOUT ANY, ABSENT FROM (or see nu/ noun/know(n))
nonfiction,nal, FACTUAL
nonsense,sical,sically,sicalness, ABSURB, GOOFY, NOT POSSIBLE, IRRATIONAL
nonserts, nonsense
nonshelont, nonsense
nonshulot, nonsense
nonsinse, nonsense
noo, new /knew
noodle,*, PASTA
noodul, noodle
nook,*, A CORNER/CREVICE/RECESSED AREA

noon, 12 O'CLOCK P.M. (or see nun)
noos, noose /new(s)
noose, SLIP-KNOT ROPE WITH A LOOPED END FOR HOLDING SOMETHING (or see new(s))
noozpaper, newspaper
nop, nob/ knob/ nope
nope, NO
norishment, nourish(ment)
nor, ANOTHER WORD FOR "NEITHER"
norm,*, SLANG FOR WHAT'S NORMAL
normal,lly,lity,lcy,lize(d),lizing,lization, MIDDLE OF THE ROAD BEHAVIOR/THOUGHT/ACTION, IN-BETWEEN, AVERAGE
normul, normal
normuly, normal(lly)
north,*,hen,hener,hern,hernmost,her,herly, herlies,herliness, ONE OF FOUR COMPASS/ MAGNETIC DIRECTIONS
northirn, north(ern)
northurly, north(erly)
nos, nose /know(s)
nosdalgek, nostalgic
nosdalgia, nostalgia
nostrel, nostril
nosdrul, nostril
nose,*,ed,sing,eless, PROBOSCUS, FACIAL FEATURE REQUIRED FOR SMELLING AND BREATHING (or see know(s))
nosel, nozzle
noseus, nauseous
noshen, notion
noshes, nauseous
noshus, nauseous
nosil, nozzle
nosle, nozzle
nost, nose(d)
nostalgea, nostalgia
nostalgia,ic,cally, REMINISCE/REFER TO THE PAST

nostalgic,cally, REMINISCE/REFER TO THE PAST
nostrel, nostril
nostril,*, ORIFICES ON NOSE WHICH EMPLOYS AIR MOVEMENT
nostrul, nostril
nosul, nozzle
nosy,sier,siest,sily,siness, FOLLOW THE NOSE, TO PRY/SNOOP AROUND OTHERS BUSINESS
not, THIS ONE OR THAT ONE, NO (or see note /knot/ naught)
notary,ries,rized,rizing,rization, HAVE OFFICIAL RECOGNIZE A SIGNATURE
notch,hes,hed,hing, TO CUT/KNOCK OUT A WEDGE IN SOMETHING, TO CARVE OUT OF
note,*,ed,ting, WRITE TEXT ON PAPER, TAKE A MENTAL NOTE, OBSERVE AND REMEMBER (or see node /knot /naught)
notee, naughty /knot(ty)
notefication, notify(fication)
notefikashen, notify(fication)
notefy, notify
notekul, nautical
notelus, nautilus
noterize, notarize
notes, notice /note(s)
notheng, nothing
nothing, NOT A THING
notice,*,ed,cing, TO TAKE NOTE OF, OBSERVE A DISCREPANCY
notiest, naughty(tiest)
notifacation, notify(fication)
notify,fies,fied,fying,fication, TO INFORM, COMMUNICATE TO SOMEONE BY VARIOUS MEANS
notikal, nautical
notilus, nautilus
notion,*, AN INKLING/VIEW/OPINION
notis, notice
notorious,sly,sness,iety,ieties, WIDELY KNOWN BUT WITHOUT POSITIVE REGARD

noxious, *HARMFUL TO HEALTH(or see nauseous*

notufikashen, notify(fication)
notufy, notify
notukul, nautical
noturize, notarize
notus, notice
noty, naughty /knot(ty)
noun,*, *A WORD REFERRING TO PEOPLE PLACE/THING/ TIME/PROPER NAME (or see known)*
nourish,hed,hes,her,hing,hment, *TO PROVIDE NECESSARY NUTRIENTS*
nouse, noose
nova,*, *STAR FLARE-UPS/BURSTS, NEW STAR*
novel,*, list,listic,ette,lize,lization,lla, *FICTITIOUS WRITING, IMAGINED PLOT AND CHARACTERS, A CREATIVE IDEA OR DESIGN*
novela, novel(lla)
novelty,ties, *UNUSUAL AND CREATIVE*
November, *NAME OF A MONTH IN THE YEAR*
noves, novice
novice,*, *A BEGINNER*
novil, novel
novildy, novelty
novimber, November
novis, novice
novle, novel
novlety, novelty
novu, nova
novul, novel
novulest, novel(ist)
novulty, novelty
novus, novice
now, *IN THE MOMENT/PRESENT*
nowar, nowhere
noweesy, noise(sy)
nowere, nowhere
nowese, noise
nowhere, *NO WHERE, NOT HERE NOW*
nowleg, knowledge
nown, noun /know(n)

noxus, noxious
noyse, noise
noze, nose /knows
nozeate, nausea(te)
nozel, nozzle
nozy, nosy
nozzle,*, *AN APERTURE FOR SPRAYING*
nu, new /knew
nuborn, newborn
nubshuel, nuptial
nucle, nucleo, *PREFIX INDICATING "NUCLEUS/ NUCLEAR" MOST OFTEN MODIFIES THE WORD*
nuclear, *HAVING TO DO WITH A NUCLEUS*
nucleus,ei, *CENTRAL HUB, PRIMARY CONTROL*
nuddy, nut(ty) /nude(ies)
nude,*, ely,eness,dism,dity,dities, *WITHOUT COVERINGS*
nudel, noodle
nuder, neuter
nudesm, nude(dism)
nudety, nude(dity)
nudge,*, ed,ging, *TO GENTLY POKE OR PUSH*
nudil, noodle
nudl, noodle
nudmeg, nutmeg
nudril, neutral
nudul, noodle
nudy, nut(ty)
nue, new /knew
nuer, new(er)
nufember, November
nuge, nudge
nuget, nugget
nugget,*, *A SMALL CHUNK OF SOMETHING*
nugit, nugget
nuglekt, neglect
nuglere, nuclear
nugleus, nucleus

nugosheate, negotiate
nugoshiable, negotiable
nugotiable, negotiable
nugotiate, negotiate
nuisance, *ANNOYING, OBNOXIOUS, CONTINUOUS IRRITATION*
nuist, new(est)
nujt, nudge(d)
nuk, nook
nukle, knuckle
nukleir, nuclear
nukleus, nucleus
nukul, knuckle
nul, null
nulefy, nullify
nulewed, newlywed
nulify, nullify
null, *OF NO VALUE*
nullify,fied,fying,fier, fication,ity,ities, *TO RENDER NOT VALUABLE OR NECESSARY*
nuly, new(l)
nulywed, newlywed
num, numb
numadik, pneumatic /nomad(ic)
numarader, numerator
numaril, numeral
numatic, pneumatic /nomad(ic)
numb,*, bed,bing,bness, *VOID OF FEELING, INABILITY TO FEEL ANYTHING*
number,*, red,ring, *A UNIT/SYMBOL WHICH REPRESENTS AN AMOUNT*
numeral,*, lly,ate,ated,ating,ation,rical, *ONE NUMBER/DIGIT, OF A DIGIT*
numerator,*, *NUMBER ABOVE THE LINE IN FRACTIONS*
numerology, *SCIENCE OF NUMBERS/FREQUENCY*
numerous,sly,osity, *MANY IN NUMBER*
numirator, numerator
numirology, numerology
numirus, numerous

numonia, pneumonia
numper, number
numpir, number
numrul, numeral
numurus, numerous
nun,*, *RELIGIOUS WOMAN WHO VOWS TO OBEY RULES AS A NUN (or see none/know(n)/noun/noon)*
nune, noon
nupshuel, nuptial
nuptial,lly, *CONCERNS WEDDING/RITUAL*
nuradic, neurotic
nurcher, nurture
nuresh, nourish
nurfus, nervous
nurish, nourish
nurishment, nourish(ment)
nurodic, neurotic
nuron, neuron
nurosis, neurosis
nurotic, neurotic
nurse,*,es,ed,sing,er,ery,eries, *TO NURTURE AND/OR PROTECT VULNERABLE THINGS/PEOPLE*
nurture,*, *PROVIDE NECESSARY NOURISHMENT TO AND/OR PROTECT VULNERABLE THINGS/PEOPLE*
nurve, nerve
nurvis, nervous
nurvus, nervous
nus, new(s) /noose
nusdalgik, nostalgic
nuse, noose /new(s)
nusel, nuzzle
nusense, nuisance
nusesidy, necessity
nusesitate, necessitate
nusil, nuzzle
nusinse, nuisance
nusle, nuzzle
nuspaper, newspaper
nustalgek, nostalgic
nusul, nuzzle

nut,*,tty, *HIGH PROTEIN WOODY FRUIT, SOMEONE WHO DOESN'T BEHAVE LOGICALLY*
nute, nude
nutedy, nude(dity)
nutel, noodle
nuter, neuter
nutesm, nude(dism)
nuthen, nothing
nuthing, nothing
nutil, noodle
nutle, noodle
nutmeg, *A SPICE*
nutoreus, notorius
nutral, neutral
nutrality, neutral(ity)
nutralize, neutral(ize)
nutreant, nutrient
nutreno, neutrino
nutreshen, nutrition
nutreshus, nutritious
nutrient, *FOOD THAT NOURISHES LIVING THINGS*
nutril, neutral
nutrino, neutrino
nutrishen, nutrition
nutrishenal, nutrition(al)
nutrition,nal,nally,nist,ous,ously,ousness,ive, ively,iveness, *GIVES/PROVIDES NOURISHMENT*
nutritious,sly,sness, *PROVIDES NOURISHMENT*
nutron, neutron
nuty, nut(ty)
nuvember, November
nuvimber, November
nuwkleus, nucleus
nuwlewed, newlywed
nuz, new(s)
nuzle, nuzzle
nuzpaper, newspaper
nuzzle,*,ed,ling, *TO SNUGGLE /DIG IN /THRUST GENTLY INTO*

nve, envy
nylon, *A MANMADE CHEMICAL FIBER*
nymph,hes, *ENTITIES, DEITIES, A STAGE IN THE DEVELOPMENT OF AN INSECT*
nymphomania,ac, *CONTINUAL/INTENSE FOCUS ON SEXUAL ACTIVITY*
nyn, nine
nyte, night /knight /knit

"O"

o, oh
O, *SYMBOL FOR OXYGEN*
O.K.,*, *OKAY*
oak,*, *A DECIDUOUS TREE WITH ACORNS*
oar,*,red, *USED TO ROW A BOAT (or see "or")*
oases, oasis
oasis, *SPOT OF TREES/WATER IN THE DESERT, COMFORT AMIDST AN UNCOMFORTABLE ENVIRONMENT*
oat,*, *A GRAIN (or see ode)*
oath,*, *PLEDGE/OBLIGATE TO CERTAIN RULES/LAWS*
oatmeal, *EDIBLE OAT GRAIN*
ob, oc, of, op, *PREFIX INDICATING "AGAINST/ TOWARDS/IN THE WAY OF" MOST OFTEN MODIFIES THE WORD*
obay, obey
obecity, obese(sity)
obedience,*,nt,ntly, *TO COMPLY/OBEY*
obees, obese
obese,seness,sity,ely, *OVERLY HEAVY, EXCESSIVELY OVERWEIGHT*
obetchuery, obituary
obeteinse, obedience
obey,*,yed,ying, *COMPLY, FOLLOW RULES AND LAWS*
obfeus, obvious
obgectif, object(ive)
obgectivity, object(ivity)

obgekshen, object(ion)
obgektif, object(ive)
obichuery, obituary
obideinse, obedience
obituary,ries, *LIST OF PEOPLE WHO HAVE TRANSPIRED FROM THIS PHYSICAL PLANE*
object,*,tion,tive,tively,tion,tionable,tionability, tionableness,tionably,tivity,tivism, *PHYSI-CAL/TANGIBLE THINGS, TO ARGUE IN DEFENSE OF, NEUTRAL POSITION*
oblagation, obligate(tion)
oblederate, obliterate
oblegate, obligate
obleterate, obliterate
oblevion, oblivion
obligate,*, ed,ting,tion,tory,toriness, *ACCEPT TERMS/RESPONSIBILITY TO PERFORM*
obliterate,*, ed,ting,tion,tive, *TO DESTROY COMPLETELY*
oblivion,ous,ously,ousness, *COMPLETELY FORGET*
oblong,gness, *LONGER LENGTH THAN SIDES, LONG/ROUND WITHOUT EDGES*
oblugashen, obligate(tion)
oblugate, obligate
obnoksheus, obnoxious
obnoxious,sly,sness, *OFFENSIVE, ROUGH FREQUENCY, DISHARMONIC IN NATURE*
obsalesent, obsolescent
obscene,ely,eness,nity,nities, *VERY UNDESIRABLE, INDECENT*
obscure,*, ed,edly,eness,ring,rity, *VAGUE, UN-FOCUSED, DIFFICULT TO EXPLAIN/UNDERSTAND*
obselesent, obsolescent
obselete, obsolete
obsene, obscene
observe,*, ed,edly,ving,vingly,vant,vantly, vance,vation,vational,edly,er, *TO WATCH/ SEE AND STUDY*
obseshen, obsess(ion)

obsesive, obsess(ive)
obsess,sses,ssed,ssive,ssively,ssion,ssional, ssionally, *TO BECOME OVERWHELMED WITH THOUGHT ABOUT ONE THING, COMPULSIVE*
obshen, option
obsilete, obsolete
obsinety, obscene(nity)
obsolescent,nce,tly, *NOT MODERN, OUT OF DATE*
obsolete,ely,eness, *NO LONGER MODERN*
obsquire, obscure
obstacle,*, *OBSTRUCTION, SOMETHING IN THE PATH*
obstatrician, obstetrician
obstatrishen, obstetrician
obstetric,*, cal,cally, *SCIENCE INVOLVING WOMEN IN CHILDBEARING PROCESS (or see obstetrician)*
obstetrician,*, *PERSON PRACTICING MEDICINE ON WOMEN IN THE CHILDBEARING PROCESS*
obstikul, obstacle
obstinate,ely,acies,acy,ateness, *RESOLVED IN PURPOSE/OPINION, UNABLE TO ARGUE WITH*
obstruct,*, ted,ting,tion,tive,tor, *GET INTO THE PATH OF, PREVENT FROM TRAVELING FURTHER*
obstukel, obstacle
obstunint, obstinate
obsulesense, obsolescent
obsulete, obsolete
obsurvashen, observe(vation)
obt, opt
obtain,*,ned,ning,nment, *ACQUIRE, COME INTO POSSESSION OF*
obtametry, optometry
obtamist, optimist
obtamize, optimize
obtane, obtain
obtek, optic
obtekul, optic(al)
obtemist, optimist
obtemize, optimize
obtemum, optimum

obteshen, optician
obtience, obedience
obtik, optic
obtikul, optic(al)
obtimesum, optimist(sm)
obtimum, optimum
obtishen, optician
obtometrist, optometry(rist)
obtometry, optometry
obtomitrist, optometry(rist)
obtreshen, optician
obtumem, optimum
obtumist, optimist
obtumistek, optimist(ic)
obtumize, optimize
obtumizum, optimist(sm)
obulent, opulent
obulint, opulent
obusev, abuse(sive)
obusif, abuse(sive)
obveus, obvious
obvious,sly,sness, *MOST APPARENT, PLAIN TO SEE/INTERPRET*
obzurvashen, observe(vation)
oc, ob, of, op, *PREFIX INDICATING "AGAINST"/ TOWARDS/ IN THE WAY OF" MOST OFTEN MODIFIES THE WORD*
ocashen, occasion
ocasional, occasion(al)
occasion,*,ned,nal,nally,nalism, *NOT FREQUENTLY OR OFTEN*
occularist, ocular(ist)
occult,*,tism, *A SCHOOL OF THOUGHT OUTSIDE OF SOCIETAL NORMS, KNOWLEDGE CONCERNING THE ESOTERIC SCIENCES*
occupancy,cies, *SPECIFIC NUMBER OF SPACES SET ASIDE FOR PEOPLE TO OCCUPY*
occupy,pies,pied,pying,pation,pational, pationally,piable,pier, *SPACE TO FILL*

occur,*,rred,rring,rrence, *TO TAKE PLACE/HAPPEN*
occurinse, occur(rrence)
ocean,*,nic, *LARGEST BODIES OF WATER*
ocen, ocean
ocerents, occur(rrence)
o'clock, *SHORT FOR "ON THE CLOCK"*
ocra, *A COLOR (or see okra)*
oct, octa, octo, *PREFIX INDICATING "EIGHT" MOST*
OFTEN MODIFIES THE WORD
octagon,nal(ly), *8 SIDED SHAPE WITH ANGLES*
octahedron,*,ra,ral, *8-FACED SOLID*
octane,*, *METHANE HYDROCARBON*
octave,*, *SECTION OF 8 TONES*
octif, octave
octihedron, octahedron
octo, octa, oct, *PREFIX INDICATING "EIGHT" MOST*
OFTEN MODIFIES THE WORD
October,*, *A MONTH OF THE YEAR*
octopus,pi, *SEA CREATURE WITH 8 ARMS*
octuf, octave
octugon, octagon
octuhedron, octahedron
octupus, octopus
ocular,rist,rly,ulist, *OF THE EYE AND EYESIGHT*
ocult, occult
ocupancy, occupancy
ocupashen, occupy(pation)
ocupied, occupy(pied)
ocupy, occupy
ocurence, occur(rrence)
ocurinse, occur(rrence)
od, odd /ode /ought
odamin, ottoman
odd,*,ddly,ddish,ddness,ddity, *NOT EVEN OR*
NORMAL (or see ode or ought)
oddesy, odyssey
ode, *POEM (or see odd or ought)*
odeanse, audience
odeble, audible

odeinse, audience
odem, autumn
odeo, audio
oder, odor/ otter/ outer
odeshen, audition
odesy, odyssey
odet, audit
odete, odd(ity)
odetion, audition
odetoreum, auditorium
odety, odd(ity)
odible, audible
odim, autumn
odio, audio
odir, odor/ otter/ outer
odishun, audition
odissy, odyssey
odisy, odyssey
odit, audit
odite, odd(ity)
odition, audition
oditorium, auditorium
odity, odd(ity)
odle, odd(ly)
odly, odd(ly)
odmeal, oatmeal
odnes, odd(ness)
odobiaugrufe, autobiography
odograf, autograph
odomashen, automatic(ion)
odomatik, automatic
odomen, ottoman
odometer,*, *INSTRUMENT THAT MEASURES NUMBER*
OF REVOLUTIONS OF A WHEEL AND DISTANCE
odomobeel, automobile
odor,*,rous,less, *SMELL (or see otter or udder)*
oduble, audible
odum, autumn
odumin, ottoman

odur, odor/ odor/ otter/ outer
odyssey,*, *A JOURNEY*
oel, oil
oeng, owe(wing)
oestur, oyster
oeul, oil
oeuly, oil(y)
of, *A WORD WHICH HELPS TO PULL SENTENCE*
STRUCTURE TOGETHER (or see off)
of, ob, oc, op, *PREFIX INDICATING "AGAINST/*
TOWARDS/IN THE WAY OF" MOST OFTEN
MODIFIES THE WORD
ofashen, ovation
ofation, ovation
ofecial, official
ofel, awful /oval
ofem, ovum
ofen, oven /often
ofend, offend
ofense, offense
ofensive, offense(sive)
ofer, offer /over
oferbering, overbearing
ofercast, overcast
ofercot, overcoat
ofercum, overcome
oferien, ovary(rian)
oferkame, overcame
oferkast, overcast
oferkot, overcoat
oferkum, overcome
oferly, over(ly)
oferot, overwrought
ofery, ovary
ofes, office
ofeser, office(r)
ofeshul, official
ofewlate, ovulate
off, *NOT OPERATING, NOT ON (or see of)*

offend,*,ded,ding, *IRRITATE/ANNOY, BREAK RULES*
offense,*,eless,sive,sively,siveness, *INITIATE,*
  MAKE THE FIRST MOVE
offer,*,red,ring, *TO GRANT/GIVE*
offes, office
office,*,er, *A PLACE/PERSON CONDUCTING BUSINESS*
official,*,lly,lism, *ASSIGNED BY DUTY, CONFIRMED BY*
  AUTHORITY
ofice, office
oficer, office(r)
oficial, official
ofil, awful /oval
ofim, ovum
ofin, oven /often
ofind, offend
ofinse, offense
ofinsuf, offense(sive)
ofir, offer /over
ofirbering, overbearing
ofircame, overcame
ofircast, overcast
ofircot, overcoat
ofircum, overcome
ofirkame, overcame
ofirkast, overcast
ofirkot, overcoat
ofirkum, overcome
ofirly, over(ly)
ofirot, overwrought
ofiry, ovary
ofis, office
ofiser, office(r)
ofishul, official
ofishuly, official(lly)
ofol, oval
often, *FREQUENTLY, DO SOMETHING MORE THAN NOT*
oftin, often
oful, awful /oval
ofulashen, ovulate(tion)

ofulate, ovulate
ofulation, ovulate(tion)
ofum, ovum
ofur, offer /over
ofurbering, overbearing
ofurcame, overcame
ofurcast, overcast
ofurly, over(ly)
ofurot, overwrought
ofury, ovary
ofus, office
ofuser, office(r)
ofvir, over
ofvur, over
oger, auger /ogre
ogern, adjourn
ogest, August
ogir, ogre /auger
ogirn, adjourn
ogist, August
ogment, augment
ogmint, augment
ogorn, adjourn
ogre,*, *UGLY AND MEAN* (or see auger)
ogur, ogre /auger
ogust, August
ogzelery, auxiliary
ogzilery, auxiliary
oh, *AN EXCLAMATION OF SURPRISE OR SUDDENNESS*
oil,*,led,ler,ling,ly,lier,liest, *SLIPPERY/ LUBRICATING*
  SUBSTANCE
oing, owe(wing)
ointment,*, *A SALVE/LOTION APPLIED TO THE SKIN*
  FOR HEALING
oister, oyster
ojern, adjourn
ojorn, adjourn
ok, okay /oak
okashenul, occasion(al)

okashiun, occasion
okay, *O.K., YES, FINE*
okerinse, occur(rrence)
okest, August
okewpansy, occupancy
okewpie, occupy
okist, August
o'klok, o'clock
okra, *A VEGETABLE* (or see ocra)
oks, ox
oksadashen, oxidant(ation)
oksadate, oxidant
oksagen, oxygen
oksedation, oxidant(ation)
oksejin, oxygen
oksen, ox(en)
okshin, auction
oksid, oxide
oksidashen, oxidant(ation)
oksidation, oxidant(ation)
oksigen, oxygen
oksijen, oxygen
oksilery, auxiliary
oksin, ox(en)
oksudashen, oxidant(ation)
oksudation, oxidant(ation)
oksugen, oxygen
oktahedron, octahedron
oktane, octane
oktegon, octagon
oktehedron, octahedron
oktev, octave
oktif, octave
oktihedron, octahedron
oktober, October
oktopus, octopus
oktuf, octave
oktugon, octagon
okularest, ocular(ist)

okult, occult
okupashen, occupy(pation)
okupensy, occupancy
okupit, occupy(pied)
okupy, occupy
okur, occur
okurinse, occur(rrence)
okust, August
okwa, aqua
okwadukt, aqueduct
okwafer, aquifer
okward, awkward
okwefer, aquifer
okword, awkward
okwu, aqua
okwurd, awkward
okzilary, auxiliary
ol, owl /all /awl /old
olastick, elastic
old, der,dest, PAST ITS PRIME, OF THE PAST
ole, old /all /awl
olef, olive
olempek, Olympic
olempic, Olympic
oleve, olive
olfebet, alphabet
olif, olive
olimpic, Olympic
olive,*, A FRUIT FROM A TREE
oll, all
olmenak, almanac
olmost, almost
olone, alone
olso, also
olt, old
oltegether, altogether
olter, altar /alder /alter
olternativ, alternative
olternutev, alternative

oltigether, altogether
oltirnutev, alternative
olugethur, altogether
oltur, altar /alder /alter
olturnativ, alternative
olturnutev, alternative
oluf, aloof /olive
oluv, olive
olwaz, always
olympic,*, RELATING TO GAMES/COUNTRY/ MOUNTAIN
omaga, omega
omed, omit /emit
omeded, omit(tted) /emit(tted)
omega, LAST, AT THE END
omeka, omega
omenus, ominous
omeshin, omission /emission
omet, omit /emit
ometion, omission /emission
ominous, sly,sness, A SIGN, THREATENING DUE TO LACK OF UNDERSTANDING, FOREBODING
ominus, ominous
omishen, omission /emission
omission,*, THE ACT OF LEAVING SOMETHING OUT (or see emission)
omit,*, tted,tting, TO LEAVE OUT (or see emit)
omition, omission /emission
omne, omni
omnefurus, omnivore(ous)
omnevore, omnivore
omnevorus, omnivore(ous)
omni, ALL AS ONE, HAVING IT ALL, ALL OF IT
omni, PREFIX INDICATING "ALL" MOST OFTEN MODIFIES THE WORD
omniferus, omnivore(ous)
omniverus, omnivore(ous)
omnivore,*, rous,rously,rousness, EATS ANYTHING DIGESTIBLE
omnivore, omnivore

on, OPERATING, FUNCTIONING, PERFORMING (or see own or one)
onarary, honorary
once, ONLY ONE TIME, FORMER (or see want(s))
oncore, encore
ond, own(ed)
one,*, eness, SINGLE, NUMERAL MEANING LESS THAN TWO BUT MORE THAN ZERO(or see won or own)
oneng, awning /own(ing)
oner, honor /own(er)
onerable, honor(able)
onest, honest
oning, awning /own(ing)
onion,*, A VEGETABLE
onir, honor /owner
onirable, honor(able)
onist, honest
onkore, encore
onle, only
only, NO EXCEPTIONS, EXCLUSIVELY, MERELY
onor, honor /owner
onoruble, honor(able)
onre, ornery
onry, ornery
onse, once /one(s) /own(s)
ont, own(ed)
onto, ON/TO, ABOUT/TOWARDS
ontra, entree
ontrapreneur,*, entrepreneur
ontre, entree
ontrupreneur,*, entrepreneur
ontu, onto
onurary, honorary
onward,*, FORWARD
onwurd, onward
onyen, onion
onyun, onion
oos, ooze
ooserp, usurp

oosurp, usurp

ooze,*,ed,zing, GENTLE FLOW, GENERAL OVERALL APPEARANCE OF EXCESSIVE, HEAVY MOISTURE

op, of, oc, ob, PREFIX INDICATING "AGAINST/ TOWARDS/IN THE WAY OF" MOST OFTEN MODIFIES THE WORD

opake, opaque

opal,*, AN IRRIDESCENT STONE

opalescence,nt, HAVING A COATING OR APPEARANCE OF RAINBOW COLORED/ IREDESCENT LIGHT, FILMY/ COLORFUL

opaque,*,ely, NON-TRANSPARENT, DULL, DENSE

oparade, operate
oparate, operate
opasit, oppose(site)
opazeshen, oppose(sition)
opeate, opiate

open,*,ned,ning,nable,ness,ner, INVITING, ALLOWING, PENETRABLE, ACCEPTING

openeun, opinion
openyun, opinion

opera,*,retta, PLAY/DRAMA WITH MUSIC/SINGING

operade, operate
operader, operate(tor)
operashen, operate(tion)

operate,*,ed,ting,tion,tional,tive,tively,tiveness, tor, TO MAKE FUNCTION, PUT INTO EFFECT, MAKE ACTIVE, REMEDY WITH ACTION

operater, operate(tor)
opertune, opportune
opertunedy, opportune(nity)
opertunest, opportune(st)
opertunity, opportune(nity)
opesishen, oppose(sition)
opesit, oppose(site)
opeum, opium
opeute, opiate
opewlent, opulent
opezit, oppose(site)

opfeis, obvious
opfeus, obvious
ophil, awful
ophul, awful

opiate,*, DRUG/NARCOTIC USED TO DULL PAIN AND INDUCE SLEEP

opilesent, opalescence(nt)
opilesinse, opalescence
opilessence, opalescence
opin, open

opinion,*,ned,nated, A JUDGEMENT/THOUGHT

opirashen, operate(tion)
opirate, operate
opirtune, opportune
opirtunedy, opportune(nity)
opirtunist, opportune(st)
opirtunity, opportune(nity)
opisit, oppose(site)

opium, JUICE FROM FLOWERING POPPY FRUIT

opizit, oppose(site)
oplagashen, obligate(tion)
opligate, obligate
opliveus, oblivion(ous)
oplivion, oblivion
oplong, oblong
oplugashen, obligate(tion)
oplugate, obligate
opnokshes, obnoxious
oponent, opponent
oponit, opponent
oporashin, operate(tion)
oporate, operate
oportune, opportune
opose, oppose

opossum, A MARSUPIAL ANIMAL

opozishen, oppose(sition)
oppasite, oppose(site)

opponent,*, THE OTHER SIDE IN COMPETITION, ONE OF TWO SIDES COMPETING

opportune,ely,eness,nism,nist,nistic,nistically, nity,nities, FAVORABLE MOMENT TO ACT OR MAKE A CHANGE

oppose,*,ed,sing,site,sitely,siteness,sition, sitional, ADVERSE/CONTRARY/CONTRASTING

opposishen, oppose(sition)
opposum, opossum
oppreshen, oppress(ion)

oppress,sses,ssed,ssing,ssible,ssion,ssive, ssively, ssiveness,ssor, CONTROL OTHER'S FREEWILL BEYOND A REASONABLE EXTENT, TYRANNIZE, CRUEL/UNUSUAL PUNISHMENT

opptomistic, optimist(ic)
oppusite, oppose(site)
opra, opera
oprater, operate(tor)
opres, oppress
opreshen, oppress(ion)
opresif, oppress(ive)
opress, oppress
opru, opera
opsalesent, obsolescent
opscure, obscure
opseen, obscene
opselete, obsolete
opsenity, obscene(nity)
opserve, observe
opshin, option
opsilesent, obsolescent
opsilete, obsolete
opsirvashen, observe(vation)
opskure, obscure
opsolete, obsolete
opstatrishen, obstetrician
opstekul, obstacle
opstenit, obstinate
opstikul, obstacle
opstinesy, obstinate(acy)
opstitrishen, obstetrician

opstrukshen, obstruct(ion)
opstrukt, obstruct
opstukel, obstacle
opstunint, obstinate
opstutrishen, obstetrician
opsulesense, obsolescent
opsulete, obsolete
opsurvashen, observe(vation)
opt, optico, opto, PREFIX INDICATING "EYE/ VISION"
   MOST OFTEN MODIFIES THE WORD
opt,ted,ting, THE ACT OF MAKING A CHOICE
optametry, optometry
optamism, optimist(sm)
optamist, optimist
optamistek, optimist(ic)
optamisum, optimist(sm)
optamize, optimize
optane, obtain
optek, optic
optemist, optimist
optemistic, optimist(ic)
optemisum, optimist(sm)
optemum, optimum
opteshen, optician
optic,*,cal,cally, CONCERNING THE EYE
optician,*, DOCTOR WHO WORKS WITH EYES
optico, opt, opto, PREFIX INDICATING "EYE/VISION"
   MOST OFTEN MODIFIES THE WORD
optimesm, optimist(sm)
optimist,tic,tically,sm,ize,ization, TO BELIEVE
   BASED ON HOPE/ FAITH, ONE WHO LOOKS ON
   THE BRIGHT SIDE, HOPE FOR A BRIGHTER FUTURE
optimize,*,ed,zing,zation, TO MAXIMIZE, REAP
   GREATEST BENEFIT FROM
optimum,*, OPTIMAL, HOPE FOR THE GREATEST,
   FAITH FOR THE BEST
option,*,ned,nal,nally, A CHOICE
optishen, optician

opto, opt, optico, PREFIX INDICATING "EYE/ VISION"
   MOST OFTEN MODIFIES THE WORD
optometry,rist,ric,rical, DOCTOR OF THE EYES
optumem, optimum
optumist, optimist
optumistek, optimist(ic)
opul, opal
opulent,tly,nce, OVER ACCUMULATION OF WEALTH
   AND/OR POWER
opulesense, opalescence
opulesent, opalescence(nt)
opulessence, opalescence
opulint, opulent
opun, open
opura, opera
opurader, operate(tor)
opurashen, operate(tion)
opurate, operate
opurtune, opportune
opurtunedy, opportune(nity)
opurtunest, opportune(st)
opurtunity, opportune(nity)
opusishen, oppose(sition)
opusit, oppose(site)
opuzishen, oppose(sition)
opuzit, oppose(site)
opveus, obvious
opzerve, observe
oqua, aqua
oquelarist, ocular(ist)
oquepy, occupy
oqupensy, occupance
oqupied, occupy(pied)
oqupy, occupy
oqwa, aqua
or, WORD USED AS A CONJUNCTION, OTHERWISE (or
   see oar /ore /are)
oracle,*,lar,larity,larly, PERSON/THING WHO HOLDS
   GREAT/SECRET WISDOM (or see auricle)

orador, orator
orafes, orifice
orafus, orifice
oragen, origin
orageno, oregano
oragin, origin
orajin, origin
orajinate, originate
orakul, oracle /auricle
oral,lly, OF/FROM THE MOUTH
orange,*, COLOR, FRUIT
orashen, orator(tion)
orator,tion,tor,torical,torically,ry,ries, SPOKEN
   FROM THE MOUTH, PUBLIC SPEAKING
orb,*, bit,biter,bitary,bicular,bicularly,biculate,
   SPHERE, GLOBE, CIRCULAR
orbet, orb(it)
orbut, orb(it)
orcanek, organic
orcanekly, organic(ally)
orcasem, orgasm
orcestra, orchestra
orchard,*, FIELD OF FRUIT TREES
orchart, orchard
orchastra, orchestra
orchen, organ
orcherd, orchard
orchestra,*,al,ally,ate,ator,ation, GROUPS OF
   PEOPLE WITH INSTRUMENTS PERFORMING MUSIC
   TOGETHER IN SYNCHRONICITY
orchid,*, A FLOWER
orchird, orchard
orchistra, orchestra
orchurt, orchard
orcid, orchid
ordain,*,ned,ning,ner,nment, APPOINT
ordane, ordain
ordaninse, ordinance
ordeal,*, MORE DRAMA THAN NECESSARY

ordel, ordeal
ordenense, ordinance
order,*, red,ring,rly,rliness, ORGANIZED, PUT INTO ITS PROPER PLACE, PROPER PLACEMENT, FOLLOWING SET OF RULES/LAWS
ordervs, h'ordeuvres
ordinance,*, A LAW
ordinence, ordinance
ordir, order
ordirves, h'ordeuvres
ordinnse, ordinance
ordur, order
ordurvs, h'ordeuvres
ore,*, ROCK CONTAINING METAL (or see oar)
orefis, orifice
orefus, orifice
oregano, AN HERB/SPICE
oregenate, originate
oregeno, oregano
oreginate, originate
orbint, orient
oreintul, orient(al)
orejen, origin
orejenal, origin(al)
orejenashen, originate(tion)
orejenat, origin(ate)
orejin, origin
orejinul, origin(al)
orel, oral
orenge, orange
orenj, orange
oreter, orator
oretor, orator
oreundashen, orient(ation)
oreunt, orient
oreuntashen, orient(ation)
orfan, orphan
orfun, orphan

organ,*,nist, A MUSICAL INSTRUMENT, A MAJOR INTERNAL BODY/WORKING PART
organek, organic
organic,*,cally, ALL NATURAL SUBSTANCE, FROM THE EARTH
organism,*,mic,mically, A LIFE FORM
organization,*,nal,nally, SYSTEM/ METHOD OF OPERATION WHICH KEEPS A BODY/HOST ALIVE, COLLECTION OF WORKING PARTS WHICH MAKE UP THE WHOLE
organize,*,ed,zing,zable,er, TO CREATE/USE A METHOD/SYSTEM WHICH CREATES ORDER/FUNCTION BETWEEN MOVING PARTS
orgasm,*,mic,mically, THE ELEVATED POINT/HEIGHT OF AN EMOTIONAL/PHYSICAL EXPERIENCE/EVENT
orgazem, orgasm
orge, orgy
orgen, organ
orgenise, organize
orgenism, organism
orgenuzashen, organization
orgin, organ /origin
orginazation, organization
orginesm, organism
orginise, organize
orginuzashen, organization
orgon, organ
orgunise, organize
orgunism, organism
orgy,gies, COMBINING OF NUMBERS OF BODIES WHO EXCESSIVELY INDULGE THEMSELVES
oriendul, orient(al)
orient,*,ted,ting,tates,tation,tational,tive, DE-FINITE POSITION/BEARING IN REFERENCE TO SPECIFIC POINTS, OF THE EAST
oriental,lly,lism,list,lize, EASTERN PLACE IN RELATION TO THE REST OF THE WORLD
orifice,*, , OPENINGS

origin,*, nal,nally,nality,nalities, BEGINNING OF CREATION, FIRST THOUGHT, THE BEGINNING
originate,*,ed,ting,tion,tor,tively, FROM WHERE IT BEGAN, FIRST THOUGHT
orijenal, origin(al)
orijenate, originate
orijinal, origin(al)
orikul, oracle /auricle
oril, oral
oringe, orange
orinj, orange
orivul, arrive(val)
orje, orgy
orjy, orgy
orkan, organ
orkanek, organic
orkanekly, organic(ally)
orkanik, organic
orkanism, organism
orkanize, organize
orkanusashen, organization
orkastra, orchestra
orkasum, orgasm
orkazim, orgasm
orked, orchid
orken, organ
orkenasashen, organization
orkenism, organism
orkenize, organize
orkenuzashen, organization
orkestra, orchestra
orkestrete, orchestra(ate)
orket, orchid
orkid, orchid
orkin, organ
orkinasation, organization
orkinazashen, organization
orkinism, organism
orkinize, organize

orkinuzashen, organization
orkistra, orchestra
orkit, orchid
orkunise, organize
orkunism, organism
orkustra, orchestra
ornade, ornate
ornament,*,tal,tally,tation, *DECORATIONS, ACCESSORIZE, BEAUTIFY*
ornamental, ornament(al)
ornate,ely,eness, *ARTISTICALLY DETAILED, EMBELLISHED*
ornement, ornament
ornemintal, ornament(al)
ornery,riness, *STUBBORN/ADVERSE DISPOSITION OR ATTITUDE*
onge, orange
ornry, ornery
ornument, ornament
ornumentul, ornament(al)
orocle, oracle
orofes, orifice
orp, orb
orpet, orb(it)
orphan,*,nage,nhood, *ONE LEFT WITHOUT PARENTS, PLACE FOR THOSE WITHOUT PARENTS*
orphen, orphan
orpit, orb(it)
orput, orb(it)
orshed, orchard
orshurd, orchard
ortenanse, ordinance
orter, order
orthridus, arthritis
orth, ortho, *PREFIX INDICATING "NORMAL" MOST OFTEN MODIFIES THE WORD*
ortinanse, ordinance
ortir, order
orthense, ordinance

ortunense, ordinance
ortur, order
orufis, orifice
orugin, origin
orujin, origin
orukle, oracle /auricle
orukul, oracle /auricle
orul, oral
orunj, orange
orupt, erupt /irrupt
oryent, orient
oryentashen, orient(ation)
oryentul, orient(al)
oryindashen, orient(ation)
osalate, oscillate
osanefurus, ozone(niferous)
oscillate,*,ed,ting,tion,tor,tory, *VOLUME OF MOVE-MENT/VIBRATION IN BETWEEN, MOVE TO/ FRO*
osculate, oscillate
osdrege, ostrich
osdrich, ostrich
osdrije, ostrich
ose, owe(s)
oselate, oscillate
osheanic, ocean(ic)
oshin, ocean
osilate, oscillate
osmose,ed,sing,sis,otic,otically, *PENETRATION OF A BARRIER WHERE TWO SHARE THE SAME AS ONE, SHARING OF INFORMATION BETWEEN TWO*
osmoses, osmose(sis)
osone, ozone
osonic, ozone(nic)
osonusfere, ozone(nosphere)
ost, oste, osteo, *PREFIX INDICATING "BONE" MOST OFTEN MODIFIES THE WORD*
ostracize,ed,zing,ism, *TO EXPEL OR EXCLUDE FROM A GROUP*
ostrech, ostrich

ostreje, ostrich
ostresize, ostracize
ostrich,hes, *A LARGE BIRD*
ostrisize, ostracize
ostrusize, ostracize
osulashen, oscillate(tion)
osulate, oscillate
osum, awesome /assume
osuniferus, ozone(niferous)
ot, *PREFIX INDICATING "EAR" MOST OFTEN MODIFIES THE WORD (or see oat/ odd/ ought/ ode)*
otej, outage
otem, autumn
otemin, ottoman
oteo, audio
oter, odor/ otter/ outer
otesm, autism
otesy, odyssey
otezum, autism
oth, oath
othentik, authentic
other,*, *THAT ONE NOT THIS ONE, THE FURTHER ONE, THE ALTERNATIVE (or see author)*
othoruterein, authoritarian
othintik, authentic
othir, author
othoretarean, authoritarian
othorety, authority
othoritarean, authoritarian
othority, authority
otim, autumn
otiman, ottoman
otimobil, automobile
otir, odor/ otter/ outer
otism, autism
otisum, autism
otisy, odyssey
otitoreum, auditorium
otizum, autism

otle, odd(ly)
otluk, outlook
otmel, oatmeal
oto, ot, PREFIX INDICATING "EAR" MOST OFTEN MODIFIES THE WORD
otobiografe, autobiography
otograf, autograph
otomadik, automatic
otoman, ottoman
otomashen, automatic(ion)
otomobel, automobile
otoneme, autonomy
otonume, autonomy
otopse, autopsy
otter,*, WATER MAMMAL
ottoman,*, FOOTSTOOL/COUCH WITHOUT BACK/ARMS
otur, odor / otter
ouch, SOUND ASSOCIATED WITH PAIN/GETTING HURT
ouder, outer
ouding, outing
ought, SHOULD/WOULD/COULD TAKE ACTION/ DO SOMETHING
ourle, hour(ly)
out, NOT IN, EXIT, NOT THERE ANYLONGER, BEYOND THE MAIN OR OBJECT, DOESN'T EXIST AS IT ONCE DID (or see ought)
out, PREFIX INDICATING "OUT/OUTWARDS/EXTERNAL/ EXTERIOR/TO A GREATER DEGREE" MOST OFTEN MODIFIES THE WORD
outage,*, QUIT WORKING, LACKING WITHOUT
outer, BEYOND THE MAIN AREA OR BODY, NOT PART OF THE WHOLE ANY LONGER, EXTERIOR
outfit,*, tted,tting, EXTERNAL GEAR/CLOTHING
outgo,oes,oing, AWAY FROM THE CENTER, LEAVING THE AREA, REMOVED FROM THE PREVIOUS PLACE
outii, outage
outing,*, TAKE A SMALL EXCURSION AWAY, TO GO AWAY BRIEFLY

outlaw,*, PEOPLE WHO PERFORM ACTS OUTSIDE OF THE LAW
outlet,*, A WAY TO GET OUT
outline,*, ed,ning, BOUNDARIES OF, DEFINING PRINCIPLES, SKETCH OR WORDS DESCRIBING THE INSIDE
outlook, PERSPECTIVE OF THE OBSERVER, WAY OF PERCEPTION
outluk, outlook
outlying, ON THE OUTSKIRTS, OUTSIDE OF, BEYOND
outpost,*, A STATION OR POST OUTSIDE OF THE MAIN CONFINES, A REMOTE SETTLEMENT
output, THE RESULT OF MANUFACTURING, WHAT IS PRODUCED
outrage,*, ed,ging,eous,eously,eousness, EXCESSIVE EMOTIONAL REACTION, SUDDEN OUTBURST
outright, WITHOUT CONCEALMENT OR RESTRAINT, OPEN, STRAIGHT OUT
outset, AT THE BEGINNING
outside,er, NOT IN THE MAIN PORTION, REMOTE FROM THE CENTER
outskirt,*, AT THE EDGES OF TOWN, BORDER DISTRICTS
outskurt, outskirt
outsmart,*,*,ted,ting, OUTWIT
outstand,ding, STANDS OUT, PROTRUDES, APART FROM THE REST, LEAVE PORT
outward,*,dly,dness, AWAY FROM CENTER, TOWARDS THE EXTERIOR, ON THE OUTSIDE
outwit,*,tted,tting, OUTSMART, THINK FASTER THAN
ovaelable, available
oval,*,lly,lness, ELONGATED CIRCLE, SHAPE OF EGG
ovary,ries,rian,rial,ritis,riotomy,riectomy, REPRODUCTIVE GLANDS
ovashen, ovation
ovashin, ovation
ovation,*, ENTHUSIASTIC APPLAUSE
ovekt, evict

ovel, oval
ovem, ovum
oven,*, CONTAINER BUILT FOR HIGH HEAT TO COOK/ BAKE THINGS
ovent, event
oventful, eventful
over, PREFIX INDICATING "EXCESSIVELY/COMPLETELY/ UPPER/ABOVE/OUTER" MOST OFTEN MODIFIES THE WORD
over,rly, ABOVE AND BEYOND, MORE THAN NORMAL
overbearing,gly, DOMINATING, OPPRESSING, TYRANNICAL, FORCEFUL
overbering, overbearing
overcame, PAST TENSE OF "OVERCOME"
overcast,ting, SHADOWING, GLOOMS OVER, SEWING ROUGH EDGES
overcoat,*, TO APPLY A COAT OVER ANOTHER
overcome,ming,came, TO RISE ABOVE AN OBSTACLE, TO MANAGE THROUGH A PROBLEM, RISE ABOVE OPPOSITION
overcum, overcome
overien, ovary(rian)
overkame, overcame
overkast, overcast
overkot, overcoat
overkum, overcome
overot, overwrought
overwrot, overwrought
overwrought, EMOTIONAL DISTRESS, TOO MUCH TO HANDLE GRACEFULLY
overy, ovary
oveulate, ovulate
ovewlate, ovulate
ovil, oval
ovim, ovum
ovin, oven
ovint, event
ovintful, eventful
ovir, over

ovirbering, overbearing
ovircast, overcast
ovircot, overcoat
ovircum, overcome
ovirkast, overcast
ovirkot, overcoat
ovirkum, overcome
ovirly, over(ly)
ovirot, overwrought
oviry, ovary
ovul, oval
ovulashen, ovulate(tion)
ovulate,*,ed,ting,tion, TO RELEASE AN EGG (OVUM) FROM THE OVARY
ovum,*, AN EGG
ovur, over
ovurbering, overbearing
ovurcast, overcast
ovurcoat, overcoat
ovurcum, overcome
ovure, ovary
ovurkame, overcame
ovurkast, overcast
ovurkot, overcoat
ovurkum, overcome
ovurly, over(ly)
ovurot, overwrought
ovury, ovary
ow, owe
owch, ouch
owd, out/ ought/ owe(d)
owdege, outage
owdeng, outing
owdfit, outfit
owdir, outer
owdishun, audition
owdition, audition
owdline, outline
owdrage, outrage

owdsmart, outsmart
owe,*,ed,wing, TO BE INDEBTED FOR
owl,*, NOCTURNAL BIRD (or see oil)
own,*,ned,ning,ner, ONE WHO HOLDS RIGHTS/TITLE TO PROPERTY (or see one or on)
owr, are/hour/our
owra, aura
owrie, awry
owrle, hour(ly)
owry, awry
owsh, ouch
owt, out /ought
owtege, outage
owtej, outage
owtfit, outfit
owtige, outage
owting, outing
owtir, outer
owtlaw, outlaw
owtlet, outlet
owtline, outline
owtluk, outlook
owtput, output
owtragus, outrage(ous)
owtrite, outright
owtset, outset
owtside, outside
owtskurt, outskirt
owtwet, outwit
owtwit, outwit
owtwurd, outward
owur, hour / our
ox,xen,xes, TYPE OF BOVINE (CATTLE)
oxa, PREFIX INDICATING "OXYGEN/ ADDITIONAL OXYGEN" MOST OFTEN MODIFIES THE WORD
oxajen, oxygen
oxajin, oxygen
oxedate, oxidant
oxedation, oxidant(ation)

oxejen, oxygen
oxejin, oxygen
oxidant,*,ation,adative,adatively, OXYGEN ACTIVELY PARTICIPATING WITH OTHER ELEMENTS
oxidashen, oxidant(ation)
oxidate, oxidant
oxide,*,dic,dize,dizer,dizing,dizable, INTERACTION BETWEEN OXYGEN AND OTHER ELEMENTS
oxijen, oxygen
oxilery, auxiliary
oxin, ox(en)
oxo, PREFIX INDICATING "OXYGEN/ADDITIONAL OXYGEN" MOST OFTEN MODIFIES THE WORD
oxsadashen, oxidant(ation)
oxsagen, oxygen
oxsigen, oxygen
oxsudashen, oxidant(ation)
oxudiz, oxide(dize)
oxugen, oxygen
oxujin, oxygen
oxy, PREFIX INDICATING "OXYGEN/ADDITIONAL OXYGEN" MOST OFTEN MODIFIES THE WORD
oxydate, oxidant
oxygen,nic,nicity,nate,nation, A GAS, GAS USED FOR RESPIRATION OF ALL LIVING THINGS
oyle, oil /oil(y)
oyntment, ointment
oyster,*, MARINE SHELLFISH, MOLLUSK
oystur, oyster
ozmosis, osmose(sis)
ozone,*,nic,niferous,nous,nide,nize,nized,nizing, nizer,nosphere, PURE AIR, FORM OF OXYGEN, LAYER AROUND THE EARTH

"P"

pa, paw /pay
paber, paper /papier mache'

pabreka, paprika
pabur, paper /papier mache'
pace,*,ed,cing,er, *RATE OF PROGRESS/ MOVEMENT, A GAIT/STEP*
pach, patch
pachen, passion
pachendly, patient(ly)
pachense, patience /patient(s)
pachin, passion
pachindly, patient(ly)
pachints, patience /patient(s)
pacific, *OF PEACE/THE PACIFIC OCEAN*
pacify,*,fies,fied,fying,fication,ficatory,fism, *TO CODDLE/APPEASE/SETTLE/ SOOTHE*
pack,*,ked,king,kage,kaged,kaging, *PLACE STUFF/FILL A CONTAINER FOR MOVING*
packet,*, *SMALL COLLECTION OF DATA/MATERIAL PROVIDING INFORMATION*
packit, packet
pact,*, *AN AGREEMENT* (or see pack(ed))
pacterul, pectoral
pad,*,dded,dding,ddy, *LAYER OF MATERIAL OF VARYING THICKNSSES FOR PROTECTION, A RESIDENCE, BOTTOM OF PAW* (or see pat /paid)
pada, pate
paddle,*,ed,ling,er, *TO USE OARS/FEET FOR MOBIL-IZATION, ITEM USED FOR ROWING, A SPANKING*
paddock,*, *SMALL AREA TO CONFINE ANIMALS/VEHICLES TEMPORARILY*
paddy,dies, *HAVING TO DO WITH RICE* (or see patty)
pade, paid/ paddy/ patty/ pate'
paded, pad(dded) /pat(tted)
padel, paddle
paden, patent
padeo, patio
padern, pattern
padestrein, pedestrian

padid, pad(dded) /pat(tted)
padik, paddock
padil, paddle
padin, patent
padio, patio
padirn, pattern
padled, paddle(d)
padlock,*, *LOCK WITH KEY OR COMBINATION DIAL*
padok, paddock
padreark, patriarch
padrearkul, patriarch(al)
padreit, patriot
padren, patron
padrenize, patron(ize)
padreodic, patriot(ic)
padreut, patriot
padriarch, patriarch
padrin, patron
padrinize, patron(ize)
padrun, patron
padrunize, patron(ize)
padryet, patriot
padsee, patsy
padthological, pathology(gical)
padtult, paddle(d)
paduk, paddock
paduled, paddle(d)
padurn, pattern
pady, paddy /patty
pae, pay /pay(ee)
pael, pail / pale
paer, pay(er)
paet, paid
pafd, pave(d)
paf, pave
pafeleon, pavilion
paferty, poverty
pafileon, pavilion
pafmint, pave(ment)

paft, pave(d)
pafurted, pervert(ed)
pagamus, pajamas
pagan,*,nish,nism,nize,nizer, *PEOPLE WHO SUPPORT NATURE AS THEIR DEITY*
page,*,ed,ging,ginate,gination,er, *SHEET IN A BOOK, TO CALL FOR (TOO MANY DEFINITIONS, PLEASE SEE STANDARD DICTIONARY)*
pageant,*,try,tries, *A SHOWY DISPLAY*
pagen, pagan
pagenashen, page(gination)
pagenate, page(ginate)
pagense, patience /patient(s)
pagent, pageant
pagentre, pageant(ry)
pagin, pagan
paginashen, page(gination)
pagint, pageant
pagonism, pagan(ism)
pagun, pagan
pai, pay
paibul, pay(yable)
paid,*, *PAST TENSE OF "PAY"* (or see pay)
pail,*,lful, *BUCKET TYPE VESSEL* (or see pal/pale/pall)
pain,*,ned,nful,nfully,nfulness,nless, *INTER-PRETATION BY THE BRAIN FROM NERVE ENDINGS SENSING HARM/THREAT* (or see pane)
paint,*,ted,ting,ter, *MANMADE OR NATURAL BASED COLORANT, VIVID DESCRIPTION*
pair,*,red,ring, *TWO IDENTICAL/SIMILAR ITEMS TOGETHER* (or see par/ parr/ pare/ pear)
pairadox, paradox
pairalise, paralyze
pairalyze, paralyze
pairudox, paradox
pait, paid
paj, page
pajamas, *SLEEPING GARMENTS*
pajenashen, page(gination)

pajenate, page(ginate)
pajense, patience /patient(s)
pajent, pageant
pajinashen, page(gination)
pajint, pageant
pakd, pact /pack(ed)
pakeg, pack(age)
paket, packet
pakij, pack(age)
pakt, pact /pack(ed)
pakut, packet
pal, PREFIX FROM SANSKRIT MEANING BROTHER/OF THE BROTHER
pal,,*,lled,lling, A FRIEND, SOMEONE YOU ENJOY HANGING OUT WITH (or see pail/ pale/ pail)
palace,,*, DWELLING OF ROYALTY
palase, palace
palate,table,tableness,tability,tably,tal,tally, talize,talization, ROOF OF THE MOUTH AS A SENSOR (or see pallet /palette /pallid)
pale,,*,ed,ling,lish,ly,eness,lid,lidly,lidness, DIM/WAN,STAKE WITH SHARP END, SPACE WITHIN A FIXED BOUNDARY (or see pail/pal/pall)
paled, pale(d)/ palate/ palette/ pallet /pallid
paleduble, palate(table)
paleintology, paleontology
palenate, pollinate
paleo, palaeo, PREFIX INDICATING "EARLY/ANCIENT/PREHISTORIC" MOST OFTEN MODIFIES THE WORD
paleontology,gies, SCIENCE CONCERNED WITH ALL LIFE IN THE PAST
paleredy, polar(ity)
palerity, polar(ity)
pales, palace /police
palesh, polish
palesy, policy
palet, palate /palate/ palette /pallet /pallid
palette,,*, PAINTER'S BOARD, VARIETY OF COLORS (or see pallet or palate)

paleuntology, paleontology
palid, pallid /palate /palette /pallet
paliduble, palate(table)
paligamus, polygamy(mous)
paligemy, polygamy
paligine, polygyny
palin, pollen
palip, polyp
palise, palace
palish, polish
palsy, policy
palit, palate/ palate/ pallet / polite /pallid
palitasize, politic(ize)
palite, palate/ palate/ pallet / polite /pallid
palituble, palate(table)
pall,,*, EVOKES A DULL/OPPRESSIVE ATMOSPHERE, COVERING FOR A COFFIN(or see pal /pale /pail /pail)
pallet, PLATFORM USED TO HOLD GOODS, A TOOL, IN A CLOCK/WATCH, POTTER'S TOOL(or see palette /palate /pallid)
pallid,dly,dness, LACKS COLOR (or see palette/ palate/ pallet)
palm,,*, the hand, A PLANT (TOO MANY DEFINITIONS, PLEASE SEE STANDARD DICTIONARY)
palpitate,,*, ed,ting,tion, PULSATE, TREMBLE
palt, pale(d)
palud, pallid
paluduble, palate(table)
paluse, palace
palushen, pollute(tion)
palut, palate/ palate/ pallet/ pallet/ pollute
palutent, pollute(tant)
palutics, politic(s)
palution, pollute(tion)
palygamus, polygamy(mous)
palyginy, polygyny
palyintology, paleontology
pamendo, pimento
pament, pay(ment)

pamento, pimento
pamflet, pamphlet
pamint, pay(ment)
pamphlet,,*, PUBLICATION CONSISTING OF FOLDED PIECES OF PAPER WITH TEXT
pamplet, pamphlet
pamunt, pay(ment)
pan, panto, PREFIX INDICATING "ALL" MOST OFTEN MODIFIES THE WORD
pan,,*,,nned,nning, FLAT METAL WITH SIDES, A COOKING UTENSIL (TOO MANY DEFINITIONS, PLEASE SEE STANDARD DICTIONARY) (OR SEE PANE OR PAIN)
pancreas,atic,atin, PART OF THE STOMACH
pancreus, pancreas
panda,,*, A BLACK/WHITE BEAR
pandees, pant(ies)
pandilunes, pantaloon(s)
pandre, pantry
pandulunes, pantaloon(s)
pane,,*, FRAME TO PLACE GLASS/PHOTOGRAPHS, DIAMOND FACE (or see pain)
panek, panic
panel,,*,led,ling,list, FLAT SHEET USED FOR COVER/DECORATION, PEOPLE WORKING AS A GROUP TO MAKE A DECISION (TOO MANY DEFINITIONS, PLEASE SEE STANDARD DICTIONARY)
panemine, pantomime
panensula, peninsula
paneramic, panorama(mic)
panic,,*,ced,cing, SUDDEN OVERWHELMING FEAR WHICH CAUSES REACTION
panik, panic
panil, panel
panimine, pantomime
paninsula, peninsula
paniramic, panorama(mic)
pankreus, pancreas
panol, panel

panomine, pantomime
panorama,*,mic,mically, ABILITY TO VIEW/OBSERVE ENTIRE EVENT/SCENE WITHOUT OBSTRUCTION
panoramic, panorama(mic)
pant,*,ted,ting,ties, BREATH/GASP HEAVILY, ARTICLE OF CLOTHING FOR LEGS/LOWER TORSO, UNDERWEAR (or see paint or pan(nned))
pantaloon,*, LOOSE FITTING PANTS
pantees, pant(ies)
panteloons, pantaloon(s)
pantemime, pantomime
panther,*, LARGE WILD CAT
panthur, panther
pantilunes, pantaloon(s)
pantimime, pantomime
pantomime,*,ed,ming,mist,mical,mically,miery, COMMUNICATE WITH GESTURES/NO SPEAKING
pantre, pantry
pantry,ries, A FOOD STORAGE CLOSET/ROOM
pantu, panda
pantulunes, pantaloon(s)
pantumime, pantomime
pantys, pant(ies)
panul, panel
panulist, panel(ist)
panumine, pantomime
paode, peyote
paodur, powder
paond, pound
paonse, pounce
paote, peyote
papaya,*, A FRUIT
paper,*,red,ring,rer,riness,ry, A USABLE SHEET OF MATERIAL FOR INK/PAINT, MADE OF WOOD/HEMP PULP, TO APPLY PAPER
papier mache', DIFFERENT TYPES OF PAPER PUT TOGETHER, COLLAGE OF PAPER (or see paper)
papir, paper /papier mache'

papreka, paprika
paprika,*, a spice
papur, paper /papier mache'
papyu, papaya
par,*,rity, TO TAKE AN AVERAGE, BALANCE EQUALLY, NORMAL/AVERAGE, A PREFIX (or see parr/ pear/ pair/ pare)
para, PREFIX INDICATING "BESIDE/BEYOND" MOST OFTEN MODIFIES THE WORD
parable,*,list,bolic, SHORT STORY/SENTENCES WHICH REFLECTS HUMAN EMOTIONAL WISDOMS (or see parabola)
parabola,*,lic, BOWL SHAPE (or see parable)
parachute,*,ed,ting,tist, DEVICE FOR DROPPING FROM GREAT HEIGHT/PLANES
parade,*,ed,ding, AN ORGANIZED CEREMONIAL MARCH DOWN STREETS OF A CITY
paradigm,*,matic, MAKING RELATIVE COMPARISONS, CATEGORIZING INTO A DEFINED SET
paradox,xes,xical,xically,xicalness, A CONTRADITION OF TERMS, WORDS/ACTIONS WHICH CANCEL EACH OTHER OUT
paraffin,nic, MELTABLE/WAXY SUBSTANCE
paragraph,*, SEVERAL SENTENCES TOGETHER SUPPORTING A THEME
parakeet,*, A TROPICAL BIRD
paralasis, paralysis
paralel, parallel
parallel,*,led,ling, EACH GOING THE SAME DIRECTION, SIDE BY SIDE, BELONG TOGETHER
parallyzed, paralyze(d)
paralusis, paralysis
paralysis,ytic,yze,yzed,zying,yzation,yzer, TO LOOSE ABILITY TO MOVE VOLUNTARILY
paralyze,*,ed,zing,zation,er, TO LOOSE ABILITY TO MOVE VOLUNTARILY
paramater, parameter / perimeter
paramedic,*, cal, MEDICAL PROFESSIONAL WHO TRAVELS TO GATHER INJURED/SICK PEOPLE

parameter,*,ric,rical, A DEFINED BOUNDARY WHICH BELONGS AS A UNIT, A MATH EXPRESSION
parametic, paramedic
paramiter, parameter / perimeter
paramount,tcy,tship,tly, UPMOST IN IMPORTANCE, AT THE TOP, SUPERIOR TO ANYTHING ELSE
paranoia,id,oeac, FEAR WITHOUT APPARENT REASON
paranoyd, paranoia(id)
paraplegia,ic, PARALYSIS OF LOWER TORSO, LOWER HALF OF BODY CANNOT BE MOVED VOLUNTARILY
parasite,*,tic,tical,tically,ticide,ticidal,tism,tize,tology,tosis, TAKES NOURISHMENT FROM ANOTHER WITHOUT PERMISSION/WILLINGNESS FROM HOST
parate, parade
paratrooper,*, ONE WHO JUMPS FROM PLANE WITH A PARACHUTE
parcel,*,led,ling, A SMALL PACKAGE, BOXED ITEMS, SMALL SECTION OF LAND, TO SECTION OFF
parch,hed,hment, DRY, NEEDS MOISTURE
parcht, parch(ed)
parcle, parcel
pard, part /pair(ed) /pare(d)
pardake, partake
parde, party
pardekul, particle
pardes, party(ties)
pardesapate, participate
pardesubate, participate
pardezan, partisan
pardikul, particle
pardisubant, participate(ant)
pardisupate, participate
pardizan, partisan
pardner, partner
pardnur, partner
pardon,*,ned,ning,nable,nableness,nably, TO FORGIVE
pardukle, particle

parfa, parfait
pari, PREFIX INDICATING "EQUAL" MOST OFTEN MODIFIES THE WORD
paribolic, parabola(lic) /parable(lic)
paride, parity /parody /paroty
paridime, paradigm
paridokical, paradox(ical)
paridoks, paradox
parifen, paraffin
parifuril, peripheral
parigraf, paragraph
parikeet, parakeet
parilel, parallel
parilize, paralyze
parimiter, perimeter /parameter
parimount, paramount
parind, parent
parinoid, paranoia(id)
parinse, parent(s)
parint, parent
parintal, parent(al)
parinthases, parenthesis
paripheral, peripheral
pariplegic, paraplegia(ic)
pariscope, periscope
parish,hes,hioner, CHURCH CONGREGATION (or see perish)
parishute, parachute
parisite, parasite
paritrooper, paratrooper
paritruper, paratrooper
parity,*, THE ACT OF CUTTING/DIVIDING (or see parody or paroty)
park,*,ked,king,ker, LAND FOR PUBLIC REST/ RECREATION, SITUATE A VEHICLE WHERE IT WILL BE IMMOBILE FOR A PERIOD OF TIME
parka,*, HEAVY COAT WITH FUR
parkay, parquet
parkeet, parakeet

parket, parquet
parkt, park(ed)
parku, parka
parodoks, paradox
parody,dies,died,dying,dic,dist, A STORY MAKING LIGHT OF A SERIOUS DRAMA/SITUATION (or see parity or paroty)
parogative, prerogative
parokside, peroxide
parole,ed,ling, UNDER COURT SUPERVISION
parona, piranha
paroose, peruse
parot, parrot
paroxside, peroxide
parportional, proportion(al)
parquet,*,try, TYPE OF WOOD FLOORING
parr, YOUNG FISH (or see par/ pare/ pear/ pair)
parrot,*,ty, A TROPICAL BIRD, TO REPEAT LIKE THE BIRD (or see parody)
parsel, parcel
parsen, parson
parshal, partial
parshul, partial
parsil, parcel
parsin, parson
parsle, parcel
parsley, AN EDIBLE HERB
parsly, parsley
parsnip,*, VEGETABLE
parson,*,nage,nic(al), IN CHARGE OF CHURCH PARISH
parsul, parcel
parsun, parson
part,*,ted,ting,tition,titioning,titioned, SELECT PART OF THE WHOLE/SOMETHING LARGER
partake,*,king,partook, TAKE PART, BE INVOLVED IN AN ASPECT OF
partekul, particle
partekularly, particular(ly)

pardun, pardon
parduzen, partisan
parduzey, party
pare,*,ed,ring, TRIM, CUT-OFF (or see par/ parr/ pair/ pear)
parebolic, parabola(lic) /parable(lic)
paredime, paradigm
paredoks, paradox
parefen, paraffin
pareferul, peripheral
paregraf, paragraph
paragraph, paragraph
parakeet, parakeet
parel, peril
parelel, parallel
parelize, paralyze
paremedic, paramedic
paremeter, perimeter /parameter
paremider, perimeter /parameter
paremount, paramount
parend, parent
parendul, parent(al)
pareneul, perennial
parenial, perennial
parenoid, paranoia(id)
parense, parent(s)
parent,*,ted,ting,tal,tage, PROVIDER OF DNA TO BIRTHED OFFSPRING
parenthesis,es,etic,tical,tically,ize, TWO MARKS (SHAPED LIKE CRESCENT MOONS) ON EITHER SIDE OF WORDS INSERTED INTO A SENTENCE
parepheral, peripheral
pareplegic, paraplegia(ic)
parescope, periscope
paresh, parish /perish
paretruper, paratrooper
parews, peruse
parfae, parfait
parfait, dessert

parten, pardon
partequler, particular
partequlurly, particular(ly)
partesan, partisan
partesapate, participate
parteshen, partition
partial,*,led,ling,lly,lity,lities,lness, PORTION/
   SECTION FROM THE WHOLE, FOCUS ON ONE
participate,*,ed,ting,tion,ant,tive,tor, TO WORK/
   PLAY WITH A GROUP, BE A PART OF
particle,*, OF SMALL PIECE/FRAGMENT IN SCIENTIFIC
   TERMS, PERTAINS TO ENGLISH GRAMMAR
particular,rate,rity,rities,rism,rist,ristic,rize,
   rization,rly,ate, REFERRING SPECIFICALLY TO A
   SMALL PIECE/FRAGMENT/PART
partiel, partial
partikquler, particular
partikul, particle
partikularly, particular(ly)
partin, pardon
partiquler, particular
partisan,*, SUPPORTS A SPECIFIC POLITICAL DOGMA
partisapate, participate
partisapunt, participate(ant)
partishen, partition
partisupent, participate(ant)
partition,*,ned,ning,ner,nment, TO SEGMENT OFF,
   DIVIDE UP INTO PARTS
partner,*,red,ring, ASSOCIATE, RELATIONS BETWEEN
   TWO PEOPLE/GROUPS, ONE OF TWO PEOPLE
partook, PAST TENSE OF "PARTAKE", BE INVOLVED IN
partreg, partridge
partridge,*, A GAME BIRD
partrij, partridge
partucle, particle
partuk, partook
partukle, particle
partun, pardon
partusen, partisan

party,ties,tied,tying, PEOPLE GATHERING FOR FUN/
   LAUGHTER/SPORT/SPECIFIC CAUSE/REASON
paruchute, parachute
parudime, paradigm
parudoks, paradox
parugraf, paragraph
parukeet, parakeet
parul, peril
parulel, parallel
parulize, paralyze
parumont, paramount
parunt, parent
paruplegic, paraplegia(ic)
paruse, peruse
parushute, parachute
parusite, parasite
paruskope, periscope
parutruper, paratrooper
paruze, peruse
parzly, parsley
parznip, parsnip
pasable, pass(able)
pasage, passage
pascripshen, prescript(ion)
pasd, past /paste /pass(ed)
pasdasheo, pistachio
pasdel, pastel
pasder, pastor /pasture
pasderize, pasteurize
pasdirize, pasteurize
pasdor, pastor /pasture
pasdrame, pastrami
pasdree, pastry
pasdrome, pastrami
pasdre, pastry
pasdur, pastor /pasture
pasduresashen, pasteurize(zation)
pasdurize, pasteurize
pase, pace

paseble, pass(able)
pasedge, passage
pasef, passive
pasefikashen, pacify(fication)
pasefy, pacify
paseg, passage
pasej, passage
pasenger, passenger
pases, possess /pass(es) /pause(s)
paseshen, position /possession
pasesuf, possess(ive)
paseve, passive
pashen, passion
pashendly, patient(ly)
pashenit, passion(ate)
pashens, patience /patient(s)
pasheon, passion
pashin, passion
pashindly, patient(ly)
pashins, patience /patient(s)
pashinute, passion(ate)
pashun, passion
pashunit, passion(ate)
pasif, passive
pasific, pacific
pasification, pacify(fication)
pasify, pacify
pasig, passage
pasij, passage
pasinger, passenger
pasinjur, passenger
pasion, passion
pasionate, passion(ate)
pasishen, position
pasition, position
pasive, passive
paskrepshen, prescript(ion)
paskripshen, prescript(ion)
paskription, prescript(ion)

pass,sses,ssed,ssing,ssable,ssably, SKIP FROM ONE TO THE NEXT, MOVE ALONG WITHOUT STOPPING, TO GO AROUND WITHOUT STOPPING

passage,*,ged,ging,eway, A NARROW WAY THROUGH, INTERCHANGE, CORRIDOR

passenger,*, PEOPLE RIDING ON/IN A VEHICLE/ VESSEL TO SOME DESTINATION

passion,*,nate,nately,nal,nless,nateness, A DEEPLY DEVOTED DESIRE FOR SOMETHING

passive,ely,eness,vity, HAS NO REACTION TO ACTION, DOESN'T GENERATE ACTION

past, PAST TENSE OF "PASS", YESTERDAY AND BEYOND, BACK THERE (or see pass(ed) or paste)

pasta, PASTE USED TO MAKE NOODLES

pastachio, pistachio

pastasheo, pistachio

paste,*,ed,ting,ty, A THICK/VISCOUS LIQUID TEXTURE MADE OF A VARIETY OF MATERIAL (or see past)

pastel,*,list, PALE IN COLOR, TYPE OF PAINTING

paster, pastor /pasture

pasteurize,*,ed,zing,zation,zer, HIGH TEMPERA- TURE OVER PERIOD OF TIME TO KILL BACTERIA

pastirize, pasteurize

pastor,*,rship, ONE IN CHARGE OF A CHURCH CONGREGATION (or see pasture)

pastrami, PICKLED BEEF

pastrome, pastrami

pastry,ries, DESSERT, BAKED GOODS

pasture,*,ed,ring,rage,rer, GRASS FIELD USED FOR GRAZING ANIMALS (or see pastor)

pasturesashen, pasteurize(zation)

pasturize, pasteurize

pasuble, pass(able)

pasuf, passive

pasufi, pacify

pasuges, passage(s)

pasuj, passage

pasuve, passive

pat,*,tted,tting, TO LIGHTLY/GENTLY SLAP/ STROKE USING THE HANDS/FEET (or see paid or pate)

pata, pate

patado, potato

pataseum, potassium

patato, potato

patch,hes,hed,hing,hy, TO COVER A HOLE WITH SOMETHING, PROTECTION FOR OPENING

pate,*, A PASTE (or see paid or pat(ty))

pateet, petite

patel, paddle

paten, patent

patenchul, potential

patenshil, potential

patent,*,ted,ting,ncy,tly,tability,table,tor, LEGAL OWNERSHIP OF A PROPERTY/IDEA/INVENTION

potential, potential

pateo, patio

paterbed, perturb(ed)

patern, pattern

paternal,lly,lism,list,listic,nity, MALE PARENT

pateshen, petition

patet, petite

path,*,hway, A DEFINED TRAIL

pathalogical, pathology(gical)

pathetic,cal,cally, MISERY, INHUMANE QUALITY, UNAGREEABLE CONDITION

patho, PREFIX INDICATING "DISEASE" MOST OFTEN MODIFIES THE WORD

pathology,gies,gic,gical,gically, SCIENCE OF STUDY OF DISEASE

patience, RELAX AND ALLOW A NATURAL COURSE (or see patient(s))

patient,*,tly, PAST TENSE OF "PATIENCE", PERSON UNDERGOING MEDICAL CARE (or see patience)

patil, paddle

patina,*, CHEMICAL APPLICATION FOR METAL

patinchul, potential

patint, patent

patintial, potential

patio,*, OUTSIDE AREA NEAR DOOR INTO DWELLING

patirn, pattern

patirnal, paternal

patishen, petition

patite, petite

patition, petition

patle, paddle

patlok, padlock

patreark, patriarch

patrearkul, patriarch(al)

patreit, patriot

patren, patron

patrenize, patron(ize)

patreotic, patriot(ic)

patreut, patriot

patriarch,hal,hship,hy,hies, MALE WHO IS HEAD OF HOUSEHOLD, DOMINANT MALE

patrinize, patron(ize)

patriot,*,tic,tically,tism, SOMEONE WITH STRONG EMOTIONAL TIES TO THEIR COUNTRY

patrol,ler,lled,lling, ONE WHO COVERS PRESCRIBED/ DESIGNATED AREA FOR SECURITY, TO PATROL

patroleum, petrol(eum)

patron,*,nal,nage,nize,nized,nizing,nizingly, SOMEONE WHO PROVIDES SUPPORT FOR GROUPS OF PEOPLE IN NEED, CLIENT

patronise, patron(ize)

patrude, protrude

patrun, patron

patrunize, patron(ize)

patrushen, protrude(usion)

patryarkle, patriarch(al)

patse, patsy

patsy,sies, THE SCAPEGOAT, TAKES THE BLAME

pattern,*,ned,ning, A SHAPE MADE TO REPRESENT AN ORIGINAL TO BE REPRODUCED, ORIGINAL TO BE REPRODUCED

patty,tties, FLAT/ROUND SHAPE (or see paddy)

patunia, petunia
patunya, petunia
paturbed, perturb(ed)
paturn, pattern
paternal, paternal
paty, patty /paddy
pauble, pay(yable)
pauder, powder
pauer, power
paulen, pollen
pauletics, politic(s)
paulip, polyp
paum, palm
paun, pawn
paur, pay(er) /power
paus, pause /paw(s)
pauschur, posture
pause,*,ed,sing,er, *A BRIEF MOMENT OF SILENCE BETWEEN, BRIEF HESITATION (or see paw(s))*
paut, pout
pauvurde, poverty
pave,*, ed,ving,ement, *TO LAY/PREPARE A TRAIL/ ROAD/PATH FOR SMOOTHER TRAVEL, APPLY A COMPOSITE ON TOP OF THE GROUND*
paverdy, poverty
pavershen, pervert(rsion)
pavilion,*, *SMALL ADDITION TO A LARGER BUILDING WHICH IS NORMALLY EXPOSED TO THE ELEMENTS*
pavillion, pavilion
pavmint, pave(ment)
pavt, pave(d)
pavurted, pervert(ed)
paw,*,wed,wing, *FEET BOTTOM OF ANIMALS, TO PERFORM GESTURES AS IF AN ANIMAL USING THEIR FEET (or see pow)*
pawlen, pollen
pawn,*,ned,ning, *TO BORROW MONEY AGAINST AN ARTICLE FOR LATER RETRIEVAL, TO PLEDGE*
paxs, pack(s)

pay,es,paid,ying,yment,yable,yably,yee,yer, *TO GIVE MONEY IN EXCHANGE FOR GOODS/SERVICES (or see pad or paid)*
payd, paid
payleontology, paleontology
payode, peyote
payote, peyote
payst, paste
payt, paid
pazd, past/ paste/ pass(ed)
pazdel, pastel
pazdry, pastry
pazefy, pacify
pazenjer, passenger
pazinger, passenger
pazishen, position
pazt, past/ paste/ pass(ed)
pea,*, *LEGUME/FOOD (or see pee/ peace/ piece)*
peace,*,eful,efully,efulness,eable,eableness,eably, *ATTITUDE/AIRE OF CALM/QUIET (or see piece)*
peach,hes,hy, *A FRUIT*
peacock,*, *A COLORFUL BIRD*
peak,*,ked,king,kedness, *THE CLIMAX/HIGHEST POINT OF A WAVE/OBJECT, MAXIMUM POINT (or see peek or pique)*
peakok, peacock
peal, *SOUNDS/RINGS (or see peel)*
peano, piano
peanut,*, *A LEGUME, SMALL NUT*
pear,*, *A FRUIT (or see pare or pair)*
pearl,*,ly,lized, *PRODUCED BY OYSTER, HAVING THE QUALITIES OF A PEARL*
peasant,*, try, *SIMPLE PERSON WHO LIVES OFF THE LAND (or see pheasant)*
peasful, peace(ful)
peat,ty, *DRIED PLANTS PARTIALLY DECAYED*
peave, peeve
pebble,*, *TINY ROCKS/STONES*
pebel, pebble

peber, pepper
pebil, pebble
pebir, pepper
pebul, pebble
pebur, pepper
pec, peck /pick /pig /pique /peak /peek
pecalo, picolo
pecan,*, *AN EDIBLE NUT*
pecdorul, pectoral /pictorial
pech, peach /pitch
peched, pitch(ed)
pecher, pitcher /picture
peck,*,ked,king,ky,ker, *BIRDS USING THEIR BILLS TO STAB/JAB, A MEASUREMENT OF WEIGHT (or see pick /pig /pique /peak /peek)*
pecnic, picnic
pecok, peacock
pecs, *SHORT FOR PECTORAL MUSCLES(or seepeck(s))*
pecsher, picture /pitcher
pect, pick(ed)/ peck(ed)/ peak(ed)
pecten,*, *A SCIENTIFIC PROCESS (or see pectin)*
pectin, *WAXY SUBSTANCE COLLECTED FROM WALLS OF PLANTS, USED TO STIFFEN (or see pecten)*
pecton, pectin /pecten
pectoral,*, *OF THE CHEST/BREAST, FINS ON FISH*
pectorial, pectoral /pictorial
pectun, pectin /pecten
pecturul, pectoral
peculiar,rly,rity,rities,ry,rily, *STRANGE, UNUSUAL*
ped, peat / pet
ped, pedi, pedo, *PREFIX INDICATING "FOOT/CHILD" MOST OFTEN MODIFIES THE WORD*
pedagogy,gies,gogue,gic,gicical,gically,gics, *ART/ SCIENCE OF TEACHING, AN EDUCATOR*
pedagree, pedigree
pedakure, pedicure
pedal,*,lled,lling,ller, *USE FOOT/LEVER TO CREATE MOVEMENT/ACTION (or see petal/peddle)*

peddle,*,ed,ling,er, MOVING/GOING ABOUT SELLING
    WARES/GOODS (or see petal or pedal)
pede, petty /pity
pedeatrician, pediatrician
pedeatrics, pediatrics
pedeatrishen, pediatrician
pedecoat, petticoat
pedegogy, pedagogy
pedegree, pedigree
pedekote, petticoat
pedekure, pedicure
pedel, pedal/ petal/ peddle
peder, peter
pedestal,*,led,ling, A BASE/STAND/PODIUM
pedestle, pedestal
pedestrian,*,, ONE WHO TRAVELS BY FOOT/ON THEIR
    FEET, SOMEONE WHO IS WALKING
pedeutrishen, pediatrician
pedi, ped, pedo, PREFIX INDICATING "FOOT/CHILD"
    MOST OFTEN MODIFIES THE WORD
pediatrician,*, DOCTOR FOR CHILDREN
pediatrishen, pediatrician
pediatrics, SCIENCE THAT WORKS WITH CHILDREN
pediatrishen, pediatrician
pedicoat, petticoat
pedicure,*,rist, WORKING WITH THE FEET
pedid, pet(tted)
pedigogy, pedagogy
pedigree,*,ed, HAS LEGAL PAPERS SHOWING
    ANCESTRY
pedikote, petticoat
pedil, pedal/ petal /peddle
pedir, peter
pedistal, pedestal
pedle, pedal/ petal/ peddle
pedo, pedi, ped, PREFIX INDICATING "FOOT/CHILD"
    MOST OFTEN MODIFIES THE WORD
pedrafication, petrify(fication)
pedrify, petrify
pedrol, petrol

pedroleim, petrol(eum)
pedrufy, petrify
peds, pet(s)
pedugogy, pedagogy
pedugree, pedigree
pedul, pedal/ petal/ peddle
pedur, peter
pedustal, pedestal
pedy, petty /pity
pee,*,ed,eing, TO URINATE (or see pea)
peech, peach
peed, peat /pee(d)
peek,*,ked,king, TO GET A QUICK GLIMPSE OF, TO
    SEE QUICKLY (or see peak)
peekt, peek(ed)
peel,*,led,ling,ler, TO REMOVE OUTER LAYER/SKIN
peenk, pink
peep,*,ped,ping,per, LOOK/GLIMPSE INTO
peeple,people
peer,*,rless,rlessly,rlessness, OF THE SAME AGE/
    RANK/STATUS, TO FOCUS YOUR GAZE FARAWAY,
    LOOK INTO (or see pyre/ pier/ pierce /pier(s))
peeroet, pirouette
peers, pier(s)/ peer(s)/ pierce
pees, pea(s)/ peace/ piece/ pee(s)
peeve,*,, vish,vishly,vishness, IRRITATE/AGGRAVATE
pef, peeve
pefs, peeve(s)
peg,*,gged,gging, A SPIKE OF ANY MATERIAL USED TO
    HOLD UP/HOLD DOWN SOMETHING
pegamus, pajamas
pegated, picket(ed)
pegen, pigeon
peget, picket
pegul, pickle
pegy, pig(ggy) /pick(y)
peiny, peony
peir, pier/ peer/ pyre
peirce, pierce

peirse, pierce /pier(s) /peer(s)
pejamus, pajamas
pejen, pigeon
pek, peck /pick /pig /pique /peak /peek
pekalo, picolo
pekan, pecan
pekel, pickle
peker, pick(er) /peck(er)
pekewler, peculiar
pekit, picket
peknik, picnic
pekok, peacock
pekol, pickle
pekon, pecan
peksher, picture /pitcher
pekten, pectin / pecten
pektin, pectin / pecten
pektoral, pectoral /pictorial
pektorul, pectoral /pictorial
pektun, pectin / pecten
pekture, picture /pitcher
pekul, pickle
pekuler, peculiar
pekuleur, peculiar
pekur, pick(er) /peck(er)
peky, pick(y)
pel, peel/ peal/ pill
pelacan, pelican
pelaf, pilaf
pelage, pillage
pelakan, pelican
pelar, pillar
pelaredy, polar(ity)
pelej, pillage
pelekan, pelican
peler, pillar
pelese, police
pelet, pellet
pelgrem, pilgrim

pelgremege, pilgrim(age)
pelgrim, pilgrim
pelican,*, *A LARGE BIRD WHO EATS FISH*
peligamus, polygamy(mous)
peligamy, polygamy
pelit, pellet /polite
pellet,*, *ANYTHING SMALL/ROUND/HARD*
pellow, pillow
pelminary, pulmonary
pelof, pilaf
pelot, pellet
pelow, pillow
pelt,*, ,ted,ting, *ANYTHING SMALL/ROUND/HARD*
HITTING SOMETHING, THE HIDE AND HAIR FROM A
SMALL ANIMAL
peluge, pillage
pelukin, pelican
pelushen, pollute(tion)
pelut, pellet / pollute
pelutent, pollute(tant)
pelution, pollute(tion)
pelvek, pelvic
pelves, pelvis
pelvic, *LARGE BONE ON LOWER TORSO WHERE LEGS*
ARE ATTACHED
pelvis,es,ic, *LARGE BONE ON LOWER TORSO WHERE*
LEGS ARE ATTACHED
pelygamus, polygamy(mous)
pelygamy, polygamy
peminto, pimento
pemp, pimp
pempul, pimple
pemt, pimp(ed)
pen,*, ,nned,nning, *INSTRUMENT WITH INK FOR WRIT-*
ING, HAVING BEEN WRITTEN/COMPOSED, FEMALE
SWAN, CAGE FOR PIGS (or see pin/pent)
penacle, pentacle / pinnacle
penada, pinata
penagon, pentagon

penagram, pentagram
penakle, pinnacle /pentacle
penal,*,lize,lization,lly,lity,lties, *PUNISHMENT*
penasilen, penicillin
penatrable, penetrable
penatrashen, penetrate(tion)
penatrate, penetrate
pench, pinch
penchant, *DESIRE MOSTLY, STRONG LIKING FOR, BIAS*
penchers, pinch(ers) or pincers
pencil,*, ,led,ling, *WOODEN/GRAPHITE WRITING*
INSTRUMENT, TO USE TO WRITE
pendalum, pendulum
pendant,dent,*, *ITEM HANGING FROM SOMETHING,*
SUSPENDED ITEM
pendelum, pendulum
pendulum, pendulum
pending, *ACTION IN PROCESS AIMED FOR COMPLETION*
pendo, pinto
pendulum,*,lar, *SUSPENDED FROM A FIXED POINT,*
ENDS FREE TO SEEK BALANCE/EQUILIBRIUM
peneal gland, pineal gland
penecilin, penicillin
penecle, pinnacle / pentacle
penegram, pentagram
penensula, peninsula
peneol gland, pineal gland
penes, penis
penetrable,*,bility,eness,ly, *ABLE/ EXPOSED TO*
ACCEPT/EXPERIENCE INCOMING/ PENETRATION,
BOUNDARIES ALLOW FOR INFILTRATION
penetrate,*, ,ed,ting,tion,ant,tive,tively,tiveness,
TO ENTER/PIERCE/AFFECT
pengalum, pendulum
pengilum, pendulum
penguin,*, , *BIRD OF THE ANTARCTIC*
pengwen, penguin
penial gland, pineal gland
penicillin,ium,ia, *ANTIBIOTIC DERIVED FROM A MOLD,*
USED FOR KILLING BACTERIA

penikul, pentacle / pinnacle
peninsula,*,ar, *FINGER/PORTION OF LAND JUTTING*
FROM THE MAINLAND, SURROUNDED BY WATER
penis, *MALE ORGAN USED FOR COPULATION/URINATION*
penjalum, pendulum
penjulem, pendulum
penk, pink
penkwen, penguin
penky, pink(y)
penny,nnies, *A U.S. COIN*
pennyul gland, pineal gland
pensel, pencil
pensers, pincers / pinch(ers)
penshen, pension
penshent, penchant
pensil, pencil
pension,*,nable,nary,naries,ner, *A REGULARLY*
ALLOTTED ALOWANCE
pensul, pencil
pent, *CLOSED OFF, SHUT IN (or see pen(ned)/ pint)*
pent, penta,peta, *PREFIX INDICATING "FIVE" MOST*
OFTEN MODIFIES THE WORD
pentacle,*, *A FIVE POINT STAR*
pentagon,nal,nally, *U.S. OFFICE OF DEFENSE*
pentagram,*, , *A PENTACLE, FIVE POINT STAR*
pentalum, pendulum
pentegram, pentagram
pentigon, pentagon
pentilum, pendulum
penting, pending
pento, pinto
pentucle, pentacle / pinnacle
pentugon, pentagon
pentulem, pendulum
penud, peanut
penugon, pentagon
penugram, pentagram
penukel, pentacle / pinnacle
penulize, penal(ize)

penulty, penal(ty)
penus, penis
penusilen, penicillin
penut, peanut
penutrashen, penetrate(tion)
penutruble, penetrable
peny, penny
penyada, pinata
penyoda, pinata
peode, peyote
peony,nies, A FLOWER
people,*, HUMANS
peote, peyote
pep,*, pped,pping,ppy, VIGOR/ENERGY ENERGETIC
(or see peep)
pepal, people
pepe, pep(ppy)
peper, pepper
pepil, people
pepir, pepper
pepiu, papaya
peple, people
peporshenal, proportion(al)
pepul, people
pepur, pepper
pepy, pep(ppy)
pequleur, peculiar
per, BY/THROUGH/EACH (or see peer or purr)
per, PREFIX INDICATING "COMPLETELY/ THOROUGHLY"
MOST OFTEN MODIFIES THE WORD
perabolic, parabola(lic)/ parable(lic)
perabul, parable
perade, parade
peradime, paradigm
peradox, paradox
perafen, paraffin
peragative, prerogative

peragraf, paragraph
perakeet, parakeet
peralasis, paralysis
peralel, parallel
peralises, paralysis
peralusis, paralysis
peramedur, parameter /perimeter
perametic, paramedic
perametur, parameter /perimeter
peramid, pyramid
peramitur, parameter /perimeter
peramount, paramount
peranoid, paranoia(id)
peranoyd, paranoia(id)
perant, parent
peraplegic, paraplegia(ic)
perascope, periscope
perashute, parachute
perasite, parasite
perate, parade
peratruper, paratrooper
peraty, parody/ parity/ parot(y)
perbendikuler, perpendicular
perceive,*, ed,ving,er, TO SEE/UNDERSTAND/KNOW
percent,*, tage,tages,tile,tum, PORTION OF THE
WHOLE AMOUNT
percept,tion,tional,tive,tively,tiveness,tivity,tual
tually, TO KNOW/PERCEIVE WITH THE SENSES
perceptible,bility,bly,KNOW/PERCEIVE WITH SENSES
perceive, perceive
perch,hes,hed,hing, A FISH, WHERE BIRDS ROOST,
TINY BUILDING OUTCROP (or see purge)
perchus, purchase /perch(es)
percieve, perceive
percintage, percent(age)
percipatation, precipitate(tion)
percivere, persevere
percrastination, procrastinate
percushen, percussion

percussion,*,nist,ive,ively,iveness, IMPACT BET-
WEEN TWO BODIES OF MATTER, MUSICAL
INSTRUMENT GROUP
pereadontek, periodontic
pereadontist, periodontist
perebolic, parabola(lic)/ parable(lic)
perebul, parable
perechute, parachute
peredime, paradigm
peredox, paradox
peredy, parody/ parity/ parot(y)
pereferul, peripheral
perefin, paraffin
peregraf, paragraph
perekeet, parakeet
perel, peril
perelel, parallel
perelize, paralyze
peremedic, paramedic
peremont, paramount
peremownt, paramount
perend, parent
perenial, perennial
perennial,*,lly, EXISTS/GROWS ALL YEAR LONG
perenoya, paranoia
perens, parent(s)
perent, parent
pereod, period
pereodic, periodic /periotic
pereot, period
pereotecul, periodic(al)
pereotic, periodic / periotic
pereotical, periodic(al)
perepheral, peripheral
pereple, parable
pereplegic, paraplegia(ic)
perescope, periscope
peresh, parish /perish
pereshute, parachute

peresite, parasite
peret, parrot
peretruper, paratrooper
pereud, period
pereudonteks, periodontic(s)
pereudontest, periodontist
perfect,ted,ting,tion,ter,tness,tible,tible,tibilist, tibility,tionism,tionist,tionistic,tive,tively, tiveness,tivity,tly,to,tos, *GREAT AT THE MOMENT, SYNCHRONOUS, HARMONIC*
pefekshen, perfect(ion)
perfeted, pervert(ed)
perfikt, perfect
perform,*,med,ming,mance,mances,mable, mer, *ACT/PLAY OUT/MOTION/FUNCTIONABLE*
performence, perform(ance)
perfume,*,ed,ming,ery,eries, *A SCENT/SMELL WHICH COMES NATURALLY OR IS APPLIED*
pergatory, purgatory
perge, purge
perger, perjure
pergery, perjure(ry)
pergitory, purgatory
pergury, perjure(ry)
pergutory, purgatory
perhaps, could be, likely, possible
peri, *PREFIX INDICATING "AROUND/ABOUT" MOST OFTEN MODIFIES THE WORD*
periadontist, periodontist
peribolic, parabola(lic)/ parable(lic)
peribul, parable
perichute, parachute
peridime, paradigm
peridox, paradox
perifen, paraffin
perifuril, peripheral
perigraf, paragraph
perikeet, parakeet

peril,*, led,ling,lous,lously,lousness, *CAUTION, GREAT DANGER, HAZARDOUS (OR SEE PEARL)*
perilel, parallel
perilize, paralyze
perimed, pyramid
perimedic, paramedic
perimeter,*,tric,trical,trically,ry, *AROUND A PARTICULAR AREA, CIRCUMFERENCE, BOUNDARY/SIDES* (or see parameter)
perimetic, paramedic
perimider, perimeter /parameter
perimiter, perimeter /parameter
perimount, paramount
perind, parent
perinoid, paranoia(id)
perinoya, paranoia
perinse, parent(s)
perint, parent
period,*, , *A PUNCTUATION MARK, SPAN OF TIME, MOMENT, MENSTRUATION*
periodic,cal,cally,city, *RECURRING, PREDICTABLE PATTERN* (or see periotic)
periodontic,*,tal,ia,ium, *SCIENCE/STUDY OF THE TEETH/GUMS*
periodontist, *DENTIST/DOCTOR, OF TEETH*
periotic, *OF THE EAR* (or see periodic)
peripheral,ric,rally,ry,ries, *GENERAL EXTERIOR AREA AROUND A NUCLEUS/CENTER/TOWN, CIRCUMFERENCE*
periple, parable
periplegic, paraplegia(ic)
periscope,*,pic,pical, *USED IN SUBMARINES/TANKS FOR VIEWING ABOVE THE VESSEL/WATER*
perish,hes,hed,hing,hable,hability,hableness, hably, *STOP BEING ALIVE, END OF GROWING/ BREATHING, BEGIN TO ROT* (or see parish)
perisite, parasite
perit, parrot
perituper, paratrooper

perity, parody/ parity/ parot(y)
perje, purge
perjure,ed,ring,er,ry,ries,rious,riously, *KNOW-INGLY MAKE A FALSE STATEMENT UNDER OATH*
perkeet, parakeet
perkrastination, procrastinate
perkushen, percussion
perkusion, percussion
perl, pearl
permanence,cy,cies,nt,ntly,ntness, *THE STATE OF BEING PERMANENT/FIXED*
permanent,tly,tness, *CHEMICAL TREATMENT DONE TO HAIR, A FIXED POSITION, NONMOVING*
permanins, permanence
permeable,ly,bility, *FILTERS/SPREADS/ABSORBS, FILLS SPACE IN BETWEEN*
permeate,*,ed,ting,tion,tive,ance,able,ableness, ably,ability, *FILTERS/SPREADS/ABSORBS, FILLS SPACE IN BETWEEN*
permenant, permanent
permenence, permanence
permeuble, permeable
permiate, permeate
permishen, permission
permisive, permission(ive)
permissible,bility,ly, *HAVE APPROVAL FOR/OF, ALLOWABLE*
permission,ible,ibility,ibleness,ibly,ive,ively, iveness, *HAVE APPROVAL FOR/OF*
permisuf, permission(ive)
permit,*,tted,tting,tter, *RECEIPT/LICENSE/ALLOWING APPROVAL* (or see pyramid)
permited, permit(tted)
permition, permission
permunint, permanent
permunins, permanence
perodox, paradox
perody, parody/ parity/ parot(y)
peroet, pirouette

perogative, prerogative
perograf, paragraph
perokside, peroxide
perole, parole
perona, piranha
peront, parent
peroose, peruse
perosity, porosity
peroty, parody/ parity/ parot(y)
peroxide,ed,ding, A CHEMICAL
perpel, purple
perpendicular,rity,rly, RIGHT ANGLE TO A PLANE
perpes, purpose
perpesly, purpose(ly)
perpetrate,*,ed,ting,tion,tor, EXECUTE, COMMIT
perpetshuate, perpetual(ate)
perpetual,lly,ate,able,ation,ator,uity,uties, ONGOING, FOREVER, CONTINUOUS
perpetuity,uties, ongoing, FOREVER, CONTINUOUS
perpil, purple
perpindicular, perpendicular
perpis, purpose
perpisly, purpose(ly)
perplex,xes,xed,xing,xingly,xity,xities, NOT UNDERSTANDING, CONFUSED
perpol, purple
perporshenal, proportion(al)
perportional, proportion(al)
perpos, purpose
perposly, purpose(ly)
perposterus, preposterous
perpostirus, preposterous
perpul, purple
perpus, purpose
perpusle, purpose(ly)
perputrate, perpetrate

perrenial, perennial
pers, pierce/ purse/ pier(s)/ peer(s)
persacute, persecute
persafere, persevere
persanu, persona
persarverance, persevere(rance)
persavere, persevere
persbektif, perspective
persbiration, perspiration
persbire, perspire
perscripshen, prescript(ion)
perse, purse
persebduble, perceptible
persebtef, percept(ive)
persecute,*,ed,ting,tion,tive,tor, TO AGGRAVATE/HARASS/PUNISH (or see prosecute)
persede, precede / proceed
persenality, personality
persenaly, personal(lly)
persenel, personnel
persent, percent
persentige, percent(age)
persentil, percent(ile)
persenuble, person(able)
persenulize, personal(ize)
persepatashen, precipitate(tion)
persepshen, percept(ion)
perseptable, perceptible
perseptef, percept(ive)
perseption, percept(ion)
perseptive, percept(ive)
perserverance, persevere(rance)
perservere, persevere
perseshen, precision / procession /precession
persest, persist
persestince, persist(ence)
perseve, perceive
persevere,*,ed,ring,ringly,rance, TO PERSIST, CONTINUE ON DESPITE ODDS/OBSTACLES

persh, perch /purge
pershis, purchase /perch(es)
persikute, persecute
persin, person
persinaledy, personality
persinel, personnel
persint, percent
persinuble, person(able)
persinul, personal
persinulize, personal(ize)
persinuly, personal(lly)
perspipetashen, precipitate(tion)
perspipitation, precipitate(tion)
persirverance, persevere(rance)
perskripshen, prescript(ion)
persishen, precision
persist,*,ted,ting,tence,tency,tent,tently, CONSISTENT IN FOCUS, TENACIOUS
persition, precision
persivere, persevere
persiverense, persevere(rance)
perskripshen, prescript(ion)
persokut, persecute
person,*,na,nal,nate,nalty,nalties,nation,native,native, nator,nification,nify,nifier,nify,nification, PEOPLE, ONE HUMAN BEING
personal,*,able,ableness,age,ly,lism,lty,lity, lities,lize, AURA/ESSENCE/ATTITUDE/BEHAVIOR OF A PERSON, CAN RELATE TO OTHERS
personality,ties, A PERSON'S ATTITUDE/BEHAVIOR
personefication, person(ification)
personel, personnel /personal
personify,fier,fies,fied,fying,fication, TO REPRESENT AS HUMAN, ACT LIKE, ACT AS IF
personnel, GROUP/BODY OF PEOPLE, DEPARTMENT WHICH HANDLES EMPLOY OF PEOPLE
persoo, pursue
perspective,*,ely, FROM A CERTAIN POINT OF VIEW
persperashen, perspiration

perspiration, TO SWEAT, RELEASE WATER FROM THE PORES TO COOL OFF
perspire,*,ed,ring,tion,tory, TO SWEAT, RELEASE WATER FROM THE PORES TO COOL OFF
persuade,*,ed,ding,asion,dible,asive,asively, asiveness, COERCE/SWAY/IMPRESS SOMEONE/ SOMETHING TO COMMIT TO YOUR IDEALS
persuasion, COERCE/SWAY/IMPRESS SOMEONE
persude, pursue(d)
persu, pursue
persun, person
persunal, personal
persunality, personality
persunaly, personal(lly)
persunel, personnel
persute, pursue(uit)
persuvere, persevere
perswade, persuade
perswaseve, persuade(asive)
perswashen, persuade(asion)
perswasif, persuade(asive)
pert,tly,tness, chic, BRIGHT, LIVELY
pertain,*,ned,ning, ASSOCIATED WITH, BELONGS TO
pertane, pertain
pertishen, partition
pertrayal, portray(al)
pertrude, protrude
perturb,*,bed,bing,bable,bation,bational, BOTHERED BY, DISTURBED
peruble, parable
perudime, paradigm
perudox, paradox
perufin, paraffin
perugraf, paragraph
perukeet, parakeet
perul, peril
perulel, parallel
perulised, paralyze(d)
perulize, paralyze

perumedic, paramedic
perumid, pyramid
perumount', paramount
perund, parent
perunoid, paranoia(id)
perunoya, paranoia
perunt, parent
peruphen, paraffin
peruplegic, paraplegia(ic)
perupul, parable
peruse,*,ed,sing,sal, TO READ/EXAMINE CAREFULLY
perushute, parachute
perusite, parasite
peruskope, periscope
perut, parrot
perutruper, paratrooper
pervade,*,ed,ding,er,asion,asive,asively, asiveness, TO PERMEATE, SPREAD THROUGH
pervashen, pervade(asion)
pervasif, pervade(asion)
pervert,*,ted,tedly,dness,ter,tibility,tible,tibly, rse,rsely,rseness,rsion,rsity,rsities,rsive, DEVIANT BY SOCIETAL NORMS
perzakute, persecute
perzaverinse, persevere(rance)
perzuverinse, persevere(rance)
pes, peace/ piece/ pee(s)/ pea(s)
pesa, pizza
pesamist, pessimism(st)
pesamistic, pessimism(stic)
pesamisum, pessimism
pesant, peasant
pesd, pest
pesdalense, pestilence
pesdasheo, pistachio
pesdaside, pesticide
pesdrome, pastrami
pesdulinse, pestilence
pesebly, peace(ably)

pesel, pestle
pesemisum, pessimism
pesent, peasant
peses, possess
pesesuf, possess(ive)
pesful, peace(ful)
pesher, pitcher /picture
pesibly, peace(ably)
pesific, pacific
pesil, pestle
pesimesum, pessimism
pesimist, pessimism(st)
pesimistic, pessimism(stic)
pesint, peasant
pesishen, position
position, position
peskripshen, prescript(ion)
pesol, pestle
pessimism,st,stic,stically, CONTRARY TO, THE DOWNSIDE
pessimistic,tically, CONTRARY TO, THE DOWNSIDE
pest,*,ty, ANNOYANCE, BOTHERSOME
pestachio, pistachio
pestal, pestle /pistol /pistil
pestalinse, pestilence
pestasheo, pistachio
pestaside, pesticide
pestel, pistil/ pistol/ pestle
pestelinse, pestilence
pesten, piston
pesticide,*,dal, HARMFUL/POISONOUS CHEMICALS USED TO KILL INSECTS/ANIMALS/PLANTS
pestil, pistil/ pistol/ pestle
pestilence, DISEASE WHICH SPREADS THROUGHOUT
pestin, piston
pestle,*,ed,ling, GRIND/PULVERIZE/CRUSH/SMASH AGAINST A SURFACE WITH THIS AS A TOOL, NORMALLY ASSOCIATED WITH MORTAR/PESTLE
pestrome, pastrami

pestul, pistil/ pistol/ pestle
pestuled, pestle(d)
pestun, piston
pestuside, pesticide
pesuble, peace(able)
pesubly, peace(ably)
pesul, pestle
pesumisem, pessimism
pesumistic, pessimism(stic)
pet,*,tted,tting, AN ANIMAL KEPT CONFINED AND FED BY HUMANS, TO STROKE (or see peat)
peta, pent, penta, PREFIX INDICATING "FIVE" MOST OFTEN MODIFIES THE WORD
petado, potato
petagogy, pedagogy
petagojik, pedagogy(gic)
petagree, pedigree
petakure, pedicure
petal,*,led, PART OF FLOWER(or see pedal/peddle)
petaseum, potassium
petasium, potassium
petato, potato
petch, pitch
petcher, pitcher /picture
pete, petty /pity
peteatriks, pediatrics
peteatrishen, pediatrician
petecoat, petticoat
peted, pet(tted)
petegree, pedigree
petekote, petticoat
petekure, pedicure
petel, pedal/ petal/ peddle
petena, patina
peteness, petty(ttiness)
peter,*,red,ring, TO GET TIRED, RUN OUT OF ENERGY
petestul, pedestal
peteutrishen, pediatrician
pethetic, pathetic

peti, petty
petiatrics, pediatrics
peticoat, petticoat
peticure, pedicure
petier, petty(ttier)
petiest, petty(ttiest)
petigree, pedigree
petikote, petticoat
petikure, pedicure
petil, pedal/ petal/ peddle
petina, patina
petinchul, potential
petiness, petty(ttiness)
petinshul, potential
petir, peter
petistul, pedestal
petite,eness, SMALL WITH NORMAL PROPORTIONS
petition,*,ned,ning, SOLICIT/APPROACH/REQUEST SOMETHING
petle, pedal/ petal/ peddle
petnik, picnic
petr, petri, petro, PREFIX INDICATING "STONE/ PETROLEUM" MOST OFTEN MODIFIES THE WORD
petrafikashen, petrify(fication)
petrafy, petrify
petrefication, petrify(fication)
petrefy, petrify
petrewd, protrude
petrify,fies,fied,fying,fication,factive,faction, BE FROZEN WITH HORROR, TURNED TO STONE
petro, petri, petr, PREFIX INDICATING "STONE/ PETROLEUM" MOST OFTEN MODIFIES THE WORD
petrol, patrol
petrol,*,leum, HYDROCARBON/OIL/FUEL
petrolium, petrol(eum)
petrude, protrude
petrushen, protrude(usion)
petsa, pizza
petticoat,*, , UNDERGARMENT, LAYERED SLIP

petty,ttier,ttiest,ttily,ttiness, SMALL/RESTRICTIVE/ HABITUAL OUTLOOK LOOK FOR FLAWS
petugogy, pedagogy
petugree, pedigree
petul, pedal/ petal/ peddle
petunia,*, , A FLOWER
petur, peter
peturbed, perturb(ed)
peturnol, paternal
petustel, pedestal
pety, petty /pity
peu, pew
peub, pube
peuberdy, puberty
peubik, pube(bic)
peuburdy, puberty
peuk, puke
peunatef, punitive
peune, peony /puny
peunutive, punitive
peuny, peony /puny
peupul, pupil
peur, pier/ peer/ pyre/ pure
peuraficashen, purify(fication)
peure, puree'
peurefide, purify(fied)
peurfy, purify
peurly, puree(ly)
peury, puree'
peutrid, putrid
pev, peeve
pevurted, pervert(ed)
pew,*, , BENCH SEATS IN CHURCH
pewder, pewter
pewding, pudding /putt(ing)
pewdur, pewter
pewne, puny
pewpul, pupil
pewt, put

pewter,rer, MOLDABLE METAL MADE WITH LEAD, USED AS DISHES/VESSELS
pewtrid, putrid
pex, pick(s) /peck(s)
peyer, pure
peyeree, puree'
peyerify, purify
peyerly, pure(ly)
peyir, pure
peyote,*,tle, CACTUS, PRODUCES MESCALINE
peyur, pure
peyuree, puree'
peyurefide, purify(fied)
peyurify, purify
peyurly, pure(ly)
pez, pea(s) /peace /piece
peza, pizza
pezamistic, pessimism(stic)
pezd, pest
pezdalense, pestilence
pezdaside, pesticide
pezent, peasant
pezes, possess
pezful, peace(ful)
pezt, pest
pezubly, peace(ably)
pezunt, peasant
phalanthropy, philanthropy
phalek, philli(c)
philli,ic,icism,ism,icist,luses, OF THE PENIS
phalosify, philosophy
phanetik, phonetic
phanik, phonic
phantem, phantom
phantom,*, AN ILLUSIVE/SURREAL APPARITION, NOT PHYSICAL
pharaoh,*,onic(al) EGYPTIAN KINGS
pharmac, pharmaco, PREFIX INDICATING "DRUGS/ MEDICINES" MOST OFTEN MODIFIES THE WORD

pharmaceutic,*,cal,cally, DISPENSING OF MANMADE CHEMICALS/DRUGS
pharmacist,*, ONE WHO DISPENSES MANMADE CHEMICALS/DRUGS/MEDICINE
pharmasutical, pharmaceutic(al)
pharmicist, pharmacist
pharmusutical, pharmaceutical(al)
pharoh, pharaoh
phase,*, ed,sing, AN ASPECT/PORTION OF AN OVERALL PROJECT/DESIGN, CHANGES/MOVEMENT
phasek, physique
phasic, physique
phasishen, physician
phasphate, phosphate
phausfate, phosphate
phaze, phase
pheasant,*, GAME BIRD
pheladendron, philodendron
phelanthrapist, philanthropy(pist)
phelanthropek, philanthropy(pic)
phelarmonic, philharmonic
phelodendron, philodendron
phelosofy, philosophy
pheludindron, philodendron
phenaminan, phenomenon
phenomenal,ly,lism,list,listic,listically, INCREDIBLE, EXTRAORDINARY
phenomenon,*, STRANGE/UNCHARACTERISTIC BEHAVIOR/EVENT, GIVEN TO THE INVISIBLE
phenominon, phenomenon
pheroh, pharaoh
phesant, pheasant
phesasist, physicist
phesek, physique /physic
phesent, pheasant
pheseology, physiology
phesesist, physicist
phesic physic /physique
phesint, pheasant

phesod, facade
phesunt, pheasant
phil, philo, PREFIX INDICATING "LOVE" MOST OFTEN MODIFIES THE WORD
philadendron, philodendron
philanthrapist, philanthropy(pist)
philanthropek, philanthropy(pic)
philanthropy,pies,pic,pical,pically,pist, GIVE TO MANKIND VIA A KIND ACT/MONEY, A BENEFACTOR
philarmonic, philharmonic
philasofical, philosophy(hical)
philasophical, philosophy(hical)
philermonic, philharmonic
philharmonic,*, LOVE OF HARMONICS, ENJOYMENT OF HARMONIC MUSICAL INSTRUMENTS
philodendron,*, A TROPICAL PLANT
philosofy, philosophy
philosophy,hies,her,hic,hical,hically,hize,hizer, ACQUISITION/ACCUMULATION OF WISDOM WHETHER PHYSICAL OR METAPHYSICAL
philudindron, philodendron
philurmonic, philharmonic
phinaminan, phenomenon
phinaumenun, phenomenon
phinetik, phonetic
phinomenal, phenomenal
phinominan, phenomenon
phisasist, physicist
phisecal, physical
phisek, physique /physic
phiseks, physics
phiseologikul, physiology(gical)
phiseology, physiology
phisesist, physicist
phishen, fission
phisic physic /physique
phisical, physical
phisiks, physics
phisiology, physiology

phisisist, physicist
phisyological, physiology(gical)
phisyologist, physiology(gist)
phlabadumist, phlebotomy(mist)
phlabitis, phlebitis
phlabodumist, phlebotomy(mist)
phlabotomy, phlebotomy
phlebitis,ic, *VEIN INFLAMMATION/SWELLING*
phlebodomist, phlebotomy(mist)
phlebotomy,mic,mist,mize, *OPENING VEINS TO RELIEVE PRESSURE*
phlegm,my, *MUCUS*
phlem, phlegm
phlibites, phlebitis
phlibodumist, phlebotomy(mist)
phlibotomy, phlebotomy
phlim, phlegm
phlubotomy, phlebotomy
phnegraf, phonograph
phobea, phobia
phobia,bic, *UNFOUNDED FEAR, NO APPARENT REASON FOR FEAR/DREAD*
phodagraf, photo(graph)
phodasinthesis, photosynthesis
phodegraf, photo(graph)
phodesinthesis, photosynthesis
phodo, photo
phodograf, photo(graph)
phodon, photon
phodosynthesis, photosynthesis
phodugraf, photo(graph)
phon, phono, *PREFIX INDICATING "SOUND" MOST OFTEN MODIFIES THE WORD*
phone,*,ed,ning, *SPEAKING/HEARING COMMUNICATION DEVICE*
phonegraph, phonograph
phonetic,*,cal,cally, *METHOD OF HOW WORDS ARE HEARD/SPOKEN AND TRANSMITTED, THE SOUND/AUDIO CONCERNING WORDS*

phonic,*, *IDENTIFYING/SPELLING WORDS ACCORDING TO THEIR SOUNDS*
phonigraf, phonograph
phonograph,*, *hic,hical,hically, RECORD PLAYER*
phony,ney, *fake/not real (also spelled phoney)*
phosfade, phosphate
phosfate, phosphate
phosphate,*, *A CHEMICAL/SALT*
phot, photo, *PREFIX INDICATING "LIGHT" MOST OFTEN MODIFIES THE WORD*
photagraf, photo(graph)
photasinthesis, photosynthesis
photigraf, photo(graph)
photo,*,ograph,ographer,ography,ographic, ographical,ographically, *PICTURE CREATED IN A PROCESS USING LIGHT*
photograf, photo(graph)
photon,*,nic, *A QUANTUM PARTICLE WITH NO MASS/CHARGE*
photosinthesis, photosynthesis
photosynthesis,ize,etic,etically, *PROCESS WHERE PLANTS TURN LIGHT INTO ENERGY*
photugraf, photo(graph)
phsycist, physicist
phulanthrapy, philanthropy
phulosefy, philosophy
phunamina, phenomenon
phunomenal, phenomenal
phuzek, physique
phycisian, physician
phycisist, physicist
physasist, physicist
physecal, physical
physek, physique /physic
physeks, physics
physekul, physical
physeological, physiology(gical)
physeology, physiology
physeshan, physician

physesist, physicist
physi, physio, physico, *PREFIX INDICATING "PHYSICAL/NATURAL" MOST OFTEN MODIFIES THE WORD*
physic,*, *OF NATURE (or see physique or physics)*
physical,*,lly,lity,lities, *CAN BE SEEN/SENSED WITH THE EYE, AN EXAM*
physician,*, *LICENSED TO PRACTICE MEDICINE*
physicist,*, *ONE WHO STUDIES PHYSICS*
physico, physio, physi, *PREFIX INDICATING "PHYSICAL/NATURAL" MOST OFTEN MODIFIES THE WORD*
physics, *THE STUDY OF SUBATOMIC PARTICLES, A SCIENCE (or see physic or physique)*
physik, physique /physic
physiology,gist,gical,gically,gist, *CONCERNING PLANTS/ANIMALS, SCIENCE OF NATURE*
physique, *PHYSICAL BODY/STRUCTURE*
physisist, physicist
phyt, phyto, *PREFIX INDICATING "PLANT" MOST OFTEN MODIFIES THE WORD*
pi, *GREEK LETTER WHICH STANDS FOR MATHEMATICAL RATIO 3.141592 (or see pie)*
pial, pile
pianeer, pioneer
piano,*, *USING KEYS TO STRIKE STRINGS OF THIS INSTRUMENT HOUSED IN A LARGE WOODEN BOX*
pibe, pipe
pic,*, *A SMALL TRIANGULAR/FLAT/RIGID ITEM USED TO STRUM STRINGS OF A MUSICAL INSTRUMENT (or see pick/ pig/ pique/ peak/ peek/ pike)*
picalo, picolo
picdorul, pectoral /pictorial
pich, pitch
pichur, pitcher /picture
pichy, pitch(y)
pick,*,ked,king,kier,kiest,ky, *CHOOSE/SELECT FROM AMONGST OTHERS, ACQUIRE (or see pic/ pig/ pique/ peak/ peek/ pike)*

pickalo, picolo
picket,*,,ter,ted,ting, *WOODEN POST WITH SHARP-ENED END, BARRIER/FENCE AS IN A UNION STRIKE, POST GUARD*
pickle,*,,ed,ling, *TO SOAK/MARINATE FOOD IN A BRINE/SALT SOLUTION*
picknic, picnic
pickul, pickle
picnic,*, *A LUNCH OUTDOORS*
picolo,*, list, *INSTRUMENT/FLUTE*
picsher, picture /pitcher
pict, pick(ed) /pig(gged)
picter, picture /pitcher
pictorial,*,,lly,lness, *VISION/ENVISIONED AS A PICTURE*
picture,*,,ed,ring, *A VISUAL REPRESENTATION OF A SCENE*
piculear, peculiar
pid, pit
pide, pity
pidestreun, pedestrian
pidy, pity
pie,*, *FOOD ITEM INCORPORATING A CRUST AND FILLING* (or see pi)
piece,*,,ed,cing,er, *A PART OF A WHOLE, ONE AMONGST MANY* (or see peace)
piel, pile
pieneer, pioneer
pieno, piano
pier,*, *MANMADE OUTCROP ABOVE THE WATER FOR DOCKING BOATS/FISHING* (or see peer/ pierce/ pyre)
pierce,*,,ed,cing,cingly, *TO PENETRATE/ PUNCTURE* (or see peer(s) or pier(s))
pies, pious
piethon, python
pig,*,,gged,gging,ggish,ggy, *DOMESTICATED SWINE/BOAR* (or see peg/ pick/ pic)
pigal, pickle

pigamus, pajamas
pigated, picket(ed)
pigen, pigeon
pigeon,*, *A CITY BIRD, OF THE DOVE FAMILY*
piget, picket
pigeted, picket(ed)
pigil, pickle
pigin, pigeon
pigit, picket
pigle, pickle
pigme, pygmy
pigul, pickle
pigy, pig(ggy)
pijamas, pajamas
pijen, pigeon
pik, pic/ pick/ pike/ pig
pikal, pickle
pikalo, picolo
pikd, pick(ed) /pique(d)
pike,*,,ed,king, *A FISH, STAFF WITH POINTED TIP USED AS A WEAPON/TOOL, A POINT, TURNPIKE* (or see pick /pig /pique /peak /peek)
pikel, pickle
piker, pick(er)
piket, picket
pikeust, pick(iest)
pikir, pick(er)
pikit, picket
pikle, pickle
piknik, picnic
pikol, pickle
pikon, pecan
piksher, picture /pitcher
pikt, pick(ed) /pique(d)
piktorul, pectoral /pictorial
pikture, picture /pitcher
pikul, pickle
pikuleur, peculiar
pikur, pick(er)

piky, pig(ggy) /pick(y)
pil, pill /pile
pilaf,*, *ASIAN STYLE OF RICE*
pilage, pillage
pilar, pillar
pilaredy, polar(ity)
pile,*,,ed,ling, *A MOUND/ACCUMULATION OF SOMETHING, A POST/TIMBER/PILLAR WITH POINTED END, NAP OF FABRIC, HEMORRHOIDS*
pilej, pillage
piler, pillar
pilerity, polar(ity)
pilese, police
pilet, pilot
pilgrim,*,,mage,maged,maging, *ORIGINAL SETTLERS IN AMERICA FROM EUROPE, THOSE WHO TRAVEL TO UNSEEN PLACES*
pilig, pillage
pilij, pillage
pilite, polite /pilot
pill,*, *tablet/capsules*
pillage,*,,ed,ging, *TO GO THROUGH OTHER PEOPLES STUFF, TO PLUNDER/TAKE AWAY/STEAL*
pillar,*, *A POST/MONUMENT/SUPPORT*
pillow,*, *A CUSHION, HEAD SUPPORT WHEN LYING DOWN, CUSHION TO PROTECT FROM HARM*
pilot,*,,ted,ting,tless, *ONE WHO NAVIGATES/ OPERATES A VESSEL, ONE THAT STEERS, A FLAME ON A GAS APPLIANCE*
pilow, pillow
pils, pill(s) /pile(s)
piluge, pillage
pilur, pillar
pilushen, pollute(tion)
pilt, pilot /pollute
pilutent, pollute(tant)
pilution, pollute(tion)
pimento,*, *A SWEET PEPPER*

pimp,*,ped,ping, ONE WHO CAPITALIZES FROM PROSTITUTES, INSIGNIFICANT, PETTY, COOL
pimpel, pimple
pimple,*, INFLAMED SKIN PORES
pimpul, pimple
pin,*,nned,nning,nner, TO FASTEN, SHARP TIPPED THIN OBJECT (or see pen /pent /pine)
pinacle, pentacle /pinnacle
pinada, pinata
pinagon, pentagon
pinagram, pentagram
pinakle, pinnacle /pentacle
pinalty, penal(ty)
pinaple, pineapple
pinapple, pineapple
pinasilun, penicillin
pinata,*, A PAPIER MACHE PARTY DECORATION FILLED WITH GOODIES FOR CHILDREN
pinatrate, penetrate
pinatruble, penetrable
pincers, USED FOR GRIPPING, CLAWLIKE (or see pinch(ers))
pinch,*,hes,hed,hing,her, SQUEEZE TOGETHER FOR HOLDING SOMETHING, TWO SIDES COMING TOGETHER (or see pincers)
pinchent, penchant
pinchers, pinch(ers) /pincers
pind, pine(d) /pin(nned)
pindalem, pendulum
pindent, pendant /pendent
pinding, pending
pindo, pinto
pine,*,ed,ning, AN EVERGREEN TREE, TO PAINFULLY LONG FOR SOMEONE/ SOMETHING
pineal gland, PINE CONE SHAPED ORGAN IN THE BODY WHICH SECRETES MELATONIN
pineapple,*, A TROPICAL FRUIT
pinecillin, penicillin
pinecle, pinnacle /pentacle

pineer, pioneer
pinegon, pentagon
pineng, pine(ning) /pin(nning)
pinetrate, penetrate
pingalum, pendulum
pingwen, penguin
pinjalum, pendulum
pinjulim, pendulum
pink,*,ky, A COLOR, THE LITTLE FINGER ON THE HAND
pinkwen, penguin
pinnacle,*, PEAK /POINT /CREST /CONE (or see pentacle)
pinsel, pencil
pinsers, pincers /pinch(ers)
pinshen, pension
pinshent, penchant
pinsil, pencil
pinsion, pension
pinsul, pencil
pint,*, A U.S. FORM OF MEASUREMENT FOR LIQUIDS (or see pine(d))
pintacle, pentacle /pinnacle
pintagon, pentagon
pintagram, pentagram
pintalum, pendulum
pintegon, pentagon
pinting, pending
pinto,*,oes, SPOTTED HORSE/ BEAN
pintucle, pentacle /pinnacle
pintulem, pendulum
pinugram, pentagram
pinukle, pinnacle /pentacle
pinulize, penal(ize)
pinulty, penal(ty)
pinusilun, penicillin
pinutrashen, penetrate(tion)
pinutrate, penetrate
pinutruble, penetrable
piny, penny /pine(y)

pinyada, pinata
pioneer,*,red,ring, ONE WHO DISCOVERS NEW TERRITORY/THE UNKNOWN
pious,sly,sness, HOLIER THAN THOU, INTENSELY MOTIVATED ABOUT THEIR GOD, REVERENCE FOR
pipe,*,ed,ping, TUBULAR/HOLLOW FORM
piporshenal, proportion(al)
pique,*,ed,uing, HEIGHTEN/STIMULATE, RIBBED/ RAISED EFFECT (or see peak or peek)
piquleur, peculiar
pir, per /purr
pirade, parade
piraet, pirouette
piralusis, paralysis
piramid, pyramid
pirana, piranha
piranha,*, A FLESH EATING FRESH WATER FISH (or see prana)
pirate,*,ed,ting, ONE WHO TRAVERSES THE SEAS STEALING FROM OTHERS, TO TAKE FROM OTHERS WITHOUT PERMISSION
pirbendikuler, perpendicular
pirceive, perceive
pircent, percent
pirceptible, perceptible
pirch, perch /purge
pirchus, purchase /perch(es)
pircushen, percussion
pircusion, percussion
pirdly, pert(ly)
piremid, pyramid
pireneal, perennial
pireod, period
pireodic, periodic /periotic
pireodontic, periodontic
pireodontist, periodontist
pireot, period
pireoticul, periodic(al)
piret, pirate

pireud, period
pireut, period
pirews, peruse
pirfect, perfect
pirfekd, perfect
pirferted, pervert(ed)
pirfikt, perfect
pirform, perform
pirformence, perform(ance)
pirfume, perfume
pirgatory, purgatory
pirge, purge
pirger, perjure
pirgery, perjure(ry)
pirgetory, purgatory
pirgury, perjure(ry)
pirgutory, purgatory
pirhaps, perhaps
piright, pyrite
pirit, pirate /pyrite
pirje, purge
pirjury, perjure(ry)
pirkrastination, procrastinate
pirkushen, percussion
pirmanence, permanence
pirmaneat, permanent
pirmeate, permeate
pirmenant, permanent
pirmesabul, permissible
pirmet, permit
pirmeuble, permeable
pirmishen, permission
pirmisive, permission(ive)
pirmisuf, permission(ive)
pirmit, permit
pirmition, permission
pirmnent, permanent
piro, pyro
piroet, pirouette

pirogative, prerogative
pirokside, peroxide
pirole, parole
pirona, piranha
pirosedy, porosity
pirosity, porosity
pirot, pirate
pirouette,*, *TO TWIRL ABOUT ON THE TIPS OF TOES*
piroxside, peroxide
pirpechuel, perpetual
pirpendicular, perpendicular
pirpes, purpose
pirpeshual, perpetual
pirpesly, purpose(ly)
pirpetrate, perpetrate
pirpetshuate, perpetual(ate)
pirpetual, perpetual
pirpetuate, perpetual(ate)
pirpetuity, perpetuity
pirpis, purpose
pirpisly, purpose(ly)
pirple, purple
pirpleksity, perplex(ity)
pirplexity, perplex(ity)
pirporshenal, proportion(al)
pirportional, proportion(al)
pirpos, purpose
pirposful, purpose(ful)
pirposly, purpose(ly)
pirpus, purpose
pirpusly, purpose(ly)
pirputrate, perpetrate
pirs, purse
pirsacute, persecute
pirsavere, persevere
pirsbektif, perspective
pirsbiration, perspiration
pirsbire, perspire
pirscripshen, prescript(ion)

pirscription, prescript(ion)
pirsebtef, percept(ive)
pirsecute, persecute
pirsen, person
pirsenal, personal
pirsenaledy, personality
pirsenaly, personality
pirsenality, personality
pirsenaly, personal(lly)
pirsenel, personnel
pirsent, percent
pirsentage, percent(age)
pirsenuble, person(able)
pirsenulize, personal(ize)
pirseptable, perceptible
pirseptive, percept(ive)
pirseshen, precision
pirseve, perceive
pirseverense, persevere(rance)
pirsh, perch /purge
pirshes, purchase /perch(es)
pirsikute, persecute
pirsinuble, person(able)
pirsinulize, personal(ize)
pirsistence, persist(ence)
pirskripshen, prescript(ion)
pirson, person
pirsona, persona
pirsonality, personality
pirsonefication, person(ification)
pirsonel, personnel /personal
pirsonification, person(ification)
pirsonifikashen, person(ification)
pirsonify, personify
pirsonuble, person(able)
pirsoo, pursue
pirspective, perspective
pirspektif, perspective
pirspiration, perspiration
pirspire, perspire

pirsu, pursue
pirsuade, persuade
pirsuasion, persuade(asion)
pirsuasive, persuade(asive)
pirsude, pursue(d)
pirsunal, personal/ personnel
pirsunel, personnel/ personal
pirsute, pursue(uit)
pirsuvere, persevere
pirswade, persuade
pirswaseve, persuade(asive)
pirswashen, persuade(asion)
pirswasif, persuade(asive)
pirt, pert
pirtain, pertain
pirtane, pertain
pirtly, pert(ly)
pirtray, portray
pirtrayal, portray(al)
pirturb, perturb
pirumid, pyramid
piruse, peruse
pirut, pirate
pirvade, pervade
pirvashen, pervade(asion)/provision
pirvasif, pervade(asion)
pirvershen, pervert(rsion)
pirvert, pervert
piryte, pyrite
pirzukewt, persecute
pisa, pizza
pisdachio, pistachio
pisdasheo, pistachio
pisdrome, pastrami
pises, possess
piseshen, position
pisesif, possess(ive)
pisher, pitcher /picture
piskrepshin, prescript(ion)

pistachio,*, *AN EDIBLE NUT*
pistasheo, pistachio
pisten, piston
pistil,*, llate, *PART OF A FLOWER (or see pistol)*
pistol,*, led,ling, *HANDGUN/FIREARM (or see pistil)*
piston,*, *PART OF AN ENGINE*
pistrome, pastrami
pistul, pistil/ pistol/ pestle
pistun, piston
pit,*, tted,tting, *THE SEED OF A FRUIT, A HOLLOWED*
    DEPRESSION (or see pet)
pitado, potato
pitaseum, potassium
pitasium, potassium
pitato, potato
pitch, hes,hed,hing,hy, *A TAR, BASEBALL MANEUVER*
    (too many definitions, please see standard
    dictionary)
pitcher,*, *POSITION IN THE GAME OF BASEBALL, A*
    VESSEL FOR HOLDING LIQUIDS (or see picture)
pitena, patina
pitenchul, potential
pitenshil, potential
pithon, python
pitina, patina
pitinshil, potential
pitnik, picnic
pitrol, patrol
pitroleum, petrol(eum)
pitrood, protrude
pitrude, protrude
pitrushen, protrude(usion)
pitsa, pizza
pituitary,ries, *A PERTAINING TO A GLAND WHICH*
    PRODUCES HORMONES
pitunia, petunia
piturbed, perturb(ed)

pity,tier,tiful,tifully,tifulness,tiless,tilessly,
    tilessness,yied,ying,yingly, *HAVE SYMPATHY/*
    GRIEF/COMPASSION FOR SOMEONE
piul, pile
piuneer, pioneer
piuny, puny
pius, pious
pivurted, pervert(ed)
piwrite, pyrite
piwro, pyro
pix, pick(s) /pic(s)
piyuree, puree'
pizdromy, pastrami
pizes, possess
piztacheo, pistachio
pizza,*, *A FLAT BREAD WITH OTHER FOODS COOKED ON*
    TOP OF IT
pla, play
placard,*, *A FLAT CARD DISPLAYING INFORMATION*
placate,*, ed,ting,er,tion,tive,tory, *TO PACIFY/*
    APPEASE/LET THEM HAVE THEIR WAY
place,*, ed,cing,ement, *POSITION/AREA*
placebo,*, *AN IMITATION/FAKE, PRETENDING TO BE*
    THE REAL THING
placed, placid /place(d)
placenta,*, al,ary,ation, *THE LINING OF A MAMMALS*
    WOMB/UTERUS WHICH HOLDS THE FETUS
placerd, placard
placid,dity,dness,dly, *CALM/GENTLE/QUIET*
plack, plaque
placment, place(ment)
placurd, placard
plad, plaid/ plait/ play(ed)/ plate
pladenum, platinum
plader, platter
pladform, platform
pladinum, platinum
pladir, platter
pladnum, platinum

pladur, platter
plaeng, play(ing)
plag, plague
plagerism, plagiarism
plagiarism,st,stic,ize,izer, TO COPY SOMEONE ELSES WORK WITHOUT PERMISSION
plagiresm, plagiarism
plague,*,ed,uing, A SPREADING DISEASE WHICH CAUSES HARM, A NUISANCE (or see plaque)
plagurism, plagiarism
plaid,*,ded, A CROSS WEAVING PATTERN (or see plait or play(ed))
plaigerism, plagiarism
plain,*,nly,nness, WITHOUT ACCENTS/ORNAMENTS, NO OUTSTANDING FEATURES (or see plane)
plait,*,ter,ting, BRAID/FOLD OVER/INTERWOVEN (or see plate or plaid)
plajerism, plagiarism
plajurism, plagiarism
plak, plaque
plakard, placard
plakate, placate
plakurd, placard
plan,*,nned,nning,nner,nless,lessly,nlessness, TO CONTRIVE/DREAM/CONJURE/DESIGN (or see plane or plain)
planaterium, planetary(rium)
plancton, plankton
plane,*,ed,ning,er, A FLAT/LEVEL SURFACE, A FLYING VESSEL (or see plan or plain)
planet,*, A SPHERICAL BODY IN SPACE
planetary,rium(s), OF/CONCERNING BODIES OF MATTER IN SPACE
planit, planet
planitareum, planetary(rium)
plank,*,king, FLAT/WIDE BOARD
plankton,nic, TINY WATER ORGANISMS

plant,*,ted,ting,ter, ORGANISM WHICH TRANSFORMS LIGHT ENERGY AND HAS NO NERVOUS SYSTEM, TO TAKE A STAND, TAKE ROOT
plantain,*,*, ANTI- BACTERIAL/INFLAMMATORY/VIRAL/ HEALING PLANT
plantane, plantian
plantashen, plantation
plantation,*, LARGE ESTATE WHICH GROW LARGE FIELDS OF CROPS
planter,*, VESSEL/CONTAINER WHICH HOLDS PLANTS/DIRT
planut, planet
plaque,*, A COATING OF SOMETHING, A FLAT BOARD WITH TEXT COMMEMORATING SOMEONE
plasa, plaza
plasdur, plaster
plasebo, placebo
plased, placid
plasible, plausible
plasinta, placenta
plasit, placid
plasma,mic, CONCERNS THE BLOOD (TOO MANY DEFI-NITIONS, PLEASE SEE STANDARD DICTIONARY)
plasment, place(ment)
plastek, plastic
plaster,*,red,ring,ry, A GYSUM OR OTHER PASTE MATERIAL THAT SPREADS, TO COAT WITH
plastic,*, MOLDABLE/VERSATILE SUBSTANCE
plasu, plaza
plasuble, plausible
plat,*,tted,tting, MAP/CHART/PLOT, A BRAID (or see plate /plait /play(ed))
platau, plateau
plate,*,ed,ting, FLAT/ROUND VESSEL (TOO MANY DEFINITIONS, PLEASE SEE STANDARD DICTIONARY) (or see plat /plait /plait /play(ed))
plateau,*, ELEVATED AREA OF LAND WITH A FLAT TOP
platepus, platypus
plater, platter

platform,*, ELEVATED FORM WITH A FLAT TOP/AREA
platibus, platypus
platinum,*, A METAL
platipus, platypus
platir, platter
platnum, platinum
plato, plateau
platonic,ism,ist,istic,ize, LOVE/FRIENDSHIP WITHOUT SEX, SPIRITUAL, OF Plato
platoon,*, A GROUP/UNIT IN MILITARY
platter,*, A FLAT PLATE/VESSEL
platur, platter
platypus,ses, UNDERWATER MAMMAL THAT HAS BIRD-LIKE QUALITIES
plausible,bility,eness,ly,ive, POSSIBLE/CONVINCING
plaw, plow
play,*,yed,ying,yer,yful,yfully,yfulness, BEHAVE CHEERFULLY/JOYFUL/HAPPY
playkate, placate
plaza, A SQUARE CITY CENTER/TOWN
plazma, plasma
plaztek, plastic
plea,*,ad,aded,ading,adable,ader, TO BEG/ DECLARE/ARGUE FOR (or see pleat)
pleasant,try,tly,tness,try,tries, AMIABLE/ ENJOYABLE/NON-DRAMATIC EXPERIENCE
please,*,ed,sing,singly,singness,surable, surableness,surably,sure(s), sured, TO SATISFY QUENCH/APPEASE/ PROVIDE COMFORT
pleat,*,ted,ter, FOLDS/CREASES (or see plea(d))
plecebo, placebo
plecenta, placenta
plech, pledge
plecht, pledge(d)
pleksiglass, plexiglass
pleded, plea(ded)
pledge,*,ed,ging,ger,gor, TO OFFER A PROMISE/ GUARANTEE
pledonic, Platonic

pliable,bility,eness,ly, BENDABLE/FLEXIBLE
plicebo, placebo
plieble, pliable
plight,*, SITUATION/CONDITION (or see polite)
plintaful, plenty(tiful)
plinty, plenty
plirul, plural
plisebo, placebo
plisenta, placenta
plite, plight /polite
plitonic, Platonic
plitune, platoon
pliuble, pliable
pliwood, plywood
pliwute, plywood
plod,*,dded,dding,ddingly,dder, TO MOVE ABOUT
    WITH NO ENTHUSIASM, IN THE DOLDRUMS,
    HEAVY/SLOW WALKING (or see plot)
ploe, ploy
ploom, plume
plop,*,pped,pping, SOUND/MOVEMENT RESEMBLING
    DROPPING SOMETHING HEAVY/FLAT
plopt, plop(pped)
ploseble, plausible
plosible, plausible
plot,*,tted,tting,tter,ttage, TO MAP/PLAN/CHART
    OUT (or see plod)
ploted, plot(tted)
ploter, plot(tter)
plotoon, platoon
plotune, platoon
plow,*,wed,wing,wable,wer, TO PHYSICALLY CAUSE
    TO TURN OVER/ROLL/REARRANGE
plowee, ploy
ploy,*, A TRICK
plozible, plausible
plucenta, placenta

pluck,*,ked,ker,king,ky,kily,kiness, PULL
    STRINGS ON INSTRUMENT, REMOVE FEATHERS
pludonic, Platonic
plug,*,gged,gging, AN OBJECT WHICH FILLS/FITS
    INTO HOLES, SHOOT, BULLET (or see pluck)
pluk, pluck /plug
plum,*, A FRUIT (or see plumb or plume)
plumb,*,bed,ber,bing, USE PIPES TO TRANSPORT
    WATER/LIQUIDS/GAS, TO SQUARE, MAKE LEVEL
    (or see plum)
plume,ed,ming,my, A BILLOWY CLOUD OF MATTER
    FROM A VOLCANO, BIRD'S FEATHERS (or see
    plum or plumb)
plumer, plumber
plumit, plummet
plummet,*,ted,ting, TO FALL STRAIGHT DOWN, USED
    TO TEST FOR PERPENDICULAR LEVEL
plump,ply,pish, round/full/chubby, A HEAVY
    FALLING SOUND (or see plumb)
plunch, plunge
plunder,*,red,ring,rer,rable,rous,rage, TO
    FORCIBLY ROB
plunge,*,ed,ging,er, TO DIVE/DELVE/THRUST INTO
plunje, plunge
plunter, plunder
plural,lly,lism,list,listic,lity,lities,lize,lized,lizing,
    lization, MORE THAN ONE
plus,ses, TO ADD/GAIN/POSITIVE
plusebo, placebo
plusenta, placenta
plush,hier,hiest,hy,hly, THICK/SOFT/LUXURIOUS
plusinta, placenta
pluto, plateau
plutonic, Platonic
plutonium, A CHEMICAL ELEMENT
plutoon, platoon
plutune, platoon
pluwrel, plural
ply,lies,lied,ying, TO DO/FURNISH/WORK AT, LAYERS

pleduble, plea(dble)
pleed, plea(d)
plees, please /plea(s)
pleet, pleat /plea(d)
plege, pledge
plegeurism, plagiarism
plegt, pledge(d)
pleje, pledge
plejur, pleasure
pleksaglass, plexiglass
pleksiglass, plexiglass
plendiful, plenty(tiful)
plendy, plenty
plentaful, plenty(tiful)
plenty,tiful,tifully,tifulness,ties, ENOUGH/AMPLE
    AMOUNT
pleral, plural
pleril, plural
ples, please /plea(s)
plesant, pleasant
plesebo, placebo
plesent, pleasant
plesinta, placenta
plesunt, pleasant
plet, pleat /plead
pleted, plea(ded)
pleto, plateau
pletonic, Platonic
pletoon, platoon
pletune, platoon
plewm, plume
plewrel, plural
plewtonium, plutonium
plexaglass, plexiglass
plexiglass, CLEAR SHEET OF PLASTIC
plez, please /plea(s)
plezent, pleasant
plezint, pleasant
pli, ply

plyible, pliable
plyt, plight /polite
plyuble, pliable
plywood, FORMED SHEET CONSISTING OF LAYERS OF WOOD/COMPOSITE
plywude, plywood
plywute, plywood
pneumatic,*,cally, USING COMPRESSION TO OPERATE TOOLS, AIR/GAS SCIENCE
pneumonia,ic, LUNG INFLAMMATION
pnewmatic, pneumatic
pnumatic, pneumatic
pnumonia, pneumonia
poach,hes,hed,hing,her, WAY TO COOK EGGS, TO UNLAWFULLY TAKE/KILL ANIMALS/ FISH
poatry, poetry
poch, poach
pocht, poach(ed)
pock, SCAR/PIT/ERUPTION ON THE SKIN (or see poke)
pocker, poker
pocket,*,ted,ting,tful, A FOLD IN CLOTHING WHICH HOLDS THINGS, TO CONCEAL INTO CLOTHING
pocks, pox
pocrate, procreate
pod,*,dded,dding, THAT WHICH ENVELOPES SOME OF MANY (or see pot)
podable, potable
podary, potter(y)
pode, potty
podebul, potable
poded, pot(tted) /pod(dded)
podel, puddle /poodle
podend, potent
podensy, potent(ncy)
podent, potent
poder, potter
podery, potter(y)
podestrein, pedestrian

podeum, podium
podibul, potable
podid, pot(tted) /pod(dded)
podind, potent
podinsy, potent(ncy)
podir, potter
podiry, potter(y)
podium,*, A PLATFORM FOR SPEAKERS, PEDESTAL
podlach, potlatch
podlage, potlatch
podluk, potluck
podpory, potpourri
poduble, potable
podunsy, potent(ncy)
podur, potter
podury, potter(y)
pody, potty
poed, poet
poedik, poet(ic)
poem,*, TEXT/WRITINGS WHICH DEPICT A STORY/ THOUGHT/EMOTION
poenseda, poinsetta
poenseta, poinsetta
poent, point
poenyent, poignant
poenzeda, poinsetta
poes, poise /pose
poesin, poison
poet,*,tic,tical,tically,ticize,ticized,ticising,tics, SOMEONE WHO WRITES/ IS GIVEN TO POETRY
poetry, LITERARY VERSE PROJECTING EMOTIONS/AN EVENT/IDEA
poez, poise
poezun, poison
poferdy, poverty
pofirty, poverty
pofurdee, poverty
poger, poker
poid, poet

poignant,tly,ncy, TO THE POINT, PRECISE, EXACT
poim, poem
poinant, poignant
poinseda, poinsetta
poinsettia,*,*, A SEASONAL FLOWERING PLANT
point,*, ,ted,ter,ting,te,ty, THE TIP, DIRECT/AIM/ SHOW, PRIMARY THEME/ISSUE(TOO MANY DE-FINITIONS, PLEASE SEE STANDARD DICTIONARY)
poinyent, poignant
poinzeta, poinsetta
poise,ed, IN POSITION TO, SUSPENDED ACTION, IN EQUILIBRIUM
poison,*,ned,ning,nous,nously, TOO HIGH A DOSE OF THIS WILL KILL, ABILITY TO HARM
poit, poet
poitry, poetry
poizen, poison
pok, poke /pock
pokd, poke(d)
poke,*,ed,king,ey, TO PUSH/PRY/MOVE SOMETHING USING NOSE/FINGER/TOOL/IMPLEMENT, TO BE SLOW (or see pock)
poker, A CARD GAME, A TOOL
poket, pocket
pokit, pocket
pokreate, procreate
poks, pox
pokut, pocket
poky, poke(y)
pol, pole/ poll/ pool
polar,rity,rities,rization,rize,rizable,rizer, ENDS OPPOSITE OF ONE ANOTHER, HAVING TO DO WITH THE EARTH/ENERGY POLES
polaredy, polar(ity)
polatics, politic(s)
pold, poll(ed)
poldes, poultice
poldis, poultice
poldre, poultry

poldus, poultice
pole,*, ROD, STAFF, (TOO MANY DEFINITIONS, PLEASE SEE STANDARD DICTIONARY) (or see poll)
polegimy, polygamy
polegon, polygon
polegraf, polygraph
polegraph, polygraph
polehedron, polyhedron
polemur, polymer
polen, pollen
polenade, pollinate
polenate, pollinate
polenation, pollinate(tion)
poleo, polio
polep, polyp
poler, polar
polerize, polar(ize)
polese, police
polesh, polish
polester, polyester
polesy, policy
polet, pullet
poletics, politic(s)
poleticul, politic(al)
poletishen, politic(ian)
poley, pulley
police,*,ed,cing, KEEP WATCH OVER A DESIGNATED AREA, ONE WHO KEEPS WATCH
policy,cies, RULES ESTABLISHED BY PRINCIPLES WHICH GUIDE BUSINESS AFFAIRS
polie, pulley
poliester, polyester
poligamus, polygamy(mous)
poligamy, polygamy
poligine, polygyny
poligon, polygon
poligraf, polygraph
poligraph, polygraph
polihedron, polyhedron

polimer, polymer
polin, pollen
polinate, pollinate
polination, pollinate(tion)
polio, POLIOMYELITIS, A CRIPPLING DISEASE
polip, polyp
polir, polar
polise, police
polish,hes,hed,hing,her, USE CHEMICAL OR FRICTION TO REMOVE OXYDATION, A NATIONALITY
polit, pullet
polite,ely,eness, CONSIDERATE, RESPECTFUL
politecal, politic(al)
politeshen, politic(ian)
politic,*,cal,cally,cian,cize,cized,cizing, CONCERNING GOVERNMENT
poll,*,lled,lling, USED TO TAX/SURVEY/VOTE, PART OF HEAD WITH HAIR (or see pole)
pollen,*, MICROSCOPIC SPORES PRODUCED BY PLANTS
pollenate, pollinate
pollinate,*,ed,ting,tion,tor,niferous,nium,nia, nize(r), POLLEN TRANSMITTED FROM ONE PLANT TO ANOTHER
pollute,*,ed,er,tant,ting,tion, HARMFUL (BYPRODUCTS) RELEASED INTO THE ENVIRONMENT
polm, palm
polre, polar
polse, pulse
polt, poll(ed)
poltes, poultice
poltice, poultice
poltis, poultice
poltree, poultry
poltry, poultry
poltus, poultice
polup, polyp
polur, polar
polurize, polar(ize)
polusee, policy

polushen, pollute(tion)
polusy, policy
polut, pullet /pollute
polutent, pollute(tant)
poluteshen, pollute(tion)
polutics, politic(s)
polution, pollute(tion)
poly, PREFIX INDICATING "MANY" MOST OFTEN MODIFIES THE WORD
poly, pulley
polyester,rification, CHEMICAL CHAIN WHICH IS USED TO MAKE PRODUCTS
polygamus, polygamy(mous)
polygamy,mist,mous,mously, MAN/ WOMAN HAVING MORE THAN ONE LEGAL PARTNER/ SPOUSE AT A TIME (or see polygyny)
polyginy, polygyny
polygon,*,nal,nally, THREE OR MORE STRAIGHT SIDES
polygraph,*,hic, VERSATILE INSTRUMENT FOR REPLICATING/RECORDING
polygyny,nous, HAVING MORE THAN ONE WIFE AT A TIME (or see polygamy)
polyhedron, polyh•dron
polyhedron,*,ra,ral, A SOLID SURROUNDED BY MANY PLANED SURFACES
polymer,*,ric,rism,rization,rize, COMPOUNDS OF TWO OR MORE WITH A SIMILAR RELATIONSHIP
polymir, polymer
polyp,*,pous,pary, MANY GROWTHS/TUMORS
pom, palm /poem
pomagranate, pomegranate
pombus, pompous
pomegranate,*, A FRUIT
pomel, pummel
pomigranate, pomegranate
pomil, pummel
pompis, pompous

pompous,sly,sness, *EXAGGERATED EXPRESSION TO SHOW SELFIMPORTANCE*
pompus, pompous
pomugranate, pomegranate
pomul, pummel
pon, pawn
poncho,*, *BLANKET/COAT*
pond,*, *SMALL BODY OF WATER* (or see pawn(ed))
ponder,*,red,ring,rable,rer,rous,rously,rousness, *TAKE TIME TO CONTEMPLATE ON A DECISION*
pondificate, pontificate
pondir, ponder
pondoon, pontoon
pondune, pontoon
pondur, ponder
pone, pony
ponsho, poncho
pont, pond /pawn(ed)
pontcho, poncho
ponteficate, pontificate
ponter, ponder
pontificate,*,ed,ting,tion,tor, *TO HAVE DOGMATIC CHARACTERISTICS, RELIGIOUS EXPRESSION*
pontoon,*, *FLOATS ON A PLANE IN PLACE OF WHEELS, A TYPE OF BOAT*
pontune, pontoon
pontur, ponder
pony,nies, *YOUNG/SMALL HORSE*
pooch,hes, *DOG*
pood, put
pooding, pudding /putt(ing)
poodle,*, *A BREED OF DOG* (or see puddle)
pool,*, led,ling, *PLACE TO SWIM, GAME USING BALLS/ STICKS, COLLECTION/ ACCUMULATION OF LIQUID*
poold, pull(ed) /pool(ed)
poolt, pull(ed) /pool(ed)
poor,rish,rly,rness, *LACKING BASIC NECESSITIES* (or see pore or pour)
poos, puss

poosh, push
pooshis, push(es)
pooshy, push(y)
poosy, pussy
poot, put
pootal, poodle
pooting, pudding /putt(ing)
pootle, poodle
pop,*,pped,pping,pper, *A SOUND, A SOFT DRINK, SOMETHING BURSTING*
popalashen, populate(tion)
popaler, popular
popcorn,*, *COOKED CORN KERNEL*
popkorn, popcorn
popelashen, populate(tion)
popelur, popular
popery, potpourri
popewlashen, populate(tion)
popewler, popular
popilashen, populate(tion)
popiler, popular
poping, pop(pping)
popiry, potpourri
poplar,*, *A TREE* (or see popular)
poplashen, populate(tion)
poplur, poplar /popular
poporshenal, proportion(al)
poppy,ppies, *FLOWER*
popree, potpourri
popt, pop(pped)
populachen, populate(tion)
popular,ly,rity,rize,rization,rizer, *DESIRABLE BY MANY* (or see poplar)
populashen, populate(tion)
populate,*,ed,ting,tion,list,lous,lously,lousness, *TWO OR MORE THINGS THRIVING TOGETHER*
populus, populate(lous)
popury, potpourri
popy, poppy

popya, papaya
por, poor/ pour/ pore
porcalin, porcelain
porcelain, *A FINE/TRANSLUCENT CERAMIC*
porcepine, porcupine
porch,hes, *A PLATFORM/STOOP/LANDING ADDED TO THE OUTSIDE OF A STRUCTURE*
porcipine, porcupine
porcupine,*, *LARGE RODENT WITH EXTERIOR QUILLS*
pordable, portable
pordal, portal
pordeble, portable
pordel, portal
porder, porter
pordfolio, portfolio
pordible, portable
porduble, portable
pordul, portal
pordur, porter
pore,*,ed,ring,ring, *ONE OF MANY LOCATION ON THE SKIN/SURFACE FOR RESPIRATION, LOOK/ EXAMINE WITH PERSERVERANCE* (or see poor /pour)
pores, porous /pore(s)
poris, porous
pork,ky,ker, *MEAT/OF PIGS/BOAR*
porkepine, porcupine
porkewpine, porcupine
porkipine, porcupine
porkupine, porcupine
porogative, prerogative
porole, parole
porosity,sities, *NUMBER/AMOUNT OF OPENINGS/PORES*
porous,sly,sness, *MANY OPENINGS/ PORES*
porpis, porpoise
porpoise,*, *LARGE FISH THAT LOOKS LIKE A DOLPHIN, A CETACEAN*
porpus, porpoise
porqupine, porcupine

porsalin, porcelain
porselan, porcelain
porsh, porch
porshin, portion
porshon, portion
porsilan, porcelain
porslin, porcelain
port,*,tly, A PLACE ON LAND WHERE VESSELS DOCK,
    TYPE OF WINE (TOO MANY DEFINITIONS, PLEASE
    SEE STANDARD DICTIONARY)
portable,bility,bly, ABLE TO BE MOVED ABOUT EASILY
portal,*, OPENING ALLOWING ABILITY TO MOVE FROM
    ONE PLACE TO ANOTHER, PART OF THE LIVER
porteble, portable
porteon, portion
porter,*, AN ATTENDANT ON RAILCARS
portfolio,*, A DELIBERATE COLLECTION OF SPECIFIC
    PAPERS FOR PRESENTATION
portible, portable
portil, portal
portion,*,ned,ning, PART OF THE WHOLE
portir, porter
portle, portal
portrait,*,tist, PAINTING/PHOTO OF A PERSON
portrat, portrait
portray,*,yed,ying,yal,yer, ATTEMPT TO
    PERSONIFY/DESCRIBE
portret, portrait
portuble, portable
portul, portal
portur, porter
porus, porous
poruse, peruse
porusness, porous(ness)
pos, pause /paw(s) /pose
posabiledy, possible(bility)
posability, possible(bility)
posative, positive
posatron, positron

posbone, postpone
poscher, posture
posd, post /pose(d)
posda, pasta
posdal, postal
posdchur, posture
posdel, postal
posder, poster /posture
posderety, posterior(ity)
posderior, posterior
posderity, posterior(ity)
posdil, postal
posdir, poster /posture
posdle, postal
posdmark, postmark
posdpardum, postpartum
posdu, pasta
posdul, postal
posdulate, postulate
posdur, poster /posture
pose,*,ed,sing,er, STRIKE/HOLD AN ATTITUDE/
    POSTURE (or see posse or posy)
posebiledy, possible(bility)
posebly, possible(ly)
posebul, possible
posee, posy /posse
posem, opossum
poses, possess /pose(s) /posy /posse
posesuf, possess(ive)
posetef, positive
posetive, positive
posetron, positron
posey, posse /posy
poshin, potion
poshon, potion
posibiledy, possible(bility)
posibly, possible(ly)
posibul, possible
posie, posse /posy

posim, opossum
posishen, position
positef, positive
position,*,ned,ning,nal,ner, POSTURE/
    ATTITUDE/PLACEMENT/STANCE
positive,*, ely,eness,vism,vist,vistic, TYPE OF
    CHARGE, ON THE UP SIDE, OPTIMISTIC
positron,*, PARTICLE OF POSITIVE CHARGE
posmordum, postmortem
posmortem, postmortem
posom, opossum
posotive, positive
pospartum, postpartum
pospone, postpone
posse, A GROUP OUT TO COLLECT JUSTICE
possess,ses,sed,sing,sive, OWN/HAVE
possesuf, possess(ive)
possible,bility,bilities,ly, MOST LIKELY COULD BE
    DONE/PERFORMED
possum, opossum
post, PREFIX INDICATING "AFTER IN ORDER OR TIME"
    MOST OFTEN MODIFIES THE WORD
post,*,ted,ting, MAKE INFORMATION PUBLIC, A
    VERTICAL SUPPORT TO ATTACH SOMETHING TO
    (or see pose(d))
posta, pasta
postage, PRICE TO SHIP/FREIGHT SOMETHING TO A
    MAILBOX
postaj, postage
postal,age, TO MAIL BY POST, PAY TO MAIL
postasheo, pistachio
postcher, posture
postege, postage
postej, postage
postel, postal
poster,*, LARGE/BLOWN-UP PICTURE WITH OR
    WITHOUT INFORMATION (or see posture)
posterety, posterior(ity)
posterior,ly, THE REAR, FOLLOWS

posterity, *CONCERNING THE FUTURE*
postige, postage
postij, postage
postil, postal
postir, poster / posture
postireor, posterior
postle, postal
postmark,*,ked,king, *AN INKED STAMP SHOWING DATE SOMETHING WAS MAILED*
postmordem, postmortem
postmortem, *A BODY ONCE THE SPIRIT IS REMOVED, AFTER DEATH*
postpartum, *AFTER GIVING BIRTH*
postpone,*,ed,ning,nable,ement,er, *TO PUT OFF UNTIL ANOTHER TIME*
postu, pasta
postuge, postage
postulate,*,ed,ting,tion,tor, *TO CLAIM/ PETITION, ASSUME WITHOUT TRUTH*
postur, poster / posture
posture,*,ed,ring, *STANCE/PHYSICAL ATTITUDE*
posubel, possible
posubility, possible(bility)
posubly, possible(ly)
posum, opossum
posutron, positron
posy,sies, *A FLOWER* (or see posse)
pot,*,tted,tting,table,tability,tableness, *ROUND/ FLAT BOTTOM CONTAINER FOR COOKING/PLANTS* (or see pod)
potable, *WATER YOU CAN DRINK*
potary, potter(y)
potaseum, potassium
potassium,ic, *METALLIC CHEMICAL ELEMENT*
potato,oes, *A STARCHY VEGETABLE*
poteble, potable
poted, pot(tted) /pod(dded)
potee, potty
poten, potent

potenchul, potential
potend, potent
potenshul, potential
potensy, potent(ncy)
potent,ncy,ncies,tly, *AMOUNT/DEGREE OF STRENGTH*
potential,*,lly,lity,lities, *STRONG POSSIBILITY*
poter, potter
potery, potter(y)
poteum, podium
potible, potable
potid, pot(tted) /pod(dded)
potin, potent
potintiale, potential(lly)
potinchul, potential
potind, potent
potinshul, potential
potinsy, potent(ncy)
potint, potent
potintial, potential
potion,*, *LIQUID WITH SPIRITUAL POWERS*
potir, potter
potiry, potter(y)
potium, podium
potlach, potlatch
potlatch,hes, *FESTIVAL/PARTY EXCHANGING GIFTS/GOODS*
potlege, potlatch
potluck,*, *A GATHERING OF PEOPLE WHERE EACH BRINGS A DISH OF FOOD TO SHARE*
potluk, potluck
potpery, potpourri
potpourri,*, *DRIED PLANTS COMBINED FOR THEIR AROMATHERAPY*
potrude, protrude
potrushen, protrude(usion)
potter,*, *ONE WHO WORKS WITH CLAY*
pottery,ries, *THINGS MADE OF CLAY THEN FIRED IN A KILN*
potty,tties, *A TOILET*

potuble, potable
potun, potent
potunsy, potent(ncy)
potury, potter(y)
poty, potty
pouch,hes,hed, *BAG/SACK/CAVITY FOR HOLDING THINGS*
poud, pout
pouder, powder
poudir, powder
pouer, power
poultes, poultice
poultice,*,ed,cing, *CRUSHED PLANTS/ HERBS MIXED WITH A BASE FOR APPLICATION*
poultry,ries, *EDIBLE BIRDS/FOWL*
poum, poem
pounce,*,ed,cing, *JUMP/LEAP TOWARDS AS IF TO GRAB/ATTACK, A POWDER*
pound,*,ded,ding, *U.S. MEASUREMENT FOR SOLIDS, TO HAMMER/STRIKE, BRITISH MONEY, AN AREA OF CONFINEMENT/HOLDING*
pounse, pounce
pount, pound
pour,*,red,ring, *WHEN TRANSFERRING LIQUID, A STREAMING FROM ONE PLACE TO ANOTHER* (or see poor or pore)
pourus, porous
pout,*,ted,ter,ting, *TO SULK, BE SULLEN, A FISH* (or see poet)
pouwir, power
pouwur, power
poverdy, poverty
poverty, *WITHOUT BASIC NEEDS BEING FULFILLED*
povileon, pavilion
povirty, poverty
povurty, poverty
powar, power
powch, pouch
powd, pout

powder,*,red,ring,rer,ry, *FINELY CRUSHED*
   MINERAL/PLANT, PULVERIZED
powdir , powder
powdur , powder
power,*,red,ring,rful,ringfully,rfulness,rless,
   rlessly,rlessness, *A CHARGE, RAISING OF*
   FREQUENCY, EUPHORIC SENSE OF SUPREMACY/
   MASTERY (or see poor or pour)
powir , power
pownd , pound
pownse , pounce
pownt , pound
powt , pout
powtch , pouch
powtur , powder
powur , power
pox, *INDICATION THAT ONE IS DISTURBED BY A VIRUS*
   IN THE BODY
poynt , point
poynyent , poignant
poyse , poise
poysin , poison
poz , pause /paw(s) /pose
pozd , pose(d) /pause(d)
pozda , pasta
pozderedy , posterior(ity)
pozdmark , postmark
pozdmordum , postmortem
pozdu , pasta
pozdul , postal
poze , pose /pose /pause /posy /paw(s)
pozeble , possible
pozebly , possible(ly)
pozee , posy
pozetron , positron
pozible , possible
pozishen , position
pozitef , positive
pozpardum , postpartum

pozpone , postpone
pozt , post /pose(d) /pause(d)
pozta , pasta
poztaj , postage
poztej , postal
pozter , poster /posture
poztereur , posterior
pozterior , posterior
poztij , postage
poztir , poster /posture
poztmordum , postmortem
poztpardim , postpartum
poztu , pasta
poztul , postal
poztur , poster /posture
pozuble , possible
pozubly , possible(ly)
pozutif , positive
pozy , posy
pra , pray /prey
prabared , prepare(d)
prabebly , probably
praberty , property
prabibly , probably
prabirty , property
prablum , problem
prabozkus , proboscis
prabubilety , probable(bility)
prabubly , probably
prabugate , propagate
prabur , proper
praburly , proper(ly)
praburty , property
pracareus , precarious
pracaushen , precaution
pracawshen , precaution
pracedure , procedure
praceedure , procedure
pracess , process

pracipitashen , precipitate(tion)
pracise , precise
pracisly , precise(ly)
pracktus , practice
praclame , proclaim
praclemashen , proclamation
praclevity , proclivity
praclimation , proclamation
praclivedy , proclivity
praclivity , proclivity
praclution , preclude(usion)
pracoshus , precocious
pracrastination , procrastinate(tion)
pracrastunate , procrastinate
practekul , practice(cal)
practes , practice
practeshener , practitioner
practice,*,ed,cer,cing,cal,cally,cality,calness,
   cality, *PERFORM REPEATEDLY TO ACHIEVE*
   MASTERY
practishener , practitioner
practitioner,*, *ONE WHO PRACTICES*
practus , practice
pradasheus , predacious
pradatious , predacious
pradecament , predicament
pradector , predict(or)
pradegul , prodigal
pradegy , prodigy
pradekament , predicament
pradekshen , predict(ion)
pradekt , predict
pradektability , predict(ability)
pradektable , predict(able)
pradicament , predicament
pradict , predict
pradiction , predict(ion)
pradictor , predict(or)
pradigul , prodigal

pradigy , prodigy
pradikament , predicament
pradikshen , predict(ion)
pradiktability , predict(ability)
pradiktable , predict(able)
pradomenate , predominate
pradomenatly , predominate(ly)
pradominate , predominate
pradukshen , product(ion)
praduktion , product(ion)
prae , pray /prey
praer , pray(er)
prafale , prevail
prafanedy , profane(nity)
prafanity , profane(nity)
prafedik , prophet(ic)
prafes , profess
prafeser , professor
prafeshenul , profession(al)
prafeshinul , profession(al)
prafesy , prophecy/ prophesy
prafet , profit / prophet
prafetable , profit(able)
prafetek , prophet(ic)
prafetible , profit(able)
prafetik , prophet(ic)
prafide , provide
prafiduble , provide(dable)
prafishent , proficient
prafit , profit /prophet
prafiteer , profit(eer)
prafoundly , profound(ly)
prafusy , prophecy/ prophesy
prageks , project(s)
pragekshin , project(ion)
pragektile , project(ile)
pragektor , project(or)
pragesterone , progesterone
pragmadik , pragmatic

pragmatic , *,cal,cally,calness,cism,ism,ist,istic,
  BUSINESSLIKE, OFFICIAL ACTIVITY, OF
  PRACTICALITY AND TRUTH
pragmatism , pragmatic(ism)
pragmitist , pragmatic(ist)
pragmutism , pragmatic(ism)
pragmutist , pragmatic(ist)
pragreshen , progress(ion)
pragresive , progress(ive)
pragress , progress
pragretion , progress(ion)
prahebatif , prohibit(ive)
prahebit , prohibit
prahibative , prohibit(ive)
prahibetory , prohibit(ory)
prahibit , prohibit
praink , prank
prairie , *, LARGE AREA OF LAND MOSTLY VOID OF
  TREES
praise , *,ed,er,sing, TO CONDONE/COMPLIMENT
  SOMEONE/SOMETHING
prajection , project(ion)
prajeks , project(s)
prajekshun , project(ion)
prajektile , project(ile)
prajektor , project(or)
prajesterone , progesterone
prakawshen , precaution
praklaim , proclaim
praklemashen , proclamation
praklemation , proclamation
praklevity , proclivity
praklimation , proclamation
praklivity , proclivity
praklude , preclude
praklumation , proclamation
prakoshen , precaution
prakoshious , precocious
prakotius , precocious

prakrastenate , procrastinate
prakrastination , procrastinate(tion)
praktekul , practice(cal)
praktes , practice
prakteshener , practitioner
praktetioner , practitioner
praktical , practice(cal)
praktikul , practice(cal)
praktis , practice
praktishener , practitioner
praktitioner , practitioner
praktus , practice
praleminary , preliminary
pralene , praline
pralimenary , preliminary
praline , *, CANDY
pralong , prolong
pralongate , prolong(ate)
pralood , prelude
pralude , prelude
pramenant , prominent
pramenit , prominent
pramere , premiere
prames , promise
prameskuis , promiscuity(uous)
pramesuble , permissible
praminade , prom(enade)
praminent , prominent
pramis , promise
pramisable , permissible
pramiskuis , promiscuity(uous)
pramisquety , promiscuity
pramisquos , promiscuity(uous)
pramoder , promote(r)
pramonishen , premonition
pramoshen , promote(tion)
pramoter , promote(r)
pramotion , promote(tion)

prana, *ONE OF MANY WORDS FOR THE LIFE/ENERGY OF THE BREATH (or see piranha)*
pranaunse, pronounce
prance,*,ed,cing,er, *TO LIGHTLY DANCE ABOUT, TO WALK A GAIT WITH A PROUD/ BOLD POSTURE*
prank,*,kish,kster, *TO PULL A TRICK ON SOMEONE, A SHOWFUL TRICK*
pranounce, pronounce
pranownse, pronounce
pranse, prance /prawn(s)
pranunseashen, pronunciate(tion)
pranunsiate, pronunciate
pranunsiation, pronunciation(tion)
prapablee, probably
prapare, prepare
praparidness, prepare(dness)
prapegate, propagate
prapel, propel
prapeler, propel(ller)
prapelint, propel(llant)
praper, proper /prepare
praperedness, prepare(ness)
praperly, proper(ly)
praperty, property
praphisy, prophecy /prophesy
praphut, prophet /profit
prapigate, propagate
prapir, proper
prapirty, property
praplum, problem
prapogate, propagate
praponint, proponent
praporshen, proportion
praportion, proportion
praposal, propose(sal)
prapose, propose
praposition, proposition
praposterus, preposterous
praposturis, preposterous

prapoze, propose
prapozishen, proposition
praprietor, proprietor
prapubly, probably
prapuganda, propaganda
prapugashen, propagate(tion)
prapugate, propagate
prapur, proper
prapurty, property
prare, prairie
prarogative, prerogative
prary, prairie
prascribe, prescribe /proscribe
prascription, prescript(ion)
prascriptive, prescript(ive)
prasdeje, prestige
prasdrate, prostrate /prostate
prase, praise
prasechen, precision /procession /precession
prasecute, prosecute
prasede, precede /proceed
prasedger, procedure
praseet, precede
prasejur, procedure
prasekushen, prosecute(tion)
prasekute, prosecute
prasentuble, present(able)
praserve, preserve
prases, process /precess
praseshen, precision /procession /precession
prasetchur, procedure
prasetion, precision /procession /precession
prasetyur, procedure
prasicute, prosecute
praside, preside
prasidger, procedure
prasijer, procedure
prasikushen, prosecute(tion)
prasintable, present(able)

prasipatate, precipitate
prasise, precise
prasishen, precision /procession /precession
prasisly, precise(ly)
prasited, preside(d)
praskrepshen, prescript(ion)
praskribe, prescribe /proscribe
praskribshen, prescript(ion)
praskript, prescript /prescribe(d)
prasomtif, presume(mptive)
praspect, prospect
praspective, prospect(ive)
praspekt, prospect
praspektif, prospect(ive)
prasperus, prosper(ous)
praspur, prosper
prastate, prostate /prostrate
prastegis, prestige(gious)
prasteje, prestige
prastejus, prestige(gious)
prastetute, prostitute
prasthesis, prosthesis
prasthesus, prosthesis
prastrate, prostrate /prostate
prasukushen, prosecute(tion)
prasum, presume
prasumptive, presume(mptive)
prasumshen, presume(mption)
prasumtif, presume(mptive)
prasumtion, presume(mption)
prasumtuis, presume(mptuous)
prasurve, preserve
pratect, protect
pratection, protect(ion)
pratekshen, protect(ion)
pratekt, protect
pratektuf, protect(ive)
pratend, pretend
pratended, pretend(ed)

pratind, pretend
pratrude, protrude
pratrugin, protrude(usion)
pratrusef, protrude(usive)
pratrusion, protrude(usion)
praud, proud
praudly, proud(ly)
praukse, proxy
praul, prowl
praun, prawn
prauses, process
praustat, prostate /prostrate
praut, proud
prautly, proud(ly)
pravale, prevail
pravense, province
pravenshen, prevent(ion)
pravent, prevent
praventable, prevent(able)
praventive, prevent(ive)
praverb, proverb
praverbeul, proverb(ial)
pravide, provide
praviduble, provide(dable)
pravinse, province
pravinshen, prevent(ion)
pravinshul, province(cial)
pravint, prevent
pravintable, prevent(able)
pravirb, proverb
pravirbeal, proverb(ial)
pravock, provoke
pravocative, provocative
pravokative, provocative
pravoke, provoke
pravurb, proverb
pravurbeul, proverb(ial)
prawdly, proud(ly)
prawess, prowess

prawl, prowl
prawn,*, *LARGE SHRIMP*
prawt, proud
prawtly, proud(ly)
pray,*,yed,ying,yer, *FOCUS A THOUGHT ON A DESIRE TO BE PHYSICALLY MANIFEST IN THE FUTURE, FAITHFULLY PROJECT (or see praise or prey)*
praylene, praling
prayree, paririe
praze, praise /pray(s)
prazent, present
prazentuble, present(able)
prazerve, preserve
prazint, present
prazumtues, presume(mptuous)
prazurve, preserve
pre, *PREFIX INDICATING "BEFORE" MOST OFTEN MODIFIES THE WORD*
preach,hes,hed,hing,hingly,her,hify,fy, *TO VOCALLY TEACH A LESSON*
preamble, *BRIEF INTRODUCTION, PREFACE*
preample, preamble
prebozkus, proboscis
precarious,sly,sness, *UNCERTAIN ABOUT STABILITY OR FIRM POSITION, NOT SECURE*
precastine, procrastinate
precaushen, precaution
precaution,*,nary,ous, *TAKE STEPS TO PREPARE TO AVERT DANGER/HARM*
precede,*,ed,ding,ence,ency,nt, *GOING/BEING BEFORE, SETS GUIDELINES FOR ALL THAT FOLLOWS (or see proceed)*
precipitate, precipitate
precersory, precursor(y)
precess,ssion,ssional, *FIRST IN ORDER/RANK/TIME, BEHAVIOR OF PLANETS/AXIS/MOTION*
precession,ssional, *FIRST IN ORDER/RANK/TIME, BEHAVIOR OF PLANETS/AXIS/MOTION (or see procession or precision)*

prech, preach
precher, preach(er)
precidense, precede(nce) /president(s)
president, precede(nt) /president
precinct,*, *AREAS DIVIDED FOR VOTING/CONTROL*
precious,ly,ness, *HIGHLY ENRICHED, VALUABLE*
precipitate,*,ely,eness,tive,tor,toud,toudly, tousness,tion, *FALLING MOISTURE, BRING ABOUT (TOO MANY DEFINITIONS, PLEASE SEE STANDARD DICTIONARY)*
precise,ely,eness,sion,sionist, *EXACT/ CLOSE TO PERFECT, CAREFUL ATTENTION TO DETAIL*
precision, *EXACT/CLOSE TO PERFECT, CAREFUL ATTENTION TO DETAIL (or see procession or precession)*
precishen, precision /procession /precession
precius, precious
preclame, proclaim
preclude,*,ed,ding,usion,usive,usively, *DO NOT ALLOW OPERATION OF, TO REJECT, HINDER*
preclushen, preclude(usion)
preclution, preclude(usion)
precocious,ly,ness,ity, *MATURING EARLY/QUICKLY*
precognative, precognitive
precognishen, precognition
precognition,ive, *ABLE TO SENSE/KNOW THE FUTURE*
precognitive, *ABILITY TO SENSE/KNOW THE FUTURE*
precoshen, precaution
precoshus, precocious
precotion, precaution
precotious, precocious
precrastination, procrastinate
precrastination, procrastination
precugnishen, precognition
precursor,ry,sive, *COMES BEFORE*
predacious,ness,ity,ation, *PREDATORY/PREYS, ATTACKING/KILLING/HUNTING*
predacity, predacious(ity)
predasesor, predecessor
predasheus, predacious

predater , predator
predatious , predacious
predator,rial,rily,ry, *ATTACKING/KILLING/HUNTING*
predatoreul , predator(ial)
predatorial , predator(ial)
prede , pretty
predecesor , predecessor
predecessor,*, *WHO LIVED/CAME BEFORE,ANCESTOR*
predekshen , predict(ion)
predekt , predict
predesesor , predecessor
predesor , predecessor
predespazishen , predispose(sition)
predespose , predispose
predetor , predator
predetorial , predator(ial)
predeur , pretty(ttier)
prediar , pretty(ttier)
predicament,*,tal, *TO BE IN AN AWKWARD/ CHALLENGING/DIFFICULT POSITION*
predicesor , predecessor
predict,*,ted,ting,table,tably,tability,tion,tive, tively,tor, *TO FORETELL THE FUTURE*
predier , pretty(ttier)
prediest , pretty(ttiest)
predikament , predicament
prediktable , predict(able)
predisesor , predecessor
predispazishen , predispose(sition)
predispose,*,ed,sing,sition, *TENDENCY TOWARDS BEFOREHAND*
preditor , predator
preditorial , predator(ial)
predlude , preclude
predomenashen , predominate(tion)
predominate,ely,tion,nant,nantly,ance,ncy, *DOMINATE/AUTHORITY/ CONTROL OVER*
predsul , pretzel
preduction , product(ion)
predukshen , product(ion)

predusesor , predecessor
predutoreul , predator(ial)
predutor , predator
predutory , predator(y)
predy , pretty
predyest , pretty(ttiest)
preech , preach
preechy , preach(y)
preempt,tor,ption,ptive,ptively, *TO OCCUPY/SEIZE/ ACQUIRE BEFORE ANYONE ELSE CAN ACQUIRE OWNERSHIP*
preemshen , preempt(ion)
preemt , preempt
preface,ed,cing, *REMARKS/INTRODUCTION BEFORE A BOOK/LITERARY WORK*
prefale , prevail
prefanedy , profane(nity)
prefanity , profane(nity)
prefeks , prefix
prefer,*,red,ring,rence(s),rable,rableness, rability,rably,rential,rentially,rment, *TO CHOOSE OVER OTHERS, MOST DESIRABLE*
preferinse , prefer(ence)
preferuble , prefer(able)
prefese , preface
prefeshenul , profession(al)
prefesur , professor
prefex , prefix
preficks , prefix
prefide , provide
prefiduble , provide(dable)
prefiks , prefix
prefir , prefer
prefirability , prefer(ability)
prefirable , prefer(able)
prefirense , prefer(ence)
prefirenshul , prefer(ential)
prefirential , prefer(ential)
prefis , preface

prefix,xes,xal,xally, *LETTERS BEFORE A BASE WORD THAT MODIFIES IT'S MEANING, EXISTS PRIOR TO*
preforenshul , prefer(ential)
prefound , profound
prefoundly , profound(ly)
prefur , prefer
prefurabiledy , prefer(ability)
prefurable , prefer(able)
prefurenshul , prefer(ential)
prefurential , prefer(ential)
prefurinse , prefer(ence)
prefuse , preface
prefy , privy
pregadis , prejudice
pregedis , prejudice
pregekshin , project(ion)
pregesterone , progesterone
pregidis , prejudice
pregnant,tly,ncy,ncies,able,ability, *BODY CARRYING AN EMBRYO*
pregnensy , pregnant(ncy)
pregnint , pregnant
pregnonsy , pregnant(ncy)
pregnunt , pregnant
pregnut , pregnant
pregodis , prejudice
pregreshen , progress(ion)
pregretion , progress(ion)
pregudis , prejudice
preimshen , preempt(ion)
preimt , preempt
preimtif , preempt(ive)
preimtive , preempt(ive)
prejadis , prejudice
prejekshin , project(ion)
prejidis , prejudice
prejodis , prejudice

prejudice,*,ed,cing,cial,cially,cialness, *TO HAVE AN OPINION OR ATTITUDE ABOUT SOMETHING/ SOMEONE WITHOUT BASIS OF FULLKNOWLEDGE*
prek, prick
prekareus, precarious
prekarius, precarious
prekastinate, procrastinate
prekaution, precaution
prekawshen, precaution
preked, prick(ed)
prekersery, precursor(y)
prekirsor, precursor
prekirsory, precursor(y)
preklame, proclaim
preklewd, preclude
preklushen, preclude(usion)
preklution, preclude(usion)
preknet, pregnant
preknit, pregnant
preknut, pregnant
prekognative, precognitive
prekognishen, precognition
prekognition, precognition
prekoshious, precocious
prekoshus, precocious
prekotius, precocious
prekrastination, procrastinate
prekrastination, procrastinate
prekursor, precursor
prekursory, precursor(y)
preleminary, preliminary
prelene, praline
prelewt, prelude
preliminary, preliminary
preliminary,ries,rily, *INTRODUCTION TO THE MAIN THEME/EVENT/PRESENTATION, COMES BEFORE*
prelong, prolong
prelongate, prolong(ate)
prelood, prelude

prelude,*,ded,ding,er,usion,usive, *LEADING UP/INTRODUCTORY TO*
prelute, prelude
prem, prim
premachure, premature
premanishen, premonition
premanition, premonition
prematif, primitive
prematively, primitive(ly)
premature,ely,eness,rity, *BEFORE RIPE/MATURE/ FULLY FORMED*
premear, premiere
premecure, premature
premedatate, premeditate
premeditate,*,ed,ting,tion,tive, *TO PLAN OUT BEFORE THE ACT OF*
premeim, premium
premeneshen, premonition
premenishen, premonition
premenstrual,llly, *PRIOR TO/BEFORE MENSTRUATION*
premenzdrul, premenstrual
premere, premiere
premese, premise
premetetate, premeditate
premetitate, premeditate
premeum, premium
premichure, premature
premiere,*, *PLAY/OPERA/MOVIE FIRST PUBLIC EXPOSURE*
preminishen, premonition
preminstral, premenstrual
preminstrul, premenstrual
premiom, premium
premisabul, permissible
premise,es, *ASSUMPTION, BEFOREHAND, LAND WITH TENANTS, BEGINNING OF, PROPOSITION*
premiskues, promiscuity(uous)
premitive, primitive
premiture, premature

premium,*, bonus, additionally
premoder, promote(r)
premoneshen, premonition
premonition, premonition
premonition,*, *SENSE/FEELING BEFORE AN EVENT*
premose, premise
premoshen, promote(tion)
premote, promote
premotion, promote(tion)
premoture, premature
premp, primp
prempt, primp(ed)
premuchure, premature
premunishen, premonition
premunition, premonition
premuse, premise
premutif, primitive
premuture, premature
prence, prince /print(s)
prenceses, princess(es)
prencess, princess
prenciple, principle /principal
prend, print
prendable, print(able)
prender, print(er)
prendible, print(able)
prenduble, print(able)
prenoense, pronounce
prenounce, pronounce
prensabul, principle /principal
prensaple, principle principal
prense, prince /print(s)
prenses, princess /prince(s)
prensibul, principle /principal
prensipul, principle /principal
prensis, princess /prince(s)
prensuple, principle /principal
prent, print
prentabul, print(able)

prenter, print(er)
prentible, print(able)
prentr, print(er)
prentur, print(er)
prenus, apprentice
prenunseate, pronunciate
prenunsiation, pronunciate(tion)
prep,*,pped,pping,pper,ppy, *TO PREPARE/MAKE READY FOR*
prepare,*,ed,edness,ring,ration,rative,ratively, rator,ratory,rer,rily, *TO EQUIP/COMPOSE/ ASSEMBLE/MANUFACTURE/CONDITION SOMETHING/SOMEONE FOR ACTIVITY/EVENT*
prepaseshen, preposition /proposition
prepazishen, preposition /proposition
preperashen, prepare(ration)
preperatory, prepare(ratory)
preperidness, prepare(ness)
prepiration, prepare(ration)
prepiratory, prepare(ratory)
prepiseshen, preposition /proposition
preponent, proponent
preporashen, prepare(ration)
preporshen, proportion
preportion, proportion
preposal, propose(sal)
prepose, propose
preposishen, preposition /proposition
preposition, proposition
preposition,*,ned,ning,nal,nally, *ENGLISH LANGUAGE TERM (or see proposition)*
preposterous,sly,sness, *BEYOND RATIONAL, GOES AGAINST COMMON SENSE*
preposturis, preposterous
prepoze, propose
prepozishen, preposition /proposition
prepozle, propose(sal)
prepriator, proprietor
prepurashen, prepare(ration)

prepuration, prepare(ration)
prepusition, proposition
prepuzishen, preposition /proposition
prer, pray(er)
preree, prairie
prerogative,*, , *PRIVILEDGED*
prery, prairie
pres, press
presadense, precede(nce) /president(s)
presadenshul, president(ial)
presadinse, precede(nce) /president(s)
presadint, precede(nt) /president
prescrebshin, prescript(ion)
prescribe,*,ed,bing,er, *RULE/COURSE/ACTION TO BE FOLLOWED (or see prescript/proscribe)*
prescripshen, prescript(ion)
prescript,tible,tion,tive,tively,tiveness,tivism, *CLAIM/CUSTOM/RULE/RIGHT/TITLE TO (or see prescribe)*
prescrishen, prescript(ion)
presd, press(ed)
presdeje, prestige
presdo, presto
presede, precede /proceed
presedent, precede(nt) /president
presedential, president(ial)
presedger, procedure
presedintial, president(ial)
presedyur, procedure
preseet, prissy
preseet, precede
preseger, procedure
presejur, procedure
presence, *OF BEING PRESENT, IN IMMEDIATE VICINITY OF (or see present)*
presenked, precinct
presenkt, precinct
presense, presence

present,*,ted,ter,ting,tly,tness,table,tableness, tability,tably,tment, *GIFT,ABLE TO BE GIVEN, ACCEPTABLE,TO OFFER SOMETHING,IN IMMEDIATE VICINITY OF,MAKE VISIBLE (or see presence)*
presentation,*,nal,ive, *TO OFFER/ EXHIBIT/ PRESENT SOMETHING*
preser, pressure /press(er)
preservashen, preserve(vation)
preserve,*,ed,er,vable,vation,ving, *TO PROTECT FROM, PREVENT CONDITION FROM BEING ALTERED/EXPLOITED/CHANGED*
preses, precess
preseshen, precision /procession /precession
presetgur, procedure
presetion, precision /procession /precession
presh, preach
presher, pressure
presherize, pressure(rize)
preshes, precious
preshir, pressure
preshis, precious
preshorize, pressure(rize)
preshur, pressure
preshurize, pressure(rize)
preshus, precious
preside,*,ed,ding,er, *ONE IN A HIERARCHAL POSITION OVER, THE AUTHORITY OF THE GROUP, OVERSEEING*
presidense, precede(nce)/ president(s)
presidenshul, president(ial)
president,*,ncy,ncies,tial, *LEADERSHIP POSITION (or see precedent)*
presishen, precision /procession /precession
presiger, procedure
presijur, procedure
presim, prism
presin, prison
presinct, precinct
presiner, prison(er)

previlent, prevalent
previnshun, prevent(ion)
previntion, prevent(ion)
previntive, prevent(ive)
previous, sly, sness, *HAPPENED/OCCURRED BEFORE*
previus, previous
previusly, previous(ly)
prevlig, priviledge
prevlej, priviledge
prevocative, provocative
prevok, provoke
prevokative, provocative
prevokt, provoke
prevulense, prevalent(nce)
prevulent, prevalent
prevulinse, prevalent(nce)
prevy, privy
prey, *, yed, ying, yer, *TO STALK/HUNT DOWN SOME-*
    ONE/SOMETHING FOR SATISFACTION/
    NOURISHMENT (or see pray)
prezadinshul, president(ial)
prezadint, precede(nt) /president
prezedinshul, president(ial)
prezedint, precede(nt) /president
prezent, present
prezentashen, presentation
prezents, presence /present(s)
prezervashen, preserve(vation)
prezerve, preserve
prezident, precede(nt) /president
preziner, prison(er)
prezint, present
prezintly, present(ly)
prezints, presence /present(s)
prezodent, precede(nt) /president
prezomtuis, presume(mptuous)
prezt, priest
prezudenshul, president(ial)
prezudent, precede(nt) /president

prezum, prism
prezumtues, presume(mptuous)
prezunt, present
prhaps, perhaps
pri, pry
priboskus, proboscis
pric, prick /price
pricarius, precarious
pricashen, precaution
pricastinate, procrastinate
pricaushen, precaution
pricaution, precaution
price, *, ed, cing, ey, eless, *COST OF/ FOR SOMETHING*
pricede, precede /proceed
pricise, precise
pricisely, precise(ly)
prick, *, ked, king, kley, klier, kliest, kliness, *TO*
    PIERCE WITH A SHARP POINT, PUNCTURE, SLANG
    FOR MALE ORGAN, POINTED
priclame, proclaim
priclude, preclude
priclushen, preclude(usion)
priclution, preclude(usion)
pricognative, precognitive
pricoshus, precocious
pricotion, precaution
pricotious, precocious
pricy, price(y)
pridacity, predacious(ity)
pridashius, predacious
pridatious, predacious
pride, ded, ding, eful, efully, efulness, *EGO PROTECT-*
    ING ITS SELF-ESTEEM, BOASTFUL, ARROGANT
pridear, pretty(ttier)
pridect, predict
pridekter, predict(or)
pridespose, predispose
prideur, pretty(ttier)
pridful, pride(ful)

pridfulness, pride(fulness)
pridfuly, pride(fully)
pridictable, predict(able)
pridiction, predict(ion)
pridiest, pretty(ttiest)
pridikament, predicament
pridikshen, predict(ion)
pridominate, predominate
pridukshen, product(ion)
priduktion, product(ion)
pridy, pretty
pridyest, pretty(ttiest)
prieng, pry(ing)
prier, prior
prieredy, prior(ity)
priest, *, tly, tliness, thood, tess, *AN ASSIGNED*
    PERSON TO REPRESENT A RELIGIOUS BELIEF
prifale, prevail
prifasee, private(acy)
prifatize, private(tize)
prifatlee, private(ly)
prifee, privy
prifes, profess
prifeshen, profession
prifeshinol, profession(al)
prifesor, professor
prifesy, private(acy)
prifet, private
prifetize, private(tize)
prifetlee, private(ly)
prifide, provide
prifisee, private(acy)
prifit, private
prifitize, private(tize)
prifitlee, private(ly)
prifot, private
prifotize, private(tize)
prifound, profound
prifusy, private(acy)

prifut, private
prifutize, private(tize)
prifutlee, private(ly)
prify, privy
prigekshen, project(ion)
prignostik, prognostic
prigreshen, progress(ion)
prijekshen, project(ion)
prijektile, project(ile)
prik, prick
prikareus, precarious
prikastinate, procrastinate
priked, prick(ed)
priklame, proclaim
prikle, prick(ly)
prikognishen, precognition
prikoshen, precaution
prikoshus, precocious
prikotion, precaution
prikotius, precocious
prikrastination, procrastinate
prikt, prick(ed)
prilimenary, preliminary
prilong, prolong
prilongate, prolong(ate)
prim,mmer,mmest,mmly,mmness, FORMAL/
    PROPER (or see prime)
primade, primate
primal, PRIMITIVE, BASE, FUNDAMENTAL
primary,ries,rily, MAIN ONE, CENTRAL, MOST
    IMPORTANT, FUNDAMENTAL
primate,*,eship,tial, MAMMALS, MAN/MONKEYS/APES
primatif, primitive
primative, primitive
primativly, primitive(ly)
prime,ed,ming,ely,eness,er, AT ITS PEAK, READY,
    PREPARED FOR AN EVENT, TYPE OF NUMBER
primel, primal
primer, premiere / prime(r)

primerily, primary(rily)
primery, primary
primir, prime(r)
primitive,*,ely,eness,vism,vist,vistic, SIMPLE,
    EARLIEST EXPRESSION, CRUDE, GEOMETRIC
    EXPRESSION
primle, primal
primly, prim(mmly) /prime(ly)
primoder, promote(r)
primol, primal
primoshen, promote(tion)
promote, promote
primoter, promote(r)
primotion, promote(tion)
primp,*,ped,ping, TO ADORN/GROOM/DRESS UP
primul, primal
primur, prime(r) / prim(mmer)
primutif, primitive
prinaunse, pronounce
prince,*,edom,eship, MALE POSITION OF ROYALTY
princess,sses, FEMALE POSITION OF ROYALTY
principal,*,lly,lship,lity,lities,lly, PRIMARY/FIRST IN
    IMPORTANCE/POSITION, TERM HAVING TO DO
    WITH MONEY/RULE/LAW (or see principle)
principle,*,ed,MAIN POINT, GENERAL TRUTH,ADOPTED
    METHOD/RULE/LAW (or see principal)
prind, print
prinounce, pronounce
prinownse, pronounce
prinsabul, principle /principal
prinse, prince /print(s)
prinsepul, principle /principal
prinses, princess /prince(s)
prinseses, princess(es)
prinsipul, principle /principal
prinsuple, principle /principal
print,*,ted,ting,table,tability,ter,tery,tless, USE
    OF TEXT TO COMMUNICATE
printuble, print(able)

printur, print(er)
prinunseashen, pronunciate(tion)
prinunseate, pronunciate
prinunsiation, pronunciation(tion)
prior,rly,rship,rate,rity,rities, FIRST, BEFORE,
    EARLIER, RELIGIOUS RANK
priorety, prior(ity)
prioridy, prior(ity)
pripare, prepare
pripeler, propel(ller)
priponent, proponent
priporshen, proportion
priportion, proportion
priposal, propose(sal)
pripose, propose
priposterus, preposterous
pripostirus, preposterous
pripozle, propose(sal)
pripriator, proprietor
priprogative, prerogative
pris, price /prize
priscribe, prescribe / proscribe
prisdeje, prestige
prise, price /price(y) /prize
prisechen, precision /procession /precession
prised, precede/ proceed/ proceed/ price(d)
prisedger, procedure
prisee, prissy /price(y)
priseet, precede /proceed
prisejur, procedure
prisem, prism
prisen, prison
prisener, prison(er)
prisentable, present(able)
priserve, preserve
prises, precess/ price(s)/ prize(s)
priseshen, precision /procession /precession
prisetgur, procedure
prisetion, precision /procession /precession

priside, preside
prisigur, procedure
prisim, prism
prisin, prison
prisipatate, precipitate
prisipatation, precipitate(tion)
prisise, precise
prisisly, precise(ly)
priskrepshen, prescript(ion)
priskribe, prescribe /proscribe
prisless, price(less)
prislis, price(less)
prism,*,matic,matically, GEOMETRICAL SHAPE, OPTICAL/CRYSTAL/RAINBOW EFFECT
prismadik, prism(atic)
prisom, prism
prisomtif, presume(mptive)
prison,*,ner, A BUILDING USED TO CONFINE/HOLD, A FEELING OF INVOLUNTARY RESTRAINT
prissy,ssily,ssiness, ARROGANTLY PRIM, GIRLY GIRL
prist, price(d)
pristege, prestige
pristegus, prestige(gious)
pristeje, prestige
pristene, pristine
pristine,ely, UNCONTAMINATED, PURE
prisum, prism /presume
prisumptive, presume(mptive)
prisumtion, presume(mption)
prisumtuis, presume(mptuous)
prisun, prison
prisuner, prison(er)
prisurf, preserve
prisurve, preserve
prisy, prissy / price(y)
prit, pride
pritear, pretty(ttier)
pritect, protect
pritection, protect(ion)

prited, pride(d)
pritekshen, protect(ion)
pritekt, protect
pritektif, protect(ive)
pritenshen, pretend(nsion)
priteur, pretty(ttier)
pritful, pride(ful)
pritiest, pretty(ttiest)
pritrude, protrude
pritrushen, protrude(usion)
pritrusion, protrude(usion)
prity, pretty
priur, prior
prival, prevail
privaledged, priviledge(d)
privalije, priviledge
privalt, prevail(ed)
privasee, private(acy)
private,ely,acy,tness,tize,tization,tion, BE WHERE OTHERS CANNOT ACCESS YOU, SECLUDED, U.S. MILITARY RANK, NON-GOVERNMENTAL
privatesation, private(tization)
privatisation, private(tization)
privatly, private(ly)
privecy, private(acy)
privee, privy
priveisly, previous(ly)
priveledged, priviledge(d)
privelige, priviledge
privenshen, prevent(ion)
privent, prevent
priventable, prevent(able)
priventive, prevent(ive)
priverbeul, proverb(ial)
privese, private(acy)
privet, private
privetisation, private(tization)
privetly, private(ly)
priveusly, previous(ly)

privicy, private(acy)
prividuble, provide(dable)
priviledge.*,ed,ging, SPECIAL, HONORARY, FAVORED, CHOSEN
privilige, priviledge
privit, private
privitly, private(ly)
privocative, provocative
privock, provoke
privokative, provocative
privoke, provoke
privokt, provoke(d)
privulej, priviledge
privusee, private(acy)
privut, private
privutization, private(tization)
privutly, private(ly)
privvy, privy

privy,vies,vier,viest, OUTDOOR TOILET, IN ON A PRIVATE MATTER/SECRET
privyed, privy(vied)
prize,*,ed,zing, GIFT/REWARD/AWARD FOR ACCOMPLISHMENT/WINNING (or see price/pry(s))
prizen, prison
prizener, prison(er)
prizent, present
prizerve, preserve
prizin, prison
prizis, prize(s) /price(s)
prizm, prism
prizmadik, prism(atic)
prizmatic, prism(atic)
prizomtuis, presume(mptuous)
prizoner, prison(er)
prizum, prism
prizumshen, presume(mption)
prizumtues, presume(mptuous)
prizun, prison
prizuner, prison(er)

prizus, prize(s) /price(s)
pro, PREFIX INDICATING "FOR/ON BEHALF/IN FRONT OF/ FORTH" MODIFIES THE MEANING OF THE WORD
pro,*, SHORT FOR PROFESSIONAL (or see prose)
prob, prop / probe
probabil, probable
probable, probable
probable,ly,bilism,bilist,bilistic,bility,bilities, MOST LIKELY/CHANCE TO OCCUR/HAPPEN
probably, MOST LIKELY TO OCCUR/HAPPEN
probade, probate
probaganda, propaganda
probagashen, propagate(tion)
probagate, propagate
probagation, propagate(tion)
probane, propane
probashen, probate(tion)
probashinul, probate(tional)
probate,*, ed,ting,tion,tional,tionary,tionally, tioner,tive,tory, EXAMINATION/INVESTIGATE THE TRUTH/VALIDITY/GENUINENESS/AUTHENTICITY
probatid, probate(d)
probe,*, ed,bing,er, TO DEEPLY INVESTIGATE/ OBSERVE, INSTRUMENT/ACT FOR RELAYING FACTUAL INFORMATION (or see prop)
probebly, probably
probebul, probable
probeganda, propaganda
probegashen, propagate(tion)
probegate, propagate
prober, proper
proberte, property
probibly, probably
probibul, probable
probiganda, propaganda
probigashen, propagate(tion)
probigate, propagate
probirty, property

problem,*,matic,matical,matically, CHALLENGING SITUATION/INFORMATION WHICH REQUIRES RESOLUTION/ANSWERS/RESULTS
problum, problem
probobul, probable
proboganda, propaganda
probogation, propagate(tion)
proboscis,ses,ides, SNOUT/NOSE/TRUNK
probs, probe(s) /prop(s)
probubilety, probable(bility)
probuble, probable
probuganda, propaganda
probugashen, propagate(tion)
probugate, propagate
probur, proper
proburty, property
procede, proceed
procedure,*,ral,rally, NORMAL/PROPER ACTION/ METHOD/PROCESS
proceedure, procedure
proces, process
proceshen, precision /procession /precession
procesion, precision /procession /precession
process,sses,ssing,ssor,ssion,ssionally, sser, INCREMENTAL/GRADUAL CHANGES/STEPS TO ACHIEVE A GOAL
procession,nal,nally, MOVING ALONG AS A GROUP (or see procession or precession)
prockreashen, procreate(tion)
proclaim,*,med,ming,mer, MAKE VERBAL ANNOUNCEMENT WITH AUTHORITY
proclamashen, proclamation
proclamation,*, ANNOUNCE/DECLARE TO THE PUBLIC
proclimashen, proclamation
proclimation, proclamation
proclivity,ties, a tendency towards
proclumashen, proclamation

proclumation, proclamation
procram, program
procrastinate,*,ed,ting,tion,tor, REPEATEDLY PUT OFF UNTIL LATER
procreashen, procreate(tion)
procreate,*, ed,ting,tion,tive,tor, TO REPRODUCE/ PRODUCE
prod,*,dded,dding,dder, TO POKE/JAB, A POLE/ STICK WITH POINTED END
prodakol, protocol
prodatipe, prototype
prodegul, prodigal
prodegy, prodigy
prodekol, protocol
prodest, protest
prodetipe, prototype
prodews, produce
prodicol, protocol
prodigal,lity,lly, ONE WHO SPENDS/ WASTES TOO MUCH MONEY
prodigul, prodigal
prodigy,gies, VERY YOUNG PERSON WITH REMARKABLE TALENTS/SKILLS/APTITUDE
prodikol, protocol
prodikt, predict
proditipe, prototype
prodon, proton
prodotype, prototype
produce,*, ed,cing,cible,cable,ctible,er, CREATE/ MANUFACTURE/BRING FORTH, FRUIT/VEGETABLE
producol, protocol
producshen, product(ion)
product,*, tion,tive,tively,tiveness,tivity, SOME- THING PRODUCED/MANUFACTURED/DEVELOPED AS SALEABLE GOOD, ACT OF CREATING GOODS
produgee, prodigy
produgil, prodigal
produkol, protocol
produkshen, product(ion)

produktion, product(ion)
produse, produce
produtipe, prototype
prof, proof /prove
profable, prove(vable)
profalaktik, prophylactic
profane,ely,eness,er,nity,nities, *TO MISUSE WORDS, VULGAR LANGUAGE*
profanedy, profane(nity)
profat, profit /prophet
profedik, prophet(ic)
profelaktik, prophylactic
profeser, professor
profeshen, profession
profeshenul, profession(al)
profesional, profession(al)
profesor, professor
profess,sses,ssed,ssedly,ssing, *TO VOW, CLAIM ALLEGIANCE/ACCEPTANCE*
profession,*,nal,nally,nalism,nalize, *LOYAL TO A VOCATION, ADEPT IN THEIR FIELD*
professor,*,rial,rially,rate,riate,rship, *TEACHER ON COLLEGE/UNIVERSITY STAFF*
profesy, prophecy/ prophesy
profet, profit /prophet
profetable, profit(able)
profeteer, profit(eer)
profetible, profit(able)
profetik, prophet(ic)
proficient,tly,ncy, *SKILLED/KNOWLEDGEABLE*
profide, provide
profiduble, provide(dable)
profilaktik, prophylactic
profile,*,ed,ling, *SIDE VIEW OF FACE, OUTLINE/ CONTOUR, BIOGRAPHICAL OUTLINE*
profishent, proficient
profisy, prophecy/ prophesy

profit,*,ted,ting,tless,table,tability,tableness, tably,teer, *GAIN ON THE SALE OF SOMETHING (or see prophet)*
profituble, profit(able)
profolaktik, prophylactic
profound,dly,dness, *DEEP/SIGNIFICANT IN KNOWLEDGE/INSIGHT*
profownd, profound
profowndly, profound(ly)
profownt, profound
profulaktik, prophylactic
profusy, prophecy/ prophesy
progeks, project(s)
progekshin, project(ion)
progekt, project
progektile, project(ile)
progesterone, *A CHEMICAL PRODUCED BY FEMALES HUMANS/MAMMALS*
prognastic, prognostic
prognosis,ses, *a medical opinion*
prognostic,*,cate,cative,cator,cation, *PREDICT A MEDICAL CONDITION'S OUTCOME*
program,*,mmed,mming,mmer,mmatic, mmatically, *AN OUTLINE OF EVENTS/ACTIONS/ SCHEDULES*
programt, program(mmed)
progreshen, progress(ion)
progresive, progress(ive)
progress,sses,ssed,ssing,ssion,ssional,ssionist, ssist,ssive,ssiveness,ssively, *ADVANCEMENT/ EVOLUTION/ FORWARD MOVEMENT*
progretion, progress(ion)
progris, progress
prohabeshin, prohibit(ion)
prohebatory, prohibit(ory)
prohebit, prohibit
prohebition, prohibit(ion)
prohibatif, prohibit(ive)
prohibetory, prohibit(ory)

prohibit,*,ted,ting,tive,tively,tion,tionist,tory, *FORBID/PREVENT/NOT ALLOWED TO DO*
project,*,table,tile,tion,tional,tionist,tive,tively, tivity,tor, *PLAN/OBJECTIVE/UNDERTAKING TO BE CARRIED OUT, JUT OUT/PROTRUDE, PRESENT*
projekshin, project(ion)
projeksion, project(ion)
projektile, project(ile)
projesterone, progesterone
projestirone, progesterone
prokastinate, procrastinate
proklaim, proclaim
proklame, proclaim
proklemashen, proclamation
proklevidy, proclivity
proklimation, proclamation
proklumation, proclamation
proknosis, prognosis
prokram, program
prokrastinate, procrastinate
prokrastination, procrastinate(tion)
prokreashen, procreate(tion)
prokreate, procreate
prokreation, procreate(tion)
prokriate, procreate
prokse, proxy
proksemate, proximate
proksimety, proximate(mity)
proksumit, proximate
proleminary, preliminary
prolimenary, preliminary
prolog, prologue
prologue,*,ed,uing,uize,uized,uizing,gize,gizer, *INTRO/PREFACE/SPEECH BEFORE A BOOK/PLAY/ POEM/NOVEL*
prolok, prologue
prolong,*,ged,ging,gate,gation,ger, *TO EXTEND/ LENGTHEN/ELONGATE TIME*
prolongade, prolong(ate)

prolonk, prolong
prom,*,menade,menaded,menading,menader, FORMAL DANCE
promanent, prominent
promanintly, prominent(ly)
promanitly, prominent(ly)
promd, prompt
promded, prompt(ed)
promdly, prompt(ly)
promenant, prominent
promenintly, prominent(ly)
prominet, prominent
promes, promise
promeskuis, promiscuity(uous)
promesquis, promiscuity(uous)
promesquity, promiscuity
prominade, prom(enade) / prominent
prominate, prom(enade) / prominent
prominent,ncy,tly, PRONOUNCED/DISTINCT/JUTS OUT/STANDS OUT/NOTICEABLE
prominet, prominent
promiscuity,uous,uously,uousness, GIVEN TO CONDUCTING SEXUAL/RANDOM/INDESCRIMINATE ACTIVITY WITH MANY
promise,*,ed,sing,sable,ser,see,sor,sory, PLEDGE AGREE/LOYALTY TO FOLLOW THROUGH AS STATED
promiskuis, promiscuity(uous)
promisquis, promiscuity(uous)
promisquity, promiscuity
promist, promise(d)
promote,*,ed,ting,tion,tional,tive,tiveness,er, TO ADVERTISE/PRESENT/ ENGAGE TO FURTHER A PROJECT/EVENT/SALE
prompnes, prompt(ness)
prompt,*,ted,ting,tly,tness,ter,titude, TIMELY/ EXACT/TO REMIND/PUNCTUAL
promt, prompt
promted, prompt(ed)
promtlee, prompt(ly)
promunetly, prominent(ly)

promus, promise
prona, prana /piranha
pronaun, pronoun
pronaunse, pronounce
prondo, pronto
prone,ely,eness, given/inclined to, face down
prones, prone(ness) /prawn(s)
pronnis, prone(ness)
pronoun, class of words in English grammar
pronounce,*,ed,edly,cing,eable,er,ement, articulate/annunciate speaking, define, speak with confidence/authority
pronoun, pronoun
pronto, quickly/immediately
pronu, prana / piranha
pronunciate,*,ed,ting,tion,tional, ARTICULATE, BE SPECIFIC IN SPEECH/SPEAKING
pronunseashen, pronunciate(tion)
pronunseate, pronunciate
pronunsiation, pronunciate(tion)
prood, prude
proodish, prude(dish)
proof,*,fed,fing,fer, FACTUAL EVIDENCE, TO SUPPORT THE TRUTH, TESTED (or see prove)
proon, prune
proot, prude
proove, prove
prop,*,pped,pping, THEATER STAGE SET TERM, A SUPPORT, AIRPLANE PROPELLER (or see probe)
propabel, probable
propabelity, probable(bility)
propable, probable /probably
propabul, probable
propagade, propagate
propaganda,dist,distic,distically,dism,dize, MISINFORMATION, PURPOSEFUL HALF-TRUTHS
propagashen, propagate(tion)
propagate,*,ed,ting,tion,tional,tive,tor, TO BREED/REPRODUCE/MAKE MORE OF

propain, propane
propane, A GAS
propasishen, preposition /proposition
propasterus, preposterous
propazishen, preposition /proposition
propd, prop(pped) /robe(d)
propebly, probably
proped, prop(pped) /probe(d)
propeganda, propaganda
propegashen, propagate(tion)
propegate, propagate
propegation, propagate(tion)
propel,*,lled,lling,llant,ller, EXERT/GIVE MOMEN-TUM/START INTO ACTION, MOVING PART ON A PLANE, ELEMENT USED TO CREATE MOVEMENT
propeler, propel(ller)
propelint, propel(llant)
proper,rly,rness, correct/accurate
properedness, prepare(dness)
properidness, prepare(dness)
property,ties,tied,tyless, SOMETHING TANGIBLE/ PHYSICAL TO BE OWNED BY SOMEONE
prophalaktik, prophylactic
prophecy,cies,cied, PREDICTION OF A DIRE/ UNDESIRABLE FUTURE (or see prophesy)
prophelaktik, prophylactic
prophesy,sies,sied, PREDICTION OF THE FUTURE (or see prophecy)
prophet,ecy,ecies,ecied, ONE WHO IS BELIEVED TO HAVE CONNECTION TO THE UNKNOWN SOURCE FOR PREDICTIONS/ANSWERS (or see profit)
prophilaktik, prophylactic
prophile, profile
prophisy, prophecy/ prophesy
prophit, prophet /profit
propholaktik, prophylactic
prophylactic,cally, ITEM USED FOR CONTRACEPTION
propibly, probably
propigade, propagate

propiganda, propaganda
propigashen, propagate(tion)
propigate, propagate
propigation, propagate(tion)
propiseshen, preposition/ proposition
proplem, problem
proplum, problem
propogate, propagate
proponent,*, ONE WHO MAKES A PROPOSAL
proporshen, proportion
proportion,*,nable,ned,ning,nal,nally,nality, nate,nately,nateness, PARTS EQUAL/RELATIVE IN PERSPECTIVE/SIZE
propose,*,ed,er,sing,sal,sition,sitional,sitionally, OFFER/PRESENT IDEA (or see preposition) SUGGESTION
proposterus, preposterous
proposishen, preposition /proposition
propozishen, preposition /proposition
propriater, proprietor
propriuter, proprietor
proposeshen, preposition /proposition
propt, prop(pped) /probe(d)
propubil, probable
propubiledy, probable(bility)
propubly, probably
propuganda, propaganda
propugashen, propagate(tion)
propugate, propagate
propugation, propagate(tion)
propur, proper
propurle, proper(ly)
propuzishen, preposition/ proposition
pros, prose /pro(s)
prosberity, prosper(ity)
proprietor,rship,ty,ties,LEGAL OWNER/TITLEHOLDER

proscribe,*,ed,bing,er, OUTLAW/ PROHIBIT (or see prescribe)
prosdatoot, prostitute
prosdetushen, prostitute(tion)
prosditute, prostitute
prosdition, prostitute(tion)
prosdrate, prostrate /prostate
prose, MORE LIKE NORMAL WRITTEN LANGUAGE THAN POETRY (or see pro(s))
prosechin, precision /procession /precession
prosecute,*,ed,ting,tion,tive,tor, FOLLOW THROUGH, FINAL DETERMINATION, ENFORCE THE LAW, SIDE WHO BRINGS ABOUT A LAWSUIT (or see persecute)
prosed, proceed
proseds, proceed(s)
proseger, procedure
proseets, proceed(s)
proseetsher, procedure
prosejur, procedure
prosekewt, prosecute
prosekushen, prosecute(tion)
prosekution, prosecute(tion)
proses, process
proseshen, precision /procession /precession
prosetion, precision /procession /precession
prosicute, prosecute
prosidger, procedure
prosijur, procedure
prosikushen, prosecute(tion)
prosikute, prosecute
prosis, process
prosparidy, prosper(ity)
prospect,*,ting,tor,tive,tively,tus, EXPECTING/ FUTURE/POSSIBLE EVENT/SITUATION, MINING FOR SOMETHING
prospectif, prospect(ive)
prospekt, prospect
prospektif, prospect(ive)

prosper,*,red,ring,rity,rities,rous,rously, rousness, BENEFIT GREATLY, BE SUCCESSFUL
prosperidy, prosper(ity)
prospir, prosper
prospirus, prosper(ous)
prospures, prosper(s) /prosper(ous)
prostate, prostate /prostrate
prostate,ectomy,ectomies,tism, PERTAINS TO PROSTATE GLAND AROUND MALE URETHRA (or see prostrate)
prostatution, prostitute(tion)
prostetute, prostitute
prostetution, prostitute(tion)
prosthesis,etic,rtically, ARTIFICIAL REPLACEMENT OF A BODY PART
prosthesus, prosthesis
prostitute, prostitute
prostitute,*,tion,tor, A PERSON WHO TRADES SEXUAL FAVORS FOR MONEY/GOODS
prostrade, prostrate /prostate
prostrate,*,ed,ting,tion,tive,tor, TO PLACE ONE'S BODY INTO A SUBMISSIVE POSITION/POSTURE, TO ASSUME A HUMILIATED/HELPLESS/ POWER-LESS POSITION (or see prostate)
prosukushen, prosecute(tion)
prot, prod
protacol, protocol
protaga, protege'
protagenist, protagonist
protaginest, protagonist
protagonist,*, LEADING/PRINCIPAL CHARACTER
protajay, protege'
protakol, protocol
protatype, prototype
protean, protein
protecol, protocol
protect,*,ted,ting,tingly,tion,tionism,tionist, tive,tor, GUARD/ SHIELD/PREVENT FROM DANGER/HARM/DESTRUCTION

protectif, protect(ive)
protega, protege'
protege',*, YOUNG PERSON UNDER CARE/PROTECT-
ION OF AN ELDER/MASTER (or see prodigy)
protein,*, CHEMICAL COMPOUNDS
protejay, protege'
protekol, protocol
protekshen, protect(ion)
protekt, protect
protektuf, protect(ive)
protene, protein
protes, protest
protest,*,ted,ting,ter, TAKE ACTION AGAINST A
PERCEIVED INJUSTICE TO AFFECT CHANGE
protestur, protest(er)
protetipe, prototype
protetype, prototype
proticol, protocol
protiga, protege'
protijay, protege'
protikol, protocol
prototipe, prototype
prototype, prototype
protocol,*,led,ling, GENERAL RULE WHETHER
FORMALIZED OR NOT
proton,*,nic, A MOLECULAR PARTICLE OF POSITIVE
CHARGE
protonek, proton(ic)
protonie, prototype
protonitype, prototype
prototype,*,pal,pic, A MODEL/REPLICATE OF
ORIGINAL, FIRST MODEL
protract,*,tion,tive,ted,tor, TO DRAW OUT/ LENGTHEN
TIME/SPACE/DISTANCE, A TOOL FOR DRAWING
protrakt, protract
protrakter, protract(or)
protrude,*,ed,ent,ding,usible,usion,usile,usive,
usively,usiveness, EXTENDS/PROJECTS OUT
protrugin, protrude(usion)
protrushen, protrude(usion)
protrusuf, protrude(usive)

protukol, protocol
protutipe, prototype
protutype, prototype
proud,dly,dness, PAST TENSE OF" PRIDE", HAPPY
ABOUT AN ACCOMPLISHMENT
proues, prowess
prouis, prowess
proul, prowl
provacation, provocative(ion)
provakashen, provocative(ion)
prove,*,ed,ving,vable,vably,ver, BRING FORTH
FACTS, MAKE TRUTH KNOWN (or see proof)
proveable, prove(vable)
proveble, prove(vable)
provecation, provocative(ion)
provekation, provocative(ion)
provence, province
provencial, province(cial)
provensial, province(cial)
provent, prevent
provents, province
proverb,*,bial,bially, POPULAR/WISE SAYING
proverbeil, proverb(ial)
proverbeul, proverb(ial)
proveshen, provision
provible, prove(vable)
provication, provocative(ion)
provide,*,ed,ding,er,dable, MAKE AVAILABLE/
GIVE/EXPOSE
provikation, provocative(ion)
province,*,cial,cially,ciality,cialize,cialities,cialist
cialize,cialism, DESIGNATED AREA OUTSIDE OF
MAINSTREAM GIVEN TO A SPECIFIC ORDER/RULE
provinshul, province(cial)
provint, prevent
provints, province
provirb, proverb
provirbeul, proverb(ial)
provision,*,ned,ning,ner, SUPPLIES, ALLOWANCES,
PROVIDE FOR

provocative,ely,eness,ion, TO STIMULATE/ENTICE
TO REACT
provokative, provocative
provoke,*,ed,king,kingly,ocation, ENTICE/LURE/
MANIPULATE TO REACT
provost,tship, CHURCH/EDUCATIONAL SUPERIOR
provuble, prove(vable)
provukashen, provocative(ion)
provukation, provocative(ion)
provurb, proverb
provurbeul, proverb(ial)
provurbial, proverb(ial)
prowd, proud
prowdly, proud(ly)
prowess, EXCEPTIONAL BRAVERY/SKILL
prowis, prowess
prowl,*,led,ling,ler, SOMEONE SNEAKING AROUND IN
SEARCH OF SOMETHING/SOMEONE
prowt, proud
prowtly, proud(ly)
proxamit, proximate
proxamity, proximate(mity)
proxemidy, proximate(mity)
proximate,ely,eness,mity,al, NEXT/NEAR IN
TIME/SPACE, CLOSE TO (or see approximate)
proxsemity, proximate(mity)
proxy,xies, AUTHORIZED/LEGAL TO SUBSTITUTE FOR
proxumit, proximate
prozdatute, prostitute
prozdetushen, prostitute(tion)
prozditushin, prostitute(tion)
prozdrate, prostrate /prostate
proztate, prostate /prostrate
prubaskis, proboscis
prubozkis, proboscis
prucede, precede /proceed
prucedure, procedure
pruclivity, proclivity
prude,ery,eries,dish,dishness, SOMEONE
UNCOMFORTABLE WITH SEX RELATED ISSUES

prudence,nt,ntly,ntial,ntially, *PRACTICING CAUTION/GOOD JUDGEMENT*
prudense, prudence
prudesh, prude(dish)
prudikament, predicament
prudinse, prudence
prudunt, prudence(nt)
pruf, proof /prove
prufanedy, profane(nity)
prufanity, profane(nity)
prufedik, prophet(ic)
prufeshen, profession
prufeshinul, profession(al)
prufesional, profession
prufible, prove(vable)
prufide, provide
prufiduble, provide(dable)
prufuble, prove(vable)
prugektile, project(ile)
prugnostik, prognostic
prugnoztek, prognostic
prugreshen, progress(ion)
prugresif, progress(ive)
prugresive, progress(ive)
prugretion, progress(ion)
pruhebit, prohibit
pruhibatif, prohibit(ive)
pruhibet, prohibit
prujektile, project(ile)
pruklivedy, proclivity
pruklivity, proclivity
pruleminary, preliminary
prulimenary, preliminary
prumere, premiere
prumiskues, promiscuity(uous)
prumoder, promote(r)
prumoshen, promote(tion)
prumote, promote
prumoter, promote(r)

prumotion, promote(tion)
prune,*,ed,ning, *DRIED PLUM, TRIM A SHRUB/TREE*
prunownse, pronounce
prupare, prepare
prupel, propel
prupeler, propel(ller)
prupelint, propel(llant)
prupelir, propel(ller)
prupelt, propel(lled)
pruponent, proponent
pruporshen, proportion
pruporshenate, proportion(al)
pruportion, proportion
prupose, propose
pruposition, proposition
pruposle, propose(sal)
prupoze, propose
prupozel, propose(sal)
prupozishen, proposition
prupriater, proprietor
pruprietor, proprietor
prusdej, prestige
prusdejus, prestige(gious)
prusechen, precision /procession /precession
prusede, precede /proceed
prusejur, procedure
pruseshin, precision /procession /precession
prusetgur, procedure
prusetion, precision /procession /precession
prusijer, procedure
prusiputashen, precipitate(tion)
prusishen, precision
prusisly, precise(ly)
prusition, precision /procession /precession
pruskribe, proscribe /proscribe
prusteg, prestige
prustegis, prestige(gious)
prustejus, prestige(gious)
prute, prude

prutective, protect(ive)
prutekshen, protect(ion)
prutektuf, protect(ive)
prutish, prude(dish)
prutrude, protrude
prutrushen, protrude(usion)
prutrusion, protrude(usion)
pruvale, prevail
pruv, prove
pruvencial, province(cial)
pruvenshen, prevent(ion)
pruvenshul, province(cial)
pruvent, prevent
pruventable, prevent(able)
pruventive, prevent(ive)
pruverbeul, proverb(ial)
pruvide, provide
pruviduble, provide(dable)
pruvinshul, province(cial)
pruvint, prevent
pruvintable, prevent(able)
pruvokative, provocative
pruzentuble, present(able)
pruzumshen, presume(mption)
pry,ries,ried,ying,yingly,yer, *PEEP IN, METHOD OF OPENING SOMETHING THAT'S TIGHTLY CLOSED*
pryer, prior
prymate, primate
psalm,*, *BIBLICAL SONG*
psariasis, psoriasis
pseudo, *FALSE/PRETENDED/IMITATING*
pseudo, *PREFIX INDICATING "FALSE/PRETENDED/IMITATING" MOST OFTEN MODIFIES THE WORD*
pseudonym,*, *USING ANOTHER NAME*
psicheatric, psychiatric
psichopathologist, psychopath(ologist)
psikeatric, psychiatric
psikik, psychic
psikilegekul, psychology(gical)

psikilegy, psychology
psikologekul, psychology(gical)
psikologest, psychology(gist)
psikology, psychology
psikopath, psychopath
psikopathic, psychopath(ic)
psikopathologist, psychopath(ologist)
psikosis, psychosis
psikotic, psychotic
psoriasis,atic, skin problem
psudo, pseudo
psuriesis, psoriasis
psych, PREFIX INDICATING "MIND/MENTAL" MOST
    OFTEN MODIFIES THE WORD
psychadelic, psychedelic
psyche, OVERALL ESSENCE OF THE HUMAN BEING,
    SOUL/BODY/MIND/SPIRIT (or see sic or sick)
psycheatric, psychiatric
psychedelic,*, HALLUCINATION/DELUSION/MIND
    ALTERING
psychiatric,*,cally, FIELD OF SCIENCE WHICH
    STUDIES THE MIND/EMOTIONS
psychiatry,rist, PHYSICIAN WHO STUDIES THE MIND/
    THE STUDY OF THE MIND/EMOTIONS
psychic,*,cal,cally, USE OF THE MORPHOGENIC FIELD
    TO SEE PAST/PRESENT/FUTURE EVENTS, EXTRA-
    SENSORY PERCEPTION
psychidelic, psychedelic
psychietrist, psychiatry(rist)
psychietry, psychiatry
psychiotrist, psychiatry(rist)
psycho,*, SLANG FOR SOMEONE WHO IS BEING
    LUDICROUS/CRAZY
psychodelic, psychedelic
psychology, psychology
psycholgekul, psychology(gical)
psychology,gies,gic,gical,gically,gism,gist,gize,
    FIELD OF SCIENCE RELATED TO STUDYING THE
    MIND/MENTAL

psychopath,*, hic,hology,hologist,hologic,
    hological,hy,hic,hical,hically, SOMEONE WHO
    HAS/OR WORKS WITH A PERSONALITY DISORDER
psychopathic, psychopath(ic)
psychopathologist, psychopath(ologist)
psychosis, A MENTAL DISORDER WHICH RENDERS A
    PERSON DISATTACHED FROM NORMAL REALITY
psychotic,cally, MENTAL DISORDER THAT RENDERS A
    PERSON DISATTACHED FROM NORMAL REALITY
psychudelic, psychedelic
psycik, psychic
psykadelic, psychedelic
psykapathic, psychopath(ic)
psykeatric, psychiatric
psykedelic, psychedelic
psykek, psychic
psykepathic, psychopath(ic)
psykiatric, psychiatric
psykiatrist, psychiatry(rist)
psykiatry, psychiatry
psykidelic, psychedelic
psykik, psychic
psykipathic, psychopath(ic)
psykiutry, psychiatry
psyko, psycho
psykolegy, psychology
psykoligekul, psychology(gical)
psykoligy, psychology
psykologekul, psychology(gical)
psykologest, psychology(gist)
psykology, psychology
psykopath, psychopath
psykopathic, psychopath(ic)
psykopathologist, psychopath(ologist)
psykosis, psychosis
psykotic, psychotic
psykudelic, psychedelic
psykyatric, psychiatric
pu, pew

pub,*, A TAVERN (or see pube)
pube,*, bic,escent,escence,escency, HAIR ON
    GENITALS WHICH APPEAR DURING PUBERTY, THE
    DOWN ON PLANTS
pubek, pube(bic)
puberdy, puberty
puberty, BECOMING OF AGE FOR REPRODUCTION
pubirty, puberty
publacation, publication
publacist, publicist
publakashen, publication
publakation, publication
publash, publish
publasher, publish(er)
publasist, publicist
publasize, publicity(ize)
publecation, publication
publecist, publicist
publecity, publicity(ity)
publek, public
publekashin, publication
publekation, publication
publesher, publish(er)
publeshuble, publish(able)
publesist, publicist
publesity, publicity(ity)
publesize, publicity(ize)
public,cly,cness, NOT PRIVATE
publicashen, publication
publication,*, ISSUE PRINTED MATERIAL FOR PUBLIC
publicist,ity,ize, INVOLVED IN THE PRODUCTION
    OF/DISSEMINATION OF WRITTEN TEXT
publikashen, publication
publikation, publication
publisaty, publicist(ity)
publisaty, publicist(ity)
publisety, publicity(ity)
publish,hes,hable,her, INVOLVEMENT IN THE
    PRODUCTION OF DISSEMINATING WRITTEN
    TEXT/INFORMATION

publishuble, publish(able)
publisist, publicist
publisity, publicist(ity)
publisize, publicity(ize)
publokashen, publication
publosher, publish(er)
publosist, publicist
publosize, publicity(ize)
publucation, publication
publucist, publicist
publukation, publication
publush, publish
publushable, publish(able)
publusher, publish(er)
publusist, publicist
publusize, publicity(ize)
puburdy, puberty
puch, pooch / push
puck,*, A DISC USED IN HOCKEY (or see puke)
pudal, puddle /poodle
puddil, puddle /poodle
pudding, A CREAMY DESSERT (or see putt(ing))
puddle,*,ed,ling, A SMALL POOL OF LIQUID (or see poodle)
puddul, puddle /poodle
pude, put /putty
pudel, puddle /poodle
pudeng, pudding /putt(ing)
puder, pewter /putt(er)
pudestrein, pedestrian
pudgie, pudgy
pudgy, A LITTLE BIT OVERWEIGHT
pudil, puddle /poodle
puding, pudding /putt(ing)
pudir, pewter /putt(er)
pudje, pudgy
pudul, puddle /poodle
pudur, pewter /putt(er)
pudy, putty

puer, poor/ pour/ pore
puf, puff
pufeleon, pavilion
pufer, puff(er)
puff,*, ffed,ffing,ffer, SHORT/SUDDEN BURST OF AIR, TO INHALE/EXHALE SMOKE
pufileon, pavilion
pufs, puff(s)
puft, puff(ed)
pugamus, pajamas
puge, pudgy
puir, poor/ pour/ pore
puit, put
pujamus, pajamas
puje, pudgy
pujomus, pajamas
puk, puck /puke
puke,*,ed,king, TO VOMIT/THROW-UP (or see puck)
pukon, pecan
pukuleur, peculiar
pul, pull /pool
pularity, polar(ity)
puld, pull(ed) /pool(ed)
pule, pool /pulley
puled, pull(ed) /pool(ed)
pulegimy, polygamy
puleridy, polar(ity)
pules, police /pulley(s)
pulet, pullet
pulewshen, pollute(tion)
puley, pulley
pulferise, pulverize
pulfurise, pulverize
pulies, pulley(s)
puligamus, polygamy(mous)
puligemy, polygamy
puligine, polygyny
puling, pull(ing) /pool(ing)
pulit, pullet / polite

pull,*,lled,lling,ller, TO DRAW/BRING TOWARDS/ TUG SOMETHING/SOMEONE (or see pool)
pullet,*, young domesticated hen
pulley,*, TOOL USED WITH ROPE FOR LIFTING/PULLING
pullit, pullet
pulmanery, pulmonary
pulmonary, pertaining to the lungs
pulmonery, pulmonary
pulp,piness,PY, A FIBROUS/THICK SUBSTANCE LEFT BEHIND WHEN VEGETABLE/FRUIT/PLANTS ARE COOKED/SMASHED
pulpet, pulpit
pulpit, CHURCH PLATFORM
pulsashen, pulsate(tion)
pulsate,*,ed,ting,tile,tion,tor,tory,PULSE/THROB
pulse,*,ed,sing, THROB/BEAT RYTHMICALLY
pult, pull(ed) /pool(ed)
pulushen, pollute(tion)
pulut, pollute /pullet
pulutent, pollute(tant)
pulution, pollute(tion)
pulverize,*,ed,zing,rable,zable,er, REDUCE TO POWDER/PULP
pulvirise, pulverize
pulvorise, pulverize
puly, pulley
pulygamus, polygamy(mous)
pulygamy, polygamy
pulyginy, polygyny
pulzate, pulsate
pumal, pummel
pumas, pumice
pumb, pump
pumbt, pump(ed)
pumcan, pumpkin
pumel, pummel
pumes, pumice
pumice,cite, A VOLCANIC STONE USED FOR SANDING
pumil, pummel

pumis, pumice
pumkan, pumpkin
pumkun, pumpkin
pumle, pummel
pummel,*,led,ling, *TO POMMEL/HIT REPEATEDLY/ CAUSE DAMAGE*
pumol, pummel
pumos, pumice
pump,*,ped,ping,per, *TO FORCE LIQUID/OBJECT TO MOVE IN A DESIGNATED DIRECTION*
pumpken, pumpkin
pumpkin,*, *A LARGE SQUASH*
pumpt, pump(ed)
pumul, pummel
pumus, pumice
pun,*,nned,nning, *TO USE WORDS SIMILAR BUT DIFFERENT FOR HUMOROUS INTENT*
punatef, punitive
punative, punitive
punch,hes,hed,hing,her, *STRIKE AGAINST SOME-THING WITH FORCE, TO PIERCE, DRINK MIXTURE*
puncherd, puncture(d)
puncht, punch(ed)
punchuate, punctuate
puncsher, puncture
puncshuate, punctuate
puncshuel, punctual
punctewashen, punctuate(tion)
punctual,lity,lly,lness, *ARRIVE ON TIME*
punctuashen, punctuate(tion)
punctuate,*,ed,tion,tive,tor, *USE MARKS/SYMBOLS IN TEXT FOR CLARIFICATION*
puncture,*,ed,ring,rable, *TO PIERCE/PERFORATE/ PRICK THROUGH SOMETHING*
pund, punt /pun/(nned)
punech, punish
puneched, punish(ed)
punechmint, punish(ment)
punensula, peninsula

punesh, punish
puneshmint, punish(ment)
punesht, punish(ed)
punetive, punitive
pungensy, pungent(ncy)
pungent,tly,ncy, *A STRONG/SHARP SMELL/TASTE*
punginsy, pungent(ncy)
pungunt, pungent
punich, punish
punichment, punish(ment)
puninsula, peninsula
punish,hes,hed,hing,her,hable,hability,hment, *APPLY MEASURES TO CORRECT INTOLERABLE ACT*
punishmint, punish(ment)
punisht, punish(ed)
punitive,ely,eness, *INFLICT/IMPOSE PUNISHMENT*
punjensy, pungent(ncy)
punjinsy, pungent(ncy)
punjunt, pungent
punk,*,ker, *A STICK USED FOR STARTING FIREWORKS/ FIRECRACKERS, DERAGATORY FOR BAD BEHAVIOR*
punkchashen, punctuate(tion)
punkcher, puncture
punkchewashen, punctuate(tion)
punkchewate, punctuate
punkchir, puncture
punkchuate, punctuate
punkchuation, punctuate(tion)
punkchur, puncture
punkir, punk(er)
punksher, puncture
punkshewal, punctual
punkshewashen, punctuate(tion)
punkshewate, punctuate
punkshewul, punctual
punkshir, puncture
punkshooate, punctuate
punkshooation, punctuate(tion)
punkshooel, punctual

punkshor, puncture
punkshual, punctual
punkshuashen, punctuate(tion)
punkshuate, punctuate
punkshuation, punctuate(tion)
punkshuol, punctual
punkshur, puncture
punktual, punctual
punktuate, punctuate
punotif, punitive
punsh, punch
punt,*,ted,ting,ter, *DROP/KICK A BALL, PROPEL, OF A POINTED NATURE, GAMBLE* (or see pun(ed))
punshur, puncture / punch(er)
punuched, punish(ed)
punuchment, punish(ment)
punudeve, punitive
punudive, punitive
punushed, punish(ed)
punushment, punish(ment)
punutive, punitive
puny,nier,niest, *INSIGNIFICANT/SMALL/WEAK IN SIZE/STRENGTH*
pup,*,ppy,ppies, *A NEWBORN DOG/SEAL*
pupal, pupil
pupater, puppet(eer)
pupatree, puppet(ry)
pupe, pup(ppy)
pupel, pupil
pupet, puppet
pupeteer, puppet(eer)
pupetry, puppet(ry)
pupil,*, *PART OF THE EYE, STUDENT UNDER THE TUTELAGE OF AN INSTRUCTOR/GUARDIAN*
pupit, puppet
pupiteer, puppet(eer)
pupitry, puppet(ry)
pupiya, papaya
puplasher, publish(er)

purosity, porosity
puroxside, peroxide
purpel, purple
purpendicular, perpendicular
purpes, purpose
purpeshual, perpetual
purpesly, purpose(ly)
purpetrate, perpetrate
purpetshual, perpetual
purpetshuate, perpetual(ate)
purpetual, perpetual
purpetuate, perpetual(ate)
purpetuity, perpetuity
purpil, purple
purpindicular, perpendicular
purpis, purpose
purpisly, purpose(ly)
purpitrate, perpetrate
purple,lish, *A COLOR*
purpleksity, perplex(ity)
purplex, perplex
purplexity, perplex(ity)
purporshenal, proportion(al)
purportional, proportion(al)
purpose,*,ed,sing,eful,efully,efulness,eless,ely, *REASON FOR/MISSION/GOAL, DESIGN FOR*
purposly, purpose(ly)
purpul, purple
purpus, purpose
purpusly, purpose(ly)
purr,*,rring, *A GUTTERAL SOUND COMING FROM A CATS THROAT WHEN PLEASED*
pursacute, persecute
pursavere, persevere
pursbektif, perspective
pursbiration, perspiration
pursbire, perspire
purscription, prescript(ion)

purse,*,ed,sing, *HAND BAG, PRIZE MONEY, SQUEEZE TIGHTLY TOGETHER*
pursebduble, perceptible
pursebtef, percept(ive)
pursecute, persecute
pursen, person
pursenality, personality
pursenaly, personal(lly)
pursenel, personnel
pursent, percent
pursentige, percent(age)
pursentil, percent(ile)
pursenuble, person(able)
pursenul, personal
pursenulize, personal(ize)
pursepdable, perceptible
pursepshen, percept(ion)
purseptef, percept(ive)
purseption, percept(ion)
purseptive, percept(ive)
purseshen, precision
pursest, persist
purseve, perceive
purseverense, persevere(rance)
purshis, purchase / perch(es)
pursikute, persecute
pursin, person
pursinaledy, personality
pursinel, personnel
pursint, percent
pursinuble, person(able)
pursinulize, personal(ize)
pursinuly, personal(lly)
pursipatation, precipitate(tion)
pursishen, precision
pursist, persist
pursistence, persist(ence)
purskripshen, prescript(ion)
purson, person

pursona, persona
pursonality, personality
pursonefication, person(ification)
pursonifekashen, person(ification)
pursonify, personify
pursoo, pursue
pursparashen, perspiration
purspective, perspective
pursperashen, perspiration
purspiration, perspiration
purspire, perspire
pursuade, persuade
pursuasion, persuade(asion)
pursuasive, persuade(asive)
pursude, pursue(d)
pursue,*,ed,uing,er,uant,uit, *SEEKING/STRIVING TO OVERCOME/OVERTAKE*
pursute, pursue(uit)
pursuvere, persevere
purswade, persuade
purswashen, persuade(asion)
purswasif, persuade(asive)
purt, pert
purtain, pertain
purtane, pertain
purterb, perturb
purterbt, perturb(ed)
purteshen, partition
purtishen, partition
purtrayal, portray(al)
purtrayed, portray(ed)
puruficashun, purify(fication)
purufied, purify(fied)
puruse, peruse
purvade, pervade
purvashen, pervade(asion)/provision
purvasif, pervade(asion)
purvert, pervert
purvurshen, pervert(rsion)

pury , puree'
purzakute , persecute
pus, FLUID/INFLAMMATION PRESENT AS THE RESULT OF AN INFECTION (or see puss)
pusdasheo , pistachio
pusdromy , pastrami
pusefic , pacific
pusel , puzzle
puseld , puzzle(d)
puses , possess
push,hes,her,hing,hy,hily,hiness, TO FORCE MOVEMENT, TO MOVE BY FORCE, EXERT FORCE
pushenis , push(iness)
pushir , push(er)
pusie , pussy
pusific , pacific
pusil , puzzle
pusiled , puzzle(d)
pusishen , position
puskrepshen , prescript(ion)
puss,ssy,ssies, A CAT, THE FACE WHERE THE MOUTH IS, SLANDER FOR A WHIMP (or see pus)
pustasheo , pistachio
pustrome , pastrami
pusul , puzzle
pusy , pussy
put,*,tting, TO PLACE (or see putt)
putado , potato
putal , puddle /poodle
putato , potato
putee , putty
putees , putty(tties)
putel , puddle /poodle
putena , patina
putenchul , potential
puteng , pudding /putt(ing) /put(tting)
putenshul , potential
putential , potential
puter , pewter /putt(er)

puterbd , perturb(ed)
puternol , paternal
putestrein , pedestrian
puthetic , pathetic
putil , puddle /poodle
putina , patina
putinchul , potential
puting , pudding /putt(ing) /put(tting)
putintial , potential
putir , pewter /putt(er)
putishen , petition /beautician
putition , petition
putle , puddle /poodle
putol , puddle /poodle
putoto , potato
putrid,dity,dness,dly, ROTTEN/CORRUPT/VILE
putrol , patrol
putrood , protrude
putrude , protrude
putt,*,tting,tter, A GOLF STROKE (or see put)
puttle , puddle /poodle
putty,tties,ttied,ttying, A TACKY /PASTY SUBSTANCE
putul , puddle /poodle
puty , putty
puveleon , pavilion
puvileon , pavilion
puvirted , pervert(ed)
puwding , pudding /putt(ing) /put(tting)
puzel , puzzle
puzeld , puzzle(d)
puzes , possess
puzil , puzzle
puzled , puzzle(d)
puzzle,*,ed,ling,er,ement, PROBLEM WITH ONLY ONE SOLUTION, MANY PARTS MAKE UP THE BIG PICTURE
pygme , pygmy
pygmy,mies, VERY SMALL/DWARFED IN COMPARISON TO OTHERS IN ITS SPECIES
pyis , pious

pyke , pike
pyle , pile
pype , pipe
pyramid,*, FOUR-SIDED/TRIANGULAR STRUCTURE
pyrana , piranha
pyranna , piranha
pyre,*, A MOUND OF COMBUSTIBLE MATERIAL WHERE AN EXPIRED BODY IS PLACED FOR CEREMONIAL CREMATION (or see pier /peer /pierce)
pyrite,*,tic, YELLOW COLORED METAL
pyro, PREFIX INDICATING "FIRE/HEAT" MOST OFTEN MODIFIES THE WORD
pyro,*, SLANG FOR SOMEONE WHO PLAYS WITH FIRE
pyrona , piranha
python,*, A VENOMOUS SNAKE

"Q"

qkumber , cucumber
qkwant , quaint
qords , quartz /quart(s)
qork , quark /cork
qorts , quartz /quart(s)
quack,*, SOUND A DUCK MAKES, SLANG FOR A 'NO GOOD DOCTOR'
quad,*, SHORT FOR QUADRANT, FOUR, QUADRANGLE, QUADRUPLET
quadrant,*,tal, ONE QUARTER OF A CIRCLE
quadrint , quadrant
quael , quail
quaent , quaint
quagmire,*,ed, BOG, SOFT EARTH HEAVY WITH MOISTURE
quail,*, A GAME BIRD
quaint,tly,tness, PLEASING/COMFORTABLE/ PICTURESQUE
quak , quack

quake,*,ed,king, *A TREMBLING/SHAKING*
quakmire, quagmire
qual, quail
qualedy, quality
qualefy, qualify
qualefyable, qualify(fiable)
qualetatif, quality(tative)
qualetative, quality(tative)
qualety, quality
qualidy, quality
qualify, fies,fied,fiedly,fiedness,fier,fiable,fying, fication, *IS ELIGIBLE/CAPABLE/SKILLFUL ENOUGH*
qualifyable, qualify(fiable)
qualifyer, qualify(fier)
qualitatif, quality(tative)
quality,ties,tative,tatively, *A MEASURE/ GUAGE OF THE RESULTS OF THE OUTCOME OF AN EFFORT, A SCALE WHICH RATES THE BEST/WORST*
qualm,*,mish,mishly,mishness, *FEELING OF DOUBT/TWINGE/UNEASINESS*
qualufecashen, qualify(fication)
qualufi, qualify
quandary,ries, *DIFFICULTY/HESITANCY/PERPLEXING*
quandery, quandary
quandre, quandary
quanta,tum, *SMALLEST AMOUNT OF ENERGY CAPABLE OF EXISTING ON ITS OWN, QUALITY/EXTENT*
quant, quaint
quantefy, quantify
quantefyer, quantify(fier)
quantem, quanta(tum)
quantery, quandary
quantety, quantity
quantify,fies,fied,fying,fiable,fication,fier, *TO MEASURE/DETERMINE THE AMOUNT*
quantim, quanta(tum)
quantity,ties, *MEASURE OF THE AMOUNT/FREQUENCY OF OCCURENCE*
quantom, quanta(tum)

quantry, quandary
quarantine,*,ed,ning,nable, *SECTION OFF/ISOLATE FROM EVERYTHING ELSE*
quarder, quarter
quarderly, quarter(ly)
quardur, quarter
quardurly, quarter(ly)
quarel, quarrel
quarentene, quarantine
quari, query
quaril, quarrel
quarinteen, quarantine
quark,*, *BASIC/ELEMENTARY PARTICLE* (or see cork)
quarol, quarrel
quarontene, quarantine
quarrel,*,led,ling,lsome,lsomely,lsomeness, *TO BICKER/ARGUE/BE AT ODDS WITH/ENHARMONIC, OF A SQUARE SHAPED HEAD, A TOOL*
quarry,rries,rried,ying,rrier, *TO DIG A PIT INTO THE EARTH FOR STONE/DIRT, PURSUED GAME*
quart,*, *U.S. MEASUREMENT OF LIQUID* (or see quartz)
quarter,*,red,ring,rage,rly,lies, *ONE-FOURTH OF THE WHOLE, U.S. COIN* (TOO MANY DEFINITIONS, PLEASE SEE STANDARD DICTIONARY)
quartirly, quarter(ly)
quartur, quarter
quarturly, quarter(ly)
quartz,zose,zous, *MINERAL/ROCK* (or see quart(s))
quarunteen, quarantine
quare, quarry /query
quasar,*, *ASTRONOMICAL OBJECT WITH HIGH ENERGY OUTPUT*
quasi, *SORT OF, SIMILAR, NOT CERTAIN*
quawry, quarry
quazar, quasar
qucumber, cucumber
quean, queen
queck, quick

queckest, quick(est)
queen,*,ndom,nlike,nliness,nly, *A FEMALE WHO IS GIVEN TO/OF ROYALTY*
queer,*,rly,rness, *STRANGE/ODD, HOMOSEXUAL*
quefer, quiver
quefur, quiver
quek, quick
quekest, quick(est)
quekly, quick(ly)
queke, quick(ie)
quel, quill
quelt, quilt
quemulutive, cumulative
quench,hes,hed,hing,hable,her,hless, *TO SATISFY /PUT AWAY /EXTINGUISH*
quentuplet, quintuplet
querable, curable
queri, query
querk, quirk
querky, quirk(y)
query,ries,ried,rying, *ASK OF/QUESTION/INQUIRE*
quesdun, question
quest,ter,tingly, *ON A JOURNEY/ADVENTURE SEEKING SOMETHING*
questen, question
question,*,ned,ning,nable,nableness,nably, nability,nary,naries,nless,nnaire, *TO ASK/ INQUIRE, HAVE DOUBT, NEED INFORMATION ON MATTER/SUBJECT*
questshunar, question(nnaire)
questun, question
quet, quit /quite
queter, quit(tter) /quiet(er)
quevor, quiver
quevur, quiver
quez, quiz
quezene, cuisine
quezt, quest

quick,kly,ker,kest,kness,ken,kie,kener, *FAST/*
  WITHOUT DELAY/BRIEF, SKIN UNDER NAILS
quiet,ter,test,tly,tness,tism,tude, *SILENCE/CALM/*
  STILLNESS/TRANQUIL (or see quit or quite)
qufur, quiver
quik, quick
quikest, quick(est)
quikly, quick(ly)
quiky, quick(ie)
quil, quill
quill,*, *WING/TAIL FEATHER OF LARGE BIRD (TOO MANY*
  DEFINITIONS, PLEASE SEE STANDARD DICTIONARY)
quilt,*,ted,ting,ter, *HANDMADE/STITCHED BLANKET,*
  THICKLY BLANKETED
quinch, quench
quinsh, quench
quintuplet,*, *FIVE OF ANYTHING*
quirk,*,ky,kily,kiness, *GIVEN TO IRRATIC MOVEMENT*
  JERKING/SUDDEN CHANGES
quiry, query
quisine, cuisine
quit,*,tted,tting,tter, *STOP (or see quite)*
quite,*COMPLETELY CERTAIN/CLEAR(or see quit/quiet)*
quiut, quiet
quiutly, quiet(ly)
quiver,*,red,ring, *CASE TO CARRY ARROWS, TREMBLE/*
  SHAKE/TREMOR
quivor, quiver
quiz,zzes,zzed,zzing,zzical,zzically,zzer,
  zzicality, *TO TEST/WONDER, BE CONFUSED*
qumulotive, cumulative
quochent, quotient
quochiunt, quotient
quoda, quota
quode, quote
quodrant, quadrant
quodrunt, quadrant
quodu, quota
quoledy, quality

quolm, qualm
quondery, quandary
quondry, quandary
quontefy, quantify
quontefyer, quantify(fier)
quontem, quanta(tum)
quonitery, quandary
quontety, quantity
quontify, quantify
quontim, quanta(tum)
quontity, quantity
quontre, quandary
quontum, quanta(tum)
quord, quart
quorderly, quarter(ly)
quordir, quarter
quordorly, quarter(ly)
quords, quartz /quart(s)
quordurly, quarter(ly)
quordz, quartz /quart(s)
quorel, quarrel
quorem, quorum
quorentene, quarantine
quoril, quarrel
quorim, quorum
quorintene, quarantine
quork, quark
quorol, quarrel
quorom, quorum
quort, quart
quorter, quarter
quorterly, quarter(ly)
quortir, quarter
quortirly, quarter(ly)
quorts, quartz /quart(s)
quorturly, quarter(ly)
quortz, quartz /quart(s)
quorum, *THE MAJORITY OF A SELECTED GROUP*
quoruntene, quarantine

quory, quarry
quoshent, quotient
quoshunt, quotient
quota,*, *A PERMITTED NUMBER/QUANTITY*
quotashen, quote(tation)
quote,*,ted,ting,tation,table,tability, *TO IDENTIFY/*
  CITE/REPEAT EXACTLY WHAT SOMEONE SAID,
  STATE FACTS, TO USE MARKS AROUND QUOTES
quotient,*, *A MATHEMATICAL RESULT*
quowry, quarry
qurader, curator
qureus, curious
qutikle, cuticle
qwack, quack
qwad, quad
qwadrent, quadrant
qwagmire, quagmire
qwaint, quaint
qwak, quack /quake
qwakmire, quagmire
qwale, quail
qwaledy, quality
qwalefieur, qualify(fier)
qwalefiuble, qualify(fiable)
qwaletatif, quality(tative)
qwalety, quality
qwalidy, quality
qwalifecation, qualify(fication)
qwalifikashen, qualify(fication)
qwalitative, quality(tative)
qwalitee, quality
qwalm, qualm
qwant, quaint
qwantefy, quantify
qwantefyer, quantify(fier)
qwantem, quanta(tum)
qwantety, quantity
qwantify, quantify
qwantifyer, quantify(fier)

qwantim, quanta(tum)
qwantity, quantity
qwantum, quanta(tum)
qwarder, quarter
qwards, quartz /quart(s)
qwardur, quarter
qwarel, quarrel
qwarentene, quarantine
qwaril, quarrel
qwarintene, quarantine
qwark, quark
qwarol, quarrel
qwarter, quarter
qwarts, quartz /quart(s)
qwartur, quarter
qwarul, quarrel
qwary, query
qwasar, quasar
qwasy, quasi
qwazar, quasar
qwazy, quasi
qwear, queer
qween, queen
qweer, queer
qwek, quick
qwekest, quick(est)
qwekly, quick(ly)
qweky, quick(ie)
qwel, quill
qwelt, quilt
qwench, quench
qwensh, quench
qwentuplet, quintuplet
qwerk, quirk
qwerky, quirk(y)
qwery, query
qwes, quiz
qwesden, question
qwesekal, quiz(zzical)

qweshten, question
qwest, quest
qwestchenair, question(nnaire)
qwestshun, question
qwestunair, question(nnaire)
qwet, quit / quite
qweter, quit(tter) /quiet(er)
qwevir, quiver
qwevur, quiver
qwez, quiz
qwezekal, quiz(zzical)
qwik, quick
qwikest, quick(est)
qwikly, quick(ly)
qwiky, quick(ie)
qwil, quill
qwilt, quilt
qwinch, quench
qwinsh, quench
qwintuplet, quintuplet
qwirk, quirk
qwirky, quirk(y)
qwiry, query
qwis, quiz
qwit, quit /quite
qwiter, quit(tter) /quiet(er)
qwiver, quiver
qwivur, quiver
qwiz, quiz
qwizekal, quiz(zzical)
qwochent, quotient
qwod, quad
qwoda, quota
qwodashen, quote(tation)
qwodation, quote(tation)
qwode, quote
qwodrent, quadrant
qwodrunt, quadrant
qwodu, quota

qwoduble, quote(table)
qwoledy, quality
qwolefikashen, qualify(fication)
qwolefiuble, qualify(fiable)
qwolefiur, qualify(fier)
qwoletatif, quality(tative)
qwolety, quality
qwolifekation, qualify(fication)
qwolm, qualm
qwomtum, quanta(tum)
qwondry, quandary
qwontefy, quantify
qwontefyer, quantify(fier)
qwontem, quanta(tum)
qwontery, quandary
qwontety, quantity
qwontify, quantify
qwontifyer, quantify(fier)
qwontim, quanta(tum)
qwontity, quantity
qworam, quorum
qworder, quarter
qwords, quartz /quart(s)
qwordur, quarter
qworel, quarrel
qworem, quorum
qworentene, quarantine
qworil, quarrel
qworim, quorum
qworintene, quarantine
qwork, quark
qworol, quarrel
qworom, quorum
qworter, quarter
qworts, quartz /quart(s)
qwortur, quarter
qworul, quarrel
qworum, quorum
qwoshent, quotient

qwosy, quasi
qwota, quota
qwotashen, quote(tation)
qwotation, quote(tation)
qwote, quote
qwotuble, quote(table)
qwozy, quasi
qwurentene, quarantine
qwurintene, quarantine
qwurk, quirk
qwurky, quirk(y)

ra, ray /raw
rabbi,*, *JEWISH RELIGIOUS TITLE*
rabbit,*, *LONG-EARED RODENT*
rabcity, rhapsody
rabed, rabbit /rabid /rapid
rabees, rabid(ies)
rabel, rebel
rabeleon, rebel(llion)
rabeleus, rebel(llious)
rabelius, rebel(llious)
rabet, rabbit/rabid/rapid
rabi, rabbi
rabid,dity,dly,dness,ies, *MADNESS/FURIOUSNESS/ UNREASONABLE, DISEASE* (or see rapid)
rabit, rabbit/rabid/rapid
rablie, reply
rabodek, robot(ic)
rabot, rabbit /rabid /rapid
rabotik, robot(ic)
rabsady, rhapsody
rabsudy, rhapsody
rabt, rape(d) /wrap(pped) /rap(pped)
rabud, rabbit /rabid /rapid

rabut, rabbit /rabid /rapid
racat, racket /racquet
racateer, racketeer
raccoon,*, *PLANTIGRADE CARNIVOROUS MAMMAL*
raccune, raccoon
race,*, ed,cing,er,ey, *COMPETITION WITH MORE THAN ONE, GAME WITH A PHYSICAL BEGINNING/END, CATEGORY FOR HUMAN TYPES* (or see raise)
racede, recede
raceptecle, receptacle
racepter, receptor
racepticle, receptacle
raception, reception
raceptucle, receptacle
racet, racket /racquet
raceteer, racketeer
rach, rash
rachal, racial
rachen, ration
racheo, ratio
rachet, ratchet
rachil, racial
rachin, ration
rachio, ratio
rachit, ratchet
rachon, ration
rachul, racial
rachun, ration
rachunil, rational
rachut, ratchet
racial,lly,lism,list,listic, *CHARACTERISTICS/ DIFFERENCES IN RACES/PEOPLE*
racipeint, recipient
raciprocation, reciprocate(tion)
racism,*, *HUMAN FEAR/IGNORANCE TOWARDS PEOPLE OF A DIFFERENT COLOR/RACE*
racist,*, *HUMAN FEAR/IGNORANCE TOWARDS PEOPLE OF A DIFFERENT COLOR/RACE*
racit, racket /racquet /recite

raciteer, racketeer
rack,*,ked,king,ker, *APPARATUS USED FOR HANGING/ STRETCHING THINGS* (or see rake or wrack)
racket,try, *NOISY SOUND, USED IN SPORTS TO HIT A BALL* (or see racquet)
racketeer,*, ring, *SLANG FOR SOMEONE ENGAGED IN SOMETHING ILLEGAL*
rackit, racket /racquet
rackiteer, racketeer
rackoteer, racketeer
rackut, racket /racquet
rackuteer, racketeer
raconasinse, reconnaissance
raconstitushen, reconstitute(tion)
raconstitute, reconstitute
racoon, raccoon
racrute, recruit
racruter, recruit(er)
racumbent, recumbent
racut, racket /racquet
racuteer, racketeer
rad, raid /rate
radar,*, *A RADIO WAVE FREQUENCY*
raddle, rattle
rade, raid
radeal, radial
radeant, radiance(nt)
radeashen, radiate(tion)
radeate, radiate
radeater, radiate(tor)
radeation, radiate(tion)
radecal, radical
radech, radish
radeemible, redeem(able)
radefy, ratify
radeil, radial
radeim, radium
radeinse, radiance
radeint, radiance(nt)

radeints, radiance
radekly, radical(lly)
radekul, radical
radel, rattle
rademe, redeem
rademption, redemption
rademshin, radical
rademtif, redemption(ive)
rademtion, redemption
rademtive, redemption(ive)
rademuble, redeem(able)
radeo, radio
radeol, radial
radeom, radium
radeos, radius /radio(es)
radesh, radish
radeul, radial
radeum, radium
radeunse, radiance
radeunt, radiance(nt)
radeus, radius
radial,*,lly, *CENTER WITH SPOKES/RAYS GOING OUT FROM THE CENTER, A TYPE OF TIRE*
radiance,cy,cies,nt,ntly, *BRIGHT/SHINING LIKE A STAR, GLOWING BRIGHT*
radiashen, radiate(tion)
radiate, radiate
radiate,*,ed,ting,tion,tional,tive,tor, *TO EMIT/ GIVE FORTH/EXUDE*
radiater, radiate(tor)
radical,*,lly,lness,lism, *A FAR-SWEEPING CHANGE/ ACT/ATTITUDE FROM THE EXISTING IDEALISM*
radicaly, radical(lly)
radich, radish
radicle, radical
radicly, radical(lly)
radiel, radial
radiem, radium
radify, ratify

radikle, radical
radikly, radical(lly)
radikul, radical
radil, rattle
radio, *PREFIX INDICATING "RADIO/ RADIATION" MOST OFTEN MODIFIES THE WORD, FROM ANCIENT WORD "RADIUS" (RAY)*
radio,oes,oed,oing, *WIRELESS AUDIO TRANSMITTING/ RECEIVING DEVICE*
radiol, radial
radish,hes, *A VEGETABLE*
radiul, radial
radium, *A METALLIC ELEMENT WHICH IS RADIOACTIVE*
radiunse, radiance
radius,ii,ses, *AREA WITHIN A CIRCLE, RAY EXTENDING FROM CENTER OF CIRCLE, BONE DESCRIPTIONS*
radol, rattle
radon, *A CHEMICAL ELEMENT*
rador, radar
raduction, reduce(ction)
radufy, ratify
radukle, radical
radukly, radical(lly)
radukshen, reduce(ction)
radul, rattle
radundense, redundant(ncy)
radundent, redundant
radundunse, redundant(ncy)
radusable, reduce(cible)
raduse, reduce
radush, radish
raelm, realm
raelrod, railroad
raen, rain /reign /rein
raenbo, rainbow
raenj, range
raer, rare
raesesem, racism
raf, rave

rafal, raffle /ravel
rafalee, reveille
rafan, raven
rafash, ravish
rafd, raft /waft
rafded, raft(ed)
rafdur, raft(er)
rafe, rave
rafel, raffle /ravel /reveal
rafelashen, revelation
rafen, raven /ravine
rafenge, revenge
rafenje, revenge
rafenus, raven(ous)
rafeole, ravioli
rafer, revere /refer
rafers, reverse /refer(s)
rafesh, ravish
rafeusil, refuse(sal)
rafewsel, refuse(sal)
raffle,*,ed,ling, *A GAME*
rafiew, review /revue
rafiful, revival
rafil, raffle /ravel
rafilee, reveille
rafin, raven /refine
rafinable, refine(nable)
rafinery, refine(ry)
rafinje, revenge
rafinment, refine(ment)
rafinuble, refine(nable)
rafinury, refine(ry)
rafinus, raven(ous)
rafioly, ravioli
rafirse, reverse
rafish, ravish
raflashen, revelation
rafle, raffle /ravel
raflect, reflect

raflection, reflect(ion)
raflective, reflect(ive)
raflekshen, reflect(ion)
raflektor, reflect(or)
rafol, raffle
rafolee, reveille
raformutory, reform(atory)
rafractory, refract(ory)
rafrain, refrain
rafraktory, refract(ory)
rafrane, refrain
rafregirant, refrigerate(ant)
rafregirator, refrigerate(tor)
rafresh, refresh
rafreshment, refresh(ment)
rafrigerant, refrigerate(ant)
rafrigerator, refrigerate(tor)
raft,*,ted,ting,ter, *A SMALL BOAT MADE WITH A MATERIAL FILLED WITH AIR (or see rave(d))*
raftur, raft(er) /waft(er)
rafue, review /revue
raful, raffle /ravel
rafulashen, revelation
rafulation, revelation
rafulee, reveille
rafun, raven
rafunus, raven(ous)
rafurbish, refurbish
rafurse, reverse
rafusel, refuse(sal)
rag,*,gged,ggedness,ggedly,ggedly, *TATTERED/ TORN/WORN-OUT MATERIAL OR CLOTH (or see rack or rage)*
ragalia, regal(ia)
ragardless, regard(less)
ragd, rage(d) /rag(gged)
rage,*,ed,ging,gingly, *INTENSE/VIOLENT ANGER, OF INTENSE/GREAT FORCE*
raged, rag(gged) / racket

ragedy, rag(ggedy)
rajekt, reject
ragektion, reject(ion)
rager, roger
raget, rag(gged) /racket
ragid, rag(gged) /racket
ragidy, rag(ggedy)
ragir, roger
ragit, rag(gged) /racket
ragity, rag(ggedy)
ragret, regret
ragreted, regret(tted)
ragretful, regret(ful)
ragretfully, regret(fully)
ragt, rage(d) /rake(d) /rack(ed) /wrack(ed)
ragud, rag(gged) /racket
ragudy, rag(ggedy)
ragut, rag(gged) /racket
raid,*,ded,ding,der, *A SUDDEN ENTRY/ATTACK/SALE (or see rate)*
rail,*,led,ling,ler, *METAL/WOOD BARS/POSTS, TO PUNISH/SCOLD, A BIRD (or see rale)*
railroad,*,ded,ding,der, *ROAD MADE OF RAILS, BRING A FALSE CHARGE AGAINST SOMEONE, OF LOCOMOTIVES*
rain,*,ned,ning,ny, *WATER RELEASED FROM CLOUDS (or see reign or rein)*
rainbow,*, *AN ARC/BOW OF COLORS NORMALLY CAUSED BY RAIN*
rainder, reindeer
raing, range
rair, rare
rairly, rare(ly)
raise,es,ed,sing,er, *TO LIFT/BRING/TAKE UP (or see ray(s) or razor)*
raisin,*, *A DRIED PLUM*
rait, rate
raive, rave
raj, rage

rajd, rage(d)
rajekshen, reject(ion)
rajektion, reject(ion)
rajer, roger
rajur, roger
rak, rack /rake /wrack /rag
rakat, racket / racquet
rakateer, racketeer
rake,*,ed,king, *TOOL/IMPLEMENT TO MOVE ORGANIC MATERIAL AROUND (or see rack or wrack)*
raket, racket /racquet
raketeer, racketeer
rakit, racket /racquet
rakiteer, racketeer
rakonesinse, reconnaissance
rakonstitute, reconstitute
rakonusents, reconnaissance
rakoon, raccoon
rakord, record
rakorder, record(er)
rakot, racket /racquet
rakoteer, racketeer
rakrute, recruit
rakruter, recruit(er)
rakt, rake(d) /rack(ed) /wrack(ed)
rakumbent, recumbent
rakune, raccoon
rakut, racket /racquet
rakuteer, racketeer
rakwest, request
rakwire, require
rakwirment, require(ment)
rakwrute, recruit
ralaks, relax
ralax, relax
rale, *A BREATHING SOUND (or see rail or rally)*
raleenkwish, relinquish
ralef, relief
ralejis, religion(ous)

ralek, rollick
ralenkwish, relinquish
ralenqwish, relinquish
ralentless, relentless
ralerode, railroad
ralese, release
raleve, relieve
ralevir, relieve(r)
rali, rely /rally
raliable, rely(liable)
raliant, reliance(nt)
ralick, rollick
ralie, rally
raliense, reliance
raligeon, religion
raligis, religion(ous)
raligius, religion(ous)
ralik, rollick
ralinkwish, relinquish
ralinquish, relinquish
ralintless, relentless
ralish, relish
raliubility, rely(liability)
raliuble, rely(liable)
raliunts, reliance
rally, llies,llied,ying,llier, BRING/CALL SUMMON FORTH
SPIRIT/ACTION/ENTHUSIASM
ralm, realm
ralrod, railroad
ralrot, railroad
ralrus, walrus
raluctant, reluctant
raluctinse, reluctant(nce)
raluktint, reluctant
ralwrod, railroad
raly, rally /rely
ram,*,mmed,mming,mmer, MALE SHEEP, DEVICE
USED TO STRIKE/FORCE/CRUSH/POUND
ramadik, rheumatic

ramafication, ramification
ramafikashen, ramification
ramain, remain /romaine
ramander, remain(der)
ramane, remain /romaine
ramantek, romantic
ramantic, romantic
ramantisize, romantic(ize)
ramarkible, remark(able)
ramatik, rheumatic
rambal, ramble
rambant, rampant
rambint, rampant
ramble,*,ed,ling,er, WANDER/MEANDER, STYLE OF
HOME
rambul, ramble
rambunctious,sly,sness, NOISY/BOISTEROUS/LOUD
rambunktious, rambuctious
rambunt, rampant
ramd, ram(mmed)
ramedeul, remedy(dial)
ramediashen, remedy(diation)
ramediation, remedy(diation)
ramefekashen, ramification
ramefekation, ramification
ramember, remember
ramembranxe, remember(ance)
rameshen, remission
ramet, remit
rameteul, remedy(dial)
ramidal, remit(ttal)
ramifekashen, ramification
ramification,*, THE RESULT/RESPONSE OF AN ACTION
ramifikation, ramification
ramindur, remind(er)
ramint, remind
ramintur, remind(er)
ramishen, remission
ramision, remission

ramit, remit
ramital, remit(ttal)
ramition, remission
ramituble, remit(ttable)
ramofer, remove(r)
ramorse, remorse
ramorsless, remorse(less)
ramote, remote
ramotly, remote(ly)
ramover, remove(r)
ramp,*,ped,ping,part, DEVICE TO CREATE INCLINE/
SLOPE FOR MOVING/RAISING FROM ONE LEVEL
TO ANOTHER
rampage,*,ed,ging,eous,eously,eousness,
BOISTEROUS/VIOLENT/PASSIONATE BEHAVIOR
rampaje, rampage
rampant,tly,ncy, RUN AMUCK/WILD/UNPREDICTABLY
rampel, ramble
rampent, rampant
rampint, rampant
rample, ramble
rampt, ramp(ed)
rampunkshes, rambuctious
rampunt, rampant
ramsum, ransom
ramt, ram(mmed)
ramuf, remove
ramufecation, ramification
ramufekashen, ramification
ramufel, remove(val)
ramufible, remove(vable)
ramufikation, ramification
ramufikashen, ramification
ramufil, remove(val)
ramufucation, ramification
ramuneration, remunerate(tion)
ramuvable, remove(vable)
ramuval, remove(val)
ran, PAST TENSE OF "RUN" (or see rain/rein/reign)

ranbo, rainbow
ranced, rancid
ranch,hes,her, *WHERE HORSES/CATTLE ARE RAISED/*
   BOARDED, A TYPE OF DRESSING
ranchur, ranch(er)
rancid,kity,kness,kly, *SMELL/TASTE OF FOOD THAT*
   IS SPOILED/ROTTEN
rancud, rancid
ranbow, rainbow
rand, rant / rain(ed)
randam, random
rander, reindeer
randim, random
random,mly,mness, *WITHOUT AN APPARENT/*
   RECOGNIZABLE ORDER
rane, rain /reign /rein
ranege, renege
range,*,ed,ging,er, *DEFINED/SPECIFIC AREA WHICH*
   HOLDS DATA/INFORMATION/ANIMALS (or see
   ranch)
rangel, wrangle
ranglur, wrangle(r)
rangt, range(d)
rangul, wrangle
rangur, range(r)
ranige, renege
ranik, renege
ranj, range /ranch
rank,*,ked,king,kly,kness, *A CHRONOLOGICAL/*
   LINEAR ORDER, A BAD/OFFENSIVE SMELL/ODOR
ranone, renown
ranoserus, rhinoceros
ranosirus, rhinoceros
ranouncement, renounce(ment)
ranounse, renounce
ranown, renown
ranownsment, renounce(ment)
ransack,*,ked,king,ker, *TO PLUNDER/ SEARCH*
   THROUGH PEOPLE'S BELONGINGS

ransak, ransack
ransam, ransom
ransed, rancid
ransem, ransom
ransh, ranch
ransher, ranch(er)
ransid, rancid
ransim, ransom
ransit, rancid
ransom,*,mer, *FORCE SOMEONE TO PAY FOR THE*
   RETURN OF GOODS/PEOPLE
ransud, rancid
ransum, ransom
ransut, rancid
rant,*,ted,ting,tingly,ter, *TALK/UTTER LOUD*
   AGITATED OR AGGRESSIVE WORDS
rantsum, ransom
rantum, random
ranumerate, remunerate
ranzak, ransack
ranzum, ransom
raon, rayon
rap,*,pped,pping,pper, *TYPE OF MUSIC AND THAT*
   ASSOCIATED WITH IT, TYPE OF SOUND, BLAME/
   PUNISHMENT / FOR AN ILLEGAL ACT NOT
   RESPONSIBLE FOR (or see wrap or rape)
rapad, rapid
rapar, repair
rapcher, rapture
rapcherus, rapture(rous)
rapchur, rapture
rapcity, rhapsody
rape,*,ed,ping,pist, *VIOLENTLY/FORCEFULLY/*
   PHYSICALLY PENETRATE A PERSON AGAINST THEIR
   WILL (or see rap or wrap)
rapeal, repeal
rapeat, repeat
raped, rape(d)/ rapid/ rabid
rapededly, repeat(edly)

rapeel, repeal
rapel, rappel /repeal /repel
rapelein, rebel(llion)
rapelent, repellent
rapeleon, rebel(llion)
rapelinsy, repellent(ncy)
rapelint, repellent
rapenins, repent(ance)
rapent, repent
rapentinse, repent(ance)
raper, rap(pper) /rape(r) /wrap(pper)
rapest, rape(pist)
rapete, repeat
rapetedly, repeat(edly)
rapedly, rapid(ly)
rapid,*,dly,dness,dity, *QUICK* (or see rabid)
rapinens, repent(ance)
rapint, repent
rapintense, repent(ance)
rapir, rap(pper) /rape(r) /wrap(pper)
raplacment, replace(ment)
raplase, replace
raplasmint, replace(ment)
raplenish, replenish
raplenishment, replenish(ment)
raplid, reply(lied)
raplinesh, replenish
rapor, rapport
raporder, report(er)
raport, rapport /report
raporter, report(er)
rapository, repository
rapour, rapport
rapozitory, repository
rappel,*,led,ling, *TO DESCEND FROM A HEIGHT WITH*
   A ROPE (or see repel)
rapport, *HARMONY/AFFILIATION WITH*
rapreshen, repress(ion)
rapresion, repress(ion)

rapress, repress
rapresuve, repress(ive)
raproch, reproach
raprochuble, reproach(able)
rapsety, rhapsody
rapshur, rapture
rapsuty, rhapsody
rapt, rape(d) /wrap(pped) /rap(pped)
raptcher, rapture
raptur, raptor
rapture,*,ed,ring,rous,rously,sness, *EXTREME DELIGHT/JOY/PLEASURE*
rapublek, republic
rapublekan, republic(an)
rapublikan, republic(an)
rapud, rapid
rapedutif, repetitive
rapugnense, repugnant(nce)
rapugnent, repugnant
rapulshen, repulse(ion)
rapulsif, repulse(sive)
rapulsion, repulse(ion)
rapuplekan, republic(an)
rapur, rap(pper) /rap(er) /rap(per) /wrap(pper)
rapust, rape(pist)
rapute, repute
raqet, racket /racquet
raqeteer, racketeer
raqrute, recruit
raquire, require
raquirment, require(ment)
raqut, racket /racquet
raquteer, racketeer
raqwest, request
raqwire, require
raqwirment, require(ment)
rar, rare
rare,ely,est,eness,rity, *MOST UNCOMMON/ UNNUSUAL/SCARCE, MEAT BARELY COOKED*

rarety, rare(rity)
rarist, rare(rist)
rarity, rare(rity)
rarly, rare(ly)
rarudy, rare(rity)
raruty, rare(rity)
ras, race /raise /ray(s)
rasberry, raspberry
rasbery, raspberry
rascal,*,lly,lities, *MISCHIEVOUS /PLAYFUL/ ROQUISH BEHAVIOR*
rascul, rascal
rasd, race(d) /raise(d)
raseat, receipt
rasebshenist, receptionist
rasebshin, reception
rasebter, receptor
rasebtif, receptive
rasebtive, receptive
raseed, recede
rasefe, receive
rasefible, receive(vable)
rasemblinse, resemble(lance)
rasembul, resemble
rasen, raisin/ race(cing) /raise(sing)
rasentful, resent(ful)
rasentment, resent(ment)
rasepdekle, receptacle
rasepdukul, receptacle
rasepe, recipe
rasepeunt, recipient
raseprikul, reciprocal
raseprocation, reciprocate(tion)
raseprokashen, reciprocate(tion)
raseprokate, reciprocate
rasepshenist, receptionist
rasepshun, reception
raseptacle, receptacle
raseptef, receptive

raseptikle, receptacle
raseptionest, receptionist
raseptive, receptive
raseptor, receptor
raseptukle, receptacle
raser, razor /raise(r) /race(r)
raserekshen, resurrect(ion)
rasesem, racism
raseshun, recess(ion)
rasesif, recess(ive)
rasesion, recess(ion)
rasesive, recess(ive)
rasession, recess(ion)
rasest, racist
rasestef, resist(ive)
rasestif, resist(ive)
rasestinse, resist(ance)
rasestint, resist(ant)
rasestive, resist(ive)
rasesum, racism
rasete, receipt
rasetion, recess(ion)
raseve, receive
rasevuble, receive(vable)
rash,hes, *A SKIN FORMATION*
rashal, racial
rashel, racial
rashen, ration
rashenaledy, rational(ity)
rashenality, rational(ity)
rashenalization, rational(ization)
rashent, ration(ed)
rashenul, rational
rasheo, ratio
rasheonalization, rational(ization)
rasheunolezashen, rational(ization)
rashil, racial
rashin, ration
rashinal, rational

rashinaledy, rational(ity)
rashinality, rational(ity)
rashint, ration(ed)
rashinul, rational
rashinulization, rational(ization)
rashio, ratio
rashon, ration
rashonality, rational(ity)
rashonalization, rational(ization)
rashonel, rational
rashs, rash(es)
rashul, racial
rashun, ration
rashunal, ration(al)
rashunaledy, rational(ity)
rashunality, rational(ity)
rashunalization, rational(ization)
rashund, ration(ed)
rashunil, rational
raside, reside
rasiduel, residue(ual)
rasign, resign
rasiliency, resilient(ncy)
rasilient, resilient
rasimblanse, resemble(lance)
rasimble, resemble
rasin, raisin /race(cing) /raise(sing)
rasinful, resent(ful)
rasipeant, recipient
rasipeint, recipient
rasiprikul, reciprocal
rasiprocation, reciprocate(tion)
rasiprokashen, reciprocate(tion)
rasiprokate, reciprocate
rasiprokle, reciprocal
rasiprokul, reciprocal
rasir, razor /raise(r) /race(r)
rasirekshen, resurrect(ion)
rasis, race(s) /raise(s) /racist

rasisem, racism
rasism, racism
rasist, racist /resist
rasistef, resist(ive)
rasistense, resist(ance)
rasistent, resist(ant)
rasister, resist(or)
rasistive, resist(ive)
rasisum, racism
rasite, recite
rasitle, recite(tal)
rasitul, recite(tal)
rasizm, racism
rasizum, racism
raskel, rascal
raskle, rascal
rasn, raisin/ raise(sing)/ race(cing)
rasodo, risotto
rasolve, resolve
rasolvuble, resolve(vable)
rasor, razor/raise(r)/race(r)
rasort, resort
rasoto, risotto
rasotto, risotto
rasp,*,per,pingly,py, *A TOOL WHICH ROUGHS/
   SCRAPES/SANDS, A ROUGH SOUND*
raspberry,rries, *AN EDIBLE BERRY*
respect, respect
respectful, respect(ful)
respective, respect(ive)
respectuble, respect(able)
raspekt, respect
raspektful, respect(ful)
raspektif, respect(ive)
raspektuble, respect(able)
raspite, respite
raspond, respond
rasponder, respond(er)
rasponse, response

rasponsef, response(sive)
rasponsive, response(sive)
rasponsuble, response(sible)
rast, race(d) /raise(d)
rastore, restore
rastrant, restrain(t)
rastrektif, restrict(ive)
rastrektion, restrict(ion)
rastrikshen, restrict(ion)
rastrikt, restrict
rastriktive, restrict(ive)
rasume, resume
rasun, raisin /raise(sing) /race(cing)
rasur, razor /raise(r) /race(r)
rasurekshen, resurrect(ion)
rasus, racist /race(s)
rasusatate, resuscitate
rasuscitate, resuscitate
rasusitashen, resuscitate(tion)
rasusitate, resuscitate
rasusitator, resuscitate(tor)
rasust, racist
rasy, race(y)
rat,*,tted,tting,tty, *RODENT, SOMEONE WHO REVEALS
   OTHERS PRIVATE INFORMATION WITHOUT PERMIS-
   SION, TANGLED HAIR (or see rate or raid)*
ratainer, retain(er)
rataleashen, retaliate(tion)
rataleate, retaliate
rataleation, retaliate(tion)
ratane, retain
rataner, retain(er)
ratar, radar
ratash, radish
ratchat, ratchet
ratchet,*, *A DEVICE/TOOL*
ratchut, ratchet
rate,*,ed,ting, *TO RANK/QUALIFY/QUANTIFY/PROVIDE
   A VALUE TO (or see raid)*

rateal, radial
rateant, radiance(nt)
rateashen, radiate(tion)
rateate, radiate
rateater, radiate(tor)
rateation, radiate(tion)
ratecal, radical
ratech, radish
rated, rate(d) /rat(tted) /rot(tted)
ratefy, ratify
rateil, radial
rateim, radium
rateinse, radiance
rateint, radiance(nt)
rateints, radiance
rateis, radius
ratekly, radical(lly)
ratekul, radical
ratel, rattle
ratenshun, retention
ratentif, retention(ive)
ratention, retention
ratentive, retention(ive)
rateo, ratio /radio
rateod, radio(ed)
rateol, radial
rateom, radium
ratesh, radish
rateul, radial
rateum, radium
rateunse, radiance
rateunt, radiance(nt)
rateus, radius
rath, wrath
rather, THIS OVER THAT, PREFERENCE
rathful, wrath(ful)
rathur, rather
ratiate, radiate
ratiater, radiate(tor)

ratical, radical
ratich, radish
raticly, radical(lly)
ratid, rat(tted) /rate(d)
ratiel, radial
ratiem, radium
ratify,fies,fied,fying,fication,fier, TO APPROVE/ CONFIRM/MAKE FORMAL
ratikly, radical(lly)
ratikul, radical
ratikuly, radical(lly)
ratil, rattle
ratinshun, retention
ratintion, retention
ratio,*, COMPARISON OF AMOUNTS
ratiol, radial
ration,*,ned,ning, A SPECIFIC/LIMITED AMOUNT
rational,le,ly,lness,nale,lism,list,listic,listically, lity,lities,lize,lizer,lization, FACTUAL/LEVEL- HEADED/NONEMOTIONAL THOUGHT
rationalezation, rational(ization)
rationulization, rational(ization)
ratire, retire
ratirment, retire(ment)
ratisery, rotisserie
ratish, radish
ratisury, rotisserie
ratiul, radial
ratium, radium
ratiunse, radiance
ratius, radius
ratol, rattle
raton, radon
ratorical, rhetoric(al)
ratrakshen, retract(ion)
ratrakted, retract(ed)
ratrefe, retrieve
ratrefer, retrieve(r)
ratreful, retrieve(val)

ratreve, retrieve
ratrevul, retrieve(val)
ratrevur, retrieve(r)
rattle,*,ed,ling,er,ly, INSTRUMENT/TOY WITH BEADS (OR OTHER) INSIDE MAKING SOUND/RATTLE
ratufy, ratify
ratukle, radical
ratukly, radical(lly)
ratul, rattle
ratush, radish
raty, rat(tty)
raudy, rowdy
rauk, rock
raunchy,hier,hiest, INDECENT/FOUL
raunyin, reunion
raunyun, reunion
raust, roust
raut, wrought /route
rauty, rowdy
rav, rave
ravage,*,ed,ging, TO VIOLENTLY DAMAGE/DESTROY/ DEVASTATE
ravaje, ravage
raval, ravel
ravalashen, revelation
ravalee, reveille
ravalve, revolve
ravan, raven
ravash, ravish
rave,*,ed,ving,er, DELIRIOUS/WILD/EXCESSIVE, CARRYING ON, INCESSANT ABOUT
raveel, reveal
raveer, revere
ravege, ravage
ravegen, revise(sion)
raveje, ravage
ravejen, revise(sion)
ravel,led,ling,ler,lment, BECOME FRAYED/ ENTANGLED (or see reveal)

ravelation, revelation
ravelee, reveille
ravelt, reveal(ed)
raven,*,ner,ning,ningly,nous,nously,nousness, *BIRD, PLUNDER/DEVOUR GREEDILY, VORACIOUS APPETITE (or see ravine or rave(ving))*
ravench, revenge
ravene, ravine
ravenge, revenge
ravengful, revenge(ful)
ravenje, revenge
ravenjful, revenge(ful)
ravenus, raven(ous)
raveoly, ravioli
raverberate, reverberate
raverbirate, reverberate
ravere, revere
raversuble, reverse(sible)
ravert, revert
ravesh, ravish
raveshen, revise(sion)
ravesion, revise(sion)
raview, review /revue
rafif, revive
ravige, ravage
ravigen, revise(sion)
ravije, ravage
ravijen, revise(sion)
ravil, ravel
ravilashen, revelation
ravilation, revelation
ravilee, reveille /ravel
ravin, raven /ravine
ravinch, revenge
ravine,*, *A DEEP GORGE/DRIED RIVER BED WORN AWAY BY WATER (or see raven)*
ravinge, revenge
ravingful, revenge(ful)
ravinje, revenge

ravinful, revenge(ful)
ravinous, raven(ous)
ravinus, raven(ous)
ravioli,*, *STUFFED PASTA/NOODLE*
ravirberate, reverberate
ravirse, reverse
ravirsuble, reverse(sible)
ravirt, revert
ravise, revise
ravish,hes,hed,hing,her,hment, *CARRY AWAY/ TRANSPORT/RAPE BY FORCE, OVERWHELM EMOTIONALLY*
ravishen, revise(sion)
ravision, revise(sion)
ravival, revival
ravive, revive
ravivle, revival
ravivuble, revive(vable)
ravize, revise
ravle, ravel
ravocable, revocable
ravokable, revocable
ravoke, revoke
ravokt, revoke(d)
ravol, ravel
ravolashen, revelation
ravolation, revelation
ravolee, reveille
ravolfe, revolve
ravolfer, revolve(r)
ravolt, revolt
ravolve, revolve
ravolver, revolve(r)
ravon, raven /rave(ving)
ravonous, raven(ous)
ravu, review /revue
ravuge, ravage
ravuje, ravage
ravul, ravel

ravulashen, revelation
ravulation, revelation
ravulee, reveille
ravurbarate, reverberate
ravurse, reverse
ravurt, revert
raw,wly,wness, *UNFINISHED/UNCOOKED/ UNADULTERATED, IN ITS NATURAL STATE*
raward, reward
rawdy, rowdy
rawlik, rollick
rawnd, round
rawnt, round
raword, reward
rawst, roust
rawty, rowdy
ray,*, *STREAM OF LIGHT/HOPE/ENERGY*
raybees, rabid(ies)
raydar, radar
raydon, radon
rayl, rail /rale
rayn, rain/ reign/ rein
raynbo, rainbow
rayon, *SYNTHETIC FIBER*
raysd, raise(d) /race(d)
rayunyon, reunion
razberee, raspberry
razd, race(d) /raise(d)
raze, raise /ray(s) /race
razeleant, resilient
razemble, resemble
razemblinse, resemble(lance)
razen, raisin/ raise(sing)/ race(cing)
razent, resent
razentment, resent(ment)
razer, razor
razesd, racist
razesm, racism
razest, racist /resist

razide, reside
raziduel, residue(ual)
razilyent, resilient
razimble, resemble
razimbul, resemble
razin, raisin /raise(sing) /race(cing)/ resign
razir, razor
razisd, racist
razism, racism
razist, racist /resist
razistef, resist(ive)
razistense, resist(ance)
razistent, resist(ant)
razistur, resist(or)
razite, recite
razizum, racism
razkel, rascal
razkul, rascal
razodo, risotto
razolve, resolve
razoom, resume
razon, raisin /raise(sing) /race(cing)
razor,*, *SHARP BLADE INSTRUMENT FOR CUTTING HAIR*
razort, resort
razoto, risotto
razt, raise(d) /race(d)
razume, resume
razun, raisin /raise(sing) /race(cing)
razur, razor
razust, racist
re, *PREFIX INDICATING "BACK/AGAIN/IN RESPONSE"*
   MOST OFTEN MODIFIES THE WORD
reach,hes,hed,hing, *TO STRETCH FURTHER THAN*
   NORMAL TO ACHIEVE/GRASP/ACQUIRE
reacshen, react(ion)
react,*,ted,ting,tion,tionary,tionaries,tionist,
   tive,tance,tor, *TO RESPOND/ACT/MOVE IN*
   RESPONSE TO STIMULUS
reacter, react(or)

reactur, react(or)
read,*,ding,dable,dability,dableness,dably,der,
   ABLE TO VIEW/SEE/DECIPHER TEXT/LETTERS/
   NUMBERS/ SYMBOLS (or see red)
ready,died,dying,dily,diness, *PREPARED TO ACT/*
   PERFORM/RESPOND (or see read)
reaf, reef
reaks, react(s)
reakshen, react(ion)
reakshun, react(ion)
reakt, react
reakted, react(ed)
reaktef, react(ive)
reakter, react(or)
reaktif, react(ive)
reaktion, react(ion)
reaktir, react(or)
reaktive, react(ive)
reaktor, react(or)
reaktuf, react(ive)
reaktur, react(or)
real,lness,nism,list,listic,listically,lity,lities,lly,
   lization,lize,lized,lizing,lizingly,*PHYSICAL/*
   TRUTHFUL/FACTUAL (or see reel or realty)
realdy, realty
realedy, real(ity)
realestic, real(istic)
realety, real(ity)
realidy, real(ity)
realm,*,*, *AREA OF SCOPE/INTEREST*
realty,ties,tor, *OF REAL ESTATE/PROPERTY*
ream,*,med,ming,mer, *BUNDLED PAPER, ENLARGE/*
   BORE/BEVEL/ENLARGE/SQUEEZE WITH A TOOL
reanlistment, reenlist(ment)
reap,*,ped,ping,per, *TO ACCEPT/RECEIVE/HARVEST*
   FOR YOUR EFFORTS
rear,*,red,ring, *THE END/LAST/BOTTOM OF*
   SOMETHING, TO RISE UP ON HINDQUARTERS
reary, weary

reason,*,ned,ning,nable,nableness,nably, *TO*
   WEIGH LOGIC AGAINST EMOTIONS IN MAKING
   DECISIONS, USE MODERATE JUDGEMENT
reastat, rheostat
reaultee, realty
reax, react(s)
reb, rib
rebade, rebate
rebaflavin, riboflavin
rebal, rebel
reban, ribbon
rebate,*, er, *TO RETURN BACK*
rebatishen, repetition
rebel,*,lled,lling,llion,llious,lliously,lliousness, *TO*
   RISE UP/GO AGAINST MAINSTREAM OF
   RULE/THOUGHT
rebelein, rebel(llion)
rebelion, rebel(llion)
rebelyus, rebel(llious)
reben, ribbon
reberkushen, repercussion
reberkution, repercussion
rebertwa, repertoire
rebertwor, repertoire
rebetishen, repetition
rebeut, rebut /reboot
rebeutashen, repute(tation)
rebeutel, rebut(ttal)
rebewk, rebuke
rebewt, rebut /reboot
rebewtel, rebut(ttal)
rebil, rebel
rebin, ribbon
rebirkushen, repercussion
rebirkution, repercussion
rebirtwa, repertoire
rebirtwor, repertoire
reble, rebel
rebled, rebel(lled)

recepticle, receptacle
reception,*, *AN EVENT/CEREMONY/DEVICE WHICH RECEIVE/ACKNOWLEDGE/ACCEPTS INCOMING*
receptionist,*, *SOMEONE WHO ACCEPTS INCOMING CALLS/VISITORS/CUSTOMERS*
receptive,ely,eness,vity, *ABLE TO TAKE IN/RECEIVE*
receptor,*, *THAT WHICH RECEIVES*
receptucle, receptacle
recer, recur
reces, recess
recess,sses,ssed,ssion,ssional,ssionary,sive, ssively,ssiveness, *TO TAKE A BREAK, RECEDE*
receve, receive
rech, reach /wretch /rich
rechd, reach(ed) /wretch(ed)
rechis, reach(es) /rich(es)
rechly, rich(ly)
recht, reach(ed) /wretch(ed)
rechual, ritual
rechuol, ritual
recieve, receive
recipe,*, *DIRECTIONS FOR COOKING*
recipient,*, *THOSE WHO RECEIVE/IN RECEIPT OF*
recipracate, reciprocate
reciprocal,lity,lly, *GIVE AND TAKE, BACK AND FORTH, MUTUALLY RESPONSIVE*
reciprocate,*,ted,ting,tion,tive, *MOVES BACK AND FORTH, MUTUALLY RESPONSIVE*
recir, recur
recite,*,ed,ting,tal,tation,tative,*REPEAT/RELATE GIVE ACCOUNT FROM MEMOR*
reck, wreck /wreak
reckamendation, recommend(ation)
recken, reckon
reckensile, reconcile
reckety, rickety
reckin, reckon
reckinsile, reconcile
reckits, rickets

rebut,*,tted,tting,table,ttal(s), *TO ARGUE/REFUTE/ OPPOSE/THRUST BACK* (or see reboot)
rebutal, rebut(ttal)
rebutashen, repute(tation)
rebute, reboot
rebutishen, repetition
rebutle, rebut(ttal)
recal, recall
recall,*,lled,lling,llable, *TO CALL/SOLICITE SOMETHING BACK TO THE SOURCE/CREATOR*
recamend, recommend
recansile, reconcile
recant,*,ted,ting, *TO CONTRADICT/RETRACT WHAT WAS JUST SAID*
recap,*,pped,pping,pable, *TO SUMMARIZE/ RECOAT/RESURFACE*
recaul, recall
reccomend, recommend
reccomendable, recommend(able)
reccomendation, recommend(ation)
reccomended, recommend(ed)
reccomenduble, recommend(able)
recede,*,ed,ding, *RETREAT/WITHDRAW/YIELD TO PREVIOUS/PRIOR*
receipt,*, *ACKNOWLEDGEMENT/INVOICE FOR HAVING RECEIVED SERVICES/GOODS*
receive,*,ed,ving,vable(s),er,ership, *ACCEPT/ ACQUIRE/ACCUMULATE*
recensile, reconcile
recent,tly,ncy,tness, *HAVING OCCURED NEAR/CLOSE TO THE PRESENT TIME* (or see resent)
recepe, recipe
receprocate, reciprocate
receprokul, reciprocal
recepshen, reception
recepshenist, receptionist
recepshin, reception
receptacle,*, *A PLACE TO DELIVER, A RECEIVING PLACE, ELECTRICAL SOURCE*

rebleka, replica
reblekashen, replica(tion)
reblika, replica
reblikate, replica(te)
reblikation, replica(tion)
rebluka, replica
reblukashen, replica(tion)
reblukate, replica(te)
reblukation, replica(tion)
rebof, rebuff
reboflavin, riboflavin
rebol, rebel
rebon, ribbon
reboot,*,ted,ting, *TO RESTART A COMPUTER/ MEMORY/ACTION* (or see rebut)
reborkushen, repercussion
rebotek, robot(ic)
rebound,ded,ding, *REPERCUSSION/REACTION TO A COLLISION WITH EMOTIONS/ATTITUDES/ SOMETHING PHYSICAL*
rebownd, rebound
rebownt, rebound
rebrkushen, repercussion
rebt, rib(bbed) /rip(pped)
rebtile, reptile
rebtileun, reptile(lian)
rebudal, rebut(ttal)
rebudle, rebut(ttal)
rebuf, rebuff
rebuff,*,ffed,ffing, *REFUSE/REJECT*
rebuflavin, riboflavin
rebuke,*,ed,king,er, *SEVERE/SHARP REJECT/REFUSE*
rebul, rebel
rebuled, rebel(lled)
rebun, ribbon
reburkushen, repercussion
reburkution, repercussion
reburtwa, repertoire
reburtwor, repertoire

recklaim, reclaim /reclame
recklamashen, reclamation
recklame, reclaim /reclame
reckless,ssly,ssness, *TO BE UNAWARE/CARELESS OF SURROUNDING ENVIRONMENT POSING POTENTIAL DANGER/PAIN*
reckline, recline
recklus, recluse /reckless
reckognition, recognition
reckomend, recommend
reckon,*,ned,ning, *SUPPOSE, TO BE CONSIDERED*
reckonsile, reconcile
reckumend, recommend
reckumendation, recommend(ation)
reckun, reckon
reckunsile, reconcile
reclaim,*,med,ming,mer, *TO TAKE BACK, MAKE PURE/USABLE AGAIN* (or see reclame)
reclaimable, reclamable
reclamable,*TAKE BACK, MAKE PURE/ USABLE AGAIN*
reclamashen, reclamation
reclamation,*, , *TAKE BACK, MAKE PURE/USABLE*
reclame,*, , *ADVERTISE ONESELF, PUBLIC ATTENTION/ NOTORIETY* (or see reclaim)
reclamer, reclaim(er)
recline,*,ed,ning,er, *RECUMBENT POSITION/LIE BACK*
reclumashen, reclamation
reclumation, reclamation
recluse,*,sion, *SHUT ONESELF OFF/AWAY FROM SOCIETY/SOCIAL ENVIRONMENT*
reclushen, recluse(sion)
recochet, ricochet
recogneshen, recognition
recognision, recognition
recognition,ive,tory, *TO FIND FAMILIAR, FRIENDLY ATTENTION*
recognize, recognize
recognize,*,ed,zing,zance,zable,zability,zable, er, *FIND FAMILIAR/KNOW/ACKNOWLEDGE*

recognizuble, recognize(zable)
recoil,*,led,lless, *SUDDEN JERK/DRAW BACK/ SHRINKING FROM*
recol, recoil / recall
recold, recoil(ed)
recolt, recoil(ed)
recomendable, recommend(able)
recomendashen, recommend(ation)
recomindation, recommend(ation)
recommend,*,ded,ding,dation,dable,datory, *ADVISE/SUGGEST FAVORABLY*
recommendashen, recommend(ation)
reconaisanse, reconnaissance
reconasinse, reconnaissance
reconcile,*,ed,ling,lable,lability,lableness,lably, ement,liation,liatory, *REBUILD FRIENDSHIP, RESTORE UNION, ADJUST TO DIFFERENCES*
reconnaissance, *EXAMINE PARAMETER/TERRITORY*
reconsile, reconcile
reconsileashen, reconcile(liation)
reconsileation, reconcile(liation)
reconstatute, reconstitute
reconstetushen, reconstitute(tion)
reconstetute, reconstitute
reconstitute,*,ed,ting,tion, *TO RECONSTRUCT FROM A CONDENSED/DRIED STATE*
recoop, recoup
recooped, recoup(ed)
recooperashen, recuperate(tion)
recooperate, recuperate
record,*,ded,ding,der, *DOCUMENT/TAPE/WRITE/ DEFINE AN EVENT/TEXT/SPEECH FOR POSTERITY/ PRESERVE EVIDENCE*
recorse, recourse
recoup,*,ped,ping,pable,pment, *TO REGAIN/BE COMPENSATED*
recourse, *RETURN TO FOR BACK-UP HELP*
recover,rable,ry, *TO GET BACK TO NORMAL/HEALTHY, BECOME OPERABLE AGAIN*

recreashen, recreation
recreation,nal, *AMUSEMENT/DIVERSION/PLAY*
recruit,*,ted,ting,ter,tment(s), *ORGANIZE/ENLIST/ ENTICE PEOPLE TO JOIN*
recrute, recruit
recruter, recruit(er)
rectafy, rectify
rectal,lly, *INVOLVING/PERTAINING TO THE RECTUM*
rectatude, rectitude
rectem, rectum
rectifie, rectify
rectify,fies,fied,fying,fiable,fication, *TO AMEND/ CORRECT/MAKE RIGHT*
rectil, rectal
rectim, rectum
rectitude,dinous, *RIGHTEOUS IN FORM/INTEGRITY*
rectol, rectal
rectom, rectum
rectul, rectal
rectum,*, ta, *THE LOWER LARGE INTESTINE*
rectutude, rectitude
recufer, recover
recufry, recover(y)
recumbent,ncy,tly, *RECLINING/LYING POSITION*
recumendashen, recommend(ation)
recunsile, reconcile
recupe, recoup
recuped, recoup(ed)
recuperashen, recuperate(tion)
recuperate,*,ed,ting,tion,tive,tory, *RECOVER/ REGAIN FORM ILLNESS/FINANCIAL STRESS*
recur,*,rring,rrent,rrently, *REPEATEDLY HAPPENING*
recurd, record
recuver, recover
recuvry, recover(y)
recwuzit, requisite
red,*, dder,ddest,dding,dness,dden, *A COLOR, PERTAINING TO THE COLOR* (or see read)
redabel, read(able)

redabul, read(able)
redal, riddle
redard, retard
redasent, reticent
redasint, reticent
rede, ready
redeam, redeem
redeble, read(able)
redeed, ready(died) / read
redeem, *,med,ming,mer,mable, CLEAR PAYMENT, RECOVER, FULFILL PLEDGE
redeemible, redeem(able)
redempshun, redemption
redemption, *,nal,ner,ive,tory, TO BE/ACT OF BEING REDEEMED
redemshen, redemption
redemtion, redemption
redemtive, redemption(ive)
redemuble, redeem(able)
redents, rid(ddance)
reder, red(dder) /read(er)
redern, return
redge, ridge
redi, ready
redible, read(able)
redicint, reticent
redicule, ridicule
redimtive, redemption(ive)
redin, red(dden)
redir, red(dder) /read(er)
redisent, reticent
redle, riddle
redna, retina
redniss, red(ness)
redo, oing, TO DO AGAIN/OVER
redoo, redo
redoose, reduce
redor, read(er) /red(dder)
redroactive, retroactive

redroaktif, retroactive
redrograte, retrograde
redrospection, retrospect(ion)
redrospekshin, retrospect(ion)
redubel, read(able)
redubol, read(able)
reduce, *,ed,cing,er,cible,cibly,cibility,ction, ctional,ctive, TO LOWER/DIMUTION/DIVIDE
reducshen, reduce(ction)
reduing, redo(ing)
redukshen, reduce(ction)
reduktion, reduce(ction)
redul, riddle
redun, red(dden)
redundant, tly,ncy,cies, OVER AND OVER, REPEATEDLY/REPETITION/UNNECESSARY
redundensy, redundant(ncy)
redur, red(dder) /read(er)
redurn, return
redusable, reduce(cible)
reduse, reduce
redusent, reticent
redusint, reticent
redy, ready
reech, reach
reed, *,ding,dy, A PLANT, CONVEX MOLDING, RIDGES (or see read)
reederate, reiterate
reef, *,fer, OCEAN LEDGE, PART OF A SAIL, ROLLED MARIJUANA, REFRIGERATOR
reek, *,ked,king,ker,kingly,ky, OFFENSIVE/STRONG/ AWFUL ODOR (or see wreak)
reel, *,led,ling,ler,lable, TO WIND/PULL IN, A DANCE, WOUND UP, REVOLVING TOOL (or see real)
reem, ream
reemberse, reimburse
reembersment, reimburse(ment)
reemburse, reimburse
reembursment, reimburse(ment)

reenact, *,ted,ting,tment, TO REPLICATE A PERFORMANCE/EVENT
reenaktment, reenact(ment)
reenforse, reinforce
reenforsment, reinforce(ment)
reenlestment, reenlist(ment)
reenlist, *,ted,ting,tment, TO ENLIST AGAIN
reep, reap
reept, reap(ed)
reer, rear
reeth, wreath
reeturate, reiterate
ref, reef /referee
refal, revel
refalashen, revelation
refalation, revelation
refald, revel(lled)
refalee, reveille
refar, river
refarmashen, reform(ation)
refarmation, reform(ation)
refeel, reveal
refel, revel
refelashen, revelation
refelation, revelation
refeld, revel(lled) /refilled
refelee, reveille
refer, *,rred,rring,rable,rral(s), RECOMMEND/ HAND OVER/REQUEST/ASSIGN SOMEONE ELSE, SLANG FOR REFRIGERATOR (or see reef(er) or river)
referal, refer(rral)
referbash, refurbish
referbish, refurbish
referbishment, refurbish(ment)
referd, refer(rred)
refere, referee
referee, *, eed, eeing, ASSIGNED TO SETTLE DISPUTES/MAKE JUDGEMENT CALLS
reference, *, ed,cing, DIRECTION/ALLUSION/GUIDE

referendum,*,da, MEASURE PUT BEFORE PUBLIC TO VOTE ON
referil, refer(rral)
referindum, referendum
referinse, reference
refermashen, reform(ation)
refermation, reform(ation)
referse, reverse
refeuge, refuge
refeugy, refugee
refeuje, refuge
refeuse, refuse
refeusil, refuse(sal)
refeuze, refuse
refewge, refuge /refugee
refewje, refuge
refews, refuse
refewsel, refuse(sal)
refew, review /revue
refiful, revival
refilashen, revelation
refilation, revelation
refild, revel(lled)
refilee, reveille
refine,*,ed,ning,ery,nable,ement, TO REMOVE IMPURITIES/ALLOYS, MAKE FINE
refinment, refine(ment)
refinury, refine(ry)
refir, refer /reef(er) /river
refiral, refer(rral)
refirbash, refurbish
refirbish, refurbish
refird, refer(rred)
refired, refer(rred)
refiree, referee
refirence, reference
refirendum, referendum
refirense, reference
refirmashen, reform(ation)

refirmation, reform(ation)
refirse, reverse
rifural, referral
reflashen, revelation
reflecks, reflex /reflect(s)
reflecksef, reflex(ive)
reflect,*,ted,ting,tion,tive,tively,tiveness,tively, tivity,tor,torize, TO MIRROR/CAST BACK/ REPRODUCE AN IMAGE (or see reflex)
reflectif, reflect(ive)
refleks, reflex /reflect(s)
reflekshen, reflect(ion)
refleksif, reflex(ive)
reflekt, reflect /reflex(ed)
reflektif, reflect(ive)
reflektion, reflect(ion)
reflektor, reflect(or)
reflex,xes,xed,xing,xly,xive,xively,xiveness, xivity, A REACTION/RESPONSE (or see reflect)
reflexsif, reflex(ive)
reflext, reflex(ed)
refol, revel
refolashen, revelation
refolation, revelation
refold, revel(lled)
refolee, reveille
refor, river/ refer/ reef(er)
reform,*,med,ming,mer,mation,mable,matory, matories,mative, TO CHANGE/MODIFY/RETRAIN/ REARRANGE/RESTORE
reformashen, reform(ation)
reformd, reform(ed)
reformitory, reform(atory)
reformutory, reform(atory)
refract,*,ted,ting,tion,tive,tory, TO DEFLECT/ REFLECT INTO A DIFFERENT DIRECTION/DENSITY
refrain,nment, A REPETITIVE BREAK/ INTERRUPTION, TO REPRESS/ABSTAIN
refrakt, refract

refraktory, refract(ory)
refrane, refrain
refred, referee(d)
refree, referee
refregirant, refrigerate(ant)
refregirator, refrigerate(tor)
refrendum, referendum
refrense, reference
refresh,hes,hing,her,ment, TO MAKE FRESH AGAIN/INVIGORATE
refrigerate,*,ed,ting,tion,ant, USED TO KEEP THINGS COOL/COLD
refrigerator, refrigerate(tor)
refrigerent, refrigerate(ant)
refrindum, referendum
refrinse, reference
refry, referee
reft, rift
refue, review /revue
refuge,*, A MANMADE/NATURAL SHELTER, TEMPORARY PROTECTION FROM THE ENVIRONMENT
refugee,*, ONE ESCAPING PERSECUTION IN A FOREIGN COUNTRY
refugy, refugee
refuje, refuge
reful, revel
refulashen, revelation
refulation, revelation
refulee, reveille
refund,*,ded,ding,dable, RETURN/COMPENSATE/ GIVE BACK
refundible, refund(able)
refunduble, refund(able)
refunt, refund
refur, refer /reef(er) /river
refurbeshment, refurbish(ment)
refurbish,hes,hed,hing,hment, TO RENOVATE/ MAKE FRESH AGAIN
refurd, refer(rred)

refured, refer(rred)
refuree, referee
refurendum, referendum
refurense, reference
refuril, refer(rral)
refurindum, referendum
refurmashen, reform(ation)
refurse, reverse
refuse, raffle /refuse
refuse, *,ed,sing,sal,er, *TO NOT ACCEPT, DENY/ REJECT, TO DISCARD UNUSABLES/TRASH*
refusel, refuse(sal)
refuze, refuse
reg, rig /ridge
regal, lly,lia,le,led,ling,lity,lities, *PERTAINING TO LAVISH FEASTS/ROYALTY*
regalea, regal(ia)
regaledy, regal(ity)
regamen, regime(n)
regamentashen, regime(ntation)
regamentation, regime(ntation)
regamin, regime(n)
regamint, regime(nt)
regan, region
regard, *,ded,ding,dful,dfully,dfullness,dless, dlessly,dlessness, *TO CONSIDER, SHOW CONCERN/ATTENTION/RESPECT*
regart, regard
regaster, register
regastrashen, registration
regastration, registration
regect, reject
regekshen, reject(ion)
regekt, reject
regektion, reject(ion)
regel, regal
regementation, regime(ntation)
regemin, regime(n)
regemint, regime(nt)

regemintation, regime(ntation)
regen, region
regenal, region(al)
reger, rigor
regergetate, regurgitate
regerjutate, regurgitate
regestir, register
regestrashen, registration
regestration, registration
reget, rigid
regeuler, regular
regeulerly, regular(ly)
regewlashen, regulate(tion)
regewlate, regulate
regewlation, regulate(tion)
regewlerly, regular(ly)
regewvinate, rejuvenate
regid, rigid
regil, regal
regime, *,en,ent,ental,entally,entation, *A MODE/ SYSTEM OF RULE/MANAGE*
regimentashen, regime(ntation)
regimentation, regime(ntation)
regimin, regime(min)
regimint, regime(nt)
regimintation, regime(ntation)
regin, region
reginal, region(al)
region, *,nal,nally,nalism,nalist,nalistic, *AN AREA/PART/SECTION OF*
regirus, rigor(ous)
register, *,red,ring, *SIGN UP/ENROLL TO PARTICIPATE*
registrashen, registration
registration, *,nal, *SIGN UP/ENROLL TO PARTICIPATE*
regit, rigid
reglar, regular
reglate, regulate
regle, regal
reglerly, regular(ly)
reglir, regular

reg|urly, regular(ly)
regoise, rejoice
regon, region
regonal, region(al)
regoyse, rejoice
regres, regress
regresif, regress(ive)
regresive, regress(ive)
regress, *,sses,ssed,ssing,ssion,ssive,ssively, ssiveness,ssor, *GOING BACK/REVERSION*
regresuf, regress(ive)
regret, *,tted,tting,tful,tfully,tfulness,table,tably, ter, *SENSE OF LOSS/SORROW, SORRY*
regreted, regret(tted)
regretfuly, regret(fully)
reguard, regard
reguardless, regard(less)
regul, regal
regular, *,rly,rity,rness,rize, *NORMAL/AVERAGE/ TYPICAL*
regulashen, regulate(tion)
regulate, *,ed,ting,tion,tive,tor,tory, *TO NORMALIZE/KEEP WITHIN LIMITS/STANDARDS*
reguler, regular
regulerly, regular(ly)
regulur, regular
regunal, region(al)
regurgitate, *,ed,ting,tion, *RUSH/SURGE BACK AND FORTH*
regurjitate, regurgitate
regurs, rigor(s)
regurus, rigor(ous)
regustir, register
registrashen, registration

registration, registration
reguvanashen, rejuvenate(tion)
reguvanate, rejuvenate
reguvanation, rejuvenate(tion)
reguvinate, rejuvenate
reguvination, rejuvenate(tion)
reguvunate, rejuvenate
regwasit, requisite
regwazit, requisite
rehab,bberr, SLANG FOR REHABILITATION
rehabeletashen, rehabilitate(tion)
rehabeletate, rehabilitate
rehabilitate,*,ed,ting,tion,tive, RESTORE/
  REINSTATE/REESTABLISH
rehap, rehab
rehearse,*,ed,sing,sal, TO PRACTICE REPEATEDLY
  FOR A PERFORMANCE
rehebilatation, rehabilitate(tion)
rehersal, rehearse(sal)
reherse, rehearse
rehersul, rehearse(sal)
rehirsul, rehearse(sal)
rehubelatashen, rehabilitate
rehubilatate, rehabilitate
rehubiletation, rehabilitate(tion)
rehurse, rehearse
rehursil, rehearse(sal)
reiderate, reiterate
reidurate, reiterate
reign,*,ned,ning, HAVE RULE/ POWER/SOVEREIGNTY
  (or see rain or rein)
reil, real /reel
reilistec, real(istic)
reiltee, realty
reilty, realty
reimberse, reimburse
reimbirsment, reimburse(ment)
reimburse,*,ed,sing,sable,ement,er, PAY BACK/
  REFUND/COMPENSATE

rein,*,ned,ning,nless, RESTRAINT/CURB/CONTROL
  (or see rain or rhein)
reinacment, reenact(ment)
reinacted, reenact(ed)
reinakt, reenact
reinaktment, reenact(ment)
reindeer,*, IN THE DEER FAMILY
reinforce,*,ed,cing,ement, INCREASE/STRENGTHEN
reinforse, reinforce
reinforsment, reinforce(ment)
reinlest, reenlist
reinlisment, reenlist(ment)
reinlist, reenlist
reinlistment, reenlist(ment)
reiterate,*,ed,ting,tion,tive,tively,tiveness, TO
  REPEAT/SAY AGAIN
reiturate, reiterate
rej, ridge
rejament, regime(nt)
rejamin, regime(n)
rejamintashen, regime(ntation)
rejamination, regime(ntation)
rejan, region
rejaster, register
reject,*,ted,ting,tion,ter,tive, REFUSE TO RECEIVE/
  RECOGNIZE/ACKNOWLEDGE/ACCEPT
rejekshen, reject(ion)
rejekt, reject
rejektion, reject(ion)
rejen, region
rejenul, region(al)
rejestir, register
rejestrashen, registration
rejestration, registration
rejet, rigid
rejewvinate, rejuvenate
rejid, rigid
rejimen, regime(n)
rejiment, regime(nt)

rejin, region
rejinul, region(al)
rejister, register
rejistrashen, registration
rejistration, registration
rejit, rigid
rejoese, rejoice
rejoice,*,ed,cing,er,cingly, TO DISPLAY
  JOY/GLADNESS
rejon, region
rejonal, region(al)
rejoyse, rejoice
rejumen, regime(n)
rejument, regime(nt)
rejumentashen, regime(ntation)
rejumentation, regime(ntation)
rejumin, regime(n)
rejumint, regime(nt)
rejumintashen, regime(ntation)
rejumintation, regime(ntation)
rejumintation, regime(ntation)
rejun, region
rejunal, region(al)
rejustir, register
rejustrashen, registration
rejustration, registration
rejuvanashen, rejuvenate(tion)
rejuvenate,*,ed,ting,tion,tor,nize,nescence,
  MAKE YOUTHFUL AGAIN
rejuvinashen, rejuvenate(tion)
rejuvinate, rejuvenate
rejuvination, rejuvenate(tion)
rek, wreck /wreak /reek
rekal, recall
rekamend, recommend
rekamendation, recommend(ation)
rekamenduble, recommend(able)
rekamented, recommend(ed)
rekanize, recognize
rekansile, reconcile

rekansileashun, reconcile(liation)
rekant, recant
rekap, recap
rekapt, recap(pped)
rekashay, ricochet
rekedy, rickety
rekegnise, recognize
reken, reckon
rekendil, rekindle
rekendul, rekindle
rekenize, recognize
rekensile, reconcile
rekensileashun, reconcile(liation)
reker, recur /wrecker
rekerd, record
rekety, rickety
rekeulir, regular
rekewlashen, regulate(tion)
rekewpt, recoup(ed)
rekewpurate, recuperate
rekidy, rickety
rekimented, recommend(ed)
rekin, reckon
rekindle,*,ed,ling, RENEW
rekindul, rekindle
rekinise, recognize
rekinsile, reconcile
rekir, recur /wrecker
rekird, record
rekits, rickets
rekity, rickety
reklaimuble, reclamable
reklamashen, reclamation
reklamation, reclamation
reklame, reclaim /reclame
reklamshen, reclamation
reklamuble, reclamable
reklas, reckless
reklemashen, reclamation

rekless, reckless
reklimashen, reclamation
reklimation, reclamation
rekline, recline
reklinur, recline(r)
reklir, regular
reklis, reckless
rekloos, recluse
reklumation, reclamation
reklus, reckless
rekluse, recluse
rekochet, ricochet
rekofry, recover(y)
rekogneshen, recognition
rekognise, recognize
rekognition, recognition
rekognize, recognize
rekognizuble, recognize(zable)
rekoil, recoil
rekol, recall
rekold, recoll(ed)
rekole, recoil /recall
rekolt, recoll(ed)
rekomend, recommend
rekomendashen, recommend(ation)
rekomented, recommend(ed)
rekon, reckon
rekonasents, reconnaissance
rekonisense, reconnaissance
rekonize, recognize
rekonsile, reconcile
rekonsileat, reconcile(ate)
rekonsileation, reconcile(liation)
rekonstatute, reconstitute
rekonstetushen, reconstitute(tion)
rekonstetute, reconstitute
rekonstitution, reconstitute(tion)
rekonusinse, reconnaissance
rekoop, recoup

rekooperate, recuperate
rekor, wrecker
rekord, record
rekorder, record(er)
rekorse, recourse
rekover, recover
rekoyl, recoil
rekreashen, recreation
rekreation, recreation
rekroot, recruit
rekrute, recruit
rekruter, recruit(er)
reks, reek(s)
rekt, reek(ed)
rektafy, rectify
rektal, rectal
rektatude, rectitude
rektel, rectal
rektem, rectum
rektify, rectify
rektitude, rectitude
rektol, rectal
rektom, rectum
rektufy, rectify
rektul, rectal
rektum, rectum
rekuasit, requisite
rekufer, recover
rekufry, recover(y)
rekugnise, recognize
rekugnishen, recognition
rekugnize, recognize
rekugnizuble, recognize(zable)
rekulade, regulate
rekular, regular
rekulashen, regulate(tion)
rekulate, regulate
rekulation, regulate(tion)
rekumbent, recumbent

rekumend, recommend
rekumendashen, recommend(ation)
rekumenduble, recommend(able)
rekumended, recommend(ed)
rekumind, recommend
rekun, reckon
rekunize, recognize
rekunsile, reconcile
rekunsileashen, reconcile(liation)
rekunsileation, reconcile(liation)
rekupe, recoup
rekuperate, recuperate
rekuperation, recuperate(tion)
rekupirate, recuperate
rekupurashen, recuperate(tion)
rekupt, recoup(ed)
rekur, recur /wrecker
rekurd, record
rekushet, ricochet
rekuver, recover
rekuvry, recover(y)
rekwasit, requisite
rekwest, request
rekwire, require
rekwirment, require(ment)
rekwrute, recruit
rekwuzit, requisite
rel, real /reel /rill
rela, relay
relabs, relapse
relagashen, relegate(tion)
relagate, relegate
relagation, relegate(tion)
relaks, relax
relaps, relapse
relapse,*,ed,sing,er, TO BACKSLIDE/FALL BACK
relashen, relate(tion)
relashunship, relate(tionship)

relate,*,ed,ting,tion,tional,table,tionship,edness
  BE ASSOCIATED/CONNECTED/ALLIED WITH, TO
  TELL/NARRATE
relatevity, relativity
relatif, relative
relative,*,ely,eness,vism,vist,vistic,vity,
  ASSOCIATED/SIMILAR/CLOSE/CONNECTION
relativity,vities, THAT WHICH IS RELATIVE
relativly, relative(ly)
relax,*,xes,xed,xing,xation,xedly,xedness, xer,
  xant, BECOME CALM/LOOSE/SLACK
relay,*,yed,ying, USE OF MACHINERY/ELECTRICITY/
  TECHNOLOGY/ANIMALS/PEOPLE TO
  SEND/TRANSMIT/ RETRIEVE
rele, real(lly) /reel /real
release,*,ed,sing,er,sable, TO FREE
relef, relief
relegate,*,ed,ting,tion, SEND AWAY
relese, release
relesh, relish
reletif, relative
reletivly, relative(ly)
reletivity, relativity
releve, relieve
relever, relieve(r)
relevur, relieve(r)
reli, real(lly) /rely
reliance,nt,ntly, CONFIDENCE/TRUST/DEPENDENT
  REMOVAL/ALLEVIATION FROM PAIN
reliaple, rely(liable)
relic,*, MEMENTOS/PRESERVED/KEEP SAKES
relidy, real(ity)
relief,eve,*,eved,eving,ever,evable, EASE/
  REMOVAL/ALLEVIATION FROM PAIN
relieve,*,ed,ving,er, EASED/REMOVED/ALLEVIATED
  FROM PAIN (or see relief)

religashen, relegate(tion)
religate, relegate
religation, relegate(tion)
religeon, religion
religion,*,ous,ously,ousness, BELIEF IN A GOD IN A
  SPECIFIC/PARTICULAR WAY
religon, religion
religus, religion(ous)
relik, relic
relinkwish, relinquish
relinquish,hes,hed,hing,hment, GIVE UP
  POSSESSION OF
relintless, relentless
relish,hes,hed,hing,hable, APPETIZER, PICKLED
  CONDIMENT, TO BE GRATIFIED/PLEASED/
  LIKE/SAVOR SOMETHING
relity, real(ity)
reliubility, rely(liability)
reliuble, rely(liable)
reliunse, reliance
reliunt, reliance(nt)
reliver, relieve(r)
relm, realm
relogate, relegate
relogation, relegate(tion)
reltifly, relative(ly)
reluctant,nce, APPREHENSIVE/RESISTANT/UNWILLING
reluctinse, reluctant(nce)
reluctint, reluctant
relugashen, relegate(tion)
relugate, relegate
relugation, relegate(tion)
reluktant, reluctant
reluktense, reluctant(nce)
reluktint, reluctant
relur, regular
relush, relish
relutif, relative
relutivly, relative(ly)

rely,lies,lied,lying,liable,liability,liableness,liably, TRUSTWORTHY/SUPPORTIVE/DEPENDABLE (or see really)
rem, ream/ realm/ rim
remade, remedy
remadik, rheumatic
remain, *,ned,ning,nder, STAY BEHIND/ LEFT OVER (or see romaine)
remane, remain /romaine
remanis, reminisce
remanisent, reminisce(nt)
remantisize, romantic(ize)
remar, ream(er)
remark,*,ked,king,kable,kably, COMMENT/OBSER-VATION/BRIEF STATEMENT, WORTHY OF COMMENT/OBSERVATION/NOTICE
remarkuble, remark(able)
rematik, rheumatic
rematy, remedy
rembunctious, rambunctious
rembunkshes, rambunctious
reme, ream
remede, remedy
remediashen, remedy(diation)
remedy,dies,died,dying,diable,diableness,diably, diless,dial,diation, TO FIX/IMPROVE DAMAGE/ RELIEVE DISORDER
remember,*,red,ring,rance,rancer,ACKNOWLEDGE THINK OF/RECOLLECT THE PAST
remembrinse, remember(ance)
remembur, remember
remenis, reminisce
remenisent, reminisce(nt)
remer, ream(er)
remeshen, remission
remet, remit
remety, remedy
remidal, remit(ttal)
remidy, remedy

remind, remind
remind,*,ded,ding,der,dful, CAUSE TO RECOLLECT/ REMEMBER
remindur, remind(er)
reminis, reminisce
reminisce,*,ed,cing,ent,ently, TO LONGINGLY REMEMBER/THINK OF THE PAST
reminisent, reminisce(nt)
remintur, remind(er)
remir, ream(er)
remishen, remission
remision, remission
remission, ABATEMENT, TEMPORARY REDUCTION/ DISAPPEARANCE
remit,*,tted,tting,tment,ttable,tter,ttance,ttent, ttently,ttal, TRANSMIT/ SEND/GIVE BACK
remital, remit(ttal)
remited, remit(tted)
remition, remission
remituble, remit(ttable)
remity, remedy
remnant,*, LEFT OVERS/REMAINS/SCRAPS
remnet, remnant
remnint, remnant
remofer, remove(r)
remonis, reminisce
remoof, remove
remooval, remove(val)
remoovil, remove(val)
remorse,eful,efully,efulness,eless,elessly, elessness, PAIN/GUILT WHEN LOOKING TO SOMETHING IN THE PAST
remorsful, remorse(ful)
remorsless, remorse(ful)
remote,ely, eness, REMOVED FROM SOCIAL CENTERS, FAR OFF IN DISTANCE/TIME
remotly, remote(ly)
remove, *,ed,ving,vable,vability,vableness, vably,val,ver, TAKE AWAY/ ERASE

remudy, remedy
remufe, remove
remufer, remove(r)
remufible, remove(vable)
remufil, remove(val)
remunerate, *,ed,ting,ability,able,tion,tive, tively,tiveness, TO PAY FOR LOSS/ REPAY/COMPENSATE/REWARD
remunerashen, remunerate(tion)
remuneration, remunerate(tion)
remunirate, remunerate
remuniration, remunerate(tion)
remunis, reminisce
remur, ream(er)
remutoed, rheumatic(toid)
remuty, remedy
remuvable, remove(vable)
remuve, remove
remuvel, remove(val)
remuvul, remove(val)
ren, wren
renagade, renegade
renaisance, renaissance
renaissance, PERIOD OF TIME IN EUROPE
renasance, renaissance
renasonts, renaissance
renauserus, rhinoceros
renavashen, renovate(tion)
renavate, renovate
renavation, renovate(tion)
renawserus, rhinoceros
rench, wrench
rendal, rent(al)
render, *,red,ring,rable,rer, RETURN/GIVE IN/ SUBMIT/FURNISH/SURRENDER/CAUSE (or see rent(er))
rendur, render
rendezvous, ARRANGE TO MEET, MEET UP WITH
renegade, *,do, ONE WHO DESERTS, A TRAITOR

renege,*,ed,ging,er, *TO FAIL/GO BACK ON WORD, VIOLATE CARD GAME RULE*
renevashen, renovate(tion)
renevate, renovate
renevation, renovate(tion)
renew,*,wed,wing,wability,wable,wably,wer, wal, *REFRESH/MAKE LIKE NEW/ REFURBISH*
reng, ring /wring /rink /wring
renger, ring(er)
renigade, renegade
renige, renege
renik, renege
renisance, renaissance
renissance, renaissance
renk, ring /rink /wring
renkle, wrinkle
renkul, wrinkle
renlistment, reenlist(ment)
renone, renown
renoserus, rhinoceros
renosirus, rhinoceros
renosonse, renaissance
renounce,*,ed,cing,eable,ement,er, *DISOWN/ REJECT/CAST OFF*
renounse, renounce
renounsment, renounce(ment)
renovaded, renovate(d)
renovashen, renovate(tion)
renown,ned, *ACHIEVEMENTS/REPUTATION KNOWN FAR AND WIDE*
renownse, renounce
renownsment, renounce(ment)
rens, rinse /wren(s) /rent(s)
rensd, rinse(d)
rensur, rinse(r)
rent,*,tal,ted,ting,table,ter, *TO PAY SOMEONE TO BORROW THE USE OF PROPERTY*

rentel, rent(al)
renter, render /rent(er)
rentible, rent(able)
rentil, rent(al)
rentuble, rent(able)
rentul, rent(al)
renu, renew
renuable, renew(able)
renuel, renew(al)
renugade, renegade
renuil, renew(al)
renumerate, remunerate
renumeration, remunerate(tion)
renusanse, renaissance
renussance, renaissance
renuvadid, renovate(d)
renuvashen, renovate(tion)
renuvate, renovate
renuvation, renovate(tion)
reol, real /reel
reolistic, real(istic)
reoltee, realty
reolty, realty
reostat, rheostat
rep, rip /ripe /reep
repair,*,red,ring,rable,rer, *TO FIX/RESTORE TO A USABLE CONDITION*
repal, rebel /ripple
reparable, *ABLE TO BE REPAIRED*
reparashen, reparation
reparation,able,ative, *ABLE TO BE REPAIRED*
reparcushen, repercussion
repare, repair
reparkushen, repercussion
repateshen, repetition
repatishus, repetition(ous)
repatition, repetition
repatitious, repetition(ous)
repd, rip(pped) /reep(ed)

repeal,*,led,ling, *TO END/ABOLISH A LAW (or see repel or rappel)*
repeat,*,ted,ting,ter,tedly,table,tability, *TO SAY/DO/HAPPEN AGAIN, MORE THAN ONCE*
reped, rip(pped) /reep(ed)
repedatif, repetitive
repededly, repeat(edly)
repedutif, repetitive
repeel, repeal
repeet, repeat
repel,*,lled,lling,ller,llency, *TO KEEP SOMETHING AWAY/OFF OF, REJECTS/RESISTS (or see rappel/ repeal/ ripple)*
repelent, repellent
repelinsy, repellent(ncy)
repellent,*,tly,ncy, *REJECT/RESIST, KEEP OFF OF*
repellinsy, repellent(ncy)
repense, repent(s)
repent,*,ted,ting,tance,tant,ter, *TO REALIZE/ REMEDY WRONGDOING*
repentinse, repent(ance)
reperable, reparable
reperashen, reparation
reperation, reparation
repercushen, repercussion
repercussion,*,ive, *THE EFFECTS/DEVELOPMENT ACHIEVED/RESULTING FROM AN ACTION*
reperkushen, repercussion
reperkution, repercussion
repertoire,*, *LIST OF DRAMAS/PERFORMANCES/ TALENTS/AVAILABLE RESOURCES*
repertwa, repertoire
repertwor, repertoire
repete, repeat
repetedly, repeat(edly)
repetishen, repetition
repetishus, repetition(ous)
repetition,*,ous,ously,ousness, *REPEAT/SAY/DO SOMETHING OVER AND OVER, ROUTINE*

repetitive, ely, eness, *REPEAT OVER AND OVER*
repetitous , repetition(ous)
reputashen , repute(tation)
reputation , repute(tation)
repeutuble , repute(table)
rephund , refund
repil , rebel /ripple
repint , repent
repintense , repent(ance)
repirable , reparable
repirashen , reparation
repiration , reparation
repircushen , repercussion
repirkushon , repercussion
repirtoire , repertoire
repirtwor , repertoire
repitishen , repetition
repitishus , repetition(ous)
repitition , repetition
repititious , repetition(ous)
repl , repel /ripple /rebel
replace, *, ed, cing, ement, eable, er, *TO PUT SOMETHING IN PLACE OF SOMETHING ELSE*
replacment , replace(ment)
replakation , replica(tion)
replasmint , replace(ment)
reple , rebel or ripple
repleca , replica
replecation , replica(tion)
repleka , replica
replekate , replica(te)
replenish, hes, hed, hing, her, hment, *TO RESTOCK/ REFILL*
repleneshment , replenish(ment)
replica, *, ate, ated, ating, ation, *TO MAKE AN EXACT COPY OF*
replika , replica

replikate , replica(te)
replucation , replica(tion)
repluka , replica
replukate , replica(te)
replukation , replica(tion)
reply, lies, lied, lying, lier, *TO ANSWER BACK/RESPOND*
repoflavin , riboflavin
repoire , rapport
repol , rebel /ripple
repor , rapport
reporashen , reparation
reporation , reparation
reporder , report(er)
reporkushen , repercussion
report, *, ted, tedly, ting, ter, table, tage, torial, torially, *GIVE ACCOUNT OF AN EVENT/OCCURRENCE*
repository, ries, *A PLACE/SHELTER/DWELLING WHICH STORES/PRESERVES/ SAFEKEEPS*
reposutory , repository
reposteshen , repetition
repour , rapport
repozitory , repository
reprable , reparable
repraduction , reproduce(ction)
repradukshen , reproduce(ction)
repraduse , reproduce
repramand , reprimand
reprasent , represent
reprazintation , represent(ation)
repreble , reparable
repreduction , reproduce(ction)
repremand , reprimand
represent, *, ted, ting, table, ter, tation, tational, tationalism, tative, tatively, tativeness, *TO ACT ON BEHALF OF SOMEONE/SOMETHING ELSE*
represhin , repress(ion)
represif , repress(ive)
represion , repress(ion)
represive , repress(ive)

repress, sses, ssed, ssing, ssion, sser, *TO PREVENT/ SUPPRESS/BLOCK NATURAL EXPRESSION (or see oppress)*
represuve , repress(ive)
reprible , reparable
reprimand, *, ded, ding, *TO BE REPRESSED/ REPROVED/FORMALLY REBUKED*
reprisent , represent
reprkushen , repercussion
reproach, hes, hed, hing, hingly, hable, hableness, hably, her, *BLAMED/CRITICIZED FOR WRONGDOING*
reproch , reproach
reprochuble , reproach(able)
reproduce, *, ed, cing, cible, cibility, er, ction, ctive, ctively, ctiveness, ctivity, *PRODUCE ANEW, DUPLICATE/REPEAT/REMEMBER*
reprodukshen , reproduce(ction)
reproduse , reproduce
repruble , reparable
repruction , reproduce(ction)
reprudukshen , reproduce(ction)
reprumand , reprimand
reprusent , represent
repruzentation , represent(ation)
rept , reap(ed)/rip(pped) /reep(ed)
repteleun , reptile(lian)
reptile, *, lian, *COLD BLOODED VERTEBRATE*
reptilein , reptile(lian)
reptishus , repetition(ous)
republek , republic
republekin , republic(an)
republic, *, can, *A TYPE OF POLITICAL SYSTEM*
republikan , republic(an)
repugnant, tly, nce, ncy, *STRONG OPPOSITION/ DISLIKE/AVERSION*
repugnense , repugnant(nce)
repugnent , repugnant
repul , ripple / rebel
repuld , ripple(d)

repulse,*,ed,sing,sion,sive,sively,siveness, *REPEL/AVERT/REBUFF/FORBID*
repulshen, repulse(ion)
repulsif, repulse(sive)
repult, ripple(d)
repurable, reparable
repurashen, reparation
repuration, reparation
repurcushen, repercussion
repurkution, repercussion
repurtoire, repertoire
repurtwa, repertoire
repurtwor, repertoire
reputashen, repute(tation)
repute,ed,edly,table,tably,tability,tation, *TYPE OF CHARACTER*
reputeshen, repetition
reputishus, repetition(ous)
reputition, repetition
reputitious, repetition(ous)
reqrute, recruit
reqest,*,ted,ting, *ASK/PETITION/SOLICIT FOR*
require,*,ed,ring,ement, *ESSENTIAL/ NECESSARY*
requisite,*,ely,eness, *REQUIRED/ NECESSARY*
requpe, recoup
reqwasit, requisite
reqwest, request
reqwire, require
reqwirement, require(ment)
rer, rear /rare
rerd, rear(ed)
rere, weary
reridy, rare(rity)
rerity, rare(rity)
resadenshul, reside(ntial)
resadensy, reside(ncy)
resadential, reside(ntial)
resadinshul, reside(ntial)
resadinsy, reside(ncy)

resadue, residue
resal, wrestle
resalushen, resolute(tion)
resan, reason /resin /rise(n)
resanate, resonate
resandly, recent(ly)
resanense, resonance
resanent, resonance(nt)
resaninse, resonance
resanuble, reason(able)
resape, recipe
resarektion, resurrect(ion)
resatashen, recite(tion)
rescue,*,ed,uing,er, *TO SAVE/SPARE FROM DANGER/HARM*
resdrane, restrain
research,hes,hed,hing,her, *TO STUDY/OBSERVE/ DERIVE FOR FACTS*
resebshen, reception
resebshinist, receptionist
resebter, receptor
resebtif, receptive
resebtive, receptive
resede, recede
reseded, recede(d)
resedenshul, reside(ntial)
resedinse, residence(cy)
resedential, reside(ntial)
resedue, residue
reseed, recede
reseef, receive
reseet, receipt
reseeve, receive
resefe, receive
resefuble, receive(vable)
resegnation, resign(ation)
reselute, resolute
resemble,*,ed,ling,lance,lant, *SIMILAR/LIKENESS*
resemblinse, resemble(lance)

resen, reason/ resin/ rise(n)
resenate, resonate
resenation, resonate(tion)
resenator, resonate(tor)
resendly, recent(ly)
reseninse, resonance
resent,*,ted,ting,tful,tfulness,tment, *FEEL SORRY FOR ONESELF, DOESN'T FEEL APPRECIA- TED FOR A DEED DONE (or see recent)*
resenuble, reason(able)
resepdekle, receptacle
resepe, recipe
resepunt, recipient
reseprocal, reciprocal
reseprocation, reciprocate(tion)
reseprokashen, reciprocate(tion)
resepshen, reception
resepshenist, receptionist
resepshun, reception
reseptacle, receptacle
reseptcle, receptacle
reseptif, receptive
reseption, reception
reseptionest, receptionist
reseptive, receptive
reseptor, receptor
reseptukle, receptacle
reserch, research
reserect, resurrect
reserection, resurrect(ion)
reserf, reserve
reserfd, reserve(d)
reserginse, resurgent(nce)
resergint, resurgent
reserve,*,ed,ving,edly,edness,vist, *TO HAVE EXTRA/TO SPARE/STORED UP*
reservoir,*, *WHERE WATER IS COLLECTED/STORED*
reservor, reservoir
reses, recess

respiration,*,nal,tor,tory, INHALE/EXHALE OF THE
BREATH IN PLANTS/ANIMALS
respite,ed,ting, REST/RELIEF FROM LABOR/
SUFFERING/FEAR
respond,*,ded,ding,dent,der, TO ANSWER/REPLY/
CORRESPOND
respondint, respond(ent)
response,*,sibility,sibilities,sible,sibleness,
sibly,sive,sively,siveness, TO ANSWER/
REPLY/CORRESPOND
responsef, response(sive)
responsive, response(sive)
responsuble, response(sible)
respont, respond
respurashen, respiration
respurater, respiration(tor)
respuration, respiration
resque, rescue
resqwu, rescue
resrektion, resurrect(ion)
rest,*,ted,ting,tful,tfully,tfulness, TIME/TRANQUIL-
ITY/PEACE BETWEEN MOMENTS OF MENTAL/
PHYSICAL EXERTION (or see wrest or wrist)
restaraunt, restaurant
restaront, restaurant
restatushen, restitution
restatution, restitution
restatutive, restitution(ive)
restaurant,*, A PUBLIC EATERY
restauront, restaurant
resterashen, restore(ration)
resteration, restore(ration)
restetushen, restitution
restetution, restitutions
restfuly, rest(fully)
restid, rest(ed) /wrest(ed)
restirashen, restore(ration)
restiration, restore(ration)
restitushen, restitution

restitution,*, COMPENSATING/GIVING BACK
FOR A LOSS
restorashen, restore(ration)
restore,*,ed,ring,er,ration,rative, TO REFURBISH/
RECONSTRUCT BACK TO NEAR ORIGINAL
restrain,*,ned,ning,nt,nable, STOP/CONTROL
SOMETHING/SOMEONE FROM DOING SOMETHING
restrane, restrain
restrant, restaurant /restrain(t)
restrektif, restrict(ive)
restrict,*,ted,ting,tion,tive, TO CONTROL/LIMIT
THE FLOW OF
restrikshen, restrict(ion)
restrikt, restrict
restriktion, restrict(ion)
restriktive, restrict(ive)
restront, restaurant
resturashen, restore(ration)
resturation, restore(ration)
restutushen, restitution
restutution, restitution
resucitate, resuscitate
resudenshul, reside(ntial)
resudensy, reside(ncy)
resudent, resident
resudential, reside(ntial)
resudinshul, reside(ntial)
resudinsy, reside(ncy)
resudue, residue
resudy, residue
resugnashin, resign(ation)
resugnation, resign(ation)
resul, wrestle
result,*,ted,ting,tant, THE OUTCOME/REACTION/
CONDITION OF AN ACTION
resulushin, resolute(tion)
resulute, resolute
resuma, resume
resume,*, resume',*, CONTINUE/CARRY ON, A
SUMMARY OF SOMEONE'S WORK HISTORY

resun, reason /resin /rise(n)
resunate, resonate
resunation, resonate(tion)
resunator, resonate(tor)
resundly, recent(ly)
resunense, resonance
resunent, resonance(nt)
resuninse, resonance
resuntly, recent(ly)
resunuble, reason(able)
resupe, recipe
resurch, research
resurect, resurrect
resurection, resurrect(ion)
resurfs, reserve(s)
resurgense, resurgent(nce)
resurgent,*,nce, TO RISE UP/STRENGTHEN AGAIN
resurginse, resurgent(nce)
resurgint, resurgent
resurrect,*,ted,ting,tion,tional,tionist,tionism,
RAISE FROM THE DEAD, TO REINSTATE/RESTORE
resurvd, reserve(d)
resurve, reserve
resurvor, reservoir
resusatashen, resuscitate(tion)
resusatator, resuscitate(tor)
resuscitate,*,ed,ting,tion,tive,tor, TO RESTORE
LIFE/BREATHING AGAIN
resuscitator, resuscitate
resusitator, resuscitate(tor)
ret, red / read
retabul, read(able)
retail,*,led,ling,ler, SALE OF GOODS IN SMALL
QUANTITIES TO CONSUMERS
retain,*,ned,ner,nable,nability,nment, TO
CONTINUE/HOLD/KEEP IN POSSESSION
retal, retail
retaleashen, retaliate(tion)
retaleate, retaliate

retaleation, retaliate(tion)
retaler, retail(er)
retaliate,*,ed,ting,tion, *TO RETURN A PUNISHMENT/*
    DELIBERATE HARM IN REVENGE
retan, retain
retaner, retain(er)
retanse, rid(ddance)
retard,*,ded,ding,dant,dation,date,der,
    DEVELOPMENT/GROWTH IS SLOWED DOWN/
    CURBED/DELAYED
retardashen, retard(ation)
retardat, retard(ate)
retardint, retard(ant)
retardir, retard(er)
retardunt, retard(ant)
retaric, rhetoric
retasense, reticent(nce)
retasent, reticent
retashin, rotate(tion)
retasint, reticent
retch, rich /wretch
reted, ready(died) /read
retee, ready
retenshun, retention
retentif, retention(ive)
retention,ive,ivity,ivities, *TO HOLD/MAINTAIN/*
    REMEMBER
retentive, retention(ive)
reter, red(dder) /read(er)
retern, return
reternd, return(ed)
reth, wreath
rethem, rhythm
rethum, rhythm
reti, ready
reticent,nce,ncy,tly, *RESERVED/APPREHENSIVE IN*
    SPEAKING FREELY
reticint, reticent
retina,*,al,nitis, *ASSOCIATED WITH THE EYE*

retinse, rid(ddance)
retinshun, retention
retintion, retention
retir, read(er) /retire
retire,*,ed,ring,ringly,ringness,rement, *REMOVE/*
    RETREAT/WITHDRAW FROM SOME FORM OF
    ACTIVITY/ CIRCULATION/WORK
retirec, rhetoric
retirment, retire(ment)
retirn, return
retirndt, return(ed)
retisense, reticent(nce)
retisent, reticent
retisint, reticent
retna, retina
retnu, retina
retor, read(er)
retorec, rhetoric
retoric, rhetoric
retorical, rhetoric(al)
retract,*,ted,ting,tion,tability,table,tation,
    WITHDRAW/REMOVE/TAKE BACK
retraction, retract(ion)
retrakshen, retract(ion)
retrakted, retract(ed)
retrefe, retrieve
retrefer, retrieve(r)
retreful, retrieve(val)
retrevul, retrieve(val)
retrevur, retrieve(r)
retrieve,*,ed,ving,val,er, *RESTORE/REMEDY/SAVE/*
    GET SOMETHING BACK, A TYPE OF DOG
retro, *PREFIX INDICATING "BACKWARDS" MOST OFTEN*
    MODIFIES THE WORD
retroactif, retroactive
retroactive,ely, *EFFECTIVE PRESENTLY BACK TO SOME*
    POINT IN THE PAST
retroaktif, retroactive
retroaktive, retroactive

retrograde,*,ed,ding,dation,ely, *MOVING*
    CONTRARY/BACKWARDS/REVERSE/INVERSE
retrogratashen, retrograde(dation)
retrogreat, retrograde
retrosbekt, retrospect
retrospect,tion, *RECOLLECTION/REVIEW OF THE PAST*
retrospekt, retrospect
retrospektion, retrospect(ion)
retsee, ritzy
retsy, ritzy
retual, ritual
retubil, read(able)
retuble, read(able)
retul, riddle
retur, red(dder) /read(er)
returec, rhetoric
returic, rhetoric
return,*,ned,ning, *TO GO BACK TO PLACE OF*
    ORIGINATION/BEGINNING/THE MOMENT
returndt, return(ed)
retusense, reticent(nce)
retusent, reticent
retusint, reticent
rety, ready
retzy, ritzy
reul, real /reel
reuldee, realty
reuldy, realty
reulestic, real(istic)
reulistic, real(istic)
reulty, realty
reum, realm
reunacment, reenact(ment)
reunactment, reenact(ment)
reunakt, reenact
reunaktment, reenact(ment)
reunforse, reinforce
reunforsment, reinforce(ment)
reunion,*,, *GATHERING, COMING TOGETHER*

reunyun, reunion
reustat, rheostat
reval, revel
revalation, revelation
revalee, reveille
revaler, revel(er)
revalve, revolve
revaly, reveille
revar, river
reveal,*,,led,ling,ler,lingly, *EXPOSE/MAKE KNOWN/ UNCOVER, BE FRANK* (or see revel)
reveelt, reveal(ed)
reveer, revere
reveille,*,, *MILITARY WAKE-UP CALL/SIGNAL*
revejen, revise(sion)
revel,*,,lled,lling,ler, *PLEASURE/ENJOYMENT IN SOMETHING* (or see reveal)
revelashen, revelation
revelation,*,,nal,tory, *A SUDDEN REALIZATION/ UNDERSTANDING OF VALUABLE/SURPRISING INFORMATION*
reveld, revel(lled) /reveal(ed)
revelee, reveille
revelir, revel(er)
revelly, reveille
revench, revenge
revene, ravine
revenge,eful,efully,er, *TO BE RETALIATORY/HARMFUL WITH INTENT*
revengful, revenge(ful)
rever, revere /river
reverberate,*,,ed,ting,ant,tion,tive,tor, *AN ECHO, REFLECTION OF WAVES OFF A SURFACE*
reverbirate, reverberate
revere,*,,ed,ring, *DEEPLY ADMIRE/RESPECT SOMEONE*
reverse,*,,ed,sing,sal,sely,er,sible,sibility,sibly, *CHANGE TO OPPOSITE, INSIDE OUT/BACKWARD*
reversuble, reverse(sible)

revert,*,,ted,ting,ter,tible, *GO BACK TO PREVIOUS/ FORMER/ORIGINAL*
reveshen, revise(sion)
revesion, revise(sion)
revew, review /revue
review,*,,wed,wing,wable,wer, *EXAMINE/INSPECT/ CRITIQUE/SURVEY/ASSESS* (or see revue)
revigen, revise(sion)
revil, revel /reveal
revilashen, revelation
revilation, revelation
revild, revel(lled)
revilee, reveille
reviler, revel(er)
revily, reveille
revinch, revenge
revine, ravine
revingful, revenge(ful)
revir, river
revirbarate, reverberate
revirberate, reverberate
revirse, reverse
revirsuble, reverse(sible)
revirt, revert
revise,*,,ed,sing,sion,sable,er,sory, *ADJUST/ UPDATE/ALTER/IMPROVE*
revishen, revise(sion)
revision, revise(sion)
revival,*,, *RENEWAL/RECOVERY/REESTABLISHMENT OF FLOURISH/VIGOROUS AGAIN*
revive,*,,ed,ving,vable,er, *BECOME CONSCIOUSE/ RELIVE, REVIVAL*
revivle, revival
revivuble, revive(vable)
revlashen, revelation
revocable,bility,ly,, *ABILITY TO BE CANCELLED/ CALLED BACK IN*
revokability, revocable(bility)
revokable, revocable

revoke,*,,ed,king,er, *MAKE NULL AND VOID, CANCEL, SUMMON SOMEONE/SOMETHING BACK*
revol, revel
revolashen, revelation
revolation, revelation
revold, revolt /revel(lled)
revolee, reveille
revolfe, revolve
revolt,*,,ted,ting, *REBEL/DEFY AUTHORITY, REPULSED*
revoltid, revolt(ed)
revolve,*,,ed,ving,er,vable, *CIRCULAR MOVEMENT/ RECURRING, A TYPE OF GUN*
revue,*,, *MUSICAL EVENT* (or see review)
revul, revel
revulashen, revelation
revulation, revelation
revuled, revel(lled)
revulee, reveille
revuler, revel(er)
revuly, reveille
revur, river
revurbarate, reverberate
revurse, reverse
revursuble, reverse(sible)
revurt, revert
rew, rue /roux
reward,*,,ded,ding, *SOMETHING RECEIVED FOR HAVING DONE SOMETHING COMMENDABLE*
rewbe, ruby
rewd, rude
rewdest, rude(st)
rewf, roof
rewge, rouge
rewje, rouge
rewl, rule
rewlet, roulette
rewm, room
rewmer, rumor
rewmur, rumor

reword, reward
rewral, rural
rewralee, rural(lly)
rewrul, rural
rewrulee, rural(lly)
rewsdir, rooster
rewsdur, rooster
rewse, ruse
rewstur, rooster
rewt, route /root /rude
rewteen, routine
rewthles, ruthless
rewtlee, rude(ly)
reyewnyin, reunion
reyunyon, reunion
rezadenshul, reside(ntial)
rezadensy, reside(ncy)
rezadinsy, reside(ncy)
rezadue, residue
rezalushen, resolute(tion)
rezalute, resolute
rezalution, resolute(tion)
rezan, reason/ resin/ rise(n)
rezand, recent
rezandly, recent(ly)
rezanense, resonance
rezanent, resonance(nt)
rezant, recent
rezanuble, reason(able)
rezarection, resurrect(ion)
rezarektion, resurrect(ion)
rezedue, residue
rezegnation, resign(ation)
rezelute, resolute
rezen, reason/ resin/ rise(n)
rezenator, resonate(tor)
rezend, recent
rezendly, recent(ly)
rezent, recent /resent

rezenuble, reason(able)
rezerf, reserve
rezervor, reservoir
rezide, reside
rezidensy, reside(ncy)
rezidinsy, reside(ncy)
rezidual, residue(ual)
rezidue, residue
rezignashin, resign(ation)
rezilute, resolute
rezin, reason /resin /rise(n)
rezinator, resonate(tor)
rezind, recent
rezindly, recent(ly)
rezine, resign
rezinent, resonance(nt)
rezint, recent /resent
rezinuble, reason(able)
rezirvor, reservoir
rezist, resist
rezistense, resist(ance)
rezistent, resist(ant)
rezistif, resist(ive)
rezistor, resist(or)
reznuble, reason(able)
rezodo, risotto
rezolushin, resolute(tion)
rezolve, resolve
rezom, resume
rezon, reason /resin /rise(n)
rezonate, resonate
rezondly, recent(ly)
rezonense, resonance
rezontle, recent(ly)
rezoom, resume
rezort, resort
rezorvor, reservoir
rezoto, risotto
rezrekshen, resurrect(ion)

rezt, rest /wrist /wrest
rezudensy, reside(ncy)
rezudinsy, reside(ncy)
rezudue, residue
rezult, result
rezultent, result(ant)
rezultunt, result(ant)
rezulushen, resolute(tion)
rezulute, resolute
rezulution, resolute(tion)
rezuma, resume'
rezume, resume
rezun, reason /resin /rise(n)
rezunate, resonate
rezunation, resonate(tion)
rezund, recent
rezundly, recent(ly)
rezunense, resonance
rezunent, resonance(nt)
rezunt, recent
rezunuble, reason(able)
rezurection, resurrect(ion)
rezurekshen, resurrect(ion)
rezurf, reserve
rezurve, reserve
rezurvor, reservoir
rezuvor, reservoir
rhain, rain /reign /rein
rhanoceros, rhinoceros
rhanosirus, rhinoceros
rhapsady, rhapsody
rhapsedy, rhapsody
rhapsody, dies, *IRREGULAR/INTENSE IMPROVISATION*
IN REGARD TO MUSIC/EXPRESSION/LITERATURE
rhapsuty, rhapsody
rhatorecal, rhetoric(al)
rhatorical, rhetoric(al)
rhedaric, rhetoric
rheduric, rhetoric

rhein, rain /reign /rein
rheindeer, reindeer
rhen, rain /reign /rein
rhenoceros, rhinoceros
rhenosirus, rhinoceros
rheostat,*,tic, ELECTRONIC DEVICE
rhetarec, rhetoric
rheteric, rhetoric
rhethm, rhythm
rhethym, rhythm
rhetoric,*,cal,cally, THE ART OF SPEAKING/WRITING EFFECTIVELY/PERSUASIVELY
rheturec, rhetoric
rheumatic,*,cally,ism,toid,toidal,toidally, ASSO-CIATED WITH STIFF JOINTS/MUSCLES IN BODY
rhime, rhyme
rhinasurus, rhinoceros
rhinauserus, rhinoceros
rhinestone,*, FAKE GEMS
rhino,*, SHORT FOR RHINOCEROS
rhinoceros,ses, A MAMMAL/ANIMAL
rhinosurus, rhinoceros
rhinstone, rhinestone
rhisome, rhizome
rhithm, rhythm
rhithum, rhythm
rhitorecal, rhetoric(al)
rhitorical, rhetoric(al)
rhiz, rhizo, PREFIX INDICATING "ROOT" MOST OFTEN MODIFIES THE WORD
rhizome,*, TYPE OF PLANT ROOT
rhod, PREFIX INDICATING "RED" MOST OFTEN MODIFIES THE WORD
rhodadendron, rhododendron
rhodidendron, rhododendron
rhodo, PREFIX INDICATING "RED" MOST OFTEN MODIFIES THE WORD
rhododendron,*,rhododendrum,*, CAN BE SPELLED EITHER WAY, FLOWERING PLANT/BUSH

rhodudindron, rhododendron
rhotorical, rhetoric(al)
rhubarb, AN EDIBLE PLANT
rhunoceros, rhinoceros
rhunosirus, rhinoceros
rhutorecal, rhetoric(al)
rhutorical, rhetoric(al)
rhyme,*,ed,ming,er, PUT WORDS TOGETHER IN SPEECH WHICH SOUND LIKE EACH OTHER
rhysome, rhizome
rhythm,*,mic,mical,mically, A REPETITIOUS BEAT/FREQUENCY/PATTERN
rhyzome, rhizome
ri, rye /wry
rib,*,bbed,bbing, BONES IN TORSO (TOO MANY DEFI-NITIONS, PLEASE SEE STANDARD DICTIONARY)
ribaflavin, riboflavin
riban, ribbon
ribbin, ribbon
ribbon,*,ny, THIN STRIP OF SOMETHING, A DECORATION USED AS AN AWARD
ribbun, ribbon
ribeled, rebel(lled)
ribeleon, rebel(llion)
ribeleus, rebel(llious)
riben, ribbon
ribin, ribbon
riblase, replace
riblie, reply
ribodek, robot(ic)
riboflavin,*, A CHEMICAL COMPOUND/VITAMIN
ribon, ribbon /rib(bbing)
ribt, rib(bbed) /rip(pped)
ribullican, republic(an)
ribun, ribbon /rib(bbing)
ributle, rebut(ttal)
ricachet, ricochet
ricashay, ricochet
rice, A GRAIN (or see rise)

riced, recede
ricepter, receptor
rich,hes,her,hest,hly, ABUNDANT/PLENTIFUL/FERTILE/PRODUCTIVE
richewul, ritual
richuol, ritual
ricipient, recipient
rickets, VITAMIN DEFICIENCY DISEASE
rickety, UNSTABLE CONDITION
rickidy, rickety
rickits, rickets
rickity, rickety
rickliner, recline(r)
rickonusinse, reconnaissance
riclusion, recluse(sion)
ricochet,*,ted,ting, THE ACTION OF REBOUNDING/ BOUNCING OFF AN OBJECT
riconstitushen, reconstitute(tion)
riconstitute, reconstitute
ricoshay, ricochet
ricruter, recruit(er)
ricumbent, recumbent
ricushay, ricochet
rid,*,dded,dding,ddance, TO BE DISPOSED OF/DONE AWAY WITH (or see ride /red /read /right)
ridakeul, ridicule
ridakule, ridicule
ridal, riddle
ridanse, rid(ddance)
ridar, ride(r) /write(r)
riddle,*,ed,ling,er, PUZZLE OF WORDS
ride,*,ding,rode,er, TO BE CARRIED/MOVED ALONG IN/ON SOMETHING (or see write or right)
ridecule, ridicule
rideemible, redeem(able)
rideme, redeem
ridekule, ridicule
rideme, redeem
ridempshun, redemption
ridemtion, redemption

ridemuble, redeem(able)
ridense, rid(ddance)
ridents, rid(ddance)
ridge,*,ed, *RAISED AREA*
ridicule,*,ed,ling,er, *TO MAKE FUN OF*
ridikule, ridicule
ridinse, rid(ddance)
ridle, riddle
ridol, riddle
ridoose, reduce
riduction, reduce(ction)
ridukeul, ridicule
ridukshen, reduce(ction)
riduktion, reduce(ction)
ridul, riddle
ridundensy, redundant(ncy)
ridundent, redundant
ridundinsy, redundant(ncy)
ridundint, redundant
ridusable, reduce(cible)
riduse, reduce
rie, rye /wry
riel, rile
riestat, rheostat
riet, riot
rifal, rifle
rifar, river
rifeel, reveal
rifeelt, reveal(ed)
rifel, rival /rifle
rifenge, revenge
rifenje, revenge
rifer, river
riferbishment, refurbish(ment)
riferse, reverse
rifeusil, refuse(sal)
rifewsel, refuse(sal)
rifful, revival
rifl, rival /rifle

rifinable, refine(nable)
rifine, refine
rifinery, refine(ry)
rifinje, revenge
rifinment, refine(ment)
rifinury, refine(ry)
rifle,*, *A GUN, TO PILLAGE*
riflect, reflect
riflection, reflect(ion)
riflective, reflect(ive)
riflector, reflect(or)
riflekshen, reflect(ion)
riflekt, reflect
riflektif, reflect(ive)
riflektor, reflect(or)
rifletive, reflect(ive)
rifol, rifle
rifor, river
riformitory, reform(atory)
rifract, refract
rifractory, refract(ory)
rifrain, refrain
rifrakt, refract
rifraktory, refract(ory)
rifrane, refrain
rifresher, refresh(er)
rifreshment, refresh(ment)
rifrigerator, refrigerate(tor)
rift,*,ted,ting, *TO SLOWLY SPREAD APART, GROWING CHASM*
riful, rival /rifle
rifur, river
rifurbishment, refurbish(ment)
rifurse, reverse
rifusel, refuse(sal)
rig,*,gged,gging,gger, *ASSEMBLE DEVICES TOGETHER (TOO MANY DEFINITIONS, PLEASE SEE STANDARD DICTIONARY) (or see ridge)*
rigal, wriggle

rigaledy, regal(ity)
rigalia, regal(ia)
rigality, regal(ity)
rigard, regard
rigardless, regard(less)
rige, ridge
rigect, reject
riged, rigid
rigekshen, reject(ion)
rigekt, reject
rigektion, reject(ion)
riger, rigor
riget, rigid
right,*,ted,tness,teous,teously,teousness,tful, tfully,tfulness,tism,tist,tly, *TO BE CORRECT, SPECIFIC DIRECTION/ORIENTATION, OTHER SIDE OF LEFT (or see rite /write /wright /writ)*
rigid,dly,dness,dity,dizer,dify,ification, *STIFF/ UNYIELDING*
rigirs, rigor(s)
rigit, rigid
rigle, wriggle
rigol, wriggle
rigor,*,rous,rously, *CONDITIONS INVOLVING HARDSHIP/SEVERITY/TOUGH DEMANDS*
rigres, rigor(ous)
rigresif, regress(ive)
rigresive, regress(ive)
rigress, regress
rigret, regret
rigreted, regret(tted)
rigretful, regret(ful)
rigretfully, regret(fully)
rigrus, rigor(ous)
rigul, wriggle
rigurs, rigor(s)
rigurus, rigor(ous)
riji, ridge
rijed, rigid

rijekshen, reject(ion)
rijekt, reject
rijektion, reject(ion)
rijet, rigid
rijid, rigid
rijit, rigid
rikachet, ricochet
rikashay, ricochet
rikedy, rickety
rikerus, rigor(ous)
rikeshay, ricochet
rikete, rickety
rikets, rickets
rikidy, rickety
rikishay, ricochet
rikity, rickety
rikliner, recline(r)
riklinur, recline(r)
rikochet, ricochet
rikonasinse, reconnaissance
rikonstitute, reconstitute
rikonusins, reconnaissance
rikord, record
rikorder, record(er)
rikrute, recruit
rikruter, recruit(er)
rikumbent, recumbent
rikurus, rigor(ous)
rikwest, request
rikwire, require
rikwirment, require(ment)
ril, real /reel /rile /rill
rilaks, relax
rilax, relax
rile,*,ed,ling, *TO PROVOKE INTO ACTION* (or see rill)
rilef, relief
rilegeon, religion
rilegon, religion
rilegous, religion(ous)

rilenquish, relinquish
rilese, release
rilevar, relieve(r)
rileve, relieve
rilevir, relieve(r)
rili, rely
riliaple, rely(liable)
rilients, reliance
riligen, religion
riliubility, rely(liability)
riliuble, rely(liable)
riliunse, reliance
riliunt, reliance(nt)
rill,*, *NARROW VALLEY/CHANNEL* (or see real/reel/rile)
rilly, real(lly)
riluctanse, reluctant(nce)
riluctant, reluctant
riluktense, reluctant(nce)
riluktint, reluctant
rily, real(lly) /rely
rim,*,mmed,mming,*CURVED/CIRCULAR OUTER EDGE*
rimadik, rheumatic
rimander, remain(der)
rimane, remain /romaine
rimanis, reminisce
rimanisent, reminisce(nt)
rimantek, romantic
rimantisize, romantic(ize)
rimark, remark
rimarkible, remark(able)
rimarkt, remark(ed)
rimarkuble, remark(able)
rimatik, rheumatic
rimaty, remedy
rimbunctious, rambuctious
rimbunkshes, rambuctious
rime, rhyme
rimedeul, remedy(dial)

rimedial, remedy(dial)
rimediashen, remedy(diation)
rimediation, remedy(diation)
rimembranse, remember(ance)
rimembur, remember
rimenis, reminisce
rimenisent, reminisce(nt)
rimet, remit
rimeted, remit(tted)
rimetuble, remit(table)
rimety, remedy
rimidy, remedy
rimind, remind
rimindur, remind(er)
rimintur, remind(er)
rimishen, remission
rimission, remission
rimit, remit
rimital, remit(ttal)
rimition, remission
rimity, remedy
rimnent, remnant
rimnet, remnant
rimnint, remnant
rimofer, remove(r)
rimonis, reminisce
rimonisent, reminisce(nt)
rimorse, remorse
rimorsful, remorse(ful)
rimorsless, remorse(less)
rimote, remote
rimotly, remote(ly)
rimover, remove(r)
rimudy, remedy
rimufel, remove(val)
rimufer, remove(r)
rimufible, remove(vable)
rimunerashen, remunerate(tion)
rimunerate, remunerate

rimunirate, remunerate
rimuniration, remunerate(tion)
rimunis, reminisce
rimunisent, reminisce(nt)
rimuty, remedy
rimuvable, remove(vable)
rin, wren
rinagade, renegade
rinasonse, renaissance
rinasonts, renaissance
rinasurus, rhinoceros
rinauserus, rhinoceros
rinavashen, renovate(tion)
rinavate, renovate
rinavation, renovate(tion)
rinevate, renovate
rinevation, renovate(tion)
rinch, wrench
rind,*, *THE EXTERIOR COVERING/SKIN OF SOME*
    FRUIT/TREES/CHEESE
rinder, render
rindur, render
rinegade, renegade
rinege, renege
rinesonse, renaissance
rinestone, rhinestone
rinevashen, renovate(tion)
rinevate, renovate
rinevation, renovate(tion)
ring,*,ged,ging,ger,ger,rung, *A SOUND, ARTICLE OF*
    JEWELRY, CIRCULAR SHAPE (or see wring /rink)
ringur, ringer
rinige, renege
rink,*, *PLACE FOR SKATING* (or see ring)
rinkle, wrinkle
rinkul, wrinkle
rino, rhino
rinone, renown
rinoserus, rhinoceros
rinosonse, renaissance

rinosurus, rhinoceros
rinounce, renounce
rinouncement, renounce(ment)
rinovadid, renovate(d)
rinovashen, renovate(tion)
rinovate, renovate
rinovation, renovate(tion)
rinown, renown
rinownse, renounce
rinownsment, renounce(ment)
rinoz, rhino(s)
rinsd, rinse(d)
rinse,*, ed,sing,er, *TO WASH/CLEAN WITH A LIQUID*
rinoserus, rhinoceros
rinstone, rhinestone
rinsur, rinse(r)
rint, rind
rinter, render
rintible, rent(able)
rintuble, rent(able)
rinu, renew
rinuable, renew(able)
rinual, renew(al)
rinuel, renew(al)
rinugade, renegade
rinumerate, remunerate
rinusonts, renaissance
rinuvadid, renovate(d)
rinuvashen, renovate(tion)
rinuvate, renovate
rinztone, rhinestone
riol, rile
riostat, rheostat
riot,*,ted,ting,ter, *ANGRY CROWD/MOB OF PEOPLE*
    WHO MAY OR MAY NOT BE VIOLENT
rip,*,pped,pping,pper, *TO TEAR/SLICE SOMETHING*
    OPEN/APART (or see ripe)
ripaflavin, riboflavin
ripair, repair

ripal, ripple
ripar, repair
ripd, rip(pped)
ripe,*,en,ened,er,est,ening,ely,eness, *FULLY*
    MATURE/PRIME IN DEVELOPMENT (or see rip)
ripeal, repeal
ripeat, repeat
riped, rip(pped)
ripededly, repeat(edly)
ripeel, repeal
ripeet, repeat
ripel, rappel /repeal /repel
ripelent, repellent
ripeleon, rebel(llion)
ripelinsy, repellent(ncy)
ripelint, repellent
ripellinsy, repellent(ncy)
ripend, ripe(ned)
ripenins, repent(ance)
ripense, repent(s)
ripent, repent
ripete, repeat
ripetedly, repeat(edly)
ripin, ripe(n) /rip(pping)
riplace, replace
riplacement, replace(ment)
riplase, replace
riplasmint, replace(ment)
riple, ripple
riplenesh, replenish
riplenish, replenish
riplenishment, replenish(ment)
riplid, reply(lied)
riplied, reply(lied)
riply, reply
ripnes, ripe(ness)
ripoflavin, riboflavin
ripoire, rapport
ripol, ripple

ripold, ripple(d)
ripon, ribbon /ripe(n)
ripor, rapport /rip(pper)
riporder, report(er)
riport, report
riporter, report(er)
ripository, repository
riposutory, repository
ripozitory, repository
ripple,*,ed,ling, *A SMALL WAVE*
ripreshen, repress(ion)
ripresif, repress(ive)
ripresion, repress(ion)
ripresive, repress(ive)
ripress, repress
ripresuve, repress(ive)
riproch, reproach
riprochuble, reproach(able)
ripublek, republic
ripublekan, republic(an)
ripublic, republic
ripublican, republic(an)
ripugnense, repugnant(nce)
ripugnent, repugnant
ripul, ripple /rebel
ripuld, ripple(d)
ripulse, repulse
ripulshen, repulse(ion)
ripulsif, repulse(sive)
ripulsion, repulse(ion)
ripult, ripple(d)
ripun, ripe(n)
ripund, ripe(ned)
ripunt, ripe(ned)
ripuplecan, republic(an)
ripuplican, republic(an)
ripur, ripe(r)
ripust, ripe(st)
riqrute, recruit

riquire, require
riquirment, require(ment)
riqwire, require
riqwirment, require(ment)
risdrane, restrain
rise,*,sing,en,er, *ASSOCIATED WITH UPWARDS/ MOVING UP/UPWARD BOUND* (or see rice)
riseat, receipt
risebtif, receptive
risebtive, receptive
riseed, recede
riseef, receive
riseet, receipt
risefe, receive
risemblanse, resemble(lance)
risentful, resent(ful)
risentment, resent(ment)
risepdekle, receptacle
risepdikul, receptacle
risepeant, recipient
risepeunt, recipient
risepshun, reception
riseptacle, receptacle
riseptef, receptive
riseptekle, receptacle
risepter, receptor
riseption, reception
riseptive, receptive
riseptukle, receptacle
riseshun, recess(ion)
risesif, recess(ive)
risesion, recess(ion)
risesive, recess(ive)
risession, recess(ion)
risestanse, resist(ance)
risestor, resist(or)
risete, receipt
risetion, recess(ion)
risevuble, receive(vable)

rishuel, ritual
riside, reside
risign, resign
risilyent, resilient
risipeunt, recipient
risir, rise(r)
risitle, recite(tal)
risitul, recite(tal)
risk,*,ked,king,ky, *TAKE A CHANCE/ GAMBLE*
riskt, risk(ed)
risodo, risotto
risolve, resolve
risolvuble, resolve(vable)
risome, rhizome
risor, rise(r)
risort, resort
risoto, risotto
risotto, *TYPE OF EDIBLE DISH/FOOD*
rispect, respect
rispectful, respect(ful)
rispective, respect(ive)
rispectuble, respect(able)
rispekt, respect
rispektful, respect(ful)
rispektive, respect(ive)
rispektuble, respect(able)
rispite, respite
rispond, respond
rispondent, respond(ent)
risponder, respond(er)
rispose, response
risponse, response
risponsive, response(sive)
risponsuble, response(sible)
rispont, respond
rist, wrist
ristore, restore
ristrain, restrain
ristraint, restrain(t)
ristrane, restrain

ristrant, restrain(t)
ristrikt, restrict
ristriktive, restrict(ive)
risuma, resume
risume, resume
risurs, rise(rs)
risusatator, resuscitate(tor)
risusetate, resuscitate
risusitashen, resuscitate(tion)
rit, rite /write /wright /writ /right /rid
ritacule, ridicule
ritainer, retain(er)
ritakeul, ridicule
ritakule, ridicule
rital, riddle
ritaleashen, retaliate(tion)
ritaleate, retaliate
ritaleation, retaliate(tion)
ritaliation, retaliate(tion)
ritane, retain
ritaner, retain(er)
ritanse, rid(ddance)
ritashen, rotate(tion)
ritch, rich
ritchly, rich(ly)
ritchuil, ritual

rite,*, A CEREMONY/OBSERVANCE (or see right/
    write/white/writ/wright)
ritense, rid(ddance)
ritenshun, retention
ritentif, retention(ive)
rith, writhe
rithem, rhythm
rithm, rhythm
rithum, rhythm
ritinshun, retention
ritire, retire
ritirment, retire(ment)
ritle, riddle

ritorical, rhetoric(al)
ritracted, retract(ed)
ritraction, retract(ion)
ritrakshen, retract(ion)
ritrakted, retract(ed)
ritrefe, retrieve
ritrefer, retrieve(r)
ritreful, retrieve(val)
ritreve, retrieve
ritrevul, retrieve(val)
ritrevur, retrieve(r)
ritsee, ritzy
ritsy, ritzy
ritual,*,lly,lism,list,listic,listically,lize,lization,
    CEREMONY
rituil, ritual
ritukeul, ridicule
ritul, riddle
ritzy,zier,ziest, SWANKY/ELEGANT
riul, rile
riunyen, reunion
riunyun, reunion
riuse, ruse
riut, riot
riuted, riot(ed)
riuter, riot(er)
rival,*,led,ling,lry,lries, COMPETITOR
rivalfe, revolve
rivalree, rival(ry)
rivalve, revolve
riveel, reveal
riveelt, reveal(ed)
riveer, revere
rivegen, revise(sion)
rivejen, revise(sion)
rivel, rival /arrival
rivench, revenge
rivenge, revenge
rivengful, revenge(ful)

rivenje, revenge
river,*, TRIBUTARY/CHANNEL OF WATER, SOMETHING
    FLOWING
riverberate, reverberate
rivere, revere
riverse, reverse
riversuble, reverse(sible)
rivert, revert
riview, review /revue
rivigen, revise(sion)
rivijen, revise(sion)
riving, revenge
rivingful, revenge(ful)
rivinje, revenge
rivirbarate, reverberate
rivirse, reverse
rivirt, revert
rivise, revise
rivishen, revise(sion)
rivision, revise(sion)
rivival, revival
rivive, revive
rivivuble, revive(vable)
rivivul, revive(val)
rivize, revise
rivlree, rival(ry)
rivocability, revocable(bility)
rivocable, revocable
rivokability, revocable(bility)
rivokable, revocable
rivoke, revoke
rivokt, revoke(d)
rivol, rival /arrival
rivolfe, revolve
rivolfer, revolve(r)
rivolree, rival(ry)
rivolt, revolt
rivolve, revolve
rivolver, revolve(r)

rivul, rival /arrival
rivulree, rival(ry)
rivurbarate, reverberate
rivurse, reverse
rivurt, revert
riward, reward
riword, reward
riyewnyen, reunion
riyunyun, reunion
rizalfe, resolve
rize, rise /rice
rizelyent, resilient
rizemblanse, resemble(lance)
rizemble, resemble
rizent, resent
rizentful, resent(ful)
rizentment, resent(ment)
rizer, rise(r)
rizid, reside
rizilyent, resilient
rizine, resign
rizist, resist
rizite, recite
rizodo, risotto
rizolve, resolve
rizolvuble, resolve(vable)
rizom, resume
rizome, rhizome
rizoom, resume
rizort, resort
rizoto, risotto
rizultent, result(ant)
rizultunt, result(ant)
rizum, resume
rizuma, resume'
rizume, resume /resume'
rizur, rise(r)
ro, row /raw
roach, es, *AN INSECT, BUTT END OF HERB CIGARETTE*

road,*,dy, *A PATH/PASSAGE/WIDE TRAIL TO TRAVEL ON (or see rode or wrote)*
roam,*,,med,ming,mer, *TO WANDER/MOVE ABOUT AIMLESSLY (or see room)*
roar,*,red,ring, *LOUD/DEEP SOUND/ EXPRESSION COMING FROM THE THROAT*
roast,*,ted,ting,ter, *TO SLOWLY COOK IN AN OVEN, BAKE WITHOUT A FLAME*
rob,*,bbed,bbing,bber, *TO STEAL, TAKE AWAY FROM WITHOUT PERMISSION (or see robe or rope)*
robd, rob(bbed) /rope(d)
robe,*,ed,bing, *A LONG/LOOSE/SLEEVED GARMENT (or see rob or rope)*
robed, robe(d) /rob(bbed)
robeled, rebel(lled)
robeleus, rebel(llious)
roben, robin /rob(bbing)
rober, rob(bber)
robin,*, , *A TYPE OF BIRD (or see rob(bbing))*
robodezashen, robot(ization)
robost, robust
robot,*,tic,tism,tize,tization, *A MACHINE WHICH WORKS FOR PEOPLE*
robotisashen, robot(ization)
robotizashen, robot(ization)
robt, rob(bbed) /rope(d) /robe(d)
robudezashin, robot(ization)
robun, robin /rob(bbing)
robushus, robust(ious)
robust,*,tly,tness,tious,tiously,tiousness, *FULL/ HEALTHY/STRONG*
robustus, robust(ious)
robutesation, robot(ization)
robuzd, robust
roch, roach
rocher, roger
roches, roach(es)
rochir, roger
rochur, roger

rock,*,ked,king,ker,ky, *A HARD MINERAL, A BACK AND FORTH MOTION*
rockateer, rocket(eer)
rocket,*,try,teer, *A FUELED CYLINDER WITH A POINTED TIP*
rod,*,dded,dding,dless, *A THIN ROUND/CYLINDRICAL STAFF/POLE/STICK SHAPE (or see rot/ road/ rode/ wrote)*
rodadendron, rhododendron
rodadindron, rhododendron
rodant, rodent
rodar, rotor
rodaree, rotary
rodary, rotary
rodatelir, rototiller
rodatilur, rototiller
rode, *PAST TENSE OF "RIDE" (or see road or wrote)*
rodedendron, rhododendron
rodedindron, rhododendron
rodent,*, , *A SMALL MAMMAL*
rodeo,*,oed,oing, *GAME IN ARENA USING HORSES/ COWS/ROPES*
roder, rotor
rodery, rotary
roditilur, rototiller
rodidendron, rhododendron
rodidindron, rhododendron
rodint, rodent
rodio, rodeo
rodir, rotor
roditelur, rototiller
rododendrem, rhododendron
rodotiler, rototiller
rodudindron, rhododendron
rodunt, rodent
rodur, rotor
roduree, rotary
rodury, rotary
rodutiler, rototiller

roeal, royal	rolik, rollick	romited, remit(tted)
roeul, royal	rolir, roll(er)	romition, remission
roeyul, royal	**roll**,*,lled,lling,ller, *A BREAD SHAPE, MOVES/GOES*	romituble, remit(ttable)
rof, rove /rough	*AROUND IN CIRCULAR FASHION* (or see role)	**romp**,*,ped,ping,per, *PLAYFULLY FROLIC/JUMP/*
rofeelt, reveal(ed)	**rollick**,*,ked,king, *TO PLAYFULLY ROLL/TUMBLE/*	*BOUNCE AROUND*
rofer, revere/ refer/ rove(r)	*JUMP/SKIP AROUND*	rompt, romp(ed)
roferse, reverse	rolor, roll(er)	roms, room(s) /roam(s)
rofeusil, refuse(sal)	rolres, walrus	romufel, remove(val)
rofiew, review / revue	rolrus, walrus	romufible, remove(vable)
rofiful, revival	rolur, roll(er)	romufil, remove(val)
rofir, rove(r) /rough(er)	rom, roam / oom	romunerate, remunerate
rofirst, reverse	romadik, rheumatic	romunirashen, remunerate(tion)
rofue, review /revue	**romaine**, *TYPE OF LETTUCE* (or see remain)	romunirate, remunerate
rofur, rove(r) /rough(er)	**romance**,*,ed,cing,er, *FANCIFUL/WHIMSICAL/*	romuvable, remove(vable)
rofurse, reverse	*EXTRAVAGANT EXPERIENCE WITH INFATUATION/*	romuver, remove(r)
rog, rogue /rouge	*LOVE BETWEEN TWO PEOPLE*	romy, room(y)
roger, *RADIO COMMUNICATION WHICH MEANS "OKAY",*	romane, romaine /remain	ronchee, raunchy
SOMEONE'S NAME	romanek, romantic	ronchy, raunchy
rogir, roger	romanse, romance	rondavous, rendezvous
rogue,*,uish,uishly,uishness,ery,eries,*SWINDLER/*	**romantic**,cally,cism,cist,cize,cization, *INVOLVES*	rondavu, rendezvous
TRICKY/DEVIANT BEHAVIOR (or see rouge)	*ROMANCE*	ronduvu, rendezvous
rogur, roger	romantisize, romantic(ize)	ronege, renege
roiel, royal	romark, remark	rong, wrong
roiul, royal	romatik, rheumatic	rongle, wrong(ly)
rojer, roger	romatoyd, rheumatic(toid)	ronige, renege
rojur, roger	romb, romp	ronk, wrong
rok, rock /rogue	rombed, romp(ed) / roam(ed)	ronouncement, renounce(ment)
rokateer, rocket(eer)	romediashen, remedy(diation)	ronounse, renounce
roket, rocket	romediation, remedy(diation)	ronownse, renounce
roketeer, rocket(eer)	romeshen, remission	ronownsment, renounce(ment)
rokut, rocket	rometeul, remedy(dial)	ronshy, raunchy
rokuteer, rocket(eer)	romidal, remit(ttal)	rontavu, rendezvous
rol, roll /role	romind, remind	rontchy, raunchy
rolar, roll(er)	romindur, remind(er)	rontivu, rendezvous
role,*, *A PART/CHARACTER IN A PLAY* (or see roll)	romintur, remind(er)	roobarb, rhubarb
roleck, rollick	romishen, remission	rood, rude /root
roled, roll(ed)	romision, remission	roodly, rude(ly)
rolek, rollick	romission, remission	rooen, ruin
roler, roll(er)	romital, remit(ttal)	rooenus, ruin(ous)

roof,*,fed,fing,fer, *THE TOP/COVER OF A DWELLING/ STRUCTURE*
rooin, ruin
rooinus, ruin(ous)
roold, rule(d)
rooler, rule(r)
roolet, roulette
roolir, rule(r)
roolt, rule(d)
roolur, rule(r)
room,*,med,ming,mer,ful,my,miness,mily, *A CUBICLE/SPACE/PLACE WITH WALLS WITHIN A LARGER DWELLING/STRUCTURE (or see roam)*
rooman, rumen
roomanu, rumina
roomatoyd, rheumatic(toid)
roomen, rumen
roomena, rumina
roomenate, rumina(te)
roomenator, rumina(tor)
roomin, rumen
roominate, rumina(te)
roominator, rumina(tor)
roomon, rumen
roon, rune
roonashen, ruin(ation)
roonation, ruin(ation)
roose, ruse
roost,*,ted,ting, *TO SIT ATOP OF SOMETHING TO REST/SLEEP, NORMALLY A PLACE WHERE BIRDS SLEEP (or see roast or rust)*
rooster,*, *A MALE CHICKEN*
root,*,ted,ting,tertage,tless,ty, *PART OF PLANT THAT'S UNDERGROUND*
rop, rope /rob
ropair, repair
ropare, repair
rope,*,ed,ping,er, *MANY STRANDS WOVEN TOGETHER INTO ONE (or see robe)*

ropeel, repeal
ropeet, repeat
ropel, rappel /repeal /repel
ropelinsy, repellent(ncy)
ropent, repent
ropete, repeat
roplenish, replenish
roposutory, repository
rore, roar
ros, rose /row(s)
rosaree, rosary
rosary,ries, *A STRAND OF BEADS WITH A CROSS ON IT*
rosdrane, restrain
rose,*,eate,eately,ette, *A FLOWER/COLOR, PAST TENSE FOR "RISE" (or see row(s))*
rosebshin, reception
rosebshinist, receptionist
rosebtif, receptive
rosefe, receive
rosefible, receive(vable)
rosen, rosin
rosepdekle, receptacle
rosepdikul, receptacle
rosepeunt, recipient
roseprikul, reciprocal
rosepshen, reception
rosepshenist, receptionist
roseptekle, receptacle
roseptif, receptive
roseptionest, receptionist
roseptive, receptive
roseree, rosary
roseshun, recess(ion)
rosesive, recess(ive)
rosetion, recess(ion)
roseve, receive
rosevuble, receive(vable)
rosin,*,ned,ny, *OIL FROM TURPENTINE*
rosipeant, recipient

rosipeint, recipient
rosiprekul, reciprocal
rosiree, rosary
rosodo, risotto
rosoto, risotto
rospective, respect(ive)
rospektif, respect(ive)
rost, roast
rostar, roster/roaster/rooster
roster,*, *LIST OF NAMES/EVENTS (or see roaster or rooster)*
rostir, roster /roaster /rooster
rostore, restore
rostrain, restrain
rostrane, restrain
rostrektif, restrict(ive)
rostrikshen, restrict(ion)
rostrikt, restrict
rostriktion, restrict(ion)
rostriktive, restrict(ive)
rostur, roster /roaster /rooster
rosun, rosin
rosuree, rosary
rot,*,tted,tting, *DETERIORATE/DISINTEGRATE (or see rod /rod /wrote /rote /wrought)*
rotade, rotate
rotaleation, retaliate(tion)
rotaliation, retaliate(tion)
rotan, rotten
rotaree, rotary
rotary,ries, *A SPINNING/ROTATION ON AN AXIS/HUB*
rotashen, rotate(tion)
rotashenul, rotate(tional)
rotashun, rotate(tion)
rotate,*,ed,ting,table,tably,tatory,tion,tional, tive,tor, *TAKE TURNS, REVOLVE/ALTERNATE*
rotatelur, rototiller
rotatiller, rototiller

rote, *REPETITION/OVER AND OVER* (or see wrote/rot/ road/rode)
roten, rotten
roteo, rodeo
roter, rotor
rotery, rotary
rotesaree, rotisserie
rotesuree, rotisserie
rotetiller, rototiller
rotin, rotten
rotio, rodeo
rotir, rotor /retire
rotiry, rotary
rotisaree, rotisserie
rotisserie, *, A FOOD COOKER
rotisuree, rotisserie
rotitelir, rototiller
rotor, *, TO DO WITH ROTATION/HUB
rototiler, rototiller
rototiller, *, MACHINE TO TILL GROUND
rotten, PAST TENSE FOR "ROT"
rotun, rotten
rotur, rotor
rotury, rotary
roudy, rowdy
rouf, rough
rouge, RED MAKE-UP FOR FACE (or see rogue)
rough, hen,her,hest,hly,hness,hage,hen,hish, *ABRASIVE/FIBROUS/UNREFINED/UNEVEN*
ruj, rouge
roulette, GAME WITH SPINNING DISK/BALL
rounation, ruin(ation)
round, *,ded,ding,der,dest,der,dish,dly,dness, *CIRCULAR SHAPE, AROUND, MAKE MORE EVEN/SMOOTH TO SHAPE*
rount, round
roust, TO WAKEN/AROUSE, FORCE TO ACTION
route, *,ed,ting,er, *SPECIFIC/PARTICULAR PATH/ NETWORK/LINES* (or see root)

routeen, routine
routine, *,ely,nize,nized,nizing, *PERFORM SPECIFIC FUNCTION ON CONTINUOUS BASIS*
routy, rowdy
roux, *A PASTE FOR SAUCE/GRAVY* (or see rue)
rovalfe, revolve
rove, *,ed,ving,er, *TO WANDER/MOVE AIMLESSLY SEEKING FOR SOMETHING*
roveel, reveal
roveelt, reveal(ed)
rovegen, revise(sion)
rovejen, revise(sion)
rovench, revenge
rovene, ravine
rovenge, revenge
rovengful, revenge(ful)
rovenjful, revenge(ful)
roverberate, reverberate
roverbirate, reverberate
rovere, revere
roverse, reverse
rovert, revert
roveshen, revise(sion)
rovesion, revise(sion)
roview, review / revue
rovigen, revise(sion)
rovijen, revise(sion)
rovinch, revenge
rovinjful, revenge(ful)
rovir, rove(r)
rovirbarate, reverberate
rovirberate, reverberate
rovirse, reverse
rovirsuble, reverse(sible)
rovirt, revert
rovise, revise
rovishen, revise(sion)
rovision, revise(sion)
rovival, revival

rovive, revive
rovivle, revival
rovivuble, revive(vable)
rovize, revise
rovocability, revocable(bility)
rovolfe, revolve
rovolfer, revolve(r)
rovolve, revolve
rovue, review / revue
rovur, rove(r)
rovurse, reverse
rovurt, revert
row, wed,wer,wing, *USE OF TWO OARS PADDLES/ ARMS/DEVICES TO NAVIGATE THROUGH WATER*
roward, reward
rowbot, robot
rowch, roach
rowdy, dier,diest, *TO TALK/BE LOUD/ROUGH*
rowmane, romaine
rowmanse, romance
rownd, round
rownt, round
roword, reward
rowp, rope
rowst, roust
rowtee, rowdy
rowty, rowdy
royal, lty,ties,lly,lism,list, *OF KINGS/QUEENS, A SOVEREIGN POWER/RIGHT*
royel, royal
royul, royal
roz, rose /row(s)
rozaree, rosary
roze, rose /row(s)
rozen, rosin
rozeree, rosary
rozin, rosin
roziree, rosary
rozodo, risotto

rozt, roast
rozter, roster
roztur, roster
rozun, rosin
rozuree, rosary
rub,*,bbed,bbing,bber, *TO USE MOTION/MASSAGE TO WORK AN AREA*
rubal, rubble
rubar, rubber
rubarb, rhubarb
rubash, rubbish
rubber,*,rize, *A MATERIAL DERIVED FROM PETROLEUM*
rubbish, *GARBAGE/TRASH, WORTH REJECTING/ ELIMINATING*
rubble, *ROCKS/DEBRIS LAYING AROUND*
rube, ruby
rubed, rub(bbed)
rubee, ruby
rubel, rubble
rubeled, rebel(lled)
rubelein, rebel(llion)
rubeleus, rebel(llious)
rubelyon, rebel(llion)
ruber, rubber
ruberize, rubber(ize)
rubesh, rubbish
rubil, rubble
rubir, rubber
rubirize, rubber(ize)
rubish, rubbish
rublase, replace
ruble, rubble
rublie, reply
rubodek, robot(ic)
rubodizashen, robot(ization)
ruborb, rhubarb
rubotek, robot(ic)
rubotiks, robot(ics)
rubt, rub(bbed)

rubul, rubble
rubur, rubber
ruby, ruby
ruby,bies, *A GEMSTONE*
rucede, recede
rucepter, receptor
ruch, rush
ruciprocation, reciprocate(tion)
ruck, rug
ruclaimuble, reclamable
rucumbent, recumbent
rudder,*,rless, *A BLADE ON A BOAT WHICH STEERS BEHAVIOR OR WORDS, UNREFINED/RAW*
rude,er,est,dly,eness, *TO OFFEND SOMEONE WITH BEHAVIOR OR WORDS, UNREFINED/RAW*
rudeemible, redeem(able)
rudeme, redeem
rudemption, redemption
rudemshen, redemption
ruder, rudder
rudir, rudder
rudist, rude(st)
rudur, rudder
ruduse, reduce
rudusible, reduce(cible)
rue,*, *AN HERB (or see roux)*
ruebarb, rhubarb
ruel, rule
ruelur, rule(r)
ruen, ruin
ruenashen, ruin(ation)
ruenation, ruin(ation)
ruenus, ruin(ous)
ruf, roof /rough /ruff
rufag, rough(age)
rufal, ruffle
rufeel, reveal
rufeelt, reveal(ed)
rufeer, revere
rufeg, rough(age)

rufej, rough(age)
rufel, ruffle
rufen, ravine /rough(en)
rufenge, revenge
rufenje, revenge
rufer, roof(er) /rough(er) /refer
rufere, revere /refer
ruferse, reverse /refer(s)
rufest, rough(est)
ruff,*,ffed, *ELABORATE COLLAR, CARD GAME TERM (or see rough or roof)*
ruffle,*,ed,ling, *TO MESS UP/DISTURB*
rufiew, review revue
rufiful, revival
rufig, rough(age)
rufij, rough(age)
rufil, ruffle
rufinable, refine(nable)
rufine, refine
rufinery, refine(ry)
rufinje, revenge
rufinment, refine(ment)
rufinuble, refine(nable)
rufinury, refine(ry)
rufir, rough(er) /roof(er) /refer
rufirse, reverse
rufist, rough(est)
rufle, ruffle
ruflection, reflect(ion)
ruflee, rough(ly)
ruflekshen, reflect(ion)
ruflekt, reflect
ruflektion, reflect(ion)
ruflektor, reflect(or)
rufly, rough(ly)
rufol, ruffle
rufor, rough(er) /roof(er) /refer
rufractory, refract(ory)
rufrain, refrain

rufraktory, refract(ory)
rufrane, refrain
rufregirant, refrigerate(ant)
rufregirator, refrigerate(tor)
rufresher, refresh(er)
rufreshment, refresh(ment)
rufrigerant, refrigerate(ant)
rufrigerator, refrigerate(tor)
rufs, roof(s) /ruff(s)
ruft, roof(ed) /rough(ed)
rufue, review /revue
ruful, ruffle
rufur, rough(er) /roof(er) /refer
rufurse, reverse
rufursuble, reverse(sible)
rufust, rough(est)
rug,*, NONATTACHED FLOOR COVERING
rugard, regard
ruge, rouge
ruged, rugged
rugged,dly,dness, ROUGH/COARSE/UNREFINED/
    IRREGULAR
rugit, rugged
rugresif, regress(ive)
rugresive, regress(ive)
rugret, regret
rugreted, regret(tted)
rugretful, regret(ful)
rugretfuly, regret(fully)
rugud, rugged
rugut, rugged
ruil, rule
ruin,*,ned,ning,nation,nous, BREAK/DESTROY,
    COMPLETE FAILURE/DECAY
ruje, rouge
ruk, rug /rook
ruklamuble, reclamable
rukliner, recline(r)
rukord, record

rukorder, record(er)
rukumbent, recumbent
rukwest, request
rukwire, require
rukwirment, require(ment)
rulaks, relax
rular, rule(r)
rulax, relax
ruld, rule(d)
rule,*,ed,ling,er, A LAW/COMMAND/ METHOD, PERIOD
    OF GOVERNING, DEVICE TO MEASURE
rulegis, religion(ous)
rulejis, religion(ous)
rulenquish, relinquish
rulentless, relentless
rulese, release
rulet, roulette
rulette, roulette
ruleve, relieve
rulever, relieve(r)
ruli, rely
ruliability, rely(liability)
rulianse, reliance
ruliense, reliance
ruligeon, religion
ruligous, religion(ous)
rulijes, religion(ous)
rulinkwish, relinquish
rulinqish, relinquish
rulintless, relentless
rulir, rule(r)
rulit, rule(d)
ruluktense, reluctant(nce)
ruluktint, reluctant
rulur, rule(r)
ruly, rely
rum,*,mmer,mmy, LIQUOR, UNUSUAL
rumach, rummage
rumadik, rheumatic

rumadoed, rheumatic(toid)
rumage, rummage
rumain, remain /romaine
rumaje, rummage
rumanater, rumina(tor)
rumander, remain(der)
rumane, remain /romaine
rumanek, romantic
rumantek, romantic
rumanticize, romantic(ize)
rumantisize, romantic(ize)
rumanu, rumina
rumar, rumor
rumared, rumor(ed)
rumark, remark
rumarkt, remark(ed)
rumarkuble, remark(able)
rumatezum, rheumatic(ism)
rumatik, rheumatic
rumatism, rheumatic(ism)
rumatizum, rheumatic(ism)
rumatoed, rheumatic(toid)
rumb, rump
rumbal, rumble
rumble,*,ed,ling,er,ly, DEEP/ROLLING SOUND, A
    FIGHT (or see rumple)
rumbul, rumble
rume, room
rumech, rummage
rumedeal, remedy(dial)
rumedge, rummage
rumedial, remedy(dial)
rumediashen, remedy(diation)
rumediation, remedy(diation)
rumedoed, rheumatic(toid)
rumege, rummage
rumeje, rummage
rumember, remember

rumen,*, STOMACH IN RUMINANT ANIMALS (many stomachs)
rumena, rumina
rumenate, rumina(te)
rumenator, rumina(tor)
rumer, rumor /room(er)
rumered, rumor(ed)
rumert, rumor(ed)
rumes, room(s)
rumeshen, remission
rumet, remit
rumetisem, rheumatic(ism)
rumetism, rheumatic(ism)
rumetoid, rheumatic(toid)
rumich, rummage
rumidal, remit(ttal)
rumidoed, rheumatic(toid)
rumige, rummage
rumije, rummage
rumina,al,ant,antly,ate,ation,ative,atively,ator, PERTAIN TO CHEWING OF CUD/MANY STOMACHS
rumind, remind
rumindur, remind(er)
rumintur, remind(er)
rumir, rumor /room(er)
rumired, rumor(ed)
rumishen, remission
rumission, remission
rumit, remit
rumitable, remit(ttable)
rumited, remit(tted)
rumitezum, rheumatic(ism)
rumition, remission
rumitizum, rheumatic(ism)
rumitoed, rheumatic(toid)
rumitoid, rheumatic(toid)
rummage,*,ed,ging, GO THROUGH/SEARCH/ RANSACK
rummige, rummage

rumofer, remove(r)
rumor,*,red, GOSSIP/HEARSAY/GENERAL TALK
rumorse, remorse
rumorsful, remorse(ful)
rumorsless, remorse(ful)
rumote, remote
rumotisem, rheumatic(ism)
rumotism, rheumatic(ism)
rumotly, remote(ly)
rumovable, remove(vable)
rumover, remove(r)
rump,*, REAR/TAIL END, BUTTOCKS
rums, room(s)
rumuch, rummage
rumufer, remove(r)
rumufible, remove(vable)
rumuge, rummage
rumun, rumen
rumunerashen, remunerate(tion)
rumunerate, remunerate
rumuneration, remunerate(tion)
rumunirashen, remunerate(tion)
rumunirate, remunerate
rumur, rumor
rumurt, rumor(ed)
rumutezim, rheumatic(ism)
rumutizem, rheumatic(ism)
rumy, room(y)
run,*,nning,nner,nny, TO MOVE AWAY QUICKLY USING LEGS, MOVING LIQUID (or see rune)
runar, run(nner)
rund, runt
rune,*,nic, SYMBOLS/ALPHABET (or see run/ruin/ run(nny))
runege, renege
runer, run(nner)
rung,*, PAST TENSE OF "RING", STEPS/LEVELS OF A LADDER, STEERING FOR SHIP (or see wrung)
runige, renege

runik, renege
runir, run(nner)
runone, renown
runoserus, rhinoceros
runosirus, rhinoceros
runounsment, renounce(ment)
runown, renown
runownse, renounce
runownsment, renounce(ment)
runre, run(nner)
runt,*,tier,tiest,tiness,ty, SMALLEST OF A GROUP/ LITTER/SPECIES
runumerate, remunerate
runur, run(nner)
rup, rip /ripe /rub
rupair, repair
rupal, rubble
rupare, repair
rupcher, rupture
rupchur, rupture
rupeal, repeal
rupeat, repeat
rupedidly, repeat(edly)
rupedutif, repetitive
rupee, ruby
rupeel, repeal
rupeet, repeat
rupel, rappel /repeal /repel /rubble
rupelein, rebel(llion)
rupelent, repellent
rupelinsy, repellent(ncy)
rupelint, repellent
rupense, repent(s)
rupent, repent
rupentinse, repent(ance)
ruper, rubber
rupesh, rubbish
rupete, repeat
rupetedly, repeat(edly)

ruversuble, reverse(sible)
ruvurt, revert
ruveshen, revise(sion)
ruvesion, revise(sion)
ruview, review / revue
ruvigen, revise(sion)
ruvijen, revise(sion)
ruvinch, revenge
ruvine, ravine
ruving, revenge
ruvingful, revenge(ful)
ruvinje, revenge
ruvinjful, revenge(ful)
ruvirbarate, reverberate
ruviberate, reverberate
ruvirse, reverse
ruvirsuble, reverse(sible)
ruvirt, revert
ruvise, revise
ruvishen, revise(sion)
ruvision, revise(sion)
ruvival, revival
ruvive, revive
ruvivle, revival
ruvivuble, revive(vable)
ruvize, revise
ruvocability, revocable(bility)
ruvocable, revocable
ruvokability, revocable(bility)
ruvokable, revocable
ruvoke, revoke
ruvokt, revoke(d)
ruvolfe, revolve
ruvolfer, revolve(r)
ruvolt, revolt
ruvoltid, revolt(ed)
ruvolve, revolve
ruvolver, revolve(r)
ruvue, review /revue

ruvurse, reverse
ruvurt, revert
ruward, reward
ruword, reward
ruwul, rural
ruzemblinse, resemble(lance)
ruzentful, resent(ful)
ruzentment, resent(ment)
ruzerved, reserve(d)
ruzestif, resist(ive)
ruzestir, resist(or)
ruzide, reside
ruziduil, residue(ual)
ruzileant, resilient
ruzilient, resilient
ruzimble, resemble
ruzimblense, resemble(lance)
ruzine, resign
ruzintful, resent(ful)
ruzintment, resent(ment)
ruzist, resist
ruzistanse, resist(ance)
ruzistant, resist(ant)
ruzistef, resist(ive)
ruzistense, resist(ance)
ruzistent, resist(ant)
ruzister, resist(or)
ruzodo, risotto
ruzolfe, resolve
ruzolve, resolve
ruzort, resort
ruzoto, risotto
ruzt, rust / oost
ruztek, rustic
ruztid, rust(ed)
ruztuk, rustic
ruzty, rust(y)
ruzurfs, reserve(s)
ry, rye / wry

rye, *A GRAIN* (or see wry)
ryle, rile
ryme, rhyme
ryno, rhino
rynstone, rhinestone
rysome, rhizome
ryth, writhe
rythem, rhythm
rythom, rhythm
ryut, riot
ryzome, rhizome

"S"

sa, saw /say
sabal, sable
sabateur, saboteur
sabatoj, sabotage
sabature, saboteur
saber,*,red,ring, *A BROADSWORD, LIGHT SWORD WITH BLUNT TIP*
sabereoredy, superior(ity)
sabereority, superior(ity)
sabereur, superior
sabetaje, sabotage
sabetoge, sabotage
sabeture, saboteur
sabil, sable
sabir, saber
sabitaje, sabotage
sabiteur, saboteur
sabitoge, sabotage
sabitoj, sabotage
sabiture, saboteur
sable,*, *CARNIVOROUS ANIMAL*
sableng, sapling
sabling, sapling

sabol, sable
sabor, saber
sabotage,*,ed,ging, _TO HINDER/DAMAGE_
SOMEONE'S ATTEMPTS/POSSESSIONS/EFFORTS
sabotaje, sabotage
saboteur,*, _COMMITS SABOTAGE_
saboture, saboteur
sabre, saber
sabul, sable
sabur, saber
sabutaje, sabotage
sabuteur, saboteur
sabutoge, sabotage
sabutoj, sabotage
saccaren, saccharin
saccerin, saccharin
saccharin,ne,nely,nity, _MANMADE SUGAR_
saccuren, saccharin
sacede, secede
sacha, sachet
sachal, satchel
sacharate, saturate
sacharation, saturate(tion)
sachay, sashay /sachet
sache, sachet
sacheable, sate(tiable)
sacheatid, sate(tiated)
sachel, satchel
sacherashen, saturate(tion)
sacherate, saturate
sacheration, saturate(tion)
sacherin, saccharin
sacheuble, sate(tiable)
sachil, satchel
sachirashen, saturate(tion)
sachirate, saturate
sachiration, saturate(tion)
sachiren, saccharin

sachol, satchel
sachul, satchel
sachurate, saturate
sachuration, saturate(tion)
sack,*,ked,king,ker,kful, _A BAG MADE OF VARIOUS_
MATERIALS USED TO CONTAIN/HOLD SOMETHING,
TO BAG/TACKLE (or see sax)
sackarin, saccharin
sackralegus, sacrilege(gious)
sackralijes, sacrilege(gious)
sackrament, sacrament
sackrul, sacral
sackrument, sacrament
sackuren, saccharin
saclusion, seclusion
sacrafise, sacrifice
sacral, _ASSOCIATED WITH RITES_
sacraleje, sacrilege
sacraligous, sacrilege(gious)
sacrament,*,tal,tally,talism,talist,tarianism,
THAT WHICH IS SACRED
sacrasankt, sacrosanct
sacred,dly,dness, _OF REVERENCE/WORSHIPPED_
sacrefise, sacrifice
sacrel, sacrum(ral)
sacreleje, sacrilege
sacreligus, sacrilege(gious)
sacrem, sacrum
sacremint, sacrament
sacresanct, sacrosanct
sacreshen, secrete(tion)
sacresion, secrete(tion)
sacrete, secrete /sacred
sacretion, secrete(tion)
sacrid, sacred
sacrifice,*,ed,cing,er,cial,cially, _TO GIVE UP_
WITHOUT PROFIT/RETURN, DENY ONESELF
sacril, sacrum(ral)

sacrilege,gious,giously,giousness, _VIOLATION OF_
SACRED
sacrim, sacrum
sacrosanct,tily,tness, _TOO HOLY TO BE CRITICIZED_
OR SLANDERED
sacrud, sacred
sacrufise, sacrifice
sacrul, sacrum(ral)
sacruleje, sacrilege
sacruligus, sacrilege(gious)
sacrum,ral, _LUMBAR VERTEBRAE ON THE SPINE_
sacrument, sacrament
sacumb, succemb
sacure, secure
sad,dly,dness,dden,dder,ddest, _SORROWFUL/_
MOURNFUL, UNHAPPY WITH RESULTS (or see sat)
sadalight, satellite
sadalite, satellite
sadarday, Saturday
sadasfaction, satisfy(faction)
sadasfakshen, satisfy(faction)
sadasfy, satisfy
sadashen, sedate(tion)
sadasion, sedate(tion)
sadate, sedate
sadation, sedate(tion)
saddle,*,ed,ling,er, _A DEVICE/SEAT USED TO GO FOR_
A RIDE ON A FOUR LEGGED ANIMAL
sadel, saddle
sadelite, satellite
sademize, sodomy(mize)
saden, sad(dden) /satin
sadeny, satin(y)
saderday, Saturday
sadesfaction, satisfy(faction)
sadesfakshen, satisfy(faction)
sadesfy, satisfy
sadesum, sadism
sadews, seduce

sadil, saddle
sadilight, satellite
sadilite, satellite
sadimize, sodomy(mize)
sadin, sad(dden) /satin
sadiny, satin(y)
sadirday, Saturday
sadisfaction, satisfy(faction)
sadisfakshen, satisfy(faction)
sadisfy, satisfy
sadism,stic,st,stically, *SEXUALLY AROUSED BY PAIN/ TORTURE*
sadisum, sadism
sadle, saddle
sadnes, sad(ness)
sadnis, sad(ness)
sadolite, satellite
sadomasakisum, sadomasochism
sadomasochism,st,stic, *ASSOCIATED WITH SADISM*
sadomasukezim, sadomasochism
sadoose, seduce
sadosfaction, satisfy(faction)
sadosfakshen, satisfy(faction)
saducshen, seduce(ction)
saductive, seduce(ctive)
saduktion, seduce(ction)
saduktive, seduce(ctive)
sadul, saddle
saduld, saddle(d)
sadulite, satellite
sadun, sad(dden) /satin
sadurday, Saturday
saduse, seduce
sadusfakshen, satisfy(faction)
sadusfy, satisfy
sae, say
saed, said /set
saen, sane /sain
saend, sound

saent, saint
safari,*, *HUNTING EXPEDITION*
safd, save(d)
safe,ely,er,est,eness,ety, *PROTECT FROM HARM (or see salve)*
safekate, suffocate
safekation, suffocate(tion)
safeks, suffix
safestikashen, sophisticate(tion)
safestikated, sophisticate(d)
safestikation, sophisticate(tion)
safex, suffix
safflower, *FLOWERS WHICH PRODUCED OIL*
saffron, *A FLOWER/COLOR*
saficashen, suffocate(tion)
saficate, suffocate
safication, suffocate(tion)
safichent, sufficient
saficient, sufficient
safikashen, suffocate(tion)
safikate, suffocate
safikation, suffocate(tion)
safiks, suffix
safinth, seventh
safir, safe(r)/ savor/ sapphire
safire, sapphire
safise, suffice
safishent, sufficient
safishently, sufficient(ly)
safishunt, sufficient
safist, safe(st)
safistakashen, sophisticate(tion)
safistakated, sophisticate(d)
safistakation, sophisticate(tion)
safix, suffix
saflawur, safflower
saflee, safe(ly)
saflour, safflower
saflower, safflower

safly, safe(ly)
safmore, sophomore
safocashen, suffocate(tion)
safocate, suffocate
safocation, suffocate(tion)
safron, saffron
safrun, saffron /sovereign
saftee, safe(ty)
safucashen, suffocate(tion)
safucate, suffocate
safucation, suffocate(tion)
safukashen, suffocate(tion)
safukate, suffocate
safur, safe(r) / savor
safy, savvy
safyur, savior
sag,*,gged,gging,ggy, *TO BOW/BEND IN A CERTAIN AREA (or see sack or sage)*
sagd, sag(ged) /sage(d)
sage,*,ed,ging,ely,eness, *AN HERB/PLANT, SOMEONE WISE*
saged, sag(gged) /sage(d)
sagee, sage(ggy)
sagis, sage(s)
saguaro,*, *A CACTUS*
sagus, sage(s)
sagy, sag(ggy)
said, *PAST TENSE OF "SAY"* (or see set)
sail,*,led,ling,ler, *OF/GIVEN TO A BOAT WITH SAILS, USING THE WIND TO NAVIGATE A BOAT/VESSEL (or see sale or sailor))*
sailor,*, *PEOPLE WHO OPERATE SEAGOING VESSELS (or see sail(er))*
saim, same
sain, *TO MAKE THE SIGN OF THE CROSS (or see sane or say(ing))*
sainkshuary, sanctuary

salmun, salmon
salod, salad
salomander, salamander
salomantur, salamander
salomee, salami
salon,*, *CUTS/STYLES HAIR*
saloon,*, *TYPE OF DRINKING ESTABLISHMENT*
saloot, salute
salt,*,ted,ting,ty,tier,tiest,ter, *SODIUM/ CHEMICAL COMPOUND* (or see sail(ed))
salud, salad
saludid, salute(d)
saludness, solid(ness)
salum, solemn
salumandur, salamander
salumantur, salamander
salumly, solemn(ly)
salune, saloon
salunization, saline(nization)
salur, sail(er) /sailor
saluree, salary /celery
salus, solace
salushen, solution
salut, salad
salutashen, salute(tation)
salute,*,ed,ting,tary,tarily,tariness,tation, tational,torian,tor,tories,ter, *METHOD OF GREETING*
salutid, salute(d)
salution, solution
saluvate, saliva(te)
salvage,ed,ging,gable,er, *THOUGH DAMAGED, IS STILL WORTHY OF SAVING*
salvashen, salvation
salvation,nal,nism, *PRESERVE/PROTECT FROM DANGER/HARM*
salve,*,ed,ving, *AN OINTMENT/BALM USED FOR HEALING SORES* (or see solve)
salvech, salvage

saleree, salary celery
salesteal, celestial
salet, salad
saleutation, salute(tation)
salevate, saliva(te)
salewtashen, salute(tation)
salfent, solvent
salfint, solvent
salicit, solicit
salicitation, solicit(ation)
saliciter, solicit(er)
salid, salad
salidarity, solidarity
salidefy, solid(ify)
salidness, solid(ness)
salilakwy, soliloquy
salilaqwy, soliloquy
salim, solemn
salimandur, salamander
salimly, solemn(ly)
saline,na,nity,nization, *PERTAINS TO SALT*
salinidy, saline(nity)
salir, sail(er) /sailor
saliry, salary /celery
salis, solace
saliset, solicit
saliseter, solicit(er)
salisit, solicit
salisitation, solicit(ation)
salisiter, solicit(er)
salit, salad
salitefy, solid(ify)
saliva,ary,ate,ation, *FLUID SECRETED BY GLANDS IN THE MOUTH*
salm, psalm
salmin, salmon
salmon, a fish
salmonela, salmonella
salmonella, *BACTERIA WHICH POISONS FOOD*

salved, solve(d)
salvige, salvage
salvije, salvage
salvuble, solve(vable)
salvug, salvage
salyutashen, salute(tation)
saman, salmon
samanela, salmonella
samantics, semantics
same,eness, *ALIKE/SIMILAR*
samen, salmon
samenela, salmonella
samesdur, semester
samester, semester
sametrek, symmetry(ric)
sametric, symmetry(ric)
samin, salmon
saminela, salmonella
samonela, salmonella
sampal, sample
sample,*,ed,ling,er, *A SMALL AMOUNT/TASTE OF SOMETHING*
samplir, sample(r)
sampul, sample
samun, salmon
samunela, salmonella
san, sane /sain /sand
sanada, sonata
sanareo, scenario
sanatarium, sanitorium
sanatate, sanitate
sanatesation, sanitize(zation)
sanatezashen, sanitize(zation)
sanatization, sanitize(zation)
sanatize, sanitize
sanatoreum, sanitorium
sanatu, sonata
sancshen, sanction
sancshin, sanction

sancshuary, sanctuary
sancshuery, sanctuary
sancshun, sanction
sanctafie, sanctify
sanctify,fies,fied,fying,fication,fier, *MAKE HOLY*
sanction,*,ned,ning,ner,nable, *FORMAL/BINDING PERMISSION*
sanctofie, sanctify
sanctofy, sanctify
sanctuary,ries, *REPRIEVE FROM PROBLEMS, PLACE OF IMMUNITY*
sanctuery, sanctuary
sanctufy, sanctify
sand,*,ded,ding,dy,der, *TINY ROCKS, TO SMOOTH A SURFACE BY THE ACT OF SANDING*
sandal,*, *TYPE OF SHOE*
sandee, sand(y)
sandel, sandal
sandul, sandal
sandur, sand(er)
sandwech, sandwich
sandwich,hes,hed,hing, *MEAT/VEGETABLES BETWEEN TWO PIECES OF BREAD, TO PHYSICALLY BE BETWEEN TWO THINGS*
sandwitch, sandwich
sane,ely,eness,nity,nities, *OF SOUND MIND/JUDGEMENT* (or see sain or sand)
sanedy, sanity
sanek, sonic
sanelity, senile(lity)
sanereo, scenario
sanerist, scenario(ist)
sanetareum, sanitorium
sanetary, sanitary
sanetate, sanitate
sanetery, sanitary
sanetize, sanitize
sanetoreum, sanitorium
sanetorium, sanitorium
sanety, sanity

sanidy, sanity
sanility, senile(lity)
sanitareum, sanitorium
sanitarium, sanitorium
sanitary,ries,rily,riness, *CLEAN/FREE OF MOST HARMFUL BACTERIA*
sanitate,*,ed,ting, *TO CLEAN/FREE FROM HARMFUL BACTERIA*
sanitery, sanitary
sanitezation, sanitize(zation)
sanitised, sanitize(d)
sanitize,*,ed,zing,zation,er, *TO CLEAN/FREE OF HARMFUL BACTERIA*
sanitizer, sanitize(r)
sanitorium,*, *RESORT/FACILITY FOR LONG-TERM CARE OF ILLNESS/HEALTH*
sanity,ties, *RELATED TO A SOUND MIND/JUDGEMENT*
sankchuery, sanctuary
sankdefide, sanctify(fied)
sankdefy, sanctify
sankdify, sanctify
sankdufide, sanctify(fied)
sankdufy, sanctify
sankshen, sanction
sankshin, sanction
sankshuery, sanctuary
sankshun, sanction
sanktafi, sanctify
sanktify, sanctify
sanktion, sanction
sanktofie, sanctify
sanktuary, sanctuary
sanktuery, sanctuary
sanktufie, sanctify
sanoda, sonata
sanografee, scenography
sanopsis, synopsis
sanota, sonata
sant, saint

sante, sand(y)
santels, sandal(s)
santly, saint(ly)
santuls, sandal(s)
santur, sand(er)
santwech, sandwich
santwitch, sandwich
sanuc, sonic
sanudy, sanity
sanuk, sonic
sanut, sonnet
sanutareum, sanitorium
sanutary, sanitary
sanutate, sanitate
sanutery, sanitary
sanutezashen, sanitize(zation)
sanutisation, sanitize(zation)
sanutised, sanitize(d)
sanutize, sanitize
sanutizer, sanitize(r)
sanuty, sanity
sanwech, sandwich
saons, se'ance
sap,*,pped,pping,ppy, *THE LIFEBLOOD OF PLANTS*
saped, sap(pped)
sapenid, subpoena(ed)
sapenud, subpoena(ed)
saperb, superb
saperblee superb(ly)
sapereor, superior
sapereoredy, superior(ity)
sapereority, superior(ity)
saperlative, superlative
saperlutif, superlative
saphire, sapphire
saphmore, sophomore
sapinud, subpoena(ed)
sapirb, superb
sapirblee superb(ly)

sapireor, superior
sapireority, superior(ity)
sapirlutif, superlative
sapleminul, subliminal
sapleng, sapling
sapli, supply
saplier, supply(lier)
sapling,*, *YOUNG TREES*
sapliur, supply(lier)
saply, supply
saport, support
saportef, support(ive)
saportive, support(ive)
sapose, suppose
sapository, suppository
saposubly, suppose(dly)
sapoze, suppose
sapozetory, suppository
sapozitory, suppository
sapozubly, suppose(dly)
sapphire,*, *A GEM STONE*
sappresion, suppress(ion)
saprechen, suppress(ion)
sapreem, supreme
sapremacy, supremacy
sapreme, supreme
sapremusist, supremacy(cist)
sapremusy, supremacy
sapreno, soprano
sapres, suppress
sapreshen, suppress(ion)
sapretion, suppress(ion)
saprino, soprano
sapt, sap(pped)
sapurb, superb
sapurblee, superb(ly)
sapurlative, superlative
sapurlitef, superlative
sapurlutif, superlative

sapy, sap(ppy)
saquential, sequence(ntial)
saquer, secure
saquir, secure
saquoia, sequoia
sar, czar
saran, *A THIN PLASTIC*
sarandipity, serendipity
sarape, serape
sarcafagus, sarcophagus
sarcasm,*, *REMARKS MEANT TO BE DEMEANING/ MOCKERY TO ANOTHER*
sarcastecly, sarcastic(ally)
sarcastek, sarcastic
sarcastekly, sarcastic(ally)
sarcastic,cness,calness,cally, *REMARKS MEANT TO BE DEMEANING/MOCKERY TO ANOTHER*
sarcastikly, sarcastic(ally)
sarcastuk, sarcastic
sarcazum, sarcasm
sarcophagus,es,gi, *STONE COFFIN*
sardeen, sardine
sardene, sardine
sardine,*, *TINY EDIBLE FISH*
sarel, sorrel /surreal
sarench, syringe
sarender, surrender
sarendipity, serendipity
sarene, serene
sarenge, syringe
sarenity, serene(nity)
sarenje, syringe
sarenk, saw(ing)
sargent, sergeant
sargint, sargeant
sari, sorry
sarinch, syringe
sarinder, surrender
sarindipity, serendipity

saring, saw(ing)
saringe, syringe
sarinje, syringe
sarink, saw(ing)
sariosis, psoriasis
sariusis, psoriasis
sarjent, sargeant
sarjint, sargeant
sarkafigus, sarcophagus
sarkasem, sarcasm
sarkasim, sarcasm
sarkastek, sarcastic
sarkastiklee, sarcastic(ally)
sarkastuk, sarcastic
sarkawfegus, sarcophagus
sarkazum, sarcasm
sarkofigus, sarcophagus
sarkofugus, sarcophagus
sarkophagus, sarcophagus
saro, sorrow
saroful, sorrow(ful)
sarong,*, *MATERIAL/CLOTH USED TO WRAP AROUND THE LOWER TORSO*
sarope, serape
saroredy, sorority
sarority, sorority
saround, surround
sarow, sorrow
sarowful, sorrow(ful)
sarownd, surround
sarrated, serrate(d)
sarration, serrate(tion)
sarro, sorrow
sarundipity, serendipity
sarundipudy, serendipity
sary, saury /sorry
sas, sass
sasafras, sassafras
sascha, sashay /sachet

sass,sses,ssing,ssy, *SPEAK IMPUDENTLY, SMART BACK AT*
sassafras, *USEFUL TREE ROOTBARK*
sasufras, sassafras
sasur, saucer
sasy, saucy /sass(y)
sata, saute' /sate
satalite, satellite
satanek, satanic
satanic,cal,cally,ism,ist, *MOCKERY OF CHRISTIAN RITUAL*
satanuk, satanic
satanukel, satanic(al)
satarate, saturate
satarday, Saturday
satasfaction, satisfy(faction)
satasfakshen, satisfy(faction)
satasfy, satisfy
satay, saute' /sate
satchal, satchel
satcharashen, saturate(tion)
satcharate, saturate
satchel,*, *BAG/CARRYING CASE*
satcherashen, saturate(tion)
satcherate, saturate
satchil, satchel
satchirashen, saturate(tion)
satchirate, saturate
satchul, satchel
satchurashen, saturate(tion)
satchurate, saturate
sate,ed,ting,tiable,tiably,tiability,tiableness, tiate,tiated,tiation,tiety, *TO BE COMPLETELY SATISFIED* (or see saute)
sateable, sate(tiable)
satel, saddle
satelite, satellite
satellite,*, *A PLANET OR MANMADE DEVICE WHICH ORBITS THE EARTH*

satemize, sodomy(mize)
saten, sad(dden) /satin
sateny, satin(y)
saterate, saturate
saterday, Saturday
saterikul, satirical
satesfaction, satisfy(faction)
satesfakshen, satisfy(faction)
satesfy, satisfy
satesm, sadism
satiaty, sate(tiety)
satilite, satellite
satimize, sodomy(mize)
satin,ny, *A SOFT FABRIC*
satirate, saturate
satirday, Saturday
satire,*,ric,rical,rically,ricalness,rist,rize,rizer, *EMPLOY IRONY/WIT/SARCASM* (or see satyr)
satirest, satire(rist)
satisfakshen, satisfy(faction)
satisfy,fies,fied,fying,fiable,fier,fyingly, *NEEDS/DEMANDS/EXPECTATIONS FULFILLED*
satisum, sadism
satle, saddle
satlee, sad(ly)
satnis, sad(ness)
satolite, satellite
satomasakisum, sadomasochism
satomasochism, sadomasochism
satosfaction, satisfy(faction)
satosfakshen, satisfy(faction)
satul, saddle
satulite, satellite
saturate,*,ed,ting,tion,tor, *LIQUID WILL PENETRATE UNTIL IT CAN PENETRATE NO MORE*
Saturday,*, *A DAY OF THE WEEK*
satusfakshen, satisfy(faction)
satusfy, satisfy
satyerashen, saturate(tion)

sased, sass(ed) /secede
sasede, secede
sasefras, sassafras
saseg, sausage
sasej, sausage
sasenked, succinct
sasenkt, succinct
sasenktly, succint(ly)
saseptible, susceptible
saseptif, suceptive
saseptive, suceptive
saseptuble, susceptible
saseptuf, suceptive
saser, saucer
saseshen, secession
sasesion, secession
saset, secede
sasetion, secession
sasha, sachet
sashay,*, *TO WISPILY WALK AS IF DANCING* (or see sachet)
sasheable, sate(tiable)
sasheated, sate(tiated)
sashet, sashay /sachet
sasheuble, sate(tiable)
sasifras, sassafras
sasig, sausage
sasij, sausage
sasinked, succinct
sasinkt, succinct
sasinktly, succint(ly)
sasir, saucer
sasofras, sassafras
sasor, saucer
saspekt, suspect
saspend, suspend
saspender, suspender
saspeshus, suspicious
saspishus, suspicious

satyirate, saturate
satyr,*,ric, *MYTHOLOGICAL CREATURE (or see satire)*
satyurate, saturate
satyuration, saturate(tion)
sauble, say(able)
sauce,*,ed,cing, *A THICK LIQUID WITH SPICES/*
   HERBS/FLAVORINGS ADDED
saucer,*,, *A SMALL PLATE, SHAPE OF A PLATE*
sauciur, saucy(cier)
saucy,cier,ciest,cily,ciness, *OF BEING IMPUDENT/*
   FLIPPANT TOWARD SUPERIORS
sauder, solder
sauderd, solder(ed)
saudumize, sodomy(mize)
saudumy, sodomy
sauer, sour
sauerkraut, *FERMENTED CABBAGE*
saufari, safari
saufen, soft(en)
saufet, soffit
saufiner, soft(ener)
saufit, soffit
saufmore, sophomore
saufunir, soft(ener)
saugee, soggy
sauir, sour
sauirkraut, sauerkraut
sauirkrowt, sauerkraut
saulder, solder
saulesmint, solace(ment)
saulid, solid
saulis, solace
saulisment, solace(ment)
saulitare, solitaire /solitary
sauliderity, solidarity
saulus, solace
saulutare, solitaire /solitary
saulutude, solitude
sauna,*,, *ROOM WITH MOIST HEAT/STEAM*

saund, sound
saunek, sonic
saunet, sonnet
saunik, sonic
saunit, sonnet
saunt, sound
saunter,*,red,ring,rer, *A LEISURLY WALK/STROLL*
saunu, sauna
saunut, sonnet
saur, sour
sauree, sorry
sauro, sorrow
saury,ries, *A FISH (or see sorry)*
sausage,*,, *MINCED MEAT WITH FLAVORINGS*
sauseur, saucy(cier)
sausier, saucy(cier)
saute,*,eed,eing, *TO QUICKLY FRY IN A PAN/WOK*
   (or see sate)
sauter, solder
sautered, solder(ed)
sauren, sovereign
sauvter, soft(er)
sauvuble, solve(vable)
sauyubil, soluble
sav, save / salve/ solve
savach, savage
savage,*,ely,eness,ery,eries,gism, *BEASTLY/*
   RUDE/BARBARIAN
savagly, savage(ly)
savana, savanna
savanna, *MEADOW/PLAIN WITH SHRUBS/TREES*
savant,*,, *A WISE/LEARNED PERSON*
savar, savor /save(r)
savaren, sovereign
savd, save(d)
save,*,ed,ving,er, *RESCUE FROM DANGER/HARM/*
   ALTERCATION (or see safe or salve)
savech, savage
savechry, savage(ry)

savee, savvy
savege, savage
savegly, savage(ly)
savegry, savage(ry)
saveje, savage
saver, save(r) /savor
saveridy, severe(rity)
saverin, sovereign
saverity, severe(rity)
savich, savage
savichry, savage(ry)
savier, savvy(vvier) /savior
savigly, savage(ly)
savigry, savage(ry)
savije, savage
savinth, seventh
savior,*,, *ONE CHOSEN BY PEOPLE TO LEAD THEM*
   FROM IGNORANCE INTO ENLIGHTENMENT
savir, savor /save(r)
savird, savor(ed)
saviren, sovereign
savlawur, safflower
savlee, safe(ly)
savont, savant
savor,*,red,ring,rer,ry, *FOOD WITH MOST*
   PALATABLE FLAVOR/SMELL/TASTE
savree, savor(y)
savren, sovereign
savron, saffron /sovereign
savrun, sovereign
savry, savor(y)
savtee, safe(ty)
savuch, savage
savugly, savage(ly)
savugry, savage(ry)
savuje, savage
savur, savor /save(r)
savurd, savor(ed)
savuren, sovereign

savurin, sovereign
savvy,viek,ying,vier,viest, *INTELLIGENT/SHREWD UNDERSTANDING*
savy, savvy
savyer, savior
savyur, savior
saw,*,wed,wing,wer, *PAST TENSE OF "SEE", A BLADE WITH TEETH THAT CUTS* (or see sauce)
sawarkrowt, sauerkraut
sawaro, saguaro
sawdemise, sodomy(mize)
sawdemy, sodomy
sawder, solder
sawdered, solder(ed)
sawdimy, sodomy
sawdumize, sodomy(mize)
sawdur, solder
sawer, sour
sawerkraut, sauerkraut
sawfenir, soft(ener)
sawfet, soffit
sawfin, soft(en)
sawfinur, soft(ener)
sawfit, soffit
sawfmore, sophomore
sawfun, soft(en)
sawfuner, soft(ener)
sawgee, soggy
sawir, sour
sawirkraut, sauerkraut
sawirkrowt, sauerkraut
sawker, soccer
sawled, solid
sawlesmint, solace(ment)
sawletare, solitaire /solitary
sawlf, solve
sawlid, solid
sawlidness, solid(ness)
sawlis, solace

sawlisment, solace(ment)
sawlitness, solid(ness)
sawlud, solid
sawludness, solid(ness)
sawlutare, solitaire /solitary
sawlutude, solitude
sawnek, sonic
sawnet, sonnet
sawnik, sonic
sawnut, sonnet
sawor, sour
saworo, saguaro
sawp, sop / sob
sawpee, sop(ppy)
sawree, saury /sorry
sawrely, sorry(rily)
sawrench, syringe
sawri,sorry
sawro, saguaro /sorrow
sawrong, sarong
sawry, sorry
saws, saw(s)/ sauce/ souse
sawsege, sausage
sawseje, sausage
sawser, saucer
sawsige, sausage
sawsor, saucer
sawst, souse(d)
sawsuge, sausage
sawsuje, sausage
sawsur, saucer
sawsy, saucy
sawt, saw(ed)
sawtay, saute' /sate
sawte, saute' /sate
sawtemy, sodomy
sawtered, solder(ed)
sawtimise, sodomy(mize)
sawtumy, sodomy

sawur, sour
sawurkraut, sauerkraut
sawurkrowt, sauerkraut
sawvuble, solve(vable)
sawyebul, soluble
sawyubil, soluble
sawzy, saucy
sax, *SLANG FOR SAXOPHONE* (or see sack(s))
saxophone,*,nic,nist, *HORN INSTRUMENT*
saxsifone, saxophone
saxsuphone, saxophone
say,*,yable,yer,ying, *WHAT HAS BEEN SPOKEN, TO SPEAK VERBALLY*
sayabil, soluble
sayans, se'ance
sayn, sain/ sane/ say(ing)
sayons, se'ance
sayulose, cellulose
sbase, space /space(y)
sbaser, space(r)
sbast, space(d)
sbasur, space(r)
sbasy, space(y)
sbegut, spigot
sbekit, spigot
sbekot, spigot
sbidel, spittle
sbidul, spittle
sbiget, spigot
sbikit, spigot
sbikot, spigot
sbital, spittle
sbitul, spittle
sblash, splash
sblat, splat
sblendur, splinter /splendor
sblent, splint
sblerge, splurge
sblerje, splurge

sblet, split
sbletur, split(tter)
sblices, splice(s)
sblindur, splinter /splendor
sblint, splint
sblirge, splurge
sblirje, splurge
sblise, splice
sbliser, splice(r)
sblist, splice(d)
sblisur, splice(r)
sblit, split
sbliter, split(tter)
sblitur, split(tter)
sbloch, splotch
sblochy, splotch(y)
sblotch, splotch
sblotchee, splotch(y)
sblurje, splurge
sboel, spoil
sboeld, spoil(ed) /spoilt
sboeleg, spoil(age)
sboil, spoil
sboild, spoil(ed) /spoilt
sboiled, spoil(ed) /spoilt
sboileg, spoil(age)
sbore, spore
sboyl, spoil
sbre, spree
sbree, spree
sbreg, sprig
sbrews, spruce
sbrig, sprig
sbroose, spruce
sbruse, spruce
sbun, spun
sburd, spur(rred)
sburt, spur(rred)

scab,*,bbed,bbing,bby, CRUST FORMED ON SKIN OVER OPEN WOUND, TERM FOR STRIKE WORKERS
scabard, scabbard
scabbard,*, SWORD SHEATH
scabburd, scabbard
scabed, scab(bbed)
scabees, scabies
scaberd, scabbard
scabies,etic,ious, SKIN DISEASE
scaburd, scabbard
scaby, scab(bby)
scad,*, EDIBLE FISH, LARGE NUMBER/QUANTITY
scader, skate(r) / scatter
scadered, scatter(ed)
scadir, skate(r) / scatter
scadured, scatter(ed)
scaffold,*,ding, TEMPORARY FRAMEWORK WITH PLANKS USED TO CONDUCT WORK
scafold, scaffold
scair, scare
scairslee, scarce(ly)
scairsness, scarce(ness)
scalar, A PHYSICS EXPRESSION, OF MASS AND TIME
scald,*,ded,ding, SURFACE BURN
scale,*,ed,ling,eless,eliness, INSTRUMENT FOR MEASURING WEIGHT, MUSICAL LADDER, TO CLIMB (or see scaly)
scaleness, scaly(liness)
scaleon, scallion
scalep, scallop
scaleun, scallion
scaley, scaly
scalion, scallion
scalip, scallop
scallion,*, TYPE OF ONION
scallop,*,per, SHELLFISH, TYPE OF DISH/SHAPE
scalop, scallop
scalor, scalar

scalp,*,ped,ping,per, SKIN ON HUMAN SKULL, WAY OF SELLING TICKETS (or see scallop)
scalpal, scalpel
scalpel,*, A SURGICAL KNIFE
scalpul, scalpel
scalup, scallop
scaly,liness, SIMILAR/SAME AS SCALES ON A FISH
scalyin, scallion
scalyun, scallion
scamatic, scheme(matic)
scan,*,nned,nning,nner, A MACHINE WHICH COPIES/TAKES DIGITAL IMAGES
scandal,*,lize,lous,lously,lousness, EVENT WHICH DEGRADES/OFFENDS A SOCIAL VALUE/IDEA
scandel, scandal
scandelus, scandal(ous)
scandil, scandal
scandolus, scandal(ous)
scandul, scandal
scandulus, scandal(ous)
scaner, scan(nner)
scanerio, scenario
scanir, scan(nner)
scanography, scenography
scant,tily,tness, LIMITED RESOURCE
scantuly, scant(ily)
scanur, scan(nner)
scapala, scapula
scapel, scalpel
scapeula, scapula
scapewla, scapula
scapil, scalpel
scapila, scapula
scapul, scalpel
scapula,*, SHOULDER BLADE
scar,*,rred,rring, A PHYSICAL MARK LEFT AFTER A BODILY INJURY HAS HEALED (or see scare)
scarce,ely,city,eness, IN DEMAND/RARE
scarcedy, scarce(city)

scare,*,ed,ring,ey, FRIGHTEN/ALARM
scared, scare(d) /scar(rred)
scarf,rves,fless, A LIGHTWEIGHT MATERIAL WORN ON THE HEAD, TO WOLF DOWN FOOD/DRINK
scarfd, scarf(ed)
scarfs, scarf(rves)
scarft, scarf(ed)
scarlet, A COLOR
scarlut, scarlet
scarse, scarce
scarsedy, scarce(city)
scarsity, scarce(city)
scarsly, scarce(ly)
scarsness, scarce(ness)
scarsudy, scarce(city)
scart, scar(rred) /scare(d)
scary, scare(y)
scat,tted,tting, SINGING IMPROVISATION, TO HURRY AWAY, FISH, ANIMAL FECAL (or see skat /skate)
scater, scatter
scathe,ed,hing,eless, TO INJURE/HARM
scatir, scatter
scatter,*,red,ring,rable,rer, DISPERSED ABOUT IRREGULARLY (or see skate(r))
scatur, scatter
scauler, scholar
scaulerly, scholar(ly)
scavage, scavenge
scavager, scavenge(r)
scavenge,ed,ging,er, TO SEARCH/SEEK FOR USABLE MATERIAL (TOO MANY DEFINITIONS, PLEASE SEE STANDARD DICTIONARY)
scavuge, scavenge
scavunjer, scavenge(r)
scawler, scholar
scawlerly, scholar(ly)
scem, scheme /skim
scenac, scene(nic)

scenario,*,ist, TO OUTLINE SCENES/CHARACTERS FOR PLAY/MOVIE
scenary, scene(ry)
scene,*, ery,eries,nic, A VISUAL PRESENTATION OF A PLACE/EVENT
scenic, scene(nic)
sceniry, scene(ry)
scenography,hic,hically, RULES IN CREATING PERSPECTIVE
scent,*,ted,tless,tlessness,ODOR/FRAGRANCE
scenur, skinner
sceptacism, skeptic(ism)
sceptasisum, skeptic(ism)
scepter,*,red,ring, ROD OF AUTHORITY/ROYALTY
scepticism, skeptic(ism)
sceptik, skeptic
sceptir, scepter
sceptisitum, skeptic(ism)
sceptor, scepter
sceptuk, skeptic
sceptur, scepter
sceptusisum, skeptic(ism)
scer, scare
scerfy, scurvy
sceris, scirrhus /cirrus
scersity, scarce(city)
scersly, scarce(ly)
scersudy, scarce(city)
scerus, scirrhus /cirrus
scery, scurry
scesurs, scissors
scewbu, scuba
scewp, scoop
scewper, scoop(er)
schalastic, scholastic
schaler, scholar
schalerly, scholar(ly)
schamatic, scheme(matic)
schaulerly, scholar(ly)

schedewl, schedule
schedule,*,ed,ling, AN ITEMIZED LIST CONCERNING TIME AND APPOINTMENTS
scheem, scheme
schelastic, scholastic
scheme,*,ed,ming,er,ma,mata,matic,matically, matism,matist,matize,matization,matizer, A PLAN/ PLOT/ PROJECT
schemir, skim(mmer) /scheme(r)
schemur, skim(mmer) /scheme(r)
schilastic, scholastic
schimatic, scheme(matic)
schist,tose,tous, ROCK TYPE DETERMINED BY THE WAY IT EXFOLIATES
schitzophrenia, schizophrenia
schizofrenia, schizophrenia
schizoid, PERTAINING TO SCHIZOPHRENIA
schizophrenia,ic, MENTAL PROBLEM
schizoyd, schizoid
scholar,*,rly,rism,rless,rliness, ONCE WHO HAS STUDIED/LEARNED A GREAT DEAL
scholastic,*,cal,cally,cate,cism, RELATED/ CONCERNING SCHOOL
scholer, scholar
scholerly, scholar(ly)
school,*,led,ling, A PLACE TO LEARN
schooner,*,*, TYPE OF SAILING VESSEL
schuel, school
schulastic, scholastic
schule, school
schumatic, scheme(matic)
schuner, schooner
sciadeca, sciatic(a)
sciadica, sciatic(a)
scianse, science
sciantifek, scientific
sciantifekaly, scientific(ally)
sciantificly, scientific(ally)
sciatek, sciatic

sciatic,ca,cally, *MAJOR NERVES IN THE BODY NEAR THE HIPS*
sciatik, sciatic
science,*, *FIELDS OF GENERAL LAWS CONCERNING EVERYTHING IN OUR REALITY*
scientest, scientist
scientifek, scientific
scientific,cally, *GIVEN TO THE FIELD OF SCIENCE*
scientifikaly, scientific(ally)
scientist,*,sm, *MAJORS IN FIELD OF SCIENCE*
scif, skiff
scikyatrus, psychiatry(rist)
scimatic, scheme(matic)
scinario, scenario
scinerio, scenario
scinography, scenography
scint, scent
scinur, skinner
scirfy, scurvy
scirhus, scirrhus /cirrus
scirus, scirrhus /cirrus
sciry, scurry
scisers, scissors
scissor,*, *TOOL TO CUT/SEVER*
scisurs, scissors
scith, scythe
sciuntefikaly, scientific(ally)
sciuntist, scientist
scizurs, scissors
scof, scoff
scofed, scoff(ed)
scoff,*,fed,fing,fingly,fer, *TO SHOW MOCKERY/ DISTASTE/RIDUCULE*
scold,*,ded,ding,der, *TO FIND FAULT/REPRIMAND SOMEONE FOR THEIR BEHAVIOR (or see scald)*
scoleosis, scoliosis

scoliosis,ic, *CURVATURE OF THE SPINE*
scolt, scold / scald
sconce,*,ed,cing, *LIGHTS ON THE WALL, FORT, SKULL*
scone,*, *A BREAD CAKE*
scons, scone(s) / sconce
sconts, sconce
scooba, scuba
scooder, scoot(er)
scoop,*,ped,ping,per,pful, *GATHER UP QUANTITY OF SOMETHING ALL AT ONCE*
scoopir, scoop(er)
scoot,*,ted,ting,ter, *TO GO/SEND HASTILY ALONG, TO SLIDE OVER (or see scute)*
scorch,hes,hed,hing,her, *LIGHTLY BURN*
score,*,ed,ring,er,eless, *MARK BY GOUGING/ SCRATCHING, EARNING POINTS IN COMPETITION*
scorlis, score(less)
scorn,*,ned,ning,ningly,nful,nfully,nfulness, *EXPRESS DISTATE/CONTEMPT*
scornfuly, scorn(fully)
scorpeon, scorpion
scorpion,*, *AN ARACHNOID*
scoul, scowl
scouled, scowl(ed)
scoundrel,*,lly, *A MEAN/BASE PERSON WHO HAS NO HONOR FOR OTHERS*
scoundril, scoundrel
scoundrle, scoundrel
scour,*,red,ring,rer, *TO SCRUB CLEAN, GO OVER, PURGE*
scourd, scour(ed)
scourge,*,ed,ging,er, *TO TORMENT/TORTURE/ SEVERLY PUNISH*
scout,*,ted,ting,ter, *TO HUNT/SEARCH FOR*
scouwl, scowl
scower, scour
scowl,*,led,ling,ler, *WEARING A LOOK OF BEING IRRATABLE/ANGRY*
scowndrel, scoundrel

scowr, scour
scowt, scout
scowrd, scour(ed)
scrach, scratch
scrag,*,gged,gging,ggy,gily,giness, *JAGGED/ DISHEVELED/SKINNY/BONEY/SCRAWNY/LEAN*
scraggly,lies,lier,liest,gily,giness, *SPLINTERED/ SHATTERED/JAGGED/CRAGGY*
scragleur, scraggly(lier)
scragliest, scraggly(liest)
scragly, scrag(ily) / scraggly
scrakly, scrag(ily) / scraggly
scram,*,mmed,mming, *GO AWAY QUICKLY*
scrambal, scramble
scrambil, scramble
scramble,*,ed,ling,er, *TO MIX UP/TOGETHER, TO CLUMSILY TAKE ACTION*
scrambul, scramble
scrap,*,pped,pping,pper,ppage, *SMALL PARTICLE/ PIECE/FRAGMENT, LEFT OVERS, TO PICK A FIGHT (or see scrape)*
scrape,*,ed,ping,er,pable, *TO RASP/GRATE/MOVE BY DRAGGING TO CAUSE NOISE/ DAMAGE/MARKS (or see scrap)*
scrapt, scrap(pped) / scrape(d)
scrapuble, scrap(able)
scratch,hes,hed,hing,hy, *TO MARK/CUT/CROSS-OUT*
scrawl,*,led,ling,ly,ler, *AWKWARD/ IRREGULAR MARKS AS IF DONE HASTILY*
screach, screech
scream,*,med,ming,mer,mingly, *A LOUD/SHRILL/ HARSH OUTCRY FROM THE THROAT*
screan, screen
screanable, screen(able)
screbul, scribble
screch, screech
scred, screed
screech,hes,hed,hing, *A SHARP/GRATING/SHRILL LOUD SOUND*

screed,*,ded,ding, *TO SEPARATE PARTICLES FROM ONE ANOTHER, PLASTER/MORTAR TECHNIQUE*
screem, scream
screen,*,ned,ning,ner,nable, *MATERIAL FOR WINDOWS , SORT/SIFT THROUGH*
scremp, scrimp
scremshaw, scrimshaw
scren, screen
screped, script
screpsher, scripture
scrept, script
screpture, scripture
screw,wed,wing,wer,wy, *SMALL CYLINDRICAL OBJECT WITH POINTED TIP/SLOTTED HEAD*
screwdhee, scrutiny
screwge, scrooge
screwje, scrooge
screwpul, scruple
screwpulus, scrupulous
screwtney, scrutiny
scribble,*,ed,ling,er, *TO SCRAWL/MAKE UNDECIPHERABLE MARKS*
scribe,*,ed,bing,er,bal, *A WRITER*
scribd, scribe(d) /script
scrible, scribble
scribul, scribble
scrimage, scrimmage
scrimmage,*,ed,ging, *A PHYSICAL ROUGH ABOUT WITH OTHERS IN A GAME*
scrimp,*,ped,ping,py, *HAVE TIGHT BUDGET/ SPENDING HABIT TO SAVE FOR SOMETHING ELSE*
scrimshaw, *IVORY CARVING*
scrimuge, scrimmage
scrimuje, scrimmage
scripshur, scripture
script,*,ted,ting, *THE CHARACTERS/TEXT OF A PLAY/ MOVIE/BROADCAST/PROGRAM*
scripture,*,ral,rally,ralness, *RELIGIOUS WRITING*
scroge, scrooge

scroje, scrooge
scrol, scrawl /scroll
scroll,*,lled,lling, *PARCHMENT/PAPER ROLLED UP*
scrooge, *A MISER, TIGHTWAD*
scrooje, scrooge
scrooteny, scrutiny
scrounge,*,ed,ging,ey, *FORAGE AROUND, A DISHEVELED/UNKEPT LOOK*
scroungy, scrounge(y)
scrowl, scrawl
scrowngy, scrounge(y)
scrownje, scrounge /scrounge(y)
scru, screw
scrub,*,bbed,bbing,bber,bby, *TO RUB/SCOURGE BRISKLY, LOW GROWTH TREE/SHRUBS*
scrudnee, scrutiny
scruf, scruff
scruff,ffy, *BACK/NAPE OF NECK*
scrufy, scruff(y)
scruge, scrooge
scruje, scrooge
scruny, scrutiny
scrup, scrub
scrupel, scruple
scrupewlus, scrupulous
scruple,*,ed,ling, *TO REMAIN CONSCIOUSLY AWARE/ALERT*
scrupol, scruple
scrupulous,osity,sness,sly, *BEING CAREFUL CONCERNING WHAT IS RIGHT/PROPER*
scrut, screw(ed)
scruteny, scrutiny
scrutiny,nize,nizes,nized,nizing,nization,nizer, nizingly, *CLOSELY EXAMINE/EVALUATE*
scruwy, screw(y)
scruy, screw(y)
scuba,*, *UNDERWATER DEVICE FOR BREATHING*
scuder, scoot(er)
scuf, scuff

scufel, scuffle
scuff,*,ffed,ffing, *TO LEAVE MARKS BY WEARING/ USAGE/WALKING*
scuffle,*,ed,ling, *DISORDERLY PHYSICAL STRUGGLE/ FIGHT*
scufil, scuffle
scuful, scuffle
sculbed, sculpt
sculbshir, sculpt(ure)
sculpshir, sculpt(ure)
sculpt,*,ted,ting,ter,ture,tural,turally, *FORM BY HUMAN/NATURAL PROCESS TO CREATE 3D IMAGES*
sculpter, sculpt(ure)
scum,*,mmed,mming,mmy, *NASTY/ VILE/ WORTHLESS, RESIDUE LEFT BEHIND*
scumatic, scheme(matic)
scumy, scum(mmy)
scunario, scenario
scuner, schooner
scupe, scoop
scurfy, scurvy
scurry,rries,rried,rrying, *TO SCAMPER/HURRY*
scurvy,vies,vier,viest,vily,viness, *A DISEASE*
scury, scurry
scute,*, *BONY PLATE/SHIELD* (or see scoot)
scuter, scoot(er)
scwaled, squalid
scwolid, squalid
scythe,*,ed,hing, *A TOOL WITH LONG BLADE USED IN SWEEPING MOTIONS TO CUT GRASS/GRAIN*
sdaroyd, steroid
sdash, stash
sdemulashen, stimulate(tion)
sdemulate, stimulate
sdemulation, stimulate(tion)
sderdy, sturdy
sdergen, sturgeon
sderjon, sturgeon
sderoed, steroid

sderoet, steroid
sderoyd, steroid
sderty, sturdy
sdewdeo, studio
sdewdeus, studious
sdewpendus, stupendous
sdewper, stupor
sdewpid, stupid
sdewpir, stupor
sdewpur, stupor
sdifel, stifle
sdiful, stifle
sdil, style /still
sdilesh, style(lish)
sdilest, style(list)
sdilist, style(list)
sdilush, style(lish)
sdime, stymie
sdimulashen, stimulate(tion)
sdimulate, stimulate
sdimulation, stimulate(tion)
sdirafom, styrofoam
sdirdy, sturdy
sdirefom, styrofoam
sdirty, sturdy
sdirufom, styrofoam
sdo, stow /store
sdoe, stow
sdoek, stoic
sdogee, stogy
sdogy, stogy
sdoik, stoic
sdol, stole
sdolen, stole(n)
sdolun, stole(n)
sdon, stun
sdools, stool(s)
sdooped, stupid
sdoopid, stupid

sdoopidudy, stupid(ity)
sdoopiduty, stupid(ity)
sdoopir, stupor
sdoopufid, stupefy(fied)
sdoopur, stupor
sdopid, stupid
sdored, story(ried)
sdoree, story
sdoreg, storage
sdorej, storage
sdores, story(ries)
sdorig, storage
sdorij, storage
sdorm, storm
sdormee, storm(y)
sdow, stow
sdowek, stoic
sdowik, stoic
sdra, straw /stray
sdradagee, strategy
sdradajist, strategy(gist)
sdrade, stray(ed) /straight
sdrades, stratus
sdradis, stratus
sdradugee, strategy
sdradugist, strategy(gist)
sdradus, stratus
sdrae, stray
sdrain, strain
sdrand, strain(ed) /strand
sdrane, strain
sdrap, strap
sdras, stress
sdratagee, strategy
sdrategek, strategic
sdrategekly, strategic(ally)
sdrategist, strategy(gist)
sdrategy, strategy
sdratejik, strategic

sdratejikly, strategic(ally)
sdratejist, strategy(gist)
sdrates, stratus
sdratesfere, stratosphere
sdratesphere, stratosphere
sdratigek, strategic
sdratigekly, strategic(ally)
sdratis, stratus
sdratosfere, stratosphere
sdratosphere, stratosphere
sdratugee, strategy
sdratugist, strategy(gist)
sdratus, stratus
sdratusfere, stratosphere
sdratusphere, stratosphere
sdraw, straw
sdrayd, stray(ed) /straight
sdreakee, streak(y)
sdrech, stretch
sdrecher, stretch(er)
sdrechr, stretch(er)
sdrechur, stretch(er)
sdreek, streak
sdreem, stream
sdreet, street
sdrek, streak
sdrekd, strict /streak(ed)
sdreke, streak(y)
sdreknine, strychnine
sdrekun, stricken
sdreky, streak(y)
sdrem, stream
sdremer, stream(er)
sdremur, stream(er)
sdreneus, strenous
sdrenewus, strenous
sdreng, string
sdrengee, string(y)
sdrengint, stringent

sdrenjint, stringent
sdrenkth, strength
sdrenth, strength
sdrenues, strenous
sdrep, strep/ strip/stripe
sdrepd, stripe(d) /strip(pped)
sdreped, stripe(d) /strip(pped)
sdreper, stripe(r) /strip(pper)
sdrepur, stripe(r) /strip(pper)
sdres, stress
sdresh, stretch
sdret, street
sdreun, strewn
sdrew, strew
sdriashen, striate(tion)
sdriate, striate
sdriation, striate(tion)
sdrife, strife /strive
sdrik, strike
sdrikd, strict
sdriked, strict
sdriken, stricken
sdriknin, strychnine
sdrikun, stricken
sdrinewus, strenous
sdring, string
sdringee, string(y)
sdrinjint, stringent
sdrinkth, strength
sdrinth, strength
sdrinues, strenous
sdrip, strep/ strip/stripe
sdriped, stripe(d) /strip(pped)
sdriper, stripe(r) /strip(pper)
sdripur, stripe(r) /strip(pper)
sdrivd, strive(d)
sdrive, strive /strife
sdro, straw
sdrobe, strobe

sdroganoff, stroganoff
sdroginof, stroganoff
sdroke, stroke
sdrol, stroll
sdroler, stroll(er)
sdrolur, stroll(er)
sdrong, strong
sdrongist, strong(est)
sdrongur, strong(er)
sdroodel, strudel
sdroodul, strudel
sdroon, strewn
sdrope, strobe
sdru, strew
sdrudel, strudel
sdrudid, strut(tted)
sdrudil, strudel
sdrudul, strudel
sdrueng, strew(ing)
sdrugel, struggle
sdrugul, struggle
sdruk, struck
sdrukchur, structure
sdrukshur, structure
sdrukul, struggle
sdrum, strum
sdrumer, strum(mmer)
sdrun, strewn
sdrut, strut
sdrutegek, strategic
sdrutegekly, strategic(ally)
sdrutejik, strategic
sdrutigekly, strategic(ally)
sdruz, strew(s)
sdryate, striate
sdubee, stub(bby)
sdubel, stubble
sdubern, stubborn
sduble, stubble

sduborn, stubborn
sdubul, stubble
sduburn, stubborn
sduby, stub(bby)
sduded, study(died) /stud(dded)
sdudee, study
sdudeo, studio
sduder, stutter
sdudes, study(dies)
sdudeus, studious
sdudio, studio
sdudir, stutter
sdudius, studious
sdudur, stutter
sdudy, study
sduel, stool
sdufee, stuff(y)
sduil, stool
sduko, stucco
sdule, stool
sdump, stump
sdumpee, stump(y)
sdun, stun
sdunk, stunk
sdunt, stunt /stun(nned)
sduol, stool
sdupafid, stupefy(fied)
sduped, stub(bbed) /stupid
sdupedudy, stupid(ity)
sdupeduty, stupid(ity)
sdupefy, stupefy
sdupel, stubble
sdupendus, stupendous
sduper, stupor
sdupidudy, stupid(ity)
sdupiduty, stupid(ity)
sdupify, stupefy
sdupil, stubble
sdupindus, stupendous

secrutary, secretary
secrutereul, secretary(rial)
secrutery, secretary
secrutive, secret(ive)
secrutly, secret(ly)
secshen, section
secshenul, section(al)
secshun, section
secshunal, section(al)
sect,*, *A SEGMENT/SECTION OF SOMETHING*
secter, sector
section,*, ned,ning,nal,nally,nalism, *ONE PART OF THE WHOLE*
sectir, sector
sector,*,rial, *A PART/DIVISION OF THE WHOLE*
sectur, sector
secular,rly,rism,rist,ristic,rity,rities,rize,rizer, rization, *UNBIND FROM RELIGIOUS BELIEF*
seculir, secular
secumb, succemb
secund,dly, *BOTANICAL TERM (or see second or secant)*
secundery, second(ary)
secundly, second(ly)
secure,*,ed,ring,rable,ely,eness,ement,er,rity, ties, *PROTECT FROM CERTAIN ELEMENTS, KEEP FIRMLY IN PLACE*
securety, secure(rity)
securidy, secure(rity)
sed, said/ set/ seed
sedalment, settle(ment)
sedam, sedum
sedamentary, sedament(ary)
sedamint, sediment
sedan,*,, *TYPE OF VEHICLE*
sedashen, sedate(tion)
sedasion, sedate(tion)
sedate,*,ed,ting,ely,eness,tion,tive, *TO APPEASE/ SUBSIDE/CALM*

sedelment, settle(ment)
sedem, sedum
sedemint, sediment
sedews, seduce
sedge,*,,gy, *A SWAMP GRASS WITH EDGES*
sedil, settle
sedilment, settle(ment)
sedim, sedum
sediment,*, tary,tal,tation, *ACCUMULATION OF NON-LIQUID MATTER SEPARATED FROM LIQUID*
sedle, settle
sedlers, settle(rs)
sedling, seedling /settle(ling)
sediment, settle(ment)
sedol, settle
sedom, sedum
sedoose, seduce
seduce,*, ed,cing,er,cible,cable,ction,ctive, cement,ctively,ctiveness, *COERCED/ENTICED AWAY FROM NORMAL PATTERN OF BEHAVIOR*
seducshen, seduce(ction)
seductif, seduce(ctive)
seduktion, seduce(ction)
seduktive, seduce(ctive)
sedul, settle
sedulers, settle(rs)
sedulment, settle(ment)
sedum,*,, *A PLANT*
sedumentary, sedament(ary)
sedumint, sediment
seduse, seduce
sedy, seed(y)
see,*,eeable,eeableness,eeing,een,eeing,eer, *USE OF THE EYES, VISUAL IMAGING (or sea or seize)*
seed,*,ded,ding,dless,dful,der,dy, *SOMETHING THAT HOLDS THE FUTURE, DNA BLUEPRINTS*
seedling,*,, *GROWTH BURSTING FROM A SEED*
seefood, seafood

seefud, seafood
seeg, siege
seej, siege
seek,*,ked,king,ker, *TO SEARCH FOR*
seekratif, secret(ive)
seekrutif, secret(ive)
seel, seal
seeld, seal(ed)
seem,*,,med,ming,mingly,mingness,mly,mliness *APPEARS TO BE TRUTHFUL/ FACTUAL/REAL, COULD BE (or see seam)*
seemstras, seamstress
seemstrus, seamstress
seen, *PAST TENSE OF "SEE" (or see scene or seine)*
seena, sienna
seengle, single
seengul, single
seengulerety, singular(ity)
seep,*,,ped,ping,py,page, *THE OOZING OF LIQUID THROUGH A BARRIER*
seepige, seep(age)
seepuge, seep(age)
seer,*,, *ONE WHO SEES/HAS SPIRITUAL INSIGHT/ PREDICTOR OF THE FUTURE (or see "sear")*
seera, sierra
sees, seize/ cease/ sea(s)/ see(s)
seesan, season
seeshell, seashell
seesin, season
seesta, siesta
seesun, season
seethe,*,,ed,hing,hingly, *STATE OF AGITATION/ EXCITEMENT THAT CANNOT BE CONTAINED*
seety, seed(y)
seez, seize/ cease/ sea(s)/ see(s)
sef, sieve
sefalis, syphilis
sefan, seven
sefanteen, seventeen

segir, seize(zure)
segis, sedge(s)
segjest, suggest
segjestion, suggest(ion)
segjestshen, suggest(ion)
segma, sigma
segment,*,ted,ting,tary,tal,tally, *ONE PORTION/*
SECTION OF THE WHOLE
segmentul, segment(al)
segmintul, segment(al)
segmu, sigma
segnafiable, signify(fiable)
segnafier, signify(fier)
segnature, signature
segnifukent, significant
segnucher, signature
segnul, signal
segnushure, signature
segragashen, segregate(tion)
segragate, segregate
segregate,*,ed,ting,tion,tive,tionist, *TO SET*
APART, SEPARATE/DIVIDE FROM THE WHOLE
segrigate, segregate
segrugashen, segregate(tion)
segrugate, segregate
segur, seize(zure)
segus, sedge(s)
seible, see(able)
seige, siege
seine, *A NET (or see "seen" or scene)*
seing, see(ing)
seir, sear /seer
seira, sierra
seism,mic,mical,mically,city,cities,mism, *FREQUENCY/WAVES OF THE EARTH, EARTHQUAKE*
seista, siesta
seize,*,ed,zing,zure,zer, *TO GRAB/ CONFISCATE*
FORCEFULLY/QUICKLY (or see cease)
sej, sedge /siege

sejd, siege(d)
sejer, seize(zure)
sejes, sedge(s)
sejt, siege(d)
sejur, seize(zure)
sejus, sedge(s)
sek, sic/ sick/ seek
sekal, sickle
sekamore, sycamore
sekand, secant /second /secund
sekandery, second(ary)
sekandly, second(ly)
sekendly, second(ly)
sekent, secant /second /secund
sekently, second(ly)
sekeuridy, secure(rity)
sekewlir, secular
sekewlur, secular
sekewr, secure
sekewrity, secure(rity)
sekiatrist, psychiatry(rist)
sekiatry, psychiatry
sekil, sickle
sekind, secant /second /secund
sekindery, second(ary)
sekindly, second(ly)
sekintly, second(ly)
sekir, seek(er)
sekle, sickle
seklushen, seclusion
seklusion, seclusion
seklution, seclusion
sekma, sigma
sekment, segment
sekmentul, segment(al)
sekmint, segment
seknafiur, signify(fier)
seknafy, signify
seknashure, signature

sefanth, seventh
sefaree, safari
sefenteith, seventieth
sefestikashen, sophisticate(tion)
sefestikation, sophisticate(tion)
sefichent, sufficient
sefichunt, sufficient
sefin, seven
sefinteen, seventeen
sefinteith, seventieth
sefinth, seventh
sefise, suffice
sefishent, sufficient
sefishunt, sufficient
sefistukashen, sophisticate(tion)
sefistukation, sophisticate(tion)
seflus, syphilis
sefon, seven
sefonteen, seventeen
sefood, seafood
sefral, several
sefrense, severance
sefril, several
sefrinse, severance
sefrul, several
sefrunse, severance
sefud, seafood
sefules, syphilis
sefun, seven
sefunteen, seventeen
sefunteith, seventieth
sefunth, seventh
seg, siege /sedge
segar, cigar
segaret, cigarette
sege, sedge /siege
seged, siege(d)
seger, seize(zure)
seges, sedge(s) /siege(s)

seknifukent, significant
seknishure, signature
seknol, signal
seknucher, signature
seknul, signal
sekol, sickle
sekondery, second(ary)
sekragashen, segregate(tion)
sekragate, segregate
sekragation, segregate(tion)
sekrat, secret
sekratary, secretary
sekratereul, secretary(rial)
sekratery, secretary
sekratif, secret(ive)
sekrative, secret(ive)
sekregate, segregate(tion)
sekreshen, secrete(tion)
sekresion, secrete(tion)
sekret, secret /secrete
sekrete, secrete /secrete
sekretive, secret(ive)
sekretly, secret(ly)
sekrigashen, segregate(tion)
sekrigate, segregate
sekrigation, segregate(tion)
sekrit, secret
sekritary, secretary
sekritereul, secretary(rial)
sekritery, secretary
sekritive, secret(ive)
sekritly, secret(ly)
sekrogate, segregate
sekrtly, secret(ly)
sekrugashen, segregate(tion)
sekrugate, segregate
sekrugation, segregate(tion)
sekrut, secret
sekrutary, secretary

sekrutef, secret(ive)
sekrutereul, secretary(rial)
sekrutery, secretary
sekrutive, secret(ive)
sekrutly, secret(ly)
seks, seek(s) /sex
sekshen, section
sekshenul, section(al)
sekshin, section
sekshinul, section(al)
sekshuel, sexual
sekshuil, sexual
sekshun, section
sekshunal, section(al)
sekshwal, sexual
seksion, section
seksis, sex(es)
seksless, sex(less)
sekst, sex(ed)
sekstant, sextant
sekste, sixty
seksteen, sixteen
seksteenth, sixteen(th)
sekstent, sextant
sekstet, sextet
seksteuth, sixtieth
seksth, sixth
sekstile, sextile
sekstileon, sextillion
sekstillion, sextillion
sekstiuth, sixtieth
sekstuple, sextuple
sekstuplet, sextuplet
sekstupul, sextuple
seksty, sixty
seksualedy, sexual(ity)
seksuality, sexual(ity)
seksus, sex(es)
seksy, sex(y)

sekt, sect /seek(ed)
sekter, sector
sekth, sixth
sektion, section
sektional, section(al)
sektir, sector
sektur, sector
sekul, sickle
sekular, secular
sekulir, secular
sekum, succumb
sekund, secant/ second/ secund
sekundery, second(ary)
sekundly, second(ly)
sekuntly, second(ly)
sekure, secure
sekuridy, secure(rity)
sekurity, secure(rity)
sekwal, sequel
sekwel, sequel
sekwen, sequin
sekwense, sequence
sekwenshul, sequence(ntial)
sekwential, sequence(ntial)
sekwents, sequence
sekwil, sequel
sekwin, sequin
sekwinse, sequence
sekwoia, sequoia
sekwoya, sequoia
sekwul, sequel
sekwunts, sequence
sel, seal/ sell/ sale/ cell
selabent, celibant
selabil, syllable
selable, syllable
selabrate, celebrate
selabus, syllabus
selafane, cellophane

selakit, silica(te)
selal, salal
selami, salami
selanoid, solenoid
selaphane, cellophane
selareum, solarium
selary, celery
selawet, silhouette
seld, seal(ed) /sold
seldem, seldom
seldemly, seldom(ly)
seldom,mly,mness, RARELY/INFREQUENTLY
seldumly, seldom(ly)
selebrety, celebrity
selebusy, celibacy
select,*,ted,ting,tion,tness,tor,tee,tive,tively, tiveness,tivity, CHOOSE ONE AMONG MANY
selee, silly
selk, silk
selekshen, select(ion)
selekt, select
selektif, select(ive)
selektion, select(ion)
selektive, select(ive)
seleng, ceiling /seal(ing)
selenium,iferous, CHEMICAL ELEMENT
selenoid, solenoid
seler, cellar/ seal(er)/ sell(er)
selery, celery
self,lves, fless,flessly,flessness, FIRST PERSON FOR SELF
selfer, silver
selferware, silverware
selfesh, selfish
selfeshly, selfish(ly)
selfir, silver
selfish,hly,hness, LESS THOUGHT FOR OTHERS THAN FOR SELF
selfishlis, selfish(less)
selfis, self(less)

selflisness, self(lessness)
selfs, self(lves)
selfurware, silverware
selfury, silver(y)
selfush, selfish
seli, silly
selibent, celibant
selibrate, celebrate
selibuse, celibacy
selicon, silicon /silicone
selilaquy, soliloquy
selines, silly(lliness)
seling, ceiling/ sell(ing)/ seal(ing)
selinoid, solenoid
selir, cellar/ seal(er)/ sell(er)
seliset, solicit
selisetation, solicit(ation)
seliseter, solicit(er)
selivu, saliva
selkun, silk(en)
selky, silk(y)
sell,*,lling,ller, TO TRADE GOODS/SERVICES FOR MONEY (or see sail/ sale/ sill)
seller, cellar /sell(er)
sellfish, selfish
selluler, cellular
sellur, cellar /sell
seloet, silhouette
selomee, salami
selon, salon
selonoid, solenoid
seloon, saloon
seloot, salute
selor, cellar/ seal(er)/ sell(er)
sels, sell(s) /seal(s)
selseus, celsius
selt, seal(ed) /sold /silt
seltashen, silt(ation)
seltation, silt(ation)

seltem, seldom
seltum, seldom
selty, silt(y)
selubasy, celibacy
selubel, syllable
selubent, celibant
selubrate, celebrate
selubus, syllabus
selufane, cellophane
selukon, silicon /silicone
selular, cellular
selulite, cellulite
selulose, cellulose
selune, saloon
selunoid, solenoid
selur, cellar/ sell(er)/ seal(er)
selure, celery
selushen, solution
selute, salute
selution, solution
selverware, silverware
selvir, silver
selvurware, silverware
selvury, silver(y)
sely, silly
semalarity, similar(ity)
semaler, similar
semalerly, similar(ly)
semanar, seminar
semantics,cal,cally,cist, STUDY OF LANGUAGE/ WORDS
semar, simmer
semashen, sum(mmation)
semation, sum(mmation)
sematry, symmetry
sembal, symbol
sembalism, symbol(ism)
sembeodik, symbiotic
sembeosis, symbiosis

sembeotek, symbiotic
sembilism, symbol(ism)
sembiosis, symbiosis
semblance, *, *SIMILARITY/RESEMBLANCE*
semble, symbol
semblents, semblance
semblinse, semblance
sembolek, symbol(ic)
sembolik, symbol(ic)
sembul, cymbal /symbol
sembulism, symbol(ism)
semdum, symptom
semecolon, semicolon
semekolun, semicolon
semelur, similar
semelurly, similar(ly)
semen, *SUBSTANCE CONTAINING MALE SPERM*
semenal, seminal
semenar, seminar
sement, cement
semenul, seminal
semesder, semester
semester, *, tral,trial, *SIX MONTH PERIOD OF TIME*
semetric, symmetry(ric)
semetry, symmetry
semeulate, simulate
semewlation, simulate(tion)
semfeny, symphony
semfonic, symphony(nic)
semfune, symphony
semi, *PREFIX INDICATING "HALF/PARTLY" MOST OFTEN*
MODIFIES THE WORD
semicolon, *, *A PUNCTUATION MARK*
semikolin, semicolon
semilarity, similar(ity)
semiler, similar
semilerly, similar(ly)
semin, semen

seminal, lly, niferous, *CAPABLE OF CREATING LIFE/*
FUTURE DEVELOPMENT
seminar, *, *A GROUP OF PEOPLE CONVERGING*
TOGETHER TO LEARN ONE THING IN PARTICULAR
semingly, seem(ingly)
semir, simmer
semitary, cemetary
semliness, seem(liness)
semly, seem(ly)
semon, semen
semonal, seminal
semonar, seminar
semoolader, simulate(tor)
sempal, simple
sempalest, simple(st)
sempaly, simple(ly)
sempathee, sympathy
sempathetic, sympathy(hetic)
sempathize, sympathy(hize)
sempathy, sympathy
sempdum, symptom
sempel, simple
sempelist, simple(st)
sempethy, sympathy
semphonek, symphony(nic)
semphonic, symphony(nic)
semphuny, symphony
sempithize, sympathy(hize)
sempithy, sympathy
semple, simple
sempler, simple(r)
semplest, simple(st)
semplisity, simple(licity)
semplistec, simple(listic)
sempol, simple
sempoler, simple(r)
sempolest, simple(st)
semposeum, symposium

sempozeum, symposium
semptem, symptom
semptum, symptom
sempul, simple
sempuler, simple(r)
sempulest, simple(st)
sempuly, simple(ly)
semputhee, sympathy
semputhetic, sympathy(hetic)
semputhize, sympathy(hize)
semstras, seamstress
semstrus, seamstress
semtem, symptom
semtum, symptom
semulader, simulate(tor)
semularly, similar(ly)
semulashen, simulate(tion)
semulate, simulate
semulation, simulate(tion)
semulator, simulate(tor)
semuler, similar
semulerly, similar(ly)
semullarety, similar(ity)
semun, semen
semunal, seminal
semunar, seminar
semur, simmer
semutare, cemetary
semutree, symmetry
semwat, somewhat
semwere, somewhere
semwhat, somewhat
semwhere, somewhere
semwot, somewhat
sen, seen/ scene/ seine/ sin
senada, sonata
senak, scene(nic)
senamon, cinnamon
senanem, synonym

senapse, synapse
senapsis, synapsis
senaptek, synaptic
senaptic, synaptic
senareo, scenario
senary, scene(ry)
senaster, sinister
senate, *A BODY/HOUSE OF U.S. GOVERNMENT*
senator,*,rial,rially,rship, *ELECTED MEMBER OFTHE*
U.S. GOVERNMENT
senatoriel, senator(ial)
senatu, sonata
senc, sync /sink
sence, since
sench, cinch
senched, singe(d) /cinch(ed)
senchro, syncro
senchronus, synchrony(nous)
sencht, singe(d) /cinch(ed)
sencro, syncro
sencronize, synchrony(nize)
sencrony, synchrony
send,*,ding,der,nt, *PUSH/ENCOURAGE SOMETHING*
TO LEAVE YOUR VICINITY,HAVE DELIVERED
sendamental, sentiment(al)
sendamintal, sentiment(al)
sender, cinder /send(er)
sendicate, syndicate
sendication, syndicate(tion)
sendikation, syndicate(tion)
sendiket, syndicate
sendral, central
sendrem, syndrome
sendrum, syndrome
sendukit, syndicate
sendumentil, sentiment(al)
sendumeter, centimeter
sene, scene /seen
sened, sin(nned)

senek, scene(nic)
senema, cinema
seneority, senior(ity)
sener, sin(nner)
senerist, scenario(ist)
senery, scene(ry)
senete, senate
senetor, senator
senew, sinew
senful, sin(ful)
senfuly, sin(fully)
seng, sing/ sink/ singe/ cinch
sengal, single
senge, singe /cinch
senged, singe(d) /cinch(ed)
sengel, single
senger, sing(er)
sengewler, singular
sengle, single
sengs, sing(s) /sink(s)
sengt, singe(d) /cinch(ed)
sengul, single
sengularedy, singular(ity)
sengularly, singular(ly)
senguled, single(d)
senguler, singular
senguleridy, singular(ity)
senguly, single(ly)
senical, cynical
senik, cynic /scene(nic)
senile,lity, *WHEN THE MIND CEASES TO STAY SHARP/*
ALERT DUE TO AGING
senilidy, senile(lity)
senior,*,rity, *UPPER RANK, OLDER THAN MOST,*
HIGHER IN CLASS
senir, sin(nner)
senirgy, synergy
seniry, scene(ry)
senistur, sinister

senite, senate
senitor, senator
senitoreul, senator(ial)
senj, singe /cinch
senjt, singe(d) /cinch(ed)
senk, sync /sink
senker, sink(er) /sing(er)
senkewler, singular
senkil, single
senkir, sink(er) /sing(er)
senkle, single(ly)
senkranes, synchrony(nous)
senkro, syncro
senkrone, synchrony
senkronize, synchrony(nize)
senkrunus, synchrony(nous)
senkt, sink(ed)
senkul, single
senkularedy, singular(ity)
senkularly, singular(ly)
senkuler, singular
senkur, sink(er) /sing(er)
senles, sin(less)
senoda, sonata
senodu, sonata
senografee, scenography
senography, scenography
senonemus, synonym(ous)
senonim, synonym
senonimus, synonym(ous)
senonym, synonym
senopsis, synopsis
senota, sonata
senotor, senator
sens, sense /since /cent(s) /sin(s)
sensability, sensible(bility)
sensable, sensible
sensaridy, sincere(rity)
sensarity, sincere(rity)

sensashen, sensation
sensation, *, nal,nally,nalism,nalist,nalistic, *A FEELING /SENSE /KNOWINGNESS OF AN AFFECT*
sensative, sensitive
sensd, sense(d)
sense, *,ed,sing,er,eless, *TO FEEL/KNOW, OF THE SIX SENSES; HEAR/SEE/SMELL/TASTE/TOUCH/ FEEL* (or see sent or cent(s))
sensebility, sensible(bility)
senseble, sensible
senseer, sincere
senseerly, sincere(ly)
sensere, sincere / censor
senseredy, sincere(rity)
senserity, sincere(rity)
senserly, sincere(ly)
senshewality, sensual(ity)
senshewus, sensuous
senshual, sensual
senshuality, sensual(ity)
senshues, sensuous
senshuil, sensual
senshury, century
sensible,eness,ly,bility,bilities, *TO BE NORMAL/ PREDICTABLE TO OTHERS*
sensir, sensor /censor
sensitive,ely,eness,vity,vities,ize,ization,izer, *READILY RESPONDS TO STIMULUS*
sensitivity, sensitive(vity)
sensless, sense(less)
sensor, censor /censure
sensor,*,red,ring,ry,rial, *ABLE TO RESPOND TO A PARTICULAR STIMULUS, SENSE IMPULSES*
sensoreal, sensor(ial)
sensual,lity,lly,lism,list,listic,lize,lization, *OPEN TO THE BODY'S EXPRESSION/DESIRE/FEELING, UNINHIBITED*
sensuble, sensible
sensuous,sly,sness, *OF BEING SENSUAL*

sensur, sensor /censor
sensus, censes /sense
sensutive, sensitive
sensutivity, sensitive(vity)
sent,PAST TENSE OF "SEND"(or see scent/sin(nned)
sentaks, syntax
sentamental, sentiment(al)
sentax, syntax
sentchuous, sensuous
sentchuwos, sensuous
sented, scent(ed)
senteince, sentient(ncy)
senteint, sentient
sentekit, syndicate
sentement, sentiment
sentemental, sentiment(al)
sentence,*,ed,cing,ntial,ntially, *COMPLETE THOUGHT GRAMMATICALLY, A FORMAL JUDGEMENT/ DECISION*
senteneul, centennial
sentennial, centennial
sentense, sentence
senter, center
senthasis, synthesis
senthedek, synthetic
senthedik, synthetic
senthesis, synthesis
senthetic, synthetic
senthusis, synthesis
sentient,tly,nce,ncy, *ABILITY/FACULTY TO PERCEIVE CONSCIOUSLY*
sentigrade, centigrade
sentiment,*,tal,tally,tality,talities,talism,talist, talize,talization, *EMOTIONALLY SWAYED BY THE PAST*
sentimeter, centimeter
sentineol, centennial
sentinse, sentence
sentipede, centipede

sentless, scent(less)
sentrul, central
sentry,ries, *A GUARD FOR GATE/ENTRY*
sents, since/ sense/ cent(s)/ scent(s)
sentument, sentiment
sentumental, sentiment(al)
sentury, century
senu, sinew
senuee, sinew(y)
senuk, scene(nic)
senunem, synonym
senupeded, centipede
senur, sin(nner)
senurgy, synergy
senury, scene(ry)
senuster, sinister
senute, senate
senutor, senator
senutoreul, senator(ial)
senutorial, senator(ial)
senuw, sinew
senuy, sinew(y)
senyer, senior
senyority, senior(ity)
senyuee, sinew(y)
senyur, senior
seonse, se'ance
sep, seep /sip
sepage, seep(age)
sepal, *,led,lled,lous,loid, *PART OF A FLOWER*
separable,bility,eness,bly, *ABLE TO BE SEPARATED*
separador, separator
separashen, separate(tion)
separate,*,ed,ting,tion,ely,eness,tist,tism,tistic, tive, *DIVIDE/BREAK APART FROM THE WHOLE*
separator,*, *THAT WHICH ENCOURAGES SEPARATION*
separet, separate
separite, separate
sepausatory, suppository

sepd, sip(pped)
sepea, sepia
sepege, seep(age)
sepej, seep(age)
seperabul, separable
seperader, separator
seperashen, separate(tion)
seperate, separate
seperately, separate(tly)
seperation, separate(tion)
seperatly, separate(tly)
seperator, separator
seperible, separable
seperubil, separable
sepeu, sepia
sephelis, syphilis
sephules, syphilis
sepia, *A COLOR/PIGMENT, A FISH*
sepige, seep(age)
sepij, seep(age)
sepil, sepal
sepirable, separable
sepirador, separator
sepirashen, separate(tion)
sepirate, separate
sepiration, separate(tion)
sepirator, separator
sepirlative, superlative
sepiruble, separable
sepkonshes, subconsciouse
sepkontrakt, subcontract
seplant, supplant
seple, sepal
sepli, supply
seplier, supply(lier)
sepling, sibling
sepliur, supply(lier)
seply, supply
sepol, sepal
seport, support
seportive, support(ive)
sepose, suppose
seposetory, suppository
seposubly, suppose(dly)
sepozatory, suppository
sepoze, suppose
sepozubly, suppose(dly)
seprabul, separable
seprashen, separate(tion)
seprat, separate
sepratisem, separate(tism)
seprative, separate(tive)
sepratly, separate(tly)
seprator, separator
seprechen, suppress(ion)
sepreem, supreme
sepreme, supreme
sepres, suppress
sepreshen, suppress(ion)
sepret, separate
sepretion, suppress(ion)
sepretism, separate(tism)
sepretive, separate(tly)
sepretly, separate(tly)
sepribul, separable
seprino, soprano
seprit, separate
sepritesm, separate(tism)
sepritly, separate(tly)
sepruble, separable
seprubul, separable
seprut, separate
seprutly, separate(tly)
septar, scepter
septek, septic /styptic
September, *A MONTH OF THE YEAR*
septer, scepter
septic,*,cally,city, *THAT WHICH CAUSES PUTREFACTION OR SEPSIS, OF BEING ROTTEN*
septik, styptic
septimber, September
septir, scepter
septisity, septic(ity)
septor, scepter
septupil, septuple
septuple,ed,ling, *SEVEN TIMES/FOLD*
septur, scepter
sepuge, seep(age)
sepuj, seep(age)
sepul, sepal
sepurabul, separable
sepurador, separator
sepurashen, separate(tion)
sepurate, separate
sepurately, separate(tly)
sepurater, separator
sepuration, separate(tion)
sepurb, superb
sepurblee superb(ly)
sepurible, separable
sepurlative, superlative
sequel,*, *CONTINUATION ON THE STORY*
sequence,cy,er,ntial,ntially, *SERIES/PARTS ALIGNED IN ORDER/PATTERN*
sequenshil, sequence(ntial)
sequer, secure
sequill, sequel
sequin,*,ned, *SMALL REFLECTIVE DECORATIONS USED ON CLOTHING*
sequir, secure
sequoia,*, *TYPE OF TREE, A TRIBE*
seqwen, sequin
ser, seer/ sir/ sear
seraget, surrogate
seran, saran
seranade, serenade

serandipity, serendipity
serandipudy, serendipity
serap, syrup
serape,*, , *OUTER GARMENT/BLANKET/SHAWL*
serashen, serrate(tion)
serated, serrate(d)
seration, serrate(tion)
serbent, serpent
sercafigus, sarcophagus
serch, search
sercharj, surcharge
serchuble, search(able)
sercle, circle
sercophagus, sarcophagus
sercumfurens, circumference
sercumsize, circumcise
sercumstans, circumstance
sercut, circuit
serdufy, certify
sereal, serial/ cereal/ surreal
serealism, surrealism
serees, series
serel, sorrel /surreal
serelism, surrealism
serenade,*,ed,ding,er, *SOLITARY PERFORMANCE BY*
SOMEONE FOR SOMEONE IN PARTICULAR
serender, surrender
serendipity,tous, *UNEXPECTED/ACCIDENTAL HAPPY*
ENDING
serene,ely,eness,nity,nities, *TRANQUIL/PEACEFUL*
sereol, serial /cereal
serep, syrup
sereul, serial /cereal
sereulizum, surrealism
sereus, serious
sereusly, serious(ly)
serf,fage,fdom,fhood,fism,fish, *WORKER WHO BE-*
LONGED WITH THE LAND (or see surf or serve)
serface, surface

serfdum, serf(dom)
serfee, surf(y)
serfej, serf(age)
serfes, surface
serfis, surface /service
serfuge, serf(age)
serfunt, servant
serfur, surf(er)
serfus, surface /service
sergd, surge(d)
serge, *A TWILLED FABRIC (or see surge)*
sergeant,*,ncy, *A RANK/POSITION WITHIN THE U.S.*
MILITARY/POLICE
sergen, surgeon
sergent, sargeant
sergeon, surgeon
sergery, surgery
sergikul, surgical
sergin, surgeon
sergiry, surgery
sergon, surgeon
sergree, surgery
sergukle, surgical
serguree, surgery
serial,lly,list,lize,lization, *SUCCESSIVE NUMBER/*
SERIES (or see cereal)
seriasis, psoriasis
series, *CORRESPONDING/SUCCESSIVE EVENTS/ITEMS*
serim, serum
serimony, ceremony
serinade, serenade
serinder, surrender
serindipity, serendipity
serindipudy, serendipity
serious,sly,sness, *EARNEST/SOLEMN/GRAVE*
serip, syrup
seris, scirrhus /cirrus
seriulesm, surrealism
serius, serious

seriusis, psoriasis
serjakle, surgical
serjaree, surgery
serje, surge /serge
serjen, surgeon
serjikul, surgical
serjon, surgeon
serjree, surgery
serjukle, surgical
serkemsize, circumcise
serkimstans, circumstance
serkimsize, circumcise
serkis, circuis
serkit, circuit
serkle, circle
serkofegus, sarcophagus
serkofigus, sarcophagus
serkulate, circulate
serkuler, circular
serkumfurense, circumference
serkumsize, circumcise
serkumstans, circumstance
serkus, circus
serlee, surly
serloin, sirloin
serly, surly
serman, sermon
sermize, surmise
sermon, *,nic,nize,nizer, *A RELIGIOUS DISCOURSE*
sermun, sermon
serogate, surrogate
serondipity, serendipity
serong, sarong
serope, serape
seroredy, sorority
serority, sorority
seros, scirrhus /cirrus
seround, surround
serownd, surround

serpas, surpass
serpent,*, A SNAKE
serpentene, serpentine
serpentine, SHAPED/MOVEMENT OF A SNAKE
serpint, serpent
serpintene, serpentine
serplus, surplus
serprize, surprise
serrate,ed,ting,tion, MANY TEETH, HAVING THE
    OUTLINE OF MANY JAGGED TEETH
serrender, surrender
sersharge, surcharge
sertification, certificate(tion)
sertificut, certificate
sertifucate, certificate
sertifikashen, certificate(tion)
sertin, certain
sertufie, certify
seruget, surrogate
serum,*, A FLUID OF INOCULATION
serumony, ceremony
serunade, serenade
serundipety, serendipity
serundipudy, serendipity
serup, syrup
serus, cirrus /scirrhus
serva, survey
servaer, survey(or)
servailense, surveillance
servailinse, surveillance
servant,*, ONE EMPLOYED/OWNED TO PERFORM
    DOMESTIC CHORES/WORK
servatood, servitude
servatude, servitude
servaur, survey(or)
servayer, survey(or)
serve,*,ed,ving,er, ONE WHO PUTS A BALL INTO
    PLAY, TO PERFORM DUTIES FOR OTHERS
serveilinse, surveillance

servent, servant
serveor, survey(or)
serves, service
serveyor, survey(or)
service,*,ed,cing,eable,eability,eableness,eably,
    ACCOMODATE/PROVIDE SOMEONE/SOMETHING
servife, survive
serviks, cervix
servint, servant
servisuble, service(cable)
servitude, TO BE IN THE SERVICE OF OTHERS
servive, survive
serviver, survive(vor)
servivul, survive(val)
servunt, servant
servusable, service(cable)
servutude, servitude
ses, see(s) sea(s)/ seize /cease
sesal, sizzle
sesame,*, AN EDIBLE SEED
sesan, season
sesdamadik, system(atic)
sesdamatic, system(atic)
sesdan, sustain
sesdum, system
sesdumadik, system(atic)
sesdumatic, system(atic)
sesede, secede
sesee, sissy
sesel, sizzle
sesen, season
seseptif, suceptive
seseptive, suceptive
sesers, scissors
seset, secede
sesetion, secession
seshell, seashell
seshon, session
sesil, sizzle

sesime, sesame
sesin, season
sesion, session
sesirs, scissors
sesle, sizzle
sesmek, seism(ic)
sesmic, seism(ic)
sesmical, seism(ical)
sesmik, seism(ic)
sesome, sesame
seson, season
sesors, scissors
sespend, suspend
sespishus, suspicious
session,*,nal, A PERIOD/COURSE/SPECIFIC OF TIME
sest, cyst
sestain, sustain
sestane, sustain
sestanuble, sustain(able)
sester, sister
sestim, system
sestir, sister
sestum, system
sestumatic, system(atic)
sestur, sister
sesturly, sister(ly)
sesul, sizzle
sesume, sesame
sesun, season
sesurs, scissors
sesy, sissy
set,*,tting,ttee,tter, SET OF ITEMS, PUT INTO PLACE
    (TOO MANY DEFINITIONS, PLEASE CONSULT
    STANDARD DICTIONARY) (or see seat or said)
setal, settle
setalment, settle(ment)
setament, sediment
setamentary, sedament(ary)
setamint, sediment

setanic, satanic
setanikul, satanic(al)
setchuashen, situate(tion)
setee, set(ttee)
setel, settle
setelment, settle(ment)
setemint, sediment
seteminary, sedament(ary)
seter, set(tter)
seterical, satire(rical)
seth, seethe /scythe
setil, settle
setilment, settle(ment)
setion, session
setir, set(tter)
setle, settle
setling, seedling /settle(ling)
setlment, settle(ment)
settle,*,ed,ling,ement,er, FINAL AGREEMENT, BECOME STATIONARY
setuashen, situate(tion)
setuation, situate(tion)
setul, settle
setulers, settle(rs)
setulment, settle(ment)
setumentary, sedament(ary)
setur, set(tter)/ seat(er)/ seed(er)
sety, city
seubil, see(able)
seuble, see, see(able)
seuler, cellular
seur, sear /seer
sev, sieve
sevan, seven
sevandy, seventy
sevant, savant
sevanteen, seventeen
sevanteith, seventieth
sevanth, seventh

sevanty, seventy
sevanu, savanna
sevarul, several
seven,*, A NUMBER
sevendeith, seventieth
sevendy, seventy
seventeen, A DOUBLE DIGIT NUMBER
seventh, A PLACE IN THE NUMBER SEQUENCE, COMES AFTER THE SIXTH
seventieth, COMES AFTER THE 69TH IN NUMBER SEQUENCE
seventy,ties, COMES AFTER 69 IN NUMBER SEQUENCE
sever,*,red,ring,rable,ralty,rance, TO CUT OFF, SEPARATE FROM HOST (or see severe)
several,lly, MORE THAN TWO
severance, SEPARATION/SPLIT/PARTING, FROM THE WORD "SEVER"
severe,ely,eness,rity,rities, EXTREME/ HARSH/ PUNISHING (or see sever)
severedy, severe(rity)
severt, sever(ed)
severinse, severance
severly, severe(ly)
severul, several
severunse, severance
sevik, civic
sevil, civil
sevilean, civilian
sevin, seven
sevindeith, seventieth
sevindy, seventy
sevinteen, seventeen
sevinteith, seventieth
sevinth, seventh
sevinty, seventy
seviral, several
seviranse, severance
sevird, severe(d)

sevire, severe /sever
sevirly, severe(ly)
sevirt, sever(ed)
sevirunse, severance
sevon, seven
sevondeith, seventieth
sevondy, seventy
sevont, savant
sevonteen, seventeen
sevonteith, seventieth
sevor, sever
sevral, several
sevrense, severance
sevrul, several
sevrunse, severance
sevt, sift /sieve(d)
sevun, seven
sevundeith, seventieth
sevundy, seventy
sevunteen, seventeen
sevunteith, seventieth
sevunth, seventh
sevunty, seventy
sevur, sever
sevural, several
sevuranse, severance
sevurd, sever(ed)
sew,*,wer,wed,wing,wn, TO JOIN/UNITE PIECES WITH STITCHES (or see "so / sow")
sewage, WASTE MATTER
sewaro, saguaro
sewd, sue(d) /sew(ed)
sewdanim, pseudonym
sewdo, pseudo
sewdonim, pseudonym
sewer,*,rage, A CHANNEL FOR WASTE/WATER (or see sew(er))
sewfaner, souvenir
sewfineer, souvenir

sewflay, souffle'
sewfuner, souvenir
sewkrose, sucrose
sewn, PAST TENSE OF "SEW" (or see son or sown)
seworo, saguaro
sewpee, soup(y)
sewperb, superb
sewpurb, superb
sewpy, soup(y)
sewt, soot /suit
sewtanim, pseudonym
sewto, pseudo
sewtonim, pseudonym
sewture, suture
sex,xes,xed,xing,xless,xy, CONCERNING THE
    REPRODUCTIVE AREAS
sexis, sex(es)
sexshen, section
sexshin, section
sexshinul, section(al)
sexshualedy, sexual(ity)
sexshuality, sexual(ity)
sexshunol, section(al)
sexshwal, sexual
sextant, SIXTH PART OF A CIRCLE, AN INSTRUMENT
sexteen, sixteen
sexteenth, sixteenth
sextet,*, SIX IN A COLLECTION
sexth, sixth
sextile, ASTRONOMICAL/STATISTICAL EXPRESSION
sextileon, sextillion
sextilion, sextillion
sextillion,nth, A VERY LARGE NUMBER
sextint, sextant
sextion, section
sextional, section(al)
sextuple,ed,ling, SIX FOLD/PARTS/TIMES
sextuplet,*, SIX EQUAL
sexual,lly,lity, PERTAINING TO THE FIRST SEAL/SEX

sexuol, sexual
sexuoly, sexual(lly)
sexus, sex(es)
sexyewality, sexual(ity)
sexyewul, sexual
sexyuality, sexual(ity)
sexyuol, sexual
seyer, sear /seer
seyons, se'ance
seyur, sear /seer
sez, seize/ cease/ sea(s)/ see(s)
sezal, sizzle
sezen, season
sezil, sizzle
sezin, season
sezle, sizzle
sezmek, seism(ic)
sezmic, seism(ic)
sezmical, seism(ical)
sezors, scissors
sezul, sizzle
sezun, season
sezurs, scissors
sfarekil, sphere(rical)
sfeer, sphere
sfencks, sphinx
sfencter, sphincter
sfenktur, sphincter
sfenx, sphinx
sfer, sphere
sferakil, sphere(rical)
sfere, sphere
sferekul, sphere(rical)
sferical, sphere(rical)
sferukle, sphere(rical)
sfincter, sphincter
sfinks, sphinx
sfinktur, sphincter
sfinx, sphinx

sgoundrel, scoundrel
sgowndrul, scoundrel
sgragliest, scraggly(liest)
sgrakleur, scraggly(lier)
shabby,bily,biness, WORN/THREADBARE
shabely, shabby(bbily)
shabiness, shabby(bbiness)
shaby, shabby
shack,*,ked,king, A SHANTY/PRIMITIVE HUT/CABIN
    (or see shag or shake)
shackle,*,ed,ling,er, A FASTENER/CUFFS
shade,*,ed,ding,dy,eless, OVERHEAD PROTECTION
    FROM THE SUN
shader, shatter
shadey, shade(dy)
shadir, shatter
shado, shadow
shadow,*,wed,wing,wy, AREA WHERE THE LIGHT
    DOESN'T PENETRATE, SCREEN/PROTECT
shadur, shatter
shaem, shame
shaemful, shame(ful)
shaenk, shank
shafd, shaft/ shave(d)/ chafe(d)
shafe, shave /chafe
shafed, shaft /shave(d)
shaft,*,ted,ting, NARROW COLUMN/CYLINDER (or
    see chafe(d) or shave(d))
shag,gged,gging,ggy,ggier,ggiest, CARPET, TO
    RETRIEVE, LOOSE THREADS (or see shack)
shagier, shag(ggier)
shagiest, shag(ggiest) /shake(kiest)
shagy, shag(ggy)
shaim, shame
shaimless, shame(less)
shaink, shank
shak, shack /shake

shake,*,ed,king,er,ky,kier,kiest, *JUMBLE/JOSTLE/ VIBRATE, MOVE UP AND DOWN, BUILDING MATERIAL* (or see shack)
shaked, shack(ed) /shake(d)
shakel, shackle
shakul, shackle
shakult, shackle(d)
shakyest, shake(kiest)
shal, shall /shale /shawl
shale,*, *TYPE OF CLAY-ROCK* (or see shell)
shalet, shallot
shalit, shallot
shall, *COULD, ALLOWED/ABLE TO* (or see shell)
shallot,*, *PLANT BULBS USED IN COOKING*
shallow,wly,wness, *OF LITTLE DEPTH, SUPERFICIAL*
shalo, shallow
shaloness, shallow(ness)
shalot, shallot
shalow, shallow
shalowness, shallow(ness)
shalut, shallot
sham,,mmed,mming,mmer, *COVER-UP FOR THE TRUTH* (or see shame)
shaman,*, nic,nism,nist,nistic, *WISE ONE WITH SPIRITUAL POWERS*
shambal, shamble
shamble,,ed,ling, *UNSTEADY, DISORDER*
shambul, shamble
shame,*,,ed,ming,eful,efully,efulness,eless, *OF DISGRACE/DISHONORED* (or see sham)
shamed, shame(d) /sham(mmed)
shamen, shaman
shamer, sham(mmer)
shamful, shame(ful)
shamin, shaman
shaminesm, shaman(ism)
shamless, shame(less)
shamonek, shaman(ic)
shamonism, shaman(ism)

shample, shamble
shampoo,*,ooed,ooing,ooer, *USE SOAP TO CLEAN HAIR/CARPET/UPHOLSTERY*
shampoor, shampoo(er)
shampu, shampoo
shampuir, shampoo(er)
shampul, shamble
shamrock,*, *PLANT*
shamrok, shamrock
shananigen, shenanigan
shananugin, shenanigan
shandalere, chandelier
shandulere, chandelier
shange, change
shank,*, *PART OF THE BODY*
shanty,ties, *ROUGH/FRONTIER STRUCTURE*
shantys, shanty(ties)
shape,*,ed,ping,pable,eless,elessness,elessly, eliness,ely,er, *OF FORM/FIGURE*
shapeable, shape(pable)
shaperd, shepherd
shaplis, shape(less)
shaply, shape(ly)
shapuble, shape(pable)
shapuer, shampoo(er)
sharade, charade
shard,*, *FRAGMENT*
share,*,ed,ring,er, *TO DIVIDE INTO PORTIONS*
sharee, sherry
sharef, sheriff
shari, sherry
sharif, sheriff
shark,*, *MARINE FISH, LIKE A SHARK*
sharp,ply,pness,pen,pens,pened,pener,per,pie, *DISTINCT POINT/TIP*
sharpin, sharp(en)
sharpind, sharp(ened)
sharpinur, sharp(ener)

sharpnis, sharp(ness)
sharpuner, sharp(ener)
sharpy, sharp(ie)
sharry, sherry
sharuf, sheriff
shate, shade
shater, shatter
shatir, shatter
shato, shadow
shatord, shatter(ed)
shatoy, shadow(y)
shatter,*,red,ring, *REDUCE TO PIECES/FRAGMENTS*
shaturd, shatter(ed)
shauk, chalk/ choke/ shock/ chock
shavar, shave(r)
shave,*,ed,ving,er, *TO REDUCE THE SURFACE/ OUTCROP, SCRATCH/GRAZE THE SURFACE*
shavir, shave(r)
shavur, shave(r)
shawer, shower
shawir, shower
shawl,*, *EXTERIOR GARMENT FOR SHOULDERS*
shawmen, shaman
shawmonism, shaman(ism)
shawur, shower
she,*, *THAT FEMALE*
sheaf,aves, *BOUND STALKS, QUIVER OF ARROWS*
shear,*,red,ring,rer,shorn, *TO CUT WITH CLIPPERS* (or see sheer)
sheath,hes,hed,her, *CASE/COVERING FOR A SWORD* (or see sheer)
sheberd, shepherd
sheburd, shepherd
shechul, special
she'd,, *CONTRACTION OF THE WORDS "SHE HAD/WOULD"* (or see shed)
shed,*,dded,dding, *A SMALL STRUCTURE* (or see she'd or sheet)
sheef, sheaf
sheek, chic

sheeld, shield
sheen,*,ned,ning,nier,niest,ny, RADIANT/BRIGHT/ LIGHT
sheengul, shingle
sheep,pish, A RUMINANT ANIMAL
sheer,*,red,ring,rer,rly,rness, NAUTICAL TERM, NEAR TRANSPARENT, OF LITTLE BODY/SUBSTANCE (or see shear)
sheet,*,ting, THIN/FLAT SUBSTANCE/MATERIAL
sheeth, sheath
shef, chief /chief /sheaf
shefor, shiver
sheft, shift
shefur, shiver
sheild, shield
sheilt, shield
shel, she'll /shell
shelak, shallac
sheld, shield /shell(ed)
sheld, shield
sheldur, shelter
sheldurless, shelter(less)
shelf, HORIZONTAL LEDGE TO PLACE THINGS ON (or see shelve)
shelfs, shelve(s)
she'll, CONTRACTION OF THE WORDS "SHE WILL" (or see shell)
shell,*,lled,lling, HOUSING/PROTECTION FOR CREATURES, LAYERS OF ATOM, HAND OVER (or see she'll)
shellac, A CHEMICAL SOLUTION
shelt, shell(ed)
shelter,*,red,ring,rless,COVER/PROTECTION/REFUGE
sheltired, shelter(ed)
sheltur, shelter
shelturd, shelter(ed)
shelturless, shelter(less)
shelve,*,ed,ving,er, PLURAL FOR SHELF, LEDGE TO PLACE ITEMS

shem, shim
shemed, shim(mmed) /shimmy(mmied)
shemee, shimmy
shemir, shimmer
shemmiry, shimmer(y)
shemonic, shaman(ic)
shemur, shimmer
shemury, shimmer(y)
shemy, shimmy
shen, sheen/ shin/ chin
shenanigan,*, NONSENSE TRICKERY
shengle, shingle
shengul, shingle
shep, sheep /ship
shepard, shepherd
sheper, ship(pper)
sheperd, shepherd
shepherd,*, THAT WHICH GUARDS/PROTECTS
shepird, shepherd
shepish, sheep(ish)
sheprek, shipwreck
shept, ship(pped)
shepur, ship(pper)
shepurd, shepherd
shepwreck, shipwreck
sher, sure/ share/ chair
sherba, sherbet
sherbet,*, FRUIT FLAVORED ICE DESSERT
sherbirt, sherbet
sherburt, sherbet
sherd, shear(ed) /sheer(ed) /share(d)
shered, shear(ed) /sheer(ed) /share(d)
sheredy, surety
sheri, sherry
sheridy, surety
sheriff, sheriff
sheriff,*, LAW ENFORCEMENT OFFICIAL
sherir, shear(er)

sherity, surety
sherly, sure(ly)
sheror, shear(er)
sherrif, sheriff
sherry,ries, TYPE OF WINE
shert, shear(ed) /sheer(ed) /shirt
sheruf, sheriff
sherur, shear(er)
shery, sherry
shet, shed/ sheet/ she'd
shethd, sheath(ed)
sheult, shield
shevir, shiver
shevt, shift
shevtur, shift(er)
shevulry, chivalry
shevur, shiver
shew, shoe /chew
shewr, sure
shews, shoe(s)
shewt, chute /shoot /chew(ed)
shi, shy
shid, shy(hied)
shield,*,ded,ding, USED FOR DEFENSE/PROTECTION
shier, shy(er)
shift,*,ted,ting,tingly,tingness,ter,tless,tlessly, tlessness,ty,tily,tiness, LEAVE ONE GEAR/ FOCUS/PLACE/POINT TO GO TO ANOTHER
shiftur, shift(er)
shifur, shiver
shil, she'll /shell
shilak, shellac
shild, shield
shilee, shy(ly)
shily, shy(ly)
shim,*,mmed,mming, A THIN STRIP OF SOME MATERIAL USED TO FILL GAPS
shimanik, shaman(ic)
shimee, shimmy

shimer, shimmer
shimery, shimmer(y)
shimes, shimmy(mmies) /shim(s)
shimmer,*,ry, *LIGHT/GLEAMING*
shimmy,mmies,mmied,mmying, *VIBRATION/ WOBBLING*
shimonic, shaman(ic)
shimur, shimmer
shimury, shimmer(y)
shimy, shimmy
shimyd, shimmy(mmied)
shimys, shimmy(mmies)
shin,*,nned,nning, *PART OF THE LEG, SPLINT OF WOOD* (or see shine or chin)
shinanigan, shananigan
shinanugan, shenanigan
shind, shine(d) /shin(nned)
shine,*,ed,ning,er,ny,nier,niest,niness, *RADIANT/ REFLECTIVE* (or see chin /shin /shiny)
shineist, shiny(niest)
shiness, shy(ness)
shineur, shiny(nier)
shingle,*,ed,ling, *ROOF COVERING, PAINFUL VIRAL INFECTION*
shingul, shingle
shinguled, shingle(d)
shinie, shiny
shinyest, shiny(niest)
shinyness, shiny(niness)
ship,*,pped,pping,pper, *A WATER/NAUTICAL VESSEL, SEND SOMETHING BY ROAD/SEA/AIR*
shipd, ship(pped)
shiper, ship(pper)
shiprek, shipwreck
shipur, ship(pper)
shipwreck,*,ked, *BOAT WHICH WRECKS IN THE SEA*
shir, sure /shy(er)
shirbert, sherbet

shirbet, sherbet
shirburt, sherbet
shiredy, surety
shirety, surety
shirly, sure(ly)
shirt,*, *UPPER TORSO GARMENT*
shister, shyster
shistur, shyster
shiur, shy(er)
shiver,*,red,ring, *SHAKE/TREMBLE FROM COLD/FEAR*
shivt, shift
shivulry, chivalry
shivur, shiver
sho, show
shoal,*, *SHALLOW AREA ASSOCIATED WITH A BODY OF WATER, SCHOOL OF FISH*
shoar, shore /chore
shock,*,ked,king,ker,kingly, *SUDDEN/ABRUPT/ UNPREDICTABLE EVENT, JOLT OF ELECTRICITY, SUDDEN IMPACT*
shod,*, *TO SHOE A HORSE* (or see show(ed)/shoot/ shoe(d) /should)
shode, shoddy
shoddy,ddies, *INFERIOR PRODUCT/SERVICE PRODUCED TO MOCK FINE QUALITY*
shody, shoddy
shoe,*,er, *FOOT COVERING, ONE WHO SHOES HORSES*
shofel, shovel
shofer, chauffeur
shok, chalk/ choke/ shock/ chock
shoked, shock(ed) /choke(d) /chock(ed)
shol, shawl /shoal
sholak, shallac
sholder, shoulder
sholdur, shoulder
shole, shoal /shawl
sholtur, shoulder
shoman, shaman
shomenism, shaman(ism)

shomin, shaman
shoo, shoe
shood, should /shoe(d)
shook, *PAST TENSE OF "SHAKE", A SET OF PREFABRICATED PARTS* (or see shuck)
shoot,*,ting,ter, *AIM AT SOMETHING TO DISCHARGE INTO/PIERCE OR CAPTURE AN IMAGE* (or see shut or should)
shop,*,pped,pping,pper, *SEEK TO PURCHASE GOODS ITEMS, A PLACE TO MANUFACTURE/PERFORM RETAIL ACTIVITIES* (or see chop)
shoper, shop(pper)
shopur, shop(pper)
shor, shore/ chore/ sure
shord, shore(d) /short
shordist, short(est)
shore,*,ed,ring, *PLACE WHERE BODY OF WATER MEETS LAND* (or see chore)
shork, shark
shorn, *PAST TENSE OF "SHEAR"*
shorp, sharp
shors, shore(s) /chore(s)
short,*,ted,ter,test, *BRIEF/ABRUPT, SMALLER/LESS THAN NORMAL* (or see shore(d))
shortir, short(er)
shortist, short(est)
shortur, short(er)
shos, shoe(s)
shot,*, *PAST TENSE OF "SHOOT", TAKE A HIT OF/FROM SOMETHING, TO FILM* (or see shod)
shoty, shoddy
shoud, shout
shoul, shawl
should, *PAST TENSE OF "SHALL"*
shoulder,*,red,ring, *BODY PART HOLDING THE ARM, TO USE THE SHOULDER*
shout,*,ted,ting, *TO SPEAK/VOICE WORDS LOUDLY*
shove,*,ed,ving, *TO PUSH/RAM AGAINST*

shus, shoe(s)
shush, TO ENCOURAGE TO BE QUIET
shut,*,tting, TO CLOSE/STOP (or see should /shoot /chute)
shutal, shuttle
shute, chute /shoot
shuter, shutter /shudder /shoot(er)
shutir, shutter /shudder /shoot(er)
shutled, shuttle(d)
shutol, shuttle
shutter,*, A HINGED FLAP/COVER OVER AN OPENING (or see shudder)
shuttle,*,ed,ling, CARRY/TRANSPORT TO ANOTHER PLACE
shutur, shutter /shudder /shoot(er)
shuve, shove
shuvel, shovel
shuvul, shovel
shuw, shoe
shuz, shoe(s)
shy,hies,hied,ying,yer,yly,yness,yer, LESS THAN WILLING TO ACCEPT/FACE HEAD-ON/CONFRONT
shyster,*, ONE WHO IS UNETHICAL
shystur, shyster
si, sigh
siadeka, sciatic(a)
siadika, sciatic(a)
sianide, cyanide
sianse, science
siantifek, scientific
siantist, scientist
siants, science
siatek, sciatic
siateka, sciatic(a)
siatic, sciatic
siatika, sciatic(a)
sibkonchus, subconsciouse
sibkontrakt, subcontract
siblengs, sibling(s)

sibling,*, LEGAL BROTHERS/SISTERS
siborg, cyborg
siburnetiks, Cybernetics
sic, WORD USED FOR REPLACEMENT IN TEXT, TO ENCOURAGE SOMETHING TO ATTACK (or see sick or psyche)
sicede, secede
sicheatric, psychiatric
sichek, psychic
sichewashen, situate(tion)
sichewation, situate(tion)
sichiatric, psychiatric
sichic, psychic
sicholegist, psychology(gist)
sichologekul, psychology(gical)
sichologest, psychology(gist)
sichology, psychology
sichopath, psychopath
sichopathologist, psychopath(ologist)
sichosis, psychosis
sichuaded, situate(d)
sichuashen, situate(tion)
sichuate, situate
sichuation, situate(tion)
sichudelic, psychedelic
sick,kish,kishness,kly,kliness, PHYSICALLY/MENTALLY ILL (or see psyche)
sickal, sickle /cycle
sickle,*,ed,ling, TOOL USED FOR CUTTING GRASS/GRAIN, CRESCENT MOON SHAPE (or see cycle)
sicks, six
sickstee, sixty
sickteith, sixtieth
sickth, sixth
siclone, cyclone
sicreshen, secrete(tion)
sicrete, secrete
sicretion, secrete(tion)
sicumb, succumb

sicure, secure
sid, sigh(ed) /side /sight
sidan, sedan
sidar, sit(tter) /cider /side(r)
sidashen, sedate(tion)
sidasion, sedate(tion)
sidate, sedate
sidation, sedate(tion)
side,*,ed,ding,er, BE NEAR/BESIDE BUT NOT ON, A POSITION ASIDE FROM CENTER (or see site or sight)
sideng, side(ding) /site(ting) /sight(ing)
sidewse, seduce
sidir, sit(tter) /cider /side(r)
sidokshen, seduce(ction)
sidoose, seduce
sidor, sit(tter)/ cider/ side(r)
sids, sit(s)/ set(s)/ side(s)
siducshen, seduce(ction)
sidukshen, seduce(ction)
siduktion, seduce(ction)
siduktive, seduce(ctive)
sidur, sit(tter)/ cider/ side(r)
siduse, seduce
siduzen, citizen
siege,*,ed,ging, TAKE/STEAL CONTROL OF FUNCTIONS
siegur, seize(zure)
siejur, seize(zure)
sienna, A COLOR/PIGMENT
siense, science
sienses, science(s)
sientifekly, scientific(ally)
sientific, scientific
sientifikly, scientific(ally)
sientist, scientist
sier, sigh(er)
siera, sierra
sierra, SECTION OF HILLS/RANGE, A FISH
siesta,*, AFTERNOON NAP

sieve, *, ed,ving, *A STRAINER/NET FOR SOLIDS/LIQUIDS*
sieze, seize
sif, sieve
sifalis, syphilis
sifaree, safari
sifd, sieve(d) /sift
sifen, siphon
sifenul, siphon(al)
sifinal, siphon(al)
sifise, suffice
siflus, syphilis
sifon, siphon
sift, *, ted,ting,ter, *SEPARATE VARIOUS GRAIN SIZES FROM ONE ANOTHER, SORT FOR A SPECIFIC THING* (or see sieve(d))
siftur, sift(er)
sifules, syphilis
sifunil, siphon(al)
sigar, cigar
sigaret, cigarette
siger, seize(zure)
siggesdeve, suggest(ive)
siggestion, suggestion
sigh, *, hed,hing,her, *A DEEP/RELEASING BREATH*
sight, *, ted,ting,table,ter,tless,tlessly,tlessness, tly,tliness, *VISUAL, ABLE TO SEE* (or see site)
sigjesdeve, suggest(ive)
sigjestion, suggest(ion)
sigjestive, suggest(ive)
sigjestshen, suggest(ion)
sigma, *GREEK ALPHABET LETTER*
sigmu, sigma
sign, *, ned,ning, *WRITTEN TEXT, SYMBOL WITH MEANING, A PLACARD/BOARD WITH WORDS/ SYMBOLS, A SIGNATURE* (or see sine)
signacher, signature
signafiable, signify(fiable)
signafier, signify(fier)

signafy, signify
signal, *, led,ling,ler,lly,lize,lized,lizing, *IMAGE/ GESTURE USED TO COMMUNICATE*
signature, *, tory,tories, *A PERSON'S NAME/MARK, TO SIGN SOMETHING*
signefiable, signify(fiable)
signefukent significant
signeture, signature
signifacantly, significant(ly)
significant, tly,nce,ncy,ncies,ation,ative,atively, ativeness, *OF IMPORTANCE/OUTSTANDING*
signify, fied,fying,fiable,fier, *INDICATE/POINT OUT*
signuchur, signature
signufy, signify
signul, signal
signushure, signature
sigur, seize(zure)
sijur, seize(zure)
sik, sick /psyche
sikadelic, psychedelic
sikal, sickle /cycle
sikamore, sycamore
sike, psyche/ sick/ sic
sikeatree, psychiatry
sikeatric, psychiatric
sikedelic, psychedelic
sikek, psychic
sikel, sickle /cycle
sikepath, psychopath
sikeurety, secure(rity)
sikewr, secure
sikgest, suggest
sikgestion, suggest(ion)
sikiatree, psychiatry
sikiatrist, psychiatry(rist)
sikik, psychic
sikil, sickle /cycle
sikiotrist, psychiatry(rist)
sikiutrest, psychiatry(rist)

sikiutry, psychiatry
sikjest, suggest
sikjestion, suggest(ion)
sikjestshen, suggest(ion)
sikle, sickle
siklude, seclude
siklushen, seclusion
siklution, seclusion
sikma, sigma
siknacher, signature
siknafier, signify(fier)
siknashure, signature
siknature, signature
siknefakent significant
siknefy, signify
sikneture, signature
siknifakent significant
siknify, signify
siknishure, signature
siknol, signal
siknufy, signify
siknul, signal
siknuture, signature
siko, psycho
sikodelic, psychedelic
sikodik, psychotic
sikology, psychology
sikologekul, psychology(gical)
sikologest, psychology(gist)
sikology, psychology
sikopath, psychopath
sikopathic, psychopath(ic)
sikopathologist, psychopath(ologist)
sikosis, psychosis
sikotic, psychotic
sikreshen, secrete(tion)
sikresion, secrete(tion)
sikrete, secrete
siks, six

sikstee , sixty
siksteen , sixteen
siksteenth , sixteen(th)
sikstelth , sixtieth
siksteuth , sixtieth
sikstiuth , sixtieth
siksty , sixty
sikteith , sixtieth
sikth , sixth
sikudelic , psychedelic
sikul , sickle /cycle
sikulest , cyclist
sikum , succumb
sikumore , sycamore
sikure , secure
sekuredy , secure(rity)
sikurity , secure(rity)
sikwenshul , sequence(ntial)
sikwential , sequence(ntial)
sikwoia , sequoia
sikwoya , sequoia
siky , psyche /sick
silabes , syllabus
silabil , syllable
silacon , silicon /silicone
silakit , silica(te)
silakon , silicon /silicone
silal , salal
silami , salami
silanoid , solenoid
silanse , silence
silant , silent
silantly , silent(ly)
silantness , silent(ness)
silareum , solarium
silawet , silhouette
sild , silt
sildashen , silt(ation)
silebus , syllabus

sileca , silica
silecate , silica(te)

silective , select(ive)
silee , silly
sileka , silica
silekshen , select(ion)
silekt , select
silektif , select(ive)
silektion , select(ion)
silektive , select(ive)
silence ,*,ed,cing,er, OF BEING QUIET, NO SOUND
silendur , cyclinder
sileness , silly(lliness)
sileng , ceiling /seal(ing)
silenium , selenium
silenoid , solenoid
silense , silence
silensur , silence(r)
silent ,tly,tness, BEING QUIET, NO SOUND
silerium , solarium
silesit , solicit
silesitation , solicit(ation)
silesiter , solicit(er)
silesteul , celestial
sileur , silly(llier)
silewet , silhouette
silfer , silver
silferware , silverware
silfur , silver
silfurware , silverware
silfury , silver(y)
silhouete , silhouette
silhouette ,*,ed,ting, THE SHAPE/OUTLINE OF SOMETHING
silica ,ate, A NATURAL CHEMICAL COMPOUND
silicon , A NATURALLY OCCURING ELEMENT (or see silicone)

silicone ,*, A SILICON SUBSTITUTE, MANMADE CHEMICAL (or see silicon)
siliest , silly(lliest)
siliness , silly(lliness)
siling , ceiling /seal(ing)
silinoid , solenoid
silins , silence
silinser , silence(r)
silivu , saliva
silk ,*,ken,ky,kily,kiness, A THREAD/FABRIC MADE FROM SILKWORMS
silkee , silk(y)
silkeness , silk(iness)
silkun , silk(en)
sill ,*, A HORIZONTAL SHELF (or see sell)
silly ,lier,liest,lies,liness, GOOFY/FUNNY, NOT SERIOUS
silo ,*,oed,oing, A STRUCTURE/HOUSING FOR GRAIN/ MISSILES/ROCKETS
siloet , silhouette
silomee , salami
silon , salon
siloon , saloon
siloot , salute
silow , silo
silt ,tation,ty, A VERY FINE DIRT/SEDIMENT
siltashen , silt(ation)
silubel , syllable
silubes , syllabus
silubil , syllable
siluca , silica
silucone , silicon /silicone
siludid , salute(d)
siluet , silhouette
siluka , silica
siluket , silica(te)
silukon , silicon /silicone
silune , saloon
silunoid , solenoid

simulerity, similar(ity)
simulerly, similar(ly)
simultaneous,sly,eity, *HAPPENING AT SAME TIME*
simultaniously, simultaneous(ly)
simur, simmer
simurd, simmer(ed)
simurt, simmer(ed)
simutary, cemetary
simutree, symmetry
sin,*,nned,nning,nner,nful,nless, *COMMIT IMMORAL*
ACT KNOWING IT IS IMMORAL (or see sine/
sign(s)/ since)
sinada, sonata
sinanem, synonym
sinapse, synapse
sinapsis, synapsis
sinaptek, synaptic
sinaptic, synaptic
sinareo, scenario
sinas, sinus
sinaster, sinister
sinata, sonata
sinatorial, senator(ial)
sinatur, senator
sinc, sync /sink
since, *REFERRING TO THE PAST, FROM THEN UP UNTIL*
NOW, BECAUSE OF (or see sense/ cent(s)/
sin(s)/ scent(s))
sincere,ely,rity,eness, *HONEST/GENUINE*
sincerly, sincere(ly)
sinch, cinch
sinched, singe(d) /cinch(ed)
sinchro, syncro
sinchronus, synchrony(nous)
sincht, singe(d) /cinch(ed)
sincronize, synchrony(nize)
sincrony, synchrony
sind, send/ sign(ed)/ sin(nned)
sinder, cinder / send(er)

sindicate, syndicate
sindication, syndicate(tion)
sindikation, syndicate(tion)
sindiket, syndicate
sindrem, syndrome
sindrum, syndrome
sindukit, syndicate
sindur, send(er)
sine, *MATHEMATICAL FUNCTION* (or see sign or sin)
sined, sign(ed) /sin(nned)
sinegrade, centigrade
sinek, cynic
sinekal, cynical
sinema, cinema
sinemin, cinnamon
sineority, senior(ity)
sinepede, centipede
siner, sin(nner)
sinereo, scenario
sinergy, synergy
sinerist, scenario(ist)
sines, sign(s) /sin(s) /sinus
sinester, sinister
sinetor, senator
sinetorial, senator(ial)
sinew,wy, *TENDONS, TO STRENGTHEN*
sinfuly, sin(fully)
sing,*,ging,ger, *TO CREATE MELODIC NOTES/SONGS*
WITH THE VOICE/THROAT(or see singe/sink)
singal, single
singar, sing(er)
singe,*,ed,ging, *TO SCORCH/SLIGHTLY BURN*
SOMETHING (or see sing or cinch)
singel, single
singewlerety, singular(ity)
singil, single
singir, sing(er)
single,*,ed,ling,ly, *ONE, NOT WITH OTHERS*
singul, single

singular,rly,rness,rize,rity,rities, *OF BEING ONE/*
ONCE, INDIVIDUAL
singuler, singular
singulerety, singular(ity)
singuleridy, singular(ity)
singulerly, singular(ly)
singuly, single(ly)
singur, sing(er)
singus, singe(s) /cinch(es)
sinima, cinema
sinir, sin(nner)
sinister,rous,rly,rness, *SOMETHING EVIL/*
FOREBODING
sinj, singe /cinch
sinjd, singe(d) /cinch(ed)
sinjt, singe(d) /cinch(ed)
sink,*,ked,king,ker,kage, *TO DESCEND/LOWER/*
RECLINE/SUBMERGE, A BASIN (or see sync)
sinkd, sink(ed)
sinkewler, singular
sinkil, single
sinkir, sink(er) /sing(er)
sinkle, single
sinkly, single(ly)
sinkranes, synchrony(nous)
sinkrenus, synchrony(nous)
sinkro, syncro
sinkronee, synchrony
sinkronize, synchrony(nize)
sinkronus, synchrony(nous)
sinkrony, synchrony
sinkt, sink(ed)
sinkul, single
sinkularedy, singular(ity)
sinkularly, singular(ly)
sinkuler, singular
sinkur, sink(er) /sing(er)
sinles, sin(less)
sinnless, sin(less)

sinoda, sonata
sinodu, sonata
sinografee, scenography
sinography, scenography
sinome, tsunami
sinonemus, synonym(ous)
sinonim, synonym
sinonimus, synonym(ous)
sinonym, synonym
sinopsis, synopsis
sinota, sonata
sinoter, senator
sinsable, sensible
sinsaredy, sincere(rity)
sinsaridy, sincere(rity)
sinsashen, sensation
sinsation, sensation
sinsative, sensitive
sinsativity, sensitive(vity)
sinse, since /sense /cent(s) /scent(s)
sinseer, sincere
sinseerly, sincere(ly)
sinsere, sincere
sinseredy, sincere(rity)
sinserity, sincere(rity)
sinserly, sincere(ly)
sinsery, sensor(y)
sinsetive, sensitive
sinseur, sincere
sinshere, century
sinshewality, sensual(ity)
sinshewus, sensuous
sinshual, sensual
sinshuality, sensual(ity)
sinshuos, sensuous
sinshure, century
sinsiry, sensor(y)
sinsless, sense(less)
sinsor, censor /censure

sinsoreal, sensor(ial)
sinsory, sensor(y)
sinst, sense(d)
sinsual, sensual
sinsuble, sensible
sinsus, census /sense
sinsutive, sensitive
sinsutivity, sensitive(vity)
sint, sent /cent /scent /sin(nned)
sintaks, syntax
sintament, sentiment
sintamental, sentiment(al)
sintax, syntax
sintchuis, sensuous
sintekit, syndicate
sintement, sentiment
sinteneul, centennial
sintense, sentence
sinter, center
sinthasis, synthesis
sinthedik, synthetic
sinthesis, synthesis
sinthetek, synthetic
sinthusis, synthesis
sintimental, sentiment(al)
sintineul, centennial
sintinse, sentence
sintrie, sentry
sintrul, central
sintry, sentry
sintrys, sentry(ries)
sintugrade, centigrade
sintumental, sentiment(al)
sintury, century
sinu, sinew
sinuee, sinew(y)
sinugrade, centigrade
sinumeter, centimeter
sinumon, cinnamon

sinunem, synonym
sinupede, centipede
sinur, sin(nner)
sinurgy, synergy
sinus,ses,sitis, *RESPIRATORY CAVITIES/PASSAGES IN THE FACE, BOTANICAL TERM*
sinuster, sinister
sinutor, senator
sinutorial, senator(ial)
sinuy, sinew(y)
sinyor, senior
sinyority, senior(ity)
sinyuee, sinew(y)
siontefikly, scientific(ally)
siontest, scientist
siontifek, scientific
siontist, scientist
sip,*,pped,pping,pper,ppingly, *TO PURSE THE LIPS TO DRINK, SMALL DRINKS* (or see sipe)
sipasetory, suppository
sipausatory, suppository
sipereor, superior
sipereority, superior(ity)
sipereur, superior
siperlitef, superlative
siphelis, syphilis
siphen, siphon
siphenul, siphon(al)
siphilis, syphilis
siphon,nal,nic,nless, *TO USE PRESSURE/SUCTION TO RELOCATE FLUIDS* (also spelled syphon)
siphules, syphilis
sipkonchus, subconsciouse
siplant, supplant
sipli, supply
siplier, supply(lier)
sipling, sibling
sipliur, supply(lier)
siply, supply

siport, support
siportef, support(ive)
sirportive, support(ive)
siposatory, suppository
sipose, suppose
siposubly, suppose(dly)
sipoze, suppose
sipozubly, suppose(dly)
sipreem, supreme
sipreno, soprano
sipres, suppress
sipreshun, suppress(ion)
siptek, styptic
siptik, styptic
sipur, sip(pper)
sipurb, superb
sipurblee, superb(ly)
sipurlitef, superlative
siquential, sequence(ntial)
siquer, secure
siquir, secure
siquoia, sequoia
sir,*, TITLE OF A MAN (or see sire)
siraded, serrate(d)
siraget, surrogate
siragit, surrogate
siramik, ceramic
siran, saran /siren
sirape, syrup /serape
sirashen, serrate(tion)
sirated, serrate(d)
siration, serrate(tion)
sircharge, surcharge
sirchuble, search(able)
sircle, circle
sircomfurinse, circumference
sircophagus, sarcophagus
sircumferenc, circumference
sircumpherence, circumference

sircumsize, circumcise
sircumstans, circumstance
sircus, circus
sircut, circuit
sirdify, certify
sire,*,ed,ring, MALE PARENT OF A MAMMAL (or see sir)
sireal, serial/ cereal/ surreal
sirealism, surrealism
sirelisum, surrealism
sirel, sorrel /surreal
sirelism, surrealism
sirem, serum
siren,*, LOUD/PIERCING SOUNDS FROM A DEVICE, SEA NYMPHS
sirench, syringe
sirendur, surrender
sirene, serene
sireng, syringe
sirenidy, serene(nity)
sirenity, serene(nity)
sirenj, syringe
sireol, serial /cereal
sireous, serious
sirep, syrup
sires, series /sire(s) /cirrus /scirrhus
sireul, cereal /serial
sireulizum, surrealism
sireus, serious
sireusly, serious(ly)
sirf, surf/ serf/ serve
sirface, surface
sirfdum, serf(dom)
sirfege, serf(age)
sirfeje, serf(age)
sirfes, surface /service
sirfibul, surf(able)
sirfis, surface
sirfunt, servant

sirfur, surf(er)
sirgakle, surgical
sirge, surge /serge
sirgekul, surgical
sirgen, surgeon
sirgeon, surgeon
sirgon, surgeon
sirgree, surgery
sirgukle, surgical
sirguree, surgery
siriasis, psoriasis
sirim, serum
sirin, siren
siriosly, serious(ly)
sirius, serious
sirjakle, surgical
sirje, surge /serge
sirjekul, surgical
sirjen, surgeon
sirjon, surgeon
sirjree, surgery
sirjukle, surgical
sirjuree, surgery
sirkawfigus, sarcophagus
sirkewler, circular
sirklar, circular
sirkofegus, sarcophagus
sirkulate, circulate
sirkumferinse, circumference
sirkumsize, circumcise
sirlee, surly
sirloin,*, A CUT OF BEEF
sirly, surly
sirman, sermon
sirmize, surmise
sirmon, sermon
sirogate, surrogate
siron, siren
sirong, sarong

sirope, serape /syrup
siroredy, sorority
sirority, sorority
siros, scirrhus /cirrus
siround, surround
sirownd, surround
sirpas, surpass
sirpent, serpent
sirpentene, serpentine
sirpint, serpent
sirpintent, serpentine
sirplus, surplus
sirprize, surprise
sirrated, serrate(d)
sirrus, cirrus /scirrhus
sirtin, certain
sirum, serum
sirun, siren
sirup, syrup
sirus, cirrus /scirrhus
sirv, serve
sirva, survey
sirvailense, surveillance
sirvalense, surveillance
sirvatood, servitude
sirvatude, servitude
sirvaur, survey(or)
sirvayer, survey(or)
sirve, serve /survey
sirveillinse, surveillance
sirveor, survey(or)
sirves, service /survey(s) /serve(s)
sirvesable, service(cable)
sirveyor, survey(or)
sirvife, survive
sirvint, servant
sirvis, service
sirvitude, servitude
sirvive, survive

sirvivul, survive(val)
sirvont, servant
sirvunt, servant
sirvusable, service(cable)
sirvutude, servitude
sirys, series
sisabul, size(zable)
sisal, sizzle
sisd, size(d) /cyst
sisdamadik, system(atic)
sisdamatic, system(atic)
sisdan, sustain
sisdem, system
sisdum, system
sisdumadik, system(atic)
sisdumatic, system(atic)
sise, size
siseble, size(zable)
sisede, secede
siseded, secede(d)
sisee, sissy
sisel, sizzle
siseptible, susceptible
siseptif, suceptive
siseptive, suceptive
siseptuble, susceptible
siseptuf, suceptive
sisers, scissors
siseshen, secession
sisesion, secession
siset, secede
sisetion, secession
sisle, sizzle
sismec, seism(ic)
sismic, seism(ic)
sismical, seism(ical)
sismik, seism(ic)
sisors, scissors
sispend, suspend

sissy, sies,sified,siness,yness,yish, *BEHAVE LIKE A COWARD, UNMASCULINE*
sist, cist /cyst
sistain, sustain
sistane, sustain
sistanuble, sustain(able)
sistem, system
sister,*,rly, *FEMALES WHO HAVE A STRONG AFFINITY OR RELATIONSHIP, LAWFUL FEMALE SIBLING*
sistre, sister
sistum, system
sistumatic, system(atic)
sistur, sister
sisturly, sister(ly)
sisturn, cistern
sisubil, size(zable)
sisuble, size(zable)
sisul, sizzle
sisurs, scissors
sisus, size(s)
sisy, sissy
sit,*,tting,tter, *POSITION RESTING ON THE BUTTOCKS, WHAT SOMETHING OCCUPYING SPACE/POSITION DOES (or see set /site /side)*
sitanic, satanic
sitanikul, satanic(al)
sitashun, citation
sitation, citation
sitchuashen, situate(tion)
sitchuate, situate
site,*, *AREA OF SIGNIFICANCE (or see sight or side)*
siter, sit(tter)/ cider/ side(r)
siterical, satire(rical)
sitesin, citizen
sith, scythe
sitir, sit(tter)/ cider/ side(r)
sitor, sit(tter)/ cider/ side(r)
sitrek, citric
sitrik, citric

sitrus, citrus
situashen, situashe(tion)
situate,ed,ting,tion,tional,tionally, LOCATION/
    POSITION OF OBJECTS/EVENTS
situatid, situate(d)
situr, sit(tter) /cider
situzin, citizen
sity, city
siunide, cyanide
siunse, science
siuntest, scientist
siuntifek, scientific
siuntifekaly, scientific(ally)
siuntist, scientist
siur, sigh(er)
siv, sieve
sivana, savanna
sivant, savant
sivd, sieve(d) /sift
sivear, severe
sived, sieve(d) /sift
sivere, severe
siverity, severe(rity)
siverly, severe(ly)
sivic, civic
sivilean, civilian
sivont, savant
sivt, sift /sieve(d)
sivted, sift(ed)
sivter, sift(er)
sivul, civil
siworo, saguaro
six,xes, AN ENGLISH NUMBER AFTER FIVE
sixis, six(es)
sixstenth, sixteen(th)
sixtee, sixty
sixteen,nth, AN ENGLISH NUMBER AFTER FIFTEEN, 16
    PARTS OF A WHOLE
sixteith, sixtieth

sixten, sixteen
sixth,*, AN ENGLISH NUMBER AFTER THE FIFTH, OF SIX
    EQUAL PARTS
sixtieth, AN ENGLISH NUMBER AFTER 59, OF 60
    EQUAL PARTS
sixty,ties, AN ENGLISH NUMBER AFTER 59
sixtyn, sixteen
sixus, six(es)
sizabil, size(zable)
sizal, sizzle
sizars, scissors
sizd, size(d) /seize(d)
size,*,ed,zing,zable,zably,zableness, AREA/
    DIMENSION OF SOMETHING
sizebul, size(zable)
sizel, sizzle
sizers, scissors
sizible, size(zable)
sizis, size(s)
sizle, sizzle
sizmek, seism(ic)
sizmekul, seism(ical)
sizmik, seism(ic)
sizmikul, seism(ical)
sizold, sizzle(d)
sizors, scissors
siztur, sister
sizuble, size(zable)
sizul, sizzle
sizurs, scissors
sizus, size(s)
sizzle,*,ed,ling,er, A COOKING/FRYING/SIZZLING
    SOUND
skab, scab
skabard, scabbard
skabbard, scabbard
skabed, scab(bbed)
skabees, scabies
skaburd, scabbard

skaby, scab(bby)
skabys, scabies
skad, scat/ skate/ skat/ scad
skader, skate(r) /scatter
skafold, scaffold
skafolding, scaffold(ing)
skair, scare
skairslee, scarce(ly)
skalar, scalar
skalastic, scholastic
skalb, scalp
skalber, scalp(er)
skald, scald /scale(d)
skale, scale
skalee, scaly
skaleness, scaly(liness)
skaleon, scallion
skalep, scallop
skaleun, scallion
skaley, scaly
skalip, scallop
skaliun, scallion
skallion, scallion
skallop, scallop
skalor, scalar
skalp, scalp
skalpel, scalpel
skalper, scalp(er)
skalpul, scalpel
skalt, scald /scale(d)
skalup, scallop
skaly, scaly
skalyin, scallion
skalyun, scallion
skamatek, scheme(matic)
skan, scan
skand, scan(nned)
skandal, scandal
skandelus, scandal(ous)

skandul, scandal
skandulus, scandal(ous)
skaner, scan(nner)
skanir, scan(nner)
skant, scant /scan(nned)
skantily, scant(ily)
skantuly, scant(ily)
skanur, scan(nner)
skapal, scalpel
skapala, scapula
skapel, scalpel
skapela, scapula
skapeula, scapula
skapil, scalpel
skapila, scapula
skapul, scalpel
skapula, scapula
skar, scar /scare
skarcedy, scarce(city)
skarcity, scarce(city)
skare, scare /scare(y)
skarf, scarf
skarlut, scarlet
skarse, scarce /scare(s)
skarsedy, scarce(city)
skarsly, scarce(ly)
skarsness, scarce(ness)
skarves, scarf(rves)
skat, *A CARD GAME* (or see scat or skate)
skat, scat /skate /skat
skatar, skate(r) /scatter
skate, *,ed,ting,er, TO MOVE ABOUT WITH ROLLERS/ BLADES ATTACHED TO SHOES, TO MOVE IN GLIDING MOTION (or see skat or scat)*
skater, scatter /skate(r)
skathe, scathe
skator, skate(r) /scatter
skattur, scatter /skate(r)
skatur, skate(r) /scatter

skauler, scholar
skaulerly, scholar(ly)
skavage, scavage
skavege, scavenge
skaveger, scavenge(r)
skavenger, scavenge(r)
skavinger, scavenge(r)
skavuge, scavenge
skavunger, scavenge(r)
skawler, scholar
skawlerly, scholar(ly)
skeam, scheme
skeat, skeet
skech, sketch
skechily, sketch(ily)
skechis, sketch(es)
skecht, sketch(ed)
skechuly, sketch(ily)
skechus, shetch(es)
skechwal, schedule
skechwul, schedule
sked, ski(ed) /skid
skedchewl, schedule
skedchule, schedule
skedule, schedule
skeed, ski(ed) /skid
skeem, scheme
skeemer, skim(mmer) /scheme(r)
skeen, skein
skeet, *TYPE OF TRAPSHOOTING*
skef, skiff
skein, *FLOCK OF WILD BIRDS, BUNDLE OF THREAD/YARN*
skeing, ski(iing)
skeir, skier
skel, skill /skull/ school
skelastic, scholastic
skelaten, skeleton
skelatul, sketal

skelatun, skeleton
skeld, skill(ed)
skeled, skill(ed)
skeletal,tally, *BONES OF A BODY, BASIC FRAMEWORK*
skeletin, skeleton
skeleton, *,tal,tally,nize,nizer, *BONES OF A BODY, BASIC FRAMEWORK*
skeletun, skeleton
skelful, skill(ful)
skelit, skillet
skeliton, skeleton
skelitul, skeletal
skelitun, skeleton
skelut, skillet
skelutin, skeleton
skem, scheme /skim
skematik, scheme(matic)
skemd, skim(mmed) /scheme(d)
skeme, scheme
skemer, skim(mmer) /scheme(r)
skemur, skim(mmer) /scheme(r)
sken, skein /skin
skenee, skinny
skenir, skinner
skeniur, skinny(nier)
skeniust, skinny(niest)
skenlus, skin(less)
skenur, skinner
skeny, skinny
skeor, skier
skep, skip
skepir, skipper
skeps, skip(s)
skept, skip(pped)
skeptacism, skeptic(ism)
skeptak, skeptic
skeptic, *,cal,cally,calness,cism, *ONE WHO DOUBTS/ CHALLENGES DOCTRINATED BELIEFS (also spelled "sceptic")*

skepticism, skeptic(ism)
skeptuk, skeptic
skeptusisum, skeptic(ism)
sker, scare /skier
skerd, skirt /scare(d)
skerfy, scurvy
skerge, scourge
skerje, scourge
skers, skier(s) /scare(s) /scarce
skersedy, scarce(city)
skersity, scarce(city)
skersly, scarce(ly)
skersness, scarce(ness)
skersudy, scarce(city)
skert, skirt /scare(d)
skervy, scurvy
skery, scurry
skeryd, scurry(ried)
skeshily, sketch(ily)
sket, skeet /skit
sketch,hes,hed,hing,her,hy,hily,hiness, *A BRIEF/ ROUGH OUTLINE/DRAWING/ IDEA*
sketchewl, schedule
sketsh, sketch
skeu, skew
skeuer, skewer
skeuner, schooner
skeur, skier /skewer
skew,*,wed,wing,wness, *SLANTED/SLOPED/ DISTORTED/OBLIQUE POSITION*
skewbu, scuba
skewdur, scoot(er)
skewer,*, *THIN/LONG INSTRUMENT FOR HOLDING MEAT/VEGETABLES FOR GRILLING*
skewir, skewer
skewp, scoop
skewpur, scoop(er)
skewtur, scoot(er)
skewur, skewer

skezafrinea, schizophrenia
ski,*,ied,iing, *TO USE LONG DEVICES ATTACHED TO FEET TO ACHIEVE SPEED/ GLIDING ON VARIOUS SURFACES* (or see sky)
skid,*,dded,dding,ddingly, *FRAMEWORK TO MAKE SOMETHING SLIDE ALONG, SLIDE WHEN COMING TO A STOP* (or see ski(ed) or skit)
skidesh, skittish
skidush, skittish
skier,*,*, *SOMEONE WHO SKIS*
skif, skiff
skiff,*, *SMALL BOAT*
skiier, skier
skiir, skier
skiis, ski(s)
skil, skill
skilastic, scholastic
skilet, skillet
skilful, skill(ful)
skilfuly, skill(fully)
skill,*,led,lful,lfully,lfulness,lless, *HAVING GAINED AN APTITUDE FOR PERFORMING A CRAFT/TRADE*
skillet,*, *LONG HANDLED FRYING PAN*
skilut, skillet
skim,*,mmed,mming,mmer, *BE ON/GLANCE OVER A SURFACE,REMOVE THE SURFACE* (or see scheme)
skimatik, scheme(matic)
skimer, skim(mer) /skim(mmer)
skimur, skim(mer) /skim(mmer)
skin,*,nned,nning,nner,nless,nny, *SURFACE ORGANISM THAT PROTECTS BODILY FLUIDS/ CONTENTS, TO REMOVE COVER/LAYER OF PROTECTION FROM SOMETHING* (or see skein)
skinee, skinny
skiner, skinner
skineust, skinny(niest)
sking, ski(iing)
skinles, skin(less)
skinner,ry, *ONE WHO REMOVES SKIN*

skinny,nnier,nniest, *BONEY, NOT MUCH MUSCLE OR FAT ON THE BODY*
skinur, skinner
skiny, skinny
skip,*,pped,pping, *PASS OVER/MISS A BEAT/LEVEL*
skiper, skipper
skipir, skipper
skipper,*, *CAPTAIN OF A SHIP/BOAT, AN INSECT, ONE WHO SKIPS*
skipur, skipper
skir, skier
skireed, scurry(ried)
skirfy, scurvy
skirt,*,ted,ting,ter, *A GARMENT WORN TO COVER/ PROTECT THE LOWER TORSO, TO EVADE/PASS AROUND AND ISSUE/EVENT*
skirvy, scurvy
skiry, scurry
skisoed, schizoid
skisophrenea, schizophrenia
skit,*, *A BRIEF/SHORT PLAY*
skitesh, skittish
skitish, skittish
skitsafrenea, schizophrenia
skitsophrenia, schizophrenia
skittish,hly, *EASILY FRIGHTENED*
skitush, skittish
skitzafrenea, schizophrenia
skiur, skewer
skizoed, schizoid
skizofrenea, schizophrenia
skizoid, schizoid
skizophrenia, schizophrenia
skof, scoff
skolar, scholar
skolarly, scholar(ly)
skolastic, scholastic
skold, scold /scald
skoleoses, scoliosis

skowntrel, scoundrel
skowr, scour
skowt, scout
skowter, scout(er)
skowurd, scour(ed)
skquer, skewer
skquir, skewer
skrabs, scrap(s) /scrape(s)
skrach, scratch
skrag, scrag
skragliest, scraggly(liest)
skragly, scrag(ily) /scraggly
skrakleur, scraggly(lier)
skrakly, scrag(ily) /scraggly
skram, scram
skrambul, scramble
skrampul, scramble
skrap, scrap / scrape
skraper, scraper /scrap(pper)
skrapuble, scrap(able)
skratch, scratch
skreach, screech
skream, scream
skrean, screen
skreblur, scribble(r)
skrebul, scribble
skrech, screech
skred, screed
skreech, screech
skreed, screed
skreem, scream
skreen, screen
skreenuble, screen(able)
skremage, scrimmage
skremije, scrimmage
skremp, scrimp
skremshaw, scrimshaw
skremuge, scrimmage
skremuje, scrimmage

skren, screen
skrenuble, screen(able)
skreped, script
skrepshur, scripture
skrept, script
skrepture, scripture
skrew, screw
skrewge, scrooge
skrewje, scrooge
skrewpal, scruple
skrewpel, scruple
skrewpils, scruple(s)
skrewpewlis, scrupulous
skrewpul, scruple
skrewpules, scrupulous
skrewpulisle, scrupulous(ly)
skrewteny, scrutiny
skrewtiney, scrutiny
skrewy, screw(y)
skribe, scribe
skrible, scribble
skribler, scribble(r)
skribul, scribble
skrimage, scrimmage
skrimije, scrimmage
skrimp, scrimp
skrimshaw, scrimshaw
skrimuge, scrimmage
skrimuje, scrimmage
skriped, script
skripshur, scripture
skript, script
skripture, scripture
skripuld, scribble(d)
skrol, scrawl /scroll
skroo, screw
skrooge, scrooge
skrooje, scrooge
skrooy, screw(y)

skoleosis, scoliosis
skoler, scholar
skolerly, scholar(ly)
skoliosis, scoliosis
skolir, scholar
skolirly, scholar(ly)
skolt, scold /scald
skolur, scholar
skolurly, scholar(ly)
skomatik, scheme(matic)
skone, scone
skons, scone(s) /sconce
skonts, sconce
skoobu, scuba
skooder, scoot(er)
skool, school
skooner, schooner
skoop, scoop
skooper, scoop(er)
skoot, scoot /scute
skooter, scoot(er)
skor, scar
skorch, scorch
skore, score
skorles, score(less)
skorn, scorn
skornfuly, scorn(fully)
skorpeon, scorpion
skorpeun, scorpion
skorsh, scorch
skorur, score(r)
skoul, scowl
skour, scour
skout, scout
skouter, scout(er)
skower, scour
skowir, scour
skowl, scowl
skowndrel, scoundrel

skroul, scrawl
skrounge, scrounge
skrowl, scrawl
skrownge, scrounge/ scrounge(y)
skrowngy, scrounge(y)
skrownje, scrounge/ scrounge(y)
skru, screw
skrub, scrub
skrud, screw(ed)
skrudnee, scrutiny
skruf, scruff
skrufy, scruff(y)
skruge, scrooge
skruje, scrooge
skrup, scrub
skrupel, scruple
skrupeulus, scrupulous
skrupul, scruple
skrupules, scrupulous
skrupulous, scrupulous
skruteny, scrutiny
skrutiny, scrutiny
skruwe, screw(y)
skruy, screw(y)
sku, skew
skual, squal
skuar, skewer
skuba, scuba
skuder, scoot(er)
skued, squid
skueel, squeal
skuegul, squiggle
skuel, school
skuelched, squelch(ed)
skuelsh, squelch
skuer, skewer
skuesh, squish
skueshy, squish(y)
skuf, scuff

skufel, scuffle
skuful, scuffle
skuid, squid
skuigul, squiggle
skuir, skewer
skuish, squish
skuishy, squish(y)
skulastic, scholastic
skulbd, sculpt
skulbsher, sculpt(ure)
skulbshir, sculpt(ure)
skulbt, sculpt
skul, school /skull
skull,*, THE HEAD'S BONE (or see school)
skulpsher, sculpt(ure)
skulpshur, sculpt(ure)
skulpt, sculpt
skum, scum
skumatek, scheme(matic)
skumy, scum(mmy)
skuner, schooner
skunk,*, OMNIVOROUS BLACK/WHITE MAMMAL WITH
      STRONG SCENT GLANDS
skupe, scoop
skuper, scoop(er)
skurage, scourge
skuraje, scourge
skured, scurry(ried) /skewer(ed)
skureed, scurry(ried)
skurfy, scurvy
skurge, scourge
skurige, scourge
skurje, scourge
skurt, skirt
skurvy, scurvy
skury, scurry
skuryd, scurry(ried)
skut, skew(ed)
skute, scoot /scute

skuter, scoot(er)
skwabil, squabble
skwabul, squabble
skwad, squad / squat
skwader, squat(ttor)
skwadir, squat(ttor)
skwadrin, squadron
skwadron, squadron
skwadur, squat(ttor)
skwair, square
skwairly, square(ly)
skwal, squal
skwaled, squalid
skwalid, squalid
skwalor, squalor
skwander, squander
skwantur, squander
skwapel, squabble
skwapul, squabble
skward, square(d)
skware, square
skwarlee, square(ly)
skwart, square(d) /squirt
skwash, squash
skwat, squad /squat
skwater, squat(ttor)
skwatir, squat(ttor)
skwatrin, squadron
skwaudren, squadron
skwauled, squalid
skwaulid, squalid
skwaulir, squalor
skwaulur, squalor
skwaut, squad /squat
skwautrin, squadron
skwautron, squadron
skweak, squeak
skwed, squid
skweegee, squeegee

skweeje, squeegee
skweek, squeak
skweel, squeal
skweemish, squeamish
skwees, squeeze
skweesir, squeeze(r)
skweeze, squeeze
skwegal, squiggle
skwegee, squeegee
skwegul, squiggle
skwegy, squeegee
skwejee, squeegee
skwel, squeal
skwelch, squelch
skweler, squeal(er)
skwelir, squeal(er)
skwelsh, squelch
skweltch, squelch
skwelur, squeal(er)
skwemesh, squeamish
skwemish, squeamish
skwent, squint
skweral, squirrel
skwerl, squirrel
skwerly, squirrel(y)
skwerm, squirm
skwermy, squirm(y)
skwerol, squirrel
skwert, squirt
skwerul, squirrel
skwes, squeeze
skweser, squeeze(r)
skwesh, squish
skweshy, squish(y)
skwesir, squeeze(r)
skwesur, squeeze(r)
skwet, squid
skweze, squeeze
skwezur, squeeze(r)

skwiarly, square(ly)
skwid, squid
skwigal, squiggle
skwigul, squiggle
skwint, squint
skwire, squire
skwirl, squirrel
skwirm, squirm
skwirmy, squirm(y)
skwirt, squirt
skwirul, squirrel
skwish, squish
skwishy, squish(y)
skwobil, squabble
skwobul, squabble
skwod, squad /squat
skwodir, squat(ttor)
skwodrin, squadron
skwodron, squadron
skwodur, squat(ttor)
skwol, squal
skwoled, squalid
skwolid, squalid
skwolor, squalor
skwondur, squander
skwontur, squander
skwopel, squabble
skwopil, squabble
skwosh, squash
skwot, squad /squat
skwoter, squat(ttor)
skwotir, squat(ttor)
skwotrin, squadron
skwotron, squadron
skwotur, squat(ttor)
skwural, squirrel
skwurl, squirrel
skwurly, squirrel(y)
skwurm, squirm

skwurmt, squirm(ed)
skwurmy, squirm(y)
skwurt, squirt
sky, kies, *THE FIRMAMENT/FIELD ABOVE A PLANET (or see ski)*
sla, slay /sleigh
slab, *, bbed, bbing, *A LARGE/FLAT/SOLID MATERIAL (or see slap)*
slabt, slept /slap(pped)
slack, *, ked, king, ker, ken, *NOT TAUT/TIGHT, PAIR OF DRESS PANTS, NOT SHARP/ALERT/ ON THE BALL (or see slag)*
slade, slay(ed) /slate
slader, slaughter
slae, slay /sleigh
slafe, slave
slafree, slave(ry)
slafry, slave(ry)
slag hamer, sledge hammer
slag, *WASTE REMNANTS FROM METALS (or see slack)*
slai, slay /sleigh
slain, *PAST TENSE OF "SLAY", KILL VIOLENTLY*
slak, slack
slaker, slack(er)
slakur, slack(er)
slam, *, mmed, mming, mmer, *SHUT/CLOSE/STRIKE SEVERLY/HARSHLY/LOUDLY, A JAIL*
slamur, slam(mmer)
slan, slain
slander, *, red, ring, rer, rous, rously, rousness, *FALSE/UNTRUE REMARKS/WORDS*
slanderus, slander(ous)
slandured, slander(ed)
slanduris, slander(ous)
slang, *, gily, giness, gy, *NON-STANDARD USAGE OF WORDS, SHORT-LIVED WORDS*
slank, slang
slant, *, ted, ting, *A SLOPING/OBLIQUE STANCE, NOT LEVEL, BIASED*

slantur, slander
slap,*,pped,pping,pper, TO STRIKE WITH AN OPEN HAND, A CRISP/SHORT BLOW
slapir, slap(pper)
slapt, slap(pped) /slept
slas, sleigh(s) /slay(s) /slaw(s)
slash,hes,hed,hing,her, TO DRIVE A SWEEPING STROKE OR BLOW, TO CUT/OPEN WITH A BLADE
slashur, slash(er)
slat,*,ted,ting, THIN STRIPS OF WOOD/METAL (or see slate or slay(ed))
slate,*,ed,ting,ty, CLAY/SHALE/COAL TYPES OF ROCK, AN APPOINTMENT (or see slat or slay(ed))
slath, sloth
slau, slaw
slaudir, slaughter
slaudur, slaughter
slaughter,*,red,ring,rer,rous,rously, TO VIOLENTLY KILL/DESTROY
slauterus, slaughter(ous)
slave,*,ed,ving,ery, ONE WHO IS FORCED TO WORK FOR SOMEONE WITHOUT PAY, TO WORK HARDER THAN REASONABLE
slaven, sloven
slavenly, sloven(ly)
slavry, slave(ry)
slaw,*, COLD CABBAGE/VEGETABLE DISH
slawb, slob
slawderus, slaughter(ous)
slawdur, slaughter
slawter, slaughter
slawterus, slaughter(ous)
slay,*,yed,ying,yer,slew,slain, KILL VIOLENTLY (or see sleigh)
sleak, sleek
sleaken, sleek(en)
sleaknes, sleek(ness)
sleat, sleet

sleave,*,ed,ving, SEPARATE/DISENTANGLE THREADS/ FILAMENTS (or see sleeve)
sleazy,zier,ziest,zily,ziness, CHEAP/POOR CHARACTER/QUALITY
sleber, sleep(er)
slebir, sleep(er)
slebry, slip(ppery)
slebt, slept
slebur, sleep(er)
sleck, slick
slecker, slick(er)
sleckly, sleek(ly)
sled,*,dded,dding,dder, TO SLIDE/GLIDE SMOOTHLY ALONG THE GROUND (or see sleigh or slid)
sledge hammer, LARGE/HEAVY HAMMER
sledir, sled(dder)
sledur, sled(dder)
sleef, sleeve /sleave
sleek,ken,ker,kly,kness, SHINY/ SMOOTH/ SOOTHING
sleeknis, sleek(ness)
sleep,*,ping,slept,per,pless,py,piness,pily, SLOW DOWN BASIC FUNCTIONS TO REST, BECOME UNCONSCIOUS, PLACE TO SLEEP
sleepee, sleep(y)
sleeseist, sleazy(ziest)
sleesy, sleazy
sleet,*,ted,ting, ICY SNOW, FROZEN PRECIPITATION
sleeve,*, COVER FOR MANY THINGS (TOO MANY DEFI- NITIONS, PLEASE SEE STANDARD DICTIONARY)
sleezee, sleazy
sleezyest, sleazy(ziest)
slefs, sleeve(s) /sleave(s)
slefur, sliver
sleg, slick
slege hamer, sledge hammer
sleigh,*,hing, A CONTRAPTION DESIGNED TO GLIDE/SLIDE ALONG THE GROUND (or see sled)
sleight,ted,ting, ADROIT/NIMBLE OF BODY/MIND, "SLEIGHT OF HAND", (or see slight)

sleje hamer, sledge hammer
slek, slick /sleek
sleker, slick(er) /sleek(er)
slekly, sleek(ly) /slick(ly)
sleknis, slick(ness) /sleek(ness)
slekur, slick(er) /sleek(er)
slem, slim
slemd, slim(mmed) /slime(d)
slemest, slim(mmest)
slemir, slim(mmer)
slemt, slim(mmed) /slime(d)
slemur, slim(mmer)
slemust, slim(mmest)
slender,rly,rness,rize, SLIM
slendir, slender
slendirness, slender(ness)
slendur, slender
slendurness, slender(ness)
sleng, sling
slenger, sling(er)
slengur, sling(er)
slenk, sling /slink
slenky, slink(y)
slenter, slender
slentur, slender
slep, sleep /slip /slept
slepd, slept /slip(pped)
sleper, sleep(er)
slepir, sleep(er)
slepless, sleep(less)
slepry, slip(ppery)
sleps, sleep(s) /slip(s)
slept, PAST TENSE OF "SLEEP", TO TAKE A DEEP REST WITH EYES CLOSED
slepur, sleep(er)
slepy, sleep(y)
sler, slur
sleried, slurry(ried)
slerp, slurp

slerpt, slurp(ed)
slert, slur(rred)
slery, slurry
sleryed, slurry(ried)
slesee, sleazy
sleseer, sleazy(zier)
sleseist, sleazy(ziest)
sleseur, sleazy(zier)
slesy, sleazy
slet, sled /slid
sleter, sled(dder)
sletir, sled(dder)
slets, sleet(s)
sletur, sled(dder)
sleuth, *, TRACK /TRAIL /DETECTIVE
sleve, sleeve / sleave
sleved, sleeve(d) /sleave(d)
slever, sliver
slevir, sliver
slevs, sleeve(s) /sleave(s)
slevur, sliver
slew, PAST TENSE OF "SLAY", LARGE AMOUNT/NUMBER OF SOMETHING, TO PIVOT, ALSO "SLUE" (or see slue or slough)
slewth, sleuth
sley, slay /sleigh
slezee, sleazy
slezeist, sleazy(ziest)
slezeur', sleazy(zier)
slezy, sleazy
sli, sly
slibree, slip(ppery)
slibry, slip(ppery)
sliburee, slip(ppery)
slice, *, ed,cing,er, TO CUT
slick, kly,kness,ker, SLIPPERY/SMOOTH
slid, PAST TENSE OF "SLIDE", GLIDE/MOVE ALONG SMOOTHLY WITHOUT TRACTION (or see sled/ slide/ slit/ sleight/ slight)

slide, *, ding,er,slid, GLIDE/MOVE ALONG SMOOTHLY WITHOUT TRACTION (or see slid /slit /slight / sleight)
slided, slide(d) /slight(ed)
slidlee, slight(ly)
slifur, sliver
slig, slick
slight, *, ted,test,ting,ter,tingly,tly,tness, BARELY/PETTY/SLENDER/FRAIL/ NEGLIGENT/ DISRESPECTFUL (or see sleight)
slightist, slight(est)
slik, slick
sliker, slick(er)
slikness, slick(ness)
sliknis, slick(ness)
slikur, slick(er)
slily, sly(lly)
slim, *, mmer,mmest,mmed,mming,mly, UNDER PROPORTION, UNSUBSTANTIAL, SMALL (or see slime)
slimd, slim(mmed) /slime(d)
slime, *, ed,ming,my,mier,miest,mily,miness, VISCOUS /MUCOUS /OOZEY SECRETION (or see slim)
slimed, slim(mmed) /slime(d)
slimee, slime(y)
slimely, slim(ly)
slimeness, slime(miness)
slimur, slim(mmer)
slimeur, slime(mier)
slimiest, slime(miest)
slimiur, slime(mier)
slimt, slim(mmed) /slime(d)
slimur, slim(er)
slimy, slime(y)
slimyest, slime(miest)
slinder, slender
slindurness, slender(ness)
sliness, sly(ness)

sling, *, slung,ged,ging,ger, A DEVICE DESIGNED TO STRADLE/HOLD, TO FLING (or see slink)
slingt, sling(ed) /slink(ed)
slingur, sling(er)
slink, *, ked,slunk,king,ky, MOVE/CREEP/WALK QUIETLY/SECRETIVELY, BORN PREMATURELY
slinkd, slink(ed) /sling(ed)
slinkey, slink(y)
slinkt, slink(ed) /sling(ed)
slinter, slender
slip, *, pped,pping,ppery, SLIDE/GLIDE/FALL AWAY, LOSS OF TRACTION/FOOTING, AN UNDERGARMENT
sliparee, slip(ppery)
slipry, slip(ppery)
slipt, slip(pped)
slipuree, slip(ppery)
slirp, slurp
sliry, slurry
slise, slice
sliser, slice(r)
slit, *, tting,ter, CUT SLOTS/OPENINGS INTO (or see slid /slide /slight /sleight)
slited, sleight(ed)/ slight(ed)/ slide(d)
slither, *, red,ring,ry, TO SNAKE/SLIDE ALONG
slithry, slither(y)
slithur, slither
slitly, slight(ly)
sliver, *, red,ring,rer, SMALL/THIN PIECE OF MATTER WHICH SPLINTERED/SEPARATED FROM LARGER OBJECT
slivir, sliver
slivur, sliver
slo, slaw /slow
slob, *, bbed,bbing, SOMEONE WHO IS UNKEPT/ UNCLEAN/UNHEALTHY (or see slab or slop)
slobber, *, red,ring,ry, DROOL/WET SECRETION FROM THE MOUTH
slober, slobber
slobery, slobber(y)

slobur, slobber
slobury, slobber(y)
slod, slot /slow(ed)
slodder, slaughter
slode, slot /slow(ed)
sloder, slaughter
slods, slot(s)
slodur, slaughter
slodurus, slaughter(ous)
sloe, slough /slow
sloer, slow(er)
sloest, slow(est)
slof, slough
slofenly, sloven(ly)
slofun, sloven
slofunly, sloven(ly)
slogan,*, *A CATCHWORD/PHRASE/ MOTO/BATTLE CRY*
slogun, slogan
sloir, slow(er)
sloist, slow(est)
sloken, slogan
slokun, slogan
sole, slow(ly)
soly, slow(ly)
slonis, slow(ness)
sloo, slew /slue /slough
sloose, sluice
slooth, sleuth
slop,*, pped,pping,ppy,ppier,ppiest, ppily, ppiness, *CARELESS, SPILLED LIQUID, NASTY FOOD, SLUSHY/MUDDY (or see slob or slope)*
slopd, slope(d) / slop(pped)
slope,*, ed,ping,er,pingly,pingness, *AN INCREASE/ DECREASE IN ANGLE ALONG A HORIZONTAL/ VERTICAL PLANE (or see slop)*
slopee, slop(ppy)
slopeir, slop(ppier)
slopely, slop(ppily)
slopery, slobber(y)

slopeur, slop(ppier)
slopily, slop(ppily)
slopiness, slop(ppiness)
slopry, slobber(y)
slopt, slope(d) /slop(pped)
slopule, slop(ppily)
slopury, slobber(y)
slopy, slop(ppy)
slopyer, slop(ppier)
slopyest, slop(ppiest)
slopyness, slop(ppiness)
slos, sloth(es)
slosh,*, es,ed,hing,hy, *LIQUID SPLASHING AROUND*
sloshee, slosh(y)
slot,*, tted,tting, *NARROW OPENING/CUT CREATED TO ALLOW INSERTION OF SOMETHING (or see slow(ed))*
sloted, slot(tted)
sloter, slaughter
sloth,hes, *SLOW TREE-DWELLING MAMMAL*
slouch,hes,hed,hing,hier,hily,hiness,hier,hiest, *DROOPS INTO A NON-ERECT POSITION*
slough,hy,hiness,hy, *TO SHED/CAST OFF, MARSHY/ SWAMPY AREA, CONDITION OF DEGRADATION (or see slew or slue)*
slour, slow(er)
sloutsh, slouch
sloutshed, slouch(ed)
sloven,*, nly,liness,nlier,nliest, *UNTIDY/CARELESSLY CLAD*
slovin, sloven
slovinly, sloven(ly)
slovun, sloven
slovunliness, sloven(liness)
slovunly, sloven(ly)
slow,*, wed,wing,wer,west,wly,wish,wness, *TO PERFORM AT LESS THAN NORMAL/AVERAGE SPEED (or see slough)*
slowb, slob

slowch, slouch
slowcheur, slouch(ier)
slowchily, slouch(ily)
slowist, slow(est)
slowur, slow(er)
slu, slew/ slue/ slough
sluce, sluice
slud, slue(d)/ slough(ed)/ slew(ed)
sludch, sludge
sludchy, sludge(gy)
sludge,gier,giest,gy, *A THICK/VISCOUS LIQUID WITH HEAVY SEDIMENT*
sludgeur, sludge(gier)
sludje, sludge
slue,ed,uing, *TO PIVOT/SWING AROUND, HAVING TO DO WITH SLEW (or see slew or slough)*
sluee, slough(y)
slueness, slough(iness)
sluf, slough
slug,*,gged,gging,ggish,ggishly,ggishness, *REMNANT OF BULLET THAT'S BEEN SHOT, HIT/ LUG SOMETHING,GASTROPOD THAT EATS PLANTS*
slugar, slugger
sluge, sludge
sluger, slugger
slugesh, slug(ggish)
slugeshness, slug(ggishness)
slugeur, sludge(gier)
slugger,*, *ONE WHO HITS HARD/HEAVY*
slugir, slugger
slugish, slug(ggish)
slugishness, slug(ggishenss)
slugt, slug(gged)
slugur, slugger
slugush, slug(ggish)
slugy, sludge(gy)
sluice,ed,cing, *A CHANNEL/CANAL OF WATER, ITEM USED TO PAN FOR GOLD*
sluje, sludge

slujeir, sludge(gier)
slujy, sludge(gy)
sluk, slug
sluker, slugger
slukesh, slug(ggish)
slukir, slugger
slukishnes, slug(ggishness)
slukur, slugger
slum,*,mmed,mming,mmer, *POOR/HIGHLY POPULATED/DIRTY AREA*
slumber,*,red,ring,rer,rless,rous,ry,rously, rousness, *TO SLEEP, BE QUITE INACTIVE, LIGHT SLEEP/DOZE*
slumbir, slumber
slumbrus, slumber(ous)
slumbrusly, slumber(ously)
slumbrusness, slumber(ousness)
slumbry, slumber(y)
slumbur, slumber
slumd, slum(mmed)
slump,*,ped,ping, *A DIP IN PRODUCTION/ A SURFACE/VALUE*
slumper, slumber
slumpur, slumber
slumur, slum(mmer)
slung, *PAST TENSE FOR "SLING"*
slunk, slung
slur,*,rred,rring, *TO SMEAR/SMUDGE WORDS/ SPEECH, INARTICULATE/ CARELESS*
slureng, slurry(ing) /slur(rring)
slurp,*,ped,ping, *LOUD SIPPING SOUNDS WITH MOUTH*
slurry,ried,ying, *SOFT/ORGANIC MATERIAL CHOPPED UP IN LIQUID*
slury, slurry
sluryed, slurry(ried)
slurz, slur(s)
slus, sluice
sluse, sluice

slush,hy,hiness, *BETWEEN LIQUID AND SOLID*
slushyness, slush(iness)
slutch, sludge
slutge, sludge
sluth, sleuth
slutje, sludge
sluy, slough(y)
sly,yly,yness, *SMOOTH/DISCREET/QUIET*
slym, slim /slime
slynis, sly(ness)
slynke, slink(y)
slyse, slice
slyt, slight/ slide/ slid
smack,*,ked,king,ker,*TO DO WITH THE MOUTH, A SHARP BLOW, DIRECT/STRAIGHT, SAILING VESSEL*
smak, smack
smaker, smack(er)
smal, small
smaler, small(er)
smalest, small(est)
smalist, small(est)
small,*,ler,lest,ness, *NOT AS LARGE COMPARED WITH NORMAL/AVERAGE*
smard alik, smart aleck
smarden, smart(en)
smardest, smart(est)
smardin, smart(en)
smart aleck,ky, *SOMEONE WHO IS SMARTING OFF/CONCEITED/SHOWOFF*
smart alik, smart aleck
smart,*,ted,ten,tly,tness,ter,test,ty, *SHARP/ QUICK/ALERT/PRACTICAL*
smartie, smart(y)
smartist, smart(est)
smash,hes,hed,hing,her, *BLAST/CRUSH/DEMOLISH TO PIECES, DESTROY BY VIOLENT BLOWS*
smashur, smash(er)
smear,*,red,ring,rY, *TO SPREAD/WIPE INTO, CAUSE TO RUN TOGETHER, SLANDER*

smedin, smite(ten)
smeer, smear
smeery, smeer(y)
smel, smell
smeld, smell(ed) /smelt
smelder, smelter
smeldur, smelter
smelee, smell(y)
smell,*,led,ling,ly, *TO PERCEIVE WITH THE NOSE/OLFACTORY*
smelt, *FISH (or see smell(ed))*
smelter,*, *METAL MELTING PROCESS*
smely, smell(y)
smer, smear
smerk, smirk
smerker, smirk(er)
smethureens, smithereens
smetin, smite(ten)
smiden, smite(ten)
smil, smile
smile,*,ed,ling,ly, *A FACIAL EXPRESSION WHICH STATES THAT ALL IS WELL, FRIENDLY EXPRESSION*
smily, smile(y)
smirk,*,ked,king,ker,kingly, *SMUG SMILE EXPRESSING SUPERIORITY/CONCEIT*
smirkd, smirk(ed)
smit, smite
smite,ting,tten, *SERIOUSLY/DEEPLY STRUCK/ AFFECTED, EXACT*
smiten, smite(tten)
smitin, smite(ten)
smiwree, smeer(y)
smithereens, *BLOW/SMASH TO PIECES/BITS*
smithureens, smithereens
smock,*, *OUTER GARMENT LOOSELY COVERING MAIN TORSO* (or see smoke)
smog,ggy, *HEAVY AIRBORNE POLLUTION* (or see smock or smoke)
smogy, smog(ggy)

smok, smock/ smog/ smoke
smokd, smoke(d) /smog(gged)
smoke,*,ed,king,er,eless,ey, *CLOUD OF GAS RESULTING FROM BURNED MATERIAL (or see smock)*
smokir, smoke(r)
smokless, smoke(less)
smoklus, smoke(less)
smokt, smoke(d) /smog(ed)
smokur, smoke(r)
smoky, smoke(y) /smog(ggy)
smol, small
smold, smolt
smolder,*,red,ring, *TO SLOWLY COOK IN SMOKE/ WITHOUT FLAME*
smoler, small(er)
smolir, small(er)
smolt, *A STAGE IN SALMON/FISH GROWTH*
smolter, smolder
smoltur, smolder
smolur, small(er)
smoth, smooth
smooch,hes,hed,hing, *TO HUG/KISS*
smooth,hes,hed,hing,her,hest,hly,hness,hen, *LACKS ROUGHNESS/HESITATION, PLEASANT TO THE SENSES*
smoothie,*, *A FRUIT SLUSH/DRINK*
smoothin, smooth(en)
smoothnis, smooth(ness)
smoothy, smoothie
smord alek, smart aleck
smorgasboard,*, *BUFFET WITH CONGLOMERATION/ SELECTION OF FOODS*
smorgusboard, smorgasboard
smort, smart
smuch, smooch /smudge
smuched, smooch(ed) /smudge(d)
smuches, smooch(es) /smudge(s)
smudeist, smut(ttiest)

smudeness, smut(ttiness)
smudeur, smut(ttier)
smudge,*,ed,ging,er, *SMEAR/STAIN, A SMOLDERING FIRE/SMOKE FOR PROTECTION*
smudy, smut(tty)
smug,gly,gness, *SELF-SATISFIED/CONCEITED (or see smooch)*
smugal, smuggle
smugaler, smuggle(r)
smuge, smudge
smuggle,*,ed,ling,er, *TO TRANSPORT SOMETHING ACROSS A LAWFUL BORDER WITHOUT PERMISSION*
smuglir, smuggle(r)
smugul, smuggle
smuj, smudge
smuk, smug
smukil, smuggle
smuklee, smug(ly)
smukler, smuggle(r)
smukly, smug(ly)
smuknes, smug(ness)
smukul, smuggle
smukuler, smuggle(r)
smurk, smirk
smut,tted,tting,tty,ttier,ttiest,ttily,ttiness,*SOOTY/ SMUDGED, INDECENT LANGUAGE, PLANT AFFECTED BY FUNGUS SPORES*
smuteir, smut(ttier)
smuteist, smut(ttiest)
smuteness, smut(ttiness)
smuth, smooth
smuthen, smooth(en)
smuther, smooth(er) /smother
smuthie, smoothie
smuthir, smooth(er) /smother
smuthist, smooth(est)
smuthly, smooth(ly)
smuthness, smooth(ness)
smuthy, smoothie

smuty, smut(tty)
snabur, snap(pper)
snach, snatch
snachir, snatch(er)
snack,*,ked,king, *LITTLE BIT OF FOOD BETWEEN MEALS (or see snake or snag)*
snael, snail
snafoo, snafu
snafu,ued,uing, *UNEXPECTED/CHAOTIC TURN OF EVENTS*
snag,*,gged,gging,ggy,ggier,ggiest, *TO BE CAUGHT UP/ENTANGLED (or see snack)*
snageist, snag(ggiest)
snaggier, snag(ggier)
snail,*, *GASTROPOD MOLLUSK WITH SHELL*
snair, snare
snak, snack/ snake/ snag
snakd, snack(ed)/ snake(d)/ snag(gged)
snake,*,ed,king,ky,kily, *REPTILE WITH NO LIMBS (ARMS/LEGS) (or see snack)*
snakey, snake(ky)
snaks, snack(s) /snake(s) /snag(s)
snakt, snack(ed) /snake(d) /snag(gged)
snale, snail
snap,*,pped,pping,pper, *A QUICK/BITING MOTION, CRISP BREAK, BRITTLE/TENSE*
snaper, snap(pper)
snapper,*, *A FISH*
snapur, snap(pper)
snard, snare(d)
snare,*,ed,ring,er, *A TRAP/NOOSE FOR CATCHING THINGS, USED FOR INSTRUMENT*
snarl,*,led,ling,ler,ly,lingly, *TO ENTANGLE/ COMPLICATE, A THREATENING SOUND*
snarlee, snarl(y)
snart, snare(d)
snasee, snazzy
snaseur, snazzy(zier)
snasiest, snazzy(ziest)

snasy, snazzy
snatch,hes,hed,hing,her, *SUDDEN/SWIFT MOVE TO GRASP/SEIZE SOMETHING*
snaul, snail
snawt, snout
snazeir, snazzy(zier)
snazeist, snazzy(ziest)
snazeur, snazzy(zier)
snazy, snazzy
snazzy,zzier,zziest, *FANCY*
sneak,*,ked,king,kingly,kily,kiness,ky, *ENGAGE IN AN ACTIVITY IN A SECRETTIVE MANNER*
sneaker,*, *TENNIS SHOES, SOMEONE WHO SNEAKS AROUND*
sneakey, sneak(y)
sneakir, sneak(er)
sneakuly, sneak(ily)
snear, sneer
sneaze, sneeze
sneazy, sneeze(zy)
snech, snitch
snechur, snitch(er)
sneek, sneak
sneeker, sneaker
sneeky, sneak(y)
sneesy, sneeze(zy)
sneeze,*,ed,zing,zy, *AN INVOLUNTARY GUST OF AIR FORCED THROUGH THE NASAL PASSAGES TO RELIEVE THEM OF AN IRRITANT*
snef, sniff
snefdur, snifter
snefel, sniffle
snefer, sniff(er)
sneftur, snifter
sneful, sniffle
snefur, sniff(er)
snek, sneak
sneker, sneaker

snekily, sneak(ily)
snekir, sneaker
snekuly, sneak(ily)
snekur, sneaker / snicker
sneky, sneak(y)
snep, snip
snepee, snip(ppy)
snepit, snip(ppy)
snept, snip(pped)
sner, snare /sneer
snert, snare(d) /sneer(ed)
snesy, sneeze(zy)
snetch, snitch
sneveler, snivel(ller)
snevil, snivel
snevlur, snivel(ller)
snevul, snivel
snevult, snivel(lled)
snewdy, snooty
snewp, snoop
snews, snooze
sneze, sneeze
snezy, sneeze(zy)
snibt, snip(pped) /snipe(d)
snich, snitch
snicher, snitch(er)
snicker,*,red,ring,rer,ringly, *EMOTE A NEGATIVE SNEERING LAUGH OUT OF DISRESPECT*
snide,er,est,ely, *INSINUATING/SARCASTIC LAUGH OUT OF DISRESPECT*
snidly, snide(ly)
snif, sniff
snifal, sniffle
snifd, sniff(ed)
snifdur, snifter
snifer, sniff(er)
sniff,*,ffed,ffing,ffer, *TO SMELL FOR, SEARCH FOR AS A DOG DOES BY SMELLING*
sniffle,*,ed,ling,er, *A NASAL SOUND*
snifter,*, *STYLE OF GLASS DRINKING VESSEL*

sniftur, snifter
sniful, sniffle
snifur, sniff(er)
sniker, snicker
snikur, snicker
snip,*,pped,pping,ppy, *CUT OFF A SMALL PORTION OF SOMETHING (or see snipe)*
snipe,*,ed,ping,er, *TYPE OF BIRD, TO SHOOT FROM A CAMOUFLAGED POSITION (or see snip)*
sniped, snip(pped) /snipe(d)
snipee, snip(ppy)
snipet, snippet
snippet,*, *SMALL BITS/FRAGMENTS/PARTS*
snipur, snipe(r)
sniput, snippet
snitch,hes,hed,hing,her, *TO FINK/RAT ON SOMEONE, BE AN INFORMANT*
snite, snide
snitly, snide(ly)
snivel,*,lled,lling,ller, *TO WHINE/CRY WHILE EXCREMENTING SNOT/MUCOUS FROM NOSE*
snivlur, snivel(ller)
snivul, snivel
sno, snow
snob,*,bby,bbery,bberies,bbish,bbishly, bbishness, *SOMEONE DISPLAYING SUPERIORITY/ SMUGNESS/SELF-RIGHTEOUSNESS*
snobeshnis, snob(bbishness)
snobish, snob(bbish)
snoby, snob(bby)
snod, snow(ed) /snot
snody, snot(tty)
snoker, snooker
snoodeist, snooty(tiest)
snoody, snooty
snooker,*, *GAME OF BILLIARDS*
snoop,*,ped,ping,per,pier,piest,py, *SOMEONE WHO IS NOSEY/PRYING/PROWLING*
snoose, snooze

snooty,tier,tiest,tily,tiness, *SNOBBISH, BELIEVE*
THEY'RE EXCLUSIVE
snooze,*,ed,zing,er, *SLEEP/NAP*
snop, snob
snopee, snob(bby)
snopy, snob(bby)
snore,*,ed,ring,er, *EMIT LOUD BREATHING SOUND*
DURING SLEEP, TO SLEEP WITH THE MOUTH OPEN
snorkel,*,led,ling, *UNDERWATER BREATHING*
APPARATUS
snorkul, snorkel
snorl, snarl
snorlingly, snarl(lingly)
snort,*,ted,ting, *LOUD/QUICK BURST OF AIR FORCED*
FROM THE NOSE
snot,tty, *MUCOUS EXCREMENTED IN THE SINUS*
CAVITIES, SOMEONE WHO CARRIES AN AIR OF
SUPERIORITY/CALLOUSNESS
snotee, snot(tty)
snoud, snout
snout,*,ted,tish,ty, *THE NOSE/MUZZLE OF ANIMALS*
snow,*,wed,wing,wy, *WHITE/LIGHT PRECIPITATION*
FALLING FROM CLOUDS, BURY/COVER/FOOL
SOMEONE LIKE SNOW AS A BLANKET
snowd, snow(ed) /snout
snowee, snow(y)
snowt, snout /snow(ed)
snub,*,bbed,bbing,bber,bness,bby,bbiness,
TURNED UP NOSE WITH ATTITUDE, TO REBUKE/
REBUFF/NEGLECT (or see snoop)
snube, snub(bby) /snoop(y)
snubed, snoop(ed) /snub(bbed)
snubiness, snub(bbiness)
snubt, snoop(ed)
snuby, snub(bby)
snudy, snooty
snuf, snuff
snuff,*,ffer,ffy, *PAST TENSE OF "SNIFF", PUT OUT/*
EXTINGUISH/END, POWDERED TOBACCO

snuffely, snuffle(ly)
snuffle,ed,ling,er,ly, *SNIFFLE/NASAL CONGESTION*
snufil, snuffle
snufir, snuff(er)
snufuly, snuffle(ly)
snufur, snuff(er)
snug,gger,ggest,gged,gging,gness,ggery,
FIRMLY/COMFORTABLY IN PLACE
snugelt, snuggle(d)
snuger, snug(gger)
snuggle,*,ed,ling,ly, *TO COZY/NESTLE UP*
COMFORTABLY AGAINST SOMETHING/SOMEONE
snugle, snuggle
snugly, snuggle(ly)
snugnis, snug(ness)
snugul, snuggle
snuker, snooker
snukle, snuggle
snuklee, snuggle(ly)
snupe, snoop
snuper, snoop(er)
snupy, snoop(y)
snuse, snooze
snuteir, snooty(tier)
snuteist, snooty(tiest)
snuty, snooty
snuze, snooze
snyd, snide
so, *THAT WHICH IS APPROXIMATE (TOO MANY*
DEFINITIONS, PLEASE CONSULT STANDARD
DICTIONARY) (or see sew or sow)
soak,*,ked,king,ker,kingly, *TO EXPOSE TO*
MOISTURE UNTIL SATURATED
soap,*,ped,ping,py,piness, *MANMADE COMPOUND*
USED FOR CLEANING (or see sop)
soar,*,red,ring,rer, *RISE TO GREAT HEIGHTS EITHER*
LITERALLY OR FIGURATIVELY (or see sore)
soaside, suicide

sob,*,bbed,bbing,bber, *TO CRY WITH DEEP*
GASPS/EMOTION (or see sop or soap)
sobed, sob(bbed) /soap(ed) /sop(pped)
sober,red,ring,ringly,rness, *NOT INTOXICATED/*
DRUNK, INFORMATION WHICH IS SERIOUS/GRAVE
IN NATURE
sobir, sober
sobirnes, sober(ness)
sobriaty, sobriety
sobriety, *being sober, FREE FROM EXCESS/*
EXTRAVAGANCE, SERIOUS/GRAVE
sobriudy, sobriety
sobt, sop(pped) /sob(bbed)
sobur, sober
soburnes, sober(ness)
soccer, *A TYPE OF FOOTBALL GAME*
socer, soccer
sochably, sociable(ly)
sochalist, social(ist)
sochaly, social(lly)
sochealugist, sociology(gist)
sochebul, sociable
sochel, social
sochelize, social(ize)
sochely, social(lly)
socheology, sociology
socheolugist, sociology(gist)
socher, soldier
sochibly, sociable(ly)
sochibul, sociable
sochil, social
sochilest, social(ist)
sochilize, social(ize)
sochily, social(lly)
sochioligy, sociology
sochuble, sociable
sochubly, sociable(ly)
sochul, social
sochulee, social(lly)

soky, soggy
sokynis, soggy(gginess)
sol, sole /soul
solace,ed,cing,ement,er, *COMFORT, ALLEVIATION*
   FROM WORRY/SORROW/GRIEF
solad, solid /salad
soladerity, solidarity
solami, salami
solar,rize,rization, *HEAT/LIGHT PRODUCED BY SUN*
solarium,*, *ENCLOSURE WHICH ALLOWS MAXIMUM*
   PENETRATION OF THE SUNS RAYS
solas, solace/ soul(ess)/ sole(eless)
solatare, solitaire /solitary
solatarily, solitary(rily)
solatary, solitary
solatood, solitude
solatude, solitude
solcher, soldier
solchur, soldier
solder,*,red,ring,rer, *USE OF FLUX/SOFT METAL TO*
   MELD SEVERAL PIECES OF METAL TOGETHER
soldier,*,rly,rship,ry,ries, *PEOPLE TRAINED TO*
   PARTICIPATE IN WAR/BATTLE
soldir, solder /soldier
soldired, solder(ed)
sole,*,ely,eness,eless, *ONE AND ONLY, THE BOTTOM*
   OF FEET/SHOES (or see soul)
solective, select(ive)
soled, solid
soledarity, solidarity
soledify, solid(ify)
soledness, solid(ness)
solee, sole(ly)
solelukwy, soliloquy
solem, solemn
solemly, solemn(ly)
solemn,nly,nness,nity,nities,nize,nization,
   nisation, *OBSERVANCE OF CELEBRATIONS/RITES,*
   OF A GRAVE/SERIOUS DISPOSITION/ACTIVITY

solen, sullen
solenium, selenium
solenoid,*,dal,dally, magnetically controlled
   device
soler, solar
solereum, solarium
solerize, solar(ize)
soles, solace/ soul(ess)/ sole(eless)
solesit, solicit
solesitation, solicit(ation)
solesiter, solicit(er)
solesment, solace(ment)
solet, solid
soletare, solitaire /solitary
soletarily, solitary(rily)
soletary, solitary
soletness, solid(ness)
soletood, solitude
soletude, solitude
solf, solve
solfely, soul(fully)
solfint, solvent
solfuly, soul(fully)
solfunt, solvent
solger, soldier
solgur, soldier
solinoid, solenoid
soljur, soldier
solicit,*,ted,ting,tor,tation,tous,tously,tousness,
   tude, *TO SEEK/REQUEST/APPLY/INFLUENCE/*
   PETITION FOR AN ACTION/OPPORTUNITY/FUNDING
solid,*,dly,dify,difiable,dification,dness,dity,
   dities, *GIVING THE IMPRESSION OF BEING*
   HARD/FIRM/COMPACT/THICK
solidarity,ties, *PEOPLE WHO FORM SOLID*
   RELATIONSHIPS BASED ON COMMONALITIES
solidefy, solid(ify)
soliderity, solidarity
solilaquy, soliloquy

soliloquy,uies,uist,uizer, *TALK TO ONESELF, SHARE*
   THOUGHTS OUTLOUD BEFORE AN AUDIENCE
solim, solemn
solimly, solemn(ly)
solin, sullen
solir, solar
solirise, solar(ize)
solis, solace /soul(ess) /sole(eless)
soliset, solicit
solisetation, solicit(ation)
soliseter, solicit(er)
solisment, solace(ment)
solit, solid
solitaire, *CARD GAME PLAYED ALONE*
solitary,ries,rily,riness, *OF BEING COMPLETELY*
   ALONE, SECLUDED
solitness, solid(ness)
solitude, *ALONE/REMOTE/LONELY*
solivu, saliva
soljer, soldier
soljur, soldier
solm, psalm
solo,*,oed,oing,oist, *TO PERFORM ALONE*
solomi, salami
solon, salon
solonoid, solenoid
soloon, saloon
soloot, salute
solstce, solstice
solstice,itial,itially, *TIME OF THE YEAR BASED UPON*
   SUN'S POSITION
solstis, solstice
solt, salt /sold
soluble,eness,ly,bility, *ABLE TO DISSOLVE IN WATER*
solud, solid
solum, solemn
solumly, solemn(ly)
solun, sullen
solune, saloon

solunoid, solenoid
solur, solar
solurize, solar(ize)
soluse, solace /soul(ess) /sole(eless)
solutare, solitaire /solitary
solutarily, solitary(rily)
solutary, solitary
solute, salute
solution,*, *A COMBINATION OF CHEMICAL FORMS, THE ANSWER TO A PROBLEM, SETTLEMENT*
solutood, solitude
solutude, solitude
solvant, solvent
solvashin, salvation
solve,*,ed,ving,vable,vability,vableness,er,*TO REMEDY/FIX/UNDERSTAND (or see salve)*
solvent,ency,ently, *ABLE TO BE DISSOLVED*
solvuble, solve(vable)
solvunt, solvent
soly, sole(ly)
solyubel, soluble
som, psalm /sum /some
somber,rly,rness, *MELANCHOLY/GRAVE/DEPRESSING IN MOOD/ATTITUDE*
sombir, somber
sombirly, somber(ly)
sombreo, sombrero
sombrero,*, *A WIDE BRIM HAT*
sombur, somber
somburly, somber(ly)
some, *PARTIAL/A FEW OF, AN INDEFINITE AMOUNT/ DISTANCE (or see sum)*
somersault,*,ted,ting, *AN ENTIRE BODY MANEUVER WITH HEELS GOING OVER HEAD*
somester, semester
something, *WANT FOR, INDETERMINABLE AMOUNT/ TYPE/OBJECT OF, OPPOSITE OF NOTHING*
sometime,*, *UNSPECIFIED TIME*
somewat, somewhat

somewere, somewhere
somewhat, *INDETERMINATE MEASURE*
somewhere, *UNSPECIFIED PLACE*
somewot, somewhat
somewut, somewhat
somirsalt, somersault
somirsolt, somersault
somper, somber
sompur, somber
somtheng, something
somthing, something
somtime, sometime
somting, something
somware, somewhere
somwat, somewhat
somwer, somewhere
somwhare, somewhere
somwhere, somewhere
somwot, somewhat
somwut, somewhat
son,*,nless,nny, *PARENT'S MALE OFFSPRING (or see sun/ sown/ sewn)*
sona, sauna
sonar, *ACRONYM FOR SOUND NAVIGATION AND RANGING (or see soon(er))*
sonareo, scenario
sonata, *A FORM FOR INSTRUMENTS IN MUSIC*
sonda, Sunday
sondree, sundry
sondrys, sundry(ries)
sonec, sonic
sonek, sonic
sonereo, scenario
sonet, sonnet
song,*,gful,gless, *COLLECTION/ARRANGEMENT OF MUSICAL NOTES AND/OR ACCOMPANYING WORDS*
sonic,cally, *SOUNDWAVE/FREQUENCY*
sonik, sonic
sonit, sonnet

sonk, song
sonkles, song(less)
sonks, song(s)
sonnet,*,teer,tize,tization, *A COMPLETE IDEA WRITTEN POETICALLY IN 14 LINES*
sonor, sonar
sonseer, sincere
sonter, saunter
sontir, saunter
sontre, saunter
sontree, sundry
sontres, sundry(ries)
sontur, saunter
sonu, sauna
sonuk, sonic
sonut, sonnet
sooaside, suicide
soodar, suitor
soodir, suitor
soodo, pseudo
soodor, suitor
soody, soot(y)
sooet, suet
soofaneer, souvenir
soofineer, souvenir
soofla, souffle'
sooflay, souffle'
soofuneer, souvenir
sooit, suet
sookrose, sucrose
soon,ner,nest, *BEFORE IT'S TOO LATE, CLOSE TO NOW, READILY PREFER (or see sun or son)*
soopereur, superior
sooperfishul, superficial
sooperioredy, superior(ity)
soopireur, superior
soopifishul, superficial
soopurb, superb
soopurfishul, superficial

soot, sue(d) /suit
soot,ty, *BLACK CARBON RESULTANT OF BURNED MATERIAL* (or see suit)
sooter, suitor
sooth,hes,hed,hing,hingly,hingness,her, *TO CALM, RELIEVE AGITATION*
sootir, suitor
sootor, suitor
soour, sewer
soovaneer, souvenir
soovneer, souvenir
sop,*,pped,pping,ppy, *ABSORB/SATURATE SOME-THING WITH LIQUID*(or see soap /soup /sob /sap)
sopd, sop(pped)/ sob(bbed)/ soap(ed)
sope, soap/ sop/ soap(y)/ sop(ppy)
soped, sop(pped)/ sob(bbed)/ soap(ed)
sopee, soap(y)
soper, sober /sob(bber)
soperioredy, superior(ity)
soperiority, superior(ity)
sophisticate,ed,edly,tion, *IMPROVED QUALITY OF*
sophomore, sophomore
sophomore,*,ric,rical,rically, *STUDENT IN THE SECOND YEAR OF A FOUR-YEAR COURSE*
soprano,*,, *HIGHEST OCTAVE ABLE TO BE OBTAINED BY VOICE OR INSTRUMENT*
soprechen, suppress(ion)
sopreno, soprano
sopres, suppress
sopreshen, suppress(ion)
sopretion, suppress(ion)
soprietee, sobriety
soprino, soprano
sopt, sop(pped)/ sob(bbed)/ soap(ed)
sopy, soap(y) /sop(ppy)
soquer, secure
sor, sore /soar
soran, saran

sorape, serape
sorce, source
sorcerur, sorcery(rer)
sorcery,rer,rous, *USING THE "SOURCE" OR INVISIBLE FIELD TO CREATE PHYSICAL THINGS/ACTIONS*
sord, soar(ed)/ sword/ sort
sorded, sordid /sort(ed)
sordedly, sordid(ly)
sordeen, sardine
sordene, sardine
sorder, sort(er)
sordid,dly,dness, *OF BEING DIRTY/MEAN* (or see sort(ed))
sordir, sort(er)
sordud, sordid /sort(ed)
sordudly, sordid(ly)
sordur, sort(er)
sore,*,,er,est,ely,eness, *PAIN/INFLAMMA-TION/PERTURBED* (or see soar or sorry)
sored, soar(ed) / sword
soree, sorry
sorel, sorrel /surreal
sorene, serene
sorenidy, serene(nity)
sorenity, serene(nity)
soresury, sorcery
sorgem, sorghum
sorgent, sargeant
sorghum, *GRAIN USED FOR MANY PURPOSES*
sorgint, sargeant
sorgum, sorghum
sori, sorry
soriasis, psoriasis
sorily, sorry(rily)
sorir, sore(r)
sorist, sore(st)
soriusis, psoriasis
sorkazem, sarcasm
sorkem, sorghum

sorkum, sorghum
sorly, sore(ly)
sorness, sore(ness)
sornis, sore(ness)
soro, sorrow
soroful, sorrow(ful)
sorority,ties, *FEMALE COLLEGE ORGANIZATIONS*
sorow, sorrow
sorowful, sorrow(ful)
sorrel, *AN EDIBLE PLANT* (or see surreal)
sorro, sorrow
sorrow,*,,wful,wfully,wfulness, *GRIEF/SADNESS/ REGRET*
sorry,rrier,rriest,rrily,rriness, *APOLOGETIC/ REGRETFUL/RESENTFUL* (or see saury)
sors, source /sore(s) /czar(s)
sorseree, sorcery
sorserer, sorcery(rer)
sorsuree, sorcery
sorsurer, sorcery(rer)
sort,*,ted,ting,ter,table, *CATEGORIZE/ARRANGE/ COMPARTMENTALIZE BY ASSOCIATION* (or see sword or sordid)
sortar, sort(er)
sorted, sordid /sort(ed)
sortedly, sordid(ly)
sortidly, sordid(ly)
sortir, sort(er)
sortud, sordid /sort(ed)
sortudly, sordid(ly)
sortur, sort(er)
sorur, sore(r)
sory, saury /sorry
sorz, source /sore(s)
sos, sauce/ saw(s)/ sew(s)
sose, saucy
sosege, sausage
soseje, sausage
soseptif, suceptive

soser, saucer
soseshen, secession
sosetion, secession
soseur, saucy(cier)
soshable, sociable
soshaly, social(lly)
soshealegy, sociology
soshebul, sociable
soshel, social
soshelize, social(ize)
sosheolugest, sociology(gist)
sosheolugy, sociology
soshible, sociable
soshibly, sociable(ly)
soshibul, sociable
soshil, social
soshilist, social(ist)
soshilize, social(ize)
soshily, social(lly)
soshubil, sociable
soshubly, sociable(ly)
soshul, social
soshulist, social(ist)
soshulize, social(ize)
soshuly, social(lly)
sosiatal, society(tal)
sosiaty, society
sosiedle, society(tal)
sosier, saucy(cier)
sosietal, society(tal)
sosiety, society
sosige, sausage
sosije, sausage
sosiology, sociology
sosir, saucer
sosiudil, society(tal)
sosiudy, society
sosiutul, society(tal)
sosoge, sausage

sosojle, sausage
sospishus, suspicious
sosuge, sausage
sosuje, sausage
sosur, saucer
sosy, saucy
sot, sought /suite /soot
sota, soda
sotame, sodomy
sotanic, satanic
sotay, saute' / sate
sote, saute' / sate
soted, saute'(d)
soteim, sodium
sotemy, sodomy
soteum, sodium
sotiably, sociable(ly)
sotiabul, sociable
sotialy, social(lly)
sotu, soda
sotume, sodomy
souffle',*,eed, *A BAKED FLUFFY DISH*
soufle', souffle'
soul,*,lful,lfully,lfulness,less, *INVISIBLE FIELD/ DESTINY/SPIRIT THOUGHT TO EXIST WITHIN THE BODY (or see sole or sol)*
sound,*,ded,ding,der,dless,dlessly,dly,dness, *A WAVE/FREQUENCY/INTERPRETED WITH THE EARS/EQUIPMENT, A CHANNEL OF LAND/WATER, SAFE/SECURE/STABLE*
sought, *PAST TENSE OF "SEEK"*
soup,*,py, *EDIBLE LIQUID BASE WITH BROTH AND/OR VEGETABLES/MEAT, TO BE LIKE SOUP*
sour,*,red,ring,rish,rly,rness, *GONE BAD/RANCID, TYPE OF TASTE REGISTERED ON A CERTAIN PLACE ON THE TONGUE*
source,*,ed, *POINT OF ORIGINATION OF SOMETHING, BEGINNING/PRIMARY*
sourkraut, sauerkraut

sourkrowt, sauerkraut
souse,*,ed,sing, *TO BE IMMERSED/DRENCHED/ SATURATED IN, INTOXICATED*
soust, souse(d)
souted, saute'(d)
south,hern,herner,hernly,herly,herlies, *A NAVIGATIONAL DIRECTION*
souvaneer, souvenir
souvenir,*, *A TOKEN WHICH REMINDS/SHOWS WHAT YOU HAVE DONE OR WHERE YOU HAVE BEEN*
souvuneer, souvenir
sovana, savanna
sovant, savant
sovaren, sovereign
sovereign,nly,nty,nties, *SELF-SUFFICIENT, FREE OF OUTSIDE CONTROL*
soverin, sovereign
soverity, severe(rity)
soviren, sovereign
sovont, savant
sovren, sovereign
sovrenedy, sovereign(ity)
sovrin, sovereign
sovrinedy, sovereign(ity)
sovrun, sovereign
sovt, soft
sovtur, soft(er)
sovurin, sovereign
sow,*,wed,wing,wer,wn, *TO PLANT/IMPLANT/ PROPOGATE, FEMALE PIG (or see "so"/ sewn/ son/ sun/ souse)*
sowarkraut, sauerkraut
sowd, sew(ed) /sow(ed)
sower, sour
sowerkrowt, sauerkraut
sowir, sour
sowirkraut, sauerkraut
sowitare, solitaire / solitary
sown, *PAST TENSE OF "SOW" (OR SEE SEWN)*

sownd, sound
sowndlis, sound(less)
sownt, sound
sowpee, sop(ppy)
sowr, sour /sow(er)
sowree, saury /sorry
sows, sauce/ sow(s)/ souse/ saw(s)
sowsd, souse(d) /sauce(d)
sowt, sew(ed)/ sow(ed)/ sought
sowth, south
sowur, sour
sowurkraut, sauerkraut
sowurkrowt, sauerkraut
soy, *A SOYBEAN SAUCE/CONDIMENT*
soybean,*, *A PLANT/LEGUME*
soybeen, soybean
soyible, soluble
soyl, soil
soyul, soil
soz, sauce /saw(s)
sozy, saucy
spa,*, *RETREAT/RESORT/HOT TUB/MINERAL SPRINGS FACILITY* (or see spay)
space,*,ed,cing,er,eless,ey, *PLACE WHERE NO APPARENT MATTER EXISTS*
spachela, spatula
spachula, spatula
spacious,sly,sness, *OPEN/VAST/BROAD AREA*
spackel, spackle
spackle,*,ed,ling,er, *PASTE FOR REPAIRING DAMAGE*
spacy, space(y)
spad, spade /spay(ed)
spadchewla, spatula
spadchula, spatula
spade,*,eful,er, *A SHOVEL/SYMBOL/SHAPE*
spadshewlu, spatula
spadshula, spatula
spaenk, spank
spagem, sphagnum

spagnem, sphagum
spagnum, sphagnum
spagum, sphagnum
spaink, spank
spaircity, sparse(sity)
spairs, sparse /spare(s)
spairsly, sparse(ly)
spakel, spackle
spakil, spackle
spakul, spackle
span,*,nned,nning,nner, *A TOOL, MATCHED PAIR, SPACE/DISTANCE BETWEEN*
spangle,*,ed,ling, *SPARKLING/GLITTERY ORNAMENTS ON SOMETHING*
spank,*,ked,king, *OPEN HANDED SWATS ON BUTTOCKS, SPRITELY/LIVELY/NEW*
spar,*,rred,rring, *PHYSICAL DISPUTE WITH, CRYSTAL- LINE MINERAL (TOO MANY DEFINITIONS, PLEASE SEE STANDARD DICTIONARY)* (or see spare)
sparadik, sporadic
sparadikly, sporadic(ally)
sparcity, sparse(sity)
sparckul, sparkle
spare,*,ed,ring,eable,ely,eness,er,ringly, ringness, *LEFT OVER/EXTRA, TO SAVE/REFRAIN FROM, BOWLING EXPRESSION* (or see spar)
sparengly, spare(ringly)
spark,*,ked,king,ker,kish, *RESULT BETWEEN TWO ELECTRICAL CHARGES COLLIDING, PARTICLES OF GLOWING MATTER*
sparkal, sparkle
sparkil, sparkle
sparkle,*,ed,ling,er, *GLITTERY/FLASHING LIGHT*
sparkul, sparkle
sparo, sparrow
sparrow,*, *A BIRD*
sparse,er,est,ely,eness,sity, *RARE/NOT MANY OF/MEAGER* (or see spare(s))
sparsedy, sparse(sity)

sparsidy, sparse(sity)
sparsly, sparse(ly)
sparsudy, sparse(sity)
spart, spare(d) /spar(rred)
spas, spa(s) / space /spay(s)
spasam, spasm
spasdek, spastic
spasdik, spastic
spase, space
spasee, space(y)
spasefik, specific
spasefikly, specific(ally)
spasem, spasm
spaser, space(r)
spashel, spatial
spashely, spatial
spashes, spacious
spashesness, spacious(ness)
spasheus, spacious
spashewla, spatula
spashil, spatial
spashily, spatial(lly)
spashis, spacious
spashisnes, spacious(ness)
spashius, spacious
spashle, spatial
spashul, spatial
spashula, spatula
spashuly, spatial(lly)
spashus, spacious
spashusnes, spacious(ness)
spasifek, specific
spasifekly, specific(ally)
spasific, specific
spasim, spasm
spasiousness, spacious(ness)
spasir, space(r)
spasm,*,modic,modical,dically, *MUSCLE CONTRACTION*

spasom, spasm
spastek, spastic
spastic,cally, OCCURENCE OF MUSCLE SPASMS
spastuk, spastic
spasum, spasm
spasur, space(r)
spasy, space(y)
spat,*, PAST TENSE OF "SPIT" (or see spay(ed) or spade)
spatchela, spatula
spatchula, spatula
spate, spade/ spat/ spay(ed)
spatial,llity,lly, SPACE WITH NO PHYSICAL MATTER APPARENT (or see special)
spatialy, spatial(lly)
spatiuly, spatial(lly)
spatshewla, spatula
spatshula, spatula
spatula,*, FLAT/BROAD BLADE HAND IMPLEMENT/TOOL
spatulu, spatula
spause, spouse
spaut, spout
spautles, spot(less)
spaw, spa
spawn,*,ned,ning, TO INCUBATE, GIVE BIRTH TO, PRODUCE OFFSPRING
spaws, spouse
spawt, spout
spawtles, spot(less)
spay,*,yed,ying, TO NEUTER/PREVENT FROM CREATING OFFSPRING
spazam, spasm
spazdek, spastic
spazduk, spastic
spazem, spasm
spazim, spasm
spaztek, spastic
spaztuk, spastic
spazum, spasm

speach, speech
speachless, speech(less)
spead, speed
speady, speed(y)
speak,*, spoke,ker,king,kable,kingly, TO MAKE VERBAL SOUNDS WITH INTENT TO COMMUNICATE (or see speck)
speakible, speak(able)
speakuble, speak(able)
speal, spiel
spear,*,red,ring,rer, A LONG SHAFT WITH SHARP POINTED/PIERCING INSTRUMENT ON ONE END
spec, speech /speak /speck
specafy, specify
specamen, specimen
specemin, specimen
specewlate, speculate
specewlum, speculum
spech, speech
spechal, special
spechalist, special(ist)
spechalize, special(ize)
spechelty, special(ity)
speches, speech(es)
spechil, special
spechilist, special(ist)
spechilize, special(ize)
spechis, speech(es)
spechle, special
spechles, speech(less)
spechlist, special(ist)
spechlize, special(ize)
spechlus, speech(less)
spechol, special / speckle
specholist, special(ist)
specholize, special(ize)
specholty, special(ity)
spechulist, special(ist)
spechulize, special(ize)

spechulty, special(ity)
special,llly,list,lty,lties,lism,list,listic,lization,lize, lizes,lized,lizing,lity, UNLIKE THE OTHERS, RARE/UNUSUAL, SPECIFIC CATEGORY
species, A CLASSIFICATION
specific,*,cally,city,cation, TO CLEARLY/DISTINCTLY STATE/DEFINE/MAKE KNOWN
specifide, specify(fied)
specify,fies,fied,fying,fier,fiable, TO CLEARLY/ DISTINCTLY STATE/DEFINE/MAKE KNOWN/REVEAL
specimen,*, SAMPLE/EXAMPLE OF SOMETHING
speck,*, kle,kles,kled,kling, TINY FLECKS/SPOTS (or see specs or speak)
specktrem, spectrum
specktrum, spectrum
speckulashen, speculate(tion)
speckulation, speculate(tion)
specs, SHORT FOR SPECTACLES/GLASSES/DRAWINGS (or see speck)
specs, speak /speck
spectacle,*,ed, GLASSES FOR THE EYES, FOR PUBLIC EXHIBITION/VIEW
spectacul, spectacle
spectacular,rly,rity, MOST IMPRESSIVE EVENT/ ACTIVITY/OCCURENCE
spectader, spectator
spectadur, spectator
spectakewler, spectacular
spectator,*, SOMEONE WATCHING AN EVENT WITHOUT PARTICIPATING
spectecul, spectacle
specter,*, A SPIRIT/GHOST APPEARANCE/APPARITION
specticle, spectacle
specticul, spectacle
spectir, specter
spector, specter
spectral,lity,lness,lly, GIVEN TO BE LIKE A SPIRIT/GHOST
spectrim, spectrum

spectrol, spectral
spectrom, spectrum
spectrul, spectral
spectrum,*, *A RANGE OF SOMETHING BETWEEN TWO GIVEN POINTS*
spectucle, spectacle
spectur, specter
specufy, specify
speculashen, speculate(tion)
speculate,*,ed,ting,tor,tion,tive,tiveness,tory, *THEORIZE BASED UPON FACTS/KNOWINGNESS*
speculim, speculum
speculum,*, *MEDICAL INSTRUMENT USED TO LOOK AT/EXAMINE MORE CLOSELY, MIRROR*
sped, *PAST TENSE OF "SPEED"*
spede, speed(y)
spedeness, speed(iness)
speder, speed(er)
spedeur, speed(ier)
spedily, speed(ily)
spedir, speed(er)
spedul, spittle
speduly, speed(ily)
spedur, speed(er)
spedy, speed(y)
speech,hes,hless,hlessness, *TO VOCALLY EMPHASIZE SOUNDS/WORDS*
speed,*,ded,ding,dier,diest,der,dy,dily,diness, *THE RATE/VELOCITY OF MOVEMENT, TO TRAVEL FASTER THAN NORMAL*
speedeness, speed(iness)
speeker, speak(er)
speekt, speak
speel, spiel
speer, spear
speer, sphere /spear
speget, spigot
spegit, spigot
spegot, spigot

spekabul, speak(able)
spekal, speck(le)
speker, speak(er)
spekeulate, speculate
spekeulatif, speculate(tive)
spekewlashen, speculate(tion)
spekewlate, speculate
spekewlation, speculate(tion)
spekewlative, speculate(tive)
spekewlem, speculum
spekible, speak(able)
spekil, speck(le)
spekir, speak(er)
spekol, speck(le)
spekor, speak(er)
speks, specs/ speak(s)/ speck(s)
spekt, spoke
spektadur, spectator
spektakewler, spectacular
spektakle, spectacle
spektakul, spectacle
spektakuler, spectacular
spektar, specter
spektator, spectator
spektekul, spectacle
spekter, specter
spektikul, spectacle
spektir, specter
spektor, specter
spektrality, spectral(ity)
spektram, spectrum
spektrel, spectral
spektrem, spectrum
spektrul, spectral
spektrum, spectrum
spektukul, spectacle
spektur, specter
spekuble, speak(able)
spekul, speck(le)

spekulashen, speculate(tion)
spekulate, speculate
spekulation, speculate(tion)
spekulative, speculate(tive)
spekulem, speculum
spekulotif, speculate(tive)
spekulum, speculum
spekulutive, speculate(tive)
spekur, speak(er)
spekyewlem, speculum
spekyulate, speculate
spekyulatif, speculate(tive)
spel, spiel/ spell/ spill
spelar, spell(er)
speld, spill(ed)/ spelt/ spell(ed)
spelor, spell(er)
spell,*,led,ling,ler, *FORMULATE LETTERS INTO ACCEPTABLE FORMAT, BE SUBCONSCIOUSLY CONTROLLED*
spellur, spell(er)
spelor, spell(er)
spelt, *PAST TENSE OF "SPELL", A TYPE OF WHEAT (or see spell(ed)/spill(ed)/spiel(ed))*
spelur, spell(er)
spen, spin /spend
spenatch, spinach
spend,*,spent,ding,der,dy, *TRADE OUTGO FOR INCOME (or see spent or spin(nned))*
spendal, spindle
spended, spent
spendir, spend(er)
spendle, spindle
spendly, spindle(y)
spendul, spindle
spenech, spinach
spenich, spinach
spent, *PAST TENSE OF "SPEND" (or see spend)*
spentle, spindle
spentul, spindle

spenuch, spinach
spenur, spin(nner)
spenutch, spinach
speol, spiel
sper, spare/ spear/ spur
speradik, sporadic
spercity, sparse(sity)
sperd, spear(ed) /spur(rred)
sperds, spurt(s)
sperichual, spiritual
sperichualidy, spiritual(ity)
speringly, spare(ringly)
sperit, spirit
speritshuality, spiritual(ity)
sperm,*, A METHOD OF CARRYING MALE DNA FOR PROCREATION, SEMEN
spero, sparrow
sperow, sparrow
spers, sparse/ spare(s)/ spear(s)/ spur(s)
spersity, sparse(sity)
sperslee, sparse(ly)
spersly, sparse(ly)
spersudy, sparse(sity)
spert, spurt /spare(d)/ spear(ed)
spesaficashen, specify(fication)
spesafide, specify(fied)
spesafikation, specify(fication)
spesafy, specify
spesamen, specimen
spesamin, specimen
spesefakation, specify(fication)
spesefide, specify(fied)
spesefukation, specify(fication)
spesefy, specify
spesemin, specimen
speshal, special
speshalist, special(ist)
speshalize, special(ize)
speshelty, special(ity)

speshez, species
speshil, special
speshilest, special(ist)
speshilty, special(ity)
speshis, species
speshle, special
speshlist, special(ist)
speshlize, special(ize)
speshol, special
spesholty, special(ity)
speshul, special
speshulist, special(ist)
speshulize, special(ize)
speshulty, special(ity)
spesial, special
spesies, species
spesifakation, specify(fication)
spesifek, specific
spesifcashen, specify(fication)
spesification, specify(fication)
spesifide, specify(fied)
spesifik, specific
spesifucashen, specify(fication)
spesifukation, specify(fication)
spesify, specify
spesimen, specimen
spesimin, specimen
spesofecashen, specify(fication)
spesofecation, specify(fication)
spesofide, specify(fied)
spesufication, specify(fication)
spesufide, specify(fied)
spesufy, specify
spesumen, specimen
spesumin, specimen
spet, sped
spetil, spittle
spetle, spittle
spetoon, spittoon

spetul, spittle
spetune, spittoon
spetur, spit(tter)
speu, spew
speul, spiel /spill
spew,*,wed,wing, TO RUN/FLOW FORTH, EJECT FROM WITHIN, VOMIT
sphagnum,nous, VARIETY OF MOSS
spharikul, sphere(rical)
spharukil, sphere(rical)
sphenctur, sphincter
sphenktur, sphincter
spherakil, sphere(rical)
sphere,*,ed,ring,ral,rical,rics,ry, A CIRCLE/AREA EXTENDED AROUND THE CENTER WHERE DISTANCE IS EQUAL FROM THE CENTER
spherekil, sphere(rical)
spherikul, sphere(rical)
sphincter,ral,rial,rate,ric, MUSCLE WHICH CONTRACTS THE ORIFICE ON THE LOWER TORSO
sphinkter, sphincter
sphinx,xes,xian, A FIGURE WITH THE HEAD OF ONE THING AND BODY OF SOMETHING DIFFERENT
sphire, sphere
spice,*,ed,cing,ery,cy, OF OR GIVEN TO SPICES, CULINARY PLANTS
spictacular, spectacular
spictakuler, spectacular
spid, spy(pied) /spite
spide, spite / spit / spy(pied)
spider,*,ry, EIGHT LEGGED ARACHNID
spidful, spite(ful)
spidul, spittle
spidur, spider
spidury, spider(y)
spiel,*, TALK/EXPLAIN AT LENGTH WITH PERSUASION
spiget, spigot
spigot,*, A DEVICE/FAUCET FOR ALLOWING/STOPPING THE FLOW OF LIQUIDS

spigut, spigot
spike,*,ed,king,ky,ker, *STIFF/SHARP, USED TO IMPALE/ PIERCE, SHAPED LIKE A NAIL*
spikt, spike(d)
spiktakewler, spectacular
spiktakuler, spectacular
spiky, spike(ky)
spil, spill
spill,*,lled,lling,llage, *SOMETHING LOOSE/LIQUID TO FLOW FROM CONTAINER/SOURCE, TO DIVULGE (or see spiel or spell)*
spin,*,nned,nning,nner, *TO WEAVE/TWIST/WRAP AROUND, TELL A STORY, PERFORM CIRCULAR MOTION (or see spine or spend)*
spinach, *VEGETABLE/PLANT*
spinal,lly, *ASSOCIATED WITH THE SPINE*
spinatch, spinach
spind, spend /spin(nned)
spinded, spent
spinder, spend(er)
spindil, spindle
spindle,*,ed,ling,ly, *A ROD/PIN TO WOUND/SPIN/ TWIST SOMETHING AROUND*
spindly, spindle(y)
spindul, spindle
spindur, spend(er)
spine,*,eless,elessly,elessness,ny,escent, escence, *BACKBONE/VERTEBRATE OF BODIES, A LONG CREST/SET OF PEAKS*
spinech, spinach
spinel, spinal
spiner, spin(nner)
spinlesness, spine(lessness)
spinless, spine(less)
spinol, spinal
spinor, spin(nner)
spint, spent
spinter, spend(er)
spintil, spindle

spintir, spend(er)
spintul, spindle
spintur, spend(er)
spinuch, spinach
spinul, spinal
spinur, spin(nner)
spinutch, spinach
spiny, spine(y)
spir, spur /spire
spiradek, sporadic
spiradic, sporadic
spiradik, sporadic
spiradikly, sporadic(ally)
spiral,*,lled,lling,lly, *REPEATED CIRCULAR CURVE WHOSE EVOLUTION AROUND CONSISTENTLY ASCENDS OR DESCENDS, CONTINUOUS CIRCULAR MOTION IN ONE DIRECTION OR ANOTHER*
spiraly, spiral(lly)
spird, spire(d) /spur(rred) /spurt
spire,ed,ring,ry, *COMING TO A POINT, PYRAMID SHAPE*
spirechualedy, spiritual(ity)
spirechuil, spiritual
spirel, spiral
spireshuil, spiritual
spiret, spirit
spiretshualety, spiritual(ity)
spirichual, spiritual
spirichualidy, spiritual(ity)
spirichuel, spiritual
spiril, spiral
spirit,*,ted,tism,tist,tistic, *CHARACTER/DISPOSITION ESSENCE OF ENERGY/ANIMATION, THAT WHICH MAKES THINGS LIFELIKE/ALIVE, ALCOHOL*
spiritchuel, spiritual
spiritual,lly,lness,lism,list,listic,lity,lities,lize, lized,lizing,lty,lties, *IMMATERIAL ESSENCE/ SPIRIT/LIFE, OF THE UNKNOWN, NOT PHYSICAL*
spirm, sperm
spirt, spurt /spire(d)

spirul, spiral
spiruly, spiral(lly)
spisd, spice(d)
spise, spice /spy(pies)
spised, spice(d)
spisury, spice(ry)
spisy, spice(y)
spit,*,tted,tting,spat,tter, *SALIVA WHICH IS FORCED FROM THE MOUTH, ROD/PIN FOR HOLDING MEAT WHILE COOKING, NARROW POINT OF LAND*
spital, spittle
spite,ed,ting,eful,efully,efulness, *MALICIOUS INTENT/DISPOSITION*
spitel, spittle
spiter, spider /spit(tter)
spitful, spite(ful)
spitle, spittle
spitoon, spittoon
spittle, *SECRETION BY INSECTS*
spittoon,*, *VESSEL FOR SPIT*
spittune, spittoon
spitul, spittle
spitune, spittoon
spitur, spider /spit(tter)
spiz, spy(pies) /spice
spize, spice/ spy(pies)/ spice(y)
spla, splay
splach, splotch
splachy, splotch(y)
splad, splat /splay(ed)
splader, splatter
spladur, splatter
splaer, splay(er)
splash,hes,hed,hing,her,hy,hily,hiness, *PARTICLES OF LIQUID SCATTERED INTO THE AIR*
splat, *BACK OF A CHAIR, A TYPE OF SOUND*
splater, splatter
splator, splatter
splatter,*,red,ring, *TO SPLASH A LIQUID*

splatur, splatter
splaur, splay(er)
splay,*,yed,yer, TO SPREAD OUT/FLARE/FAN, CREATE CURVE
splean, spleen
spledur, split(tter)
spleen,*,nful,ny,nier,niest, AN ORGAN IN THE BODY, ILL HUMOR/IRRITABLE
splendant, splendent
splendedly, splendid(ly)
splendent, BRILLIANT/RADIANT IN APPEARANCE
splender, splendor /splinter
splendid,*,dly,dness, GRAND/MAGNIFICENT/
splendint, splendent
splendir, splendor /splinter
splendit, splendid
splendor,*,rous, BRILLIANCE/LUSTER (or see splinter)
splendris, splendor(ous)
splendrus, splendor(ous)
splendunt, splendent
splendur, splendor /splinter
splene, spleen /spleen(y)
splent, splint
splented, splendid
splentor, splendor /splinter
splentrus, splendor(ous)
splentur, splendor /splinter
spleny, spleen(y)
splerge, splurge
splerje, splurge
splet, split
spletor, split(tter)
splice,*,ed,cing,er, TO GRAFT/PIECE TOGETHER PERFECTLY, CUT AND JOIN
splider, split(tter)
splindant, splendent
splinded, splendid
splindedly, splendid(ly)

splindint, splendent
splindir, splendor /splinter
splindit, splendid
splindrus, splendor(ous)
splindud, splendid
splindunt, splendent
splindur, splendor /splinter
splint,*, REPAIR FOR A FRACTURE
splinted, splinter(ed)
splinter,*,red,ring,ry, A SMALL SLICE/PIECE BROKEN/CUT OFF LENGHTWISE, A SLIVER
splintird, splinter(ed)
splintor, splendor /splinter
splintrus, splendor(ous)
splintur, splendor /splinter
splirge, splurge
splirje, splurge
splisur, splice(r)
split,*,tted,tting,tter, BROKEN/TORN APART/ SEPARATED (TOO MANY DEFINITIONS, PLEASE SEE STANDARD DICTIONARY)
splitor, split(tter)
sploch, splotch
sploche, splotch(y)
splotch,hes,hed,hing,hy,hier,hiest, AN IRREGULAR SPOT/SPLASH OF LIQUID/COLOR/STAIN
splurgd, splurge(d)
splurge,*,ed,ging, TO OVER SPEND
spo, spa
spock, spoke
spod, spot
spodable, spot(able)
spoded, spot(tted)
spodee, spot(tty)
spodible, spot(able)
spodid, spot(tted)
spodlis, spot(less)
spoduble, spot(able)
spoel, spoil

spoeld, spoil(ed) /spoilt
spoeleg, spoil(age)
spoelij, spoil(age)
spoelt, spoil(ed) /spoilt
spoeluj, spoil(age)
spoil,*,led,ling,lage,ler,lable,spoilt, TO GO BAD, DAMAGE, RENDER UNFIT
spoild, spoil(ed) /spoilt
spoileg, spoil(age)
spoilej, spoil(age)
spoilt, PAST TENSE OF "SPOIL" (or see spoil(ed))
spoiluje, spoil(age)
spoke,*,en, PAST TENSE OF "SPEAK", RODS/WIRES RADIATING FROM THE HUB OF A WHEEL
spokun, spoke(n)
spon, spawn
sponge,*,ed,ging,gy,gier,giest,giness,er, SEA ANIMAL, SKELETON OF SEA ANIMALS USED TO CLEAN/ABSORB LIQUIDS
sponser, sponsor
sponsor,*,red,ring,rial,rship, SOMEONE WHO PAYS/SUPPORTS SOMEONE ELSE
sponsur, sponsor
spont, spawn(ed) /spoon(ed)
spontaineus, spontaneous
spontaneity,eities, ABLE TO ACT QUICKLY ON IMPULSE WITHOUT CONSTRAINT
spontaneous,sly,sness, ABLE TO ACT QUICKLY ON IMPULSE WITHOUT CONSTRAINT
spontaneus, spontaneous
spontenaity, spontaneity
spontinaedy, spontaneity
spontinaity, spontaneity
spontunaity, spontaneity
sponzur, sponsor
spoof,*, TO TEASE/DECEIVE WITH GOOD INTENT
spook,*,ked,king,ky,kish, TO ACT LIKE OR BE A GHOST/SPECTER/APPARITION
spool,*,led,ling, ROUND/CYLINDER SHAPE HOLDING LENGTHS OF SOMETHING WOUND AROUND IT

spoon,*,ned,ning,nful, UTENSIL WITH HANDLE AT
   ONE END AND A BOWL SHAPE ON THE OTHER
spor, spar /spore
sporadic,cal,cally, IRRATIC/UNPREDICTABLE
   OCCURENCES
sporadikly, sporadic(ally)
sporded, sport(ed)
spordee, sport(y)
spordid, sport(ed)
spordy, sport(y)
spore,*,red,ring,ral,roid,riferous,rulate, REPRO-
   DUCTIVE SEEDS OF BACTERIA AND SOME PLANTS
sporol, spore(ral)
sport,*,ted,ting,tive,tively,tiveness,ty, ATHLETIC/
   OUTDOOR GAMES, TO CARRY, GOOD ATTITUDE
sportee, sport(y)
sportef, sport(ive)
sportif, sport(ive)
sportud, sport(ed)
sporul, spore(ral)
spot,*,tted,tting,tty,ttier,ttiest,tter,table,tless,
   tlessly,tlessness, FLAW/MARK/BLEMISH, A
   PARTICULAR/SPECIFIC PLACE
spoted, spot(tted)
spotee, spot(tty)
spotible, spot(able)
spotid, spot(ted)
spotuble, spot(able)
spoty, spot(tty)
spouse,*,sal, ONE WHO IS ENGAGED OR VOWED/
   MARRIED TO ANOTHER
spout,*,ted,ting,ter, PIPE/NOZZLE PROJECTING FROM
   VESSEL FOR LIQUID
spown, spawn
spowse, spouse
spowsul, spouse(sal)
spowt, spout
spoyl, spoil
spoyleg, spoil(age)

spoylej, spoil(age)
spra, spray
sprae, spray
spraer, spray(er)
spraget, sprocket
spragit, sprocket
sprain,*,ned,ning, TO TWIST/WRENCH/OVER
   STRETCH A MUSCLE IN THE BODY
spraket, sprocket
spral, sprawl
spran, sprain
spraor, spray(er)
sprat, spray(ed)
spraukit, sprocket
spraur, spray(er)
spraut, sprout
sprawl,*,led,ling, TO EXTEND/SPREAD OUT IN
   IRREGULAR POSITION/MANNER
sprawt, sprout
spray,*,yed,ying,yer, PARTICLES OF LIQUID
   RELEASED/FORCED INTO THE AIR
spre, spree
spread,*,ding,der, FORCE/EXTEND INTO A THIN
   LAYER OVER SUBSTANTIAL DISTANCE/TIME/SPACE
spred, spread
spredur, spread(er)
spree,*, FROLICING/MERRY TIME
spreg, sprig
spreng, spring
sprengee, spring(y)
sprengy, spring(y)
sprenk, spring
sprenkal, sprinkle
sprenkil, sprinkle
sprenkler, sprinkle(r)
sprenklor, sprinkle(r)
sprenkul, sprinkle
sprenkuler, sprinkle(r)
sprent, sprint

sprentur, sprint(er)
spret, spread
spreter, spread(er)
spretur, spread(er)
sprews, spruce
spri, spry
sprig,*, SMALL BRANCH FROM PLANT
sprilee, spry(ly)
sprily, spry(ly)
spring,*,ged,ging,sprang,gy,gily,giness, A
   RIVULET OF WATER, COILED DEVICE (TOO MANY
   DEFINITIONS, PLEASE SEE STANDARD DICTIONARY)
springey, spring(y)
sprinis, spry(ness)
sprink, spring
sprinkel, sprinkle
sprinkle,*,ed,ling,er, TO SHOOT/RELEASE/SPRAY
   HEAVY DROPS OF LIQUID
sprinklor, sprinkle(r)
sprinkul, sprinkle
sprinkuler, sprinkle(r)
sprint,*,ting,ter, RACE/SPEED A SHORT DISTANCE
sprintor, sprint(er)
sprintur, sprint(er)
sprocket,*, PART OF A WHEEL/CHAIN
sprogit, sprocket
sprokut, sprocket
sprol, sprawl
sproose, spruce
sprout,*,ted,ting, TO GERMINATE, GROW INTO THE
   DAYLIGHT, SHOW GROWTH
sprowt, sprout
spruce,*,ed,cing,ely,eness, TYPE OF TREE, TO GET
   DRESSED UP
spruse, spruce
spry,yly,yness, LIVELY/NIMBLE
sprynis, spry(ness)
spud,*,dded,dding, POTATOE, TOOL, TO WEED OUT
spuder, sputter

spudor, sputter
spue, spew
spufe, spoof
spuk, spook
spuky, spook(y)
spule, spool
spun, *PAST TENSE OF "SPIN"* (or see spoon)
spunch, sponge
spune, spoon / spun
spunful, spoon(ful)
spung, sponge /spunk
spungee, sponge(gy)
spungenis, spunk(iness)
spungy, sponge(gy)
spunj, sponge
spunjy, sponge(gy)
spunk, *ky,kily,kiness, SPIRITED/COURAGEOUS, TINDER FROM FUNGUS*
spunkenis, spunk(iness)
spur, **,rred,rring,rious,riously,riousness, TO STIMULATE/ENCOURAGE TO GO ON, DEVICE FOR BOOTS/RIDING (TOO MANY DEFINITIONS, PLEASE SEE STANDARD DICTIONARY)* (or see spurt)
spuradek, sporadic
spuradikly, sporadic(ally)
spurm, sperm
spurt, **,ted,ting, SUDDEN JOLT/GROWTH/MOVEMENT, SHORT PERIOD OF TIME*
spusefikly, specific(ally)
spusifikly, specific(ally)
sput, spud
sputer, sputter
sputter, **,red,ring,rer, TO RAPIDLY/INCOHERENTLY SPEAK, IRRATIC/HALTING MOTION/SOUND*
sputur, sputter
spy, *pies,pied,pying, SECRET SURVEILLANCE/ MONITORING/WATCHING*
spyd, spy(pied)
spyder, spider

spydful, spite(ful)
spydur, spider
spyeng, spy(ing)
spyke, spike
spyse, spy(pies) /spice
spytur, spider
sqeek, squeak
squabble, **,ed,ling,er, MINOR SCUFFLE/DISPUTE*
squad, **, A SMALL GROUP OF SPECIFIC PEOPLE* (or see squat)
squadir, squat(tter)
squadron, **, SMALL MILITARY/POLICE GROUP*
squadur, squat(tter)
squaemish, squeamish
squal, **,ller,lly, SUDDEN/STRONG GUSTS OF WIND/ RAIN/SLEET*
squaled, squalid
squalid, *dly,dness,dity, NEGLECTED/FOUL/FILTHY*
squalor, *NEGLECTED/FOUL/FILTHY*
squander, **,red,ring, TO RECKLESSLY LET GO OF/ USE/WASTE*
square, **,ed,ring,ely,eness,rish,rishly, OF BEING FOUR EQUAL SIDES, TO BE PROPORTIONAL, SOMEONE DULL, A MATH OPERATION*
squarly, square(ly)
squash, *hes,hed,hing, A VEGETABLE/GAME, TO SMASH/CRUSH SOMETHING*
squat, **,tted,tting,tter, REST ON HAUNCHES, LOWER THE UPPER TORSO, TO SIT* (or see squad)
squator, squat(tter)
squeak, **,ked,king,kingly,ker,ky, A SHORT/SHRILL SOUND*
squeal, **,led,ling,ler, A LOUD/SHRILL SOUND PRO-DUCED BY GLEE/HAPPINESS, TO TELL A TRUTH ABOUT SOMEONE WITHOUT THEIR PERMISSION*
squeamish, *hly,hness, UNEASY/UNSETTLING, DISGUSTED ABOUT SOMETHING*
squed, squid

squeegee, **,ed,eing, AN INSTRUMENT/IMPLEMENT FOR REMOVING WATER/LIQUID*
squeejy, squeegee
squeek, squeak
squeel, squeal
squeelur, squeal(er)
squeemish, squeamish
squeese, squeeze
squeeze, **,ed,zing,er,zingly,zable, TO FORCE BY TIGHTENING GRIP*
squegy, squeegee
squejy, squeegee
squel, squeal
squelch, *hed,hing,her, SILENCE/CRUSH/SUPPRESS, A SOUND*
squelur, squeal(er)
squemish, squeamish
squent, squint
squerl, squirrel
squerm, squirm
squermy, squirm(y)
squert, squirt
squesh, squish
squeshy, squish(y)
squesur, squeeze(r)
squeze, squeeze
squid, **, A CEPHALOPOD FOUND IN SALT WATER*
squiggle, **,ed,ling, SQUIRM/TWIST*
squigy, squeegee
squint, **,ted,ting, TO CLOSE EYES TO A NARROW OPENING FOR PROTECTION*
squire, **,ed,ring, MAN OF ARISTOCRATIC BIRTH, MAN WHO ESCORTS*
squirel, squirrel
squirl, squirrel
squirm, **,med,ming,mer,my,mier,miest, TO WRITH/WRIGGLE LIKE A WORM*
squirrel, **,lly, A RODENT, TO BEHAVE LIKE A SQUIRREL*

squirt,*,ted,ting, A NARROW STREAM OF LIQUID EMITTED FROM AN ORIFICE
squrt, squirt

squish,hes,hed,hing,hy,hier,hiest, SQUASH/SMASH
sqwal, squal
sqwalid, squalid
sta, stay

stab,*,bbed,bbing,bber, TO POKE/THRUST A BLADE WITH SHARP TIP INTO SOMETHING/SOMEONE
stabalize, stabilize
stabelity, stability
stabilise, stabilize

stability,ties, OF FIRM GROUND/FORM/FOUNDATION

stabilize,*,ed,zing,er,zation, TO PROVIDE/ENSURE FIRM GROUND/FORM
stabiludy, stability
stablize, stabilize
stabulize, stabilize

staccato,*, , SHARP/BRIEF MUSICAL NOTE (or see stoccado)
stachur, stature
stachitorty, statue(utory)
stad, staid/ stay(ed)/ state
stadeim, stadium
stadek, static
stades, status
stadeum, stadium
stadiem, stadium
stadik, static
stadis, status

stadium,*, A LARGE ARENA FOR PEOPLE TO GATHER
stadus, status
staf, staff/ staph/ stave
stafed, staff(ed)

staff,*,ffed,ffing, GROUP OF HIRED PEOPLE, TALL POLE/ STICK TO BE CARRIED/USED BY HAND (or see staph)
staft, staff(ed) /stave(d)

stag,*,gged,gging,gger, MALE IN THE DEER FAMILY, MALE UNACCOMPANIED AT A GATHERING (or see stage or stack)
stagd, stag(gged) / stage(d)

stage,*,ed,ging,er,ey, PLATFORM DESIGNED FOR PLAYS/THEATER, TO PERFORM (or see stag)
staged, stag(gged) /stage(d)
stagee, stodgy
stageer, stagger

stagger,*,red,ring,rer,ringly, TO SWAY/WAVER/ WALK UNSTEADILY, SHOCKED, HORSE/COW HIT BY A DISEASE
stagir, stagger
stagnade, stagnate

stagnant,tly,ncy, NO MOVEMENT/MOTION
stagnashen, stagnate(tion)

stagnate,*,ed,ting,tion, QUIT MOVING, BECOME DULL/QUIET
stagnatid, stagnate(d)
stagnit, stagnant
stagnunt, stagnant
stagnut, stagnant
stager, stagger
stagred, stagger(ed)
stagt, stag(gged) /stage(d)
stagur, stagger
stagy, stodgy

staid,dly,dness, IN PLACE OF, FIXED/STEADY (or see stead or stay(ed))

stain,*,ned,ning,nable,ner,nless,nlessly,UN- DESIRABLE MARK,PERMANENTLY PLACE/AFFIX COLOR

stair,*, STEPS MAKING A RISE IN ELEVATION (or see stare)
stak, stack /stake /steak
stakabul, stack(able)
stakado, staccato /stoccado
stakato, staccato /stoccado
stakd, stack(ed) /stake(d)

stake,*,ed,king, LEVERAGE/PLEDGE/WAGER SUP-PORT FOR SOMETHING, HAVE A VESTED INTEREST IN, BROAD POINTED POST FOR STRIKING/DRIVING INTO GROUND (or see steak)
staked, stack(ed) /stake(d)
staker, stagger /stack(er)
stakibel, stack(able)
stakibul, stack(able)
stakir, stagger /stack(er)
staknade, stagnate
staknashen, stagnate(tion)
staknate, stagnate
staknation, stagnate(tion)
staknunt, stagnant
stakodo, staccato /stoccado
stakoto, staccato /stoccado
stakt, stack(ed) /stake(d)
stakubil, stack(able)
stakuble, stack(able)
stakur, stagger /stack(er)
stal, stall /stale

stale, LOSS OF ACTION/TASTE/FLAVOR (or see stall)
staleon, stallion
stalium, stallion

stalk,*,ked,king,ker, FOLLOW SOMEONE/SOME-THING WITH INTENT WITHOUT THEIR KNOWING, MAIN PORTION OF A POLE SHAPED PLANT

stall,*,lled,lling, A DWELLING FOR HORSES, TO HESITATE/QUIT/PAUSE (or see stale)

stallion,*, MALE HORSE CAPABLE OF BREEDING

stalwart,tly,tness, UNCOMPROMISING/STRONG IN RESOLUTION
stalwort, stalwart
stalyun, stallion

stamen,*,nal, PLANT ORGAN
stamenu, stamina
stamer, stammer
stamin, stamen

stamina, LONGEVITY IN STRENGTH

stamir, stammer
stammer,red,ring,ringly, *PAUSE/HESITATE IN SPEECH*
stamp,*,ped,ping,per, *AFFIXED TO A POSTAL LETTER, A MARK LEFT BY PRESSING*
stampede,*,ed,ding,dingly, *A MAD/SUDDEN RUSH IN ONE DIRECTION BY MANY*
stampet, stampede
stampir, stamp(er)
stampur, stamp(er)
stamun, stamen
stamur, stammer
stan, stain
stance, *A STAND/ATTITUDE/POSITION*
stancheon, stanchion
stanchion,*, *BEAM/POST FOR SUPPORT*
stand,*,ding,der,stood, *PARTICULAR POSITION, BE UPRIGHT IN FOOTING (TOO MANY DEFINITIONS, PLEASE SEE STANDARD DICTIONARY)*
standard,*,dize,dized,dization, *A GENERAL CONSENSUS ON METHODOLOGY/DIMENSIONS/ DEGREE OF MEASURMENT*
standerd, standard
standerdazation, standard(ization)
standurd, standard
standurdize, standard(ize)
stane, stain
staneble, stain(able)
stanible, stain(able)
stank, *PAST TENSE OF "STINK"*
stans, stance /stain(s) /stand(s)
stansa, stanza
stanshen, stanchion
stanshon, stanchion
stansu, stanza
stant, stand
stanuble, stain(able)
stanza,*, *FOUR OR MORE IN A VERSE/POEM*
stap, stab

stapel, staple
staph, *SHORT FOR STAPHYLOCOCCUS (or see staff)*
staple,*,ed,ling,er, *FASTENER MADE OF METAL, BASIC REQUIREMENTS FOR SURVIVAL*
stapul, staple
star,*,rred,rring,rless,rry, *CELESTIAL/SHINING BODY IN SPACE, PERSON WHO ACHIEVES THE LIMELIGHT, GEOMETRIC SHAPE (or see stare or star)*
staralize, steril(lize)
starch,hes,hed,hing,hiness,hy, *NATURALLY OCCURING CHEMICAL USED TO MAKE THINGS STIFF*
starchenes, starch(iness)
stard, start /stare(d) /star(rred)
starder, starter
stardil, startle
stardul, startle
stardur, starter
stare,*,ed,ring, *TO AFFIX EYES ONTO A SINGLE POINT WITHOUT MOVING (or see star/stair/star(rry)*
stared, stare(d) /star(rred)
stareledy, steril(lity)
starelidy, steril(lity)
stareo, stereo
starf, starve
staril, sterile
starilety, steril(lity)
starilize, steril(lize)
stark,kly,kness, *GRIM/DESOLATE SCENE WITH LITTLE TO ENTERTAIN THE EYE*
starling,*, *A BIRD*
staroed, steroid
staroid, steroid
stars, stair(s) /stare(s) /star(s)
start,*,ted,ting,ter, *BEGIN, INITIAL ACTION (or see stare(d))*
starter,*, *ELECTRIC MOTOR, BEGIN/INITIATE ACTION*
startil, startle
startir, starter

startle,*,ed,ling, *TO BE ALARMED/SURPRISED BY SUDDEN ACTION/EVENT*
startul, startle
startur, starter
starul, sterile
starulize, steril(lize)
starvashen, starvation
starvation, *SERIOUSLY LACK NOURISHMENT/BASIC ESSENTIALS*
starve,*,ed,ving, *SERIOUSLY LACK NOURISHMENT/ BASIC ESSENTIALS*
stas, stay(s)
stases, stasis
stash,hes,hed,hing, *TO HIDE/PUT SOMETHING AWAY*
stashen, station
stashenary, stationary /stationery
stasher, stature
stashewesk, statue(sque)
stashewtory, statute(tory)
stashin, station /stash(ing)
stashinary, stationary /stationery
stashir, stature
stashonery, stationary /stationery
stashoot, statute
stashu, statue
stashuary, statuary
stashuery, statuary
stashuesk, statue(sque)
stashun, station
stashunery, stationary /stationery
stashur, stature
stashute, statute
stashutory, statute(tory)
stasis, *EQUILIBRIUM, FROZEN IN TIME/MOVEMENT, INACTIVITY*
stasus, stasis
stat,*, *HOSPITAL EMERGENCY EXPRESSION, SHORT FOR STATISTICS (or see state or stay(ed))*
statchuesk, statue(sque)

state, *, ed, ting, PORTION OF LAND WITH SPECIFIC/ DECISIVE BORDER, CURRENT CONDITION
statek, static
statement, *, SUMMARY/REVIEW OF EXISTING CONDITION/STATUS
states, status /state(s)
stateur, stature
stateutory, statute(tory)
static, *, cal, cally, NO MOVEMENT/ACTION, AT REST
statik, static
station, *, A PLACE TO MOMENTARILY REST/RECEIVE SERVICES
stationary, REST/STOP/BE STILL(or see stationery)
stationery, ENVELOPE/PAPER FOR WRITING (or see stationary)
statis, status
statistic, *, cal, cally, A MATHEMATICAL ACCOUNT OF CURRENT SITUATION/CONDITION
statiur, stature
statment, statement
statmunt, statement
stats, state(s) /stat(s)
statshu, statue
statshuery, statuary
statuary, ries, COLLECTION OF STATUES
statue, *, esque, ette, SOLID/STATIONARY FORM CARVED/MOLDED TO RESEMBLE SOMETHING/ SOMEONE
statuery, statuary
statuesk, statue(sque)
stature, PHYSICAL DIMENSIONS OF A LIVING THING
status, CURRENT POSITION/STANDING
statute, *, tory, A FIXED PERMANENT LAW
stauk, stock
staunch, hly, hness, RIGID/FIRM STRUCTURE/FORM, LIQUID RESILLIENT
staut, stout
stave, *, ed, ving, FIGHT OFF AN ATTACK, A ROD/POLE/ STICK

stawgines, stodgy(giness)
stawk, stock /stalk
stawked, stock(ed) /stoke(d)
stawt, stout
stay, *, yed, ying, TO REMAIN BEHIND/IN ONE PLACE, DON'T FOLLOW/MOVE
stead, TO BE IN SOMEONE'S PLACE/POSITION WHILE THEY'RE AWAY (or see steed or staid)
steadeness, steady(diness)
steadfast, tly, tness, HOLDING FIXED /FIRM/ UNWAVERING (also stedfast)
steady, dies, dier, diest, died, dying, dily, diness, FIXED/FIRM/CONSTANT
steak, *, A CUT OF BEEF (or see stake)
steal, *, ling, stole, TAKE SOMETHING FROM SOME- ONE WITHOUT THEIR PERMISSION (or see steel/ stile /still)
stealth, hy, hily, hiness, SECRECY
steam, *, med, ming, mer, mily, miness, THE USE OF HOT WATER TURNED TO GASEOUS STATE
stear, steer
stebel, steeple /stipple
stebul, steeple /stipple
stebulashen, stipulate(tion)
stebulation, stipulate(tion)
stebulatory, stipulate(tory)
stech, stitch
sted, SHORT FOR "INSTEAD" (or see stead or steed)
stede, steady
stedeness, steady(diness)
stedes, steady(dies)
stedfast, tly, tness, HOLDING FIXED /FIRM/ UNWAVERING (also steadfast)
stedfastnes, steadfast(ness)
stedily, steady(dily)
stediness, steady(diness)
stedness, staid(ness) /stead(ness)
steduly, steady(dily)
stedy, steady

steed, *, HORSE WITH SPIRIT, STALLION (or see stead)
steel, ly, lier, liest, liness, TYPE OF METAL (or see steal /stile /still)
steenkur, stink(er)
steenky, stink(y)
steep, *, ped, ping, ply, pness, per, pen, SHARP SLOPE SOAK/IMMERSE (or see step or steppe)
steeple, *, TALL ROOF COMING TO A POINT AT THE TOP
steer, *, red, ring, rable, rer, rage, TO MANIPULATE/ CONTROL INTO PARTICULAR DIRECTION, CASTRATED BOVINE
steerible, steer(able)
steeruble, steer(able)
stef, stiff
stefin, stiff(en)
stefnis, stiff(ness)
stegma, stigma
stegmadik, stigma(tic)
stegmatist, stigma(tist)
stein, *, BEER MUGS
stek, stick / steak /stake
stekado, staccato /stoccado
stekato, staccato /stoccado
stekir, stick(er)
stekler, stickler
steklur, stickler
stekmu, stigma
stekodo, staccato /stoccado
stekor, stick(er)
stekoto, staccato /stoccado
stekur, stick(er)
steky, stick(y)
stel, steel/ steal/ still/ stile
stelar, stellar
stelir, stellar
stellar, OF THE STARS
stelnis, still(ness)
stelnus, still(ness)

stipeulutory, stipulate(tory)
stipewlate, stipulate
stiplur, stipple(r)
stipple,ed,ling,er, *MANY DOTS TO CREATE A SCENE/ PICTURE*
stiptek, styptic
stiptik, styptic
stipulashen, stipulate(tion)
stipulate,*,ed,ting,tion,tive,tory, *AN AGREEMENT WITH GUIDELINES*
stir,*,rred,rring,rrer,rringly, *TO CREATE MOTION/ MOVEMENT*
stirafom, styrofoam
stird, stir(rred)
stirdy, sturdy
stirefoam, styrofoam
stirgen, sturgeon
stirgeon, sturgeon
stirjun, sturgeon
stirleng, sterling
stirn, stern
stirnem, sternum
stirnly, stern(ly)
stirnness, stern(ess)
stirnum, sternum
stirrup,*, *PART ON A HORSES SADDLE*
stirt, stir(rred)
stirty, sturdy
stirufoam, styrofoam
stirup, stirrup
stish, stitch
stitch,hes,hed,hing,her, *TO SEW TOGETHER, USE OF A NEEDLE*
stiulize, style(lize)
stive, stiff
sto, stow /store
stoakul, stoic(al)
stob, stop
stobur, stop(pper)

stocado, staccato /stoccado
stocato, staccato /stoccado
stoccado, *TO STAB/THRUST WITH A WEAPON (ALSO SPELLED STOCCATA) (or see staccato)*
stoccato, staccato/stoccado
stock,*,ked,king,ker,ky, *TO COLLECT/AMASS/ ACCUMULATE SOMETHING, HOLDING INTEREST IN A COMPANY (or see stalk/ stoke/ stocking)*
stocking,*, *MATERIAL FOR COVERING LEGS/FEET*
stodgeness, stodgy(giness)
stodgy,gily,giness,gier,giest, *DULL/NOT INTERESTING, HEAVY/THICK (or see stogy)*
stodgyest, stodgy(giest)
stoec, stoic
stoecul, stoic(al)
stoeg, stow(age)
stoej, stow(age)
stoek, stoic
stoekul, stoic(al)
stof, stove / stuff
stofs, stove(s) /stuff(s)
stoge, stogy/ stodgy/ stooge
stogeist, stodgy(giest)
stogenis, stodgy(giness)
stogey, stogy
stogiest, stodgy(giest)
stogines, stodgy(giness)
stogy, *CIGAR, BOOT (or see stodgy)*
stogyest, stodgy(giest)
stogyness, stodgy(giness)
stoic,*,cal,cally,calness,cism, *SECT WHO BELIEVES FREEDOM FROM PASSION/GRIEF/JOY IS A VIRTUE*
stoicul, stoic(al)
stoig, stow(age)
stoij, stow(age)
stoikal, stoic(al)
stok, stock /stoke
stokada, staccato /stoccado
stokato, staccato /stoccado

stokd, stock(ed) /stoke(d)
stoke,*,ed,king,er, *TO STIR/FEED/POKE (or see stock(y) or stalk)*
stoked, stock(ed) /stoke(d)
stokee, stock(y) /stogy
stoker, stock(er) /stalk(er)
stokur, stock(er) /stalk(er)
stoky, stock(y) /stogy
stol, stall
stold, stall(ed)
stole,en, *PAST TENSE OF "STEAL", WOMAN'S FUR ACCESSORY FOR THE SHOULDERS*
stolin, stole(n)
stolk, stalk /stock
stolker, stalk(er)
stolun, stole(n)
stolwart, stalwart
stolwort, stalwart
stomach,*,hic,hically,hy, *POUCH IN THE BODY WHICH HOLDS FOOD FOR DIGESTION*
stomek, stomach
stomik, stomach
stomp,*,ped,ping,per, *USING THE FOOT FOR FORCEFUL/HEAVY STEPS*
stompur, stomp(er)
stomuk, stomach
ston, stun /stone
stonch, staunch
stone,*,ed,ning,er,ny,nier,niest,nily,niness,*ROCK UNDER HEAVY INFLUENCE OF SOMETHING*
stoney, stone(ny)
stonsh, staunch
stonshly, staunch(ly)
stooart, steward
stoobid, stupid
stooerd, steward
stooge,*, *TO BE TRICKED/FOILED, A COMEDIAN*
stool,*,lie, *SMALL SEAT WITH NO BACK/ARMS, FECES, AN INFORMER*

stoole, stool(ie)
stoop,*,ped,ping, *TO BEND OVER, TO LOWER IN STATUS/EXPECTATIONS, SMALL PORCH*
stooped, stoop(ed) /stupid
stoopedity, stupid(ity)
stooper, stupor
stoopir, stupor
stoopud, stupid
stoopufid, stupefy(fied)
stoopur, stupor
stop,*,pped,pping,page,pper, *PUT AN END TO, HALT PROGRESS OF, BLOCK*
stopud, stupid
stopur, stop(pper)
stor, store /star
storach, storage
storage,*, *KEEP/STOCKPILE THINGS/INFORMATION*
storck, stork
stord, store(d) /star(rred)
stor, store /star
store,*,ed,ring,er,eable, *PUT AWAY FOR SAFE KEEPING, RETAIL ESTABLISHMENT (or see story)*
storech, storage
storeg, storage
storij, storage
stork,*, *A BIRD*
storm,*,med,ming,my, *CLASHING/MEETING OF TWO DIFFERENT ENERGY FRONTS AND THE REPERCUSSIONS AS A RESULT*
stormee, storm(y)
stort, store(d) /star(rred)
storuch, storage
storug, storage
storuj, storage
story,ries,ried, *A TALE/EXPLANATION OF AN EVENT/ OCCURENCE, VARIOUS FLOOR LEVELS WITHIN A BUILDING/ HOME*
storyd, story(ried)
storys, story(ries)

stot, stow(ed) /stood
stoug, stow(age)
stouj, stow(age)
stout,*, *SOLID/HARDY/ROBUST/STRONG/RESISTANT*
stove,*, *AN APPLIANCE/APPARATUS FOR COOKING/ HEATING*
stovs, stove(s) /stuff(s)
stow,*,wed,wing,wage, *TO PUT SOMETHING/CARGO AWAY/PLACE*
stoweg, stow(age)
stowej, stow(age)
stowek, stoic
stowgee, stogy
stowic, stoic
stowig, stow(age)
stowij, stow(age)
stowik, stoic
stowt, stout /stow(ed)
stra, straw /stray
stradagee, strategy
stradajist, strategy(gist)
straddle,*,ed,ling,er, *SIT ATOP OF SOMETHING, BE IN BETWEEN/THE MIDDLE OF, BE ON BOTH SIDES OF SOMETHING AT THE SAME TIME*
strade, stray(ed) /straight /strait
stradegist, strategy(gist)
stradejist, strategy(gist)
stradel, straddle
straden, straight(ened)
strades, stratus
stradigest, strategy(gist)
stradil, straddle
stradin, straight(ened)
stradis, stratus
stradle, straddle
strados, stratus
straduge, strategy
stradugist, strategy(gist)
stradujist, strategy(gist)

stradul, straddle
stradun, straight(ened)
stradus, stratus
strae, stray
stragel, straggle
strageler, straggle(r)
stragely, straggle(ly)
straggle,er,ly,lier,liest, *WANDER OFF COURSE IN IRREGULAR PATTERN, DISORGANIZED/ DISHEVELED/UNTIDY*
straght, straight /strait
stragil, straggle
stragiler, straggle(r)
stragily, straggle(ly)
stragle, straggle
straglee, straggle(ly)
stragleist, straggle(st)
straglur, straggle(r)
stragul, straggle
straguly, straggle(ly)
straight,ten,tened,tening,tener, *BE LINEAR/LEVEL/ TRUE, WITHOUT DEVIATION BETWEEN POINT A AND B (or see strait)*
strain,*,ned,ning,ner, *TO STRETCH/PUSH/PULL TO MAXIMUM CAPACITY, SIFT/SIEVE OUT LARGER PARTICLES, REMOVE PARTICULATE MATTER*
strainly, strange(ly)
strainj, strange
strait,*,ten,tly,tness, *NARROW PASSAGEWAY BETWEEN TWO BODIES OF WATER, DIFFICULT/DESPERATE POSITION, CLOSE/STRICT/TIGHT (or see straight)*
strakly, straggle(ly)
stran, strain
stranch, strange
strand,*,ded,ding, *ONE ALL ALONE, BE SINGLED OUT AWAY FROM OTHERS*
straner, strain(er)
strangal, strangle

stream,*,med,ming,mer, GENTLE/FLOWING/
CONSISTENT MOVEMENT
strech, stretch
strecher, stretch(er)
strechnine, strychnine
strechur, stretch(er)
streekee, streak(y)
streem, stream
streemer, stream(er)
streengy, string(y)
street,*, A ROADWAY/PATH WIDE ENOUGH FOR ALL
TYPES OF TRAVEL
strek, streak
strekd, strict /streak(ed)
streke, streak(y)
strekin, stricken
strekly, strict(ly)
streknine, strychnine
strekt, strict /streak(ed)
strekun, stricken
streky, streak(y)
strem, stream
stremer, stream(er)
stremur, stream(er)
streneus, strenous
strenewus, strenuous
streng, string
strengee, string(y)
strengensees, stringent(ncies)
strengently, stringent(ly)
strengint, stringent
strength,*,hen,hened,hening,hener,hlessness,
STRONG ENOUGH, ENDURANCE
strenjint, stringent
strenkth, strength
strenth, strength
strenthin, strength(en)
strenues, strenous
strenuous,sity,sness, STRAINING POINT/CHALLENGE

strategy,gies,gist, HAVE A METHOD /PLAN TO
PERFORM AN ACTION/EVENT/PLAY
stratejik, strategic
stratejikly, strategic(ally)
stratel, straddle
straten, straight(en)
stratend, straight(ened)
strates, stratus
stratesfere, stratosphere
stratesphere, stratosphere
stratigek, strategic
stratigekly, strategic(ally)
stratigest, strategy(gist)
stratil, straddle
stratin, straight(en)
stratis, stratus
stratle, straddle
stratnur, straight(ener)
straton, straight(en)
stratoned, straight(ened)
stratos, stratus
stratosfere, stratosphere
stratosphere,ric, LAYER SEVEN MILES ABOVE EARTH
stratugee, strategy
stratugist, strategy(gist)
stratugy, strategy
stratul, straddle
stratun, straight(ened)
stratuned, straight(ened)
stratus, UNIFORM/WEAK LAYER OF CLOUDS
stratusfere, stratosphere
stratusphere, stratosphere
straw,*, STALK OF GRAIN, A TUBE TO SIP LIQUIDS
stray,*,yed,ying,yer, WANDER FROM THE GROUP/
CENTER
strayd, stray(ed) /straight
streak,*,ked,king,ky,kily,kiness, SMEARED AS IF
WIPED, A BLURRED IMAGE

strange,ely,er,est,eness, UNFAMILIAR/ODD/WEIRD
strangeulat, strangulate(tion)
strangel, strangle
strangir, strange(r)
strangist, strange(st)
strangle,*,ed,ling,er, TO CHOKE/HINDER/STOP/
CLOSE OFF
strangor, strange(r)
strangul, strangle
strangulashen, strangulate(tion)
strangulate,*,ed,ting,tion, TO CHOKE /HINDER/
STOP /CLOSE OFF
strangur, strange(r)
stranir, strain(er)
stranj, strange
stranjer, strange(r)
stranjest, strange(st)
stranjly, strange(ly)
stranjur, strange(r)
strankel, strangle
strankler, strangle(r)
strankul, strangle
strankulate, strangulate
stranor, strain(er)
stransh, strange
strant, strand
stranur, strain(er)
strap,*,pped,pping, NARROW/THIN STRIP OF
SOMETHING, TIE DOWN/FASTEN/SECURE WITH
strapeng, strap(pping)
stras, stray(s) /stress
strat, straight /strait /stray(ed)
stratagee, strategy
stratagist, strategy(gist)
strategek, strategic
strategekly, strategic(ally)
strategic,*,cal,cally, PERFORM ALONG A GUIDELINE/
METHODOLOGY, HAVE A PLAN

strep, SHORT FOR STREPTOCOCCAL, BACTERIA AFFECTING THE THROAT (or see strip or stripe)
streptdokokus, streptococcus
strepir, stripe(r) /strip(pper)
streptococcus,cal, BACTERIA AFFECTING THE THROAT
streptokokus, streptococcus
strepur, stripe(r) /strip(pper)
stres, stress
stresh, stretch
stress,sses,ssed,ssing,ssful,ssfully,ssless, slessness, STRETCHED NEAR TO THE LIMIT OF ACCEPTANCE, CHALLENGE TO DEAL WITH
stret, street
stretch,hes,hed,hing,her,hability,hable, REACH TO MAXIMUM, PULL AGAINST, EXTEND OUT
streu, strew
strew,*,wed,wing,strewn, SCATTER/SPREAD ABOUT
strewn, PAST TENSE OF "STREW", SCATTER /THROW
striashen, striate(tion)
striate,*,ed,ting,tion, PARALLEL STREAKS/SMEARS/ FURROWS
strichnine, strychnine
stricken, PAST TENSE OF "STRIKE", AFFLICTED WITH/ CHALLENGED, DEALT A BLOW (or see strike)
strict,tly,tness, EXTREMELY FIRM /GUARDED/ DISCIPLINED
stride,*,ed,ding,er, LARGE /LONG STEPS, A TYPE OF GAIT WHEN WALKING
strife,eless,eful, OPPOSITION /QUARREL /CONFLICT (or see strive)
strikd, strict
strike,*,king,kingly,struck, DEALT A SHARP/FORCE- FUL BLOW, TERM IN SPORTS, TO IGNITE (or see stricken)
striken, stricken
strikly, strict(ly)
striknine, strychnine
strikon, stricken
strikt, strict

strikun, stricken
strinewus, strenuous
string,*,ged,ging,ger,gy, THIN ROPE, A LONG/ THIN/TWISTED SUBSTANCE
stringensees, stringent(ncies)
stringent,tly,ncy,ncies, NARROW/THIN/BOUND/ TIGHT, STRICT/SEVERE
stringth, strength
strinjint, stringent
strinkth, strength
strinth, strength
strinues, strenuous
strip,*,pped,pping,pper, TO REMOVE EXCESS/ EXTERNAL LAYER, REMOVE CLOTHES (or see stripe)
stripd, stripe(d) /strip(pped)
stripdokokus, streptococcus
stripe,*,ped,ping,per,py,pier,piest, THIN/ NARROW/LONG UNIFORM SHAPE (or see strip)
stript, stripe(d) /strip(pped)
striptokokus, streptococcus
stripur, stripe(r) /strip(pper)
strite, stride
strive,*,ed,ving,er, TO WORK/EXERT TO ACCOMPLISH A GOAL/END RESULT (or see strife)
strivt, strive(d)
stro, straw
strobe,*, STROBOSCOPE, TYPE OF LIGHT
stroganoff, A TYPE OF COOKED DISH WITH PASTA
stroginof, stroganoff
stroke,*,ed,king,er, FORCE/BLOW TO MOVE SOME- THING, SWEEPING MOVEMENT, MEDICAL TERM
strol, stroll
stroler, stroll(er)
stroll,*,lled,lling,ller, A CASUAL GAIT IN WALKING, MOVE ABOUT WITH WHEELS
strolur, stroll(er)
strong,ger,gest,gly,gness, GREAT IN STRENGTH FORCE/MASS/POSITION/MOVEMENT

strongist, strong(est)
strongur, strong(er)
stronkist, strong(est)
stronkur, strong(er)
stroodel, strudel
stroon, strewn
strope, strobe
strow, straw
stru, strew
struck, PAST TENSE OF "STRIKE", A SHARP/FORCEFUL BLOW, TERM IN SPORTS, TO IGNITE
structure,*, ed,ring,rless,rlessness,ral,rally, PLANNED/SPECIFIC/FORM/SHAPE/ARRANGEMENT, A DWELLING
strudel, TYPE OF PASTRY
strudul, strudel
struen, strewn
strugel, struggle
struggle,*,ed,ling,er,lingly, TO RESIST/FIGHT/ CONTEND WITH
strugle, struggle
strugul, struggle
struk, struck
strukcher, structure
strukel, struggle
strukle, struggle
struksher, structure
strukture, structure
strukul, struggle
strum,*,mmed,mming,mmer, USE FINGERS TO LIGHTLY TRAVEL OVER SEVERAL STRINGS OF AN INSTRUMENT
strumer, strum(mmer)
strun, strewn
strut,*,tted,tting, A DEVICE USED TO BRACE/ SUPPORT, TO WALK WITH A PROUD GAIT
strutegek, strategic
strutejik, strategic
strutejikly, strategic(ally)

strutigekly, strategic(ally)
struz, strew(s)
stryate, striate
strychnine, POISON ORIGINATING FROM A PLANT
stryknine, strychnine
stu, stew
stualee, stool(ie)
stuardes, steward(ess)
stuart, steward
stuartes, steward(ess)
stub, *,bbed,bbing,bby, A KNOB/STUMP, OF A THEATER TICKET, RECEIVE A STRIKING BLOW
stubble, *,ed,ly, SHORT STALKS REMAINING AFTER CUTTING OFF TIP/TOPS
stubborn,nly,ness, FIRMLY UNREASONABLE
stubed, stupid /stub(bbed)
stubee, stub(bby)
stubel, stubble
stubelidy, stability
stubelity, stability
stubern, stubborn
stubid, stupid
stubil, stubble
stubiledy, stability
stubility, stability
stubirn, stubborn
stuble, stubble
stuborn, stubborn
stubud, stupid
stubul, stubble
stuburn, stubborn
stucado, staccato /stoccado
stucato, staccato /stoccado
stucco, *,oed,oing, CEMENT/PLASTER APPLIED FOR COVERING ON WALLS
stuch, stooge /stuck
stuco, stucco

stud, *,dded,dding, STALLION, A GOOD QUALITY/ BREEDING MALE, BEAM/POST/BOARD IN WALLS/ ROOF OF STRUCTURE (or see stew(ed) /stood)
stude, study
studed, study(died) /stud(dded)
studeis, studious
studens, student(s)
student, *, tship, PERSON WHO IS LEARNING/FORMING KNOWLEDGE ABOUT SOMETHING
studeo, studio
studer, stutter
studes, study(dies)
studeus, studious
studid, study(died) /stud(dded)
studint, student
studio, *, SPACE/ROOM FOR CREATING ARTWORK OF ANY MEDIUM
studious,sly,sness, DEVOTED TO GAINING KNOWLEDGE ABOUT SOMETHING
studir, stutter
studunt, student
studur, stutter
study,dies,died,ying, TO TAKE MENTAL NOTE OF, LEARN, READ UP ON, A ROOM TO READ/WRITE
stue, stew
stuel, stool
stuelee, stool(ie)
stuepiduty, stupid(ity)
stuerd, steward
stuerdes, steward(ess)
stuerdis, steward(ess)
stuf, stuff
stufee, stuff(y)
stuff, *,ffed,ffing,ffy,ffier,ffiest, CRAM/FORCE/PACK SOMETHING INTO CONTAINMENT, REFERENCE TO A BUNCH OF THINGS, TIGHTLY CONFINED
stufy, stuff(y)
stuge, stooge
stuil, stool

stuird, steward
stuirdes, steward(ess)
stuje, stooge
stukado, staccato /stoccado
stuko, stucco
stule, stool
stulie, stool(ie)
stumach, stomach
stumb, stump
stumbel, stumble
stumble, *,ed,ling,er,lingly, TO FAULTER/TRIP/ BUMBLE/FALL INTO
stumbul, stumble
stumek, stomach
stump, *,ped,ping,per,py,pier,piest, THE END OF SOMETHING WITH MAIN PORTION CUT OFF/ ELIMINATED/REMOVED, TO BE AT A LOSS
stumpee, stump(y)
stumpul, stumble
stumuk, stomach
stun, *,nned,nning,nningly, TO BE SURPRISED OR IMMOBILIZED PHYSICALLY/MENTALLY/ PSYCHOLOGICALLY OR EMOTIONALLY
stund, stun(nned) /stunt
stunk, PAST TENSE OF "STINK", TO SMELL FOUL
stunt, *,ted,ting,tedness, A SHORT /UNDEVELOPED OR QUICK ACT/MOVEMENT, A STINT (or see stun(nned))
stuol, stool
stup, stoop
stupafid, stupefy(fied)
stupafie, stupefy
stuped, stupid /stub(bbed) /stoop(ed)
stupedity, stupid(ity)
stupee, stub(bby)
stupefy,fied,fying,fiedness,fyingly,faction,factive SHOCK/OVERWHELM/MAKE STUPID
stupendous,sly,sness, GREAT/GRAND/ASTONISHING
stupendus, stupendous

stuper, stupor
stupid,dly,dness,dity,dities, BEHAVIOR GIVEN TO BE DULL/BORING
stupify, stupefy
stupindus, stupendous
stupir, stupor
stupor,rous, MENTAL LACK OF STABILITY/SENSIBILITY
stupt, stoop(ed) /stub(bbed)
stupfie, stupefy
stupy, stub(bby)
stur, stir
sturdes, stewardess /stewards
sturdy,dily,diness, OF FIRM/STABLE/STRONG STATURE/FORM
sturep, stirrup
sturgen, sturgeon
sturgeon, A FISH
sturgon, sturgeon
sturip, stirrup
sturjen, sturgeon
sturjun, sturgeon
sturling, sterling
sturn, stern
sturnem, sternum
sturnim, sternum
sturnly, stern(ly)
sturnness, stern(ess)
sturnum, sternum
sturor, stir(rrer)
sturty, sturdy
sturty, sturdy
stutter, stutter
stutestiks, statistic(s)
stutir, stutter
stutistiks, statistic(s)
stutor, stutter
stutter,*,red,ring,rer,ringly, TO STAMMER/REPEAT SECTIONS OF WORDS IN SPEAKING
stuwardes, steward(ess)
sty,ties, SWINE ENCLOSURE, EYE INFLAMMATION

style,*,ed,ling,er,eless,elessness,lish,lishly, lishness,list,listic,listical,listically,lize, lization,lizer, FORM/EXPRESSION/MANNER OF, ONE WHO MAINTAINS FORM/EXPRESSION/ MANNER OF THE ERA
styles, style(s) /stylus
stylest, style(list)
stylis, stylus
stylus,ses,li, A POINTED INSTRUMENT FOR THE HAND TO USE FOR WRITING/ ENGRAVING/DRAWING (or see style(list))
stymed, stymie(d)
stymie,*,ed,eing,stymy, A DIFFICULT SITUATION/ POSITION, BALL POSITION IN SPORTS
styn, stein
stype, stipe
styptic,cal,city, STOPS BLEEDING
styrafom, styrofoam
styrofoam, MANMADE SPONGEY MATERIAL WITH VARIOUS USES
styrufoam, styrofoam
su, sue
suad, suede /sway(ed) /swat
suade, suede /sway(ed)
suafe, suave
suafly, suave(ly)
suage, sewage
suaje, sewage
suar, sewer
suareje, sewer(age)
suaside, suicide
suasidul, suicide(dal)
suasite, suicide
suate, suede/ sway(ed)/ swat
suave,ely,eness,vity, SMOOTH/PLEASANT/ SOPHISTICATED
suavidy, suave(vity)
suavly, suave(ly)

sub, PREFIX INDICATING "BELOW/UNDER/NEAR/IN PLACE OF SECONDARY/" MOST OFTEN MODIFIES THE WORD
sub,*, SHORT FOR SUBSTITUTE, SUBMARINE, TYPE OF SANDWICH
subcity, subsidy
subconshes, subconsciouse
subconchisly, subconsciouse(ly)
subconchus, subconsciouse
subconsciouse,sly,sness, NOT CONSCIOUS/FULLY AWARE OF, UNDERLYING CONSCIOUSNESS
subconshus, subconsciouse
subcontract,*,ted,ting,tor, TO CARRY OUT ANOTHER PERSON'S CONTRACT
subdavejen, subdivision
subdevide, subdivide
subdevishen, subdivision
subdew, subdue
subdivide,*,ed,ding,dable,er, TO DIVIDE UP INTO PARTS UNDER A CATEGORY
subdivision,*, HOUSING DEVELOPMENT
subdo, subdue
subdue,*,ed,uing,uable,uer,ual, TO OVERCOME/ OVERPOWER/INFLUENCE
subduvide, subdivide
subduvigun, subdivision
subduvishen, subdivision
subee, soup(y)
suber, super /supper
suberb, suburb /superb
suberbea, suburb(ia)
suberben, suburb(an)
suberentendent, superintendent
subereur, superior
suberfishul, superficial
suberintendint, superintendent
subfert, subvert
subgegate, subjugate
subgekdif, subject(ive)

subgekt, subject
subgektive, subject(ive)
subgektivedy, subject(ivity)
subgigate, subjugate
subgugate, subjugate
subir, super /supper
subirb, suburb /superb
subirbea, suburb(ia)
subirben, suburb(an)
subirentendent, superintendent
subjagashen, subjugate(tion)
subjagate, subjugate
subjagation, subjugate(tion)
subject, *, ted,ting,tion,tive,tively,tiveness,
tivity,tivism,tivist,tivistic, *UNDER RULE/*
AUTHORITY/SCRUTINY, OPEN TO CRITERIA
subjegate, subjugate
subjekt, subject
subjektef, subject(ive)
subjektivety, subject(ivity)
subjugate, *, ed,ting,tion,tor,tive, *TO CONQUER/*
DOMINATE/ENSLAVE
subjugation, subjugate(tion)
subkonshus, subconsciouse
subkonshusly, subconsciouse(ly)
subkontrakt, subcontract
sublamashen, sublime(mation)
sublamate, sublime(mate)
subleminaly, subliminal(lly)
subleminul, subliminal
sublimashen, sublime(mation)
sublime, er,est,ed,ming,ely,eness,er,mate,tion,
mity,mities, *LOFTY/ELEVATED/SUPERIOR/*
EXALTED/HIGHER STATE OF BEING
sublimenaly, subliminal(lly)
sublimenul, subliminal
subliminal,lly, *UNDERLYING, NOT FULLY AWARE OF*
sublumashen, sublime(mation)
sublyme, sublime

submareen, submarine
submaren, submarine
submarine, *, *BULLET SHAPED/OCEAN GOING VESSEL*
WHICH CAN SUBMERGE/GO UNDER WATER
submechen, submission
submerge, *,ed,ging,ence,gible, *BE UNDER LIQUID*
submerj, submerge
submerjebul, submerge(gable)
submerse, *,ed,sing,sible,sion, *GO INTO LIQUID*
submershen, submerse(sion)
submersible, submerse(sible)
submertion, submerse(sion)
submeshen, submission
submesif, submissive
submesive, submissive
submet, submit
submetid, submit(tted)
submetion, submission
submichen, submission
submirj, submerge
submirse, submerse
submirshen, submerse(sion)
submirtion, submerse(sion)
submisefly, submissive(ly)
submisevly, submissive(ly)
submishen, submission
submisive, submissive
submisivly, submissive(ly)
submission,*,*RELINQUISH TO, AGREE TO, ABIDE BY,*
UNDER THE AUTHORITY OF
submissive,ely,eness, *CAPABLE/GIVEN TO SUBMIT/*
COMPLIANCE/SURRENDER
submisuf, submissive
submit, *,tted,tting,ttal, *TO COMPLY/SURRENDER/*
COMMIT/YIELD
submitid, submit(tted)
submition, submission
submoren, submarine
submuren, submarine

submurg, submerge
submurj, submerge
submurjebul, submerge(gable)
submurs, submerse
submurshen, submerse(sion)
submurtion, submerse(sion)
subordenation, subordinate(tion)
subordenit, subordinate
subordinashen, subordinate(tion)
subordinate, *, ed,ting,ely,eness,tion,tive,
LESSER IN RANK/ORDER/SECONDARY/DEPENDANT
subordnet, subordinate
subpenu, subpoena
subpoena, *,aed,aing, *A LAWFUL PROCESS/MANDATE*
OF CALLING SOMEONE FORTH FOR INFORMATION
subregation, subrogate(tion)
subriedy, sobriety
subriety, sobriety
subrigate, subrogate
subrigation, subrogate(tion)
subriode, sobriety
subrogashen, subrogate(tion)
subrogate,*,ed,ting,tion, *REPLACE/SUBSTITUTE*
SOMEONE/SOMETHING
subsadize, subsidy(dize)
ubsakwenty, subsequent(ly)
subsaqwenty, subsequent(ly)
subscrebshen, subscription
subscreption, subscription
subscription, subscription
subscribe,*,ed,bing,er, *TO COMMIT PAYMENT FOR*
RECEIPT OF SOMETHING, A SIGNED STATEMENT
subscribshen, subscription
subscription, *, *AGREE TO COMMIT MONEY IN EX-*
CHANGE FOR GOODS, SIGNATURE OF COMMITMENT
subsdanshul, substantial
subsdatushen, substitute(tion)
subsdutut, substitute
subsdents, substance
subsdratem, substrate(tum)

subsdutoot, substitute
subsdutushin, substitute(tion)
subsede, subsidy
subsedens, subsidy(dence)
subsediary, subsidiary
subsedize, subsidy(dize)
subsedy, subsidy
subsekwint, subsequent
subsekwintly, subsequent(ly)
subsequent,nce,tly,tness, *AFTER/FOLLOWING IN A CERTAIN SEQUENCE/ORDER*
subseqwint, subsequent
subserveint, subservient
subservient, subservient
subserveintly, subservient(ly)
subserveints, subservient(nce)
subservient,nce,ncy,tly, *FACILITATES PROMOTION OF/ACT TO CREATE, TO SERVE*
subsestense, subsistence
subsestense, subsistence
subside,*,ed,ding,ence, *TO SETTLE/SINK/FALL TO A LOWER LEVEL*
subsidens, subsidy(dence)
subside, subsidy
subsidiary,ries,rily,diariness, *TO AID/ASSIST/HELP WITH A CONTRIBUTION*
subsidy,dies,dize,dization,dizer, *ORGANIZATION/ GOVERNMENT WHO HELPS OTHERS BY PROVIDING MONEY/SERVICES TOWARD OVERALL NEEDS OF SPECIFIC PEOPLE*
subsikwent, subsequent
subsikwently, subsequent(ly)
subsirveint, subservient
subsirveins, subservient(nce)
subsistence,nt, *THE BASIC FOUNDATION WHICH SUPPORTS LIFE*
subsite, subside
subsitearee, subsidiary
subsitinse, subside(nce)
subsity, subsidy

subskrebshin, subscription
subskreption, subscription
subskrib, subscribe
subskripshen, subscription
subskription, subscription
substance,*, *MATTER, FIRMNESS, REAL*
substancheate, substantiate
substanchel, substantial
substanchely, substantial(lly)
substanchiative, substantiate(tive)
substanchil, substantial
substanchuly, substantial(lly)
substansheate, substantiate
substansheative, substantiate(tive)
substanshul, substantial
substantial,lity,lly,lness, *OF ENOUGH, MORE THAN A LITTLE, REWARDING AMOUNT*
substantiate,*,ed,ting,tion,tive, *OF SUBSTANCE, FACTUAL/REAL*
substashial, substantial
substatushen, substitute(tion)
substatute, substitute
substatution, substitute(tion)
substechuent, substituent
substense, substance
substetuent, substituent
substetute, substitute
substetution, substitute(tion)
substichuent, substituent
substinse, substance
substishuent, substituent
substitoot, substitute
substituent,*, *REPLACE ONE PERSON FOR ANOTHER*
substitushen, substitute(tion)
substitute,*,ed,ting,tion,table,tional,tionally, tionary,tive,tively, *REPLACE ONE FOR ANOTHER*
substrade, substrate
substradem, substrate(tum)
substrate,*,tum,tums, *LAYER BELOW*

subsstutushen, substitute(tion)
subsukwently, subsequent(ly)
subsuquently, subsequent(ly)
subsurveanse, subservient(nce)
subsurveint, subservient
subsurviently, subservient(ly)
subtavigen, subdivision
subtle,eness,ety,ily, *NOT OBVIOUS, SLIGHT HINT OF, SUGGESTIVE WITHOUT SPECIFICS*
subtract,*,ted,ting,ter,tive, *TAKE AWAY FROM THE WHOLE/ORIGINAL PART*
subtrakshin, subtract(ion)
subtrakshun, subtract(ion)
subtrakt, subtract
subtraktion, subtract(ion)
subur, super /supper
suburb,*,bia,ban,banite, *DISTRICT JUST OUTSIDE OF MAJOR POPULATED AREA*
suburbea, suburb(ia)
suburben, suburb(an)
suburintendent, superintendent
subversef, subversive
subvershen, subversion
subversion,ary, *REMOVE THE BASIS/FOUNDATION OF ANYTHING IN ORDER TO DESTROY IT*
subversive,rsively,rsiveness, *REMOVE THE BASIS/ FOUNDATION OF ANYTHING TO DESTROY IT*
subvert,*,ted,ting,ter, *REMOVE BASIS/FOUNDATION OF ANYTHING IN ORDER TO DESTROY IT*
subvertion, subversion
subvirsef, subversive
subvirshen, subversion
subvirsion, subversion
subvirt, subvert
subvursef, subversive
subvurshen, subversion
subvursive, subversive
subvurt, subvert
subvurtion, subversion

sucrete, secrete
sucretion, secrete(tion)
sucrose, SUGAR OBTAINED FROM PLANTS
succeed, succeed
sucses, success
sucesful, success(ful)
sucesif, successive
sucesiflee, successive(ly)
suction, TO FORCEFULLY DRAW SOMETHING FROM ITS SOURCE, CREATE A VACUUM/ADHERENCE
suculent, succulent
suculint, succulent
sucumb, succumb
sucure, secure
sud, sue(d) /suds
sudan, sedan
sudanem, pseudonym
sudanim, pseudonym
sudar, suitor
sudashen, sedate(tion)
sudasion, sedate(tion)
sudate, sedate
sudation, sedate(tion)
sudden,nly,nness, IMMEDIATELY, NO TIME LAPSE
sude, sue(d) /soot(y)
suden, sudden
sudenim, pseudonym
sudenly, sudden(ly)
suder, suitor
sudews, seduce
sudin, sudden
sudinem, pseudonym
sudinly, sudden(ly)
sudir, suitor
sudo, pseudo
sudon, sudden
sudonem, pseudonym
sudonim, pseudonym
sudonly, sudden(ly)

sudoose, seduce
sudor, suitor
suds,SY, BUBBLES/FOAMY/LATHER/FROTH
suduchen, seduce(ction)
suductive, seduce(ctive)
suduktion, seduce(ction)
suduktive, seduce(ctive)
sudun, sudden
sudunly, sudden(ly)
suduse, seduce
sudy, soot(y)
sue,*,ed,uing,er, TO LEGALLY ATTEMPT TO FORCE SOMEONE TO PAY MONEY FOR A WRONGDOING
suecher, suture
suede, LEATHER (or see sway(ed))
suege, sewage
sueje, sewage
suenome, tsunami
suer, sewer
suereje, sewer(age)
sueside, suicide
suesidul, suicide(dal)
suesite, suicide
suet, PART OF ANIMALS WHICH YIELDS TALLOW (or see suit or sweet)
sufaneer, souvenir
sufaree, safari
sufary, safari
sufecashen, suffocate(tion)
sufecate, suffocate
sufecation, suffocate(tion)
sufeer, severe
sufeerly, severe(ly)
sufekashen, suffocate(tion)
sufekate, suffocate
sufeks, suffix
sufeneer, souvenir
sufer, suffer
suferd, suffer(ed)

subwa, subway
subway,*, UNDERGROUND ELECTRIC TRAIN, A SANDWICH
succeed,*,ded,ding, IMPROVE/GAIN/OVERCOME
succeses, success(es)
succesful, success(ful)
succesion, succession
success,es,ssful,ssfully,ssfulness, IMPROVING/GAINING/OVERCOMING/ADVANCING
succession,nal,nally, SEQUENCE/SERIES/ONE AFTER THE OTHER OF SOMETHING/SOMEONE
successive,ely,eness, FOLLOWING IN ORDER WITHOUT INTERRUPTION
succinct,tly,tness, BRIEF/SHORT/SUMMARY
succor,rer, OFFER RELIEF/SUPPORT/AID IN TIMES OF NEED (or see suck(er))
succsed, succeed
succulent,*,tly,nce,ncy, JUICY/DELICIOUS TO THE PHYSICAL SENSES
succumb,*,bed, SURRENDER/RETIRE TO, FALL FOR, YIELD/GIVE WAY TO
sucdhen, suction
sucede, secede
sucenct, succinct
sucer, succor /suck(er)
sucession, succession
such, USED TO MAKE A COMPARISON WITH SOMETHING IMPLIED BY CONTEXT
sucher, suture /suck(er)
suchur, suture /suck(er)
sucinct, succinct
suck,*,ked,king,ker, FORCEFULLY PULL/DRAW SOMETHING AWAY FROM ITS SOURCE, A FISH, LOLLIPOP (or see succor)
suckle,*,ed,ling, THE ACT OF BREAST FEEDING
suckshun, suction
sucor, succor /suck(er)
sucour, succor /suck(er)
sucreshen, secrete(tion)

sufere, severe
suferly, severe(ly)
sufestikashen, sophisticate(tion)
sufestikated, sophisticate(d)
sufestikation, sophisticate(tion)
sufex, suffix
suffer,*,red,ring,rable,rableness,rably,rer, ringly,rance, *REACTION TO PAIN/ INFLICTION*
suffice,ed,cing, *SUFFICIENT, ADEQUATE, SATISFIED*
sufichent, sufficient
sufficient,tly,ncy, *ENOUGH, ADEQUATE, SATISFIED*
suffishent, sufficient
suffix,xes,xed,xal,xion,xation, *AN END ATTACHED TO SOMETHING/WORD*
suffocate,*,ed,ting,tion,tive,tingly, *SMOTHER, CHOKE OFF, REMOVE OXYGEN*
suffrage,ette,gist, *VOTING AND RIGHTS TO VOTE*
suficashen, suffocate(tion)
suficate, suffocate
sufication, suffocate(tion)
sufice, suffice
suficent, sufficient
sufichent, sufficient
suficient, sufficient
suficiently, sufficient(ly)
sufikashen, suffocate(tion)
sufikate, suffocate
sufikation, suffocate(tion)
sufiks, suffix
sufiksis, suffix(es)
sufir, suffer
sufird, suffer(ed)
sufirly, severe(ly)
sufise, suffice
sufishent, sufficient
sufishintly, sufficient(ly)
sufishunt, sufficient
sufistakashen, sophisticate(tion)
sufistakation, sophisticate(tion)

sufix, suffix
sufixes, suffix(es)
sufla, souffle'
suflay, souffle'
sufocashen, suffocate(tion)
sufocate, suffocate
sufocation, suffocate(tion)
sufor, suffer
suford, suffer(ed)
sufrage, suffrage
sufragist, suffrage(gist)
sufraje, suffrage
sufranse, suffer(ance)
sufrech, suffrage
sufreje, suffrage
sufrige, suffrage
sufrigest, suffrage(gist)
sufrije, suffrage
sufrinse, suffer(ance)
sufrugist, suffrage(gist)
sufucashen, suffocate(tion)
sufukate, suffocate
sufukation, suffocate(tion)
sufuner, souvenir
sufur, suffer
sufurd, suffer(ed)
sugar,rless,red,ry,rlike, *SUCROSE, SUBSTANCE OBTAINED FROM PLANTS*
sugchestshen, suggest(ion)
suggesdiv, suggest(ive)
suger, sugar
sugest, suggest
suggest,*,ted,ting,ter,tion,tive,tible,tibility, tively,tiveness, *A FACT/THEORY TO CONSIDER*
suggestshen, suggest(ion)
sugjesdiv, suggest(ive)
sugjest, suggest
sugjestion, suggest(ion)
sugjestive, suggest(ive)

sugnefakent, significant
sugnifukent, significant
suicide,*,ed,ding,dal,dally, *TAKE ONE'S OWN LIFE*
suicidul, suicide(dal)
suige, sewage
suir, sewer
suireje, sewer(age)
suiside, suicide
suisidul, suicide(dal)
suisite, suicide
suit,*,ted,ting,table,tability,tableness,tably, *PANTS/JACKET SET, IN A CARD GAME, PROPER/ AGREEABLE/FITTING* (or see suite /sweet)
suite,*, *TYPE OF ROOM (TOO MANY DEFINITIONS, PLEASE CONSULT STANDARD DICTIONARY)* (or see suit)
suitor,*, *ONE WHO SUES, MAN COURTING A WOMAN*
sujest, suggest
suk, suck
sukal, suckle
sukchen, suction
sukchest, suggest
sukchun, suction
sukel, suckle
suker, succor /suck(er)
sukewlent, succulent
sukewlunt, succulent
sukewr, secure
sukewrity, secure(rity)
sukgeshin, suggest(ion)
sukgest, suggest
sukgestion, suggest(ion)
sukgestshen, suggest(ion)
sukiatrist, psychiatry(rist)
sukiatry, psychiatry
sukil, suckle
sukir, succor /suck(er)
sukiutrest, psychiatry(rist)
sukjesdev, suggest(ive)

sukjest, suggest
sukjestion, suggest(ion)
sukjestshen, suggest(ion)
sukle, suckle
suklushen, seclusion
suklusion, seclusion
sukol, suckle
sukor, succor /suck(er)
sukour, succor/ secure/ suck(er)
sukqulent, succulent
sukreshen, secrete(tion)
sukresion, secrete(tion)
sukrete, secrete
sukrose, sucrose
suksed, succeed
sukses, success
suksesful, success(ful)
sukseshen, succession
suksesif, successive
suksesiflee, successive(ly)
sukshen, suction
sukshun, suction
sukul, suckle
sukulent, succulent
sukum, succumb
sukur, suck(er)/ succor/ secure
sukurity, secure(rity)
sukwenshul, sequence(ntial)
sukwential, sequence(ntial)
sukwoya, sequoia
sulal, salal
sulami, salami
sulareum, solarium
suldree, sultry
sulebrity, celebrity
sulective, select(ive)
suledify, solid(ify)
suleks, select(s)
sulekshen, select(ion)

sulekt, select
sulektion, select(ion)
sulektive, select(ive)
sulektof, select(ive)
suleluquy, soliloquy
sulen, sullen
sulenity, saline(nity)
sulenium, selenium
sulerium, solarium
sulesit, solicit
sulesitation, solicit(ation)
sulesiter, solicit(er)
sulesteul, celestial
sulewshen, solution
sulewtion, solution
sulfade, sulfate
sulfate,*,ed,ting, *ALSO SULPHATE, A SULFURIC ACID SALT*
sulfats, sulfate(s)
sulfer, sulfur
sulferik, sulfur(ic)
sulfide,*, *A SULFUR CHEMICAL COMPOUND*
sulfir, sulfur
sulfirek, sulfur(ic)
sulfite, sulfide
sulfur,ric,rize,rous,rously,rousness, *ALSO SULPHUR, NON-METALLIC ELEMENT*
sulfurik, sulfur(ic)
sulicit, solicit
sulicitation, solicit(ation)
suliciter, solicit(er)
sulidefy, solid(ify)
sulilakwee, soliloquy
sulin, sullen
sulinidy, saline(nity)
sulisetation, solicit(ation)
sulisit, solicit
sulisiter, solicit(er)
sulitefy, solid(ify)

sulivu, saliva
sulk,*,ked,king,ker,ky,kies,kier,kiest,kily,kiness, *UPSET AT NOT GETTING ENOUGH ATTENTION, REACTION TO BEING OFFENDED*
sulkey, sulk(y)
sullen,nly,nness, *ALONE/GLOOMY/DISMAL*
sulomee, salami
sulon, salon
suloon, saloon
suloot, salute
sulowl, salal
sulphade, sulfate
sulphate, sulfate
sulpher, sulfur
sulpherik, sulfur(ic)
sulphide, sulfide
sulphir, sulfur
sulphurek, sulfur(ic)
sultan,*,nic, *DOMESTICATED FOWL, DESPOT/TYRANT*
sultin, sultan
sultree, sultry
sultry,rily,riness, *SWEATY/HEAVY/HOT, OVER-POWERING COMBINATION*
sultun, sultan
sulun, sullen /saloon
sulushen, solution
sulute, salute
sulution, solution
sum,*,mmed,mming,mmation,mmational, *TOTAL OF, ALTOGETHER, CONCISE/SIMPLE*
sumachin, sum(mmation)
suman, summon
sumantics, semantics
sumarely, summary(rily)
sumarize, summary(rize)
sumaruly, summary(rily)
sumary, summary /summer(y)
sumashen, sum(mmation)
sumation, sum(mmation)

sumb, sump
sumbreo, sombrero
sumbrero, sombrero
sumchewus, sumptuous
sumchuis, sumptuous
sumd, sum(mmed)
sumding, something
sumedul, summit(ttal)
sumen, summon
sumener, summon(er)
sument, cement
sumer, summer
sumerily, summary(rily)
sumerise, summary(rize)
sumersolt, somersault
sumeruly, summary(rily)
sumery, summary /summer(y)
sumesder, semester
sumester, semester
sumet, summit
sumetal, summit(ttal)
sumetrek, symmetry(ric)
sumetric, symmetry(ric)
sumfing, something
sumidul, summit(ttal)
sumin, summon
sumint, cement
sumir, summer
sumiry, summary /summer(y)
sumit, summit /submit
sumitul, summit(ttal)
summary,ries,rized,rizing,rizer,rist,rily,riness, *CONCISE/SIMPLIFIED SHORT VERSION*
summen, summon
summer,*,red,ring,rly,ry, *SEASON FROM JUNE THROUGH SEPTEMBER*
summin, summon
summit,*,ttal, *THE HIGHEST PART/PEAK/POINT/ RANK OF (or see submit)*

summon,*,ned,ning,ner, *TO PETITION/CALL/SEND/ ORDER FOR ATTENDANCE*
sumon, summon
sumoner, summon(er)
sump, *DEPRESSION WHERE POOL OF LIQUID CAN COLLECT*
sumpchewus, sumptuous
sumpshues, sumptuous
sumptues, sumptuous
sumptuous,sly,sness, *IMPRESSIVE/LUXURIOUS/ MAGNIFICENT*
sumshuis, sumptuous
sumt, sum(mmed)
sumthing, something
sumtime, sometime
sumur, summer
sumuree, summary /summer(y)
sumurees, summary(ries)
sumurize, summary(rize)
sumursolt, somersault
sumury, summary /summer(y)
sumut, summit
sumware, somewhere
sumwat, somewhat
sumwer, somewhere
sumwhat, somewhat
sumwhere, somewhere
sumwot, somewhat
sumwut, somewhat
sun,*,nned,nning,nny, *THE SOLAR PLANET WHICH ALL PLANETS IN OUR SOLAR SYSTEM REVOLVE AROUND (or see "son /sunn /soon")*
sunada, sonata
suname, tsunami
sunapsis, synapsis
sunaptek, synaptic
sunaptic, synaptic
sunareo, scenario
sunatu, sonata

sunda, Sunday
Sunday,*, *MONTH OF THE WEEK*
sundiket, syndicate
sundree, sundry
sundres, sundry(ries)
sundry,ries, *MANY SMALL THINGS*
sundukit, syndicate
sune, sun(nny) /son(y)
sunelity, senile(lity)
sunereo, scenario
sunerist, scenario(ist)
sunility, senile(lity)
sunn, *A SHRUB (or see sun or son)*
sunoda, sonata
sunografee, scenography
sunome, tsunami
sunonimus, synonym(ous)
sunopsis, synopsis
sunota, sonata
sunseer, sincere
sunseerly, sincere(ly)
suntree, sundry
suny, sun(nny) /son(y)
suoge, sewage
suor, sewer
suosidel, suicide(dal)
suove, suave
sup, soup
sup,*,pped,pping, *SHORT FOR HAVING SUPPER/ DINNER, TO SIP (or see sub)*
supal, supple
suparlatif, superlative
suparlutif, superlative
suparstishus, superstitious
supasetory, suppository
supasition, supposition
supasitory, suppository
supausatory, suppository
supazishen, supposition

supcity, subsidy
supconchesly, subconsciousce(ly)
supconshus, subconsciousce
supcontrakt, subcontract
supdavide, subdivide
supdavijin, subdivision
supdevide, subdivide
supdew, subdue
supdevid, subdivide
supdo, subdue
supdu, subdue
supduvide, subdivide
supe, soup(y)
supel, supple
supenu, subpoena
super, PREFIX INDICATING "OVER/ABOVE/TO A VERY HIGH DEGREE," MOST OFTEN MODIFIES THE WORD
super,rable,rably,rableness, GREAT/EXCESSIVE/ HIGH UP/STRONG (or see supper)
superb,bly,bness, GRAND/SPLENDID (or see suburb)
superbea, suburb(ia)
superentendent, superintendent
supereoredy, superior(ity)
supereority, superior(ity)
supereur, superior
superfichul, superficial
superficial,lity,lities,lly,lness, UNREAL/ILLUSION/ FAUX/FALSE LAYER
superfishul, superficial
superflewus, superfluous
superflues, superfluous
superfluous,sly,sness, EXCESS
superintendent,*, ONE WHO OVERSEES/MANAGES
superior,*,rity,rly, RANK/AUTHORITY OVER ANOTHER, ELEVATED, BETTER QUALITY/GRADE
superioridy, superior(ity)
superlatif, superlative

superlative,*,ely,eness, SURPASSES ALL DEGREES/ RANK BY COMPARISON
superlutif, superlative
supersdishen, superstition
supersteshus, superstitious
superstition,*,ous,ously,ousness, ALLOW SOME- THING SEEMINGLY IRRATIONAL TO FORETELL FUTURE EVENTS
superstitious,sly,sness, ALLOW SOMETHING SEEM- INGLY IRRATIONAL TO FORETELL FUTURE EVENTS
supervise,*,ed,sing,sor,sory,sion, PROVIDE OVERSIGHT/DIRECTION TO OTHERS
supervishen, supervise(sion)
supervizury, supervise(sory)
supesition, supposition
supgekt, subject
supgektif, subject(ive)
supil, supple
supina, subpoena
supir, super /supper
supirb, suburb / superb
supirblee, superb(ly)
supirentendent, superintendent
supireority, superior(ity)
supireur, superior
supirfichul, superficial
supirfishul, superficial
supirflewus, superfluous
supirfluis, superfluous
supirlatif, superlative
supirlative, superlative
supirlutif, superlative
supirsdishen, superstition
supirsteshus, superstitious
supirstition, superstition
supirveshin, supervise(sion)
supirvise, supervise
supirvisery, supervise(ry)
supirvishen, supervise(sion)

supirvision, supervise(sion)
supizeshen, supposition
supjekt, subject
supjektid, subject(ed)
supjektif, subject(ive)
supkonchisly, subconsciousce(ly)
supkonchus, subconsciousce
supkonsheslly, subconsciousce(ly)
supkonshus, subconsciousce
supkontrakt, subcontract
suplamashen, sublime(mation)
suplament, supplement
suplamentul, supplement(al)
suplamint, supplement
suplant, supplant
suple, supple
suplement, supplement
suplementul, supplement(al)
suplemint, supplement
supleminul, subliminal
supli, supply
suplier, supply(lier)
suplime, sublime
supliment, supplement
suplimentul, supplement(al)
suplimenul, subliminal
suplument, supplement
suplumentul, supplement(al)
suply, supply
suplyer, supply(lier)
supmareen, submarine
supmaren, submarine
supmerg, submerge
supmerjebul, submerge(gable)
supmerse, submerse
supmersible, submerse(sible)
supmet, submit
supmeted, submit(tted)
supmichen, submission

supmirj, submerge
supmit, submit
supmited, submit(tted)
supmureen, submarine
supmurg, submerge
supmurjebul, submerge(gable)
supmurs, submerse
supmursabul, submerse(sible)
supmurshen, submerse(sion)
supol, supple
supor, super /supper
supordenate, subordinate
supordinet, subordinate
supordunet, subordinate
suport, support
suportef, support(ive)
suportive, support(ive)
suporvise, supervise
supose, suppose
suposetory, suppository
suposidly, suppose(dly)
suposition, supposition
supository, suppository
suposubly, suppose(dly)
supozatory, suppository
supozetory, suppository
supoze, suppose
supozeshin, supposition
supozetory, suppository
supozitory, suppository
supozubly, suppose(dly)
supper, *DINNER, MEAL IN EVENING* (or see super)
supplament, supplement
supplamentul, supplement(al)
supplant,*,ting,tation,ter, *FORCEFUL/UNDER-*
  HANDED REMOVAL OF SOMETHING/ SOMEONE
supple,ely,ly,eness, *FLEXIBLE/GRACEFULLY*
  CONFORMING (or see supply)
supplement,*,ted,ting,tal,tary,tation,tary, *IN*
  ADDITION TO THE BASIC

supplimentul, supplement(al)
supplment, supplement
supplmentul, supplement(al)
supply,lies,lied,lying,lier, *TO SUPPORT/PROVIDE*
  GOODS/SERVICES
support,*,ted,ting,tive,ter,table,tableness,
  tably, *ENABLE/EMPOWER/SUSTAIN/ASSIST/*
  STRUCTURE SOMETHING/SOMEONE
suppose,*,ed,sing,edly,sable,sably, *PROPOSE/*
  SUGGEST/IMPLY THE WAY SOMETHING IS TO BE
supposition,*,nal,nally, *HYPOTHESIS/ ASSUMPTION*
suppository,ries, *PREPARATION FOR INSERTION INTO*
  ORIFICE ON THE LOWER HALF OF THE BODY
suppreshun, suppress(ion)
suppresion, suppress(ion)
suppress,sses,ssed,ssing,ssible,ssor,ssion,ssive,
  PREVENT/RESTRAIN
suprechen, suppress(ion)
supreem, supreme
supreem, supreme
supremacy,macist, *ONE WHO BELIEVES THEY ARE*
  SUPERIOR OVER OTHERS
supremasist, supremacy(cist)
supreme,ely,eness, *HIGHEST OF QUALITY/DEGREE*
supremusee, supremacy
supremusist, supremacy(cist)
supremusy, supremacy
supreno, soprano
supres, suppress
supreshen, suppress(ion)
supress, suppress
supression, suppress(ion)
supretion, suppress(ion)
suprino, soprano
suprogate, subrogate
suprogate, subrogate
suprveshin, supervise(sion)
suprvishen, supervise(sion)
supsakwently, subsequent(ly)
supsdents, substance
supsditushen, substitute(tion)

supsedy, subsidy
supsekwint, subsequent
supsekwintly, subsequent(ly)
supseqwint, subsequent
supserveint, subservient
supsestinse, subsistence
supside, subside
supsideary, subsidiary
supsidinse, subside(nce)
supsikwent, subsequent
supsikwently, subsequent(ly)
supsirveint, subservient
supsistense, subsistence
supsite, subside
supskrepshen, subscription
supskrib, subscribe
supskription, subscription
supstanchily, substantial(lly)
supstansheate, substantiate
supstanshul, substantial
supstanshulee, substantial(lly)
supstantiate, substantiate
supstatoot, substitute
supstatushen, substitute(tion)
supstense, substance
supstetoot, substitute
supstichuent, substituent
supstinse, substance
supstishuent, substituent
supstitoot, substitute
supstitushen, substitute(tion)
supstitute, substitute
supstradem, substrate(tum)
supstrate, substrate
supstratem, substrate(tum)
supsurveint, subservient
suptrakchin, subtract(ion)
suptrakshun, subtract(ion)
suptrakt, subtract

supul, supple
supur, super /supper
supurb, suburb /superb
supurblee superb(ly)
supurfichul, superficial
supurfishul, superficial
superintendent, superintendent
superlative, superlative
supurlutif, superlative
supurstishus, superstitious
supurstition, superstition
supurveshin, supervise(sion)
supurvise, supervise
supurvision, supervise(sion)
supusition, supposition
supuzishen, supposition
supvert, subvert
supvurt, subvert
supwa, subway
supy, soup(y)
suquential, sequence(ntial)
suquir, secure

sur, PREFIX INDICATING "OVER/ABOVE/TO A VERY HIGH DEGREE," MOST OFTEN MODIFIES THE WORD (or see sir or sure)
suraget, surrogate
suragit, surrogate
suramik, ceramic
suran, saran
surape, serape
suratid, serrate(d)
surbent, serpent
surch, search

surcharge,*,ed,ging, AN EXCESS CHARGE/TAX OVER AND ABOVE THE NORM
surcharj, surcharge
surchuble, search(able)
surcle, circle
surcumcise, circumcise

surcumfirense, circumference
surcut, circuit

sure,ely,eness, MOST CERTAINLY, OF COURSE, INEVITABLE, CONFIDENTLY (or see surly)
sureal, surreal
surealism, surrealism
suree, surrey
sureilisum, surrealism
surel, sorrel /surreal
surelism, surrealism
surender, surrender
surene, serene
surenge, syringe
surenidy, serene(nity)
surenity, serene(nity)
surenje, syringe
sureolesum, surrealism

surety,ties, ONE WHO IS BOUND/LIABLE/RESPONSIBLE
sureulist, surrealism(st)
sureulizum, surrealism

surf,*,fed,fing,fable,fer,fy,fier,fiest, WHERE THE OCEANS WAVES BREAK, CRUISE THE INTERNET/TV (or see serf or serve)

surface,*,ed,cing,eless,er, THE TOP/EXTERNAL/OUTSIDE PORTION OF (or see service)
surfase, surface
surfd, surf(ed)
surfeje, serf(age)
surfent, servant
surfes, surface
surfibul, surf(able)
surfis, surface /service
surft, serve(d) /surf(ed)
surfunt, servant
surfur, surf(er)
surgakle, surgical
surgaree, surgery
surgarge, surcharge
surgd, surge(d)

surge,*,ed,ging, ENERGETIC SWELLING/BURST/FLUCTUATION OF SOMETHING (or see search(ed))
surgen, surgeon
surgeon,*,ncy,ncies, NAME FOR DOCTOR WHO PERFORMS SURGICAL PROCEDURES
surgery,ries, PERFORM A MEDICAL OPERATION
surgical,lly, ASSOCIATED WITH MEDICAL OPERATIONS
surgikul, surgical
surgin, surgeon
surgis, surge(s)
surgon, surgeon
surgree, surgery
surgukle, surgical
suriasis, psoriasis
suringe, syringe
surinje, syringe
surjakle, surgical
surjaree, surgery
surje, surge
surjen, surgeon
surjikul, surgical
surjon, surgeon
surjree, surgery
surjukle, surgical
surkawfigus, sarcophagus
surkewlate, circulate
surkofegus, sarcophagus
surkulir, circular
surkumfurens, circumference
surkumstans, circumstance
surkus, circus
surlee, surly
surly, surly
surloen, sirloin
surloin, sirloin
surly,lily,liness, ROUGH/RUDE (or see sure(ly))
surmin, sermon
surmise,*,ed,sing, ASSUME/GUESS
surmize, surmise
surmon, sermon

surogate, surrogate
surong, sarong
surope, serape
suroredy, sorority
surority, sorority
suround, surround
surownd, surround
surpass,sses,ssed,ssing,ssable,ssingly, *TO GO BEYOND EXPECTATIONS*
surpent, serpent
surpentene, serpentine
surpint, serpent
surpintene, serpentine
surplus,sage, *MORE THAN NEEDED /NECESSARY, OVERABUNDANCE OF*
surprise,*,ed,sing,sal,ser,singly, *UNEXPECTEDLY SHOWING UP /APPEARING /OCCURING*
surprize, surprise
surrated, serrate(d)
surreal,lism,list,listic,listically, *NOT OF THIS PLANE/ WORLD, UNREAL, TIME PERIOD IN ART*
surrealism,st,stic,stically, *NOT OF THIS PLANE/ WORLD, UNREAL, TIME PERIOD IN ART*
surrender,*,red,ring, *GIVE UP, RELINQUISH POWER*
surrey, *SMALL HORSE DRAWN CARRIAGE*
surrogate,*,ed,ting, *TO SUBSTITUTE SOMEONE AND THEIR DUTIES*
surround,*,ded,ding, *ENCOMPASS/ENCIRCLE/ ENCLOSE AROUND*
surry, surrey
surten, certain
surthener, south(erner)
surtifecate, certificate
surtify, certify
surva, survey
survalinse, surveillance
survas, survey(s) /service
survatood, servitude
survatude, servitude

survaur, survey(or)
survayer, survey(or)
survd, serve(d)
surveilance, surveillance
surveillance,nt, *TO OBSERVE/WATCH OVER SOMEONE/SOMETHING, SPYING*
survent, servant
surveor, survey(or)
surves, service
survesable, service(cable)
survesuble, service(cable)
survey,*,yed,ying,yor, *TO CAPTURE FACTS/VIEW/ DOCUMENT AN AREA/SITUATION*
survife, surviv
surviks, cervix
survint, servant
survis, service
survisable, service(cable)
survive,*,ed,ving,val,vor, *TO REMAIN ALIVE AFTER AN ORDEAL/TRAGIC EVENT*
survivul, survive(val)
survont, servant
survunt, servant
survus, service
sury, surrey
susceptible,eness,ly,bility, *PRONE/LIKELY/GIVEN TO BE AFFECTED*
susceptive,eness,vity, *ABLE/LIKELY TO BE AFFECTED TO BE AFFECTED*
susdan, sustain
susdanuble, sustain(able)
susdeninse, sustenance
susdinense, sustenance
susede, secede
susenked, succinct
susenktly, succint(ly)
suseptible, susceptible
suseptif, suceptive
suseptive, suceptive
suseptuble, susceptible

suseptuf, suceptive
suseshen, secession
susesion, secession
susete, secede
sush, such
susiadul, society(tal)
susiete, society
susietul, society(tal)
susiety, society
susinkt, succinct
susinktly, succint(ly)
susiudil, society(tal)
susiuty, society
suspect,*,ted,ting, *LIKELY TO BE INVOLVED IN AN EVENT*
suspekt, suspect
suspend,*,ded,ding, *TEMPORARILY BAR/RELIEVE FROM DUTIES/REMOVE, HANG IN THE AIR*
suspender,*,*, *SHOULDER HOLDERS FOR PANTS, ONE WHO SUSPENDS*
suspense,eful,sive,sively,siveness, *TO WAIT WITH UNCERTAINTY*
suspensful, suspense(ful)
suspenshen, suspension
suspension, *HANGING/FLOATING IN LIQUID*
suspent, suspend
suspention, suspension
suspeshen, suspicion
suspeshesly, suspicious(ly)
suspeshus, suspicious
suspicion,*, *SUSPECT TO/OF, TO SUPPOSE WITHOUT CLEAR EVIDENCE*
suspicious,sly,sness, *SUSPECT TO/OF, TO SUPPOSE WITHOUTH CLEAR EVIDENCE*
suspind, suspend
suspinder, suspender
suspinse, suspense
suspinsful, suspense(ful)
suspinshen, suspension

suspintion, suspension
suspishesly, suspicious(ly)
suspishes, suspicious
suspishun, suspicion
suspitious, suspicious
sustain,*,ned,ning,nable,ner,nment, ENDURE/
    CONFIRM
sustane, sustain
sustanense, sustenance
sustanible, sustain(able)
sustanuble, sustain(able)
sustenance, BASIC PROVISIONS FOR SURVIVAL
susteninse, sustenance
sustunense, sustenance
sut, soot /suit
sutal, subtle
sutaltee, subtle(ty)
sutanic, satanic
sutanikul, satanic(al)
sutar, suitor
sutcher, suture
sutchur, suture
sutel, subtle
suteltee, subtle(ty)
suten, sudden
sutenly, sudden(ly)
suter, suitor
suterical, satire(rical)
suth, soothe
sutherly, south(erly)
suthirnur, south(erner)
suthurn, south(ern)
sutil, subtle
sutiltee, subtle(ty)
sutin, sudden
sutinly, sudden(ly)
sutir, suitor
sutle, subtle
sutly, subtle(ly)

suto, pseudo
sutol, subtle
sutoltee, subtle(ty)
suton, sudden
sutonem, pseudonym
sutonim, pseudonym
sutor, suitor
suts, suds
sutultee, subtle(ty)
sutun, sudden
sutunly, sudden(ly)
suture,*,ed,ring,rally, STITCHES USED IN SURGERY
suty, soot(y)
suvana, savanna
suvaner, souvenir
suvant, savant
suvear, severe
suvearly, severe(ly)
suveleun, civilian
suveneer, souvenir
suvere, severe
suverity, severe(rity)
suverly, severe(ly)
suviner, souvenir
suvire, severe
suvont, savant
suvuneer, souvenir
suvunir, souvenir
suwar, sewer
suwaro, saguaro
suwer, sewer
suwerige, sewer(age)
suwero, saguaro
suwir, sewer
suworo, saguaro
suwrench, syringe
suwurege, sewer(age)
svenks, sphinx
svenkter, sphincter

svenx, sphinx
svinks, sphinx
svinktur, sphincter
svinx, sphinx
swa, sway
swab,*,bbed,bbing, AN ABSORBENT MATERIAL TO
    DAB/MOP/CLEAN (or see swap)
swabed, swap(pped) /swab(bbed)
swabt, swap(pped) /swab(bbed)
swach, swatch
swad, suede /sway(ed)
swaddle,ed,ling, TO WRAP WITH STRIPS OF CLOTH
swade, suede /sway(ed)
swadul, swaddle
swae, sway
swaf, suave
swafly, suave(ly)
swag,*,gged,gging, HANG LOOSE (or see swage)
swage,ed,ging, BLACKSMITHS TOOL (or see swag)
swager, swagger
swagger,*,red,ring,rer,ringly, STRUT LIKE A BULLY
    OR AS A DRUNK
swagur, swagger
swair, swear
swak, swag
swaker, swagger
swallow,*,wed,wing, TO TAKE DOWN THE THROAT
    WILLINGLY, A BIRD
swalo, swallow
swalow, swallow
swam, PAST TENSE OF "SWIM"
swamp,*,ped,py,pier,piest,piness,per, MARSHY/
    WATERY LAND
swan,*, A LONG-NECKED BIRD
swang, PAST TENSE OF "SWING" (or see swank)
swank,ker,kily,kiness,ky, SOMEONE WHO MOVES
    WITH AN AIR OF DASHING SMARTNESS (or see
    swang)
swankee, swank(y)

swap,*,pped,pping, TRADE/BARTER (or see swab)
swaped, swap(pped) /swab(bbed)
swapt, swap(pped) /swab(bbed)
swar, swear
swarm,*,med,ming,mer, GROUP OF MANY BEES/
   ZOOSPHORES/PEOPLE, SHIN UP TREE
swarn, sworn
swasteka, swastika
swastika,*, A SYMBOLIC SHAPE
swat,*,tted,tting,tter, A STRIKING BLOW (or see
   sway(ed) or suede)
swatch,hes, PIECE/SAMPLE OF MATERIAL
swate, suede/ sway(ed)/ swat
swath,hes, TRAVEL IN LONG STRIPS GOING BACK AND
   FORTH IN SEQUENTIAL PARALLEL MOVEMENTS
swatul, swaddle
swave, suave
swavedy, suave(vity)
swavity, suave(vity)
swavly, suave(ly)
sway,*,yed,ying,yable,yer, TO SWING BACK AND
   FORTH, TO SAG
swayd, suede /sway(ed)
sweap, sweep
swear,*,ring,swore,sworn,rer, PROFANITY/PLEDGE/
   PROMISE
sweat,*,ted,ting,ty, MOISTURE COMING THROUGH
   PORES OF SKIN TO COOL BODY DOWN, BE
   ANXIOUS, HEAT TO MELTING (or see sweet)
sweater,*, A KNITTED ARTICLE OF CLOTHING
swebt, swept
swech, switch
sweder, sweater/ sweet(er)
swedur, sweater/ sweet(er)
swedy, sweat(y)/ sweet(ie)
sweep,*,ped,ping,per,swept, TO MOVE DIRT ON
   FLOOR/GROUND, A GESTURE/STROKE/MOTION
sweet,*,tly,tness,ten,tie,tish, PALATABLE/PLEASANT
   TASTE, WITH SUGAR (or see sweat/suit/suite)

sweft, swift
sweg, swig
swek, swig
swel, swell
sweld, swell(ed)
swelder, swelter
sweldur, swelter
swell,*,lled,lling,swollen, TEMPORARILY BECOME
   LARGER/HIGHER/INCREASED, A WAVE, AN
   EXPRESSION OF APPROVAL
swelt, swell(ed)
swelter,*,red,ring,ringly, AFFECTED BY OPPRESSIVE
   HEAT
sweltir, swelter
sweltur, swelter
swem, swim
swemur, swim(mmer)
swendul, swindle
sweng, swing
swengur, swing(er)
swep, sweep /swept
sweper, sweep(er)
swept, PAST TENSE OF "SWEEP"
swepur, sweep(er)
swerf, swerve
swerl, swirl
swerve,*,ed,ving, SUDDENLY SWAY/VEER DIRECTION
swesh, swish
swet, sweet /sweat
swete, sweet(ie) /sweat(y)
swetch, switch
sweten, sweet(en)
sweter, sweater /sweet(er)
swetin, sweet(en) /sweat(ing)
swetir, sweater /sweet(er)
swetle, sweet(ly)
swetur, sweater /sweet(er)
swevel, swivel
swevul, swivel

swich, switch
swifd, swift
swifdly, swift(ly)
swifdnes, swift(ness)
swift,tly,tness, RAPID MOVEMENT
swig,*,gged,gging,gger, TAKE LARGE DRINKS OF
   ALCOHOLIC LIQUID
swik, swig
swill,ller, FOOD FOR SWINE, TO GUZZLE
swim,*,mmed,mming,mmer,swam, USE APPEN-
   DAGES OF BODY TO MOVE THROUGH WATER
swimd, swim(mmed)
swimt, swim(mmed)
swimur, swim(mmer)
swin, swine
swindal, swindle
swindle,*,ed,ling,er, ONE WHO CHEATS/SCHEME'S/
   MANIPULATES MONEY FRAUDULENTLY
swindul, swindle
swine,*,nish,nishly,nishness, DOMESTICATED
   PIG/BOAR
swing,*,ging,ger,swang,gable, GLIDE/MOVE/SWAY
   BACK AND FORTH, TYPE OF DANCE/RELATIONSHIP
swip, swipe
swipe,*,ed,ping, TAKE/STRIKE/HIT, MOVE ACROSS A
   SCANNER
swirf, swerve
swirl,*,led,ling,lingly,ly,lier,liest, MOVE IN
   CIRCULAR MOTION, TWIST/CURL
swirve, swerve
swish,her,hy,hingly, A SOUND, A WISPY/QUICK/
   SWEEPING MOVEMENT
switch,hes,hed,hing,her,CHANGE/FLIP/DIVERT FROM
   ONE WAY/SOURCE TO ANOTHER, STICK
swivel,*,led,ling, MOVEMENT CONSTRAINED TO A
   SINGLE PIVOT POINT
swivle, swivel
swivul, swivel
swob, swap /swab

swobed, swap(pped) /swab(bbed)
swobt, swap(pped) /swab(bbed)
swoch, swatch
swodel, swaddle
swodul, swaddle
swof, suave
swofly, suave(ly)
swolen, swollen
swollen, PAST TENSE OF "SWELL"
swolo, swallow
swolun, swollen
swomp, swamp
swompe, swamp(y)
swomper, swamp(er)
swompy, swamp(y)
swon, swan /swoon
swond, swoon(ed)
swoon,*,ned,ning,ner,ningly, FAINT/DIZZY FROM
    LACK OF OXYGEN OR FROM FEELINGS OF ELATION
swoop,*,ped,ping,per, DESCEND TO CAPTURE AND
    ASCEND, BIRD'S MOVEMENT
swoosh,hing, FAST/RUSHING SOUND/MOVEMENT
swop, swap /swab
swopt, swap(pped) /swab(bbed)
swor, swore
sword,*, A POINTED/LONG/SHARP DOUBLE-EDGED
    WEAPON
swore, PAST TENSE OF "SWEAR"
sworm, swarm
swormer, swarm(er)
sworn, PAST TENSE OF "SWEAR"
swosteku, swastika
swostiku, swastika
swot, swat
swotch, swatch
swoth, swath
swov, suave
swovity, suave(vity)
swovly, suave(ly)

swoztiku, swastika
swune, swoon
swup, swoop
swurf, swerve
swurl, swirl
swurve, swerve
swush, swoosh
sy, sigh
syanide, cyanide
sybernetics, cybernetics
syborg, cyborg
sycadellic, psychedelic
sycamore,*, A TREE/FRUIT
sycek, psychic
sychadelic, psychedelic
syche, psyche/ sick/ sic
sychic, psychic
sycho, psycho
sychologekul, psychology(gical)
sychology, psychology
sychopath, psychopath
sychosis, psychosis
sychotic, psychotic
syclone, cyclone
syfalis, syphilis
syfen, siphon
syflus, syphilis
syfules, syphilis
syfun, siphon
sykadelic, psychedelic
sykamore, sycamore
syke, psyche/ sick/ sic
sykeatric, psychiatric
sykek, psychic
sykiatrist, psychiatry(rist)
sykik, psychic
sykilogekul, psychology(gical)
sykle, cycle
syklist, cyclist

syko, psycho
sykodik, psychotic
sykologee, psychology
sykologest, psychology(gist)
sykopath, psychopath
sykopathic, psychopath(ic)
sykopatholagist, psychopath(ologist)
sykosis, psychosis
sykotic, psychotic
syksteen, sixteen
syl, PREFIX INDICATING "TOGETHER/UNITED/ALIKE"
    MOST OFTEN MODIFIES THE WORD
sylable, syllable
sylabus, syllabus
syllable,*,ed,ling, WORD THAT CAN BE DIVIDED INTO
    PARTS BASED UPON PHONETIC SOUNDS
syllabus,ses, AN OUTLINE/SUMMARY
    LECTURE/TEACHINGS
sym, PREFIX INDICATING "TOGETHER/UNITED/ALIKE"
    MOST OFTEN MODIFIES THE WORD
symatry, symmetry
symbal, symbol
symbalism, symbol(ism)
symbeotic, symbiotic
symbiosis,(plural = symbioses) WHERE TWO LIVE
    BODIES CO-EXIST WITH MUTUAL BENEFITS
symbiotic,cally, WHERE TWO LIVE BODIES CO-EXIST
    WITH MUTUAL BENEFITS
symbol,*,lic,lical,lically,lism,list,lize,lization,lizer
    logy, LETTER/SHAPE WHICH HAS MEANING
symbolek, symbol(ic)
symbulism, symbol(ism)
symdum, symptom
symetrik, symmetry(ric)
symetry, symmetry
symfeny, symphony
symfonic, symphony(nic)
symfuny, symphony

symmetry, ries, ric, rical, rically, ricalness, rize, rization, *MATHEMATICAL EXPRESSION, WHERE LINES ARE CONSISTENT WITHIN GUIDELINES*

sympathy, hies, hetic, hetically, hize, hizes, hized, hizing, her, hizingly, *ABILITY TO RELATE/ REVERBERATE IN FREQUENCY/FEELINGS*

sympthy, sympathy

symphonek, symphony(nic)

symphony, nies, nic, nically, nious, niously, *HARMONIC WAVES/FREQENCY, ORCHESTRA*

symphuny, symphony

symphoseum, symposium

sympl, simple / symbol

symposium,*, *CONFERENCE/MEETING WHERE VIEWS ARE DISCUSSED*

sympozeum, symposium

symposm, symptom

symptom, symptom

symptom,*, matic, matical, matically, *REACTION TO SOME UNSEEN AFFECTATION*

symptum, symptom

symputhee, sympathy

symputhize, sympathy(hize)

symtem, symptom

symtum, symptom

symutree, symmetry

syn, *PREFIX INDICATING "TOGETHER/UNITED/ALIKE" MOST OFTEN MODIFIES THE WORD*

synanem, synonym

synapse, *WHERE TWO NERVE ENDINGS COMMUNICATE (or see synapsis/synaptic)*

synapsis, *MEIOSIS PHASE WITH CHROMOSOMES (or see synapse)*

synapsus, synapsis

synaptek, synaptic

synaptic, *MEIOSIS PHASE WITH CHROMOSOMES (or see synapse)*

sync, *SHORT FOR SYNCHRONIZE (or see sink)*

synchro, syncro

synchronus, synchrony(nous)

synchrony, nal, nic, nical, nically, nism, nistic, nistical, nistically, nize, nized, nizing, nizer, nization, nous, nously, nousness, *WHEN HARMONY BETWEEN THINGS/PEOPLE/WAVES/ FREQUENCY HAPPENS SIMULTANEOUSLY*

syncro, *SHORT FOR SYNCHRONIZE*

syncronize, synchrony(nize)

syncrony, synchrony

syndecate, syndicate

syndicashen, syndicate(tion)

syndicate,*, tion, tor, *COMPANIES/CORPORATIONS JOINING FOR A FINANCIAL VENTURE*

syndikation, syndicate(tion)

syndiket, syndicate

syndrem, syndrome

syndrome,*, mic, *COMBINATION OF CIRCUMSTANCES SYMPTOMS HAPPENING AT THE SAME TIME*

syndrum, syndrome

synducate, syndicate

syndukit, syndicate

synergy, gies, getic, gism, gist, gistic, gistically, *PARTS WORKING TOGETHER COOPERATIVELY*

synik, cynic

synikal, cynical

synirgy, synergy

synkrenus, synchrony(nous)

synkronee, synchrony

synkronize, synchrony(nize)

synkrunus, synchrony(nous)

synonemus, synchrony(ous)

synonim, synonym

synonimus, synonym(ous)

synonym,*, mic, mical, mity, mize, mized, mizing, mous, mously, *IS ABOUT THE SAME, SIMILAR CHARACTERISTICS*

synopses, synopsis

synopsis, *CONCENTRATED VERSION OF SOMETHING WRITTEN, A SUMMARY*

syntaks, syntax

syntax, *A GRAMMAR RULE*

syntekit, syndicate

synthasis, synthesis

synthedik, synthetic

synthesis, ses, size, *BRINGING OF PARTS/ELEMENTS TOGETHER CREATING A MORE COMPLEX WHOLE*

synthetek, synthetic

synthetic,*, cal, cally, *MAN MADE CHEMICAL COMPOUNDS*

synthusis, synthesis

synunem, cinnamon

synunem, synonym

syphelis, syphilis

syphen, siphon

syphilis, itic, *A VENEREAL DISEASE*

syphin, siphon

syphon, siphon

syphules, syphilis

syrenge, syringe

syrinch, syringe

syringe,*, *A TUBE WITH A PISTON FOR PULLING/ EXPELLING LIQUIDS*

syrinje, syringe

syrip, syrup

syrup, ped, ping, py, *A VISCOUS/THICK SUGAR BASED LIQUID*

sysdamadik, system(atic)

sysdamatic, system(atic)

sysdem, system

sysdum, system

sysdumadik, system(atic)

sysdumatic, system(atic)

syst, cist / cyst

system,*, mless, matic, matical, matically, maticness, matism, matist, matize, matization, matizer, mic, mically, mize, mization, mizer, *OF OR PERTAINING TO A PLAN/METHODOLOGY WITH PARTICULAR ORDER/ARRANGEMENT, A CLASSIFICATION*

systumatic, system(atic)
syterical, satire(rical)
syth, scythe

t-shirt,*, *SHORT SLEEVE/COLLARLESS SHIRT*
tab,*,bbed,bbing, *BILL FOR SERVICE PERFORMED, A SPACER (TOO MANY DEFINITIONS, PLEASE CONSULT STANDARD DICTIONARY) (or see tap or tape)*
tabaco, tobacco
tabako, tobacco
tabal, table
tabby,bbies,bbied,ying, *STYLE OF FUR ON A CAT*
tabd, tab(bbed) /tap(pped)
tabe, tabby
tabel, table
tabernacle,*,ed,ling,cular, *A NICHE/DWELLING FOR SYMBOLIC STATUE, PART OF A BOAT*
taberqulosis, tuberculosis
tabeulate, tabulate
tabew, taboo
tabewlashen, tabulate(tion)
tabewlate, tabulate
tabewlation, tabulate(tion)
tabewler, tabular
tabil, table
tabirnakle, tabernacle
tablau, tableau
table,*,ed,ling, *GET RID OF, USUABLE SURFACE TO SET ITEMS (TOO MANY DEFINITIONS, PLEASE CONSULT STANDARD DICTIONARY)*
tableau,*, *PRESENTATION/ARRANGEMENT WITH PICTURES*
tablet,*, *BOUND COMPILATION OF PAPERS, PILL SHAPE, FLAT WRITING SURFACE*
tablit, tablet

tablo, tableau
tabloed, tabloid
tabloid,*, *GOSSIP NEWSPAPER WITH PICTURES*
tabloyd, tabloid
tablut, tablet
tabogin, toboggan
taboo,*,ooed,ooing, *PROHIBITED/BANNED/ DISCRIMINATED AGAINST*
tabt, tape(d) /tab(bbed) /tap(pped)
tabu, taboo
tabul, table
tabular,rly, *RESEMBLING/CAN BE USED AS A TABLE*
tabulashen, tabulate(tion)
tabulate,*,ed,ting,tion,tor, *ENTER/LIST/FORMULATE ONTO A TABLE*
tabuld, table(d)
tabuler, tabular
tabulir, tabular
taburnakle, tabernacle
taby, tabby
tacd, tact /tack(ed)
tacdil, tactile
tacdul, tactile
tacet, *MUSICAL TERM/ACTION (or see tacit)*
tachometer,rically,ry, *A DEVICE TO MEASURE LIQUID VELOCITY/MOVEMENT*
tachomitur, tachometer
tachy, *PREFIX INDICATING "RAPID" MOST OFTEN MODIFIES THE WORD*
tacit,tly,tness, *IMPLIED WITHOUT SPEAKING IN WORDS (or see tacet)*
tack,*,ked,king,ky,ker, *ATTACH/AFFIX TO, SAILING TERM, POINTED OBJECT WITH A BROAD HEAD FOR AFFIXING THINGS (or see take or tact)*
tackle,*,ed,ling,er,*PURSUE/OVERCOME/ACCOMPLISH*
tacksonamy, taxonomy
tacky,kiness, *STICKY, DISORDERLY/SHABBY (or see tachy)*
taco,*, *SHAPED CORN TORTILLA FILLED WITH FOODS*

tacshoal, tactual
tacshuel, tactual
tact,*,tful,tfully,tfulness,tless,tlessly,tlessness, *DIPLOMATIC/APPROPRIATE IN PRESENTATION (or see tack or take)*
tactakul, tactic(al)
tactek, tactic
tactekil, tactic(al)
tactic,*,cal,cally,cian, *STRATEGY/PLAN TO PERFORM A MANEUVER/EXPERIMENT/ACTION*
tactick, tactic
tactikel, tactic(al)
tactile,lity, *PERTAINING TO THE SENSE OF TOUCH*
taction, *ACT OF TOUCHING*
tactual,lly, *PERTAINING/GIVEN TO SENSE OF TOUCH*
tactukil, tactic(al)
tada, today
tader, tater /tatter
tadir, tater /tatter
tador, tater /tatter
tadpole,*, *YOUNG FROG LARVAE*
tadpowl, tadpole
tadur, tater /tatter
tael, tail/ tale/ towel
taelur, tailor
taent, taint
tafe, taffy
tafedu, taffeta
tafee, taffy
tafeta, taffeta
taffeta, *TYPE OF WOVEN FABRIC*
taffy, *A CANDY*
tafy, taffy
tag,*,gged,gging, *TO LABEL/IDENTIFY SOMETHING, A GAME OF CHASE (or see tack or take)*
tagethur, together
tagle, toggle
tail,*,led,ling,lless, *APPENDAGE ON THE REAR OF SOMETHING ALIVE, TO FOLLOW SOMEONE CLOSELY (or see tale /tell /tall /towel)*

tailor,*,red,ring, CUSTOM MAKES CLOTHING
taim, tame
taingo, tango
taint,*,ted,ting,tless, DISTRACTING IMPREFECTION, CORRUPT/POLLUTED
tak, tack/ take/ tact
takal, tackle
takamidur, tachometer
takchen, taction
takchun, taction
takd, tact/ talk(ed)/ tack(ed)
takdel, tactile
take,*,took,king,en,kingly,kingness, ACQUIRE FOR ONE'S SELF, REMOVE FROM SOMETHING/SOMEONE (TOO MANY DEFINITIONS, PLEASE CONSULT STANDARD DICTIONARY) (or see tack or tag)
taked, tact/ tack(ed)/ took
takee, tacky / take
takel, toggle
takela, tequila
taken, PAST TENSE OF "TAKE"
takil, tackle /toggle
takila, tequila
takin, taken /tack(ing)
takle, tackle /toggle
tako, taco
takol, tackle
takomeder, tachometer
takomitur, tachometer
taks, take(s) /tack(s)
taksachen, tax(ation)
taksation, tax(ation)
taksebul, tax(able)
taksed, taxi(ed)
taksedermy, taxidermy
taksee, taxi
takseng, taxi(iing) /tax(ing)
takshen, taction
takshuil, tactual

takshun, taction
taksibul, tax(able)
taksidermy, taxidermy
taksieng, taxi(iing)
taksobel, tax(able)
taksonimy, taxonomy
taksuble, tax(able)
taksudirmy, taxidermy
taksy, taxi
takt, tact /tack(ed)
taktakil, tactic(al)
taktek, tactic
taktekul, tactic(al)
taktik, tactic
taktikul, tactic(al)
taktil, tactile
taktion, taction
taktuk, tactic
taktukel, tactic(al)
taktul, tactile
takul, tackle /toggle
takun, taken /tack(ing)
taky, tacky /tachy
tal, tall /towel /tale /tail
talasman, talesman /talisman
talaspore, teliospore
talc, A CHEMICAL COMPOUND (or see talk)
tale,* A STORY (or see tail /tall /towel)
talee, tally
talen, talon
talent,*,ted,HAVE NATURAL ABILITY FOR SOMETHING
taleology, teleology
talepathee, telepathy
taleputhee, telepathy
taler, tailor /tall(er)
talerible, tolerable
tales, tail(less)
talesman, SOMEONE PICKED FROM A COURTROOM TO SERVE ON A JURY (or see talisman)

talin, talon
talint, talent
talir, tailor /tall(er)
talirate, tolerate
talirense, tolerance
talisman, A CHARM/FIGURINE FOR GOOD LUCK (or see talesman)
talk,*,ked,king,ker,kative,kativeness,kie,ky, USE THE MOUTH/VOICE TO EXPRESS THOUGHT/FEELING
talkatif, talk(ative)
tall,ler,lest,lish,lness, MORE THAN AVERAGE HEIGHT (or see tale/ tail/ towel)
tallow,wy, ANIMAL FAT
tally,lied,lying, REGISTER/RECORD/LABEL, KEEP SCORE/COUNT
talness, tall(ness)
talo, tallow
talon,*,ned, CLAWS OF A BIRD OF PREY
talor, tailor
talosman, talesman /talisman
talow, tallow
talr, tailor
talun, talon
talunt, talent
talur, tailor /tall(er)
talurashen, tolerate(tion)
talurate, tolerate
talurense, tolerance
talurent, tolerant
talurible, tolerable
talurint, tolerant
talusman, talesman /talisman
taly, tally
tambaren, tambourine
tamburen, tambourine
tambourine,*, A MUSICAL INSTRUMENT
tamp,*,ped,ping,per,pered,pering,perer,HAMMER/ STRIKE LIGHT BLOWS, DISRUPT/CORRUPT
tampan, tampon

tampon,*, FEMININE HYGIENE PRODUCT
tampurd, tamp(ered)
tamulchuous, tumult(uous)
tamult, tumult
tan,*, PREFIX INDICATING "EXTEND/EXPAND/SPREAD/ CONTINUE/SPIN OUT/WEAVE/PUT FORTH/ SHOW/ MANIFEST" MOST OFTEN MODIFIES THE WORD
tan,*,nned,nning,nnish,nner, TO ENCOURAGE CHANGE/MODIFY SKIN
tanage, tannage
tand, tan(nned)
tandem, ONE BEFORE THE OTHER
tandim, tandem
tandrem, tantrum
tandrum, tantrum
tandum, tandem
tanej, tannage
tanel, tunnel
taner, tan(nner)
tang,ged,gy,gier,giest, A SHARP SOUND/TASTE, A CHISEL STYLE TOOL
tangabul, tangible
tangarene, tangerine
tangebul, tangible
tangee, tang(y)
tangel, tangle
tanger, tanker
tangerine,*, A CITRUS FRUIT
tangeur, tang(ier)
tangible,*,bility,eness,ly, ABLE TO BE FELT/ ACQUIRED/ACCOMPLISHED PHYSICALLY
tangibul, tangible
tangil, tangle
tangint, tangent
tangirene, tangerine

tangle,*, ed,ling,er,ly,ement, TWISTED/ PERPLEXING/CONFUSING
tanglee, tangle(ly)
tanglmint, tangle(ment)
tango,*,oed,oing, A DANCE
tangol, tangle
tangubul, tangible
tangul, tangle
tangur, tanker
tangurene, tangerine
tanige, tannage
tanil, tunnel
tanir, tan(nner)
tanjable, tangible
tanjarene, tangerine
tanjebul, tangible
tanjent, tangent
tanjerine, tangerine
tanjibul, tangible
tanjint, tangent
tanjubul, tangible
tanjurene, tangerine
tank,*, CONTAINER FOR LIQUIDS, A CONTAINER
tanker, CONTAINER WHICH TRANSPORTS LIQUIDS OVER A DISTANCE
tanko, tango
tankur, tanker
tannage, ACT/RESULT OF TANNING HIDES
tanol, tunnel
tanpon, tampon
tansy,sies, A BITTER HERB
tant, taunt /taint /tan(nned)
tantalize,*,ed,zing,er,zingly, ENCOURAGED/TEASED TORMENTED WITHOUT HOPES OF RECEIVING THE END RESULT
tantamount, EQUIVALENT/SIMILAR TO
tantelize, tantalize
tantem, tandem
tantilize, tantalize

tantim, tandem
tantimount, tantamount
tantra,rism,rist, RITUAL INVOLVING MOVEMENT OF FIRST LEVEL ENERGY
tantrem, tantrum
tantrest, tantra(rist)
tantrim, tantrum
tantru, tantra
tantrum,*, ANGRY/EMOTIONAL OUTBURST
tantulise, tantalize
tantum, tandem
tantumownt, tantamount
tanuj, tannage
tanul, tunnel
tanur, tan(nner)
tap,*,pped,pping,pper, LIGHT BLOWS, A FAUCET/ VALVE USED TO ACCESS LIQUIDS FROM A CONTAINER (or see tape)
tapastre, tapestry
tape,*,ed,ping,er, STICKY PLASTIC USED TO SECURE/ WRAP/MEND, LONG FLAT FLEXIBLE DEVICE/ MATERIAL (or see tap)
tapek, topic
tapekul, topical
tapeoka, tapioca
taper,*,red,ring, DESCRIPTION FOR SOMETHING LONG THAT DECREASES IN WIDTH AS IT REACHES THE END/ TIP/POINT
tapestry,ries, LARGE WOVEN FABRIC/THREADS ILLUSTRATING A DESIGN/PICTURE
tapik, topic
tapioca, PUDDING DERIVED FROM STARCHY PLANT
tapir, taper / tap(pper)
tapistre, tapestry
taploed, tabloid
taploid, tabloid
taployd, tabloid
taps, A MUSICAL SIGNAL USED FOR LIGHTS OUT IN MILITARY (or see tap(s) or tape(s))

tapt, tape(d) /tap(pped)
tapuk, topic
tapur, taper /tap(pper)
tapustree, tapestry
taquela, tequila
taquila, tequila
tar,*,rred,rring, A WOOD/COAL COMBINATION BY-
   PRODUCT (or see tare)
tara, terra
tarafy, terrify
taragen, tarragon
taragon, tarragon
tarain, terrain / terrane
taranchula, tarantula
tarane, terrain /terrane
taranshula, tarantula
tarantula,*, A LARGE SPIDER
tararium, terrarium
taraso, terrazzo
tarazo, terrazzo
tard, tar(rred) /tart /tare(d) /tear(ed)
tardee, tardy
tardenes, tardy(diness)
tardur, tartar
tardy,dier,diest,dily,diness, LATE
tare,*, ed,ring, METHOD OF WEIGHING GOODS (or
   see tar /tear /tarry)
tarebly, terrible(ly)
tarebul, terrible
tared, tarif(d)/ tar(rred)/ tear(ed)/ tarry(ried)
taref, tariff
tarefic, terrific
tarefy, terrify
tarereim, terrarium
taresdreul, terrestrial
tarestrial, terrestrial
tareur, terrier
target,*,ted,ting, A POINT/AREA TO AIM AT/FOR
targit, target

targut, target
taribul, terrible
tarier, terrier
tarif, tariff
tarifek, terrific
tariff,*, A TAX
tarific, terrific
tarify, terrify
tarit, terret
tariur, terrier
tarlatan,*, LOOSELY WOVEN MATERIAL
tarletin, tarlatan
tarluten, tarlatan
tarmac,*, MATERIAL USED FOR ROADS/LANDING
   PADS/PARKING
tarmak, tarmac
tarnesh, tarnish
tarnish,hes,hed,hing,hable, OXYDATION WHICH
   DISCOLORS, CAUSE TO LOOSE LUSTER/SHINE/
   STATE OF BEING
tarnush, tarnish
tarp,*,ped,ping, A LARGE/WOVEN MATERIAL FOR
   COVERING/OVERHEAD PROTECTION
tarpalene, tarpaulin
tarpaulin,*, A WEATHERPROOF MATERIAL USED FOR A
   COVERING
tarpeline, tarpaulin
tarpin, tarpon
tarpon,*, LARGE OCEAN FISH
tarpulene, tarpaulin
tarpun, tarpon
tarragon, AN HERB/PLANT
tarrazzo, terrazzo
tarrif, tariff
tarry,rries,rried,ying,rrier, LOITERING/LINGERING,
   NOT MOVING ALONG, COVERED IN TAR
tars, tarso, PREFIX INDICATING "EYELID/ANKLE/
   BONES" MOST OFTEN MODIFIES THE WORD

tart,*,tish,tishly,tly,tness, SOUR TASTE, PASTRY (or
   see tar(rred)/ tear(ed)/ tare(d)/ tort/ torte)
tartar, CALCIUM PHOSPHATE DEPOSIT, DEPOSIT FROM
   WINEMAKING, A SAUCE
tartir, tartar
tartoof, tartuffe
tartuffe or tartufe, COMIC DEPICTING A HYPOCRITE
tartur, tartar
taru, terra
taruf, tariff
tarufy, terrify
tarutoree, territory
tary, tarry
taryd, tarry(ried)
tasc, task
tasd, taste
tasde, taste(ty)
tasel, tassel
taset, tacet /tacit
tasil, tassel
tasit, tacet /tacit
task,*,ked,king, CHORE/WORK TO BE DONE,
   CHALLENGE INVOLVING HARDSHIP
tasles, taste(less)
tasol, tassel
tassel,*, HANGING THREADED ORNAMENT
taste,*,ed,ting,er,eful,efully,efulness,eless,
   elessly,elessness,ty,tier,tiest,tily,tiness,
   SENSE/ FEELING WITHIN THE MOUTH
tastee, taste(ty)
tasteir, taste(tier)
tastenes, taste(tiness)
tasteur, taste(tier)
tastful, taste(ful)
tastfule, taste(fully)
tastfuly, taste(fully)
tastur, taste(r)
tasul, tassel
tatel, tattle

te, tea /tee

tea,*, DRIED PLANTS STEEPED IN WATER (or see tee)

teach,hes,hed,hing,her,hable,hability,hableness, hably, TRAIN/COACH/INSTRUCT, INFORMATION/ KNOWLEDGE BEING PASSED ON TO OTHERS

teachs, teach(es)

teachuble, teach(able)

teachur, teach(er)

teak,*, A TREE

teal, A COLOR (or see teil)

team,*,med,ming, GROUP WHO ATTEMPTS TO SYNCHRONOUSLY WORK/PLAY/ PERFORM TOGETHER (or see teem)

tear,*,red,ring,ry,rful,rfully,rfullness,rless, rlessly,rier,riest,rer, TO RIP, LIQUID COMING FROM THE EYES RELATED TO AN EMOTIONAL THOUGHT/EVENT (or see tier)

tearu, tiara

tease,*,ed,sing,er,sable,singly, TAUNT/PROVOKE/ ANNOY AS A DISTRACTION

teat,*, TIT/NIPPLE/UDDER

tebaco, tobacco

tebagen, toboggan

tebako, tobacco

tebea, tibia

tebogin, toboggan

tebse, tip(sy)

tech, teach

techable, teach(able)

techer, teach(er)

teches, teach(es)

techi,*, SHORT FOR TECHNICIAN

techible, teach(able)

techir, teach(er)

techis, teach(es)

technalogical, technology(gical)

technawlugee, technology

technecal, technical

tavern,*,ner, A PLACE WHICH SELLS SPIRITS/ ALCOHOLIC BEVERAGES

tavurn, tavern

tawer, tower

tawir, tower

tawn, town

tawp, taupe /top

tawt, taught /taut /tout

tax,xes,xed,xing,xable,xability,xation, CHARGE ADDED ON TO GOODS/RESOURCES/SERVICE COLLECTED BY THE CITY/STATE/FEDERAL GOVERNMENTS, A CHALLENGE (or see taxi)

taxadermy, taxidermy

taxashen, tax(ation)

taxe, taxi

taxed, taxi(ed) /tax(ed)

taxedirmy, taxidermy

taxi,*,ied,iing, VEHICLE TO HIRE FOR TRANSPORTA- TION, NAVIGATE A PLANE/BOAT AT SLOW SPEED, MEDICAL TERM (or see tax)

taxidermy,mist, ONE WHO EMBALMS/STUFFS ANIMALS

taxieng, taxi(iing)

taxonimy, taxonomy

taxonomy,nic,mical,mically,mist, METHOD TO CATEGORIZE/CLASSIFY ANIMALS/PLANTS

taxs, tax(es)

taxsachen, tax(ation)

taxsashen, tax(ation)

taxse, taxi

taxsedermy, taxidermy

taxsible, tax(able)

taxsuble, tax(able)

taxsudermy, taxidermy

taxudermy, taxidermy

taxus, tax(es)

tayler, tailor

taylur, tailor

taynt, taint

tater,*, SHORT FOR POTATOE (or see tatter)

tatewist, tattoo(ist)

tatil, tattle

tatir, tater /tatter

tatle, tattle

tatlur, tattle(r)

tatoist, tattoo(ist)

tatol, tattle

tatoo, tattoo

tator, tater /tatter

tatter,*,red,ring, WORN/SHREDDED MATERIAL (or see tater)

tattle,*,ed,ling,er, TO RAT/FINK/TELL/EXPOSE SOMEONE'S WORDS/BEHAVIOR/ACT

tattoo,*,ooed,ooing,ooer,ooist, TO APPLY PERMANENT INK INTO THE SKIN WITH A NEEDLE

tatuist, tattoo(ist)

tatul, tattle

tatur, tatter /tatter

taturd, tatter(ed)

tauer, tower

taught, PAST TENSE OF "TEACH" (or see taut/tout)

taugt, taught /taut /tout

tauko, taco

tauksik, toxic

taul, towel /tall

tauler, tall(er)

taulir, tall(er)

taulk, talk /talc

taulky, talk(y)

taulur, tall(er)

taulurinse, tolerance

taun, town

taunt,*,ted,ting,ter, TEASE/PROVOKE/MANIPULATE SOMEONE TO REACT (or see tout)

taupe, A COLOR (or see toupe)

taupikul, topical

taut,ten,tly,tness, HOLD/STRETCH TIGHT (or see taught/ taunt/ tout)

technek, technique
tecneque, technique
technical,lly,lness,lity,lities, DETAILED/SPECIFIC,
    SPECIFIC TO THE LANGUAGE/SCHOOL/TRADE
technikality, technical(ity)
technilogikul, technology(gical)
technique,*, METHOD OF PERFORMING SOMETHING
    FOR SPECIFIC END RESULTS
technology,gist,gic,gical,gically, INDUSTRIAL
    SCIENCE/ART
technolugee, technology
technukality, technical(ity)
techuble, teach(able)
techur, teach(er)
techus, teach(es)
tectonic,*, SCIENCE/ART O FCONSTRUCTING/STUDYING
    FORMS/SHAPES
teda, today
tedbet, tidbit
tedbit, tidbit
teder, teeter
tedeus, tedious
tedeusly, tedious(ly)
tedious,sly,sness, DETAILED/SLOW/MONOTONOUS
tedius, tedious
tediur, teeter
tedir, teeter
tee,*,ed,eing, A TERM IN THE GAME OF GOLF, TO BE
    IRRITATED, SHAPE/LETTER, ALL COMES TOGETHER
    SUITABLY/PERFECTLY (or see tea)
teecher, teach(er)
teechuble, teach(able)
teechur, teach(er)
teek, teak
teel, teal /teil
teem,*,med,ming, OVERFLOWING/ABUNDANT/
    COMING FORTH (or see team)
teen,*,ny,nier,niest, SHORT FOR TEENAGER,
    SOMETHING VERY SMALL

tene, teen(y)
teeneur, teen(ier)
teenksher, tincture
teenkur, tinker
teenyer, teen(ier)
teepee,*, A CONICAL SHAPED DWELLING COMMON TO
    NATIVE AMERICANS
teers, tear(s) /tier(s)
teery, tear(y)
tees, tease / tea(s)/ tee(s)
teet, teat /tit
teeter,*,red,ring, TO SHIFT WEIGHT BACK AND FORTH
    AS IN A ROCKING MOTION, A HORIZONTAL
    BALANCING MOVEMENT, BALANCING MANEUVER
teeter-totter,*, SEESAW/TOY, LONG BOARD ON A
    FULCRUM WHICH MOVES UP/DOWN WITH
    SHIFTING OF WEIGHT
teeth,he,hed,hing,her, MORE THAN ONE TOOTH, ACT
    OF GROWING FIRST SET OF TEETH
teetur, teeter
tef, tiff
teil, A LIME TREE (or see teal)
teird, tier(ed) /tear(ed)
tek, teak
tekal, tickle
tekdile, textile
teke, tiki
tekel, tickle
tekela, tequila
teket, ticket
teki, techi /tiki
tekil, tickle
tekit, ticket
tekle, tickle
teklech, tickle(lish)
teklish, tickle(lish)
teknakaledy, technical(ity)
teknalogical, technology(gical)
teknalugee, technology

teknek, technique
teknekality, technical(ity)
teknekul, technical
tekneque, technique
teknikul, technical
teknilogikul, technology(gical)
teknolugee, technology
teknowlugee, technology
teknukalety, technical(ity)
teknukil, technical
teknulogical, technology(gical)
tekol, tickle
tekot, ticket
teksd, text
teksdeur, texture
teksdile, textile
teksdure, texture
tekst, text
tekster, texture
tekstile, textile
teksture, texture
tekt, text / tick(ed)
tektonek, tectonic
tektonic, tectonic
tekil, tickle
tekul, tickle
tekut, ticket
teky, tiki
tel, PREFIX INDICATING "END/FAR" MOST OFTEN
    MODIFIES THE WORD (or see teil or teal)
tel/ tell/ tale/ tail/ teil/ teal
telacast, telecast
telafase, telophase
telafone, telephone
telafoto, telephoto
telagraf, telegraph
telagram, telegram
telagraph, telegraph
telakanesis, telekinesis

telakast, telecast
telakenetek, telekinetic
telakinetic, telekinetic
telakunesis, telekinesis
telaphase, telophase
telaphone, telephone
telaphoto, telophoto
telapromptur, teleprompter
telapromtur, teleprompter
telar, teller
telaskope, telescope
telaskopic, telescope(pic)
telathon, telethon
telatipe, teletype
telavichen, television
telavision, television
telavize, televise
teld, tell/ told/ till(ed)
tele, PREFIX INDICATING "DISTANCE" MOST OFTEN MODIFIES THE WORD
tele, telly
telealogy, teleology
teleaspore, teliospore
telecast,*,ted,ting,ter, BROADCAST BY TELEVISION
telefone, telephone
telefoto, telephoto
telegraf, telegraph
telegram,*, SEND MESSAGE/MONEY BY WIRE
telegraph,her,hist,hic,hically, MESSAGE/TRANS-MISSION SENT BY USING AN INSTRUMENT, WIRE TRANSFER
telekinesis, OBJECTS MOVING WHICH HAVE NO VISIBLE EXPLANATION AS TO CAUSE
telekinetic,*, OBJECTS MOVING WHICH HAVE NO VISIBLE EXPLANATION AS TO CAUSE
telekunesis, telekinesis
telekunetic, telekinetic
teleology,gism,gist, SCIENCE WHICH STUDIES ETHICS/CAUSES/ACTS IN NATURE

telepathee, telepathy
telepathy,hic,hically,hist, COMMUNICATE BY WAVE-LENGTH, MIND COMMUNICATION
telephone,*,nic,nically, INSTRUMENT FOR VERBAL COMMUNICATION
telephoto,ography,ographic, TAKING PHOTOS AT LONG DISTANCE
teleprompter,*, A DEVICE WHICH ENLARGES TEXT FOR THOSE ON CAMERA TO READ FROM
teleputhee, telepathy
teler, teller
telescope,*,ed,ping,pic,pically, INSTRUMENT THAT SEEMINGLY REDUCES DISTANCE BY USE OF LENSES (or see microscope)
telethon,*, A TELEVISION BROADCAST WHICH LASTS A LONG TIME
teletipe, teletype
teletype, DEVICE USED TO TRANSMIT MESSAGES
teleupromtur, teleprompter
teleuspore, teliospore
televigen, television
televijan, television
televise,*,ed,sing, USING TELEVISION TO TRANSMIT/ BROADCAST
television,*,nally,nary, VISUAL IMAGES SENT BY WAVES THROUGH DEVICE WHICH INTERPRETS THEM
teli, telly
telialegy, teleology
teliaulugy, teleology
telicast, telecast
telifone, telephone
telifoto, telephoto
teligraf, telegraph
teligram, telegram
teligraph, telegraph
telikanesis, telekinesis
telikast, telecast
telikunesis, telekinesis
teliology, teleology

teliospore,*,ric, METHOD OF FUNGI GERMINATION
teliphone, telephone
teliphoto, telephoto
telipromptur, teleprompter
telipromtur, teleprompter
telir, teller
teliskope, telescope
teliskopic, telescope(pic)
telithon, telethon
telitipe, teletype
teliuspore, teliospore
telivishen, television
television, television
televize, televise
tell,*,ling,told, TO COMMUNICATE INFORMATION ALONG (or see teal or teil)
teller,*, ONE WHO DEALS DIRECTLY WITH CUSTOMERS AT A BANK, NARRATOR, ONE WHO FACILITATES COMMUNICATION BETWEEN OTHERS
telltale,er, TATTLER, ONE WHO PASSES ALONG GOSSIP/HERESAY, A TOOL FOR NAVIGATION
telly, SHORT FOR TELEVISION
telo, PREFIX INDICATING "END/FAR" MOST OFTEN MODIFIES THE WORD
telofase, telophase
telokanesis, telekinesis
telokunesis, telekinesis
telophase,sic, BIOLOGICAL TERM
telor, teller
teloskope, telescope
teloskopic, telescope(pic)
telothon, telethon
telovishen, television
telt, till(ed) /told /tilt
teltail, telltale
teltale, telltale
telufase, telophase
telufone, telephone
telufoto, telophoto

telugraf, telegraph
telugram, telegram
telugraph, telegraph
telukanesis, telekinesis
telukast, telecast
telukenetick, telekinetic
telukinetik, telekinetic
telukunesis, telekinesis
teluphase, telophase
teluphone, telephone
teluphoto, telephoto
telupromtur, teleprompter
telur, teller
teluskope, telescope
teluskopic, telescope(pic)
teluthon, telethon
telutipe, teletype
teluvegun, television
teluvision, television
teluvize, televise
tem, team /teem
tembir, timber
tembor, timber
tembr, timber
tembrachure, temperature
tembramentul, temper(mental)
tembruchure, temperature
tembrumentul, temper(mental)
tembrushure, temperature
tembur, timber
temd, team(ed) /teem(ed)
temet, timid
temidly, timid(lly)
temod, timid
tempal, temple
tempararely, temporary(rily)
temparary, temporary
temparize, temporize

temper,*,red,ring,rment,rmentally, rance,rate,rately,rateness,rability,rable, rer, *EMOTIONS WORKED INTO AN ANGRY STATE, HEATING UP CARBON MATERIAL TO FORCE MOLECULAR REALIGNMENT*
tempera, tempura
temperarily, temporary(rily)
temperary, temporary
temperature,*, , *A MEASUREMENT OF HOT/COLD VARIANCES*
temperize, temporize
tempermint, temper(ment)
tempershues, tempest(uous)
tempest,tuous,tuously,tuousness, *OF BEING STORMY /WINDY /TURBULENT*
tempil, temple
tempir, temper
tempirashure, temperature
tempiriment, temper(ment)
tempirushure, temperature
templat, template
template,*, , *SOMETHING TO SUPPORT/ALLOW THE FORM OF SOMETHING, FOR MAKING REPLICAS*
temple,*,ed,eless, *RELIGIOUS STRUCTURE FOR WORSHIP, SPOT ON THE HEAD OF THE BODY*
templut, template
tempo,*, , *THE RHYTHM OF A WAVE, RATE /SPEED/ PACE OF MOVEMENT*
tempol, temple
tempor, *PREFIX INDICATING "TIME/TEMPLES" MOST OFTEN MODIFIES THE WORD*
tempor, temper
temporal,lly,lness,lity,lities, *OF OR GIVEN TO THIS TIME/SPACE/DISTANCE*
temporarely, temporary(rily)
temporary,rarily,riness, *SHORT DURATION IN TIME*
temporely, temporal(lly)
temporize,*,ed,zing,zer,zation,zingly, *GAIN/ DELAY/YIELD/MANIPULATE TIME*

temporment, temper(ment)
temporo, *PREFIX INDICATING "TIME/TEMPLES" MOST OFTEN MODIFIES THE WORD*
temporul, temporal
tempra, tempura
temprachure, temperature
tempral, temporal
tempramentul, temper(mental)
temprary, temporary
temprashure, temperature
temprature, temperature
tempremintul, temper(mental)
tempreruly, temporary(rily)
temprery, temporary
tempru, tempura
temprumintul, temper(mental)
tempt,*,ted,ting,tingly,table,ter,tingness,tress, *TO ENTICE/ALLURE/SEDUCE/INVITE*
temptashen, temptation
temptation,*, , *APPREHENSION IN RESPONDING TO INVITATION/ENTICEMENT/SEDUCTION*
tempul, temple
tempur, temper
tempura, *BATTER DIPPED VEGETABLES/FISH*
temporarily, temporary(rily)
temporary, temporary
temporely, temporal(lly)
temporery, temporary
tempureruly, temporary(rily)
tempurize, temporize
tempurment, temper(ment)
tempust, tempest
temt, tempt/ team(ed)/ teem(ed)
temtashen, temptation
temtation, temptation
temted, tempt(ed)
temtres, tempt(ress)
temulchuis, tumult(uous)
temulchuous, tumult(uous)

temult, tumult
temut, timid
ten,*, ENGLISH NUMBER AFTER NINE/BEFORE ELEVEN
    (or see tin or teen)
tenabel, tenable
tenable,tility,eness,ly, CAN SURVIVE ATTEMPT AT
    BEING TAKEN/CARRIED AWAY
tenachus, tenacious
tenacious,sly,sness, PERSISTENT/CONSISTENT,
    WITHOUT FAULTER
tenacity, OF BEING TENACIOUS
tenakle, tentacle
tenament, tenement
tenansy, tenant(ncy)
tenant,*,ncy,cies,try, BORROWER OF LAND/
    STRUCTURE PROPERTY HELD/OWNED BY ANOTHER
tenasedy, tenacity
tenasuty, tenacity
tenashus, tenacious
tenasity, tenacity
tenat, tenet /tenant
tenatef, tentative
tenatious, tenacious
tenative, tentative
tencity, tense(sity)
tend,*,ded,ding,dance,dentious,dencious,
    dentiously,dentiousness,denciousness,
    HAVE LEANING/AFFINITY/TENDENCY TOWARDS,,
    TAKE CARE OF (or see tin(nned)/ tent/ tint)
tendatev, tentative
tendency,cies, HAVE LEANING/INCLINATION
    TOWARDS, DISPOSITION/CAPABILITY OF
tendenus, tendon(dinous)
tender,rly,rness,rer,rize,rization,rizer, SOFTENED
    FIBERS, SOFT/GENTLE IN NATURE/TEMPERAMENT,
    OFFER TOWARDS DEBT (or see tinder)
tenderloin,*, CUT OF BEEF
tendid, tend(ed) /tint(ed)
tendin, tendon

tendinsy, tendency
tendir, tender /tinder
tendirloin, tenderloin
tendon,*,dinous,nitis, PART OF A MUSCLE
tendorize, tender(ize)
tendril,*, CURLING OF A PLANT/HAIR
tendrul, tendril
tendun, tendon
tendunitus, tendon(itis)
tendunus, tendon(dinous)
tendur, tender /tinder
tendurize, tender(ize)
tendurloin, tenderloin
tendurly, tender(ly)
tendutif, tentative
tene, teeny /tin(nny)
tenekle, tentacle
tenement,*,tary, DWELLING WHERE PEOPLE LIVE AS
    TENANTS, PERMANENT PROPERTY
tenen, tenon
tenensy, tenant(ncy)
tener, tenor
tenet,*, DOCTRINE/BELIEF/DOGMA HELD TO BE TRUE
    (or see tenant)
tenetif, tentative
tenetive, tentative
teneur, tenure /teen(ier)
teneust, teen(iest)
tenewus, tenuous
tenfold, TEN TIMES OVER/GREATER
teng, ting /tinge
tenible, tenable
teniest, teen(iest)
tenikle, tentacle
teniment, tenement
tenin, tenon
tenir, tenor
tenis, tennis
tenit, tenet /tenant

tenite, tonight
tenj, tinge
tenkchur, tincture
tenker, tinker
tenkil, tinkle
tenkir, tinker
tenkol, tinkle
tenkshir, tincture
tenkture, tincture
tenkul, tinkle
tenkur, tinker
tennis, A RACQUET GAME
tenon, A CARPENTRY TOOL
tenor,*, A PITCH/LEVEL OF SOUND (TOO MANY DEFINI-
    TIONS, PLEASE CONSULT STANDARD DICTIONARY)
tenos, tennis
tens, ten(s) /tent(s) /tense /tint(s) /tend
tense,*,ed,sing,ely,eness,sity,eless,sion,sional,
    sionless,sive, STRETCHED/PUSHED/STRAINED
    BEYOND A COMFORTABLE POSITION, TIGHT, IN
    RELATION TO TIME (or see tent(s))
tensul, tinsel
tent,*,ted, SHARP PEAK WITH TWO EQUAL SLOPES,
    TEMPORARY/PORTABLE SHELTER, SURGICAL
    PROCEDURE (or see tint/ tend/ tin(nned))
tentacle,*,ed,cular, LONG/FLEXIBLE APPENDAGES ON
    A LIVING THING
tentakle, tentacle
tentative,ely,eness, TEMPORARY PLAN/TIME, NOT
    CERTAIN AS OF YET
tented, tint(ed)/ tent(ed)/ tend(ed)
tentekle, tentacle
tentetive, tentative
tenth,*, ONE PART OUT OF TEN
tentikle, tentacle
tentukle, tentacle
tentutive, tentative
tenuble, tenable
tenues, tenuous

tenukle, tentacle
tenument, tenement
tenunsy, tenant(ncy)
tenunt, tenant
tenuous,sly,sness, *DELICATE/WEAK/FINE/DILUTED*
tenure,rial,rially, *HOLDING/POSSESSING PROPERTY*
OR POSITION
tenus, tennis
tenutef, tentative
tenutive, tentative
teny, teen(y) /tin(nny)
tenyewr, tenure
tenyewus, tenuous
tenyir, tenure
tenyur, tenure
tenzul, tinsel
tep, tip
tepakle, typical
tepd, tip(pped)
tepe, teepee
teped, tepid
tepekul, typical
teper, tip(pper)
tepid,dity,dness,dly, *LUKEWARM, WARM TO TOUCH*
tepikul, typical
tepod, tepid
tepor, tip(pper)
tepse, tip(sy)
tepud, tepid
tepufy, typify
tepukle, typical
tepur, tip(pper)
tequila, *A LIQUOR/ALCOHOL*
ter, *PREFIX INDICATING "THREE" MOST OFTEN MODIFIES*
THE WORD
ter, tear / tier
tera, *PREFIX INDICATING "ONE TRILLION/MONSTER"*
MOST OFTEN MODIFIES THE WORD

tera, terra
terable, terrible
terace, terrace
terafy, terrify
teragen, tarragon
teragin, tarragon
terain, terrain /terrane
teranchula, tarantula
terane, terrain / terrane
teranshulu, tarantula
terantula, tarantula
terareim, terrarium
terarium, terrarium
teras, terrace
terastrial, terrestrial
terat, terret
teratoreul, territory(rial)
teratory, territory
terazo, terrazzo
terazzo, terrazzo
terben, turban /turbine
terbin, turban /turbine
terbo, turbo
terbulens, turbulent(nce)
terbulent, turbulent
terbun, turban /turbine
terd, tier(ed)/ tear(ed)/ tour(ed)
terdle, turtle
tere, tear(y)
tereble, terrible
terefic, terrific
terefy, terrify
terene, tyranny
terer, terror
terereim, terrarium
teres, terrace
teresdreul, terrestrial
teresm, tour(ism)
terest, tour(ist)

terestrial, terrestrial
teret, turret /terret
tereur, tarry(rier) /terrier
tereur, terrier
terf, turf
terfil, tear(ful)
terful, tear(ful)
terible, terrible
teribly, terrible(ly)
teribul, terrible
terif, tariff
terifek, terrific
terify, terrify
teriny, tyranny
terir, terror
teris, terrace
terism, tour(ism)
terist, tour(ist)
terit, turret / terret
teritoree, territory
teritoreul, territory(rial)
teritory, territory
teriur, terrier
terkoes, turquois
terkois, turquois
term,*,med,mless, *INVOLVING A SPECIFIC PERIOD OF*
TIME, FIXED/SPECIFIC QUANTITY/VALUE
termarek, turmeric
termd, term(ed)
termenal, terminal
termenashen, terminate(tion)
termenate, terminate
termenation, terminate(tion)
termenator, terminate(tor)
termenology, terminology
termenul, terminal
termerik, turmeric
terminal,*,lly,able,ableness,ably, *A STATION/*
CONDUIT/CIRCUIT, TERMINATES/COMES TO AN END

terminate,*,tive,tively,tor,tion,tional, TO END
terminology,gies,gical,gically, SPECIFIC WORDS/ LANGUAGE WITHIN A SCIENCE/ART TO EXPLAIN PROCESSES
terminul, terminal
termite,*, WOOD EATING INSECT
termoel, turmoil
termole, turmoil
termonel, terminal
termunate, terminate
terminology, terminology
tern, turn
tern,*, A BIRD (or see turn)
ternament, tournament
ternd, turn(ed)
ternep, turnip
terniment, tournament
ternip, turnip
ternument, tournament
teror, terror
terpentin, turpentine
terpewlent, turbulent
terpintin, turpentine
terpulent, turbulent
terpuntine, turpentine
terra, PLANETS MOUNTAINOUS AREA
terrace,*, ed,cing, VARIOUS LEVEL AREAS CUT INTO A SLOPE
terrain, THE NATURALLY SHAPED LANDSCAPE (or see terrane)
terrane, GROUP OF NATURAL FORMATIONS PARTICULARLY ROCK (or see terrain)
terrarium,*, CONTAINER FOR PLANTS/ANIMALS TO LIVE/VIEWED
terrazzo, MOSAIC PIECES OF STONE/TILE
terrestrial,lly, PERTAINING TO THE EARTH/WORLD
terret,*, ON A SADDLE/HARNESS (or see turret)
terreur, terrier

terrible,eness,ly,HORRIBLE/AWFUL/UNCOMFORTABLE/ STRESSFUL
terrier,*, BREED OF DOG
terrif, tariff
terrific,cally, EXCELLENT/EXCITING/WONDERFUL
terrify,fies,fied,ying,yingly, STRICKEN WITH TERROR, HORRIFY/FRIGHTEN
terrir, terror
territory,ries,rial,rially,rialism,rialist,riality, rialize,rialization, A SPECIFIC REGION/AREA OF TURF/ LAND
terror,*,rism,rist,ristic,rless,rize,rization,rizer, EXTREME FEAR/HORROR
terrur, terror
ters, tear(s) /tier(s)
terse,er,est,ely,eness, FREE OF FRIVOLTIES/ SUPERFICIALITY
tersheary, tertiary
tershury, tertiary
tert, tier(ed) /tear(ed)
tertiary,ries, THREE/THIRD/THIRDS OF SOMETHING
tertil, turtle
tertul, turtle
teru, terra
terubil, terrible
terubly, terrible(ly)
teruf, tariff
terufy, terrify
terugen, tarragon
terugin, tarragon
terur, terror
terus, terrace
terut, turret
terutoree, territory
terutoreul, territory(rial)
terutory, territory
tery, tear(y) /tarry
terz, tear(s) /tier(s)
tes, tease

tesabel, tease(sable)
tesdamoneul, testimony(nial)
tesdee, testy
tesdekle, testicle
tesdi, testy
tesdukle, testicle
tesdumoneul, testimony(nial)
teseble, tease(sable)
tesh, teach
teshu, tissue
tesible, tease(sable)
test,*,ted,ting,ter, TO CHALLENGE, EXPERIMENT FOR REACTION, A SHELL
testafide, testify(fied)
testafy, testify
testament,*,tary,tal, WITNESS, CREATE A WILL
testamint, testament
testamoneul, testimony(nial)
teste, testy
testefide, testify(fied)
testefy, testify
testekle, testicle
testemint, testament
testemony, testimony
testicle,*,cular,culate, MALE REPRODUCTIVE GLANDS
testify,fies,fied,fying,fier, TO DECLARE AS A WITNESS, DECLARE UNDER OATH
testikle, testicle
testikuler, testicle(cular)
testiment, testament
testimony,nies,ial, TO PROVIDE WRITTEN/VERBAL ACCOUNT AS A WITNESS
testir, test(er)
testufid, testify(fied)
testufy, testify
testukle, testicle
testument, testament
testumint, testament
testumoneul, testimony(nial)

testumony, testimony
testur, test(er)
testy,tily,tiness, *TOUCHY/IRRITABLE*
tesu, tissue
tesubil, tease(sable)
tesuble, tease(sable)
tesy, tizzy
tetanus, *A BACTERIA WHICH ENTERS OPEN WOUNDS*
tetbet, tidbit
tetbit, tidbit
teter, teeter
teth, teeth
tether,*,red,ring, *CORD/ROPE/STRANDS TO SECURE*
  SOMETHING FROM GOING AWAY(or see teeth(er)
tethur, tether
tetir, teeter
tetnus, tetanus
tetra, *PREFIX INDICATING "FOUR" MOST OFTEN*
  MODIFIES THE WORD
tetra,*, *FRESH WATER TROPICAL FISH*
tetru, tetra
tetunes, testanus
tetur, teeter
teuburkwulosis, tuberculosis
teul, teal /tell /teil
teurd, tier(ed) /tear(ed)
teurism, tour(ism)
teusday, Tuesday
tewb, tube
tewbles, tube(less)
tewbuler, tube(bular)
tewl, tool
tewm, tomb
tewnik, tunic
tewt, toot
tewth, tooth
tewthles, tooth(less)
texder, texture
texdile, textile

texdir, texture
texsdure, texture
text,tual,tually,tualism,tualist, *PRINTED/WRITTEN*
  LETTERS TO FORM WORDS
textile,*, *ANY MATERIAL THAT CAN BE WOVEN*
texture,*,ed,ring,ral,rally, *ANY RAISED/VARIANT*
  PORTION OF A FLAT/SMOOTH SURFACE
tez, tease
tezzy, tizzy
tha, thaw /they
thad, they'd
thael, they'll
thair, there/ their/ they're
thalamus,mi,mic,mically, *PART OF A BRAIN/FLOWER*
thalas, thallus
thalimus, thalamus
thalumus, thalamus
thalus, thallus
thamadik, theme(matic)
than, *WORD USED TO COMPARE/CONTRAST*
thanck, thank
thang, thong /thing
thank,*,ked,king,ker,kful,kfully,kfullness,kless,
  klessly,klessness, *APPRECIATION/ GRATITUDE*
thanklis, thank(less)
thar, there/ their/ they're
tharbi, thereby
thare, there/ their/ they're
tharepist, therapy(pist)
tharepudik, therapy(peutic)
tharepy, therapy
tharfor, therefor /therefore
tharfour, therefor /therefore
tharipist, therapy(pist)
tharipudik, therapy(peutic)
tharipy, therapy
tharof, thereof
tharuf, thereof

tharupest, therapy(pist)
tharupist, therapy(pist)
tharupudik, therapy(peutic)
tharupy, therapy
thasares, thesaurus
thasoris, thesaurus
that,*, *SOMEONE/SOMETHING NOT IN THE*
  IMMEDIATE AREA/TIME FRAME, PREVIOUSLY
  MENTIONED, A PRONOUN
thatch,hes,hed,hing,her, *MATTED/LAYERED*
  ORGANIC MATERIAL, SURFACE COVERING
thau, thaw /thou
thaud, thaw(ed) /thought
thaung, thong
thausend, thousand
thausund, thousand
thaw,*,wed,wing, *TEMPERATURE WARMING AWAY*
  FROM FREEZING, UNFREEZING (or see thou)
thawt, thaw(ed) /thought
thayd, they'd
thayl, they'll
the, *AN IDENTIFYING/SPECIFYING WORD PRIOR TO A*
  NOUN (or see thee)
theader, theater
theadir, theater
theadrekul, theatric(al)
theadrikal, theatric(al)
theadur, theater
thealegy, theology
theam, theme
theater,*, or theatre, *A STRUCTURE FOR*
  PERFORMING AND OTHER ARTS
theatir, theater
theatrek, theatric
theatrekul, theatric(al)
theatric,*,cal(s),calism,cality,calize,cally, *THE*
  ART OF PERFORMING, DRAMATIC
theatur, theater
thee, *REFERS TO A PERSON* (or see "the")

theef, thief
theem, theme
theesm, theism
thef, thief
thefd, theft
theft,*, STEALING
theif, thief
theil, they'll
their,*, REFERS TO PEOPLE, POSSESSIVE PLURAL PRONOUN (or see there or they're)
theism,st,stic,stical,stically, BELIEF IN ONE DEITY
theive, thieve
thek, thick
thekin, thick(en)
thekinur, thick(ener)
thekist, thick(est)
thekit, thicket
theknur, thick(ener)
thekun, thick(en)
thekuner, thick(ener)
thekust, thick(est)
thekut, thicket
them, PRONOUN REFERRING TO MORE THAN ONE (or see theme)
themadik, theme(matic)
themble, thimble
thembul, thimble
theme,*,matic,matically, A SPECIFIC TOPIC/SUBJECT
themselves, PLURAL PRONOUN POSSESSIVE
then, SIGNIFIES TIME/PLACE (or see thin or than)
thener, thin(nner)
theng, thing
thenir, thin(nner)
thenk, think
thenkar, think(er)
thenkur, think(er)
thenly, thin(ly)
thenur, thin(nner)

theo, PREFIX INDICATING "GOD" MOST OFTEN MODIFIES THE WORD (or see thio)
theology,gies,gian,gic,gical,gically,gize,gizer, PHILOSOPHY CONCERNING RELIGION
theolugy, theology
theory,ries,rize,rized,rizing,rem,rematic, rematically,retic,retics,retical,retically, PRINCIPLES/TECHNIQUES/BELIEF IN AN ATTEMPT TO EXPLAIN/UNDERSTAND EVENTS
ther, there/ their/ they're
therapudik, therapy(peutic)
therapy,pies,pist,peutic,peutical,peutically, peutics,peutist, TREATMENT TO REMEDY A MALADY
therasik, thoracic
therbi, thereby
therd, third
therdly, third(ly)
there,*, FOLLOWS NOUN/PRONOUN TO DESCRIBE PLACE/TIME/EMPHASIS (or see their /they're)
thereby, IN WHICH CASE/INSTANCE
therefor, FOR IT/THIS/THAT (or see therefore)
therefore, IN REFERENCE TO BEFORE MENTIONED (or see therefor)
thereof, BECAUSE OF THAT
therepeudik, thrapy(peutic)
therfor, therefor /therefore
therfour, therefor /therefore
therm, PREFIX INDICATING "HEAT" MOST OFTEN MODIFIES THE WORD
therm,mic, CALORIES/HEAT
thermal,*,lly, RELATED TO HEAT
thermamedur, thermometer
thermamiter, thermometer
thermometer,*,tric,trical,trically,try,INSTRUMENT WHICH MEASURES HOT/COLD VARIANCES
thermomuder, thermometer
thermul, thermal
thero, thorough

therof, thereof
therogh, thorough
thorough, thorough
therow, thorough
thers, there(s) /their(s)
thersd, thirst
Thersday, Thursday
thersdy, thirst(y) /Thursday
therst, thirst
thersty, thirst(y) /Thursday
thert, third
theruf, thereof
therupist, therapy(pist)
therupudik, therapy(peutic)
therupy, therapy
thery, theory
Therzday, Thursday
thes, this or these
thesal, thistle
thesares, thesaurus
thesaurus,ses, BOOK OF SYNONYMS
thesbein, thespian
these, PLURAL TENSE OF "THIS" (or see this)
thesis,theses, SET/PUT DOWN/DOCUMENT/PROVE
thesle, thistle
thespein, thespian
thespian,*, ACTOR/ACTRESS
thesul, thistle
thesus, thesis
theury, theory
thev, thieve
thevaree, thieve(ry)
thevury, thieve(ry)
thewre, theory
they, PLURAL OF "PERSONS IN GENERAL"
they'd, CONTRACTION OF THE WORDS "THEY HAD/ WOULD"
they'll, CONTRACTION OF THE WORDS "THEY SHALL/ WILL"

they're, CONTRACTION OF OF THE WORDS "THEY ARE" (or see there or their)
they've, CONTRACTION OF THE WORDS "THEY HAVE"
theyl, they'll
thi, PREFIX INDICATING "SULFUR" MOST OFTEN MODIFIES THE WORD (or see thigh or thy)
thiadur, theater
thiamen, thiamine
thiamine, VITAMIN COMPOUND
thiazine, CHEMICAL COMPOUND
thick,ken(s),kened,kening,kener,ker,kest,kness, kly,kish, WITHNOTICCABLE DEPTH/VISCOSITY/ DENSITY, EXCESSIVE/EXAGGERATED
thicket,*,ted,ty, DENSE/THICK SHRUBS
thief,*, ONE WHO STEALS
thieve,*, ed,ving,ery,eries,vish,vishly,vishness, OF STEALING
thiezene, thiazine
thigh,*, PORTION OF LEG ABOVE THE KNEE
thik, thick
thiken, thick(en)
thiket, thicket
thikist, thick(est)
thikit, thicket
thiknur, thick(ener)
thikuner, thick(ener)
thikust, thick(est)
thikut, thicket
thim, them
thimadek, theme(matic)
thimadik, theme(matic)
thimas, thymus
thimatik, theme(matic)
thimble,*, DEVICE FOR PROTECTION OF FINGERTIPS
thimbul, thimble
thimes, thymus
thimomedur, thermometer

thimple, thimble
thimpul, thimble
thimselfs, themselves
thimselvs, themselves
thimus, thymus
thin,*,nned,nning,nner,nly,nness,nnish, LESS VISCOSITY/WEIGHT/THICKNESS/DEPTH THAN PREFERRED/NORMAL (or see then/than/thine)
thind, thin(nned)
thine, thou, thy, THIRD PERSON PRONOUN MEANING YOU OR YOURS (or see thin)
thiner, thin(nner)
thing,*, GENERIC TITLE FOR THAT WHICH IS NOT KNOWN/UNDERSTOOD, WITHOUT A NAME (or see think)
think,*,king,ker,thought,kable,kableness,kably, kingly, TO ENGAGE THE MIND, TO SUPPOSE/ CONTEMPLATE/CONSIDER (or see thing)
thinkur, think(er)
thinur, thin(nner)
thio, PREFIX INDICATING "SULFUR" MOST OFTEN MODIFIES THE WORD (or see theo)
thirasik, thoracic
third,*,dly, ENGLISH NUMBER AFTER TWO, AFTER THE SECOND, ONE THIRD OF THE WHOLE
thirdlee, third(ly)
thirm, therm
thirmal, thermal
thirmamedur, thermometer
thirmamiter, thermometer
thirmek, therm(ic)
thirmel, thermal
thirmometur, thermometer
thirmomuder, thermometer
thirmul, thermal
thiro, thorough
thiroed, thyroid
thirogh, thorough
thiroed, thyroid

thiroid, thyroid
thirough, thorough
thirow, thorough
thiroyd, thyroid
Thirsday, Thursday
thirst,ty,tier,tiest,tily,tiness,ter, STRONG DESIRE FOR LIQUIDS, CRAVE SENSORY/MENTAL INPUT
thirsdy, thirst(y) /Thursday
thirt, third
thiry, theory
this, PRONOUN/POSSESSIVE PRESENT TIME
thisal, thistle
thisares, thesaurus
thisel, thistle
thises, thesis
thisle, thistle
thisoris, thesaurus
thistle,*, A PLANT
thisul, thistle
thisus, thesis
thiumen, thiamine
thiumin, thiamine
thiuzene, thiazine
thiwroed, thyroid
thiz, this
tho, though /thou /thaw
thogh, though
thoght, thought
thoghtles, thought(less)
thong,*, SHOES, UNDER GARMENT, LEATHER STRAP
thonk, thong
thoracic, THE CHEST AREA
thoraks, thorax
thorasik, thoracic
thorax,xes, THE CHEST AREA
thorn,*,ny,less, A SHARP/PRICKLY POINT ON A PLANT/TREE
thornee, thorn(y)
thornlis, thorn(less)

thoro, thorough

thorogh, thorough

thorough,hly,hness, COMPLETE/DETAILED/ACCURATE

thorow, thorough

thos, those

those, PRONOUN FOR REMOTE

thosend, thousand

thosund, thousand

thot, thaw(ed) /thought

thotful, thought(ful)

thotles, thought(less)

thou, thy, thine, THIRD PERSON PRONOUN MEANING YOU OR YOURS (or see though)

though, PLURAL ADJECTIVE MEANING THAT/BUT/ HOWEVER

thought,*,tfull,tfully,tfullness,tless,tlessly, PAST TENSE OF THE WORD "THINK"/ CONTEMPLATE

thousand,*,dth, ENGLISH NUMBER AFTER 999

thousend, thousand

thousind, thousand

thousnd, thousand

thow, thou/ thaw/ though

thowsand, thousand

thowsund, thousand

thowsunth, thousand(th)

thoz, those

thrab, throb

thral, thrall

thrall, ENSLAVED/SLAVE/BONDAGE

thraul, thrall

thre, three

thread,*,ded,ding,der,dless,dy,diness, A THIN STRAND/FILAMENT/CORD

threat,*,ten,tened,tening,tener,teningly, to CHALLENGE AGAINST SOMEONE/SOMETHINGS IDEALS/EXPECTATIONS

threch, thresh

threchhold, threshold

threchold, threshold

thred, thread /threat

threden, threat(en)

thredin, threat(en)

thredined, threat(ened)

thredun, threat(en)

thredund, threat(ened)

three,*, ENGLISH NUMBER AFTER TWO

threfd, thrift

threft, thrift

threfty, thrifty

threl, thrill

threlur, thrill(er)

thresh,hes,hed,hing,her, BEAT GRAIN

threshhold, threshold

threshold,*, A DOOR WAY/SILL, ENTRANCE

thret, thread /threat

thretind, threat(ened)

thretund, threat(ened)

threw, PAST TENSE OF "THROW" (or see thru through)

thrice, THREE TIMES

thrif, thrive

thrifd, thrift /thrive(d)

thrifdee, thrifty

thrifs, thrive(s)

thrift,ty,tily,tiness, MINDS/WATCHES/CONTROLS SPENDING/USE OF RESOURCES (or see thrive(d)

thril, thrill

thriler, thrill(er)

thrill,*,lled,lling,ller, EMOTION EXAGERRATED IN A POSITIVE FASHION, DELIGHT

thrilor, thrill(er)

thrilur, thrill(er)

thrise, thrice

thrive,*,ed,ving,vingly,er, TO EXIST SUCCESSFULLY

thro, throe /throw /through

throat,*,ted,ty,tily,tiness, CONICAL/HOLLOW ENTRANCE/PASSAGEWAY, FRONT PART OF NECK

throb,*,bbed,bbing,bber, PULSATE/VIBRATE

throd, throat /throw(n)

throdel, throttle

throdul, throttle

throe,*, AMIDST STRONG PAIN/AGONY/EMOTIONAL TURMOIL (or see throw)

throl, thrall

throne,*,ed,ning,eless, SOVEREIGN/AUTHORITATIVE PLACEMENT, A CHAIR (or see thrown)

throng,*, IN A CROWD/MULTITUDE OF PEOPLE/THINGS (or see thong)

thronk, throng

throsd, thrust

throst, thrust

throt, throat /throw(n)

throtal, throttle

throtil, throttle

throttle,*,ed,ling,er, CONTROL OF FLOW THROUGH AN ORIFICE/OPENING/THROAT

throtul, throttle

through, or thru, TO PENETRATE/PASS/MAKE IT TO THE END (or see threw)

throw,wn, TO TOSS, ELIMINATE, GET RID OF (or see throe or throne)

thrown, PAST TENSE OF "THROW" (or see throne)

thrownt, throw(n) /throat

thru, or through, TO PENETRATE/PASS/MAKE IT TO THE END (or see threw)

thruch, thrush

thrusd, thrust

thrush, A BIRD, A CHILDRENS DISEASE

thrust,*,ted,ting,ter, TO PLUNGE/DRIVE/FORCE FORWARD

thruzd, thrust

thud,*,dded,dding, A SOLID/HEAVY/DROPPING/ FALLING SOUND

thug,*, ROBBERS/IMMORAL PEOPLE

thuk, thug
thum, thumb
thumadik, theme(matic)
thumatik, theme(matic)
thumb,*,bed,bing, *OPPOSABLE DIGIT ON THE HAND, USE OF THE THUMB* (or see thump)
thumbt, thumb(ed) /thump(pped)
thump,*,pped,pping, *A FALLING/HEAVY SOUND, SOUND OF HEARTBEAT* (or see thumb)
thumpt, thumb(ed) /thump(pped)
thumselfs, themselves
thunder,*,red,ring,ringly,rer, *THE RUMBLING SOUND IN A RAIN STORM*
thuntur, thunder
thurasik, thoracic
thurd, third
thurdly, third(ly)
thurm, therm
thurmal, thermal
thurmamiter, thermometer
thurmic, therm(ic)
thurmil, thermal
thurmometer, thermometer
thurmomuder, thermometer
thuro, thorough
thurow, thorough
thursd, thirst
Thursday,*, *ENGLISH DAY OF THE WEEK*
thursdy, thirst(y)/ Thursday
thurst, thirst
thursty, thirst(y)/ Thursday
thurt, third
thurtly, third(ly)
Thurzda, Thursday
thus, *WORD TO MEAN "IN EFFECT/THEREFORE, AS A RESULT"*
thusares, thesaurus
thusores, thesaurus

thwart,*,ted,tedly,ting,ter, *TO INTERVENE/WARD OFF/DISTRACT A MISSION/ EVENT/ACTION FROM ACCOMPLISHMENT/ GOAL*
thwort, thwart
thy, thine, thou, *THIRD PERSON PRONOUN MEANING YOU OR YOURS* (or see thigh)
thymas, thymus
thyme, *AN HERBAL PLANT* (or see time)
thymis, thymus
thymus,ses,mi, *A GLAND IN THE BODY*
thyroid,dless, *GLAND/CARTILAGE IN THE THROAT OF A BODY*
thyuzene, thiazine
ti, tie
tiara,*, *SMALL CROWN/CORONET FOR HEAD*
tibaco, tobacco
tibagen, toboggan
tibako, tobacco
tibea, tibia
tiberqulosis, tuberculosis
tibia,al, *SHIN BONE IN LEG*
tibogin, toboggan
tibogon, toboggan
tibse, tip(sy)
tic, *A TWITCHING IN THE BODY/FACE* (or see tick)
tick,*,ked,king,ker, *SMALL BLOOD SUCKING INSECT, RYTHMIC CLOCK SOUND, A MARK ETCHED INTO SOMETHING, MATTRESS/PILLOW COVERING, TELEGRAPH INSTRUMENT* (or see tic)
ticket,*,ted,ting, *PIECE OF PAPER ISSUED WHICH BEARS INFORMATION SOLICITING YOUR PERSONAL APPEARANCE/VISIT*
tickle,*,ed,ling,er,lish,lishly,lishness, *SENSATION TO SKIN/EMOTIONS WHICH GENERATES SMILE/ LAUGHTER/RESPONSE*
tid, tide/ tied/ tight
tida, today
tidal,lly, *CONCERNING THE EBB AND FLOW OF THE SEA/OCEAN* (or see title)

tiday, today
tidbet, tidbit
tidbit,*, *A SNIPPET/SMALL PORTION OF SOMETHING GREATER/LARGER*
tide,*,ed,ding,eful,eless, elessness,elike, *CONCERNING THE RISE/FALL OF OCEAN/SEA/ ECONOMICS* (or see tight/ tied/ tidy)
tided, tidy/ tide(d)/ tied
tidel, tidal /title
tiden, tight(en)
tideness, tidy(diness)
tidil, tidal /title
tidin, tight(en)
tidings, *INFORMATION/KNOWLEDGE SHARING*
tidol, tidal /title
tidon, tight(en)
tidond, tight(ened)
tidul, tidal /title
tidun, tight(en)
tidy,dies,died,dying,dily,diness, *GET/KEEP THINGS ORGANIZED/IN ORDER*
tie,*,ed,tying, *TO HOLD/BUNDLE/TIGHTEN THINGS TOGETHER USING twine/string/rope*
tied, *PAST TENSE OF "TIE"* (or see tight or tide)
tieng, tying
tier,*,red,ring, *TO ELEVATE IN INCREMENTAL STEPS, RISERS, A LAYERED ARRANGEMENT OF ROWS* (or see tear)
tiera, tiara
tif, tiff
tifes, typhus
tiff, small argument
tifis, typhus
tifoed, typhoid
tifoid, typhoid
tifoon, typhoon
tifun, typhoon
tifus, typhus
tigar, tiger

tiger,*,rish, *LARGE WILD FELINE*
tigethur, together
tight,tly,tness,ten,tened,tening, *APPLY PRESSURE/ RESTRAINT/SUPPRESSION*
tights, *SNUG FITTING OUTER WEAR*
tigor, tiger
tigress, *FEMALE WILD FELINE*
tigur, tiger
tikal, tickle
tike,*, *SMALL/YOUNG CHILD* (or see tiki)
tikel, tickle
tiker, tiger /tick(er)
tiket, ticket
tiki, *A CARVED MYTHOLOGICAL FIGURE, OF POLYNESIAN CULTURE*
tikil, tickle
tikir, tiger
tikit, ticket
tikle, tickle
tiklech, tickle(lish)
tiklush, tickle(lish)
tikol, tickle
tikor, tiger
tikot, ticket
tikres, tigress
tikt, tick(ed)
tikul, tickle
tikur, tiger
tikut, ticket
tiky, tiki
til, tile /till
tild, tile(d)/ till(ed)/ tilt
tile,*,ed,ling,er, *FLAT/THIN SLAB OF VARIOUS MATERIAL, TO STACK* (or see till)
tilepathee, telepathy
tileputhee, telepathy
tilerean, telurian

till,*,lled,lling,ller,llage, *PERFORM LABOR, PLACE FOR MONEY IN A BANK, ROTATING SOIL (TOO MANY DEFINITIONS, PLEASE SEE STANDARD DICTIONARY) (or see tile)*
tilt,*,ted,ting,ter, *TO ROTATE OFF-CENTER, LEAN ONE WAY OR ANOTHER* (or see till(ed) or tile(d))
tilurean, telurian
tim, time
timado, tomato
timados, tomato(es)
timato, tomato
timber, *TREES VIEWED AS LUMBER* (or see timbre)
timbrachure, temperature
timbrashure, temperature
timbre, *A TONAL QUALITY* (or see timber)
timbruchure, temperature
timbrushure, temperature
timbur, timber
timd, time(d)
time,*,ed,ming,er,ely,elier,eliest,eliness, *HUMAN CONSTRUCT TO DIFFERENTIATE BETWEEN PLACE/ SPACE, TO QUAGE HOW MUCH SECONDS/MINUTES/ HOURS/DAYS/ MONTHS/YEARS* (or see thyme)
timed, timid /time(d)
timedly, timid(ly)
timet, timid
timid,dly,dity,dness, *HESITANT/CAUTIOUS*
timly, time(ly)
timod, timid
timpal, temple
timparary, temporary
timparize, temporize
timper, temper
timperary, temporary
timperashure, temperature
timperize, temporize
timperushure, temperature
timpeshues, tempest(uous)
timpest, tempest

timpestuous, tempest(uous)
timpil, temple
timplat, template
timplut, template
timpo, tempo
timpol, temple
timporarely, temporary(rily)
timporul, temporal
timprachure, temperature
timpral, temporal
timpramentul, temper(mental)
timprary, temporary
timprashure, temperature
timprature, temperature
timprery, temporary
timpromintal, temper(mental)
timprumental, temper(mental)
timptashen, temptation
timptation, temptation
timptres, tempt(ress)
timpul, temple
timpur, temper
timpura, tempura
timpurarely, temporary(rily)
timpurary, temporary
timpurize, temporize
timpust, tempest
timt, tempt
timtashen, temptation
timtation, temptation
timted, tempt(ed)
timtres, tempt(ress)
timud, timid
timulchuis, tumult(uous)
timulchuous, tumult(uous)
timult, tumult
timur, time(r)
timut, timid

tin,*,nned,nning,nnier,nniest,nny,nnilly,nniness, TYPE OF METAL, USE OF METAL, TINSMITH (or see ten /tine /tint /tiny /tend)
tinable, tenable
tinachus, tenacious
tinacity, tenacity
tinakle, tentacle
tinament, tenement
tinamint, tenement
tinansy, tenant(ncy)
tinant, tenant
tinasedy, tenacity
tinashus, tenacious
tinasity, tenacity
tinatef, tentative
tinatif, tentative
tinatious, tenacious
tinative, tentative
tinchd, tinge(d)
tincity, tense(sity)
tincture,*, HERBS/PLANTS SUBMERGED IN ALCOHOL FOR MEDICINAL USE
tind, tin(nned) / tend
tindatev, tentative
tinded, tend(ed) /tint(ed)
tinden, tendon
tindensy, tendency
tindenus, tendon(dinous)
tinder,ry, USED FOR KINDLING (or see tender)
tinderize, tender(ize)
tinderloin, tenderloin
tinderly, tender(ly)
tindernes, tender(ness)
tindinsy, tendency
tindirloin, tenderloin
tindon, tendon
tindorize, tender(ize)
tindrel, tendril
tindrul, tendril

tindun, tendon
tindur, tender /tinder
tindurize, tender(ize)
tindurloin, tenderloin
tindurly, tender(ly)
tindutif, tentative
tine,*, A POINT ON A TOOL/INSTRUMENT/HORN/FORK (or see tin or tiny)
tinekle, tentacle
tinemint, tenement
tinen, tenon
tinensy, tenant(ncy)
tinent, tenant
tiner, tenor
tines, tennis /tine(s)
tinet, tenet /tenant
tineur, tenure
tinewus, tenuous
tinfold, tenfold
ting, A SOUND (or see tinge)
tinge,*,ed,ging, A HINT/TRACE/SMALL BIT OF CHANGE IN COLOR/QUALITY (or see ting)
tinible, tenable
tinikle, tentacle
tinir, tenor
tinit, tenet /tenant
tinite, tonight
tinj, tinge
tink, ting
tinkal, tinkle
tinkchur, tincture
tinker,*,red,ring,rer, TO TOY/FONDLE/MEND/HANDLE SOMETHING
tinkle,*,ed,ling,ly,er,est, A FAINT LITTLE SOUND
tinkol, tinkle
tinksher, tincture
tinkture, tincture
tinkul, tinkle
tinkur, tinker

tinon, tenon
tinor, tenor
tins, tin(s) /tent(s) /tense /tint(s) /tend
tinse, tense /tent(s)
tinsel,*,lled,lling,lly, SHINY/METALLIC STRIPS FOR DECORATION
tinsil, tinsel
tinsity, tense(sity)
tinsle, tinsel
tinsness, tense(ness)
tinsul, tinsel
tint,*,ted,ting,tless, CHANGE/APPLY SHADE OF COLOR (or see tent /tense /tin(nned) /tend)
tintakle, tentacle
tintative, tentative
tinted, tint(ed)/ tent(ed)/ tend(ed)
tintetive, tentative
tinth, tenth
tintid, tint(ed)/ tent(ed)/ tend(ed)
tintikle, tentacle
tintuckle, tentacle
tintud, tint(ed)/ tent(ed)/ tend(ed)
tintukle, tentacle
tintutive, tentative
tinuble, tenable
tinuis, tenuous
tinukle, tentacle
tinument, tenement
tinunsy, tenant(ncy)
tinunt, tenant
tinur, tenor
tinus, tennis
tinutef, tentative
tinutive, tentative
tiny,nier,niest,nily,niness, LITTLE, VERY SMALL IN SCALE (or see tin(nny))
tinyewr, tenure
tinyewus, tenuous
tinyir, tenure

tinyur, tenure
tinzul, tinsel
tip,*, pped,pping,pper,ppable,pless,psy, *TO LEAN TOP OFF-CENTER OF GRAVITY*
tipakle, typical
tipd, tip(pped) /type(d)
tipe, type /tip
tipekul, typical
tiper, tip(pper) /type(r)
tiphoon, typhoon
tiphune, typhoon
tipikul, typical
tipist, type(pist)
tipo, typo
tipography, topography
tipogrufe, topography
tipse, tip(sy)
tipt, tip(pped) /type(d)
tipufy, typify
tipukle, typical
tipur, tip(pper) /type(r)
tiquila, tequila
tir, tire

tirade,*, *VERBAL/VIOLENT OUTBURST*
tiranchula, tarantula
tirane, terrain /terrane
tiranekul, tyrant(nnical)
tiranikul, tyrant(nnical)
tiranshulu, tarantula
tirant, tyrant
tirantula, tarantula
tirate, tirade
tirazo, terrazzo
tirben, turban /turbine
tirbo, turbo
tirbulens, turbulent(nce)
tirbulent, turbulent
tirbun, turban /turbine
tird, tire(d)

tirdle, turtle
tire,*, ed,ring,eless,elessly,elessness,edly, edness,esome,esomely,esomeness, *TO RUN OUT OF ENERGY, USED ON WHEELS*
tirene, tyranny
tirent, tyrant
tireny, tyranny
tiresdreul, terrestrial
tirf, turf
tirit, turret
tirkoes, turquois
tirkoys, turquois
tirles, tire(less)
tirlis, tire(less)
tirm, term
tirmenashen, terminate(tion)
tirmenate, terminate
tirmenation, terminate(tion)
tirmenator, terminate(tor)
tirmenology, terminology
tirmenul, terminal
tirminate, terminate
tirmination, terminate(tion)
tirminator, terminate(tor)
tirminology, terminology
tirminul, terminal
tirmite, termite
tirmoel, turmoil
tirmonel, terminal
tirmunology, terminology
tirn, tern /turn
tirnament, tournament
tirnep, turnip
tirnument, tournament
tirpentine, turpentine
tirpewlent, turbulent
tirpulent, turbulent
tirpuntine, turpentine
tirrazo, terrazzo

tirse, terse
tirsheary, tertiary
tirsnes, terse(ness)
tirsum, tire(some)
tirtil, turtle
tirtul, turtle
tirunt, tyrant
tirut, turret
tise, tizzy
tishew, tissue
tissue,*, *A SMALL/LIGHTWEIGHT PIECE OF PAPER*
tissue, tissue
tisy, tizzy
tit,*, *NIPPLE ON FEMALE OF SPECIES, TEAT* (or see tied/tight/tights)
tital, title / tidal
titan, tight(en)
titbet, tidbit
titbit, tidbit
tite, tidy /tight /tied
titel, title /tidal
titen, tight(en)
titend, tight(ened)
titenes, tidy(diness)
tithe,*, ed,hing,hable,eless, *A PERCENTAGE TO BE GIVEN AWAY TO SOMEONE/SOMETHING*
titil, title /tidal
titind, tight(ened)
title,*, ed,ling, *A NAME* (or see tidal or tight(ly))
titly, tight(ly)
titond, tight(ened)
titul, title /tidal
titun, tight(en)
titund, tight(ened)
tity, tidy
tiung, tying
tizzy, *A FRENZIED STATE, A DITHER*

to, PREPOSITION IN THE ENGLISH LANGUAGE TO SHOW RELATIONSHIP BETWEEN PERSON/PLACE/THING (or see toe/ too/ tow)

toad,*, AN AMPHIBIAN MOSTLY FOUND IN DRY TERRAIN (or see told or toe(d))

toagrife, topography

toast,*,ted,ting,ter, TO BROWN FOOD WITH A HEAT SOURCE, HONORING SOMETHING/SOMEONE BEFORE HAVING A DRINK

tobacco, PLANT WHOSE LEAVES CONTAIN NICOTINE

tobaco, tobacco
tobagen, toboggan
tobako, tobacco
toberkulosis, tuberculosis
tobogan, toboggan

toboggan,*,ner,nist, TYPE OF SLED

tobogin, toboggan
tod, toad /toe(d) /tow(ed)
toda, today
todal, total
todel, total
todem, totem
todil, total
todim, totem
todler, toddler
todlur, toddler
todom, totem
todul, total
todum, totem
tody, toddy

toe,*, ed,eless,eing, INDEX ON A FOOT (TOO MANY DEFINITIONS, PLEASE SEE STANDARD DICTIONARY) (or see to /tow /toy)

toel, toil

toeld, toil(ed) /told
toelet, toilet
toeng, toe(ing) /toy(ing) /tow(ing)

tofu, A SOYBEAN BASED FOOD

toga,*, A WRAP AS WORN BY ROMANS

togal, toggle
togel, toggle

together,rness, BROUGHT/COLLECTED/ROUNDED UP INTO ONE PLACE

toggle,*, ed,ling, LEVER/SWITCH FOR ALTERING ELECTRICAL CURRENT, A SYSTEM DEVISED TO FACILITATE MOVEMENT

toght, taught /taut /tout
togle, toggle
togu, toggle
togul, toggle
toi, toy
toid, toy(ed)

toil,*, led,ling,ler, TO LABOR/WORK VERY HARD

toild, toil(ed)

toilet,*, A FIXTURE FOR CAPTURING URING/FECES

toka, toga
tokel, toggle
tokela, tequila

token,*, A SMALL DISK/COIN/PAPER RESEMBLING SOMETHING OF VALUE

tokik, toxic
tokil, toggle
tokila, tequila
tokin, token
tokle, toggle
toko, taco
toksakology, toxicology
toksek, toxic
toksen, toxin
toksikology, toxicology
toksukology, toxicology
toksun, toxin
toku, toga

tokul, toggle
tokun, token
tol, tall /toll
tolarense, tolerance
tolarent, tolerant
tolarible, tolerable
tolarinse, tolerance

told, PAST TENSE OF "TELL" (or see toll(ed))

tole, toll
toler, tall(er)

tolerable,eness,bility,ly, BE PATIENT WITH DESPITE THE IRRITATION

tolerance, BE PATIENT WITH DESPITE THE IRRITATION

tolerant,ntly, BE PATIENT WITH DESPITE IRRITATION

tolerashen, tolerate(tion)

tolerate,*, ed,ting,tion,tive,tor, BE PATIENT WITH DESPITE THE IRRITATION

tolerinse, tolerance
tolerint, tolerant
tolir, tall(er)
tolirashen, tolerate(tion)
tolirate, tolerate
tolirense, tolerance
toliruble, tolerable
tolk, talk /talc

toll,*, lled,lling, BELL RINGING, A REQUIRED FEE (or see tall)

tolness, tall(ness)
tolorinse, tolerance
tolur, tall(er)
tolurashen, tolerate(tion)
tolurate, tolerate
toluration, tolerate(tion)
tolurense, tolerance
tolurent, tolerant
toluribe, tolerable
tolurinse, tolerance
tolurint, tolerant
tomado, tomato

tomato,*,oe,oes, *A FRUIT/VEGETABLE*
tomb,*, *STONE ENCLOSURE FOR A LIFELESS BODY*
ton,*,nnage, *2,000 POUNDS* (or see tone or toon)
tonaledy, tone(nality)
tone,*,ed,ning,nal,nality,nally,eless,elessly,eless ness, *SOUND FREQUENCY, MAKE FIRM/STRONG*
tonej, ton(nnage)
tonek, tonic
tong,*, *A TOOL USED FOR GRASPING/PICKING THINGS UP* (or see tongue)
tongue,*,ed,uing, *MOVABLE ORGAN IN THE MOUTH, PART OF A HITCH, POINT ON LAND* (or see tong)
tonic,*,cally, *A MIXTURE, RELATED TO TONE*
tonight, *THE NIGHT OF PRESENT TENSE*
tonij, ton(nnage)
tonik, tonic
tonite, tonight
tonk, tong /tongue
tonles, tone(less)
tons, taunt(s) /ton(s) /tone(s)
tonsalodemy, tonsillotomy
tonsel, tonsil
tonselodemy, tonsillotomy
tonsil,*, *TISSUE HANGING IN THE THROAT*
tonsillotomy, *ACT OF REMOVING THE TONSILS*
tonsilotomy, tonsillotomy
tonsul, tonsil
tonsulodemy, tonsillotomy
tont, taunt
tonul, tone(nal)
too, *PREPOSITION MEANING ALSO/MORE THAN ENOUGH* (or see to /toe /tow /two)
took, *PAST TENSE OF "TAKE", TO TAKE SOMETHING*
tool,*, *A DEVICE DESIGNED TO HELP WITH WORK*
toolip, tulip
toob, tube
tooba, tuba
tooch, tush
toocha, touche'

toom, tomb
toomer, tumor
toomur, tumor
toon,*, *SHORT FOR CARTOON* (or see tune)
toona, tuna
toonek, tunic
toonik, tunic
toonu, tuna
toopa, toupee
toopay, toupee
toosday, Tuesday
toosh, tush
toot,*,ted,ting, *A SOUND FROM A HORN*
tooth,hed,hing,hless,hlessly,hy,hily, hiness,teeth, *ENAMELED BONE PROJECTILES IN THE MOUTH, AN OUTCROP ON GEARS*
tootoo, tutu
top, *PREFIX INDICATING "PLACE" MOST OFTEN MODIFIES THE WORD*
top,*,pped,pping,pper,pless, *THE HEAD/TIP/ UPPERMOST PART OF, SPINNING TOY* (or see taupe /toupe)
topa, toupee
topagrafik, topography(hic)
topagraphical, topography(hical)
topagraphy, topography
topal, topple
topalegy, topology
tope, toupee /taupe
topeary, topiary
topek, topic
topekul, topical
toper, top(pper)
topiary,ries, *THE SCIENCE OF TRIMMING PLANTS*
topic,*, *SUBJECT/TITLE/THEME*
topical,lity,lities, *THE SURFACE/SHALLOW*
topiery, topiary
topigrafik, topography(hic)

topigrafikul, topography(hical)
topigraphic, topography(hic)
topigraphical, topography(hical)
topil, topple
tople, topple
toples, top(pless)
topo, *PREFIX INDICATING "PLACE" MOST OFTEN MODIFIES THE WORD*
topography,hies,hic,hical,hically,her, *A SCIENCE WHICH IDENTIFIES ELEVATIONS/DEPRESSION ON THE EARTH*
topol, topple
topolegy, topology
topoligy, topology
topology,gic,gical,gically,gist, *SCIENCE THAT CAN IDENTIFY ELEVATION/DEPRESSION ON THE EARTH*
topple,*,ed,ling, *OVERTHROWN, COME DOWN, FALL OVER*
topugrafik, topography(hic)
topugrafikul, topography(hical)
topugraphical, topography(hical)
topuk, topic
topukil, topical
topul, topple
tor, tar / tore
torch,hes,hed,hing, *A STAFF/BRANCH WHICH HAS FIRE ON THE END*
torcher, torture
torcherus, torture(rous)
torchirus, torture(rous)
torchur, torture
tord, toward /tour(ed) /tar(rred) /tore
tordis, tortoise
tordus, tortoise
tore, *PAST TENSE OF "TEAR"*
torenshil, torrent(ial)
torenshul, torrent(ial)
torent, torrent
torential, torrent(ial)

tores, torus
torget, target
torgut, target
torifek, terrific
torinshul, torrent(ial)
torint, torrent
toris, torus
tork, torque
torment,*,ted,ting,ter,tor, *TO EXTEND/APPLY CRUELTY/PAIN TO SOMETHING/SOMEONE*
tormint, torment
tornado,*,oes,dic, *A HIGH/SWIRLING WIND WHICH BEGINS IN THE SKY THEN TOUCHES THE GROUND*
tornados, tornado(es)
tornato, tornado
tornesh, tarnish
tornushd, tarnish(ed)
toros, torus
torp, tarp
torpedo,*,oed,oing, *A CONICAL/BULLET-SHAPED MISSILE THAT PROPELS ITSELF THROUGH WATER*
torpedod, torpedo(ed)
torque, *AN EXERTED FORCE, AN ORNAMENT*
torrent,*,tial,tially, *A VIOLENT/SUDDEN GUSH/RUSH OF GREAT VOLUME*
torsh, torch
torshen, torsion
torsher, torture
torshun, torsion
torshur, torture
torsion,nal,nally, *TO TWIST SOMETHING OPPOSINGLY*
torso,*,si, *THE MAIN PORTION/TRUNK OF A BODY*
tort,*,*, *WRONG/IMPROPER* (or see torte or tart)
torte,*,*, *A HEAVILY MADE CAKE* (or see tort or tart)
torteu, tortilla
tortelu, tortilla
tortes, tortoise
torteus, tortuous
tortila, tortilla

tortilla,*,*, *CORN BASED ROUND/FLAT CAKE*
tortilu, tortilla
tortis, tortoise
tortoise, *A TURTLE LIVING ON LAND*
tortuous,uously,uousness, *OF BEING TWISTED/CROOKED/BENT BY NATURE*
torture,*,ed,ring,rable,edly,er,esome,ringly,rouse,sly, *PURPOSEFUL INFLICTION OF PAIN*
tortus, tortoise
torus, *RING SHAPED/BULGE/RIDGE*
tos, toss / toe(s) / two(s) / tow(s)
tosd, toast / toss(ed)
tosday, Tuesday
tosder, toast(er)
tosdur, toast(er)
toss,sses,ssed,ssing, *GENTLY THROW WITH UPWARD MOTION*
tost, toast / toss(ed)
tostur, toast(er)
tot,*,*, *SMALL, YOUNG CHILD* (or see taught /taut/ tout /tote)
total,*,led,ling,lly,lity,lize,lizer, *SUM OF ALL PARTS, COMPLETELY*
tote,*,ed,ting, *TO CARRY* (or see tot/taught/taut/ tout)
totel, total
totem,mic,mism,mist,mistic, *A CARVED/SYMBOLIC REPRESENTATION*
toten, taut(en)
totil, total
totile, total(lly)
totin, totem
totin, taut(en)
totler, toddler
totlur, toddler
totnes, taut(ness)
totom, totem
totule, total(lly)
totum, totem

toty, toddy
touch,hes,hed,hing,hable,hableness,her,hy,hily,hiness, *CONTACT/PRESSURE/EFFECT/SENSATION AFFECTING SOME PART OF THE BODY* (or see touche' /tush)
touche', *FENCING/SPORT EXPRESSION* (or see touch/ tush)
tough,her,hest,hen,hener,hly,hness,hie,hy, *DIFFICULT/CHALLENGING TO PENETRATE/AFFECT/ CONVINCE/ASSUME*
taught, tuft
toul, towel /tool
toun, town
toupee, *FALSE HAIR PIECE* (or see taupe)
tour,*,red,ring,rism,rist,tie,ty, *PERUSE/VISIT/ TRAVEL TO SITES WITHIN A SPECIFIC TIME FRAME*
tournament,*,*, *COMPETITION IN SPORTS*
tousil, tousle
tousle,*,ed,ling, *RUFFLE/MESS UP*
tout,*,ted,ting, *TO SOLICIT FOR VOTES/SALES/ INFORMATION* (or see taut /taught)
tow,*,wed,wing, *TO HAUL/PULL BEHIND* (or see toe /two /too /to /toe(d))
toward,*,dly,dliness, *IN THE DIRECTION OF, EXPRESSING DIRECTION*
towd, tow(ed) /toe(d) /toad
towel,*,led,ling, *CLOTH/MATERIAL FOR USE IN DEALING WITH LIQUID*
tower,*,red,ring, *VERTICAL RISE, STRUCTURE WITH GREAT HEIGHT*
towir, tower
town,*,nie, *A DESIGNATED AREA WHERE PEOPLE COHABITATE/LIVE/CONDUCT BUSINESS*
towsil, tousle
towst, toast
towt, tout /taut /taught
towur, tower
tox, *PREFIX INDICATING "POISON" MOST OFTEN MODIFIES THE WORD*

toxakology, toxicology
toxek, toxic
toxen, toxin
toxi, PREFIX INDICATING "POISON" MOST OFTEN MODIFIES THE WORD
toxic,*,cal,cally,cant,cation,city, POISONOUS
toxico, PREFIX INDICATING "POISON" MOST OFTEN MODIFIES THE WORD
toxicology,gic,gical,gically,cologist,cosis, SCIENCE/STUDY OF POISONS
toxik, toxic
toxikology, toxicology
toxin,*, POISON
toxun, toxin
toy,*,yed,ying, PLAYTHING
toyl, toil
toylet, toilet
tozdur, toast(er)
tozt, toast
tra, PREFIX INDICATING "ACROSS/OVER/BEYOND" MOST OFTEN MODIFIES THE WORD (or see tray)
trac, track /trace
trace,*,ed,cing,er,eable,eableness,eably,eless, PATH/LINE/SCENT/CLUES LEADING TO ORIGINA-TION/BEGINNING POINT (or see tray(s) /track)
trach, trash
trachea,al,ate,eitis, TUBE PLACED IN THE THROAT FOR AIR/FOOD
trachoma,atous, EYELID INFLAMMATION/INFECTION
track,*,ked,king,ker,kable,kless,klessly, klessness, PATH/RAILS TO TRANSPORT/NAVIGATE ALONG (or see tract)
trackshen, traction
tract,*, A STRETCH/AREA OF SPACE/TIME/DISTANCE (or see track(ed))
tractable,tability,tableness,tably,EASILY MANIPU-LATED/FORMED (or see track(able))
tracter, tractor

traction,nal,tive, FIRM GRIP FOR MOMENTUM, METHOD TO RELIEVE STRESS ON THE BODY
tractor,*, EQUIPMENT USED FOR WORK
tractur, tractor
tracuble, trace(able)
tracur, trace(r)
trade,*,ed,ding,er, EXCHANGE ONE THING FOR ANOTHER (or see trait)
traden, trod(dden) /trot(tting)
tradeshenul, tradition(al)
tradeshin, tradition
tradetion, tradition
tradin, trod(dden) /trot(tting)
tradir, trade(r) /traitor
tradishenul, tradition(al)
tradition,*, nal,nally,nalism,nalist,nalistic, PRACTICED REPEATEDLY THROUGHOUT TIME
tradur, trade(r) /traitor
trae, tray
trael, trail
traf, trough
trafek, traffic
trafel, travel
traffic,cked,cking, MANY PEOPLE USING SAME ROADWAY/PATH/AVENUE/METHOD ROUTINELY
trafik, traffic
trafil, travel
trafler, travel(er)
trafuk, traffic
traful, travel
tragedy,dies, A GREAT CATASTROPHIC/DISASTROUS EVENT
tragek, tragic
tragekle, tragic(ally)
tragekt, traject
tragektery, traject(ory)
tragety, tragedy
tragic,cal,cally,calness, A TRAGEDY
tragide, tragedy

tragik, tragic
tragude, tragedy
trail,*,led,ling,ler, A PATH/ROUTE
trailer,*, CONTAINER ON WHEELS WITH HITCH, MOVIE PREVIEW (or see trail(er))
trailor, trawler(er) /trail(er) /trailer
train,*,ned,ning,ner,nable, LOCOMOTIVE/RAILWAY CARS, DISCIPLINE TO FOLLOW DIRECTIONS AS COMMANDED/INSTRUCTED
trainkwol, tranquil
trainqwil, tranquil
trainuble, train(able)
traipse,*,ed,sing, TO WALK AROUND WITHOUT PURPOSE
trait,*, SPECIFIC QUALITIES/FEATURES (or see trade)
traitor,*,rous,rously, ONE WHO BETRAYS ANOTHER
traject,tion,tory,tories, THE CURVE/ARC OF DIRECTION WHEN AIMING/CASTING/SHOOTING
trajectery, traject(ory)
trajek, tragic
trajekle, tragic(ally)
trajekt, traject
trajektery, traject(ory)
trajide, tragedy
trajik, tragic
trajude, tragedy
trak, track /tract
trakd, track(ed) /tract
trakea, trachea
traker, track(er)
trakia, trachea
trakible, track(able) /tract(able)
trakiu, trachea
traklis, track(less)
trakomu, trachoma
trakshen, traction
trakshun, traction
trakt, track(ed) /tract
traktor, tractor

trakuble, track(able) /tract(able)
trakur, track(er)
tral, trawl /troll /trowel
trale, trail /trolley
traler, trawl(er) /trail(er) /trailer
traley, trolley
tralur, trawler(er) /trail(er) /trailer
tram,*,mmed,mming, MECHANICALLY ADJUST, TRANSPORTER ON RAILS, WOVEN SILK TECHNIQUE
tramadik, trauma(tic)
tramatis, trauma(tize)
tramb, tramp
trambalen, trampoline
trambon, trombone
trambulen, trampoline
tramel, trommel
tramendus, tremendous
tramil, trommel
tramindus, tremendous
tramol, trommel
tramp,*, STEP HEAVILY, TRAVEL ON FOOT FROM PLACE TO PLACE FOR SUBSTINENCE WITHOUT A HOME
trampalen, trampoline
trampil, trample
trample,*,ed,ling, STEP/STOMP HEAVILY CAUSING HARM/INJURY
tramplen, trampoline
trampol, trample
trampoline,*,er,nist, MATERIAL STRETCHED ACROSS A FRAME SUPPORTED BY SPRINGS TO JUMP ON
trampul, trample
trampulen, trampoline
tramu, trauma
tramul, trommel
tramutize, trauma(tize)
tran, PREFIX INDICATING "ACROSS/OVER/BEYOND" MOST OFTEN MODIFIES THE WORD (or see train)
trance,*,ed,cing, A SUBCONSCIOUS STATE OF MIND
trancefigurashen, transfigure(ration)

trancefushen, transfuse(sion)
trane, train
traneble, train(able)
tranes, train(s) /tran(s) /trance
trangretion, transgress(ion)
tranible, train(able)
tranir, train(er)
trankwel, tranquil
tranquil,lly,lness,lize,lizes,lizer,lizing,lity, PEACEFUL/CALM/RELAXING
tranqwul, tranquil
trans, trance /train(s) /tran(s)
transacshun, transact(ion)
transact,ted,ting,tion,tional, CARRY OUT/MAKE EXCHANGE IN BUSINESS
transaktion, transact(ion)
transatif, transit(ive)
transbertashen, transport(ation)
transbir, transpire
transbirtashen, transport(ation)
transblant, transplant
transbonder, transponder
transbort, transport
transburtachen, transport(ation)
transcend,*,ded,ding,dent,dence,dency,dently, dental,dentally,dentalism,dentalist, NOT OF THE MATERIAL/PHYSICAL PLANE/FREQUENCY
transcrepshen, transcription
transcribe,*,ed,bing,er, PHYSICALLY/LITERALLY MAKE NOTATION/COPY, AVAILABLE FOR VIEWING
transcripshen, transcription
transcription,*,tional,tive, PHYSICALLY/LITERALLY MAKE NOTATION/COPY, AVAILABLE FOR VIEWING
transdews, transduce
transdewsur, transduce(r)
transduce,*,er, CHANGE ONE TYPE OF FREQUENCY/ ENERGY INTO ANOTHER
transduction,*,nal, CHANGE TYPE OF FREQUENCY/ ENERGY INTO ANOTHER BIOLOGICALLY

transduse, transduce
transduxshin, transduction
transeant, transeint
transechen, transit(ion)
transect,*,ted,ting,tion, DIVIDE/SEVER/CUT ACROSS
transeint, transeint
transekt, transect
transem, transom
transend, transcend
transend, transcend
transendense, transcend(ence)
transendent, transcend(ent)
transendentul, transcend(ental)
transendul, transcend(ental)
transent, transcend
transeshenul, transit(ional)
transestur, transistor
transet, transit
transetif, transit(ive)
transetional, transit(ional)
transetory, transit(ory)
transeunt, transeint
transexshen, transect(ion)
transfeks, transfix
transfer,*,red,ring,ral,rable,ree,rence,rntial,ror, MOVE/SHIFT FROM ONE PLACE TO ANOTHER
transfermashen, transform(ation)
transfeugin, transfuse(sion)
transfews, transfuse
transfex, transfix

transfigure,*,ed,ring,rement,ration, TO CHANGE APPEARANCE OF
transfirens, transfer(ence)
transfirmation, transform(ation)
transfiruble, transfer(able)
transfix,xed,xing,xion, HOLD/FROZEN IN PLACE
transfor, transfer
transform,*,med,ming,mer,mation,mational, mationally,mative,mable, CHANGE FROM ONE TO ANOTHER, AN EVOLUTION

transformur, transform(er)
transfujen, transfuse(sion)
transfurens, transfer(ence)
transfurmashen, transform(ation)
transfuruble, transfer(able)
transfuse,ed,sing,sible,sable,sion,*TRANSMISSION/
    MOVEMENT OF LIQUID/BLOOD*
transgreshen, transgress(ion)
transgresif, transgress(ive)
transgress,sive,sor,sion, *VIOLATING A LAW*
transgretion, transgress(ion)
transichenul, transit(ional)
transient,tly,nce,ncy, *PHYSICALLY TEMPORARY/
    PASSING*
transim, transom
transind, transcend
transindense, transcend(ence)
transindentul, transcend(ental)
transishen, transit(ion)
transistor,*,rize, *ELECTRONIC DEVICE*
transkribe, transcribe
translachen, translate(tion)
translade, translate
transladuble, translate(table)
transladur, translate(tor)
translate,*,ed,ting,tion,tionally,tive,tively,
    tiveness,tivity,tory,torily,toriness, *PASSING
    OVER/THROUGH/ACROSS*
trans'atir, translate(tor)
translatuble, translate(table)
translewsed, translucid
translewsins, translucent(nce)
translewsint, translucent
transloused, translucid
translucent,nce,ncy,ntly, *LIGHT CAN PENETRATE*
translucid, *LIGHT CAN PENETRATE*

translusent, translucent
translusinse, translucent(nce)
translusit, translucid
transmechen, transmission
transmedable, transmit(ttable)
transmedal, transmit(ttal)
transmedur, transmit(tter)
transmesable, transmissible
transmeshen, transmission
transmetuble, transmit(ttable)
transmewt, transmute
transmewtuble, transmute, transmute(table)
transmichen, transmission
transmiduble, transmit(ttable)
transmidul, transmit(ttal)
transmidur, transmit(tter)
transmisability, transmissible(bility)
transmision, transmission
transmissible,bility, *PASSED ALONG, MOVEABLE,
    ABLE TO TRANSMIT*
transmission,*, *GEARS WHICH ENCOURAGE
    MOVEMENT, EFFECTIVE COMMUNICATION*
transmisuble, transmissible
transmit,*,tted,tting,ttable,ttal,ttance,ttancy,
    tter, *PASS FROM ONE TO ANOTHER*
transmitable, transmit(ttable)
transmiter, transmit(tter)
transmition, transmission
transmitle, transmit(ttal)
transmutachen, transmute(tation)
transmute,*,ted,ting,ter,table,tableness,
    tability,tably,tation,tative, *TRANSFORM/
    CHANGE FROM ONE FORM TO ANOTHER*
transmutible, transmute(table)
transmutuble, transmute(table)
transom,*,med, *A BEAM/CROSSBOAR, VENTILATION
    WINDOW*
transparensy, transparent(ncy)

transparent,tly,tness,ncy,ncies, *CLEAR, ALLOWS
    VISUAL PENETRATION*
transparint, transparent
transperinsy, transparent(ncy)
transperint, transparent
transpertashen, transport(ation)
transpire,*,ed,ring,rable,ratory, *SWEAT/PERSPIRE,
    TO HAPPEN, COME ABOUT*
transpirtachen, transport(ation)
transpirtasion, transport(ation)
transplant,*,ted,ting,table,tation,ter, *MOVE/
    TRANSFER FROM ONE LOCATION TO ANOTHER*
transplantuble, transplant(able)
transponder,*, *A RADIO*
transporduble, transport(able)
transport,*,ted,ting,tability,table,ter,tation,
    tional, *CARRY/RELOCATE*
transportashen, transport(ation)
transportuble, transport(able)
transpose,*,ed,sing,sable,sition,sitional, *MOVE*
transpoz, transpose
transpurtachen, transport(ation)
transpuzishen, transpose(sition)
transum, transom
transutif, transit(ive)
transutory, transit(ory)
transverse,ely,sal,sally, *LYING ACROSS THE SAME
    LINE TWICE, CROSSING*
transvurs, transverse
tranuble, train(able)
tranur, train(er)
tranzacktion, transact(ion)
tranzakt, transact
tranzatef, transit(ive)
tranzbirtashen, transport(ation)
tranzblant, transplant
tranzbonder, transponder
tranzbort, transport
tranzbortuble, transport(able)

tranzdukshen, transduction
tranzdusir, transduce(r)
tranzeant, transeint
tranzechen, transit(ion)
tranzekt, transect
tranzendentul, transcend(ental)
tranzeshenul, transit(ional)
tranzeshin, transit(ion)
tranzestur, transistor
tranzet, transit
tranzetory, transit(ory)
tranzfeks, transfix
tranzfermashen, transform(ation)
tranzfeugen, transfuse(sion)
tranzfewshen, transfuse(sion)
tranzfewz, transfuse
tranzfex, transfix
tranzfikyerashen, transfigure(ration)
tranzfir, transfer
tranzfix, transfix
tranzform, transform
tranzformashen, transform(ation)
tranzformur, transform(er)
tranzfujin, transfuse(sion)
tranzfur, transfer
tranzfuruble, transfer(able)
tranzgres, transgress
tranzgreshen, transgress(ion)
tranzgresif, transgress(ive)
tranzichen, transit(ion)
tranzishenul, transit(ional)
tranzit, transit
tranzitional, transit(ional)
tranzitory, transit(ory)
tranzkribe, transcribe
tranzlachen, translate(tion)
tranzlade, translate
tranzladuble, translate(table)
tranzladur, translate(tor)

tranzlate, translate
tranzlater, translate(tor)
tranzlatible, translate(table)
tranzlation, translate(tion)
tranzlewsed, translucid
tranzlewsense, translucent(nce)
tranzlewsint, translucent
tranzlousent, translucent
tranzlousid, translucid
tranzlused, translucid
tranzlusense, translucent(nce)
tranzlusent, translucent
tranzmedable, transmit(table)
tranzmedur, transmit(tter)
tranzmeshin, transmission
tranzmesuble, transmissible
tranzmet, transmit
tranzmetuble, transmit(ttable)
tranzmetur, transmit(tter)
tranzmeut, transmute
tranzmewtashen, transmute(tation)
tranzmichen, transmission
tranzmidul, transmit(ttal)
tranzmidur, transmit(tter)
tranzmishen, transmission
tranzmision, transmission
tranzmisuble, transmissible
tranzmit, transmit
tranzmition, transmission
tranzmitur, transmit(tter)
tranzmutachen, transmute(tation)
tranzmutasion, transmute(tation)
tranzmute, transmute
tranzmutuble, transmute(table)
tranzpazichen, transpose(sition)
tranzperint, transparent
tranzplant, transplant
tranzplantuble, transplant(able)
tranzponder, transponder

tranzporduble, transport(able)
tranzport, transport
tranzportashen, transport(ation)
tranzpoz, transpose
tranzutif, transit(ive)
tranzvurs, transverse
trap,*,pped,pping,pper, *CATCH/HOLD/PREVENT SOMETHING FROM ITS NORMAL MOVEMENT/ACTION MUSICAL INSTRUMENT, DEVICE FOR TRAPPING*
trapazoed, trapezoid
trapekul, tropic(al)
traper, trap(pper)
trapes, trapeze
trapeze,zist, *A TYPE OF SWING*
trapezoid,dal, *A GEOMETRIC SHAPE*
traphek, traffic
trapickul, tropic(al)
trapik, tropic
trapikul, tropic(al)
trapir, trap(pper)
trapizoed, trapezoid
trapse, traipse
trapur, trap(pper)
trapuzoed, trapezoid
tras, tray(s) /trace
trasabul, trace(able)
trase, trace /tray(s)
trash,hes,hed,hing,hily,hiness,hy, *GARBAGE, DISPOSABLE/DISCARDED ITEMS*
trashd, trash(ed)
trashe, trash(y)
trasible, trace(able)
trasuble, trace(able)
trat, trade /trait
trater, trade(r) /traitor
trats, trait(s) /trade(s)
tratur, trade(r) /traitor
trau, trough /trowel
traudishen, tradition

traudition, tradition
trauf, trough
traul, trawl/ troll/ trowel
traule, trolley
trauma,*,tic,tical,tism,tize,tized,tizing, *SUDDEN/ VIOLENT SHOCK TO THE SYSTEM*
trausers, trousers
travail,*, *ENDURE A HARDSHIP*
travel,*,led,ling,ler, *PHYSICALLY MOVE ABOUT/ AWAY (or see travail)*
traverse,*,ed,sing,sable,sal,ser, *TO CROSS/ ACCOMPLISH A BARRIER/BOUNDARY*
travesty,ties,tied,tying, *RIDICULE BY DISTORTING/ DEBASING/MOCKING AN ACTUAL EXPERIENCE*
travil, travel
travirs, traverse
travisty, travesty
travler, travel(er)
travoste, travesty
travul, travel
travusde, travesty
trawl,ler, *BAITED HOOKS IN A LONG LINE/NET FOR CATCHING FISH (or see troll or trowel)*
trawmu, trauma
trawpek, tropic
trawpekul, tropic(al)
trawpik, tropic
trawsers, trousers
trawt, trot /trout
tray,*, *SHALLOW PAN WITH SIDES FOR CARRYING/ HOLDING ITEMS*
traykoma, trachoma
tre, tree /tray
treachery,ries,rous,rously,rousness, *RISKY, OF TREASON/BETRAYAL/TRICKERY*
tread,*,ded,ding,der,trod,trodden, *HEAVY/SLOW WALK, SWIM IN PLACE, TIRE IMPRINT (TOO MANY DEFINITIONS, PLEASE SEE STANDARD DICTIONARY) (or see tree(d))*

tready, treaty
treason,nable,nous,nably, *BEFRIEND THE ENEMY*
treasure,*,ed,ring,rable,er, *SOMETHING WORTHY/ VALUABLE*
treasury,ries, *PLACE WHERE MONEY IS MANAGED*
treat,*,ted,ting,ter, *A TASTY MORSEL TO EAT, TO PAY THE CHARGE/BILL FOR SOMEONE, TAKE FINANCIAL RESPONSIBILITY AS AN ACT OF KINDNESS*
treaty,ties,tise, *WRITTEN SETTLEMENT OF AGREEMENT BETWEEN TWO POWERS/FACTIONS*
treazen, treason
trebel, treble
trebeulashen, tribulation
trebeun, tribune
trebeut, tribute
trebeutery, tributary
trebewlashen, tribulation
trebewn, tribune
trebil, treble
treble,ed,ling, *TREBLE CLEF, MUSICAL PITCH/NOTES, OF TRIPLE/THREE, SYMBOL*
trebul, treble
trebulashen, tribulation
trebun, tribune
trebute, tribute
trebutery, tributary
trechirus, treachery(rous)
trechury, treachery
treck, trek
tred, tread /tree(d)
trede, treaty
tredid, tread(ed) /treat(ed) /trade(d)
tree,*,eed,eeing,eeless,eelessness, *LARGE WOODY PLANT, TO FORCE UP A TREE (or see tread)*
treety, treaty
treezin, treason
trefea, trivia
treger, treasure /trigger
tregery, treasury

tregunometry, trigonometry
tregur, treasure /trigger
trejere, treasury
trejur, treasury
trek,*,kked,kking,kker,kkie, *TO JOURNEY/TRAVEL/ MIGRATE SLOWLY*
trekal, trickle
treked, trek(kked) /trick(ed)
trekil, trickle
trekinoses, trichinosis
trekir, trigger
trekol, trickle
trekoma, trachoma
trekt, trek(kked) /trick(ed)
trekul, trickle
trekur, trigger
trel, trill
trelege, trilogy
treleim, trillium
treleon, trillion
treles, trellis
treleum, trillium
trelion, trillion
trellis,sed, *DECORATIVE LATTICE*
treluge, trilogy
trelus, trellis
trelyen, trillion
trem, trim
tremadik, trauma(tic)
tremar, tremor
trematik, trauma(tic)
trembil, tremble
tremble,*,ed,ling,er,lingly, *TO VIBRATE/SHAKE INVOLUNTARILY*
trembul, tremble
tremd, trim(mmed)
tremendous,sly,sness, *SUBSTANTIAL IN SIZE/ AMOUNT*

tremendus, tremendous
tremer, trim(mmer) /tremor
tremindus, tremendous
tremor,*,rous, INVOLUNTARY VIBRATION/SHAKING, RESULT OF EARTH CRUST MOVEMENT (or see trim(mmer))
trempul, tremble
tremur, trim(mmer) /tremor
trench,hes,hed,hing,her, A DITCH/FURROW DUG INTO A FLAT SURFACE
trend,*,dy, A TEMPORARY MOVEMENT IN DESIGN/ CLOTHING/STYLE
trende, trend(y)
trenidy, trine(nity)
trenity, trine(nity)
trenket, trinket
trenkit, trinket
trensh, trench
trent, trend
trente, trend(y)
trenute, trine(nity)
treo, trio
trep, trip
trepul, triple /treble
tresal, trestle
tresen, treason
treser, treasure
tresere, treasury
treshery, treachery /treasury
treshure, treachery /treasure
treshures, treachery(rous)
tresil, trestle
tresin, treason
tresir, treasure
tresle, trestle
treson, treason
trespas, trespass
trespass,sses,ssed,ssing,sser, TO ENTER ONTO PROPERTY WITHOUT INVITATION/PERMISSION

tresspas, trespass
trestle,*, SUPPORT FRAME/BEAM
tresul, trestle
tresun, treason
tresure, treasure /treasury
tret, treat
trete, treaty
tretid, tread(ed) /treat(ed)
treuth, truth
trevail, travail
trevet, trivet
treveul, trivia(l)
trevia, trivia
trevit, trivet
treviul, trivia(l)
trew, true
trewant, truant
trewbador, troubadour
trewent, truant
trewezm, true(uism)
trewint, truant
trewly, true(uly)
trewp, troop /troupe
trewpur, troop(er)
trews, truce
trewth, truth
trezen, treason
trezer, treason
trezery, treasury
trezpas, trespass
trezun, treason
trezure, treasure /treasury
tri, PREFIX INDICATING "THREE" MOST OFTEN MODIFIES THE WORD (or see try)
tri, tri /try
triad,*,dic,dically, CONSISTING OF THREE PARTS/ ELEMENTS
trial, A MOMENT/PERIOD/PLACE OF CONSIDERATION/ REVIEW/JUDGEMENT

triamverite, triumvirate
triangewlate, triangular(ate)
triangewlur, triangular
triangle,*, THREE SIDED GEOMETRIC SHAPE
triangul, triangle
triangular,rity,rly,ate,ated,ating,ation, TO MAKE INTO THREE SIDES/PARTS/AREAS
triankl, triangle
triankulate, triangular(ate)
triankuler, triangular
triat, triad
trib, tribe
tribe,*,bal,bally,balism,listic, PEOPLE OF A SOCIETY WHO SHARE COMMON BELIEFS/VALUES/MORALS
tribel, tribe(bal)
tribeun, tribune
tribeunul, tribune(nal)
tribeut, tribute
tribeutary, tributary
tribewlashen, tribulation
tribewn, tribune
tribewnul, tribune(nal)
tribewtery, tributary
tribul, tribe(bal)
tribulation,te, TRIAL/STRESS/TROUBLE
tribune,*,nal,eship,nate, THAT WHICH CHAMPIONS PEOPLES RIGHTS, COURT OF LAW, A PLATFORM
tribunel, tribune(nal)
tribunul, tribune(nal)
tributary,ries,rily, FLOWING/STREAMING OF LIQUID/ WATER/RESOURCES/MONEY WHICH FEEDS/MOVES INTO A LARGER BODY
tribute, TO OFFER/SUPPLY GRATITUDE/MONEY
triceps, ARM MUSCLES
trichanosis, trichinosis
trichinosis, DISEASE IN INTESTINES CAUSED BY WORMS
trichunosis, trichinosis

trick,*,ked,king,ker,kery,keries,kish,kishly,ky, kishness, PRANK/HOAX (or see trek)
trickle,*,ed,ling, TINY FLOWING STREAM
trickunosis, trichinosis
tricycle,*,ed,ling, THREE WHEELED BIKE
tricd, tried /trite
trident,*,tate,tal, THREE PRONGED FORK/BARB, BALLISTIC MISSILE SYSTEM
tridint, trident
tried, PAST TENSE OF "TRY", INSIGHTED FOR A CRIME, TESTED (or see trite)
triel, trial
triemverat, triumvirate
triemverint, triumvirate
trieng, try(ing)
trifea, trivia
trifil, trifle
trifle,*,ed,ling,er,lingly,lingness, SMALL /MINIMAL AMOUNT, NOT TAKE SERIOUSLY, IDLE TIME
triful, trifle
trigar, trigger
trigenometry, trigonometry
trigger,*,red,ring,rless, PART OF GUN WHICH RELEASES BULLET
trigonometry, MATH WITH SYMBOLS /DESIGNS
trigur, trigger
trihedras, OF THREE INTERSECTING LINES
trihedril, trihedron(ral)
trihedron,*,ras,ral, THREE INTERSECTING LINES
trihedrul, trihedron(ral)
trik, trick
trikal, trickle
trikanosis, trichinosis
trikel, trickle
trikenoses, trichinosis
trikery, trick(ery)
trikul, trickle
trikure, trick(ery)
triky, trick(y)

tril, trial /trill
trilabit, trilobite
triladerul, trilateral
trilateral,lity,lly, THREE SIDED
trilaturil, trilateral
trilebit, trilobite
trilege, trilogy
trilengwul, trilingual
trileon, trillion
trileum, trillium
trilingual,lly, THREE LANGUAGES
trilingwul, trilingual
trilion, trillion
trilium, trillium
trill, TYPE OF SOUND
trillion, ONE MILLION TIMES ONE MILLION
trillium, A LAWFULLY PROTECTED PLANT
trilobite,*,tic, EXTINCT ARTHROPOD, THREE LOBES
trilogy, THREE PARTS TOGETHER IN A MUSICAL/ LITERARY/FILMED DRAMATIC WORK
trilubit, trilobite
triluge, trilogy
trilyun, trillion
trim,*,mmed,mming,mmer, TO REMOVE EXCESS, CREATE A CLEAN/TIDY/FINISHED APPEARANCE
trimer, trim(mmer) /tremor
trimur, trim(mmer) /tremor
trin, trine
trinch, trench
trind, trend
trine,*,nal,nity, OF THREE PARTS
trinedy, trine(nity)
trinket,*, SMALL KNICK KNACK/ORNAMENT
trinsh, trench
trint, trend
trio,*, THREE PARTS

trip,*,pped,pping,pper,ppingly,pper, JOURNEY AWAY FROM, STUMBLE (TOO MANY DEFINITIONS, PLEASE SEE STANDARD DICTIONARY) (or see tripe)
tripal, triple
tripd, trip(pped)
tripe, COW/SHEEP STOMACH, POOR IN QUALITY
tripel, triple
tripewlashen, tribulation
triple,*,ed,ling,ly,let,licate,lication, THREE OF, THREE TIMES/FOLD
tripod,*, THREE LEGGED
tripol, triple
tripot, tripod
tripul, triple
tripuld, triple(d)
tripulashen, tribulation
trisebs, triceps
trisekel, tricycle
triseps, triceps
trisycle, tricycle
trit, tried /trite
trite,ely,eness, OF LITTLE INTEREST IN (or see tried)
tritle, trite(ly)
tritly, trite(ly)
tritnes, trite(ness)
triul, trial
triumf, triumph
triumfent, triumph(ant)
triumph,*,hal,hally,hant,hantly,her, A GAIN/ VICTORY/SUCCESS
triumphent, triumph(ant)
triumvaret, triumvirate
triumvirate, GROUP OF THREE
triveal, trivia(l)
trivet,*, STAND WITH THREE LEGS
triveu, trivia
triveul, trivia(l)

trivia,al,ality,alities,alization,alize,ally, *INSIGNIFICANT/UNIMPORTANT*
trivit, trivet
trod,*,dden, *PAST TENSE OF "TREAD", WALK HEAVILY/ SLOWLY WITH NO AMBITION (OR SEE TROT)*
troden, trod(dden) /trot(tting)
trodeshinul, tradition(al)
trodin, trod(dden) /trot(tting)
trodishinul, tradition(al)
trodition, tradition
troditional, tradition(al)
troe, troy
trof, trough /trove
trofe, trophy
trofy, trophy
trogectery, traject(ory)
troi, troy
trojektery, traject(ory)
trol, trawl /troll /trowel
trole, trolley /troll
troll,*,ler, *TYPE OF SINGING, DRAGGING A HOOK, IMAGINARY CREATURE (or see trawl)*
troly, trolley
troma, trauma
tromatizd, trauma(tized)
trombone,*,*, *A MUSICAL INSTRUMENT*
tromel, trommel
trommel, *ROUND SCREEN FOR SEPARATING VARIOUS SIZES OF ORGANIC MATERIAL*
tromu, trauma
tromul, trommel
tromutize, trauma(tize)
troobudor, troubadour
troop,*,ped,ping,per, *AN ASSEMBLY/GROUP/FLOCK (or see troupe)*
troos, truce
tropeckul, tropic(al)
tropek, tropic
tropekul, tropic(al)

tropes, trapeze
trophe, trophy
trophy,hies,hic, *MOUNTED HEAD OF ANIMAL, A FIGURINE/COIN DESIGNED FOR AWARD/ ACHIEVEMENT*
tropic,*,cal,cally, *CONTINUOUS WARM WEATHER CLIMATE*
tropickul, tropic(al)
tropik, tropic
tropikul, tropic(al)
trot,*,tted,tting,tter, *TYPE OF WALKING/RUNNING (or see trout or trod)*
trotin, trod(dden) /trot(tting)
troubadour, *POETS OF ANTIQUITY*
trouble,*,ed,ling,er,esome,esomely,esomeness, lous,lously,lousness, *CHALLENGING/DIFFICULT*
trouf, trough
trough,*, *VESSEL FOR ANIMALS TO FEED/DRINK, RECTANGULAR/SHALLOW CHANNEL/SHAPE*
troul, trowel /troll
troupe,*,ped,ping, *THEATER GROUP/PERFORMERS (or see troop)*
trousers, *PANTS*
trout, *TYPE OF FISH*
trouwl, trowel
trove,*, *A FIND /DISCOVERY*
trovers, traverse
trowel,*,led,ling,ler, *HAND TOOL TO WORK PLASTER/ MUD/MORTAR*
trowsers, trousers
trowt, trout
trowzurs, trousers
troy, *MEASUREMENT FOR WEIGHT OF PRECIOUS METALS*
tru, true
truant,tly, *NOT AT SCHOOL WITHOUT GOOD REASON*
trubador, troubadour
trubel, trouble
trubidor, troubadour
trubudor, troubadour

trubul, trouble
truce, *COME TO AGREEMENT AFTER FIGHT/ARGUMENT*
truch, trudge
truck,*,ked,king,ker, *VEHICLE FOR HAULING/MOVING*
trudeshin, tradition
trudeshinul, tradition(al)
trudge,*,ed,ging,er, *WALK SLOWLY WITH HEAVY FEET*
trudishenul, tradition(al)
trudition, tradition
truditional, tradition(al)
true,eness,uism,uly, *ACCURATE/FACTUAL/REAL/ STRAIGHT UP/ON THE LEVEL*
truent, truant
truews, truce
truezm, true(uism)
trufal, truffle
truffle,*,ed, *AN EDIBLE FUNGI, A CANDY*
truful, truffle
trug, trudge
trugekt, traject
trugektery, traject(ory)
truint, truant
truizm, true(uism)
truj, trudge
trujd, trudge(d)
trujectery, traject(ory)
trujekt, traject
trujektery, traject(ory)
truk, truck
truker, truck(er)
trule, true(uly)
trumadik, trauma(tic)
trumendus, tremendous
trumindus, tremendous
trump,*,ped,ping,per,pery, *OVERRANK/SURPASS/ DECEIVE*
trumpd, trump(ed)
trumpet,*,ter, *A HORNED INSTRUMENT, PITCH OF THE SOUND OF A HORN*

trumput, trumpet
truncate,*,,ed,ting,tion, *CUT OFF TIP/END/PART OF, CUT SHORT*
trunck, trunk
trundel, trundle
trundle,er, *CIRCLE/WHEEL FOR ROTATION*
trundul, trundle
trunk,*,, *MAIN BODY/PART FROM WHICH ALL THINGS EXTEND BEYOND, CONTAINER FOR ITEMS, ELEPHANT NOSE*
trunkate, truncate
trupe, troop /troupe
trupel, trouble
truper, troop(er)
trupes, trapeze
trupir, troop(er)
trupl, trouble
trups, troop(s) /troupe(s)
trupul, trouble
trupur, troop(er)
trus, truce /truss
truse, truce
truss,sses,sser, *TO BOLSTER/SECURE/SUPPORT WITH BEAMS/TIES/ROPE*
trust,*,,ted,ting,tee,tful,tfully,tfulness,ty,tiness, *TO PLACE HOPE/FAITH/BELIEF/CONFIDENCE IN*
truste, trust(y)
truth,*,,hless,hful,hfully,hfulness, *ACCEPTED AS FACT/CONSTANCY/ACTUAL*
truvale, travail
truvers, traverse
truwent, truant
truz, truce
try,ries,ried,ying,yingly,yingness,*PUT TO THE TEST, ATTEMPT, DIFFICULT/CHALLENGE TO ACCOMPLISH*
tryd, tried /trite
trydent, trident
tryeng, try(ing)
tryn, trine

tsunami,ic, *GIGANTIC TIDAL WAVE*
tsunome, tsunami
tub,*,,bbable,bber,bby,bbier,bbiest,bbiness, *LARGE VESSEL/CONTAINER FOR LIQUID, ROUND LIKE A TUB (or see tube)*
tuba,*,, *HORNED INSTRUMENT*
tubaco, tobacco
tubagen, toboggan
tubako, tobacco
tube,*,,ed,bing,er,eless,erous,erously,bular, bularly,bularity,bule,bulous,bulously,bulure *CYLINDER/ROUND SHAPE (or see tub)*
tubequlosis, tuberculosis
tuberculosis,ous,ously, *DISEASE OF THE LUNGS*
tuberquelosis, tuberculosis
tubeulur, tube(bular)
tubir, tube(ber)
tubirquelosis, tuberculosis
tubles, tube(less)
tubogin, toboggan
tubu, tuba
tubur, tube(ber)
tuby, tub(bby)
tuch, touch /tush
tucha, touche'
tuche, touch(y) /touche
tuchible, touch(able)
tuck,*,,ked,king,ker,kered, *TO PULL/SECURE EDGES, PLACE AWAY SAFELY, WEARY/TIRED FROM WORKING*
tuda, today
tuder, tutor
tudur, tutor
tuel, tool
Tuesday,*, *DAY OF THE WEEK*
tuf, tough
tufen, tough(en)
tufer, tough(er)
tufest, tough(est)
tuff, tough

tufin, tough(en)
tufir, tough(er)
tufist, tough(est)
tuft,*,,ter,ty,tier,tiest, *CLUMP/CLUSTER/BUNCH OF THREADS/HAIR/MATERIAL/FUR*
tufun, tough(en)
tufur, tough(er)
tug,*,gged,gging,gger, *TO PULL/DRAG/HAUL*
tugethur, together
tugt, tug(gged)
tuil, tool
tuk, tuck/ tug/ took
tukd, tuck(ed) /tug(gged)
tuke, took
tukela, tequila
tukila, tequila
tuksedo, tuxedo
tuksido, tuxedo
tukt, tuck(ed) /tug
tukurd, tuck(ered)
tule, tool
tulep, tulip
tuleputhee, telepathy
tulip,*, *A FLOWER*
tum, tomb
tumato, tomato
tumbel, tumble
tumble,*,ed,ling,er, *BE TOSSED ABOUT, A DRINKING VESSEL, A CAM, LOCKING PART, BOLT ACTION, ACROBATICS*
tumblir, tumble(r)
tumbul, tumble
tumer, tumor
tumerus, tumor(ous)
tumor,*,,rous,rlike, *A CLUMP/MASS OF TISSUE*
tumulchewus, tumult(uous)
tumulchuis, tumult(uous)
tumult,tuary,tuous,tuously,tuousness, *DISTRUBANCE /AGITATED/DISORDER*

tumures, tumor(ous)
tun, tune /toon /ton
tuna,*, *SALT WATER FISH*
tunacity, tenacity
tunaledy, tone(nality)
tunasedy, tenacity
tunasity, tenacity
tundra, *ARCTIC PLAINS AROUND NORTH/SOUTH POLES*
tundru, tundra
tune,*,ed,ning,er,eful,efully,efulness,eless, *SET/ADJUST HARMONY/FREQUENCY (or see toon)*
tuneg, ton(nnage)
tunej, ton(nnage)
tunek, tunic
tunel, tunnel
tungsten,nic, *METAL ELEMENT, TYPE OF FILAMENT IN LIGHT BULBS*
tungstin, tungsten
tunic,*, *LONG GARMENT, A COVERING*
tunig, ton(nnage)
tunij, ton(nnage)
tunil, tunnel
tunir, tune(r)
tunite, tonight
tunl, tunnel
tunnel,*,led,ling,ler, *TUBULAR SHAPED OPENING GOING INTO A SURFACE*
tunor, tune(r)
tuns, tune(s) /ton(s) /toon(s)
tunsten, tungsten
tunstun, tungsten
tunt, tune(d)
tuntru, tundra
tunu, tuna
tunuk, tunic
tunul, tunnel
tunur, tune(r)
tup, tub
tupa, toupee

tupagrufe, topography
tupay, toupee
tupe, tube /tub(bby)
tupht, tuft
tupography, topography
tupogrufe, topography
tupuler, tube(bular)
tuquela, tequila
tuquila, tequila
turain, terrain /terrane
turanchula, tarantula
turane, terrain /terrane
turanshulu, tarantula
turantula, tarantula
turareum, terrarium
turazo, terrazzo
turban,*, *LONG SCARF WRAPPED AS A HEADDRESS (or see turbine)*
turben, turban /turbine
turbeulent, turbulent
turbin, turban /turbine
turbine,*, *MOTOR WITH ROTORS SUPPLIED BY A CONSTANT FLOW (or see turban)*
turbo,*, *POWERED BY/AS IF BY A TURBINE MOTOR*
turbon, turban /turbine
turbulens, turbulent(nce)
turbulent,tly,nce, *ROUGH/IRRATIC/RANDOM FLOW*
turcoys, turquois
turd, tour(ed)
turdul, turtle
ture, tour
turefic, terrific
turenshul, torrent(ial)
turereum, terrarium
turesdreul, terrestrial
turet, turret
turf,*,fy,fier,fiest, *GRASS/ORGANIC MATERIAL FORMING A SURFACE BLANKET*
turifek, terrific

turific, terrific
turist, tour(ist)
turisum, tour(ism)
turit, turret
turkes, turkey(s)
turkey,*, *EDIBLE BIRD*
turkie, turkey
turkois, turquois
turky, turkey
turm, term
turmaric, turmeric
turmenashen, terminate(tion)
turmenate, terminate
turmenator, terminate(tor)
turmenology, terminology
turmenul, terminal
turmeric,*, *SPICE FROM A PLANT*
turmeruk, turmeric
turminashen, terminate(tion)
turminate, terminate
turmination, terminate(tion)
turminator, terminate(tor)
turminolegy, terminology
turminul, terminal
turmite, termite
turmoel, turmoil
turmoil, *STATE OF STRESS/CONFUSION*
turmonel, terminal
turn,*,ned,ning,*CHANGE DIRECTION, ROTATE/CURVE/ BEND IN COURSE (TOO MANY DEFINITIONS, PLEASE SEE STANDARD DICTIONARY)*
turnado, tornado
turnament, tournament
turnato, tornado
turnep, turnip
turniment, tournament
turnip,*, *A VEGETABLE*
turnument, tournament
turpentine, *MINERAL SPIRIT WITH VOLATILE OIL*

turpewlent, turbulent
turpulent, turbulent
turpuntine, turpentine
turquois,*, *BLUE/GREEN GEMSTONE*
turret,*, *CYLINDRICAL OUTCROP AS SEEN ON CASTLES (TOO MANY DEFINITIONS, PLEASE SEE STANDARD DICTIONARY)*
turse, terse
tursheare, tertiary
turshury, tertiary
tursnes, terse(ness)
turtle,*, *REPTILE WITH A SHELL*
turut, turret
tusday, Tuesday
tush,hes, *REAR END, BUTTOCK* (or see touch)
tusha, touche'
tusk,*,ked,ker, *LARGE EXTERIOR TOOTH*
tusled, tousle(d)
tute, toot
tuter, tutor
tuth, tooth
tuthee, tooth(y)
tuthles, tooth(less)
tutir, tutor
tutor,*,red,ring,rage,rship,rial, *TO MENTOR/TEACH OR BE A GUARDIAN OF SOMEONE*
tutur, tutor
tutu,*, *OUTER GARMENT DANCERS WEAR*
tuxedo, *FORMAL ATTIRE FOR MEN*
twain, *RIVERBOAT TERM*
twalth, twelfth
twan, twain
twang,gy, *A VIBRATIONAL TONE*
twank, twang
twead, tweed
tweak,*,ked,king,ky, *TO ADJUST*
tweat, tweet
tweazer, tweezer
twed, tweed

twede, tweed(y)
tweder, tweeter
twedul, twiddle
twedur, tweeter
tweed,*,dy,dier,diest,diness,*TYPE OF WOOL/WEAVE*
tweek, tweak
tweenkul, twinkle
tweet,*, *SOUND OF A BIRD*
tweeter, *TYPE OF SPEAKER FOR SOUND EQUIPMENT*
tweezer,*, *TOOL FOR PLUCKING/PINCHING*
tweg, twig
twek, tweak /twig
tweke, tweak(y)
twelf, twelve
twelfth,*, *ONE OUT OF TWELVE*
twelth, twelfth
twelve,*, *ENGLISH NUMBER AFTER ELEVEN*
twelvth, twelfth
twen, twin
twench, twinge
twende, twenty
twenge, twinge
twenj, twinge
twenkul, twinkle
twenteith, twentieth
twentes, twenty(ties)
twentie, twenty
twentieth, *ONE PART OF TWENTY PARTS*
twenty,ties, *ENGLISH NUMBER AFTER NINETEEN*
twentys, twenty(ties)
twerl, twirl
twerp, *A DEROGATORY SLANG*
tweser, tweezer
twest, twist
twesur, tweezer
twet, tweet
twetur, tweeter
twezer, tweezer
twhirl, twirl

twice, *TWO TIMES*
twidal, twiddle
twiddle,*,ed,ding,er, *TO ROTATE ONE AROUND ANOTHER, IDLY TOY WITH SOMETHING*
twidul, twiddle
twig,*,ggy, *PART OF A WOODY BRANCH*
twik, twig
twilid, twilight
twilight, *SUNSET/SUNRISE*
twilite, twilight
twin,*, *TWO IDENTICAL/SIMILAR* (or see twine)
twinch, twinge
twindy, twenty
twine,*,ed,ning,er, *BRAIDED/TWISTED ROPE OR THREAD* (or see twin)
twinge,*,ed,ging, *SHARP/SUDDEN JERK RELATED TO PAINFUL SCENE/EXPERIENCE*
twinj, twinge
twinkal, twinkle
twinkle,*,ed,ling,er, *SPARKLE/GLEAM OF LIGHT*
twinkul, twinkle
twinteith, twentieth
twintieth, twentieth
twinty, twenty
twirl,*,led,ling,ler, *SPIN/WHIRL AROUND*
twirp,*, *DEROGATORY SLANG*
twis, twice
twist,*,ted,ting,ter, *COILED ROTATION IN ACTION*
two,*, *ENGLISH NUMBER AFTER ONE* (or see too/to)
twoberkeuloses, tuberculosis
twobu, tuba
twobuler, tube(bular)
twocha, touche'
twonik, tunic
twonu, tuna
twopa, toupee
tworl, twirl
twotwo, tutu
twurl, twirl

twurp, twerp /twirp
ty, tie
tydengs, tidings
tyeng, tying
tyfoed, typhoid
tyfus, typhus
tyk, tike
tynkshur, tincture
type,*,ed,ping,er,eable,pist, *USE OF A MACHINE TO CREATE TEXT (TOO MANY DEFINITIONS, PLEASE SEE STANDARD DICTIONARY) (or see tip)*
typecul, typical
typefy, typify
typhis, typhus
typhoid, *DISEASE OF THE INTESTINES*
typhoon,*, *HURRICANE*
typhus,hous, *A DISEASE CAUSED BY FLEAS*
typical,lly,lness,lity, *PREDICTABLE/CHARACTERISTIC*
typicul, typical
typify,fication, *SYMBOLIZES*
typikul, typical
typo,*, *TEXT ERROR*
typukle, typical
tyranekal, tyrant(nnical)
tyranikul, tyrant(nnical)
tyranny,nnies, *OF BEING CRUEL/PREDATORY*
tyrant,*,nny,nnies,nous,nously,nousness,nize, nizer,nic,nical,nically,nicalness,nicide, *CRUEL VICIOUS PREDATOR, ONE WHO EXPLOITS VICTIMS*
tyreny, tyranny

"U"

ubikwety, ubiquity
ubiquity,tous,tary,tously,tousness, *OMNIPRESENT, EXISTS EVERYWHERE*
ubolesh, abolish

ubord, aboard
uborded, abort(ed)
ubort, abort
ubreveat, abbreviate
ubreveashen, abbreviate(tion)
ubriged, abridged
ubrod, abroad
ubserd, absurd
ubsesd, obsess(ed)
ubseshen, obssess(ion)
ubset, upset
ubstane, abstain
ubstrakshen, obstruct(ion) /abstract(ion)
ubstrukt, obstruct
ubtane, obtain
ubzerd, absurd
ubzerve, observe
ubzorb, absorb
ubzurv, observe
udalize, utilize
udapt, adapt
udder,*, *TEATS ON A MILKING ANIMALS* (or see utter)
uder, udder /utter
uderus, uterus
udeshen, edition /add(ition)
udir, udder /utter
udirens, utter(ance)
udirus, uterus
udishen, edition /add(ition)
udopt, adopt
udor, udder /utter /adore
udulize, utilize
udur, udder /utter
ufermutif, affirm(ative)
ufileate, affiliate
ufileashen, affiliate(tion)
ugilede, agile(ty)
ugilety, agile(ty)
ugle, ugly

ugleist, ugly(liest)
ugleur, ugly(lier)
ugly,lies,lier,liest, *UNATTRACTIVE*
ugre, agree
ugresev, aggressive
ugreshen, aggression
ugretion, aggression
ugresuv, aggressive
uhsumpshen, assumption
uhsumshen, assumption
ujiledy, agile(lity)
ujilety, agile(lity)
ukalale, ukulele
ukews, accuse
ukilale, ukulele
ukle, ugly
ukomplesh, accomplish
ukomplis, accomplise
ukount, account
ukresif, aggressive
ukulale, ukulele
ukulayle, ukulele
ukulele,*, *SMALL FOUR STRING GUITAR*
ukustemed, accustom(ed)
ukuz, accuse
ukwire, acquire
ulcer,*,red,rate,rated,rating,ration,rative,rous, rousness, *FESTERED SORES IN THE LINING OF THE STOMACH*
ulceradid, ulcer(ated)
ulcir, ulcer
ulcirashen, ulcer(ation)
ulcur, ulcer
uldamitle, ultimate(ly)
uldimetle, ultimate(ly)
uldrusonek, ultrasonic
uldumetle, ultimate(ly)
ule, you'll /yule
uliens, alliance

ulif, alive
ulike, alike
ulin, align
ulinment, align(ment)
ulions, alliance
uliv, alive
ulowanse, allowance
ulow, allow
ulser, ulcer
ulseradid, ulcer(ated)
ulserashen, ulcer(ation)
ulsirashen, ulcer(ation)
ulsur, ulcer
ulsurashen, ulcer(ation)
ulsurated, ulcer(ated)
ultamatem, ultimatum
ultamet, ultimate
ultametle, ultimate(ly)
ultemit, ultimate
ultereur, ulterior
ulterior,rly, *UNDERLYING, SECRETIVE, NOT UP FRONT (or see alterior)*
ultimate,ely,eness, *THE GREATEST OF ALL*
ultimetly, ultimate(ly)
ultireor, ulterior
ultra, *THE GREATEST/MOST/BEST/EXTREME*
ultrasonic,*, *ABOVE 20,000 VIBRATIONS PER SECOND*
ultru, ultra
ultrusonek, ultrasonic
ultumetle, ultimate(ly)
ultumint, ultimate
ultumit, ultimate
umaunt, amount
umbelikul, umbilical
umbilical,ate,ated,tion, *RELATING TO THE NAVEL*
umeba, amoeba
umend, amend
umindment, amend(ment)
umonea, ammonia

umount, amount

=================
UN......If the word is not listed, remove the first 2 letters -**UN**- then look up the remainder of the word!!
Example: "unfavorable", "**un**" means "not/reversal" then look up the word "**favorable**".
=================

un, *PREFIX INDICATING THAT "NOT/REVERSAL" MOST OFTEN MODIFIES THE WORD (or see prefix "in" or "en")*
unable, *NOT ABLE/CAPABLE(or see enable/inability)*
unabridged, *IN ITS FULL-LENGTH*
unabriged, unabridged
unacorn, unicorn
unacycle, unicycle
unadime, anatomy
unafekachen, unify(fication)
unafi, unify
unafid, unify(fied)
unafiuble, unify(fiable)
unaform, uniform
unaformety, uniform(ity)
unaformly, uniform(ly)
unakorn, unicorn
unapel, unable
unapl, unable
unasen, unison
unasikle, unicycle
unasycle, unicycle
unate, unity
unaterein, unitary(rian)
unatery, unitary
unatize, unite(tize)
unaty, unity
unavers, universe
unaversal, universal

unaversity, university
unaversule, universal(lly)
unavirs, universe
unavirsity, university
unavirsul, universal
unavurs, universe
unavursal, universal
unavursity, university
unbanone, unbeknown
unbanonst, unbeknown(st)
unbeknown,nst, *NOT KNOWN*
unbenon, unbeknown
unbenonst, unbeknown(st)
unbenownst, unbeknown(st)
unbinone, unbeknown
unbinonst, unbeknown(st)
unbunownst, unbeknown(st)
uncal, uncle
uncane, uncanny
uncanily, uncanny(nily)
uncanines, uncanny(niness)
uncanny,nily,nniness, *NOT FORESEEN/ORDINARY*
uncanuly, uncanny(nily)
uncany, uncanny
uncel, uncle
uncil, uncle
uncle,*, *THE BROTHER OF A FATHER/MOTHER*
under, *PREFIX INDICATING THAT "BELOW/INCOMPLETE" MOST OFTEN MODIFIES THE WORD*
underhand,ded,dedly,dedness, *DISHONEST*
undermine,*,ed,ning,er, *REMOVE CREDIBILITY OF SOMEONE, ETCH AWAY AT THE FOUNDATION/ SOMEONE BASE/FOOTING OF SOMETHING/SOMEONE*
underneath, *BELOW/UNDERSIDE/LOWER, NOT VISIBLE*
underneeth, underneath
underneth, underneath
understand,*,ding,dability,dable,dably,dingly, *COMPREHEND/KNOW/PERCEIVE*
understood, *PAST TENSE OF "UNDERSTAND"*

underway, ACTIVELY MOVING ALONG, IN THE PROCESS TOWARDS COMPLETION

underwear, UNDER CLOTHING

undes, undies
undeulate, undulate
undewlashen, undulate(tion)
undewlate, undulate
undewlated, undulate(d)
undewly, unduly

undies, SHORT FOR UNDERWEAR

undirhand, underhand
undirhandedly, underhand(edly)
undirhandid, underhand(ed)
undirmind, undermine(d)
undirmine, undermine
undirneth, underneath
undirstand, understand
undirstood, understood
undirstude, understood
undirwa, underway
undole, unduly
undoly, unduly
undoole, unduly
undulashen, undulate(tion)

undulate,*,ed,ting,tion,tory, WAVE MOTION

unduly, BEYOND MODERATION, UNLAWFUL

undurhand, underhand
undurhandidly, underhand(edly)
undurmind, undermine(d)
undurmine, undermine
undurneth, underneath
undurstand, understand
undurstood, understood
undurstude, understood
undurwa, underway
uneak, unique

unearth,*,hed,hing,hly,hliness, REMOVE FROM THE EARTH/DIRT, SOLVE A MYSTERY, NOT OF THIS PLANE/REALITY

unebriged, unabridged
unecorn, unicorn
unecycle, unicycle
uneek, unique
uneekle, unique(ly)
uneeknes, unique(ness)
unefi, unify
unefid, unify(fied)
unefikashen, unify(fication)
uneform, uniform
uneformedy, uniform(ity)
uneformety, uniform(ity)
uneformly, uniform(ly)
unefy, unify
unegma, enigma / enema
unek, unique
unekle, unique(ly)
uneknes, unique(ness)
unekorn, unicorn
unekwul, inequal
unema, enema /anemia
unemea, anemia /enema
unemek, anemic
uneonize, union(ize)
uneque, unique
unerth, unearth
unerthd, unearth(ed)
unesikul, unicycle
uneson, unison
unesunus, unison(ous)
unesycle, unicycle
unet, unit
unetarean, unitary(rian)
unetary, unitary
unety, unity
uneversal, universal
unevursal, universal

uni, PREFIX INDICATING THAT "ONE/SINGLE" MOST OFTEN MODIFIES THE WORD

==============
UNI......If the word is not listed, remove the first 3 letters -**UNI**- then look up the remainder of the word!!
Example: "unilateral", "**uni**" means "one/single" then look up the word "**lateral**".
==============

unicorn,*, A MYTHOLOGICAL HORSE WITH A HORN COMING FROM IT'S FOREHEAD

unicycle,*, ONE-WHEELED CYCLE (or monocycle)

unifekachen, unify(fication)
unifi, unify
unifid, unify(fied)
unifikashen, unify(fication)

uniform,*,med,mly,mity,mness,mitarian, mitarianism, NEAR EXACT IN SHAPE/FORM/ APPEARANCE/CHARACTER

uniformedy, uniform(ity)
uniformety, uniform(ity)

unify,fies,fied,fier,fying,fiable,fication, ABLE TO BE BROUGHT TOGETHER AS ONE/UNIFIED PART

unifyable, unify(fiable)
unigma, enigma /enema
unikle, unique(ly)
unimea, anemia / enema

union,*,nism,nist,nize,nized,nizing,nization, TO BRING/FORM TOGETHER AS ONE, ALL PARTS COMING TOGETHER WORKING AS ONE

unique,ely,eness, UNMATCHED, ONE OF A KIND

unirth, unearth
unirthd, unearth(ed)
unisen, unison
unisikul, unicycle

unison,nal,nous, ONE IN SOUND

unisycle, unicycle

unit,*,tage, ONE PART/COMPONENT OF THE WHOLE

unitarein, unitary(rian)

unitary,rian,rarianism, CHARACTER WITHIN A UNIT, AS A UNIT
unite,*,ed,ting,table,er,edly,tive,tize,ty, ALL PARTS/SECTIONS/FACTIONS COMING TOGETHER/ FUNCTIONING AS ONE/WHOLE (or see unity)
uniterein, unitary(rian)
unituble, unite(table)
unity, ALL AS ONE, A JOINING (or see unite)
universal,*,lly,lness,lism,list,lity,lities,lize, lization, APPLIES/ACCEPTED/RELATING TO EVERYWHERE/EVERYONE/EVERYTHING
universe,*, OF ONE, ALL TOGETHER
university,ties, A PLACE OF HIGHER EDUCATION
univrs, universe
univursal, universal
univursity, university
univursuly, universal(lly)
unkal, uncle
unkanely, uncanny(nily)
unkanenes, uncanny(niness)
unkany, uncanny
unkel, uncle
unkul, uncle
unles, unless
unless, OR, IN PLACE OF, AN EXCEPTION
unoint, anoint
unovers, universe
unoversity, university
unoy, annoy
unroole, unruly
unruly,lier,liest,liness, NOT OBEDIENT/CONFORMING
unsanitere, insanitary
untel, until
until, TIME BETWEEN NOW AND THE FUTURE/NEXT TIME
unto, SAME AS "UNTIL", SOMETHING ACCOMPLISHED
untwo, unto
unubriged, unabridged
unucorn, unicorn
unufikachen, unify(fication)

unufikashen, unify(fication)
unformady, uniform(ity)
unukorn, unicorn
unurth, unearth
unurthd, unearth(ed)
unusin, unison
unut, unit
unuvers, universe
unuversity, university
unuversule, universal(lly)
unuvirs, universe
unweting, unwitting
unwetingly, unwitting(ly)
unwitting,gly, NOT KNOWING/AWARE
unwrule, unruly
unyen, union
unyon, union
unyunize, union(ize)
up, DIRECTION TOWARDS THE SKY
up, PREFIX INDICATING THAT "MOST RECENTLY/HIGHER" MOST OFTEN MODIFIES THE WORD
upar, upper
upbeat, HIGHER NOTE/FREQUENCY/ATTITUDE
upbet, upbeat
uper, upper
upheave,ed,ving,ver,val, A LIFTING/RISING OF
upheeve, upheave
uphev, upheave
uphevel, upheave(val)
uphevul, upheave(val)
upholestury, upholstery
upholsdure, upholstery
upholstery,ries, FABRICS FOR COVERING
upholsture, upholstery
upir, upper
upland, HIGHER REGION/GROUND
uplend, upland
uplod, applaud
uplos, applause

upon, VERY CLOSE TO, UP ON
upper, THE HIGHER LEVEL
uprasul, appraisal
uprazel, appraisal
upreveate, abbreviate
upright,tly,tness, TO BE VERTICAL, BE IN THE RIGHT
uprite, upright
uproar,rious,riously,riousness, A COMMOTION/ DISTURBANCE, ELEVATED EMOTIONAL STATE
uproch, approach
uproot,*,ted,ting,ter, TO MOVE, TO REMOVE ROOTS FROM THE GROUND
upror, uproar
uprut, uproot
uprutid, uproot(ed)
upserd, absurd
upset,*,tting, A DISTURBANCE/IMBALANCE
upstag, upstage
upstage,*,ed,ging, TO DISTRACT THE AUDIENCE FROM SOMEONE ELSE, BACK OF THE STAGE
upstairs, GO TO UPPER LEVEL BY MEANS OF STAIRS
upstaj, upstage
upstajd, upstage(d)
upstars, upstairs
upsters, upstairs
upsurd, absurd
uptane, obtain
upur, upper
upward,*, MOVE UP
upwerd, upward
upwholstery, upholstery
upwird, upward
upwort, upward
upwright, upright
upwrite, upright
upwror, uproar
upwruted, uproot(ed)
upwurd, upward
uradik, erotic /erratic

uralogy, urology
uran, urine
uraneum, uranium
uranium, *A METAL CHEMICAL*
uranology,gies,gical, *STUDY OF ASTRONOMY/THE HEAVENS*
urater, ureter
uraudik, erotic
urban,nism,nist,nistic,nistically,nite,nity,nities, nize,nization, *LIFE ON THE OUTSKIRSTS OF CITY*
urben, urban
urbenite, urban(ite)
urbon, urban
urbonite, urban(ite)
urchen, urchin
urchin,*, *A SEA CREATURE*
urea,al,eic, *CHEMICAL IN URINE*
ureik, urea(eic)
urek, uric
uren, urine
urenaded, urinate(d)
urenary, urinary
urenate, urinate
urenology, uranology
urenul, urinal
ureter,ral,ric, *CANAL FROM KIDNEY TO BLADDER CONTAINED WITHIN THE BODY*
uretha, urethra
urethane, *A MANMADE CHEMICAL*
urethra,*,al, *TUBE IN THE BODY WHICH FUNNELS URINE FOR DISCHARGE*
urgd, urge(d)
urge,*,ed,ging,er,gingly,ency,ent,ently, *OVER-WHELMING DESIRE TO ACCOMPLISH/FULFILL*
urgint, urge(nt)
urgis, urge(s)
uria, urea
uric, *OF THE URINE*
urik, uric

urin, urine
urinal, *A DEVICE/VESSEL FOR MALE'S TO URINATE INTO*
urinary, *OF THE URINE*
urinate,*,ed,ting,tion, *THE ACT OF RELEASING/ DISCHARGING URINE*
urine, *LIQUID WASTE SECRETION*
urinery, urinary
urinology, uranology
urinul, urinal
uriter, ureter
urithane, urethane
urithra, urethra
urj, urge
urjd, urge(d)
urjent, urge(nt)
urjinse, urge(ncy)
urjint, urge(nt)
urn,*, *A VESSEL USED TO MAKE BUTTER/HOLD CONTENTS (or see earn)*
urodik, erotic
urolegy, urology
urology, *FIELD OF SCIENCE WHICH STUDIES THE URINARY TRACT*
urulogy, urology
uron, urine
uronate, urinate
urunal, urinal
urunate, urinate
urunery, urinary
urunology, uranology
us, *PEOPLE INCLUDING SELF (or see use or yew(s))*
usd, use(d)
use,*,ed,sing,sage,sance,eful,efully,efulness, eless,elessly,elessness,er, *EMPLOY/EXPLOIT/ UTILIZE TO ACCOMPLISH/ACHIEVE SUCCESS, EXPLOITS OTHERS (or see yew(s))*
useful,lly,lness, *ABLE TO BE UTILIZED EASILY*
useless,slly,sness, *NOT ABLE TO BE UTILIZED EASILY*
uselis, useless

user,*, *ONE WHO EXPLOITS OTHERS/RESOURCES, THOSE WHO USE DRUGS*
userp, usurp
userped, usurp(ed)
usert, assert
usertev, assert(ive)
usery, usury
usfekseat, asphyxiate
usfikseat, asphyxiate
usfixeat, asphyxiate
usful, useful
usher,*,red,ring, *TENDS TO GUESTS AT PUBLIC GATHERING, INDUCE/ESCORT/BRING ABOUT*
ushir, usher
ushwaly, usual(lly)
ushwule, usual(lly)
usir, user
usiry, usury
usirtif, assert(ive)
uslis, useless
uslus, useless
usofegus, esophagus
usry, usury
usual,lly,lness, *MOST COMMON/PREDICTABLE*
usumshen, assumption
usumpshen, assumption
usur, user
usurp,*,ped,ping,pation,per, *TO ASSUME POSSESSION OF UNLAWFULLY*
usury,ries,rer,rious,riously,riousness, *CHARGE EXORBITANT/UNLAWFUL AMOUNT OF INTEREST FOR A LOAN*
uteludy, utility
utensil,*, *DEVICE/INSTRUMENT/TOOL FOR WORK/ PURPOSE*
utensul, utensil
uter, utter /udder
uterus,ri, *HOME FOR EMBRYO IN FEMALE MAMMALS*
uther, other

utilatarian, utilitarian
utilety, utility
utilitarian,*,nism, FOCUS ON USEFUL/PRACTICALITY
utility,ties, A USEFUL SERVICE FOR THE COMMON GOOD OF THE PEOPLE
utilize,*,ed,zing,zable,zation,zer, MAKE USE OF
utilude, utility
utiluty, utility
utinsel, utensil
utinsul, utensil
utir, utter /udder
utmost, BEST /HIGHEST IN ORDER OF IMPORTANCE
utopia,an, IDEAL SITUATION
utor, utter /udder
utter,*,red,ring,rance,rable,rer, TO SPEAK (or see udder)
utur, utter /udder
uturd, utter(ed)
uwil, awhile
uzd, use(d)
uzre, usury

"V"

vacabeulery, vocabulary
vacant,ncy,ncies,tly,tness, DWELLING WITH NO ONE CURRENTLY LIVING IN IT, LEFT UNOCCUPIED
vacancy,ncies, UNOCCUPIED DWELLING
vacashend, vacation(ed)
vacashun, vacation
vacate,*,ed,ting, TO LEAVE PERMANENTLY
vacation,*,ned,ning,nless,ner,nist, TO GO AWAY FOR A BRIEF VISIT/EXCURSION WITH THE INTENT OF ENJOYMENT/RELAXATION
vaccen, vaccine
vaccilate, vacilate

vaccinate,*,ned,tion,tor, TO INOCULATE WITH A CHEMICAL/MEDICINE TO AFFECT THE BODY AGAINST DISEASE/INFECTION
vaccine,nal, USED TO STIMULATE THE BODY TO PRODUCE ANTIBODIES, USED TO PROTECT AGAINST A VIRUS
vaccum, vacuum
vacenity, vicinity
vacensy, vacancy
vacent, vacant
vacilate,*,ed,ting,tingly,tion,tor,tory, TO MOVE BACK AND FORTH/TO AND FRO, FLUCTUATE BETWEEN TWO POINTS
vacinate, vaccinate
vacine, vaccine
vacinity, vicinity
vacsinate, vaccinate
vacsination, vaccinate(tion)
vacum, vacuum
vacuole,*,, BIOLOGICAL EXPRESSION
vacuum,*,med,ming, A MACHINE USED TO PULL/SUCK/PICK UP, DEAD/EMPTY SPACE CREATED BY REMOVING PARTICLES
vad, vat
vag, vague
vagabond,*,,dish,dism, ONE WHO ROAMS WITHOUT A PERMANENT HOME AND SUSTENANCE
vagary,ried,rious,riously, WHIMSICAL, UNPREDICTABLE IN MOVEMENT/BEHAVIOR
vage, vague
vagebond, vagabond
vagenul, vagina(l)
vagery, vagary
vagina,*,al, TUBULAR SHAPED CANAL FOUND IN PLANTS/FEMALE BODIES
vaginul, vagina(l)
vagiry, vagary
vagist, vague(st)
vagle, vague(ly)

vagly, vague(ly)
vagobond, vagabond
vagrant,*,tly,ncy,ncies, HOMELESS WHO WANDER/ROAM
vagre, vagary
vagrense, vagrant(ncy)
vagrent, vagrant
vagrunse, vagrant(ncy)
vagry, vagary
vagrybond, vagabond
vague,er, est, ely,eness, HAZY, UNCLEAR
vagury, vagary
vagust, vague(st)
vahement, vahemence(nt)
vahemins, vehemence
vail,*, TO LOWER/REMOVE (or see vale or veil)
vain,nly,ness, TO ATTEMPT WITHOUT HAVING SUCCESS, TO BE SELF ABSORBED WITH ONE'S OWN SHALLOW VALUES (or see vane or vein)
vajenul, vagina(l)
vajina, vagina
vajinul, vagina(l)
vajunal, vagina(l)
vak, vague
vakabeulery, vocabulary
vakabulery, vocabulary
vakachend, vacation(ed)
vakachun, vacation
vakadid, vacate(d)
vakashen, vacation
vakashend, vacation(ed)
vakashun, vacation
vakat, vacate
vakatid, vacate(d)
vakchenashin, vaccinate(tion)
vakchunashen, vaccinate(tion)
vake, vague
vakense, vacant(ncy)
vakent, vacant

valedictorian, *ONE WHO SPEAKS AT A SCHOOL COMMENCEMENT*

valedictory,ries,*SCHOOL FINAL/FAREWELL CEREMONY*

valediktorian, valedictorian
valediktory, valedictory
valedity, valid(ity)
valeint, valiant

valence,CY, *A WAY TO MEASURE THE STRENGTH OF AN ATOM (or see valance)*

valens, valance

valentine,*, *TO HONOR ONE WHOM YOU ARE ATTRACTED TO IN A ROMANTIC WAY*

valer, valor
valerean, valerian
valerian, *AN HERB*
valerus, valor(ous)

valet, *ONE WHO PARKS CARS FOR GUESTS AT AN EVENT/PUBLIC PLACE*

valet, valid
valeubul, value(uable)
valeunt, valiant
valeuntly, valient(ly)
valey, valley
valf, valve

valiant,tly,tness, *OF COURAGE/STRONG/BRAVE*

valid,dly,dness,date,dated,dating,dation,dity, dities, *REAL/FACTUAL/ACTUAL, TO ACKNOWLEDGE AUTHENTICITY*

validectory, valedictory
validete, valid(ity)
validety, valid(ity)
validiction, valediction
validictorian, valedictorian
validiktory, valedictory
valie, valley
valins, valance /valence
valintine, valentine
valir, valor
valirus, valor(ous)

valit, valid
valitel, volatile
valkano, volcano

valley,*, *AREA BETWEEN THE MOUNTAINS AT THE LOWEST POINTS*

valoor, velour /velure /valor

valor,rous,rously,rousness, *QUALITY ATTRIBUTED TO MALE WHO DISPLAYS BRAVERY/FIRM RESOLVE (or see velour/ velure)*

valosedy, velocity
valosety, velocity
valotel, volatile
valu, value
valubel, value(uable)
valubul, value(uable)
valud, valid /value(d)
valudectory, valedictory
valudikshen, valediction
valudiktory, valedictory

value,*, ed,uing,eless,elessness,er,uable, uableness,uably,uate,uator,uation,uational, uationally, *WHAT SOMETHING IS WORTH*

valules, value(less)
valum, volume
valuns, valance
valuntery, voluntary
valuntine, valentine
valur, velour /velure /valor
valut, valid
valutel, volatile

valve,*, eless, *AN APETURE/OPENING TO REGULATE FLOW OF AIR/LIQUID/MOLECULES*

valy, valley
valyant, valiant
valyently, valient(ly)
valyew, value
valyewbul, value(uable)
valyint, valiant
valyu, value

vakently, vacant(ly)
vakeum, vacuum
vakinse, vacant(ncy)
vakint, vacant
vakle, vague(ly)
vakly, vague(ly)
vakoum, vacuum
vakrent, vagrant
vakrint, vagrant
vakseen, vaccine
vaksen, vaccine
vaksenate, vaccinate
vakshenashin, vaccinate(tion)
vaksinate, vaccinate
vaksination, vaccinate(tion)
vaksine, vaccine
vaksunashen, vaccinate(tion)
vakual, vacuole
vakum, vacuum
vakumt, vacuum(ed)
vakunse, vacant(ncy)
vakunt, vacant
vakuol, vacuole
vakyewm, vacuum
vakyewol, vacuole
vakyual, vacuole
vakyum, vacuum
vala, valet
valacity, velocity
valadectory, valedictory
valadiction, valediction
valadiktorean, valedictorian

valance,es,ed, *SHORT CURTAIN (or see valence)*

valans, valance /valence
valantine, valentine

vale, *A VALLEY (or see vail /veil /valley)*

valed, valid /veil(ed)

valediction, *A VALEDICTORY*

valyubil, value(uable)
valyuble, value(uable)
valyum, volume
valyunt, valiant
valyuntle, valiant(ly)
vamb, vamp
vambir, vampire
vamp,*,ped,ping, TO MOVE BITS/PIECES AROUND TO CHANGE FLOW/DIRECTION OF SOMETHING, IMPROVISE
vampire,*,ric,rism, ONE THAT DWELLS IN THE NIGHT AND USES BLOOD FOR SUSTENANCE
van,*,nned,nning, TYPE OF VEHICLE (or see vane/ vain /vein)
vandal,*,lic,lism,listic,lize,lized,lizing, TO BREAK IN AND DESTROY ANOTHERS PROPERTY
vandel, vandal
vandelism, vandal(ism)
vandelize, vandal(ize)
vandiktif, vindictive
vandil, vandal
vandilize, vandal(ize)
vandulism, vandal(ism)
vandulize, vandal(ize)
vane,*,ed,eless, DEVICE MOUNTED TO DISPLAY WIND DIRECTION, FEATHER ON AN ARROW (or see van/vain/vein)
vanech, vanish
vanedy, vanity
vaneer, veneer
vaneer, veneer
vanela, vanilla
vaner, veneer
vanesh, vanish
vaneshd, vanish(ed)
vanesht, vanish(ed)
vanety, vanity
vangard, vanguard
vangart, vanguard
vanguard, THE FEW WHO ARE AHEAD OF THE GROUP

vanich, vanish
vanide, vanity
vanila, vanilla
vanilla, TYPE OF FRUIT/BEAN
vanish,hes,hed,hing,her, TO DISAPPEAR
vanishd, vanish(ed)
vanity,ties, OF BEING VAIN, SELF-ABSORBED WITH SHALLOW VALUES
vankuesh, vanquish
vankwesh, vanquish
vankwish, vanquish
vankwishd, vanquish(ed)
vanquesh, vanquish
vanqueshd, vanquish(ed)
vanquish,hes,hed,hing,hable,her, TO OVERCOME/ SUBDUE/DEFEAT
vanqwesh, vanquish
vanqweshd, vanquish(ed)
vanqwish, vanquish
vantage,*, A SUPERIOR POSITION/LOCATION
vantech, vantage
vantej, vantage
vantich, vantage
vantig, vantage
vantuj, vantage
vanude, vanity
vanush, vanish
vanushd, vanish(ed)
vanute, vanity
vaper, vapor
vaperize, vapor(ize)
vapir, vapor
vapirize, vapor(ize)
vapor,*,rer,rish,rishness,rific,ring,rize,rizable, rization,rizer,rous,rously,rousness,rosity,ry, FUMES/CLOUD EMITTED/GIVEN OFF BY SOMETHING WHEN EXPOSED TO THE AIR
vapur, vapor
vapurize, vapor(ize)

varashis, veracious /voracious
varcity, varsity
vare, vary /very
vareagashen, variegate(tion)
vareashen, variate(tion)
vareation, variate(tion)
vared, vary(ried)
varefication, verify(fication)
varefy, verify
vareins, variant(nce)
vareint, variant
vares, vary(ries)
vareuble, variable
vareuns, variant(nce)
vareunt, variant
vareus, vary(rious)
vari, vary /very
variable,*,bility,eness,ly, THE CHANGE IN VALUE OF SOMETHING, THE GIVENS IN AN EQUATION, RATE OF SPEED/FLOW/FREQUENCY
variant,*,nce, RANGE OF SPEED/FLOW/FREQUENCY
variate,tion,tional,tionally,tive,tively, THE RATE OF CHANGE/FLOW/SPEED/DIRECTION/FREQUENCY
variedy, variety
variegate,*,ed,ting,tion, OF A VARIETY
variety,ties,tal,tally, A RANGE OF CHOICES
varificashen, verify(fication)
varify, verify
varis, vary(ries)
variuble, variable
variugashen, variegate(tion)
variuns, variant(nce)
variuty, variety
varment, A TROUBLESOME ANIMAL
varmint, varment
varmun, varment
varnesh, varnish
varneshd, varnish(ed)

varnish,hes,hed,hing,her,hy, *AN APPLIED TRANSPARENT/CHEMICAL COATING FOR PROTECTION*
varnush, varnish
varsedy, varsity
varsety, varsity
varsity,ties, *MOST ATHLETICALLY FIT ON A SCHOOL SPORTS TEAM*
varsudes, varsity(ties)
varsuty, varsity
varufi, verify
vary,ries,ried,ying,yingly,rier,rious,riously, riousness, *MOVEABLE RANGE/RATE OF CHANGE/ CHOICES/SELECTION (or see very)*
varyd, vary(ried)
varys, vary(ries)
vas, vase
vasalashen, vacilate(tion)
vasalate, vacilate
vasalation, vacilate(tion)
vascular,rity, *FLOW WITHIN A SYSTEM*
vasd, vast
vase,*, *a container*
vasectomy,mies, *SURGICAL PROCEDURE FOR MALES*
vasektumy, vasectomy
vaselashen, vacilate(tion)
vaselate, vacilate
vaselation, vacilate(tion)
vasenedy, vicinity
vasenety, vicinity
vasilashen, vacilate(tion)
vasilate, vacilate
vasilation, vacilate(tion)
vasinedy, vicinity
vasinety, vicinity
vaskeuler, vascular
vaskewler, vascular
vaskuler, vascular
vasnes, vast(ness)

vasqueler, vascular
vasquler, vascular
vast,tly,tness,ty,tier,tiest,titude,tity, *GREAT AMOUNT IN RANGE/DEGREES/FREQUENCY/AREA*
vasul, vessel
vasulashen, vacilate(tion)
vasulate, vacilate
vasulation, vacilate(tion)
vat,*, *A VESSEL FOR LIQUIDS*
vau, vow
vauch, vouch
vaucher, vouch(er)
vaud, vow(ed)
vaudku, vodka
vaul, vowel
vaulatil, volatile
vaulcano, volcano
vaulee, volley
vaulenteer, volunteer
vaulie, volley
vaulinter, volunteer
vaulkano, volcano
vault,*,ted,ting,ter, *A HOLDING/CONTAINER TO PROTECT VALUABLES, ARCHED HEIGHT WITHIN A DWELLING/SPACE/CONTAINER, TO LEAP HIGH (or see volt)*
vaulume, volume
vauluntery, voluntary
vaulutil, volatile
vauly, volley
vaumet, vomit
vaumit, vomit
vaush, vouch
vausher, vouch(er)
vautku, vodka
vauz, vase
vaw, vow
vawch, vouch
vawcher, vouch(er)

vawd, vow(ed)
vawl, vowel
vawle, volley
vea, via
veakul, vehicle
vecenity, vicinity
vechen, vision
vechenary, vision(ary)
veches, vicious
vechualize, visual(ize)
vechulante, vigil(ante)
vechun, vision
vechunary, vision(ary)
vechus, vicious
vecinity, vicinity
vecks, vex
vectomize, victim(ize)
vectumizashen, victim(ization)
vectumize, victim(ize)
vedeo, video
vederan, veteran
vedio, video
vedo, veto
vedod, veto(ed)
vedran, veteran
vedurin, veteran
veer,*,red,ring,ringly, *SWERVE IN MOVEMENT, MOVE TOWARDS PARTICULAR DIRECTION*
vegatashen, vegetate(tion)
vegatate, vegetate
vegatuble, vegetable
vegduble, vegetable
vegel, vigil
vegelante, vigil(ante)
veger, vigor
vegerus, vigor(ous)
vegetable,*, *CATEGORY OF EDIBLE PLANTS*
vegetal, *OF BEING A VEGETABLE*

vegetuble, vegetable
vegetul, vegetal
vegil, vigil
vegilante, vigil(ante)
vegilent, vigil(ant)
veginu, vagina
vegir, vigor
vegirus, vigor(ous)
vegitashen, vegetate(tion)
vegitate, vegetate
vegiterean, vegetarian
vegitel, vegetal
vegituble, vegetable
vegitul, vegetal
vegolante, vigil(ante)
vegorus, vigor(ous)
vegtable, vegetable
vegtuble, vegetable
vegual, visual
vegulante, vigil(ante)
veguol, visual
veguolize, visual(ize)
vegur, vigor
vegurus, vigor(ous)
vegutarean, vegetarian
vegutashen, vegetate(tion)
vegutate, vegetate
vehecle, vehicle
vehekul, vehicle
vehikul, vehicle
veikle, vehicle

veil,*,led,ling, A THIN/TRANSPARENT/REMOVABLE COVER (or see vail or vale)

vein,*,ned,ning,nal,ny,nlet, TUBE/CHANNEL THAT ALLOWS FLOW OF LIQUID (or see vane or vain)

veiwed, view(ed)
vejalante, vigil(ante)
vejalent, vigil(ant)
vejatashen, vegetate(tion)
vejatate, vegetate
vejaterean, vegetarian
vejdible, vegetable
vejduble, vegetable
vejetarean, vegetarian
vejetashen, vegetate(tion)
vejetul, vegetal
vejewelize, visual(ize)
vejinu, vagina
vejitarean, vegetarian
vejitashen, vegetate(tion)
vejitate, vegetate
vejitul, vegetal
vejolent, vigil(ant)
vejituble, vegetable
vejual, visual
vejulante, vigil(ante)
vejulent, vigil(ant)
vejuolize, visual(ize)
vejutarean, vegetarian
vejutashen, vegetate(tion)
vejutate, vegetate
vekabeulery, vocabulary
vekabulery, vocabulary
veker, vigor
vekir, vigor
vekor, vigor
veks, vex
veksashen, vex(ation)

veksation, vex(ation)
vektem, victim
vektemize, victim(ize)
vektumize, victim(ize)
vekur, vigor
vela, villa
velafy, vilify
velage, vill(age)
velanus, villain(ous)
velarean, valerian
velefy, vilify
velege, vill(age)
velej, vill(age)
velenus, villain(ous)
velidety, valid(ity)

velocity, RATE/AMOUNT OF MOVEMENT/SPEED

velon, villain

velour,*, TYPE OF FABRIC/VELVET (or see velure)

velu, villa
veluch, vill(age)
velufy, vilify
velug, vill(age)
veluj, vill(age)
velun, villain
velunus, villain(ous)

velure,*,ed,ring, TYPE OF FABRIC (or see velour)

velutch, vill(age)

velvet,*,ted,ting,teen,ty, THICK/SILKY/SOFT FABRIC

velvity, velvet(y)
velvude, velvet(y)
velvut, velvet
vem, vim
vemens, vehemence
venager, vinegar
venagrey, vinaigrette
venaker, vinegar
venam, venom
venamus, venom(ous)
venasin, venison

vegetarian,*,nism, ONE WHO EATS PRIMARILY VEGETABLES

vegetate,*,ed,ting,tion,tional,tionless,tive, tively,tiveness, TO SIT/AGE/ RIPEN LIKE A VEGETABLE WITHOUT MOVEMENT

vegetuble, vegetable
vegetul, vegetal
vegil, vigil
vegilante, vigil(ante)
vegilent, vigil(ant)
veginu, vagina
vegir, vigor
vegirus, vigor(ous)
vegitashen, vegetate(tion)
vegitate, vegetate
vegiterean, vegetarian
vegitul, vegetal
vegolante, vigil(ante)
vegorus, vigor(ous)
vegtable, vegetable
vegtuble, vegetable
vegual, visual
vegulante, vigil(ante)
veguol, visual
veguolize, visual(ize)
vegur, vigor
vegurus, vigor(ous)
vegutarean, vegetarian
vegutashen, vegetate(tion)
vegutate, vegetate
vehecle, vehicle
vehekul, vehicle

vehemence,cy,nt,ntly, STRONG/FORCEFUL FEELINGS BROUGHT ON BY AN EMOTIONAL STATE/PASSION, STRONG/FORCEFUL EVENT

vehemint, vehemence(nt)

vehicle,*, MOVING/POWERED VESSELS

vehicul, vehicle

vencher, venture
venchurd, venture(d)
vend, *, ded,ding,der,dition, TO SELL (or see vent)
vendacation, vindicate(tion)
vendalashen, ventilate(tion)
vendalate, ventilate
vendalation, ventilate(tion)
vendecate, vindicate
vendecation, vindicate(tion)
vendedu, vendetta
vendekduf, vindictive
vendektif, vindictive
vendetta, *, A STRONG/DEEP GRUDGE/DISPUTE/ DISAGREEMENT
vendicashen, vindicate(tion)
vendicate, vindicate
vendiktif, vindictive
venducation, vindicate(tion)
vendulashen, ventilate(tion)
veneer, *, red,ring,rer,rable,rability,rableness, rably, THIN OVERLAYMENT USED FOR SURFACING
venegrey, vinaigrette
venela, vanilla
venem, venom
venemus, venom(ous)
venerate, *, ed,ting,tor,tion,able,ability,ableness, ably, TO WORSHIP/PUT IN HIGH ESTEEM OVER ONESELF, TO CANONIZE
venew, venue
venge, *, ed,ging,eance,eful,efully,efulness,SEEK AVENGE FOR A WRONG, BE VINDICTIVE/ RELENTLESS IN PURSUIT OF SATISFACTION
vengens, venge(ance)
vengful, venge(ful)
venguns, venge(ance)
veniger, vinegar
venigrey, vinaigrette
venila, vanilla
venim, venom

venimus, venom(ous)
venirate, venerate
venison, TERM FOR THE MEAT OF THE DEER FAMILY
venj, venge
venjens, venge(ance)
venjful, venge(ful)
venjuns, venge(ance)
veno, vino
venom, mous,mously,mousness, POISON
venomus, venom(ous)
venorate, venerate
venosen, venison
vensable, vincible
vensher, venture
vensubul, vincible
vent, *, ted,ting, ALLOWS THE RELEASE OF AIR/STEAM/ HEAT/EMOTIONS (or see vend)
ventage, vintage
ventalashen, ventilate(tion)
ventalate, ventilate
ventalation, ventilate(tion)
ventej, vintage
ventilashen, ventilate(tion)
ventilate, *, ed,ting,tion,tive,tor,tory, ENCOURAGE THE FLOW OF AIR
ventricle, *, cular,culus,culi, TUBES/ARTERIES
ventrikul, ventricle
ventriloquist, tic,sm,uy,ial,ially,ize, TO THROW/ PROJECT THE VOICE WITHOUT MOVING THE LIPS
ventrilukwist, ventriloquist
ventrukle, ventricle
ventuge, vintage
ventuj, vintage
venture, *, ed,ring, GO ON BRAVE/DARING ADVEN- TURE, MOVE TOWARDS UNKNOWN TERRITORY
venu, venue
venue, *, WAYS/PATHS, A LEGAL TERM
venuger, vinegar
venugray, vinaigrette

venuker, vinegar
venumus, venom(ous)
venurate, venerate
venusin, venison
venyou, venue
ver, veer
veracious,sly,sness, TRUTHFUL/UNERRING (or see voracious)
veracity,ties, EAGERNESS/SUPPORT FOR THE TRUTH
verafecation, verify(fication)
verafikashen, verify(fication)
verafy, verify
verashes, voracious /veracious
verasious, voracious /veracious
verasity, veracity
verb, *, AN ENGLISH WORD WHICH DENOTES ACTION
verbadum, verbatim
verbal,lly,lism,list,listic,lize,lized,lizing,lization, lizer, FROM THE MOUTH/VOICE/SPEAK, MAKE THOUGHTS HEARD
verbatim, EXACT WORDS
verbatum, verbatim
verble, verbal /verbal(lly)
verblize, verbal(ize)
verboly, verbal(lly)
verbose,ely,eness,sity, TOO WORDY, USES TOO MANY WORDS TO DESCRIBE/COMMUNICATE
verbosity, verbose(sity)
verbosudy, verbose(sity)
verbule, verbal /verbal(lly)
verbulize, verbal(ize)
verchen, version /virgin
verchew, virtue
verchewul, virtual
verchoo, virtue
verchualedy, virtual(ity)
verchuality, virtual(ity)
verchuol, virtual
verd, veer(ed)

verdabra, vertebra
verdago, vertigo
verdekly, vertical(lly)
verdekt, verdict
verdekul, vertical
verdibra, vertebra
verdict,*, *FINAL DECISION/JUDGEMENT*
verdigo, vertigo
verdikly, vertical(lly)
verdikul, vertical
verdubra, vertebra
verdukil, vertical
vere, very
vereability, variable(lity)
vereashen, variate(tion)
vereate, variate
vereation, variate(tion)
vered, vary(ried)
verefukashen, verify(fication)
verefy, verify
verefikashen, verify(fication)
veres, vary(ries)
vereuble, variable
vereugate, variegate
vereuns, variant(nce)
vereunt, variant
vereus, vary(rious)
verge,*, ed,ging, *EDGE/RIM/PIVOT/PEAK PRIOR TO*
vergen, version /virgin
vergun, version /virgin
veri, very
veriagashen, variegate(tion)
veriagate, variegate
veriant, variant
veriants, variant(nce)
veriate, variate
verient, variant
verietal, variety(tal)
veriety, variety

verifikashen, verify(fication)
verifucation, verify(fication)
verify,*, fies,fied,fying,fication,ficative,ficatory,
fiability,fiable,fiableness,fier, *AUTHENTICATE/
ACKNOWLEDGE/RECOGNIZE FOR TRUTH*
veriibility, variable(lity)
veriuble, variable
veriugate, variegate
veriuns, variant(nce)
verius, vary(rious)
verj, verge
verjen, version / virgin
vermekulite, vermiculite
vermen, vermin
vermiculite, *TYPE OF ROCK*
vermikewlite, vermiculite
vermin,nous,nously, *ANNOYING/PESTY LIVING THING
IN GREAT QUANTITIES*
vermiqulite, vermiculite
vermooth, vermouth
vermouth, *ALCOHOLIC APERITIF*
vermuth, vermouth
vernacular,rly,rism, *WORD USED AS IT ORIGINATED,
NATIVE USE OF WORD*
vernakular, vernacular
verp, verb
verply, verbal(lly)
verpul, verbal
vers, verse /veer(s)
versatile,ely,eness,lity, *ABLE TO CONFORM TO MANY
GIVEN SITUATIONS*
versatilety, versatile(lity)
verse,*, ed,sing,sify,sifies,sified,sifying,sifier,
sification, *ONE PART/STANZA OF A GREATER
PIECE/STORY, TO MAKE VERSE* (or see versus)
versetul, versatile
vershin, version
vershu, virtue
vershuality, virtual(ity)

version,*, *ONE PART/VIEW/PERSPECTIVE OF A
STORY/EVENT*
versis, verse(s) /versus
versital, versatile
versitlety, versatile(lity)
versus, *AGAINST, TWO PERSPECTIVES IN OPPOSITION*
(or see verse(s))
versutil, versatile
versutlety, versatile(lity)
vert, veer(ed)
vertabra, vertebra
vertebra,*, al,ally,ate,ation, *A BONE IN THE SPINE*
vertego, vertigo
vertekul, vertical
vertibra, vertebra
vertical,lity,lness,lly, *OPPOSED TO THE HORIZONTAL,
AN UPRIGHT POSITION*
verticly, vertical(lly)
vertigo,oes, *DIZZY*
vertikul, vertical
vertucly, vertical(lly)
vertue, virtue
vertugo, vertigo
verufecation, verify(fication)
verufikashen, verify(fication)
verufy, verify
verul, virile
very, *MUCH/LOTS, GREAT AMOUNT* (or see vary)
veryus, vary(rious)
vesa, visa
vesabul, visible
vesatashen, visit(ation)
vesater, visit(or)
vesatir, visit(or)
vesatude, vicissitude
vescosedy, viscous(ity)
vescosity, viscous(ity)
vescosudy, viscous(ity)
vesdabule, vestibule

vesdubule, vestibule
vesectomy, vasectomy
vesel, vessel
vesenedy, vicinity
vesenety, vicinity
vesetashen, visit(ation)
veseter, visit(or)
veshen, vision
veshenary, vision(ary)
veshes, vicious
veshuel, visual
veshun, vision
veshunary, vision(ary)
veshus, vicious
vesil, vessel
vesinedy, vicinity
vesinety, vicinity
vesit, visit
vesitashen, visit(ation)
vesiter, visit(or)
vesitude, vicissitude
veskes, viscous
veskosedy, viscous(ity)
veskosity, viscous(ity)
veskus, viscous
vesle, vessel
vessel,*, A CONTAINER
vest,ted,ting, SLEEVELESS OUTER GARMENT, POSSESS POWER/POSITION
vestábule, vestibule
vestibule,*,ed,ling,lar,late, A CHAMBER/CAVITY
vestubule, vestibule
vesu, visa
vesubel, visible
vesubiledy, visibility
vesuble, visible /visible(ly)
vesul, vessel
vesut, visit
vesutashen, visit(ation)

vesuter, visit(or)
vesutude, vicissitude
vet,*, SHORT FOR VETERINARIAN AND VETERAN
vetaren, veteran
veteran,*, ONES WHO SURVIVED A WAR/BATTLE OR GAINED WISDOM THROUGH STUDY/ SERVICE
vetiren, veteran
veto,oes,oed,oing,oer, TO REJECT/FORBID
vetod, veto(ed)
vetos, veto(es)
vetran, veteran
veturen, veteran
veu, via / view
veud, view(ed)
veukle, vehicle
veva, viva
veved, vivid
vevidly, vivid(ly)
vevu, viva
vew, view
vex,xed,xing,xingly,xer,xation,xatious,xatiously, xatiousness,xedly,xedness, TO PLAGUE/ IRRITATE/CAUSE COMMOTION
vexashen, vex(ation)
veyude, view(ed)
vezabel, visible
vezabelity, visibility
vezabiledy, visibility
vezatashen, visit(ation)
vezibiledy, visibility
vezit, visit
vezitashen, visit(ation)
vezubelity, visibility
vezubiledy, visibility
vezutashen, visit(ation)
via, BY WAY/MEANS OF
viable,bility,ly, POSSIBLE/CAPABLE
viabul, viable
viaduct,*, CHANNELS WHICH ALLOW FLOW/TRANSPORT

viaduk, viaduct
vial,*,led,ling, SMALL BOTTLE (or see vile)
vialashen, violate(tion)
vialate, violate
vialation, violate(tion)
vialen, violin
vialens, violent(nce)
vialet, violet
vialin, violin
vialint, violent
vialunt, violent
vibe,*,ed, SHORT FOR VIBRATION, A RYTHMIC SYNCHRONICITY, RESOUNDS WELL TOGETHER
vibrachun, vibrate(tion)
vibraded, vibrate(d)
vibrant,ncy,tly, PULSING WITH ENERGY/LIFE
vibrashen, vibrate(tion)
vibrate,*,ed,ting,tion, PULSATING RYTHM/WAVES
vibratid, vibrate(d)
vibrator,*,ry, MACHINE WHICH PRODUCES PULSES OF WAVES/FREQUENCY
vibrensy, vibrant(ncy)
vibrent, vibrant
vibrently, vibrant(ly)
vibrinsy, vibrant(ncy)
vibrutory, vibrator(y)
vicabulary, vocabulary
vice,*, REPLACING ONE INFERIOR WITH ANOTHER, INSTEAD OF (or see vise)
vicenity, vicinity
vichen, vision
vichenary, vision(ary)
viches, vicious
vichualize, visual(ize)
vichulante, vigil(ante)
vichun, vision
vichunary, vision(ary)
vichus, vicious

vichwal, visual
vichwulize, visual(ize)
vicinity,*,ties, WITHIN THE AREA
vicious,*,sly,sness, HATEFUL DISPOSITION, LASHING OUT WITH DARK/NEGATIVE EMOTION
vicissitude, vicissitude
vicissitude,dinary,dinous, TO MOVE FROM ONE FREQUENCY TO ANOTHER, A MUTATION
victamize, victim(ize)
victem, victim
victim,*,*,mize,mized,mizing,mization,mizer, BE ON THE RECEIVING SIDE OF ILL WILL ,HELPLESS, INABILITY TO GAIN POWER IN A SITUATION
victomizashen, victim(ization)
victomize, victim(ize)
victum, victim
victumizashen, victim(ization)
victumize, victim(ize)
vidal, vital
vidamen, vitamine
videl, vital
videmen, vitamine
video,*,od, A MOVING/VISUAL FILM WITH MANY FRAMES/PICTURES
vidio, video
vidl, vital
vidul, vital
vidumen, vitamine
vidumin, vitamine
vieble, viable
viebul, viable
vieduk, viaduct
vielashen, violate(tion)
vielate, violate
view,*,wed,wing,wer, TO SEE WITH THE EYES
vigalanty, vigil(ante)
vigalent, vigil(ant)
vigel, vigil
vigelent, vigil(ant)

vigeng, viking
viger, vigor
vigerus, vigor(ous)
vigil,la,lance,lant,lantly,lante,lantism, TO WATCH OVER, PAY CAREFUL ATTENTION TO
viging, viking
viginu, vagina
vigir, vigor
vigirus, vigor(ous)
vigolante, vigil(ante)
vigor,*,rous,roso,rously,rousness, OF VITALITY/ STRENGTH
vigorus, vigor(ous)
vigual, visual
vigulante, vigil(ante)
vigulent, vigil(ant)
viguol, visual
vigur, vigor
vigurus, vigor(ous)
vijalante, vigil(ante)
vijalent, vigil(ant)
vijewelize, visual(ize)
vijinu, vagina
vijolent, vigil(ant)
vijual, visual
vijulante, vigil(ante)
vijulent, vigil(ant)
vijwel, visual
vijwul, visual
vijwulize, visual(ize)
vikabeulery, vocabulary
vikabulery, vocabulary
vikeng, viking
viker, vigor
viking,*, SCANDINAVIAN WARRIOR
vikir, vigor
vikor, vigor
viktem, victim
viktemizashen, victim(ization)

viktemize, victim(ize)
viktim, victim
viktumizashen, victim(ization)
viktumize, victim(ize)
vikur, vigor
vila, valet /villa
vilafy, vilify
vilage, vill(age)
vilan, villain
vilanus, villain(ous)
vilarean, valerian
vile,*,ely,eness, DISGUSTING (or see vial /villa / valet)
vilefy, vilify
vilege, vill(age)
vilej, vill(age)
vilen, villain /violin
vilenus, villain(ous)
vilerean, valerian
vilet, valet
vilify,fied,vying,fication,fier, TO DEFACE/SLANDER/ DEGRADE
vilij, vill(age)
vilin, villain /violin
vilinus, villain(ous)
villa,age,ager,agery, A RURAL/COUNTRY TOWN (or see valet)
villain,*,nous,nously,nousness,ny,nies, THE BAD GUY/ANTAGONIST, OF EVIL CHARACTER
villian, villain
vilofi, vilify
vilon, villain
vilosedy, velocity
vilosety, velocity
vilu, villa
viluch, vill(age)
vilufy, vilify
vilug, vill(age)
viluj, vill(age)

vilun, villain
vilunus, villain(ous)
vilure, velour /velure
vilutch, vill(age)
vim, *OF STRENGTH/ENTHUSIASM*
vin, vine
vinager, vinegar
vinagra, vinaigrette
vinagrette, vinaigrette
vinaigrette, *SALAD DRESSING WITH MOSTLY VINEGAR*
vinaker, vinegar
vinal, vinyl
vinamus, venom(ous)
vinasin, venison
vincher, venture
vinchurd, venture(d)
vincible,lity,eness, *CAN BE OVERCOME/CONQUERED*
vind, vend /vent
vindalashen, ventilate(tion)
vindalate, ventilate
vindecate, vindicate
vindedu, vendetta
vindekdef, vindictive
vindektif, vindictive
vindeta, vendetta
vindetta, vendetta
vindicashen, vindicate(tion)
vindicate,*,ed,ting,able,ation,ator,atory, *TO BE LIBERATED BY AVENGING*
vindictef, vindictive
vindictive,ely,eness, *HAS A REVENGE*
vindikduv, vindictive
vindiktif, vindictive
vinducation, vindicate(tion)
vindulashen, ventilate(tion)
vindulate, ventilate
vine,*,ey, *A TRAILING PLANT SUCH AS IVY/GRAPE*
vineer, veneer
vinegar,ry,rish, *RESULT OF FERMENTATION*

vinegre, vinaigrette
vinegrette, vinaigrette
vinel, vinyl
vinemus, venom(ous)
viner, veneer
vinerate, venerate
vinew, venue
ving, venge
vingents, venge(ance)
vingful, venge(ful)
viniger, vinegar
vinigre, vinaigrette
vinigrette, vinaigrette
vinil, vinyl
vinila, vanilla
vinj, venge
vinjents, venge(ance)
vinjful, venge(ful)
vino, *WINE*
vinol, vinyl
vinosen, venison
vinsable, vincible
vinsher, venture
vinsuble, vincible
vint, vint /vend
vintage, *RESULT OF A SUPERIOR CROP SEASON*
vintalashen, ventilate(tion)
vintalate, ventilate
vintalation, ventilate(tion)
vinteg, vintage
vintuj, vintage
vintrecular, ventricle(cular)
vintrelukwist, ventriloquist
vintrikul, ventricle
vintrikuler, ventricle(cular)
vintrilukwist, ventriloquist
vintrukle, ventricle
vintuge, vintage
vintuj, vintage

vintulate, ventilate
vintured, venture(d)
vinu, venue
vinuger, vinegar
vinugrey, vinaigrette
vinuker, vinegar
vinul, vinyl
vinumus, venom(ous)
vinurate, venerate
vinusen, venison
viny, vine(y)
vinyl, *TYPE OF PLASTIC*
vinyou, venue
viola, *STRINGED INSTRUMENT*
violadid, violate(d)
violashen, violate(tion)
violate,*,ed,ting,tive,tor,tion, *TO BASH BOUNDARIES/LAWS SET FORTH BY PEOPLE/NATURE*
violen, violin
violens, violent(nce)
violent,tly,nce, *USE OF AGGRESSIVE FORCE*
violet, *DARK COLOR OF RED/BLUE*
violin,*, *STRINGED INSTRUMENT*
violint, violent
violunt, violent
vipe, vibe
viper,*,rish,rous,rously, *POISONOUS SNAKE*
vipir, viper
viporus, viper(ous)
viprus, viper(ous)
vipur, viper
viracious, voracious /veracious
viral, *OF A VIRUS (or see virile)*
viralent, virulent
viralint, virulent
virashes, voracious /veracious
virasious, voracious /veracious
virasity, veracity
virb, verb

virbadum, verbatim
virbatum, verbatim
virble, verbal
virblize, verbal(ize)
virbly, verbal(lly)
virboly, verbal(lly)
virbos, verbose
virbosity, verbose(sity)
virbosudy, verbose(sity)
virbul, verbal
virbule, verbal(lly)
virbulize, verbal(ize)
virchen, version
virchew, virtue
virchewul, virtual
virchoo, virtue
virchual, virtual
virchualedy, virtual(ity)
virchuality, virtual(ity)
virchuil, virtual
virchuol, virtual
viidabra, vertebra
virdago, vertigo
virdego, vertigo
virdek, verdict
virdekly, vertical(lly)
virdekul, vertical
virdibra, vertebra
virdict, verdict
virdigo, vertigo
virdikly, vertical(lly)
virdikt, verdict
virdikul, vertical
virdubra, vertebra
virdugo, vertigo
virdukil, vertical
virdukly, vertical(lly)
virel, viral /virile
vires, virus

virge, verge
virgen, version / virgin
virgin,*,nal, PRISTINE/NATURAL, HASN'T BEEN EXPLOITED/ALTERED (or see version)
virgun, version / virgin
virile,lity,lism, OF HEALTHY MASCULINE QUALITIES (or see viral)
viris, virus
viriudy, variety
viriuty, variety
virje, verge
virjen, virgin
virjin, version /virgin
virmeculite, vermiculite
virmen, vermin
virmikewlite, vermiculite
virmikulite, vermiculite
virmin, vermin
virmiqulite, vermiculite
virmooth, vermouth
virmuth, vermouth
virnakuler, vernacular
virol, viral /virile
virolent, virulent
viros, virus
virp, verb
virply, verbal(lly)
virpul, verbal
virs, verse
virsatil, versatile
virsatilety, versatile(lily)
virsetal, versatile
virshen, version
virshuality, virtual(ity)
virsutil, versatile
virsutilety, versatile(lily)
virtebra, vertebra
virtego, vertigo
virtekul, vertical

virtibra, vertebra
virtigo, vertigo
virtikul, vertical
virtual,lity,llv, NOT PHYSICAL TO THE TOUCH
virtue,uosity,uosities,uoso,uous,uously, KNOWS OF EXCELLENCE, ONE WITH SUPRA KNOWLEDGE
virtugo, vertigo
virtukle, vertical(lly)
virul, viral / virile
virulent, VERY BITTER/POISONOUS/DANGEROUS
virulint, virulent
virus,ses, LIVING ORGANISM
visa,aed,aing, A PASS/PASSPORT
visabelity, visibility
visabil, visible
visabiledy, visibility
visabilety, visibility
visably, visible(lly)
visatashen, visit(ation)
visater, visit(or)
visatude, vicissitude
viscos, viscous
viscosedy, viscous(ity)
viscosity, viscous(ity)
viscous,sly,sness,osity, TEXTURE/CONSISTENCY OF SYRUP
viscus, viscous
vise,*, ed,sing, A TOOL/PRESS FOR GRIPING/HOLDING ITEMS IN PLACE (or see vice)
visectomy, vasectomy
visekteme, vasectomy
visenedy, vicinity
visenety, vicinity
viser, visor
viset, visit
visetashen, visit(ation)
visetation, visit(ation)
viseter, visit(or)

vocul, vocal
voculize, vocal(ize)
voded, vote(d)
vodef, votive
voder, vote(r)
vodev, votive
vodid, vote(d)
vodif, votive
vodir, vote(r)
vodiv, votive
vodka, *ALCOHOLIC SPIRITS*
vodur, vote(r)
voed, void
voeg, voyage
voej, voyage
voes, voice
voezd, voice(d)
vog, vogue
vogue, *IN FASHION*
voice,*,ed,cing,eful,efulness,eless,elessly, elessness, *SOUND COMING FROM THE MOUTH*
void,*,ded,ding,dable,der,dness, dance, *ONE VAST NOTHING MATERIALLY YET ALL THINGS POTENTIALLY, RETURN TO NOTHING/NULL*
voig, voyage
voij, voyage
vois, voice
voist, voice(d)
vok, vogue
vokabeulery, vocabulary
vokabulery, vocabulary
vokalize, vocal(ize)
vokashen, vocation
vokashenul, vocation(al)
vokation, vocation
vokationul, vocation(al)
vokel, vocal
vokelize, vocal(ize)
vokil, vocal

vokilize, vocal
vokul, vocal
vokulize, vocal(ize)
volanteer, volunteer
volanterd, volunteer(ed)
volatel, volatile
volatile,eness,lity,lize,lization, *ABLE TO CHANGE SUDDENLY IN COMPOSITION, EXPLOSIVE*
volcano,*,nic,cally,nism,nicity,nist,nize,nized, nizing, *MOUNTAIN ERUPTION FROM ITS CORE*
volcher, vulture
vold, vault /volt
vole, volley
volee, volley
volenter, volunteer
volenterd, volunteer(ed)
volentery, voluntary
voleum, volume
voli, volley
volinter, volunteer
volisity, velocity
volitel, volatile
volkano, volcano
volley,*,yed,ying,yer, *TO GO BACK AND FORTH, DISCHARGE OF MANY THINGS AT ONCE*
volly, volley
volnerable, vulnerable
volnirable, vulnerable
volosedy, velocity
volshur, vulture
volt,*, *ELECTRICAL MEASUREMENT OF POWER* (or see vault)
voltaec, voltaic
voltaic,*, *TYPE OF ELECTRICAL ACTION*
voltauk, voltaic
voltshur, vulture

volume,*,ed,ming,minous,minously,minosity, minousness, *LEVEL OF SOUND/FREQUENCY, MANY THINGS BROUGHT TOGETHER, FORM OF MEASUREMENT*
voluntary,rism,rist,ristic,ries,rily,riness,ryism, *TO FREELY OFFER SERVICE WITHOUT EXPECTING PAY/ MONEY/EXCHANGE*
volunteer,*,red,ring, *TO FREELY OFFER SERVICE WITHOUT EXPECTING PAY/MONEY/EXCHANGE*
volunter, volunteer
volunterd, volunteer(ed)
voluntery, voluntary
volutel, volatile
volutil, volatile
volva,ate, *FUNGI MEMBRANE* (or see vulva)
voly, volley
volyewm, volume
vomet, vomit
vomit,*,ted,ting,ter,tous,tory,tories,turition,tus, tuses, *THE ENERGETIC DISCHARGE OF CONTENTS OF THE STOMACH THROUGH THE MOUTH*
vomut, vomit
voner, veneer
voodoo, *FICTITIOUS PRACTICE OF SORCERY*
voracious,sly,sness, *DEVOUR WITH EXTREME ENTHUSIASM/GREED*
vorashus, voracious / veracious
vorasity, veracity
vorteks, vortex
vortesis, vortex(es)
vortex,xes,tices,tical,tically,ticose, *A SWIRLING/ SPIRAL MOVEMENT*
vortisus, vortex(es)
vos, vase
vosektumy, vasectomy
vot, vote
vote,*,ed,ting,er,eless, *TO MAKE A CHOICE/ DECISION BETWEEN TWO OR MORE THINGS*
votef, votive

voteve, votive
votid, vote(d)
votif, votive
votive, DEDICATED WITH A VOW
votka, vodka
votku, vodka
votuve, votive
vouch,hes,hed,hing,her,hee, TO CONFIRM/ATTEST/ UPHOLD LEGITIMACY/VALIDITY OF SOMEONE/SOMETHING
vouchd, vouch(ed)
voug, voyage
vouj, voyage
voul, vowel
vow,*,*,wed, TAKE AN OATH, TO SWEAR TO UPHOLD
vowch, vouch
vowchur, vouch(er)
vowel,*, ONE OF SIX LETTERS OF THE ENGLISH ALPHABET WITH CERTAIN CHARACTERISTICS
vowl, vowel
voyage,*,ed,ging,er, A JOURNEY/TRIP BY SEA
voyd, void
voyg, voyage
voyj, voyage
voyst, voice(d)
voz, vase
vucabeulery, vocabulary
vucinity, vicinity
vud, view(ed)
vudu, voodoo
vue, view
vugina, vagina
vuhemint, vahemence(nt)
vujina, vagina
vukabulery, vocabulary
vula, valet
vularean, valerian
vulchur, vulture

vuledity, valid(ity)
vulerean, valerian
vulerian, valerian
vulet, valet
vulfa, vulva /volva
vulgar,rly,rness,rian,rism,rity,rities,rize,rization, rizer, OFF COLOR IN BEHAVIOR/LANGUAGE, RUDE/ OFFENSIVE IN MANNERISM
vulgaredy, vulgar(ity)
vulger, vulgar
vulgeredy, vulgar(ity)
vulgurly, vulgar(ly)
vulidete, valid(ity)
vulnerable,bility,eness,bly, NOT WELL PROTECTED
vulnuruble, vulnerable
vulosedy, velocity
vulosety, velocity
vulsher, vulture
vulture,*, A LARGE SCAVENGER BIRD
vulur, velour /velure
vulva, EXTERNAL FEMALE GENITALIA (or see volva)
vuneer, veneer
vunela, vanilla
vuner, veneer
vunila, vanilla
vuracious, voracious /veracious
vurashes, voracious /veracious
vurasity, veracity
vurb, verb
vurbadum, verbatim
vurbatum, verbatim
vurbelize, verbal(ize)
vurblize, verbal(ize)
vurbose, verbose
vurbuliz, verbal(ize)
vurchen, version /virgin
vurchew, virtue
vurchewul, virtual
vurchoo, virtue

vurchual, virtual
vurchuol, virtual
vurdabra, vertebra
vurdago, vertigo
vurdekly, vertical(lly)
vurdekt, verdict
vurdekul, vertical
vurdibra, vertebra
vurdigo, vertigo
vurdikly, vertical(lly)
vurdikt, verdict
vurdikul, vertical
vurdubra, vertebra
vurdukil, vertical
vurge, verge
vurgen, version /virgin
vurgun, version /virgin
vuriedy, variety
vurietal, variety(tal)
vuriety, variety
vurje, verge
vurjen, version /virgin
vurjun, version /virgin
vurmeculite, vermiculite
vurmikulite, vermiculite
vurmouth, vermouth
vurmuth, vermouth
vurnaculer, vernacular
vurnakuler, vernacular
vurp, verb
vurple, verbal /verbal(lly)
vurs, verse
vursatilety, versatile(lity)
vursitelity, versatile(lity)
vurtabra, vertebra
vurtego, vertigo
vurtekul, vertical
vurtibra, vertebra
vurtigo, vertigo

vurtikul, vertical
vurtue, virtue
vurtugo, vertigo
vusectemy, vasectomy
vusekteme, vasectomy
vusenedy, vicinity
vusinity, vicinity
vyle, vial /vile

"W"

wa, way /weigh /whey
wabel, wobble
wabul, wobble
wach, wage /wash /watch
wacher, washer /wage(r)
waches, wage(s) /watch(es)
wachir, washer /wage(r)
wachis, wage(s) /watch(es)
wachus, wage(s) /wash(es)
wack, wake /whack /wok
wacks, wax /whack(s)
wacky,kily,kiness, SILLY, ERRATIC, CRAZY
wackyness, wacky(kiness)
wad,*,dded,dding, CRUMPLE/CRINKLE/ROLL SOME-
    THING UP INTO A BALL SHAPE (or see wade/
    what /watt /wait /weight)
waddle,*,ed,ling,er,ly, MOVE BACK AND FORTH IN
    MOVEMENT SUCH AS A PENGUIN WALKING
wade,*,ed,ding,er, TO WALK/NAVIGATE THROUGH
    SHALLOW WATER/LIQUID/RESISTANT MATERIAL (or
    see wait /wad /weight)
wadel, waddle /what'll
wader, wader /water /waiter
waderproof, waterproof
waderpruf, waterproof

waders, LONG RUBBER BOOTS FOR FEET TO PROTECT
    AGAINST DEEP WATER (or see waiters)
wadertite, watertight
wadid, wad(dded) /wait(ed) /wede(d)
wadil, waddle /what'll
wadir, wader /water /waiter
wadirproof, waterproof
wadirpruf, waterproof
wadirs, waders /waiter(s) /water(s)
wadirtite, watertight
wadle, waddle /what'll
wadol, waddle /what'll
wador, wader /water /waiter
wadres, waitress
wadrus, waitress
wadud, wad(dded) /wait(ed) /wade(d)
wadul, waddle /what'll
wadur, wader /water /waiter
wadurd, water(ed)
wadurfol, waterfall
wadurproof, waterproof
wadurpruf, waterproof
wadurs, waders /waiter(s) /water(s)
wae, way /weigh /whey
wael, whale /wail /wale
waen, wain /wane
waest, waist /waste
waet, wait /weight
waf, wave
wafd, waft /raft /wave(d) /waive(d)
wafe, wave /wave(vy)
wafel, waffle
wafer,*, THIN SLICE OF SOMETHING (or see waiver)
waffle,*,ed, BATTER COOKED IN A WAFFLE MAKER
wafil, waffle
wafir, wafer /waiver
wafle, waffle
waflis, wave(less)
wafor, wafer /waiver

waft,*,tage,ter, SMALL PENNANT SHAPED FLAG, BE
    CARRIED ALONG ,FLOAT (or see raft/wave(d)/
    waive(d))
waful, waffle
wafur, wafer /waiver
wag,*,gged,gging,gger,ggle,ggles,ggled,ggling,
    ggly,ggingly, QUICKLY MOVE BACK AND FORTH
    SUCH AS A DOGS TAIL (or see wage)
wagd, wag(gged) /wage(d)
wage,*,ed,ging,eless,er,erer, MONEY EARNED BY
    WORKING,MAKE A BET, CREATE CONFLICT/WAR (or
    see wag)
wagen, wagon
wagil, waggle
wagin, wagon
wagir, wage(r)
wagle, waggle /waggle(ly)
wagly, waggle(ly)
wagon,*,ner, VESSEL WITH A BOX SHAPE BASE AND
    FOUR WHEELS FOR CARRYING THINGS
wagul, waggle
wagun, wake(n) /wagon
wagur, wage(r)
wail,*,led,ling,ler,lingly,lful,lfully, VERY HEAVY/
    LOUD/PAINFUL CRY (or see wale or whale)
wain, type of wagon (or see wane)
wainscot,ted,ting, WOOD/SUBSTANCE ONLY
    COVERING LOWER HALF OF A WALL
wainskot, wainscot
waist, THE MIDDLE SECTION/MIDRIFF OF A BODY
    BETWEEN RIBCAGE AND HIPS (or see waste)
wait,*,ted,ting,ter, TO PAUSE/STOP MOMENTUM
    TEMPORARILY, TO SERVICE ANOTHER'S NEEDS (or
    see wade or weight)
waiter,*, ONE WHO SERVES PATRONS FOOD AT A
    RESTAURANT/CAFE/DINER (or see waders)
waitress,ses, FEMALES WHO SERVE PATRONS FOOD AT
    A RESTAURANT/CAFE/DINER

waive,*,ed,ving, TO RELINQUISH/LET GO OF YOUR
  RIGHTS TO SOMETHING (or see wave or wife)
waiver,*, A TEMPORARY PASS, TO GIVE UP RIGHTS
wajd, wage(d)
wajer, wage(r)
wajur, wage(r)
wak, walk /whack /wake /wok
wake,*,ed,en,woke,eful,efully,efulness,eless, BE
  AWARE OF PHYSICAL REALITY AFTER BEING ASLEEP,
  WAVE CAUSED BY MOVEMENT, RITUAL PERFORMED
  FOR DECEASED (or see whack /wok /wacky)
waken, wake(n) /wagon
wakenes, wacky(kiness)
wakin, wake(n) /wagon
wakon, wake(n) /wagon
waks, wax /whack(s) /wake(s)
wakse, wax(y)
wakser, wax(er)
waksy, wax(y)
wakun, wake(n) /wagon
waky, wacky
wakynes, wacky(kiness)
wal, wall /wail /whale
wald, wail(ed) /wale(d) /wall(ed)
wale,*,ed,ling, A WELT CAUSED BY A WHIPPING,
  SUPPORT FOR OUTSIDE PLANKING OF A BOAT (or
  see wail /whale /wall)
walep, wallop
walet, wallet
walip, wallop
walit, wallet
walk,*,ked,king,ker, MOVING/TRAVELING ON FOOT
walker,*, A DEVICE TO HELP PEOPLE WALK (or see
  walk(er))
walkor, walk(er) /walker
wall,*,lled, VERTICAL SECTION OF A DWELLING/
  STRUCTURE (or see wail or wale)
wallet,*, HOLDER FOR MONEY AND I.D.
wallit, wallet

wallop,*,ped,ping,per, THRASH/STRIKE A BLOW TO
wallow,*,wed,wing,wer, LIKE A PIG SQUIRMING IN
  THE MUD, TO LIE/BE DEEP INTO SOMETHING
wallut, wallet
walnut,*, A NUT
walo, wallow
walod, wallow(ed)
walop, wallop
waloped, wallop(ed)
walow, wallow
walowed, wallow(ed)
walres, walrus
walrus,ses, A CARNIVOROUS/MARINE MAMMAL
wals, whale /wall(s) /wale /wail
walts, waltz
waltsd, waltz(ed)
waltz,zes,zed,zing,zer, DANCE TO 3/4 TIME MUSIC
walup, wallop
waluped, wallop(ed)
walupt, wallop(ed)
walut, wallet
walz, waltz
walzed, waltz(ed)
wamp, whomp
wan,*, WASHED OUT/WEAK IN COLOR/ENERGY/MOTION
  (or see wain /wane /won /one)
wand,*, A SLENDER STICK USED FOR MANY PURPOSES
  (or see want or won't)
wander,*,red,ring,ringly,rer, TO MOVE/TRAVEL
  AIMLESSLY ABOUT (or see wonder)
wandurer, wander(er)
wane,*,ed,ning,eY, ON THE DOWNSIDE OF A
  PEAK/WAVE, TO DIMINISH (or see wan or wain)
wanscoat, wainscot
wanskot, wainscot
want,*,ted,ting,ter, TO DESIRE FOR SOMETHING (or
  see won't or wand)
wanten, wanton

wanton,nly,nness, WANTS FOR NOTHING, FREE/
  UNBOUND/UNRESTRAINED
wantun, wanton
wantunes, wanton(nness)
wantunle, wanton(ly)
wapen, weapon
wapun, weapon
war,*,rred,rring,rless, DISPLAY OF HOSTILITY/
  OPPOSITION BETWEEN FORCES (or see wore/
  wear /where /ware /we're /weir)
warale, weary(rily)
warant, warrant
warante, warrant(y)
waras, whereas
warbil, warble
warble,*,ed,ling, TYPE OF VIBRATION/SOUND, A
  TUMOR/SWELLING
warbler,*, A BIRD
warbul, warble
ward,*,ded,ding,der, TERRITORY/AREA, FEND OFF,
  DEFEND AGAINST (or see wart /war(rred)/
  where'd)
warden,*, A PAID OVERSEER IN A PRISON SYSTEM
wardon, warden
wardrobe,*, COLLECTION OF CLOTHING, PLACE
  WHERE CLOTHING IS KEPT
wardun, warden
ware,*, BE WATCHFUL OF, SPECIAL ITEMS OF USE/
  VALUE (or see war /wear /where /weary)
warefur, wherever
wareir, warrior
warele, weary(rily)
waren, warren
warent, warrant
warente, warrant(y)
warenty, warrant(y)
wareur, warrior
warevur, wherever
warf, wharf

warier, warrior
warily, weary(rily)
warin, warren
warint, warrant
warinte, warrant(y)
warinted, warrant(ed)
warinty, warrant(y)
warl, where'll
warm,*,med,ming,mer,mest,mth,mly,mish, mness, TEMPERATURE BETWEEN HOT/COLD, BECOME COMFORTABLE WITH (or see worm)
warmist, warm(est)
warn,*,ned,ning,ner,ningly, TO CAUTION SOMEONE AGAINST HARM/PUNISHMENT (or see worn)
warp,*,ped,ping, TO BECOME TWISTED/BENT/ BOWED IN SHAPE
warrant,*,ted,ting,ty,ties,ter, A GUARANTEE/ AUTHORIZATION/CONTRACT
warren,*,, ENCLOSURE FOR BREEDING GAME
warrior,*,, BRAVE/PUTS UP A FIGHT IN WARFARE
warrun, warren
warsh, wash
warshd, wash(ed)
wart,*,ted,ty, A BUMPY SKIN GROWTH
wartrobe, wardrobe
warule, weary(rily)
warun, warren
warunt, warrant
warunte, warrant(y)
warunted, warrant(ed)
warunty, warrant(y)
warwithal, wherewithal
wary,rier,riest,rily,riness, BE CAUTIOUS/CAREFUL OF (or see weary)
was, PAST TENSE OF "IS" (or see weigh(s)/way(s))
wasd, waist /waste
wash,hes,hed,hing,her,hable,hy, TO CLEANSE WITH WATER/LIQUID
washe, wash(y)

washeble, wash(able)
washepl, wash(able)
washer, AN APPLIANCE TO WASH CLOTHES, SOMEONE WHO WASHES
washible, wash(able)
washipl, wash(able)
washir, washer
washt, wash(ed)
washuble, wash(able)
washur, washer
wasn't, CONTRACTION OF THE WORDS "WAS NOT", PAST TENSE OF "IS NOT"
wasp,*, A STINGING/FLYING INSECT
waste,*,ed,ting,er,tage,eness,tingly, MORE THAN NECESSARY, LEFTOVERS, REMAINS OF SOMETHING (or see waist)
wastid, waste(d)
wat, wait /weight /what /watt /wade /wad
watch,hes,hed,hing,hful,hgully,hfulness, TO BE MONITORED/OBSERVED/FOLLOWED/LOOKED AFTER, A DEVICE WORN ON THE WRIST
wated, wade(d) /wait(ed) /wad(dded)
watel, waddle /what'll
water,*,red,ring,ry,rless,rish, CLEAR/NATURAL SOLUTION THAT CONFORMS TO ICE/LIQUID/GAS
watercress, AN EDIBLE PLANT
waterd, water(ed)
waterfall, A DOWNFLOWING OF WATER
waterfaul, waterfall
waterfol, waterfall
waterkres, watercress
waterproof,fed,fing,fer, WATER CANNOT PENETRATE
waterpruf, waterproof
waters, waders /waiter(s) /water(s)
watertight,tness, SEALS AGAINST WATER ENTERING
watertite, watertight
watever, whatever
watevur, whatever

watid, wade(d) /wait(ed) /wad(dded)
watil, waddle /what'll
watir, wader /water /waiter
watird, water(ed)
watirfal, waterfall
watirfol, waterfall
watirkres, watercress
watirproof, waterproof
watirpruf, waterproof
watirs, waders /waiter(s) /water(s)
watle, waddle /what'll
wator, wader /water /waiter
watres, waitress
watrus, waitress
watt,*,ttage, MEASURE OF ELECTRIC POWER (or see what or wad)
watud, wade(d) /wait(ed) /wad(dded)
watul, waddle /what'll
watur, wader /wate /waiter
waturcres, watercress
waturfal, waterfall
waturfol, waterfall
waturproof, waterproof
waturpruf, waterproof
waturs, waders /waiter(s) /water(s)
waubel, wobble
waubil, wobble
wauch, watch
wauchful, watch(ful)
wauded, wade(d)/wait(ed)/wad(dded)
waudel, waddle /what'll
wauder, water
waudertight, watertight
waudid, wade(d)/wait(ed)/wad(dded)
waudil, waddle /what'll
waudul, waddle /what'll
waufel, waffle
wauful, waffle
wauk, wok /walk

waul, whale /wail /wale /wail
waulep, wallop
waulet, wallet
waulk, walk
waulker, walk(er) /walker
waulkur, walk(er) /walker
waulnut, walnut
waulo, wallow
waulop, wallop
waulow, wallow
waults, waltz
waulup, wallop
waulut, wallet
waun, won /one
waund, wound
waunder, wander /wonder
waunt, want
wauper, whopper
waupur, whopper
waurl, where'll
waurp, warp
waut, watt /what /wad
wautercres, watercress
wautertite, watertight
wavd, wave(d) / waive(d)
wave,*,ed,ving,eless,vy,vily,viness, SERPENTINE
    ACTION WHICH DISPLAYS UP/DOWN/BACK/FORTH
    MOVEMENTS
wavenes, wave(viness)
waver, TO FLUCTUATE UP/DOWN/BACK/FORTH (or see
    waiver or wafer)
wavir, waiver /wafer
wavles, wave(less)
wavur, waiver /wafer
wavynes, wave(viness)
wax,xes,xed,xing,xer,xen,xy,xiness, INCREASE
    IN INTENSITY/SIZE/STRENGTH, MATTER PRODUCED
    BY BEE/PETROLEUM (or see whack(s)/wake(s))
waxin, wax(en)

waxse, wax(y)
way,*,yless, THE METHOD/FASHION/STYLE/DIRECTION
    (or see weigh or whey)
wayv, wave
waz, way(s) /weigh(s) /was
wazp, wasp
we, MORE THAN ONE WITH SELF INCLUDED (or see
    wee /whee /whey)
weak,*,ker,kest,ken,kened,kening,kish,kishly,
    kishness,kener,kling,kly,kliness,kness,
    LACKING IN SKILL/STRENGTH/KNOWLEDGE (or
    see week)
weald,*, PRISTINE/UNCULTIVATED FIELD IN AMIDST A
    FOREST (or see wield or wheel(ed))
wealth,hy,hier,hiest,hily,hiness, AN OVER-
    ABUNDANCE, MORE THAN ONE NEEDS
wean,*,ned,ning,ner,nling, TO SLOWLY REDUCE
    NEED FOR NOURISHMENT FROM THE MOTHER/
    PRIMARY FOOD SOURCE (or see ween)
weane, weeny
weapan, weapon
weape, weep(y)
weaped, weep(ed) /wept /reap(ed)
weapen, weapon
weapon,*,nry,nless, A TOOL/INSTRUMENT FOR
    PROTECTION OR TO USE TO HURT/KILL
weapun, weapon
weapy, weep(y)
wear,*,ring,wore,worn,rable,rer, USE SOMETHING
    UNTIL IT DOESN'T LOOK NEW,COVERING,CLOTHING
    (or see ware /where /we're /weir)
weard, weird
weary,rier,riest,ried,rying,rily,riness,riful,rifully,
    rifulness,riless,risome,risomely,risomeness,
    TIRED/EXHAUSTED/FATIGUED (or see wary)
weasel,*, led,ling, CARNIVOROUS/SLINKY/RODENT/
    MAMMAL

weather,*,red,ring,rability,rly,rliness, ELEMENTS/
    ATMOSPHERE AROUND THE EARTH (or see
    whether/ wether)
weathur, weather /whether /wether /wither
weave,*,ed,ving,er, CRISS-CROSS PERPENDICULAR
    FIBERS ONE INTO/THROUGH/ACROSS THE OTHER
    (or see we've)
web,*,bbed,bbing,bby, INTERCONNECTING STRANDS
    CRISSCROSSING ONE ANOTHER, A NET, STRETCHED
    SKIN ON DUCK FEET (or see wept)
webd, web(bbed) /wept /weep(ed)
webt, web(bbed) /wept /weep(ed)
wech, which /witch /wedge
wechd, wedge(d)
wecht, wedge(d)
we'd, CONTRACTION OF THE WORDS "WE WOULD/HAD"
    (or see wed /weed /wheat /whet)
wed,*,dded,dding, GET MARRIED (or see wet/
    we'd /weed /whet /wheat)
weded, wed(dded)/weed(ed)/wet(tted)
wedeir, weed(er) /wet(tter)
wedel, whittle
weder, weed(er) /wet(tter)
wedge,*,ed,ging,gy,gier,giest,gie, A TRIANGULAR
    SHAPE, METHOD FOR RAISING/LEVELING
wedible, wet(able)
wedid, wed(dded) /weed(ed) /wet(tted)
wediest, weed(iest)
wedil, wheedle /whittle
wedir, weed(er) /wet(tter)
wedle, wheedle /whittle
wedlock, MARRIAGE
wedlok, wedlock
Wednesday, DAY OF THE WEEK
wedo, widow
wedol, wheedle /whittle
width, width
wedud, wed(dded) /weed(ed) /wet(tted)
wedul, wheedle /whittle

wedur, weed(er) /wet(tter)

wee, *TINY/SMALL* (or see we or whee)

weed,*,ded,ding,dy,dier,diest,dless,der,dily, diness, *A PLANT NOT UNDERSTOOD/APPRECIATED FOR MEDICINAL QUALITIES* (or see we'd/wheat)

week,*,kly, *SEVEN DAYS IN A ROW* (or see weak)

weekle, week(ly)

ween,*,ned,ning, *DESIRE/EXPECT SOMETHING* (or see wean)

weeny,nies,nier,niest,nsy, *TINY/SMALL, A TYPE OF HOTDOG/WEINER*

weep,*,ped,ping,py,pier,piest, *PASSIONATE/SAD /INTENSE CRYING, AN OOZING/LEAKING/DRIPPING OF FLUIDS* (wept or reap)

weery, weary

weevil,*,led,ly, *AN INSECT/BEETLE WHICH BORES INTO PLANTS*

wef, weave /we've

weful, weevil

weg, wedge /wig

wegal, wiggle

wegd, wedge(d)

wege, wedge /wedge(gy)

weged, wedge(d) /wig(gged)

wegis, wedge(s)

wegle, wiggle

wegul, wiggle

wegus, wedge(s)

weigh,*,hed,hing,hable,her, *THE ACT OF MEASUR- ING THE WEIGHT OF SOMETHING, TO FEEL WEIGHT* (or see way or whey)

weight,ty,tier,tiest,ted,tless,tlessness,ty, tier,tiest,tily,tiness, *THE MEASUREMENT OF VOLUME/DENSITY/MASS* (or see wait or whet)

weild, wield /weald /weld

weir,*, *A WALL/DAM BUILT TO SLOW DOWN FLOW OF WATER* (or see were /we're /wear /where)

weird,der,dest,dly,dness, *STRANGE/UNCOMMON/ UNKNOWN/UNLIKELY*

wej, wedge

wejt, wedge(d)

wek, weak /week /wick

weked, wicked / wick(ed)

weker, wicker

wekle, week(ly)

wekur, wicker /weak(er)

wel, well /we'll /wheel

welcome,*,ed,ming,ely,eness,er, *TO INVITE/ HONOR/ENCOURAGE/ACKNOWLEDGE THE ARRIVAL OF SOMETHING/SOMEONE*

welcomnes, welcome(ness)

welcum, welcome

weld,*,ded,ding,der,dability,dable,dment, *FUSE TWO PIECES OF SUBSTANCE TOGETHER USING A FILLER, HERB* (or see wheel(ed)/wield/weald)

weldid, weld(ed) /wield(ed)

weldir, weld(er) /wield(er)

weldmint, weld(ment)

welduble, weld(able) /wield(able)

weldur, weld(er) /wield(er)

weldurnes, wilderness

weler, wheel(er)

welfare,rism, *ABLE TO FARE WELL AND FUNCTION NORMALLY/PROPERLY*

welfer, welfare

welkem, welcome

welkumd, welcome(d)

welkumt, welcome(d)

we'll, *CONTRACTION OF THE WORDS "WE WILL"* (or see well or wheel)

well,*,lled,lling, *FIT/HEALTHY, A DEEP HOLE WHERE WATER SEEPS INTO, WORD POSED AS A QUESTION, ALSO/IN ADDITION TO* (or see will/we'll/wheel)

wellth, wealth

welo, willow

welt,*, *A DISCOLORED/RAISED AREA ON THE SKIN WHERE DAMAGE OCCURED* (or see weld /weild/ wheel(ed) /weald /wilt)

welter, weld(er) /wield(er)

welth, wealth

welthe, wealth(y)

weltheist, wealth(iest)

welthenes, wealth(iness)

weltheur, wealth(ier)

welur, wheel(er)

wem, whim

weman, women

wemin, women

wempe, wimp(y)

wemped, wimp(ed)

wemper, whimper

wempur, whimper

wemsekul, whimsical

wemsukil, whimsical

wen, wean /ween /win /when

wence, wince

wench,hes,hed,hing, *DEROGATORY WORD FOR A WOMAN WHO IS FROM THE COUNTRY/ PROMISCUOUS* (or see winch or wrench)

wenchis, wench(es) /winch(es) /wrench(es)

wencht, wench(ed) /winch(ed) /wrench(ed)

wend,*,ded,ding, *TURN/CURVE WHILE PROCEDING FORWARD* (or see wean(ed)/ween(ed)/wind)

wende, wind(y)

wendeur, wind(ier)

wendy, wind(y)

wene, weeny

wenefer, whenever

wenefur, whenever

wener, wean(er) /winner

wenie, weeny

wenir, wean(er) /winner

wens, whence /win(s) /wince

wensda, Wednesday

wensday, Wednesday

wensh, wench /winch /wrench

wenshd, wench(ed) /winch(ed) /wrench(ed)

went, *PAST TENSE OF "GO"* (or see wind)
wenter, winter
wentre, wintry
wentur, winter
wenur, wean(er) /winner
weny, weeny
wenzda, Wednesday
wep, web /weep /whip
wepd, web(bbed)/wept /weep(ed)
wepe, weep(y)
weped, weep(ed)/wept /reap(ed)
wepen, whip(pping) /weapon
wepenre, weapon(ry)
weperwil, whipporwill
wepeur, weep(ier)
wepin, weapon
wepinre, weapon(ry)
wept, *PAST TENSE OF "WEEP"* (or see web(bbed))
wepun, weapon
wepunre, weapon(ry)
wepurwil, whipporwill
wepy, weep(y)
wepyer, weep(ier)
wer, wear /ware /where /we're /were /weir
werable, wear(able)
werafir, wherever
weras, whereas
werd, word /word /weird /where'd /weird
werder, weird(er)
werdest, weird(est)
werdist, weird(est)
werdly, weird(ly)
werdnes, weird(ness)
we're, *CONTRACTION OF THE WORDS "WE ARE"* (or see were /where /weir /whirr)
were, *PAST TENSE OF "WAS/IS"* (or see where/ we're /whirr /weary /wire /weir /worry)
wereble, wear(able)
werefur, wherever

weren't, *CONTRACTION OF THE WORDS "WERE NOT"*
werever, wherever
werible, wear(able)
werie, weary
werkd, work(ed)
werkt, work(ed)
werkuble, work(able)
werl, whirl /whorl /where'll
werld, whirl(ed) /world /whorl(ed)
werlpool, whirlpool
werlpul, whirlpool
werlwend, whirlwind
werlwind, whirlwind
werm, worm
wernt, weren't
wers, where's /wear(s) /ware(s) /worse /worst
wershep, worship
wership, worship
wert, weird /word /word /where'd
werth, worth
werubel, wear(able)
weruble, wear(able)
werwithal, wherewithal
wery, weary /wary /worry
wes, wheeze
wesal, weasel
wesd, whiz(zzed)
wesdim, wisdom
wesdum, wisdom
wesdwurd, west(ward)
wesel, whistle
weseld, weasel(ed)
wesenes, wheeze(ziness)
weserd, wizard
weses, whiz(zzes)
wesh, wish
weshd, wish(ed)
wesil, weasel
wesk, whisk

weskd, whisk(ed)
weske, whiskey
wesker, whisker
weskur, whisker
wesky, whiskey
wesol, weasel /whistle
wesp, wisp
wespe, wisp(y)
wesper, whisper
wesperd, whisper(ed)
wespur, whisper
wespurd, whisper(ed)
wespy, wisp(y)
west, terly,tern,ternize,ting,tward, *ONE OF THE FOUR DIRECTIONS ON THE EARTH*
westirea, wisteria
westirly, west(erly)
westirn, west(ern)
westirnise, west(ernize)
westle, whistle
westorn, west(ern)
westornize, west(ernize)
westurle, west(erly)
westurly, west(erly)
westurn, west(ern)
westurnise, west(ernize)
westwerd, west(ward)
westwurd, west(ward)
wesul, weasel /whistle
wesuld, weasel(ed) /whistle(d)
wesuls, weasel(s) /whistle(s)
wesurd, wizard
wesus, whiz(zzes)
wet, *, tting,tter,ttest,tly,tness,table,ttish, *BATHED/COATED/AFFECTED BY A LIQUID* (or see wheat /wed /whet /we'd /weed /wit)
wetch, which /witch
wetel, whittle
weter, wet(tter) /whet(tter)

wherd, where'd /weird

where'd, *CONTRACTION OF THE WORDS "WHERE DID"* (or see weird)

where'll, *CONTRACTION OF THE WORDS "WHERE WILL" SLANG WORD* (or see whirl)

where's, *CONTRACTION OF THE WORDS "WHERE IS"* (or see ware(s) or wear(s))

where,,*, *IN REFERENCE TO PLACE* (or see ware/ were /we're /whirr)

whereas, *ALTHOUGH, EXCEPT THAT, OTHER THAN*

wherever, *NO SPECIFIC PLACE*

wherewithal, *TO HAVE THE RESOURCES/TIME*

wherl, whirl /whorl /whirlpool

whirlpool, whirlpool

whirlwind, whirlwind

whers, where's /wear(s) /ware(s)

whert, where'd /weird

wherwithal, wherewithal

whesk, whisk

whesky, whiskey

whet,,*,tted,tting,tter, *SMALL AMOUNT REMOVED/ ADDED/CARVED OUT* (or see wet /wheat/ wit /wed)

whether, *WHEN ONE OF SEVERAL CHOICES HASN'T BEEN DECIDED, REFERRING TO CHOICE* (or see weather/wether/wither)

whetle, whittle

whetlok, wedlock

whetul, whittle

whew, *DEEP SIGH OF RELIEF AFTER A STRESSFUL MOMENT* (or see woo/hue/who)

whey, *INGREDIENT IN WARM-BLOODED ANIMALS MILK* (or see way or weigh)

whez, whiz /wheeze

wheze, wheeze(zy)

whezines, wheeze(ziness)

which, *CHOICE BETWEEN/CHOOSE ONE* (or see witch)

whid, wide /white

while, *REFERENCE TO TIME,IN THE MEANTIME, DURING/AT THE SAME TIME*

whim,msy,msies, *SPONTANEOUS, WITHOUT MUCH FORETHOUGHT*

whimper,,*,red,ring,rer, *SOFT CRYING/WHINING SOUND*

whimsical,lity,lness,lly, *WITH A FRIVOLOUS NATURE, ADVENTUROUS/FANTASY*

whine,,*,ed,ning,ey,er, *A NASAL/NEEDY/PLEADING/ WANTING SOUND* (or see wine or whinny)

whinefur, whenever

whinevur, whenever

whinny,nnies,nnied,nnying, *SOUND A HORSE MAKES* (or see whine(y))

whint, went

whiny, whine(y) /whinny

whip,,*,pped,pping,pper, *TO BEAT/WORK INTO A LATHER, LONG DEVICE MADE OF WOVEN LEATHER STRIPS* (or see wipe)

whiperwil, whipporwill

whipporwill, *A BIRD*

whipurwil, whipporwill

whirl,,*,led,ling,ler,ly, *SPIN AROUND* (or see whorl)

whirlpool,,*, *A CIRCULAR/SPIRAL MOTION IN THE WATER*

whirlwind,,*, *CIRCULAR/SPIRAL MOTION IN THE WIND*

whirr,,*,rred,rring, *TYPE OF SOUND LIKE A MOTOR/ SPIRAL* (or see were /we're /where /whirl)

whisel, whistle

whisk,,*,ked,king, *BRUSH AWAY AS IF BY THE WIND*

whisker,,*,ry, *LONG SENSITIVE/SENSORY HAIRS AROUND ANIMALS NOSE/SNOUT, FACIAL HAIR*

whiskey, *ALCOHOL FERMENTATION*

whisky, whiskey

whisol, whistle

whisper,,*,red,ring,rer,ry, *SPEAK QUIETLY/FAINTLY*

whistle,,*,ed,ling,er, *FORCED AIR FROM BETWEEN PURSED LIPS PRODUCING SOUND*

whisul, whistle

whit, white /wit /wide

white,,*, ed,ting,er,est,en,ener,eness,ening, *COLOR PRODUCED BY ALL COLORS OF THE LIGHT SPECTRUM, CALCIUM CARBONATE*

whitle, whittle

whittle,,*,ed,ling,er, *SHAVE OFF SMALL PORTIONS/ SLIVERS OF WOOD*

whitul, whittle

whity, wit(tty)

whiz,zzes,zzed,zzing, *TO STREAK BY QUICKLY AS IF BLOWN BY A STRONG WIND*

who,,*, *TO REFER TO "IN GENERAL" WITHOUT USING A NAME/TITLE/DESCRIPTION OF* (or see whoa/ hue /whew /woo)

whoa, *"STOP" WORD FOR A HORSE* (or see woo/ whew /woe)

who'd, *CONTRACTION OF THE WORDS "WHO HAD/ WOULD/COULD"*

whodel, waddle /what'll

whodul, waddle /what'll

whoever, *IN REFERENCE TO ANYBODY, SOMEONE WHOSE NAME/TITLE IS NOT KNOWN AT THE TIME*

whole,,*,ey,eness,esome, *ENTIRE THING, ALL OF IT, WELL-ROUNDED, COMPLETE* (or see hole/holy/ wholly)

wholesale,ed,ling,er, *SELL WITHOUT PRICE MARK-UP*

wholesome,ely,eness, *COMPLETE, WELL-ROUNDED*

wholly, *COMPLETE IN ITS ENTIRETY* (or see holy)

wholsail, wholesale

wholsel, wholesale

wholsem, wholesome

wholsum, wholesome

wholupt, wallop(ed)

wholy, wholly /whole(y)

whom, *OBJECTIVE PRONOUN OF "WHO"*

whomever, *OBJECTIVE CASE OF "WHOEVER"*

whomp,,*,ped,ping, *A SOUND, COMPLETE VICTORY*

wilow, willow
wilt,*,ted,ting, *TO DROOP FROM LACK OF NOURISHMENT AS A PLANT DOES* (or see welt)

wim, whim
wiman, women
wimon, women
wimp,*,ped,ping,py, *LACK OF COURAGE/STRENGTH*
wimpur, whimper
wimsecal, whimsical
wimsikul, whimsical
win,*, nning,nner,won,nnable, *ADVANTAGE IN COMPETITION* (or see when)
wince,*,ed,cing, *TO FLINCH* (or see whence)
winch,hes,hed,hing, *PULL/HOIST SOMETHING BY MEANS OF A DEVICE* (or see wench or wrench)
winchd, wench(ed) /winch(ed) /wrench(ed)
winchis, wench(es) /winch(es) /wrench(es)
wind,*,ded,ding,dy,dier,diest, *AIR MOVING FASTER THAN A BREEZE,TURN SOMETHING UNTIL TIGHT/ TAUT* (or see went)
wined, wine(d) /whine(d) /wind
winefer, whenever
winefur, whenever
winer, winner
winey, whine(y) /whinny
winsday, Wednesday
winsh, wench /winch /wrench
winshd, wench(ed) /winch(ed) /wrench(ed)
wint, went /wend /whine(d) /wind
winter,*,red,ring, *SEASON BETWEEN FALL/AUTUMN AND SPRING* (or see winter)
wintre, winter / wintry
wintry,rier,riest, *LIKE WINTER*
wintur, winter
winur, winner
winy, whine(y) /whinny
wip, whip / wipe
wipd, whip(pped) /wipe(d)

wide,er,est,en,eness,ener,ely,dish, *DIMENSION OF GIRTH/BREADTH, EXTENT/SPREAD OF* (or see white or width)
widel, whittle
widl, whittle
wido, widow
widow,*, wer, *SPOUSE WHO LOST MATE TO DEATH*
width,*, *THE MEASUREMENT/DISTANCE OF ONE SIDE OF SOMETHING*
widul, whittle
wield,*,ded,ding,dable,der,dy, *TO USE/GIVEN TO POWER/COMMAND* (or see weld)
wife,eves,ely, *FEMALE LEGALLY BONDED IN MARRIAGE*
wifes, wives
wifs, wives
wig,*,gged,gging, *FALSE HAIR FOR THE HEAD, TO FREAK OUT/ACT NUTS, BE UNCHARACTERISTICALLY UNPREDICTABLE* (or see wick)
wiged, wig(gged)
wiggle,*,ed,ling, *TO MOVE QUICKLY FROM SIDE TO SIDE* (or see wriggle)
wigul, wiggle
wik, wick
wiked, wicked
wiker, wicker
wikur, wicker
wil, while /will /well
wild,der,dest,dly, *UNCONTROLLABLE, NO RESTRAINT IN ACTIONS*
wilderness, *UNTAMED/NATURAL FOREST*
wildist, wild(est)
wildurnes, wilderness
will,*, lled,lling,llful,llfully,llfulness,llingly, llingness, *DESIRE/INCLINATION TO MAKE HAPPEN, LEGAL DOCUMENT OUT-LINING DIVISION OF PROPERTY AFTER DEATH* (or see well)
willdernes, wilderness
willow,*,wy, *A TREE, LIKE THE TREE*
wilo, willow

whoop,*,ped,ping, *A TYPE OF SOUND USED IN WAR CRIES, GET A SPANKING/BEATING*
whoosh,hes,hed,hing, *AN ACTION/SOUND AS IF SWEPT UP BY THE WIND*
wush, whoosh
whoper, whopper
whopper,*, *GREAT/GIANT/HUGE*
whore,*,ed,ring, *A DEROGATORY TERM FOR A PROMISCUOUS FEMALE*
whorf, wharf
whorl,*,led,ling, *LIKE A WHIRL/SWIRL AS IF TURNED ABOUT BY THE WIND, SPIRAL* (or see whirl)
who's, *CONTRACTION OF THE WORDS "WHO IS/HAS"* (or see whose or hose)
whose, *BELONGS TO SOMEONE/SOMETHING IN PARTICULAR* (or see who's)
whot, what /watt
whud, what /would
whudel, what'll /waddle
whudevur, whatever
whudul, what'll /waddle
whuever, whoever
whup, whoop
whurlwind, whirlwind
whut, what /would
whutel, what'll /waddle
whutever, whatever
whutul, what'll /waddle
why, *A GENERAL QUESTION DESIRING AN ANSWER*
wi, why
wic, wick
wich, which /witch
wicked,dly,dness, *EVIL* (or see wick(ed))
wicker, *FURNITURE BUILT OF WOODY/WOVEN MATERIAL*
wick,*,ked,king,ker, *SLOWLY SOAK UP LIQUID, A WOVEN COTTON FOR LAMP OIL, EVIL/ MALICIOUSNESS INTENT* (or see wig)
wid, wide /ride /white

wipe,*,ed,ping,er, REMOVE CONTAMINANT/SURFACE DEBRIS/MATERIAL TO CREATE SMOOTH PLANE/ SURFACE (or see whip)
wipen, whip(pping) /wipe(ping)
wiperwil, whipporwill
wipon, whip(pping) /wipe(ping)
wipt, whip(pped) /wipe(d)
wipun, whip(pping) /wipe(ping)
wipurwil, whipporwill
wir, wire /were /wear /ware /where /we're
wird, word /wire(d)
wire,*,ed,ring,eless, METAL STRAND
wirk, work
wirkeble, work(able)
wirkt, work(ed)
wirkuble, work(able)
wirkur, work(er)
wirl, whirl /whorl
wirld, whirl(ed) /world /whorl(ed)
wirles, wire(less)
wirlpul, whirlpool
wirlwind, whirlwind
wirm, worm
wirnt, weren't
wirpool, whirlpool
wirs, worse /worst
wirshep, worship
wirshup, worship
wirth, worth
wirthe, worth(y)
wirthy, worth(y)
wis, wise /whiz
wisd, whiz(zzed)
wisdem, wisdom
wisdom, KNOWLEDGE GAINED BY EXPERIENCE
wisdum, wisdom
wise,er,est,ely, KNOWLEDGE GAINED BY EXPERIENCE
wisel, whistle
wiserd, wizard

wises, whiz(zzes) /wise(s)
wish,hes,hed,hing,HOPE/IMAGINE FOR THE FUTURE
wishus, wish(es)
wisk, whisk
wiskd, whisk(ed)
wiske, whiskey
wisker, whisker
wiskur, whisker
wisky, whiskey
wisol, whistle
wisp,*,py, LIGHT/AIRY, OF LITTLE WEIGHT
wispe, wisp(y)
wisper, whisper
wisperd, whisper(ed)
wispur, whisper
wispurer, whisper(er)
wisteria, A FLOWERING BUSH
wistle, whistle
wisul, whistle
wisurd, wizard
wisus, whiz(zzes)
wit,*,tted,tting,tty,ttier,ttiest, QUICK IN MIND/ RESPONSE (or see wet /white /write)
witch,hes,hing,hy,hery, TERM FOR A FEMALE WHO GIVES IMPRESSION THEY HAVE SUPER POWER (or see which)
wite, wit(tty) /white
witel, whittle
with,* PREFIX INDICATING "BACK/AWAY/AGAINST" MOST OFTEN MODIFIES THE WORD (or see width)
withaut, without
withdrau, withdraw
withdraw,*,wing,wal,wn,withdrew, PULL/MOVE BACK, RETREAT
withdro, withdraw
withdron, withdraw(n)
witheld, withheld
withen, within

wither,*,red,ring, SHRIVEL/SHRINK FROM LACK OF NOURISHMENT/MOISTURE
withheld, PAST TENSE OF "WITHHOLD", TO HOLD BACK
withhold,*,ded,ding, THE ACT OF HOLDING BACK, REFRAIN FROM MAKING VISIBLE/APPARENT
within, CONTAINED, NOT VISIBLE/APPARENT
witholb, withhold
withor, wither
without, LACKING, NOT HAVING
withstand,*,ding,withstood, TO STAND AGAINST, TOLERATE
withstood, PAST TENSE OF "WITHSTAND"
withstud, withstood
withur, wither
witle, whittle
witness,sses,ssed,ssing, HAVE KNOWINGNESS OF, HAVING SEEN
witnus, witness
witol, whittle
witul, whittle
wity, wit(tty)
wives, WORD THAT IS PLURAL FOR "WIFE", MORE THAN ONE WIFE
wiz, wise /whiz
wizard,*,dry, A PERSON WHO PARTAKES IN ACTIONS INVOLVING MYSTICAL POWER
wizd, whiz(zzed)
wizer, wise(r)
wizerd, wizard
wizest, wise(st)
wizur, wise(r)
wizurd, wizard
wo, whoa /woo /woe /whew
wobble,*,ed,ling,ly, LACKS STABILITY IN POSITION, NOT STEADY
wobul, wobble
woch, wash /watch
wochd, watch(ed)
woches, watch(es)

wochful, watch(ful)
wocht, watch(ed)
wochus, watch(es)
wod, wad/ wood/ would/ what/ wait
wodent, wouldn't
woder, water
wodercres, watercress
wodere, water(y)
woderfol, waterfall
woderkres, watercress
wodertite, watertight
wodery, water(y)
wodid, wad(dded) /wait(ed) /wade(d)
wodil, waddle /what'll
wodint, wouldn't
wodir, water
wodirfal, waterfall
wodirkres, watercress
wodirtite, watertight
wodul, waddle /what'll
wodur, water
wodurkres, watercress
wodurtite, watertight
woe,*,eful,efully,efulness, *SORROW/LAMENT (or see woo or whoa)*
wofel, waffle
woful, waffle
wok, walk /woke /wok
wok,*, *VESSEL FOR COOKING (or see woke or walk)*
woke, *PAST TENSE FOR "WAKE" (or see wok /walk)*
woken, *PAST TENSE FOR "WAKE", BRING TO CONSCIOUSNESS FROM A DEEP SLEEP*
wokin, woken
wokun, woken
wol, wall /wool
wold, wall(ed)/ wail(ed)/ /would
wolen, wool(en)
wolep, wallop
wolet, wallet

wolf,lves,fing, *OF THE WILD CANINE/CANID FAMILY*
wolin, wool(en)
wolip, wallop
wolipd, wallop(ed)
woliped, wallop(ed)
wolit, wallet
wolk, walk /woke
wolken, walk(ing)
wolker, walk(er) /walker
wolkur, walk(er) /walker
wolnut, walnut
wolo, wallow
wolod, wallow(ed)
wolopd, wallop(ed)
wolopt, wallop(ed)
wolres, walrus
wolrus, walrus
wolsem, wholesome
wolst, waltz(ed)
wolts, waltz
woltsd, waltz(ed)
woltz, waltz
wolup, wallop
wolupt, wallop(ed)
wolut, wallet
wolveren, wolverine
wolverine,*,, *ANIMAL IN THE WEASEL FAMILY, NOT RELATED TO A WOLF*
wolves, *PLURAL FOR "WOLF", IN THE CANID FAMILY*
wolwrus, walrus
wolz, waltz
woman,women, *AN ADULT FEMALE*
womanhood, *GROWING INTO ADULT FEMALE HUMAN*
women, *PLURAL FOR "WOMAN"*
womin, woman /women
wominhud, womanhood
womp, whomp
womun, woman /women
won, *PAST TENSE WORD FOR "WIN"(or see one/wan)*

wond, wand /won /wane(d) /wan(ed)
wonder,*,red,ring, *TO QUESTION/PONDER/MARVEL (or see wander)*
wonderd, wander(ed) /wonder(ed)
wonderful,lly,lness, *FULL OF AWE, IMPRESSED*
wondurd, wander(ed) / wonder(ed)
wonderer, wander(er)
won't, *CONTRACTION OF THE WORDS "WILL NOT" (or see want)*
wonten, wanton
wontenes, wanton(nness)
wonter, wander /wonder
wonton, wanton
wontunes, wanton(nness)
wontunle, wanton(ly)
woo,*,oed,oing,oingly, *ACTS PERFORMED TO GAIN ATTENTION/AFFECTION/APPROVAL FROM SOMEONE (or see whew/woe/whoa)*
wood,*,ded,den,dy,dsy, *A FIBROUS/NATURAL MATERIAL, STEM/BASE OF A TREE/BUSH, HEAVILY TREED/BUSHY AREA (or see would)*
woofer,*,, *LOUDSPEAKER IN SOUND SYSTEM*
woofur, woofer
wool,*,len,ly, *HAIR FROM THE FLEECE OF ANIMALS*
woolvs, wolves
woop, whoop
woose, woozy
woosh, whoosh
woozy,zily,ziness, *FEELING OUT OF SORTS/ UNSTABLE/SLIGHTLY DRUNK*
woper, whopper
wopur, whopper
wor, war / wore
worant, warrant
worbeld, warble(d)
worbild, warble(d)
worbler, warbler
worblur, warbler
worbuld, warble(d)

word,*,ded,ding,dy,dily,diness,dless,dlessly, dlessness, *LETTERS ARRANGED TOGETHER TO CREATE MEANING, USING TOO MANY WORDS TO DESCRIBE* (or see war(rred)/ward)
worden, warden
wordon, warden
wordrob, wardrobe
wordun, warden
woreir, warrior
wore, *PAST TENSE OF "WEAR"* (or see war)
woren, warren
worent, warrant
worented, warrant(ed)
worentes, warrant(ies)
worenty, warrant(y)
woreur, warrior
worf, wharf
worier, warrior
worin, warren
worint, warrant
worinte, warrant(y)
worinted, warrant(ed)
worinty, warrant(y)
work,*,ked,king,ker,kable,kability,kableness, *PERFORM ACTIONS/TASKS TO ACCOMPLISH A DESIRED RESULT*
workuble, work(able)
worl, whirl / whorl
world,*,dly,dliness, *OF/BELONGS TO THIS PLANET*
worm,*,med,ming,mer,my, *AN INVERTEBRATE WHICH LIVES MOSTLY CONCEALED FROM VIEW*
wormd, warm(ed) / worm(ed)
wormer, warm(er) /worm(er)
wormest, warm(est)
wormle, warm(ly)
wormth, warm(th)
wormur, warm(er)
wormust, warm(est)
worn, *PAST TENSE OF "WEAR", USED MANY TIMES, OVERWORKED, AS A COVERING* (or see warn)
wornd, warn(ed)
wornt, warn(ed) /weren't
worp, warp
worpd, warp(ed)
worry,*,rries,rried,rying,rrisome,yingly,rrier, *BE CONCERNED/FEARFUL ABOUT SOMETHING WHICH MAY OR MAY NOT HAPPEN*
worse,st,en, *MORE THAN BAD, MORE TROUBLE THAN EXPECTED/ANTICIPATED* (or see worst)
worsen,*,ned,ning, *CONTINUES TO GET WORST/ DETERIORATE*
worsh, wash
worshep, worship
worship,*,pped,pping,pper, *ONE WHO IDOLIZES/ ADORES SOMEONE/SOMETHING*
worst, *MORE EXTREME THAN WORSE, MORE TROUBLE THAN EXPECTED/ANTICIPATED* (or see worse)
wort, wart /word /ward
worth,hies,hier,hiest,hiness,hless,hlessly, hlessness,hy,hily, *THE VALUE/QUALITY OF SOMETHING/SOMEONE*
worun, warren
worunt, warrant
worunty, warrant(y)
wory, worry
wos, was /woe(s)
wosh, wash
woshd, wash(ed)
woshepl, wash(able)
wosher, washer
woshir, washer
wosht, wash(ed)
woshuble, wash(able)
woshur, washer
wosnt, wasn't
wosp, wasp
wot, watt /what /wad
wotch, watch

wotertite, watertight
woturd, water(ed)
would, *PERHAPS WILL BE DONE/ACCOMPLISHED, POSSIBLE* (or see wood)
wouldn't, *CONTRACTION OF THE WORDS "WOULD NOT", WILL NOT BE DONE/ACCOMPLISHED*
wound,*,ded,ding,dless, *PHYSICALLY HARMED, PAST TENSE OF "WIND"*
woz, was
wozp, wasp
wozy, woozy
wra, ray /raw
wrack,*,ked,king,kful, *WRECKED/RUINED, PERTAIN- ING TO CLOUDS* (or see rack)
wrak, rack /rake /wrack /rag
wrangle,*,ed,ling,er, *BE CONFRONTATIONAL/ ARGUMENTATIVE, TO ROUND UP CATTLE*
wrangul, wrangle
wrap,*,pped,pping,pper, *COVER/SURROUND SOME- THING, TO PACKAGE UP* (or see rap)
wrased, raise(d) /race(d) /erase(d)
wrath,hful,hfully,he, *EXTREMELY ANGRY/PUNISHING/ REVENGEFUL*
wreak,*, *CAUSE CONFUSION/DAMAGE AS IF BY MEANS OF RAGE/VENGEANCE* (or see reek or wreck)
wreath,*, *CIRCULAR GARLAND OF VARIOUS PLANT/ ORGANIC MATERIAL*
wreck,*,ked,king, *CRASH/ALTER/DESTROY* (or see wreak)
wrecker,*, *A TRUCK THAT TOWS VEHICLES*
wreek, wreak /reak
wreeth, wreath
wregul, wriggle
wreker, wrecker
wrekur, wrecker
wren,*, *A SMALL BIRD*
wrench,hes,hed,hing, *A HAND TOOL USED FOR TURNING/TWISTING, TO TWIST SOMETHING AROUND* (or see winch or wench)

wrer, rear /rare /wear
wresil, wrestle
wresl, wrestle
wrest,*,ted,ting,ter, *TO FORCIBLY TWIST/WRING/ REMOVE FROM GRASP/POWER (or see wrist)*
wrestle,*,ed,ling,er, *TO FORCIBLY ATTEMPT TO MANEUVER/MANIPULATE*
wresul, wrestle
wriggle,*,ed,ling,ly, *TO SQUIRM/WRITHE/MOVE IN TWISTING/TURNING MOTIONS (or see wiggle)*
wright, *PROFESSIONAL INVOLVED IN ART/HAND WORK, AN ARTISAN(or see right/rite/writ)*
wrigle, wriggle
wrigul, wriggle
wrin, wren
wrinch, wrench
wring,*,ging,wrung, *TO TWIST SOMETHING AROUND TIGHTLY CREATING/COMPRESSION (or see ring)*
wrinkle,*,ed,ling,ey, *LINES/CREASES*
wrist, *A JOINT THE ARM (or see wrest)*
writ, *WRITTEN COURT ORDER (or see write /right/ rite)*
write,*,en,tting,wrote, *PUT WORDS/MUSIC INTO PHYSICAL FORM/MAKE VISIBLE (or see writ/ right/ rite /wright)*
writhe,*,ed,hing,er, *TO TWIST/SQUIRM EMOTIONALLY/PHYSICALLY*
wrong,*,ged,ging,ger,gly,gness, *NOT SUITABLE/ CORRECT/PROPER/NORMAL*
wrot, wrought /wrote /rote
wrote, *PAST TENSE OF "WRITE" (or see rote/ wrought /rot)*
wrought, *DECORATIVE METALWORK, PAST TENSE OF "WREAK", TWISTED WITH WORRY/PAIN*
wrout, wrought
wrung, *PAST TENSE OF "WRING" (or see rung)*
wry,rier,riest,yly,yness, *TWISTEDLY IRONIC, OUT OF SHAPE (or see rye)*
wryth, writhe

wu, whew /woo
wud, would /wood /what
wudal, what'll /waddle
wudent, wouldn't
wudever, whatever
wudil, what'll /waddle
wudint, wouldn't
wudul, what'll /waddle
wue, whew / woo
wufer, woofer
wufir, woofer
wufs, wolves
wul, wool
wulen, wool(en)
wulf, wolf
wulferene, wolverine
wulin, wool(en)
wulveren, wolverine
wulviren, wolverine
wulvs, wolves
wumen, woman /women
wumin, woman /women
wuminhud, womanhood
wunderful, wonderful
wundurful, wonderful
wunefur, whenever
wunevur, whenever
wup, whoop
wur, were /whirr
wurd, word
wure, worry
wuri, worry
wurk, work
wurkd, work(ed)
wurkebul, work(able)
wurker, work(er)
wurkt, work(ed)
wurl, whirl / whorl
wurld, whirl(ed) /world /whorl(ed)

wurlpool, whirlpool
wurlpul, whirlpool
wurls, whirl(s) /whorl(s)
wurlt, whirl(ed)/world /whorl(ed)
wurlwend, whirlwind
wurlwind, whirlwind
wurm, worm
wurnt, weren't
wurs, worse /worst
wursen, worsen
wurshep, worship
wurshup, worship
wurst, worst
wurth, worth
wurthe, worth(y)
wurthy, worth(y)
wury, worry
wus, was
wuse, woozy
wusnt, wasn't
wut, what /would /wood
wutefer, whatever
wutel, what'll /waddle
wutever, whatever
wutil, what'll /waddle
wutul, what'll /waddle
wuz, was
wuznt, wasn't
wuzy, woozy
wy, why

"X"

xagurate, exaggerate
xajurate, exaggerate
xakut, execute

xam, exam
xamen, examine
xamin, examine
xampel, example
xampul, example
xamun, examine
xaspurate, exasperate
xaust, exhaust
xchang, exchange
xekute, execute
xempt, exempt
xen, xeno, *PREFIX INDICATING "STRANGE" MOST OFTEN MODIFIES THE WORD*
xenon, *A GAS*
xenophobe,bia,bic, *IRRATIONAL/EXTREME HATRED/ CONTEMPT FOR FOREIGN PEOPLE*
xer, *PREFIX INDICATING "DRY" MOST OFTEN MODIFIES THE WORD*
xerafit, xerophyte
xeraphyte, xerophyte
xero, *PREFIX INDICATING "DRY" MOST OFTEN MODIFIES THE WORD*
xerophily,lous, *SURVIVES IN DRY/HOT REGIONS*
xerophyte,*,tic,tically,tism, *DROUGHT/HEAT RESISTANT PLANT*
xet, exit
xhale, exhale
xibit, exhibit
xil, exile
xilene, xylene
xiraphyte, xerophyte
xist, exist
xit, exit
xklud, exclude
xklumashen, exclamation
xkurshen, excursion
xkuse, excuse
xkuvate, excavate
xodik, exotic

xpand, expand
xpekt, expect
xpel, expel
xpens, expense
xpereins, experience
xperumint, experiment
xpir, expire
xplan, explain
xplod, explode
xplor, explore
xployt, exploit
xport, export
xpoz, expose
xpres, express
xpudeshin, expedition
xpurt, expert
xsalint, excellent
xsed, exceed
xsel, excel /accel /axle
xsept, except
xses, excess
xsit, excite /exit
xsulent, excellent
xsurpt, excerpt
xsursiz, exercise
xtend, extend
xtereur, exterior
xtinkt, extinct
xtrakt, extract
xtrem, extreme
xtru, extra
xturnol, external
xukute, execute
xurt, exert
xyl, xylo, *PREFIX INDICATING "WOOD" MOST OFTEN MODIFIES THE WORD*
xylafon, xylophone
xylagraf, xylograph
xylaphone, xylophone

xylatomy, xylotomy
xylaudomy, xylotomy
xylem, *THAT WHICH FORMS WOODY FIBER/TISSUE/ STEM IN PLANTS*
xylene,*lol, *A CHEMICAL*
xyl, xylo, *PREFIX INDICATING "WOOD" MOST OFTEN MODIFIES THE WORD*
xylofon, xylophone
xylograph,*,her,hy,hic,hical,hically, *WOOD CARVINGS USED TO EMBOSS SOMETHING ELSE*
xylophone,*,nist, *MUSICAL INSTRUMENT*
xylose, *A CHEMICAL*
xylotomy,mic,mical,mous,mist, *THE ART OF CUTTING WOOD*
xylum, xylem

"Y"

ya, yaw /ye /yea /yeah
yacht,*,ting, *PLEASURE SHIP*
yahoo,*, *EXPRESSION OF JOY, ROWDY PEOPLE*
yal, yawl /y'all /yowl /you'll
y'all, *CONTRACTION OF THE WORDS "YOU ALL"* (or see you'll /yawl /yowl)
yam,*, *TYPE OF POTATO*
yank,*,ked,king, *TO SWIFTLY JERK/PULL*
yard,*,dage, *ENGLISH MEASUREMENT OF DISTANCE/ LENGTH,THREE FEET, AREA FOR SPECIAL USE*
yareu, urea
yareul, urea(l)
yarn,*, *SPUN THREADS*
yarrow, *A WILD HERB*
yart, yard
yau, yaw /ye /yea /yeah
yaul, yawl /y'all /yowl /you'll
yaupon, *SHRUB HOLLY*

yaurd, yard
yaw,*,wed,wing, VERTICAL ROLL/TILT ON A SHIP/VESSEL /CRAFT
yawl,*, TYPE OF BOAT (or see y'all or yowl)
yawn,*,ned,ning, EXAGERRATED STRETCHING OF JAW WHILE DEEPLY INHALING
ye, ANOTHER EXPRESSION OF "YOU"
yea,*, VERBAL VOTE OF "YES" (or see yeah)
yeah, SAME MEANING AS "YES" (or see yea)
year,*,rly, 365 DAYS
yearling,*, AN ANIMAL IN ITS SECOND YEAR OF LIFE
yearn,*,ned,ning, LONG FOR/WANT SOMETHING
yeast,*,ted,ting,ty, A FUNGUS THAT ACTIVATES FOOD TOWARD FERMENTATION
yel, yell
yeld, yell(ed) /yield
yell,*,lled,lling, TO VOICE/VOCALIZE LOUDLY (or see yield)
yellow,*,wed,wing, A COLOR
yelp,*,ped,ping, HIGH-PITCHED SOUND DOG MAKES ASSOCIATED WITH PAIN
yelt, yell(ed) / yield
yeoman,*,nly,yoemen, A NAVAL TERM/POSITION
yep, yip /yes
yepe, yippee
yeraneum, uranium
yerater, ureter
yerathan, urethane
yereik, urea(eic)
yerek, uric
yerethu, urethra
yerin, urine
yerinary, urinary
yerinate, urinate
yerology, urology
yerolugy, urology
yers, your's
yerun, urine
yerunal, urinal

yerunolegy, uranology
yes,ses, AFFIRMATIVE/CONFIRM/APPROVE
yesterday, THE DAY BEFORE TODAY
yet, EXCEPT/BUT, IN REFERENCE TO TIME
yeu, ewe /you /yew
yeuld, yield / yell(ed)
yew,*, A TREE (or see you or ewe)
yewbikwite, ubiquity
yewcaliptus, eucalyptus
yewderis, uterus
yewdirus, uterus
yewdulize, utilize
yewjuale, usual(lly)
yewkalale, ukulele
yewkulale, ukulele
yewnafid, unify(fied)
yewnaform, uniform
yewnaformedy, uniform(ity)
yewnasen, unison
yewnasikul, unicycle
yewnatery, unitary
yewnaversul, universal
yewnek, unique
yewnekorn, unicorn
yewnesikul, unicycle
yewnet, unit
yewnety, unity
yewnevers, universe
yewnikorn, unicorn
yewnit, unit
yewnitary, unitary
yewnite, unite
yewnufikashen, unify(fication)
yewnusen, unison
yewnusikul, unicycle
yewnutarean, unitary(rian)
yewnuversul, universal
yewnyun, union
yewsd, use(d)

yewshwul, usual
yewtensul, utensil
yewtilutarean, utilitarian
yewtilute, utility
yewtinsil, utensil
yewtopea, utopia
yewtulize, utilize
yewturis, uterus
yield,*,ded,ding, GIVE WAY TO, GAIN/PRODUCE
yip,*,pped,pping, SOUND/BARK FROM A DOG (or see yep)
yipe, yippee
yippee, JUBILANT SOUND OF JOY
yipy, yippee
yiraneum, uranium
yirathan, urethane
yirek, uric
yiren, urine
yirenary, urinary
yirenate, urinate
yirenul, urinal
yirethu, urethra
yiruter, ureter

yo, yaw /ye /yea /yeah
yodel,*,led,ling,ler, FALSETTO SOUND COMING FROM THE THROAT
yoga, FORM OF MEDITATIVE EXERCISE
yogi,ic, TEACHES/PRACTICES THE ART OF YOGA
yogurt, FOOD WITH PUDDING TEXTURE/CONSISTENCY
yoke,*,ed,king, HARNESS (or see yolk)
yokel,*, A LOCAL/COUNTRY TYPE PERSON
yol, yawl /y'all /yowl /you'll
yolk,*,, YELLOW PART OF EGG, EMBRYO (or see yoke)
yonder, WAY OVER THERE
yoni, FEMALE GENITALIA
yord, yard
yorn, yarn
you, REFERRING TO A PERSON OTHER THAN SELF (or see yew or ewe)

youbikwite, ubiquity
you'd,* *CONTRACTION OF THE WORDS "YOU WOULD/ SHOULD/COULD"*
youdulize, utilize
youduris, uterus
you'll,* *CONTRACTION OF THE WORDS "YOU WILL"* (or see yule)
younaversul, universal
younavirsity, university
younevirsul, universal
younevursity, university
young,ger,gest,gish, *YOUTHFUL, EARLIER YEARS*
youngster,* , *YOUNG PEOPLE/CHILDREN*
youniversity, university
youniversul, universal
younivurs, universe
younuvers, universe
your,* , *IN REFERENCE TO SOMEONE ELSES POSSESSION* (or see you're)
you're,* *CONTRACTION OF THE WORDS "YOU ARE"* (or see your)
your's, *BELONGS TO YOU*
yourself,lves, *MAKING REFERENCE TO SOMEONE ELSE*
yous, use
yousd, use(d)
youser, user
youserp, usurp
yousery, usury
yousful, useful
youshwule, usual(lly)
yousles, useless
youslus, useless
youtensul, utensil
youth,* , *YOUNG*
youthful,lly,lness, *OF BEING YOUNG*
youtilady, utility
youtilutarean, utilitarian
youtilute, utility
youtopea, utopia

youtulize, utilize
youturis, uterus
you've,* *CONTRACTION OF THE WORDS "YOU HAVE"*
youz, use
yowl,*,led,ling,ler, *MOURNFUL CRY OF A DOG/CANID*
yu, you /yew /ewe
yubikwite, ubiquity
yuderus, uterus
yuduris, uterus
yue, ewe /you /yew
yukaliptus, eucalyptus
yukulale, ukulele
yule, *PAGAN FESTIVAL AROUND CHRISTMAS* (or see you'll)
yup, yip /yes
yuraneum, uranium
yuranium, uranium
yurathen, urethane
yureik, urea(eic)
yurek, uric
yuren, urine
yurenal, urinal
yurenary, urinary
yurenat, urinate
yurethu, urethra
yureu, urea
yureul, urea(l)
yurin, urine
yuritur, ureter
yurology, urology
yurolugy, urology
yuron, urine
yurs, your's
yurt,* , *TENT/DOME STRUCTURE/DWELLING*
yusd, use(d)
yuser, user
yuserp, usurp
yusful, useful
yushuel, usual

yushwul, usual
yusir, user
yusirp, usurp
yusiry, usury
yuslus, useless
yust, use(d)
yutopea, utopia
yutulize, utilize
yuturis, uterus
yuwl, yawl /y'all /yowl /you'll
yuze, use
yuzer, user
yuzir, user
yuzur, use

"Z"

zar, czar
zderty, sturdy
zdirdy, sturdy
zdurdee, sturdy
zdurty, sturdy
zeal,lous,lously,lousness, *PASSIONATE/ EXUBERANT/EAGER EMOTIONS*
zealot,* , *ONE WHO IS FANATICAL/GETS CARRIED AWAY BY EMOTIONS*
zebra,* , *AFRICAN STRIPED HORSE*
zebru, zebra
zefir, zephyr
zel, zeal
zeleon, zillion
zeles, zeal(ous)
zelet, zealot
zelis, zeal(ous)
zelit, zealot
zelus, zeal(ous)
zelut, zealot

zenafobia, xenophobe(bia)
zeneth, zenith
zeng, zing
zenge, zing(y)
zenith,hal, *HIGHEST/FARTHEST PEAK/POINT*
zenk, zinc
zenofob, xenophobe
zenofobic, xenophobe(bic)
zenon, xenon
zenuth, zenith
zenya, zinnia
zep, zip
zephir, zephyr
zephyr,*, *FRAGILE/GENTLE WIND/FABRIC*
zepur, zipper
zerafit, xerophyte
zeraufilus, xerophily(lous)
zerconium, zirconium
zero,oes,oed,oing, *NUMBER INDICATING NIL/ NOTHING, TO TARGET IN ON*
zerofele, xerophily
zerofelus, xerophily(lous)
zerofit, xerophyte
zerofule, xerophily
zerofulus, xerophily(lous)
zest,ty,tful,tfrully,tfulness, *WITH ENERGY/SPICE/ GUSTO*
zethur, zither
zig-zag,*, *TO GO BACK AND FORTH WHILE MOVING IN ONE SPECIFIC DIRECTION*
zilafon, xylophone
zilagraf, xylograph
zilaudime, xylotomy
zilaugrafur, xylograph(er)
zilauteme, xylotomy
zilefon, xylophone
zilegraf, xylograph
zilem, xylem
zilen, xylene

zileon, zillion
zilion, zillion
ziliphone, xylophone
zillion,*, *EXTREMELY HIGH NUMBER*
zilodeme, xylotomy
zilograf, xylograph
zilom, xylem
zilos, xylose
ziloteme, xylotomy
zilufon, xylophone
zilugraf, xylograph
zilum, xylem
ziluphone, xylophone
zimerge, zymurgy
zimolege, zymology
zimurge, zymurgy
zinafobia, xenophobe(bia)
zinafobic, xenophobe(bic)
zinc,ced,cing,cic,cous,cky,cy,cite, *A METAL*
zing,*,ged,ging,gy, *A SPEEDY/SHRILL SOUND/ACTION WHICH HAPPENS VERY QUICKLY, FAST, SPEEDY*
zinia, zinnia
zink, zinc
zinnia,*, *A FLOWER*
zinya, zinnia
zip,*,pped,pping,ppy, *FAST/SWIFT*
zipd, zip(pped)
zipe, zip(ppy)
ziped, zip(pped)
ziper, zipper
zipper,*,red,ring, *A CLOSING DEVICE*
zipur, zipper
zirafule, xerophily
zirconium, *ON THE PERIODIC TABLE OF ELEMENTS*
zirkoneum, zirconium
zirofit, xerophyte
ziruphyte, xerophyte
zither,*, *AN INSTRUMENT*
zithur, zither

zoademy, zootomy
zoagrafe, zoography
zodeak, zodiac
zodiac,cal, *DEPICTION OF CONSTELLATIONS AND HOW THEY RELATE TO HUMANS*
zoezu, zoysia
zolsa, zoysia
zombe, zombie
zombie,*, *SOMEONE WHO IS ROBOTIC/CONTROLLED BY A NON-HUMAN FORCE*
zone,*,ed,ning,nal,nate,nated,nation, *A SPECIFIC AREA DESIGNATED FOR SPECIFIC PURPOSES*
zoo, *PREFIX INDICATING "ANIMAL" MOST OFTEN MODIFIES THE WORD*
zoo,*, *PLACE WHERE ANIMALS ARE AVAILABLE FOR VIEWING PUBLIC*
zoodeme, zootomy
zoofit, zoophyte
zoography,her,hic,hical,hically, *RELATED TO THE STUDY OF ANIMALS AND THEIR BEHAVIOR*
zoogrufe, zoography
zoology,gical,gically,gist, *SCIENCE OF STUDYING ANIMALS AND THEIR BEHAVIOR*
zoom,*,med,ming, *TO DECREASE DISTANCE BETWEEN OBSERVER AND THE OBSERVED*
zoometry,ric,rical,rist, *SCIENCE WHICH STUDIES ANIMALS AND THEIR SIZES/PROPORTIONS*
zoomorfik, zoomorphic
zoomorphic,ism, *TO PORTRAY/ASCRIBE ANIMALS AS HAVING HUMAN FEELINGS/BEHAVIORS/ CHARACTERISTICS*
zoophyte,*,tic,tical, *ANIMALS THAT RESEMBLE PLANTS*
zootomy,mic,mical,mist, *STUDY/DISSECTION OF THE ANATOMY OF ANIMALS*
zorgem, sorghum
zorgum, sorghum
zorkum, sorghum
zoysa, zoysia